P9-BZS-868

> Management Skill Builder©

International Business

Strategy, Management,
and the New Realities

S. Tamer Cavusgil
Michigan State University

Gary Knight
Florida State University

John R. Riesenberger
Executive in Residence, CIBER
Michigan State University

PEARSON

Prentice
Hall

Upper Saddle River, New Jersey, 07458

Library of Congress Cataloging-in-Publication Data

Cavusgil, S. Tamer.
  International business : strategy, management, and the new realities / S. Tamer Cavusgil, Gary
Knight, John R. Riesenberger.
    p. cm.
  Includes bibliographical references and index.
  ISBN 0-13-173860-7 (alk. paper)
  1. International business enterprises--Management. I. Knight, Gary, 1939- II. Riesenberger, John R.,
1948- III. Title.
  HD62.4.C389 2008
  658'.049--dc22

            2007041181

Editor-in-Chief: David Parker
Acquisitions Editor: Jennifer Collins
Senior Development Editor: Lena Buonanno
Product Development Manager: Ashley Santora
Assistant Editor: Kristen Varina
Editorial Assistant: Elizabeth Davis
Director of Development: Steve Deitmer
Media Project Manager: Ashley Lulling
Marketing Manager: Patrice Jones
Senior Managing Editor: Judy Leale
Project Manager, Production: Kevin H. Holm
Permissions Project Manager: Charles Morris
Senior Operations Supervisor: Arnold Vila
Senior Art Director: Maria Lange

Interior Design: Rob Aleman
Cover Illustration/Photo: Imagebroker/Alamy
Director, Image Resource Center: Melinda Patelli
Manager, Rights and Permissions: Zina Arabia
Manager: Visual Research: Beth Brenzel
Manager, Cover Visual Research & Permissions:
Karen Sanatar
Image Permission Coordinator: Angelique Sharps
Photo Researcher: Sheila Norman
Composition: Prepare
Full-Service Project Management: Prepare Inc.
Printer/Binder: R.R. Donnelly; Phoenix Color Corp.
Typeface: 10/12 Palatino

Credits and acknowledgments borrowed from other sources and reproduced, with permission, in this text-book appear on appropriate page within text (or on page 640).

Copyright © 2008 by Pearson Education, Inc., Upper Saddle River, New Jersey, 07458.
Pearson Prentice Hall
All rights reserved. Printed in the United States of America. This publication is protected by Copyright and permission should be obtained from the publisher prior to any prohibited reproduction, storage in a retrieval system, or transmission in any form or by any means, electronic, mechanical, photocopying, recording, or likewise. For information regarding permission(s), write to: Rights and Permissions Department.

Pearson Prentice Hall™ is a trademark of Pearson Education, Inc.
Pearson® is a registered trademark of Pearson plc
Prentice Hall® is a registered trademark of Pearson Education, Inc.

Pearson Education, LTD.
Pearson Education Singapore, Pte. Ltd
Pearson Education Canada, Ltd.
Pearson Education–Japan

Pearson Education Australia PTY, Limited
Pearson Education North Asia Ltd
Pearson Educación de Mexico, S.A. de C.V.
Pearson Education Malaysia, Pte. Ltd

10 9 8 7 6 5 4 3 2 1

ISBN-13: 978-0-13-173860-7

ISBN-10: 0-13-173860-7

Dedicated to...

This book is dedicated to: my parents, Mehmet and Naciye Cavusgil, who never received much formal education but passed on a deep sense of appreciation for knowledge to their children; my wife Judy, and my children Erin and Emre Cavusgil who graciously provided much-needed understanding, support, and encouragement; and my students whom I had the opportunity to mentor over the years.

S. Tamer Cavusgil
East Lansing, Michigan

This book is dedicated to my wife Mari, for her patience, intellect and adventurous spirit, and to Bill and Audrey, for being great parents and role models.

Gary Knight
Tallahassee, Florida

This book and the accompanying knowledge portal are dedicated to my parents, Richard and Marie Riesenberger, for their example, many sacrifices and love. To my wife and best friend, Pat, for her enthusiasm and loving support. To my daughters Jenny and Chris and their husbands, Martijn and Byron, of whom I am so very proud and thankful. To my amazing grandchildren Ryan and Paige—the future of the New Realities.

John R. Riesenberger
Basking Ridge, New Jersey

About the Authors

S. Tamer Cavusgil

Michigan State University, University Distinguished Faculty, The John William Byington Endowed Chair in Global Marketing, Executive Director, Center for International Business Education and Research (CIBER)

Professor Cavusgil has been mentoring students, executives, and educators in international business for the past three decades. A native of Turkey, Professor Cavusgil's professional work has taken him to numerous other emerging markets.

Professor Cavusgil has authored over 160 refereed journal articles and three dozen books including *Doing Business in the Emerging Markets* (Sage). His work is among the most cited contributions in international business. He is the founding editor of the *Journal of International Marketing* and *Advances in International Marketing*. He serves on the editorial review boards of professional journals.

Professor Cavusgil is an elected Fellow of the *Academy of International Business*, a distinction earned by a select group of intellectual leaders in international business. He also served as Vice President of the AIB, and on the Board of Directors of the *American Marketing Association*. Michigan State University bestowed him with its highest recognition for contributions to the international mission: the Ralph H. Smuckler Award for Advancing International Studies. He was named "International Trade Educator of the Year" in 1996 by the *National Association of Small Business International Trade Educators (NASBITE)*. At Michigan State University, he also earned the distinction of University Distinguished Faculty, the highest award given to a faculty member. In 2007, he was named an Honorary Fellow of the Sidney Sussex College at the University of Cambridge.

Professor Cavusgil holds MBA and Ph.D. degrees in business from the University of Wisconsin. Previously, he held positions at the Middle East Technical University in Turkey, University of Wisconsin-Whitewater, and Bradley University. He also served as Senior Fulbright Scholar to Australia and taught at Monash University and other Australian institutions. He served as a visiting Professor at Manchester Business School, and as Gianni and Joan Montezemolo Visiting Chair at the University of Cambridge, the United Kingdom.

Gary Knight

Florida State University
Associate Professor
Director of Program in International Business

Professor Knight has extensive experience in international business in the private sector. In his position as Export Manager for a medium-sized enterprise, he directed the firm's operations in Canada, Europe, Japan, and Mexico, supervising the business activities of some 50 distributors in these regions. Previously, he worked for a leading manufacturer of electrical machinery at its headquarters in Tokyo, Japan, and for the Japan office of the State of Washington.

At Florida State University, Professor Knight developed the study abroad programs in business in Britain, France, Japan, and Spain, as well as FSU's online courses in international business. He has won several awards for research and teaching, including best teacher in the MBA program and the Hans B. Thorelli Best Paper Award for his article "Entrepreneurship and Strategy: The SME Under Globalization." His research emphasizes regional integration, international business strategy, international services, and internationalization of small and medium-sized firms.

Professor Knight is a member of the Academy of International Business. He has authored three books and nearly one hundred refereed articles in academic journals and conference proceedings, including *Journal of International Business Studies, Journal of World Business, International Executive,* and *Management International Review.* He is on the editorial review boards of several international journals. The United States House of Representative's Committee on Small Business recently invited Professor Knight to provide expert testimony on terrorism's effects on international business.

Professor Knight earned his MBA at the University of Washington and Ph.D. at Michigan State University, both in international business. Earlier degrees were in Finance and Modern Languages. He also attended the University of Paris in France and Sophia University in Japan, and is fluent in French, Japanese, and Spanish.

John R. Riesenberger
Michigan State University
Executive in Residence
Center for International Business Education and Research

John's international business career spans over three decades in the global pharmaceutical industry. He has conducted business transactions in 21 countries. His passion is to help students develop the managerial skills frequently required of new graduates entering careers in international business.

Currently, John is a Principal in a "born global" science-branding communications agency with clients that include the majority of the leading global pharmaceutical companies headquartered in Europe, Japan, and the United States.

John worked with Pharmacia & Upjohn and The Upjohn Company as a senior executive. His experience covers a diverse range of divisional, geographic, and functional accountabilities. His most recent position was Vice-President, Business Intelligence, Global Business Management. Previous assignments included: Vice-President of The Upjohn Company of Canada, Vice-President of Business Information, Executive Director-Worldwide Strategic Marketing Services, Executive Director-Worldwide Medical Sciences Liaison, and Director of Sales. Prior to joining The Upjohn Company, he served as a Customer Service Supervisor with the Chase Manhattan Bank.

John served as a member of the Global Advisory Board of the American Marketing Association and as a member of the Business Advisory Board of the Michigan State University Center for International Business Education and Research. He served as Chairman, Industry Advisory Board, "Value of Marketing Program," SEI Center for the Advanced Studies in Management, The Wharton School of the University of Pennsylvania. He is the former Chairman of the Pharmaceutical Manufacturing Association Marketing Practices Committee. John is the co-author, with Robert T. Moran, of *The Global Challenge: Building the New Worldwide Enterprise* (McGraw-Hill, London).

John holds a Bachelor of Science degree in Economics-Business and a Masters of Business Administration in Management from Hofstra University. He attended the Harvard Business School's International Senior Management Program (ISMP 89).

> Brief Contents

Contents

> Preface

Why We Created This Book And Teaching System

The book you are holding, **International Business: Strategy, Management, and the New Realities**, is a component of an innovative educational system we have been developing over the past several years. The system represents an innovative and exciting approach to teaching international business. The insights we gained from comprehensive research and discussions with hundreds of practitioners, students, and faculty have been instrumental in refining our pedagogical philosophy and resources. The book attempts to impart the core body of knowledge in international business in an interesting and lively manner. Our teaching system works from the ground up, where cases, exercises, and management skill builders are seamlessly integrated and matched to the topics covered in each chapter. The accompanying knowledge portal, the C/K/R Educator's Consortium©, is designed as a clearinghouse for learning, networking, and sharing for International business educators worldwide.

The C/K/R Educational System is based on the following guiding principles:

New Realities

There are new realities in international business that are critical for today's students to embrace. We are witnessing remarkable changes in the cross-border flow of products, services, capital, ideas, and people. Today's volume of international trade, ease of communication and travel, and technological advances compel, and help, large and small firms to internationalize. We designed the content, organization, and features of the book and other resources to motivate and prepare future managers to grasp these new realities. These include: global sourcing, the impact of technological advances on globalization, globalization of finance, and the success of the smaller firm in international markets. Three other new realities are worth elaborating here: emerging markets, the diversity of international business participants, and corporate social responsibility.

Emerging Markets Students need an improved understanding of the changing nature of the international business landscape, not just the Triad regions (Europe, North America, and Japan). Over the past two decades, some 30 high-growth, high-potential countries have sprung into the forefront of cross-border business with rapid industrialization, privatization, and modernization.

We introduce emerging markets in Chapter 1, "Introduction: What is International Business" and, discuss how companies such as Renault and Microsoft achieve efficiencies by sourcing to countries such as Romania and India. In Chapter 9, "Understanding Emerging Markets," we explain what makes emerging markets attractive for international business and the risks and challenges of doing business in these markets. In Chapter 9 we also discuss Mexico's Cemex, Egypt's Orascom Telecom, and China's Shanghai Automotive.

The Diversity of International Business Participants Multinational enterprises (MNEs) have historically been the most important type of focal firm. However, students need to be familiar with a variety of firms active in international business. We therefore provide balanced coverage of MNEs, small and medium-sized enterprises (SMEs), and born globals. We introduce these three types of firms in Chapter 1 and revisit them throughout the book. Here are a few examples of the firms we discuss:

- Diesel, a fashion design company that grew from an SME into an MNE (Chapter 1, "Introduction: What is International Business?")

- Electrolux, a Swedish MNE in the kitchen appliance industry
  (Chapter 2, Globalization of Markets and the Internationalization of the Firm")

- Geo Search, a Japanese born global in the electronics industry
  (Chapter 3, "Organizational Participants that Make International Business Happen")

- L'Oreal, a French MNE in the cosmetic industry
  (Chapter 5, "The Cultural Environment of International Business")

- The challenges MNEs and SMEs encounter in Russia
  (Chapter 6, "Political and Legal Systems in National Environments")

- How trade barriers affect SMEs
  (Chapter 7, "Government Intervention in International Business")

- IKEA, a Swedish MNE in the furniture industry
  (Chapter 11, "Global Strategy and Organization")

- PMI Mortgage Insurance Co., a U.S. service firm
  (Chapter 13, "Exporting and Countertrade")

Corporate Social Responsibility Firms are increasingly aware of their role as good corporate citizens. We introduce corporate social responsibility in Chapter 1, "Introduction: What is International Business?" and provide examples from firms such as Starbucks and McDonald's. In Chapter 6, "Political and Legal Systems in National Environments," we summarize ethical practices and values. In Chapter 9, "Understanding Emerging Markets," we cover how firms foster economic development with profitable projects. In Chapter 16, "Global Sourcing," we address ethical and social implications of global sourcing. In Chapter 18, "International Human Resource Management," we discuss how firms can create more equitable working environments for foreign employees.

Educator's Consortium©

Instructors need an innovative educational solution that goes beyond the textbook and its traditional supplements. We address this need with the C/K/R Educator's Consortium©. The Educator's Consortium© is the first online, global community to bring together international business instructors who are dedicated to preparing today's students to be creative, open-minded, and socially responsible.

The CKR Educator's Consortium© is a dynamic virtual library of pedagogical content and tools: It is designed to make every instructor look good in the classroom, as well as to save them time. The Educator's Consortium© offers these advantages:

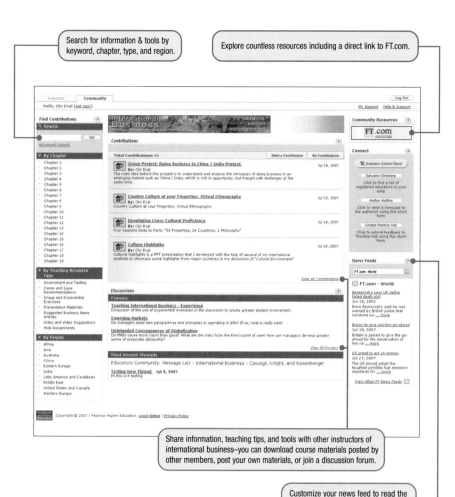

Search for information & tools by keyword, chapter, type, and region.

Explore countless resources including a direct link to FT.com.

Share information, teaching tips, and tools with other instructors of international business—you can download course materials posted by other members, post your own materials, or join a discussion forum.

Customize your news feed to read the latest developments around the world.

- Connects IB educators all over the world, providing opportunities for collaboration through the Educator's Directory.
- Gives the instructor the ability to customize material to suit his or her own needs and teaching style by searching through community-generated material that is constantly updated.
- Offers an asynchronous bulletin board, inviting all adopters to exchange teaching ideas, post questions, and dialog through threaded discussions with one another and with the author team. The authors ensure quality content by screening contributed material.
- Includes unlimited access to ft.com, the portal of the *Financial Times*.

FINANCIAL TIMES

globalEDGE™ Knowledge Portal

globalEDGE™ was developed at Michigan State University's Center for International Business Education and Research (CIBER) under the direction of S. Tamer Cavusgil. globalEDGE™ has become the leading knowledge portal for professionals in international business, providing a gateway to specialized knowledge on countries, cross-border transactions, culture, and firm practice. In each chapter, the authors provide several globalEDGE™ exercises as the basis for student assignments and projects.

Textbook Features of Special Note

Maps

In today's globalized world, it is more important than ever for students to understand world geography. Our maps are large, easy to read, and colorful. Below is an example of a map from Chapter 9. Note the clear labeling of countries, the use of color coding, and the cut-out of Europe to make countries easy to identify:

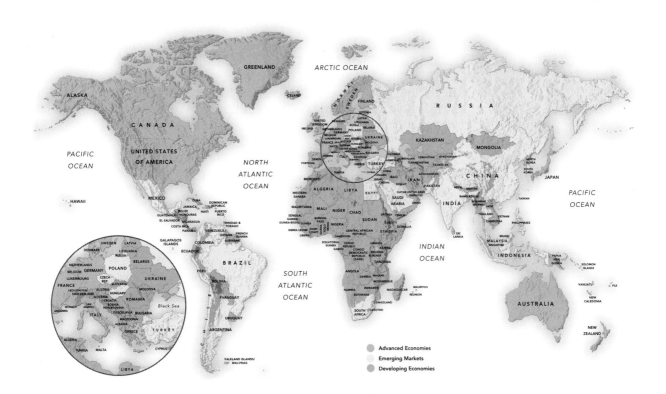

Recent Grad in IB

Select chapters include a special feature entitled *Recent Grad in IB*, which highlights IB graduates now working in exciting international careers. We hope this feature will motivate today's students to travel, learn another language, and be open to working internationally.

Closing Case

Each chapter closes with an extensive case study that is new, developed specifically to address the learning objectives in the chapter and written by the authors. The cases help students build their managerial skills by applying what they have learned in the chapter to a situation faced by a real-world manager. Questions accompany the case for assignment as homework. Class discussion helps students sharpen their analytical and decision-making skills. Here are a few examples of the closing cases:

- Chapter 1: Whirlpool's Dramatic Turnaround through Internationalization
- Chapter 4: Hyundai: The Struggle for International Success
- Chapter 5: Hollywood and the Rise of Cultural Protectionism
- Chapter 6: Pillaging Patents: The New War on Pharmaceutical Drugs
- Chapter 7: Airbus Versus Boeing: When is Intervention Not Intervention?
- Chapter 11: Carlos Ghosn and Renault-Nissan: Leading for Global Success
- Chapter 12: Advanced Biomedical Devices: Assessing Readiness to Export
- Chapter 14: AUTOLATINA: A Failed International Partnership
- Chapter 15: Subway and the Challenges of Franchising in China
- Chapter 17: MTV India: Balancing Global and Local Marketing

Additional cases are provided at the Educator's Consortium©.

C/K/R Management Skill Builder©

As future managers, students must learn how to gather and analyze market information. We have devised an entirely new educational tool—the *C/K/R Management Skill Builder (MSB)©*. The MSB is a practical exercise that helps students gain familiarity with key managerial challenges they are likely to encounter as entry-level professionals. Students complete their *C/K/R MSBs©* by starting out with author-provided guidelines and a suggested presentation template available on the student knowledge portal. The MSBs will give students practical, real-world skills that will help them perform well in their careers. Here are a few examples of the MSBs:

- Chapter 2: Corporate Social Responsibility: Coffee, Ethiopia, and Starbucks

- Chapter 5: Developing an Incentive Plan for Sales Personnel from Different Cultures

- Chapter 6: Performing a Preliminary Country Risk Analysis
- Chapter 9: Learning About and Assessing Emerging Markets
- Chapter 12: Global Market Opportunity Assessment for Cancer Insurance
- Chapter 14: Selecting a Site for a Foreign Manufacturing Plant

This Book Supports Association to Advance Collegiate Schools of Business (AACSB) International Accreditation

Each chapter ends with a collection of exercises: Closing Case, Test Your Comprehension, Apply Your Understanding, globalEDGE™ Internet Exercises, and C/K/R Management Skill Builder©. In every chapter, next to each exercise, we provide a specific AACSB tagging logo to help instructors identify those exercises that support AACSB learning goals. We also provide AACSB tagging for all the questions in the Test Item File that accompanies the textbook.

What is the AACSB? AACSB is a not-for-profit corporation of educational institutions, corporations and other organizations devoted to the promotion and improvement of higher education in business administration and accounting. A collegiate institution offering degrees in business administration or accounting may volunteer for AACSB accreditation review. The AACSB makes initial accreditation decisions and conducts periodic reviews to promote continuous quality improvement in management education. Pearson Education is a proud member of the AACSB and is pleased to provide advice to help you apply AACSB Learning Standards.

What are AACSB Learning Standards? One of the criteria for AACSB accreditation is the quality of the curricula. Although no specific courses are required, the AACSB expects a curriculum to include learning experiences in such areas as:

- Communication
- Ethical reasoning
- Analytical skills
- Use of information technology
- Multiculturalism and diversity
- Reflective thinking

These six categories are AACSB Learning Standards. Questions that test skills relevant to these standards are tagged with the appropriate standard. For example, a question testing the moral questions associated with externalities would receive the Ethical Reasoning tag.

How can I use these tags? Tagged exercises help you measure whether students are grasping the course content that aligns with AACSB guidelines noted above. In addition, the tagged exercises may help to identify potential applications of these skills. This, in turn, may suggest enrichment activities or other educational experiences to help students achieve these goals.

Resources in Support of the Text

Instructor's Resource Center

At **www.prenhall.com/irc**, instructors can access a variety of print, digital, and presentation resources available with this text in downloadable format. Registration is simple and gives you immediate access to new titles and new editions. As a registered faculty member, you can download resource files and receive immediate access and instructions for installing course management content on your campus server.

If you ever need assistance, our dedicated technical support team is ready to help with the media supplements that accompany this text. Visit **www.247.prenhall.com** for answers to frequently asked questions and toll-free user support phone numbers.

The following supplements are available to adopting instructors

- **Instructor's Resource Center (IRC) on CD-ROM**—ISBN: 0-13-156318-1

All instructor resources in one place. It's your choice. The Instructor's Resource Center on CD-Rom includes the following supplements:

- **Instructor's Manual**
- **Test Item File**
- **Image Bank**
- **PowerPoints**
- **Printed Instructor's Manual**—ISBN: 0-13-232241-2

Authored by Professor Carol Sanchez of Grand Valley State University and Professor Marta Szabo White of George State University, the Instructor's Manual offers much more than just the traditional, limited chapter outline and answers to the end-of-chapter materials. In addition to these basic items, you will find suggested teaching strategies for 45-, 90-, and 180-minute sessions, chapter coverage suggestions for semester and quarter-length courses, and modular suggestions for courses focused on general management, strategy, and/or organizational behavior. The coverage for each chapter includes a variety of resources such as exercises, critical-thinking assignments, debate topics, and research assignments. Two appendices contain complete PowerPoint slides and an in-depth Video Guide.

- **Printed Test Item File**—ISBN: 0-13-156319-X

The test bank, authored by Cara Cantarella of Acumen Enterprises, Inc., contains approximately 75 questions per chapter, including multiple-choice, true/false, short answer, and essay questions based on a short business scenario. Cara is an assessment expert with extensive experience in test authoring. Each question for each chapter has been carefully reviewed and edited by the authors and Professor Candan Celik of Michigan State University to ensure accuracy and appropriateness.

Test questions are annotated with the following information:

- Page number from the main text of where the question's topic is covered
- Learning Objective from the main text
- Difficulty level: Easy for straight recall, Moderate for some analysis, or Analytical for complex analysis
- Topic: the term or concept the question supports
- Skill: concept or application

For each question that tests a standard from the Association to Advance Collegiate Schools of Business (AACSB), we use one of the following annotations:

- Communication
- Ethical Reasoning
- Analytical Skills
- Use of Information Technology
- Multicultural and Diversity
- Reflective Thinking

TestGen Test Generating Software—Available at the IRC online

This easy-to-use software allows instructors to custom design, save, and generate classroom tests. Instructors can edit, add, or delete questions from the test bank; edit existing graphics and create new graphics; analyze test results; and organize a database of tests and student results. It provides many flexible options for organizing and displaying tests, along with a search-and-sort feature.

- **PowerPoint Slides**—created by the authors—are available at the IRC (online or on CD-ROM).
- **Image Bank**—Visit the IRC on CD-ROM for this resource

All of the exhibits from the textbook are available electronically for instructors to download, print, display in class, or produce customized materials.

- **Custom Videos on DVD**—ISBN: 0-13-232207-2

The new DVD (ISBN: 0-13-232207-2) accompanying *International Business: Strategy, Management, and the New Realities*, contains both short and full-length clips highlighting international business issues. The Instructor's Manual offers the complete Video Guide.

Knowledge Portal Online Courses

The Knowledge Portal online courses offer the best teaching and learning online resources all in one place. It is all that instructors need to plan and administer their courses and all that students need for anytime, anywhere access to online course material. All of the materials for *International Business: Strategy, Management, and the New Realities*, are conveniently organized by chapter in the Knowledge Portal. The Knowledge Portal online courses are available in three course management platforms: *BlackBoard*, *CourseCompass*, and *WebCT* and features the following materials:

- **For the Student:** Student PowerPoints
- Link to FT.com for an additional $25 six-month subscription
- Market Entry Strategy Project
- Chapter quizzes
- Link to **www.globaledge.msu.edu**
- Selection of short video clips
- Management Skill Builder exercises
- **For the Instructor:** All of the instructor's supplements, including the materials from the Instructor's Resource Center—(Test Bank, Instructor's Manual, and PowerPoint® slides)—have been pre-loaded into the Knowledge Portal online courses. Instructors choose can easily modify these materials for their online courses.

The Knowledge Portal online courses require an access code, which can be shrink-wrapped free of charge with new copies of this text. Please contact your local sales representative for the correct ISBN.

Knowledge Portal Companion Website

The Knowledge Portal Companion Website (for those who do not desire course management functionality) at **www.prenhall.com/cavusgil** contains valuable resources for both students and professors. This content is open access except as indicated. An access code is shipped with each copy of the book.

- Student PowerPoints
- Link to FT.com for an additional $25 six-month subscription
- Market Entry Strategy Project (Pass Code Protected)
- Chapter quizzes
- Link to **www.globaledge.msu.edu**
- Selection of short video clips (Pass Code Protected)
- Management Skill Builder exercises (Pass Code Protected)

Vango Notes

Study on the go with VangoNotes (**www.VangoNotes.com**), detailed chapter reviews in downloadable MP3 format. Now wherever you are and whatever you're doing, you can study on the go by listening to the following for each chapter of your textbook:

- Big Ideas: Your "need to know" for each chapter
- Key Terms: Audio "flashcards"—help you review key concepts and terms
- Rapid Review: Quick-drill session—use it right before your test

VangoNotes are **flexible**: Download all the material (or only the chapters you need) directly to your player. And *VangoNotes* are **efficient**: Use them in your car, at the gym, walking to class, wherever you go. So get yours today, and get studying.

CourseSmart eTextbooks Online

CourseSmart is an exciting new choice for students looking to save money. As an alternative to purchasing the print textbook, students can purchase an electronic version of the same content at a savings of up to 50 percent off the suggested list price of the print text. With a CourseSmart eTextbook, students can search the text, make notes online, print out reading assignments that incorporate lecture notes, and bookmark important passages for later review. For more information, or to purchase access to the CourseSmart eTextbook, visit **www.coursesmart.com**.

Feedback

The authors and the product team would appreciate hearing from you! Let us know what you think about this textbook by writing to college_marketing@pren-hall.com. Please include "Feedback about Cavusgil/Knight/Riesenberger 1e" in the subject line.

For any questions related to this product, please contact our customer service department online at **www.247.prenhall.com**.

Acknowledgments

Our Reviewers

Through three drafts of the manuscript, we received guidance and insights at several critical junctures from many trusted reviewers who provided specific recommendations on how to improve and refine the content, presentation, and organization. Their contributions were invaluable in crystallizing our thinking. We extend our gratitude to:

Raj Aggarwal, University of Akron
Richard Ajayi, University of Central Florida
Allen Amason, University of Georgia
Bulent Aybar, Southern New Hampshire University
Nizamettin Aydin, Suffolk University
Peter Banfe, Ohio Northern University
Eric Baumgardner, Xavier University
Lawrence Beer, Arizona State University
David Berg, University of Wisconsin-Milwaukee
Jean Boddewyn, Baruch College, City University of New York
Kirt Butler, Michigan State University
Tom Cary, City University, Seattle
Aruna Chandra, Indiana State University
Tim Curran, University of South Florida
Madeline Calabrese Damkar, California State University-East Bay
Seyda Deligonul, St. John Fisher College
Peter Dowling, Victoria University of Wellington, New Zealand
Bradley Farnsworth, University of Michigan
David Griffith, Michigan State University
Tom Head, Roosevelt University
Bruce Heiman, San Francisco State University
Ali Kara, Pennsylvania State University-University Park
Daekwan Kim, Florida State University
Ahmet Kirca, Michigan State University

Tatiana Kostova, University of South Carolina
Chuck Kwok, University of South Carolina
Yikuan Lee, San Francisco State University
Bijou Lester, Drexel University
Barbara Moebius, Waukesha County Technical College
Bruce Money, Brigham Young University
Bill Murray, University of San Francisco
Matthew B. Myers, University of Tennessee
Jeffrey W. Overby, Belmont University
Susan Peterson, Scottsdale Community College
Iordanis Petsas, University of Scranton
Zahir Quraeshi, Western Michigan University
Roberto Ragozzino, University of Central Florida
Hakan Saraoglu, Bryant University
Carol Sanchez, Grand Valley State University
Kurt Stanberry, University of Houston-Downtown
John Stanbury, George Mason University
Philip Sussan, University of Central Florida
Charles Ray Taylor, Villanova University
Deanna Teel, Houston Community College
Thuhang Tran, Middle Tennessee State University
Cheryl Van Deusen, University of North Florida
Linn Van Dyne, Michigan State University
William Walker, University of Houston
Marta Szabo White, Georgia State University
Betty Yobaccio, Bryant University

Focus Group Participants

We were also fortunate that so many colleagues generously gave their time and offered perspectives on our teaching resources and the Educator's Consortium. We met with these colleagues in person, teleconferenced with them, or otherwise received their input. The insights and recommendations of these educators were instrumental in the design and format of the C/K/R Portal. We extend our gratitude and thanks to the following reviewers and colleagues:

Yusaf Akbar, Southern New Hampshire University
Victor Alicea, Normandale Community College
Gail Arch, Curry College
Anke Arnaud, University of Central Florida
Choton Basu, University of Wisconsin, Whitewater
Paula Bobrowski, Auburn University

Teresa Brosnan, City University, Bellevue
Nichole Castater, Clark Atlanta University
Mike C.H. (Chen-Ho) Chao, Baruch College, City University of New York
David Chaplin, Waldorf College
Dong Chen, Loyola Marymount University

Chen Oi Chin, Lawrence Technological University
Patrick Chinon, Syracuse University
Farok J. Contractor, Rutgers University
Christine Cope Pence, University of California, Riverside
Angelica Cortes, University of Texas-Pan American
Michael Deis, Clayton State University
Les Dlabay, Lake Forest College
Gary Donnelly, Casper College
Gideon Falk, Purdue University-Calumet
Marc Fetscherin, Rollins College
Charles Fishel, San Jose State University
Frank Flauto, Austin Community College
Georgine K. Fogel, Salem International University
Frank Franzak, Virginia Commonwealth University
Debbie Gilliard, Metropolitan State College
Robert Goddard, Appalachian State University
Kenneth Gray, Florida A&M University
Andy Grein, Baruch College, City University of New York
Andrew C. Gross, Cleveland State University
David Grossman, Florida Southern College
Seid Hassan, Murray State University
Xiaohong He, Quinnipiac University
Wei He, Indiana State University
Christina Heiss, University of Missouri-Kansas City
Guy Holburn, University of Western Ontario
Anisul Islam, University of Houston-Downtown
Basil Janavaras, Minnesota State University
Raj Javalgi, Cleveland State University
Yikuan Jiang, California State University-East Bay
Ken Kim, University of Toledo
Anthony C. Koh, The University of Toledo
Ann Langlois, Palm Beach Atlantic University
Michael La Rocco, University of Saint Francis
Romas A. Laskauskas, Villa Julie College
Shaomin Li, Old Dominion University

Ted London, University of Michigan
Peter Magnusson, Saint Louis University
Charles Mambula, Suffolk University
David McArthur, Utah Valley State College
Ofer Meilich, Bradley University
Lauryn Migenes, University of Central Florida
Mortada Mohamed, Austin Community College
Robert T. Moran, Thunderbird
Carolyn Mueller, Stetson University
Kelly J. Murphrey, Texas A&M University
William Newburry, Florida International University
Stanley Nollen, Georgetown University
Augustine Nwabuzor, Florida A&M University
David Paul, California State University-East Bay
Christine Pence, University of California Riverside
Heather Pendarvis-McCord, Bradley University
Kathleen Rehbein, Marquette University
Liesl Riddle, George Washington University
John Rushing, Barry University
Mary Saladino, Montclair State University
Carol Sanchez, Grand Valley State University
Camille Schuster, California State University-San Marcos
Eugene Seeley, Utah Valley State College
Mandep Singh, Western Illinois University
Rajendra Sinhaa, Des Moines Area Community College
John E. Spillan, Pennsylvania State University-DuBois
Uday S. Tate, Marshall University
Janell Townsend, Oakland University
Sameer Vaidya, Texas Wesleyan University
Robert Ware, Savannah State University
Marta Szabo White, Georgia State University
Steve Williamson, University of North Florida
Lynn Wilson, Saint Leo University
Attila Yaprak, Wayne State University
Rama Yelkur, University of Wisconsin-Eau Claire
Christopher Ziemnowicz, Concord University

Our Colleagues, Doctoral Students, and Practitioners

Numerous individuals have contributed to our thinking over the years. Through conversations, conferences, seminars, and writings, we have greatly benefited from the views and experience of international business educators and professionals from around the world. The senior author also had many rich conversations with the doctoral students whom he mentored over the years. Their names appear below if they have not been previously mentioned above. Directly or indirectly, their thoughtful ideas and suggestions have had a significant impact on the development of this book. Some have also contributed specific content to the Educator's Consortium. Our appreciation goes to many individuals including:

Billur Akdeniz, Michigan State University
Lyn Amine, Saint Louis University
Catherine N. Axinn, Ohio University
Ted Bany, The Upjohn Company
Nigel Barrett, University of Technology Sydney, Australia

Christopher Bartlett, Harvard Business School
Simon Bell, University of Cambridge
Daniel C. Bello, Georgia State University
Muzaffer Bodur, Bogazici University, Istanbul, Turkey
Nakiye Boyacigiller, Sabanci University

John Brawley, The Upjohn Company
Roger Calantone, Michigan State University
Erin Cavusgil, Michigan State University
Brian Chabowski, University of Tulsa
Emin Civi, University of New Brunswick, St. John, Canada
Tevfik Dalgic, University of Texas at Dallas
Guillermo D'Andrea, Universidad Austral-Argentina
Angela da Rocha, Universidad Federal do Rio de Janeiro, Brazil
Deniz Erden, Bogazici University, Istanbul, Turkey
Felicitas Evangelista, University of Western Sydney, Australia
Cuneyt Evirgen, Sabanci University
Richard Fletcher, University of Western Sydney, Australia
Harold Fishkin, The Upjohn Company
Esra Gencturk, Koc University
Pervez Ghauri, University of Manchester, U.K.
Tracy Gonzalez, Michigan State University
Sangphet Hanvanich, Xavier University
Tomas Hult, Michigan State University
Destan Kandemir, Bilkent University
Irem Kiyak, Michigan State University
Tunga Kiyak, Michigan State University
Phillip Kotler, Northwestern University
Tiger Li, Florida International University
Karen Loch, Georgia State University
Mushtaq Luqmani, Western Michigan University
Robert McCarthy, The Upjohn Company
Myron Miller, Michigan State University (ret.)
Vincent Mongello, The Upjohn Company
Robert T. Moran, Thunderbird
G.M. Naidu, University of Wisconsin-Whitewater

Robert Nason, Michigan State University
John R. Nevin, University of Wisconsin
Glenn Omura, Michigan State University
Gregory Osland, Butler University
Aysegul Ozsomer, Koc University
Morys Perry, University of Michigan-Flint
Alex Rialp, Universidad Autonoma de Barcelona, Spain
Tony Roath, University of Oklahoma
Carol Sanchez, Grand Valley State University
Peter Seaver, The Upjohn Company
Steven Seggie, Bilkent University
Linda Hui Shi, University of Victoria
Rudolf R. Sinkovics, The University of Manchester
Carl Arthur Solberg, Norwegian School of Management, Norway
Elif Sonmez-Persinger, Eastern Michigan University
Douglas Squires, The Upjohn Company of Canada
Barbara Stoettinger, Wirtschaftuniversitaet Wein, Austria
Berk Talay, Michigan State University
David Tse, University of Hong Kong
Nukhet Vardar, Yeditepe University, Istanbul, Turkey
Kathy Waldie, Michigan State University
Marta Szabo White, Georgia State University
Fang Wu, University of Texas-Dallas
Shichun (Alex) Xu, University of Tennessee
Goksel Yalcinkaya, University of New Hampshire
Ugur Yavas, East Tennessee State University
Sengun Yeniyurt, Rutgers University
Poh-Lin Yeoh, Bentley College
Eden Yin, University of Cambridge
Chun Zhang, University of Vermont
Shaoming Zou, University of Missouri

Our Prentice Hall Team

This book would not have been possible without the tireless efforts of many dedicated professionals at our publisher, Prentice Hall. We are especially grateful to David Parker who was an acquisitions editor when we started this project three years ago. His positive outlook, professional demeanor, and good sense of humor provided the motivation for us to persist with this effort. We were also very fortunate to have highly competent and professional assistance of Lena Buonanno throughout the entire project. Her careful editing and creative ideas were instrumental in enhancing the content and composition of the final product. Gina Huck Siegert provided able and cheerful coordination through two rounds of revisions with our reviewers. Kathleen McLellan helped organize numerous focus groups with insightful educators and assisted with marketing efforts. Our appreciation goes to many other individuals at Prentice Hall, including: Linda Albelli, Robert Aleman, Alvelino Alves, Cara Cantarella, Elizabeth Davis, Stephen Deitmer, Jerome Grant, Kevin Holm, Patrice Jones, Brian Kibby, Maria Lange, John LaVacca, Judy Leale, Patrick Leow, Ben Paris, Ashley Santora, and Kristen Varina.

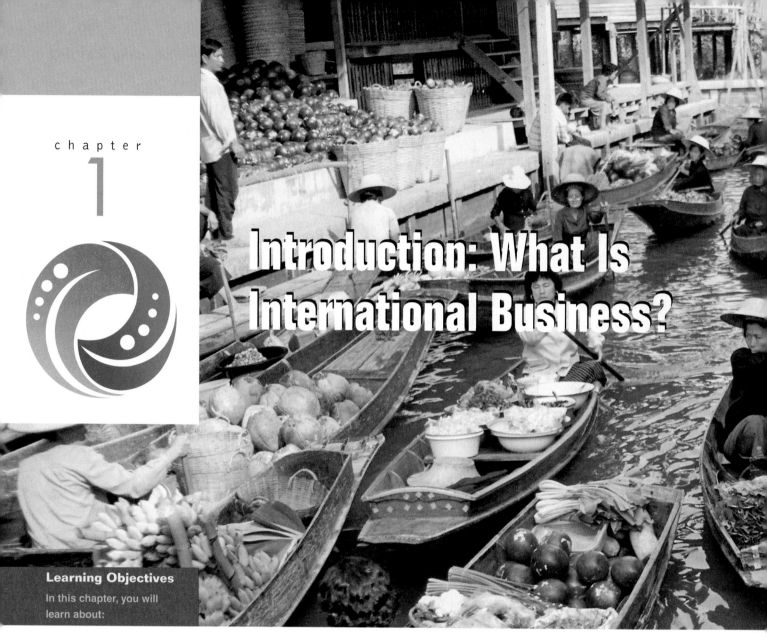

Introduction: What Is International Business?

Learning Objectives

In this chapter, you will learn about:

1. What is international business?
2. What are the key concepts in international trade and investment?
3. How does international business differ from domestic business?
4. Who participates in international business?
5. Why do firms pursue internationalization strategies?
6. Why should you study international business?

> A Day in the Global Economy

Julie Valentine is a college junior majoring in business. On a recent Saturday, she went shopping at a local mall. First, she ordered a big breakfast, unaware that most of her meal was imported from abroad: bacon from Spain, fruit from Costa Rica, juice from Brazil, French-branded yogurt, and bread made from wheat grown in Argentina. Julie then headed to the department store to buy a gift for her dad. She perused neckties with Italian and French brand names, and others made in China, Mexico, and Romania. She also considered electric shavers made by Braun (a German brand) and Philips (a Dutch brand). She eventually bought a Panasonic (a Japanese brand). Next, she headed to the perfume counter, where she tried various brands, including Chanel (France), French Connection (UK), Eau de Gucci (Italy), and Shiseido (Japan).

Julie was dreaming of buying a laptop computer. At the electronics store, she explored several models made in China, Ireland, Malaysia, and Taiwan. As she passed a travel agency, she remembered that her spring vacation was just around the corner and decided to consult her best friend Melissa. Whipping out her Nokia cell phone (a Finnish brand, but made in Hungary, Mexico, and South Korea), she

reached Melissa. Melissa answered on her Motorola phone (a U.S. firm, but made in Malaysia and other Asian locations). The two chatted about their dream trip to the beaches of southern Spain, considered Mexico, but decided they will probably end up in Panama City, Florida. Julie looked at a blouse made in Vietnam, but hesitated to purchase it because she had read that some products from southeast Asia are made by child labor.

Julie left the mall and drove away in her Hyundai (a Korean brand, but made in China). She was envious of Melissa's car, a BMW (German, but made in the United States from Asian, European, and South African components). Over the following weeks, Julie and her exchange-student friend, Anders (her favorite Norwegian import), meet up several times at restaurants featuring food from various nations, including France, India, Lebanon, and Mexico. On Friday night, they watched the latest movie in the Matrix series (made in Australia and the United States, financed by the Japanese) on a friend's big-screen TV (a Dutch brand, but made in Indonesia). Over dinner, Julie and Anders enjoyed pasta from Italy and shrimp from El Salvador, and chatted about their future. Julie was dreaming of an international career.

What Is International Business?

International business
Performance of trade and investment activities by firms across national borders.

As you can see from the opening vignette, international business touches our daily experiences. **International business** refers to the performance of trade and investment activities by firms across national borders. Since the most conspicuous aspect of international business is the crossing of national boundaries, we also refer to international business as *cross-border business*. Firms organize, source, manufacture, market, and conduct other value-adding activities on an international scale. They seek foreign customers and engage in collaborative relationships with foreign business partners. While international business is primarily carried out by individual firms, governments and international agencies also engage in international business transactions.[1] Firms and nations exchange many physical and intellectual assets including products, services, capital, technology, know-how, and labor. In this book, we are concerned primarily with the international business activities of the individual firm.

While international business has been around for centuries, it has gained much speed and complexity over the past two decades. Firms seek international market opportunities more today than ever before, touching the lives of billions of people around the world. Daily chores such as shopping and leisure activities such as listening to music, watching a movie, or surfing the Internet involve international business transactions that connect you to the global economy. International business gives you access to products and services from around the world and profoundly affects your quality of life and economic well-being.

Globalization of markets
Ongoing economic integration and growing interdependency of countries worldwide.

The growth of international business activity coincides with the broader phenomenon of globalization of markets. The **globalization of markets** refers to the ongoing economic integration and growing interdependency of countries worldwide. While internationalization of the firm refers to the tendency of companies to systematically increase the international dimension of their business activities, globalization refers to a macrotrend of intense economic interconnectedness between countries. In essence, globalization leads to compression of time and space. It allows many firms to internationalize and has substantially increased the volume and variety of cross-border transactions in goods, services, and capital flows. It has also led to more rapid and widespread diffusion of products, technology, and knowledge worldwide, regardless of origin.

In practical terms, the globalization of markets is evident in several related trends. First is the unprecedented growth of international trade. In 1960, cross-border trade was modest—about $100 billion per year. Today, it accounts for a substantial proportion of the world economy, amounting to some $10 trillion annually—that is, $10,000,000,000,000! Second, trade between nations is accompanied by substantial flows of capital, technology, and knowledge. Third is the development of highly sophisticated global financial systems and mechanisms that facilitate the cross-border flow of products, money, technology, and knowledge. Fourth, globalization has brought about a greater degree of collaboration among nations through multilateral regulatory agencies such as the World Trade Organization (WTO) and the International Monetary Fund (IMF).

Globalization both compels and facilitates companies to pursue cross-border business activities and international expansion. Simultaneously, going international for a firm has become easier than ever before. A few decades ago, international business was largely the domain of large, multinational companies. Recent developments have created a more level playing field that allows firms of any size to benefit from active participation in international business. In this text, you will read about the international activities of smaller firms, along with those of large multinational enterprises. In addition, where cross-border business was once mainly undertaken by manufacturing firms, this is no longer the case. Companies in the services sector are also internationalizing, in such industries as banking, transportation, engineering, design, advertising, and retailing.

We will study the globalization of markets in greater detail in Chapter 2. Let's now review key concepts and trends associated with international business as practiced by firms.

What Are the Key Concepts in International Trade and Investment?

The most conventional forms of international business transactions are international trade and investment. **International trade** refers to an exchange of products and services across national borders. Trade involves both products (merchandise) and services (intangibles). Exchange can be through **exporting**, an entry strategy involving the sale of products or services to customers located abroad, from a base in the home country or a third country. Exchange can also take the form of **importing**, or **global sourcing**—the procurement of products or services from suppliers located abroad for consumption in the home country or a third country. Therefore, exporting is an outbound activity, while importing is an inbound flow of products and services. Both finished products and intermediate goods, such as raw materials and components, are subject to importing and exporting.

International investment refers to the transfer of assets to another country, or the acquisition of assets in that country. These assets include capital, technology, managerial talent, and manufacturing infrastructure. Economists refer to such assets as *factors of production*. With trade, products and services cross national borders. With investment, by contrast, the firm itself crosses borders to secure ownership of assets located abroad.

The two essential types of cross-border investment are portfolio investment and foreign direct investment. **International portfolio investment** refers to the passive ownership of foreign securities such as stocks and bonds for the purpose of generating financial returns. It does not entail active management or control over these assets. The foreign investor has a relatively short-term interest in the ownership of these assets. **Foreign direct investment (FDI)** refers to an internationalization strategy in which the firm establishes a physical presence abroad through acquisition of productive assets such as capital, technology, labor, land, plant, and equipment. It is a foreign-market entry strategy that gives investors partial or full ownership of a productive enterprise dedicated to manufacturing, marketing, or research and development activities. Firms usually have a long-term plan to invest such resources in foreign countries.

The Nature of International Trade

Exhibit 1.1 contrasts the growth of total world exports to the growth of total world gross domestic product (GDP) since 1970. GDP is the total value of products and services produced in a country over the course of a year. The growth of export activity by nations has continued to outpace the growth of domestic production during the last few decades, illustrating the fast pace of globalization. In fact, world exports grew more than thirty-fold during this period, while world GDP grew more than tenfold. This difference is in part due to advanced economies such as Canada and Japan now sourcing many of the products that they consume from low-cost manufacturing locations such as China and Mexico. For example, although the United States once produced most of the products that it consumes, today it has become much more dependent on imports. Rapid integration of world economies is fueled by such factors as advances in information and transportation technologies, the decline of trade barriers, liberalization of markets, and the remarkable economic growth of emerging market countries.

International trade Exchange of products and services across national borders; typically through exporting and importing.

Exporting Sale of products or services to customers located abroad, from a base in the home country or a third country.

Importing or global sourcing Procurement of products or services from suppliers located abroad for consumption in the home country or a third country.

International investment The transfer of assets to another country or the acquisition of assets in that country.

International portfolio investment Passive ownership of foreign securities such as stocks and bonds for the purpose of generating financial returns.

Foreign direct investment (FDI) An internationalization strategy in which the firm establishes a physical presence abroad through acquisition of productive assets such as capital, technology, labor, land, plant, and equipment.

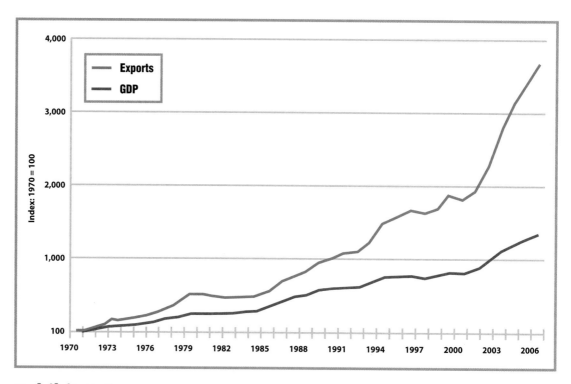

Exhibit 1.1   Comparing the Growth Rates of World GDP and World Exports

SOURCE: International Monetary Fund, *World Economic Outlook* database, April 2006 (www.imf.org).

Exhibit 1.2 identifies the leading nations involved in the exporting and importing of products (but not services)— that is, international merchandise trade. Panel (a) shows the total value of products traded in billions of U.S. dollars. Panel (b) shows the annual value of products traded as a percentage of each nation's GDP. While the United States is the leading country in terms of the absolute value of total merchandise trade, trade accounts for only 19 percent of its GDP. In contrast, merchandise trade is a much larger component of economic activity in countries such as Belgium (167 percent), the Netherlands (117 percent), and Germany (59 percent). These percentages show that some economies are very dependent on international trade relative to the value of all goods and services produced domestically. The same is true for countries such as Singapore, Hong Kong, South Korea, and Malaysia, because trade accounts for more than 100 percent of their GDPs. These countries are known as *entrepôt* economies because they import a large volume of products, some of which they process into higher value-added products, and some they simply re-export to other destinations. For example, Singapore is a major entrepôt, or depot, for petroleum products received from the Middle East, which it then exports to China and other destinations in Asia.

The Nature of International Investment

Of the two types of investment flows between nations—portfolio investment and foreign direct investment—we are concerned primarily with FDI, because it is the ultimate stage of internationalization, and encompasses the widest range of international business involvement. FDI is the foreign entry strategy practiced by the most internationally active firms. Companies usually engage in FDI for the long term, and retain partial or complete ownership of the assets they acquire.

Firms undertake FDI for a variety of strategic reasons, including: (1) to set up manufacturing or assembly operations, or other physical facilities; (2) to

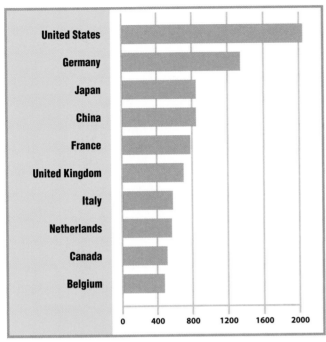

(a) Total annual value of products trade (exports + imports) in billions of U.S. dollars

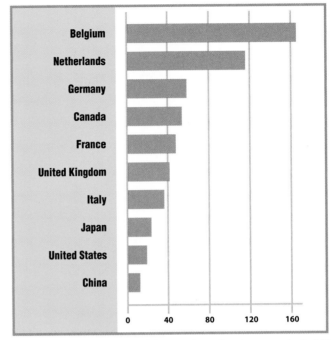

(b) Total annual value of products trade (exports + imports) as a percentage of nation's GDP

Exhibit 1.2 Leading Countries in International Merchandise Trade

SOURCE: World Trade Organization (www.wto.org); data for 2005. © 2006 World Trade Organization.

open a sales or representative office or other facility to conduct marketing or distribution activities; or (3) to establish a regional headquarters. In the process, the firm establishes a new legal business entity, subject to the regulations of the host government.

FDI is especially common among large, resourceful companies with substantial international operations. For instance, many European and U.S. firms have invested in China, India, and Russia to manufacture or assemble products, taking advantage of low-cost labor and other resources in these countries. At the same time, companies from these rapidly developing economies have begun to invest in western markets. For example, India's Mittal Steel Co. acquired the Luxembourg-based Arcelor SA in 2006, creating a $38 billion conglomerate—the world's largest steel company. Also, the Russian oil and gas firm Lukos recently established thousands of service stations in the United States and Europe.

Exhibit 1.3 shows the dramatic growth of FDI into various world regions since the 1980s. The exhibit reveals that the dollar volume of FDI has grown immensely since the 1980s, especially into advanced (or developed) economies such as Japan, Europe, and North America. FDI inflows were interrupted in 2001 by the worldwide panic that ensued following the September 11 terrorist attacks in the United States, but the trend remains strong and, over time, is growing. Of particular significance is the growth of FDI into *developing economies*, nations with lower incomes, less-developed industrial base, and less investment capital than advanced economies. Most of the developing economies are located in parts of Africa, Asia, and Latin America. Despite poor income levels, developing economies collectively comprise a substantial and growing proportion of international trade and investment activities. The ability to invest in other countries provides customers in both developing and advanced economies with a wider selection of products and services at lower prices. Living standards of billions of people are better because of international trade and investment activities.

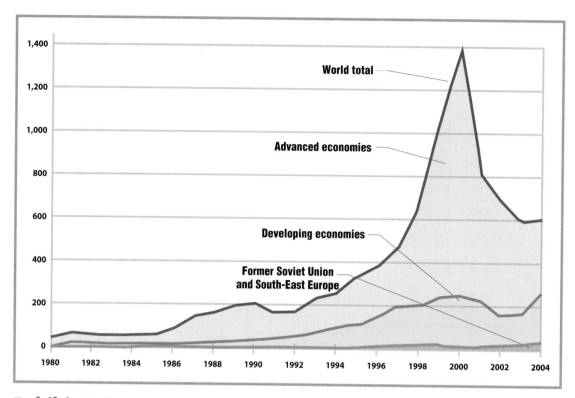

Exhibit 1.3   Foreign Direct Investment (FDI) Inflows into World Regions (in Billions of U.S. Dollars per Year)

SOURCE: UNCTAD, World Investment Report, United Nations, New York, 2005 at www.unctad.org. The United Nations is the author of the original material. Used with permission.

Services as Well as Products

Traditionally, international trade and investment have been regarded as the domain of companies that make and sell products—tangible merchandise such as clothing, computers, and cars. Today, firms that produce *services* (intangibles) are key international business players as well. Services are deeds, performances, or efforts performed directly by people working in banks, consulting firms, hotels, airlines, construction companies, retailers, and countless other firms in the services sector. For instance, advertising for the Procter & Gamble products that you purchased may have been created by Saatchi & Saatchi, headquartered in the United Kingdom. If you own a house, the mortgage may be underwritten by the Dutch bank ABN Amro. Perhaps you eat lunch in a cafeteria owned by the French firm Sodexho, which manages the food and beverage operations on numerous university campuses. In the United States and several European countries, travel and tourism are now the number one source of revenue from foreigners.

International trade in services accounts for about one quarter of all international trade and is growing rapidly. In recent years, services trade has been growing faster than products trade. Exhibit 1.4 identifies the leading countries in total international services trade, including both exports and imports. Panel (a) shows the total annual value of services trade in billions of U.S. dollars. Panel (b) shows the total annual value of services trade as a percentage of each nation's GDP. As with products, larger advanced economies account for the greatest proportion of world services trade. This is expected, because these tend to be postindustrial, service-based economies. Compare the value of mer-

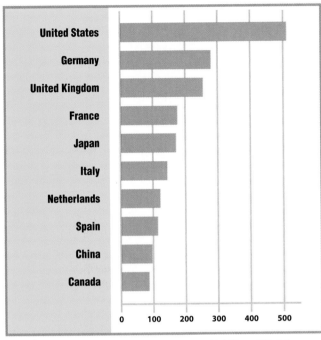

(a) Total annual value of services trade (exports + imports) in billions of U.S. dollars

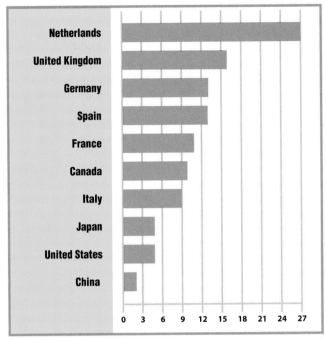

(b) Total annual value of services trade (exports + imports) as a percentage of nation's GDP

Exhibit 1.4 Leading Countries in International Services Trade

SOURCE: © 2006 World Trade Organization.

chandise trade in Exhibit 1.2 with the value of services trade in Exhibit 1.4 for each country. Even though trade in services is rapidly rising, the absolute value of merchandise trade is still several times larger than the value of services trade. One reason is that services face greater challenges and barriers in cross-border trade than merchandise goods.

Not all services can be exported. As examples, you cannot export the construction work to build a house, repair work done on your car, or the experience of eating a meal in a restaurant—even though some services can be digitized and moved across borders. Most services can be offered internationally only by establishing a physical presence abroad through direct investment. Firms employ FDI to set up restaurants, retail stores, and other physical facilities, through which they sell trillions of dollars worth of services abroad every year.

There are numerous industries in the services sector with strong potential for internationalization. The largest auction-based retailer on the Internet is eBay. The firm earned over 6 billion dollars in 2006, of which about 40 percent came from international sales. The company expects most future revenue growth will come from abroad. When developing its business in India, eBay acquired the Mumbai-based e-retailer Baazee. This acquisition followed eBay's expansion into China, Korea, and Europe.[2] With more than 1 billion people, India is the world's second most populous nation (China is the first, with 1.3 billion). There are an estimated 40 million Internet users in India, compared with 132 million in China and 210 million in the United States. However, the number of Indian consumers who shop online is growing rapidly.

Exhibit 1.5 illustrates the diversity of service sectors that are internationalizing—extending their reach beyond the countries where they are based. If you are considering a career in international business, keep these industries in mind.

Exhibit 1.5

Service Industry Sectors That Are
Rapidly Internationalizing

SOURCE: International Trade Administration,
Washington, DC: U.S. Department of Commerce.

Industry	Representative Activities	Representative Companies
Architectural, construction, and engineering	Construction, electric power utilities, design, engineering services for airports, hospitals, dams	ABB, Bechtel Group, Halliburton, Kajima, Philip Holzman, Skanska AB
Banking, finance, and insurance	Banks, insurance, risk evaluation, management	Citigroup, CIGNA, Barclays, HSBC, Ernst & Young
Education, training, and publishing	Management training, technical training, English language training	Berlitz, Kumon Math & Reading Centers, NOVA, Pearson, Elsevier
Entertainment	Movies, recorded music, Internet- based entertainment	Time Warner, Sony, Virgin, MGM
Information services	E-commerce, e-mail, funds transfer, data interchange, data processing, network services, professional computer services	Infosys, EDI, Hitachi, Qualcomm, Cisco
Professional business services	Accounting, advertising, legal, management consulting	Leo Burnett, EYLaw, McKinsey, A.T. Kearney, Booz Allen Hamilton, Cap Gemini
Transportation	Aviation, ocean shipping, railroads, trucking, airports	Maersk, Sante Fe, Port Authority of New Jersey, SNCF (French railroads)
Travel and tourism	Transportation, lodging, food and beverage, recreation, travel on aircraft, ocean carriers, and railways	Carlson Wagonlit, Marriott, British Airways

The International Financial Services Sector

International banking and financial services are among the most internationally active service industries. The explosive growth of investment and financial flows beginning in the 1970s led to the development of capital markets worldwide. Much of this growth is due to two factors: money flowing across national borders into portfolio investments and pension funds, and the internationalization of banks. The activities of banks and other financial institutions help increase economic activity in developing economies by increasing the amount of cheap, local investment capital, stimulating development of local financial markets, and encouraging people to save money.

International banking is flourishing in such regions as the Middle East, where the return on equity in Saudi Arabia, for instance, exceeds 20 percent (as compared to 15 percent in the United States and much less in France and Germany). Citibank, Deutsche Bank, BNP Paribas, and other international banks are thriving because of high oil prices, a boom in consumer banking, and low taxes. National Commercial Bank, the biggest bank in the region, calculates that non interest-bearing deposits comprise nearly 50 percent of total deposits in Saudi Arabia. Banks lend this free money to companies and consumers at high margins. Banks bypass Islamic rules against paying interest by structuring loans as partnerships.[3]

How Does International Business Differ from Domestic Business?

Firms engaged in international business operate in business environments characterized by unique economic conditions, political systems, laws and regulations, and national culture. For example, the economic environment of India differs sharply from that of Germany. The legal environment of Saudi Arabia does not resemble that of Japan. The cultural environment of China is very distinct from that of Canada. Not only does the firm find itself in less familiar surroundings than it does domestically, it encounters many *uncontrollable variables*—factors over which the firm has little control. These factors introduce new or elevated types of business risks for the firm.

The Four Risks in Internationalization

Internationalizing firms are routinely exposed to four major types of risk, as illustrated in Exhibit 1.6: cross-cultural risk, country risk, currency risk, and commercial risk. The firm must manage these risks to avoid financial loss or product failures.

Cross-cultural risk refers to a situation or event where a cultural miscommunication puts some human value at stake. Cross-cultural risk is posed by differences in language, lifestyles, mindsets, customs, and/or religion. Values unique to a culture

Cross-cultural risk A situation or event where a cultural miscommunication puts some human value at stake.

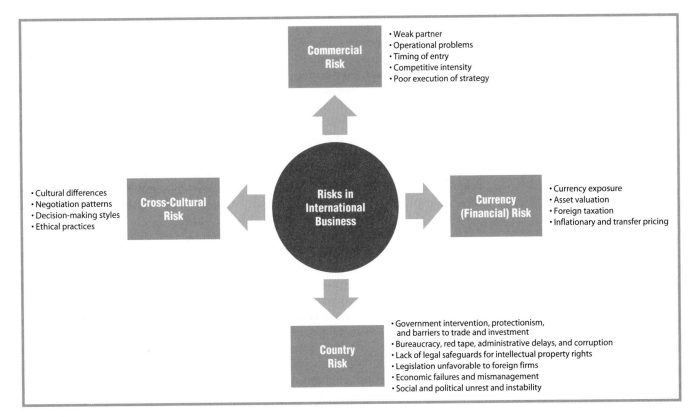

Exhibit 1.6 The Four Risks of International Business

tend to be long-lasting and transmitted from one generation to the next. These values influence the mindset and work style of employees and the shopping patterns of buyers. Foreign customer characteristics differ significantly from those of buyers in the home market. Language is a critical dimension of culture. In addition to facilitating communication, language is a window on people's value systems and living conditions. For example, Eskimo languages have various words for "snow" while the South American Aztecs used the same basic word stem for snow, ice, and cold. When translating from one language to another, it is often difficult to find words that convey the same meanings. For example, a one-word equivalent to *aftertaste* does not exist in many languages. Such challenges impede effective communication and cause misunderstandings. Miscommunication due to cultural differences gives rise to inappropriate business strategies and ineffective relations with customers. We examine cross-cultural risk in greater detail in Chapter 5.

Country risk Potentially adverse effects on company operations and profitability caused by developments in the political, legal, and economic environment in a foreign country.

Country risk (also known as *political risk*) refers to the potentially adverse effects on company operations and profitability caused by developments in the political, legal, and economic environment in a foreign country. Country risk includes the possibility of foreign government intervention in firms' business activities. For example, governments may restrict access to markets, impose bureaucratic procedures on business transactions, and limit the amount of earned income that firms can bring home from foreign operations. The degree of government intervention in commercial activities varies from country to country. For instance, Singapore and Ireland are characterized by substantial economic freedom—that is, a fairly liberal economic environment. By contrast, the Chinese and Russian governments intervene regularly in business affairs.[4] Country risk also includes laws and regulations that potentially hinder company operations and performance. Critical legal dimensions include property rights, intellectual property protection, product liability, and taxation policies. Nations also experience potentially harmful economic conditions, often due to high inflation, national debt, and unbalanced international trade. We examine country risk in greater detail in Chapter 6.

Currency risk Risk of adverse fluctuations in exchange rates.

Currency risk (also referred to as *financial risk*) refers to the risk of adverse fluctuations in exchange rates. Fluctuation is common for exchange rates, or the value of one currency in terms of another. Currency risk arises because international transactions are often conducted in more than one national currency. When Frankfort, Michigan-based fruit processor Graceland Fruit, Inc. exports dried cherries to confectioneries in Japan, it will normally be paid in Japanese yen. When currencies fluctuate significantly, however, the value of the firm's assets, earnings, and operating income can be reduced. The cost of importing parts or components used in manufacturing finished products can increase dramatically if the value of the currency in which the imports are denominated rises sharply. Inflation and other harmful economic conditions experienced in one country may have immediate consequences for exchange rates due to the growing interconnectedness of national economies. We elaborate on country risk in Chapters 10, 17, and 19.

Commercial risk Firm's potential loss or failure from poorly developed or executed business strategies, tactics, or procedures.

Commercial risk refers to the firm's potential loss or failure from poorly developed or executed business strategies, tactics, or procedures. Managers may make poor choices in such areas as the selection of business partners, timing of market entry, pricing, creation of product features, and promotional themes. While such failures also exist in domestic business, the consequences are usually more costly when they are committed abroad. For example, in domestic business a company may terminate a poorly performing distributor simply with advance notice. In a foreign market, however, terminating business partners can prove costly due to regulations that protect local firms. Marketing inferior or harmful products, falling short of customer expectations, or failing to provide adequate customer service may harm the firm's reputation and international performance.

The four types of international business risks are omnipresent; the firm may encounter them around every corner. While these risks cannot be avoided, they can be anticipated and managed. Experienced international firms conduct research to anticipate potential risks, understand their implications, and take proactive action to reduce their effects. In fact, this book is dedicated to providing you, the future manager, with a good understanding of the risks as well as managerial skills and strategies to effectively counter them.

Some international risks are extremely challenging. An example is the East Asian economic crisis of the late 1990s. Between January and July of 1998, the currencies of several East Asian countries lost between 35 and 70 percent of their value, leading to the collapse of national stock markets, deepening trade deficits, and suspension of normal business activity. Political and social unrest soon followed in Indonesia, Malaysia, South Korea, Thailand, and the Philippines. In all, the East Asian economic crisis generated substantial commercial, currency, and country risks. Nevertheless, some farsighted firms foresaw these challenges and proactively redeployed key resources to minimize their negative effects.

National differences require managers to formulate approaches tailored to conditions in each country where the firm does business. Differences typically require firms to substantially alter their products and services. For instance, Citibank varies its banking practices around the world; approaches for loaning funds must conform to unique regulatory and cultural conditions from Africa, to Asia, to the Middle East. Nestlé must alter the packaging and ingredients it uses for the breakfast cereals that it sells abroad. For example, compared to North Americans, Asians generally prefer less sugar in their cereals. McDonald's varies the type of menu items that it sells in its restaurants around the world.

Who Participates in International Business?

What types of organizations are active in international business? Among the most important are *focal firms*, the firms that directly initiate and implement international business activity. Let's briefly highlight two types of focal firms in international business: the multinational enterprise (MNE) and small and medium-sized enterprise (SME).

Multinational Enterprise (MNE)

Multinational enterprises (also known as multinational corporations) have historically been the most important type of focal firm. A **multinational enterprise** is a large company with substantial resources that performs various business activities through a network of subsidiaries and affiliates located in multiple countries. One of the hallmarks of MNEs is that they tend to carry out R&D, procurement, manufacturing, and marketing activities wherever in the world it makes most economic sense. In addition to a home office or headquarters, the typical MNE owns a worldwide network of subsidiaries. It collaborates with numerous suppliers and independent business partners abroad (sometimes termed *affiliates*).

Typical MNEs include Caterpillar, Kodak, Nokia, Samsung, Unilever, Citibank, Vodafone, Carrefour, Bechtel, Four Seasons Hotels, Disney, DHL, and Nippon Life Insurance. The most well-known multinational firms are ranked, based on international sales revenue, in annual listings such as *Fortune* magazine's *Global 500*. In recent years, the largest MNEs are found in the oil industry (such as Exxon Mobil, Royal Dutch Shell, and BP) and the automotive industry (General Motors, Renault-Nissan, Toyota, and Ford), as well as retailing (Wal-Mart). Exhibit 1.7 shows the geographic distribution of the world's leading MNEs. The size of each circle is indicated by the total revenues of the MNEs headquartered in a particular country, as ranked in Fortune *Global 500*. For example, the United States hosts 170 MNEs, whose combined revenues amount to $6,645 billion.

While MNEs are among the leading participants, international business is not the domain of large, resourceful firms alone. Many **small and medium-sized enterprises (SMEs)** participate as well. In the United States, an SME is a company

Multinational enterprise (MNE) A large company with substantial resources that performs various business activities through a network of subsidiaries and affiliates located in multiple countries.

Small and Medium-sized Enterprise (SME) A company with 500 or fewer employees in the United States, although this number may need to be adjusted downward for other countries.

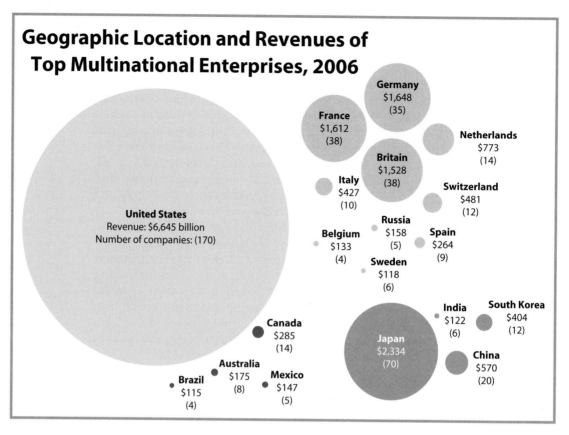

Geographic Location and Revenues of Top Multinational Enterprises, 2006

Germany
$1,648
(35)

France
$1,612
(38)

Netherlands
$773
(14)

Britain
$1,528
(38)

Italy
$427
(10)

Switzerland
$481
(12)

United States
Revenue: $6,645 billion
Number of companies: (170)

Russia
$158
(5)

Belgium
$133
(4)

Spain
$264
(9)

Sweden
$118
(6)

India
$122
(6)

South Korea
$404
(12)

Canada
$285
(14)

Japan
$2,334
(70)

China
$570
(20)

Australia
$175
(8)

Mexico
$147
(5)

Brazil
$115
(4)

Exhibit 1.7   Geographic Location of Multinational Enterprises, 2006

SOURCE: *Fortune*, "Fortune Global 500" (money.cnn.com/fortune). FORTUNE graphic by Samuel Vesasco/5W Infographic from "Tale of 229 Cities," pages 96–97, *Fortune*, July 24, 2007. © 2007 Time Inc. All rights reserved.

with 500 or fewer employees, although this number may need to be adjusted downward for other countries. In addition to being smaller players in their respective economies, SMEs tend to have limited managerial and other resources, and primarily use exporting to expand internationally. In most nations, SMEs constitute between 90 and 95 percent of all firms.

With the globalization of markets, advances in various technologies, and other facilitating factors, more and more SMEs are pursuing business opportunities around the world. SMEs account for about one third of exports from Asia and about a quarter of exports from the affluent countries in Europe and North America. In selected countries such as Italy, South Korea, and China, SMEs contribute more than 50 percent of total national exports.[5]

Born global firm A young entrepreneurial company that initiates international business activity very early in its evolution, moving rapidly into foreign markets.

One type of contemporary international SME is the **born global firm**, a young entrepreneurial company that initiates international business activity very early in its evolution, moving rapidly into foreign markets. Born globals are found in advanced economies, such as Australia and Japan, and in emerging markets, such as China and India. One example is DLP, Inc., a leading manufacturer of disposable medical products for heart surgery. DLP began international operations as a young firm, acquiring nearly a third of total sales from abroad. The founder spent much of DLP's early years traveling around Europe and Asia, doggedly developing markets. From their earliest days, born globals established much of their business activities overseas.

The main difference between born globals and large MNEs is that born globals internationalize at or near their founding, despite the scarce resources typical of new firms. The emergence of born globals has been facilitated by information and communications technologies, and globe-spanning transportation systems that make international trade easier for all firms.

International business requires specialized knowledge, commitment of resources, and considerable time to develop foreign business partnerships. How do SMEs succeed in international business despite resource limitations? First, compared to large MNEs, smaller firms are often more innovative, more adaptable, and have quicker response times when it comes to implementing new ideas and technologies and meeting customer needs. Second, SMEs are better able to serve niche markets around the world that hold little interest for MNEs. Third, smaller firms are usually avid users of new information and communication technologies, including the Internet. Fourth, as they usually lack substantial resources, smaller firms minimize overhead or fixed investments. Instead, they rely on external facilitators such as FedEx and DHL, as well as independent distributors in foreign markets. Fifth, smaller firms tend to thrive on private knowledge that they possess or produce. They access and mobilize resources through their cross-border knowledge networks, or their international social capital.[6]

In each chapter, the feature entitled *Global Trend* profiles an important new development in international business. The first *Global Trend* features Diesel, an SME that eventually grew into a large firm.

> GLOBAL TREND

DIESEL S.p.A.: A Smaller Firm's Smashing Success in International Markets

For the global youth culture, Diesel's fashions are highly preferred to other brands. Founded in Italy in 1978, Diesel started out as an SME, and eventually grew to achieve annual sales of more than $1 billion (U.S.), 85 percent of which come from abroad. Diesel produces unusual but popular men's and women's casual wear. Competing with Donna Karan and Tommy Hilfiger, Diesel wear is futuristic. Its jeans come in exotic shades and styles. Diesel management sees the world as a single, borderless macroculture, and Diesel staff includes an assortment of personalities from all parts of the globe who create an unpredictable, dynamic vitality and energy. The firm focuses on design and marketing, leaving the production of jeans to subcontractors.

Diesel is Europe's hottest blue jeans brand, and has expanded its distribution to over 80 countries through department stores and specialty retailers, as well as some 200 Diesel-owned stores from Paris to Miami to Tokyo. At over $100 a pair,

Diesel jeans are expensive for many, but controversial advertising has propelled the company to huge international success. The company's advertising has featured sumo wrestlers kissing, a row of chimpanzees giving the fascist salute, and inflatable naked dolls in a board meeting with a hugely overweight CEO. Its ads poke fun at death, obesity, murder, and do-gooders. Some people in the United States see the prankish campaigns as politically incorrect. For instance, under pressure from activists, Diesel withdrew ads that applauded smoking and gun ownership with slogans such as "145 cigarettes a day will give you that sexy voice and win new friends." Another ad featured nuns in blue jeans below the copy: "Pure, virginal 100% cotton. Soft and yet miraculously strong."

If Starbucks can charge several dollars for coffee, then Diesel executives believe they can persuade consumers to pay $108 for its jeans. Diesel was one of the first companies to have a major Internet presence

(www.diesel.com), selling jeans via an online virtual store. Diesel's web advertising is hip, with a powerful, market-friendly message that drives its popularity to youth worldwide. The firm introduces some 1,500 new designs every 6 months, and employs a multicultural team of young designers who travel the globe for inspiration and weave their impressions into the next collection.

Diesel is a classic success story in international business by a smaller firm. Its strategy is instructive for other marketers of jeans such as Kitson, Lucky Brand, Mavi Jeans, and 7 For All Mankind.

Sources: Diesel's online Web site at www.diesel.com; Edmondson, Gail. (2003). "Diesel is Smoking But Can Its Provocative Ads Keep Sales Growth Hot?", *Business Week*, February 10, p. 64; Hoover's online Web site for Whirlpool Corporation, www.hoover's.com; Helliker, Kevin. (1998). "Teen Retailing: The Underground Taste Makers—Is Diesel Apparel a Bit Too Trendy for Its Own Good?, *Wall Street Journal*, December 9, p. B1; OECD. (1997). *Globalization and Small and Medium Enterprises (SMEs)*. Paris: OECD; Sansoni, Sylvia. (1996). "Full Steam Ahead for Diesel; Will Its Pricey Jeans and Outrageous Ads Succeed in the U.S.?" *Business Week*, April 29, pp. 58–60.

Non-governmental Organizations (NGOs)

In addition to profit-seeking focal firms in international business, there are numerous *non-profit organizations* that conduct cross-border activities. These include charitable groups and *non-governmental organizations (NGOs)*. They pursue special causes and serve as an advocate for the arts, education, politics, religion, and research. They operate internationally to either conduct their activities or raise funds. Examples of nonprofit organizations include the Bill and Melinda Gates Foundation and the British Wellcome Trust, which support health and educational initiatives. CARE is an international non-profit organization dedicated to reducing poverty.

Many MNEs operate charitable foundations that support various initiatives worldwide. GlaxoSmithKline (GSK), the giant pharmaceutical firm, operates a number of small country-based foundations in Canada, the Czech Republic, France, Italy, Romania, Spain, and the United States. GSK developed Barretstown in Ireland and L'Envol in France as residential camps where seriously ill children can have fun and develop self-confidence. GSK promotes healthy eating and exercise to Slovakian children living on urban housing estates; healthcare for homeless and abandoned children in Spain; and the integration of children with disabilities into Russian society. GSK developed the Integrated Management of Childhood Illnesses initiative in Ethiopia, aiming to reduce childhood deaths from preventable and treatable conditions such as malaria, measles, and malnutrition. In Vietnam, GSK supports the "500 Ethnic Midwives" initiative to provide birthing support to communities in poor rural areas with limited access to health care services.

Why Do Firms Pursue Internationalization Strategies?

Firms pursue internationalization strategies for a variety of reasons. Firms often have more than one motive for international expansion. Some motives are strategic in nature, while others are reactive. An example of a strategic, or proactive, motive is to tap foreign market opportunities or acquire new knowledge. An example of a reactive motive is the need to serve a key customer who has expanded abroad. Nine specific motivations include:

The drive for market diversification beyond London led to ATMs appearing throughout the world, including Japan.

1. *Seek opportunities for growth through market diversification.* Substantial market potential exists outside the home country. Many large and small companies, including Gillette, Siemens, Sony, and Biogen, derive more than half of their sales from abroad. When they diversify into foreign markets, firms can generate sales and profit opportunities that cannot be matched at home. Internationalization can also extend the marketable life of products or services that have reached their maturity in the home country. One example is the internationalization of automatic teller machines (ATMs). The first ATM was installed outside a north London branch of Barclays Bank in 1967. The machines were next adopted in the United States and Japan. As the growth of ATMs began to slow in these countries, they were marketed throughout the rest of the world. Today there are more than 1.5 million ATMs worldwide, with one installed somewhere every seven minutes or so.

2. *Earn higher margins and profits.* For many types of products and services, market growth in mature economies is sluggish or flat. Competition is often intense, forcing firms to get by on slim profit margins. By contrast, most foreign markets may be underserved (typical of high-growth emerging markets) or not served at all (typical of developing economies). Less intense competition, combined with strong market demand, implies that companies can command higher margins for their offerings. For example, compared to their respective home markets, bathroom fixture manufacturers American Standard and Toto (of Japan) have found a more favorable competitive environment in rapidly industrializing countries such as Indonesia, Mexico, and Vietnam. Just imagine the demand for bathroom fixtures in the thousands of office buildings and residential complexes that are going up from Shanghai to Singapore!

3. *Gain new ideas about products, services, and business methods.* International markets are characterized by tough competitors and demanding customers with various needs. Unique foreign environments expose firms to new ideas for products, processes, and business methods. The experience of doing business abroad helps firms acquire new knowledge for improving organizational effectiveness and efficiency. For example, just-in-time inventory techniques were refined by Toyota and then adopted by other manufacturers all over the world. Several of Toyota's foreign suppliers learned about just-in-time practices from the Japanese firm, and then applied those methods to their own manufacturing operations.

4. *Better serve key customers that have relocated abroad.* In a global economy, many firms internationalize to better serve clients that have moved into foreign markets. For example, when Toyota opened its first factory in the United Kingdom, many Japanese auto parts suppliers followed, establishing their own operations there.

5. *Be closer to supply sources, benefit from global sourcing advantages, or gain flexibility in the sourcing of products.* Companies in extractive industries such as petroleum, mining, and forestry establish international operations where these raw materials are located. One example is the aluminum producer Alcoa, which locates mining operations abroad to extract aluminum's base mineral bauxite from mines in Brazil, Guinea, Jamaica, and elsewhere. In addition, some firms internationalize to gain flexibility from a greater variety of supply bases. For instance, Dell Computer has assembly facilities in Asia, Europe, and the Americas that allow management to quickly shift production from one region to another. Compared to less agile rivals, this flexibility provides Dell with *competitive advantages*—a distinctive competency that provides the firm with superior competitive positioning. In particular, it allows the firm to skillfully manage currency exchange rate fluctuations.

6. *Gain access to lower-cost or better-value factors of production.* Internationalization enables the firm to access capital, technology, managerial talent, labor, and land at lower costs, higher-quality, or better overall value at locations worldwide. For example, some Taiwanese computer manufacturers have established subsidiaries in the United States to access low-cost capital. The United States is home to numerous capital sources in the high-tech sector, such as stock exchanges and venture capitalists, which have attracted countless firms from abroad seeking funds. More commonly, firms venture abroad in search of skilled or low-cost labor. For instance, the Japanese firm, Canon, relocated much of its production to China to profit from that country's inexpensive, productive workforce.

7. *Develop economies of scale in sourcing, production, marketing, and R&D.* Economies of scale refer to the reduction of the per-unit cost of manufacturing and marketing due to operating at high volume. For example, manufacturing the 100,000th DVD player on a production line is always cheaper than manufacturing the first one. By expanding internationally, the firm greatly increases the size of its customer base, thereby increasing the volume of products that it manufactures. On a per-unit-of-output basis, the greater the volume of production, the lower the total cost. Economies of scale are also present in R&D, sourcing, marketing, distribution, and after-sales service.

8. *Confront international competitors more effectively or thwart the growth of competition in the home market.* International competition is substantial and increasing, with multinational competitors invading markets worldwide. The firm can enhance its competitive positioning by confronting competitors in international markets or preemptively entering a competitor's home markets to destabilize and curb its growth. One example is Caterpillar's preemptive entry into Japan just as its main rival in the earthmoving equipment industry, Komatsu, was getting started in the early 1970s. Caterpillar's preemptive move hindered Komatsu's international expansion for at least a decade. Had it not moved proactively to stifle Komatsu's growth in Japan, Komatsu's home market, Caterpillar would certainly have had to face a more potent rival sooner.

9. *Invest in a potentially rewarding relationship with a foreign partner.* Firms often have long-term strategic reasons for venturing abroad. Joint ventures or project-based alliances with key foreign players can lead to the development of new products, early positioning in future key markets, or other long-term, profit-making opportunities. For example, Black and Decker entered a joint venture with Bajaj, an Indian retailer, to position itself for expected long-term sales in the huge Indian market. The French computer firm Groupe Bull partnered with Toshiba in Japan to gain insights for developing the next generation of information technology.

At the broadest level, companies internationalize to enhance competitive advantage and to seek growth and profit opportunities. Throughout this book, we explore the environment within which firms seek these opportunities, as well as discuss the strategies and managerial skills necessary for achieving international business success.

Why Should You Study International Business?

There are many reasons to study international business. We can examine the reasons from the perspectives of the global economy, the national economy, the firm, and you as a future manager.

Facilitator of the Global Economy and Interconnectedness

A young workforce in China and other emerging markets is causing faster integration of these economies with the rest of the world.

International business is transforming the world as never before. The decades following the establishment of the General Agreement on Tariffs and Trade (GATT) in 1947 witnessed unprecedented growth in international trade and investment. Companies focused more and more on the mass production of products and services to meet insatiable world demand.

Since the 1980s, *emerging markets* provided new impetus to worldwide economic interconnectedness. These fast-growth developing economies—some two dozen countries including Brazil, India, China, and Poland—are experiencing substantial market liberalization, privatization, and industrialization, which are fueling global economic transformation. These emerging markets, located on every continent, are gradually breaking away from the stagnation typical of developing economies. Collectively, the emerging markets are home to the largest proportion of world population and participate increasingly in foreign trade. In the opening vignette, Julie sampled products from several emerging markets, including Argentina, Hungary, and Mexico.

Along with market globalization, another megatrend, *advances in technology*, has also served to transform the global economy. The rise of information and communication technologies, as well as production and process technologies, has dramatically reduced the cost of conducting business with customers located abroad. The Internet and e-commerce make international business increasingly imperative for firms of all sizes and resource levels. Technological advances both facilitate, and are facilitated by, globalization. They allow globalization to progress more rapidly. Globalization, in turn, accelerates the development of the latest technologies.

Contributor to National Economic Well-Being

International business contributes to economic prosperity and standards of living, provides interconnectedness to the world economy and access to a range of valuable intermediate and finished products and services, and helps countries use their resources more efficiently. Consequently, governments have become more willing to open their borders to foreign trade and investment.

International trade is a critical engine for job creation. It is estimated that every $1 billion increase in exports creates more than 20,000 new jobs. In the United States, cross-border trade directly supports at least 12 million jobs. One of every seven dollars of U.S. sales is made abroad. One of every three U.S. farm acres and one of every six U.S. jobs is producing for export markets. Generally, exporting firms create jobs faster than nonexporting firms. Wages and benefits for export-related jobs are better, on average, than those for nonexporting jobs.[7]

There is a strong relationship between a nation's level of prosperity and its participation in cross-border trade and investment. International business is both a cause and a result of increasing national prosperity. It is helping to spread national prosperity and abundance beyond advanced economies into developing economies. Nations once suffering from economic stagnation are now increasingly prosperous. For instance, China, India, and Eastern European nations are active international traders. The proportion of affluent citizens in these countries is rapidly growing. In terms of material gain, households in many developing economies have recently experienced huge increases in the ownership of televisions, refrigerators, and other mass-produced products. While these gains are attributable to various causes, the benefits of free exchange of products, services, capital, and technology among nations are paramount.

International trade and investment can also help reduce poor economic conditions in developing economies. The rapid economic growth of emerging countries is stimulating solid gains in living standards. Growing prosperity is accompanied by gains in literacy rates, nutrition, and health care. Trade and investment help to promote freedom and democracy and may reduce the likelihood of cross-border conflict. The world has recently entered a new era of international tension, sometimes accompanied by terrorism. International business can help to limit such tension, by reducing world poverty and increasing interactions that help soothe relations among nations.[8]

The development of the European Union (EU) is helping to raise living standards of millions of EU citizens, particularly in Eastern Europe. The EU is making international trade

International trade is causing faster diffusion of consumer products and brands.

and investment much easier for European businesses. It is transforming Europe into a new powerhouse in global trade.

Cross-border business also helps integrate world economies. The North American Free Trade Agreement (NAFTA), launched in 1994, integrates the economies of Canada, Mexico, and the United States in a giant market of roughly 450 million consumers. Multicountry collaboration in the automobile industry and other sectors created good-paying jobs and helped make Mexico one of the top U.S. trading partners. Following NAFTA's launch, the volume of trade among the three countries increased dramatically, helping to improve living standards for millions of people. In Mexico, NAFTA led to substantially higher wages, better social systems, and higher employment rates.[9] Recently, a new accord was launched between the United States and Costa Rica, El Salvador, Guatemala, Honduras, Nicaragua, and the Dominican Republic. Known as the Dominican Republic Central American Free Trade Agreement (DR-CAFTA), it promises to invigorate the economies of the member countries.

A Competitive Advantage for the Firm

To sustain a competitive advantage in the global economy, firms must readily participate in cross-border business and acquire the necessary skills, knowledge, and competence. Procter & Gamble sells shampoo, disposable diapers, and other consumer products in more than 150 countries. MTV broadcasts its programming in some 140 countries. Nestlé sells its food and beverage products worldwide, obtaining nearly all its revenue from foreign operations. As these examples imply, going international offers countless opportunities for firms to increase revenue. Young companies can achieve substantial growth by targeting new markets and opportunities to earn additional profits. Foreign markets are likely to generate favorable outcomes for the firm in terms of sales, profit margins, growth, and new knowledge.

In addition, firms can maximize the efficiency of their operations through international business. Companies secure cost-effective factor inputs by establishing manufacturing in emerging markets like Brazil, Mexico, and Poland, or sourcing from foreign suppliers. For example, Microsoft cuts the costs of its operations by having much of its software written in India. Renault achieves efficiency by assembling cars at low-cost factories in Romania.

International business also allows firms to access critical resources that may be unavailable at home. It helps firms reduce the costs of new product development, after-sales service, and other critical business activities. Companies access foreign sources of information and knowledge that provide the basis for future R&D, improved production and administrative processes, and other innovations. Internationalization broadens the options for dealing with competitors, offering opportunities to make globally strategic moves and countermoves that help the firm compete more effectively with domestic and foreign rivals.[10]

An Opportunity for Global Corporate Citizenship

As firms increasingly venture into international markets, they need to learn how to become global citizens. Beyond delivering value-added products, technology, and other benefits to their customers, they need to be responsive to the needs of other stakeholder groups, including the media, local communities, academics, and the nonprofit sector. In foreign markets, firms must try in earnest to meet local expectations with respect to labor and environmental standards, accepted codes of conduct, and the overall welfare of the society that hosts them.

As businesses operating in a host society, internationalizing firms are always under public scrutiny. Their actions are closely monitored and held to local ethical standards. Firms with iconic global brands such as Coca-Cola, McDonald's, and Citibank are especially conspicuous. When consumers or other groups wish to express their discontent, say, with United States foreign policy, these firms may become favorite targets of public protests. Actions of internationalizing firms can also raise nationalistic sentiments. For example, when the news of United Arab Emirates-controlled firm Dubai Ports World winning a contract to operate some United States ports hit the media in 2006, the U.S. Congress acted swiftly to block the deal in response to strong disapproval from the public.

Rather than being caught red-handed or off guard, firms are proactively developing socially responsible policies and practices. For example, Starbucks recently announced that it will sell only coffee from growers certified by the Rain Forest Alliance, a global nonprofit organization that promotes the interests of coffee growers and the environment. Such multinational enterprises as Philips, Unilever, and Wal-Mart have announced practices that would help to enforce sustainable development. McDonald's has announced that it will only purchase beef from farmers who meet special standards on animal welfare and environmental practices. The firm also recently implemented a global ban on growth-promoting antibiotics in the poultry that it purchases. McDonald's is now publishing the nutritional content of its products in all the markets it operates. Its outlets in Britain, Germany, Sweden, and Austria sell only organic milk.[11] Clearly, internationally active firms must embed corporate citizenship into their strategic decisions, as well as their ongoing processes and practices.

Conspicuous global brands such as Coca-Cola are constantly under scrutiny.

A Competitive Advantage for You

Julie, the student in the opening vignette, is touched every day by a variety of international business transactions. She is considering a career in international business because she is starting to grasp its growing importance. She is beginning a path full of intrigue and excitement. While most international careers are based in one's home country, managers travel the world and meet people from various cultures and backgrounds. Traveling to countries such as Argentina, China, India, Poland, or South Africa can lead to exciting learning experiences and provide challenges.

Managers rising to the top of most of the world's leading corporations—AIG, ABB, Citigroup, Coca-Cola, Kellogg, McDonald's, Oracle, Nissan, and SAP—honed their managerial skills in international business. Working across national cultures exposed these managers to a range of enlightening experiences, new knowledge, novel ways of seeing the world, and various unusual challenges. Managers with extensive international experience are generally more confident, cosmopolitan, and better suited to meet the variety of challenges they may encounter throughout their careers. In short, acquiring knowledge and managerial skills in international business is not only exciting, challenging, and fun, but it is also a unique professional development opportunity.

In this text you will learn more about the merits of gaining international business proficiency, through the experiences of people like you, in a special feature called *Recent Grad in IB*. Read about Ashley Lumb, a recent graduate who is enjoying her early experiences in international business.

In Ashley Lumb's senior year in college, a six-week study abroad program to Europe sparked a strong desire for an international career. Following graduation, she worked as a Junior Analyst at KPMG in London, where she gained technical training and analytical skills. She wanted to work in the luxury goods industry in Europe and eventually took a 6-month contract job at Vins Sans Frontieres. VSF enrolled Ashley in its wine courses at company headquarters in the south of France. VSF imports wine from around the world and sells it exclusively to private yachts along the Cote D'Azur (French Riviera). Ashley gained experience in various innovative marketing methods. For instance, VSF attends yacht trade fairs and hosts wine tastings. The primary method for reaching the yachts, however, is by foot. VSF's marketing reps like Ashley scour the ports from San Remo, Italy, to St. Tropez, France, daily, speaking with yacht chefs, stewards, or captains about wine and distributing wine catalogs.

Ashley next worked as an account representative for The Ultimate Living Group in Monte Carlo, Monaco. The company caters to the corporate jet set that travels to Cannes for meetings and conferences. The key event of the year is the Cannes Film Festival.

Next, Ashley worked as a marketing associate at Made in Museum (MIM) in Rome, Italy. MIM specializes in the design, production, and delivery of authorized museum reproductions. It markets jewelry, sculptures, mosaics, and Etruscan pottery. Ashley organized the products into groups, and restructured the inventory and web site.

While in Italy, Ashley developed a passion for the fashion industry, so she decided to move to New York. Before leaving Italy, Ashley took a course at the prestigious Polimoda International Institute of Design and Marketing in Florence entitled "Business and Marketing in the Fashion Industry." In New York, Ashley worked at the headquarters of fashion houses Hermes and J. Crew. After two months, she leveraged the services of a bilingual recruiting agency, Euromonde Inc., to land a job at *Italian Vogue* magazine in Times Square to work as the U.S. advertising/marketing coordinator.

Ashley's Advice for an International Business Career

"Working abroad helped me sort through my career goals, as Europe offered a view into other industries that the United States lacked. I had the opportunity to sample different environments, and although they might seem far apart, I clearly saw a shared passion for exceptional products and dynamism. Back in the United States, my international experience is an impressive asset to prospective employers because it is valued as proof of one's ability to handle challenging assignments and work with people from diverse cultures and backgrounds."

Success Factors

"The two most important factors in working abroad were hard work and networking. I had to cast a wide net and meet a lot of people, send a lot of résumés, ask a lot of questions, and research the market. To keep myself afloat between assignments, I worked in jobs that were not quite as glamorous."

Ashley's majors: Finance, Marketing, and International business

Objectives: Adventure, international perspective, career growth, self-understanding, and the opportunity to learn foreign languages

Internships during college: Merrill Lynch

Jobs held since graduating:

- Junior Analyst at KPMG, London, England
- Marketing Representative, Vins Sans Frontieres; Nice, France
- Account Representative, The Ultimate Living Group: Monte Carlo, Monaco
- Marketing Associate, Made in Museum: Rome, Italy
- Advertising/Marketing Coordinator, Italian Vogue: New York, United States

Challenges

"The decision to work abroad carries some risks. After all, you're leaving much of what you know behind. What's more, I was stepping outside a clearly defined career path. The language barrier was always present. The work was almost always in English, though I did pick up Italian and a bit of French through classes and immersing myself in the culture."

What's Ahead?

"I'd like to continue my path in the fashion magazine industry and work in a merchandising, special events, or promotions capacity. I'm also studying French and eventually I would like to attend the graduate school ESSEC, Paris, to pursue an MBA program that specializes in international luxury goods management."

Whirlpool's Dramatic Turnaround Through Internationalization

Home appliance maker Whirlpool Corporation, headquartered in Benton Harbor, Michigan, generated over $19 billion in annual sales in 2006, an increase of 26 percent from the previous year. Key factors influencing this performance include the acquisition of the Maytag Corporation in 2006 and an increased global demand for its brands and innovative products. During the next several years, the company expects growth in Asia and Latin America to be significantly higher than in North America and Europe.

Whirlpool employs more than 80,000 employees in over 60 manufacturing and technology centers worldwide. The firm manufactures washers, dryers, refrigerators, dishwashers, freezers, ranges, compactors, and microwave ovens in 13 countries and sells them in 170 others under brand names such as Whirlpool, Maytag, Magic Chef, Jenn-Air, Amana, KitchenAid, Kenmore, Brastemp, and Bauknecht. Whirlpool generates almost 60 percent of its sales from North America, 25 percent from Europe, 15 percent from Latin America, and just 2 percent from Asia.

International Expansion

As the U.S. appliance market matured in the 1990s, Whirlpool faced intense domestic competition and more demanding buyers, resulting in lower profit margins. Meanwhile, international market trade barriers fell, consumer affluence grew, and capitalism flourished. Management realized that it could best deal with these threats and opportunities by undertaking a systematic program of internationalization. As a result, Whirlpool engaged in a series of moves over the next decade.

Whirlpool acquired the appliance business of Philips in Europe, 65 percent of Italian cooling compressor manufacturer Aspera, and purchased Poland's second largest appliance maker. In Eastern Europe, Whirlpool created subsidiaries to sell and service appliances in Bulgaria, Hungary, Romania, Russia, Slovakia, and the Czech Republic.

In China, Whirlpool formed a joint venture to produce air conditioners and established a corporate headquarters and product development/technology center in Shanghai. The company also opened regional offices in Hong Kong, New Delhi, and Singapore. In Mexico, Whirlpool acquired Vitromatic, a former joint venture partner in Mexico. It also developed low-cost versions of popular models to target customers in low-income markets in Latin America, China, and India.

Three factors have driven this global expansion. First, Whirlpool sought to reduce its costs of R&D, manufacturing, and service by locating plants and other operations in lower-cost locations such as China, Mexico, and Poland. Second, flat to declining sales growth in the United States pressured management to target sales in new markets abroad. Third, Whirlpool realized the firm's manufacturing and assembly operations would benefit from a more global approach. Management redesigned products with more standardized parts and ramped up marketing to make Whirlpool a globally recognized brand. The company integrated the activities of regional subsidiaries so that Whirlpool's most advanced expertise in appliance technology, production, and distribution could be shared with the firm's divisions worldwide.

Innovation

Whirlpool conducted an internal critical assessment in the late 1990s. It became apparent that a consumer walking into any appliance store anywhere in the world would witness a "sea of white" appliances with little differentiation, even between manufacturers. The industry became known as the "white goods business." Consumers perceived the products as commodities, which offered little differential advantage and commanded ever lower prices due to increasing competition.

In 1999, Whirlpool management launched a major campaign to differentiate the firm's offerings by emphasizing innovative, value-added products. In early 2000, Whirlpool enlisted 75 employees from almost every job classification and assigned them in groups to Benton Harbor, Italy, and Brazil. Training lasted nearly a year and was conducted by an outside consulting group.

The next step was to get the rest of the global workforce involved. Whirlpool established an intranet site and created a do-it-yourself course in innovation. Throughout 2001 and 2002 Whirlpool's "knowledge management" intranet site recorded up to 300,000 hits per month. The company established a rating system to identify high potential, innovative ideas. Since 2003, revenue has quadrupled annually. Whirlpool estimates that the new appliances in development from this system, once marketed, could produce $3 billion in annual sales, up from projections of $1.3 billion in 2003. Whirlpool developed microwave ovens that can grill steaks, bake pizzas, or come in the form of a drawer that slides out for easy access to large dishes. The firm invented a washer with a built-in sensor that detects the size of the load and automatically picks the water level, spin speed, and type of wash cycle, essentially making all decisions for the user.

Local Preferences

Cross-regional R&D teams also collaborate on innovations to adapt offerings to meet local demands in diverse international environments. For example, due to very different climates, Italians often line-dried their clothing, while the Danes need to spin-dry their clothes. Capacity requirements vary greatly for refrigerators. The Spanish care about capacity for meats, the British want well-constructed units, and the French are more concerned about the capacity for keeping fruits and vegetables fresh. Germans are particularly concerned about environmental features, while child safety features are very important to the Italians. In India, Whirlpool developed a washing machine that delivers a higher level of cleanliness for consumers who believe whiteness of clothing expresses purity. The washer's gentle hand-scrub movement and unique "hot wash technology" maximize the effectiveness of laundry detergent.

Whirlpool has benefited immensely from international business. The firm is a leading example of how internationalization can revive declining sales and optimize cost structures. It has developed international distribution that reduces expenses, leading to higher profits, and has positioned itself to challenge competitors on a global scale. The firm has thrived through sensitivity and commitment to consumers in diverse cultural and economic settings around the world.

Growing Competitive Threat from Abroad

Yet not all is bright and sparkling on Whirlpool's horizon. Haier, China's largest appliance maker, established a production base and a distribution center in South Carolina in the United States. The firm also bought a six-story landmark structure in New York, dubbed the Haier Building, to house its U.S. headquarters. The world's fifth-largest kitchen appliance maker, Haier has captured nearly 20 percent and 50 percent of the markets for window air conditioners and small refrigerators, respectively. Now it is expanding into full-size refrigerators. Haier's moves are especially troubling given that Whirlpool generates very little of its sales from Asia, the world's most populous region, where Haier already has a strong presence.

Ironically, Haier's South Carolina factory is creating new jobs in a state that witnessed a mass exodus of tex-

tile jobs to factories in China. South Carolina receives foreign direct investment from various countries and is home to four Japanese and 18 European facilities. These trends show that globalization both benefits and poses new threats to Whirlpool's international ambitions.

As it struggles to remain a world-class player in a key industry, Whirlpool faces new challenges. Management wants to expand sales in emerging markets while defending the home market from global rivals from China and elsewhere. The firm seeks to continue to leverage and enjoy all the benefits of international business.

AACSB: Reflective Thinking, Analytical Skills

Case Questions

1. What is the nature of Whirlpool's domestic and international business environments? What types of risk does the firm face?

2. How can Whirlpool benefit from going international? What types of advantages can the firm obtain? What advantages acquired abroad can help management improve Whirlpool's performance in its home market?

3. What actions has Whirlpool management taken to ensure that the firm succeeds in local markets throughout the world? To what extent is the appliance business local/regional rather than global?

4. How can Whirlpool effectively compete with new rivals originating from low-cost countries, such as Haier from China? Should Whirlpool's response differ in its home and foreign markets? If so, how?

5. The "Careers" section at Whirlpool's website (www.whirlpool.com/) advertises "opportunities you never knew existed . . . everywhere across the globe." Visit the site and report on the types of jobs available at Whirlpool and the locations of these positions worldwide. What positions interest you most? Would you like to work in Whirlpool's international operations? Why or why not?

Sources: Association of Home Appliance Manufacturers Web site, www.aham.org/News; Cavusgil, Tamer. (2001). "Globalization Headaches at Whirlpool" *Global Marketing 3rd Edition.* Boston: McGraw-Hill. Hoover's online Web site for Whirlpool Corporation www.hoovers.com; Spors, Kelly. (2004). "Against the Grain: A Chinese Appliance Maker has Placed Its Bet on a Counter-intuitive Strategy: It's Bringing Jobs to the U.S." *Wall Street Journal*, September 27, p. R6; Stepanek, Marcia. (2000). "As I Was Saying to My Refrigerator. . .," *Business Week*, September 18, p. 40; Stevens, James. (2002). "In Hot pursuit of Mexico: Whirlpool," *Appliance Manufacturer*, October 50(10), pp. 12–13; *Whirlpool Corporation Annual Report 2005.* Whirlpool's corporate Web site; press release, February 7, 2007, www.whirlpoolcorp.com; May 8, 2006. "Creativity Overflowing" www.businessweek.com; May 8, 2006. "Whirlpool's Future Won't Fade" www.businessweek.com

CHAPTER ESSENTIALS

Key Terms

born global firm, p. 14
commercial risk, p. 12
country risk, p. 12
cross-cultural risk, p. 11
currency risk, p. 12
exporting, p. 5
foreign direct investment (FDI), p. 5

globalization of markets, p. 4
importing or global sourcing, p. 5
international business, p. 4
international investment, p. 5
international portfolio
    investment, p. 5
international trade, p. 5

multinational enterprise
    (MNE), p. 13
small and medium-sized enterprise
    (SMEs), p. 13

Summary

In this chapter, you learned about:

1. What is international business?

International business refers to the performance of trade and investment activities by firms across national borders. **Globalization of markets** is the ongoing economic integration and growing interdependency of countries worldwide. International business is characterized by international trade and investment.

2. What are the key concepts in international trade and investment?

International trade refers to exchange of products and services across national borders, typically through exporting and importing. **Exporting** is the sale of products or services to customers located abroad, from a base in the home country or a third country. **Importing** or **global sourcing** refers to procurement of products or services from foreign suppliers for consumption in the home country or a third country. **International investment** refers to international transfer or acquisition of ownership in assets. **International portfolio investment** is passive ownership of foreign securities such as stocks and bonds for the purpose of generating financial returns. **Foreign direct investment** is an internationalization strategy in which the firm establishes a physical presence abroad through acquisition of productive assets such as capital, technology, labor, land, plant, and equipment.

3. How does international business differ from domestic business?

International firms are constantly exposed to four major categories of risk that must be managed. **Cross-cultural risk** refers to a situation or event where some human value has been put at stake due to a cultural miscommunication. **Country risk** refers to the potentially adverse effects on company operations and profitability caused by developments in the political, legal, and economic environment in a foreign country. **Currency risk** refers to the risk of adverse fluctuations in exchange rates. **Commercial risk** arises from the possibility of a firm's loss or failure from poorly developed or executed business strategies, tactics, or procedures. The risks are ever-present in international business and firms take proactive steps to reduce their effects.

4. Who participates in international business?

A key participant in international business is the **multinational enterprise (MNE)**—a large company with many resources whose business activities are performed by a network of subsidiaries located in multiple countries. Also very active in international business are **small and medium-sized enterprises (SMEs)**—companies with 500 or fewer employees. **Born globals** are entrepreneurial firms that initiate international business from or near their founding. Non-governmental organizations (NGOs) are non-profit organizations that pursue special causes and serve as an advocate for the arts, education, politics, religion, and research.

5. Why do firms pursue internationalization strategies?

Companies internationalize for various reasons. These include the ability to increase sales and profits, better serve customers, access lower-cost or superior production factors, optimize sourcing activities, develop economies of scale, confront competitors more effectively, develop rewarding relationships with foreign partners, and gain access to new ideas for creating or improving products and services.

6. Why should you study international business?

There are many reasons to study international business. It enhances a firm's competitive positioning in the global market, facilitates development of the global economy and of the interconnectedness among nations, and contributes to national economic well-being. International business also compels firms to act as a socially responsible corporate citizen in the host country. From a career standpoint, learning about international business will provide you with a competitive edge and enhance your ability to thrive in the job market.

Test Your Comprehension AACSB: Reflective Thinking

1. Distinguish between international business and globalization of markets.

2. What is the difference between exporting and foreign direct investment?

3. What makes international business different from domestic business?

4. What are the various types of risks that firms face when they conduct international business?

5. Who are the major participants in international business?

6. What is the difference between a multinational enterprise (MNE) and a small and medium-sized enterprise (SME)?

7. What are some of the key motivations for firms to engage in international business?

8. Why should you care about international business?

Apply Your Understanding AACSB: Communication, Reflective Thinking

1. Richard Bendix is the marketing manager at a firm that makes and sells high-quality prefabricated houses. He believes there is little difference between his home-country market and foreign markets, and that he can use the same methods for selling in Asia or Latin America as he does in his home country. Write a memo in which you explain to Richard the differences between domestic and international business. Explain the risks and other differences that Richard's firm will likely encounter if it expanded abroad.

2. After graduation, suppose you get a job with Beck Corporation, a small firm that does business only in its domestic market. You have just completed coursework in international business, are aware of various business opportunities abroad, and believe that Beck should internationalize. Write a memo to your boss in which you explain why your company should pursue international business. What are the benefits to Beck of venturing abroad? Explain why firms internationalize.

3. You have become the president of the International Business Club at your school. You are trying to recruit new members and find that many students do not recognize the importance of international business or the career opportunities available to them. You decide to give a presentation on this theme. Prepare an outline of a presentation in which you explain what types of companies participate in international business, why students should study international business, and possible career opportunities.

globalEDGE™ is a leading knowledge portal for professionals in international business. It is a gateway to specialized knowledge on countries, international business transactions, culture, and firm practice. globalEDGE™ has been developed at

Michigan State University's Center for International Business Education and Research (CIBER) under the direction of Professor S. Tamer Cavusgil.

Consult the globalEDGE™ portal to complete the Internet exercises at the end of each chapter.

Internet Exercises

AACSB: Communication, Use of Information Technology, Analytical Skills

1. You can gain valuable insights into international business by examining how countries compare to each other. Various research groups and international agencies systematically examine economic, political, and other features of nations and provide annual rankings. Visit globalEDGE Resource Desk, click on "Research: Rankings." You will find more than two dozen country rankings based on: degree of globalization, attractiveness with respect to FDI or global sourcing, retail development, extent of E-readiness, degree of economic freedom, quality of living, global competitiveness, and many other factors. Choose the ranking study that is of most interest to you. Learn about the methodology and the specific indicators used to rate countries. Then, examine how the following three countries rank in this study: Germany, Singapore, and South Africa. Based on your examination of their relative standing, provide an explanation of why they rank where they do. Indicate whether their relative positions makes sense to you.

2. In this chapter, we reviewed the four major risks that firms face in international business: cross-cultural risk, country risk, currency risk, and commercial risk. Identify one or more countries that interest you, then visit globalEDGE™ and research the countries to uncover examples of each of the four types of risks. For example, China is characterized by various cultural differences and a national government that tends to intervene in business. Research by entering the country name into the search engine. Then, under Quick Links, visit links such as the Country Commercial Guide and Economist Country Briefing. Illustrate each risk with examples.

3. You have recently been hired by a smaller firm that is beginning to expand internationally. When first starting out, most firms choose exporting as their main foreign market entry strategy. However, no one in your firm knows how to conduct exporting. Therefore, your boss has given you an assignment: Prepare a presentation for your coworkers on how to engage in exporting. Using globalEDGE™, your task is to find and review a "Guide to Exporting" that you can use to create your presentation.

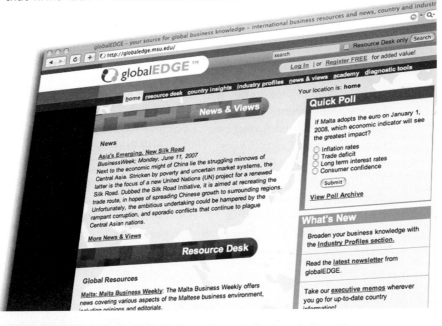

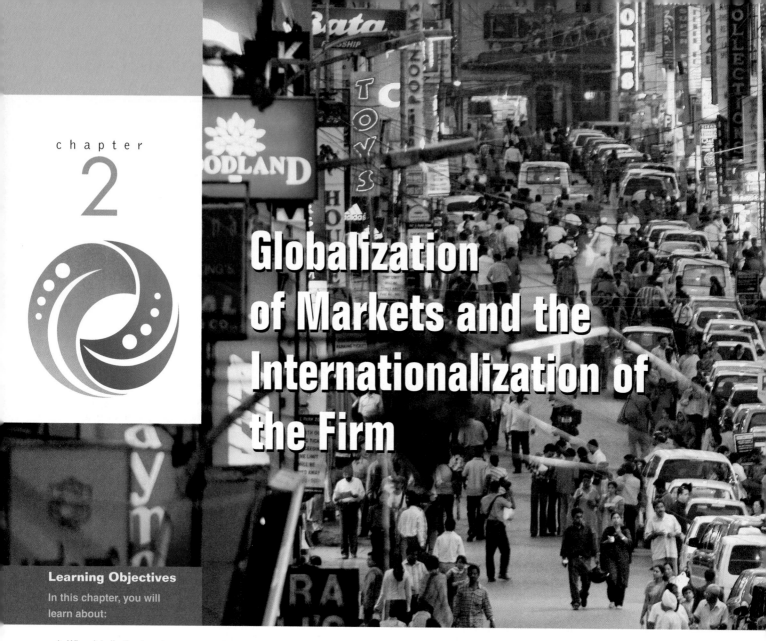

Globalization
of Markets and the
Internationalization of
the Firm

Learning Objectives

In this chapter, you will learn about:

1. Why globalization is not a new phenomenon

2. An organizing framework for market globalization

3. Dimensions of market globalization

4. Drivers of market globalization

5. Technological advances as a driver of market globalization

6. Societal consequences of market globalization

7. Firm-level consequences of market globalization: internationalization of the firm's value chain

> ## Bangalore: The New Silicon Valley

Weekday evenings in Bangalore, thousands of young men and women commute by bus to the call centers that characterize this city, the fifth largest in India. As the business day begins in Eastern Canada and the United States, these young Indians put on their telephone headsets to begin the overnight shift. They assist North American customers with service problems regarding credit cards, product purchases, and Internet transactions. Over 100,000 people are employed in Bangalore writing software, designing chips, running computer systems, reading X-rays, processing mortgages, preparing tax forms, and tracing lost luggage for firms in Australia, China, Europe, Japan, and North America. You can observe the same pattern in Delhi, Chennai, Hyderabad, and other emerging high-tech centers across India. Accenture, AOL, Intel, Cisco, Oracle, Philips, and Ernst & Young all have located operations in the country.

The number of people working in outsourced information technology (IT) services in India surpassed one million in 2008. What is the attraction? First, Indians are paid roughly one-quarter of what Westerners receive for similar work, and in many cases they do a better job. Second, India is home to several million highly

educated knowledge workers. Third, English is widely spoken. Finally, being located in a different time zone from Europe and the United States allows the Indians to take advantage of time-sharing. When North Americans are ending their work-day, Indians are arriving at the office to start their day. Because of instant data trans-mission via the Internet, Europeans and North Americans can e-mail the projects they are working on to their Indian counterparts, who then submit the completed work by the next morning. For companies in the knowledge economy, welcome to the 24-hour workday.

Infosys is the leading software firm in India. Infosys CEO Nandan Nilekani boasts of his global video conference room with a wall-size flat screen TV. Infosys regularly holds virtual meetings with its key global value-chain players on the super-size screen. The company's American designers can be on the screen speaking with their Indian software writers and their Asian manufacturers, simultaneously. "That's what globalization is all about today," says Nilekani. Above the screen are eight clocks that sum up the Infosys workday: 24/7/365. The clocks are labeled U.S. West, U.S. East, London, India, Singapore, Hong Kong, Japan, and Australia.[1]

Nilekani explains that computers are becoming cheaper and commonplace around the world, and there is an explosion of e-mail software and search engines like Google. Proprietary software can chop up any piece of work and send one part to Boston, one part to Bangalore, and one part to Beijing, making it easy for anyone to do remote development. "When all these things came together, they created a platform for intellectual work that could be delivered from anywhere. It could be disaggregated, delivered, distributed, produced and put back together again. What you see in Bangalore today is really the culmination of all these things coming together." Emerging markets like India, Brazil, and China can compete equally for global knowledge work as never before.[2]

Ravi Patel is typical of the knowledge workers Bangalore IT firms employ. He drives a Suzuki car, uses a Sony Ericsson mobile phone, and banks with Citibank. He hangs out with friends drinking Starbucks coffee, or Bacardi and Sprite. He watches American movies on a Samsung TV, brushes his teeth with Colgate, and owns a pair of Reeboks. At work Ravi uses an Acer computer with Microsoft software, a Lucent telephone, a Mita copy machine, and drinks Coca-Cola.

Ravi's life illustrates the phenomenon of *globalization*. Globalization has several implications:

- It is increasingly difficult to distinguish where you are in the world based on the products and services that you consume.

- The most important technologies can be developed in most locations worldwide.

- Jobs in the knowledge sector are being performed wherever the firm can extract maximal advantages, anywhere in the world.

- In the long run, by emphasizing free trade and global sourcing, globalization allows consumers worldwide to receive maximum quality at minimum price. Buyers in both producer and consumer nations increase their discretionary income and quality of life.[3]

Sources: John Heilemann (2004). "In Through the Outsourcing Door." *Business 2.0*, November; (2003). "Where Is Your Job Going?" *Fortune*, November; Friedman, Thomas. (2005). "It's a Flat World, After All." *The New York Times Magazine*, April; Siegel, Jeremy. (2005). *The Future for Investors*. New York: Crown Business.

Globalization of markets
The gradual integration and growing interdependence of national economies.

The opening vignette highlights two megatrends that, more than any other, have altered the business environment: the globalization of markets and technological advances. As we discussed in Chapter 1, **globalization of markets** refers to the gradual integration and growing interdependence of national economies. Globalization allows firms to view the world as an integrated marketplace. Initially, scholars used the term *market globalization* to refer to the emergence of global markets for standardized products and services and the growth of world-scale companies that serve those markets. However, the term has a broader meaning, and also refers to the interconnectedness of national economies and the growing interdependence of buyers, producers, suppliers, and governments in different countries. Market globalization is manifested by the production and marketing of branded products and services worldwide. Declining trade barriers, and the ease with which international business transactions take place due to the Internet and other technologies, are contributing to a gradual integration of most national economies into a unified market.

Ongoing technological advances characterize the other megatrend that has transformed contemporary business. Developments in information, manufacturing, and transportation technologies, as well as the emergence of the Internet, have facilitated rapid and early internationalization of countless firms, such as Neogen (www.neogen.com). The firm's founders developed diagnostic kits to test for food safety. Compared to test kits then available from other firms, Neogen's products were more accurate, more efficient, and easier to use. As word spread about the superiority of the products Neogen was able to internationalize quickly, and acquired a worldwide clientele. Farmers use Neogen test kits to test for pesticide residue; veterinarians use them for pharmaceuticals, vaccines, and topicals; and the USDA's Food Safety Inspection Service has used Neogen's rapid test for E. coli. Today, Neogen is a highly successful international firm.

Modern technology is promoting a higher level of international business activity than ever before. For example, many companies in software, gaming, or entertainment maintain a presence only on the Web. Advances in transportation and communication technologies have greatly aided express delivery service providers such as DHL, UPS, and FedEx to serve clients around the world.

The twin trends of market globalization and technological advances now permit firms to more readily engage in both marketing and *procurement* activities on a global scale. Companies increasingly sell their offerings throughout the world. More firms source raw materials, parts, components, and service inputs from suppliers located around the globe. These trends also serve to transform national economies. Growing world trade and foreign direct investment, coupled with the spread of technology, provide consumers and industrial buyers with a much greater choice of products and services. The competitive and innovative activities of internationally active firms are helping to reduce the prices that consumers and firms pay for products and services. Job creation by internationally active firms is contributing to higher living standards for people around the world. At the same time, preferences for some consumer products appear to be converging across markets, exemplified by the universal popularity of certain music, entertainment, consumer electronics, and food. Globalization is helping to disseminate values from liberalized economies about free trade and respect for intellectual property rights to an ever-widening international audience.[4]

 # Why Globalization Is Not a New Phenomenon

Advanced technologies, such as the Internet and modern transportation systems, have accelerated the pace of globalization. However, globalization is not a new phenomenon; it has simply accelerated and gained complex character in recent decades. Early civilizations in the Mediterranean, Middle East, Asia, Africa, and Europe have all contributed to the growth of cross-border trade over time. Globalization evolved out of a common, shared international heritage of all civilizations, no matter where they developed, to reach out and touch one another.[5] It is a culmination of the wonders of difference and discovery that people recognized thousands of years ago. Exchange with others gave societies the opportunity to expand and grow. Trade through the ages fostered civilization; without it, we would be a world of warring tribes bent on getting what we need through combat.[6] Cross-border trading opened the world to innovations and progress.

Phases of Globalization

Since the 1800s, we can identify four distinct phases in the evolution of market globalization. Each phase is accompanied by revolutionary technological developments and international trends. These are illustrated in Exhibit 2.1. Let's briefly review these stages.

The first phase of globalization began about 1830 and peaked around 1880.[7] International business became widespread during this period due to the growth of railroads, efficient ocean transport, and the rise of large manufacturing and trading companies. Invention of the telegraph and telephone in the late 1800s facilitated information flows between and within nations, and greatly aided early efforts to manage companies' supply chains.

Phase of Globalization	*Approximate Period*	*Triggers*	*Key Characteristics*
First phase	1830 to late 1800s, peaking in 1880	Introduction of railroads and ocean transport	Rise of manufacturing: cross-border trade of commodities, largely by trading companies
Second phase	1900 to 1930	Rise of electricity and steel production	Emergence and dominance of early multinational enterprises (primarily European and North American) in manufacturing, extractive, and agricultural industries
Third phase	1948 to 1970s	Formation of General Agreement on Tariff and Trade (GATT); conclusion of World War II; Marshall Plan to reconstruct Europe	Concerted effort on the part of industrializing Western countries to gradually reduce barriers to trade; rise of multinational companies from Japan; cross-border trade of branded products; cross-border flow of money paralleling the development of global capital markets
Fourth phase	1980s to present	Radical advances in information, communication, manufacturing, and consultation technologies; privatization of state-owned enterprises in transition countries; remarkable economic growth in emerging markets	Unprecedented rate of growth in cross-border trade of products, services, and capital; participation in international business of small and large companies originating from many countries; focus on emerging markets for export, FDI, and sourcing activities

Exhibit 2.1 Phases of Globalization Since the Early 1800s

The second phase of globalization began around 1900 and was associated with the rise of electricity and steel production. The phase reached its height just before the Great Depression, a worldwide economic downturn that began in 1929. In 1900, Western Europe was the most industrialized region in the world. Europe's colonization of countries in Asia, Africa, the Middle East, and beyond led to the establishment of some of the earliest subsidiaries of multinational firms. European companies such as BASF, British Petroleum, Nestlé, Shell, and Siemens had established foreign manufacturing plants by 1900.[8] In the years before World War I (pre-1914), many firms were already operating globally. The Italian manufacturer Fiat supplied vehicles to nations on both sides of the war.

The third phase of globalization began after World War II. At war's end, in 1945, substantial pent-up demand existed for consumer products, as well as for input goods to rebuild Europe and Japan. The United States was least harmed by the war and became the world's dominant economy. Substantial government aid helped stimulate economic activity in Europe. Before the war, tariffs and other trade barriers had been high, and there had been strict controls on currency and capital movements. Several industrialized countries, including Australia, Britain, and the United States, systematically sought to reduce barriers to international trade. The result of this effort was the *General Agreement on Tariffs and Trade* (GATT). Emerging from the Bretton Woods Conference of 23 nations in 1947, the GATT served as a global negotiating forum for liberalizing trade barriers.

The GATT marked the beginning of a series of annual negotiating meetings aimed at reducing barriers to international trade and investment. Participating governments recognized that liberalized trade would stimulate industrialization, modernization, and better living standards. The GATT eventually transformed into the World Trade Organization (WTO) as more countries joined this multinational agency. The **World Trade Organization** is a multilateral governing body empowered to regulate international trade and investment. The WTO aims to ensure fairness and efficiency in international transactions. Some 149 nations are now members of the WTO. Additional global cooperation in the post-war era gave birth to other international organizations such as the International Monetary Fund and the World Bank.

Early multinationals from this third phase of globalization originated from the United States, Western Europe, and Japan. The Europeans often expanded into former colonies. Firms like Unilever, Philips, Royal Dutch-Shell, British Petroleum, and Bayer organized their businesses by establishing independent subsidiaries in each of the foreign countries where they did business. Numerous companies developed internationally recognized trade names, including Nestlé, Kraft, John Deere, Kellogg, Lockheed, Caterpillar, Coca-Cola, Chrysler, Pepsi-Cola, Singer (sewing machines), and Levi's. American multinationals such as IBM, Boeing, Texas Instruments, Xerox, and McDonnell Douglas spread out across the globe on the strength of technological and competitive advantages. Gillette, Kodak, and Kellogg succeeded by offering unique products. Foreign subsidiaries of these firms were formed along a clone model, wherein they produced and sold the same products as the parent firm and operated miniature, autonomous versions of those firms. Gradually, multinational firms began to seek cost advantages by locating factories in developing countries with low labor costs.

Growing MNE activities and early efforts at trade liberalization resulted in substantial increases in international trade and investment beginning in the 1960s. Recovered from World War II, MNEs in Europe and Japan began to challenge the global dominance of U.S. multinationals. With the easing of trade barriers and currency controls, capital began to flow freely across national borders, leading to integration of global financial markets.[9]

The fourth and current phase of globalization began in the early 1980s. This period witnessed enormous growth in cross-border trade and investment. The current phase was triggered by key trends, including the commercialization of the personal computer, the development of the Internet and the Web browser, advances in communication and manufacturing technologies, the collapse of the Soviet Union and ensuing market liberalization in central and Eastern Europe, and the industrialization and modernization efforts of East Asian economies, including China.

Growing international prosperity began to reach emerging markets such as Brazil, India, and Mexico. The 1980s witnessed huge increases in FDI, especially in capital- and technology-intensive sectors. Technological advances in information, communications, and transportation made it feasible for managers to organize far-flung operations around the world, geographically distant yet electronically interconnected. These technologies also facilitated the globalization of the service sector in areas such as banking, entertainment, tourism, insurance, and retailing. The merger of major firms once viewed as strongholds of national corporate power exemplified the growing integration of the world economy. For example, GM acquired Saab in Sweden, Ford acquired Mazda in Japan, and Daimler Benz bought Chrysler in the United States.

In the contemporary era, countless firms configure and coordinate trade and investment activities in a giant global marketplace. In their own way, globalization and technological advances are resulting in the "death of distance."[10] That is, the geographic and, to some extent, cultural distances that separate nations are shrinking. Exhibit 2.2 reveals the progression of this trend. The ensuing phases of globalization have gradually shrunk the world into a manageable global marketplace.

World Trade Organization A multilateral governing body empowered to regulate international trade and investment.

Exhibit 2.2

The Death of Distance

SOURCE: Adapted from P. Dicken (1992), *Global Shift*. New York: Guilford, p. 104.

In this time period. . .	Fastest transportation was via. . .	At a speed of. . .
1500 to 1840s	• Human-powered ships and horse-drawn carriages	10 miles per hour
1850 to 1900	• Steamships • Steam locomotive trains	36 miles per hour 65 miles per hour
Early 1900s to today	• Motor vehicles • Propeller airplanes • Jet aircraft	75 miles per hour 300– 400 miles per hour 500– 700 miles per hour

An Organizing Framework for Market Globalization

Exhibit 2.3 presents an organizing framework for examining market globalization. The exhibit makes a distinction between the: (1) drivers or causes of globalization; (2) many dimensions or manifestations of globalization; (3a) societal consequences of globalization; and (3b) firm-level consequences of globalization—factors compelling companies to proactively internationalize. The exhibit's double arrows point to the interactive nature of the relationship between market globalization and its consequences. For example, as market globalization intensifies, individual business enterprises are compelled to respond to challenges and exploit new advantages. Keep in mind, however, that firms do not pursue internationalization strategies solely as a reaction to market globalization. As we discussed in Chapter 1, firms seek internationalization proactively also as a result of various internal forces (e.g., pursuit of growth, customers, or to minimize dependence on the domestic market through geographic diversification). Often adverse conditions in the home market, such as regulation or declining industry sales, compel firms to proactively seek international expansion.

Given the intensity of global competition, many firms proactively pursue internationalization as a strategic move. That is, they display a more aggressive attitude toward identifying foreign market opportunities, seeking partnerships with foreign firms, and building organizational capabilities to enhance their competitive advantage. Firms with such a proactive stance tend to be more successful in global competition than those firms that engage in international business as a reactive move.

Vodafone, one of the leading wireless phone services providers, is a good example of firms pursuing internationalization as a strategic growth alternative. The firm's main offerings include telecommunications and data services, multimedia portals, cellular operations, satellite services, and retail shops. Vodafone has annual sales of over $40 billion and some 200 million customers in 30 countries. Founded in 1982 in Britain, by 1993 Vodafone had interests in mobile phone networks in Australia, Greece, Hong Kong, Malta, and Scandinavia. The firm launched or bought stakes in operations throughout Europe, the Americas, and parts of Asia and Africa. Vodafone has internationalized mainly through foreign direct investment by drawing funds from global capital markets.

Vodafone took advantage of other important trends in the globalization era, including harmonization of communications technologies, converging buyer characteristics, and reduced trade and investment barriers. As emerging markets develop economically, they leapfrog older telecom technologies (typically landline systems) and embrace cell phone technology instead—a boon to Vodafone. In

1. Drivers of Market Globalization

- Worldwide reduction of barriers to trade and investment
- Transition to market-based economies and adoption of free trade in China, former Soviet Union countries, and elsewhere
- Industrialization, economic development, and modernization
- Integration of world financial markets
- Advances in technology

2. Dimensions of Market Globalization

- Integration and interdependence of national economies
- Rise of regional economic integration blocs
- Growth of global investment and financial flows
- Convergence of buyer lifestyles and preferences
- Globalization of firms' production activities

3a. Societal Consequences of Market Globalization

- Loss of national sovereignty
- Offshoring and the flight of jobs
- Effect on the poor
- Effect on the natural environment
- Effect on national culture

3b. Firm-level Consequences of Market Globalization: Internationalization of the Firm's Value Chain

- Countless new business opportunities for internationalizing firms
- New risks and intense rivalry from foreign competitors
- More demanding buyers, who source from suppliers worldwide
- Greater emphasis on proactive internationalization
- Internationalization of firm's value chain

Exhibit 2.3 The Drivers and Consequences of Market Globalization

Turkey, Vodafone acquired Telsim, the country's second biggest mobile phone operator. In 2007, Vodafone acquired much of India's cell phone business, a move that leverages the country's rapid economic growth and need for modern telephony.

Vodafone's proactive global strategy emphasizes selling standardized products and services and pursuing standardized marketing programs across the globe. To minimize costs and project a global image, many of Vodafone's cell phones are largely identical worldwide, with adaptations made to accommodate local regulations and telephone standards. Vodafone spends considerable resources on advertising every year, with a focus on developing and maintaining a global brand that people recognize everywhere. The convergence of buyer lifestyles and economic levels worldwide help facilitate the global approach. Management coordinates operations on a global scale and strives to implement common business processes in procurement and quality control. The strategies of product standardization, global branding, and maximizing sales to customers worldwide owe much of their success to the globalization of markets. Vodafone's strategic internationalization allows the firm to benefit from economies of scale, which helps make its products more price-competitive.[11]

 Dimensions of Market Globalization

As a broad phenomenon, globalization has been investigated from the perspective of various disciplines, including economics, history, anthropology, political science, sociology, and technology. In terms of international business, market globalization can be viewed simultaneously as a: (1) consequence of economic, technological, and government policy trends; (2) driver of economic, political, and social phenomena; and (3) driver and consequence of firm-level internationalization. Globalization of markets is a multifaceted phenomenon, with five major dimensions:

1. **Integration and interdependence of national economies.** Internationally active firms devise multicountry operations through trade, investment, geographic dispersal of company resources, and integration and coordination of **value chain** activities—the sequence of value-adding activities performed by the firm in the process of developing, producing, marketing, and servicing a product. The *aggregate* activities of these firms give rise to *economic integration*. Governments contribute to this integration by various means. First, they gradually lower barriers to international trade and investment (for example, by negotiating trade agreements). Second, they increasingly harmonize their monetary and fiscal policies within *regional economic integration blocs* (also known as *trade blocs*), such as the European Union. Third, they devise and supervise *supranational* institutions—such as the World Bank, International Monetary Fund, and the World Trade Organization—that seek further reductions in trade and investment barriers.

2. **Rise of regional economic integration blocs.** Closely related to the previous trend is the emergence since the 1950s of regional economic integration blocs. Examples include the North American Free Trade Agreement area (*NAFTA*), the Asia Pacific Economic Cooperation zone (*APEC*), and *Mercosur* in Latin America. These regional economic blocs incorporate groups of countries within which trade and investment flows are facilitated through the reduction of trade and investment barriers. In more advanced arrangements, such as the "common market," barriers to the cross-border flow of factors of production (mostly labor and capital) are removed. The European Union, in addition to adopting free trade among its members, is harmonizing fiscal and monetary policies and adopting common business regulations.

3. **Growth of global investment and financial flows.** In the process of conducting international transactions, firms and governments buy and sell large volumes of national currencies (such as dollars, euros, and yen). The free movement of capital around the world— the globalization of capital— extends economic activities across the globe and is fostering interconnectedness among world economies. Commercial and investment banking is a global industry. The bond market has gained worldwide scope, with foreign bonds representing a major source of debt financing for governments and firms. Information and communications networks facilitate heavy volumes of financial transactions every day, integrating national markets. Nevertheless, widespread integration can have negative effects. For example, when Thailand and Malaysia experienced a monetary crisis in 1997, it quickly spread to South Korea, Indonesia, and the Philippines, causing prolonged recession in most East Asian economies.

4. **Convergence of consumer lifestyles and preferences.** Around the world, many consumers are increasingly similar in how they spend their money and time. Lifestyles and preferences are converging. Consumers in Tokyo, New York, and Paris demand similar household goods, clothing, automobiles, and electronics. Teenagers everywhere are attracted to iPods, Nokia cell phones, and Levi's jeans. Major brands have gained a worldwide following. The trend is encouraged by greater international travel, movies, global media, and the Internet, which expose people to products, services, and living patterns from around the world. Hollywood films such as *Kill Bill* and *Lord of the Rings* receive much attention from a global audience. Convergence of preferences is also occurring in industrial markets, where professional buyers source

Value chain The sequence of value-adding activities performed by the firm in the process of developing, producing, marketing, and servicing a product.

The French supermarket Carrefour is one of many multinational enterprises that contribute to convergence of consumer lifestyles and preferences.

raw materials, parts, and components that are increasingly *standardized*—that is, very similar in design and structure. Yet, while converging tastes facilitate the marketing of highly standardized products and services to buyers worldwide, they also promote the loss of traditional lifestyles and values in individual countries.

5. **Globalization of production.** Intense global competition is forcing firms to reduce the cost of production and marketing. Companies strive to drive down prices through economies of scale and by standardizing what they sell. They seek economies in manufacturing and procurement by shifting these activities to foreign locations in order to take advantage of national differences in the cost and quality of factor inputs. Firms in the auto and textile industries, for example, have relocated their manufacturing to low labor-cost locations such as China, Mexico, and Eastern Europe. Production on a global basis is occurring in the service sector as well, in such industries as retailing, banking, insurance, and data processing. As an example, the real estate firm RE/MAX has established more than 5,000 offices in over 50 countries. The French firm Accor operates hundreds of hotels worldwide.

 # Drivers of Market Globalization

Various trends have converged in recent years as causes of market globalization. Five drivers are particularly notable:

1. **Worldwide reduction of barriers to trade and investment.** The tendency of national governments to reduce trade and investment barriers has accelerated global economic integration. For example, tariffs on the import of automobiles, industrial machinery, and countless other products have declined nearly to zero in many countries, encouraging freer international exchange of goods and services. Reduction in trade barriers is greatly aided by the WTO. China joined the WTO in 2001 and has committed to making its market more accessible to foreign companies. Reduction of trade barriers is also associated with the emergence of regional economic integration blocs, a key dimension of market globalization.

2. **Market liberalization and adoption of free markets.** Built in 1961, the Berlin Wall separated the communist East Berlin from the democratic West Berlin. The collapse of the Soviet Union's economy in 1989, the tearing down of the Berlin Wall that same year, and China's free-market reforms all signaled the end of the 50-year Cold War between autocratic communist regimes and democracy, and smoothed the integration of former command economies into the global economy. Numerous East Asian economies, stretching from South Korea to Malaysia and Indonesia, had already embarked on ambitious market-based reforms. India joined the trend in 1991. These events opened roughly one-third of the world to freer international trade and investment. China, India, and Eastern Europe have become some of the most cost-effective locations for producing goods and services worldwide. Privatization of previously state-owned industries in these countries encouraged economic efficiency and attracted massive foreign capital into their national economies.

3. **Industrialization, economic development, and modernization.** Industrialization implies that emerging markets—rapidly developing economies in Asia, Latin America, and Eastern Europe—are moving from being low value-adding commodity producers, dependent on low-cost labor, to sophisticated competitive producers and exporters of premium products such as electronics, computers, and aircraft.[12] For example, Brazil has become a leading producer of private aircraft, and the Czech Republic now excels in the production of automobiles. As highlighted in the opening vignette, India is now a leading supplier of computer software. Economic development is enhancing standards of living and discretionary income in emerging markets. Perhaps the most important measure of economic development is *Gross National Income (GNI)* per head.[13] Exhibit 2.4 maps the levels

Exhibit 2.4

Gross National Income in U.S. Dollars

SOURCE: World Bank (2006) World Bank Development Indicator database. Numbers are based on the Atlas Methodology of the World Bank, a three-year average of the official exchange rate, adjusted for inflation.

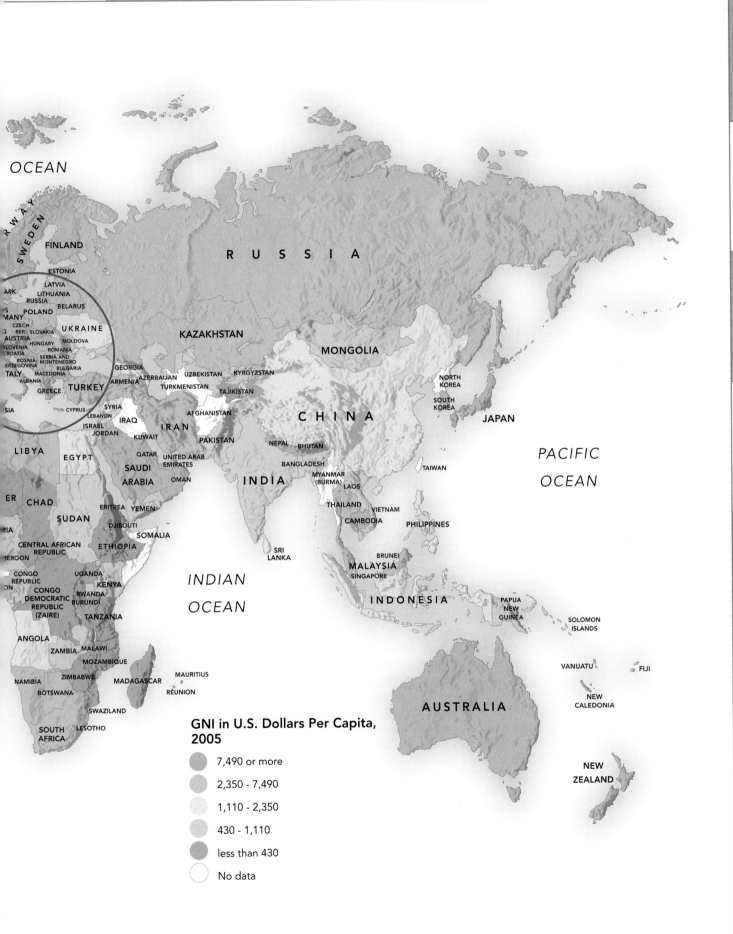

OCEAN

NORWAY
SWEDEN
FINLAND
ESTONIA
ARK LATVIA
LITHUANIA
RUSSIA
MANY BELARUS
POLAND
S CZECH UKRAINE
3 REP. SLOVAKIA
AUSTRIA HUNGARY MOLDOVA
SLOVENIA ROMANIA
CROATIA SERBIA AND
BOSNIA MONTENEGRO
ERZEGOVINA BULGARIA
ITALY MACEDONIA
ALBANIA
GREECE TURKEY
SIA CYPRUS SYRIA
LEBANON
ISRAEL IRAQ
JORDAN KUWAIT
LIBYA QATAR
EGYPT UNITED ARAB
EMIRATES
SAUDI OMAN
ARABIA

RUSSIA

KAZAKHSTAN

MONGOLIA

GEORGIA
ARMENIA AZERBAIJAN UZBEKISTAN KYRGYZSTAN
TURKMENISTAN TAJIKISTAN
AFGHANISTAN CHINA
IRAN
PAKISTAN
NEPAL BHUTAN
BANGLADESH
MYANMAR LAOS
(BURMA)
INDIA THAILAND VIETNAM
CAMBODIA

NORTH
KOREA
SOUTH
KOREA
JAPAN

PACIFIC
OCEAN

TAIWAN

ER CHAD YEMEN
ERITREA
SUDAN DJIBOUTI
CENTRAL AFRICAN SOMALIA
REPUBLIC ETHIOPIA
EROON
CONGO UGANDA
REPUBLIC KENYA
ON CONGO RWANDA
DEMOCRATIC BURUNDI
REPUBLIC
(ZAIRE) TANZANIA
ANGOLA
ZAMBIA MALAWI
MOZAMBIQUE
NAMIBIA ZIMBABWE
BOTSWANA MADAGASCAR
SWAZILAND
SOUTH LESOTHO
AFRICA

SRI
LANKA

INDIAN

OCEAN

PHILIPPINES

BRUNEI
MALAYSIA
SINGAPORE

INDONESIA

PAPUA
NEW
GUINEA

SOLOMON
ISLANDS

MAURITIUS
RÉUNION

AUSTRALIA

VANUATU FIJI

NEW
CALEDONIA

NEW
ZEALAND

GNI in U.S. Dollars Per Capita, 2005

- 7,490 or more
- 2,350 - 7,490
- 1,110 - 2,350
- 430 - 1,110
- less than 430
- No data

of GNI worldwide. The exhibit reveals that Africa is home to the lowest-income countries, along with India and a few other countries in Asia and Nicaragua. These areas are also characterized by low levels of market globalization. The adoption of modern technologies, improvement of living standards, and adoption of modern legal and banking practices are increasing the attractiveness of emerging markets as investment targets and facilitating the spread of ideas, products, and services across the globe.

4. **Integration of world financial markets.** Integration of world financial markets makes it possible for internationally active firms to raise capital, borrow funds, and engage in foreign currency transactions. Financial services firms follow their customers to foreign markets. Cross-border transactions are made easier partly as a result of the ease with which funds can be transferred between buyers and sellers, through a network of international commercial banks. For example, as an individual you can transfer funds to a friend in another country using the Society for Worldwide Interbank Financial Telecommunication (SWIFT) network. Connecting over 7,800 financial institutions in some 200 countries, SWIFT facilitates the exchange of financial transactions. The globalization of finance contributes to firms' ability to develop and operate world-scale production and marketing operations. It enables companies to pay suppliers and collect payments from customers worldwide.

5. **Advances in technology.** Technological advances are a remarkable facilitator of cross-border trade and investment. Let's elaborate on this important driver of globalization and company internationalization in greater detail.

Technological Advances as a Driver of Market Globalization

Perhaps the most important drivers of market globalization since the 1980s have been technological advances in communications, information, manufacturing, and transportation. While globalization makes internationalization an imperative, technological advances provide the *means* for internationalization. Initially, technological advances have greatly eased the management of international operations. Firms now interact more efficiently with foreign partners and value-chain members than ever before. Firms transmit all variety of data, information, and vital communications that help ensure the smooth running of their operations worldwide. In addition, companies use information technology to improve the productivity of their operations, which provides substantial competitive advantages. For example, information technology allows firms to more efficiently adapt products for international markets, or produce goods in smaller lots to target international niche markets.

In addition, technological advances have made the cost of international operations affordable for all types of firms, explaining why so many small- and medium-sized enterprises (SMEs) have internationalized during the past two decades. Panel (a) of Exhibit 2.5 shows how the cost of international communications has plummeted over time. Panel (b) shows how the number of Internet users has grown dramatically in recent years.

Technological advances have also spurred the development of new products and services that appeal to a global audience. Leading examples include Walkman, PlayStation 3, and personal digital assistants (PDAs). Emerging markets and other developing country economies also benefit from technological advances, due in part to technological leapfrogging. For instance, Hungary and Poland went directly from old-style analog telecommunications (with rotary dial telephones) to cell phone technology, bypassing much of the early digital technology (push-button telephones) that characterized advanced economy telephone systems.

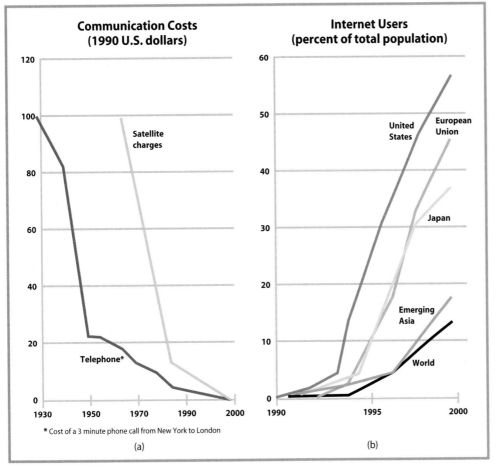

Exhibit 2.5

Declining Cost of Global
Communication and Growing
Number of Internet Users

SOURCE: IMF (2005), *World Economic Outlook.*
Washington, DC: International Monetary Fund,
from *World Economic Outlook,* 2005, Washington
DC: International Monetary Fund.
Copyright © 2005. Used with permission.

China and India are the new beachheads of technological advances. The opening vignette revealed how India has become a focus of global Internet- and knowledge-based industries. Top management at Intel and Motorola, two of the world's premier technology companies, agree that China is the place to be when it comes to technological progress. Both firms receive a substantial portion of their revenue from sales in China. Management predicts double-digit increases in demand for technology products in China far into the future. Intel's CEO commented, "I come back from visiting China and feel as if I've visited the fountain of youth of computing."[14]

The most important activity underlying technological advances is *innovation.* Societies and organizations innovate in various ways, including new product designs, new production processes, new approaches to marketing, and new ways of organizing or training. Innovation results primarily from research and development.[15] Today, more scientists and engineers are engaged in R&D activities worldwide than ever before. For example, the Japanese introduced quartz technology in clock making. The technology allowed greater accuracy and significantly lowered production costs, allowing Japanese manufacturers to establish their leadership in the clock-making industry within a few years. Among the industries most dependent on technological innovation are biotechnology, information technology, new materials, pharmaceuticals, robotics, medical equipment and devices, lasers and fiber optics, and various electronics-based industries.

Technological advances have had the greatest impact in several key areas: information technology, communications, manufacturing, and transportation.

Information Technology

The effect of information technology (IT) on business has been nothing short of revolutionary. IT is the science and process of creating and using information resources. The cost of computer processing fell by 30 percent *per year* during the past two decades, and continues to fall. The remarkable performance of the U.S. economy in the 1990s was due in large part to aggressive integration of IT into firms' value-chain activities, which accounted for 45 percent of total business investments at the time. IT alters industry structure and, in so doing, changes the rules of competition. By giving companies new ways to outperform rivals, IT creates competitive advantage.[16] For example, geographically distant country subsidiaries of a multinational company can be interconnected via intranets, facilitating the instant sharing of data, information, and experience across the firm's operations worldwide.[17] MNEs also use collaboration software that connects global product development teams scattered around the world, enabling them to work together. IT provides benefits for smaller firms as well, allowing them to design and produce customized products they can target to narrow, cross-national niches.

IT has spawned new products, such as cell phones, and new processes, such as automated factory controls. Online search engines such as Google and Yahoo allow anyone access to unlimited data in order to research markets, customers, competitors, and countries' economic conditions. At a higher level, IT supports managerial decision making—such as selection of qualified foreign business partners—based on accessing key information and intelligence.

Communications

It took five months for Spain's Queen Isabella to learn about Columbus' voyage in 1492; two weeks for Europe to learn of President Lincoln's assassination in 1865; and only seconds for the world to witness the collapse of New York's World Trade Center towers in 2001. The most profound technological advances have occurred in communications, especially telecommunications, satellites, optical fiber, wireless technology, and the Internet. At one time, people and companies used expensive phone calls, slow postal service, and clunky telex machines to communicate with foreign suppliers. In 1930, a 3-minute phone call between New York and London cost $3,000. By 1980, the cost had fallen to $6. Today, the call costs only a few cents. Scanners and fax machines send documents worldwide practically for free. Banking transactions are relatively costly when performed via ATM machines or telephones, but are virtually free when handled via the Internet.

The Internet, and Internet-dependent communications systems such as intranets, extranets, and e-mail, connect millions of people across the globe. The dot-com boom of the 1990s led to massive investment in fiber optic telecommunications. Today, the widest range of products and services—from auto parts to bank loans—is marketed online. Transmitting voices, data, and images is essentially costless, making Boston, Bangalore, and Beijing next door neighbors, instantly. South Korea, where Internet access is nearly 100 percent, is leading the way. South Korea's broadband networks for home are among the fastest in the world. Korean schoolchildren use their cell phones to get homework from their teachers and play games online with gamers worldwide. Adults use their phones to pay bills, do banking, buy lottery tickets, and check traffic conditions.

Widespread availability of the Internet and e-mail makes company internationalization cost-effective. For instance, Amdahl, a manufacturer of large-scale computers, uses the Internet to order circuit boards from factories in Asia and to arrange international shipments of parts and components via firms like DHL and Federal Express. Search engines, databases, reference guides, and countless government and private support systems assist managers to maximize knowledge and skills for international business success. The Internet opens up the global marketplace to companies that would normally not have the resources to do international business, including countless SMEs. By establishing a presence on the Web, even tiny enterprises take the first step in becoming multinational firms. Thanks to the Internet, services as diverse as designing an engine, monitoring a security camera, selling insurance, or secretarial work have become easier to export than car parts or refrigerators. The *Global Trend* feature highlights the emergence of e-commerce and its effect on international company operations and performance.

The Internet is stimulating economic development and a massive global migration of jobs, particularly in the services sector.[18] As Netscape cofounder Marc Andreesson observed, "A 14-year-old in Romania or Bangalore or Vietnam has all the information, all the tools, all the software easily available to apply knowledge however they want. Communications and information technology are now in the process of connecting all of the knowledge pools in the world together."[19] In the not-too-distant future, much of what has ever been written and recorded on paper, tape, or film will be accessible online.

> GLOBAL TREND

Globalization and E-Business in the Online World

Information technology and the Internet are transforming international business by allowing firms to conduct e-commerce online, as well as integrate e-business capabilities for activities such as sourcing and managing customer relations. E-business drives the firm's globalization efforts by helping it beat geography and time zones. The modern firm, small or large, does business around the world all day, every day. E-business levels the playing field for all types of firms. Thanks to e-technologies, even new companies can be active abroad. Born-global firms are among the most intensive users of the Web for global selling, procurement, and customer service.

E-business provides at least three types of benefits. First, it *increases productivity* and *reduces costs* in worldwide value-chain activities through online integration and coordination of production, distribution, and after-sale services. Second, it

creates value for existing customers and uncovers new sales opportunities by increasing customer focus, enhancing marketing capabilities, and launching entrepreneurial initiatives. A key benefit is the ability to implement marketing strategy on an international scale and integrate customer-focused operations worldwide. Virtual interconnectedness facilitates the sharing of new ideas and best practices for serving new and existing international markets. Third, it *improves the flow of information and knowledge throughout the firm's worldwide operations*. The Internet allows the firm to move information quickly throughout its operations worldwide, and to interact more effectively with customers, suppliers, and partners. Managers can make instantaneous changes to strategies and tactics in the firm's value-chain activities. The firm can accommodate real-time changes in market conditions almost as quickly as they occur.

For example, Cisco uses e-business solutions to minimize costs and maximize operational effectiveness in its international supply chain. The firm uses the Internet to remain constantly linked to suppliers and distributors. This helps Cisco manage inventory, product specifications, and purchase orders, as well as product life cycles. *E-procurement* systems help Cisco save money on transaction processing, reduce cycle times, and leverage supplier relations.

Customer relationship management is especially critical in foreign markets where buyers often favor local vendors. Internet-based systems provide real-time information, forecast shifting short- and long-term market needs, and increase the effectiveness of after-sales service. E-commerce enhances the means for firms to achieve competitive advantages and performance objectives in a global marketplace.

Low freight costs are one driver of market globalization.

Manufacturing

Computer-aided design (CAD) of products, robotics, and production lines managed and monitored by microprocessor-based controls are transforming manufacturing, mainly by reducing the costs of production. Revolutionary developments now permit low-scale and low-cost manufacturing. Firms can produce products in short production runs cost effectively. These developments benefit international business by allowing firms to more efficiently adapt products to individual foreign markets, profitably target small national markets, and compete more effectively with foreign competitors who already have cost advantages.

Transportation

Managers consider the costs of transporting raw materials, components, and finished products when deciding to either export or manufacture abroad. For example, if transportation costs to an important market are high, management may decide to manufacture its merchandise in the market by building a factory there. Beginning in the 1960s, technological advances led to the development of fuel-efficient jumbo jets, giant ocean-going freighters, and containerized shipping, often through the use of high-tech composites and smaller components that are less bulky and lightweight. As a result, the cost of transportation as a proportion of the value of products shipped internationally has declined substantially. Lower freight costs have spurred rapid growth in cross-border trade. Technological advances have also reduced the costs of international travel. Until 1960, it was common to travel by ship. With the development of air travel, managers quickly travel the world.

 ## Societal Consequences of Market Globalization

Our discussion so far has highlighted the far-reaching, positive outcomes of market globalization. Nevertheless, globalization has produced some harmful consequences as well. While major advances in living standards have been achieved in virtually all countries that have opened their borders to increased trade and investment, the transition to an increasingly single, global marketplace poses challenges to individuals, organizations, and governments. Low-income countries have not been able to integrate with the global economy as rapidly as others. Poverty is especially notable in Africa and in populous nations such as Brazil, China, and India. Let's now turn to some of the unintended consequences of globalization.

Loss of National Sovereignty

Sovereignty is the ability of a nation to govern its own affairs. One country's laws cannot be applied or enforced in another country. The sovereignty of nations is a fundamental principle that governs global relations. Globalization can threaten national sovereignty in various ways. MNE activities can interfere with the sovereign ability of governments to control their own economies, social structures, and political systems. Some corporations are bigger than the economies of many nations. Indeed, Wal-Mart's internal economy—its total revenues—is larger than the GDP of most of the world's nations, including Israel, Greece, and Poland. Large multinationals can exert considerable influence on governments through lobbying or campaign contributions. It is not unusual for large corporations to lobby their government, say, for devaluation of the home currency, which gives them greater price competitiveness in export markets. MNEs can also influence the legislative process and extract special favors from government agencies.

At the same time, even the largest firms are constrained by *market forces*. In countries with many competing companies, one company cannot force customers to buy its products or force suppliers to supply it with raw materials and inputs. The resources that customers and suppliers control are the result of free choices made in the marketplace. Company performance depends on the firm's skill at winning customers, working with suppliers, and dealing with competitors. Corporate dominance of individual markets is rare. In reality, market forces dominate companies. Indeed, gradual integration of the global economy and increased global competition, combined with privatization of industries in various nations, are making some companies *less* powerful within their national markets.[20] For instance, Ford, Chrysler, and General Motors once completely dominated the U.S. auto market. Today many more firms compete in the United States, including Toyota, Honda, Hyundai, Kia, Nissan, and BMW. Indeed, in annual sales, Toyota now rivals General Motors in GM's home market.

Today, globalization creates incentives for governments to pursue sound economic policies and for managers to manage their firms more effectively. To minimize globalization's harm and reap its benefits, governments should strive for an open and liberalized economic regime: freedom to enter and compete in markets; protection of persons and intellectual property; rule of law; and voluntary exchange imposed by markets rather than through political processes. Transparency in the affairs of businesses and regulatory agencies is critical.

Occasionally, governments need to scrutinize corporate activities. An example from the United States is the Sarbanes-Oxley Act of 2002 (also known as the Public Company Accounting Reform and Investor Protection Act of 2002). The legislation resulted from a decline in public trust of financial reporting practices in the wake of a series of corporate and accounting scandals involving firms such as Enron, Tyco International, and WorldCom. The legislation introduced new or enhanced standards for all U.S. public company boards, management, and public accounting firms.

Offshoring and the Flight of Jobs

Globalization has created countless new jobs and opportunities around the world, but it has also cost many people their jobs. For example, Ford, General Motors, and Volkswagen all have transferred thousands of jobs from their factories in Germany to countries in Eastern Europe. This occurred partially because mandated shorter working hours (often just 35 hours per week) and generous benefits made Germany less competitive, while Eastern Europe offers abundant low-wage workers. Recognizing this, the German government is loosening Germany's labor laws to conform to global realities. But these changes have disrupted the lives of tens of thousands of German citizens.[21] General Motors and Ford have also laid off thousands of workers in the United States, partly the result of competitive pressures posed by carmakers from Europe, Japan, and South Korea.

Offshoring is the relocation of manufacturing and other value-chain activities to cost-effective locations abroad. For example, the global accounting firm Ernst & Young has much of its support work done by accountants in the Philippines. Massachusetts General Hospital has its CT scans and X-rays interpreted by radiologists in India. Many IT support services for customers in Germany are based in the Czech Republic and Romania.[22]

Offshoring has resulted in job losses in numerous mature economies. The first wave of offshoring began in the 1960s and 1970s with the shift of U.S. and European manufacturing of cars, shoes, electronics, textiles, and toys to cheap-labor locations such as Mexico and Southeast Asia. The next wave began in the 1990s with the exodus of service sector jobs in credit card processing, software code writing, accounting, health care, and banking services. High-profile plant closures and relocation of manufacturing facilities to low-cost countries have received ample media attention in recent years. Critics have labeled many MNEs as "runaway" or "footloose" corporations—quick to relocate production to countries that offer more favorable access to inputs. For example, Electrolux, a Swedish manufacturer of home appliances, moved its Greenville, Michigan, refrigerator plant to Mexico in 2005. Electrolux had provided 2,700 jobs in this western Michigan community of 8,000. Despite repeated appeals by the local community, the labor union, and the state of Michigan, Electrolux went with its decision to shift manufacturing to Mexico. One can imagine the devastation to the economic livelihood of this community.

Effect on the Poor

Multinational firms are often criticized for paying low wages, exploiting workers, and employing child labor. Child labor is particularly troubling because it denies children educational opportunities. The International Labor Organization (www.ilo.org) estimates there are as many as 250 million children at work around the world, many working full time. Nike has been criticized for paying low wages to shoe factory workers in Asia, some of whom work in sweatshop conditions. Critics complain that while founder Phil Knight is a billionaire and Nike sells shoes for $100 or more, Nike's suppliers pay their workers only a few dollars per day.

Labor exploitation and sweatshop conditions are genuine concerns in many developing economies.[23] Nevertheless, consideration must be given to the other choices available to people in those countries. Finding work in a low-paying job may be better than finding no work at all. Recent studies suggest that banning products made using child labor may produce negative, unintended consequences.[24] Eliminating child labor can worsen living standards for children. Legislation that reduces child labor in the formal economic sector (the sector regulated and monitored by public authorities), may have little effect on jobs in the informal economic sector (sometimes called the underground economy). In the face of unrelenting poverty, abolishing formal sector jobs does not ensure that children leave the workforce and go to school.

Wages and sweatshop conditions are slowly improving in developing economies, such as those in Central America.

In many developing countries, work conditions tend to improve over time. The growth of the footwear industry in Vietnam has translated into a five-fold increase in wages in recent years. While still low by advanced economy standards, increasingly higher wages are improving the lives of millions of workers and their families. For most countries, globalization tends to support a growing economy. Exhibit 2.6 on pages 48–49 shows the GDP growth rate worldwide from 1997 to 2006. Note that most nations experienced significant, positive growth. As shown in the map, the world's fastest growing large economies are China and India. Chile, Ireland, and Vietnam are also on the fast growth track. The former Soviet Union countries in Eastern Europe suffered setbacks in the 1990s as they transitioned to market-based economic systems. Most African countries continue to suffer low or negative GDP growth and alarming poverty.

Critics insist that such workers be provided a decent wage. However, legislation to increase minimum wage levels can also reduce the number of available jobs. That is, countries that attract investment due to low-cost labor gradually lose their attractiveness as wages rise. More broadly, the evidence suggests that globalization is associated with higher wage growth over time. Exhibit 2.7 on page 50 reveals that countries that liberalize international trade and investment enjoy faster per capita economic growth. The exhibit shows how, during the 1990s, developing economies that emphasized integration with the rest of the world had faster per capita GDP growth than already integrated advanced economies, which, in turn, grew faster than nonintegrating developing economies.

Governments are responsible for ensuring that the fruits of economic progress are shared fairly, and that all citizens have access to improved welfare, living standards, and higher-value-adding, higher-paying jobs. Developing countries can engage in a number of proactive measures to reduce poverty. They can improve conditions for investment and saving, liberalize markets and promote trade and investment, build strong institutions and government to foster good governance, and invest in education and training to promote productivity and ensure worker-upward mobility. Advanced economies can play a role in reducing poverty by making their markets more accessible to low-income countries, facilitating the flows of direct investment, other private capital, and technology into low-income countries, and providing debt relief to heavily indebted nations.

Effect on the Natural Environment

Globalization can harm the environment by promoting increased manufacturing and economic activity that result in pollution, habitat destruction, and deterioration of the ozone layer. For instance, economic development in China is attracting much inward FDI and stimulating the growth of numerous industries. The construction of factories, infrastructure, and modern housing can spoil previously pristine environments. As an example, growing industrial demand for electricity led to construction of the Three Gorges Dam, which flooded agricultural lands and permanently altered the natural landscape in Eastern China.

While it is generally true that globalization-induced industrialization produces considerable environmental harm, the harm tends to decline over time. The evidence suggests that environmental destruction diminishes as economies develop, at least in the long run. To the extent that globalization stimulates rising living standards, people focus increasingly on improving their environment. Over time, governments pass legislation that promotes improved environmental conditions. For example, Japan endured polluted rivers and smoggy cities in the early decades of its economic development following World War II. But as Japan's economy grew, the Japanese passed tough environmental standards aimed at restoring natural environments.

Evolving company values and concern for corporate reputations also lead most firms to reduce or eliminate practices that harm the environment.[25] For example, with rising affluence in Mexico, big American automakers like Ford and GM have gradually improved their environmental standards. Benetton in Italy (clothing), Alcan in Canada (aluminum), and Kirin in Japan (beverages), are examples of firms that embrace practices that protect the environment, often at the expense of profits.[26] Conservation Coffee Alliance, a consortium of companies, has committed approximately $2 million to environmentally friendly coffee cultivation in Central America, Peru, and Colombia.

Effect on National Culture

Globalization exerts strong pressures on national culture. Market liberalization leaves the door open to foreign companies, global brands, unfamiliar products,

Exhibit 2.6

The Growth of World GDP, Average Annual Percent Change, 1998–2007

SOURCE: International Monetary Fund, World Economic Outlook Database

GREENLAND

ARCT

ICELAND

ALASKA

CANADA

UNITED STATES OF AMERICA

PACIFIC OCEAN

HAWAII

MEXICO

NORTH ATLANTIC OCEAN

CUBA
JAMAICA
BELIZE
HONDURAS
GUATEMALA
EL SALVADOR
COSTA RICA
NICARAGUA
PANAMA
DOMINICAN REPUBLIC
HAITI
PUERTO RICO

GALAPAGOS ISLANDS

VENEZUELA
GUYANA
COLOMBIA
ECUADOR
TRINIDAD & TOBAGO
FRENCH GUIANA
SURINAME

UNITED KINGDOM
IRELAND
NETHE
BELGI
LUXEN
FRANC
S
MONAC
ANDORRA
SPAIN
PORTUGAL

MOROCCO

WESTERN SAHARA
ALGERIA
MAURITANIA
MALI
SENEGAL
GAMBIA
GUINEA-BISSAU
GUINEA
BURKINA FASO
BENIN
SIERRA LEONE
IVORY COAST
GHANA
TOGO
LIBERIA
N
EQUATO
GUINE

BRAZIL

PERU

BOLIVIA

PARAGUAY

C
H
I
L
E

URUGUAY

ARGENTINA

SOUTH ATLANTIC OCEAN

FALKLAND ISLANDS/ MALVINAS

SWEDEN
DENMARK
LATVIA
LITHUANIA
RUSSIA
NETHERLANDS
BELGIUM
GERMANY
POLAND
BELARUS
LUXEMBOURG
CZECH REP.
UKRAINE
FRANCE
SLOVAKIA
LIECHTENSTEIN
SWITZERLAND
AUSTRIA
HUNGARY
MOLDOVA
SLOVENIA
CROATIA
ROMANIA
SAN MARINO
MONACO
BOSNIA-HERZEGOVINA
SERBIA AND MONTENEGRO
Black Sea
ANDORRA
BULGARIA
ITALY
MACEDONIA
ALBANIA
TURKEY
GREECE
ALGERIA
CYPRUS
TUNISIA
MALTA
LIBYA

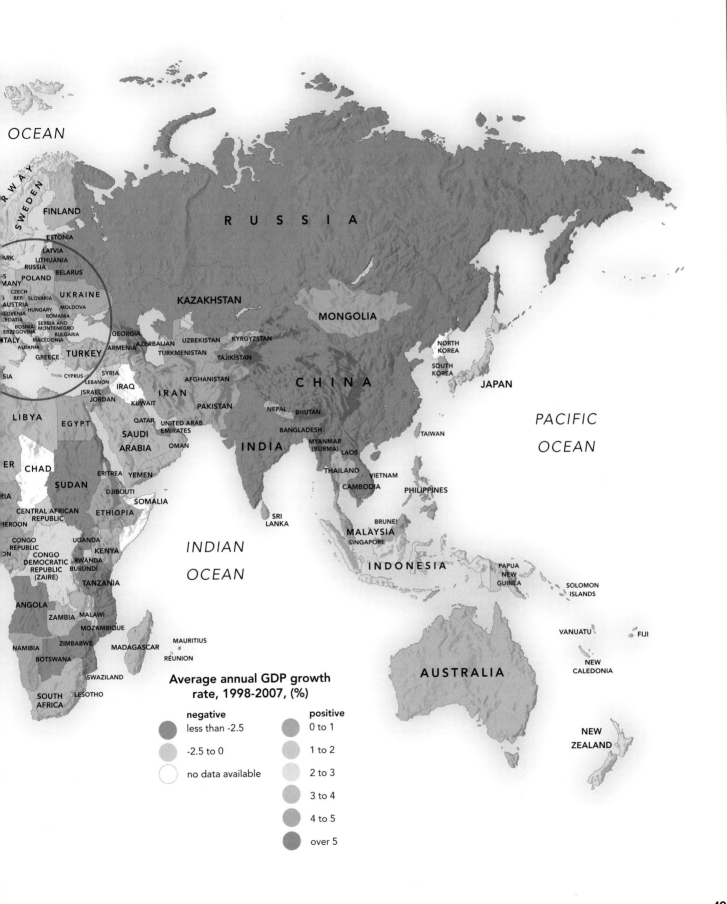

OCEAN

NORWAY
SWEDEN
FINLAND

ESTONIA
ARK
LATVIA
LITHUANIA
RUSSIA
BELARUS
POLAND
MANY
CZECH
REP. SLOVAKIA
UKRAINE
AUSTRIA
MOLDOVA
SLOVENIA
HUNGARY
ROMANIA
CROATIA
BOSNIA AND
SERBIA AND
ERZEGOVINA
MONTENEGRO
BULGARIA
ITALY
MACEDONIA
ALBANIA
GREECE
TURKEY
SIA
CYPRUS
SYRIA
LEBANON
ISRAEL
IRAQ
JORDAN
LIBYA
EGYPT
QATAR
UNITED ARAB
EMIRATES
SAUDI
ARABIA
OMAN
ER
CHAD
ERITREA
YEMEN
SUDAN
DJIBOUTI
CENTRAL AFRICAN
SOMALIA
REPUBLIC
MEROON
ETHIOPIA
CONGO
UGANDA
REPUBLIC
KENYA
ON
CONGO
RWANDA
DEMOCRATIC
BURUNDI
REPUBLIC
(ZAIRE)
TANZANIA
ANGOLA
ZAMBIA
MALAWI
MOZAMBIQUE
NAMIBIA
ZIMBABWE
MADAGASCAR
BOTSWANA
SWAZILAND
SOUTH
LESOTHO
AFRICA

RUSSIA

KAZAKHSTAN

MONGOLIA

GEORGIA
ARMENIA
AZERBAIJAN
UZBEKISTAN
KYRGYZSTAN
TURKMENISTAN
TAJIKISTAN
AFGHANISTAN
CHINA
IRAN
PAKISTAN
NEPAL
BHUTAN
BANGLADESH
INDIA
MYANMAR
(BURMA)
LAOS
THAILAND
VIETNAM
CAMBODIA

KUWAIT

NORTH
KOREA
SOUTH
KOREA
JAPAN

PACIFIC
OCEAN

TAIWAN

PHILIPPINES

SRI
LANKA

INDIAN
OCEAN

BRUNEI
MALAYSIA
SINGAPORE

INDONESIA

PAPUA
NEW
GUINEA

SOLOMON
ISLANDS

MAURITIUS
RÉUNION

VANUATU
FIJI

NEW
CALEDONIA

AUSTRALIA

NEW
ZEALAND

Average annual GDP growth rate, 1998-2007, (%)

negative
less than -2.5
-2.5 to 0
no data available

positive
0 to 1
1 to 2
2 to 3
3 to 4
4 to 5
over 5

Exhibit 2.7

Relationship Between Globalization and Growth in Per Capita Gross Domestic Product, 1990s, (adjusted for purchasing power parity)

SOURCE: Dollar, D. (2004) "Globalization, Poverty and Inequality since 1980," World Bank Policy Research Working Paper 3333, June 2004, Washington, DC: World Bank. © 2004 World Bank.

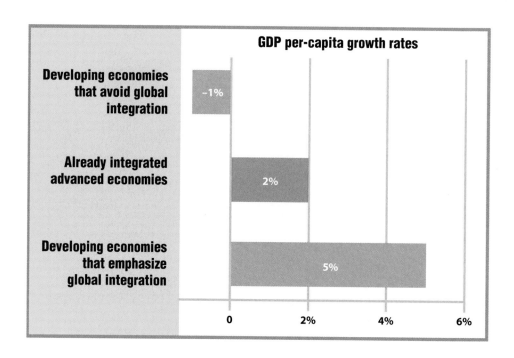

and new values. Consumers increasingly wear similar clothing, drive similar cars, and listen to the same recording stars. Advertising leads to the emergence of societal values modeled on Western countries, especially the United States. Hollywood dominates the global entertainment industry. In this way, globalization can alter people's norms, values, and behaviors, which tend to homogenize over time.

Critics call these trends the "McDonald-ization" or the "Coca-Colonization" of the world. To combat such trends, governments try to block cultural imperialism and prevent the erosion of local traditions. In Canada, France, and Germany, the public sector attempts to prevent U.S. ideals from diluting local traditions. Hollywood, McDonald's, and Disneyland are seen as Trojan horses that permanently alter food preferences, lifestyles, and other aspects of traditional life. In a globalizing world, for better or worse, such trends appear to be inevitable.

Information and communications technologies promote the homogenization of world cultures. People worldwide are exposed to movies, television, the Internet, and other information sources that promote lifestyles of people in the United States and other advanced economies. Appetites grow for "Western" products and services, which are seen to signal higher living standards. For example, despite low per-capita income, many Chinese buy consumer electronics such as cell phones and TV sets. Global media have a pervasive effect on local culture, gradually shifting it toward a universal norm.

At the same time, the flow of cultural influence often goes both ways. For instance, Advanced Fresh Concepts is a Japanese food company that is transforming fast food by selling sushi and other Japanese favorites in supermarkets throughout the United States. It sells some $250 million worth of sushi to U.S. buyers every year.[27] As the influence of the Chinese economy grows over time, Western countries will likely adopt cultural norms from China as well. Chinese restaurants and some Chinese traditions are already a way of life in much of the world outside China. Similar influences can be seen from Latin America and other areas in the developing world.

In addition, cultural anthropologists note that cultural values change at a glacial pace. Even if people from different nations appear similar on the surface, they usually hold traditional attitudes, values, and beliefs rooted in the history and culture of the country where they live. Although some tangibles are becoming more universal, people's behavior and mindsets remain stable over time. Religious differences are as strong as ever. Language differences are steadfast across national borders. While a degree of cultural imperialism may be at work, it is offset by the countertrend of nationalism. As globalization standardizes superficial aspects of life across national cultures, people are resisting these forces by insisting on their national identity and taking steps to protect it. This is evident, for example, in Belgium, Canada, and France, where laws were passed to protect national language and culture.

Firm-Level Consequences of Market Globalization: Internationalization of the Firm's Value Chain

Western companies such as McDonald's can influence people's food preferences, but cultural values remain stable over time.

The globalization of markets has opened up countless new business opportunities for internationalizing firms. At the same time, globalization implies that firms must accommodate new risks and intense rivalry from foreign competitors. Globalization results in buyers who are more demanding and who shop for the best deals from suppliers worldwide. A purely domestic focus is no longer viable for firms in most industries. Companies need to proactively internationalize their value chain in order to profit from new opportunities and reduce the harm of potential threats. Managers must increasingly adopt a worldwide orientation rather than a local focus. Internationalization may take the form of global sourcing, exporting, or investment in key markets abroad. The more proactive firms seek a simultaneous presence in all major trading regions, especially Asia, Europe, and North America. They concentrate their activities in those countries where they can achieve and sustain competitive advantage.

The most direct implication of market globalization is on the firm's value chain. Market globalization compels firms to organize their sourcing, manufacturing, marketing, and other value-adding activities on a global scale. As noted earlier, a value chain is the sequence of value-adding activities performed by the firm in the process of developing, producing, marketing, and servicing a product. In a typical value chain, the firm conducts research and product development (R&D), purchases production inputs, and assembles or manufactures a product or service. Next, the firm performs marketing activities such as pricing, promotion, and selling, followed by distribution of the product in targeted markets and after-sales service. Value chains vary in complexity and across industries and product categories. The value chain concept is useful in international business because it helps clarify what activities are performed *where* in the world. For instance, exporting firms perform most "upstream" value-chain activities (R&D and production) in the home market and most "downstream" activities (marketing and after-sales service) abroad.

Exhibit 2.8 illustrates a typical international firm's value chain. Each value-adding activity is subject to internationalization; that is, it can be performed abroad instead of at home. As the examples in Exhibit 2.8 suggest, companies have considerable latitude regarding where in the world they locate or *configure* key value-adding activities. The most typical reasons for locating value-chain activities in particular countries are to reduce the costs of R&D and production or to gain closer access to customers. The practice of internationalizing the value

Stages in the Firm's Value Chain	Research & Development	Procurement (Sourcing)	Manufacturing	Marketing	Distribution	Sales & Service
Examples	The pharmaceutical firm Pfizer conducts R&D in Singapore, Japan, and other countries to gain access to scientific talent or collaborate with local partner firms.	Office furniture manufacturer Steelcase sources low-cost parts from suppliers in China and Mexico. Dell has business processes such as data entry, call centers, and payroll processing performed in India.	Genzyme Corp. does much of the manufacturing and testing of its surgical and diagnostic products in Germany, Switzerland, and the United Kingdom. Renault produces cars via low-cost factories in eastern Europe.	BMW and Honda locate marketing subsidiaries in the United States to more effectively target their vehicles to the huge U.S. market. Carrefour and Barclays Bank establish worldwide networks of stores and offices to be near their customers.	Wolverine World Wide, marketer of popular shoe brands (e.g., Hush Puppies, Bates), contracts with independent retail stores abroad to reach its customers.	Direct sales companies such as Amway and Avon employ their own independent sales force in China, Mexico, and elsewhere, in order to reach end-users. Toyota maintains sales and customer service operations abroad in order to meet customer requirements more effectively.

Exhibit 2.8   Examples of How Firms' Value-Chain Activities Can Be Internationalized

chain is often referred to as *offshoring,* where the firm relocates a major value-chain activity by establishing a factory or other subsidiary abroad. A related trend is global sourcing, in which the firm delegates performance of the value-adding activity to an external supplier or contractor located abroad. We discuss offshoring and global sourcing in Chapter 16.

As German carmaker BMW launched a new factory in South Carolina, Jackson Mills, an aging textile plant a few miles away, closed its doors and shed thousands of workers in the same month. In both cases, globalization had created a new reality for these firms. By establishing operations in the United States, BMW found it could manufacture cars cost-effectively while more readily accessing the huge U.S. market. In the process, BMW created thousands of high-paying, better-quality jobs for U.S. workers. Simultaneously, Jackson Mills had discovered it could source textiles of comparable quality more cost-effectively from suppliers in Asia. Globalization drove these firms to relocate key value-adding activities to the most advantageous locations around the world.

Diverse Perspectives on Globalization of Markets

Recently, a major university sponsored a roundtable on the broader implications of international business. The participants were an anti-international business activist, a business executive with extensive international dealings, and a trade official from the U.S. government. Each of these individuals expressed varying views. Excerpts from the exchange present the diverse perspectives of market globalization held by different interest groups.

Activist

"One problem with international business is that it often ignores human rights and basic labor standards. Low-wage factories abroad create substandard working conditions. The activities of multinational companies result in not only job losses here at home, but also in low wages and exploited workers around the world. Just think of the sweatshops in Asia that make imported clothing. Think of the auto workers in Mexico who live in horrible conditions and make only a few dollars a day."

Business Executive

"Our country needs to participate in the global economy. Companies that export provide better-paying jobs, have more profits, pay higher taxes, and stimulate purchases from local suppliers. Foreign companies that invest here create new jobs, enhance local living standards, and pressure our firms to stay competitive in a challenging global marketplace. Exporters pay higher wages and provide better benefits than nonexporting firms. Many companies need access to foreign markets because of the huge, upfront research and development costs they accumulate. One more pill is cheap; it's the cost of research to find a cure for AIDS that is prohibitive. I think it's a pretty strong argument for the human basis of doing international business. Companies need big markets to amortize the costs of big projects. Africa is getting decimated by AIDS. But pharmaceutical firms can't do the necessary R&D unless they can amortize those costs over much larger potential markets. In the long run, uninterrupted international commerce is good."

Trade Official

"The current administration believes strongly in the value of free trade. The President strongly supported NAFTA, and this has already had a positive effect on the U.S. economy through increasing exports to Mexico, creating jobs for Americans, and leading to improved investment opportunities. Countries are forging ahead with international trade ties. Canada has completed a free trade agreement with Chile. Economic ties lead to cultural ties and more peaceful relations. Also, it is hard for our government to promote freedom and democracy around the world if we are not promoting free trade."

Activist

"We cannot overlook the detrimental effects of globalization on the natural environment. The more we trade internationally, the more irreparable harm will be done to the environment. International business means more environmentally damaging development. Companies internationalize so they can become more efficient. But if countries have weak environmental standards, then factories will be built with minimal environmental standards."

Business Executive

"If we trade internationally, then living standards will increase everywhere. As living standards rise, awareness of and care for the environment will also increase. In other words, international business is good for the world because it creates wealth. The more affluent the people, the more they will care about their environment and pass laws to protect it. Right here at home, we have shown that a good economy and a clean environment are not mutually exclusive. We can have it both ways: a clean planet and a better economic quality of life."

Trade Official

"I think part of the solution is to negotiate trade agreements that take environmental factors into account. International trade that runs roughshod over legitimate environmental concerns is counterproductive and defeats the political agendas of most governments around the world. It is clear that international trade must take environmental concerns into account."

Activist

"International trade interferes with the sovereignty of national governments. When General Motors is the nation's biggest company, like it is in Canada, it is harder for governments to manage policies regarding taxes, monetary policy, social issues, and exchange rates. And who are we, trying to impose our own cultural standards on the world? When I am in Europe or Asia, I see McDonald's all over the place. They see the United States as a dominating power that uses globalization to its own advantage, harming the economic, cultural, and environmental interests of the rest of the world."

"Global companies claim that they spread modern technologies around the world. But technology is good only if you have access to it. In most of Africa, you have no on-ramp to the Internet. To access the Internet, you need access to a computer; awfully difficult or impossible in countries where people make only a few dollars a day. When you're paid such a low wage, how can you afford technology? How can you afford to go see a doctor, even if he has the technology? Globalization is widening the gap between rich and poor. As inequality grows, people have less and less in common. Multinational companies have weakened poor countries and are exposing poor people to harmful competition. Infant industries in developing economies can't make it when they're confronted with the power of giant multinational firms."

Business Executive

"Companies increasingly recognize the importance of being good global citizens. Motorola has profited from its business in China, but it has also contributed to the development of educational systems in that country. There are a lot more literate people, especially literate women, in China than ever before. Japanese MNEs have done a great job of investing in the communities where they do business. Businesses are not all evil; they do a lot of good for the world, too. Bill Gates is going to do more than any government to get people computers and get them hooked up on the Internet. He has created the world's largest fund to combat diseases of the poor. He and Warren Buffett are tackling many of these diseases in a systematic way. GlaxoSmithKline is working with the World Health Organization to find a cure for Elephantiasis, which is a terrible disease that afflicts people in Africa."

Trade Official

"Globalization is complex and it is hard to tease out what is bad and what is good. Globalization has made rapid progress since the 1980s, a period during which global poverty has actually declined. Social indicators for many poor countries show improvement over several decades. It is true that income disparities have increased dramatically over the last 50 years while international trade has integrated the world economy. The world has experienced a generally rising tide in terms of peoples' standard of living. People everywhere today are better off than they were 50 years ago. There are some exceptions to this, of course, but it's better to live in a world in which 20 percent of the people are affluent

and 80 percent are poor, than a world in which nearly 100 percent of the people are poor, as was the case throughout most of human history. There is a strong role for government in all this. Countries benefit from trade, but governments are responsible for protecting citizens from the negative or unintended consequences that trade can bring." <

AACSB: **Reflective Thinking, Ethical Reasoning**

Case Questions

1. Do you think globalization and MNE activity are creating problems for the world? What kinds of problems can you identify? Are there some unintended consequences of international business?

2. Summarize the arguments in favor of globalization made by the business executive. What is the role of technology in supporting company performance in a globalizing business environment?

3. What are the roles of state and federal governments in dealing with globalization? Do you believe that government has a responsibility to protect its citizens from the potential negative effects of foreign MNEs conducting business in their countries? What kinds of government actions would you recommend?

4. What is the role of education in: addressing some of the problems raised in the previous discussion; creating societies in which people can deal effectively with public policy issues; creating citizens who can compete effectively in the global marketplace?

Sources: Bernard, Andrew, and J. Bradford Jensen. (1999). *Exporting and Productivity.* Cambridge, MA: National Bureau of Economic Research; International Monetary Fund. (2002). *Globalization: Threat or Opportunity?* Retrieved from www.imf.org/external/np/exr/ib/2000/041200. Washington, DC: International Monetary Fund; Lechner, Frank. (2004). *Does Globalization Cause Poverty?* Retrieved from www.sociology.emory.edu/globalization/issues03.html (Atlanta, GA: Emory University Globalization Web site); Lechner, Frank, (2004). *Does Globalization Diminish Cultural Diversity?* Retrieved from www.sociology.emory.edu/globalization/issues05.html (Atlanta, GA: Emory University Globalization Web site); Lechner, Frank, Deborah McFarland, Thomas Remington, and Jeff Rosensweig. (2004). *Is a Globalization Backlash Occurring?* Retrieved from www.emory.edu/ACAD_EXCHANGE/1999/mayjune99/global.html (Atlanta, GA: Emory University Globalization Web site); McCarty, William, Mark Kasoff, and Doug Smith. (2000). "The Importance of International Business at the Local Level," *Business Horizons* (May–June, 2000), 35–42.

CHAPTER ESSENTIALS

Key Terms

Summary

In this chapter, you learned about:

1. **Why Globalization is not a new phenomenon**

   Globalization of markets refers to the gradual integration and growing interdependence of national economies. Early civilizations in the Mediterranean, Middle East, Asia, Africa, and Europe have all contributed to the growth of cross-border trade over time. Bursts of cross-border trade have been triggered by world events and technological discoveries. The first distinct phase of market globalization ran from about 1830 to the late 1800s and was spurred by the growth of railroads, efficient ocean transport, and the rise of large manufacturing and trading firms. The second phase coincided with the rise of electricity around 1900 and peaked in the 1930s with the coming of World War II. The third phase emerged in 1945, along with the rise of economic powers such as the United States and Japan, pent-up demand, and efforts to rebuild war-torn areas. The fourth and current phase began in the 1980s and was stimulated particularly by the rise of IT, the Internet, and other advanced technologies. The **World Trade Organization** is a multilateral governing body empowered to regulate international trade and investment.

2. **An organizing framework for market globalization**

   Market globalization can be modeled in terms of its drivers, dimensions, societal consequences, and firm-level consequences. As market globalization intensifies, firms are compelled to respond to challenges and exploit new advantages. Many firms proactively pursue internationalization as a strategic move. They become more aggressive at identifying foreign market opportunities, seeking partnerships with foreign firms, and building organizational capabilities in order to enhance their competitive advantage.

3. **Dimensions of market globalization**

   Market globalization refers to the growing integration of the world economy from the international business activities of countless firms. It represents a growing global interconnectedness of buyers, producers, suppliers, and governments. Globalization has fostered a new dynamism in the world economy, the emergence of *regional economic integration blocs,* growth of global investment and financial flows, the convergence of buyer lifestyles and needs, and the globalization of production. At the business enterprise level, market globalization amounts to reconfiguration of company **value chains**—the sequence of value-adding activities including sourcing, manufacturing, marketing, and distribution—on a *global* scale.

4. **Drivers of market globalization**

   Market globalization is driven by several factors, including falling trade and investment barriers, market liberalization and adoption of free market economics in formerly closed economies, industrialization and economic development, especially among emerging markets, integration of world financial markets, and technological advances.

5. **Technological advances as a driver of market globalization**

   Advances in technology are particularly important in driving market globalization. The most important advances in technology have occurred in information technology, communications, the Internet, manufacturing, and transportation. These systems help create an interconnected network of customers, suppliers, and intermediaries worldwide. They have made the cost of international business affordable for all types of firms.

6. **Societal consequences of market globalization**

   There is much debate about globalization's benefits and harm. Critics complain that globalization interferes with national *sovereignty,* the ability of a state to govern itself without external intervention. Globalization is associated with *offshoring,* the relocation of value-chain activities to foreign locations where they can be performed less costly by subsidiaries or independent suppliers. Globalization tends to decrease poverty, but may widen the gap between the rich and the poor. Unrestricted industrialization may harm the natural environment. Globalization is also associated with the loss of cultural values unique to each nation.

7. Firm-level consequences of market globalization: Internationalization of the firm's value chain

Market globalization compels firms to organize their sourcing, manufacturing, marketing, and other value-adding activities on a global scale. Each value-adding activity can be performed in the home country or abroad. Firms choose where in the world they locate or configure key value-adding activities. Firms internationalize value-chain activities to reduce the costs of R&D and production, or to gain closer access to customers.

Test Your Comprehension

1. Define market globalization. What are the underlying dimensions of this megatrend?

2. Is globalization a recent phenomenon? Describe the four phases of globalization.

3. Summarize the five dimensions of globalization. Which of these do you think is the most visible manifestation of globalization?

4. Describe the five drivers of globalization.

5. What is the role of the World Trade Organization?

6. In what areas have technological advances had their greatest effect on facilitating world trade and investment?

7. What are the pros and cons of globalization?

8. What effect does globalization have on national sovereignty, employment, the poor, the natural environment, and national culture?

9. What are the implications of globalization for firm internationalization?

Apply Your Understanding AACSB: Communication, Reflective Thinking, Ethical Reasoning, Use of Information Technology, Analytical Skills

1. Imagine you are studying for your international business class at a local coffee shop. The manager spies your textbook and remarks: "I don't get all that foreign business stuff. I don't pay much attention to it. I'm a local guy running a small business. Thank goodness I don't have to worry about any of that." The manager's comments make you think. Despite the manager's comments, you realize there is much more to business than just local concerns. What is the likely value chain of a coffee shop? For example, how did the varieties of coffee beans get there? What is the likely effect of market globalization on coffee shops? Do technological advances play any role in the shop's value chain? Does globalization imply any negative consequences for the worldwide coffee industry? Justify your answer.

2. Suppose you get a job at Fossil Fuel, Inc., an oil company that has been severely criticized for global business practices that are seen to exacerbate economic, political, and social phenomena in some countries. Your boss directs you to increase your familiarity with market globalization, with a view to developing company strategies that are more sensitive to the firm's globalization critics. In your investigation, you discover that there are five major dimensions associated with market globalization. What are these dimensions? What are the drivers of market globalization? Structure and elaborate your answer in the form of a memo to your boss.

3. Globalization provides numerous advantages to businesses and consumers around the world. At the same time, some critics believe that globalization is harming various aspects of life and commerce. In what ways is globalization good for firms and consumers? In what ways is globalization harmful to firms and consumers?

4. Thinking in terms of the global value chain, what role does technology play in each of the value chain stages? Structure your answer by thinking about each stage of the value chain (R&D, procurement, manufacturing, marketing, distribution, sales, and service) and each major type of international technology (information technology, communications, manufacturing, and transportation). For example, today many firms use global teams to conduct R&D for new product development. The teams are linked together via intranets and other communications technologies that facilitate instantaneous interaction on daily R&D activities with team members worldwide.

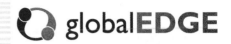
AACSB: Reflective Thinking, Ethical Reasoning, Use of Information Technology, Analytical Skills

Refer to Chapter 1, page 27, for instructions on how to access and use globalEDGE™.

1. *Foreign Policy* magazine, together with *A.T. Kearney, Inc.*, prepares an annual *Globalization Index* (enter "globalization index" at globalEDGE™), which ranks the 20 most globalized nations. The index uses four different dimensions to measure globalization:

   - *Economic integration with the rest of the world* (such as trade and FDI levels),

   - *Personal contact with the rest of the world* (such as international travel and tourism, telephone traffic),

   - *Political engagement with the rest of the world* (such as memberships in international organizations, concern about world poverty and other global issues),

   - *Technological integration with the rest of the world* (such as Internet users, hosts, secure servers).

   Visit globalEDGE™ and explain why each of these dimensions is important for a nation to have a substantial presence in the global economy and international business.

2. Service sector jobs are increasingly outsourced to lower-cost locations abroad. globalEDGE™ has various resources that detail the nature and location of jobs that have been transferred abroad. Some experts believe that the resulting foreign investment and increased demand in lower-cost countries will cause wages to rise in those countries, eliminating cost advantages from offshoring and narrowing the income gap between developed economies and low-cost countries. In other words, offshoring will help to reduce global poverty. Others believe that manufacturing jobs will be consistently moved to low-cost countries, making China and India the world's center of innovation and production. What do you think? Find three articles on outsourcing at globalEDGE™ by doing a search using the keywords "global outsourcing" or "offshoring," and write a report on the most likely consequences of these trends for your country, its workers, and consumers.

3. A key characteristic of globalization is the increasingly integrated world economy. Multinational enterprises (MNEs) and many nations have a vested interest in maintaining the globalization trend. If the trend were somehow reversed, participants in international business, such as exporters, would likely suffer big economic losses. In many ways, globalization's role in the world economy is critical. But just how big is the global economy? What is the extent of international trade relative to the size of the global economy? What is the proportion of international trade in the GDPs of each of the following countries: Australia, Canada, Sweden, United Kingdom, and the United States? Use globalEDGE™ to address these questions.

CKR Cavusgil Knight Riesenberger

Management Skill Builder©

What is a C/K/R Management Skill Builder©?

A C/K/R MSB© is a practical exercise designed to help you become familiar with key managerial challenges or decisions that entry-level professionals working in international business are likely to encounter. Completing the C/K/R MSBs© in this book will enable you to acquire practical, real-world skills that will help you perform well in your career. Each C/K/R MSB© presents:

- A managerial challenge in the context of a real-world scenario
- The skills that you will acquire in solving the challenge
- A methodology and resources to use in solving the challenge

For each *C/K/R MSB©*, the following sections are featured in the textbook:

1. Introduction
2. Managerial Challenge
3. Background
4. Managerial Skills You will Gain
5. Your Task

Each C/K/R MSB© is then continued on the C/K/R Knowledge Portal©, and features the following additional sections:

1. Expanded Background
2. Your Task and Methodology
3. Suggested Resources for this Exercise
4. Template

In order to complete each C/K/R MSB©, you need to visit the C/K/R Knowledge Portal© at **www.prenhall.com/cavusgil**.

Management Skill Builder©

Corporate Social Responsibility: Coffee, Ethiopia, and Starbucks

Corporate social responsibility refers to a management practice of making business decisions that have a positive effect on society and the environment. Management should make decisions that properly balance the business goal of profit and social issues such as education, diversity, poverty, the treatment of workers, and stewardship of the environment.

AACSB: Communication, Reflective Thinking, Ethical Reasoning, Use of Information Technology, Analytical Skills

Managerial Challenge

In international settings, the firm must establish itself as a global citizen. It must be a socially responsible corporate player. This may imply sacrificing a degree of profitability in order to make a contribution to the broader needs of the host country.

How managers resolve this trade-off between optimizing business decisions with meeting the expectations of its stakeholders (customers, employees, suppliers, taxpayers, community groups, and shareholders) is critical. The managerial challenge is one of achieving social responsibility while simultaneously meeting revenue and profitability goals.

Background

Starbucks, the international coffee vendor, contracts with farmers in Ethiopia to grow coffee beans. Acting on behalf of its coffee growers, the Ethiopian government has argued that Starbucks keeps too much of the profits from these operations: Starbucks sells coffee for $26 per pound, while it seems to overlook the fact that coffee growers in developing countries such as Ethiopia are not receiving a fair price.

Consider that many coffee experts and many coffee drinkers believe Ethiopian coffee to be the best in the world. Starbucks certainly wants to offer Ethiopian coffee, which enjoys such a great reputation, to its customers. For example, Starbucks sells a coffee called Harer, which is the name of a particular Ethiopian coffee bean. Starbucks can charge customers a premium for the experience. But Ethiopian coffee sellers cannot charge Starbucks for using that name. By seeking registered trademark status for Harer and other Ethiopian coffee beans in the United States, the Ethiopian government believes it can bargain for better export prices on behalf of some 15 million Ethiopians who depend on coffee growing for their livelihood. The Ethiopian government has received much support in this highly publicized conflict from Oxfam, a nongovernmental organization concerned with global poverty issues (http://www.oxfamamerica.org).

For its part, Starbucks has resisted actions that would reduce its bargaining power with Ethiopian coffee growers. The firm has also argued that trademarking coffee beans might introduce legal complexities that will force coffee buyers to turn to other countries. Starbucks management said that it favors a geographic certification model (similar to Florida Orange Juice or Napa Valley Wines), which provides a point of origin and establishes standards of quality.

Managerial Skills You Will Gain

In this C/K/R/ Management Skill Builder©, as a prospective manager, you will:

1. Learn the complexity of appropriately balancing the needs for corporate profitability and social responsibility.
2. Research the power of activist groups such as Oxfam.
3. Develop a systematic process through which a firm can reconcile competing demands of corporate and societal objectives.

Your Task

In this C/K/R Management Skill Builder©, assume that you are a manager at Starbucks assigned to advise senior management on whether to proceed with the endorsement of trademark rights in the United States.

In light of recent negative publicity and actions of activist groups, should Starbucks maintain its position that trademarking coffee beans might compel coffee buyers like itself to turn to alternative coffee growing nations?

Your assignment is to research the issue of Starbucks's corporate social responsibility with regard to coffee profit sharing in Ethiopia. What actions should Starbucks take in this regard?

Go to the C/K/R Knowledge Portal©

www.prenhall.com/cavusgil

Proceed to the C/K/R Knowledge Portal© to obtain the expanded background information, your task and methodology, suggested resources for this exercise, and the presentation template to use.

Organizational Participants that Make International Business Happen

> ## Born Global Firms

Established in 1989, Geo Search Ltd. is a Japanese company that develops high-technology equipment to help engineers survey ground surfaces for cavities and build safe roads, highways, airports, and underground utility lines. At the request of the United Nations, Geo Search designed the world's first land mine detector, called Mine Eye, in 1997. The firm had an immediate international market because of millions of mines buried in countries like Kuwait, Cambodia, Afghanistan, and Lebanon. The firm works with non-governmental organizations (NGOs) to search for mines worldwide. Removing land mines is a risky undertaking, particularly plastic mines that cannot be found with metal detectors. Geo Search's electromagnetic radar can distinguish between mines and other objects buried underground. Images appear in three dimensions on a liquid crystal display, and there is no need to touch the ground surface.

Geo Search is one example of an increasing number of small- and medium-sized enterprises (SMEs) that are active in international business. SMEs make up the majority of all firms in a typical country and account for about 50 percent of economic activity. Compared to large multinational enterprises (MNEs) that historically

were the most common types of international firms, the typical SME has far fewer financial and human resources. In the past, international business was beyond the reach of most SMEs. But globalization and technological advances have made venturing abroad much less expensive, and created a global commercial environment in which there are many more small firms doing international business than ever before. Since the 1980s, companies that internationalize at or near their founding, *born-global firms*, have been springing up all over the world.

Despite the scarce resources that characterize most SMEs, managers in born globals tend to see the world as their marketplace from or near the firm's founding. The period from domestic establishment to initial foreign market entry is often three years or less. By internationalizing as early and rapidly as they do, born globals develop a borderless corporate culture. Management targets products and services to a dozen or more countries within a few years after launching the firm. Compared to MNEs, smaller size provides born globals with a high degree of flexibility, which helps them serve their foreign customers better. Born globals usually internationalize through exporting.

Some firms internationalize early for various reasons. Management may perceive big demand for the firm's products abroad. Management may also have a strong international orientation, and push the firm into foreign markets. In addition, firms sometimes specialize in a particular product category for which demand in the home market is too small. When this happens, management must seek markets abroad. For example, Neogen Corporation is a born global in the United States that manufactures chemicals that kill harmful bacteria and toxins in food crops. The fact that certain toxins are more common in foreign locations led Neogen to internationalize shortly after its founding.

The widespread emergence of born global firms is an exciting trend because it shows that *any* company, regardless of its size, age, or resource base, can participate actively in international business. We therefore need to revisit the traditional view of the large multinational corporation as the dominant player in international business. Today, born globals and other SMEs that are fairly active exporters make up a sizable proportion of internationally active firms. Their relative inexperience and limited financial resources no longer prevent them from succeeding in foreign markets. The trend is particularly relevant to college students who specialize in international business, because SMEs provide many new job opportunities as they aggressively pursue international ventures. ◄

Sources: da Costa, Eduardo. (2001). *Global E-Commerce Strategies for Small Businesses.* Cambridge, MA: The MIT Press; Knight, G., and S. T. Cavusgil. (2004). "Innovation, Organizational Capabilities, and the Born-Global Firm." *Journal of International Business Studies* 35(2): 124–41; Mambula, C. J. (2004). "Relating External Support, Business Growth and Creating Strategies for Survival: A Comparative Case Study Analysis of Small Manufacturing Firms (SMFs) and Entrepreneurs." *Small Business Economics* 22:83–109; Oviatt, B., and P. McDougall. (1994). "Toward a Theory of International New Ventures," *Journal of International Business Studies* 25 (1): 45–64; OECD. (1997). *Globalization and Small and Medium Enterprises (SMEs).* Paris: Organisation for Economic Co-operation and Development; McDougall, P., and B. Oviatt. (2000). "International Entrepreneurship: The Intersection of Two Research Paths." *Academy of Management Journal* 43 (5): 902–6; Rahman, Bayan. (1999). "Extra Eye on Land Mines." *Financial Times* (July): 19; Rennie, M. (1993). "Born Global." *McKinsey Quarterly* (4): 45–52.

In Chapter 2, we learned that market globalization is the growing integration of the world economy through the activities of firms. Factors that drive globalization include falling trade and investment barriers and technological advances. In this chapter, we discuss the people and organizations that make globalization happen and their role in the value chain.

 ## Three Types of Participants in International Business

International business is a complex undertaking and requires numerous organizations to work together as a coordinated team. These organizations, or participants, contribute various types of expertise and inputs that facilitate international business. The participants vary in terms of their motives for going international, modes of entry, and types of operations. There are three major categories of participants:

1. A **focal firm** is the initiator of an international business transaction, including MNEs and SMEs, that conceives, designs, and produces the offerings intended for consumption by customers worldwide. Focal firms take the center stage in international business. They include large multinational enterprises (MNEs; also known as Multinational Corporations or MNCs) and small- and medium-sized enterprises (SMEs). Some are privately owned companies, others are public, stock-held firms, and still others are state enterprises owned by governments. Some focal firms are manufacturing businesses, while others are in the service sector.

2. A **distribution channel intermediary** is a specialist firm that provides a variety of logistics and marketing services for focal firms as part of the international supply chain, both in the home country and abroad. Intermediaries such as dis-

Focal firm The initiator of an international business transaction, including MNEs and SMEs, that conceives, designs, and produces the offerings intended for consumption by customers worldwide.

Distribution channel intermediary A specialist firm that provides a variety of logistics and marketing services for focal firms as part of the international supply chain, both in the home country and abroad.

tributors and sales representatives are typically located in foreign markets and provide distribution and marketing services on behalf of focal firms. Intermediaries are independent businesses in their respective markets, and work for focal firms on a contractual basis.

3. A **facilitator** is a firm or an individual with special expertise in legal advice, banking, customs clearance, or related support services, that assists focal firms perform international business transactions. Facilitators include logistics service providers, freight forwarders, banks, and other support firms that assist focal firms perform specific functions. A **freight forwarder** is a specialized logistics service provider that arranges international shipping on behalf of exporting firms, much like a travel agent for cargo. Facilitators are found in both home and foreign markets.

International business transactions require the participation of numerous focal firms, intermediaries, and facilitators, all working closely together. The activities of the three groups of participants overlap to some degree. The focal firm performs certain activities internally and delegates other functions to intermediaries and facilitators when their special expertise is needed. In other words, the focal firm becomes a client of intermediaries and facilitators who provide services on a contractual basis.

While these three types of participants make up the international business landscape, keep in mind that international business transactions take place within political, legal, and regulatory environments. Nations also have a strong influence over their own economic development and the progress of their industries and firms. Governments create commercial environments that encourage the development of strong industries and technological prowess. Most nations have a trade infrastructure that consists of industry associations, chambers of commerce, universities, and helpful government agencies. For example, Japan registered exemplary economic growth (what was labeled an "economic miracle") during the 1980s through careful planning and a strong partnership between government and industry that skillfully mobilized technology, capital, and skilled labor.

While the focal firms, intermediaries, and facilitators represent the supply side of international business transactions, customers or buyers make up the demand side. Customers constitute the ultimate target of international business activity. For the most part, customers comprise individual *consumers and households, retailers* (businesses that purchase finished goods for the purpose of resale), and *organizational buyers* (businesses, institutions, and governments that purchase goods and services as inputs to a production process, or as supplies needed to run a business or organization). Governments and nonprofit organizations such as CARE and UNICEF are among major international customer groups.

Participants Organized by Value-Chain Activity

It is useful to think of the three categories of participants in terms of the firm's value chain we discussed in Chapter 2. The focal firms, intermediaries, and facilitators all are involved in one or more critical value-adding activities such as procurement, manufacturing, marketing, transportation, distribution, and support—configured across several countries. The value chain can be thought of as the complete business system of the focal firm. It comprises all of the activities that the focal firm performs.

In international business, the focal firm may retain core activities such as production and marketing within its own organization and delegate distribution and customer service responsibilities to independent contractors, such as foreign-market based distributors. Therefore, the resulting business system is subject to

Facilitator A firm or an individual with special expertise in legal advice, banking, customs clearance, or related support services, that assists focal firms in the performance of international business transactions.

Freight forwarder A specialized logistics service provider that arranges international shipping on behalf of exporting firms, much like a travel agent for cargo.

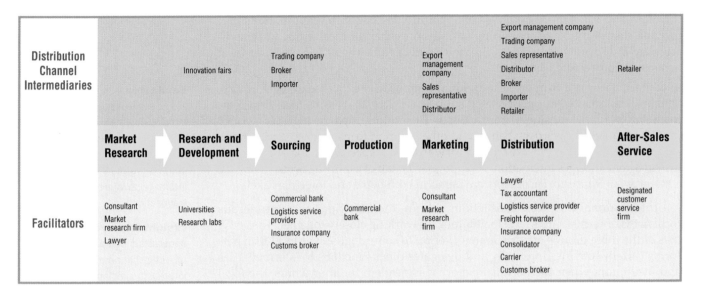

Exhibit 3.1

Typical Positions of Intermediaries and Facilitators in the International Value Chain

internationalization; that is, individual value-adding activities can be configured in multiple countries. Exhibit 3.1 shows the stages in the value chain where channel intermediaries and facilitators typically operate. It also identifies intermediaries and facilitators critical to the functioning of international business transactions that we discuss in this chapter.

In exporting firms, much of the value chain is concentrated within one nation—the home country. In highly international firms, management may perform a variety of value-chain activities—production, marketing, distribution—within several countries. In highly internationalized focal firms, the value chain is configured in numerous countries and often from multiple suppliers. Multinational enterprises strive to rationalize their value chain by locating each activity in a country with the most favorable combination of cost, quality, logistical considerations, and other criteria.

Exhibit 3.2 illustrates the national and geographic diversity of suppliers that provide content for an automobile. When General Motors redesigned the Chevrolet Malibu for the 2004 model year, it purchased key components from several dozen primary (so-called *tier one*) suppliers, such as alternators from Valeo, transmission chains from BorgWagner, door panels from Johnson Controls, and tires from Bridgestone/Firestone. These suppliers are headquartered in such countries as Germany, Japan, France, Korea, and the United Kingdom, in addition to the United States, but the components they sell are manufactured in typically low-cost countries and then shipped to the General Motors plant in Fairfax, Kansas. As you can see, manufacturing of products such as automobiles involves a truly international value chain.

An Illustration of an International Value Chain: Dell Inc.

Dell makes a variety of products, each with its own value chain. Depending on the number of products offered and the complexity of operations, companies may develop and manage numerous value chains. Exhibit 3.3 illustrates the value chain for the production and marketing of Dell notebook computers. Let's take the example of Tom, a Dell customer who placed an order for a notebook. Such orders can be placed online at Dell.com or by telephone with a Dell sales representative. After Tom placed his order, the representative input it into Dell's order management system, verified his credit card through Dell's work-flow connection with Visa, a global financial services facilitator, and released the order into Dell's production system.

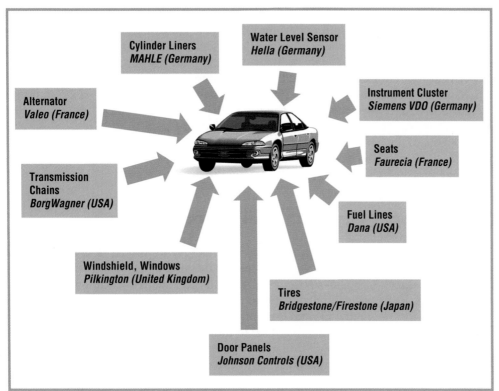

Exhibit 3.2

Sample Suppliers of Components for the Chevrolet Malibu
SOURCE: *Automotive News.*

Tom's order was processed at the Dell notebook factory in Malaysia, where the employees access parts that comprise the 30 key components of Dell notebooks from nearby suppliers. The total supply chain for Tom's computer, including multiple tiers of suppliers, involves about 400 companies, primarily in Asia, but also in Europe and the Americas.

Exhibit 3.3

Dell's International Value Chain

SOURCES: Adapted from Friedman, Thomas (2005). *The World Is Flat.* New York: Farrar, Straus, & Giroux; Lashinsky, A. (2004). "Where Dell is Going Next," *Fortune*, October 18, pp. 115–20.

Upstream Value-Chain Activities				Downstream Value-Chain Activities		
Market Research	**R&D**	**Sourcing**	**Production**	**Marketing**	**Distribution**	**After-Sales Service**
Dell conducts continuous market research, through direct interaction with thousands of customers everyday, worldwide.	R&D allows Dell to develop new notebook models and improve existing ones. Notebooks are completely redesigned every twelve months. Dell engineers in the United States conduct R&D jointly with specialized notebook designers in Taiwan.	The parts for the notebook are sourced worldwide, but mainly from suppliers in Asia. For example, Intel microprocessors are sourced from Intel factories in China, Costa Rica, and Malaysia; LCD displays are sourced from factories in South Korea, Japan, and Taiwan.	The notebook is assembled and software installed at one of Dell's six factories in Brazil, China, Ireland, Malaysia, or the United States.	Dell sells computers to buyers worldwide, but especially in the United States, where it holds one-third of the PC market, and online sales are common. Outside the United States, Dell has about 12 percent of total market share.	For its U.S. sales, Dell uses air transport to ship notebooks from its factories to the express delivery firm UPS, in Nashville, Tennessee. UPS then ships the notebooks to final customers. For sales in other countries, Dell uses local express delivery firms. The time period from order submission to final order delivery is typically less than two weeks.	Dell performs service and technical support in its major markets, especially Europe, Japan, and the United States. It employs technical support personnel in Europe, India, Japan, and the United States.

On a typical day, Dell processes orders for 150,000 computers, which are sold and distributed to customers around the world. Although based in Texas, non-U.S. sales account for roughly 40 percent of Dell's total sales (about $56 billion in 2006). As growth in U.S. sales flattens over time, the proportion of non-U.S. sales will grow. Shipping is handled via air transport. For instance, from the Dell Malaysia factory to the United States, Dell charters a China Airlines 747 that flies to Nashville, Tennessee six days a week. Each jet carries 25,000 Dell notebooks that weigh a total of 110,000 kilograms, or 242,500 pounds.

One of the hallmarks of Dell's value chain is collaboration. CEO Michael Dell and other members of top management constantly work with their suppliers to make process improvements in Dell's value chain.

 Focal Firms in International Business

Imagine a typical theatrical production on Broadway in New York or on London's West End. There are script writers, stage managers, lighting technicians, musicians, set directors, business managers, and publicity staff, in addition to performing actors. Each participant contributes to the production in different ways. Much coordination among the players is required. Advance planning, preparation, timeliness, and synchronization are critical to ultimate success. Fulfillment of international business transactions similarly requires the participation of many specialist organizations, exact timing, and precision.

As we saw early in this chapter, focal firms initiate an international business transaction by conceiving, designing, and producing offerings intended for consumption by customers worldwide. Focal firms are the most prominent international players, partly because they include well-known multinational enterprises and small- and medium-sized exporting firms, including contemporary organizations such as the born globals discussed in the opening vignette. Let's learn more about each of these key actors in international business.

The Multinational Enterprise

Multinational enterprise (MNE) Is a large company with substantial resources that performs various business activities through a network of subsidiaries and affiliates located in multiple countries.

A **Multinational enterprise (MNE)** is a large company with substantial resources that performs various business activities through a network of subsidiaries and affiliates located in multiple countries. Leading MNEs are listed on the *Fortune Global 500* (www.fortune.com). Examples include well-known companies like Nestlé, Sony, Unilever, Nokia, Ford, Citibank, ABB, and Shell Oil. Although such firms employ a range of foreign market entry modes, MNEs are best known for their direct investment activities. They operate in multiple countries, especially in Asia, Europe, and North America, by setting up production plants, marketing subsidiaries, and regional headquarters. MNEs such as Exxon, Honda, and Coca-Cola derive a substantial portion of their total sales and profits, often more than half, from cross-border operations. Exhibit 3.4 highlights a sample of MNEs and illustrates the diverse industry sectors these focal firms represent.

Some focal firms operate in the services sector, including airlines, construction companies, and management consultancies. Examples include Citibank in banking, CIGNA in insurance, Bouygues in construction, Accor in hospitality, Disney in entertainment, Nextel in telecommunications, and Best Buy in retailing. Although retailers are usually classified as intermediaries, some large ones such as IKEA, Wal-Mart, and Gap are considered focal firms themselves. In addition, nontraditional *Internet*-mediated businesses that deliver knowledge-based offerings like music, movies, and software online have joined the ranks of global focal firms. Amazon and Netflix are examples.

Sector	2005 Market Value (U.S. $ billions)	Percentage of World Total	Representative Firms
Financials	$ 5,832	24.3%	Capital One, Danske Bank, Royal Bank of Scotland
Consumer discretionary	2,667	11.1	Coach, Adidas, Salomon, Matsushita Electric
Information technology	2,635	11.0	Microsoft, Oracle, Hoya, Taiwan Semiconductor Manufacturing
Industrials	2,431	10.1	Landstar Systems, Shenzhen Expressway, Haldex
Energy	2,316	9.7	Mobil, Total, China Oilfield Services
Health care	2,274	9.5	GlaxoSmithKline, Novartis, Baxter International
Consumer staples	2,134	8.9	Procter & Gamble, Unilever, China Mengniu Dairy, Honda
Telecom services	1,394	5.8	AT&T, China Mobile, Royal KPN
Materials	1,316	5.5	Dow Chemical, Alcan, Vitro SA
Utilities	956	4.0	Duke Energy, Empresa Nacional de Electricidad SA, Hong Kong and China Gas, Ltd.
Total	**23,955**	100.0	

Exhibit 3.4

Multinational Enterprises as Focal Firms (Ranked by Industry Sector Size)

SOURCES: Business Week Global 1200, www.businessweek.com, "Breaking It Down by Industry".

Not all focal firms are private businesses. In developing countries and centrally planned economies, some focal firms are partly or wholly owned by the government. For example, Lenovo Group is China's leading computer maker. It owns the former PC business of IBM and is 50 percent government-owned. CNOCC is a huge oil company that tried to buy Unocal in the United States in 2005. It is 71 percent government-owned. Numerous other leading Chinese MNEs—Sinopec and PetroChina in oil, China Mobile and China Netcom in telephony, First Auto Works and Shanghai Automotive in cars, China Minmetals in mining, and China Life in insurance—are wholly or partially owned by the Chinese government.

MNEs have played a major role in the current phase of globalization. In the years following World War II, most multinationals, typically from the United States and the United Kingdom, went abroad in search of raw materials, production efficiencies, and foreign-based customers. Today, these firms undertake sourcing, manufacturing, servicing, and marketing activities that span all areas of the world.

A typical MNE, and one whose products you may have sampled, is Sodexho, a French firm that is the world's second-largest contract foodservice provider. Its 300,000 employees provide cafeteria-style food to universities, hospitals, corporations, and public institutions in more than 75 countries. Typical Sodexho customers include the United Kingdom's Unilever, Germany's Ministry of Foreign Affairs, and the U.S. Marine Corps. Sodexho is the food source for numerous college cafeterias in Australia, Canada, and the United States. Chances are, if you eat in a university cafeteria, it is a Sodexho operation. In the 1990s, Sodexho expanded into Japan, Africa, Russia, and Eastern Europe.

Small and Medium-Sized Enterprises

Small and medium-sized enterprise (SME) A company with 500 or fewer employees in the United States, although this number may need to be adjusted downward for other countries

Another type of focal firm that initiates cross-border business transactions is the **small and medium-sized enterprise (SME)**. SMEs are typically small (with 500 or fewer employees in the United States) manufacturers or service providers and now comprise the majority of firms active in international business. Nearly all firms, including the large MNEs, started out small. Compared to the large multinationals, SMEs can be more flexible and quicker to respond to global business opportunities if they have less bureaucracy and fewer fixed assets tied up in foreign markets. SMEs can also be more innovative, more adaptable, and more entrepreneurial. They are often seen as the backbone for entrepreneurship and innovation in national economies.

Being smaller organizations, SMEs are constrained by limited financial and human resources. This explains why most smaller firms choose exporting as their major international business mode. Their limited resources prevent them from undertaking direct investment, which is an expensive entry mode. To compensate, SMEs leverage the services of intermediaries and facilitators to succeed abroad. As their operations grow, some gradually establish company-owned sales offices or subsidiaries in their key target markets.

Because of their size and relative inexperience, SMEs often target specialized products to market niches that MNEs consider too small to service. Smaller firms increasingly serve neglected global market segments because they have access to direct marketing, globe-spanning logistics specialists such as FedEx and DHL, and local distributors. Internationally active SMEs are typically avid users of information and communications technologies that allow management to segment customers into narrow global market niches and efficiently serve highly specialized needs of buyers around the world. As a result, SMEs are gaining equal footing with large multinationals in the marketing of sophisticated products for sale around the world.

In Eastern Europe, the development of emerging market countries is driven increasingly by the rise of small and midsize fast-growth firms. These firms range from Latvian coffee shop chain Double Coffee to Hungarian employment recruiter CVO Group. Many of Eastern Europe's small firms are not in manufacturing, but in intellectual, knowledge-intensive industries, such as software and consulting. The rise of small firms in Eastern Europe is the result of two trends: recent, growing access to the affluent markets of the European Union, and the interest on the part of foreign direct investors in such liberalizing economies.[1]

Born Global Firms

Born global firm A young entrepreneurial company that initiates international business activity very early in its evolution, moving rapidly into foreign markets.

Born global firms, such as Geo Search Ltd., featured in the opening vignette, represent a relatively new breed of the international SME—those that undertake early and substantial internationalization. Despite the scarce resources typical of most small businesses, born globals achieve considerable foreign sales early in their evolution. One example is History and Heraldry, a born global in England that specializes in gifts for history buffs and those with English ancestry. In its first five years, the firm expanded its sales into 60 countries, exporting about 70 percent of total production. The firm's biggest markets include France, Germany, Italy, Spain, and the Americas. It recently opened a North American subsidiary in Florida.[2] Indeed, some successful born globals grow large enough to be considered an MNE.

Another example is QualComm. Founded in California in 1985, the firm eventually grew to become a major MNE on the strength of substantial international sales. QualComm initially developed and launched the e-mail software, Eudora. The firm's early international success was OmniTRACS, a two-way satellite message and position reporting system used in the global transportation industry. QualComm's first international launch was to Europe, just four years after founding. The firm was soon exporting to Europe, Brazil, China, India, Indonesia, and Japan. QualComm's founders were entrepreneurs who, from the beginning, made little distinction between domestic and international markets. Technological prowess and managerial vision were strong factors in making the firm an early international success.

The born-global phenomenon represents a new reality in international business. In such diverse countries as Australia, Denmark, Ireland, and the United States, born globals account for a substantial proportion of national exports. In many cases, born globals offer leading-edge products with substantial potential for

ERG Group is an Australian-born global firm that produces fare management systems for the public transit industry worldwide.

generating international sales. They are typically avid users of the Internet and modern communications technologies, which further facilitate early and efficient international operations.

The emergence of born globals is associated with *international entrepreneurship*, in which innovative, smaller firms increasingly pursue business opportunities everywhere, regardless of national borders. Communications and transportation technologies, falling trade barriers, and the emergence of niche markets worldwide make it possible for many contemporary entrepreneurial firms to view the world as their marketplace. Entrepreneurial managers are creative, proactive, have a strong feel for the business environment, and are ready to pursue new opportunities. They are comfortable dealing with risk and have the flexibility to make changes to company strategies as circumstances evolve. The appearance of born globals is heartening because it implies that any firm, regardless of size or experience, can succeed in international business.[3]

 ## Foreign Market Entry Strategies of Focal Firms

One way to analyze focal firms in international business is in terms of the entry strategies that they typically use to expand abroad. Earlier, we noted that the larger MNEs tend to expand abroad through foreign direct investment. Smaller firms, including born globals, tend to be exporters. Both MNEs and SMEs rely on contractual relationships such as franchising and licensing.

A Framework for Classifying Market Entry Strategies

Exhibit 3.5 shows the array of foreign market entry modes that focal firms use and the foreign partners they seek. The exhibit helps us understand the diversity of foreign market entry strategies.

The first column in Exhibit 3.5 lists three categories of international business transactions: transactions that involve the trade of products, transactions that involve contractual exchange of services or intangibles; and transactions based on investing equity ownership in foreign-based enterprises. Therefore, firms are generally involved in one or more of three major types of cross-border transactions: buying or selling products, buying or selling services, and producing or selling products or services abroad by establishing a foreign presence through direct investment.

Nature of International Transaction	Types of Focal Firm	Foreign Market Entry Strategy	Location of Major Activities	Typical Foreign Partners
Trade of products	Small manufacturer	Exporting	Home country	Distributor, agent, or other independent representative
	Large manufacturer	Exporting	Mainly abroad	Company-owned office or subsidiary
	Manufacturer	Importing (e.g., sourcing)	Home	Independent supplier
	Importer	Importing	Home	Trader or manufacturer
	Trading company	Exporting and Importing	Home	Trader or manufacturer
Contractual exchange of services or intangibles	Service provider	Exporting	Usually abroad	Agent, branch, or subsidiary
	Supplier of expertise or technical assistance	Consulting services	Abroad (temporarily)	Client
	Licensor with patent	Licensing	Home	Licensee
	Licensor with know-how	Licensing (technology transfer)	Home	Licensee
	Franchisor	Franchising	Home	Franchisee
	Service contractor	Management/Marketing service contracting	Abroad	Business owner or sponsor
	Construction/Engineering/ Design/ Architectural Firm	Turnkey contracting or Build-Own-Transfer	Abroad (temporarily)	Project owner
	Manufacturer	Non-equity, project-based, partnerships	Home or abroad	Manufacturer
Equity ownership in foreign-based enterprises	MNE	FDI via greenfield investment	Abroad	None
	MNE	FDI via acquisition	Abroad	Acquired company
	MNE	Equity joint venture	Abroad	Local business partner(s)

Exhibit 3.5 International Business Transactions, Types of Focal Firms, and Foreign Market Entry Strategies

Licensor A firm that enters a contractual agreement with a foreign partner that allows the latter the right to use certain intellectual property for a specified period of time in exchange for royalties or other compensation.

Franchisor A firm that grants another the right to use an entire business system in exchange for fees, royalties, or other forms of compensation.

Turnkey contractors Focal firms or a consortium of firms that plan, finance, organize, manage, and implement all phases of a project and then hand it over to a foreign customer after training local personnel.

The second column in Exhibit 3.5 identifies the types of focal firms engaged in international business. Some focal firms are manufacturing businesses such as Ford, Sharp, and John Deere. They use manufacturing processes to produce tangible products that they sell in foreign markets. Trading companies are brokers of goods and services. Service providers are firms in the services sector, such as insurance companies and theme parks. Some services firms, suppliers of expertise, provide purely intangible offerings such as advice and teaching, often one-on-one, to clients. Examples include lawyers, teachers, and consulting firms.

The second column also identifies licensors of various types of intellectual property, including patents and know-how. A **licensor** is a firm that enters a contractual agreement with a foreign partner that allows the latter the right to use certain intellectual property for a specified period of time in exchange for royalties or other compensation. A **franchisor** is a firm that grants another the right to use an entire business system in exchange for fees, royalties, or other forms of compensation. Franchisors are sophisticated licensors that provide an entire business system to a foreign franchisee, such as McDonald's and Hertz Car Rental. In addition, many firms in the construction, engineering, design, or architectural industries provide their offerings via turnkey contracting. **Turnkey contractors** are focal firms or a consortium of firms that plan, finance, organize, manage, and implement all phases of a project and then hand it over to a foreign customer after training local personnel.

The third column in Exhibit 3.5 identifies the foreign market entry strategy, or the mode of internationalization. A foreign market entry strategy refers to the manner in which the focal firm internationalizes, whether through exporting, importing, licensing, or FDI. The type of entry mode depends on the nature of the business as well as the nature of the focal firm, its products, and goals. When the nature of business is dealing in intangibles, such as professional services, the focal firm may enter into agency relationships with a foreign partner. This is common among banks, advertising agencies, and market research firms. Licensing and franchising are common in the international transfer of intangibles. A franchisor makes a contract with a foreign franchisee; a supplier of expertise makes a contract with a foreign client, and so forth.

In undertaking international business, firms have the option of serving customers either through foreign investment, or relying upon the support of independent intermediaries located abroad. In the former case, the company will set up *company-owned* manufacturing and distribution facilities. Accordingly, another key characteristic of focal firms is whether the firm maintains a physical presence in the market of interest. The fourth column in Exhibit 3.5 identifies the location of major activities. For example, most exporters carry out major activities—manufacturing, marketing, and sales—in their home country; they produce goods at home and ship them to customers abroad. MNEs and other large firms, however, tend to carry out major activities in multiple countries; they produce goods and sell them to customers primarily located abroad.

The last column in Exhibit 3.5 identifies the nature of the foreign partner. In almost all cases, the focal firm will rely upon intermediaries as well as support firms located in foreign markets. Significant activities are typically delegated to these foreign partners, including marketing, distribution, sales, and customer service. MNEs have seen a strong trend in recent years away from fully integrated operations toward the delegation of certain noncore functions to outside vendors, a practice known as *outsourcing*. Outsourcing involves the firm in a variety of foreign partnerships. For example, Nike maintains its design and marketing operations within the firm, but outsources production to independent suppliers located abroad. We explore outsourcing and offshoring more fully in Chapter 16.

Focal Firms other Than the MNE and SME

Let's develop a full understanding of focal firms other than the MNEs and SMEs that are highlighted in Exhibit 3.5. Some focal firms expand into foreign markets by entering into contractual relationships with foreign partners. Licensing and franchising are examples of contractual relationships. Occasionally, the licensor sells essential components or services to the licensee as part of their ongoing relationship. Licensing allows companies to internationalize rapidly while remaining in their home market. For instance, Anheuser-Busch signed a licensing agreement with the Japanese beer brewer Kirin, under which Kirin produces and distributes Budweiser beer in Japan. The agreement has substantial potential, given Japan's $30 billion-a-year beer market.[4] In another example, Canadian toymaker Mega Bloks signed an agreement with Disney that gives the SME the right to produce toys that feature Disney characters such as Winnie the Pooh and the Power Rangers. The toys are aimed at preschoolers and boys aged 4 to 7.[5]

Like licensors, the franchisor remains in its home market and permits its foreign partners to carry on local activities. The franchisor assists the franchisee in setting up its operation, and then maintains ongoing control over aspects of the franchisee's business, such as operations, procurement, quality control, and marketing. The franchisee benefits by gaining access to a proven business plan and substantial expertise.

Franchising is well accepted around the world and is popular among many types of service industry firms. For many successful service firms such as Subway or KFC, it is a relatively practical way to expand into many foreign markets. Exhibit 3.6 profiles some of the leading global franchisors. In China, Subway is the third-largest U.S. fast food chain, where its fish and tuna salad sandwiches are top sellers. Other

Franchisor	Type of Business	International Profile	Major International Markets
Subway	Submarine sandwiches and salads	24,838 shops in 82 countries	Canada, Australia, UK, New Zealand, China
Curves	Women's fitness and weight loss	9,000 centers in 17 countries	Canada, Mexico, Australia, Ireland, UK
UPS Store/Mail Boxes Etc.	Postal, business, and communications services	13 million packages in 200 countries	Canada, Germany, China
Pizza Hut	Pizza	12,500 outlets in 90 countries	China, Brazil
WSI Internet	Internet services	1,700 franchises in 87 countries	Canada, UK
KFC	Chicken	13,000 outlets in 90 countries	China, UK
RE/MAX	Real estate	100,000 agents in 50 countries	Canada, Australia, UK, New Zealand
Jani-King	Commercial cleaning	9,000 franchisees in 16 countries	Canada, Australia, Brazil, France, Turkey, New Zealand, Malaysia
McDonald's	Fast food restaurant	30,000 restaurants in 119 countries	Canada, France, UK, Australia, China
GNC	Vitamin and nutrition stores	5,000 stores in 38 countries	Canada, Mexico, Puerto Rico, Australia

Exhibit 3.6 Examples of Leading International Franchisors

SOURCES: Entrepreneur.com; Hoovers.com; company web sites and reports.

firms, such as The Athlete's Foot and Century 21, have been steadily growing in foreign markets through franchising. China recently passed its first laws that require franchisees to adhere closely to contractual obligations in the franchisor agreement.[6]

Turnkey contractors specialize in international construction, engineering, design, and architectural projects, typically involving airports, hospitals, oil refineries, and campuses. In a typical turnkey contract, the contractor plans, finances, organizes, manages, and implements all phases of a construction project. The contractors provide hardware and know-how to build a factory, power plant, railway, or some other integrated system that is capable of producing the products or services that the project sponsor requires. Hardware includes buildings, equipment, and inventory that comprise the tangible aspects of the system. Know-how is the knowledge about technologies, operational expertise, and managerial skills that the contractor transfers to the customer during and upon completion of the project.

These projects are typically awarded on the basis of open bidding, in which many potential contractors participate. Some contracts are highly publicized megaprojects, such as the European Channel Tunnel, the Three Gorges Dam in China, and the Hong Kong Airport. Typical examples of turnkey projects include upgrades to public transportation networks such as bridges, roadways, and rail systems. Financed largely from public budgets, most metro projects are in Asia and Western Europe, where demand is driven by intensifying urbanization and worsening congestion. One of the world's largest publicly funded heavy rail projects is underway in Delhi, India. Delhi Metro Rail Ltd. commissioned the estimated $2.3 billion turnkey project to build roads and tunnels that run through the city's central business district. The turnkey consortium includes numerous local firms as well as Skanska AB, Stockholm, one of the world's largest construction companies.[7] In Hong Kong, a private toll road operator awarded a $550-million turnkey contract to a French and Japanese joint venture for a new highway running into China. The team includes the Hong Kong subsidiary of the French giant Bouygues SA.[8] Bouygues has over 40 subsidiaries and affiliates in 80 countries.

ABB and Alstom are among the international construction contractors that have built the Three Gorges Dam on the Yangtze River in China's Hubei province. The project, which aims to control the country's mighty Yangtze River and tame the floods, is thought to have cost more than any other single construction project in China's history, with unofficial estimates as high as $75 billion.

An increasingly popular type of turnkey contract in the developing economies is the *build-own-transfer* venture. In this arrangement, the contractors acquire an ownership in the facility for a period of time until it is turned over to the client. In addition to owning a stake in the project, the contractors provide ongoing service in the form of advice, training, and assistance navigating regulatory requirements and obtaining needed approvals from government authorities. At some point after a successful period of operation, the contractors will divest their interest in the project.

Exhibit 3.7 identifies the top construction contractors in the world based on contracting revenues from projects outside their home countries. A quick perusal of the list reveals the highly global nature of the large-scale construction industry. The top firms in this industry come from various European countries, Japan, China, and the United States. These firms derive a considerable share of their total revenues from international projects. Many have established reputations in specialized project areas such as airports, steel plants, refineries, high-speed rail, and environmental projects.

International collaborative ventures represent a cross-border business alliance where partnering firms pool their resources and share the costs and risks of the new venture. Collaborative ventures are a middle ground between FDI-based foreign market entry and home country-focused operations such as exporting. In effect, a collaborative arrangement allows the focal firm to *externalize* some of its value-chain activities. Collaborative arrangements help the focal firm increase international business, compete more effectively with rivals, take advantage of complementary technologies and expertise, overcome trade barriers, connect with customers abroad, configure value chains more effectively, and generate economies of scale in production and marketing.

Joint ventures (JV) and project-based, nonequity ventures are both examples of international collaborative ventures. A **joint venture partner** is a focal firm that creates and jointly owns a new legal entity through equity investment or pooling of assets. Partners form JVs to share costs and risks, gain access to needed resources, gain economies of scale, and pursue long-term strategic goals.

Joint venture partner A focal firm that creates and jointly owns a new legal entity through equity investment or pooling of assets.

As an example, Hitachi formed a joint venture with MasterCard to promote a smart card system for banking and other applications. The Japanese electronics giant invested $2.4 million to take an 18 percent stake in the JV established in San Francisco. The firms created the venture to manage the brand and other operations of the *Multos* smart card worldwide.[9] In another instance, British Petroleum (BP) entered a joint venture in India in one of several deals intended to boost energy output in the Asian subcontinent. BP partnered with

Rank Based on 2006 Revenues	Contractor	2006 Revenue (U.S.$ millions)		Example of a Recently Completed Mega-Construction Project
		International	Total	
1	Hochtief AG, Essen, Germany	$17,598	$19,795	Berlin's new mega-airport at the Schönefeld site, Germany
2	Skanska AB, Solna, Sweden	12,347	15,722	Øresund Bridge, Denmark
3	Vinci, Rueil-Malmaison, France	11,065	32,699	Channel Tunnel, France-Great Britain
4	Strabag SE, Vienna, Austria	10,799	13,502	Xiaolangdi Multi-Purpose Dam, China
5	Bouygues, Paris, France	9,576	24,960	Groene Hart Tunnel, The Netherlands
6	Bechtel, San Francisco, CA, U.S.A.	8,931	15,367	Hong Kong Airport, China
7	Technip, Paris-La Dèfense, France	8,084	8,245	Hong Kong New Airport Passenger Terminal Building, China
8	KBR, Houston, Texas, U.S.A.	7,426	8,150	The Great Man-Made River Project (GMRP), Libya
9	Bilfinger Berger AG, Mannheim, Germany	6,553	9,967	Taipei–Kaohsiung High Speed Railway, Taiwan
10	Fluor Corp., Irving, Texas, U.S.A.	6,338	11,273	Shell Rayong Refinery, Thailand

Exhibit 3.7 Top International Construction Contractors. Based on Contracting Revenues from Projects Outside Home Country.

SOURCE: Reprinted from Engineering News-Record. Copyright © McGraw-Hill Companies, Inc. August 20, 2007. All rights reserved.

Project-based, nonequity venture partners Focal firms that collaborate through a project, with a relatively narrow scope and a well-defined timetable, without creating a new legal entity.

the state-controlled Hindustan Petroleum Corporation. The new venture built a $3 billion refinery in Punjab and established a joint marketing business, including a network of retail service stations around India. BP is developing similar ventures in China.[10]

Partners in a project-based, nonequity venture are focal firms that collaborate through a project, with a relatively narrow scope and a well-defined timetable, without creating a new legal entity. In contrast to JVs, which involve equity investment by the parent companies, project-based partnerships are less formal nonequity ventures, and are intended for a fixed duration. The partners pool their resources and expertise to perform some mutually beneficial business task, such as joint R&D or marketing, but they do not invest equity to form a new enterprise. Firms often form project-based ventures to share the enormous fixed costs involved in knowledge-intensive research and development projects. Partners may share know-how and intellectual property to develop a new technological standard.

Cisco Systems is the worldwide leader in Internet networking technology, and has expanded much of its operations through strategic alliances with key foreign players. It formed an alliance with Japan's Fujitsu to jointly develop routers and switches that enable clients to build Internet protocol networks for advanced telecommunications. In Italy, Cisco teamed with the telecommunications company Italtel to jointly develop network solutions for the convergence of voice, data, and video to meet growing global demands. In China, Cisco formed an alliance with telecommunications company ZTE to tap the Chinese and Asian markets. The two companies are collaborating to provide equipment and services to telecommunications operators in the Asia-Pacific region.[11]

Distribution Channel Intermediaries in International Business

A second category of international business participant is the distribution channel intermediary. Intermediaries are physical distribution and marketing service providers in the value chain for focal firms. They move products and services in the home country and abroad, and perform key downstream functions in the target market on behalf of focal firms, including promotion, sales, and customer service. They may organize transportation of goods and offer various logistics services such as warehousing and customer support. Intermediaries are of many different types, ranging from large international companies to small, highly specialized operations. For most exporters, relying on an independent foreign distributor is a low-cost way to enter foreign markets. The intermediary's intimate knowledge, contacts, and services in the local market can provide a strong support system for exporters that are inexperienced in international business or too small to undertake market-based activities themselves. There are three major categories of intermediaries: those based in the foreign target market, those based in the home country, and those that operate through the Internet.

Intermediaries Based in the Foreign Market

Most intermediaries are based in the exporter's target market. They provide a multitude of services, including market research, appointing local agents or commission representatives, exhibiting products at trade shows, arranging local transportation for cargo, and clearing products through customs. Intermediaries also orchestrate local marketing activities, including product adaptation, advertising, selling, and after-sales service. Many intermediaries finance sales and extend credit, facilitating prompt payment to the exporter. In short, intermediaries based in the foreign market can function like the exporter's local partner, handling all needed local business functions.

A **foreign distributor** is a foreign market-based intermediary that works under contract for an exporter, takes title to, and distributes the exporter's products in a national market or territory, often performing marketing functions such as sales, promotion, and after-sales service. Foreign distributors are essentially independent wholesalers that purchase merchandise from exporters (at a discount) and resell it after adding a profit margin. Because they take title to the goods, foreign distributors are often called *merchant distributors*. The distributor promotes, sells, and maintains an inventory of the exporter's products in the foreign market. The distributor typically maintains substantial physical resources and provides financing, technical support, and after-sales service for the product, relieving the exporter of these functions abroad. Distributors may carry a variety of noncompeting complementary products, such as home appliances and consumer electronics. For consumer goods, the distributor usually sells to retailers. For industrial goods, the distributor sells to other businesses and/or directly to end users. Compared to sales representatives, distributors are usually a better choice for firms that seek a more stable, committed presence in the target market. A key advantage of using a foreign distributor is that they typically have substantial knowledge of the exporter's products and the nature of the local market.

An **agent** is an intermediary (often an individual or a small firm) that handles orders to buy and sell commodities, products, and services in international business transactions for a commission. Also known as a *broker*, an agent may act for either buyer or seller but does not assume title or ownership of the goods. The typical agent is compensated by commission, expressed as a percentage of the price of the product sold. In economic terms, the agent brings buyers and sellers

Foreign distributor A foreign market-based intermediary that works under contract for an exporter, takes title to, and distributes the exporter's products in a national market or territory, often performing marketing functions such as sales, promotion, and after-sales service.

Agent An intermediary (often an individual or a small firm) that handles orders to buy and sell commodities, products, and services in international business transactions for a commission.

together. Agents operate under contract for a definite period of time (often as little as one year), which is renewable by mutual agreement. The contract defines territory, terms of sale, compensation, as well as grounds and procedures for terminating the agreement.[12]

The function of the agent is especially important in markets made up of many small, widely dispersed buyers and sellers. For example, brokers on the London Metal Exchange (LME) deal in copper, silver, nickel, and other metals sourced from mining operations worldwide. The volume of metal buying and selling is huge (around $5 billion per year) and the suppliers are widely dispersed worldwide. The LME greatly increases the efficiency with which manufacturing firms access the metal ingredients they need to conduct manufacturing operations. Agents are common in the international trade of commodities, especially food products and base minerals. In the services sector, agents often transact sales of insurance and securities.

Manufacturer's representative An intermediary contracted by the exporter to represent and sell its merchandise or services in a designated country or territory.

A **manufacturer's representative** is an intermediary contracted by the exporter to represent and sell its merchandise or services in a designated country or territory. Manufacturer's representatives go by various names, depending on the industry in which they work—agents, sales representatives, or service representatives. In essence, they act as contracted sales personnel in a designated target market on behalf of the exporter, but usually with broad powers and autonomy. Manufacturer's representatives may handle various noncompetitive, complementary lines of products or services. They do not take title to the goods they represent and are most often compensated by commission. With this type of representation, the exporter usually ships merchandise directly to the foreign customer or end user. Manufacturer's representatives do not maintain physical facilities, marketing, or customer support capabilities, so these functions must be handled primarily by the exporter.

In consumer markets, the foreign firm must get its products to end users through *retailers* located in the foreign market. A retailer represents the last link between distributors and end-users. Some national retail chains have expanded abroad and are now providing retail services in multiple countries. For example, Seibu, Carrefour, Royal Ahold, Tesco and Sainsbury are major retail store chains based in Japan, France, the Netherlands, and the United Kingdom, respectively. Rolex and Ralph Lauren sell their products directly to these retailers. This type of transaction has emerged from the international growth of major retail chains. Often, a traveling sales representative facilitates such transactions. Large international retailers such as Carrefour and Wal-Mart maintain purchasing offices abroad. Wal-Mart and Toys "R" Us have opened hundreds of stores around the world, especially in Mexico, Canada, Japan, China, and Europe. IKEA, a Swedish company, is the world's largest furniture retailer. Dealing directly with foreign-based retailers is efficient because it results in a much shorter distribution channel and reduced channel costs.

Retailer Tesco's delivery vans distribute products to end-users throughout Britain.

Intermediaries Based in the Home Country

In contrast to those intermediaries located abroad, a select group of intermediaries are domestically based. For one, a variety of wholesaler *importers* bring in products or commodities from foreign countries for the purpose of selling them in the home market, re-exporting them, or for use in the manufacture of finished products. Manufacturers and retailers are also important importers. Manufacturers import a range of raw materials, parts, and components used in the production of higher value-added products. They may also import a complementary collection of products and services to supplement or augment their own product range. Retailers such as department stores, specialized stores, mail order houses, and catalogue firms import many of the products that they sell. A trip to retailers such as Best Buy, Home Depot, or Staples, for instance, quickly reveals that most of their offerings are sourced from abroad, especially low labor-cost countries. (You can learn more about the world's largest retailers from various studies, including those by PriceWaterhouseCoopers: www.pwc.com).

Wholesalers import input goods that they in turn sell to manufacturers and retailers. A typical importer in this category is Capacitor Industries Inc., an SME in Chicago that imports low-cost electronic components from China and sells them to motor makers and other manufacturers in the United States and other countries. Capacitors are tiny devices that store electrical charges, keep motors running, and protect computers from surges. Capacitor Industries' strategy is simple—buy from a low-cost country and sell at a profit in an advanced economy. Importing from China and other low-cost suppliers means that the prices of domestic suppliers can be undercut by up to 30 percent.

For exporting firms that prefer to minimize the complexity of selling internationally, a **trading company** serves as an intermediary that engages in import and export of a variety of commodities, products, and services. A trading company assumes the international marketing function on behalf of producers, especially those with limited international business experience. Large trading companies operate much like agents and may deal in thousands of products that they sell in markets worldwide. Typically, they are high-volume, low-margin resellers, and are compensated by adding profit margins to what they sell.

Trading companies are very common in commodities and agricultural goods such as grain. Companies such as Minneapolis, Minnesota-based Cargill provide a useful service as international resellers of agricultural goods. With annual sales of more than $50 billion, Cargill is often listed as the largest private firm in the United States. The company employs roughly 150,000 employees in more than 60 countries. Cargill controls about 25 percent of U.S. grain exports and one-fifth of the corn-milling capacity. It buys, sorts, ships, and sells a wide range of commodities, including coffee, sugar, cotton, oil, hemp, rubber, and livestock. Most of its profits come from turning these commodities into value-added products, including oils, syrups, and flour. The company also processes all the ingredients that many food companies use to produce cereal, frozen dinners, and cake mixes.

Exhibit 3.8 provides a list of the largest trading companies in the world. What strikes you about these firms? First, note that these companies work with remarkably low margins in international trading; they tend to be high-volume, low-margin resellers. This is due to the trading companies' dealing largely in commodities such as grains, minerals, coal, and metals. Second, note that five of the ten largest trading companies are based in Japan. This is because trading companies have historically played a very important role in Japan's external trade. Being an island economy and lacking most raw materials needed for industrialization, Japan has to import them. Trading companies are also more common in South Korea, India, and Europe.

In Japan, large trading companies are known as *sogo shosha*. The sogo shosha are usually involved in both exporting and importing, and are specialists in low-margin, high-volume trading. They may also supply a range of manufacturing, financial, and logistical services. To stay close to foreign markets, managers of the sogo shosha use extensive networks of local offices, travel, and participate in trade shows, and establish business relationships with agents and distributors worldwide.

Trading company An intermediary that engages in import and export of a variety of commodities, products, and services.

Exhibit 3.8

World's Largest Trading Companies

SOURCE: "Ten Largest companies by revenue" FORTUNE Global 500, July 24, 2006 issue, FORTUNE. Copyright © 2006 Time, Inc. All rights reserved.

Rank Based on Annual Revenues	Company (Home Country)	Revenues (U.S.$ millions)	Profits (U.S.$ millions)	Profits as Percentage of Total Revenues
1	Mitsubishi (Japan)	$42,633	$3,092	7.3%
2	Mitsui (Japan)	36,349	1,788	4.9
3	Marubeni (Japan)	27,732	652	2.4
4	Sumitomo (Japan)	22,800	1,415	6.2
5	Sinochem (China)	21,089	260	1.2
6	Itochu (Japan)	19,592	1,282	6.5
7	SHV Holdings (Netherlands)	18,826	444	2.4
8	Samsung (South Korea)	15,114	77	0.5
9	COFCO (China)	14,654	199	1.4
10	SK Networks (South Korea)	14,571	467	3.2

The sogo shosha include giant firms that are little known in the West, such as Mitsui, Mitsubishi, Sumitomo, Itochu, and Marubeni, all firms on the Fortune magazine Global 500. In the 1990s, total trade of the nine top sogo shosha averaged about 25 percent of Japan's total GDP. They typically have extensive global operations. For instance, Marubeni has 23 corporate subsidiaries and a total of 121 offices in 72 countries. It owns 502 companies, of which 285 are outside Japan. The firm has about 27,000 employees, of which roughly 14,000 are overseas. Marubeni is consistently ranked in the upper end of the Global 500 and had recent annual sales of about $28 billion.

In the United States, trading companies have had a relatively negligible impact on the volume of export activity. The U.S. Congress passed the Export Trading Company (ETC) Act in 1982, providing firms with two important incentives to engage in joint exporting through the formation of export trading companies. First, immunity from antitrust legislation could allow firms to collaborate for export marketing purposes without the fear of being prosecuted for collusion. Second, U.S. bank holding companies could hold equity interest in ETCs and facilitate the formation of financially strong trading companies like the Japanese sogo shosha. This represented a significant departure from the longstanding policy of separating banking from commercial activities. Despite these incentives, trading companies are not forming to act on behalf of a group of manufacturers with limited international business experience. One of the deterrents has been the preference of U.S. firms to pursue international business expansion independently of other firms.[13]

In the United States, a more common type of domestically based intermediary is the **export management company (EMC)**, which acts as an export agent on behalf of a (usually inexperienced) client company. In return for a commission, an EMC finds export customers on behalf of the client firm, negotiates terms of sale, and arranges for international shipping. While typically much smaller than a trading company, some EMCs have well-established networks of foreign distributors in place that allow exported products immediate access to foreign markets. EMCs are often supply driven, visiting the manufacturer's facilities regularly to learn about new products and even to develop foreign-market strategies. But because of

Export management company (EMC) An intermediary that acts as an export agent on behalf of (usually inexperienced) a client company.

the indirect nature of the export sale, the manufacturer runs the risk of losing control over how its products are marketed abroad, with possible negative consequences for its international image.

Online Intermediaries

The Internet has triggered much disintermediation—the elimination of traditional intermediaries. Some focal firms now use the Internet to sell products directly to customers rather than going through traditional wholesale and retail channels. By eliminating traditional intermediaries, companies can sell their products cheaper and faster. This benefits SMEs in particular because they typically have limited resources for international operations.[14]

Just when people thought disintermediation would be an important consequence of the Internet, another trend emerged: reintermediation. This occurs when a new firm—usually an online intermediary—injects itself between buyers and suppliers in the online buying and selling environment.[15] For example, consumers can buy high-definition TVs directly from Sony at its Web site or from an online intermediary, such as CompUSA.com or Tesco.com.

Today, countless online intermediaries are brokering transactions between myriad buyers and sellers worldwide. Intermediaries survive by adding value in the distribution process. If changes in the marketplace render an intermediary's role less valuable, then the intermediary must adapt. Emergent technologies offer—and sometimes require—new roles that intermediaries have not taken previously. Many traditional retailers establish Web sites or link with online service providers to create an electronic presence. The electronic sites of stores like Tesco and Wal-Mart complement existing physical distribution infrastructure and bring more customers into retail outlets. In total, countless intermediaries and support services provide a wide range of buyer-seller functions online. They have shifted the landscape of retailing and intermediation in the global marketplace. Read more about the new Internet-based international intermediaries in the *Global Trend* feature on the next page.

More broadly, intermediaries as well as focal firms and facilitators employ the Internet and information technology (IT) tools to achieve various tasks. The Internet and IT provide enormous opportunities to transform, manage, and communicate within value chains. The technologies have triggered fundamental changes in core aspects of global business processes, including supply-chain management, procurement, and manufacturing. Information systems, electronic data interchange networks, shared databases, and other electronic links connect firms with suppliers and buyers in unprecedented ways. These links are particularly beneficial to multinational firms, whose customers may be spread around the globe. The Internet allows suppliers to be more in touch with buyers, in more direct ways.

Nevertheless, easy accessibility of the Internet has also led many shady online marketers to cause harm to unsuspecting consumers. For example, a recent *Business Week* investigation has found that only 11 percent of Web pharmacies require a prescription.[16] An astounding 89 percent, scattered largely in developing countries, appear to operate illegally. By sending billions of spam e-mail messages a day for pharmaceuticals, unscrupulous companies generate millions of dollars of drug sales. Unfortunately, these drugs are often fake products with foreign substances that may cause serious harm to users. Phony Viagra made in Thailand was found to contain vodka; bogus Tamiflu has been manufactured with vitamin C and lactose; and sometimes a medication contains lethal amounts of dangerous chemicals. Even though the pharmaceutical industry, together with various governments have been actively identifying and pursuing these companies, they seem to be elusive and often out of the reach of legal prosecution.

Online Retailers: Contemporary Global Intermediaries

Online retailing is experiencing explosive growth. The leading online auctioneer, eBay, is attracting some 70 million buyers and sellers to its Web site in a typical month. Amazon.com is a leading online retailer with 40 million visitors. Offerings at eBay and Amazon resemble online versions of vast department stores. Amazon now sells more consumer electronics than books. The Web sites of conventional retailers—once considered stuck in the bricks-and-mortar era of retailing—are growing fast. The number of shoppers using Wal-Mart's Web site now exceeds those visiting Amazon. In the United Kingdom, popular e-retailers include Argos, a catalogue merchant, and Tesco, Britain's biggest supermarket chain. The hottest online products include toys, computer games, clothing, and jewelry.

Consumers like e-retailing because they can compare products and prices, and save time. For retailers, laws and restrictions that apply to retail stores are not as strict online, and selling online is cheap. Wal-Mart and Tesco use the Web to test the market for new products before offering them in their stores. Such advantages explain why traditional retailers have made the move to become major online sellers.

EBay's cross-border business is surging, with more than 30 sites straddling the globe, from Brazil to Germany. International transactions now generate half of eBay's overall trading revenues and are growing twice as fast as domestic operations. Roughly half of eBay's 125 million registered users are located outside the United States. EBay shoppers buy a soccer jersey every five minutes in Britain, a bottle of wine every three minutes in France, a garden gnome every six minutes in Germany, and a skincare product every 30 seconds in China. EBay has managed to rapidly transplant its business model around the world. Local managers adapt to local conditions without losing the core competencies at the heart of eBay. Germany is by far the biggest international site, generating roughly one-third the sales of the U.S. market. Germany boasts a far higher percentage of active users than any other country, with roughly three-quarters of registered users trading regularly.

The internationalization of online selling indicates an interesting trend: Most of the business of international online retailers occurs *within* individual countries. At eBay's Germany site, nearly all the products, information, and chat boards are created by local buyers and sellers. The site and conversations are nearly all in German, and virtually all the users are German citizens. The same is true for India and Italy. Only about 12 percent of eBay's total gross merchandise sales involve cross-border transactions. In most countries, eBay has acquired a strong local flavor as buyers and sellers create a local community. Each country is a self-contained marketplace.

Yet international online retailers must adapt to local conditions. A big challenge is getting global markets to accept online payment systems, such as PayPal. In much of Asia, electronic payment systems remain a mystery, and online deals often require face-to-face cash payments. Cultural differences play a role, too. Asians are typically reluctant to buy used goods. Even among siblings, it is uncommon to pass down clothing. Nevertheless, more and more Asians are acquiring online trading habits. With more than 90 million Internet users, China is a fast-growing market. Within a few years, more people will be surfing the Web in China than in the United States.

One challenge for online retailers is the fact that most of the world lacks access to the Internet. The success of international online retailers depends on the availability of IT infrastructure. Countries can be ranked in terms of *electronic readiness (e-readiness),* the degree to which its citizens can participate in the advantages and opportunities of a knowledge-based economy. By this measure, Denmark is the most e-ready country in the world, followed by the United States, Sweden, Switzerland, the United Kingdom, Hong Kong, Finland, and the Netherlands. By contrast, countries such as Russia, China, Indonesia, and India score relatively low on e-readiness. In such places, online retailers can target only a small portion of the local population. In Africa and parts of South Asia, poverty is prevalent and the level of e-readiness is even lower.

Sources: *Economist.* (2005). "E-readiness," May 7, p. 98; *Economist.* (2005). "Clicks, Bricks and Bargains," December 3, pp. 57–58; Schonfeld, Erick. (2005). "The World According to eBay," *Business 2.0* (January/February): 77–84.

Facilitators in International Business

The third category of participant in international business is the facilitator. While focal firms take center stage in global business, facilitators make it possible for international business transactions to occur efficiently, smoothly, and in a timely manner. They are independent individuals or firms that assist the internationalization and international operations of focal firms. Examples include banks, international trade lawyers, freight forwarders, customs brokers, and consultants. The number and role of facilitators have grown in recent years due to the complexity of international business operations, intense competition, and technological advances. Facilitators provide many useful services, ranging from conducting market research to identifying potential business partners and providing legal advice. They typically rely heavily on IT and the Internet to carry out their facilitating activities.

Some facilitators are supply-chain management specialists, responsible for physical distribution and logistics activities of their client companies. In the *Recent Grad in IB* feature on the next page, read about Cynthia Asoka, who is developing a career in global supply-chain management.

An important facilitator of international trade is the logistics service provider. A **logistics service provider** is a transportation specialist that arranges for physical distribution and storage of products on behalf of focal firms, also controlling information between the point of origin and the point of consumption. Companies such as DHL, FedEx, UPS, and TNT provide a cost-effective means for delivering cargo virtually anywhere in the world. They also increasingly provide traditional distributor functions such as warehousing, inventory management, and order tracking. FedEx, a leading express shipping company, delivers several million packages per day and offers supply-chain management services. The firm delivers to more than 210 countries and territories, covering virtually the entire planet with its fleet of over 640 aircraft and nearly 50,000 cars, trucks, and trailers. FedEx's business in Brazil, China, and India has grown rapidly.

Recently Red Wing, a U.S. shoe manufacturer, has taken advantage of UPS's supply chain services to bypass its own Salt Lake City distribution center, which is normally used to consolidate and repackage goods for shipment to retail stores. Red Wing produces some of its shoes in China, and sorts and repackages them at a UPS facility in southern China. Shoes are then delivered directly to Red Wing retail stores around the United States. By using outside express delivery firms, Red Wing gets its product to market faster and at lower cost. To serve the international distribution needs of companies like Red Wing, UPS has built over 50 warehouses in China.

Red Wing and countless other international manufacturers use *common carriers*, companies that own the ships, trucks, airplanes, and other transportation equipment used to transport goods around the world. Common carriers play a vital role in international business and global trade. A *consolidator* is a type of shipping company that combines the cargo of more than one exporter into international shipping containers for shipment abroad.

Most exporters utilize the services of freight forwarders because they are a critical facilitator in international business. Usually based in major port cities, freight forwarders arrange international shipments for the focal firm to a foreign entry port, and even to the buyer's location in the target foreign market. They are experts on transportation methods and documentation for international trade, as well as the export rules and regulations of the home and foreign countries. They arrange for clearance of shipments through customs on the importing side of the transaction. Freight forwarders are an excellent source of advice on shipping requirements such as packing, containerization, and labeling.

Logistics service provider

A transportation specialist that arranges for physical distribution and storage of products on behalf of focal firms, also controlling information between the point of origin and the point of consumption.

Cynthia Asoka

While growing up in the Detroit area in the 70s and 80s, you couldn't help but be aware of globalization while watching the local auto industry struggle to compete with Japanese imports. With hiring freezes on at the "Big 3" automakers, area graduates often headed right back to school. After getting her undergraduate business degree in 1990 from Oakland University (with a minor in International Management), Cynthia Asoka did just that.

After a semester in Vienna as an exchange student piqued an interest in language learning, Cynthia began a graduate program in linguistics studying Chinese and Spanish. She interrupted her studies to serve as a Peace Corps microenterprise development volunteer in the Dominican Republic, working on community projects funded by the Agency for International Development and teaching English in the evenings. She returned to graduate school to complete coursework in teaching English as a second language, then worked for Samsung for two years as a corporate trainer.

When Cynthia returned from Korea, she spent 18 months working for the Korean government's Trade Promotion Organization (KOTRA) in its Chicago office, sourcing Korean products for U.S. importers as well as promoting U.S. exports to Korea. Hoping to sharpen her skills so she could open her own trading company one day, she once again returned to graduate school to pursue her MBA degree in Supply-Chain Management.

Cynthia graduated in 1999 and was recruited by International Business Machines (IBM) to join its Supply Chain Leadership Training program. After completion of the two-year program, Cynthia sourced memory chips from Korean, German, and Taiwanese manufacturers, and then managed buyers of IT equipment and software. Acknowledging her company's increased emphasis on services, Cynthia switched to sourcing services for IBM's internal use in 2004, and now uses that expertise to source for IBM's customers who have outsourced that function to her firm's Business Transformation organization.

Cynthia's Advice for an International Business Career

Constantly seek out opportunities to learn new global skills. In multinational corporations, all solutions or processes you design should be applicable across many countries, forcing you to think and act globally, as well as work in teams (most often virtually) across the world. Although my dream was to open my own trading company, the skills and experience I have acquired working at a multinational corporation have served as an education I could never have acquired on my own.

Cynthia's major: Business
Internships during college: GM auto plants in Argentina and Brazil
Jobs held since graduating:

- Peace Corps volunteer in the Dominican Republic
- Samsung in Korea
- Trade Promotion Organization (KOTRA) of Korea, Chicago office
- IBM

Success Factors

Don't be afraid to be the trainee. When I found myself as an intern working at the GM auto plants in Argentina and Brazil, I struggled to carry on a conversation in my mediocre Spanish and practically non-existent Portuguese. After graduation the next year, I again spent two years as a trainee, moving every six months to work in different roles in various IBM plants across the United States and Canada. While your former classmates may already have become managers and directors at their companies, try to focus on skill acquisition rather than titles. Ultimately, a broad understanding of issues will help you identify better solutions and put global processes in place that will last.

Governments typically charge tariffs and taxes and devise complex rules for the import of products into the countries that they govern. **Customs brokers** are specialist enterprises that arrange clearance of products through customs on behalf of importing firms. They prepare and process the required documentation to get goods cleared through customs. They are to importing what freight forwarders are to exporting, specializing in getting goods cleared through customs in the country to which the goods are shipped. Also known as *customs house brokers*, customs brokers are specifically licensed to transact customs clearance procedures, with substantial expertise in navigating complex import procedures. They understand the regulations of the national customs service, as well as other governmental agencies that affect the import of products. Usually, the freight forwarder, based in the home country, works with a customs house broker based in the destination country in handling importing operations.

Various other players facilitate the financial operations of international business. *Commercial banks* are an important player in the international activities of all firms by facilitating the exchange of foreign currencies and providing financing to buyers and sellers who usually require credit to finance transactions. The process of getting paid usually takes longer in international than in domestic transactions, so a focal firm may need a loan from a commercial bank. Commercial banks can also: transfer funds to individuals or banks abroad, provide introduction letters and *letters of credit* to travelers, supply credit information on potential representatives or foreign buyers, and collect foreign invoices, drafts, and other foreign receivables. Within each country, large banks located in major cities maintain correspondent relationships with smaller banks spread around the nation. Large banks also maintain correspondent relationships with banks throughout the world, or operate their own foreign branches, thus providing a direct channel to foreign customers.

Banking is one of the most multinational sectors. Barclays, Citicorp, and Fuji Bank have as many international branches as any of the largest manufacturing MNEs. These banks frequently provide consultation and guidance, free of charge, to their clients since they derive income from loans to the exporter and from fees for special services. They may be knowledgeable about particular countries and their business practices or industries.

When it comes to SMEs, however, banks are often reluctant to extend credit, as these smaller firms usually lack substantial collateral and experience a higher failure rate than large MNEs. When this occurs, smaller firms in the United States can turn to the *Export Import Bank* (Ex-IM Bank; www.exim.gov), a federal agency that assists exporters in financing sales of their products and services in foreign markets. The Ex-Im Bank provides direct loans, working capital loans, loan guarantees, and other financial products aimed at supporting the exporting activities of smaller firms.

In other countries, particularly in the developing world, it is commonplace for governments to provide financing, often through public *development banks* and agencies. Money is routinely available in developing countries to finance the construction of infrastructure projects such as dams and power plants. Government bank loans are

Customs brokers Specialist enterprises that arrange clearance of products through customs on behalf of importing firms.

Commercial banks such as this one at the Mall of the Emirates in Dubai are key facilitators in international commercial transactions.

generally offered at very favorable rates, and therefore attract various types of borrowers. Host governments provide loans, even to foreign firms, to the extent the incoming investment is likely to result in new jobs, technology transfer, or substantial foreign exchange. Governments in Australia, Canada, Ireland, France, Spain, the United Kingdom, and numerous other countries similarly provide financing to MNEs for the construction of factories and other large-scale operations in their countries. In the United States, several state development agencies have provided loans to MNE automakers such as BMW, Honda, Mercedes, and Toyota to establish plants in their regions.

Focal firms and other participants also use the services of *international trade lawyers* to help navigate international legal environments. The best lawyers are knowledgeable about their client's industry, the laws and regulations of target nations, and the most appropriate means for international activity in the legal/regulatory context. Foreign lawyers are familiar with the obstacles involved in doing business with individual countries, including import licenses, trade barriers, intellectual property concerns, and government restrictions in specific industries.

Firms need international trade lawyers to negotiate contracts for the sales and distribution of goods and services to customers, intermediaries, or facilitators. Lawyers play a critical role when negotiating joint venture and strategic alliance agreements, or for reaching agreement on international franchising and licensing. International trade lawyers also come into play when disputes arise with foreign business partners. When the firm needs to hire foreign employees, a good lawyer can explain labor law and employment rights and responsibilities. Internationalizing firms often apply for patents for their products and register their trademarks in the countries where they do business, which requires the services of a patent attorney. In addition, lawyers can help to identify and optimize tax benefits that may be available from certain entry modes or within individual countries.

Insurance companies provide coverage against commercial and political risks. Losses tend to occur more often in international business because of the wide range of natural and man-made circumstances to which the firm's products are exposed as they make their way through the value chain. For example, goods shipped across the ocean are occasionally damaged in transit. Insurance helps to defray the losses that would otherwise result from such damage.

International business *consultants* advise internationalizing firms on various aspects of doing business abroad and alert them to foreign market opportunities. Consultants help companies improve their performance by analyzing existing business problems and helping management develop future plans. Particularly helpful will be *tax accountants,* who can advise companies on minimizing tax obligations resulting from multicountry operations. *Market research firms* are a potential key resource for identifying and targeting foreign buyers. They possess or can gain access to information on markets, competitors, and the methods of international business.

DHL International: An Ambitious Competitor in Global Logistics Services

When Adrian Dalsey, Larry Hillbolm, and Robert Lynn founded DHL as a door-to-door express service between San Francisco and Honolulu in 1969, no one could have imagined the business evolving into a cross-border express delivery group linking 120,000 destinations in more than 220 countries and territories. Now owned by the German company Deutsche Post World Net, DHL offers express services, international air and ocean freight, contract logistics, and value-added services. While DHL is the market leader for courier express delivery in Europe and Asia, the brand struggled to develop a reputation for quality service in the United States.

Global Supply Chain and Logistics Industry

To address the needs of customers who want simple and convenient solutions at competitive prices, the supply-chain and logistics industry has changed dramatically since the early seventies. The industry includes companies that move raw materials, finished goods, packages, and documents throughout the world. Four trends are affecting the industry: globalization, deregulation, digitization, and outsourcing. Growing cross-border trade has increased the complexity of the supply chain, creating demand for professional management of the logistics activities of a focal firm. Focal firms clearly recognize the benefits of moving goods through a supply chain faster and more efficiently. As a result, specialized logistic service providers such as DHL, UPS, and FedEx have emerged to organize, coordinate, and control supply chains through technological advancements and a global presence. These facilitating firms developed global networks of offices and warehouses, acquired trucks and aircraft, and invested in extensive information tracking systems.

DHL's Internationalization

DHL entered the international express arena in 1971 with services to the Philippines. The next year, DHL initiated services to Japan, Hong Kong, Singapore, and Australia. The Asia-Pacific focus was further developed in 1980, when DHL entered China through an agency agreement with Sinotrans that was later upgraded to a 50/50 joint venture in 1986, making it the first international joint venture express company in China. In 1973 DHL expanded into Europe, with later entry in the Middle East and Africa. DHL was the first company to offer international air express services to Eastern European countries in the 1980s. To support customers worldwide, DHL established hub operations in Brussels, Cincinnati, and Manila from 1985 to 1995. Strategically positioned facilities were located in Athens, Bombay, Hong Kong, Kuala Lumpur, Moscow, Osaka, Sydney, and Bahrain. DHL formed alliances with Japan Airlines, Lufthansa, and trading company Nissho Iwai.

In 2002, the German-based company Deutsche Post acquired 100 percent ownership of DHL for $2.7 billion. Deutsche Post AG, formerly owned and operated by the German government, became a publicly traded company in 2000. Deutsche Post provides national and international services in four corporate divisions (mail, express, logistics, and financial services) under three brand names—Deutsche Post, DHL, and Postbank. Since 2002, Deutsche Post has focused on integrating its express delivery and logistics units, which include Euro Express and Danzas, under the DHL umbrella. DHL maintains five main brands: DHL Exel Supply Chain, DHL Express, DHL Freight, DHL Global Forwarding, and DHL Global Mail.

Global Positioning

In the courier, express, and parcel market, DHL International is ahead of competitors in Europe due to its efficient national express networks. With a 35 percent share of the international express segment in the Asia Pacific region, DHL is the market leader in Japan and China. A major advantage in China is its dedicated air network of more than 20 aircraft in dedicated freighter operations. DHL is investing heavily on upgrading capabilities in the China area, committing close to $1 billion dollars since 2002 to upgrade ground and air capabilities. DHL's 2005 acquisition of 81 percent of the Indian express company Blue Dart strengthens the company's ability to offer customers domestic and international express services in the key Asian markets of China and India.

In the growing logistics industry, the DHL brand has experienced double-digit increases in volume. It is the global leader in airfreight ahead of Nippon Express. DHL is able to offer airfreight in regions not served by competitors through its internal freight carrier and air fleet. It is also the leading provider of ocean freight and contract logistics.

As the express delivery service is traditionally low margin, DHL focuses on bundling services with the more lucrative, value-added contract logistics management in automotive, pharmaceutical, healthcare, electronics, telecommunications, consumer goods, and textiles/fashion sectors. These contracts are long term, an average of three years. With the acquisition of Exel, DHL has been able to extend a great majority of its existing agreements. Client companies that have recently awarded contracts to DHL include Standard Chartered Bank, Deutsche Telekom, Philips, PepsiCo, Ford, BMW, Sun Microsystems, Unisys, and Electrolux.

The Importance of the U.S. Market for DHL

The United States is an important strategic market for DHL as a global logistics service provider offering customers a global network. North American express traffic accounts for nearly half the worldwide total with highly attractive margins, reaching $46.9 billion in 2004. In 2004, 20 percent of DHL express volumes flowed into the United States or moved from there around the globe. More than one third of all global Fortune 500 companies are headquartered in the United States, where decisions on logistics and transport orders are increasingly made.

The courier service market in the United States is highly competitive and relatively consolidated, with the top five companies in the market accounting for about 47 percent of the total market value. The largest sector is ground courier service, accounting for 61 percent of sales and worth about $30 billion. The U.S. Postal Service, with a monopoly on delivering all nonurgent letters in the United States, remains the largest provider. The U.S. Postal Service and FedEx continue to broaden their range of nondelivery services, including logistics, supply-chain management, and e-commerce. By 2005, FedEx and UPS together commanded 78 percent of the U.S. parcel market, with DHL obtaining only a 7 percent share of the express delivery market. With the acquisition of Exel, DHL is the market leader of logistics in the United States.

Challenges in the U.S. Market

DHL has performed well in two other NAFTA (North American Free Trade Agreement) markets. In Canada, DHL purchased a national business to complement international activities and was able to reach break even in less than two years. In Mexico, DHL is number one in the overall express and parcel market, with a strong market position. Yet it faces considerable challenges in the United States market.

In the United States, DHL's ambition is to be a strong number three in the market after UPS and FedEx. Focusing on the small and medium-sized U.S. businesses that are increasingly involved in cross-border trade, the company aims to raise its market share. A significant move

towards that goal began with the $1.1 billion acquisition in 2003 of Airborne Express, the nation's number three express service. However, the parcel market in the United States is shifting toward ground transport, due to high fuel prices making air shipment costly. DHL's limited ground network has hurt its ability to attract domestic customers who want to send parcels overland. DHL announced plans to invest $1.2 billion in its North American network to expand the company's ground delivery capacity by 60 percent. These efforts resulted in losses of $630 million in 2004 and $380 million in 2005.

DHL is facing various challenges in its operations as well. It experienced start-up difficulties when opening a central air hub in Wilmington, Ohio, that led to delivery delays and lost customers. In November of 2005, the company was responsible for losing a computer tape with the personal information of two million ABN AMRO residential mortgage customers. Although the tape later turned up in the Ohio facility, the damage to DHL's reputation was widespread. After extensive media coverage, and incurring the cost of providing all customers access to credit reporting services, ABN announced plans to use a "secure courier system" by FedEx, in which drivers stay with the computer tape the entire time.

DHL is also experiencing challenges by FedEx and UPS on regulatory grounds. These competitors have repeatedly contested Deutsche Post's operation in the United States by petitioning the U.S. Department of Transportation to cancel DHL's registration as a foreign-owned freight forwarder. UPS argued that Deutsche Post would use its monopoly profits to engage in predatory pricing in the United States. FedEx and UPS also called for a formal enforcement investigation of DHL Airways' citizenship, alleging that foreign nationals, including Germany's postal system Deutsche Post, would control DHL Airways. Under U.S. law, citizens of the United States must own at least 75 percent of the voting stock of a U.S. airline, and U.S. citizens must manage the operations. These debates generated much discussion regarding competition in the parcel delivery market. After years of motions and hearings, regulators denied the petitions and ruled in favor of DHL.

Marketing strategy in the United States includes spending $150 million in an identity rollout with a yellow and red logo. DHL had to repaint more than 17,000 trucks, purchase 20,000 worker uniforms, paint 467 service centers, replace 16,000 drop boxes and create the packaging, envelopes, and air bills used by employees and clients. These efforts coincided with the launch of an ad campaign intended to reintroduce the company to potential customers, attacking UPS and FedEx directly. The new look contributed to a 1 percent rise in market share in the United States, about $600 million in revenue.

AACSB: **Reflective Thinking**

Case Questions

1. DHL is integrating international express and logistic services. What value-added services does DHL provide? How do the services tie in to an organization's value chain activities? Can you anticipate changes to the supply chain that would further alter the express and logistic industry?

2. Who are the target clients for a company like DHL? What factors would influence the customer to choose a particular express courier and logistics provider?

3. Given the importance of the U.S. market to the global express industry, what would you recommend to DHL for changing its position in the United States? Do you feel that DHL's current strategies will be successful?

4. It appears that DHL needs to focus on improved customer satisfaction through better service quality and a more customer-friendly workforce. In this increasingly competitive industry, personalized service and investment in a trained sales force seems to be critical in attracting clients. Would customers in the United States be willing to risk critical shipping activities to a fledgling operation? Will patience run out for the parent company Deutsche Post?

Note: This case was written by Tracy Gonzalez-Padron, under the supervision of Professor S. Tamer Cavusgil.

Sources: Berman, J. (2006). "Survey Indicates DHL Is Closing the Gap on U.S. competitors." Retrieved September 15, 2006, from www.logisticsmgmt.com; Boyd, J. (2006). "Deutsche Post Ag." (2006), in Hoover's company records, retrieved April 1, 2007, at <proquest.umi.com/pqdweb?index=0&did= 168275191&SrchMode=1&sid=1&Fmt=3&VInst=PROD&VType=PQD&RQT=30 9&VName=PQD&TS=1177706376&clientId=20174>; "Couriers in the USA." *Euromonitor International* (October 2005); "Deutsche Post AG." (June 2006) Retrieved from www.datamonitor.com; Deutsche Post Worldwide Net. (2005). Annual Report. Retrieved from www.dpwn.de; "DHL International Limited." (June 2006). Retrieved from www.datamonitor.com; "DHL Parent DPWN Restructures." *Traffic World* 1; "DHL Worldwide Network S.A./N.V.," (2006). Hoover's company records, retrieved April 1, 2007, at <proquest.umi.com/pqd-web?index=4&did=168173401&SrchMode=1&sid=2&Fmt=3&VInst=PROD&VT ype=PQD&RQT=309&VName=PQD&TS=1177706548&clientId=20174>; Ewing, Jack, Dean Foust, and Michael Eidam. "DHL's American Adventure," *Business Week* November 29, 2004, 126; Introduction to the Transportation and Logistics Industry. Retrieved October 15, 2006, from Plunkett Research, Ltd. Web site: www.plunkettresearch.com; Mucha, T. (2005). "Pouring It On to Compete with UPS and FedEx, DHL Underwent a Corporate Makeover, with New Colors, New Commercials, and 17,000 Newly Painted Trucks." *Business 2.0*, 6 (2):60; Yerak, B. (2005). "USA Finance: Shipper Locates Missing Tape with Mortgage Data." *Chicago Tribune* (December 21, 2005); Zumwinkel, Klaus. (2006). Speech presented at the annual general meeting of Deutsche Post AG on May 10, 2006, in Cologne, Germany. Retrieved from www.dpwn Media Relations.

CHAPTER ESSENTIALS

Key Terms

agent, p. 75

born global firm, p. 68

customs brokers, p. 83

distribution channel intermediary, p. 62

export management company (EMC), p. 78

facilitator, p. 63

focal firm, p. 62

foreign distributor, p. 75

franchisor, p. 70

freight forwarder, p. 63

joint venture partner, p. 73

licensor, p. 70

logistics service provider, p. 81

manufacturer's representative, p. 76

multinational enterprise (MNE), p. 66

project-based, nonequity venture partners, p. 74

small and medium-sized enterprise, p. 68

trading company, p. 77

turnkey contractors, p. 70

Summary

In this chapter, you learned about:

1. Three types of participants in international business

International business transactions require the participation of numerous focal firms, intermediaries, and facilitators. A **focal firm** is the initiator of an international business transaction that conceives, designs, and produces the offerings for customers worldwide. A **distribution channel intermediary** is a specialist firm that provides a variety of logistics and marketing services for focal firms as part of the international supply chain, both in the home country and abroad. A **facilitator** is a firm or individual with special expertise such as legal advice, banking, and customs clearance that assists focal firms in the performance of international business transactions. The three types of participants bring various types of expertise, infrastructure, and inputs that make international business take place.

2. Participants organized by value-chain activity

Focal firms, intermediaries, and facilitators all make up participants in global value chains. The value chain is the complete business system of the focal firm. It comprises all of the focal firm's activities, including market research, R&D, sourcing, production marketing, distribution, and after-sales service. Channel intermediaries and facilitators support the focal firm by performing value-adding functions. In focal firms that export, most of the value chain is concentrated in the home country. In highly international firms, value-chain activities may be performed in various countries.

3. Focal firms in international business

Focal firms include MNEs, large global corporations such as Sony and Ford. MNEs operate in multiple countries by setting up production plants, marketing subsidiaries, and regional headquarters. SMEs now comprise the majority of internationally active firms. They are relatively flexible firms that tend to emphasize exporting and leverage the help of intermediaries and facilitators to succeed in international business. **Born globals** are a category of international SMEs that internationalize at or near the firm's founding.

4. Foreign market entry strategies of focal firms

Focal firms include a **licensor**, a firm that enters a contractual agreement with a foreign partner that allows the latter the right to use certain intellectual property for a specified period of time in exchange for royalties or other compensation. A **franchisor** is a firm that grants another the right to use an entire business system in exchange for fees, royalties, or other forms of compensation. A **turnkey contractor** is a focal firm or a consortium of firms that plans, finances, organizes, manages, and implements all phases of a project, and then hands it over to a foreign customer after training local personnel. A **joint venture partner** is a focal firm that creates and jointly owns a new legal entity through equity investment or pooling of assets. **Project-based, nonequity venture partners** are focal firms that collaborate through a project with a relatively narrow scope and a well-defined timetable, without creating a new legal entity.

5. Distribution channel intermediaries in international business

Distribution channel intermediaries move products and services across national borders and eventually to end-users. They perform key downstream functions in the target market on behalf of focal firms, including marketing. A **foreign distributor** is a foreign market-based intermediary that works under contract for an exporter, takes title to, and distributes the exporter's products in a national market or territory, often performing marketing functions such as sales, promotion, and after-sales service. An **agent** is an intermediary that handles orders to buy and sell commodities, products, and services in international business transactions for a commission. A **manufacturer's representative** is an intermediary contracted by the exporter to represent and sell its merchandise or services in a designated country or territory. A **trading company** is an intermediary that engages in import and export of a variety of commodities, products, and services. An **export management company (EMC)** is an intermediary that acts as an export agent on behalf of client companies.

6. Facilitators in international business

Facilitators assist with international business transactions. A **logistics service provider** is a transportation specialist that arranges for physical distribution and storage of products on behalf of focal firms, also controlling information between the point of origin and the point of consumption. A **freight forwarder** is a specialized logistics service provider that arranges international shipping on behalf of exporting firms, much like a travel agent for cargo. A **customs broker** is a specialist enterprise that arranges clearance of products through customs on behalf of importing firms. Other facilitators include *banks, lawyers, insurance companies, consultants,* and *market research firms.*

Test Your Comprehension

1. Identify and briefly define the three major categories of participants in international business.

2. In the stages of a typical international value chain, what role does each of the three categories of participants typically play?

3. What are the specific characteristics of focal firms? Distinguish the characteristics of international MNEs, SMEs, and born-global firms.

4. What is unique about such focal firms as franchisors, licensors, and turnkey contractors?

5. What role do distribution channel intermediaries provide?

6. What are major distribution channel intermediaries based in the home country and those based abroad?

7. What are online intermediaries? How do focal firms use the Internet to carry out international activities?

8. What are the characteristics of facilitators? List and define the major types of facilitators.

Apply Your Understanding AACSB: Reflective Thinking, Communication

1. The international business landscape is occupied by focal firms, distribution channel intermediaries, and facilitators. Each group of participants assumes a different and critical role in the performance of international business transactions. Think about the degree of interdependency that exists among the three groups. What would happen if distribution channel intermediaries could not provide competent services to the focal firm? What if adequate facilitators were not available to the focal firm? To what degree would the focal firm's international business performance be hampered? Under what circumstances would the focal firm choose to internalize its value-chain activities in international business rather than delegate them to channel intermediaries and facilitators? What would be the consequences of retaining distribution and support activities within the firm?

2. Think about a company for which you would like to work following graduation. Perhaps it is in one of the following industries: music (such as Virgin), banking (Citibank), engineering (Skanska AB), food (Kraft),

automobiles (BMW), or another. Next, using the framework outlined in Exhibit 3.1 on page 64, sketch out the value chain that your chosen firm most likely uses in a particular product or service category. To complete this exercise, do library research or visit the Web site of this firm. Your value chain should include all of the major international business activities in which the firm is engaged. Next, develop a list of the intermediaries and facilitators that your company is likely to engage to configure its value chain. Indicate along your value chain where these participants are most likely to be located.

3. Following graduation, assume that you get a job at Kokanee Corporation, an SME that manufactures collars, leashes, grooming supplies, and other products for dogs and other household pets. Your boss, Mr. Eugene Kimball, wants to begin exporting Kokanee's products to foreign markets. Prepare a memo for Mr. Kimball in which you briefly describe the kinds of intermediaries and facilitators with whom Kokanee is likely to consult and work to maintain successful export operations.

 **globalEDGE** Internet Exercises

(http://globalEDGE.msu.edu)

AACSB: Reflective Thinking, Use of Information Technology

Refer to Chapter 1, page 27, for instructions on how to access and use globalEDGE™.

1. Visit the government agency or ministry in your country responsible for supporting international business. For example, in the United States, visit, the Department of Commerce (www.doc.gov). In Canada, visit Industry Canada (www.ic.gc.ca). In Denmark, visit the Ministry of Economic and Business Affairs (www.oem.dk). Identify and describe the most important support functions that the agency provides to companies that do international business. One approach is to sketch out a typical value chain, and then systematically identify the support services that the agency offers. For example, for the distribution link in the value chain, numerous governments provide "matchmaker" services, trade missions, and commercial services that link manufacturing firms with appropriate distributors located abroad.

2. Visit the Whirlpool Corporation (www.Whirl pool.com) and click on "International Sites" (under "Corporate Information"). Whirlpool has a complex value chain. Based on the information provided at the Web site address the following questions: What types of upstream value-chain activities does Whirlpool perform? What types of downstream value-chain activities does Whirlpool perform? Identify the types of participants (mainly intermediaries and facilitators) that Whirlpool is likely to use at each stage of the value chain.

3. Your company is about to initiate export activities in a country of your choice. You will need to identify distribution channel intermediaries and freight forwarders in order to have your products reach end-users in this country. Now visit the Resource Desk and Diagnostic Tools directories of globalEDGE™. What sources of information are especially helpful to you in identifying suitable foreign distributors and freight forwarders? What do you learn from these sources?

CKR Cavusgil Knight Riesenberger

Management Skill Builder©

Finding and Evaluating Freight Forwarders

As you learned in the chapter, a freight forwarder is a company that organizes the shipment of cargo via transportation modes including ships, airplanes, trucks, and railroads for manufacturers that export products. Freight forwarders do not ship cargo themselves but instead arrange for its transport by common carriers. Freight forwarders also prepare and process the documentation required for international shipments and arrange for transportation insurance and clearance through foreign customs. Freight forwarders charge a fee for their services that covers the total transport cost. Transportation is arranged from the exporter's factory or from a port in the exporter's country, to the customer's destination abroad, typically involving two or more transportation modes. UPS and DHL Worldwide Forwarding are two of the largest freight forwarders.

AACSB: Reflective Thinking, Use of Information Technology

Managerial Challenge

Evaluating and selecting a qualified freight forwarder is a critical strategic decision for managers in international operations. Freight forwarders are concentrated in large cities, and port cities, typically close to port facilities, transportation companies, and customs operations. By looking in the telephone directory of any such city, a manager can find dozens or even hundreds of freight forwarders. Freight forwarders vary widely in terms of their resources, capabilities, experience, and knowledge.

Background

It is estimated that more than 90 percent of all exporting firms have used the services of a freight forwarder. Roughly 75 percent of all international shipments involve the services of a freight forwarder. The rise of internationally active SMEs makes the services and expertise of freight forwarders even more important because smaller firms usually lack the resources or knowledge to conduct international shipping themselves.

Increased competition in both domestic and foreign markets has made the services of freight forwarders more important to exporters. First, on-time delivery can put an exporter ahead of many others. Second, firms exporting to emerging markets and developing economies need third parties with experience in these new markets or ports. Finally, parent companies that have increased trade with their foreign affiliates need reliable freight forwarders that facilitate timely transportation services, helping to ensure that production lines operate smoothly.

Managerial Skills You Will Gain

In this C/K/R Management Skill Builder©, as a prospective manager, you will:

1. Learn about freight forwarders and their role in international trade.

2. Learn the most important criteria for evaluating freight forwarders.

3. Research information to find the most appropriate freight forwarder for company needs.

Your Task

Assume that you are a manager in a small or medium-sized manufacturing firm. You are about to begin exporting your firm's products abroad. Choose a product category such as machinery or musical instruments to be shipped to foreign customers. Your task is to gather information on three different freight forwarders and then choose the best forwarder for your company.

Go to the C/K/R Knowledge Portal©

www.prenhall.com/cavusgil

Proceed to the C/K/R Knowledge Portal© to obtain the expanded background information, your task and methodology, suggested resources for this exercise, and the presentation template.

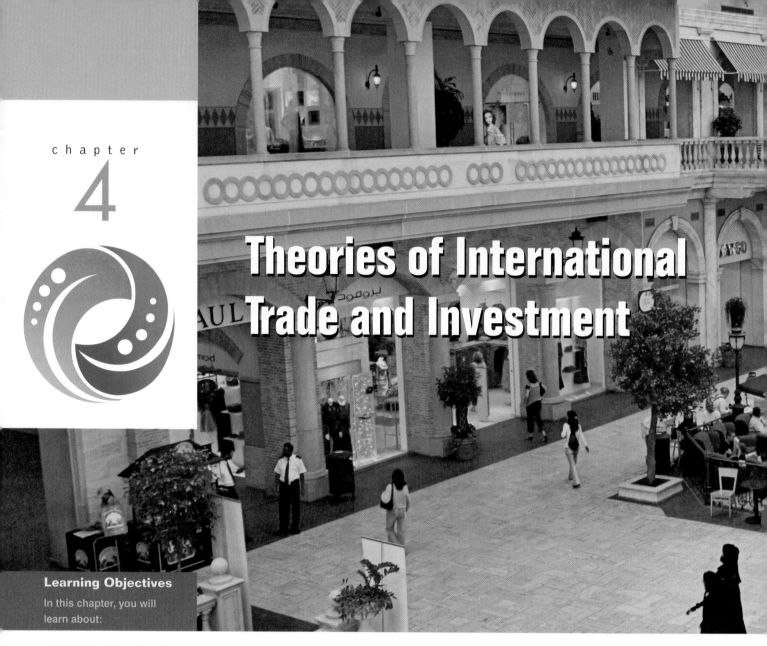

Learning Objectives

In this chapter, you will learn about:

1. Theories of international trade and investment

2. Why nations trade

3. How nations enhance their competitive advantage: contemporary theories

4. Why and how firms internationalize

5. How firms gain and sustain international competitive advantage

Theories of International Trade and Investment

> ## Dubai's Successful Transformation into a Knowledge-Based Economy

Dubai is an oil-rich country located on the Persian Gulf in the southern Arabian Peninsula. Home to roughly one million people, Dubai's per-capita GDP is over US$25,000. Dubai is one of the seven emirates that make up the United Arab Emirates. The region's wealth is based on oil and gas output, which accounts for about one-third of the emirate's GDP.

Dubai and the other emirates have a *comparative advantage* in oil because this natural resource is abundant in this region compared to other countries. These oil reserves allow Dubai to develop non-oil economic sectors that require a large infusion of capital. Dubai is developing as a multidimensional, international commercial hub. Beginning in the 1980s, the government of Dubai began collaborating with private businesses to reposition the country as a center for international trade, finance, tourism, education, and e-commerce.

The public-private partnership allows Dubai to develop national *competitive advantage* in specific industrial sectors—advantages that are difficult for competitors to replicate. Dubai's ambitious initiatives include the following:

- *State-of-the-Art Commercial Infrastructure.* Dubai built the world's biggest artificial harbor to accommodate the global shipping industry, international trade, and cruise ships. Every year, tens of millions of passengers pass through Dubai's modern international airport, which serves 80 airlines. The country created the Jebel Ali Free Trade Zone, a massive business center that hosts and provides tax incentives to more than 2,000 firms. As an example, Houston, Texas- based company Halliburton announced in early 2007 that it would move its headquarters to Dubai.

- *State-of-the-Art Infrastructure in Information and Communications Technology (ICT).* Dubai created an ICT *industrial cluster*, an oasis for firms in software development, business services, training, consulting, and e-commerce. Dubai Internet City offers foreign companies (such as Canon, IBM, Microsoft, Oracle, and Siemens) such incentives as no income tax, no currency restrictions, and minimal bureaucracy. Because few other countries have such cutting-edge ICT infrastructure, Dubai is developing a *monopoly advantage*, leading to superior performance for its companies.

■ *State-of-the-Art Financial Infrastructure.* To nurture new business, the partnership developed "Dubai Ideas Oasis," a community of entrepreneurs and venture capitalists. It also established the Dubai International Financial Center, home to dozens of global banks and financial services firms.

■ *Attractive Urban Environment.* The partnership developed Burj al Arab, a stunning hotel and one of the most recognized landmarks worldwide. It also developed the Creek, an eight-mile waterway lined with dazzling buildings, monuments, restaurants, and retail stores.

■ *Educational Infrastructure.* The country also launched The Dubai Knowledge Village, inviting foreign universities and training institutes to offer their services. Other educational initiatives ensure a pool of trained knowledge workers. English is the official language of most Dubai schools.

■ *Progressive Labor Laws.* The government devised labor laws to ensure that industry

needs for part-time and temporary requirements are quickly met. A fast-track immigration process and 24-hour visa service guarantee quick access to needed international talent.

Dubai is among the leading examples of countries that have been able to successfully reposition their economy and create comparative advantages. Dubai's transformation into a knowledge-based economy is remarkable, with oil and gas production now contributing less than 10 percent of the nation's GDP. It is all part of a plan to transform the nation into what might be termed "Dubai Inc." ◄

Sources: Arthur Andersen. (2000/2001). Dubai Makes a Bid for E-Business. *International Tax Review*, Dec/Jan, 12 (1):47; Binbyat, Ahmed. (2001). "Dubai Internet City: Open for Business," *The OECD Observer* (Jan.) 224:9; Central Intelligence Agency. (2005). *CIA World Factbook*, at www.cia.gov/cia/publications/factbook; Dubai Internet City Web site: www.dubaiinternetcity.com; *Euromoney Institutional Investor PLC*, (2000/2001); International Monetary Fund. (2005). United Arab Emirates: Selected Issues and Statistical Appendix. IMF Country Report no. 05/268 (August), retrieved from www.imf.org; Pope, Hugh. (2001). "Why is the Tech Set Putting Down Roots in the Desert? Dubai, of Course—Du-What? With Low Taxes And High Transparency, Cyber-Sheikdom Beckons," *Wall Street Journal*, Jan 23, p. A18.

In Chapter 2, we saw how the globalization of markets compels companies to pursue international business. In Chapter 3, we highlighted key participants engaged in international business. The question we need to address next is: what is the underlying economic rationale for international business activity? Why does trade take place, and what are the gains from trade and investment? In this chapter, we explain why firms and nations, such as Dubai (in the opening vignette), trade and invest internationally, and how firms acquire and sustain competitive advantage in the global marketplace. We review leading theories of why nations and individual enterprises pursue internationalization strategies as exporters, importers, investors, franchisors, or licensors.

 Theories of International Trade and Investment

For centuries economists, managers, and academic scholars have offered theories (that is, logical explanations), of the economic rationale for international trade and investment. They have debated why nations should promote trade and investment with other nations, and how nations create and sustain comparative advantage. **Comparative advantage** refers to superior features of a country that provide it with unique benefits in global competition, typically derived from either natural endowments or deliberate national policies. Also known as *country-specific advantage,* comparative advantage includes acquired resources, such as labor, climate, arable land, or petroleum reserves, as in the case of the Gulf nations. Other types of comparative advantages evolve over time, such as entrepreneurial orientation, availability of venture capital, and innovative capacity.

Over time, to understand why *companies* engage in cross-border business, the focus shifted from the nation to the individual firm. Later explanations gave rise

Comparative advantage
Superior features of a country that provide it with unique benefits in global competition typically derived from either natural endowments or deliberate national policies.

to the concept of competitive advantage, which emphasizes the role of competencies that help firms enter and succeed in foreign markets. **Competitive advantage** refers to distinctive assets or competencies of a firm—typically derived from cost, size, or innovation strengths—that are difficult for competitors to replicate or imitate. Competitive advantage is also known as *firm-specific advantage*.

While distinctions do exist between the two terms, in recent years business executives and academics such as Michael Porter have used the term *competitive advantage* to refer to the advantages possessed both by nations *and* individual firms in international trade and investment. To be consistent with the recent literature, in this text we adopt this convention as well. Exhibit 4.1 categorizes leading theories of international trade and investment into two broad groups. The first group includes nation-level theories. These are classical theories that have been advocated since the 18th century. Nation-level explanations, in turn, address two questions: (1) *why* do nations trade? and (2) *how* can nations enhance their competitive advantage?

The second group includes firm-level theories. These are more contemporary theories of how firms can create and sustain superior market position. Firm-level explanations address two additional questions: (3) *why* and *how* do firms internationalize, and (4) *how* can internationalizing firms gain and sustain competitive advantage?

We organize the remainder of our discussion according to the four fundamental questions.

Competitive Advantage

Distinctive assets or competencies of a firm—typically derived from cost, size, or innovation strengths—that are difficult for competitors to replicate or imitate.

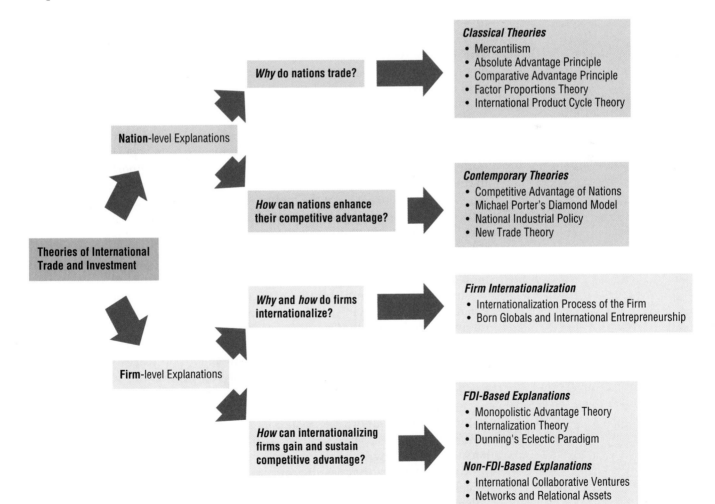

Exhibit 4.1 Theories of International Trade and Investment

Why Nations Trade

Why do nations trade with one another? The short answer is that trade allows countries to use their national resources more efficiently through *specialization*. Trade allows industries and workers to be more productive. Trade also allows countries to achieve higher living standards and keep the cost of many everyday products low. Without international trade, most nations would be unable to feed, clothe, and house their citizens at current levels. Even resource-rich countries like the United States would suffer immensely without trade. Some types of food would become unavailable, or obtainable only at very high prices. Coffee and sugar would become luxury items. Petroleum-based energy sources would dwindle. Vehicles would stop running, freight would go undelivered, and people would not be able to heat their homes in the wintertime. In short, not only do nations, companies, and citizens benefit from international trade, but modern life is virtually impossible without it.

Classical Theories

There are five classical perspectives that explain the underlying rationale for trade among nations: the mercantilist view, the absolute advantage principle, the comparative advantage principle, factor proportions theory, and the international product cycle theory.

The Mercantilist View The earliest explanations of international business emerged with the rise of European nation states in the 1500s. At that time, gold and silver were the most important sources of wealth and nations sought to amass as much of these treasures as possible. **Mercantilism** emerged in the 16th century as a dominant perspective of international trade. In simple terms, mercantilism suggests that exports are good and imports are bad. Mercantilists believed that national prosperity results from a positive balance of trade, achieved by maximizing exports and minimizing imports. They argued that the nation's power and strength increase as its wealth increases. At a time when precious metals were the main medium of exchange, gold was particularly valued because it could be used to protect and extend the nation's interests. The nation received payment for exports in gold, so exports increased the nation's gold stock. Conversely, imports reduced the gold stock because the nation paid for the imports with gold. Thus, nations desired and promoted exports but disapproved of, and impeded, imports.

In essence, mercantilism underlies the rationale for a nation's attempt to run a *trade surplus*, that is, to export more goods than it imports. Even today many people believe that running a trade surplus is beneficial, and subscribe to a view known as *neo-mercantilism*. Labor unions (that seek to protect home-country jobs), farmers (who want to keep crop prices high), and certain manufacturers (those that rely heavily on exports) all tend to support neo-mercantilism.

Yet mercantilism tends to harm the interests of firms that import, especially those that import raw materials and parts used in the manufacture of finished products. Mercantilism also harms the interests of consumers, because restricting imports reduces the choices of products they can buy. Product shortages that result from import restrictions may lead to higher prices—that is, inflation. When taken to an extreme, mercantilism may invite "beggar thy neighbor" policies, promoting the benefits of one country at the expense of others.

Mercantilism The belief that national prosperity is the result of a positive balance of trade, achieved by maximizing exports and minimizing imports.

By contrast, **free trade**—the relative absence of restrictions to the flow of goods and services between nations—is preferred because:

- Consumers and firms can more readily buy the products they want.
- The prices of imported products tend to be lower than for domestically produced products (because access to world-scale supplies forces prices down, mainly from increased competition, or because the goods are produced in lower-cost countries).
- Lower-cost imports help reduce the expenses of firms, thereby raising their profits (which may be passed on to workers in the form of higher wages).
- Lower-cost imports help reduce the expenses of consumers, thereby increasing their living standards.
- Unrestricted international trade generally increases the overall prosperity of poor countries.

Absolute Advantage Principle In the landmark book published in 1776, *An Inquiry into the Nature and Causes of the Wealth of Nations*, Scottish political economist Adam Smith attacked the mercantilist view by suggesting that nations benefit most from free trade. Smith argued that mercantilism robs individuals of the ability to trade freely and to benefit from voluntary exchanges. By trying to minimize imports, a country inevitably wastes much of its national resources in the production of goods that it is not suited to produce efficiently. Therefore, the inefficiencies of mercantilism end up reducing the wealth of the nation as a whole while enriching a limited number of individuals and interest groups. Relative to others, each country is more efficient in the production of some products and less efficient in the production of other products. Smith's **absolute advantage principle** states that a country benefits by producing only those products in which it has an absolute advantage, or can produce using fewer resources than another country. The country gains by specializing in producing those products, exporting them, and then importing the products it does not have an absolute advantage in producing. Each country increases its welfare by specializing in the production of certain products and importing others, as this allows it to be able to consume more than it otherwise could.

Exhibit 4.2 illustrates how the absolute advantage principle works in practice. Consider two nations, France and Germany, engaged in a trading relationship. France has an absolute advantage in the production of cloth, and Germany has an absolute advantage in the production of wheat. Assume that labor is the only factor of production used in making both goods. Firms employ *factors of production*—for example, labor, capital, entrepreneurship, and technology—to generate goods and services. In Exhibit 4.2, it takes an average worker in France 30 days to produce one ton of cloth and 40 days to produce one ton of wheat. It takes an average worker in Germany 100 days to produce one ton of cloth and 20 days to produce a one ton of wheat.

Compared to Germany, it is clear that France has an absolute advantage in the production of cloth, since it takes only 30 days of labor to produce one ton (compared to 100 days for Germany). Compared to France, it is clear that Germany has an absolute advantage in the production of wheat, since it takes only 20 days to produce one ton (compared to 40 days for France). If both France and Germany were to specialize, exchanging cloth and wheat at a ratio of one-to-one, France could employ more of its resources to produce cloth and Germany could employ more of its resources to produce wheat. According to Exhibit 4.2, France can import one ton of wheat in exchange for one ton of cloth, thereby "paying" only 30 labor-days for one ton of wheat. If France had produced the wheat itself, it would

Scottish political economist Adam Smith was among the first to articulate advantages of international trade.

Free trade Relative absence of restrictions to the flow of goods and services between nations.

Absolute advantage principle A country benefits by producing only those products in which it has absolute advantage, or can produce using fewer resources than another country.

	One ton of	
	Cloth	Wheat
France	30	40
Germany	100	20

Exhibit 4.2

Example of Absolute Advantage (Labor Cost in Days of Production for One Ton)

have used 40 labor-days, so it gains 10 labor-days from the trade. In a similar way, Germany also gains from trade with France.

Each country benefits by specializing in producing the product in which it has an absolute advantage and then securing the other product through trade. Thus, France should specialize in producing cloth exclusively and import wheat from Germany, and Germany should specialize in producing wheat exclusively and import cloth from France. By so doing, each country employs its labor and other resources with maximum efficiency and, as a result, living standards in each country will rise.

To employ a more contemporary example, Japan has no natural holdings of oil, but it manufactures some of the best automobiles in the world. On the other hand, Saudi Arabia produces much oil, but it lacks a substantial car industry. Given the state of their resources, it would be wasteful for each of these countries to attempt to produce both oil and cars. By trading with each other, Japan and Saudi Arabia each employ their respective resources efficiently in a mutually beneficial relationship. Japan gets oil that it refines to power its cars, and Saudi Arabia gets the cars its citizens need. Because each country uses its own resources with optimum efficiency and engages in trade, living standards for its citizens are higher than they would be if they had not engaged in trade.

By extending this example to all products that countries produce and all countries that they can trade with, it is possible to see that freely trading countries can achieve substantial gains from trade and resultant improvement in national living standards. Thus, Brazil can produce coffee more cheaply than Germany; Australia can produce wool more cheaply than Switzerland; and the United Kingdom can provide financial services more cheaply than Zimbabwe. Each of these countries is better off producing those products and services in which it is advantaged, and importing those products and services in which it is disadvantaged.

While the concept of absolute advantage provided perhaps the earliest sound rationale for international trade, it only accounted for the *absolute* advantages possessed by nations. It failed to account for more subtle advantages that nations may hold. Later studies revealed that countries benefit from international trade even when they lack an absolute advantage. This line of thinking led to the principle of *comparative advantage.*

Comparative Advantage Principle In his 1817 book, *The Principles of Political Economy and Taxation,* British political economist David Ricardo explained why it is beneficial for two countries to trade, even though one of them may have absolute advantage in the production of all products. Ricardo demonstrated that what matters is not the absolute cost of production, but rather the ratio between how easily the two countries can produce the products. Hence, the **comparative advantage principle** states that it can be beneficial for two countries to trade without barriers as long as one is more efficient at producing goods or services needed by the other. What matters is not the absolute cost of production but rather the relative efficiency with which a country can produce the product. The principle of comparative advantage remains today as the foundation and overriding justification for international trade.

To illustrate the principle of comparative advantage, let's modify the example of the trade relationship between France and Germany. As shown in Exhibit 4.3, suppose now that Germany has an absolute advantage in the production of both cloth and wheat. That is, in labor-per-day terms, Germany can produce both cloth and wheat in fewer days than France. Based on this new scenario, you might initially conclude that Germany should produce all the wheat and cloth that it needs, and not trade with France at all. However, this conclusion is not optimal. Even though Germany can produce both items more cheaply than France, it is still beneficial for Germany to trade with France.

Comparative advantage principle It can be beneficial for two countries to trade without barriers as long as one is more efficient at producing goods or services needed by the other. What matters is not the absolute cost of production, but rather the relative efficiency with which a country can produce the product.

| | One ton of | |
	Cloth	Wheat
France	30	40
Germany	10	20

Exhibit 4.3

Example of Comparative Advantage (Labor Cost in Days of Production for One Ton)

How can this be true? The answer is that rather than the *absolute* cost of production, it is the ratio of production costs between the two countries that matters. In Exhibit 4.3, Germany is comparatively more efficient at producing cloth than wheat: it can produce three times as much cloth as France (30/10), but only two times as much wheat (40/20). Thus, Germany should devote all its resources to producing cloth and import all the wheat it needs from France. France should specialize in producing wheat and import all its cloth from Germany. Each country benefits by specializing in the product in which it has a comparative, or relative, advantage and then obtaining the other product through trade.

By specializing in what they produce best and trading for the rest, Germany and France can each produce and consume relatively more of the goods that they desire for a given level of labor cost. Another way to understand the concept of comparative advantage is to consider *opportunity cost,* the value of a foregone alternative activity. In Exhibit 4.3, if Germany produces 1 ton of wheat, it forgoes 2 tons of cloth. However, if France produces 1 ton of wheat, it forgoes only 1.33 tons of cloth. Thus, France should specialize in wheat. Similarly, if France produces 1 ton of cloth, it forgoes 3/4 ton of wheat. But if Germany produces 1 ton of cloth, it forgoes only 1/2 ton of wheat. Thus, Germany should specialize in cloth. The opportunity cost of producing wheat is lower in France, and the opportunity cost of producing cloth is lower in Germany.

The concept of comparative advantage contends that trade depends on differences in *comparative* cost, and any nation can profitably trade with another even if its real costs are higher in every product that it produces. This insight is best illustrated with an example provided by Ricardo:

> "Two men can make both shoes and hats, and one is superior to the other in both employments, but in making hats he can only exceed his competitor by one fifth or 20 percent, and in making shoes he can excel him by one third or 33 percent; will it not be for the interest of both that the superior man should employ himself exclusively in making shoes and the inferior man in making hats?"[1]

While a nation might conceivably have a sufficient variety of production factors to provide every kind of product and service, it cannot produce each product and service with equal facility. The United States could produce all the coat hangers that its citizens need, but only at a high cost, because the production of coat hangers requires much labor, and wages in the United States are relatively high compared to other countries. By contrast, the production of coat hangers is a reasonable activity in a country such as China, where wages are lower than in the United States. It is advantageous, therefore, for the United States to specialize in the production of a product such as pharmaceuticals, the production of which more efficiently employs the country's abundant supply of knowledge workers and technology. The United States is then better off exporting pharmaceuticals and importing coat hangers from China. The comparative advantage view is optimistic because it implies that a nation need not be the first-, second-, or even third-best producer of particular products to benefit from international trade. Indeed, it is generally advantageous for *all* countries to participate in international trade.

Initially, the comparative advantage principle focused on the importance of natural resources in a country, or *natural advantages,* such as fertile land, abundant minerals, and favorable climate. Thus, because South Africa has extensive deposits of minerals, it produces and exports diamonds. Because Canada has much agricultural land and a suitable climate, it produces and exports wheat. Over time, however, it became clear that countries can also *create* or acquire comparative advantages. We elaborate on these so-called *acquired advantages* later in the chapter.

Limitations of Early Trade Theories While the concepts of absolute advantage and comparative advantage provided the rationale for international trade, they did not quite capture factors that make contemporary trade complex, including:

- The cost of international transportation, which is critical for cross-border trade to take place.

- Government restrictions such as tariffs (a tax on imports), import restrictions, and regulations typical of mercantilism that can hamper cross-border trade. For instance, tariffs in Japan restrict imports of certain agricultural products.

- Large-scale production in certain industries may bring about scale economies, and therefore lower prices, which can help offset weak national comparative advantage. For example, Mexico lacks advantages in the production of high-technology goods, but it compensates for this through high-volume manufacturing of various goods.

- The public sector can target and invest in certain industries, build infrastructure, or provide subsidies, all of which serve to boost firms' competitive advantages. For example, Singapore has invested heavily in developing its port infrastructure, making the country a vital depot for product import and distribution throughout Asia.

- Global telecommunications and the Internet facilitate virtually costless trade in some services and global flows of capital. The tendency has increased the ability of emerging markets such as India and Russia to access capital needed to develop key industries, even in the face of weak comparative advantages in certain areas.

- Contemporary cross-border business includes many *services* (such as banking and retailing) that cannot be traded in the usual sense and must be internationalized via foreign investment. Even nations that lack comparative advantages in service industries still develop basic services for their own citizens.

- The primary participants in cross-border trade are individual firms. Far from being homogeneous enterprises, they differ in significant ways. Some are highly entrepreneurial and innovative, or have access to exceptional human talent. As a result, some companies are more active and successful in international business than others. In other cases, firms may have a greater need to trade internationally if their home markets are too small to support their growth or revenue objectives.

In the following sections, we discuss subsequent theories that consider how these factors affect trade.

Factor Proportions Theory The next significant contribution to explaining international trade came in the 1920s, when two Swedish economists, Eli Heckscher and his student, Bertil Ohlin, proposed the *factor proportions theory* (sometimes called the *factor endowments theory*).[2] This view rests on two premises: First, products differ in the types and quantities of factors (that is, labor, natural resources, and capital) that are required for their production; and second, countries differ in the type and quantity of production factors that they possess. Thus, according to this theory, each country should export products that intensively use relatively abundant factors of production, and import goods that intensively use relatively scarce factors of production. For example, because China possesses an ample labor supply, it emphasizes the production and export of labor-intensive products, such as textiles and kitchen utensils.

Because the United States possesses much capital, it emphasizes the production and export of capital-intensive products, such as pharmaceuticals and commercial aircraft. Because Australia and Canada possess a great deal of land, they produce and export land-intensive products, such as meat, wheat, and wool.

Factor proportions theory differs somewhat from earlier trade theories by emphasizing the importance of each nation's factors of production. The theory states that, in addition to differences in the *efficiency* of production, differences in the *quantity* of factors of production held by countries also determine international trade patterns. Originally, labor was seen as the most important factor of production. This explains, for example, why China and Mexico receive huge amounts of foreign direct investment (FDI) from firms that build factories in those countries to take advantage of their inexpensive, abundant labor.

In the 1950s, Russian-born economist Wassily Leontief pointed to empirical findings that seemed to contradict the factor proportions theory. The *Leontief paradox* suggests that, because the United States has abundant capital, it should be an exporter of capital-intensive products. However, Leontief's analysis revealed that, despite the United States having abundant capital, its exports were labor-intensive and imports capital-intensive.

However, experience of the last few decades suggests that the factor proportions theory explains much of contemporary international trade. So, what accounts for the inconsistency suggested by the Leontief paradox? One explanation is that numerous factors determine the composition of a country's exports and imports. Another explanation is that labor in the United States tends to be highly skilled, giving the country substantial advantages in the production of knowledge-intensive products and services such as software and pharmaceuticals.

Perhaps the main contribution of the Leontief paradox is its suggestion that international trade is complex and cannot be fully explained by a single theory. While the factor proportions theory helps explain international trade patterns, it does not account for all trade phenomena. Subsequent refinements of the factor proportions theory suggested that other country-level assets—knowledge, technology, and capital—are instrumental in explaining each nation's international trade prowess. Taiwan, for example, is very strong in information technology and is home to a sizeable population of knowledge workers in the IT sector. These factors have helped make Taiwan one of the leading players in the global computer industry.

International Product Cycle Theory In a 1966 article entitled "International Investment and International Trade in the Product Cycle," Harvard Professor Raymond Vernon sought to explain international trade based on the evolutionary process that occurs in the development and diffusion of products around the world.[3] Vernon observed that technical innovations typically originate from advanced countries that possess abundant capital and R&D capabilities. Each product and its associated manufacturing technologies go through three stages of evolution: introduction, growth, and maturity. In the introduction stage, the new product is produced at home and enjoys a temporary monopoly. Later on, the product's inventors

Factor proportions theory describes how abundant production factors give rise to national advantages. For example, Brazil has an abundance of workers in various industries. Here, workers at the Accessorios Para Panela de Pressao in São Paulo assemble parts for pressure cookers.

mass-produce the good and seek to export it to foreign markets. As the product's manufacturing becomes more standard, foreign competitors enter the marketplace and the monopoly power of the inventors dissipates. The inventor may at this stage earn only a narrow profit margin. Companies from other countries begin producing the standardized product. Foreign competitors may even enjoy a competitive advantage in producing the mature product, and fulfill the needs of export markets as well. By now, the original innovating and exporting country may be a net importer of the product. In effect, exporting the product has caused its underlying technology to become widely known and standardized around the world.

As product standardization progresses, input requirements for production evolve. For instance, early in the product's evolution, manufacturing requires highly-skilled knowledge workers in R&D. When the product becomes standardized, mass production is the dominant activity, requiring access to less expensive raw materials and low-cost labor. Thus, as the product goes through its life cycle, comparative advantage in its production tends to shift from country to country. This type of cycle was evident in the evolution of television sets. The base technology for televisions was invented in the United States, and U.S. firms began producing TVs there in the 1940s. U.S. sales grew rapidly for many years. After becoming a standardized product, television production shifted to China, Mexico, and other countries that offer lower cost production.

Because firms around the world are constantly innovating new products, and others are constantly imitating them, the product cycle is constantly beginning and ending. In the contemporary interconnected economy, the cycle from innovation to growth to maturity is much shorter than in the 1960s to 1980s. New products with universal appeal are likely to be diffused across different countries much faster. Thanks to global media and the Internet, potential customers in distant parts of the world are likely to hear about and demand the product. Buyers in emerging markets are particularly eager to adopt new technologies as soon as they become available. This trend explains the rather rapid spread of new consumer electronics (such as digital assistants and iPods) around the world.

How Nations Enhance Their Competitive Advantage: Contemporary Theories

The globalization of markets has fostered a new type of competition—a race among nations to reposition themselves as attractive places to invest and do business. In recent decades, governments increasingly have advanced proactive policies designed to create competitive advantage, often by developing world-class economic sectors and prosperous geographic regions. These policies aim to have firms develop acquired advantages. Let's review contemporary theories aimed at enhancing the competitive advantages of national economies.

The Competitive Advantage of Nations

Just as scholars recognized that international business is good for individual nations, they increasingly sought to explain how nations can position themselves for international business success. An important contribution came from Harvard business professor Michael Porter in his 1990 book, *The Competitive Advantage of Nations*.[4] According to Porter, the competitive advantage of a nation depends on the collective competitive advantages of the nation's firms. Over time, this relationship is reciprocal: The competitive advantages held by the nation tend to drive the development of new firms and industries with these same competitive advantages.

For example, Japan is competent in high-technology industries; it is home to firms such as Toshiba and Hitachi, world-class companies in high-tech fields. Over time, Japan's national competitive advantage in high technologies has driven the development of new firms and industries in these fields. In a similar way, Britain has achieved a substantial national competitive advantage in the patent medication (prescription drug) industry due to its first-rate pharmaceutical firms, including AstraZeneca and GlaxoSmithKline. The United States has a national competitive advantage in service industries because of many leading firms, such as AIG (insurance), Merrill Lynch (financial services), Dreamworks (movies), and Accenture (consulting). U.S. prowess in the service sector, in turn, has engendered the emergence of new, innovative firms in the service industry.

An individual firm has a competitive advantage when it possesses one or more sources of distinctive competence relative to others, allowing it to perform better than its competitors. Thus, for instance, the low-cost operations of Tesco and Wal-Mart have allowed these firms to surpass other mass retailers. Nokia's superior technology and design leadership have allowed it to stay abreast and often surpass key rivals in the cell phone industry.

At both the firm and national levels, competitive advantage grows out of *innovation*.[5] Firms innovate in various ways: They develop new product designs, new production processes, new approaches to marketing, or new ways of organizing. Firms sustain innovation (and by extension, competitive advantage) by continually finding better products, services, and ways of doing things. For example, Australia's ERG Group is a world leader in fare collection equipment and software systems for the transit industry. The firm installed systems in subways, bus networks, and other mass transit systems worldwide, in major cities such as Melbourne, Rome, San Francisco, Stockholm, and Singapore. ERG has won numerous awards for its innovative products, which have allowed the firm to internationalize quickly and to numerous countries. ERG's investment in R&D has been significant, running as high as 23 percent of the company's revenue.

The aggregate innovative capacity of a nation is derived from the collective innovative capacity of its firms. The more innovative firms a nation has, the stronger that nation's competitive advantage. Innovation also promotes *productivity*, the value of the output produced by a unit of labor or capital. The more productive a firm is, the more efficiently it uses its resources. The more productive the firms in a nation are, the more efficiently the nation uses its resources. At the national level, productivity is a *key* determinant of the nation's long-run standard of living and a basic source of national per-capita (per person) income growth. Exhibit 4.4 depicts productivity levels in various nations over time. Here productivity is measured as output per hour of workers in manufacturing.

Michael Porter's Diamond Model

As part of his explanation in the *Competitive Advantage of Nations*, Michael Porter developed the *diamond model*. According to this model, competitive advantage at both the company and national levels originates from the presence and quality in the country of the four major elements summarized in Exhibit 4.5.

1. *Firm Strategy, Structure, and Rivalry* refers to the nature of domestic rivalry, and conditions in a nation that determine how firms are created, organized, and managed. The presence of strong competitors in a nation helps create and

Exhibit 4.4

Productivity Levels in Selected
Countries
Output per hour in manufacturing,
1985–2005 indices: 1992=100

SOURCE: U.S. Department of Labor, Bureau of Labor
Statistics, February 2006.

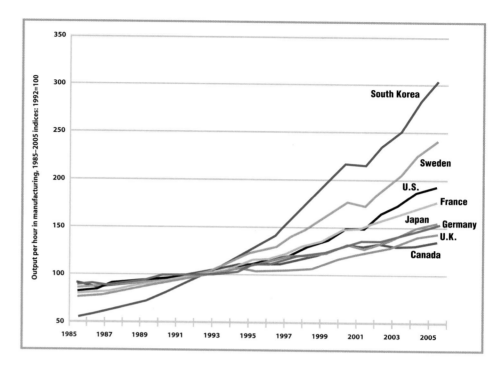

maintain national competitive advantage. For example, Italy has some of the
world's leading firms in design-intensive industries such as furniture, lighting, textiles, and fashion. Vigorous competitive rivalry puts these firms under
continuous pressure to innovate and improve. The firms compete not only for
market share, but also for human talent, technical leadership, and superior
product quality. These pressures have allowed Italy to emerge as one of the
world's leading countries in design.

2. *Factor Conditions* describes the nation's position in factors of production,
such as labor, natural resources, capital, technology, entrepreneurship, and
know-how. Consistent with the factor proportions theory, every nation has a
relative abundance of certain factor endowments, a situation that helps deter-

Exhibit 4.5

Porter's Diamond Model

SOURCE: reprinted with the permission of The Free
Press, a Division of Simon & Schuster Adult Publishing Group from The Competitive Advantage of
Nations by Michael E. Porter. Copyright © 1990,
1998 by Michael E. Porter. All rights reserved.

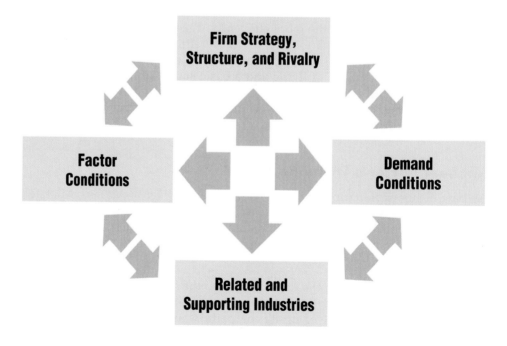

mine the nature of its national competitive advantage. For example, India's numerous low-wage knowledge workers have allowed it to develop a competitive advantage in the production of computer software. Germany's abundance of workers with strong engineering skills has propelled the country to acquire competitive advantages in the global engineering and design industry. At the same time, the scarcity of certain factors may compel countries to use them more efficiently, leading to competitive advantages. For example, today China lacks a strong base of knowledge workers in many industries. Accordingly, the Chinese government is investing in education to develop the national expertise needed to excel in various knowledge-based industries.

Bangalore, India has emerged as a world-class industrial cluster in the IT and business services industries.

3. *Demand Conditions* refers to the nature of home-market demand for specific products and services. The strength and sophistication of buyer demand facilitates the development of competitive advantages in particular industries. The presence of discerning, highly demanding customers pressures firms to innovate faster and produce better products. For example, Japan is a densely populated, hot, and humid country with very demanding consumers. These conditions led Japan to become one of the leading producers and exporters of superior, compact air conditioners. In the United States, affluence combined with an aging population encouraged the development of world-class health care companies such as Pfizer and Eli Lilly in pharmaceuticals and Boston Scientific and Medtronic in medical equipment.

4. *Related and Supporting Industries* refers to the presence of clusters of suppliers, competitors, and complementary firms that excel in particular industries. The resulting business environment is highly supportive for the founding of particular types of firms. Operating within a mass of related and supporting industries provides advantages through information and knowledge synergies, economies of scale and scope, and access to appropriate or superior inputs. For example, the Silicon Valley in California is one of the best places to launch a computer software firm, because the valley is home to thousands of knowledgeable firms and workers in the software industry. The firms in this industry generate a substantial flow of technological interchange that accelerates new product development and improvements in the software industry.

Industrial cluster refers to a concentration of businesses, suppliers, and supporting firms in the same industry at a particular location, characterized by a critical mass of human talent, capital, or other factor endowments. In addition to the Silicon Valley, other industrial clusters include the fashion industry in northern Italy, the pharmaceutical industry in Switzerland, the footwear industry in Pusan, South Korea, the IT industry in Bangalore, India, Silicon Valley North near Ottawa, Canada, and Wireless Valley, in Stockholm, Sweden.

Today, the most important sources of national advantage are the knowledge and skills possessed by individual firms, industries, and countries. More than any other factors, knowledge and skills determine where MNEs will locate economic activity around the world. Silicon Valley, California, and Bangalore, India, have emerged as leading-edge business clusters because of the availability of specialized talent. These cities have little else going for them in terms of natural industrial power. Their success derives

Industrial cluster

A concentration of businesses, suppliers, and supporting firms in the same industry at a particular location, characterized by a critical mass of human talent, capital, or other factor endowments.

Visionary national industrial policy is transforming Dubai into a high value-adding economy based on IT, biotechnology, financial services, and other knowledge-intensive industries.

National industrial policy A proactive economic development plan initiated by the public sector, often in collaboration with the private sector, that aims to develop or support particular industries within the nation.

from the knowledge of the people who work there, so-called knowledge workers. Some even argue that knowledge is now the only source of sustainable long-run competitive advantage. If this view is correct, then future national wealth will go to those countries that invest the most in R&D, education, and infrastructure that support knowledge-intensive industries.

National Industrial Policy

Perhaps the greatest contribution of Michael Porter's work has been to underscore the notion that national competitive advantage does not derive entirely from the store of natural resources that each country holds. Moreover, *inherited* national factor endowments are relatively less important than in the past. Rather, as Porter emphasized, countries can successfully *create* new advantages. Nations can develop factor conditions that they deem important for their success. The public sector can devote resources to improve national infrastructure, education systems, and capital formation. In short, Porter's diamond model implies that any country, regardless of its initial circumstances, can attain economic prosperity by systematically cultivating new and superior factor endowments.

Nations can develop these endowments through proactive **national industrial policy**. This type of policy implements an economic development plan, often in collaboration with the private sector, that aims to develop or support particular industries within the nation. Ireland, Japan, Singapore, and South Korea are examples of countries that have succeeded with national industrial policy. Policies emphasize the development of high-value adding industries that generate substantial wealth in terms of corporate profits, worker wages, and tax revenues. In the opening vignette, Dubai is pursuing a national industrial policy to develop as an international commercial center in the information and communications technology (ICT) sector. Historically, nations have favored more traditional industries, including automobiles, shipbuilding, and heavy machinery—all with long value chains that generate substantial added value. As the Dubai example illustrates, progressive nations increasingly favor high value-adding, knowledge-intensive industries such as IT, biotechnology, medical technology, and financial services. Not only do these industries provide substantial revenues to the nation, they also lead to the development of supplier and support companies that further enhance national prosperity.

National industrial policies designed to build new capacity and capabilities share the following:

- Tax incentives to encourage citizens to save and invest, which provide capital for public and private investment in plant, equipment, R&D, infrastructure, and worker skills.

- Monetary and fiscal policies, such as low-interest loans that provide a stable supply of capital for company investment needs.

- Rigorous educational systems at both the precollege and university levels that ensure a steady stream of competent workers who support high technology or high value-adding industries in areas such as the sciences, engineering, and business administration.

- Development and maintenance of strong national infrastructure in areas such as IT, communication systems, and transportation.
- Creation of strong legal and regulatory systems to ensure that citizens are confident about the soundness and stability of the national economy.[6]

National Industrial Policy in Practice: An Example

How well does national industrial policy work in practice? To address this question, let's examine the case of Ireland and the outcomes of proactive country repositioning implemented through a collaborative effort by the nation's public and private sectors.

In the 1930s, government policies limited Ireland's ability to trade with the rest of the world. Standards of living were low, young people were fleeing the country, and many wondered if Ireland had a future. Then, in the 1980s, the Irish government undertook protrade policies in cooperation with the private sector that led to the development of national advantages, helping Ireland's economy to grow rapidly and achieve high living standards. The magnitude of Ireland's accomplishment becomes clear in Exhibit 4.6, which compares the country's economic situation between 1987 and 2003.

Annual GDP growth in Ireland averaged nearly 7 percent throughout the 1990s—a fast pace. Ireland's rejuvenation was so successful that officials from around the world visit the country regularly to learn how it leaped from being one of Europe's stagnant economies to one of the most dynamic. The "Irish miracle" resulted from a combination of efforts:

- *Fiscal, monetary, and tax consolidation.* The Irish government lowered the basic corporate tax rate to zero, helping to foster entrepreneurship and increasing the nation's attractiveness for inward investment from foreign MNEs. Personal taxes were reduced, boosting consumer spending. The government substantially cut spending and borrowing, which led to lower interest rates and helped stimulate the economy.
- *Social partnership.* The government initiated earnest dialogue with labor unions. Increased coordination between government and industry improved the quality of the work force and strengthened the Irish labor pool.
- *Emphasis on high value-adding industries.* Ireland created a national infrastructure and investment climate that fosters the development of industries in high value-adding fields—pharmaceuticals, biochemistry, and IT.
- *Membership in the European Union.* The emergence of the European single market provided Ireland with a huge market for its exports. Falling trade barriers opened a giant market of 400 million consumers to Irish firms.

Statistic	Ireland in 1987	Ireland in 2003
GDP per capita	69 percent of the average of Europe	136 percent of the average of Europe
Unemployment rate	17 percent	4 percent
National debt	112 percent of the nation's GDP	33 percent of the nation's GDP

Exhibit 4.6 Transformation of Ireland's Economy from 1987 to 2003

- *Subsidies.* Ireland received subsidies from the European Union that allowed it to offset debt, invest in key infrastructure projects, and develop a range of key industries, particularly in the IT sector.
- *Education.* The country invested heavily in education, providing a steady supply of skilled workers, including scientists, engineers, and business school graduates.

Lured by the positive developments in Ireland, many foreign MNEs began investing in the country. Thanks to national industrial policy, Ireland has become a major player in world trade and is now home to more than 1,100 multinational firms. International trade, inward FDI, and economic development are dramatically raising living standards for its citizens.[7]

Read the *Global Trend* feature for additional examples of proactive nation repositioning to create new comparative advantages.

New Trade Theory

Beginning in the 1970s, economists led by Paul Krugman began to note that classical theories failed to anticipate or explain some international trade patterns. For example, they observed that trade was growing fastest between industrial countries that held similar factors of production. In some new industries, there appeared to be no clear comparative advantage. The solution to this puzzle became known as *new trade theory*. The theory argues that increasing returns to scale, especially *economies of scale*, are an important factor in some industries for superior international performance. Some industries succeed best as their volume of production increases. For example, the commercial aircraft industry has very high fixed costs that necessitate high-volume sales to achieve profitability. As a nation specializes in the production of such goods, productivity increases and unit costs fall, providing significant benefits to the local economy.

Because many national markets are relatively small, the domestic producer may not achieve economies of scale because it cannot sell products in large volume. The theory implies that firms can solve this problem by exporting, thereby gaining access to the much larger global marketplace. Similarly, some industries (for example, automobiles, aircraft, and large-scale industrial machinery) have achieved minimally profitable economies of scale by selling their output in multiple markets worldwide.

The effect of increasing returns to scale allows the nation to specialize in a smaller number of industries in which it may not necessarily hold factor or comparative advantages. The nation then imports the products that it does not make from other countries. The end result is that the nation: (1) increases the variety of products that it consumes, and (2) obtains these products at lower cost, both due to international trade and the economies of scale of its domestic industries. Thus, trade is beneficial even for countries that produce only a limited variety of products. New trade theory provides further rationale for engaging in international trade.

 # Why and How Firms Internationalize

Earlier theories of international trade focused on why and how cross-national business occurs among nations. Beginning in the 1960s, however, scholars developed theories about the managerial and organizational aspects of firm internationalization.

Internationalization Process of the Firm

The *internationalization process model* was developed in the 1970s to describe how firms expand abroad. According to this model, internationalization is a gradual process that takes place in incremental stages over a long period of time.[8] Typically, firms begin with exporting and progress to FDI, the most complex form of international activity. Initial international involvement emerges as an innovation

Repositioning to Create National Comparative Advantage

Countries that succeed at national industrial strategy have proactively created internationally competitive industries. The principle of comparative advantage and factor endowment theory imply that nations should nurture industries that use inputs that are inherent or abundant in the nation's resource endowment. Today, numerous countries that were initially poor in natural or other resources have *created* their own competitive advantages through skillful application of national industrial policies. In most industries, these *acquired advantages* have become more critical than natural endowments. Here are some examples:

Japan, a crowded island country with few natural resources, emphasized the development of various acquired advantages—skilled labor, cheap capital, and strong R&D capabilities. The systematic national strategy allowed Japan to become one of the world's strongest economies. In the decades following World War II, which had devastated the country, the Japanese government cooperated with the country's corporate and financial sectors to create a collection of leading industries in automobiles, consumer electronics, transportation equipment, and other sectors in which Japan excels today.

Silicon Valley, in California, originated when a number of high-tech firms set up shop to serve the technology needs of the U.S. military. Stanford University's creation of an industrial park led to the founding of Hewlett-Packard in 1939. In later years, high-tech firms established themselves, attracted by the area's superior factor conditions, supportive industries, and quality of life. Further growth was fueled in the 1970s by the emergence of venture capitalist firms, providing vital capital to start-up firms. Silicon Valley remains a critical center of innovation and entrepreneurship, and one of the world's leading suppliers of IT-related products and services.

Singapore is a free market economy with stable prices and a per capita GDP equal to that of the most affluent European countries. Beginning in the 1960s, the government adopted probusiness, proinvestment, export-oriented policies, combined with state-directed investments in strategic corporations. The approach stimulated economic growth that averaged 8 percent from 1960 to 1999. Singapore cut taxes and government spending, and encouraged massive inward investment in high-value industries such as electronics, chemicals, engineering, and biomedical sciences. The country boasts a highly educated labor force, as well as excellent infrastructure—including an airport and seaport that are among the best in the world—and state-of-the-art telecommunications facilities.

New Zealand's government, beginning in 1984, systematically transformed the country from an agrarian, protectionist, highly regulated economy to an industrialized, free-market economy that competes globally. The government privatized a number of former state-owned enterprises, joined various international free trade agreements, and focused on building a knowledge economy. Dynamic growth has boosted real incomes and deepened technological capabilities.

India positioned *Bangalore*, the country's third largest city, as a center of IT and business support services. In cooperation with private interests, the government reduced restrictions on foreign trade and investment, resulting in a big influx of foreign FDI. Bangalore capitalized on its large, well-educated, English-speaking workforce. The public-private partnership emphasized other high-value industries, such as biotechnology and business consulting.

The Czech Republic's recent economic reforms and successful exporting to the European Union (EU) produced economic prosperity. The Czech government harmonized its laws and regulations with those of the EU by reforming its judicial system, civil administration, financial markets regulation, intellectual property rights protection, and many other areas important to investors. The country also privatized state-owned companies. Government FDI incentives attracted firms like Toyota, ING, Siemens, Daewoo, DHL, and South African Breweries.

Vietnam's government privatized state enterprises and modernized the economy, emphasizing competitive, export-driven industries. Vietnam ramped up its exports of everything from shoes to ships. The country modernized its intellectual property regime, entered several free trade agreements, and ramped up its educational system to provide a constant stream of skilled workers. The government built infrastructure, including power stations, roads, and railways. Reforms have attracted much inward FDI from firms like Intel, and the national savings rate has increased several-fold. Economic repositioning has dramatically reduced poverty. Vietnam became one of the fastest-growing economies, averaging around 8 percent annual GDP growth in the 1990s.

Exhibit 4.7

Stages in the Internationalization Process of the Firm

in the firm, but without much rational analysis or deliberate planning on the part of managers who oversee the process. The gradual, slow, and incremental nature of internationalization results from the uncertainty and uneasiness that managers experience, mainly due to inadequate information about foreign markets and lack of experience with cross-border transactions.

A simplified illustration of the internationalization process model appears in Exhibit 4.7. A firm starts out in a *domestic focus* phase and is preoccupied with acquiring business in the home market. The firm is often unable or unwilling to engage in international business because of concerns over its readiness, or perceived obstacles in foreign markets. Eventually, the firm advances to the *pre-export stage*, often because it receives unsolicited product orders from abroad. Consequently, management investigates the feasibility of undertaking international business. The firm then advances to the *experimental involvement* stage by initiating limited international activity, typically in the form of basic exporting. As managers begin to view foreign expansion more favorably, they eventually undertake *active involvement* in international business through systematic exploration of international options and the commitment of top management time and resources toward achieving international success. Ultimately the firm may advance to the *committed involvement* stage, characterized by genuine interest and commitment of resources to making international business a key part of the firm's profit-making and value-chain activities. In this stage, the firm targets numerous foreign markets via various entry modes, especially FDI.[9]

Born Globals and International Entrepreneurship

The contemporary business environment has stimulated scholars to question the gradual and slow nature of internationalization proposed by the internationalization process model.[10] Because international business has long been the domain of large, resource-rich MNEs, earlier international business theory tended to focus on them. But during the past couple of decades, many firms have internationalized early in their evolution. Among the reasons for this shift are the growing intensity of international competition, advances in communication and transportation technologies that have reduced the cost of venturing abroad, and the integration of world economies under globalization, which makes it easier for companies of all ages and sizes to internationalize.

The new business environment represented by these trends has stimulated the widespread emergence of firms that internationalize at their founding—born globals—and the rise of a new field of scholarly inquiry, international entrepreneurship.[11] Despite the scarcity of financial, human, and tangible resources that characterize most new businesses, born globals progress to internationalization early in their evolution. Current trends imply that early internationalizing firms will gradually become the norm in international trade and investment.

 How Firms Gain and Sustain International Competitive Advantage

So far we have focused on the internationalization processes of individual firms, including smaller firms or those new to international business. Since the 1950s, multinational enterprises (MNE) such as Nestlé, Unilever, Sony, Coca-Cola, Caterpillar, and IBM have expanded abroad on a massive scale, shaping international patterns of trade, investment, and technology flows. Over time, the aggregate activities of these firms became a key driving force of globalization and ongoing integration of world economies. So important is the rise of the MNE that it ranks with the development of electric power or the invention of the aircraft as one of the major events of modern history. Let's examine these firms and their internationalization processes in more detail.

As explained in Chapter 1, an MNE is a large, resource-rich company whose business activities are performed by a network of subsidiaries located in numerous countries. The typical MNE has value chains that span multiple countries. Although an MNE originates from a home country, it establishes worldwide production facilities, marketing subsidiaries, regional headquarters, and other physical facilities directly in the countries where it does business. MNEs leverage leading-edge technologies, talented managers, large capital bases, and other advantages to succeed around the world. They take advantage of global capital markets and local resources in the countries where they operate. They are the foremost agents in disseminating new products, new technologies, and business practices worldwide, contributing to ongoing globalization of markets.

Take Sony as an example. Sony has hundreds of subsidiaries and affiliates around the world that perform the widest range of value-chain activities. Sony has annual sales of roughly $70 billion, with more than 160,000 employees worldwide. Sony's PlayStation dominates the home video game market with about 70 percent of global sales. Vaio computers are popular worldwide. The firm makes a host of other products, including PCs, digital cameras, Walkman stereos, and semiconductors. Its online music service is managed by a newly formed subsidiary of Sony Corporation of America. Sony is headquartered in Tokyo; however, Japan accounts for only about a third of its worldwide sales. It conducts business in emerging markets such as Argentina, Brazil, China, Turkey, Indonesia, Vietnam, and the Philippines. The firm is truly a borderless MNE that locates its activities wherever in the world it can maximize competitive advantages.

FDI-Based Theories

FDI stock refers to the total value of assets that MNEs own abroad via their investment activities. Exhibit 4.8 shows the stock of inward FDI and Exhibit 4.9 shows

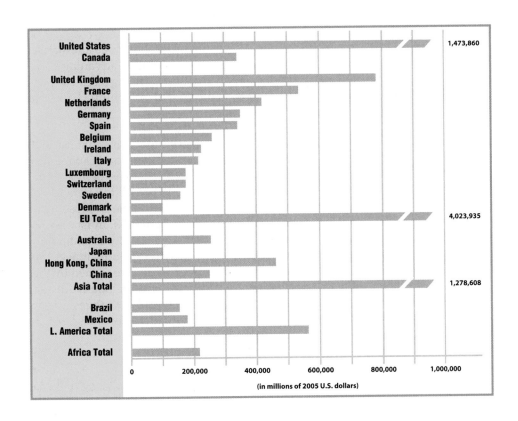

Exhibit 4.8

Stock of Inward FDI: Leading FDI Destinations (Millions of U.S. dollars)

SOURCE: UNCTAD, World Investment Report, United Nations, New York, 2005 at www.unctad.org. The United Nations is the author of the original material. Used with permission.

Exhibit 4.9

Stock of Outward FDI: Top Sources of Outward FDI (Millions of U.S. dollars)

SOURCE: UNCTAD, World Investment Report, United Nations, New York, 2005 at www.unctad.org. The United Nations is the author of the original material. Used with permission.

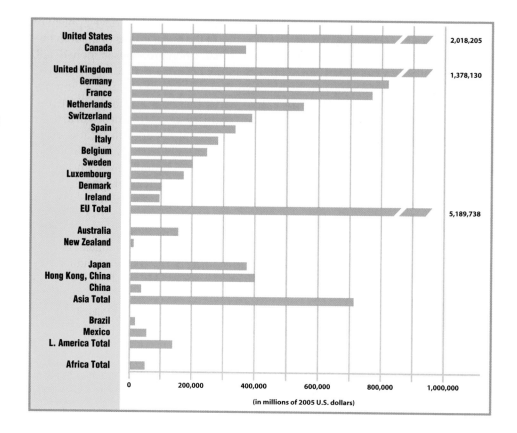

the stock of outward FDI. MNEs invest millions abroad every year to establish and expand factories and other facilities. Total FDI stock now constitutes some 20 percent of global GDP, which is a significant amount. While historically most of the world's FDI was invested both by and in Western Europe, the United States, and Japan, in recent years MNEs have begun to invest heavily in emerging markets such as China, Mexico, Brazil, and Eastern Europe.[12]

FDI is such an important entry strategy that scholars provide three alternative theories of how firms can use it to gain and sustain competitive advantage: the monopolistic advantage theory, internalization theory, and Dunning's eclectic paradigm. These theoretical perspectives are summarized in Exhibit 4.10 and described in the following sections.

Monopolistic Advantage Theory This theory suggests that firms that use FDI as an internationalization strategy tend to control certain resources and capabilities that give them a degree of monopoly power relative to foreign competitors. The advantages that arise from this monopoly power enable the MNE to operate foreign subsidiaries more profitably than the local firms that compete in those markets. A key assumption of the theory is that, to be successful, an MNE must possess monopolistic advantages over local firms in foreign markets. In addition, the firm must keep these advantages to itself by internalizing them. These advantages are specific to the MNE rather than to the location of its production, are owned by the MNE, and not easily available to its competitors. For example, the South African firm SAB Miller, the second largest beer brewer in the world, leverages a near monopoly in its home country, relying on extensive international business expertise, and offering a unique line of beers to customers around the world.[13]

The most important monopolistic advantage is superior knowledge, which includes intangible skills possessed by the MNE that provide a competitive advantage over local rivals in foreign markets. Superior, proprietary knowledge allows MNEs to create differentiated products that provide unique value to customers.[14]

Theory	Key Characteristics	Benefits	Examples
Monopolistic Advantage Theory	The firm controls one or more resources, or offers relatively unique products and services that provide it a degree of monopoly power relative to foreign markets and competitors.	The firm can operate foreign subsidiaries more profitably than the local firms that compete in their own markets.	The European pharmaceutical Novartis earns substantial profits by marketing various patent medications through its subsidiaries worldwide.
Internalization Theory	The firm acquires and retains one or more value-chain activities within the firm.	• Minimizes the disadvantages of relying on intermediaries, collaborators, or other external partners. • Ensures greater control over foreign operations, helping to maximize product quality, reliable manufacturing processes, and sound marketing practices. • Reduces the risk that knowledge and proprietary assets will be lost to competitors.	The Japanese MNE Toshiba: • Owns and operates factories in dozens of countries to manufacture laptop computers. • Controls its own manufacturing processes, ensuring quality output. • Ensures its marketing activities are carried out per headquarters' plan. • Retains key assets within the firm, such as leading-edge knowledge for producing the next generation of laptops.
Dunning's Eclectic Paradigm	• *Ownership-specific advantages*: The firm owns knowledge, skills, capabilities, processes, or physical assets. • *Location-specific advantages*: Factors in individual countries provide specific benefits, such as natural resources, skilled labor, low-cost labor, and inexpensive capital. • *Internalization advantages*: The firm benefits from internalizing foreign manufacturing, distribution, or other value-chain activities.	Provides various advantages relative to competitors, including the ability to own, control and optimize value-chain activities—R&D, production, marketing, sales distribution, after-sales service, as well as relationships with customers and key contacts—performed at the most beneficial locations worldwide.	The German MNE Siemens: • Owns factories at locations worldwide that provide optimal access to natural resources, skilled and low-cost labor. • Leverages the knowledge base of its employees in 190 countries. • Internalizes a wide range of manufacturing activities in categories such as lighting, medical equipment, and transportation machinery.

Exhibit 4.10 Theoretical Perspectives on Why Firms Choose FDI

Internalization Theory Some scholars investigated the specific benefits that MNEs derive from FDI-based entry. For instance, when Procter & Gamble entered Japan, management initially considered exporting and FDI. With exporting, P&G would have had to contract with an independent Japanese distributor to handle warehousing and marketing of soap, detergent, diapers, and the other products that P&G now sells in Japan. However, because of trade barriers imposed by the Japanese government, the strong market power of local Japanese firms, and the risk of losing control over its proprietary company knowledge, P&G chose instead to enter Japan via FDI. P&G established its own marketing subsidiary and, eventually, national headquarters in Tokyo. Such an arrangement provided various benefits that P&G would not have received had it entered Japan by contracting with Japanese distributors not owned by P&G.

Internalization theory An explanation of the process by which firms acquire and retain one or more value-chain activities "inside" the firm, minimizing the disadvantages of dealing with external partners and allowing for greater control over foreign operations.

This example reveals how MNEs *internalize* key business functions and assets within the corporate organization. **Internalization theory** explains the process by which firms acquire and retain one or more value-chain activities inside the firm, minimizing the disadvantages of dealing with external partners and allowing for greater control over foreign operations. It contrasts the costs and benefits of retaining key business activities *within* the firm against arms-length foreign entry strategies such as exporting and licensing, in which the firm contracts with *external* business partners to perform certain value-chain activities. By internalizing foreign-based value-chain activities it is the firm, rather than its products, that crosses international borders. For instance, instead of procuring from foreign independent suppliers, the MNE internalizes the supplier function by acquiring or establishing its own facilities in the foreign market. Where one firm might contract with independent foreign distributors to market its products abroad, the MNE internalizes the marketing function by establishing or acquiring its own distribution subsidiary abroad. The MNE is ultimately a vehicle for bypassing the bottlenecks and costs of the international, inter-firm exchange of goods, materials, and workers. In this way, the MNE *replaces* business activities performed in external markets with business activities performed within its own *internal* market.

As highlighted earlier, knowledge is critical to the development, production, distribution, and sale of products and services. Because competitors can easily acquire and use a firm's knowledge, firms internalize their key knowledge by internationalizing via FDI instead of other modes, such as exporting. FDI allows management to control and optimally use the firm's proprietary knowledge in foreign markets.[15]

Dunning's Eclectic Paradigm Professor John Dunning proposed the *eclectic paradigm* as a framework for determining the extent and pattern of the value-chain operations that companies own abroad. Dunning draws from various theoretical perspectives, including the comparative advantage and the factor proportions, monopolistic advantage, and internalization advantage theories.

Let's use a real firm to illustrate the eclectic paradigm. The Aluminum Corporation of America (Alcoa) has over 130,000 employees in roughly 43 countries. The company's integrated operations include bauxite mining and aluminum refining. Its products include primary aluminum (which it refines from bauxite), automotive components, and sheet aluminum for beverage cans and Reynolds Wrap®.

The eclectic paradigm specifies three conditions that determine whether or not a company will internationalize via FDI: ownership-specific advantages, location-specific advantages, and internalization advantages.

To successfully enter and conduct business in a foreign market, the MNE must possess *ownership-specific advantages* (unique to the firm) relative to other firms already doing business in the market. These consist of the knowledge, skills, capabilities, processes, relationships, or physical assets held by the firm that allow it to compete effectively in the global marketplace. They amount to the firm's *competitive advantages*. To ensure international success, the advantages must be substantial enough to offset the costs that the firm incurs in establishing and operating foreign operations. They also must be specific to the MNE that possesses them and not readily transferable to other firms. Examples of ownership-specific advantages include proprietary technology, managerial skills, trademarks or brand names, economies of scale, and access to substantial financial resources. The more valuable the firm's ownership-specific advantages, the more likely it is to internationalize via FDI.[16]

One of Alcoa's most important ownership-specific advantages is the proprietary technology that it has acquired from R&D activities. Over time, Alcoa has also acquired special managerial and marketing skills in the production and marketing of refined aluminum. The firm has a well-known brand name in the aluminum industry, which helps increase sales. Because it is a large firm, Alcoa also profits from economies of scale and the ability to finance expensive projects. These advantages have allowed Alcoa to maximize the performance of its international operations.

Alcoa has advantages in producing refined aluminum.

Location-specific advantages refer to the *comparative* advantages that exist in individual foreign countries. Each country possesses a unique set of advantages from which companies can derive specific benefits. Examples include natural resources, skilled labor, low-cost labor, and inexpensive capital. Sophisticated managers recognize and seek to benefit from the host country advantages. A location-specific advantage must be present for FDI to succeed. It must be profitable to the firm to locate abroad, that is, to utilize its ownership-specific advantages in conjunction with at least some location-specific advantages in the target country. Otherwise, the firm would use exporting to enter foreign markets.[17]

In terms of location-specific advantages, Alcoa located refineries in Brazil because of that country's huge deposits of bauxite, a mineral found in relatively few other locations worldwide. The Amazon and other major rivers in Brazil generate huge amounts of hydroelectric power, a critical ingredient in electricity-intensive aluminum refining. Alcoa also benefits in Brazil from low-cost, relatively well-educated laborers, who work in the firm's refineries.

Internalization advantages are the advantages that the firm derives from internalizing foreign-based manufacturing, distribution, or other stages in its value chain. When profitable, the firm will transfer its ownership-specific advantages across national borders *within* its own organization, rather than dissipating them to independent, foreign entities. The FDI decision depends on which is the best option—internalization versus utilizing external partners—whether they are licensees, distributors, or suppliers. Internalization advantages include: the ability to control how the firm's products are produced or marketed, the ability to control dissemination of the firm's proprietary knowledge, and the ability to reduce buyer uncertainty about the value of products the firm offers.[18]

Alcoa has internalized many of its operations instead of having them handled by outside independent suppliers for five reasons. First, Alcoa management wants to minimize dissemination of knowledge about its aluminum refining operations—knowledge the firm acquired at great expense. Second, compared to using outside suppliers, internalization provides the best net return to Alcoa, allowing it to minimize the costs of operations. Third, Alcoa needs to control sales of its aluminum products to avoid depressing world aluminum prices by supplying too much aluminum into world markets. Fourth, Alcoa wants to be able to apply a differential pricing strategy, charging different prices to different customers. The firm could not differentiate its prices very effectively without the control over the distribution of its final products that internalization provides. Finally, aluminum refining is a complex business and Alcoa wants to control it to maintain the quality of its products.

Non-FDI Based Explanations

FDI became a popular entry mode with the rise of the MNE in the 1960s and the 1970s. In the 1980s, firms began to recognize the importance of collaborative ventures and other flexible entry strategies.

International Collaborative Ventures   A collaborative venture is a form of cooperation between two or more firms. *Horizontal* collaboration occurs between partners at the same level of the value chain. Examples are manufacturer-to-manufacturer and supplier-to-supplier relationships. *Vertical* collaborations occur between partners at different levels of the value chain. An example is the relationship between a manufacturer and its distributor.

Collaborative ventures are classified into two major types: equity-based *joint ventures* that result in the formation of a new legal entity; and project-based *strategic alliances* that do not require equity commitment from the partners, but simply a willingness to cooperate in R&D, manufacturing, design, or any other value-adding activity. In both cases, collaborating firms pool resources and capabilities and generate synergy. Partners also share the risk of their joint efforts, reducing vulnerability for any one partner. To achieve international business goals, the firm sometimes has no choice but to reach out to resources and capabilities that are not available within its own organization, through collaborative ventures. In addition, occasionally a foreign government restricts the firm from entering its national market via wholly owned FDI, instead requiring the foreigner to enter via a joint venture with a local partner.[19]

By entering into a collaborative venture, the firm may gain access to foreign partners' know-how, capital, distribution channels, marketing assets, or the ability to overcome government-imposed obstacles. By partnering, the firm can better position itself to create new products and enter new markets. For example, Starbucks now boasts nearly 500 coffee shops in Japan, thanks to a joint venture with its local partner, Sazaby, Inc. The venture allowed Starbucks to internationalize rapidly in Japan and to navigate the marketplace with the help of a knowledgeable local partner.[20]

Networks and Relational Assets   Networks and relational assets represent the stock of the firm's economically beneficial long-term *relationships* with other business entities, such as manufacturers, distributors, suppliers, retailers, consultants, banks, transportation suppliers, governments, and any other organization that can provide needed capabilities. Firm-level relational assets represent a distinct competitive advantage in international business. Japanese *keiretsu* are the predecessors of the networks and alliances now emerging in the Western world. Keiretsu are complex groupings of firms with interlinked ownership and trading relationships that foster inter-firm organizational learning.[21] Like keiretsu, networks are neither formal organizations with clearly defined hierarchical structures nor impersonal, decentralized markets.

The International Marketing and Purchasing (IMP) research consortium in Europe has driven much of the theory development on networks.[22] Network theory was proposed to compensate for the inability of traditional organizational theories to account for much of what goes on in business markets. In networks, actors (buyers and sellers) become bound to one another through ongoing exchanges and linkages of products, services, finance, technology, and know-how. Continued interaction among the partners helps form stable relationships based on cooperation. Linkages through industrial networks create value and competitive advantage for firms, even among competitors. Network linkages represent a key route by which many firms expand their business abroad, develop new markets, and develop new products. In international business, mutually beneficial and enduring strategic relationships provide real advantages to partners and reduce uncertainty and transaction costs.

As we will see later in this book, in the contemporary global economy companies have increasingly shied away from making more permanent, direct investment in host countries, and opted for more flexible collaborative ventures with independent business partners.

Hyundai: The Struggle for International Success

The automotive industry is among the largest and most highly internationalized economic sectors. Hyundai Motor Company (HMC) is South Korea's number one carmaker, producing about a dozen models of cars and minivans, as well as trucks, buses, and other commercial vehicles. Popular exported models are the Accent, Elantra, and Sonata. The South Korean firm has managed to internationalize successfully, seemingly against all odds.

The Global Automobile Industry

With many competitors battling for market share, companies such as Hyundai, Ford, and Volkswagen typically operate on thin margins. The automotive industry has been suffering from excess production capacity. Although there is capacity to produce 80 million cars worldwide, total global demand runs at only about 60 million a year. Thus, automotive manufacturers typically employ only 75 percent of their production capacity. The problem has led to numerous mergers and acquisitions in recent years. Consolidations have occurred between Ford and Land Rover, Jaguar and Volvo, and DaimlerBenz with Chrysler, to name a few. In addition, the auto industry is extremely capital–intensive, and firms seek economies of scale to remain profitable. The requisite scale compels automakers to target world markets where they can generate additional sales.

South Korea and the Auto Industry

The car market in South Korea is too small on its own to sustain indigenous automakers like HMC and Kia. These firms have targeted global markets to attain the economies of scale needed to remain competitive in a tough industry. Fortunately, South Korea enjoys various national competitive advantages in the provision of cars. The country has a sizeable workforce of knowledge workers in the auto industry who drive innovations in design, features, production, and product quality. Wages in South Korea are lower than in many advanced economies, which helps keep costs down. South Korea also has a high savings rate, has received substantial inward foreign investment, and is a net exporter. These factors help ensure that South Korea enjoys a ready supply of capital, which firms in the auto industry use for R&D and product innovations. Collectively, South Korea's abundance of production factors in cost-effective labor, knowledge workers, high technology, and capital are the country's location-specific advantages.

South Korean consumers are highly demanding, so South Korean producers take great pains to produce superior products. Intense rivalry in the domestic auto industry ensures that carmakers and auto parts manufacturers focus on continuous improvement of their products. The South Korean government devised a system of close government/business ties, including directed credit, import restrictions, and sponsorship of specific industries. The government promoted the import of raw materials and technology, at the expense of consumer goods, and encouraged savings and investment over consumption. Partly due to these efforts, South Korea is home to a substantial industrial cluster for the production of cars and car parts. Gyeonggi Province is rapidly emerging as the center of South Korea's auto parts industry. The nation benefits from the presence of numerous suppliers and manufacturers in the global auto industry.

HMC's Challenges

Against this background, HMC has faced various mishaps. The South Korean economy endured a recession in the late 1990s as a result of the Asian financial crisis. The economy comprises numerous family-owned conglomerates, or *chaebol*. Combined sales of the nation's five major chaebol—Hyundai, Samsung, Daewoo, LG, and SK—account for roughly 40 percent of South Korea's GDP and total exports. Over time, these giant firms expanded rapidly, borrowing from their own banks to finance often reckless expansion into unrelated industries. Financial blunders led the South Korean government to impose greater transparency and more stringent accounting controls.

In the automotive industry, Kia Motors, South Korea's third largest automaker, went bankrupt and Daewoo was sold off to General Motors. While domestic demand in South Korea is some two million vehicles, total productive capacity had reached five million. HMC's debt burden reached five times its equity, and the firm suffered massive losses. The future was very uncertain. HMC was using less than 40 percent of its total production capacity, with a debt of around $30 billion. In 1998, HMC took control of Kia, becoming South Korea's biggest carmaker and holding three-quarters of its domestic vehicle market, as well as passing Japan's Mitsubishi and Suzuki in world ranking.

Early Internationalization Efforts

HMC was founded in 1967 by Chung Ju Yung, a visionary entrepreneur from a peasant background. His son, Chung Mong Koo, took over as chairman in 1998. The younger Mr. Chung is often quoted as saying "Quality is crucial to our survival. We have to get it right, no matter the cost."

In the late 1970s, HMC began an aggressive effort to develop engineering capabilities and new designs. In 1983 HMC launched a subsidiary in Canada, the firm's first foreign investment venture. However, the operation proved unprofitable and was shut down after only four years. Despite this outcome, HMC management learned a great deal from the experience. Instead of FDI, HMC began exporting to the U.S. market, with the Excel as an economical brand with a $4,995 price tag. The car was soon a big success, with exports rising to 250,000 units per year. Unfortunately, various problems emerged: The Excel was perceived as a low-quality vehicle, and the weak dealer network failed to produce enough sales. Consumers, including those in the United States, were losing faith in Hyundai, and the firm's brand equity began to deteriorate. The United States is the largest car market in the world, and Hyundai management had to do something drastic to turn things around.

Ultimate Success

In response to complaints about product quality, HMC introduced a 10-year warranty program. To address poor image problems, management decided it had to go beyond the typical guarantee period of only a few years and offer a very substantial warranty. The strategy was a major turning point for Hyundai, and the firm set about designing and building cars based on much higher quality standards. While still maintaining low prices, HMC has been able, over time, to provide substantial added value to consumers.

Another major step to improve quality was geographical diversification. Putting lessons learned from the failed Canadian investment into practice, HMC built a factory in Turkey in 1997, in India in 2000 (with a second plant in 2007), and in China in 2002. The main advantage of these locations is the availability of inexpensive, high-quality labor. The Turkish plant gave HMC a foothold in the Middle East, a market it wants to develop. Turkey's proximity to Western Europe is also a major advantage.

HMC uses FDI to develop key operations around the world. Management chooses foreign locations based on the advantages they can bring to the firm's global business. In 2006, HMC had more than ten production plants in locations such as Taiwan, Vietnam, Iran, Sudan, and Venezuela. It developed R&D centers in Europe, Japan, and North America. The firm has launched several distribution centers and marketing subsidiaries at locations worldwide. The distribution centers facilitate delivery of parts to HMC's expanding base of car dealers. HMC has regional headquarters in various countries in Asia, Europe, and North America. In short, to ensure control over the manufacturing and marketing of its cars around the world, HMC has internalized much of its international operations.

To gain a competitive edge, HMC must seek not only inexpensive labor—it must also source from locations that supply low-cost input goods (such as engines, tires, and car electronics). The cost-effectiveness of suppliers is a matter of life and death in the global automotive industry. HMC has entered various collaborative ventures with partners to cooperate in R&D, manufacturing, design, and other value-adding activities. These ventures have allowed the firm access to foreign partners' know-how, capital, distribution channels, marketing assets, and the ability to overcome government-imposed obstacles. For example, HMC cooperated with DaimlerChrysler to develop new technologies and improve supply-chain management. Projects include a new four-cylinder engine and a joint purchasing plan.

HMC management intends to capture 20 percent of the vehicle market in China. To that end, HMC entered a joint venture with Guangzhou Motor Group, gaining access to the commercial-vehicle market in China. HMC benefits from its proximity to China and its management's understanding of Chinese culture.

Recent Events

By 2000, HMC had become the world's fastest-growing major automaker. Sales in the United States increased more than threefold from 1998 to 2004. Currently, the firm generates about a third of its sales from North America and 10 percent from Europe. HMC's profit margins were among the highest in the industry, worldwide. It won numerous quality assurance prizes from credible organizations such as *Consumer Reports* and *J. D. Power and Associates*.

Despite successes in the early 2000s, HMC has recently suffered a series of problems. In 2004, South Korea indicted Hyundai CEO Kim Dong-Jin on charges that he violated campaign finance laws and engaged in managerial negligence. In 2007, the government fined HMC $25 million for alleged unfair market practices. Chung Mong Koo received a 3-year jail term for embezzling the equivalent of more than $100 million in company funds. These events damaged HMC's reputation with suppliers, dealers, and customers. Meanwhile, unfavorable currency exchange rates caused net profit to fall by 35 percent. Sales in HMC's domestic and foreign markets have flattened, and the firm is grappling with labor unions. Top management has been struggling to maintain HMC's great promise.

Sources: "Driving Change." *The Economist*, Sept. 2, 2004; "The Quick and the Dead." *The Economist*, Jan. 27, 2005; "Hooked on Discounts." *The Economist*, July 7, 2005; Griffiths, J. (2005). "Fiat Plans New Development Partnership", *Financial Times*, Sept. 7, 2005; "The Chaebol that Ate Korea." *The Economist*, Nov. 12, 1998; "South Korea Dumps the Past, at Last." *The Economist*, Nov. 9, 2000; "The Chaebol Spurn Change." *The Economist*, July 22, 2000; "Eureka." *The Economist*, Oct. 22, 1998; "The Last Emperor." *The Economist*, Feb. 4, 1999; Steers, R. M. (1999). *Made in Korea*. NY: Routledge; "Hyundai Revs Up." *Times Asian edition*, April 25, 2005, 27-30; Interview with Lheem Heung Soo, Vice-President, Hyundai. Assan, Turkey, on August 23, 2005; "Hyundai Grows Up." *Time*, June 27, 2005, A4-A8; *The Economist*, "The Car Company in Front." Jan. 27, 2005; Türk, E. (2005). "Yildizli Kariyer Öyküleri." *Milliyet Kariyerim*, Sept 18, 2005.

AACSB: Reflective Thinking, Analytical Skills

Case Questions

1. In the intensely competitive global automotive industry, what factors provide comparative advantage to nations? Give some examples of natural advantages and acquired advantages that nations possess in this industry.

2. Thinking in terms of factor proportions theory, what production factors are most important in the automotive industry? Based on your answer, what countries would appear to possess the most advantages for manufacturing cars? Justify your answer.

3. As a nation, what competitive advantages does South Korea offer to home-grown automakers such as HMC? What are the specific national competitive advantages that have helped HMC succeed in the global car industry?

4. Discuss HMC and its position in the global automotive industry in the context of Porter's diamond model. That is, in regards to HMC's international progress, what is the role of: firm strategy, structure, and rivalry, factor conditions, demand conditions, and related and supporting industries?

5. Discuss HMC and its position in the global automotive industry in terms of the eclectic paradigm. That is, for HMC, what is the role played by: ownership-specific advantages, location-specific advantages, and internalization advantages?

6. Visit HMC's website (http://www.hyundai-motor.com). What international collaborative ventures is HMC involved in? Does the firm appear to be a part of any networks? Describe these relationships, based on your reading of the website.

This case was written by Professor Nukhet Vardar, Yeditepe University, Istanbul, Turkey.

CHAPTER ESSENTIALS

Key Terms

absolute advantage principle, p. 97
comparative advantage, p. 94
comparative advantage principle, p. 98
competitive advantage, p. 95
free trade, p. 97
industrial cluster, p. 105
internalization theory, p. 114
mercantilism, p. 96
national industrial policy, p. 106

Summary

In this chapter, you learned about:

1. **Theories of international trade and investment**

   The basis for trade is specialization. Each nation specializes in producing certain goods and services, and then trades with other nations to acquire those goods and services in which it is not specialized. Life as we know it would be impossible without international trade.

2. **Why nations trade**

   Classical explanations of international trade began with **mercantilism**, which argued that nations should seek to maximize their wealth by exporting more than they import. **Absolute advantage principle** argues that a country benefits by producing only those products in which it has absolute advantage, or can produce using fewer resources than another country. The principle of **comparative advantage** contends that countries should specialize and export those goods in which they have a *relative* advantage compared to other countries. Nations benefit by trading with one another. Comparative advantage derives from *natural advantages* and *acquired advantages*. **Competitive advantage** derives from distinctive assets or competencies of a firm, such as cost, size, or innovation strengths, that are difficult for competitors to replicate or imitate. *Factor proportions theory* holds that nations specialize in the production of goods and services whose factors of production they hold in abundance. The *international product cycle theory* describes how a product may be invented in one country, and eventually mass-produced in other countries, with the innovating country losing its initial competitive advantage.

3. How nations enhance their competitive advantage: contemporary theories

A major recent contribution to trade theory is *Porter's diamond model*, which specifies the four conditions in each nation that give rise to national competitive advantages: *firm strategy, structure, and rivalry, factor conditions, demand conditions,* and *related and supporting industries*. An **industrial cluster** is a concentration of companies in the same industry in a given location that interact closely with one another, gaining mutual competitive advantage. *New trade theory* argues that increasing economies of scale might determine superior performance in some industries. Some industries succeed best the greater the volume of their production, which may necessitate international expansion. The competitive advantage of nations describes how nations acquire international trade advantages by developing specific skills, technologies, and industries. Firms and countries seek to increase productivity, or the amount of output produced per unit of input. **National industrial policy** describes efforts by governments to direct national resources to the development of expertise in specific industries. A government may pool resources to encourage the development of prowess in industries deemed valuable to the nation.

4. Why and how firms internationalize

The *internationalization process model* describes how companies expand into international business gradually, usually going from simple exporting to the ulti-mate, most committed stage, FDI. Born-global firms internationalize at or near their founding and are part of the emergent field of international entrepreneurship.

5. How firms gain and sustain international competitive advantage

MNEs have value chains that span geographic locations worldwide. Foreign direct investment means that firms invest at various locations to develop production, marketing, or other types of subsidiaries. *Monopolistic advantage theory* describes how companies succeed internationally by developing skills and resources that few other firms possess. The **internalization theory** explains the tendency of MNEs to internalize stages in their value chain when it is to their advantage. Internalization is the process of acquiring and maintaining one or more value chain activities inside the firm to minimize the disadvantages of subcontracting these activities to external firms. The *eclectic paradigm* specifies that the international firm should possess certain internal competitive advantages, called *ownership-specific advantages, location-specific advantages,* and *internalization advantages*. Currently, many international companies engage in *collaborative ventures*, interfirm partnerships that allow access to assets and other advantages held by foreign partners. MNEs also develop extensive networks of supportive companies such as other manufacturers, distributors, suppliers, retailers, banks, and transportation suppliers.

Test Your Comprehension AACSB: Reflective Thinking, Analytical Skills

1. Why do nations engage in international business? That is, what are the benefits of international trade and investment?

2. Describe the classical theories of international trade. Which of these theories do you believe are relevant today?

3. What is the difference between the concepts of absolute advantage and comparative advantage?

4. Summarize factor proportions theory. What factors are most abundant in the following countries: China, Japan, Germany, Saudi Arabia, and the United States? Visit globalEDGE™ for helpful information.

5. Summarize the international product cycle theory. Use the theory to explain the international evolution of automobiles and laptop computers.

6. What are the specific sources of national competitive advantage? Think of a successful product and service in your country. Which of the competitive advantage sources is most relevant for each of these?

7. Do you believe your country should adopt a national industrial policy? Why or why not?

8. How can you describe the internationalization process of the firm? Visit the websites of some major MNEs and review the history of these firms. What is the nature of internationalization in these firms? What is the nature of internationalization in born-global firms?

9. FDI-based explanations of international business evolved over time. Describe the evolution of these explanations from monopolistic advantage theory, through internalization theory, to the eclectic paradigm.

10. What are ownership-specific advantages, location-specific advantages, and internalization advantages?

Apply Your Understanding
AACSB: Reflective Thinking, Analytical Skills, Communication

1. South Africa is a nation with major mining operations and huge reserves of diamonds. It is also home to the world's biggest gold fields, in the Transvaal region. In addition to their intrinsic value, diamonds and gold have numerous industrial uses in which South Africa is the world leader. Mining precious minerals has transformed South Africa into Africa's leading industrial state. The newfound wealth financed modern transportation and communications systems. Subsequent mining activities revealed the existence of immense reserves of coal and iron ore. To handle international shipments, the government developed major ports that connect South Africa to world markets. Most recently, large quantities of natural gas were discovered offshore. South Africa is home to a large pool of low-cost workers in mining and related industries. The government has devised various plans that support particular industries, especially mining.

   These developments have led to the emergence of a cluster of highly specialized firms in the mining and extractive industries. Some of the most knowledgeable firms in the world in these industries are concentrated in South Africa, particularly De Beers S.A. De Beers has partnerships with large MNEs that hold major financial resources. The firm has substantial capabilities in marketing and international strategy. Which of the theories discussed in this chapter help explain the advantages that South Africa and De Beers SA hold?

2. Economist Lester Thurow once posed the following question: "If you were the president of your own country and could choose one of two industries in which to specialize, *computer chips* or *potato chips*, which would you choose?" When faced with this question, many people choose potato chips, because "everybody can use potato chips, but not everybody can use computer chips." But the answer is much more complex. Whether to choose computer chips or potato chips depends on several factors: the relationship between national wealth and the amount of value added in the manufacture of goods; if the country can benefit from monopoly power (few countries can make computer chips); the likelihood of spin-off industries (computer chip technology gives rise to other high technologies, such as computers); and, if technology generally makes people's lives easier and helps to raise their standard of living. In light of these considerations, which would you choose: computer chips or potato chips? Justify your answer.

3. Suppose you get a job as a consultant to Madagasland, a country in Africa. The country's minister of commerce and industry has some vague idea that Madagasland needs to be more active in international trade. The minister also recognizes that the government could help the local economy by developing a national industrial policy. Write a memo to the minister that explains: (a) how the country can leverage its comparative advantages in pursuing greater international trade, (b) what should be the elements of a national industrial policy, and (c) how the country can go about developing acquired advantages.

AACSB: Analytical Skills, Use of Information Technology

Refer to Chapter 1, page 27, for instructions on how to access and use globalEDGE.™

1. Your company is interested in importing Australian wine. As part of the initial analysis, you want to identify the strengths and possible weaknesses of the Australian wine industry. What are the conditions that make Australia a favorable location for wine cultivation? Provide a short description of the current status of Australian wine exports by variety and a list of the top importing countries of Australian wines. In addition to globalEDGE™, some useful websites for this research include www.wineaustralia.com and www.buyusa.gov.

2. Volvo (www.volvo.com) and Pilkington (www.pilkington.com) are major multinational firms with operations that span the globe. Investigate these firms by visiting their websites, as well as www.hoovers.com (a site that provides specific company information) and globalEDGE™. For each company, describe its ownership-specific advantages, location-specific advantages, and internalization advantages.

3. The main task of the World Bank is to alleviate world poverty. The Bank provides information about conditions in developing countries, which it uses to measure progress in economic and social development. *World Development Indicators* (www.worldbank.org/data/) is the Bank's premier source for data on international development. The Bank measures more than 800 indicators of national conditions regarding people, environment, and economy. Consult the website, click on World Development Indicators, and answer the following questions: (a) In countries with developing economies, what indicators are most associated with poverty? (b) What are the types of industries that most characterize impoverished countries? (c) Based on comparing development indicators in poor and affluent countries, speculate on what types of actions governments in developing countries can take to help spur economic development and alleviate poverty.

Management Skill Builder©

The Best Locations for Manufacturing

The principle of comparative advantage suggests that every country possesses specific resources that give it advantages in the production of specific products. Michael Porter's *Competitive Advantage of Nations* argues that nations become adept at certain industries due to the presence of certain resources and four conditions: firm strategy, structure, and rivalry; factor conditions; demand conditions; and related and supporting industries. Firms establish production facilities in those countries where they can obtain the most favorable resources and advantages.

AACSB: Reflective Thinking, Use of Information Technology, Analytical Skills

Managerial Challenge

In advance of locating value-chain activities abroad, management should try to ascertain the most appropriate location to achieve the advantages suggested above. A reasonable process is first to identify those factors that are most influential in determining company success, which usually varies by industry, and then conducting research to find countries that offer the best combination of these factors. Given the number of potential locations and the variables to consider, decisions about which foreign locations are best can be very challenging. The best approach is to conduct advance research and narrow the number of countries through a systematic process. This is a task you might perform regardless of whether you work for a large MNE or a smaller firm.

Background

Choosing the best foreign location for manufacturing provides numerous advantages, including the ability to: minimize the costs of producing the product, maximize the quality of finished goods, and gain access to the best factors of production and technological resources. For example, Tokyo-based Hoya, a manufacturer of eyeglass lenses, established manufacturing in the Netherlands to be close to Europe's superior technology in the lens-making industry.

These advantages translate into an increased ability of the firm to enhance its brand name, charge premium prices, gain leverage with distributors and retailers,

enhance competitive advantage, and generally earn higher profits. Manufacturing concentrated in the most favorable location provides economies of scale, which helps drive down average unit costs.

Managerial Skills You Will Gain

In this C/K/R Management Skill Builder©, as a prospective manager, you will:

1. Learn the factors to consider when locating company operations.

2. Learn how these factors relate to maximizing the firm's competitive advantage.

3. Develop research skills for planning company operations.

Your Task

Use the criteria in Porter's diamond model and online resources to identify the best countries to establish a factory in each of the following industries: dress shoes, flat-screen televisions, and pharmaceutical medicines.

Go to the C/K/R Knowledge Portal©

www.prenhall.com/cavusgil

Proceed to the C/K/R Knowledge Portal© to obtain the expanded background information, your task and methodology, suggested resources for this exercise, and the presentation template.

The Cultural Environment
of International Business

chapter

5

Learning Objectives

In this chapter, you will learn about:

1. The challenge of crossing cultural boundaries

2. The meaning of culture: foundation concepts

3. Why culture matters in international business

4. National, professional, and corporate culture

5. Interpretations of culture

6. Key dimensions of culture

7. Language as a key dimension of culture

8. Culture and contemporary issues

9. Managerial guidelines for cross-cultural success

> ## American Football . . . in Europe?

There are few things more representative of U.S. culture than American football. It is an extravaganza, complete with exciting halftime shows and peppy cheerleaders. The game exemplifies national pride. The national anthem is played, flags are unfurled, and uniformed players charge up and down the field like an army in the throes of often violent conflict. The teams' huddles divide the game into small planning sessions for the next play.

In the United States, the National Football League (NFL) oversees the sport and, like any successful business, wants to score in new markets. The NFL first tackled Europe in 1991, with plans to establish American football there. After years of failed attempts, NFL Europe emerged as six teams, five of which were based in Germany (such as the Berlin Thunder, the Cologne Centurions, and the Hamburg Sea Devils). Earlier teams established in Spain had failed.

Why did American football triumph in Germany but fail in Spain? An excellent metaphor for Spanish culture is the bullfight, an ancient pursuit. In tradition-bound Spain, bullfights are often held in 2,000-year-old Roman amphitheaters. Rather than a competitive sport, bullfighting is a ritual and an art. It is the demonstration of style and courage by the matador, the hero who fights the bulls. If the matador has per-

formed well, he receives a standing ovation by the crowds, who wave white hand-kerchiefs or throw hats and roses into the ring. The bullfight symbolizes Spanish cul-ture by combining a passionate celebration of life with an elaborate system of ritu-als, a grandiose and artistic spectacle with blood, violence, and danger. In the hearts of the Spanish people, American football cannot attain such heights.

What accounts for American football's early success in Germany? For one, the sport strongly emphasizes the traditional German traits of rules and order. In Ger-many, rules are many and conformity is valued. For instance, German parks occa-sionally have sections marked by signs where you are "permitted" to throw a stick to your dog. Germans can also be very time conscious. They know how to allocate time efficiently, and frown upon tardiness. The tendency is similar to American foot-ball, where the stop-and-go pace is timed to the second.

A popular metaphor for German culture is the symphony. In fact, two of the most revered symphonic composers—Bach and Beethoven—were German. Germans are drawn to the symmetry and order of the symphony. A conductor brings together the distinctive talents of individual performers to produce a unified sound. Like a sym-phony, football depends on a strong leader—the quarterback—who unites the distinctive talents of the players so they perform as one. At halftime, the crowd is treated to the spectacle of a huge marching band and numerous other performers, all synchronized to the highest degree. Preparation, timing, precision, conformity, and an understanding of the individual's contribution to the "score" underlie both symphonic performances and American football.

The major reason for NFL's failure in Europe has been its inability to win over Europeans shaped by ancient cultures and wedded to soccer (called *football* in most of the world). Soccer is woven into the fabric of European society. It is an outlet for inter-European rivalries that in earlier times manifested as armed conflict. Although superstars such as David Beckham emerge, soccer emphasizes a group effort—unity aimed at achieving a common goal.

The United States is a mixture of many cultures that form a multifaceted collection of ethnic identities. By contrast, Europe is home to many more ethnicities that lack the integration of the United States. Europeans have made great strides toward creating an all-encompassing European culture, but the difficulties encountered with unification reveal how individual nations are unwilling to give up their cultural identities in favor of some larger European Union ideal. Thus, the appeal of American football has varied from country to country as a function of cultural differences. Most Europeans view the sport as a perversion of soccer. It represents the American headstrong attitude, with emphasis on violent conflict. From the perspective of many Europeans, the NFL tried to push an inferior product on a market long loyal to soccer. The NFL spent countless dollars promoting its teams, largely to no avail. In the end, national culture triumphed. In 2007, the NFL closed its European franchise.

Sources: Van Bottenburg, M. (2003). Thrown for a Loss: American Football and the European Sport Space. *American Behavioral Scientist* 46 (11): 1150–62; NFL Europe. Retrieved November 2005 from en.wikipedia.org/wiki/NFL_Europe; National Football League (NFL Europe). Retrieved November 2005 from www.nfleurope.com; White, E. (2003). "Is Europe Ready for Some Football?—NFL Drafts Dolls, Actors in $1.6 Million Campaign to Promote the Super Bowl." *Wall Street Journal*, Jan. 15, B4; Gannon, M. J., and Associates. (1994). *Understanding Global Cultures: Metaphorical Journeys Through 17 Countries.* Thousand Oaks, CA: Sage.

 ## The Challenge of Crossing Cultural Boundaries

In cross-border business, we step into different cultural environments characterized by unfamiliar languages and unique value systems, beliefs, and behaviors. We encounter customers and business partners who display differing lifestyles, norms, and consumption behaviors. These differences influence all dimensions of international business. Often, they get in the way of straightforward communication, representing one of the four risks associated with international business that we introduced in Chapter 1. We highlight these risks in Exhibit 5.1. **Cross-cultural risk** is defined as a situation or event where a cultural miscommunication puts some human value at stake.

Cross-cultural risk arises routinely in international business because of the diverse cultural heritage of the participants. **Culture** refers to the learned, shared, and enduring orientation patterns in a society. People demonstrate their culture through values, ideas, attitudes, behaviors, and symbols.

Culture affects even simple greetings and partings. Greeting ceremonies are a deeply embedded cultural marker and evolve over many centuries. They specify such behaviors as how far apart to stand, what to say, and whether or not to touch or smile. The ceremonies may vary as a function of the age, gender, or status of the greeters. What people say in greeting each other also varies. For example, in China, friends express thoughtfulness by asking each other whether they have had their meal yet. In Turkey, a typical greeting is "What is new with you?" When meeting a person for the first time, the common question is "Where in the country do you come from?" in an effort to establish some commonality with the other party. The Japanese, who still exercise formal greeting and parting rituals, routinely apologize to the other party just before ending a telephone conversation.

Cross-cultural risk A situation or event where a cultural miscommunication puts some human value at stake.

Culture The learned, shared, and enduring orientation patterns in a society. People demonstrate their culture through values, ideas, attitudes, behaviors, and symbols.

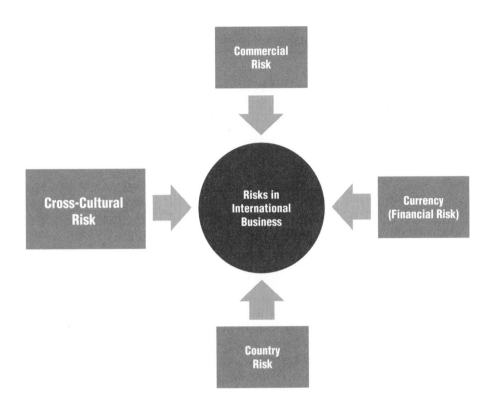

Exhibit 5.1

The Four Major Risks in
International Business

Unlike political, legal, and economic systems, culture has proven very difficult to identify and analyze. Its effects on international business are deep and
broad. Culture influences a range of interpersonal exchange as well as value-chain
operations such as product and service design, marketing, and sales. Managers
must design products and packaging with culture in mind, even regarding color.
While red may be beautiful to the Russians, it is the symbol of mourning in South
Africa. What is an appropriate gift for business partners also varies around the
world. While items such as pens are universally acceptable, others may not be
appropriate. Examples include sharp items such as knives or scissors, which
imply cutting off the relationship or other negative sentiments, chrysanthemums,
which are typically associated with funerals, and hand-
kerchiefs, which suggest sadness.

Most companies want their employees to learn about
other cultures and acquire a degree of cross-cultural proficiency. In California's Silicon Valley, where IT firms are concentrated, Intel offers a seminar to its staff called "Working
with India." The seminar aims to help employees work
more effectively with the estimated 400,000 Indian nationals
in the valley. Several other Silicon Valley firms offer similar
training. Another computer firm, AMD, flies IT workers
from India to its facilities in Texas for a month of cultural
training with U.S. managers. Workers role-play, pretending
to be native Indians, and study subjects like Indian political
history, Indian movies, and the differences between Hinduism and other Indian religions. Training includes lessons
on assigning work (Indian workers are likely to agree to
aggressive timelines and yet may not inform a manager
when falling behind, so managers should make sure

Limited interaction between societies, such as native Kenyans and
Russians or Europeans, can mag-
nify differences in values, behaviors, and symbols. In contrast,
these differences are minimized
with increased interaction.

Ethnocentric orientation
Using our own culture as the standard for judging other cultures.

Polycentric orientation A host-country mindset where the manager develops a greater affinity with the country in which she or he conducts business.

Geocentric orientation A global mindset where the manager is able to understand a business or market without regard to country boundaries.

Cross-cultural encounters are increasingly common. Maurice Dancer (far left), head concierge at The Pierre hotel in New York, interacts with a wide variety of international cultures every day, without even leaving the United States.

timelines are reasonable), preparing food (to help those who practice Jainism, company cafeterias should clearly distinguish vegan from vegetarian food), and socializing (since it's polite to initially decline an invitation to a colleague's home, managers should offer more than once).[1]

Cross-cultural risk is exacerbated by **ethnocentric orientation**—using our own culture as the standard for judging other cultures. Most of us are brought up in a single culture; we have a tendency to view the world primarily from our own perspective. Ethnocentric tendencies are a characteristic of virtually every society, and entail the belief that one's own race, religion, or ethnic group is somehow superior to others. Howard Perlmutter described ethnocentric views as "home-country orientation."[2] He argued that managers engaged in cross-border business should give up their ethnocentric orientations in favor of a polycentric or geocentric orientation. **Polycentric orientation** refers to a host-country mindset where the manager develops a greater affinity with the country in which she or he conducts business. **Geocentric orientation** refers to a global mindset where the manager is able to understand a business or market without regard to country boundaries. Geocentric tendencies can be likened to a cognitive orientation that combines an openness to, and awareness of, diversity across cultures.[3] Managers with a geocentric orientation make a deliberate effort to develop skills for successful social behavior with members of other cultures.[4] They develop new ways of thinking, learn to analyze cultures, and avoid the temptation to judge different behavior as somehow inferior. They learn to appreciate the best that humans have produced, no matter where it was developed.[5]

Unfamiliar cultures may be ever present in domestic as well as international dealings. Buyers visit from abroad to make deals, the firm may source from suppliers located in distant countries, and employees increasingly have diverse cultural backgrounds. For example, Maurice Dancer is the head concierge at The Pierre—a luxury hotel in New York City. In 2005, Taj Hotels, Resorts and Palaces, a subsidiary of Tata, the largest company in India, acquired the management contract of The Pierre. In addition to adapting his management style to fit the corporate culture of the new owners, Maurice must also adapt to certain aspects of Indian culture, demonstrated in Taj's administrative style. Maurice also manages employees from Asia, Europe, and Latin America. These employees bring idiosyncrasies to their jobs characteristic of their home countries. For example, Asians tend to be reserved when dealing with customers. In the past, Maurice had to encourage Asian subordinates to be more outgoing. Finally, much of The Pierre's clientele is foreign-born. Without even leaving the United States, Maurice interacts with a wide variety of foreign cultures every day.

The cross-cultural integration of firms like The Pierre is yet another manifestation of globalization. But globalization is leading to convergence of cultural values as well. While people around the world are not inclined to renounce their cultural values, common norms and expectations of behavior are gradually emerging. In addition, many universal values apply to cross-cultural encounters. Keep in mind that people everywhere are appreciative if you treat them with respect, try to speak their language, and show genuine interest in them.

Managers regularly risk committing embarrassing cultural blunders. Cross-cultural miscommunication can ruin business deals, hurt sales, or harm the corporate image. In this chapter, we address the risks that cultural miscommunication can pose in cross-cultural encounters. Today, developing an appreciation of, and sensitivity for, cultural differences has become an imperative for any manager.

The Meaning of Culture: Foundation Concepts

A broad definition of culture was offered by Herskovits[6] as "the human made part of the environment." Culture incorporates both objective and subjective elements. Objective or tangible aspects of culture include tools, roads, television programming, architecture, and other physical artifacts. Subjective or intangible aspects of culture include norms, values, ideas, customs, and other meaningful symbols.

Geert Hofstede,[7] a well-known Dutch organizational anthropologist, views culture as a "collective mental programming" of people. The "software of the mind," or how we think and reason, differentiates us from other groups. Such intangible orientations shape our behavior. Another scholar, Harry Triandis,[8] views culture as an interplay of sameness and differences; all cultures are simultaneously very similar and very different. While as human beings we share many commonalities and universals, as groups of people or societies we exhibit many differences. For example, some cultures are more complex than others. Some cultures are more individualistic, while others are more collectivist. Some cultures impose many norms, rules, and constraints on social behavior, while others impose very few.

Culture evolves within each society to characterize its people and to distinguish them from others. First, it captures how the members of the society live—for instance, how they feed, clothe, and shelter themselves. Second, it explains how members behave toward each other and with other groups. Third, it defines the beliefs and values of members and how they perceive the meaning of life.

Having described what culture is, it is also important to define what culture is *not*. Culture is:

- *Not right or wrong*. Culture is relative. There is no cultural absolute. People of different nationalities simply perceive the world differently. They have their particular ways of doing things, and do not fit any one standard. Each culture has its own notions of what is acceptable and unacceptable behavior. For instance, in some Islamic cultures, a wife cannot divorce her husband. In many countries, nudity is entirely acceptable on TV. In Japan and Turkey, wearing shoes in the home is taboo.

- *Not about individual behavior*. Culture is about groups. It refers to a collective phenomenon of shared values and meanings. Thus, while culture defines the collective behavior of each society, individuals often behave differently. For instance, in most countries, men wear their hair short. But a few mavericks have very long hair and stand out among their peers. In Australia, Canada, Europe, and the United States, some men wear makeup. Such nonconformist behavior does not represent the cultural values of the larger population.

- *Not inherited*. Culture is derived from the social environment. People are not born with a shared set of values and attitudes. Children gradually acquire specific ways of thinking and behaving as they are raised in a society. For example, in the United States, children usually acquire values of individualism and Christianity. But in China, children learn to depend on family members and acquire values based on Confucianism. Culture is passed from generation to generation—from parents, teachers, mentors, peers, and leaders. Modern methods of communication, including transnational media, play an enormous role in transmitting culture.

This process of learning the rules and behavioral patterns appropriate to one's society is called **socialization**. In other words, socialization is cultural learning. Through socialization, we acquire cultural understandings and orientations that are shared by society. Acquiring cultural norms and patterns is a subtle process—we adapt our behavior unconsciously and unwittingly.

Socialization The process of learning the rules and behavioral patterns appropriate to one's given society.

Acculturation The process of adjusting and adapting to a culture other than one's own.

The process of adjusting and adapting to a culture *other than one's own* is called **acculturation**. It is commonly experienced by people who live in other countries for extended periods; for example, expatriate workers.

More than any other feature of human civilization, culture signals the differences among societies on the basis of language, habits, customs, and modes of thought. Yet most of us are not completely aware of how culture affects our behavior until we come into contact with people from other cultures.

Anthropologists use the iceberg metaphor to understand the nature of culture. Culture is likened to an iceberg: Above the surface, certain characteristics are visible, but below, unseen to the observer, is a massive base of assumptions, attitudes, and values that strongly influence decision making, relationships, conflict, and other dimensions of international business. While we are conditioned by our own cultural idiosyncrasies, we are yet unaware of the nine-tenths of our cultural makeup that exist below the surface. In fact, we are often not aware of our own culture unless we come in contact with another one. Exhibit 5.2 illustrates the iceberg concept of culture. The distinction is between three layers of awareness: high culture, folk culture, and deep culture.

Exhibit 5.2

Culture as an Iceberg

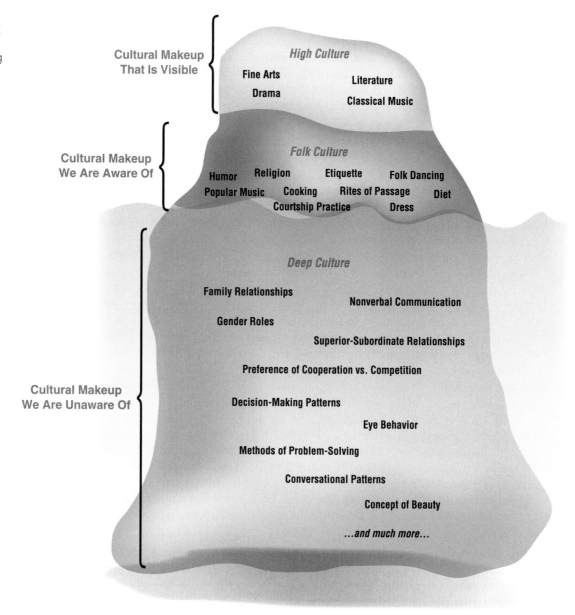

Cultural Makeup That Is Visible

High Culture

Fine Arts
Drama
Literature
Classical Music

Cultural Makeup We Are Aware Of

Folk Culture

Humor   Religion   Etiquette   Folk Dancing
Popular Music   Cooking   Rites of Passage   Diet
Courtship Practice   Dress

Cultural Makeup We Are Unaware Of

Deep Culture

Family Relationships
Nonverbal Communication
Gender Roles
Superior-Subordinate Relationships
Preference of Cooperation vs. Competition
Decision-Making Patterns
Eye Behavior
Methods of Problem-Solving
Conversational Patterns
Concept of Beauty
...and much more...

Why Culture Matters in International Business

Effective handling of the cross-cultural interface is a critical source of a firm's competitive advantage. Managers need to develop not only empathy and tolerance toward cultural differences, but also acquire a sufficient degree of factual knowledge about the beliefs and values of foreign counterparts. Cross-cultural proficiency is paramount in many managerial tasks, including:

- Developing products and services
- Communicating and interacting with foreign business partners
- Screening and selecting foreign distributors and other partners
- Negotiating and structuring international business ventures
- Interacting with current and potential customers from abroad
- Preparing for overseas trade fairs and exhibitions
- Preparing advertising and promotional materials[9]

Let's consider specific examples of how cross-cultural differences may complicate workplace issues:[10]

Teamwork. Cooperating to achieve common organizational goals is critical to business success. But what should managers do if foreign and domestic nationals don't get along with each other? Try to sensitize each group to differences and develop an appreciation for them? Rally the groups around common goals? Explicitly reward joint work?

Lifetime employment. Workers in some Asian countries enjoy a paternalistic relationship with their employers and work for the same firm all their lives. The expectations that arise from such devoted relationships can complicate dealings with outside firms. Western managers struggle with motivating employees who expect they will always have the same job regardless of the quality of their work.

Pay-for-performance system. In some countries, merit is often not the primary basis for promoting employees. In China and Japan, a person's age is the most important determinant in promoting workers. But how do such workers perform when Western firms evaluate them using performance-based measures?

Organizational structure. Some companies prefer to delegate authority to country managers, creating a decentralized organizational structure. Others are characterized by autocratic structures with power concentrated at regional or corporate headquarters. Firms may be entrepreneurial or bureaucratic. But how can you get a bureaucratic supplier to be responsive about demands for timely delivery and performance?

Union-Management relationships. In Germany, union bosses hold the same status as top-level managers and are required to sit on corporate boards. In general, European firms have evolved a business culture in which workers enjoy a more equal status with managers. This approach can reduce the flexibility of company operations if union representatives resist change.

Attitudes toward ambiguity. In each country, nationals possess a unique capacity to tolerate ambiguity. For example, some bosses give exact and detailed instructions on work to be performed, whereas others give ambiguous and incomplete instructions. If you are not comfortable working with minimum guidance or taking independent action, then you may have difficulty fitting into some cultures.

To gain a more practical perspective on culture's role in business, let's take the example of doing business in Japan. In the West, "the customer is king," but in Japan, "the customer is God." Whenever customers enter retail stores in Japan, they are greeted with vigorous cries of "Welcome" and several choruses of "Thank you very much" when they leave. In some department stores, executives and clerks line up to bow to customers at the beginning of the business day. If customers have to wait in line—which is rare—they receive a sincere apology from store personnel. Japanese firms value maintaining face, harmony, and good standing with customers and the business community. Culturally, the most important Japanese values are tradition, patience, respect, politeness, honesty, hard work, affiliation, group consensus, and cooperation.

Japan's orientation to customer service derives from its national culture. Good form, top product quality, and after-sale service are the keys to success for doing business in Japan. The Japanese put tremendous emphasis on providing excellent customer service. Japanese car dealers typically offer pickup and delivery for repair service and even make new-car sales calls to customers' homes. Nissan and Toyota use customer satisfaction surveys to evaluate their dealers. In the banking industry, personal bankers maintain relationships by calling on customers at their offices or by canvassing entire neighborhoods. They may help customers sell or buy homes, find outlets for merchandise sales, provide tax advice, or locate tenants for new buildings. Japanese taxi drivers spend spare moments shining their cabs and often wear white gloves. Trains are scheduled down to the second.

Japan is a small country (about the size of California) with nearly half the population of the United States. A densely populated and homogenous society has encouraged the development of a cohesive and polite culture. A focus on interpersonal relationships helps the Japanese avoid conflict and preserve harmony. Another key element of the Japanese culture is the emotional construct of *amae*, roughly translated as "indulgent dependence," which is a critical part of child-rearing in Japan. While Western mothers teach their children to be independent, Japanese mothers instill a sense of emotion-laden dependence in their children. Scholars believe that deeply felt *amae* guides social interactions in adulthood. The relationship between a senior and a junior is analogous to mother-child amae. Filial piety—respect for one's parents and elders—is the foundation of the Confucian ethic. Amae and the Confucian parent-child relationship provide the basis for all other relationships.

At the beginning of every working day, many firms have a group meeting intended to build harmony and team spirit, and personnel even do calisthenics together. Training of new store personnel is done in groups. The group trains together, is evaluated collectively, and may even live together. The group discovers the sources of problems and fixes them as a team. Training is very detailed. Stores provide instructions on how to greet people, what tone of voice to use, and how to handle complaints. Stores attach much weight to customer feedback; they typically make a detailed report to the manufacturer on any product defects and return the product to the manufacturer for careful analysis. Manufacturers and service suppliers design their offerings based on complaints and comments received from customers.[11]

Nevertheless, Japan is slowly changing. Modern Japan operates increasingly according to contemporary values, which Japan gradually is importing from abroad. Discount stores modeled on Carrefour, Toys "Я" Us, and Wal-Mart are beginning to displace department stores as the preferred shopping venues, especially among the younger generation. Given a choice between attentive personal service and the lowest possible prices, Japanese citizens increasingly make the trade-off.

The *Recent Grad in IB* feature highlights the cross-cultural experiences of Chinese-born Lawrence Yu, who had first-hand experience with living, studying, and working in the United States. Having an inquiring mind and being open to new experiences certainly helped Lawrence in bridging cultural gaps.

Since it opened to foreign investors in 1979, China's economy has been growing rapidly. Lawrence Yu lived in China and witnessed amazing changes there as a teenager during the 1990s. He ate at McDonald's, wore Nike shoes, and watched NBA games. He became very interested in the United States, which has a literal Chinese translation of a "beautiful country."

At the age of sixteen, Lawrence came to the United States as a foreign exchange student. After graduating from Mitchell High School, he earned a degree from Michigan State University in supply-chain management. While in college, he took a study-abroad trip to Mexico during a winter break. Lawrence practiced Spanish, lived with a Mexican family, attended business development conferences, and toured manufacturing firms.

While interning at Whirlpool Corporation in Benton Harbor, Michigan, Lawrence created an asset-tracking system for the global procurement group and conducted market research for Whirlpool in China. He also visited Whirlpool's Asia headquarters in Hong Kong and their China branch in Shenzhen. He became familiar with the local sales and marketing teams and consequently noticed opportunities for improvement and best-practice sharing, which he presented to Whirlpool executives at their U.S. headquarters. Following the summer at Whirlpool, he completed another eight-month internship with Unilever North America in Chicago.

After graduation, Lawrence worked at Dell Inc. as a master scheduler for notebook computers. He was primarily responsible for MRP forecasting, E&O (end-of-life and obsolete) planning, lead-time setting, and product transition management. Dell's notebook computer manufacturer, which ships over 7 million laptops annually, is located in Penang, Malaysia. Since Chinese is the first language of most of the Malaysian team members, Lawrence was able to communicate with them, which helped to increase communication quality and work efficiency. Dell management sent him to Dell China to work on a project with the procurement group in Shanghai. With the knowledge of Dell business that he gained in the United States, and with his language ability and strong interpersonal skills, Lawrence successfully fulfilled the mission of the trip and won praise from senior-level management.

After working as a master scheduler for over a year, Lawrence was recruited to Dell Global Logistics as a logistics program manager. His extended team managed Dell's inbound logistics business globally, with total spending over $40 million annually. In addition to daily operational tasks, his responsibilities also included weekly/monthly/quarterly business reviews, financial analysis, contract negotiations, and process-improvement projects. With the responsibility to oversee eight U.S. logistics centers and a 100-truck fleet, Lawrence gained people-management skills and learned how to make decisions under pressure, even with incomplete information.

In August 2006, Lawrence was promoted, and became the youngest Global Supply Manager at Dell, at the age of 24. He was responsible for managing Dell's $1 billion annual spending in memory (semiconductor) products. In this role, he negotiated prices with suppliers such as Samsung, Siemens, and Kingston.

Lawrence's major: Supply Chain Management

Objectives: Make a difference in the world by excelling in international business

Internships during college: Whirlpool Corporation and Unilever North America

Jobs held since graduating:

- Global Supply Manager, Dell Inc., Austin, Texas
- Logistics Program Manager, Dell Inc., Austin, Texas
- Notebook Master Scheduler, Dell Inc., Austin, Texas

Lawrence's Advice for an International Business Career

"While it was risky, I am glad that I did it. Language barriers, cultural differences, and being apart from family were all serious difficulties. Language can be improved over time, and culture can be learned while you live in that culture. I got used to living alone pretty fast. In addition to my formal education in the classroom, by living, studying, and working in another country, I was naturally learning every day. The knowledge you gain from just having been in another country cannot be learned any other way. From living on my own since the age of sixteen, I've grown a lot, physically and mentally. I now have greater confidence in whatever I pursue than I ever had before, thanks to my international experience!"

National, Professional, and Corporate Culture

While cultural idiosyncrasies influence cross-border business, we cannot attribute all difficulties to differences in national culture. Exhibit 5.3 suggests that employees are socialized into three cultures: *national culture, professional culture*, and *corporate culture*.[12] Working effectively within these overlapping cultures is a major challenge. The influence of professional and corporate culture tends to grow as people are socialized into a profession and workplace.

Most companies have a distinctive set of norms, values, beliefs, and modes of behavior that distinguish them from other organizations. Such differences are often as distinctive as the national culture. For example, Britain and the United States share a language and have a similar economic system. Two firms from the same country can have vastly different organizational cultures. The age of a company and its product portfolio both influence its corporate culture. For example, Lloyds, a large British insurance firm, has a conservative culture that may be slow to change. Virgin, the British music and travel provider, has an experimental, risk-taking culture.

These cultural layers present yet another challenge for the manager: To what extent is a particular behavior attributable to national culture? In companies with a strong organizational culture, it is hard to determine where the corporate influence begins and the national influence ends. For example, it is difficult to pinpoint the extent to which the culture of French cosmetics firm L'Oreal is due to national or corporate influences. The French have long been experienced in the cosmetics and fashion industries, but L'Oreal is a global firm staffed by managers from around the world. Their influence, combined with management's receptiveness to world culture, has shaped L'Oreal into a unique organization that is distinctive within French culture. Thus, in international business, the tendency to attribute all differences to national culture is simplistic.

Exhibit 5.3

National, Professional, and Corporate Culture

SOURCE: From *Cultural Enviroment of International Business*, 3rd edition by Terpstra, David. Copyright © 1991. Reprinted with permission of South-Western, a division of Thomson Learning.

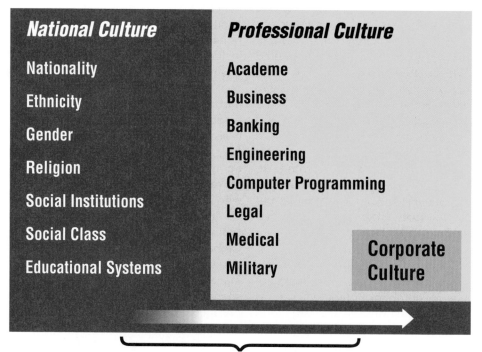

Progressive Socializations that Occur During a Person's Life

Interpretations of Culture

To explore the role of culture in international business, scholars have offered several analytical approaches. In this section, we review three such approaches: cultural metaphors, stereotypes, and idioms.

Cultural Metaphors

M. J. Gannon[13] offered a particularly insightful analysis of cultural orientations. A **cultural metaphor** refers to a distinctive tradition or institution strongly associated with a particular society. As you saw in the opening vignette, bullfighting is a metaphor for the culture of Spain. A cultural metaphor is a guide to deciphering a person's attitudes, values, and behavior.

American football, for instance, is a cultural metaphor for distinctive traditions in the United States. The Swedish *stuga* (a cottage or summer home) is a cultural metaphor for Swedes' love of nature and a desire for individualism through self-development. Other examples of cultural metaphors include the Japanese garden (tranquility), the Turkish coffeehouse (social interaction), the Israeli kibbutz (community), and the Spanish bullfight (ritual). The Brazilian concept of *jeito* or *jeitinho Brasileiro* refers to an ability to cope with the challenges of daily life through creative problem-solving or manipulating the arduous bureaucracy of the country. In the Brazilian context, manipulation, smooth-talking, or patronage are not necessarily viewed negatively, because individuals have to resort to these methods to conduct business.

Cultural metaphor A distinctive tradition or institution strongly associated with a particular society.

Stereotypes

Stereotypes are generalizations about a group of people that may or may not be factual, often overlooking real, deeper differences. The so-called *mañana* syndrome (tomorrow syndrome) refers to the stereotype that Latin Americans tend to procrastinate. To a Latin American, mañana means an indefinite future. A business promise may be willingly made but not kept since who knows what the future will bring? Many uncontrollable events may happen, so why fret over a promise?

Stereotypes are often erroneous and lead to unjustified conclusions about others. Nevertheless, virtually all people employ stereotypes, either consciously or unconsciously, because they are an easy means to judge situations and people. Despite the harm that stereotypes can cause, scholars argue that there are real differences among groups and societies. We learn about these differences by examining descriptive rather than evaluative stereotypes.[14] For example, here is a sample of widely held stereotypes of people from the United States:

Stereotype Generalization about a group of people that may or may not be factual, often overlooking real, deeper differences.

- Argumentative and aggressive, in comparison to the Japanese, who tend to be reserved and humble
- Individualistic lovers of personal freedom, in comparison to the Chinese, who tend to be group oriented
- Informal and nonhierarchical, in comparison to the Indians, who believe titles should be respected
- Entrepreneurial and risk-seeking, in comparison to the Saudi Arabians, who tend to be conservative, employing time-honored methods for getting things done
- Direct and interested in immediate returns, in comparison to the Latin Americans, who usually take time to be social and get to know their business partners

Idioms

An **idiom** is an expression whose symbolic meaning is different from its literal meaning. It is a phrase that you cannot understand by knowing only what the individual words in the phrase mean. Idioms exist in virtually every culture. People

Idiom An expression whose symbolic meaning is different from its literal meaning.

Country	Expression	Underlying Value
Japan	"The nail that sticks out gets hammered down."	Group conformity
Australia and New Zealand	"The tall poppy gets cut down." (Criticism of a person who is perceived as presumptuous, attention-seeking, or without merit.)	Egalitarianism
Sweden and other Scandinavian countries	*"Janteloven"* or *"Jante Law."* "Don't think you're anyone special or that you're better than us."	Modesty
Korea	"A tiger dies leaving its leather, a man dies leaving his name."	Honor
Turkey	"Steel that works, does not rust."	Hard work
United States	"Necessity is the mother of invention."	Resourcefulness
Thailand	"If you follow older people, dogs won't bite you."	Wisdom

Exhibit 5.4   Idioms that Symbolize Cultural Values

often use them as a short way of expressing a larger concept. For example, "to roll out the red carpet" is to extravagantly welcome a guest—no red carpet is actually used. The phrase is misunderstood when interpreted in a literal fashion. In Spanish, the idiom *"no está el horno para bolos"* literally means "the oven isn't ready for bread rolls." However, the phrase is understood as "the time isn't right." In Japanese, the phrase *"uma ga au"* literally means "our horses meet," but the everyday meaning is "we get along with each other." As with metaphors and stereotypes, managers can study national idioms to develop a better understanding of cultural values. Exhibit 5.4 offers several expressions that reveal cultural traits of various societies.

Hall's High- and Low-Context Cultures

Low-context culture A culture that relies on elaborate verbal explanations, putting much emphasis on spoken words.

Renowned anthropologist Edward T. Hall[15] made a distinction between cultures characterized as "low context" and "high context." **Low-context cultures** rely on elaborate verbal explanations, putting great emphasis on spoken words. As Exhibit 5.5 shows, the low-context countries tend to be in northern Europe and North America, which have a long tradition of rhetoric, placing central importance on the delivery of verbal messages. The primary function of speech in such cultures is to express one's ideas and thoughts as clearly, logically, and convincingly as possible. Communication is direct and explicit, and meaning is straightforward. For example, in negotiations Americans typically come to the point and do not beat around the bush. Low-context cultures tend to value expertise and performance and conduct negotiations as efficiently as possible. These cultures use specific, legalistic contracts to conclude agreements.

High-context culture A culture that emphasizes nonverbal messages and views communication as a means to promote smooth, harmonious relationships.

By contrast, **high-context cultures** such as Japan and China emphasize nonverbal messages and view communication as a means to promote smooth, harmonious relationships. They prefer an indirect and polite face-saving style that emphasizes a mutual sense of care and respect for others. They are on guard not to embarrass or offend others. This helps explain why it is difficult for Japanese people to say "no" when expressing disagreement. They are much more likely to say "it is different," an ambiguous response. In East Asian cultures, showing impatience, frustration, irritation, or anger disrupts harmony and is considered rude and offensive. Asians tend to be soft-spoken, and people typically are sensitive to context and nonverbal cues (body language). For example, at a business luncheon in Tokyo, the boss is almost always the senior-looking individual seated farthest away from the entrance to the room. In Japan, superiors are given such favored seating as a show of respect. To succeed in Asian cultures, it is critical for man-

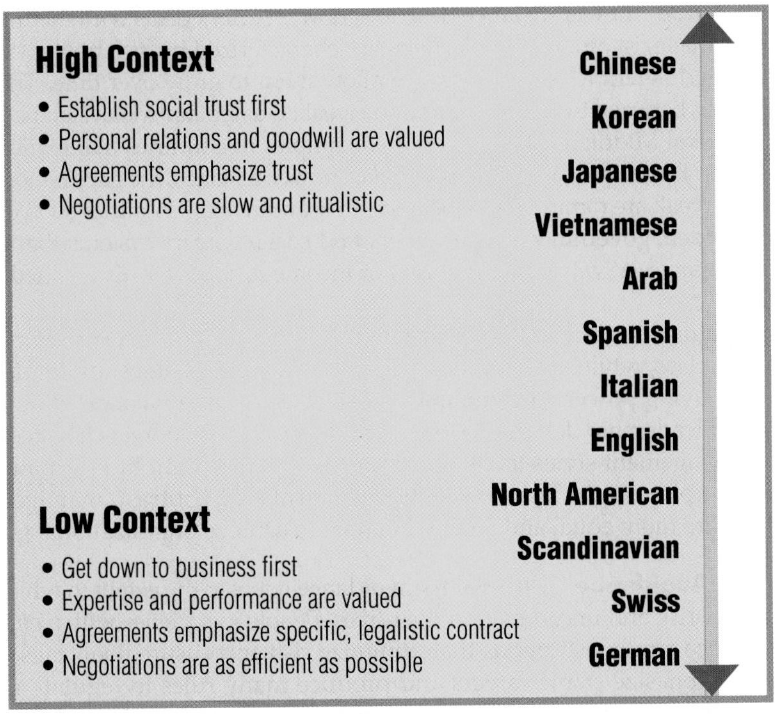

Exhibit 5.5

Hall's High and Low-Context Typology of Cultures

SOURCE: Adapted from Hall, Edward T. (1975). *Beyond Culture*, New York: Anchor.

High Context

- Establish social trust first
- Personal relations and goodwill are valued
- Agreements emphasize trust
- Negotiations are slow and ritualistic

Chinese
Korean
Japanese
Vietnamese
Arab
Spanish
Italian
English
North American
Scandinavian
Swiss
German

Low Context

- Get down to business first
- Expertise and performance are valued
- Agreements emphasize specific, legalistic contract
- Negotiations are as efficient as possible

agers to have a keen eye for nonverbal signs and body language. Negotiations tend to be slow and ritualistic, and agreement is founded on trust.

Hall's work has gained renewed importance because of the explosion of business interaction between East Asia and the rest of the world. However, the notion of high- and low-context cultures plays a role even in communications between people who speak the same language. For instance, British managers sometimes complain that presentations by U.S. managers are too detailed. Everything is spelled out, even when meanings seem perfectly obvious.

Hofstede's Research on National Culture

Dutch anthropologist Geert Hofstede conducted one of the early empirical studies of national cultural traits. He collected data on the values and attitudes of 116,000 employees at IBM Corporation, representing a diverse set of nationality, age, and gender. Hofstede conducted two surveys, one in 1968 and another in 1972. His investigation led Hofstede to delineate four independent dimensions of national culture, which we describe next.

Individualism versus Collectivism Individualism versus collectivism refers to whether a person functions primarily as an individual or within a group. In individualistic societies, ties among people are relatively loose, and each person tends to focus on his or her own self-interest. These societies prefer individualism over group conformity. Competition for resources is the norm, and those who compete best are rewarded financially. Australia, Canada, the United Kingdom, and the United States tend to be strongly individualistic societies. In collectivist societies, by contrast, ties among individuals are more important than individualism. Business is conducted in the context of a group in which others' views are strongly considered. The group is all-important, as life is fundamentally a cooperative experience. Conformity and compromise help maintain group harmony. China, Panama, and South Korea are examples of strongly collectivist societies.

Individualism versus collectivism Describes whether a person functions primarily as an individual or within a group

Power distance Describes how a society deals with the inequalities in power that exist among people.

Power Distance

Power distance describes how a society deals with the inequalities in power that exist among people. Societies characterized by *high* power distance are relatively indifferent to inequalities and allow them to grow over time. There are substantial gaps between the powerful and the weak. Guatemala, Malaysia, the Philippines, and several Middle East countries are examples of countries that exhibit high power distance. By contrast, in societies with *low* power distance, the gaps between the powerful and weak are minimal. For instance, in Scandinavian countries such as Denmark and Sweden, governments institute tax and social welfare systems that ensure their nationals are relatively equal in terms of income and power. The United States scores relatively low on power distance.

Social stratification affects power distance. In Japan, almost everybody belongs to the middle class, while in India the upper stratum controls most of the decision making and buying power. In companies, the degree of centralization of authority and autocratic leadership determines power distance. In high power-distance firms, autocratic management styles focus power at the top and grant little autonomy to lower-level employees. In low power-distance firms, by contrast, managers and subordinates are more equal and cooperate more to achieve organizational goals.

Uncertainty avoidance The extent to which people can tolerate risk and uncertainty in their lives.

Uncertainty Avoidance

Uncertainty avoidance refers to the extent to which people can tolerate risk and uncertainty in their lives. People in societies with *high* uncertainty avoidance create institutions that minimize risk and ensure financial security. Companies emphasize stable careers and produce many rules to regulate worker actions and minimize ambiguity. Managers may be slow to make decisions before they investigate the nature and potential outcomes of several options. Belgium, France, and Japan are countries that score high on uncertainty avoidance. Societies that score *low* on uncertainty avoidance socialize their members to accept and become accustomed to uncertainty. Managers are entrepreneurial and relatively comfortable about taking risks, and make decisions relatively quickly. People accept each day as it comes and take their jobs in stride because they are less concerned about ensuring their future. They tend to tolerate behavior and opinions different from their own because they do not feel threatened by them. India, Ireland, Jamaica, and the United States are leading examples of countries with low uncertainty avoidance.

Masculinity versus femininity Refers to a society's orientation, based on traditional male and female values. Masculine cultures tend to value competitiveness, assertiveness, ambition, and the accumulation of wealth. Feminine cultures emphasize nurturing roles, interdependence among people, and taking care of less fortunate people.

Masculinity versus Femininity

Masculinity versus femininity refers to a society's orientation, based on traditional male and female values. Masculine cultures tend to value competitiveness, assertiveness, ambition, and the accumulation of wealth. They are characterized by men and women who are assertive, focused on career and earning money, and may care little for others. Typical examples include Australia and Japan. The United States is a moderately masculine society. Hispanic cultures are relatively masculine and display a zest for action, daring, and competitiveness. In business, the masculinity dimension manifests as self-confidence, proactiveness, and leadership. Conversely, in feminine cultures, such as the Scandinavian countries, both men and women emphasize nurturing roles, interdependence among people, and caring for less fortunate people. Welfare systems are highly developed and education is subsidized.

The Fifth Dimension: Long-Term versus Short-Term Orientation

The four dimensions of cultural orientation that Hofstede proposed have been widely accepted. They provide us with a tool to interpret cultural differences and a foundation for classifying countries. Various empirical studies have also found relationships between the four cultural orientations and geography, suggesting that nations can be similar (culturally close) or dissimilar (culturally distant) on each of the four orientations.

Yet, the Hofstede framework suffers from some limitations. First, as noted, the study is based on data collected during the period from 1968 to 1972. Much has changed since then, including successive phases of globalization, widespread exposure to transnational media, technological advances, and the role of women in the workforce. The framework fails to account for the convergence of cultural values that has occurred during the last several decades. Second, the Hofstede findings are based on the employees of a single company—IBM—in a single industry, making it difficult to generalize. Third, the data were collected using questionnaires—not effective for probing some of the deep issues that surround culture. Finally, Hofstede did not capture all potential dimensions of culture.

Partly in response to this last criticism, Hofstede eventually added a fifth dimension to his framework: **long-term versus short-term orientation**. This dimension denotes the degree to which people and organizations defer gratification to achieve long-term success. That is, firms and people in cultures with a long-term orientation tend to take the long view to planning and living. They focus on years and decades. The long-term dimension is best illustrated by the so-called Asian values—traditional cultural orientations of several Asian societies, including China, Japan, and Singapore. These values are partly based on the teachings of the Chinese philosopher Confucius (K'ung-fu-tzu), who lived about 500 B.C. In addition to long-term orientation, Confucius advocated other values that are still the basis for much of Asian culture today. These include discipline, loyalty, hard work, regard for education, esteem for the family, focus on group harmony, and control over one's desires. Scholars often credit these values for the *East Asian miracle*, the remarkable economic growth and modernization of East Asian nations during the last several decades.[16] By contrast, the United States and most other Western countries emphasize a short-term orientation.

The Hofstede framework should be viewed as only a general guide, useful for a deeper understanding in cross-national interactions with business partners, customers, and value-chain members.

 ## Key Dimensions of Culture

We saw in Exhibit 5.2 that there are numerous dimensions of national culture. We can group them into two broad dimensions: subjective and objective. The subjective dimension of culture includes values and attitudes, manners and customs, deal versus relationship orientation, perceptions of time, perceptions of space, and religion. The objective dimension of culture includes symbolic and material productions, such as the tools, roads, and architecture unique to a society. In this section, we examine key examples of each dimension.

Values and Attitudes

Values represent a person's judgments about what is good or bad, acceptable or unacceptable, important or unimportant, and normal or abnormal.[17] People develop attitudes and preferences based on their values. Attitudes are similar to opinions except that attitudes are often unconsciously held and may not have a rational basis. Prejudices are rigidly held attitudes, usually unfavorable and usually aimed at particular groups of people.[18] Typical values in North America, northern Europe, and Japan include hard work, punctuality, and the acquisition of wealth. People from such countries may misjudge those from developing economies who may not embrace such values. They may inaccurately judge the Bolivian housekeeper for not working hard enough or the Jamaican businessman for not being on time.

Deal versus Relationship Orientation

In deal-oriented cultures, managers focus on the task at hand and want to get down to business. At the extreme, such managers may even avoid small talk and other preliminaries. They prefer to seal agreements with a legalistic contract, and follow an impersonal approach to settling disputes. Leading examples of deal-oriented cultures include Australia, northern Europe, and North America. By contrast, in relationship-oriented cultures, managers put more value on affiliations with people. To them, it is important to build trust, rapport, and get to know the other party in

Long-term versus short-term orientation Denotes the degree to which people and organizations defer gratification to achieve long-term success.

In Japan, bowing is the norm in both business and personal settings. Here, Japanese Foreign Minister Yoriko Kawaguchi and a U.S. Trade Representative (left) bow to each other before a 2004 meeting.

business interactions. For instance, it took nine years for Volkswagen to negotiate the opening of an automobile factory in China, a strongly relationship-oriented society. For the Chinese, Japanese, and many in Latin America, relationships are more important than the deal.[19] Trust is valued in business agreements. In China, *guanxi* (literally "connections") is deeply rooted in ancient Confucian philosophy, which values social hierarchy and reciprocal obligations. It stresses the importance of relationships within the family and between superiors and subordinates.

Manners and Customs

Manners and customs are ways of behaving and conducting oneself in public and business situations. Some countries are characterized by egalitarian, informal cultures, in which people are equal and work together cooperatively. In other countries, people are more formal, and status, hierarchy, power, and respect are very important. Customs that vary most worldwide are those related to eating habits and mealtimes, work hours and holidays, drinking and toasting, appropriate behavior at social gatherings, gift-giving, and the role of women. Handshaking varies across the world: limp handshakes, firm handshakes, elbow-grasping handshakes, and no handshake at all. In Southeast Asia, the handshake involves placing the palms together in front of the chest, as in praying. In Japan, bowing is the norm. In some settings it is appropriate to kiss the other's hand. In much of the world, people greet by kissing on both cheeks.[20] Gift-giving is a complex ritual practiced throughout much of the world. It is ingrained in Japanese culture, where it is usually a blunder to not offer a gift in initial meetings. The Middle East is characterized by generous gift-giving.

Perceptions of Time

In business, time dictates expectations about planning, scheduling, profit streams, and what constitutes lateness in arriving for work and meetings. For instance, Japanese managers tend to prepare strategic plans for extended periods such as the decade. The planning horizon for Western companies is much shorter, typically several years. Some societies are relatively more oriented to the past, others to the present, and still others to the future. People in past-oriented cultures believe that plans should be evaluated in terms of their fit with established traditions, customs, and wisdom. Innovation and change are infrequent and are justified to the extent they fit with past experience. Europeans are relatively past-oriented, insisting on the conservation of traditions and historical precedents.

Monochronic A rigid orientation to time, in which the individual is focused on schedules, punctuality, and time as a resource.

By contrast, young countries like Australia, Canada, and the United States are relatively focused on the present. They can be characterized as having a **monochronic** orientation to time—a rigid orientation, in which the individual is focused on schedules, punctuality, and time as a resource. People in these cultures view time as linear, like a river flowing into the future, carrying workers from one activity to the next. In such cultures, where people are highly focused on the clock, managers make commitments, set deadlines, and adhere to a strict schedule of meetings and activities. Punctuality is a virtue—time is money. Throughout the day, workers glance at their watches, their computer's clock, or the clock on the wall. Investors are impatient and want quick returns. Managers have a relatively short-term perspective when it comes to investments and making money; performance is measured on a quarterly basis. In this way, people in the United States have acquired a reputation for being hurried and impatient. Indeed, the word *business* was originally spelled *busyness*.

Polychronic A flexible, nonlinear orientation to time, in which the individual takes a long-term perspective and is capable of attending to multiple tasks simultaneously.

By contrast, cultures in parts of Africa, Asia, Latin America, and the Middle East view time as elastic. Such cultures have a **polychronic** perspective on time. In polychronic societies, people are capable of attending to multiple tasks simultaneously. Long delays are sometimes needed before taking action. Punctuality per se is relatively unimportant. Managers consider time commitments as relatively flexible. They place a higher value on relationships and spending time with other people. Managers do not adhere strictly to the clock and schedules. They are more likely to form lifelong relationships. Chinese and Japanese firms are future oriented, focusing not on how the firm will perform next quarter, but how it will perform 10 years from now. Large Japanese firms offer lifetime employment and invest heavily in employee training, expecting them to remain with the firm for 30 or 40 years. Latin Americans similarly have a flexible perception of time, and are more inclined to arrive late for appointments than people from other cultures. In the Middle East, strict Muslims view destiny as the will of God ("Inshallah" or "God willing" is a frequently used phrase) and downplay the importance of future planning. They perceive appointments as relatively vague future obligations.

Perceptions of Space

Cultures also differ in their perceptions of physical space; we have our own sense of personal space and feel uncomfortable if others violate it. Conversational distance is closer in Latin America than in northern Europe or the United States. When a North American national interacts with a Latin American, he or she may unconsciously back up to maintain personal space. Those who live in crowded Japan or Belgium have smaller personal space requirements than those who live in land-rich Russia or the United States. In Japan, it is common for employee workspaces to be crowded together in the same room, desks pushed against each other. One large office space might be used for 50 employees. North American firms partition individual workspaces and provide private offices for more important employees. In Islamic countries, close proximity may be discouraged between a man and a woman who are not married.

Religion

Religion is a system of common beliefs or attitudes concerning a being or a system of thought that people consider to be sacred, divine, or the highest truth. Religion also incorporates the moral codes, values, institutions, traditions, and rituals associated with this system. Almost every culture is underpinned by religious beliefs. Religion influences culture, and therefore business and consumer behavior, in various ways. Protestantism emphasizes hard work, individual achievement, and a sense that people can control their environment. The Protestant work ethic provided some of the basis for the development of capitalism.

In fundamentalist Islamic countries, Islam is the basis for government and legal systems as well as social and cultural order. Because people raised in Islamic cultures perceive God's will as the source of all outcomes, Muslims may be fatalistic and reactive. Islam's holy book, the Qur'an, prohibits drinking alcohol, gambling, usury, and immodest exposure. These prohibitions affect firms that deal in alcoholic beverages, resorts, entertainment, and women's clothing, as well as ad agencies, and banks and other institutions that lend money. A growing number of businesses are reaching out to Muslim communities. For example, Nokia launched a mobile phone that shows Muslims the direction toward Mecca, Islam's holiest site, when they pray. Heineken, the Dutch brewing giant, rolled out the nonalcoholic malt drink Fayrouz for the Islamic market.[21]

Exhibit 5.6 shows the dominant religions around the world. The major religions, based on number of adherents, are Christianity (2.1 billion), Islam (1.3 billion), Hinduism (900 million), Buddhism (376 million), Judaism (14 million), and Shintoism (4 million). Some people adhere to more than one belief system, such as the Japanese, who may practice both Buddhism and Shintoism. Although the exhibit displays the most common religion in each location, most countries are home to people of various beliefs.

Now that we have reviewed the subjective dimensions of culture, we turn to the objective dimensions of culture—symbolic and material productions.

Exhibit 5.6

World Religions

SOURCE: http://www.godweb.org/religionsofworld.htm
and http://www.mapsofworld.com/world-religion-map.htm

GREENLAND

ARCT

ICELAND

ALASKA

UNITED
KINGDOM

IRELAND

NE
LA

BELG
LUXE
FRANC

MONA
ANDORR

SPAIN

PORTUGAL

CANADA

MOROCCO

PACIFIC

OCEAN

UNITED STATES
OF AMERICA

NORTH

ATLANTIC

OCEAN

WESTERN
SAHARA

ALGERI

HAWAII

MEXICO

CUBA
JAMAICA
BELIZE
GUATEMALA   HONDURAS
EL SALVADOR   NICARAGUA
COSTA RICA
PANAMA

DOMINICAN
REPUBLIC
HAITI   PUERTO
RICO

MAURITANIA

MALI

SENEGAL
GAMBIA
GUINEA-BISSAU GUINEA

BURKINA
FASO

N

TRINIDAD &
TOBAGO
VENEZUELA
GUYANA   FRENCH
GUIANA

SIERRA LEONE   IVORY
COAST

GHANA
TOGO
BENIN

LIBERIA

CA

GALAPAGOS
ISLANDS

COLOMBIA
ECUADOR

SURINAME

EQUATO
GU

SWEDEN

DENMARK

LATVIA
LITHUANIA
RUSSIA

NETHER-
LANDS
BELGIUM   GERMANY
LUXEMBOURG
FRANCE
LIECHTENSTEIN
SWITZERLAND

POLAND

BELARUS

CZECH
REP.
SLOVAKIA
AUSTRIA HUNGARY
SLOVENIA
SAN   CROATIA
MONACO MARINO
BOSNIA-
ANDORRA   HERZEGOVINA
ITALY
MACEDONIA
ALBANIA

UKRAINE

MOLDOVA

ROMANIA

SERBIA AND
MONTENEGRO
BULGARIA

Black Sea

PERU

BRAZIL

BOLIVIA

SOUTH

ATLANTIC

OCEAN

PARAGUAY

ALGERIA

MALTA

TUNISIA

GREECE

TURKEY

CYPRUS

URUGUAY

ARGENTINA

C
H
I
L
E

LIBYA

FALKLAND ISLANDS/
MALVINAS

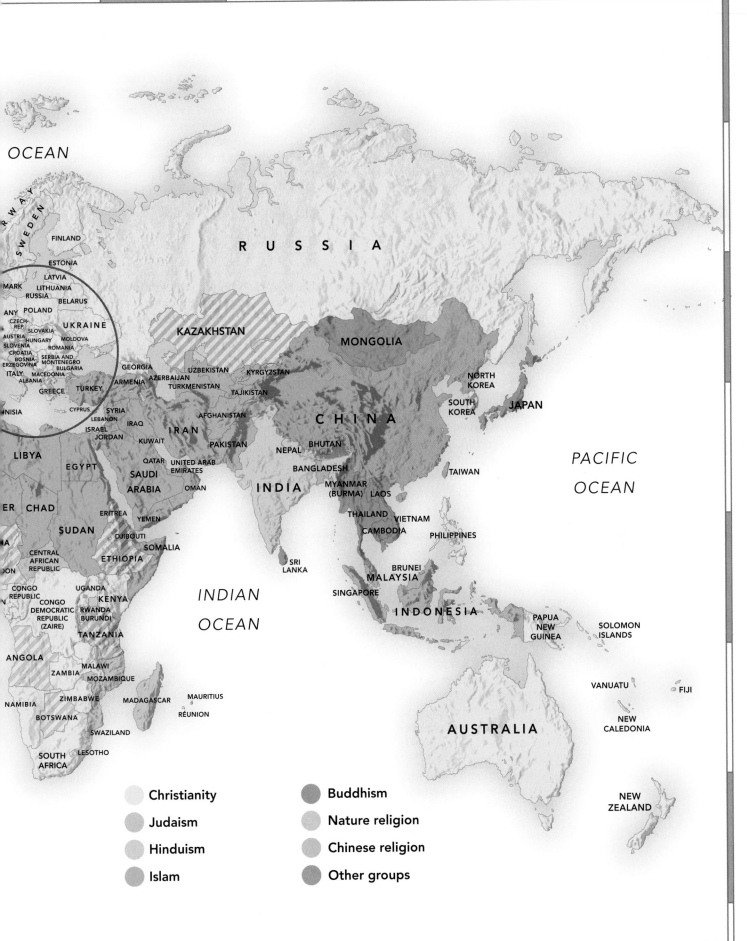

OCEAN

NORWAY

SWEDEN

FINLAND

ESTONIA

LATVIA

DENMARK

LITHUANIA

RUSSIA

BELARUS

GERMANY

POLAND

CZECH REP.

SLOVAKIA

UKRAINE

AUSTRIA

HUNGARY

MOLDOVA

SLOVENIA

CROATIA

ROMANIA

BOSNIA ERZEGOVINA

SERBIA AND MONTENEGRO

BULGARIA

ITALY

MACEDONIA

ALBANIA

GREECE

TURKEY

TUNISIA

CYPRUS

LEBANON

SYRIA

ISRAEL

IRAQ

JORDAN

LIBYA

EGYPT

GEORGIA

ARMENIA

AZERBAIJAN

TURKMENISTAN

KUWAIT

QATAR

UNITED ARAB EMIRATES

SAUDI ARABIA

OMAN

KAZAKHSTAN

UZBEKISTAN

KYRGYZSTAN

TAJIKISTAN

AFGHANISTAN

IRAN

PAKISTAN

RUSSIA

MONGOLIA

CHINA

NORTH KOREA

SOUTH KOREA

JAPAN

NEPAL

BHUTAN

BANGLADESH

INDIA

MYANMAR (BURMA)

LAOS

TAIWAN

THAILAND

VIETNAM

CAMBODIA

PHILIPPINES

PACIFIC OCEAN

NIGER

CHAD

ERITREA

YEMEN

SUDAN

DJIBOUTI

SOMALIA

CENTRAL AFRICAN REPUBLIC

ETHIOPIA

CAMEROON

CONGO REPUBLIC

UGANDA

KENYA

CONGO DEMOCRATIC REPUBLIC (ZAIRE)

RWANDA

BURUNDI

TANZANIA

SRI LANKA

INDIAN OCEAN

BRUNEI

MALAYSIA

SINGAPORE

INDONESIA

PAPUA NEW GUINEA

SOLOMON ISLANDS

ANGOLA

ZAMBIA

MALAWI

MOZAMBIQUE

ZIMBABWE

NAMIBIA

MADAGASCAR

MAURITIUS

RÉUNION

VANUATU

FIJI

BOTSWANA

SWAZILAND

NEW CALEDONIA

SOUTH AFRICA

LESOTHO

AUSTRALIA

NEW ZEALAND

Christianity

Judaism

Hinduism

Islam

Buddhism

Nature religion

Chinese religion

Other groups

143

Symbolic Productions

A symbol can be letters, figures, colors, or other characters that communicate a meaning. For instance, the cross is the main symbol of Christianity. The red star was the symbol of the former Soviet Union. National symbols include flags, anthems, seals, monuments, and historical myths. These symbols represent nations and national values, and help to unite people. Mathematicians and scientists use symbols as types of languages. Businesses have many types of symbols, in the form of trademarks, logos, and brands. Can you easily identify popular company logos such as Nike's swoosh, Apple's small apple, and Coca-Cola's unique letters?

Material Productions and Creative Expressions of Culture

Material productions are artifacts, objects, and technological systems that people construct to cope with their environments. Material productions are integral to human life and provide the means to accomplish objectives, as well as a medium for communication and exchange within and between societies. The most important technology-based material productions are the infrastructure related to energy, transportation, and communications systems. Other material productions include social infrastructure (systems that provide housing, education, and health care), financial infrastructure (systems for managing means of exchange in banks and other financial institutions), and marketing infrastructure (systems that support marketing-related activities, such as ad agencies). Creative expressions of culture include arts, folklore, music, dance, theater, and high cuisine. Food is among the most interesting cultural markers. For example, in Japan, pizza is often topped with fish and seaweed. In the United States, pizzas can be piled high with meat. In France, pizza often comes with a variety of cheeses.

 ## Language as a Key Dimension of Culture

Language is such an important dimension of culture that it requires extensive treatment.

Often described as the expression or *mirror* of culture, language is not only essential for communications, it provides insights into culture. At present the world has nearly 7,000 active languages, including over 2,000 each in Africa and Asia. But most of these languages have only a few thousand speakers. Exhibit 5.7 highlights the major languages of the world.[22] Note that while Arabic is listed in sixth place, it comprises 15 major and often highly distinct language variants across 46 countries. Linguistic proficiency is a great asset in international business because it facilitates cross-cultural understanding. Learning one or more of the frequently spoken languages can greatly enhance an international business career.

Language has both verbal and nonverbal characteristics. Much language is unspoken[23] and entails facial expressions and gestures. In fact, most verbal messages are accompanied by nonverbal ones. In this and other ways language is extremely subtle. Language is conditioned by our environment. Thus, for instance, while the language of the Inuits (an indigenous people of Canada) has several different words for "snow," English has just one; the Aztecs, moreover, used the same word stem for snow, ice, and cold. Sometimes it is difficult to find words to convey the same meaning in a different language. For instance, a one-word equivalent to "aftertaste" does not exist in many languages. There are also semantic gaps in languages. The concept and meaning of a word are not universal, even though the word can be translated well into another lan-

Rank	Language	Approximate number native speakers (millions)	Countries with substantial number of native speakers
1	Mandarin Chinese	874	China, Singapore
2	Hindi	365	India
3	English	341	United States, United Kingdom
4	Spanish	322	Argentina, Mexico, Spain.
5	Bengali	207	Bangladesh, India
6	Arabic	198	Algeria, Egypt, Saudi Arabia
7	Portuguese	176	Brazil, Portugal
8	Russian	167	Russian Federation, Ukraine
9	Japanese	125	Japan
10	German	100	Germany, Austria
11	Korean	78	South Korea, North Korea
12	French	77	France, Belgium
13	Turkish	75	Turkey, Central Asia, Eastern Europe

Exhibit 5.7 The Most Common Primary Languages in the World

SOURCE: Copyright © 2000, SIL International, from the database of Ethnologue: Languages of the World, 14th ed., www.ethnologue.com.

guage. The Japanese word "muzukashii," for example, can be variously translated as "difficult," "delicate," or "I don't want to discuss it," but in business negotiations it usually means "out of the question."

National languages, dialects, and translation have a tendency to complicate straightforward communication. Ignorance of a language can be embarrassing. Advertising themes often lose their original meaning in translation or convey unfavorable interpretations. Even those from different countries who speak the same language may experience communication problems because of unique colloquial words. The same word can convey different meanings in the two countries. Exhibit 5.8 shows how the popular slogans of some languages translate into offensive phrases in other languages. Exhibit 5.9 shows how two English-speaking countries interpret the same word in very different ways. These exhibits demonstrate how easy it is for misinterpretations to get in the way of conveying intended meaning.

Company and Location	Intended Ad Slogan	Literal Translation
Parker Pen Company in Latin America	"Use Parker Pen, avoid embarrassment"!	"Use Parker Pen, avoid pregnancy!"
Pepsi in Germany	"Come Alive with Pepsi"	"Come out of the grave with Pepsi."
Pepsi in Taiwan	"Come Alive with Pepsi"	"Pepsi brings your ancestors back from the dead."
Fisher Body (car exteriors) in Belgium	"Body by Fisher"	"Corpse by Fisher"
Salem cigarettes in Japan	"Salem—Feeling Free"	"Smoking Salem makes your mind feel free and empty."

Exhibit 5.8 Blunders in International Advertising

Exhibit 5.9

Examples of Differences in Meaning between U.S. and British English

Word	Meaning in U.S. English	Meaning in British English
Scheme	A somewhat devious plan	A plan
Redundant	Repetitive	Fired or laid off
Sharp	Smart	Conniving, unethical
To table	To put an issue on hold	To take up an issue
To bomb	To fail miserably	To succeed grandly
Windscreen	A screen that protects against wind	Automobile windshield

Business jargon that is unique to a culture can also impede communication. For example, many words and expressions that have crept into U.S. business executives' jargon from sports or military terminology pose problems for non-U.S. businesspeople. Here is some business jargon used in American English that may be puzzling for non-natives to understand: "the bottom line," "to beat around the bush," "shooting from the hip," "feather in your cap," and "get down to brass tacks." Imagine the difficulty that professional interpreters may encounter in translating such phrases!

 Culture and Contemporary Issues

We have seen that culture is relatively stable. However, contemporary issues such as globalization of markets, transnational media, technological advances, and government regulations do influence culture, and culture influences these contemporary issues. Culture is so powerful and pervasive that it continues to exert a strong effect on emergent issues. In this section, we explore the linkage between culture and key issues.

Culture and the Services Sector

Services such as lodging and retailing are increasingly international. In the most advanced economies, firms that offer services account for a greater share of FDI than firms that manufacture products.[24] Contact-based services bring service providers into direct contact with foreign customers through cross-border transactions. These service providers include architects, consultants, and lawyers. Asset-based services are those in which someone offers to establish a brick-and-mortar facility abroad, such as banks, restaurants, and retail stores.[25]

However, cultural differences create problems for services firms, leading to mishaps in the exchange process. The greater the cultural distance between the service producer and its customers, the more likely there will be cognitive and communication gaps. Imagine, for example, a Western lawyer who tries to establish a law office in China. Without a thorough knowledge of Chinese culture and language, the lawyer's efforts are largely futile. Imagine how much success a Western restaurant chain would have in Russia if it knew nothing of Russian food culture or the work customs of Russian workers!

Differences in language and national character have the same effect as trade barriers. Service firms that internationalize via FDI are particularly vulnerable, because each firm is shaped by both a national culture and an organizational culture, which originate from the source of the firm's funding.[26] For example, a Japanese bank established in New York or London remains distinctly Japanese because the capabilities that it brings with it are based on Japanese culture and the firm's Japan-based corporate culture.[27]

To overcome these challenges, services firms seek to understand the cultures and languages of the countries where they do business. For example, at the global express company FedEx, management constantly seeks to hire, train, and motivate hundreds of sales representatives who speak different languages, represent different cultures, and service different markets.[28] Without such efforts, services firms like FedEx would not likely succeed at international business.

Technology, the Internet, and Culture

Technological advances are a key determinant of culture and cultural change. These advances have led to more leisure time for culture-oriented pursuits and to the invention of computers, multimedia, and communications systems that encourage convergence in global culture. The rise of the transnational media, high-tech communications, and modern transportation systems has brought geographically separated cultures in closer contact than ever before. The *death of distance* refers to the demise of the boundaries that once separated people, due to the integrating effects of modern communications, information, and transportation technologies. Just as distinctive cultures developed in the distant past because regions had limited contact with each other, somewhat homogenized cultures are developing today due to modern technologies that increase contact among the people of the world. For example, Hollywood movies and the ability to easily travel throughout the world homogenize customs, fashions, and other manifestations of culture. Today, university students listen to much the same music and wear similar clothing styles worldwide.

Technology also provides the means to promote culture. For example, local artistic traditions from Africa, Asia, and Latin America have received a big boost from the rise of world cinema and television. Movies and TV provide artists with tools for expressing themselves and facilitate contact with consumers. In a similar way, communications technology permits us to choose our information sources. For example, people usually prefer information in their native language that represents cultural traits similar to their own. Thus, Spanish speakers in the United States increasingly select mass media sources—TV, movies, the Internet—in Spanish, limiting the homogenizing effect that would result from relying on English-speaking media. In addition, the broadening of global communications allows ethnic groups scattered around the world to remain in touch with each other.[29]

The Internet also promotes the diffusion of culture. The number of Internet users is growing rapidly worldwide, and the potential for cultural blunders arising from international e-mail use is higher than ever. To minimize such problems, international managers now access software that translates e-mail and text messages into foreign languages. After typing in a phrase, the software instantly converts messages into any of dozens of languages, including Chinese, Hebrew, and Portuguese.[30]

Globalization's Effect on Culture: Are Cultures Converging?

There is little consensus about globalization's effects on culture. While many believe that globalization is a destructive force, others see it as positive. Critics charge that globalization is harmful to local cultures and their artistic expressions and sensibilities, and is responsible for their replacement by a homogeneous, often Americanized, culture. Others argue that increased global communications is positive because it permits the flow of cultural ideas, beliefs, and values. In short, globalization is a major factor in the emergence of common culture worldwide. Many products, services, and even holidays are becoming common to world markets.

The homogenization (or the banalization) of culture is demonstrated by the growing tendency of people in much of the world to consume the same Big Macs and Coca-Colas, watch the same movies, listen to the same music, drive the same cars, and stay in the same hotels. Although food often represents a distinct culture, hamburgers, tacos, and pizza are increasingly popular around the world.[31] In Trinidad, the U.S. television series "The Young and the Restless" is so popular that in many places work effectively stops when it airs, and it has inspired calypso songs of the same name. In recent years, Baywatch and CSI Miami were among the most popular TV series worldwide. The Barbie doll has become a global phenomenon, even as the values that this icon represents may not always agree with values in more conservative cultures.[32]

However, in reality, the larger trend is more complex than these examples imply. As cross-border business integrates the world's economies, it also increases the choices available to local people by making their countries culturally richer. Cultural homogeneity and heterogeneity are not mutually exclusive alternatives or substitutes; they may exist simultaneously. Cross-cultural exchange promotes innovation and creativity. Globalization brings a wider menu of choices to consumers and increases diversity within society.[33] Cultural flows originate in many places. Just as McDonald's hamburgers have become popular in Japan, so has Vietnamese food in the United States and Japanese sushi in Europe. Integration and the spread of ideas and images tend to provoke reactions and resistance to cultural homogenization, thereby spurring individual peoples to insist on their differences. While some past customs will be eclipsed in globalization, the process is also liberating people culturally by undermining the ideological conformity of nationalism.

Managerial Guidelines for Cross-Cultural Success

Cross-cultural proficiency helps managers connect with their foreign counterparts. Seasoned managers attest to the importance of a deep knowledge of culture and language in international business. Managers can achieve effective cross-cultural interaction by keeping an open mind, being inquisitive, and not rushing to conclusions about others' behaviors.

Experienced managers acquire relevant facts, skills, and knowledge to avoid offensive or unacceptable behavior when interacting with foreign cultures. They undergo cultural training that emphasizes observational skills and human relations techniques. Skills are more important than pure information because skills can be transferred across countries, while information tends to be country specific. Various resources are available to managers for developing skills, including videotape courses, cross-cultural consultants, and programs offered by governments, universities, and training institutes. Planning that combines informal mentoring from experienced managers and formal training through seminars and simulations abroad and at home go far in helping managers meet cross-cultural challenges.

Although every culture is unique, certain basic guidelines are appropriate for consistent cross-cultural success. Let's review three guidelines managers can follow in preparing for successful cross-cultural encounters.

Cross-cultural proficiency increases the effectiveness of meetings and other encounters in international business.

Guideline 1: *Acquire factual and interpretive knowledge about the other culture, and try to speak their language.* Successful managers acquire a base of knowledge about the values, attitudes, and lifestyles of the cultures with which they interact. Managers study the political and economic background of target countries—their history, current national affairs, and perceptions about other cultures. Such knowledge facilitates understanding about the partner's mindset, organization, and objectives. Decisions and events become substantially easier to interpret. Sincere interest in the target culture helps establish trust and respect, laying the foundation for open and productive relationships. Even modest attempts to speak the local language are welcome. Higher levels of language proficiency pave the way for acquiring competitive advantages. In the long run, managers who can converse in multiple languages are more likely to negotiate successfully and have positive business interactions than managers who speak only one language.

Guideline 2: *Avoid cultural bias*. Perhaps the leading cause of culture-related problems is the ethnocentric assumptions managers may unconsciously hold. Problems arise when managers assume that foreigners think and behave just like the folks back home. Ethnocentric assumptions lead to poor business strategies in both planning and execution. They distort communications with foreigners. Managers new to international business often find the behavior of a foreigner hard to explain. They may perceive the other's behavior as odd and perhaps improper. For example, it is easy to be offended when our foreign counterpart does not appreciate our food, history, sports, or entertainment, or is otherwise inconsiderate. This situation may interfere with the manager's ability to interact effectively with the foreigner, even leading to communication breakdown. In this way, cultural bias can be a significant barrier to successful interpersonal communication.

A person's own culture conditions how he or she reacts to different values, behavior, or systems. Most people unconsciously assume that people in other cultures experience the world as they do. They view their own culture as the norm—everything else may seem strange. This is known as the **self-reference criterion**—the tendency to view other cultures through the lens of one's own culture. Understanding the self-reference criterion is a critical first step to avoiding cultural bias and ethnocentric reactions.

Critical incident analysis (CIA) refers to an analytical method for analyzing awkward situations in cross-cultural interactions by developing empathy for other points of view. It is an approach to avoiding the trap of self-reference criterion in cross-cultural encounters. Critical incident analysis encourages a more objective reaction to cultural differences by helping managers develop empathy for other points of view. The *Global Trend* feature on page 150 details how managers can learn to deliberately avoid the self-reference criterion.

Guideline 3: *Develop cross-cultural skills*. Working effectively with counterparts from other cultures requires an investment in your professional development. Each culture has its own ways of carrying out business transactions, negotiations, and dispute resolution. As an example, you will be exposed to high levels of *ambiguity;* concepts and relationships that can be understood in a variety of ways.[34] You must make an effort to gain cross-cultural proficiency to be successful in international business. Cross-cultural proficiency is characterized by four key personality traits:

- *Tolerance for ambiguity*—the ability to tolerate uncertainty and apparent lack of clarity in the thinking and actions of others.
- *Perceptiveness*—the ability to closely observe and appreciate subtle information in the speech and behavior of others.
- *Valuing personal relationships*—the ability to recognize the importance of interpersonal relationships, which are often much more important than achieving one-time goals or winning arguments.
- *Flexibility and adaptability*—the ability to be creative in devising innovative solutions, to be open-minded about outcomes, and to show grace under pressure.

As discussed earlier in the chapter, managers function better with a geocentric or cosmopolitan view of the world. Managers with this view believe they can understand and accommodate similarities and differences among cultures. Successful multinational firms seek to instill a geocentric cultural mindset in their employees and use a geocentric staffing policy to hire the best people for each position, regardless of their national origin. Over time, such firms develop a core group of managers who feel at home working in any cultural context.

One way for managers to determine the skills they need to approach cultural issues is to measure their cultural intelligence.[35] *Cultural intelligence* (CQ) is a person's capability to function effectively in situations characterized by cultural diversity. It focuses on specific capabilities that are important for high-quality personal relationships and effectiveness in culturally diverse settings and work groups.

Self-reference criterion The tendency to view other cultures through the lens of one's own culture.

Critical incident analysis (CIA) An analytical method for analyzing awkward situations in cross-cultural interactions by developing empathy for other points of view.

Minimizing Cross-Cultural Bias with Critical Incident Analysis

Firms develop and seek to maintain relationships with customers and partners that span the globe. To compete effectively, companies must continually improve ways to communicate with and manage customers, wherever they are located.

One recent trend is the rise of global account management, which puts a single manager or team in charge of a key customer and all its needs worldwide. The global account manager draws on various resources, including communication and interaction skills in cross-cultural settings, to market products and services.

Another trend is the rise of global project teams. The teams comprise members from a variety of cultural backgrounds. Global teams enable firms to profit from knowledge amassed across the organization's entire worldwide operations. Such teams function best when the members engage in high-quality communications, which involves minimizing miscommunications based on differences in language and culture.

Nevertheless, inexperienced managers often find the behavior of foreign counterparts hard to explain. They often perceive others' behavior as "odd" and perhaps improper, which hinders their ability to interact effectively with foreigners. One way to minimize cross-cultural bias and the self-reference criterion is to engage in *critical incident analysis*, a method that helps managers develop empathy for other points of view.

Consider the following scenario. Working on a joint product design, engineers from Ford (United States) and Mazda (Japan) interact intensively with each other. Ford wants to share its engineering studies and critical materials with its Japanese counterpart. Following a week of interaction, the Ford team grows increasingly uncomfortable with the seeming lack of interest from the Japanese. The Japanese engineers appear strangely indifferent and do not exhibit much reaction. When the teams meet, the Japanese appear to keep conversation among themselves and offer little feedback. Eventually, the Ford team's surprise turns into frustration and anger. They now believe that the Japanese are arrogant, uninterested in Ford's technical designs, and care little about the collaboration.

In reality, the Ford team has jumped to conclusions. They have failed to consider other plausible explanations for the Japanese behavior because they have judged the Japanese using their own culturally bound expectations. An independent observer familiar with Japanese culture and business organization could have provided alternative explanations for this situation. For one, the Japanese engineers may have not been proficient in English. They could not explain themselves easily or understand the Ford team's briefings, which all took place in English. Furthermore, Japanese usually refrain from speaking out before the entire team meets in private and reaches consensus. Japanese are generally thoughtful and typically show their respect for counterparts by listening intently while remaining quiet. These and other explanations are all plausible within the context of the Japanese culture.

So what should you do as a manager when confronted with an awkward or uncomfortable situation in a cross-cultural interaction? Critical incident analysis advocates the following steps:

Step One: Identify the situations where you need to be culturally aware to interact effectively with people from another culture. These may include socializing, working in groups, attending meetings, negotiating, and reaching agreement.

Step Two: When confronted with a seemingly strange behavior, discipline yourself not to make value judgments. Learn to suspend judgment. Instead, try to view the situation or the problem in terms of the unfamiliar culture. Make observations and gather objective information from native citizens or secondary sources. In this way, you can isolate the self-reference criterion leading you to your inaccurate conclusion.

Step Three: Learn to make a variety of interpretations of the foreigner's behavior, to select the most likely interpretation, and then to formulate your own response. By doing so, you will react to the situation without the self-reference criterion, and will likely produce the optimal response.

Step Four: Learn from this process and continuously improve.

Sources: Keller, Robert. (2001). "Cross-Functional Project Groups in Research and New Product Development." *Academy of Management Journal* 44(3): 547–55; Senn, Christoph, and Axel Thoma. (2007). "Worldly Wise: Attracting and Managing Customers Isn't the Same When Business Goes Global." *Wall Street Journal* March 3, 2007, p. R5; Solomon, C. (1998). "Building Teams Across Borders." *Workforce* 52 (4): 12–17.

Hollywood and the Rise of Cultural Protectionism

The most commercially successful filmmaker of all time, Steven Spielberg, is synonymous with American cinema. He has directed and produced international blockbusters like *ET*, *Jurassic Park*, and *War of the Worlds*. As U.S. dominance of the international film industry grows, Spielberg has been the target of complaints about how Hollywood is changing world cultures. The values represented in Spielberg's films are often viewed as part of the larger trend of the homogenization, or worse, the Americanization of global values and beliefs.

Jurassic Park ignited a storm of protest and calls for cultural protectionism. Film critics and cultural ministries around the globe found *Jurassic Park* to be a brainless film, lacking plot, and succeeding entirely through special effects and big-budget bells and whistles. French officials labeled the film a threat to their national identity. Three leading filmmakers—Pedro Almodóvar, Bernardo Bertolucci, and Wim Wenders—wrote Spielberg to reprimand him for the poor quality of the film, proclaiming he was personally responsible for undermining their efforts to keep culturally rich European cinema afloat.

Another popular American movie, *Lost in Translation*, came under fire from Los Angeles to Tokyo. Set in Japan's capital and starring Bill Murray, the film won an Academy Award for best screenplay, three Golden Globes, and was nominated for three additional Oscars. The film was criticized for its portrayal of Japanese people as robotic caricatures who mix up their L's and R's. The image-conscious Japanese were disappointed at their depiction as comic relief for foreign audiences. In a scene where Bill Murray's character is taking a shower in what is meant to be a five-star hotel, he has to bend and contort to get his head under the shower head. In reality there isn't a five-star hotel in Tokyo that hasn't accounted for the varying heights of its potential guests. Another scene, in which Murray is shown towering at least a foot above an elevator full of local businessmen, mocks the smaller physique of the Japanese. The film is seen to reinforce negative stereotypes about the Japanese.

Is the U.S. film industry overwhelming the cultures of the world? And if so, can the world really blame Hollywood? Here are some relevant statistics. Hollywood produces 80 percent of the films viewed internationally, having doubled the U.S. global market share since 1990. The European film industry is now about one-ninth the size it was in 1945. Behind aerospace, Hollywood is the United States' largest net export. The copyright-based industries, which also include software, books, music, and TV, contributed more to the U.S. economy in the early 2000s than any single manufacturing sector. While the United States imports few foreign films, Hollywood's output remains in high demand worldwide. Today, foreign films hold less than one percent of the U.S. market.

Distorting History and Religious Values

Under attack since their origin, Hollywood war films are widely accused of presenting biased accounts of history. War movies portray American soldiers as patriotic heroes, protecting all that is good from all that is evil. *Apocalypse Now* may have painted a particularly ethnocentric view of the Vietnam War, focusing on the American tragedy while ignoring that of the Vietnamese.

While many nations are steadfast in their belief of the separation of church and state, this was decidedly not the case when *The Passion of Christ* was released. The film enraged religious groups in almost every corner of the world. Mel Gibson's controversial film retells the last 12 hours of the life of Jesus Christ. The government of Malaysia found *The Passion of Christ* inappropriate for its largely Muslim population, and banned its initial release in the country. The country subsequently permitted only Christians to view the film. International organizations and individuals also attacked *The Passion of Christ* as anti-Semitic.

Crucial to U.S. dominance of world cinema are the cultural associations inherent in Hollywood films. The global recognition and acceptance of American English and cultural references are obstacles that competitors face. American stars and Hollywood directors are well established in the international movie scene, and they enjoy a drawing power that transcends national boundaries. The CEO of Time Warner attributed Hollywood's global success to the association of "American style with a way of existence that to one degree or another [people] wish to share in."

Movies and Comparative Advantage

According to the theory of comparative advantage, countries should specialize in producing what they do best and import the rest. Economists argue that this theory applies as much to films as to any industry. They argue that movies are like any other commodity, and the United States has advantages in producing entertainment and exporting it to the rest of the world. Nevertheless, critics suggest that such an assertion, while satisfying to economists, ignores the fact that movies are *unlike* other commodities. The difference lies in film's ability to influence national culture and social development. The motion picture industry is a venue for enhancing cultural identity.

The world is no longer immigrating to the United States, but the United States is attempting to emigrate to the world, through its films and the values, stereotypes, and sometimes erroneous history that they portray. As former Canadian Prime Minister Kim Campbell remarked, "Movies are culture incarnate. It is mistaken to view culture as a commodity. . . . Cultural industries, aside from their economic impact, create products that are fundamental to the survival of Canada as a society." This view highlights why governments often engage in *cultural protectionism*—that is, the application of trade barriers that aim to prevent local film industries from being swamped by U.S. imports.

Critics argue that protectionism is needed to prevent U.S. culture from being imposed on the rest of the world. Cultural protectionism is achieved by coddling the domestic industry and implementing high trade barriers, aimed especially at imports from the United States. The specific methods vary by country but usually involve subsidies, quotas, or a combination of both. Subsidies that the government gives to domestic filmmakers are often funded directly by taxes placed on box office sales of U.S. movies. But subsidies can be a crutch to a weak industry. They are employed when traditional funding sources—bank loans, stock and bond sales—prove insufficient to maintain an industry. Quotas limit the number of screens allowed to show U.S. films or require a certain number of movies to be produced domestically.

Subsidies can weaken industries. Quotas prevent consumers from seeing the films they want to see. The whole system results in the local production of films simply to fulfill government mandates. France once boasted its own booming film industry. But its complex system of quotas and subsidies has done little to slow its gradual demise. The insulation from competitive pressures provided by cultural protectionism can weaken protected industries, reducing their ability to create globally competitive films. Meanwhile, the proportion of Hollywood revenues generated from abroad continues to grow.

A Cultural Dilemma

Despite plenty of arguments on both sides of this ongoing debate, critics can no longer point a finger at Hollywood, because Hollywood is not as "American" as it once was. *The Passion of Christ*, funded by its Australian director and filmed in Italy, is a prime example of the technicolor that globalization has given to an issue that was once black and white. Two of the seven major film companies that are collectively known as Hollywood aren't even U.S. firms. Many big-budget Hollywood films these days are in fact multinational creations. Russell Crowe, Heath Ledger, Charlize Theron, Penelope Cruz, Nicole Kidman, Jude Law, and Catherine Zeta-Jones are just a few of the many stars who do not hail from the United States.

As the lines connecting Hollywood with the United States are increasingly blurred, the world needs to reconsider the methods by which to conquer this so-called beast. Protectionists should not abandon their quest to salvage the intellectual and artistic quality of films. They should heed the words of Eric Rohmer. In an interview with

the New York Times, the French director stated that his countrymen should fight back with high-quality movies, not protection. "I am a commercial film maker. I am for free competition and am not supported by the state."

AACSB: **Reflective Thinking**

Case Questions

1. Like an iceberg, most aspects of culture are largely invisible to the casual observer (for example, gender roles, ways to solve problems, conversational patterns). What aspects of culture do Hollywood films promote around the world? In what ways do Hollywood movies affect the cultural values of people outside the United States?

2. Hollywood movies are very popular in world markets, but foreign films are little viewed in the United States. What factors determine the high demand for Hollywood films in world markets? That is, why are they so popular in Europe, Japan, Latin America, and elsewhere? Why are foreign films so little demanded in the United States? What can foreign filmmakers do to increase demand for their movies in the United States?

3. Worldwide, protectionism of most goods is insignificant or declining. Do movies constitute a separate category (culture incarnate, as stated in the case study), or should they be treated like any other good? That is, given the nature of movies, is it okay for a country to shield and support its own film industry via protectionism? Are there any other cultural industries that governments should protect? Justify your answers.

4. Are subsidies and quotas the right way to protect cultural industries? What are the advantages and disadvantages of subsidies and quotas for protecting local film industries? Are there better ways to maintain and enhance home-grown film industries? Justify and elaborate your answer. ◄

This case was written by Sonia Prusaitis, under the supervision of Dr. Gary Knight.

Sources: "Moreover: Culture Wars." *Economist*, Sep, 12, 1998, pp. 97–00; Barth, Steve. (1998). "Cultural Protectionism," *World Trade*, March, 1998, p. 43; Cowen, Tyler. (1998). "French Kiss-Off: How Protectionism has Hurt French Films," *Reason Magazine* July, 1998, pp. 40–48; Day, Kiku. (2004)."Totally Lost in Translation," *The Guardian*, January 24, 2004; Delacroix, Jacques, and Julien Bornon. (2005). Can Protectionism Ever Be Respectable? *The Independent Review* 9(3): 353–65; Marvasti, Akbar, and E. Canterbery. (2005). "Cultural and Other Barriers to Motion Picture Trade," *Economic Inquiry*, January, 2005, pp. 39–55; Motion Picture Association. (2002). *U.S. Entertainment Industry*, February 5, 2005, at www.mpaa.org; Munroe, J. Richard. (1998). "Good-Bye to Hollywood: Cultural Imperialism and the New Protectionism," *Vital Speeches of the Day*, June 15; Teachout, Terry. (1998). "Cultural Protectionism: The World's Culture Czars Move to Repel the Hollywood Invasion," *The Wall Street Journal*, July 10, 1998, p. W11.

CHAPTER ESSENTIALS

Key Terms

acculturation, p. 130
critical incident analysis (CIA), p. 149
cultural metaphor, p. 135
cross-cultural risk, p. 126
culture, p. 126
ethnocentric orientation, p. 128
geocentric orientation, p. 128
high-context culture, p. 136

idiom, p. 135
individualism versus collectivism, p. 137
long-term versus short-term orientation, p. 139
low-context culture, p. 136
masculinity versus femininity, p. 138
monochronic, p. 140

polycentric, p. 128
polychronic orientation, p. 140
power distance, p. 138
self-reference criterion, p. 149
socialization, p. 129
stereotype, p. 135
uncertainty avoidance, p. 138

Summary

In this chapter, you learned about:

1. The challenge of crossing cultural boundaries

In cross-border business, we step into different cultural environments characterized by unfamiliar languages, distinctive motivations, and different values. **Culture** refers to learned, shared, and enduring orientations of a society, which are expressed in values, ideas, attitudes, behaviors, and other meaningful symbols and artifacts. **Cross-cultural risk** arises from a situation or event where a cultural miscommunication puts some human value at stake. **Ethnocentric orientation** refers to using our own culture as the standard for judging how good other cultures are. **Polycentric orientation** refers to a host country mindset where the manager develops greater affinity with the country in which she or he conducts business. **Geocentric orientation** refers to a global mindset where the manager is able to understand a business or market without regard to country boundaries.

2. The meaning of culture: foundation concepts

Culture is the collective mental programming of people. It influences consumer behavior, managerial effectiveness, and the range of value-chain operations, such as product and service design, marketing, and sales. Culture is not inherited, right or wrong, or about individual behavior. Culture is like an iceberg in that most of its elements and influence are hidden below the surface.

3. Why culture matters in international business

Managers need to develop understanding and skills in dealing with other cultures. Culture matters in international business in areas such as developing products and services; interaction with foreign business partners; selecting foreign distributors; business negotiations; dealing with customers; preparing for trade fairs; and preparing promotional materials. Cross-cultural differences complicate workplace issues such as teamwork, employment, pay-for-performance systems, organizational structures, union-management relationships, and attitudes toward ambiguity.

4. National, professional, and corporate culture

There are three layers of culture: national, professional, and corporate. Working effectively within these cultures is a major challenge. The influence of professional and corporate cultures grows as people are socialized into a profession and their workplace. Most companies exhibit a distinctive set of norms, values, and beliefs that distinguish them from other organizations. Such differences are often as distinctive as the differences in culture between nations. Managers can misinterpret the extent to which a counterpart's behavior is attributable to national, professional, or corporate culture.

5. Interpretations of culture

Culture can be interpreted through metaphors, a distinctive tradition or institution that serves as a guide or map for deciphering attitudes, values, and behavior. **Stereotypes** are generalizations about a group of people that may or may not be factual. An **idiom** is an expression whose symbolic meaning is different from its literal meaning. **Low-context cultures** rely on elaborated verbal explanations, putting much emphasis on spoken words. **High-context cultures** emphasize nonverbal communications and a more holistic approach to communication that promotes harmonious relationships. Hofstede's typology of cultural dimensions consists of **individualism versus collectivism, power distance, uncertainty avoidance, masculinity versus femininity,** and **long-term versus short-term orientation.**

6. Key dimensions of culture

The dimensions of culture include values and attitudes, which are shared beliefs or norms that individuals have internalized. Deal-versus-relationship orientation describes the intensity with which managers get down to business, as opposed to developing relationships. Manners and customs are ways of behaving and conducting oneself in public and business situations. Perceptions of time refer to the temporal focus of life, and dictate expectations about planning, scheduling, profit streams, and what constitutes lateness in arriving for work and meetings. **Monochronic** cultures tend to exhibit a rigid orientation to time in which the individual is focused on schedules, punctuality, and time as a resource. In contrast, **polychronic** cultures refers to a flexible, nonlinear orientation to time in which the individual takes a long-term perspective and is capable of multitasking. Perceptions of space represent the area or physical room within which people feel comfortable. Religion provides meaning and motivation and is very significant in defining peoples' ideals and values. Symbolic and material productions refer to the intangible and tangible meanings, institutions, and structures that individual cultures construct for themselves.

7. Language as a key dimension of culture

Language is a "mirror" of culture. It is essential for communication and provides cultural insights. There are nearly 7,000 active languages, but most have only a few thousand speakers. The major languages include Mandarin Chinese, Hindi, English, Spanish, and Arabic. Language has both verbal and nonverbal characteristics. It is conditioned by our environment. Sometimes it is difficult to find words to convey the same meaning in two different languages. Learning one or more common languages will enhance a person's international business career.

8. Culture and contemporary issues

While culture is relatively stable, contemporary issues influence culture. In contact-based services such, as found in law and architectural firms, providers interact directly with foreign nationals in culture-laden transactions. Cultural differences may lead to mishaps in the exchange process. Technological advances are a key determinant of culture and cultural change. Improved transportation and the spread of communications technology have removed the boundaries that once separated nations. Technology also promotes culture. The Internet emphasizes the role of language in communications. Globalization promotes common culture and the consumption of similar products and services worldwide.

9. Managerial guidelines for cross-cultural success

Managerial guidelines include the need to acquire factual and interpretive knowledge about the other culture, and to try to speak their language. Managers should avoid cultural bias and engage in **critical incident analysis** to avoid the **self-reference criterion**. Critical incident analysis involves being culturally aware, not making value judgments, and selecting the most likely interpretation of foreign behaviors. Experienced managers develop cross-cultural skills, including a tolerance for ambiguity, perceptiveness, valuing personal relationships, and being flexible and adaptable. Cultural intelligence is the ability to function effectively in culturally diverse situations.

Test Your Comprehension

1. Describe culture and cross-cultural risk.

2. Distinguish between socialization and acculturation.

3. Explain why culture matters in international business. In what types of contexts can cross-cultural differences cause concerns for managers?

4. Distinguish between the three layers of culture. What are the major elements of country-level and professional culture?

5. How does a manager with a deal orientation differ from a manager with a relationship orientation?

6. What are the two major perceptions of time, and how does each affect international business?

7. What are the five dimensions that make up Hofstede's model of culture?

8. Distinguish between cultural metaphors and stereotypes.

9. Summarize the three major guidelines for success in cross-cultural settings.

Apply Your Understanding
AACSB: Communication, Reflective Thinking, Multicultural and Diversity

1. Suppose you get a job at Kismet Indemnity, a life insurance company. In its 45-year history, Kismet has never done any international business. Now the president of Kismet, Mr. Randall Jay, wants to expand Kismet's business abroad. You have noted in meetings that Mr. Jay seems to lack much awareness of the role of culture. Although you have always been careful about appearing too smart around your superiors, write a memo to Mr. Jay in which you explain why culture matters in international business. In your memo, be sure to speculate on the effects of various dimensions of culture on sales of life insurance.

2. People tend to see other cultures from their own point of view. They accept their own culture and its ways as the norm—everything else seems foreign, or even mysterious. This chapter describes a technique called critical incident analysis (CIA) that encourages an objective reaction to cultural differences by helping managers develop empathy for other points of view. Using the CIA approach, define a situation that you or someone else has experienced that led to a cross-cultural misunderstanding. Perhaps it involved an interaction with a fellow student, a visit to a store in your town, or an experience you had while traveling abroad. Explain what actually happened, and how a more culturally sensitive response might have been possible if you or your fellow student had used CIA.

3. Examine the following comparison of cultural values in Mexico and the United States. Based on your analysis, use the discussion in this chapter on the dimensions and drivers of culture, as well as their management implications, to formulate a policy for marketing automobiles to consumers from each of these countries. What features should you emphasize in cars? What attributes should you emphasize in advertising cars?

Typical Values of Mexico

- Leisure considered essential for full life
- Money is for enjoying life
- Long-term orientation
- Relatively collectivist society
- Strongly male-dominated society
- Relationships are strongly valued
- Subordinates are used to being assigned tasks, not authority

Typical Values of the United States

- Leisure considered a reward for hard work
- Money is often an end in itself
- Short-term orientation
- Strongly individualistic society
- Men and women are relatively equal
- Getting the transaction done is more important than building lasting relationships
- Subordinates prefer higher degree of autonomy

globalEDGE Internet Exercises

(http://globalEDGE.msu.edu)

AACSB: Reflective Thinking

Refer to Chapter 1, page 27, for instructions on how to access and use globalEDGE™.

1. Ethnologue (www.ethnologue.com/web.asp) is a comprehensive listing of the world's known languages. It is an excellent resource for linguists, scholars, and others with language interests. Ethnologue contains statistical summaries on the number of language speakers by language size, family, and country. Visit the Ethnologue Web site and answer the following questions: (a) Visit the "Languages of China" site. What is the population of China? Of the more than 200 languages in China, which one has the largest number of speakers? Which has the second most speakers? What is the common name of the Chinese language known as *yue*? How do these figures compare to the total number of English speakers in the main English-speaking countries of Australia, Canada, the United Kingdom, and the United States? (b) Visit the "Languages of Spain" site. Most people know that Spanish originated in Spain. How many people live in Spain? How many native Spanish speakers are in Spain? How many languages altogether are spoken in Spain? (c) Switzerland is one of the smallest European countries. What are the major languages of Switzerland, and how many speakers does each have? (d) Find the table "Linguistic Diversity of Countries," which shows the population of each language as a proportion of the total population, for most countries. What are the most linguistically diversified countries in the world? What are the least diversified countries?

2. Cultural intelligence is a person's capability to function effectively in situations characterized by cultural diversity. globalEDGE ™ and other online resources feature *cultural intelligence* scales. What are the components of cultural intelligence? Answer the questions on this scale and calculate your score on cultural intelligence? Compare your score to those of your classmates.

3. Various online sites list cultural blunders or *faux pas* (false steps) that people make in their international interactions. One such site is International Education Systems (www.marybosrock.com). Neglecting to develop relationships (as in "Just sign the contract, I'm in a hurry!") and casual use of first names (as in "Just call me Bill!") are examples of the cultural blunders that seem to persist. Research online sources to identify examples of improper cultural behaviors. How can managers avoid such blunders?

CKR Cavusgil Knight Riesenberger

Management Skill Builder©

Developing an Incentive Plan for Sales Personnel from Different Cultures

Professional selling is the art of determining the needs of the client and then providing solutions for those needs in the form of appropriate products and services. Done properly, this produces satisfied customers who are motivated to buy again from the same firm. Selling is particularly important in cross-border business-to-business exchanges, which tend to be more relationship-based than business-to-consumer exchanges.

AACSB: Analytical Skills, Multicultural Diversity

Successful companies are staffed with an international sales management team that understands local country client needs and excels at understanding the social, political, regulatory, and cultural nuances of the local market. Successful international sales management teams excel at the ability to motivate in-country sales representatives, who come from various cultural backgrounds, to meet and exceed established sales goals.

Managerial Challenge

Selling across cultures requires a high level of sophistication. As emphasized throughout this text, the international environment is characterized by a range of differences in culture, economic circumstances, political systems, regulatory requirements, and other factors, all of which strongly influence the company's selling efforts. A key managerial challenge for international sales management teams is to develop proficiency in understanding foreign cultures, and to leverage these cultural skills to maximize the performance of the local, in-country sales professionals.

Background

In staffing sales personnel, firms usually prefer to hire host-country nationals because of their local knowledge and expertise and because they are less expensive to employ and house than expatriates. Employing in-country nationals poses its own challenges because of the cultural differences that characterize such personnel. To inspire a culturally diverse sales force, managers charged with sales administration must be sensitive to the needs and personality traits of the sales personnel whom they supervise. Managers often need to appeal to differ-

ing motives to induce sales personnel from various cultures to perform at their best.

Managerial Skills You Will Gain

In this C/K/R Management Skill Builder©, as a prospective manager, you will:

1. Understand the factors that motivate sales personnel in different countries.
2. Learn cultural traits in various countries and how these traits influence behaviors among sales personnel.
3. Learn how to increase company sales through more effective personnel management.
4. Gain market research skills in acquiring knowledge of social and political realities in planning company selling activities in different countries.

Your Task

Assume you are an international sales administration specialist on the management team of a firm that manufactures personal computers. Your task is to assist the international sales manager, who supervises three sales representatives from three different countries. You have been asked to design an incentive plan for each of the employees that is most likely to maximize his or her selling effort and comply with all local country rules and regulations.

Go to the C/K/R Knowledge Portal©

www.prenhall.com/cavusgil

Proceed to the C/K/R Knowledge Portal© to obtain the expanded background information, your task and methodology, suggested resources for this exercise, and the presentation template.

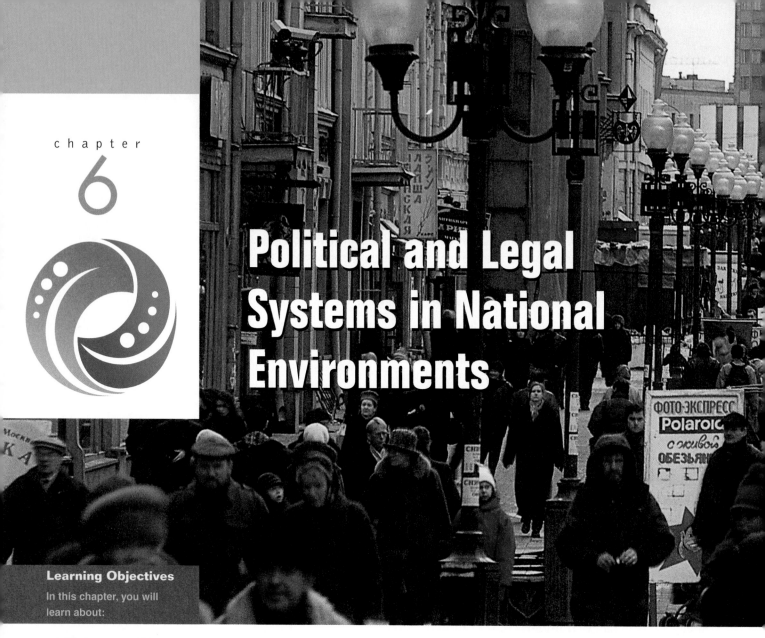

Political and Legal Systems in National Environments

> Doing Business in Russia: Evolving Legal and Political Realities

Take a walk down the open-air markets in Moscow and you will see market forces in action—vendors strewn about with stalls selling various goods. If you take a closer look, you will likely find vendors selling all variety of pirated software, music, and movie DVDs. Russian police officers are aware of these products but do not issue fines or arrest the sellers. Some corrupt officers may even get a cut of the total sales from these vendors.

Bribery is commonplace in Russia. One expert estimated that Russian small and medium-sized enterprises spend one-fifth of their net income on bribes. Because of a weak legal environment, the country is a tough place to do business. President Vladimir Putin once remarked that anyone who successfully registers a business in Russia deserves a medal. Vague and overlapping regulations enrich a host of public officials. Any new venture may necessitate dozens of government licenses, and each license may require paying a bribe. Government bureaucrats are often the most corrupt, many somehow taking expensive vacations despite receiving modest salaries. In addition to incessant bribery, there have been count-less incidents of strong-handed government interference in the private sector. Crim-

inal raiders, sometimes in collaboration with government officials, seize independently operating businesses.

One well-known example is the Russian firm Yukos—an oil company once controlled by the Russian industrialist Mikhail Khodorkovsky, who has been imprisoned by the government for alleged tax evasion. Claiming that Yukos owed back taxes, Russia's government sold part of the firm and kept the $9.3 billion in proceeds. Yukos' buyer was Baikal Finance Group, which happened to have the same address as a grocery store in a small town. This prompted many to question Baikal's existence, which led a state-owned firm known as Rosneft to announce that it had purchased Yukos for an undisclosed sum. Yukos' original buyer no longer exists, and perhaps never did. As the chain of events unfolded, so did the central government's plan to convert privatized energy firms into a patchwork of state enterprises.

Russia is also plagued by organized crime. For example, in 2006, the deputy chairman of Russia's central bank was shot dead in Moscow. He had spearheaded the country's effort to reform its corrupt banking system and had closed dozens of banks linked to organized crime, making dangerous enemies in the process.

Numerous other contract killings have taken place, as criminal organizations attempt to maintain their stronghold on much of Russia's economy. One official estimated that criminal groups control 500 large Russian firms. Foreign MNEs routinely perform background checks on employees and contractors in an effort to identify people who may be linked to organized crime or have false credentials. Foreign companies also attempt to provide for the security of staff and facilities.

Rampant corruption and crime have raised doubts about Russia's evolving legal system and its commitment to market economics. The country is transitioning from a command economy to a market economy. The shift has created much uncertainty for foreign firms doing business there. Managers must be mindful of the political and legal environments that characterize transition economies, particularly in Russia. Ambiguous regulations, nonexistent laws, inadequate

enforcement, a rudimentary court system, and a formerly totalitarian government all pose numerous difficulties. Although firms can take precautionary measures to minimize risk, not all risk is avoidable. Russia continues to improve its legal system so as to clarify business transactions and commercial law, and officials have taken tougher stances on organized crime. Numerous firms, from Boeing to IKEA, have invested billions in the country. But operating in Russia continues to pose many challenges. Potential rewards are promising for firms that plan ahead and protect their assets.

Sources: Chazan, G. (2004). "Russian Trial Opens Messy Chapter; Yukos Case Could Influence Course of Commercial Law and Business Under Putin." *Wall Street Journal*, June 16; *Economist.* (2006). "Business: The Reluctant Briber." Nov 4, p. 79; Gantz, J., and J. Rochester. (2005). "Global Fallout." In *Pirates of the Digital Millennium*. New York: Prentice Hall; Giddings, J. (2002). "Doing Business in Russia Today: Steps for Security." *BISNIS Bulletin*, February; Kvint, Vladimir. (2005). "The Scary Business of Russia." *Forbes*, May 23, p. 42.

 ## What Is Country Risk?

Every country is characterized by diverse political and legal systems that pose significant challenges for company strategy and performance. Managers must adhere to laws and regulations that govern business transactions. For example, government-imposed import tariffs lead many firms to enter foreign markets through FDI instead of exporting. At the same time, the political and legal context presents opportunities. Preferential subsidies, government incentives, and protection from competition reduce business costs and influence strategic decision making. Numerous governments encourage domestic investment from foreign MNEs by offering tax holidays and cash incentives to employ local workers. To take advantage of the opportunities and minimize the risks, managers must develop an understanding of the government sector, the political environment, and the legal framework of the countries where they conduct business. They must develop skills to interact effectively with local institutions.

The opening vignette alerts us to the risks of doing business in Russia. **Country risk** refers to exposure to potential loss or adverse effects on company operations and profitability caused by developments in a country's political and/or legal environments. Country risk is one of four major types of international business risks we introduced in Chapter 1. It is also referred to as *political risk*. Exhibit 6.1 identifies types of country risk prevalent in international business. While the immediate cause of country risk is a political or legal factor, underlying such factors may be economic, social, or technological developments.

Political or legislative actions can harm business interests, even when this is not their intent. Laws may be unexpectedly strict or may result in unintended consequences. Many laws favor host-country interests—that is, interests in foreign countries where the firm has direct operations. For example, Coca-Cola's business fell off in Germany when the government enacted a recycling plan. New laws required consumers to return nonreusable soda containers to stores for a refund of

Country risk Exposure to potential loss or adverse effects on company operations and profitability caused by developments in a country's political and/or legal environments.

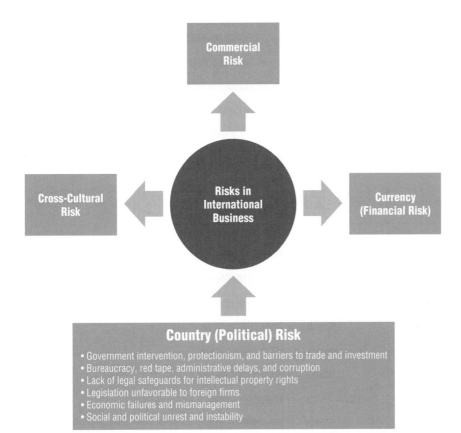

0.25 euros. Rather than cope with the unwanted returns, big supermarket chains responded by yanking Coke from their shelves, pushing their own store brands instead. In China, the government censors material that criticizes the government. Yahoo must monitor the information that appears on its Web site to prevent the Chinese government from shutting down its China operations.[1]

Just as laws and regulations can lead to country risk, their inadequate enforcement can pose challenges for the firm. Inadequate legal protection is particularly challenging in developing countries. Regulations to protect intellectual property may exist on paper but are not adequately enforced. **Intellectual property** refers to ideas or works created by people or firms, such as patents, trademarks, and copyrights. When an innovator invents a new product, produces a movie, or develops new computer software, another party can copy and sell the innovation without acknowledging or paying the inventor. As implied in the opening vignette, Russia's legal framework is relatively weak and inconsistent. Russian courts lack substantial experience ruling on commercial and international affairs. Owing to the unpredictable and potentially harmful legal environment, Western firms frequently abandon joint ventures and other business initiatives in Russia.[2]

Intellectual property Ideas or works created by people or firms, such as patents, trademarks, and copyrights.

How Prevalent Is Country Risk?

Exhibit 6.2 portrays the level of risk in various countries. Risk is measured using various indicators, such as government debt, fiscal and monetary policy, and political stability. In the wake of war and the emergence of a new political regime, Iraq is one of the riskiest countries. Zimbabwe is risky because of ongoing corruption (bribery and fraud) and political turmoil. By contrast, Singapore and Hong Kong are among the most politically stable countries.[3] Country risk may affect all

Exhibit 6.2

Country Risk in Selected Countries

On a scale of 0 to 100, the rankings combine measures of political risk (such as the threat of war) and economic risk (such as the size of fiscal deficits). They also include measures that affect a country's liquidity and solvency (for example, its debt structure and foreign-exchange reserves)

SOURCE: From *The Economist* (2005), "Country Risk, February 26, p. 102. Copyright © 2005 The Economist. Used with permission.

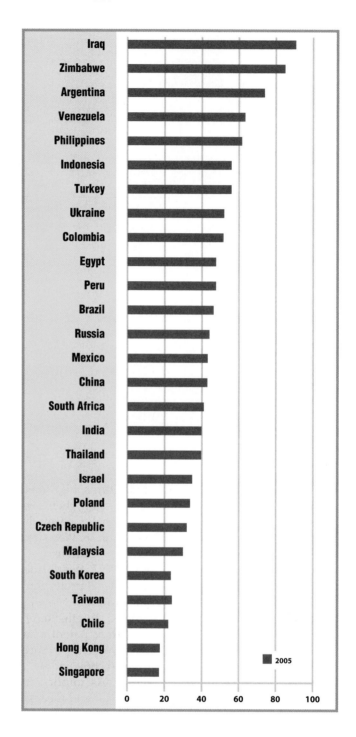

firms in a country equally, or it may affect only a subset. For instance, the civil war that occurred in the former Yugoslavia and several African countries in the 1990s tended to affect all firms. By contrast, despite the presence of several competitors in the Russian oil industry—Conoco-Phillips, Exxon Mobil, and Royal Dutch Shell—the Russian government targeted only Yukos with politically motivated persecution.[4]

India has often been characterized by high country risk. Hindu nationalists that came to political power in 1996 openly opposed foreign investment and foreign influence on Indian society. They enacted laws that targeted foreign firms for harassment. Some Indians are threatened by perceived cultural invasion from abroad. For example, the KFC restaurant chain was forced to step up security after threats by local political groups to destroy the firm's fast food outlets. About 100 farmers ransacked a KFC restaurant in Bangalore. In an earlier incident, the same restaurant was forced to close after health officials said its chicken contained excessive levels of monosodium glutamate, a flavor enhancer. KFC had long used the same ingredient abroad and won a court order to reopen the outlet.[5]

As countries develop stronger economic ties with foreign trading partners, and become better integrated with the global economy, they tend to liberalize their markets and eliminate restrictions on foreign business. This happened in India as well, with the introduction of a series of economic reforms and markets opening in 1991. Exhibit 6.2 suggests the relationship between country risk and the degree of legal and political freedom. The country risk ratings tend to be rather low in countries with a favorable legal climate and political stability. In contrast, country risk ratings are higher in countries with excessive regulatory burdens and political instability.

 ## What Are Political and Legal Systems?

A **political system** refers to a set of formal institutions that constitute a government. It includes legislative bodies, political parties, lobbying groups, and trade unions. A political system also defines how these groups interact with each other.

A **legal system** refers to a system for interpreting and enforcing laws. The laws, regulations, and rules establish norms for conduct. A legal system incorporates institutions and procedures for ensuring order and resolving disputes in commercial activities, as well as protecting intellectual property and taxing economic output. Political and legal systems are both dynamic and constantly changing. The two systems are interdependent—changes in one affect the other.

Exhibit 6.3 highlights the sources of political and legal systems that contribute to country risk. Adverse developments in political and legal systems give rise to country risk. These can result from installation of a new government, shifting values or priorities in political parties, new directions or initiatives devised by special interest groups, and the creation of new laws or regulations. Change may be gradual or sudden. Gradual change is usually easier for the firm to accommodate. By contrast, sudden change is harder to deal with and poses greater risk to the firm. Unfavorable developments give rise to new conditions that may threaten the firm's products, services, or business activities. For example, a new import tariff may increase the cost of an important component used in manufacturing a product. A modification in labor law may alter the hours that the firm's employees are allowed to work. The installation of a new political leader may lead to government takeover of corporate assets.

Country risk is *always* present, but its nature and intensity vary over time and from country to country. In China, for example, the government is in the process of overhauling the national legal system, making it increasingly consistent with Western systems. Reforms, however, have been carried out in a piecemeal manner. New regulations have been poorly formulated, confusing, or contradictory. For instance, at one point the Beijing government announced that foreign investments in China's Internet industry were illegal. By this time Western firms had already invested millions of dollars in the Chinese dot.com sector, without any indication that the investments were inappropriate. In disputes between local and foreign firms, governments are often inclined to protect local interests. Even where Western firms obtain favorable judgments in the courts, enforcement may be difficult to achieve.

Let's delve into political and legal systems in greater detail.

Political system A set of formal institutions that constitute a government.

Legal system A system for interpreting and enforcing laws.

Exhibit 6.3

Sources of Country Risk

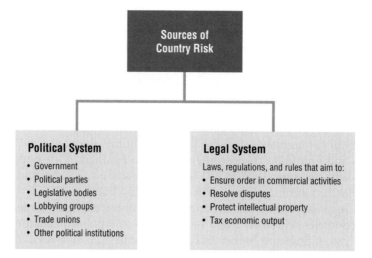

Political Systems

The principal functions of a political system are to establish stability based on laws, provide protection from external threats, and govern the allocation of valued resources among the members of a society. Each country's political system is relatively unique, having emerged within a particular historical, economic, and cultural context. Each political system evolves as a function of constituent demands and the evolution of the national and international environment. Constituents are the people and organizations that support the political regime and are the recipients of government resources.

In terms of regulating and controlling business, political systems run the gamut—from state ownership of economic enterprises and control of internal commerce to minimal government intervention in business activities. In recent history, three major types of political systems can be distinguished: totalitarianism, socialism, and democracy. Exhibit 6.4 highlights countries that exemplify these systems. Note, however, that these categories are not mutually exclusive. For example, most democracies also include some elements of socialism. Most of the totalitarian regimes of the twentieth century now embrace a mix of socialism and democracy.

Totalitarianism

Well-known totalitarian states from the past include China (1949–1980s), Germany (1933–1945), the Soviet Union (1918–1991), and Spain (1939–1975). Today, some states in the Middle East and Africa entail elements of totalitarianism. Under totalitarianism, the state attempts to regulate most aspects of public and private behavior. A totalitarian government seeks to control not only all economic and political matters but the attitudes, values, and beliefs of its citizenry. Often, the entire population is mobilized in support of the state and a political or religious ideology. Totalitarian states are generally either theocratic (religion-based) or secular (non-religion-based). Usually there is a state party led by a dictator, such as Kim Jong-il in North Korea. Party membership is mandatory for those who wish to advance within the social and economic hierarchy. Power is maintained by means of secret police, propaganda disseminated through state-controlled mass media, regulation of free discussion and criticism, and the use of terror tactics. Totalitarian states do not tolerate activities by individuals or groups such as churches, labor unions, or political parties that are not directed toward the state's goals.[6]

Elements of Totalitarianism Found in	Elements of Socialism Found in	Elements of Democracy Found in
Cuba	Bolivia	Australia
North Korea	China	Canada
Several countries in Africa (such as Eritrea, Libya, Sudan, Equatorial Guinea, Zimbabwe)	Egypt	Japan
	India	New Zealand
	Romania	United States
	Russia	Most European countries
	Venezuela	Most Latin American countries

Exhibit 6.4

Examples of Countries under Various Political Systems

Over time, most of the world's totalitarian states have either disappeared or shifted their political and economic systems toward democracy and capitalism. China initiated major reforms in the 1980s, and the Soviet Union collapsed in 1991. Agricultural lands and state enterprises were gradually sold to private interests, and entrepreneurs gained the right to establish their own businesses. However, the transition has not been easy, and former totalitarian states continue to maintain strong political control, including government intervention in business (as in the case of Russia in the opening vignette). Former Soviet states and China are still characterized by red tape that hinders the founding of new firms, bureaucratic accounting and tax regulations, inadequate legal systems to protect business interests, and weak infrastructure in transportation, communications, and information technology (see, for example, World Bank's www.doingbusiness.org).

Socialism

Socialism's fundamental tenet is that capital and wealth should be vested in the state and used primarily as a means of production for use rather than for profit. It is based on a collectivist ideology in which the collective welfare of people is believed to outweigh the welfare of the individual. Socialists argue that capitalists receive a disproportionate amount of society's wealth relative to workers. They believe that, because the pay of workers does not represent the full value of their labor, government should control the basic means of production, distribution, and commercial activity.

Socialism has manifested itself in much of the world as *social democracy,* and has been most successful in western Europe. It has also played a major role in the political systems of large countries such as Brazil and India, and today remains a viable system in much of the world. In social democratic regimes, such as France and Norway, government does intervene in the private sector and in business activities. Corporate income tax rates are also relatively higher in countries such as France and Sweden. Even robust economies like Germany have experienced net outflows of FDI as businesses seek to escape extensive regulation.

Democracy

Democracy has become the prevailing political system in much of the world's advanced economies. Democracy is characterized by two key features:

- *Private property rights:* The ability to own property and assets and to increase one's asset base by accumulating private wealth. *Property* includes tangibles, such as land and buildings, as well as intangibles, such as stocks, contracts, patent rights, and intellectual assets. Democratic governments devise laws that protect property rights. People and firms can acquire property, utilize it, buy or sell it, and bequeath it to whomever they want. These rights are important because they encourage individual

By protecting private property rights, democracies promote entrepreneurship. These women in Chetumal, Mexico, make tortillas in their small business.

initiative, ambition, and innovation, as well as thrift and the desire to accumulate wealth. People are less likely to have these qualities if there is any uncertainty about whether they can control their property or profit from it.

- *Limited government:* The government performs only essential functions that serve all citizens, such as national defense, maintaining law and order, diplomatic relations, and the construction and maintenance of infrastructure such as roads, schools, and public works. State control and intervention in the economic activities of private individuals or firms is minimal. By allowing market forces to determine economic activity, resources are allocated with maximal efficiency.[7]

Under democracy, individual pursuits of people and firms are sometimes at odds with equality and justice. Because people have differing levels of personal and financial resources, each performs with varying degrees of success, leading to inequalities. Critics of pure democracy argue that, when these inequalities become excessive, government should step in to level the playing field. In democracies such as Japan, Germany, and Sweden, the rights and freedoms associated with democracy are construed in larger societal terms rather than on behalf of individuals. Each society balances individual freedom with broader social goals.

Virtually all democracies include elements of socialism, such as government intervention in the affairs of individuals and firms. Socialistic tendencies emerge because of abuses or negative externalities that occur in purely democratic systems. For example, Japan has been striving to achieve the right balance between democracy and socialism. In the 1990s, poor management practices and an economic recession led to the bankruptcy of thousands of Japanese firms. To maintain jobs and economic stability, the Japanese government intervened to support numerous large firms and banks that, in a pure democracy, would have failed. But such policies have also led to inflexibility in the Japanese economy and a delay of needed structural improvements. Many countries, including Australia, Canada, the United States, and those in Europe, are best described as having a *mixed* political system—characterized by a strong private sector *and* a strong public sector (with considerable government regulation and control).

Democracy's Link to Economic Freedom

Compared to totalitarianism and socialism, democracy is associated with greater economic freedom and, usually, higher economic living standards. Economic freedom flourishes when governments support the institutions necessary for that freedom, such as freely operating markets and rule of law. Exhibit 6.5 reveals that the more political freedom in a nation, the more its citizens enjoy economic freedom. The extent of political freedom ranges from "free" to "not free." It is characterized by free and fair elections, the right to form political parties, fair electoral laws, existence of a parliament or other legislative body, freedom from domination by the military, foreign powers, or religious hierarchies, and self-determination for cultural, ethnic, and religious minorities. Economic freedom is related to the extent of government interference in business, the strictness of the regulatory environment, and the ease with which commercial activity is carried out according to market forces (www.freedomhouse.org).

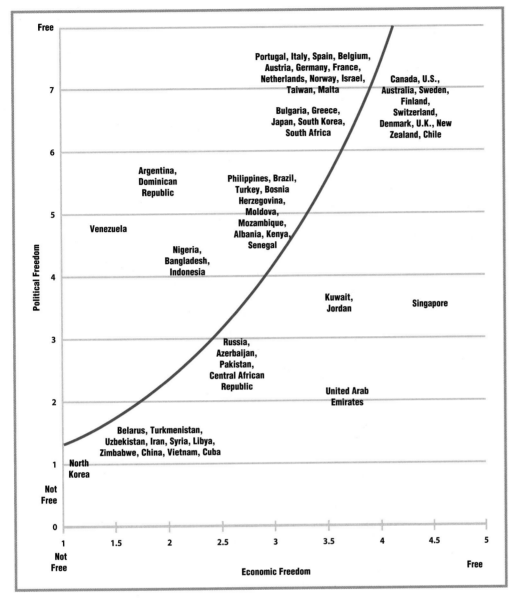

Exhibit 6.5

Relationship between Political Freedom and Economic Freedom for a Sample of Countries

SOURCE: Freedom House. Accessed at www.freedomhouse.org

How Political Systems Influence Economic Systems

Each political system tends to be associated with a particular type of economic system. Generally speaking, totalitarianism is associated with command economies, democracy is associated with market economies, and socialism is associated with mixed economies. Let's review these economic systems.

Command economy Also known as a centrally planned economy, the state is responsible for making all decisions in a command economy with respect to what goods and services the country produces, the quantity of their production, the prices at which they are sold, and the manner of their distribution. The state owns all productive wealth, land, and capital. The government allocates resources based on which industries it wants to develop. A large bureaucracy with central planners is created to manage the nation's affairs. While command economies were common in the twentieth century, they proved so inefficient that most have gradually died out. Central planning is less efficient than market forces in synchronizing supply and demand. For example, shortages were so common in the

Soviet Union that people often waited in lines for hours to buy basic goods like sugar and bread. Today many countries, especially those that embrace socialism, exhibit some characteristics of command economies. The leading examples are China, India, Russia, and certain countries in Central Asia, Eastern Europe, and the Middle East.

Market economy Decision making on levels of production, consumption, investment, and savings results from the interaction of supply and demand—that is, *market forces.* Economic decisions are left to individuals and firms. Government intervention in the marketplace is limited. Market economies are closely associated with capitalism, according to which the means of production are privately owned and operated. Participants typically exhibit a market-oriented mentality and entrepreneurial spirit. The task of the state is to establish a legal system that protects private property and contractual agreements within which people and firms can carry out their economic activity. However, the government may also intervene to address the inequalities that market economies sometimes produce.

Mixed economy A mixed economy exhibits the features of both a market economy and a command economy. It combines state intervention *and* market mechanisms for achieving production and distribution. Most industries are under private ownership, and entrepreneurs freely establish, own, and operate corporations. But the government also controls certain functions, such as pension programs, labor regulation, minimum wage levels, and environmental regulation. The state usually funds public education, health care, and other vital services. There are usually state-owned enterprises in key sectors such as transportation, telecommunications, and energy. For example, in France, the government owns key banks and some key industries, such as aluminum refining. One car company, Renault, is partially state owned, but another, Peugeot, is not. In Germany, Japan, Norway, Singapore, and Sweden, government often works closely with business and labor interests to determine industrial policy, regulate wage rates, and/or provide subsidies to support specific industries.

The last century saw a substantial increase in the number of mixed economies and a concurrent rise in government involvement in economic matters. For example, in the United States, combined government spending increased from about 3 percent of GDP in the 1930s to roughly 20 percent by the 1980s. During the same period in most other developed economies, average government spending as a percent of GDP rose from 8 to over 40 percent. Governments in Europe, Japan, and North America imposed many new regulations on private firms.[8] Regulations were adopted for workplace safety, minimum wages, pension benefits, and environmental protection.

 ## Legal Systems

Legal systems provide a framework of rules and norms of conduct that mandate, limit, or permit specified relationships among people and organizations, and provide punishments for those who violate these rules and norms. Laws require or limit specific actions, while empowering citizens to engage in certain activities, such as entering into contracts and seeking remedies for contract violations. Regulations mandate what procedures citizens and firms follow in a given context. Legal systems are dynamic; They evolve over time to represent each nation's changing social values and the evolution of their social, political, economic, and technological environments.

Prevailing political systems—totalitarianism, socialism, and democracy—tend to influence their respective legal systems as well. Democracies tend to encourage market forces and free trade. In well-developed legal systems, such as in Australia, Canada, Japan, the United States, and most European countries, laws are widely known and understood. They are effective and legitimate because they are applied to all citizens equally, issued by means of formal procedures applied by recognized government authorities, and enforced systematically and fairly by police forces and formally organized judicial bodies.

In these countries, a culture of law exists, where citizens consistently respect and follow the rule of law. **Rule of law** refers to the existence of a legal system where rules are clear, publicly disclosed, fairly enforced, and widely respected by individuals, organizations, and the government. International business flourishes in those societies where the rule of law prevails. For example, in the United States, the Securities and Exchange Act encourages confidence in business transactions by requiring public companies to frequently disclose their financial indicators to investors. Legal systems can be eroded by declining respect for the law, weak government authority, or burdensome restrictions that attempt to forbid behavior prevalent in the society. In the absence of the rule of law, economic activity can be impeded and firms have to contend with great uncertainty.

Rule of law The existence of a legal system where rules are clear, publicly disclosed, fairly enforced, and widely respected by individuals, organizations, and the government.

Five Types of Legal Systems

Nations can be characterized by one of five basic legal systems. These are: common law, civil law, religious law, socialist law, and mixed systems. These legal systems are the foundation for laws and regulations. Exhibit 6.6 provides examples of countries where these legal systems tend to prevail.

Common law (also known as case law) is a legal system that originated in England and spread to Australia, Canada, the United States, and former

Primarily Common Law	Primarily Civil Law	Primarily Religious Law	Primarily Socialist Law	Mixed Systems
Australia	Much of western	Middle East,	Russia	Much of eastern
Ireland	Europe and	North Africa,	China	Europe,
New Zealand	Latin America	and a few	Cuba	Philippines
United Kingdom	Turkey	countries in Asia	North Korea	Puerto Rico
Canada	Japan		Kazakhstan	South Africa
United States	Mexico		Uzbekistan	Thailand
India			Ukraine	Sri Lanka
Pakistan			Azerbaijan	Ethiopia
Ghana			Moldova	Hong Kong
Nigeria			Tajikistan	Bahrain
Zimbabwe			Kyrgyzstan	Qatar
Malaysia				Singapore
				Morocco
				Tunisia
				Vietnam
				Egypt

Exhibit 6.6   Dominant Legal Systems in Selected Countries

SOURCES: Accessed at wikipedia.org/wiki/Legal_systems of the world and www.droitcivil.uottawa.ca/world-legal-systems/eng-tableau.php.

members of the British Commonwealth. The basis of common law is tradition, past practices, and legal precedents set by the nation's courts through interpretation of statutes, legislation, and past rulings. The national legislature in common-law countries (such as the House of Lords in Britain and Congress in the United States) holds ultimate power in passing or amending laws. In the United States, because the U.S. Constitution is very difficult to amend, the Supreme Court and even lower courts enjoy considerable flexibility in interpreting the law. Accordingly, because common law is more open to interpretation by courts, it is more flexible than other legal systems. Thus, judges in a common-law system have substantial power to *interpret* laws based on the unique circumstances of individual cases, including commercial disputes and other business situations.

Civil law (also known as code law) is found in France, Germany, Italy, Japan, Turkey, Mexico, and in Latin America. Its origins go back to Roman law and the Napoleonic Code. Civil law is based on an all-inclusive system of laws that have been "codified"—clearly written and accessible. Civil law divides the legal system into three separate codes: commercial, civil, and criminal. Code law is considered complete as a result of catchall provisions found in most code-law systems. Rules and principles form the starting point for legal reasoning and administering justice. The codified rules emerge as specific laws and codes of conduct produced by a legislative body or some other supreme authority.

Both common law and civil law systems originated in western Europe and both represent the common values of western Europeans. A key difference between the two systems is that common law is primarily judicial in origin and based on court decisions, whereas civil law is primarily legislative in origin and is based on laws passed by national and local legislatures. Common law and civil law pose various differences for international business. These are highlighted in Exhibit 6.7. In reality, common-law systems generally contain elements of civil law, and vice versa. The two systems complement each other, and countries that employ one also tend to employ some elements of the other.

Legal Issues	Civil Law	Common Law
Ownership of intellectual property	Determined by registration.	Determined by prior use.
Enforcing agreements	Commercial agreements become enforceable only if properly notarized or registered.	Proof of agreement is sufficient for enforcing contracts.
Specificity of contracts	Contracts tend to be brief because many potential problems are already covered in the civil code.	Contracts tend to be very detailed, with all possible contingencies spelled out. Usually more costly to draft a contract.
Compliance with contracts	Noncompliance is extended to include unforeseeable human acts such as labor strikes and riots.	Acts of God (floods, lightning, hurricanes, etc.) are the only justifiable excuses for noncompliance with the provisions of contracts.

Exhibit 6.7 Examples of Differences between Common Law and Civil Law

Religious law is a legal system strongly influenced by religious beliefs, ethical codes, and moral values viewed as mandated by a supreme being. The most important religious legal systems are based on Hindu, Jewish, and Islamic law. Among these, the most widespread is Islamic law, which is found mainly in the Middle East, North Africa, and Indonesia. Islamic law is derived from interpretations of the Qur'an, the holy book of Muslims, and the teachings of the Prophet Mohammed. Also known as the *shariah*, Islamic law is nonsecular—that is, adherents generally do not differentiate between religious and secular life. Islamic law spells out norms of behavior regarding politics, economics, banking, contracts, marriage, and many other social issues. Islamic law governs relationships among people, between people and the state, and between people and a supreme being. Thus, Islamic law might be said to encompass all possible human relationships. Because it is seen as divinely ordained, Islamic law is relatively static and absolute. Unlike other legal systems, it evolves very little over time.

Saleh Nikbakht, a lawyer for university professor Hashem Aghajari, holds a copy of the court's 2004 death sentence on his client for speaking out against Iran's hardline clerical leaders.

Most Muslim countries currently maintain a dual system, where both religious and secular courts coexist. Other countries with large Muslim populations, such as Indonesia, Bangladesh, and Pakistan, now have secular constitutions and laws. Turkey, another country with a majority Muslim population, has a strongly secular constitution. Saudi Arabia and Iran are unusual in the sense that religious courts have authority over all aspects of jurisprudence.

Traditional views of religious law are opposed by modern liberal movements within Islam. For example, strict interpretation of Islamic law prohibits the giving and receiving of interest on loans or investments. Thus, to comply with Islamic law, banks charge administrative fees or take equity positions in the projects that they finance. Many Western banks—for example, Citibank, JP Morgan, and Deutsche Bank—have subsidiaries in Muslim countries that comply with shariah laws. Muslim countries such as Malaysia have issued Islamic-compliant bonds that offer revenue from an asset, such as a rental property, rather than interest.[9]

Socialist law is a legal system found mainly in the independent states of the former Soviet Union, China, and a few states in Africa. It is based on civil law, with elements of socialist principles that emphasize state ownership of property. The rights of the state are emphasized over those of the individual. Countries that adhere to socialist law tend to view property and intellectual property rights more loosely than those that apply civil or common law. With the collapse of the Soviet Union and the transition of China toward capitalism, socialist law is gradually becoming westernized. As these countries adopt free-market principles, their legal systems increasingly incorporate additional elements of civil law.

Mixed systems refers to a variation of two or more legal systems operating together. In most countries, legal systems evolve over time, adopting elements of one system or another that reflect their unique needs. The contrast between civil law and common law has become particularly blurred as many countries combine both systems. Alternatively, legal systems in Eastern Europe mix elements of civil law and socialist law. Legal systems in Lebanon, Morocco, and Tunisia share elements of civil law and Islamic law.

What about the linkage between legal systems and political systems? Socialism is most associated with socialist law, but may include elements of common law and civil law. Totalitarianism is most associated with religious law and socialist law. Democracy is associated with common law, civil law, mixed systems, and, occasionally, socialist law. Accordingly, democracy tends to be viewed as a flexible political system.

Actors in Political and Legal Systems

Political and legal systems evolve from the interplay among various societal institutions, at both the national and international levels. Five types of actors are active in transforming political and legal systems.

Government

The government, or the public sector, is the most important actor, operating at national, state, and local levels. Governments have the power to enact and enforce laws. They are particularly influential in how firms enter host countries and how they conduct business there. Governments regulate international business activity through the exercise of complex systems of institutions, agencies, and public officials. Agencies that possess such powers in the United States include the U.S. Trade Representative and the International Trade Administration. In Canada, such functions are handled by the Ministry of Foreign Affairs, the Ministry of Finance, and the Export and Import Controls Bureau. Similar agencies operate in Australia, Britain, and virtually all other countries.

International Organizations

Supranational agencies such as the World Trade Organization (www.wto.org), United Nations (www.un.org), and the World Bank (www.worldbank.org) have a strong influence on international business activities. For instance, the United Nations Conference on Trade and Development (UNCTAD) helps oversee international trade and development in the areas of investment, finance, technology, and enterprise development. Such organizations help facilitate free and fair trade by providing administrative guidance, governing frameworks, and, occasionally, financial support.

Regional Economic Blocs

Regional trade organizations, such as the European Union (EU), the North American Free Trade Agreement (NAFTA), and the Association of Southeast Asian Nations (ASEAN), aim to advance the economic and political interests of their members. The EU organization is especially well developed, with its own executive, legislative, and bureaucratic bodies. The EU enacts and enforces laws and regulations that directly affect business. For example, following new regulations forced by Lithuania's entry into the EU, the supermarket chain IKI had to spend millions to build separate entrances for fresh meat delivery in each of its 136 stores.[10]

Special Interest Groups

These organizations are formed to serve the interests of particular countries, industries, or causes. For example, the Organization for Economic Cooperation and Development (OECD) supports the economic developmental and business goals of advanced economies. The Organization of Petroleum Exporting Countries (OPEC) is a powerful cartel that controls global oil prices, which, in turn, affect the cost of doing business and consumer prices. OPEC emerged in the 1970s as a collective and powerful voice for oil-producing countries, including Saudi Arabia, Kuwait, Iran, Venezuela, Nigeria, and Indonesia. Other groups exercise similar control over the production and allocation of commodities such as sugar, coffee, and iron ore.

Special interest groups engage in political activity to advance specific causes, ranging from labor rights to environmental protection. They often influence national political processes and produce outcomes with far-reaching conse-

Organization or Group	Issues of Concern
Organized religious groups	Perceive moral violations by foreign firms
Labor organizations	Oppose imported goods and offshoring
Competing businesses	Concerned about local resource consumption
Customers	Perceived price gouging by firms
Minority groups	Perceived discrimination/sexual harassment
Conservationists	Concerned about environmental degradation
General public	Concerned about the impact of foreign firms on national culture

Exhibit 6.8

Issues of Concern to Special Interest Organizations and Groups

quences for business. Many groups target particular industries and affect individual firms accordingly. Special interest groups operate not only in host countries but also in the home country. For example, well-orchestrated U.S. interest groups forced U.S.-owned firms to reduce their investments in South Africa because of its apartheid policies.[11] Greenpeace and the Save the Waves Coalition are two environmental groups that oppose the plan of Sempra Energy, a California gas and electric utility, to build a liquefied natural gas terminal and pipeline in Mexico. They argue that Sempra's planned natural gas facility in Baja California will pollute the ocean and wipe out lobster and tuna stocks in the area. Protestors have disrupted Sempra's construction progress.[12] Exhibit 6.8 lists major interest groups and their likely stance toward various business issues.

Competing Firms

Rival domestic firms with a strong presence in the host country naturally have an interest in opposing the entry of foreign firms into the local market and may lobby their government for protection. For example, host-country competitors often complain when foreign firms receive financial support from the parent or host-country governments. This was exemplified when Asterix, a French theme park, opposed French government support for the U.S.-based Disney when the latter established Disneyland Paris. Similarly, U.S. automakers in Detroit opposed BMW's construction of a factory in South Carolina. However, the local government of South Carolina supported the BMW facility on the grounds that it would generate jobs and increase tax revenues.

Types of Country Risk Produced by the Political System

Political systems influence the activities of business in numerous ways, giving rise to various types of country risk. We discuss specific risks brought about by political systems next.

Government Takeover of Corporate Assets

Governments seize corporate assets in two major ways: confiscation and expropriation. *Confiscation* refers to the seizure of foreign assets *without* compensation. For example, in Venezuela, President Hugo Chavez confiscated a major oil field owned by the French petroleum firm Total. *Expropriation* refers to the seizure of corporate assets *with* compensation.

French farmers block the main entrance of a McDonald's fast food restaurant in Auch, south-western France during a 1999 protest. The banner translates, "No to American Orders."

A third term, *nationalization*, is also used, and it denotes government takeover of not a firm but an entire industry, with or without compensation. In 2006, the government of Bolivia nationalized much of the oil and gas industry in that country.[13] By contrast, in recent decades, numerous governments have engaged in *privatization*, the selling of state-owned enterprises to private interests. The trend has been especially notable in China and Eastern Europe, which have privatized countless state enterprises since the 1980s.

Embargoes and Sanctions

Most countries are signatories to international treaties and agreements that specify rules, principles, and standards of behavior in international business. Nevertheless, governments may unilaterally resort to sanctions and embargoes to respond to offensive activities of foreign countries. *Sanctions* are a type of ban on international trade, usually undertaken by a country, or a group of countries, against another judged to have jeopardized peace and security. *Embargoes* are official bans on exports or imports of specific products or specific modes of transport with particular countries. They are often issued during wartime or in the wake of tensions between nations. Embargoes amount to regulations that forbid trade in specific goods with specific countries. For example, the United States has enforced embargoes against Cuba, Iran, and North Korea, all at times labeled as state sponsors of terrorism. The European Union has enacted embargoes against Belarus, Sudan, and China in certain areas, such as foreign travel, to protest human rights and weapon-trading violations.

Boycotts against Firms or Nations

Consumers and special interest groups occasionally target particular firms perceived to have harmed local interests. Consumers may refuse to patronize firms that behave inappropriately. A boycott is a voluntary refusal to engage in commercial dealings with a nation or a company. Boycotts and public protests result in lost sales and increased costs related to public relations in order to improve the firm's image. Disneyland Paris and McDonald's have been the targets of boycotts by French farmers, who view these firms as symbols for venting their anger against U.S. agricultural policies and globalization. Many U.S. citizens boycotted French products following France's decision not to support the American-led invasion of Iraq in the early 2000s.

War, Insurrection, and Revolution

War, insurrection, and revolution pose big problems for business operations. While such events usually do not affect companies directly, their indirect effects can be disastrous. For example, in Mexico in the 1990s, peasants in the state of Chiapas took up arms against the government, claiming governmental oppression and indifference to poverty. Later, a presidential candidate and another political leader were assassinated. These events stimulated many firms and financiers to withdraw their investments from Mexico because they perceived heightened political instability. In order to minimize losses from warlike acts, firms can purchase war risk insurance.

Terrorism

Terrorism is the threat or actual use of force or violence to attain a political goal through fear, coercion, or intimidation.[14] In recent years, much terrorism is sponsored by national governments, making it a particularly hazardous form of country risk. Terrorism has escalated in much of the world, as exemplified by the September 11, 2001 attacks on the United States. In addition to causing tremendous loss of life, these acts severely damaged the New York financial community and disrupted the business activities of countless firms. Terrorism induces fear in consumers, who reduce their purchasing, potentially leading to economic recession. The hospitality, aviation, entertainment, and retailing industries may be particularly affected. Terrorism also affects financial markets. In the days following the 9/11 attacks, the value of the United States stock market dropped some 14 percent.[15]

 ## Types of Country Risk Produced by the Legal System

Country risk also arises due to peculiarities of national legal systems. Particularly relevant to international business are *commercial law,* which specifically covers business transactions, and *private law,* which regulates relationships between persons and organizations, including contracts, and liabilities that may arise due to negligent behavior. In many countries, the legal system favors home-country nationals. Laws are designed to promote the interests of local businesses and the local economy.

Legal systems in both the host country and the home country pose various challenges to firms.

Country Risk Arising from the Host Country Legal Environment

The host country government can impose a variety of legal stipulations on foreign companies doing business there.

Foreign investment laws These laws affect the type of entry strategy firms choose, as well as their operations and performance. Many nations impose restrictions on inward foreign direct investment (FDI). For example, Japan's *daitenhoo* (large-scale retail store law) restricted foreigners from opening warehouse-style stores such as Wal-Mart or Toys "Я" Us. The law protected smaller shops by restricting the operations of retail giants. It requires large-scale retailers to obtain the approval of local retailers, a painstaking and time-consuming process. In Malaysia, firms that want to invest in local businesses must obtain permission from the Malaysian Industrial Development Authority, which screens proposed investments to ensure they fit with national policy goals. The United States restricts foreign investments that are seen to affect national security. Major investments may be reviewed by the U.S. Committee on Investments. In 2006, the U.S. Congress fiercely opposed a pending deal granting operational control at several U.S. ports to Dubai Ports World, a firm based in the United Arab Emirates. Under strong opposition from the U.S. public and Congress, the firm eventually abandoned its investment plans.

Controls on operating forms and practices Governments impose laws and regulations on how firms should conduct production, marketing, and distribution activities within their borders. Such restrictions may reduce firms' efficiency, effectiveness, or both. For example, host countries may require companies to obtain permits to import or export. They may devise complex regulations that complicate transportation and logistical activities or limit the options for entry

In Japan, foreign-owned large-scale retail stores such as Toys "Я" Us face restrictive laws designed to protect smaller shops.

strategies. In China's huge telecommunications market, the government requires foreign investors to seek joint ventures with local firms; local operations cannot be wholly owned by foreigners. The government's goal is to ensure that China maintains control of its telecommunications industry and obtains inward transfer of technology, knowledge, and capital.

Marketing and distribution laws These laws determine which practices are allowed in advertising, promotion, and distribution. For example, Finland, France, Norway, and New Zealand prohibit cigarette advertising on television. Germany largely prohibits comparative advertising, in which one brand is touted as superior to a specific competitor. Many countries cap the pricing of critical goods and services, such as food and health care. Such constraints affect firms' marketing and profitability. Product safety and liability laws hold manufacturers and sellers responsible for damage, injury, or death caused by defective products. In the case of violations, firms and company executives are subject to legal penalties such as fines or imprisonment, as well as civil lawsuits. In contrast to advanced economies, product liability laws are generally weak in developing countries. Some firms take advantage of these weaknesses. For example, as litigants pursued tobacco companies in Europe and the United States, these companies shifted much of their marketing of cigarettes to developing countries.

Laws regarding income repatriation MNEs earn profits in various countries and typically seek ways to transfer these funds back to their home country. However, in some countries, governments devise laws that restrict such transfers. The action is often taken to preserve hard currencies, such as euros, U.S. dollars, or Japanese yen. Repatriation restrictions limit the amount of net income or dividends that firms can remit to their home-country headquarters. While such constraints often discourage inward FDI, they are common in countries experiencing shortage of hard currencies.

Environmental laws Governments also enact laws to preserve natural resources, to combat pollution and the abuse of air, earth, and water resources, and to ensure health and safety. In Germany, for example, companies must follow strict recycling regulations. The burden of recycling product packaging is placed on manufacturers and distributors. Nevertheless, governments attempt to balance environmental laws against the impact that such regulations may have on employment, entrepreneurship, and economic development. For instance, environmental standards in Mexico are looser or less well-enforced than in other countries, but the Mexican government is reluctant to strengthen these standards for fear that foreign MNEs will reduce their investment.

Contract laws International contracts attach rights, duties, and obligations to the contracting parties. Contracts are used in five main types of business transactions: (1) the sale of goods or services, especially large sales, (2) distribution of the firm's products through foreign distributors, (3) licensing and franchising—that is, a contractual relationship that allows a firm to use another company's intellectual property, marketing tools, or other assets, (4) FDI, especially where this is done in collaboration with a foreign entity, in order to create and operate a foreign subsidiary, and (5) joint ventures and other types of cross-border collaborations.

Some convergence is occurring toward an international standard for international sales contracts. In 1980, the United Nations instituted the Convention on Contracts for the International Sale of Goods (CISG), a uniform text of law for international sales contracts. More than 70 countries are now party to the CISG, covering about three-quarters of all world trade. Unless excluded by the express terms of a contract, the CISG is deemed to supersede any otherwise applicable domestic law(s) regarding an international sales transaction.

Internet and e-commerce regulations These regulations are now the new frontier in legal systems. As highlighted in this chapter's *Global Trend* feature. Internet and e-commerce laws are still evolving. Firms that undertake e-commerce in countries with weak laws face considerable risk. For example, in China, the government has developed legislation to ensure security and privacy due to the rapid spread of the Internet and e-commerce. Many consumer-privacy laws have yet to be enacted, and progress has been delayed on the development of methods to protect private data from criminal or competitive eyes. Protections for online contracting methods have been implemented with the recent adoption of e-signature laws. However, enforcement of e-commerce laws in China remains inconsistent.

Country Risk Arising from the Home-Country Legal Environment

In addition to complying with the laws of host countries, managers must adhere to the laws of their home country. Let's discuss these legal considerations. **Extraterritoriality** refers to the application of home-country laws to persons or conduct outside of national borders. In most cases, the laws are applied in an attempt to prosecute individuals or firms located abroad for some type of wrongdoing.

Extraterritoriality Application of home-country laws to persons or conduct outside of national borders.

Examples of extraterritoriality in international business abound. For example, a French court recently ordered Yahoo! to bar access to Nazi-related items on its website in France and to remove related messages, images, and literature from its sites accessible in France and the United States.[16] In 2001, the United States enacted the Patriot Act authorizing the U.S. government to seize funds held by non-U.S. banks in the United States. The European Union has pursued Microsoft for perceived monopolistic practices in the development and sale of its operating system software. Monopolies are considered harmful because they can unfairly restrain trade.

Businesses generally oppose extraterritorialty because it increases transaction costs and compliance and regulatory costs, and causes considerable uncertainty.

The Foreign Corrupt Practices Act (FCPA) Passed by the U.S. government in 1977, the FCPA made it illegal for a firm to offer bribes to foreign parties for the purpose of securing or retaining business. The FCPA came about in an era when over 400 U.S. companies admitted paying bribes to foreign government officials and politicians. The FCPA was strengthened in 1998 with additional antibribery conventions for foreign firms and managers who act in furtherance of corrupt payments while in the United States. The FCPA also requires firms with securities listed in the United States to meet its accounting provisions. All such firms must devise and maintain an accounting system that tightly controls and records all company expenditures.[17] However, the definition of a "bribe" is not clearly specified in the FCPA. For example, the act draws a distinction between bribery and "facilitation" payments, which may be permissible if they do not violate local laws.[18]

Many countries do not have antibribery laws for international transactions. Some U.S. managers have argued that the FCPA harms their interests

E-Commerce and the International Legal Environment

While still a small fraction of world trade, international e-commerce is growing fast. E-commerce operates in an electronic space not bound by geography or national borders. E-commerce reduces traditional barriers of distance from markets and the lack of information about market opportunities. The World Wide Web remains a "wild west" of international business, as most countries lack adequate legal protections. E-commerce is fraught with thorny legal issues. For example, individuals or firms that place information, photographs, or music online may be violating intellectual property laws. Although electronic contracts are in digital format, existing contract law typically covers only paper documents. Consumers who use the Internet to make purchases with credit cards may risk identity theft and fraud.

Taxation of transnational e-commerce is complex because it is often difficult to define merchandise sold online. Do software, books, and music constitute products—or services? For tax purposes, the two categories are usually treated differently. E-commerce can circumvent tariffs and other trade barriers. Most e-commerce is currently free from customs duties, largely because of the technical difficulties of applying duties to these flows. A related issue concerns the location of a sale. When a customer in Japan buys software from Microsoft's Web site—based in the United States—does the sale originate in Japan or the United States? Such questions affect not only taxation, but also legal jurisdiction, in the event of disputes between buyers and sellers.

Inadequate legal frameworks are hindering the growth of global e-commerce, and therefore international organizations are driving efforts to devise internationally appropriate laws. For example, the United Nations Commission on International Trade Law (UNCITRAL) developed the *Model Law on Electronic Commerce*. The law ensures that electronic transactions are legally recognized and that a course of action is available to enforce them. The law also provides guidelines for treating electronic legal documents (such as contracts) as equivalent to paper documents.

The UNCITRAL model is only a guide, and national governments are not bound by it. E-commerce laws are evolving differently in different countries. Individual regulations represent the values and distinctive approaches of each nation. The resultant lack of consistency creates conflicts between national jurisdictions. When creating e-commerce law, some governments favor strong control and regulation. Other governments opt for a more liberal, hands-off approach. Those who favor government intervention argue, for example, that the Internet can bring their citizens face to face with pornography, gambling, or fraud. Many want to tax e-commerce and subject it to international trade controls. By contrast, those who favor a more liberal approach argue that the Internet has the potential to transform national economies and ease global poverty. They oppose strong government intervention because it runs the risk of slowing the pace of global e-commerce and economic development.

Experts argue that evolving regulatory frameworks should be governed by consistent principles that lead to predictable results, regardless of where buyers and sellers reside. Law enforcement authorities need to cooperate cross-nationally to reduce online crime. Trust is the basis for successful e-commerce transactions, and strong legal frameworks are required to promote trustworthy online commerce. Governments must devise legal frameworks that recognize and ensure the security of electronic payment systems and the privacy of online data. Legal frameworks need to strike the right balance to ensure that international trade flourishes, but not to be so restrictive as to hinder its promise.

Sources: Primo Braga, C. (2005). "E-commerce Regulation: New Game, New Rules?," *Quarterly Review of Economics and Finance* 45(2/3): 541–58; WTO. (1999). *Seminar on Electronic Commerce and Development: Summary Report*, February 19, Geneva: World Trade Organization; United Nations. (1999). *UNCITRAL Model Law on Electronic Commerce Guide to Enactment*, New York: United Nations.

because foreign competitors often are not constrained by such laws. FCPA criminal and civil penalties have become increasingly harsh. Firms can be fined up to $2 million, while individuals can be fined up to $100,000 and face imprisonment.

Antiboycott regulations These home-country regulations prevent companies from participating in restrictive trade practices or boycotts imposed by foreign countries against other countries. Firms are not allowed to participate in boycotts to the extent they discriminate against others on the basis of race, religion, gender, or national origin. For example, some Arab nations have long boycotted trading with the state of Israel because of political disagreements, and made it a requirement for any foreign company that wishes to do business with the Arab countries to also observe this boycott. The antiboycott regulations passed by the United States Congress in 1977 effectively prohibit U.S. firms from participating in the boycott of Israel when operating in these Arab nations.

Accounting and reporting laws Accounting practices and standards differ greatly around the world. Differing standards pose difficulties for firms, but can create opportunities as well. For example, when assigning value to stocks and other securities, most countries use the lower of cost or market value. However, Brazil encourages firms to adjust their portfolio valuations because of historically high inflation there. When valuing physical assets such as plant and equipment, Canada and the United States use historical costs. Numerous countries in Latin America use inflation-adjusted market value. In the United States, firms can write off uncollectible accounts. This allowance is not permitted in France, Spain, and South Africa. Research and development costs are expensed as incurred in most of the world, but are capitalized in South Korea and Spain. Belgium, Malaysia, and Italy use both conventions.

Transparency in financial reporting The timing and transparency of financial reporting vary widely around the world. **Transparency** is the degree to which firms regularly reveal substantial information about their financial condition and accounting practices. For example, in the United States, public firms are required to report financial results to stockholders and to the Securities and Exchange Commission every quarter. In much of the world, however, financial statements may come out once a year or less often, and they often lack transparency. Not only does greater transparency improve the environment for business decision making, it also improves the ability of citizens to hold companies accountable.

In an effort to curb corruption by its firms, the United States Congress passed the 2002 Sarbanes-Oxley Act to promote greater transparency in accounting practices. This comprehensive legislation was passed to deter accounting and managerial abuses. It emerged in the wake of accounting-fraud scandals at firms such as Enron and Worldcom. The act makes corporate CEOs and CFOs personally responsible for the accuracy of annual reports and other financial data. Foreign affiliates of U.S. firms, and foreign firms with significant U.S. operations, are required to comply with the Sarbanes-Oxley provisions. European firms like Royal Dutch Shell (Netherlands and United Kingdom), Royal Ahold (Netherlands), Parmalat (Italy), and Vivendi (France) have also been accused of managerial and accounting irregularities in recent years.

However, a major drawback of the Sarbanes-Oxley reforms is the cost of compliance—estimated at tens of billions of dollars and millions of work-hours—to change or install systems for internal accounting controls. In an effort to avoid these rigid financial requirements, some European firms are reducing their business investments in the United States, and several have deregistered from U.S. stock markets.[19] In the meantime, some governments in Europe have called for stricter standards in European accounting practices.

Transparency The degree to which firms regularly reveal substantial information about their financial condition and accounting practices.

Ethical values and practices *Ethics* refers to the moral behavior of people, firms, or governments. Ethical issues often arise, or may be exacerbated, by deficiencies in legal systems. *Corruption* is an extreme form of unethical behavior. It involves the use of illegal or unethical practices, especially bribery and fraud, to achieve business objectives. Bribes may be offered to gain access to important markets and to achieve other business objectives abroad. In this chapter's opening vignette, you saw that rampant corruption has raised doubts about Russia's evolving legal system. In Germany, business managers paid $13 million in bribes during the construction of a waste incineration plant. The Yacyretá hydropower project on the border of Argentina and Paraguay, built with World Bank support, failed to meet energy-production goals, and much of the $1.87 billion in expenditures was used fraudulently.[20] Corporate corruption occurs in every society, but is particularly common in developing economies.

One study found that over 30 percent of MNEs believe that corruption is a major or very severe concern to them in their worldwide investment decisions. The United Nations estimates that the total amount of bribes paid every year is approximately $1 trillion.[21] In an effort to fight international corruption, the United States passed the Foreign Corrupt Practices Act, described earlier. In addition, in 1996 the International Chamber of Commerce adopted "Rules of Conduct to Combat Extortion and Bribery," and the United Nations issued a "Declaration against Corruption and Bribery in International Commercial Transactions." In 1998 the Organization for Economic Cooperation and Development (OECD) unveiled its own antibribery agreement. The 30 OECD members (essentially, all the advanced economies), plus several Latin American countries, have signed the accord. Finally, international organizations such as the United Nations, the World Bank, and the International Monetary Fund have launched programs to combat international corruption.

Exhibit 6.9 on pages 182–183 shows the level of corruption worldwide as perceived by executives engaged in international business. The Corruption Perceptions Index is provided by Transparency International (www.transparency.org), an organization that tracks illicit behavior worldwide. Countries with the highest scores have the lowest levels of corruption, such as Canada, Finland, New Zealand, and Denmark. Countries with the lowest scores have the highest levels of corruption, such as most countries in Africa and former Soviet Union states. Note that corruption tends to be correlated with economic development. The less economically developed a nation, the more likely it will suffer from corruption. This relationship points to a key dilemma in economic development—trade and investment can help reduce poverty, but MNEs are reluctant to do business with countries that exhibit high levels of corruption.

Corruption poses a threat to national development and internal stability and is more prevalent where transparency is lacking. Corruption harms the poorest within societies, those who may be forced to pay bribes to gain access to various products and services, such as water, electricity, and phone service. High levels of corruption are associated with low levels of inward FDI. In other words, firms tend not to invest in highly corrupt countries.[22] Corruption has been a big factor in recent construction projects in Iraq and Afghanistan and in countries devastated by the Indian Ocean tsunami disaster. Roughly 10 percent of the $4 trillion spent annually on construction procurement is wasted through bribery and corruption.[23]

Studies indicate that corruption tends to be lower in countries that are strongly integrated into the global economy, have highly transparent accounting and information systems, have consistently enforced anticorruption laws, and have governments that are committed to reducing unethical practices.[24]

Managing Country Risk

While country risk is more common in nations with substantial government intervention, in reality, country risk can occur anywhere. Thus, managers are regularly faced with the challenge of developing strategies to minimize country risk. Seasoned managers attempt to anticipate and systematically manage country risk. They take proactive measures to minimize harmful exposure and adverse effects. In the discussion that follows, we highlight five specific strategies that managers can employ to manage country risk.

Proactive Environmental Scanning

Anticipating country risk requires advance research. Initially, managers develop a comprehensive understanding of the political and legal environment in target countries. They then engage in *scanning* to assess potential risks and threats to the firm. Scanning allows the firm to improve practices in ways that conform with the goals and standards of local laws and political entities, and to create a positive environment for business success.

One of the best sources of intelligence in the scanning process is employees working in the host country. They are usually plugged in to evolving events and can evaluate them in the context of local history, culture, and politics. Embassy and trade association officials may also regularly develop and analyze intelligence on the local political scene. Some consulting firms, such as PRS Group (www.prsgroup.com) and Business Entrepreneurial Risk Intelligence (www.beri.com), specialize in country-risk assessment and provide guidelines for appropriate strategic responses. Once the firm has researched the political climate and contingencies of the target environment, it then develops and implements strategies to facilitate effective management of relations with policymakers and other helpful contacts in the host country. The firm then takes steps to minimize its exposure to country risks that threaten its performance.

Strict Adherence to Ethical Standards

Ethical behavior is essential not only for its own sake, but also because it helps insulate the firm from some country risks that other firms otherwise encounter. Those companies that engage in questionable practices, or operate outside the law, naturally invite redress from the governments of the host countries where they do business.

The trend toward corporate social responsibility (CSR) aims at improving ethical business standards. **Corporate social responsibility** refers to operating a business in a manner that meets or exceeds the ethical, legal, commercial, and public expectations of stakeholders (customers, shareholders, employees, and communities). The idea that corporations can and should be good citizens, and that good citizenship requires more than simply providing secure jobs and paying taxes, is spreading throughout the world. CSR implies that firms should behave not just to maximize their profits but in ways that benefit society.

Increasingly, companies devise business strategies that simultaneously enhance the public good and safeguard the environment.[25] There are numerous ways in which transnational firms behave responsibly. Examples of such behavior include: complying with local and international laws, not discriminating in hiring or promoting, providing fair and adequate wages, ensuring health and safety in the workplace, instituting a fair system of regular and overtime work hours, avoiding the use of child labor, and providing adequate protection of the environment.[26]

Corporate social responsibility (CSR)

Operating a business in a manner that meets or exceeds the ethical, legal, commercial, and public expectations of stakeholders (customers, shareholders, employees, and communities).

Exhibit 6.9

Corruption Perceptions Index, CPI 2006

SOURCES: Transparency International, Corruption Perceptions Index, accessed at www.transparency.org

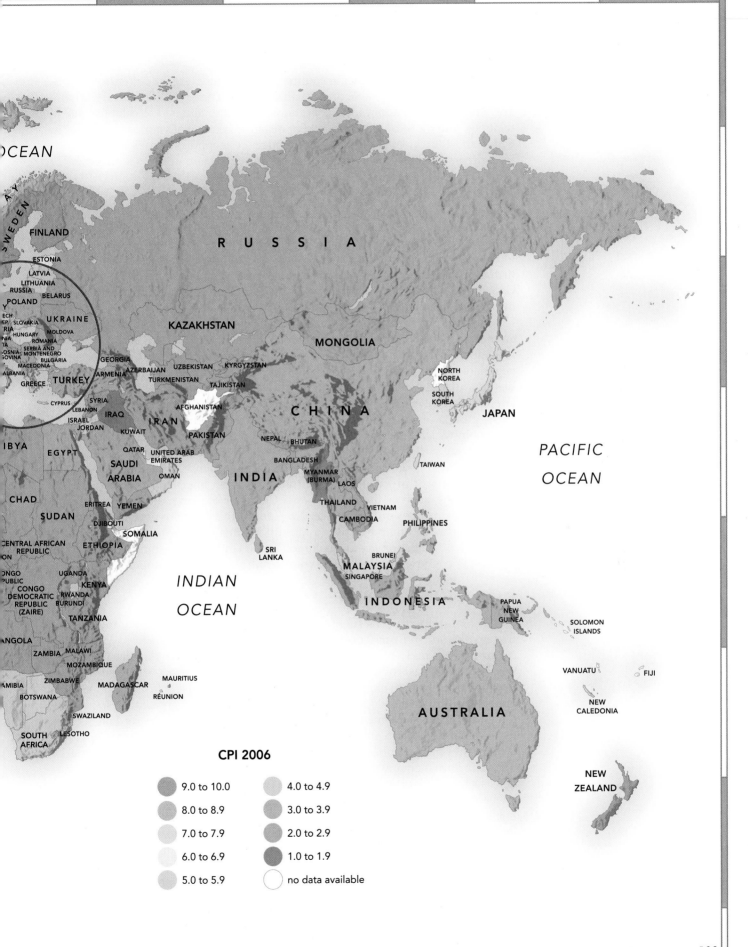

OCEAN

SWEDEN
FINLAND

ESTONIA
LATVIA
LITHUANIA
RUSSIA
BELARUS
POLAND
Y
ECH.
SLOVAKIA
UKRAINE
RIA
HUNGARY
MOLDOVA
NIA
ROMANIA
SERBIA AND
OSNIA-
MONTENEGRO
GOVINA
BULGARIA
MACEDONIA
ALBANIA
GEORGIA
GREECE
TURKEY
ARMENIA
AZERBAIJAN
CYPRUS
SYRIA
LEBANON
IRAQ
ISRAEL
JORDAN
KUWAIT
IRAN

IBYA
EGYPT
QATAR
SAUDI
UNITED ARAB
EMIRATES
ARABIA
OMAN

CHAD
ERITREA
YEMEN
SUDAN
DJIBOUTI
SOMALIA
ENTRAL AFRICAN
ETHIOPIA
REPUBLIC
ON
NGO
UGANDA
PUBLIC
CONGO
KENYA
DEMOCRATIC
RWANDA
REPUBLIC
BURUNDI
(ZAIRE)
TANZANIA
NGOLA
ZAMBIA
MALAWI
MOZAMBIQUE
AMIBIA
ZIMBABWE
BOTSWANA
SWAZILAND
SOUTH
LESOTHO
AFRICA

RUSSIA

KAZAKHSTAN

MONGOLIA

UZBEKISTAN
KYRGYZSTAN
TURKMENISTAN
TAJIKISTAN
AFGHANISTAN
CHINA
PAKISTAN

NEPAL
BHUTAN
BANGLADESH
INDIA
MYANMAR
(BURMA)
LAOS
THAILAND
VIETNAM
CAMBODIA

SRI
LANKA

INDIAN

OCEAN

NORTH
KOREA
SOUTH
KOREA
JAPAN

PACIFIC

OCEAN

TAIWAN

PHILIPPINES

BRUNEI
MALAYSIA
SINGAPORE

INDONESIA

PAPUA
NEW
GUINEA

SOLOMON
ISLANDS

MAURITIUS
MADAGASCAR
RÉUNION

VANUATU
FIJI

NEW
CALEDONIA

AUSTRALIA

NEW
ZEALAND

CPI 2006

- 9.0 to 10.0
- 8.0 to 8.9
- 7.0 to 7.9
- 6.0 to 6.9
- 5.0 to 5.9
- 4.0 to 4.9
- 3.0 to 3.9
- 2.0 to 2.9
- 1.0 to 1.9
- no data available

Allying with Qualified Local Partners

A practical approach to reducing country risk is to enter target markets in collaboration with a knowledgeable and reliable local partner. Qualified local partners are better informed about local conditions and better situated to establish stable relations with the local government. For instance, because of various challenges in China and Russia, Western firms often enter these countries by partnering with local firms who assist in navigating the complex legal and political landscape.

Protection through Legal Contracts

A legal contract spells out the rights and obligations of each party and is especially important when relationships go awry. Contract law varies widely from country to country, and firms must adhere to local standards. For example, a Canadian firm doing business in Belgium must comply with the laws of both Belgium and Canada, as well as the evolving laws of the European Union, some of which may override Belgian law.

International contractual disputes arise from time to time, and firms generally employ any of three approaches for resolving them: conciliation, arbitration, and litigation. *Conciliation* is the least adversarial method. It is a formal process of negotiation whose objective is to resolve differences in a friendly manner. The parties in a dispute employ a conciliator, who meets separately with each in an attempt to resolve their differences. Parties can also employ mediation committees—groups of informed citizens—to resolve civil disputes. *Arbitration* is a process in which a neutral third party hears both sides of a case and decides in favor of one party or the other, based on an objective assessment of the facts. Compared to litigation, arbitration saves time and expense, while maintaining the confidentiality of proceedings. Arbitration is often handled by supranational organizations, such as the International Chamber of Commerce in Paris or the Stockholm Chamber of Commerce. *Litigation* is the most adversarial approach, and occurs when one party files a lawsuit against another in order to achieve desired ends. Litigation is most common in the United States, but is eschewed in most other countries, typically in favor of arbitration or conciliation.

Safeguarding Intellectual Property Rights

Intellectual property consists of *industrial property*—that is, patents, inventions, trademarks, and industrial designs. It also includes *copyrights,* such as works of literature, music, and art, as well as books, films, and TV shows. Intellectual property is often the basis of firms' competitive advantage and long-term performance. Companies go to great expense to protect their intellectual assets in order to maintain their ability to develop and offer competitive products to customers.

Governments implement safeguards to protect intellectual property. Patents confer the exclusive right to manufacture, use, and sell products or processes. Copyright laws protect music, published works, and certain types of software. Trademarks remain in force for many years from their date of registration. International organizations such as the World Trade Organization (WTO) have devised strict standards for intellectual property protections. Other standards have been established by the World Intellectual Property Organization (WIPO) and various international treaties, such as the International Convention for the Protection of Industrial Property Rights and the Burton Convention for the Protection of Literary and Artistic Works.

Despite these protections, however, the protection of **intellectual property rights**—the legal claim that firms and individuals hold on their proprietary assets—is not guaranteed in much of the world. For one, laws enacted in one country are enforceable only within that country, conferring no protection abroad. Many countries are not members of WIPO or other treaty organizations. Practical mechanisms for

Intellectual property rights
The legal claim through which the proprietary assets of firms and individuals are protected from unauthorized use by other parties.

ensuring protection may be lacking or poorly enforced. Individual country laws and practices differ widely. As a result, firms risk local loss of their property and a decline in the value that such holdings provide. For example, widely recognized global brands—Rolex, Louis Vuitton, and Tommy Hilfiger, among others—are often victims of counterfeiting, eroding the firm's competitive advantage and brand equity.

Exhibit 6.10 summarizes losses, in millions of U.S. dollars, from illegal copying or pirating of movies, music, software, and books in various countries (see the Losses columns) and the proportion of pirated items sold as a percentage of total items sold (see the Levels columns). For example, Disney has struggled to launch its DVD movie business in China, due to rampant local counterfeiting. Legitimate Disney DVDs of films like *Finding Nemo* and *The Lion King* cost up to 10 times as much as knockoffs, restricting sales to a trickle.[27] In Russia, illicit Web sites sell popular music downloads for as little as 5 cents apiece, or less than one U.S. dollar for an entire CD. The illegal sites are popular with music fans worldwide looking for cheap downloads. The sites are easily accessed by online shoppers in countries where they are otherwise outlawed under intellectual property laws. Russia's laws regarding counterfeiting are often insufficient to thwart such crimes, and enforcement is weak.[28]

Protection of intellectual property rights is a perennial problem, especially for companies that internationalize through FDI, licensing, and collaborative modes. Particularly susceptible are firms in the pharmaceuticals, software, publishing, and music industries. Companies may file for protection under the Paris Convention for the Protection of Industrial Property, an international agreement intended to protect proprietary assets in many countries simultaneously, but the protection is limited. Ultimately, firms must apply for protection on a country-by-country basis, although patent, trademark, and copyright laws vary substantially around the world. In each country, their nature and enforcement depend on national laws, administrative practices, and treaty obligations. Enforcement is a big challenge and depends on the attitude of local courts and law enforcement agencies.

Exhibit 6.10

Estimated Losses from Copyright Piracy (Millions of U.S. Dollars) and Piracy Levels (Percentages) in Selected Countries, 2005
Losses: Illegal copying or pirating of movies, music, software, and books
Level: the proportion of pirated items sold as a percentage of total items sold

SOURCE: International Intellectual Property Alliance (IIPA), Special 301 Data Estimates, February 2007. Copyright © 2007 IIPA. Used with permission.

Country	Records and Music		Business Software		Entertainment Software		Books	Totals
	Losses	Levels	Losses	Levels	Losses	Levels	Losses	Loss
Brazil	$177	40%	$497	62%	$159	88%	$18	$851
China	203	85%	1.488	90%	510	90%	50	2,251
India	53	55%	318	70%	86	82%	40	497
Italy	48	27%	716	50%	648	40%	20	1,432
Mexico	487	67%	296	63%	182	85%	41	1,006
Philippines	50	62%	35	72%	NA	NA	49	134
Poland	24	35%	264	58%	NA	75%	NA	288
Russia	423	65%	1433	83%	282	72%	42	2,180
Saudi Arabia	20	50%	112	51%	NA	NA	8	140
Ukraine	30	60%	290	85%	NA	NA	NA	320

Pillaging Patents: The New War on Pharmaceutical Drugs
AACSB: Reflective Thinking, Ethical Reasoning

The $600 billion global pharmaceutical industry is dominated by about 10 firms; five are headquartered in Europe and five in the United States. Examples include GlaxoSmithKline (United Kingdom), Novartis AG (Switzerland), Merck (United States), Pfizer (United States), and Sanofi Aventis (France). Europe and the United States account for roughly 25 and 50 percent of worldwide pharmaceutical sales, respectively. This global industry is confronted with several major challenges.

High Cost of R&D Expenses

Pharmaceutical firms engage in large-scale, intensive research and development (R&D) to create and market drugs meant to treat everything from cancer to hair loss. Thousands of pharmaceutical drugs allow people to live longer and healthier lives. Europe and the United States are home to the major pharmaceutical firms and to industry R&D. They benefit from strong patent protection laws and abundant investment capital. According to industry statistics, it takes 12 to 15 years, and over $800 million in R&D expense, to successfully bring a new pharmaceutical compound to market. Only 1 in 10,000 investigated and tested compounds is approved for patient use. Only 3 out of every 10 new, approved compounds are successful enough to recover their R&D costs. For their successful products, pharmaceutical firms must charge prices high enough to recover not only the high costs of product development, but also to recover the cost of products that never achieve profitability.

Limited Protection for Intellectual Property

Governments grant patents and provide other types of protections for intellectual property. In practice, such protection is inadequate, especially in developing countries. India is one of the world's poorest countries, and very few of its citizens can afford health care or medications. The country has a history of weak intellectual property protection, which has discouraged R&D and innovation. In 1972, a major revision to the Indian Patent Act revoked all patents for medicines. Following this dramatic shift, foreign-branded pharmaceutical manufacturers abandoned India, and numerous pharmaceutical "chop shops" emerged. The new firms freely infringed on drug patents and engaged in a sort of selling free-for-all in the huge Indian pharmaceutical market. They reverse-engineered patented compounds developed by European and U.S. companies and began selling the pirated generics at drastically lower prices. The foreign pharmaceuticals launched legal actions against these violations but, in the absence of strict patent protection and with little local competition, the Indian generic drug manufacturers flourished.

The Challenge from Generic Brands

Under World Trade Organization (WTO) rules, a patent protects a drug inventor from competition for up to 20 years. In reality, when the lengthy testing and approval phase is factored in, the effective life of a drug patent is often less than 12 years. The manufacturer typically has only five to eight years of patent protection in which to recover its investment before generic manufacturers can legally enter the market. Once a patent expires, generic manufacturers have the right to produce medications originally invented by major pharmaceuticals. Generic manufacturers typically sell the medications that they produce at very low prices. Patent protections are important because they encourage innovation by allowing inventors a limited opportunity to recover their R&D investments. However, patent protection laws governing pharmaceuticals differ substantially around the world.

A *branded compound* is produced under patent protection by a pharmaceutical manufacturer that has undertaken expensive R&D to invent the drug. Each year, pharmaceutical firms typically invest some 20 percent of revenues into R&D to invent new compounds. "Approved generic compounds," manufactured in countries with strict bio-equivalency regulations, are comparable to branded compounds in safety, efficacy, and intended use. The main reason that generic manufacturers can charge lower prices is that they do not incur the high costs of R&D to develop new drugs. Because the medications are already established in the marketplace, generic manufacturers also incur substantially lower marketing and sales expenses.

In the world of generic drugs, Israel-based Teva Pharmaceutical is the largest manufacturer, holding about 12 percent of worldwide market share. Teva makes generic versions of about 150 brand name compounds. Teva and other generic producers have greatly increased their world market share in recent years. In the United States alone, generic medications now account for over half of all prescribed compounds. Once a branded compound's patent expires, generic manufacturers begin producing generic versions almost immediately.

Subsequently, retail prices for the compound can fall by as much as 90 percent within 12 months. The generic pharmaceutical industry is growing rapidly, partly due to rising demand for medications in developing economies and countries with weak patent protection.

Counterfeit Drugs

Many developing-country governments fail to ensure the bioequivalence of generics manufactured in their countries. As a result, a growing industry of counterfeit and bioinequivalent medications has emerged in such countries as Argentina, Brazil, China, and India. Because of the threats posed by counterfeit manufacturers, branded pharmaceutical firms spend significant resources to protect their patents and intellectual property rights around the world. Branded pharmaceutical manufacturers have pursued legal actions at the WTO and against individual nations. In 1995, the WTO's agreement on Trade-Related Aspects of Intellectual Property Rights (TRIPS) was approved by approximately 150 WTO member countries.

Neglected Therapeutic Areas

A large portion of pharmaceutical research is focused on developing treatments for diseases that can return the cost of capital and generate profits. For these reasons, pharmaceutical firms tend to target the most attractive markets. For example, these firms are much more likely to develop a drug for cancer and central nervous system diseases (such as psychiatric ailments) than for ailments common to poor countries (such as tuberculosis). Some in the pharmaceutical industry believe that R&D is too costly and risky to invest in diseases common to poor countries.

At the same time, governmental and private initiatives have begun to address these market realities by providing incentive packages and public-private partnerships. For example, the Bill and Melinda Gates Foundation is investing billions of dollars to fight AIDS, tuberculosis, and various infectious diseases that affect developing countries.

Closer to Public Scrutiny

The pharmaceutical industry's actions are often subject to public scrutiny. For example, the government of South Africa got into a tussle with several manufacturers of branded AIDS drugs. Because of high prices, the government sanctioned the importation of nonapproved generics. The reaction from branded pharmaceutical manufacturers was to sue South Africa, which created an international backlash against the firms. Not only did the episode generate much negative publicity for the branded pharmaceutical firms, it made people more aware of the generic drug industry and its potential for helping those affected by the AIDS pandemic. In the wake of the South African debacle, Brazil and several other countries threatened to break patents if pharmaceutical firms did not make their drugs more affordable. In the interest of good public relations, several branded pharmaceutical firms began to offer their AIDS drugs at lower prices in Africa. In all, the pharmaceutical firms have developed at least 88 medicines to treat AIDS and related conditions. The United States and various European governments have provided billions of dollars in subsidies to support AIDS treatment in Africa.

The Future

Without adequate protection of intellectual property rights, the pharmaceutical industry has fewer incentives to pursue drug discovery. At the same time, consumers in poor countries need access to drugs but can't afford them. Lax intellectual property laws facilitate the production of cheap generic drugs, but without these protections major pharmaceutical firms have fewer incentives to fund the R&D that results in new treatments for the diseases that plague the world.

Case Questions

1. Specify the types of country risks that pharmaceutical firms face in international business. How do the political and legal systems of countries affect the global pharmaceutical industry?

2. People need medications, but the poor often cannot afford them. Governments may not provide subsidies for health care and medications. Meanwhile, pharmaceutical firms focus their R&D on compounds likely to provide the best returns. What is the proper role of the following groups in addressing these dilemmas: national governments, branded pharmaceutical firms, and generic manufacturers?

3. Consult www.PhRMA.org, The Pharmaceutical Research and Manufacturers of America. What steps is the branded industry taking to address the various ethical issues that it faces, such as providing affordable drugs to poor countries?

4. Consult the TRIPS agreement at the WTO portal (www.wto.org). What are the latest developments regarding this treaty? What types of protection does this treaty provide to pharmaceutical firms? What enforcement mechanisms does TRIPS provide for ensuring that these protections will be carried out?

5. Recommend a strategy that management at a large pharmaceutical firm should employ in order to reduce the likelihood of political and legal risks that such firms face. What steps should management take to minimize its exposure to such risks?

Sources: Grabowski, H., H. Vernon, and J. DiMasi. (2002). "Returns on Research and Development for 1990s New Drug Introductions." *Pharmacoeconomics* 20, suppl. 3, 11–29; Trouiller, P., et al. (2002). "Drug Development for Neglected Diseases: A Deficient Market and a Public-Health Policy Failure." *The Lancet* 359 (June), 2188–94; Lofgren, H., and P. Malhotra. (2004). "India's Pharmaceutical Industry: Hype or High Tech Take-Off." *Australian Health Review* 28 (2): 182–93; Slater, J. (2003). "Indian Pirates Turned Partners; Once Copycats, Its Medication-makers Emerge As Industry Powerhouses." *Wall Street Journal*, Nov 13, 2003; Glass, G. (2005). "Patent Attack." *Pharmaceutical Executive* 25 (4): 76–81; *The Economist*. (2005). "Survey: Prescription for Change." June 18, 2005; *The Economist*. (2005). "Business: Big Generic Pharma; Pharmaceuticals." July 30, 2005; *The Economist*. (2005). *The Economist*. (2005). "Business: Corrupted; Medications and Intellectual Property." July 23, 2005; *World Trade Organization*. (1994). "Agreement on Trade-Related Aspects of Intellectual Property Rights." Retrieved from www.PhRMA.org "What Goes Into the Cost of Prescription Drugs?"

This case was written by Kevin McGarry, John Riesenberger, and Gary Knight for classroom discussion only.

CHAPTER ESSENTIALS

Key Terms

Summary

In this chapter, you learned about:

1. What is country risk?

International business is influenced by political and legal systems. **Country risk** refers to exposure to potential loss or to adverse effects on company operations and profitability caused by developments in a country's political and legal environments. Inadequate enforcement of laws can lead to loss of **intellectual property rights**. A **political system** is a set of formal institutions that constitute a government. A **legal system** is a system for interpreting and enforcing laws. Adverse developments in political and legal systems increase country risk. These can result from events such as a change in government or the creation of new laws or regulations.

2. What are political and legal systems?

A **political system** is a set of formal institutions that constitute a government. A **legal system** is a system for interpreting and enforcing laws. Adverse developments in political and legal systems increase country risk. These can result from events such as a change in government or the creation of new laws or regulations.

3. Political systems

The three existing major political systems are *totalitarianism, socialism,* and *democracy.* These systems are the frameworks within which laws are established and nations are governed. Most countries today employ some combination of democracy and socialism. Democracy is characterized by *private property rights* and *limited government.* Socialism occurs mainly as *communism* or *social democracy.* Communism proved to be ineffective for allocating resources and declined sharply with the collapse of the Soviet Union in 1991. Today, most governments combine elements of socialism and democracy. In general, totalitarianism is associated with *command economies,* socialism with *mixed economies,* and democracy with *market economies.*

4. Legal systems

There are five major legal systems: *Common Law, Civil Law, Religious Law, Socialist Law,* and *Mixed Systems.* The **rule of law** implies a legal system in which laws are clear, understood, respected, and fairly enforced.

5. Actors in political and legal systems

Actors include *government,* which exists at the national, state, and municipal levels. The World Trade Organization and the United Nations are typical of *international organizations* that influence international business. *Special interest groups* serve the interests of particular industries or country groupings, usually in pursuit of economic development. Groups exist at various levels and include labor unions, environmental organizations, and consumers that promote particular points of view. Companies deal with *competing firms* in foreign markets, who may undertake political activities aimed at influencing international entry and performance.

6. Types of country risk produced by the political system

Governments impose constraints on corporate operating methods in areas such as production, marketing, and distribution. Governments may expropriate or confiscate the assets of foreign firms. Governments or groups of countries also impose *embargoes* and *sanctions,* which restrict trade with certain countries. *Boycotts* are an attempt to halt trade or prevent business activities and are usually pursued for political reasons. War and revolution have serious consequences for international firms. *Terrorism* has become more salient recently, and reflects the use of force or violence to attain political goals via fear, coercion, and intimidation.

7. Types of country risk produced by the legal system

Foreign investment laws may restrict FDI that harm the natural environment. Controls on operating forms and practices affect firms' production, marketing, and distribution activities. Marketing and distribution laws influence the nature of international firms' promotion, and advertising. Laws regarding income repatriation restrict the transfer of profits back to the home country. Environmental laws are devised to combat practices that harm the natural environment. International contracts vary around the world in both substance and enforcement. Internet and e-commerce regulations are relatively underdeveloped in most countries. **Extraterritoriality** is the application of home-country laws to persons or conduct outside of national borders. *Antiboycott regulations* prevent companies from participating in restrictive trade practices. Accounting and reporting laws vary around the world. **Transparency** is the degree to which firms reveal substantial and regular information about their financial condition and their accounting practices. Ethical values and practices relate to the moral behavior of people, companies, and governments. Corruption involves the use of illegal or unethical practices, such as bribery and fraud, to achieve business goals. Corruption varies internationally, and may be severe in some countries.

8. Managing country risk

Successful management requires developing an understanding of the political and legal context abroad. The firm should scan the environment proactively. It should strictly adhere to ethical standards. **Corporate social responsibility (CSR)** is operating a business in a manner that meets or exceeds the ethical, legal, commercial, and public expectations of stakeholders. Country risk is also managed by allying with qualified local partners abroad. The firm should seek protection through legal contracts. To be successful, international businesses must safeguard their **intellectual property rights**.

Test Your Comprehension   AACSB: Reflective Thinking

1. What are the components of political systems? What are the components of legal systems? How do these systems lead to country risk?

2. Distinguish between totalitarianism, socialism, and democracy. What are the implications of each for internationalizing firms?

3. What are the specific characteristics of democracy? How do these characteristics facilitate international business?

4. What is the relationship between political freedom and economic freedom?

5. Describe the major types of legal systems. Which systems are most widely encountered?

6. Who are the major actors in political and legal systems? Which participant do you believe is most influential in international business?

7. Summarize how political and legal systems affect international business.

8. What are some proactive actions firms can take to minimize country risk while conducting cross-border business?

9. What are intellectual property rights? How do firms safeguard these rights?

Apply Your Understanding
AACSB: Reflective Thinking, Communication, Ethical Reasoning

1. For business enterprises to thrive, some minimum conditions must be present: recognition of private property rights and limited government intervention. To what extent may totalitarianism, socialism, and democracy interfere with the ideal commercial environment for firms?

2. Suppose you get a job at Aoki Corporation, a large firm that manufactures glass for industrial and consumer markets. Aoki is a large firm, but has little international experience. Senior managers are considering a plan to move Aoki's manufacturing to China, Mexico, or Eastern Europe, and to begin selling its glass in Latin America and Europe. However, they know little about the country risks that Aoki may encounter. How relevant are the following factors in contributing to potential country risk: foreign investment laws, controls on operating forms and practices, and laws regarding repatriation of income, environment, and contracts.

3. Royal Dutch Shell has been doing business in Nigeria since the 1920s, and has announced new plans to develop oil and gas projects there. However, over the years Shell has confronted a series of episodes involving country risk. Shell's operations are centered in Nigeria's Ogoni region, where the local citizens have protested Shell's drilling and refining activities, which are said to spoil the natural environment and reduce the amount of available farmland. Protestors also accuse Shell of extracting wealth from the region without adequately compensating local residents. Ogonis sabotaged Shell's operations to such an extent that the firm suspended parts of its Nigerian operations. Shell also came under pressure to divest its Nigerian operations and to pay reparations to the locals. Despite these problems, Shell has persisted in Nigeria. Management instituted various community development programs in the region, budgeted at $50 million per year. Describe the various types of country risk that Shell appears to face in Nigeria. What proactive steps can Shell take to anticipate future country risk? What should Shell do to deal more effectively with country risk? What steps can Shell take to be a better corporate citizen in Nigeria?

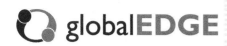
AACSB: Reflective Thinking, Communication, Use of Information Technology, Ethical Reasoning

Refer to Chapter 1, page 27, for instructions on how to access and use globalEDGE™.

1. Supranational organizations such as the World Bank (www.worldbank.org) and the World Trade Organization (www.wto.org) oversee much of the legal framework within which the world trading system operates. The political frameworks for specific industries or groupings of countries are strongly influenced by other organizations, such as the Organization of Petroleum Exporting Countries (www.opec.org) and the Organization for Economic Cooperation and Development (www.oecd.org). Using globalEDGE™ and the above online portals, address the following question: What is the goal of each organization and how does it go about achieving its goal? By viewing the news and press releases at each Web site, summarize the latest initiatives of each organization.

2. When companies venture abroad, managers need information on the nature of the legal and political environment in each country. This information is provided on various Web sources, as illustrated in the following exercises: (a) Suppose you want to sign up distributors in the European Union (EU) and want to learn about EU contract law. What would you do? Consult the globalEDGE portal to learn about trade and contract laws in Europe. Try the following: From the globalEDGE™ Resource Desk, click on Trade Law. Describe the resources there for learning about contract law in Europe. (b) The Central Intelligence Agency's portal provides up-to-date information about national governments and political environments. Go to www.cia.gov, click on "The World Factbook," and summarize the political environment in China, Colombia, France, and Russia.

3. Various organizations have devised international standards for ethical corporate behavior. These include the United Nations "Universal Declaration for Human Rights" (available at www.un.org), the OECD's "Guidelines for Multinational Enterprise" (www.oecd.org), the International Labor Organization's " Minimum Labor Standards" (www.ilo.org) and the U.S. Department of Commerce's "Model Business Principles" (www.commerce.gov). Visit these online portals and prepare a set of guidelines firms can follow in pursuing acceptable ethical standards in international business.

4. Freedom House is a nonprofit organization that monitors the state of freedom worldwide. It conducts an annual "Freedom in the World Survey," which you can view at www.freedom house.org/research. The survey compares the state of political rights and civil liberties in nearly 200 countries over time. Visit the site and answer the following questions: (a) What is the role of political rights and civil liberties in the Freedom House rankings? (b) What can governments in these countries do to facilitate more rapid social and political development? (c) What are the implications of the rankings for companies doing international business?

Performing a Preliminary Country Risk Analysis

Country risk refers to potentially adverse effects on company operations and performance caused by changes in a country's political and legal environments. Managers use country risk analysis to identify potential threats to the firm's trade and investment activities.

AACSB: Reflective Thinking, Analytic Skills

Managerial Challenge

Before venturing into any country, managers determine the likelihood and nature of country risk, and its probable effect on the operations and performance of the firm. Finding out about country risks is a task performed in MNEs and other firms with substantial international operations. As a future manager, you need to acquire market research skills that will help you understand country risk.

Background

Country risk arises primarily from government intervention. Governments may impose legal and regulatory burdens that increase business costs, delays, or lost opportunities. Governments may restrict access to important markets, impose complex bureaucratic procedures, or limit the amount of profits realizable from foreign operations. Country risk impacts management decision making regarding the strategies for entering foreign markets. By entering a market via exporting, the firm's level of market commitment and risk are relatively low, and management can rapidly withdraw or reduce its operations in the market in the event of substantial risk. By contrast, the level of risk is heightened for firms that internationalize via FDI, which results in establishing a production facility or a subsidiary in the target country.

Managerial Skills You Will Gain

In this C/K/R Management Skill Builder©, as a prospective manager, you will:

1. Learn the factors that determine country risk.
2. Learn the variables to consider when locating company operations abroad.
3. Develop market research skills for acquiring knowledge concerning country risk for planning company operations abroad.
4. Research the types of country risk that firms encounter.

Your Task

Assume you are an employee with a company that plans to build a factory abroad. Management is considering each of three countries as possible locations to build the factory. You must decide which location is best. Management prefers the country with the lowest risk. Your task is to conduct market research to investigate the degree of country risk in each of China, Mexico, and Poland. Then prepare a brief report that includes an estimate of the level of country risk in each of these countries by examining corruption, political rights, civil liberties, freedom status, and economic freedom.

Go to the C/K/R Knowledge Portal©

www.prenhall.com/cavusgil

Proceed to the C/K/R Knowledge Portal© to access the expanded background information, your task and methodology, suggested resources for this exercise, and the presentation template.

Government Intervention in International Business

> India's Path Away from Government Intervention and Bureaucracy

India is a study in contrasts. On the one hand, it is the world's leading emerging economy in IT and e-business. On the other hand, it is awash in trade barriers and business regulations. Not only does the Indian federal government impose countless regulations, standards, and administrative hurdles on businesses, each of India's 28 states imposes its own local bureaucracy and red tape. Import taxes and controls on foreign investment are substantial, with import tariffs averaging 12 percent on nonagricultural products, as compared to less than roughly 4 percent in Europe, Japan, and the United States. Hundreds of commodities, from cement to household appliances, can be imported only after receiving government approval. Licensing fees, testing procedures, and other hurdles can cost an importer thousands of dollars.

In the past, foreign firms have filed thousands of investment proposals worth hundreds of billions of dollars with the Indian government. However, bureaucratic hurdles prevented all but a fraction of these proposals from being approved. Foreign firms encountered hurdles at every turn in areas such as getting power and water connections, land use and environmental approvals, and paperwork required to demonstrate regulatory compliance. To compound matters, most regions in India

suffer from poor infrastructure—inadequate roads, bridges, airports, and telecommunications.

In 1991, to correct this situation, India began to liberalize its trading regulations and the structure of its economy. The government abolished import licenses and reduced tariffs substantially. The government also implemented numerous reforms to free the economy from state control, selling off state enterprises to the private sector and foreign investors.

Loosening bureaucracy and falling trade barriers may be paying off. The economy of the world's second-most-populous nation is expanding rapidly, averaging more than seven percent annual economic growth in the decade through 2006. Nevertheless, such transformations have not occurred without problems. In 2001, strikers opposing the Indian government's sale of an aluminum company threatened to go on a hunger strike.

India's economic revolution is helping to unleash the country's entrepreneurial potential. The Indian government is establishing Special Economic Zones (SEZs), virtual foreign territories that offer foreign firms the benefits of India's low-cost, high-skilled labor. In a typical SEZ, firms are exempt from trade barriers, sales and income taxes, licensing requirements, FDI restrictions, and customs clearance procedures. The Mahindra City SEZ, an 840-acre development, is focusing on a $277 million software development complex constructed by Infosys Technologies, India's leading IT firm.

Meanwhile, in Europe and the United States, the outsourcing of jobs to India has generated calls for protectionism—that is, trade barriers and defensive measures intended to minimize the export of jobs abroad. U.S. and European trade unions have created numerous Web sites that denounce outsourcing and offshoring. Trade barriers and government bureaucracy in India, as well as calls for protectionism in Europe and the United States, exemplify the complex world of government intervention.

Sources: Asiamoney. (2005). "India Plays Catch Up." (April): 1; Central Intelligence Agency. (2006). *World Factbook*, at *www.cia.gov/cia/publications/factbook*; *Economist* (2004). "Survey: A World of Opportunity." (November 13): 15; Evans, Bob. (2004). "Silos Of Protectionism: Raise Or Raze Them?" *InformationWeek* (March 15): 94. Irwin, Douglas. (2004). "Free-Trade Worriers" *Wall Street Journal* (August 9): A12; Solomon, Jay, and Joanna Slater. (2004). "India's Economy Gets a New Jolt from Mr. Shourie." *Wall Street Journal* (January 9): A1; United States Trade Representative. (2005). National Trade Estimate Report on Foreign Trade Barriers, at *www.ustr.gov*.

As we learned in Chapter 4, economists have long used trade theories to make the case for *free trade*, the unrestricted flow of products, services, and physical and intellectual capital across national borders. Classical trade theorists argue that countries should trade with each other in order to make optimal use of national resources and to increase living standards. FDI-based explanations reveal how firms obtain advantages by locating factories and subsidiaries in attractive locations abroad. In short, contemporary economic theory argues that international trade and investment are good for the world.

There is much empirical evidence in support of free trade. One study of over 100 countries in the 50-year period after 1945 found a strong association between market openness—that is, unimpeded free trade—and economic growth. Countries with an open economy enjoyed average annual per capita GDP growth of 4.49 percent, while relatively closed countries—those with largely unfree trade—grew at only 0.69 percent per year.[1] Other studies have confirmed that market liberalization and free trade are best for supporting economic growth and national living standards.[2]

In reality, however, there is no such thing as unimpeded free trade. Well before economists recognized the value of free trade, governments began intervening in business and the international marketplace in ways that obstruct the free flow of trade and investment. Intervention can take many forms. The government may impose tariffs and quotas, restrictions on international investment, bureaucratic procedures and red tape, and regulations that restrict types of business and value-chain activities. In addition, governments can provide subsidies and financial incentives intended to sustain domestic firms and industries.

Government Intervention in International Business

Governments intervene in trade and investment to achieve political, social, or economic objectives. Barriers are often created to benefit specific interest groups, such as domestic firms, industries, and labor unions. A key rationale is to create jobs by protecting industries from foreign competition. Governments may also intervene to support home-grown industries or firms. In various ways, government intervention alters the competitive position of companies and industries and the status of citizens. As highlighted in Exhibit 7.1, government intervention is an

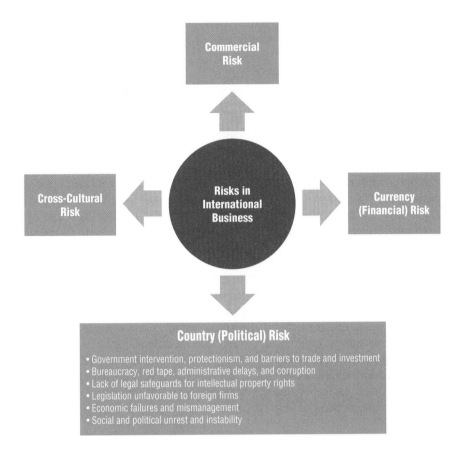

Exhibit 7.1

Government Intervention as a
Component of Country Risk

important dimension of *country risk,* which we introduced in Chapter 1 and revisited in Chapter 6.

Government intervention often results from protectionism. **Protectionism** refers to national economic policies designed to restrict free trade and protect domestic industries from foreign competition. Governments may restrain foreign investment in order to protect domestic business interests. Protectionism often leads to such specific types of intervention as tariffs, nontariff barriers such as quotas, and arbitrary administrative rules designed to discourage imports. A **tariff** (also known as a *duty*) is a tax imposed by a government on imported products, effectively increasing the cost of acquisition for the customer. A **nontariff trade barrier** is a government policy, regulation, or procedure that impedes trade through means other than explicit tariffs. Trade barriers are enforced as products pass through **customs**, the checkpoints at the ports of entry in each country where government officials inspect imported products and levy tariffs. An often-used form of nontariff trade barrier is a **quota**—a quantitative restriction placed on imports of a specific product over a specified period of time. Government intervention may also target FDI flows through *investment barriers* that restrict the operations of foreign firms.

Government intervention affects the normal operation of economic activity in a nation by hindering or helping the ability of its firms to compete internationally. Often, companies, labor unions, and other special interest groups convince governments to adopt policies that benefit them. For example, in the early 2000s, the Bush administration imposed tariffs on the import of foreign steel into the United States. This was done because competition from foreign steel manufacturers had bankrupted numerous U.S. steel firms, and the U.S. steel industry was ailing. The rationale was to give the U.S. steel industry time to restructure and revive itself. This action may have saved hundreds of jobs. On the downside, however, the barriers also increased the production cost of firms that use steel, such as Ford,

Protectionism National economic policies designed to restrict free trade and protect domestic industries from foreign competition.

Tariff A tax imposed on imported products, effectively increasing the cost of acquisition for the customer.

Nontariff trade barrier A government policy, regulation, or procedure that impedes trade through means other than explicit tariffs.

Customs Checkpoints at the ports of entry in each country where government officials inspect imported products and levy tariffs.

Quota A quantitative restriction placed on imports of a specific product over a specified period of time.

Whirlpool, and General Electric. Higher material cost made these firms less competitive and reduced prospects for selling their products in world markets.[3] The steel tariffs were removed within two years, but in the process of attempting to do good, the government also did harm.

Another example of intervention can be illustrated by the U.S. government's response to the growing threat of Japanese car imports in the 1980s, when it established "voluntary export restraints" on the number of Japanese vehicles that could be imported into the United States. This move helped insulate the U.S. auto industry for several years. In the protected environment, however, the Detroit automakers had less of an incentive to improve quality, design, and overall product appeal. Much like the athlete who performs best when faced with formidable opponents, companies also fight harder to succeed when confronted with stiff competition. Thus, government intervention motivated by protectionism has been one of several factors that, over time, weakened Detroit's ability to compete in the global auto industry.

Protectionist policies may also lead to price inflation. This results because, all else being equal, when tariffs restrict the supply of a particular product, the domestic price of the product has a tendency to rise. Tariffs may also reduce the choices available to buyers, by restricting the *variety* of imported products available for sale.

These examples illustrate that government intervention often leads to adverse *unintended consequences*—unfavorable outcomes of policies or laws. In a complex world, legislators and policymakers lack the ability to foresee all possible outcomes of an action, or the extent to which outcomes will occur. The problem of unintended consequences suggests that government intervention should be planned and implemented with great care.

 # Rationale for Government Intervention

Why does a government intervene in trade and investment activities? In the broadest terms, there are four main motives for government intervention. First, tariffs and other forms of intervention can generate a substantial amount of revenue. For example, Ghana and Sierra Leone generate more than 25 percent of total government revenue from tariffs. Second, intervention can ensure the safety, security, and welfare of citizens. For example, governments may pass laws to ensure a safe food supply and to prevent sale of products that threaten public safety. Third, intervention can help a government pursue broad-based economic, political, or social objectives. For example, a government may enact policies that aim to increase national employment or promote economic growth. Fourth, intervention can help better serve the interests of the nation's firms and industries. For example, a government may devise regulations to stimulate development of home-grown industries.

Special interest groups often serve as strong advocates for trade and investment barriers that protect their self-interests. Consider the recent trade dispute between Mexico and the United States over Mexican cement. The U.S. government imposed duties of roughly $50 per ton on the import of Mexican cement after U.S. cement makers lobbied the U.S. Congress. The stakes are huge, as Mexican imports can reach 10 percent of U.S. domestic cement consumption. The United States is one of the world's largest cement consumers and, ironically, often suffers from shortages, which are exacerbated by import restrictions. Mexico has proposed substituting import quotas in place of the high cement import tariffs. The Mexican and U.S. governments negotiated for years to resolve the dispute.[4]

Rationale for trade and investment barriers can be considered in two major categories: defensive and offensive. Governments impose *defensive* barriers to safeguard industries, workers, and special interest groups, and to promote national security. Governments impose *offensive* barriers to pursue a strategic or public policy objective, such as increasing employment or generating tax revenues.

Defensive Rationale

Four major defensive motives are particularly relevant: protection of the nation's economy, protection of an infant industry, national security, and national culture and identity. Let's address each of these motives in turn.

Protection of the national economy Proponents argue that firms in advanced economies cannot compete with those in developing countries that employ low-cost labor. In the opening vignette, labor activists have called for government intervention to prevent the outsourcing of jobs from Europe and the United States to India. Activists also call for trade barriers to curtail import of cheap products, fearing that advanced-economy manufacturers will be undersold, wages will fall, and home-country jobs will be lost. Therefore, the argument goes, governments should impose trade barriers to block imports. In response, critics counter that protectionism is at odds with the theory of comparative advantage, according to which nations should engage in *more* international trade, not less. Trade barriers interfere with country-specific specialization of labor. When countries specialize in the products that they can produce best and then trade for the rest, they perform better in the long run, delivering superior living standards to their citizens. Critics also charge that blocking imports reduces the availability and increases the cost of products sold in the home market. Industries cannot access all the input products they need. Finally, protection can trigger retaliation, whereby foreign governments impose their own trade barriers, reducing sales prospects for exporters.

Protection of an infant industry In an emerging industry, companies are often inexperienced and lack the latest technologies and know-how. They may also lack the scale typical of larger competitors in established industries abroad. Therefore, an infant industry may need temporary protection from foreign competitors. Accordingly, governments can impose temporary trade barriers on foreign imports, ensuring young firms gain a large share of the domestic market until they are strong enough to compete on their own. Protecting infant industries has allowed some countries to develop a modern industrial sector. For example, government intervention allowed Japan to become extremely competitive in automobiles early in the development of this industry. Similarly, it allowed South Korea to achieve great success in consumer electronics.

However, once in place, such protection may be hard to remove. Industry owners and workers tend to lobby to preserve government incentives indefinitely. Infant industries in many countries (especially in Latin America, South Asia, and Eastern Europe) have shown a tendency to remain dependent on government protection for prolonged periods. The industry may remain inefficient even after years of government support. Meanwhile, the nation's citizens end up paying higher taxes and higher prices for the products produced by the protected industry.[5]

National security Countries impose trade restrictions on products viewed as critical to national defense and security, such as military technology and computers. Trade barriers can help maintain domestic productive capacity in security-related products, such as computers, weaponry, and certain transportation equipment. For example, in 2005, Russia blocked a bid by German engineering giant Siemens to purchase the Russian turbine manufacturer OAO Power Machines, on grounds of national security. The Russian government has strict legislation that limits foreign investment in sectors considered vital to Russia's national interests.[6] In addition, countries impose **export controls**—government measures intended to manage or prevent the export of certain products or trade with certain countries. For instance, many countries do not allow the export of plutonium to North Korea because it can be used to make nuclear weapons.

National culture and identity Governments seek to protect certain occupations, industries, and public assets that are considered central to national

Export control A government measure intended to manage or prevent the export of certain products or trade with certain countries.

culture and identity. Consequently, government can prohibit or curtail imports of certain types of products or services. For example, Switzerland has imposed trade barriers to preserve its long-established tradition in watch-making. The Japanese restrict the import of rice because this product is central to the nation's diet and food culture. In the United States, authorities opposed Japanese investors' purchase of the Pebble Beach golf course in California, New York's Rockefeller Center, and the Seattle Mariners baseball team, because these assets are believed to be part of the national heritage. France does not allow significant foreign ownership of its TV stations because of concerns that foreign influences will taint French culture.

Offensive Rationale

Offensive rationale for government intervention fall into two categories: national strategic priorities and increasing employment.

National strategic priorities Government intervention sometimes aims to encourage the development of industries that bolster the nation's economy. It is a *proactive* variation of the infant industry rationale, and related to national industrial policy, highlighted in Chapter 4. Countries with many high-tech or high-value-adding industries—such as information technology, pharmaceuticals, car manufacturing, or financial services—create better jobs and higher tax revenues than economies based on low-value-adding industries—such as agriculture, textile manufacturing, or discount retailing. Accordingly, some governments—for example, Germany, Japan, Norway, and South Korea—devise policies that promote the development of relatively desirable industries. The government may provide financing for investment in high-tech or high-value-adding industries, encourage citizens to save money to ensure a steady supply of loanable funds for industrial investment, and fund public education to provide citizens the skills and flexibility that they need to perform in key industries.[7]

Nevertheless, such intervention is not without its challenges. It requires skillful, large-scale industrial planning and favoritism toward industries deemed critical. Deciding which industries to support is challenging because it is difficult to predict which industries will produce comparative advantages. If poor choices are made, the government may find itself continuously subsidizing industries that never reach a critical threshold of profitability and national advantage.

Increasing employment Governments often impose import barriers to protect employment in designated industries. By insulating domestic firms from foreign competition, national output is stimulated, leading to more jobs in the protected industries. The effect is usually strongest in import-intensive industries that employ much labor to produce products that are normally imported. For example, the Chinese government has traditionally required foreign companies to enter its huge markets through joint ventures with local Chinese firms. The policy creates jobs for Chinese workers. A joint venture between Shanghai Automotive Industry Corporation (SAIC) and Volkswagen created jobs in China. The SAIC later partnered with General Motors and is now producing top-selling cars in China.

This U.S. Customs Inspector uses a Vehicle Access Container Initiative System, right, a nonintrusive inspection tool, to examine a container at the Port of Los Angeles.

Instruments of Government Intervention

The main instruments of trade intervention and the classic forms of protectionism are tariffs and nontariff trade barriers. Individual countries or groups of countries, such as the European Union, can impose these barriers. In aggregate, barriers constitute a serious impediment to cross-border business. The United Nations estimates that trade barriers alone cost developing countries over $100 billion in lost trading opportunities with developed countries every year.[8] Exhibit 7.2 highlights the most common forms of government intervention and their effects.

Intervention Type	Definition	Practical Effect on Customers, Firms, or Government	Contemporary Examples
Tariff	Tax imposed on imported products	Increases cost to the importer, exporter, and usually the buyer of the product. Discourages imports of products. Generates government revenue.	Switzerland charges a tariff of 34% on agricultural product imports. Cote d'Ivoire charges a tariff on most finished products.
Quota	Quantitative restriction on imports of a product during a specified period of time	Benefits early importers, giving them monopoly power and the ability to charge higher prices. Harms late importers, who may be unable to obtain desired products. Usually results in higher prices to the buyer.	The United States imposes a quota of 120 million pairs on socks imported from China.
Local content requirements	Requirement that a manufacturer include a minimum percentage of added value that is derived from local sources	Discourages imports of raw materials, parts, components, and supplies, thereby reducing sourcing options available to manufacturers. May result in higher costs and lower product quality for importers and buyers.	The Nigerian government requires that products and services used by foreign firms in the oil industry in Nigeria must contain 50% Nigerian content.
Regulations and technical standards	Safety, health, or technical regulations; labeling requirements	May delay or block the entry of imported products, and reduce the quantity of available products, resulting in higher costs to importers and buyers.	Regulations in Honduras block imports of raw poultry from various countries. The Philippines restricts imports of certain chemicals, penicillin, and tires.
Administrative and bureaucratic procedures	Complex procedures or requirements imposed on importers or foreign investors that hinder their trade or investment activities	Slows the import of products or services. Hinders or delays firms' investment activities.	Bureaucratic delays in Costa Rica hinder or prevent the import of rice, onions, potatoes, and other agricultural products.

Exhibit 7.2 Types and Effects of Government Intervention (continues on next page)

SOURCE: Adapted from the Office of the United States Trade Representative, accessed at www.ustr.gov

Intervention Type	Definition	Practical Effect on Customers, Firms, or Government	Contemporary Examples
FDI and ownership restrictions	Rules that limit the ability of foreign firms to invest in certain industries or acquire local firms	Reduces the amount of money that a foreigner can invest in a country, and/or the proportion of ownership that a foreigner can hold in an existing or new firm in the country. May require a foreign firm to invest in the country in order to do business there.	Switzerland requires that foreign insurance firms seeking to establish a subsidiary or branch office there do so via FDI.
Subsidy	Financing or other resources that a government grants to a firm or group of firms, intended to ensure their survival or success	Increases the competitive advantage of the grantee while diminishing the competitive advantages of those that do not receive the subsidy.	Turkey grants an export subsidy of up to 20% for local producers of wheat and sugar.
Countervailing duty	Increased duties imposed on products imported into a country to offset subsidies given to producers or exporters in the exporting country	Reduces or eliminates the competitive advantage provided by subsidies.	Mexico imposes countervailing duties to offset competitive advantages enjoyed by foreign firms that receive subsidies from their governments.
Antidumping duty	Tax charged on an imported product that is priced below normal market prices or below cost	Reduces or eliminates the competitive advantage of imported products priced at abnormally low levels.	The United States has imposed antidumping duties on the import of low-cost steel in order to support U.S. based steel manufacturers.

Exhibit 7.2 Continued

Tariffs

Some countries impose *export tariffs*, taxes on products exported by their own companies. For instance, Russia charges a duty on oil exports, intended to generate government revenue and maintain higher stocks of oil within Russia. However, the most common type of tariff is the *import tariff*, a tax levied on imported products. The amount of a tariff is determined by examining a product's *harmonized code*. Products are classified under approximately 8,000 different codes in the *harmonized tariff* or *harmonized code* schedule, a standardized system used worldwide. The system is necessary because without it, firms and governments might have differing opinions on product definitions and the tariffs charged on imported products. Each is identified by a unique number that can be looked up from public sources such as the Internet.

Tariffs are usually *ad valorem*—that is, assessed as a percentage of the value of the imported product. Alternatively, the government may impose a *specific tariff*—a flat fee or fixed amount per unit of the imported product—based on weight, volume, or surface area (such as barrels of oil or square meters of fabric). A *revenue tariff* is intended to raise money for the government. A tariff on cigarette imports,

Exhibit 7.3

A Sampling of Import Tariffs

SOURCES: World Trade Organization statistics database accessed at stat.who.org; United States Trade Representative reports, accessed at www.ustr.org

	Average Import Tariff	
Country/Region	Agricultural Products	Nonagricultural Products
Australia	1.2	4.6
Canada	3.0	4.0
China	15.8	9.1
European Union	5.8	3.9
India	37.4	15.0
Japan	6.9	2.3
Mexico	24.5	17.1
United States	6.9	3.2

Note: Tariff rate expressed as percentage of the product's value (ad valorem).

for example, produces a steady flow of revenue. A *protective tariff* aims to protect domestic industries from foreign competition. A *prohibitive tariff* is one so high that no one can import any of the items.

Import tariffs can generate substantial revenue for national governments. This helps explain why tariffs tend to be fairly common in the developing economies. Even in advanced economies, tariffs provide a significant source of revenue for the government. The United States charges tariffs on many consumer, agricultural, and labor-intensive products. Interestingly, the United States often collects more tariff revenue on shoes than on cars ($1.63 billion versus $1.60 billion in 2001). The European Union applies tariffs of up to 236 percent on meat, 180 percent on cereals, and 17 percent on tennis shoes.[9]

Exhibit 7.3 provides a sample of import tariffs in selected countries. Under the terms of the North American Free Trade Agreement (NAFTA), Mexico gradually eliminated nearly all tariffs on product imports from the United States. However, Mexico maintains higher tariffs with the rest of the world, with rates of 24.5 percent for agricultural products and 17.1 percent for nonagricultural products. India's tariffs are relatively high, especially in the agricultural sector, where the rate is 37.4 percent. India's tariff system lacks transparency, and officially published tariff information is sometimes hard to find. China has reduced its tariffs significantly since joining the World Trade Organization (WTO) in 2001, but trade barriers remain high in many areas. China and India are characterized by low per capita income and high import tariffs. Ironically, as predicted by trade theory, high import tariffs tend to exacerbate national poverty.

Just as people want to avoid paying taxes, firms try to avoid paying tariffs. Because tariffs have their greatest affect on imports, firms may enter countries via nonexporting entry modes, such as FDI. In the long run, governments collect less revenue from firms if tariffs are too high. High tariffs have been known to trigger smuggling. For instance, high duties on cigarettes in Canada have led to smugglers transporting contraband tobacco across the Great Lakes of the northern United States into the Canadian frontier.

Because high tariffs inhibit free trade and economic growth, governments have tended to reduce tariffs over time. In fact, this was the primary goal of the General Agreement on Tariffs and Trade (GATT; now the WTO). Countries as diverse as Chile, Hungary, Turkey, and South Korea have liberalized their previously protected markets, lowering trade barriers and subjecting themselves to greater competition from abroad. Exhibit 7.4 illustrates trends in average world tariff rates over time. Notice that developing economies have been lowering their tariff rates since the 1980s. Continued reductions in tariffs represent a major driver of market globalization.

Exhibit 7.4

Trends over Time in Average Tariff Rates (Percentages)

Note: Rates shown are unweighted.

SOURCES: International Monetary Fund. "World Economic Outlook: Globalization and External Imbalances," April 2005 accessed at www.inf.org: United Nations Conference on Trade and Development. *UNCTAD Handbook of Statistics 2005.*

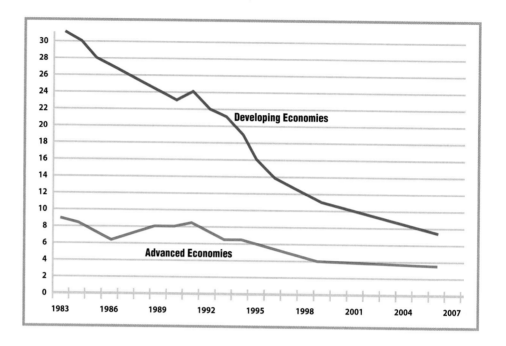

Nontariff Trade Barriers

Nontariff trade barriers are government policies or measures that restrict trade without imposing a direct tax or duty. These barriers include quotas, import licenses, local content requirements, government regulations, and administrative or bureaucratic procedures. Compared to tariffs, the use of nontariff barriers has grown substantially in recent decades. Governments sometimes prefer nontariff barriers because they are easier to conceal from the WTO and other organizations that monitor international trade. Let's now review the most common nontariff trade barriers.

Quotas restrict the physical volume or value of products that firms can import into a country. In a classic type of quota, the U.S. government imposes an upper limit of roughly two million pounds on the total amount of sugar that can be imported into the United States each year. Sugar imports that exceed this level face a tariff of several cents per pound. The upside is that U.S. sugar producers are protected from cheaper imports, giving them a competitive edge over foreign sugar producers. The downside is that U.S. consumers and producers of certain types of products—such as Hershey's and Coca-Cola—pay more for sugar. It also means that companies that manufacture products containing sugar can save money by moving production to countries that do not impose quotas or tariffs on sugar.

Governments can impose voluntary quotas, under which firms agree to limit exports of certain products. These are also known as *voluntary export restraints,* or *VERs.* For example, in 2005, import quotas in the European Union led to an impasse in which millions of Chinese-made garments piled up at ports and borders in Europe. The EU impounded the clothing because China had exceeded the voluntary import quotas it had negotiated with the EU. The action created hardship for European retailers, who had ordered their clothing stocks several months in advance. The voluntary quotas in both Europe and the United States were expected to expire in 2008.[10]

Governments occasionally require importing firms to obtain an **import license**, a formal permission to import, which restricts imports in a way that is similar to quotas. Do not confuse import licenses with the licensing strategy for entering foreign markets, in which a firm allows a foreign firms to use its intellec-

Import license Government authorization granted to a firm for importation of a product.

tual property in return for a fee. Governments sell import licenses to companies on a competitive basis or grant the licenses on a first-come, first-served basis. This process tends to discriminate against smaller firms, which typically lack the resources to purchase the licenses. Obtaining a license can be costly and very complicated. In some countries, importers must pay hefty fees to government authorities. In other countries, importers must deal with bureaucratic red tape. For instance, in Russia a complex web of licensing requirements limits imports of alcoholic beverages.

Local content requirements require manufacturers to include a minimum of local value added—that is, production that takes place locally. Local content requirements are usually imposed in countries that are members of an economic bloc, such as the European Union and NAFTA. The so called "rules of origin" requirement specifies that a certain proportion of products and supplies, or of intermediate goods used in local manufacturing, must be produced within the bloc. For a car manufacturer, the tires or windshields it purchases from another firm are intermediate goods. When the firm does not meet this requirement, the products become subject to trade barriers that member governments normally impose on nonmember countries. Thus, producers within the NAFTA zone of Canada, Mexico, and the United States pay no tariffs, as compared to countries such as China or the United Kingdom, which are not part of NAFTA. Roughly two-thirds of the value of a car manufactured within NAFTA must originate within the NAFTA member countries. If this condition is not met, the product becomes subject to the tariffs charged to non-NAFTA countries.

Government regulations and technical standards are another type of nontariff trade barrier. Examples include safety regulations for motor vehicles and electrical equipment, health regulations for hygienic food preparation, labeling requirements that indicate a product's country of origin, technical standards for computers, and bureaucratic procedures for customs clearance, including excessive red tape and slow approval processes.

In most cases, regulations and standards are legitimate efforts to protect citizens. However, occasionally governments seek to protect domestic firms by imposing red tape that creates hardships for foreign firms. For example, the European Union strictly regulates food that has been genetically modified (GM), a policy that has led to trade disagreements with the United States, whose GM food regulations are relatively lax. The United States claims that Europe's regulations violate WTO rules. GM foods such as soybeans, maize, and canola oil have been modified to make them more resistant to disease and insect pests, or to increase growth yields. Europe's strict GM food regulations are based on consumer apprehension about food safety and public distrust of government oversight of the food industry. In China, the government requires foreign firms to obtain special permits to import GM foods. China, Japan, and Taiwan require that imported agricultural products undergo strict testing, a process that may require considerable time and expense.

Some years ago, Japan prohibited the import of snow skis on the improbable grounds that Japanese snow is different from snow in other countries. Although Canada is officially bilingual (English and French), the provincial government of Quebec requires that all product labeling be in the French language. The law can be a substantial barrier to smaller firms that lack the resources to translate their labeling. Even the requirement that products clearly indicate their country of origin (for example, "Made in Costa Rica ") may constitute a barrier because people often prefer to buy domestically made products.

Governments may impose *administrative or bureaucratic procedures* that hinder the activities of importers or foreign firms. For instance, the opening vignette revealed how India's business sector is burdened by countless regulations, standards, and administrative hurdles at the state and federal levels. In Mexico, the government-imposed bureaucratic procedures led United Parcel Service to temporarily suspend its ground delivery service across the U.S.-Mexican border. Similarly, the United States barred Mexican trucks from entering the United States on the grounds that they were unsafe. Some years ago the French government restricted the import of Japanese video recording equipment by requiring that it be cleared through a single customs office in Poitiers, a town in the middle of France. This caused enormous delays and substantial additional cost to importers.

Saudi Arabia is home to various restrictive practices that hinder international commerce. For instance, every foreign business traveler to the Arab kingdom must hold an entry visa that can be obtained only by securing the support of a sponsor—a Saudi citizen who vouches for the visitor's actions. Because few Saudis are willing to assume such responsibility, foreign businesspeople who want to do business in Saudi Arabia face great difficulty.[11]

Convoluted administrative procedures are widespread in national customs agencies. The revenue generated by tariffs depends on how customs authorities classify imported products. Products often appear to fit two or more tariff categories. For example, a sport utility vehicle could be classified as a truck, a car, or a van. Each of these categories might entail a different tariff. Depending on the judgment of the customs agent, the applicable tariff might end up being high or low. Some agents try to classify products in categories that result in higher tariff revenues. Because thousands of categories exist for customs classification, a product and its corresponding tariff can be easily misclassified, either by accident or intention.

Investment Barriers

Currency control Restrictions on the outflow of hard currency from a country, or the inflow of foreign currencies.

As we saw in the opening vignette on India, countries also impose *FDI and ownership restrictions* that restrict the ability of foreign firms to invest in some industry sectors or acquire local firms. Excessive restrictions in India prevented the approval of countless investment proposals that would have resulted in billions of dollars in revenue to the local economy and government. Around the world, FDI and ownership restrictions are particularly common in industries such as broadcasting, utilities, air transportation, military technology, and financial services, as well as industries that involve major national holdings, such as oil, fisheries, and key minerals. For example, the Canadian government restricts foreign ownership of local movie studios and TV shows to protect its indigenous film and TV industry from excessive foreign influence. The Mexican government restricts FDI by

State-owned oil company PEMEX (Petroleos de Mexico) benefits from Mexico's investment barriers.

foreign investors to protect its oil industry, which is deemed critical to the nation's security. FDI and ownership restrictions are particularly burdensome in the services sector because services usually cannot be exported and providers must establish a physical presence in target markets to conduct business there. Occasionally, governments impose investment barriers aimed at protecting home-country industries and jobs.

Currency controls restrict the outflow of hard currencies (such as the U.S. dollar, the euro, and the yen), and occasionally the inflow of foreign currencies. The controls are used to conserve valuable hard currency or reduce the risk of capital flight. They are particularly common in developing countries. Some countries employ a system of dual official exchange rates in which the rate offered to exporters is relatively favorable, to encourage exports, while the rate offered to importers is relatively unfavorable, to discourage imports. Such controls both help and harm firms that establish foreign subsidiaries through FDI. The controls favor companies when they export their products from the host country, but harm companies that rely heavily on imported parts and components. Currency controls also restrict the ability of MNEs to *repatriate* their profits—that is, transfer revenues from profitable operations back to the home country.

As an example, Bangko Sentral Pilipinas (BSP), the central bank of the Philippines, required foreign portfolio investors to deposit their pesos (the Philippine currency) in local banks for a minimum of 90 days. The policy helped monetary authorities monitor the inflow and outflow of foreign investments and helped ensure that foreign funds would not be used for currency speculation that could harm the Philippine economy.

Subsidies and Other Government Support Programs

Subsidies are monetary or other resources a government grants to a firm or group of firms, usually intended either to ensure their survival by facilitating the production and marketing of products at reduced prices or to encourage exports. Subsidies come in the form of outright cash disbursements, material inputs, services, tax breaks, the construction of infrastructure, and government contracts at inflated prices. For example, the French government has provided large subsidies to Air France, the national airline. The *Closing Case* focuses on European government support of Airbus S.A.S., the leading European manufacturer of commercial aircraft. Perhaps the ultimate example of subsidized firms is in China. Several leading corporations, such as China Minmetals ($12 billion annual sales) and Shanghai Automotive ($12 billion annual sales), are in fact state enterprises wholly or partly owned by the Chinese government, which provides these firms with huge financial resources.[12]

Critics argue that subsidies reduce the cost of business for the recipient, providing it with unfair advantages. The WTO prohibits subsidies when it can be proven that they hinder free trade. However, subsidies are hard to define. For example, when a government provides the needed land, infrastructure, telecommunications systems, or utilities on behalf of firms in a corporate park, this is technically a subsidy. Yet most would agree that providing this type of support is an appropriate public function.

In Europe and the United States, governments provide agricultural subsidies to supplement the income of farmers and help manage the supply of agricultural commodities. The U.S. government grants subsidies for over two dozen commodities, including wheat, barley, cotton, milk, rice, peanuts, sugar, tobacco, and soybeans. In Europe, the Common Agricultural Policy (CAP) is a system of subsidies that represents about 40 percent of the European Union's budget, amounting to tens of billions of euros annually. The CAP and U.S. subsidies have been criticized for promoting unfair competition and high prices. The CAP and other subsidies tend to prevent developing countries from exporting their agricultural goods to the west. Subsidies encourage overproduction, and therefore lower food prices, which makes agricultural imports from developing countries less competitive.

Governments sometimes retaliate against subsidies by imposing **countervailing duties**—a duty imposed on products imported into a country to offset subsidies given to producers or exporters in the exporting country. In this way, the duty serves to cancel out the effect of the subsidy by converting it into a direct income transfer by the exporting country to the rest of the world.

Subsidies may allow a manufacturer to charge a lower price for exported products, sometimes lower than it charges its domestic or third-country customers or below manufacturing cost.[13] The practice is known as **dumping**—pricing exported products at less than their normal value, generally for less

Subsidy Monetary or other resources a government grants to a firm or group of firms, usually intended to ensure their survival by facilitating the production and marketing of products at reduced prices or to encourage exports.

Countervailing duty A duty imposed on products imported into a country to offset subsidies given to producers or exporters in the exporting country.

Dumping Pricing exported products at less than their normal value, generally for less than their price in the domestic or third-country markets, or at less than production cost.

Agencies such as Canada's Foreign Affairs and International Trade work to facilitate international activities.

Antidumping duty A tax imposed on products deemed to be dumped and causing injury to producers of competing products in the importing country.

Investment incentive Transfer payment or tax concession made directly to foreign firms to entice them to invest in the country.

than their price in the domestic or third-country markets, or at less than production cost. For example, the European Union gives a subsidy of nearly two billion euros per year to EU sugar producers, which has allowed Europe to become one of the world's largest sugar exporters. Ironically, without the subsidy Europe would be the world's biggest sugar importer. The subsidy allows EU farmers to dump massive amounts of sugar at artificially low prices onto world markets.

Dumping is against WTO rules because it amounts to unfair competition. A large MNE that charges very low prices could conceivably drive competitors out of a foreign market, thereby achieving a monopoly, and then raise its prices. Governments in the importing country often respond to dumping by imposing an **antidumping duty**—a tax imposed on products deemed to be dumped and causing injury to producers of competing products in the importing country. The WTO allows governments to impose antidumping duties on products that are deemed to be dumped and causing injury to producers of competing products in the importing country.[14] The duties are generally equal to the difference between the product's export price and their normal value. Nevertheless, dumping is hard to prove because firms usually do not reveal data on their cost structure or pricing strategies.

Government subsidies are not always direct or overt. For example, governments may support home country businesses by funding R&D initiatives, giving tax exemptions, and offering business development services, such as market information, trade missions, and privileged access to key foreign contacts. Indeed, most countries have agencies and ministries that provide such services to facilitate the international activities of their own firms. Examples include the Department of Foreign Affairs and International Trade in Canada (www.dfait-maeci.gc.ca), U.K. Trade & Investment in Britain (www.uktradeinvest.gov.uk), and the International Trade Administration of the U. S. Department of Commerce (www.doc.gov).

Related to subsidies are governmental **investment incentives**, transfer payments or tax concessions made directly to individual foreign firms to entice them to invest in the country. For example, the Hong Kong government put up most of the cash to build the Hong Kong Disney park. While the theme park and associated facilities cost about $1.81 billion, the Hong Kong government provided an investment of $1.74 billion to Walt Disney to develop the site.

In 2006, Austin, Texas and Albany, New York competed for the chance to have the Korean manufacturer Samsung Electronics build a semiconductor plant in their regions. Austin offered $225 million worth of tax relief and other concessions in its successful bid to attract Samsung's $300 million plant, estimated to create nearly 1,000 new jobs locally.

These incentives often help the economic development in a particular region or community. In the 1990s, Germany encouraged foreign companies to invest in the economically disadvantaged East German states by providing tax and investment incentives. Also in the 1990s, Ireland achieved an economic renaissance through proactive promotion by its Industrial Development Authority of Ireland as a place to do business. The group targeted foreign companies in the high-tech sector—including medical instruments, pharmaceuticals, and computer software. The Irish government offered foreign firms preferential corporate tax rates of 12 percent. These targeted efforts paid handsome dividends in terms of diversifying the Irish economy away from agricultural activities and creating substantial new employment.

Government procurement policies constitute an indirect form of nontariff trade barrier. In most countries, government purchases account for a substantial portion of GDP. Governments support domestic industries by adopting procurement policies that restrict purchases to home-country suppliers. For example, several governments require that air travel purchased with government funds be with home-country carriers. Government procurement policies are especially common in countries with large public sectors, such as China, Russia, and various Middle Eastern countries. In the United States, government agencies favor domestic suppliers unless their prices are high compared to foreign suppliers. In Japan, government agencies often do not even consider foreign bids, regardless of pricing. Public procurement agencies may impose requirements that effectively exclude foreign suppliers.

Government Intervention, Economic Freedom, and Ethical Concerns

One way of evaluating the effects of government intervention is to examine each nation's level of *economic freedom*, which is defined as the "absence of government coercion or constraint on the production, distribution, or consumption of goods and services beyond the extent necessary for citizens to protect and maintain liberty itself. In other words, people are free to work, produce, consume, and invest in the ways they feel are most productive."[15] An *Index of Economic Freedom* is published annually by the Heritage Foundation (www.heritage.org) that measures economic freedom in 161 countries.

Exhibit 7.5 shows the degree of economic freedom for each country in the Index for 2007. For each country, the Index assesses criteria such as the level of trade barriers, rule of law, level of business regulation, and protection of intellectual property rights.[16] The Index classifies virtually all the advanced economies as "free," all of the emerging markets as either "free" or "mostly free," and virtually all of the developing economies as "mostly unfree" or "repressed." The study underscores the close relationship between limited government intervention and economic freedom. Economic freedom flourishes when government supports the institutions necessary for that freedom and provides an appropriate level of intervention. Clearly, excessive regulation of business activity is detrimental to economic growth.

Government intervention and trade barriers also raise ethical concerns that affect developing economies. For example, in the United States, import tariffs on clothing and shoes often range as high as 48 percent. The resulting revenue to the U.S. government, in the billions of dollars per year, imposes a burden on clothing and shoe exporters, which tend to be concentrated in poor countries. For example, in 2001, on imports of $2.5 billion from Bangladesh (a major clothing exporter), the United States collected duties of more than $310 million. In fact, poor countries like Bangladesh—which are beginning to move from subsistence sectors such as agriculture into higher wealth-producing activities such as light manufacturing—face high tariffs, often four or five times those faced by the richest countries.[17]

Government intervention can also be used to offset harmful effects. For example, governments can use trade barriers to create or protect jobs that increase living standards for low-income groups. Governments provide subsidies that help counterbalance harmful consequences that disproportionately affect the poor. In Denmark, for example, globalization has affected thousands of workers whose jobs have been shifted to other countries with lower labor costs. The Danish government provides generous subsidies to the unemployed, aimed at retraining workers to upgrade their job skills or find work in other fields.[18]

Exhibit 7.5

Countries Ranked by Level of Economic Freedom

Source: The Heritage Foundation, accessed at www.heritage.org

Level of economic freedom

- 80-100% free
- 70-79.9% free
- 60-69.9% free
- 50-59.9% free
- 0-49.9% free
- Not ranked

Evolution of Government Intervention

At the beginning of the twentieth century, world trade was characterized by formidable trade barriers. The trading environment worsened through two world wars and the Great Depression. The United States passed the Smoot-Hawley Tariff Act in 1938, which raised U.S. tariffs to near-record heights of more than 50 percent, compared to only about three percent today. Tariffs that other countries imposed in retaliation for Smoot-Hawley choked off foreign markets for U.S. agricultural products, leading to plummeting farm prices and countless bank failures.[19] In an effort to revive trade, the U.S. government began to reduce restrictive tariffs.[20] Progressive international trade policies led to substantial tariff reductions worldwide by the late 1940s.

In 1947, 23 nations signed the General Agreements on Tariffs and Trade (GATT), the first major effort to systematically reduce trade barriers worldwide. The GATT created: (1) a process to reduce tariffs through continuous negotiations among member nations, (2) an agency to serve as a watchdog over world trade, and (3) a forum for resolving trade disputes. The GATT introduced the concept of *most favored nation* (renamed *normal trade relations* in 1998), according to which each signatory nation agreed to extend the tariff reductions covered in a trade agreement with a trading partner to all other countries. Thus, a concession to one country became a concession to all. Eventually, the GATT was superseded by the WTO in 1995 and grew to include about 150 member nations. The organization proved extremely effective and resulted in the greatest global decline in trade barriers in history. The *Global Trend* feature highlights what is perhaps the most important contemporary development in international trade, the founding and progress of the WTO.

In the 1950s, Latin America and other developing nations adopted protectionist policies aimed at industrialization and economic development. Governments imposed high tariffs and quotas on imports from the developed world, established government-supported enterprises to make the products they formerly imported, and sought to substitute local production for imports. Known as *import substitution*, the plan did not succeed. Quasi-public-private enterprises lived behind high quotas and tariffs and enjoyed big government subsidies. However, these enterprises never became competitive in world markets or raised living standards to the levels of free-trading countries. Meanwhile, the protected industries required ongoing subsidies.[21] Most countries that experimented with import substitution eventually rejected it.

By contrast, from the 1970s onward, Singapore, Hong Kong, Taiwan, and South Korea achieved rapid economic growth by encouraging the development of export-intensive industries. Their model, known as *export-led development*, proved much more successful than import substitution. These countries, along with others in East Asia, such as Malaysia, Thailand, and Indonesia, gained substantial prosperity and strong international trading links. Standards of living improved substantially, and a rising middle class helped transform these countries into competitive economies.

Elsewhere in Asia, Japan had already launched an ambitious program of industrialization and export-led development following World War II. The country's rise from poverty in the 1940s to become one of the world's wealthiest countries by the 1980s has been called the *Japanese miracle*. The feat was partly achieved with national strategic policies, including tariffs that fostered and protected Japan's infant industries—such as automobiles, shipbuilding, and consumer electronics.

Bangladesh is a major clothing exporter that faces high tariffs. Here, women work at Dhaka, a shirt exporter.

The World Trade Organization and International Services: The Doha Round

Based in Geneva, Switzerland, the World Trade Organization is the main watchdog for world trade, and counts some 150 countries as its members.

The WTO's goals include working to ensure that world trade operates smoothly, fairly, and with as few restrictions as possible. For example, since joining the WTO in 2001, China has gradually reduced import tariffs and quotas. The WTO is working to reduce trade barriers in the agricultural sector. However, more work needs to be done. For example, import tariffs exceed 100 percent on butter in Canada, fresh vegetables in the EU, and powdered milk in the United States.

The Doha Development Agenda, a WTO round of negotiations launched in Qatar in November 2001, aims for further reductions in world agricultural trade barriers, because they are particularly burdensome to developing countries, which comprise over three-quarters of WTO members. For instance, WTO negotiations led Japan to eliminate import barriers on beef, fruit juice, and apples.

The latest frontier in the WTO's battle against trade barriers is in international services. Because services are largely intangible, it is hard for governments to impose tariffs on them. Services do not pass through ports or customs stations. The "product" that a lawyer or an accountant offers is intangible—knowledge and expertise. Thus, services have become subject to an array of nontariff trade barriers. In transportation, for example, many countries require their own merchandise fleets to carry a certain proportion of their internationally traded cargo. Such laws favor home-country firms, but are a barrier to foreign-based cargo handlers. In banking, trade barriers often discriminate against foreign banks. The insurance industry in many developing economies is owned by the national government. Several European countries refuse to license foreign insurance companies.

Governments also restrict international business in services by setting technical and professional standards that may be difficult for foreign firms and individuals to meet. By requiring licenses and developing educational systems, governments ensure that professions such as law, medicine, and accounting are undertaken largely by people who are educated locally, speak the national language, and are socialized according to local standards and norms. The licensing and professional standards of one country are usually not recognized beyond its national borders. Lawyers, doctors, accountants, and numerous other professionals therefore face restrictions when they attempt to do business abroad.

Negotiations under the Doha Agenda have contributed to reducing trade and investment barriers in services. Under WTO rules, banks, insurance firms, tour operators, hotel chains, and transport companies increasingly enjoy the same trade and investment freedoms that originally applied only to products. A recent agreement significantly lowered international barriers within the telecommunications industry. Other multilateral agreements have covered computer software and financial services. The General Agreement on Trade in Services (GATS) provides new rules for trade and investment in intellectual property, covering copyrights, patents, and trademarks. Key issues the WTO-member countries are negotiating include harmonization of professional standards, acceptable levels of accreditation between member countries, movement of labor in relation to provision of services, licensing, and certification of service suppliers.

Much work remains to be done. In 2006, the trade negotiations under the Doha Development Round were suspended, primarily due to the reluctance of the United States, Japan, and the European countries to reduce farm subsidies and lower import tariffs. However, trade ministers resumed negotiations in 2007.

Sources: United States Trade Representative. (2004). "National Trade Estimate Report," available at www.ustr.gov; U.S. and Foreign Commercial Service and U.S. Department of State. (2007). *Doing Business in Japan: A Country Commercial Guide for U.S. Companies.* Washington, DC: Government Printing Office World Trade Organization. (2007). Accessed at www.wto.org

Since gaining independence from Britain in 1947, India adopted a quasi-socialist model of isolationism and strict government control. High trade and investment barriers, state intervention in labor and financial markets, a large public sector, heavy regulation of business, and central planning all contributed to the nation's poor economic performance over several decades. Beginning in the early 1990s, India began to open its markets to foreign trade and investment. Free-trade reforms, combined with privatization of state enterprises, have progressed slowly. Protectionism has declined, but high tariffs (averaging 20 percent) and FDI limitations are still in place.

Another pivotal country, China, relied on centralized economic planning since Mao Tse-Tung established a communist regime with the 1949 revolution. Agriculture and manufacturing were long controlled by inefficient state-run industries. A focus on national self-sufficiency ensured that China remained closed to international trade until the 1980s, when the nation began to liberalize its economy. In 1992, China joined the Asia-Pacific Economic Cooperation (APEC) group, a free-trade organization similar to the European Union. In 2001, China joined the WTO and committed to reducing trade barriers and increasing intellectual property protection. Trade has stimulated the Chinese economy. By 2004, China's GDP was four times the level it was in 1978, and foreign trade exceeded $1 trillion. The country has become a leading exporter of manufactured products.

How Firms Should Respond to Government Intervention

Although a manager's first inclination might be to avoid markets with high trade and investment barriers or excessive government intervention, this is not usually practical. Depending on the industry and country, firms generally must cope with protectionism and other forms of intervention. For example, in extractive industries such as aluminum and petroleum, foreign firms often enter nations that have formidable barriers. The food-processing, biotechnology, and pharmaceutical industries encounter countless laws and regulations abroad.

Strategies for Managers

Firms that want to do business in emerging markets such as China and India face seemingly endless government intervention. Developing economies in Africa, Latin America, and elsewhere feature numerous trade barriers and government involvement in business. Many firms target emerging markets and developing economies that hold long-term potential despite the challenges that they pose. Managers are not without choices, however. The following strategies are prudent.[22]

Research to gather knowledge and intelligence. Experienced managers continually scan the business environment to identify the nature of government intervention and to plan market-entry strategies, host-country operations, and government support opportunities, accordingly. Trade barriers can be costly and increase the risk of cross-border business. Managers should review their return-on-investment criteria to account for increased cost and risk. Managers should also evaluate alternative foreign market entry strategies in light of both existing and potential risks. For example, while trade barriers are low in the European Union, conditions are evolving as the member states consider a range of legislative initiatives that affect trade and investment within the single market. The European Parliament, the European Commission, and other EU bodies are devising new guidelines that affect company operations in areas ranging from product liability laws to standards for investment in European industries.

Choose the most appropriate entry strategies Tariffs and most nontariff trade barriers apply to exporting, whereas investment barriers apply to FDI. Most firms choose exporting as their initial entry strategy. However, if high tariffs are present, managers should consider other strategies, such as FDI, licensing, and joint ventures that allow the firm to produce directly in the target market, thereby avoiding import barriers. For instance, the Fuji Company built a factory in South Carolina to manufacture film for cameras. Previously, Fuji had exported film to the United States from its factories in Europe and Japan. By establishing a production base in the United States, Fuji was able to avoid U.S. tariffs and deflect claims that it was unfairly dumping Japanese-made film there.

However, even investment-based entry is affected by tariffs if it requires importing raw materials and parts to manufacture finished products in the host country. Tariffs often vary with the *form* of an imported product. For example, U.S. food processor Conagra imports cooked tuna into the United States, which it then separates and converts into canned tuna, under the Bumble Bee brand. Conagra could have the tuna canned abroad, but the tariff on canned tuna is higher than the tariff on cooked tuna. Thus, Conagra cans the tuna in the United States as a strategy to minimize paying import tariffs.[23] In the case of manufactured products, companies can ship products "knocked-down" and then assemble them in the target market. For example, in countries with relatively high tariffs on imported personal computers, importers often bring in computer parts and then assemble the computers locally.

Take advantage of foreign trade zones In an effort to create jobs and stimulate local economic development, governments establish foreign trade zones (FTZs; also known as *free trade zones* or *free ports*). A **foreign trade zone** is an area within a country that receives imported goods for assembly or other processing, and subsequent re-export. Thus, exported products receive preferential tariff treatment.[24] Products brought into an FTZ are not subject to duties, taxes, or quotas until they, or the products made from them, enter into the non-FTZ commercial territory of the country where the FTZ is located. Firms use FTZs to assemble foreign dutiable materials and components into finished products, which are then re-exported. Alternatively, firms may use FTZs to manage inventory of parts, components, or finished products that the firm will eventually need at some other location. Some firms obtain FTZ status within their own physical facilities. In the United States, for example, Japanese carmakers store vehicles at the port of Jacksonville, Florida. The cars remain in the Jacksonville FTZ, without having to pay duties, until they are shipped to U.S. dealerships.

FTZs exist in more than 75 countries, usually near seaports or airports. They can be as small as a factory or as large as an entire country. There are several hundred FTZs in the United States alone, used by thousands of firms. The Colon Free Zone, an enormous FTZ, is located on the Atlantic side of the Panama Canal. Products may be imported, stored, modified, repacked, and re-exported without being subject to any tariffs or customs regulations in the FTZ. Many private companies and warehousing operations have set up shop inside the huge zone. Most of the zone's merchandise is transshipped from Panama to other parts of the Western Hemisphere and Europe.

A successful experiment with FTZs has been the **maquiladoras**—export-assembly plants in northern Mexico along the U.S. border that produce components and typically finished products destined for the United States. Maquiladoras began emerging in the 1960s to assemble such products as electronics, clothing, plastics, furniture, appliances, and vehicles. Today, several thousand export-assembly plants in northern Mexico employ millions of Mexican workers. Later brought into the NAFTA (North American Free Trade Agreement), the collaboration enables companies from the United States, Asia, and Europe to tap low-cost labor, favorable taxes and duties, and government incentives, while serving the U.S. market.

Seek favorable customs classifications for exported products. One approach for reducing exposure to trade barriers is to have exported products classified in the appropriate harmonized product code. As we noted earlier in this chapter,

Foreign trade zone (FTZ) An area within a country that receives imported goods for assembly or other processing, and re-export. For customs purposes the FTZ is treated as if it is outside the country's borders.

Maquiladoras Export-assembly plants in northern Mexico along the U.S. border that produce components and typically finished products destined for the United States.

many products can be classified within two or more categories, each of which may imply a different tariff. For example, some telecommunications equipment can be classified as electric machinery, electronics, or measuring equipment. The manufacturer should analyze the trade barriers on differing categories to ensure that exported products are classified properly—ideally under a lower tariff code.

Alternatively, the manufacturer might be able to modify the exported product in a way that helps minimize trade barriers. For example, South Korea faced a quota on the export of nonrubber footwear to the United States. By shifting manufacturing to rubber-soled shoes, Korean firms greatly increased their footwear exports. Another strategy is to upgrade the quality of exported products, a quality-instead-of-quantity approach. For example, because Japanese automakers faced export quotas in Britain and the United States, they changed their strategy to export higher-priced, higher-quality automobiles (such as Acura and Lexus) instead of lower-priced vehicles (such as Honda and Toyota). The approach allowed the Japanese to earn higher profit margins while exporting fewer cars.

Take advantage of investment incentives and other government support programs Obtaining economic development incentives from host- or home-country governments is another strategy for reducing the cost of trade and investment barriers. For example, Mercedes built a factory in Alabama in part to benefit from reduced taxes and direct subsidies provided by the Alabama state government. Siemens established a semiconductor plant in Portugal in part to obtain subsidies from the Portuguese government and the European Union. Incentives cover nearly 40 percent of Siemens' investment and training costs. Governments in Europe, Japan, and the United States increasingly provide incentives to companies that set up shop within their national borders. In addition to direct subsidies, incentives can include reduced utility rates, employee training programs, construction of new roads and communications infrastructure, and tax holidays.

Lobby for freer trade and investment More and more nations are liberalizing markets in order to create jobs and to increase tax revenues. The Doha round of WTO negotiations in the mid-2000s aimed to make trade fairer for developing countries. Tariffs in Australia, Canada, Europe, Japan, and the United States have declined considerably over time, reaching single digits for most products. Emerging markets such as Brazil, China, India, Mexico, and various Eastern European countries are liberalizing their trade and investment restrictions.

These trends have resulted partly from the efforts of firms to petition governments, at home and abroad. Firms can lobby foreign governments to lower trade and investment barriers. This might seem far-fetched, but the Japanese, for example, have achieved considerable success with such an approach in Europe and the United States. Japanese industry officials directly lobby U.S. and European governments. In China, domestic and foreign firms have lobbied the government for relaxation of protectionist policies and regulations that make China a difficult place to do business. To increase the effectiveness of their lobbying efforts, foreign firms often hire former Chinese government officials to help lobby their former colleagues.[25] European automakers such as BMW have obtained various concessions by lobbying individual state governments in the United States. For example, the 1,039-acre site of BMW's production facilities in South Carolina is leased to the firm at an annual rent of one dollar. The private sector lobbies federal authorities to undertake government-to-government trade negotiations, aimed at lowering barriers. Private firms bring complaints to world bodies, especially the WTO, to address potentially unfair trading practices of key international markets. At a broader level, managers should take a seat at the table of public-sector decision makers who conduct negotiations with foreign governments regarding their interventionist activities. Particularly in the longer term, such efforts hold the promise of supporting company performance abroad.

Airbus versus Boeing: When is Intervention Not Intervention?

For over 50 years, many European governments have pursued public policies based on democratic socialism. Under this system, the government plays a strong role in the national economy and provides key services such as health care, utilities, mass transit, and sometimes banking and housing. Many European countries support worker and consumer cooperatives, generous social welfare policies, and strong labor unions. In Germany, labor unions are large and powerful. Layoffs and worker dismissal are complex processes that can take firms up to seven months to complete. In France, the government regulates the private sector and labor markets, and has instituted a mandatory 35-hour workweek. Corporate tax rates in France and Germany are high compared to other industrial countries. Most Europeans are accustomed to government intervention and expect government to play a significant role in guiding the national economy.

Boeing versus Airbus: The Complex Global Commercial Aircraft Industry

In the 1960s, United States companies such as Boeing and McDonnell Douglas were the dominant players in global aircraft manufacturing. Boeing was founded in 1916, in Seattle, and had many years to develop the critical mass necessary to become the world's leading aerospace manufacturer. During World War II and the subsequent Cold War years, Boeing was the recipient of many lucrative contracts from the U.S. Department of Defense.

In Europe, no single country possessed the means to launch an aerospace company capable of challenging Boeing. Manufacturing commercial aircraft is an extremely capital-intensive and complex industry that necessitates a highly skilled work force. In 1970, the governments of France and Germany formed an alliance, supported with massive government subsidies, to create Airbus S.A.S. The governments of Spain and Britain joined Airbus later. By 1981, the four-country alliance succeeded in becoming the number-two civil aircraft maker in the world. Airbus launched the A300, among the best-selling commercial aircraft of all time. Airbus also created the A320, receiving more than 400 orders before its first flight and becoming the fastest-selling large passenger jet in aviation history. By 1992, Airbus had captured roughly one-third of the global market in commercial aircraft.

Airbus has benefited from tens of billions of dollars of subsidies and soft loans from the four founding country governments and the European Union (EU). Airbus has to repay the loans only if it achieves prof-

itability. By 2005, government aid had financed, in whole or part, every major Airbus aircraft model. European governments have forgiven Airbus' debt, provided huge equity infusions, dedicated infrastructure support, and financed R&D for civil aircraft projects.

Airbus is currently a stock-held company jointly owned by the British, Germans, French, and Spanish. It is based in Toulouse, France, but has R&D and production operations scattered throughout Europe. European governments justify their financial aid to Airbus on several grounds. First, Airbus R&D activities result in new technologies of considerable value to the EU. Second, Airbus provides jobs to some 53,000 skilled and semiskilled Europeans. Third, Airbus' value-chain activities attract massive amounts of capital into Europe. Finally, Airbus generates enormous tax revenues.

Complaints about Unfair Government Intervention

Boeing and the U.S. government long have complained about the massive subsidies and soft loans that were responsible not only for Airbus' birth, but also for its ongoing success. The outcry became louder in the early 2000s, when Airbus surpassed Boeing in annual sales terms to become the world's leading commercial aircraft company. Boeing has argued that Airbus never would have gotten this far without government support. In 1992, the EU and the United States signed the Agreement on Trade in Large Civil Aircraft, which restricted European governments to providing direct support for no more than one third of the total cost of developing new aircraft. This agreement requires Airbus to repay government loans within 17 years. In return, Boeing agreed that any indirect aid it received from the U.S. Department of Defense and other government sources would be capped at four percent of its annual revenues.

However, U.S. officials eventually cancelled the agreement and demanded an end to Airbus subsidies. A key reason for the tough stance was that Airbus had begun to outsell Boeing and had launched plans for the A380, a monster aircraft likely to grab market share in the large-scale, long-haul market.

In 2005, the U.S. Trade Representative brought its case to the World Trade Organization (WTO). It arose because EU member states approved $3.7 billion in new subsidies and soft loans to Airbus. The case alleged that financial aid for the A350, A380, and earlier aircraft qualified as subsidies under the WTO's Agreement on Subsidies and Countervailing Measures (ASCM) and that the subsidies were actionable because they caused adverse effects to international trade. Under the ASCM, subsidies to specific firms or industries from a government or other public bodies are prohibited. If a WTO member provides such support, it is subject to official sanction. Airbus confirmed that it had applied to the governments of Britain, France, Germany, and Spain for launch aid for its model A350. Officials of the European Commission countered that government subsidies are permissible and that it is up to individual EU countries to decide whether to provide them.

The EU argues that the United States long has indirectly subsidized Boeing through massive defense contracts that, after all, are paid with tax dollars. The United States has given Boeing approximately $23 billion dollars in indirect government subsidies by means of R&D funding and other indirect support from the Pentagon and from NASA, the nation's space agency. Boeing is at liberty to use the knowledge acquired from such projects to produce civilian aircraft. European officials also complained that the state of Washington, Boeing's manufacturing headquarters, has provided the firm with tax breaks, infrastructure support, and other investment incentives, amounting to billions of dollars.

The EU also has a strong case at the WTO regarding Boeing's relations with its Japanese business partners. The new Boeing 787 Deamliner is built in an alliance with the heavy-industry divisions of Japanese MNEs like Mitsubishi, Kawasaki, and Fuji. The EU argues that the Japanese government provided at least $1.5 billion in soft loans, repayable only if the aircraft is a commercial success, just like the soft loans given to Airbus. In a sense, Boeing has turned the tables on Airbus subsidies by going out and getting its own subsidies, this time from the Japanese. The U.S. government does not see contracts with the military as equivalent to direct government grants.

The New Airbus A380

An experimental version of the new Airbus A380 first flew in April, 2005 from Toulouse, France. The A380's upper deck extends along the entire length of the fuselage. Its cabin provides more than 50 percent more floor space than the next largest airliner, the Boeing 747-400. The A380 provides seating for up to 853 passengers in full economy class configuration or up to 555 people with three classes of seating. It has a maximum range of 15,000 kilometers (8,000 nautical miles).

The new A380 received some $3 billion in subsidies and soft loans from various European governments. In France, a government official stated that the French state has given its financial support to the A380 program. Reports suggest that the total cost of developing and launching the A380 has reached 15 billion euros ($19.5 billion). By late 2006, the Airbus A380 was in trouble. Production had become seriously delayed, partly due to the use of two incompatible versions of computer-aided design software (one in France and one in Germany), the high degree

of customization for each airline, and managerial failures. Parts are currently manufactured in 16 plants throughout Europe and shipped to Toulouse for final assembly. The delays are estimated to have cost Airbus more than 4.8 billion euros ($6.2 billion) in profit. Meanwhile, Boeing successfully launched its Boeing 787 Dreamliner in July 2007 and appears to be six years ahead of Airbus in bringing out an innovative and fuel-efficient aircraft. The U.S. officials, on the other hand, concluding that EU subsidies and soft loans to Airbus constitute unfair trade practices, were going ahead with their action at the WTO.

AACSB: **Reflective Thinking, Ethical Reasoning**

Case Questions

1. Where do you stand? Do you think EU subsidies and soft loans to Airbus are fair? Why or why not? What advantages does Airbus gain from free financial support from the EU governments? Are complaints about the EU's government intervention fair in light of Europe's long history of democratic socialism?

2. Under the WTO Subsidies Agreement, do you think U.S. military contracts with Boeing amount to subsidies? Have these types of payments provided Boeing with unfair advantages? Justify your answer.

3. What about the infrastructure development and investment incentives provided by the state of Washington to Boeing over the years? Are these fair? Do they give Boeing unfair competitive advantages?

4. Assuming that Airbus cannot compete without subsidies and loans, is it likely that the EU will discontinue its financial support of Airbus? What are the EU's vested interests in continuing to support Airbus?

5. In the event the WTO rules against Airbus and tells it to stop providing subsidies and soft loans, how should Airbus management respond? What new approaches can they pursue to maintain Airbus' lead in the global commercial aircraft industry? <

Sources: Airbus A380. (2007). Accessed at www.wikipedia.org.; Done, Kevin. (2005). "How Airbus Flew Past Its American Rival," *Financial Times*, March 17: 6; *Economist*. (2005). "Airbus versus Boeing: The Super-jumbo of All Gambles," (January 22): 55–56; *Economist*. (2005). "Boeing versus Airbus: See You in Court," (March 26): 62–63; Frost, Laurence. (2007). *Airbus Flight Shows Troubled A380*, Accessed February 8, 2007, at www.businessweek.com; Global Business. (2006). *Wayward Airbus*, October 23, 2006, at www.businessweek.com; Lunsford, J., and D. Michaels. (2006). "Bet on Huge Plane Trips Up Airbus," *Wall Street Journal*, (June 15): A1; Malveaux, Suzanne. (2005)."U.S. takes Airbus dispute to WTO," *CNN*, May 31, accessed at edition.cnn.com; Michaels, Daniel. (2005). "Airbus Will Fete Its Giant New Jet," *Wall Street Journal*, (January 18): A8; /; U.S. Commercial Service. (2005). *Doing Business in France*, at www.buyusa.gov/france/en/; U.S. Commercial Service. (2005). *Doing Business in Germany*, accessed at www.buyusa.gov/germany/en; U.S. Trade Representative. (2005). "United States Takes Next Step in Airbus WTO Litigation," accessed at www.ustr.gov; Vives, Xavier. (2007). "Airbus and the Damage Done by Economic Patriotism," *Financial Times*, (March 7): 17.

This case was written by Dr. Gary Knight, with the assistance of Stephanie Regales.

CHAPTER ESSENTIALS

Key Terms

Summary

In this chapter, you learned about:

1. Government intervention in international business

Despite the value of free trade, governments often intervene in international business. **Protectionism** refers to national economic policies designed to restrict free trade and protect domestic industries from foreign competition. Government intervention arises typically in the form of tariffs, nontariff trade barriers, and *investment barriers*. **Tariffs** are taxes on imported products, imposed mainly to collect government revenue and protect domestic industries from foreign competition. **Nontariff trade barriers** consist of policies that restrict trade without directly imposing a tax. An example of a nontariff trade barrier is a **quota**—a quantitative restriction on imports. Managers find out what tariffs apply to their products by consulting *harmonized code* schedules, available from government agencies.

2. Rationale for government intervention

Governments impose trade and investment barriers to achieve political, social, or economic objectives. Such barriers are either defensive or offensive. A key rationale is the protection of the nation's economy, its industries, and workers. **Export controls** limit trade in sensitive products deemed critical to national security. Governments also impose barriers to protect infant industries.

3. Instruments of government intervention

Governments also impose *regulations* and *technical standards*, as well as *administrative* and *bureaucratic procedures*. Countries may also impose **currency controls** to minimize international withdrawal of national currency. *FDI* and *ownership restrictions* ensure that the nation maintains partial or full ownership of firms within its national borders. Govern-

ments also provide **subsidies**, a form of payment or other material support. Foreign governments may offset foreign subsidies by imposing **countervailing duties**. With **dumping**, a firm charges abnormally low prices abroad. A government may respond to dumping by imposing an **antidumping duty**. Governments support home-grown firms by providing **investment incentives** and biased *government procurement policies*.

4. Government intervention, economic freedom, and ethical concerns

Economic freedom refers to the extent of government intervention in the national economy. It can be accessed using the Heritage Foundation's Index of Economic Freedom. Government intervention and trade barriers can raise ethical concerns that affect developing economies and low-income consumers. However, government intervention also can be used to offset such harmful effects.

5. Evolution of government intervention

Intervention has a long history. In the late 1800s, many countries imposed substantial protectionism. From the 1930s onward, countries reduced trade barriers worldwide. In Latin America, import substitution delayed eventual transition to free trade. Following World War II, Japan embarked on industrialization and export-led development. India pursued protectionist policies, and China had little foreign involvement until the 1980s. The most important development for reducing trade barriers of the last several decades was the General Agreement on Tariffs and Trade (GATT), which was replaced in 1995 by the World Trade Organization (WTO). The 150 members of the WTO account for nearly all world trade.

6. How firms should respond to government intervention

Firms should first undertake research to understand the extent and nature of trade and investment barriers abroad. When trade barriers are substantial, FDI or joint ventures to produce products in target countries are often the most appropriate entry strategies. Where importing is essential, the firm can take advantage of **foreign trade zones**, areas where imports receive preferential tariff treatment. Management should try to obtain a favorable export classification for the firm's exported products. Government assistance in the form of subsidies and incentives helps reduce the impact of protectionism. Firms sometimes lobby the home and foreign governments for freer trade and investment.

Test Your Comprehension AACSB: **Reflective Thinking**

1. Discuss the relationship between government intervention and protectionism.

2. What are the differences among the following: tariffs, nontariff trade barriers, investment barriers, and government subsidies?

3. What are the major types of nontariff trade barriers? Suggest business strategies for minimizing the effect of nontariff trade barriers.

4. Distinguish between countervailing duties and antidumping duties.

5. In what ways do government subsidies and procurement policies amount to protectionism?

6. What is the rationale for intervention? Why do governments engage in protectionism?

7. What was the nature of government intervention in the first half of the twentieth century? How did this change in the latter half of the twentieth century?

8. Describe various company strategies to manage government intervention.

9. What is the role of FDI, licensing, and joint ventures in reducing the impact of import tariffs?

Apply Your Understanding
AACSB: **Ethical Reasoning, Reflective Thinking, Communication**

1. The United States steel industry, once the world leader, now produces less steel than either China or Japan. American steel producers have come under threat from price-competitive suppliers in Brazil, Russia, and other emerging markets. The U.S. steel industry dealt with this threat by launching a lobbying campaign aimed at persuading the U.S. government to impose barriers on the import of foreign steel. The following are excerpts from advertisements used by the steel industry in this effort:

> During the past year, America lost more than 1.1 million manufacturing jobs . . . because domestic factories have shifted their operations to low-wage countries. Manufacturing assures our national defense, our global leadership, and the living standards of more than 17 million workers.
>
> (Other nations subsidize their domestic steel industries). Longer-term, subsidized imports will destroy a vital American industry and U.S. jobs.

> In an uncertain and dangerous world, does America really want to become dependent on Russia, Japan, China, Brazil and developing countries for something so basic as steel? (*Source:* Crafted with Pride in USA Council, accessed at www.craftedwithpride.org; *Wall Street Journal*, November 9, 2001: A15).

a. Evaluate this statement. How valid is the argument?
b. Should the U.S. government impose trade barriers on the import of steel from abroad?
c. What is the effect of barriers on U.S. steel producers?
d. What is the effect of barriers on companies that use large amounts of steel in the manufacture of finished products?
e. What is the effect of barriers on consumers of products that are made with U.S. steel?

2. AgriCorp is a large trading company that exports various agricultural commodities and processed foods to developing countries. Ms. Bonnie Walters is a confident but inexperienced manager, who is often frustrated that developing countries impose high tariff and nontariff trade barriers. These barriers raise AgriCorp's cost of doing business, making the firm's pricing less competitive in its target markets. How would you explain the rationale for government intervention to Ms. Walters? Why do governments, particularly in developing economies, intervene in trade and investment activities? What are the various defensive and offensive rationale?

3. TelComm Corporation is a manufacturer of components for the cell phone industry. TelComm's founder, Mr. Alex Bell, is interested in exporting the firm's products to China. He has heard that China has the world's largest population of cell phone users, and wants to enter the market. But TelComm has little international business experience. Mr. Bell is unaware of the various types of nontariff trade barriers that TelComm might face in China and other foreign markets. How would you summarize major nontariff trade barriers to Mr. Bell? What types of investment barriers might TelComm face in the event management decided to establish a factory in China to manufacture cell phone components? What can TelComm management do to minimize the threat of these nontariff trade and investment barriers?

AACSB: Reflective Thinking, Analytical Skills, Ethical Reasoning

Refer to Chapter 1, page 27, for instructions on how to access and use globalEDGE™.

1. Your firm is considering exporting to two countries: Kenya and Vietnam. However, management's knowledge about the trade policies of these countries is limited. Conduct a search at globalEDGE™ to identify the current import policies, tariffs and restrictions in these countries. Prepare a brief report on your findings. In addition to globalEDGE™, other useful sites include UNCTAD-Trains (once there, click on Country Notes) and the U.S. Commercial Service (http://www.buyusa.gov/).

2. The Office of the U.S. Trade Representative (USTR) is responsible for developing and coordinating the international trade and investment policies of the United States. Visit the USTR Web site from globalEDGE™ or directly (www.ustr.gov). Once in Document Library, search for "National Trade Estimate Report on Foreign Trade Barriers" for the latest year. This document summarizes trade barriers around the world. See the reports for the country of your choice. What are the country's import policies and practices? What are its nontariff trade barriers? What about barriers in the services sector? Are there any sectors that seem to be particularly protected (for example, aviation, energy, telecommunications)? What is the nature of government restrictions on e-commerce? If you were a manager in a firm that wanted to export its products to the country, how would you use the USTR report to develop international business strategies?

3. Visit the following web portals and review their perspectives on the debate about free trade and government policies on trade barriers. Given the inherent conflict between national interests, special interests, asymmetries in world wage rates and other economic conditions, what is the best path forward for national governments? That is, should governments generally favor free trade, or should they intervene to protect national interests?

www.heritage.org/Research/Tradeand ForeignAid/index.cfm

www.wto.org/english/thewto_e/whatis_e/ tif_e/fact3_e.htm

www.citizen.org/trade/index.cfm

www.aflcio.org/globaleconomy/

www.sierraclub.org/trade/environment/ index.asp

www.ncpa.org/pd/trade/trade8.html

CKR Cavusgil Knight Riesenberger

Management Skill Builder©

Harmonized Code Tariffs as Trade Barriers for Developing Country Exporters

A critical step in assessing the international marketability of a company's products is to determine the extent to which they are subject to tariffs and other trade barriers. A tariff is a tax on imported products that governments impose to achieve various policy objectives. Managers must determine what tariffs they face in foreign markets. Tariff rates are particularly high for food, agricultural products, textiles, and leather. This is often a point of contention for developing countries, whose exports tend to concentrate in such primary products.

AACSB: Reflective Thinking, Analytical Skills

Managerial Challenge

Almost all countries use the system to figure out what tariffs to charge on internationally traded products. In most cases, managers use harmonized codes to find out what tariffs the firm faces in importing and exporting. Managers often use harmonized codes to determine the price competitiveness of their products in export markets and to investigate ways of differentiating or modifying their products so that they may potentially qualify for lower tariffs.

Background

The harmonized code system is necessary because, without it, firms and governments might have differing opinions on what tariffs to charge on imported goods. All products in the system are classified according to a unique six- to ten-digit number. The manager conducts research to determine what trade barriers, if any, are applicable. Data can be obtained by researching online sites, such as the U.S. Department of Commerce (www.doc.gov), ministries of commerce, and other government trade agencies worldwide.

Managerial Skills You Will Gain

In this C/K/R Management Skill Builder©, as a prospective manager, you will:

1. Learn about harmonized classification codes and how to look up tariffs, using harmonized codes.

2. Research the role of high tariffs as a trade barrier.

3. Understand the challenges faced by developing-country exporters of primary products such as food, textiles, and leather.

4. Formulate strategies for potentially reducing tariffs on exported products.

Your Task

Assume that you work for a developing-country company that exports primary products to advanced economies. Your firm is based in an emerging market or developing economy that exports various products to advanced economies. You wish to export such products as coffee, sugar, apparel, footwear, and toys. Your task is to look up the harmonized codes and applicable tariffs for each of these products. Next, you will recommend strategies to your management for possibly avoiding high tariffs by differentiating or modifying the product.

Go to the C/K/R Knowledge Portal©

www.prenhall.com/cavusgil

Proceed to the C/K/R Knowledge Portal© to obtain the expanded background information, your task and methodology, suggested resources for this exercise, and the presentation template.

Regional Economic Integration

> The European Union

At the end of World War II, Europe was economically and physically devastated. The war resulted in the destruction of much of Europe's industry and infrastructure. Soon after, at the onset of the Cold War between the United States and the Soviet Union, the European continent was physically and politically divided between Western and Eastern Europe. Many Europeans feared for their future.

To help address these concerns and generally promote peace and harmony in Europe, six western European countries—Belgium, France, Italy, Luxemburg, the Netherlands, and West Germany—formed an alliance in 1957, the European Economic Community. Its successor is the European Union (EU), which was established in 1992 and today includes 27 countries. Because the original bloc was founded in 1957, the EU in 2007 celebrated its 50th anniversary, making it one of the world's oldest regional economic blocs. A regional economic integration bloc (economic bloc) is an alliance of two or more countries that agree to eliminate tariffs and other restrictions to the cross-border flow of products, services, capital, and, occasionally, labor. Presently, the EU is the world's most advanced and largest economic bloc, with nearly a half billion people and about $14 trillion in annual GDP.

While the EU's original members were all Western European nations, it now includes Eastern European countries as well. Thirteen EU countries have adopted the

euro as their common currency, helping to lower business transaction costs and increase the transparency of pricing throughout the European area.

Trade and investment within Europe have become much easier since the 1950s. The member states allow investors from other member countries to freely establish and conduct business and transfer capital and earnings. Gradual elimination of bureaucracy at Europe's national borders has cut delivery times and reduced transportation costs. For example, the EU eliminated the need for volumes of customs clearance documents.

The EU is home to the headquarters of some of the world's most important firms. One such firm is Allianz, an insurance company founded in Germany. Allianz offers a range of insurance products and services, including life, health, and casualty insurance. In terms of market targeting and strategy development, Allianz management at one time viewed Europe as a collection of disparate countries. Since the creation of the EU, however, Allianz treats Europe increasingly as one large marketplace. Management attempts to devise pan-European strategies, an approach that reduces costs and increases the efficiency of Allianz's operations throughout Europe.

Development of the EU has allowed Allianz to internationalize faster than other insurers. The firm is present in all the new EU countries—such as Poland, Hungary, and the Czech Republic—which are proving to be among Allianz's most profitable markets. In 2006, Allianz changed its legal status from a German company to that of a Societas Europaea (SE), a company based and regulated in the EU as a whole. The legal groundwork for SE status was put in place in 2004, with passage of EU legislation that allows such firms to operate seamlessly across all 27 EU countries. By transforming into a European firm, Allianz is becoming more European than German.

Today, the EU is at a crossroads. Member countries signed the European Constitution in 2004—a treaty that aimed to improve the functioning of the EU's governing institutions. The goal of the constitution is to clarify the distribution of powers and legitimize the EU's federal authority, in much the same way the U.S. Constitution did for the United States. However, in a referendum held in 2005, France and the Netherlands rejected the constitution, which caused other countries to postpone or halt ratification. At present, the constitution's future and longer-term political integration of the EU are in

limbo. Meanwhile, in the decade through 2007, performance of the EU economy was sluggish. GDP growth and productivity stagnated and the unemployment rate hovered between 8 and 12 percent. Many Europeans are dissatisfied with the EU and are opposed to the entry of additional countries into the bloc.

The challenges facing the EU today might be typical of economic blocs in the most advanced stages of development. Nevertheless, economic blocs have become typical of the emerging landscape of international trade and investment. Today, there are roughly 200 agreements for regional trade integration around the world, some more active than others. Such alliances represent a long-term trend and are likely a stepping-stone to the emergence of worldwide free trade.

Sources: *Economist*. (2005). "Business: Limited appeal; Pan-European companies." Sept 17, p.72; *Economist*. (2007). "Fit at 50? A Special Report on the European Union." March 17, Special Section; European Commission. *The Internal Market—Ten Years without Frontiers*. Retrieved from www.ec.europa.eu; Hoovers.com. (2007). Corporate profile of Allianz at www.hoovers.com; U.S. Commercial Service. (2006). *Doing business in the European Union*. Washington, DC: U.S. and Foreign Commercial Service and U.S. Department of State.

 # Regional Integration and Economic Blocs

Regional economic integration The growing economic interdependence that results when two or more countries within a geographic region form an alliance aimed at reducing barriers to trade and investment.

The opening vignette highlights one of the most remarkable features of contemporary international business: the worldwide trend to **regional economic integration**. Also known as *regional integration*, regional economic integration refers to the growing economic interdependence that results when two or more countries within a geographic region form an alliance aimed at reducing barriers to trade and investment. Since the end of World War II, most nations have sought to collaborate, with the aim of achieving some degree of economic integration. It is estimated that about 40 percent of world trade today is under some form of preferential trade agreements signed by groups of countries. The trend is based on the premise that, by cooperating, nations within a common geographic region connected by historical, cultural, linguistic, economic, or political factors can gain mutual advantages.[1] The free trade that results from economic integration helps nations attain higher living standards by encouraging specialization, lower prices, greater choices, increased productivity, and more efficient use of resources.

To better understand regional integration, think of international business as existing along a continuum where, at one extreme, the world operates as one large free-trade area in which there are no tariffs or quotas, all countries use the same currency, and products, services, capital, and workers can move freely among nations without restriction. At the other extreme of this continuum is a world of prohibitive barriers to trade and investment where countries have separate currencies and have very little commercial interaction with each other. Regional integration is an attempt to achieve freer economic relations. Two of the most well-known examples of this trend are the European Union (EU) and the North American Free Trade Agreement area (NAFTA). The EU is composed of 27 member countries in Europe. NAFTA is composed of Canada, Mexico, and the United States.

Regional integration results from the formation of a **regional economic integration bloc**, or simply, an economic bloc, a geographic area that consists of two or more countries that agree to pursue economic integration by reducing tariffs and other restrictions to cross-border flow of products, services, capital, and, in more advanced stages, labor. (In this text, we follow the convention of using the French term, "bloc," instead of "block.") At minimum, the countries in an economic bloc become parties to a **free trade agreement**, a formal arrangement between two or more countries to reduce or eliminate tariffs, quotas, and other barriers to trade in products and services. The member nations also undertake cross-border investments within the bloc.

More advanced economic blocs, such as the EU, permit the free flow of capital, labor, and technology among the member countries. The EU is also harmonizing monetary and fiscal policies and gradually integrating the economies of its member nations. For example, in light of the faster pace of economic activity in the EU, the European Central Bank recently tightened its monetary policy by raising interest rates on the money that it loans to European banks, in an effort to reduce inflation. Cross-border merger and acquisition deals increased markedly between Austria, France, the United Kingdom, the Netherlands, and other member countries in recent years.

Why would a nation opt to be a member of an economic bloc instead of working toward a system of worldwide free trade? The primary reason is that such blocs involve a smaller number of countries and, therefore, are much easier to negotiate than a system of worldwide free trade composed of all the nations in the world. This helps explain why roughly 200 economic integration agreements have been negotiated, presenting both opportunities and challenges to internationalizing firms.

Note that the proponents of free trade on a global scale are disappointed about the proliferation of regional trade agreements. Since 1947, the General Agreement on Tariffs and Trade (GATT) and the World Trade Organization (WTO) have achieved great success in fostering economic integration on a *global* scale. The WTO recognizes that regional integration can play an important role in liberalizing trade and fostering economic development. However, existing WTO rules have been less effective in dealing with groups of countries, and the world body has failed to ensure compliance with WTO rules by all members of an economic bloc. Slow progress to liberalize trade, especially in agricultural products, has prompted many developing countries to seek alternatives to the multilateral trading system favored by the WTO. Today, the WTO remains in negotiations with economic blocs, with the aim of exercising better control over their evolution and of minimizing risks associated with regional economic integration.[2]

 Types of Regional Integration

Regional integration involves processes by which distinct national economies become economically linked and interdependent through greater cross-national movement of products, services, and factors of production. Economic integration allows member states to use resources more productively. The total output of the integrated area becomes greater than that achievable by individual states.

Exhibit 8.1 identifies five possible levels of regional integration. Regional integration is best viewed as a continuum, with economic interconnectedness progressing from a low level of integration—the free trade area— through higher levels to the most advanced form of integration—the political union. The *political union* represents the ultimate degree of integration among countries, which has not yet been achieved. The **free trade area** is the simplest and most common arrangement, in

Regional economic integration bloc A geographic area consisting of two or more countries that have agreed to pursue economic integration by reducing barriers to the cross-border flow of products, services, capital, and, in more advanced states, labor.

Free trade agreement A formal arrangement between two or more countries to reduce or eliminate tariffs, quotas, and barriers to trade in products and services.

Free trade area A stage of regional integration in which member countries agree to eliminate tariffs and other barriers to trade in products and services within the bloc.

Level of Integration	Free Trade Area	Customs Union	Common Market	Economic and (sometimes) Monetary Union	Political Union
Members agree to eliminate tariffs and non tariff trade barriers with each other but maintain their own trade barriers with non member countries. *Examples: NAFTA, EFTA, ASEAN, Australia and New Zealand Closer Economic Relations Agreement (CER)*	✔				
Common external tariffs *Example: MERCOSUR*	✔	✔			
Free movement of products, labor, and capital *Example: Pre-1992 European Economic Community*	✔	✔	✔		
Unified monetary and fiscal policy by a central authority *Example: The European Union today exhibits common trade, agricultural, and monetary policies*	✔	✔	✔	✔	
Perfect unification of all policies by a common organization; submersion of all separate national institutions *Example: Remains an ideal; yet to be achieved*	✔	✔	✔	✔	✔

Exhibit 8.1 Five Potential Levels of Regional Integration among Nations

which member countries agree to gradually eliminate formal barriers to trade in products and services within the bloc, while each member country maintains an independent international trade policy with countries outside the bloc. NAFTA is an example. The free trade area emphasizes the pursuit of comparative advantage for a group of countries rather than individual states. Governments may impose local content requirements, which specify that producers located within the member countries provide a certain proportion of products and supplies used in local manufacturing. If the content requirement is not met, the product becomes subject to the tariffs that member governments normally impose on nonmember countries.

Customs union A stage of regional integration in which the member countries agree to adopt common tariff and nontariff barriers on imports from nonmember countries.

The next level of regional integration is the **customs union**, which is similar to a free trade area except that the member states harmonize their trade policies toward nonmember countries. Unlike a free trade area, in which individual countries have their own external trade policies, the members of a customs union adopt *common* tariff and nontariff barriers on imports from nonmember countries. MERCOSUR, an economic bloc consisting of Argentina, Brazil, Paraguay, and Uruguay, is an example of this type of arrangement. Use of a common tariff system means that an exporter outside MERCOSUR faces the *same* tariffs and nontariff barriers by *any* MERCOSUR member country. Determining the most appropriate common external tariff is challenging, because member countries must agree on the tariff level. In addition, governments must agree on how to distribute proceeds from the tariff among the member countries.

At the next stage of regional integration, member countries may establish a **common market** (also known as a single market), in which trade barriers are reduced or removed, common external barriers are established and products, services, and *factors of production* such as capital, labor, and technology are allowed to move freely among the member countries. As with a customs union, the common market also establishes a common trade policy with nonmember countries. The EU is a common market. It has gradually reduced or eliminated restrictions on immigration and the cross-border flow of capital. A worker from an EU country has the right to work in other EU countries, and EU firms can freely transfer funds among their subsidiaries within the bloc.

Common markets are hard to create because they require substantial cooperation from the member countries on labor and economic policies. Moreover, because labor and capital can flow freely inside the bloc, benefits to individual members vary, because skilled labor may move to countries where wages are higher and investment capital may flow to countries where returns are greater. In the EU, for example, Germany has seen a sharp influx of workers from Poland and the Czech Republic, because workers from the latter countries can earn substantially higher wages in Germany than they can in their home countries.

An **economic union** is a stage of regional integration in which member countries enjoy all the advantages of early stages, but also strive to have common fiscal and monetary policies. At the extreme, each member country adopts identical tax rates. The bloc aims for standardized monetary policy, which requires establishing fixed exchange rates and free convertibility of currencies among the member states, in addition to allowing the free movement of capital. This standardization helps eliminate discriminatory practices that might favor one member state over another. Through greater mobility of products, services, and production factors, an economic union enables firms within the bloc to locate productive activities in member states with the most favorable economic policies.

The EU has made great strides toward achieving an economic union. For example, 13 EU countries have established a *monetary union* in which a single currency, the euro, is now in circulation. Monetary union and the euro have greatly increased the ease with which European financial institutions establish branches across the EU and offer banking services, insurance, and savings products.

Economic unions have additional characteristics. To achieve greater economic integration, member countries strive to eliminate border controls, harmonize product and labeling standards, and establish regionwide policies for energy, agriculture, and social services. An economic union also requires its members to standardize laws and regulations regarding competition, mergers, and other corporate behaviors. To facilitate free trade in services, member countries harmonize procedures for licensing of professionals so that a doctor or lawyer qualified in one country can practice in any other country.

In describing an economic union, the United States provides a good analogy. Imagine that each of the fifty states is like an individual country, but joined together in a union. The members have a common currency and a single central bank with a uniform monetary policy. Trade among the members takes place unobstructed and both labor and capital move freely among them, in pursuit of optimal returns. The federal government applies a uniform tax and fiscal policy. However, just as would occur in an economic union, the individual U.S. states also govern themselves in such areas as education, police protection, and local taxes, thereby maintaining some local autonomy. Nevertheless, the analogy only goes so far. The United States *is* a country and, unlike a real economic union, the U.S. states cannot withdraw from the union.

Common market A stage of regional integration in which trade barriers are reduced or removed, common external barriers are established, and products, services, and factors of production are allowed to move freely among the member countries.

Economic union A stage of regional integration in which member countries enjoy all the advantages of early stages, but also strive to have common fiscal and monetary policies.

Leading Economic Blocs

Examples of regional integration can be found on all continents. Leading economic blocs are illustrated in Exhibit 8.2 on pages 230–231. In this section, we discuss notable blocs in Europe, the Americas, Asia, the Middle East, and Africa.

Europe has the longest experience with regional integration and is home to several economic blocs. The most important of these are the European Union and the European Free Trade Association. Exhibit 8.3 on page 232 shows these two blocs in detail.

The European Union (EU)

Exhibit 8.4 highlights the notable features of the member countries in the European Union—the world's most integrated economic bloc. "PPP terms" in the exhibit refers to *purchasing power parity* (PPP), which means that per capita GDP figures have been adjusted for price differences. The EU traces its roots to the years following World War II, when six war-weary countries—Belgium, France, Germany, Italy, Luxembourg, and the Netherlands—sought to promote peace and prosperity through economic and political cooperation (www.europa.eu). These countries signed the Treaty of Rome in 1957, eventually leading to the formal creation of the EU in 1992. The EU has taken the following steps toward becoming a full-fledged economic union:

- *Market access.* Tariffs and most nontariff barriers have been eliminated for trade in products and services, and rules of origin favor manufacturing that uses parts and other inputs produced in the EU.
- *Common market.* The EU removed barriers to the cross-national movement of production factors—labor, capital, and technology. For example, an Italian worker now has the right to get a job in Ireland and a French company can now invest freely in Spain.
- *Trade rules.* The member countries have largely eliminated customs procedures and regulations, which streamlines transportation and logistics within Europe.
- *Standards harmonization.* The EU is harmonizing technical standards, regulations, and enforcement procedures that relate to products, services, and commercial activities. Thus, where British firms once used the imperial measurement system (that is, pounds, ounces, and inches), they have converted to the metric system, used by all the EU. Where German merchants once had a unique standard for the quality of meat and produce, they now follow procedures prescribed by the EU.

In the long run, the EU is seeking to adopt common fiscal, monetary, taxation, and social welfare policies. The 2002 introduction of the euro—the EU's common currency and now one of the world's leading currencies—simplified the process of cross-border trade and enhanced Europe's international competitiveness. Its introduction eliminated exchange rate risk in much of the bloc and forced member countries to improve their fiscal and monetary policies. Psychologically, the single currency allows consumers and businesses to think of Europe as a single national entity. Instituting the euro meant that national governments had to cede monetary power to the European Central Bank, which is based in Luxembourg and oversees EU monetary functions.

The EU has four additional institutions that perform its executive, administrative, legislative, and judicial functions. The *Council of the European Union*, based in Brussels, is the EU's main decision-making body. Composed of representatives from each member country, it makes decisions regarding economic policy, budgets, and foreign policy, as well as admission of new member countries. The *European Commission*, also based in Brussels, is similarly composed of delegates from each member state and represents the interests of the EU as a whole. It proposes legislation and policies and is responsible for implementing the decisions of the *European Parliament* and the Council of the EU. The European Parliament consists of elected representatives that hold joint sessions each month. By common agreement, the Parliament meets in three different cities (Brussels, Luxembourg, and Strasbourg, France) and can have up 732 total representatives. The Parliament has three main functions: (1) form EU legislation, (2) supervise EU institutions, and (3) make decisions about the EU budget. Finally, the *European Court of Justice,* based in Luxembourg, interprets and enforces EU laws and settles legal disputes between member states.[3]

The Global Trend feature discusses specific challenges of integrating new member states into the EU. Since 2004, 12 new states have joined the EU. The more recent addition of Bulgaria and Romania brings the total number of member countries to 27. The new member countries are important, low-cost manufacturing sites for EU firms.[4] For example, Peugeot and Citroën now produce cars at a plant in the Czech Republic. At full capacity, the factory turns out 300,000 vehicles per year. South Korea's Hyundai now produces the Kia brand of cars at a plant in

> GLOBAL TREND

Integrating Eastern Europe and Turkey into the EU

Germany's per capita GDP is $32,684. By comparison, Romania's is $10,152, Bulgaria's is $10,844, and Poland's is $14,609 (all are 2007 figures). These Eastern European countries, with their low-wage workers, make excellent manufacturing sites for firms from Western Europe and elsewhere. Just as these and other Eastern European countries have recently joined the European Union (EU), officials in Germany, France, and other long-established EU members fear losing jobs and investment to the new EU members. These same officials are reluctant to allow other low-wage countries, such as Turkey or the Ukraine, to join the EU.

In population terms, Turkey (with 71 million people) is about the same size as the 12 Eastern European countries that joined the EU since 2004. However, Turkey poses additional challenges because of cultural differences, its Islamic heritage, and historically high inflation. Some oppose Turkey joining the EU because the country is seen as too remote from current EU countries in cultural and geographic terms. Suc-

cessive Turkish governments have long sought EU membership, in part because it will help maintain economic reform in their country.

Proponents of EU enlargement are optimistic. They argue that low wages in the bloc's newest members are more an opportunity than a threat. Why? One reason is that Poland, Hungary, and other recent entrants are attracting substantial business investment that might go to China and other low-wage countries on the opposite side of the world.

The Eastern European countries will not maintain their low-cost labor advantages indefinitely. These satellites of the former Soviet Union are much richer today than they were after the collapse of communism in 1989, when Poland's per capita GDP was just $2,000. Starting from a much lower income level, these countries are relatively new to free-market economics and, as such, are growing their economies far faster than their affluent Western EU neighbors. The reason relates partly to the incremental value of inward investment in poorer countries versus richer countries. The profitability

of using additional capital or better technology is greater in an emerging market like Poland than in a high-income country like Germany. For example, while replacing an existing computer with a new, faster computer has a relatively small payoff for a German firm, installing a new computer in a Polish firm where records are kept by hand has an enormous payoff.

Rapid economic growth spurred by affiliation with the European Union implies that the newest EU members may reach economic parity with the rest of Europe within a few decades, a short time span in the life of a nation. When that day arrives, Germans, French, British, and other venerable members of the EU bloc will no longer worry about the competitive threat of their new low-wage neighbors.

Sources: *Business Week.* (1999). "How Far, How Fast? Is Central Europe Ready to Join the EU," Nov. 8, pp. 64–66; *Economist.* (2005). "Transformed: EU Membership has Worked Magic in Central Europe." June 25, pp. 6–8; *Economist.* (2004). "The Impossibility of Saying No." Sept. 18, 30–32; *Financial Times.* (2005). "Why Turks are Changing Tack on Foreign Ownership." June 28. Special report.

Exhibit 8.2

The Most Active Economic Blocs

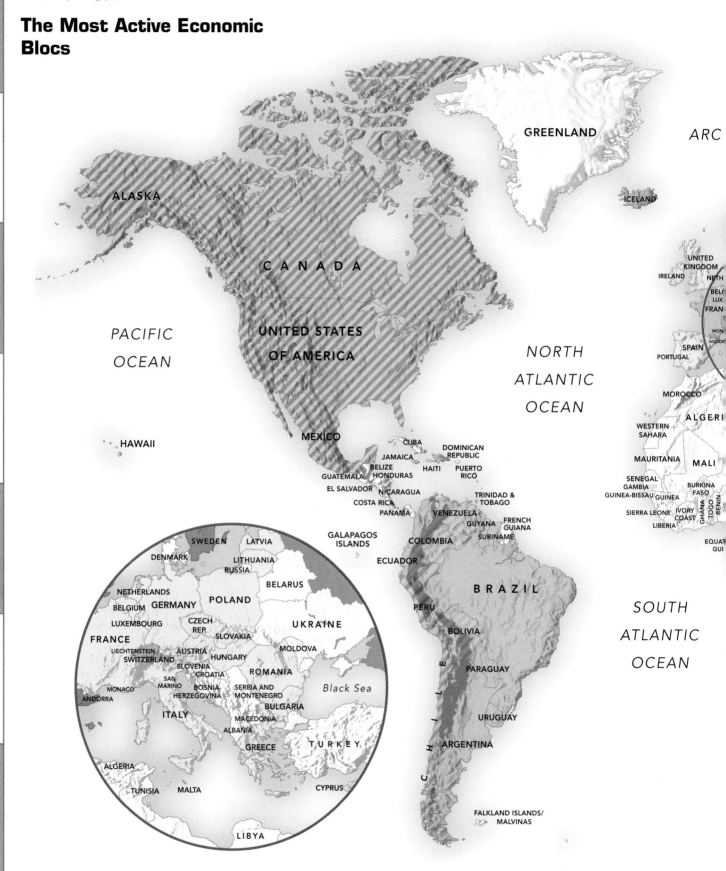

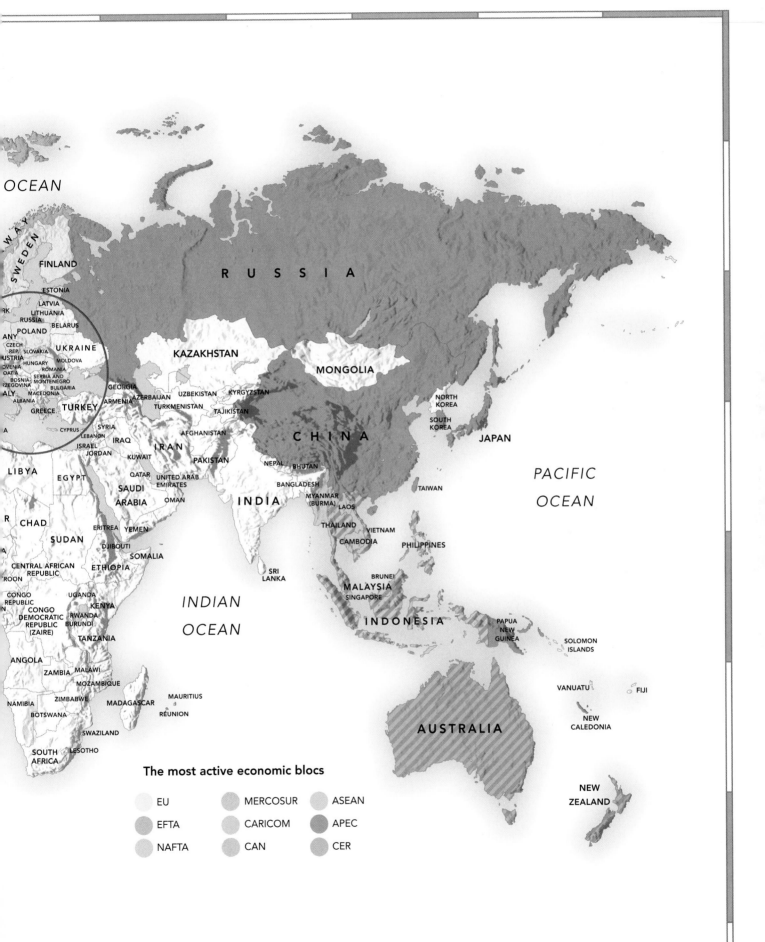

OCEAN

SWEDEN
FINLAND
ESTONIA
LATVIA
LITHUANIA
RUSSIA
BELARUS
POLAND
ANY
CZECH
REP.
SLOVAKIA
USTRIA
HUNGARY
VENIA
ROMANIA
OATIA
BOSNIA-
ZEGOVINA
SERBIA AND
MONTENEGRO
BULGARIA
ALY
MACEDONIA
ALBANIA
GREECE
TURKEY
CYPRUS
SYRIA
LEBANON
ISRAEL
JORDAN
IRAQ
IRAN

RUSSIA

KAZAKHSTAN

MONGOLIA

GEORGIA
ARMENIA
AZERBAIJAN
TURKMENISTAN
UZBEKISTAN
KYRGYZSTAN
TAJIKISTAN

NORTH
KOREA
SOUTH
KOREA

JAPAN

LIBYA
EGYPT
SAUDI
ARABIA
KUWAIT
QATAR
UNITED ARAB
EMIRATES
OMAN
YEMEN

AFGHANISTAN
PAKISTAN

NEPAL
BHUTAN

CHINA

TAIWAN

PACIFIC
OCEAN

R
CHAD
SUDAN
ERITREA
DJIBOUTI

INDIA

BANGLADESH
MYANMAR
(BURMA)
LAOS
THAILAND
VIETNAM
CAMBODIA

PHILIPPINES

CENTRAL AFRICAN
REPUBLIC
ROON
ETHIOPIA
SOMALIA

SRI
LANKA

INDIAN

OCEAN

CONGO
REPUBLIC
UGANDA
KENYA
CONGO
DEMOCRATIC
REPUBLIC
(ZAIRE)
RWANDA
BURUNDI
TANZANIA

BRUNEI
MALAYSIA
SINGAPORE

INDONESIA

PAPUA
NEW
GUINEA

SOLOMON
ISLANDS

ANGOLA
ZAMBIA
MALAWI
MOZAMBIQUE
NAMIBIA
ZIMBABWE
BOTSWANA
MADAGASCAR
MAURITIUS
RÉUNION

VANUATU

FIJI

SWAZILAND
SOUTH
AFRICA
LESOTHO

AUSTRALIA

NEW
CALEDONIA

NEW
ZEALAND

The most active economic blocs

- EU
- EFTA
- NAFTA
- MERCOSUR
- CARICOM
- CAN
- ASEAN
- APEC
- CER

Exhibit 8.3

Economic Integration in Europe

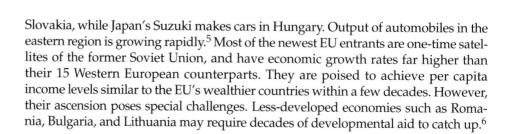

ICELAND

NORTH
ATLANTIC
OCEAN

European Union
member countries

European Free
Trade Association
member countries
(both as of July 2007)

NORWAY

FINLAND

SWEDEN

ESTONIA

RUSSIA

LATVIA

DENMARK

LITHUANIA

IRELAND

UNITED
KINGDOM

RUSSIA

BELARUS

NETHERLANDS

POLAND

BELGIUM

GERMANY

UKRAINE

LUXEMBOURG

CZECH
REP.

SLOVAKIA

LIECHTENSTEIN

MOLDOVA

FRANCE

SWITZERLAND

AUSTRIA

HUNGARY

SLOVENIA

ROMANIA

SAN
MARINO

CROATIA

BOSNIA-
HERZEGOVINA

SERBIA
AND
MONTENEGRO

Black Sea

GEORGIA

PORTUGAL

MONACO

ANDORRA

BULGARIA

ARM

SPAIN

ITALY

MACEDONIA

ALBANIA

TURKEY

GREECE

MOROCCO

SYRIA

ALGERIA

CYPRUS

IRA

TUNISIA

MALTA

LEBANON

Slovakia, while Japan's Suzuki makes cars in Hungary. Output of automobiles in the eastern region is growing rapidly.[5] Most of the newest EU entrants are one-time satellites of the former Soviet Union, and have economic growth rates far higher than their 15 Western European counterparts. They are poised to achieve per capita income levels similar to the EU's wealthier countries within a few decades. However, their ascension poses special challenges. Less-developed economies such as Romania, Bulgaria, and Lithuania may require decades of developmental aid to catch up.[6]

The EU faces other challenges as well. There is a tension in Europe between the forces for regional integration and the forces for retaining national identity. EU countries recognize that relinquishing autonomy in certain key areas and combining resources across national borders are necessary steps. However, some EU members, particularly Britain, are reluctant to surrender certain sovereign rights. They insist on maintaining their ability to set their own monetary and fiscal policies, and to undertake their own national military defense.

Finally, the Common Agricultural Policy (CAP) has long been a fixture of the European bloc. The CAP is a system of agricultural subsidies and programs that guarantees a minimum price to EU farmers and ranchers.

Members	Population (millions)	GDP (U.S.$, billions, PPP terms)	GDP per capita (U.S.$; PPP terms)	Exports as a percentage of GDP
Austria	8	$299	$36,189	29%
Belgium	10	353	33,908	52
Bulgaria	8	83	10,844	16
Cyprus	1	20	23,419	7
Czech Republic	10	210	20,539	44
Denmark	5	204	37,398	26
Estonia	1	26	19,243	36
Finland	5	179	34,162	29
France	63	1,988	31,377	17
Germany	83	2,699	32,684	26
Greece	11	274	24,733	3
Hungary	10	190	18,922	42
Ireland	4	192	45,135	53
Italy	59	1,791	30,383	17
Latvia	2	34	15,062	21
Lithuania	3	57	16,756	36
Luxembourg	0.5	35	76,025	28
Malta	0.4	8	21,081	44
The Netherlands	17	550	33,079	44
Poland	38	557	14,609	24
Portugal	11	218	20,673	18
Romania	22	219	10,152	51
Slovakia	5	101	18,705	67
Slovenia	2	49	24,459	38
Spain	42	1,203	28,810	16
Sweden	9	297	32,548	30
United Kingdom	61	2,004	32,949	14
	Total: 491	Total: $13,840		

Exhibit 8.4 Key Features of the European Union Member Countries, 2007

SOURCE: International Monetary Fund at www.imf.org

Original goals of the CAP were to provide a fair living standard for agricultural producers and food at reasonable prices for consumers. In reality, however, the CAP has increased food prices in Europe and consumes over 40 percent of the EU's annual budget. It complicates negotiations with the World Trade Organization for reducing global trade barriers. The CAP imposes high import tariffs that unfairly affect exporters in developing economies, such as Africa, that rely heavily on agricultural production. The EU has been working in recent years to reform the CAP, but progress has been slow. Meanwhile, entry into the EU of new member countries since 2004 has increased the number of bloc farmers from 7 to 11 million and increased crop production by 10 to 20 percent.

European Free Trade Association (EFTA)

The second largest free trade area in Europe is the European Free Trade Association (EFTA; see www.efta.int), which was established in 1960 by Austria, Britain, Denmark, Norway, Portugal, Sweden, and Switzerland. However, most of these countries eventually left the EFTA to join the EU. The current EFTA members are Iceland, Liechtenstein, Norway, and Switzerland. The bloc promotes free trade and strengthens economic relations with other European countries and the world. The EFTA Secretariat, headquartered in Geneva, has negotiated trade agreements with several non-European countries. EFTA members cooperate with the EU via bilateral free trade agreements, and, since 1994, through the European Economic Area arrangement, which allows for free movement of people, products, services, and capital throughout the combined area of the EFTA and the EU.

North American Free Trade Agreement (NAFTA)

Consisting of Canada, Mexico, and the United States, NAFTA is the most significant economic bloc in the Americas (see www.nafta-sec-alena.org). Exhibit 8.5 highlights key features of the NAFTA countries. The concept suggests that, in the long run, exchange rates should move toward levels that would equalize the prices of an identical basket of goods and services in any two countries. Since prices vary greatly among countries, economists adjust ordinary GDP figures for differences in purchasing power. Adjusted per capita GDP more accurately represents the amount of products that consumers can buy in a given country, using their own currency and consistent with their own standard of living.

Members	Population (millions)	GDP (U.S.$ billions, PPP terms)	GDP per capita (U.S.$; PPP terms)	Exports as a percentage of GDP
Canada	33	$1,225	$37,321	29%
Mexico	108	1,192	10,993	18
United States	302	13,678	45,257	6
	Total: 443	Total: $16,095		

Exhibit 8.5 North American Free Trade Agreement (NAFTA), 2007

SOURCE: International Monetary Fund at www.imf.org

Comparable in size to the EU, NAFTA was launched in 1994. Its passage was smoothed by the existence, since the 1960s, of the *maquiladora* program. Under this program, U.S. firms have been able to locate manufacturing facilities in an area just south of the U.S. border and access low-cost labor and other advantages in Mexico without having to pay significant tariffs.

For its member countries, the NAFTA agreement increased market access. The agreement eliminated tariffs and most nontariff barriers for products and services traded in the bloc, and made it possible for member country firms to bid for government contracts. NAFTA established trade rules and uniform customs procedures and regulations, while prohibiting the use of standards and technical regulations as trade barriers. The member countries agreed to rules for investment and intellectual property rights. NAFTA also provides for dispute settlement in areas such as investment, unfair pricing, labor issues, and the environment.

What did NAFTA accomplish for its members? Since the bloc's inception, trade among the members has more than tripled and now exceeds one trillion dollars per year. In the early 1980s, Mexico's tariffs averaged 100 percent and gradually decreased over time, eventually disappearing under NAFTA. In the 10 years following NAFTA's launch in 1994, U.S. exports to Mexico grew from about $40 billion to more than $110 billion. U.S. exports to Canada nearly doubled, to nearly $200 billion. Canada's exports to Mexico and the United States also more than doubled. In 1994, Mexican exports to the United States averaged about $50 billion per year, compared to over $160 billion by 2005.[7]

Mexico benefited greatly from NAFTA. Access to Canada and the United States helped launch numerous Mexican firms in industries such as electronics, automobiles, textiles, medical products, and services. For instance, Mexico gave birth to a $100 million-per-year dental supply industry, in which entrepreneurs export labor-intensive products such as braces, dental wax, and tools used in dental work to the United States. Annual foreign investment in Mexico rose from $4 billion in 1993 to nearly $20 billion by 2006 as United States and Canadian firms invested in their southern neighbor. In the years following NAFTA's passage, Mexico's per capita income rose substantially, to about $11,000 in 2007, making Mexico the wealthiest country in Latin America in terms of per capita income.[8]

Compared to the days before NAFTA, the member countries now trade more with each other than with former trading partners outside the NAFTA zone. Both Canada and Mexico now have some 80 percent of their trade with, and 60 percent of their FDI stocks in, the United States.[9] By increasing Mexico's attractiveness as a manufacturing location, firms like Gap Inc. and Liz Claiborne moved their factories from Asia to Mexico during the 1990s. IBM shifted much of its production of computer parts from Singapore to Mexico.

NAFTA also stimulated some restructuring in the North American labor market. Falling trade barriers triggered job losses in the North as factories were "exported" to Mexico to profit from its low-cost labor. Nevertheless, increased purchasing power of Mexican consumers meant that they could afford to buy imports from Canada and the United States. As part of the accord, the member countries were also required to strengthen their labor standards. Workers in the NAFTA zone gained the right to unionize. The accord helped to improve working conditions and compliance with labor laws. NAFTA also includes provisions that promote sustainable development and environmental protection.

Let's turn now to a collection of lesser known economic blocs, often composed of developing economies. Compared to the EU or NAFTA, the remaining blocs are less stable and have been less successful. These blocs are located in Latin America, Asia, the Middle East, and Africa.

Members	Population (millions)	GDP (U.S.$ billions, PPP terms)	GDP per capita (U.S.$; PPP terms)	Exports as a percentage of GDP
Argentina	39	$599	$15,509	6%
Brazil	189	1,758	9,286	5
Paraguay	6	32	5,264	9
Uruguay	3	38	12,012	4
Venezuela	28	182	6,614	18
Bolivia *	10	28	2,858	7
Chile *	17	225	13,588	12
Colombia *	48	380	7,975	5
Ecuador *	14	62	4,591	13
Peru *	29	190	6,609	6
	Total: 383	Total: $3,494		

* Associate members

Exhibit 8.6 El Mercado Comun del Sur (MERCOSUR), 2007

SOURCE: International Monetary Fund at www.imf.org

El Mercado Comun del Sur (MERCOSUR)

Established in 1991, MERCOSUR, or the *El Mercado Comun del Sur* (the Southern Common Market) has, become the strongest economic bloc in South America (see www.mercosur.int). Exhibit 8.6 provides the membership and key features of the MERCOSUR bloc. The four largest members alone—Argentina, Brazil, Paraguay, and Uruguay—account for some 80 percent of South America's GDP. Within its borders, MERCOSUR established the free movement of products and services, a common external tariff and trade policy, and coordinated monetary and fiscal policies. An additional priority is the construction of reliable infrastructure—roads, electricity grids, and gas pipelines—across a landmass larger than Mexico and the United States combined. MERCOSUR eventually aims to become an economic union.

MERCOSUR's early progress was impressive. It attracted much investment from nonmember countries, particularly in the auto industry. During its first six years, trade among the member countries tripled.[10] In addition to its regular members, MERCOSUR also has five associate members, which have access to preferential trade but not to the tariff benefits of full members. MERCOSUR has trade agreements with various nations outside the bloc. Some predict that MERCOSUR will be integrated with NAFTA and the Dominican Republic-Central American Free Trade Agreement (DR-CAFTA) as part of the proposed Free Trade Area of the Americas (FTAA), bringing free trade to the entire western hemisphere. If implemented, this integration would bring free trade to the entire western hemisphere.

The Caribbean Community (CARICOM)

Composed of roughly 25 member and associate member states around the Caribbean Sea, CARICOM was established in 1973 to lower trade barriers and institute a common external tariff (see www.caricom.org). However, the bloc has met with little success in stimulating economic development. Problems have resulted due to economic difficulties of the individual members and their inability to agree on basic issues. In recent years, the bloc has made much progress toward establishing the Caribbean Single Market, a common market that allows for a greater degree of free movement for products, services, capital, and labor, and gives citizens of all CARICOM countries the right to establish businesses throughout the region.

Comunidad Andina de Naciones (CAN)

Long called the Andean Pact, the Comunidad Andina de Naciones (CAN) was established in 1969 and includes Bolivia, Colombia, Ecuador, Peru, and Venezuela (see www.comunidadandina.org). The CAN countries have a population of 120 million and a combined GDP of $260 billion. CAN is expected to merge with MERCOSUR to form a new economic bloc that encompasses all of South America. The pact achieved little progress in its first 20 years, with intra-bloc trade reaching only 5 percent of the bloc members' total trade.[11] This low trade rate is partially due to geography: The Andes mountain range makes cross-border land transportation costly and cumbersome.

Association of Southeast Asian Nations (ASEAN)

One of the few examples of economic integration in Asia, ASEAN was created in 1967 with the goal of maintaining political stability and promoting regional economic and social development (see www.aseansec.org). Subsequently, ASEAN created a free trade area in which many tariffs were reduced to less than 5 percent. However, further regional integration has been slowed by large economic differences among the member countries. For instance, oil-rich Brunei has a per capita income of over $26,000, while Vietnam's is less than $4,000. The mass movement of workers from poor to prosperous countries that would likely result with further ASEAN integration reduces the likelihood that this bloc will become a common market or an economic union. In the long run, ASEAN aims to incorporate international trading powerhouses like Japan and China, whose membership would accelerate the development of extensive trade relationships. Exhibit 8.7 profiles the ASEAN. Note that Singapore's exports as a percent of its GDP exceed 100 percent. The reason is that Singapore is an entrepôt nation, an import-export platform for Asia, trading far more goods than it manufactures.

Asia Pacific Economic Cooperation (APEC)

Originally suggested by Australia, APEC aims for greater free trade and economic integration of the Pacific Rim countries. It incorporates 21 nations on both sides of the Pacific, including Australia, Canada, Chile, China, Japan, Mexico, Russia, and the United States (www.apec.org). Its members account for 85 percent of total regional trade, as well as one-third of the world's population and over half its GDP. APEC aspires to remove trade and investment barriers by 2020. Nevertheless, APEC has accomplished little. Progress has been slowed by economic and political turmoil in some member countries, as well as failure to agree on foundational issues. Members have varying national economic priorities, and the composition of less affluent Asian countries alongside strong international traders like Australia, Japan, and the United States makes it difficult to achieve agreement on a range of issues.

Members	Population millions	GDP (U.S.$ billions, PPP terms)	GDP per capita (U.S.$; PPP terms)	Exports as a percentage of GDP
Brunei	0.4	$10	$26,098	52%
Cambodia	15	41	2,673	6
Indonesia	225	1,146	5,097	8
Laos	6	15	2,402	3
Malaysia	27	341	12,703	47
Myanmar (Burma)	58	105	1,814	3
Philippines	88	474	5,409	9
Singapore	5	140	31,165	130
Thailand	66	626	9,427	16
Vietnam	86	300	3,503	10
	Total: 576	Total: $3,198		

Exhibit 8.7   Association of Southeast Asian Nations (ASEAN), 2007

SOURCE: International Monetary Fund at www.imf.org

Australia and New Zealand Closer Economic Relations Agreement (CER)

In 1966, Australia and New Zealand reached a free trade agreement that removed 80 percent of tariffs and quotas between the two nations, but was relatively complex and bureaucratic. In 1983, the Closer Economic Relations Agreement (CER) sought to accelerate free trade, leading to further economic integration of the two nations. The CER gained importance when Australia and New Zealand lost their privileged status in the British market as Britain joined the EU. Many believe the CER has been one of the world's most successful economic blocs. In 2005, the members began negotiating a free trade agreement with the ASEAN countries, a move that would further reduce Australia and New Zealand's dependence on trade with Britain.

Economic Integration in the Middle East and Africa

The Middle East and North Africa comprise a collection of primarily Islamic countries where oil is often the driving economic force. The Middle East's primary regional organization is the Gulf Cooperation Council (GCC; see www.gcc-sg.org.htm). Established in 1981 to coordinate economic, social, and cultural affairs, the GCC consists of Bahrain, Kuwait, Oman, Qatar, Saudi Arabia, and the United Arab Emirates. Specific GCC initiatives include coordination of the petroleum industry, abolition of certain tariffs, and liberalization of investment, as well as harmonization of banking, financial, and monetary policies. The GCC also wants to establish an Arab common market and increase trade ties with Asia. Although largely focused on political issues, the GCC has spawned agreements that allow its citizens to travel freely among, and establish businesses in, other member nations.

Elsewhere in the Middle East, efforts have been made for regional economic integration, such as the Arab Maghreb Union (composed of Algeria, Libya, Mauritania, Morocco, and Tunisia) and the Regional Cooperation for Development (RCD; composed of Pakistan, Iran, and Turkey). The Maghreb

Union is still struggling to become a viable economic bloc. The RCD was dissolved in 1979 and replaced by the Economic Cooperation Organization (ECO). The ECO is an international organization that now includes ten Middle Eastern and Asian countries, seeking to promote trade and investment opportunities in the region. Such regional groups are very early attempts at regional integration that may foster the development of inter-Arab trade and investment. Another grouping, the Arab League, is a longstanding political organization with 21 member states and a constitution that requires unanimous agreement in any decision making. It has been relatively unsuccessful in fostering regional economic development.

These workers harvest table grapes growing in Robertson, South Africa. External tariffs of NAFTA and the EU hinder African agricultural exports to Europe and North America.

Africa would like better access to European and North American markets for sales of farm and textile products. African countries believe they can gain clout to negotiate free trade with the developed world by forming economic blocs through regional integration. To this end, the continent has established at least nine economic blocs. Most notable are the Southern African Development Community, the Economic Community of West African States, the Economic Community of Central African States, and, most recently, the African Union for Regional Cooperation. However, these groups have not had much impact on regional trade. This failure is partially due to political turmoil and misunderstandings about free trade, as well as underdeveloped economic and transportation systems. Political instability, civil unrest and war, military dictatorships, corruption, and infectious diseases have prevented economic development in many African countries.

Why Countries Pursue Regional Integration

Economic integration contributes to corporate and industrial growth, and hence to economic progress, better living standards, and higher tax revenues for the member countries. Nations seek at least four objectives in pursuing regional integration.

Expand market size. Regional integration greatly increases the scale of the marketplace for firms inside the economic bloc. For example, while Belgium has a population of just 10 million, the absence of trade barriers with other countries in the EU gives Belgian firms easier access to a total market of roughly 490 million buyers. In a similar way, management at Allianz, the German insurance firm featured in the opening vignette, has come to view Europe as one large marketplace. When NAFTA was formed, Canadian firms gained access to the much larger markets of Mexico and the United States. In this way, consumers also gain access to a greater selection of products and services.

Achieve scale economies and enhanced productivity. Expansion of market size within an economic bloc gives member country firms the opportunity to increase the scale of operations in both production and marketing. This leads to greater concentration and increased efficiency in these activities. For instance, where a German firm may be only moderately efficient when producing 10,000 units of a product strictly for the German market, it greatly increases its efficiency by producing 50,000 units for the much larger EU market. Internalization inside the bloc helps firms learn to compete more effectively outside the bloc as well. The firms enjoy additional benefits through increased access to factors of production that now flow freely across

Members of MERCOSUR, which include Argentina, Brazil, Paraguay, and Uruguay—seek to expand market size, achieve scale economies, attract foreign direct investment, and build defensive and political posture.

national borders within the bloc.[12] Labor and other inputs are allocated more efficiently among the member countries. More efficient use of resources should lead to lower prices for consumers.

Attract direct investment from outside the bloc. Compared to investing in stand-alone countries, foreign firms prefer to invest in countries that are part of an economic bloc because factories that they build within the bloc receive preferential treatment for exports to other member countries. For example, many non-European firms—including General Mills, Samsung, and Tata—have invested heavily in the EU to take advantage of Europe's economic integration. By establishing operations in a single EU country, these firms gain free trade access to the entire EU market.

Acquire stronger defensive and political posture. One goal of regional integration is to give the member countries a stronger defensive posture relative to other nations and world regions. This was one of the motives for creating the European Community (the precursor to the EU), whose members sought to strengthen their mutual defense against the expanding influence of the former Soviet Union. Today, some view the EU as a means for Europe to counterbalance the power and international influence of the United States. Forming an economic bloc also allows countries to obtain greater bargaining power in world affairs and thereby political power. For example, the EU enjoys greater influence with the World Trade Organization in trade negotiations than any individual member country. Broadly speaking, countries are more powerful when they cooperate together than when they operate as individual entities.

 # Success Factors for Regional Integration

Experience with regional economic integration suggests that the most successful economic blocs tend to possess the following characteristics.

Economic similarity. The more similar the economies of the member countries, the more likely the economic bloc will succeed. Significant wage rate differences means that workers in lower-wage countries will migrate to higher wage countries. Significant economic instability in one member can quickly spread and harm the economies of the other members. For instance, a severe recession in one country increases the likelihood that others also experience an economic slowdown. Compatibility of economic characteristics is so important that the EU requires its current and prospective members to meet strict membership conditions, ideally low inflation, low unemployment, reasonable wages, and stable economic conditions.

Political similarity. Similarity in political systems enhances prospects for a successful bloc. Countries that seek to integrate regionally should share similar aspirations and a willingness to surrender national autonomy for the larger goals of the proposed union. In the EU, for example, Sweden has encountered difficulties in revising its fiscal policy to be more in line with other EU member countries. Sweden has attempted to lower its corporate income tax rate and other taxes to improve the country's attractiveness as a place to do business in the larger EU marketplace.

Similarity of culture and language. Cultural and linguistic similarity among the countries in an economic bloc provides the basis for mutual understanding and cooperation. This partially explains the success of the MERCOSUR bloc in Latin America, whose members share many cultural and linguistic similarities. Following the passage of NAFTA, it was easier for Canadian firms to establish trade and investment relationships in the United States than in Mexico because of the similarities between the two northern countries.

Geographic proximity. Most economic blocs are formed by countries within the same geographic region; hence the name, *regional integration.* Close geographic proximity of member countries facilitates transportation of products, labor, and other factors of production. Also, neighboring countries tend to be similar in terms of culture and language.

While the four types of similarities enhance the potential for successful regional integration, economic interests are often the most important factor. Dissimilarity in one area can be overcome by similarity in the other areas. This was demonstrated in the EU, whose member countries, despite strong cultural and linguistic differences, are able to achieve common goals based on pure economic interests.

Drawbacks and Ethical Dilemmas of Regional Integration

Regional integration is not a uniformly positive trend. The changes that result from regional integration can threaten firms and other constituents. Regional integration can give rise to ethical and moral concerns. These include:

Trade diversion. At least in the short run, regional integration gives rise to both trade creation *and* trade diversion. *Trade creation* means that trade is generated among the countries inside the economic bloc. This occurs because, as trade barriers fall within the bloc, each member country tends to favor trade with countries inside the bloc over trade with countries outside the bloc. At the same time, once the bloc is in place, member countries will discontinue some trade with nonmember countries, leading to *trade diversion.* The aggregate effect is that national patterns of trade are altered—more trade takes place inside the bloc, and less trade takes place with countries outside the bloc.

For example, suppose that before the formation of NAFTA, Canada and the United States were each self-sufficient in the production of wine. Suppose further that neither country imported wine from the other because of a 100 percent tariff. Now suppose that after the formation of NAFTA and elimination of the tariff, Canada began importing wine from the United States. This is an example of trade creation. Prior to NAFTA Canada had imported all its wine from France because Canada's tariff on wine imports from France was only 50 percent, making French wine cheaper than U.S. wine. Suppose that NAFTA's launch eliminated the higher U.S. tariff and made U.S. wine cheaper than French wine. Canada may then discontinue its wine imports from France in favor of imports from the United States. This is an example of trade diversion. Policymakers worry that the EU, NAFTA, and other economic blocs could turn into economic fortresses resulting in a decline in trade *between* blocs that exceeds the gains from trade *within* the blocs.

Reduced global free trade. In more advanced stages, regional integration can give rise to two opposing tendencies. On the one hand, a country that reduces trade barriers is moving toward free trade. On the other hand, an economic bloc that imposes external trade barriers is moving *away* from *worldwide* free trade. For instance, when countries form a customs union, the members impose common external trade

The European parliament meets in Strasbourg, France, where members of the EU make decisions about regional integration, including trade barriers and fiscal and monetary policy.

barriers and some member countries' external tariffs may actually *rise* relative to the tariffs in place prior to formation of the union.[13] Suppose that Germany, the EU's largest member, once had a 10 percent tariff on imported footwear. Assume that in the process of developing a common market, the EU countries collectively imposed a 20 percent tariff on footwear imports. In effect, Germany's external tariff on footwear has increased. In this way, regional integration results in *higher* trade barriers.

We addressed the harmful effects of import tariffs. Such trade barriers shield sellers inside the economic bloc from competitors based outside the bloc. However, buyers inside the bloc are worse off because they must pay higher prices for the products that they want to consume. Tariffs also counteract comparative advantages and interfere with trade flows that should be dictated by national endowments. All told, external trade barriers imposed by economic blocs result in a net loss in well-being to all the members of the bloc. Finally, because foreign firms sell less into a bloc that imposes restrictions, they are harmed as well. When external suppliers are based in developing economies, the consequences are significant. By limiting imports from such countries, trade barriers imposed by economic blocs threaten the ability of producers in these countries to improve their poor living conditions. This is the case, for example, of agricultural tariffs imposed by the EU and NAFTA blocs. These trade barriers do the most harm to farmers and ranchers in Africa, South America, and other areas characterized by substantial poverty. Governments need to consider the ethical consequences of such barriers when drafting regional integration agreements.[14]

Loss of national identity. When nations join together in an economic bloc, increased cross-border contact has a homogenizing effect; the members become more similar to each other and national cultural identity can be diluted. For this reason, member countries typically retain the right to protect certain industries vital to national heritage or security. For example, Canada has restricted the ability of U.S. movie and TV producers to invest in the Canadian film market. This is because Canada sees its film industry as a critical part of its national heritage and fears the dilution of its indigenous culture from an invasion of U.S. movie and TV entertainment programming. By enacting specific exclusions in the NAFTA accord, Canada has ensured that Canadian TV and movie interests remain largely in the hands of Canadians.

Sacrifice of autonomy. Later stages of regional integration require member countries to establish a central authority in order to manage the bloc's affairs. Each participating country must sacrifice to the central authority some of its autonomy, such as control over its own economy. In this way, nations that join an economic bloc run the risk of losing some of their national sovereignty. Concerns about national sovereignty have been a stumbling block in the development of the EU. In Britain, critics see the passage of many new laws and regulations by centralized EU authorities as a direct threat to British self-governance. Britain is a sovereign nation and the British electorate has little control over legislative efforts by EU federal authorities in continental Europe.[15] The British have resisted joining the European Monetary Union because such a move would reduce the power that they currently hold over their own currency, economy, and monetary regime.

Transfer of power to advantaged firms. Regional integration can concentrate economic power in the hands of fewer, more advantaged firms. Development of the regional marketplace attracts new competitors, from other bloc countries or from outside the bloc, into formerly protected national markets. Foreign invaders that are larger, have stronger brands, or enjoy other advantages can overwhelm local firms in their home markets. Moreover, regional integration encourages mergers and acquisitions within the bloc, leading to the creation of larger rivals. Over time, economic power gravitates toward the most advantaged firms in the bloc. Larger firms come to dominate smaller firms. For example, critics charged that as the

DR-CAFTA accord eliminated trade barriers that had protected Central American economies, U.S. firms entered these countries to manufacture and sell products. Because U.S. firms often enjoy advantages such as large size and better resources, some have come to dominate industries in Central America.

Failure of small or weak firms. As trade and investment barriers decline, protections are eliminated that previously shielded smaller or weaker firms from foreign competition. Companies typically find themselves battling new, often better-resourced rivals. New competitive pressures particularly threaten smaller firms, which may be absorbed or go out of business. The risk can be substantial for companies in smaller bloc countries, or in industries that lack comparative advantages. For example, under NAFTA, many U.S. companies in industries covered by the accord relocated their production to Mexico, the bloc member with the lowest wage rates. As a result, numerous firms in the U.S. tomato-growing industry went out of business as the industry shifted south to Mexico.

Corporate restructuring and job loss. Many firms must restructure to meet the competitive challenges posed in the new, enlarged marketplace of regional integration. Increased competitive pressures and corporate restructuring may lead to worker layoffs or re-assigning employees to distant locations. The resulting turmoil disrupts worker lives and, occasionally, entire communities. For example, MERCOSUR was a factor in the layoff of thousands of workers in Argentina's auto parts manufacturing sector. Low-priced auto parts from Brazil flowed into the MERCOSUR countries following implementation of the MERCOSUR agreement. The intense competition forced parts manufacturers in Argentina to cut costs, leading to worker layoffs.

In addition, regional integration compels many MNEs to centralize managerial control to regional or international headquarters. During this process, national managers may need to surrender some of their power and autonomy. For example, prior to EU unification, the Ford Motor Company maintained national headquarters in each of several European countries. Following EU unification, Ford reassigned some decision-making power from country heads to its European headquarters in Dagenham, England. The company centralized product design responsibilities, brought together pan-European design teams in Dagenham, and transferred financial controls and reporting to headquarters in the United States. Restructuring can prove difficult to managers, such as the head of Ford's subsidiary in Cologne, who resigned rather than lose power.

When they negotiate regional integration agreements, national governments have a responsibility to include provisions that reduce harmful effects such as job losses and the failure of small or weak firms. For example, NAFTA included various clauses aimed at softening the effects of economic restructuring that resulted from passage of the accord. NAFTA included provisions aimed at maintaining or improving labor conditions for workers in the member countries. Firms received long phase-in periods (often 10 years or more) to adjust to falling protectionist barriers. Funds were allocated to support the retraining of workers who lost their jobs due to NAFTA.

 # Management Implications of Regional Integration

Regional economic integration has implications for company strategy and performance. Many firms modify their strategies to take advantage of new opportunities in the enlarged marketplace or to safeguard their positions against potential threats. Choosing appropriate strategies depends largely on the firm's current position in the regional market, the characteristics of the firm's industry, and on the market's particular rules and regulations. Regional economic integration suggests at least six implications for management.

Internationalization by firms inside the economic bloc. Initially, regional integration pressures or encourages companies to internationalize into neighboring countries within the bloc. The elimination of trade and investment barriers also presents new opportunities to source input goods from foreign suppliers within the bloc. By venturing into other countries in the bloc, the firm can generate new sales and increase profits. Internationalizing into neighboring, familiar countries also provides the firm with the skills and confidence to further internationalize to markets *outside* the bloc. For example, following the formation of NAFTA, many U.S. companies entered Canada and gained valuable international experience that inspired them to launch ventures into Asia and Europe.

Rationalization of operations. Following the creation of an economic bloc, the importance of national boundaries will decrease. Instead of viewing the bloc as a collection of disparate countries, firms begin to view the bloc as a unified whole. Managers develop strategies and value-chain activities suited to the region as a whole, rather than to individual countries. *Rationalization* is the process of restructuring and consolidating company operations that managers often undertake following regional integration. When a firm rationalizes, it reduces redundancy. The goal is to reduce costs and increase the efficiency of operations. For example, management may combine two or more factories into a single production facility that eliminates duplication and generates economies of scale. Rationalization becomes an attractive option because, as trade and investment barriers decline, the firm that formerly operated factories in each of several countries reaps advantages by consolidating the factories into one or two central locations inside the economic bloc.

As an example, prior to formation of the EU, many companies operated factories in each of numerous European countries. After the EU's launch, these firms merged their plants into one or two European countries. Companies centralized plants in the EU locations that offered the lowest-cost operations and other competitive advantages. Thus, Caterpillar, the U.S. manufacturer of earth-moving equipment, was one of many companies that shifted its focus from serving individual European countries to serving the EU region. Caterpillar undertook a massive program of modernization and rationalization at its EU plants to streamline production, reduce inventories, increase economies of scale, and lower operating costs.

Companies can apply rationalization to other value-chain functions such as distribution, logistics, purchasing, and R&D. For example, following formation of the EU, the elimination of trade barriers, customs checkpoints, and country-specific transportation regulations allowed U.S. firms to restructure their EU distribution channels to make them better suited to the greatly enlarged EU marketplace. Creation of the economic bloc eliminated the need to devise separate distribution strategies for individual countries. Instead, the firms were able to employ a more global approach for the larger marketplace, generating economies of scale in distribution.

Mergers and acquisitions. The formation of economic blocs also leads to mergers and acquisitions (M&A); that is, the tendency of one firm to buy another, or of two or more firms to merge and form a larger company. Mergers and acquisitions are related to rationalization. The merger of two or more firms creates a new company that produces a product on a much larger scale. As an example, two giant engineering firms, Asea AB of Sweden and Brown, Boveri & Co. of Switzerland, merged to form Asea Brown Boveri (ABB). The merger was facilitated by regional integration of European countries in the development of the EU economic bloc. The merger allowed the new firm, ABB, to increase its R&D activities and pool greater capital funding for major projects, such as construction of power plants and large-scale industrial equipment. In the pharmaceutical industry, Britain's Zeneca purchased Sweden's Astra to form AstraZeneca. The acquisition led to the development of blockbusters such as the ulcer drug Nexium and helped transform the new company into a leader in the gastrointestinal, cardiovascular, and respiratory areas.

Regional products and marketing strategy. Regional integration can also stimulate companies to *standardize* their products and services. Companies prefer to offer relatively standardized merchandise in their various markets. The reason is that it is easier and much less costly to make and sell a few product models than dozens of models. An economic bloc facilitates the streamlining and standardization of products and marketing activities because, in more advanced stages of regional integration, the member countries tend to harmonize product standards and commercial regulations, and eliminate trade barriers and transportation bottlenecks. As conditions in the member countries become similar to each other, companies can increasingly standardize their products and marketing.[16]

For example, prior to EU unification, in order to comply with varying national regulations regarding the placement of lights, brakes, and other specifications on tractors sold in Europe, J. I. Case, a manufacturer of agricultural machinery, had produced numerous versions of its Magnum model of farm tractors. Where Case once produced 17 versions of the Magnum, the harmonization of EU product standards allowed the firm to standardize its tractor, allowing it to produce only a handful of models that were, nevertheless, appropriate for serving all the EU market.[17]

Internationalization by firms from outside the bloc. Regional integration leads to the creation of large multicountry markets, which are attractive to firms from *outside* the bloc. Such foreign firms tend to avoid exporting as an entry strategy because economic blocs erect trade barriers against imports from outside the bloc. Accordingly, the most effective way for a foreign firm to enter an economic bloc is to establish a physical presence there via FDI. By building a production facility, marketing subsidiary, or regional headquarters anywhere inside a bloc, the outsider gains access to the entire bloc and obtains advantages enjoyed by local firms based inside the bloc. As an example, since formation of the EU, Britain has become the largest recipient of FDI from the United States. U.S. firms choose Britain as the beachhead to gain access to the massive EU market. In a similar way, European firms have established factories in Mexico to access countries in the NAFTA bloc.

Collaborative ventures. Regional integration creates opportunities for cooperation among firms located inside their own bloc. For example, following creation of the European Community, the precursor to the EU, firms from France, Germany, Spain, and the United Kingdom collaborated to establish Airbus Industries, the giant commercial aircraft manufacturer. The elimination of trade and investment barriers in the EU allowed Airbus to move aircraft parts, capital, and labor among the member countries from one factory to another. In a similar way, firms from outside an economic bloc also benefit from regional integration. Outsiders ease their entry into the bloc by entering joint ventures and other collaborative arrangements with companies based inside the bloc.

In 1990, there were approximately 50 regional economic integration agreements worldwide. Today there are some 200, in various stages of development. As the growth in world trade continues apace, nations want to be part of emerging opportunities. Governments continue to liberalize trade policies, encourage imports, and restructure regulatory regimes, largely through regional cooperation. Many nations belong to several free trade agreements. Economic blocs are joining with other blocs around the world. More nations are clamoring to join the EU, which has signed trade agreements with other economic blocs worldwide. Other intercontinental blocs are underway. Empirical evidence since the 1970s suggests that regional economic integration is not slowing the progress of global free trade.[18] It is more likely that global free trade will gradually emerge as economic blocs link up with each other over time. The evidence suggests that regional economic integration is gradually giving way to a system of worldwide free trade.

CLOSING CASE

Russell Corporation: The Dilemma of Regional Free Trade

Russell Corporation is a leading manufacturer of sportswear, including sweatshirts, sweatpants, and T-shirts. Owned by Berkshire Hathaway, Russell is based in Atlanta, Georgia, in the United States, and has annual revenues of around $2 billion. Its main competitors include Adidas, Nike, Benetton, and Zara. Russell runs every step of the manufacturing process: from weaving raw yarn into fabric, to dyeing, cutting, and sewing, to selling garments through retailers. Russell's brands include JERZEES, American Athletic, Brooks, Cross Creek, Huffy Sports, Russell Athletic, and Spalding. The firm sells through mass merchandisers, department stores such as Wal-Mart, and golf pro shops. Russell sells its apparel in about 100 countries and recently restructured production. The firm closed plants, moved some manufacturing abroad, and eliminated 1,700 U.S. jobs.

Management at Russell was pleased with the passage of the Dominican Republic-Central American Free Trade Agreement (DR-CAFTA) in 2005. The pact eliminated trade barriers between the United States and six Latin American countries: Guatemala, Honduras, El Salvador, Nicaragua, Costa Rica, and the Dominican Republic. Following DR-CAFTA's passage, Central American countries experienced a significant rise in foreign direct investment (FDI) from abroad. The apparel and clothing sector—consisting of firms like Russell—were among the biggest beneficiaries.

Prior to DR-CAFTA, many North American apparel companies sourced from China and other Asian nations, where production costs are low. DR-CAFTA virtually eliminated tariffs on trade between the United States, Central America, and the Dominican Republic. Now Russell can cost-effectively source raw materials in Central America, manufacture fabric in the United States, then send the fabric to its factories in Honduras for assembly. Once the garments are completed, they are re-exported to the U.S. for distribution. Without DR-CAFTA, it would not have been cost effective to make fabric in the United States, export it to Asia, have the products manufactured there and then reexported back. Under that scenario, Russell would have shifted *all* its manufacturing to China.

Background on DR-CAFTA

In the past, Central America and the Caribbean were parties to various protectionist trade arrangements, including the worldwide Multi-Fibre Agreement (MFA) of 1974. Among its provisions, the MFA shielded the North and Central American apparel industries from foreign competition by imposing strict import quotas. When the MFA expired in 2005, many countries became exposed to the full force of cheap imports from low-cost producers in Asia. China dramatically increased its apparel exports to the United States, to the detriment of U.S. and Central American producers that long had supplied Western markets. For example, Alabama was once the world center of sock manufacturing. When the MFA expired, the sock capital shifted to Datang, China. Alabama sock workers receive an average of $10 an hour, compared to 70 cents an hour in Datang.

Since the expiration of the MFA, China has been flooding the United States with apparel. In recent years, China's share of finished clothing exports to the United States, once less than 20 percent, has leaped past 50 percent in some segments. To protect its home-grown apparel industry, the United States reimposed some trade barriers against Chinese imports. The U.S. government justified this action in part because China's currency, the yuan, is considered undervalued, which makes Chinese exports artificially cheap. However, such protection of the U.S. apparel industry is only temporary. World Trade Organization rules require the U.S. government to remove the trade barriers, at which time Chinese exports to the United States will increase.

Many in the U.S. apparel industry see DR-CAFTA as perhaps the only way to compete with China. DR-CAFTA helps maintain much apparel production in the Western Hemisphere by creating a bigger apparel market in the region and granting favorable trade status to apparel producers who manufacture their products using raw material from the DR-CAFTA region.

The United States is the biggest apparel market, importing more than $9 billion worth of apparel from the DR-CAFTA countries in each of 2004, 2005, and 2006. Honduras was the biggest shipper in dollar value, and exported products such as cotton blouses, shirts, and underwear. Meanwhile, DR-CAFTA gave U.S. producers an equal footing to sell their products to Central America. For example, the region is the second largest market for U.S. textiles and yarn, which Central American manufacturers use to produce finished apparel.

The DR-CAFTA countries are part of a large and growing trade region, and the free trade agreement is helping to improve economic conditions there. Perhaps the most important long-term benefit will be foreign investment in new technologies and a better-educated regional labor force. Some see DR-CAFTA as a further step toward development of the Free Trade Area of the Americas (FTAA), a proposed agreement that would bring free trade to all or most of North, Central, and South America.

The Situation in Honduras

Russell manufactures much of its garments in Honduras, a poor Central American country with 7 million people, one quarter of whom are illiterate. Honduras has an annual per-capita GDP of about $3,000. In 2006, the country's unemployment rate was 28 percent. The Honduras currency, the lempira, has been weakening against the U.S. dollar over time. Growth remains dependent on the U.S. economy, its largest trading partner, and on reduction of the high local crime rate. Honduras sends over 73 percent of its exported goods to the United States and receives about 53 percent of its imports from that country. The Honduran government is counting on the DR-CAFTA agreement to increase trade with the United States and the Central American region.

Few countries rely on their apparel industry more than Honduras. The Honduran government used incentives to create a large cluster of apparel firms. In addition to low-cost labor, Honduras offers a generous tax package: firms pay no income tax, value-added tax, or duties. Honduran apparel manufacturers can truck their merchandise to Puerto Cortes, Central America's biggest port, in just 30 minutes. From there, it takes only 22 hours to ship the goods to Miami by container ship. Honduras' apparel sector employs over 110,000 people, or 30 percent of the country's total industrial employment. The government is investing to improve Puerto Cortes and create a Textiles and Apparel University to train future managers and supervisors. To counter Chinese competition, the apparel industry in Honduras has begun to offer the "total package"—buying fabric, and sometimes even designing the garments, as well as final assembly.

Some Honduran apparel plants employ sophisticated technologies to increase productivity and output. For example, one supplier uses computer-aided design to cut cloth before sending it to be stitched into shirts for brands such as Jockey, Ralph Lauren, and Nautica. In 2003, the stock of U.S. FDI in Honduras was $262 million and rose to $339 million the following year. However, Honduras' legal system remains weak and corruption is a problem.

Honduran apparel producers are taking steps to survive in the evolving free trade environment. Geographic proximity to the United States is a big advantage that gives producers greater flexibility to respond quickly to rapidly evolving tastes. Honduran producers can ship finished merchandise to the United States in less than 24 hours, while similar shipments from China take up to a month.

Russell's Dilemmas

Many consumers shop for athletic clothing based on price, so even slight price increases can affect sales. Unlike Nike and Adidas, Russell does not enjoy much brand loyalty. Russell must decide whether to retain its manufacturing in Honduras or move everything to China.

An additional possibility is to establish production in Eastern Europe to gain access to the huge EU market. Meanwhile, Adidas and Nike are pursuing markets in China and other Asian countries. Labor costs for manufacturing apparel are similar in Central America and China. In both locations, workers earn around a dollar per hour and can produce over a hundred garments per day, from precut cloth. Labor costs are roughly $2 an hour in Eastern Europe, but producers are advantaged by being so close to the nearly 500 million consumers in the EU.

Management at Russell is keeping an eye on the proposed FTAA, which would widen access to the Latin American marketplace with its 500 million consumers. Maintaining a presence in Latin America would give Russell a favorable position for targeting new markets there. But progress on the FTAA has been slowed due to hostile public and governmental opposition from some South American countries. Governments in countries such as Bolivia and Venezuela argue that the FTAA will increase U.S. dominance in the region and harm local workers, subjecting them to sweatshop working conditions.

Meanwhile, regional integration is creating a larger market in the Western Hemisphere and new opportunities to source low-cost inputs from regional suppliers. While increased competition from China poses new challenges, the DR-CAFTA accord is helping to level the playing field. Russell management is concerned about manufacturing costs that are higher than competitors and is poised to consolidate much of its production into suppliers located close to its home market. At the same time, Russell is also contemplating new markets in the Americas and beyond.

AACSB: Reflective Thinking, Ethical Reasoning

Case Questions

1. Worldwide, China has the most absolute and comparative advantages in producing apparel. Free trade theory implies that retailers should import clothing from the most efficient country. Nevertheless, DR-CAFTA aims to promote Central American trade with the United States, and the United States has imposed quotas on imports from China. Given this, and the potential drawbacks of regional integration, would it be better to allow free trade to take its natural course? That is, would it be better to rescind DR-CAFTA and allow apparel retailers to import from the most cost-effective suppliers, wherever they are located worldwide?

2. What are the advantages and disadvantages of DR-CAFTA to Honduran firms? To Honduras as a nation? Should free trade be extended throughout Latin America through the proposed FTAA?

3. Honduras is a poor country that faces the loss of jobs in its apparel sector from growing foreign competition. What can the Honduran government do to help keep jobs in Honduras? The government can address some problems by attracting more foreign investment into Honduras. In what ways could foreign investment help? What steps could the government take to attract more FDI?

4. Russell Corporation is a smaller player than its formidable rivals, Adidas and Nike. What should Russell do to counter these firms? What should Russell do to counter the flood of low-cost athletic apparel now entering the United States from China? What strategic approaches should Russell follow to ensure its future survival and success? ◄

Sources: Authers, John. (2004). "Honduras Textile Groups Hope Trade Deal Will Sew Up Future." *Financial Times*, July 27, p. 8; Authers, John. (2006). "Employment Shrinks in the Textile Sector." *Financial Times*, March 10, p. 5; Borneman, Jim. (2006). "Regional Support in a Global Fight." *Textile World*, May/June, pp. 26–32; Central Intelligence Agency. (2006). *CIA World Factbook*, entry on Honduras; Colvin, Geoffrey. (2005). "Saving America's Socks—But Killing Free Trade." *Fortune*, August 22, p. 38; *Economist*. (2004). "Textiles: Losing Their Shirts," Oct. 16, pp. 59–60; *Financial Times*. (2007). "Adidas Sets Personal best in Sports Sales." March 28, p. 17; Hoovers.com. (2006). Corporate summaries of Russell, Nike, and Adidas. Retrieved from www.hoovers.com; Lapper, Richard. (2005). "Textile groups in a bind if U.S. unravels CAFTA treaty." *Financial Times*, June 7, p.18; Millman, John. (2003). "Central America Finds Impetus for Growth." *Wall Street Journal*, Dec. 8, p. A2; Morphy, Erika. (2005). "Trade Watch: CAFTA—The Rocky Path to Regional Free Trade. *Foreign Direct Investment*, Oct. 1,p. 1; Nike, Inc. (2007). "Nike, Inc. Outlines Strategies for Global Growth and Market Leadership across Core Consumer Categories." Retrieved Feb. 6, 2007, from www.nike.com; Paulson, Henry, Jr. (2005). "CAFTA Is the American Way." *Wall Street Journal*, July 14, p. A10; *Wall Street Journal*. (2005). "Russell Corp.: Profit Estimates are Lowered Because of Katrina and CAFTA." Sept. 20, p. 1.

CHAPTER ESSENTIALS

Key Terms

common market, p. 227
customs union, p. 226
economic union, p. 227
free trade agreement, p. 225

free trade area, p. 225
regional economic integration,
    p. 224

regional economic integration bloc,
    p. 225

Summary

In this chapter, you learned about:

1. Regional integration and economic blocs

Regional economic integration involves groups of countries forming alliances to promote free trade, cross-national investment, and other mutual goals. This integration results from **regional economic integration blocs** (or economic blocs), in which member countries agree to eliminate tariffs and other restrictions on the cross-national flow of products, services, capital, and, in more advanced stages, labor, within the bloc. At minimum, the countries in an economic bloc become parties to a **free trade agreement**, which eliminates tariffs, quotas, and other trade barriers.

2. Types of regional integration

For countries that become members of an economic bloc, there are various stages of regional integration. First is the **free trade area**, in which tariffs and other trade barriers are eliminated, and that emerge when nations sign a free trade agreement. Second is the **customs union**, a free trade area in which common trade barriers are imposed on nonmember countries. Third is the **common market**, a customs union in which factors of production move freely among the members. Fourth is the **economic union**, a common market in which some important economic policies are harmonized among the member states. A true *political union* does not yet exist.

3. Leading economic blocs

There are roughly 200 economic integration agreements in the world. The European Union (EU) is the most advanced of these, comprising 27 countries in Europe. The EU has increased market access, improved trade rules, and harmonized standards among its members. Europe is also home to the European Free Trade Association. In the Americas, the most notable bloc is the North American Free Trade Agreement (NAFTA). The bloc consists of Canada, Mexico, and the United States. NAFTA has reached only the free-trade-area stage of regional integration. Other economic blocs in the Americas include MERCOSUR, CARICOM, and CAN. In the Asia/Pacific region, ASEAN, APEC, and the Australia and New Zealand Closer Economic Relations Agreement (CER) are the leading blocs. Economic blocs in Africa and the Middle East have experienced only limited success.

4. Why countries pursue regional integration

Regional integration contributes to corporate and industrial growth, and hence to economic growth, better living standards, and higher tax revenues for the member countries. It increases market size by integrating the economies within a region. It increases economies of scale and factor productivity among firms in the member countries and attracts foreign investors to the bloc. Regional integration also increases competition and economic dynamism within the bloc, and increases the bloc's political power.

5. Success factors for regional integration

The most successful blocs consist of countries that are relatively similar in terms of culture, language, and economic and political structures. The countries should also be close to each other geographically. Countries can overcome major differences in any one of these factors if there are strong similarities in all the other factors.

6. Drawbacks and ethical dilemmas of regional integration

Regional integration simultaneously leads to *trade creation*, whereby new trade is generated among the countries inside the bloc, and *trade diversion*, in which member countries discontinue some trade with countries outside the bloc. Regional integration entails specific disadvantages. It can reduce global free trade, particularly when member countries form a customs union that results in substantial trade barriers to countries outside the bloc. When economic blocs involve many countries of various sizes, regional integration can concentrate power into large firms and large nations inside the bloc. Regional integration results in economic restructuring, which may harm particular industries and firms. When a country joins an economic bloc, it must relinquish some of its autonomy and national power to the bloc's central authority. Individual countries risk losing some of their national identity.

7. Management implications of regional integration

Regional integration leads to increased internationalization by firms inside their economic bloc. Firms reconfigure and rationalize their operations in line with the larger internal market. Management reconfigures value-chain activities on a pan-regional basis. The formation of economic blocs also leads to mergers and acquisitions because the emergence of a new, larger market favors the creation of larger firms. Managers revise marketing strategies by standardizing products and developing regional brands. Regional integration also leads firms from outside the bloc to expand into the bloc, often via direct investment and collaborations with bloc firms. But regional integration leads to competitive pressures and other challenges to firms inside the bloc, some of which may lay off workers or go out of business.

Test Your Comprehension AACSB: Reflective Thinking

1. What is a regional economic integration bloc (also called an economic bloc)?

2. What is the role of free trade agreements in the formation of economic blocs?

3. What are the different levels of economic integration?

4. Differentiate between a free trade area and a customs unions. Differentiate between a customs unions and a common market.

5. What are the world's leading economic blocs? Which blocs are most advanced in terms of regional integration?

6. Describe the major characteristics of the European Union and NAFTA.

7. Why do nations seek to join or form economic blocs? What are the advantages of such arrangements?

8. What national conditions contribute to the success of economic integration?

9. Explain the drawbacks of regional integration for nations. Explain the drawbacks for firms.

10. Distinguish between trade creation and trade diversion.

11. What strategies should companies employ to maximize the benefits of regional integration?

Apply Your Understanding
AACSB: Ethical Reasoning, Reflective Thinking, Communication

1. There are some 200 economic integration agreements in effect around the world already, far more than even a few years ago. Virtually every country is now party to one or more free trade agreements. Supporters argue that free trade is good for nations. What is the basis for their support? That is, what are the specific benefits that countries seek by joining an economic bloc? What is the main economic bloc for your country? From your perspective, what advantages has bloc membership brought to your country? What disadvantages has bloc membership produced?

2. The United States is in free trade agreements with Mexico, Canada (NAFTA), and several Central American countries (via the DR-CAFTA accord featured in the *Closing Case*), among others. Critics charge that these agreements are harmful because of the substantial wage differences with the partner countries. For example, a Mexican worker may earn one-fifth the hourly wage of a U.S. worker. Critics further argue it would be unwise for the United States to establish a common market or economic union with Latin American countries. They argue that a U.S. worker will be disadvantaged relative to a Mexican worker if he or she does not work with more or better natural resources than the Mexican, have a better skill set, and have access to better technology. What can U.S. firms do to maintain their competitiveness relative to Mexican firms, given Mexico's advantage in low wages? It is likely that some day the United States will form a common market with Mexico and other Latin American partners. In your view, what conditions should be in place before such an agreement is allowed to go forward?

3. Following implementation of free trade agreements, trade has grown *within* each of the CARICOM and CAN economic blocs. The growth of within-bloc trade implies that exports from your country to these blocs may be declining over time. Discuss strategies for counteracting such a shift. What recommendations would you make to a company for pursuing opportunities within these blocs? What is the role of international business research, market entry strategy, foreign direct investment, marketing strategy, and collaboration for maintaining or augmenting commerce with these blocs?

AACSB: **Reflective Thinking, Analytical Skills, Ethical Reasoning**

Refer to Chapter 1, page 27, for instructions on how to access and use globalEDGE™.

1. There has been much opposition to the Free Trade Area of the Americas (FTAA). For a sampling of arguments against this proposed pact, visit www.globalexchange.org; www.citizenstrade.org/stopftaa.php; and www.corpwatch.org. Also visit the official site of the FTAA at www.ftaa-alca.org, or get information on the proposed pact from globalEDGE™. Based on your reading of the chapter, evaluate the anti-FTAA arguments. What is your position? Do you agree or disagree with arguments made by the critics? Why or why not? Do you think the proposed FTAA would harm small Latin American countries? Would it be a boon only to large countries such as Brazil, Canada, and the United States?

2. Visit the Web sites of three major economic blocs. One way to do this is to enter the acronyms for each bloc into a globalEDGE™ search. Using the "Success Factors for Regional Integration" framework highlighted in this chapter, discuss the likely long-term prospects for success in each of these blocs. For each bloc, which of the success factors are strongest and which are weakest? Which bloc seems to have the best chances for long-term success? Why?

3. NAFTA is a free trade area, and the EU is a common market. Visit the Web sites of these two economic blocs, www.nafta-sec-alena.org and europa.eu.int, and explain the business strategy implications of each type of economic bloc. Small and medium-sized enterprises (SMEs) tend to be disadvantaged when it comes to competing against large corporations in regional economic blocs. What steps can SMEs in particular take to maximize prospects for success when doing business in a free trade area? What steps can SMEs take when doing business in a common market?

Management Skill Builder©

Entering the Retailing Sector in the New EU Member States

Retailers expand internationally primarily through foreign direct investment. Major retailers such as Wal-Mart and Tesco have been expanding abroad since the 1970s. Recently, retailers have been targeting Eastern European countries that have joined the European Union (EU) since 2004. With a population of almost a half-billion people, the EU is an impressive potential market. However, recent enlargement of the EU from 15 to 27 members has proven difficult. Challenges have arisen due to differences in the economic conditions and the developmental stage of the new members, which are mainly Eastern European countries and former satellites of the Soviet Union.

AACSB: Reflective Thinking, Analytical Skills

Managerial Challenge

Numerous retailers are making plans to take advantage of the entry of new country markets into the EU. However, choosing the best markets to locate stores is complex because there are so many locations to consider. Managers conduct research to ensure they establish stores in locations most likely to enhance company performance.

Background

As a single unit, the EU has the largest economy in the world. The countries that joined the EU since 2004 differ in many ways from the original EU members. Most are former Soviet satellites that were under a communist command economy for several decades. New entrants such as Poland, Hungary, and the Czech Republic had to adjust their economies to qualify for EU membership. There are substantial business opportunities in these countries for large-scale retailers. Income levels in the new members are growing and the countries are excellent sites from which retailers can source manufactured goods at lower cost.

Managerial Skills You Will Gain

By completing this C/K/R Management Skill Builder©, as a prospective manager, you will:

1. Learn about the EU and its expansion to include countries in Eastern Europe.

2. Examine conditions in Eastern Europe faced by potential entrants.

3. Understand the factors to consider when locating retail stores abroad.

4. Determine how country factors relate to maximizing competitive advantage in the location of retail stores.

Your Task

Assume that you work for a large retailer, such as Wal-Mart, Tesco, or Zara. Management wants to expand into new member states of the European Union. Your task is to conduct research to determine the most attractive location for establishing a large retail store and central distribution center.

Go to the C/K/R Knowledge Portal©

www.prenhall.com/cavusgil

Proceed to the C/K/R Knowledge Portal© to obtain the expanded background information, your task and methodology, suggested resources for this exercise, and the presentation template.

Understanding Emerging Markets

> ## The New Global Challengers: Newly Internationalizing MNEs from Emerging Markets

Emerging markets are countries such as Brazil, China, India, Mexico, and Turkey that, in contrast to advanced economies, are experiencing rapid economic growth, industrialization, and modernization. Most emerging markets are characterized by a young population and a growing middle-class.[1] While emerging markets represent attractive markets and low-cost manufacturing bases, they also tend to have inadequate commercial infrastructure, evolving legal systems, and a high-risk business environment. Despite their drawbacks, emerging markets have begun to produce *new global challengers,* top firms that are fast becoming key contenders in world markets. These firms pose competitive challenges to companies from the advanced economies, such as in Europe, Japan, and North America.

In a recent study, The Boston Consulting Group identified the top 100 firms from emerging markets that have successfully ventured into global markets. While many of these firms are from China and India, others hail from various other countries. For example, the Mexican firm Cemex is one of the world's largest cement producers. In Russia, Lukoil has big ambitions in the global energy sector. In Turkey, diversified conglomerate Koc Holding owns Arcelik, the giant home appliance producer.

The Brazilian food processors, Sadia and Perdigao, exemplify the international entrepreneurship of the new global challengers. These firms operate farms and market chilled and frozen foods, cereals, and ready-to-eat meals. Each firm is a $2 billion enterprise and exports about half of its annual production. Abundant production resources for pork, poultry, and grains in Brazil and ideal growing conditions for animal feed provide advantages for these firms. Both Sadia and Perdigao also take pride in their world-class global distribution and supply-chain management systems.

The new global challengers, including Sadia and Perdigao, apply business strategies, such as using home-country natural resources, low-cost sources of labor, engineering and managerial talent that sometimes exceed those of their counterparts in highly industrialized countries. Many of the firms are growing internationally by taking their established brands to global markets. For example, China's Hisense sells millions of its branded television sets and air conditioners in over 40 countries. It is the best-selling brand of flat-panel TV in France. Hisense also makes stylish consumer electronics at low prices.

Another strategy of new global challengers is to turn engineering into global innovation. Brazil's Embraer has tapped the large labor market of experienced but low-cost engineers in that country to build innovative small jets. Embraer has zipped past Canada's Bombardier to become the world's largest producer of regional jet aircraft. Some emerging market firms have assumed global leadership in specific product categories, such as Hong Kong's Johnson Electric, the world leader in small electric motors for automotive and consumer applications.

Other new global challengers have leveraged local bases of ample natural resources. Russia's Rusal is extracting the country's rich reserves of bauxite to produce aluminum for international markets. The majority of the world's natural resources are located in developing economies, and a growing number of new global challengers use those resources to their advantage. China's CNOOC, for example, has been buying into oil and gas reserves in Asia and Africa.

Rolling out new business models to multiple markets is another strategy employed by new global challengers. Some gain access to key markets by acquiring important local businesses. Others build relationships with major retailers, such as Home Depot and Wal-Mart. Still others target high-volume sales to large industrial buyers. For instance, China's BYD targets Motorola, Nokia, and Sony Ericsson to sell its cell phone batteries.

The success of new global challengers suggests that the character of international trade and investment is shifting. Today, there are many more emerging market firms active on the world stage. They possess distinct advantages and are becoming key competitors to MNEs from advanced economies, which have traditionally dominated international business. The firms identified in the Boston Consulting Group study are just the tip of the iceberg; thousands of firms from emerging markets have big global dreams and are progressing accordingly. Managers from the advanced economies who don't take these new rivals seriously risk getting blindsided.

Sources: Boston Consulting Group. (2006). *The New Global Challengers.* Boston: The Boston Consulting Group, Inc.; Engardio, Pete. (2006). "Emerging Giants." *Business Week*, July 31, pp. 40–42.

In this chapter we discuss emerging market economies and contrast them to the other two major groups of countries: advanced economies and developing economies. Our focus is on the emerging markets since they represent the most important settings for growth-minded companies today.[2] Each country group poses distinctive opportunities and risks for companies engaged in international business. By exploring a country's stage of economic development, a manager can gain insights into at least three important country characteristics: the purchasing capacity of its citizens, the sophistication of the business sector, and the adequacy of commercial infrastructure, in such areas as communications, transportation, and energy generation.

 The Distinction between Advanced Economies, Developing Economies, and Emerging Markets

Exhibit 9.1 highlights the advanced economies, developing economies, and the emerging markets. **Advanced economies** are post-industrial countries characterized by high per-capita income, highly competitive industries, and well-developed commercial infrastructure. The advanced economies are the world's richest countries and include Australia, Canada, Japan, New Zealand, the United States, and most European countries. **Developing economies** are low-income countries characterized by limited industrialization and stagnant economies. Of the developing

Advanced economies
Post-industrial countries characterized by high per-capita income, highly competitive industries, and well-developed commercial infrastructure.

Developing economies
Low-income countries characterized by limited industrialization and stagnant economies.

economies, the most numerous group includes Bangladesh, Nicaragua, and Zaire. Emerging market economies or, briefly, **emerging markets**, refer to a subset of former developing economies that have achieved substantial industrialization, modernization, and rapid economic growth since the 1980s. The economies are differentiated by degree of economic development and per-capita income. Currently, some 27 countries are considered emerging markets. These economies are found mainly in Asia, Latin America, and Eastern Europe. The largest emerging markets are China, India, Brazil, and Russia.

Exhibit 9.2 on pages 258–259 provides an overview of the key differences among the three groups of countries.

Emerging markets Subset of former developing economies that have achieved substantial industrialization, modernization, and rapid economic growth since the 1980s.

Advanced Economies

Having reached a fairly mature state of industrial development, advanced economies largely transformed from manufacturing economies into service-based economies. Home to only about 14 percent of the world's population, the advanced economies have long dominated international business. They account for about half of world GDP, over half of world trade in products, and three-quarters of world trade in services.

Advanced economies have democratic, multiparty systems of government. Their economic systems are usually based on capitalism, with relatively little government intervention in business. They have tremendous purchasing power, with few restrictions on international trade and investment. They host the world's largest MNEs. A leading example is Ireland, which has one of the world's best performing economies, a booming job market, and per-capita income higher than many of its European neighbors. Ireland succeeded through a program of strict fiscal and monetary policies. The government cut federal spending, taxes, and borrowing. Such policies gave rise to lower interest rates, more available capital, and attracted much FDI from foreign manufacturers in high-tech industries, such as Gateway and Polaroid. Over time Ireland has built up a strong educational system, producing a steady supply of skilled workers, scientists, engineers, and managers.[3]

Developing Economies

Developing country consumers have low discretionary incomes; the proportion of personal income spent on purchases other than food, clothing, and housing is very limited. Approximately 17 percent of people in developing economies live on less than $1 per day. Around 40 percent live on less than $2 per day.[4] To compound matters, birth rates in developing economies tend to be high. The combination of low income and high birth rates tends to perpetuate the poverty characteristic of developing economies. Developing economies are sometimes called *underdeveloped countries* or *third-world countries*. However, these terms are imprecise because, despite poor economic conditions, the countries tend to be highly developed in historical and cultural terms.

Developing economies are also hindered by high infant mortality, malnutrition, short life expectancy, illiteracy, and poor education systems. For example, the proportion of children who finish primary school in most African countries is less than 50 percent.[5] Because education is strongly correlated with economic development, poverty tends to persist. Lack of adequate health care is a big concern. Some 95 percent of the world's AIDS victims are found in developing economies, an additional hardship that hampers their development. Ailing adults cannot work or care for their children and require much medical care. As a result, productivity is stagnant, which means living standards deteriorate. Orphaned children are unlikely to get an education, and the vicious cycle of poverty persists.

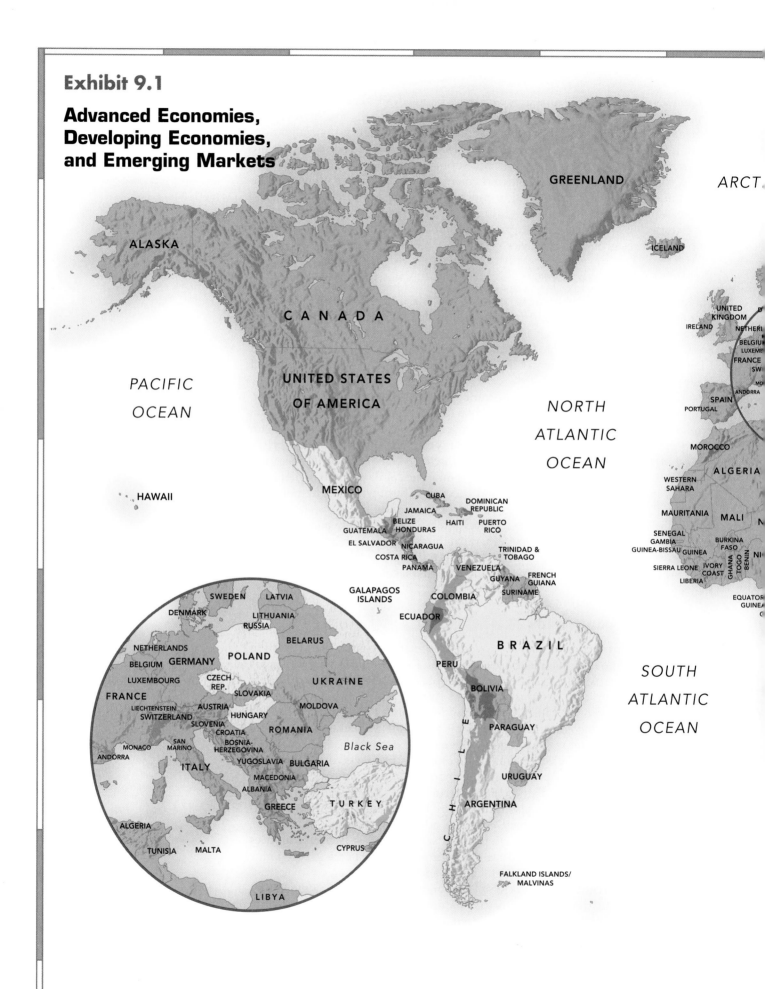

Exhibit 9.1

Advanced Economies, Developing Economies, and Emerging Markets

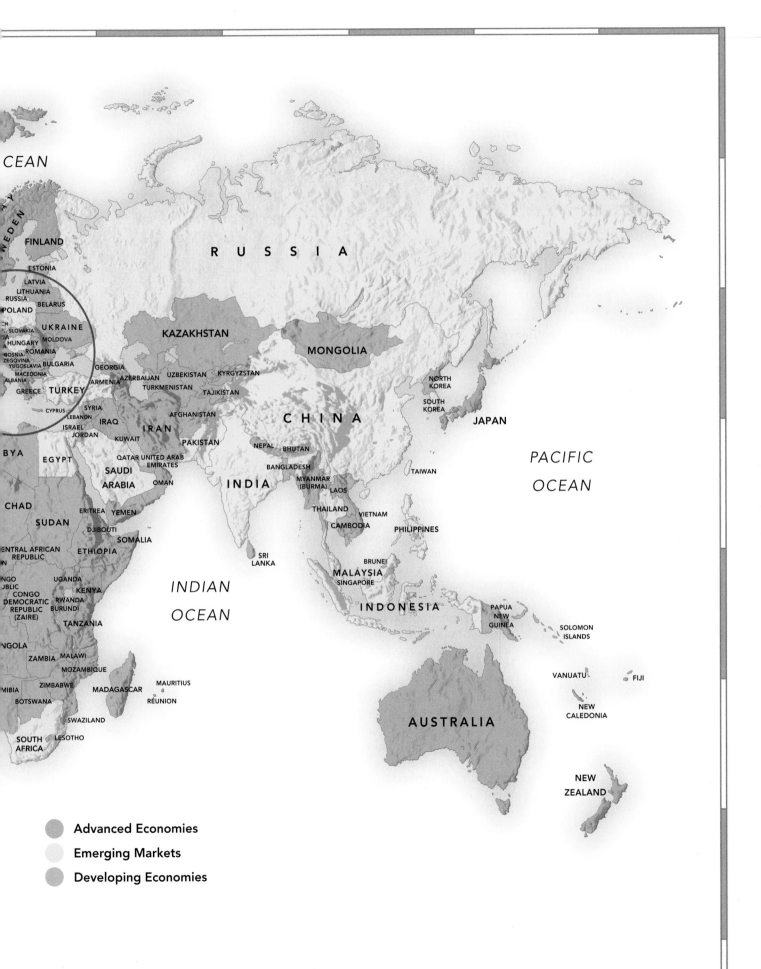

OCEAN

SWEDEN
FINLAND
ESTONIA
LATVIA
LITHUANIA
RUSSIA
BELARUS
POLAND
CH
SLOVAKIA
IA
HUNGARY MOLDOVA
A
BOSNIA ROMANIA
ZEGOVINA
YUGOSLAVIA BULGARIA
MACEDONIA
ALBANIA
GREECE TURKEY
CYPRUS SYRIA
LEBANON
ISRAEL IRAQ
JORDAN KUWAIT
BYA
EGYPT
SAUDI
ARABIA OMAN
QATAR UNITED ARAB
EMIRATES

RUSSIA

KAZAKHSTAN

MONGOLIA

GEORGIA
ARMENIA AZERBAIJAN
TURKMENISTAN
UZBEKISTAN KYRGYZSTAN
TAJIKISTAN
AFGHANISTAN
IRAN
PAKISTAN

NORTH
KOREA
SOUTH
KOREA
JAPAN

CHINA

PACIFIC
OCEAN

NEPAL BHUTAN
BANGLADESH
INDIA MYANMAR
(BURMA) LAOS
TAIWAN

CHAD
SUDAN
ERITREA YEMEN
DJIBOUTI
SOMALIA

ENTRAL AFRICAN
REPUBLIC
N
ETHIOPIA

NGO
UBLIC
CONGO
DEMOCRATIC
REPUBLIC
(ZAIRE)
UGANDA
RWANDA
BURUNDI
KENYA

TANZANIA

THAILAND
VIETNAM
CAMBODIA
PHILIPPINES

SRI
LANKA

BRUNEI
MALAYSIA
SINGAPORE

INDIAN

OCEAN

INDONESIA
PAPUA
NEW
GUINEA

SOLOMON
ISLANDS

NGOLA
ZAMBIA MALAWI
MOZAMBIQUE
MIBIA ZIMBABWE
BOTSWANA
MADAGASCAR
MAURITIUS
RÉUNION

VANUATU
FIJI

NEW
CALEDONIA

SWAZILAND
SOUTH LESOTHO
AFRICA

AUSTRALIA

NEW
ZEALAND

● Advanced Economies
● Emerging Markets
● Developing Economies

259

Dimension	Advanced economies	Developing economies	Emerging markets
Representative countries	Canada, France, Japan, United Kingdom, United States	Angola, Bolivia, Nigeria, Bangladesh	Brazil, China, India, Indonesia, Turkey
Approximate number of countries	30	150	27
Population (Percentage of world)	14	24	62
Approximate average per capita income (U.S. dollars; PPP basis)	33,750	6,450	13,250
Approximate share of world GDP (PPP basis)	48	9	43
Population (millions)	892	1,877	3,775
Telephone lines per 1,000 people (fixed and mobile)	1,369	355	724
Personal computers per 1,000 people	517	39	191
Internet users per 1,000 people	533	103	240

Exhibit 9.2 Key Differences among the Three Major Country Groups

SOURCE: World Bank at www.worldbank.com: International Monetary Fund at www.imf.com

Governments in developing economies are often severely indebted. In fact, some countries in Africa, Latin America, and South Asia have debt levels that approach or exceed their annual gross domestic product. This means it would cost a year's worth of national productive output just to pay off the national debt. Much of Africa's poverty is the result of government policies that discourage entrepreneurship, trade, and investment. For example, starting a new business in sub-Saharan countries in Africa involves an average of 11 different approvals and takes 62 days to complete. In the advanced economies, by contrast, starting a new business takes an average of six approvals and 17 days to complete.[6] Bureaucracy and red tape in developing economies often hinder the ability of firms from these countries to participate in the global economy.

International trade and investment help to stimulate economic growth, create jobs, raise incomes, and lower prices for the products and services demanded by consumers and companies. When countries are cut off from the global economy, the result is increased poverty and unemployment – conditions that can give rise to revolution, terrorism, and war. By contrast, nations that participate actively in the global economy enjoy economic stability and better living standards. As Exhibit 9.3 illustrates, there are substantial differences in critical trade conditions across the three country groups.

Emerging Market Economies

Emerging markets are found in East and South Asia, Eastern Europe, South Africa, Latin America, and the Middle East. Perhaps the most distinguishing characteristic is that these countries are enjoying rapidly improving living standards and a growing middle class with rising economic aspirations. As a result, their importance in the world economy is increasing as attractive destinations for exports, FDI, and sourcing.

Trade condition	Advanced economies	Developing economies	Emerging markets
Industry	Highly developed	Poor	Rapidly improving
Competition	Substantial	Limited	Moderate but increasing
Trade barriers	Minimal	Moderate to high	Rapidly liberalizing
Trade volume	High	Low	High
Inward FDI	High	Low	Moderate to high

Exhibit 9.3

Trade Conditions within Major Country Groups

SOURCES: International Monetary Fund at www.imf.org, World Bank at www.worldbank.org, and *CIA World Factbook 2007* at https://www.cia.gov/cia/publications/factbook/

Because of dynamic changes in these economies, the list of countries regarded as emerging markets is also evolving. For example, it can be argued that Hong Kong, Israel, Saudi Arabia, Singapore, South Korea, and Taiwan have developed beyond the emerging market stage. Several emerging markets will join the group of wealthy nations in the not-too-distant future. In 2004, emerging markets, including the Czech Republic, Hungary, and Poland, received a boost when they became members of the European Union. By joining the EU, these countries had to adopt stable monetary and trade policies. They leverage their low-cost labor to attract investment from Western Europe, thereby boosting their economies.

Similarly, some countries currently classified as developing economies have the potential to become emerging markets in the near future. These include the European countries of Estonia, Latvia, Lithuania, Slovakia; the Latin American countries of Costa Rica, Panama, and Uruguay; as well as Kazakhstan, Nigeria, Vietnam, and the United Arab Emirates. Finally, economic prosperity often varies *within* emerging markets. In these countries, there are usually two sets of economies—those in urban areas and those in rural areas: urban areas tend to have more developed economic infrastructure and consumers with greater discretionary income than rural areas.

Those emerging markets in Eastern Europe such as the Czech Republic, Hungary, and Poland have also been engaged in rapid privatization of former state enterprises since 1989 after these countries transformed from centrally planned economies into liberalized markets. Therefore, these emerging markets are also referred to as **transition economies**. China and Russia are also considered transition economies.

Privatization of state enterprises and promoting new, privately-owned businesses were important first steps in attracting foreign direct investment. **Privatization** refers to transfer of state-owned industries to private concerns. Most transition economies have been engaged in large-scale privatization of state-owned enterprises.

The transition economies hold much potential. Long burdened by excessive regulation and entrenched government bureaucracy, they are gradually introducing legal frameworks to protect business and consumer interests and ensure intellectual property rights. Yet, the changes that have been occurring in transition economies are often painful. For instance, within a few years of the collapse of the Soviet Union, the Russian economy shrunk by nearly half the size it had been at the beginning of its transformation in 1989. Russia endured high inflation with annual price increases reaching 100 percent or more, hindering foreign investment and economic development. Shaking off the Soviet legacy required the country to restructure not just institutions and firms, but also adopt new values about private ownership, profits, intellectual property, and other fundamental aspects of a free-market economy. Initially, western companies

Transition economies Subset of emerging markets that have transformed from centrally planned economies into liberalized markets.

Privatization Transfer of state-owned industries to private concerns.

Characteristic	Advanced economies	Developing economies	Emerging markets
Median age of citizens	38 years	24 years	32 years
Major sector focus	Services, branded products	Agriculture, commodities	Manufacturing, some services
Education level	High	Low	Medium
Economic and political freedom	Free or mostly free	Mostly repressed	Moderately free or mostly not free
Economic / political system	Capitalist	Authoritarian, socialist, or communist	Rapidly transitioning to capitalism
Regulatory environment	Minimal regulations	Highly regulated, burdensome	Achieved much economic liberalization
Country risk	Low	Moderate to high	Variable
Intellectual property protection	Strong	Weak	Moderate and improving
Infrastructure	Well-developed	Inadequate	Moderate but improving

Exhibit 9.4   National Characteristics of Major Country Groups

SOURCES: International Monetary Fund at www.imf.org, World Bank at www.worldbank.org, and *CIA World Factbook 2007* at https:// www.cia.gov/cia/publications/factbook/

doing business in Russia found it difficult to recruit managers who understood modern management practices. Management education in Russia is just catching up with that of developed nations.[7]

As transition economies liberalized their markets, many foreign companies initiated trade and investment relationships with them. Privatization provided many opportunities for foreign firms to enter these markets by purchasing former state enterprises. In Eastern Europe, Western companies are leveraging inexpensive labor and other advantages in the region to manufacture products bound for export markets. Hungary, Poland, the Czech Republic, and other former East Bloc countries have made great strides in political and economic restructuring. These countries are well on their way to more advanced stages of economic development.

Exhibit 9.4 contrasts the national characteristics of emerging markets with the other two country groups. Exhibit 9.5 shows that emerging markets account for over 40 percent of world GDP. Similarly, they represent over 30 percent of exports and receive over 20 percent of FDI.

In the mid-2000s, the emerging markets collectively enjoyed an average annual GDP growth rate of nearly 7 percent, a remarkable feat. As Exhibit 9.6 shows, their economies have been growing much faster than those of the advanced economies.

Emerging markets possess numerous advantages that have fostered their rise. The presence of low-cost labor, knowledge workers, government support, low-cost capital, and powerful, highly networked conglomerates have helped make these countries formidable challengers in the global marketplace. **New global challengers** are top firms from rapidly developing emerging markets that are fast becoming key contenders in world markets. One example is Orascom Telecom, an Egyptian mobile telecommunications provider that has leveraged managerial skills, superior technology, and rapid growth to become one of the leading telecoms in Africa and the Middle East. Starting in 1997, management strung together a telecom empire that stretches from North Africa to Iraq to Pakistan and

New global challengers Top firms from rapidly developing emerging markets that are fast becoming key contenders in world markets.

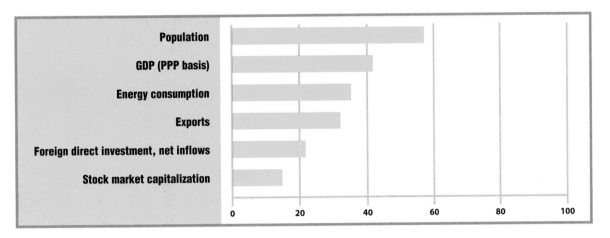

Exhibit 9.5   Why They Matter: Emerging Markets as a Percent of World Total

Note: Taiwan is not included because of insufficient data.

SOURCES: Economist. (2006). "The New Titans," September 14, survey section; International Monetary Fund at www.imf.org; Central Intelligence Agency. (2006). *World Factbook*, at www.cia.gov; World Bank at web.worldbank.org

Bangladesh. Orascom now has roughly 50 million subscribers and more than $3 billion in annual revenues. Operating expenses in Egypt are perhaps a tenth of what they are in Europe, because engineers and sales people work for less. Orascom's advantage is growth, which provides a continuous stream of capital to fund expansion plans. Management has excelled at local branding and tailoring telephone products and services to local pocketbooks.[8]

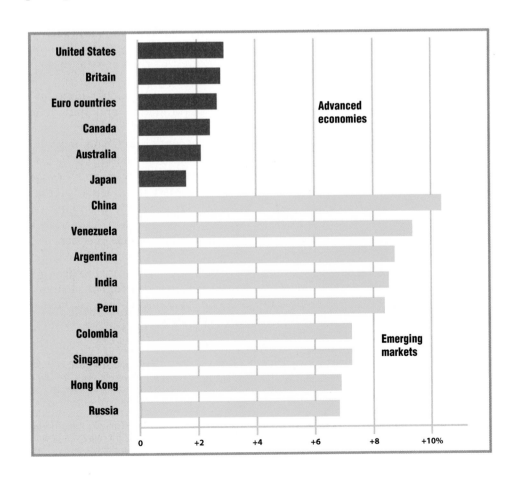

Exhibit 9.6

GDP Growth Rates in Advanced Economies and Emerging Markets

SOURCE: Norris, Floyd (2006), "Maybe Developing Nations Are Not Emerging but Have Emerged," *The New York Times*, December 30, p. 8. Copyright © 2006 New York Times Co. Reprinted with permission.

China is the largest emerging market, and its role in international business is expanding rapidly. With a population of 1.3 billion people (one-fifth of the world total), the Chinese economy continues to grow at an impressive rate of nearly 10 percent per year. The country has already produced numerous new global challengers, such as Shanghai Automotive (China's top automaker), Sinopec (a large oil company), and Shanghai Baosteel (a steel manufacturer). The *Global Trend* feature highlights China's growing role in international business.

> GLOBAL TREND

China: Growing Role in International Business

A huge population and rapidly growing economy make China a huge importer of consumer products, technology, and commodities. Long a communist regime, China began pursuing market reforms in the late 1970s. It achieved explosive economic growth, quadrupling its GDP during the succeeding 30 years. China's growth was especially fast in the 1990s—while exports amounted to just $78 billion in 1993, they surged to $974 billion by 2006. Although income per person is still modest at around $6,800, China in 2007 stood as the second-largest economy in the world (after the United States).

China's economic reforms have progressed in fits and starts, with the national government periodically loosening and tightening central controls. China has struggled to sustain job growth for tens of millions of workers laid off from state-owned enterprises, migrants, and new entrants to the workforce. Roughly one hundred million rural workers drift between villages and the huge cities, many subsisting through part-time, low-paying jobs. Poor infrastructure in communications and transportation remains a major challenge, especially in the countryside.

After joining the WTO in 2001, China's role as a global manufacturing site expanded, triggering massive exports to Europe, the United States,

and elsewhere worldwide. Investment has poured into China from MNEs who perceive a bright future for the country both as a manufacturing platform and huge consumer market. China buys roughly 20 percent of the world's aluminum, copper, washing machines, soybeans, poultry, and ice cream. It consumes roughly one-third of the world's coal, cotton, fish, rice, and cigarettes. The country buys one-quarter of the world's steel and one-half its pork. It is home to 20 percent of the world's cell phone users. Rapid industrialization means that the country needs to import aircraft, machinery, production equipment, telecommunications technology, and various raw materials.

These trends are both a boon and a bane to international business. While it is a booming new market, China also puts considerable strain on world resources, leading to higher commodity prices. It also means environmental degradation. Eight of the 10 most polluted cities in the world are now in China. The country now releases 13 percent of global carbon dioxide emissions, second only to the United States (23 percent). There are also serious problems of water pollution, deforestation, desertification, and soil problems.[9] Nevertheless, all this suggests opportunities for western firms marketing technologies and equipment for the protection of the environment.

To profit from China's low-cost labor and growing affluence, thousands of foreign companies set up sales offices and manufacturing facilities there. For most of these firms, however, success has come slowly, or not at all. The biggest problem is that China is still relatively poor. Out of a total population of 1.3 billion, the realistic target consumer segment is much smaller, perhaps 250 million middle-class residents of urban areas, largely along the more developed eastern coastal regions. Other challenges include regional differences in language, autonomous local governments, and inadequate infrastructure. Yet, many companies have succeeded in China, including Coca-Cola, General Motors, McDonald's, Motorola, Airbus, and Volkswagen. Wal-Mart saved immense sums by sourcing over $30 billion of merchandise from China in 2007. Success in China requires a deep understanding of the market and long-term commitment. The country holds huge long-term potential for firms that take the time and invest the resources to succeed there.

Sources: Central Intelligence Agency. (2007). *World Factbook*, www.cia.org; *Fortune*. (1999). "China's Tough Markets," October 11, p. 282; *Fortune*. (2004). "What China Eats (and Drinks and. . .)" October 4, pp. 151–53; Garten, Jeffrey. (1997). *The big ten: The big emerging markets and how they will change our lives.* New York: Basic Books.

What Makes Emerging Markets Attractive for International Business

Emerging markets are attractive to internationalizing firms as target markets, manufacturing bases, and sourcing destinations.

Emerging Markets as Target Markets

Emerging markets have become important for marketing a wide variety of products and services. The growing middle class in these countries implies substantial demand for a variety of consumer products such as electronics and automobiles and services such as health care. For example, roughly a quarter of Mexico's 105 million people enjoy affluence equivalent to many in the United States. Businesses in these countries also demand technology and equipment. Exports to emerging markets account for one-third of total merchandise exports from the United States. The largest emerging markets have doubled their share of world imports in the last few years.

Emerging markets are excellent targets for manufactured products and technology. For example, the textile machinery industry in India is huge, oil and gas exploration plays a vital role in Russia, and agriculture is a major sector in China. Emerging markets are also home to various niche markets. For example, Lockheed Aircraft, whose Hercules turboprop is a popular airliner in poorer countries, has developed transport planes that carry bulk commodities at relatively low costs. Novartis and Pfizer are pharmaceutical firms that reap big profits from selling vaccines and medicines that can be stored without refrigeration when shipped to distant markets. Airbus Industries is a leading commercial aircraft manufacturer based in Europe. It has developed a double-decker plane for both passengers and cargo, targeted to increasing traffic between advanced and emerging markets. For various products and services, demand is growing fastest in emerging markets. For example, for power tool companies like Black & Decker and Robert Bosch, the fastest-growing markets are in Asia, Latin America, Africa, and the Middle East.[10]

Finally, governments and state enterprises in emerging markets are major targets for sale of infrastructure-related products and services such as machinery, power transmission equipment, transportation equipment, high-technology products, and other products that countries in the middle stage of development typically need.

Emerging Markets as Manufacturing Bases

Emerging markets have long served as platforms for manufacturing by MNEs. Firms from Japan, Europe, the United States, and other advanced economies have invested vast sums to develop manufacturing facilities in emerging markets. The reason is that these markets are home to low-wage, high-quality labor for manufacturing and assembly operations. In addition, some emerging markets have large reserves of raw materials and natural resources. As examples, Mexico and China are important production platforms for manufacturing cars and consumer electronics. South Africa is a key source for industrial diamonds. Brazil long has been a center for mining bauxite, the main ingredient in aluminum. Thailand has become an important manufacturing location for Japanese MNEs such as Sony, Sharp, and Mitsubishi. Motorola, Intel, and Philips manufacture semiconductors in Malaysia and Taiwan.

These workers are assembling Audi car engines in Hungary. Emerging markets are excellent locations for global sourcing.

Outsourcing The procurement of selected value-adding activities, including production of intermediate goods or finished products, from independent suppliers.

Global sourcing The procurement of products and services from foreign locations. Procurement can be from either independent suppliers or company-owned subsidiaries.

Emerging markets also enjoy considerable success in certain industries; for example, South Korea in electronics, semiconductors, and automobiles; Taiwan and Malaysia in personal computers; and South Africa in mining. Individual firms, including those highlighted in the opening vignette, have also become world class companies. Did you know, for example, that the world's number three and four top-selling beer brands are produced by new global challengers based in Brazil (Skol, made by InBev) and Mexico (Corona, made by Grupo Modelo)? Together, these firms make more than 50 million barrels of beer annually. South Korea's Samsung is already the world's leading producer of semiconductors and flat screen TVs. It has displaced better-known MNEs in these industries in Japan and the United States, such as Sony and Motorola.

Emerging Markets as Sourcing Destinations

In recent years, companies sought ways of transferring or delegating non-core tasks or operations from in-house groups to specialized contractors. This business trend is known as **outsourcing**—the procurement of selected value-adding activities, including production of intermediate goods or finished products, from independent suppliers. Outsourcing helps foreign firms become more efficient, concentrate on their core competences, and obtain competitive advantages. When sourcing involves foreign suppliers or production bases, then the phenomenon is known as global sourcing or *offshoring*. Thus, **global sourcing** refers to the procurement of products and services from foreign locations. Procurement can be from either independent suppliers or company-owned subsidiaries. We dedicate Chapter 16 to global sourcing topics.

Emerging markets have served as excellent platforms for sourcing. For example, numerous MNEs have established call centers in Eastern Europe, India, and the Philippines. Firms in the IT industry such as Dell and IBM reap substantial benefits from the ability to outsource certain technological functions to knowledge workers in India. Intel and Microsoft have much of their programming activities performed in Bangalore, India. Investments from abroad benefit emerging markets as they lead to new jobs and production capacity, transfer of technology and know-how, and linkages to the global marketplace.

 ## Estimating the True Potential of Emerging Markets

Estimating the true potential of market demand in emerging markets poses various challenges. Unique country conditions such as limited availability of data sources or reliability of information make it challenging for western firms to gather market insights. Carrying out market research may be more costly than in advanced economies. Often firms may have to improvise.[11] To overcome these challenges, in the early stages of market research, managers emphasize three practical approaches to develop more reliable estimates of market potential. These relate to the use of per-capita income, size of middle-class, and market potential indicators.

Per-capita Income as an Indicator of Market Potential

When managers evaluate the market potential of individual markets, they often start by examining aggregate country data, such as gross national income (GNI) or per-capita GDP, expressed in terms of a reference currency, such as the U.S. dollar. The second column in Exhibit 9.7 provides per-capita GDP for a sample of emerging markets and the United States, for comparison purposes. For example, in 2007 China's per-capita GDP converted at market exchange rates was $2,310, while that of the United States was $45,490.

However, per-capita GDP converted at market exchange rates paints an inaccurate picture of market potential because it overlooks the substantial price differences that exist between advanced economies and emerging markets. Prices are usually lower for a wide variety of products and services in emerging markets. As an example, a U.S. dollar exchanged and spent in China will buy much more than a dollar spent in the United States.

So what should managers do to accurately estimate market potential? The answer lies in using per-capita GDP figures *adjusted* for price differences. Economists estimate real buying power by calculating GDP statistics based on *purchasing power parity* (PPP). As you learned in Chapter 8, the PPP concept suggests that, in the long run, exchange rates should move toward levels that would equalize the prices of an identical basket of goods and services in any two countries. Since prices vary greatly among countries, economists adjust ordinary GDP figures for differences in purchasing power. Adjusted per-capita GDP more accurately represents the amount of products that consumers can buy in a given country, using *their own currency* and consistent with *their own standard of living*.

Now examine per-capita GDP, adjusted for purchasing power parity, for the same sample of countries in the third column in Exhibit 9.7. Note that a more accurate estimate of China's per-capita GDP is $8,486—more than three times higher the per-capita GDP at market exchange rates. Compare the two figures for other countries as well. These estimates are a more realistic indicator of purchasing power of consumers in emerging and developing economies. This helps explain why firms increasingly target emerging markets despite the seemingly low income levels indicated in conventional income statistics.

Country	Per-capita GDP, Converted using market exchange rates (U.S.$)	Per-capita GDP, Converted using PPP exchange rates (U.S.$)
Argentina	$6,278	$17,062
Brazil	6,220	9,531
Bulgaria	4,704	10,677
China	2,310	8,486
Hungary	12,433	20,701
South Korea	19,485	25,403
Mexico	8,530	11,761
Russia	8,209	13,210
Turkey	5,882	9,629
United States	45,490	45,176

Exhibit 9.7

Difference in Per Capita GDP, in Conventional and Purchasing Power Parity (PPP) Terms, 2007

SOURCE: International Monetary Fund, *World Economic Outlook Database*, April 2007, at www.imf.org

Another way to illustrate the PPP concept is to examine the *Big Mac Index* available at globalEDGE™ and developed by the *Economist* (www.economist.com). The Big Mac Index first gathers information on the price of hamburgers at McDonald's restaurants worldwide. It then compares the prices based on actual exchange rates to those based on the PPP price of Big Macs to see whether a nation's currency is under- or over-valued. The Index reveals that the currencies of most European countries (mainly the euro) are overvalued, while those for most developing economies or emerging markets are undervalued. If you are hungry for a Big Mac, go to China where you can get it for as little as 1.31 in U.S. dollars. You should avoid Norway, where the Big Mac will cost you 7.05 in U.S. dollars.

Even when adjusted for purchasing power parity, managers should exercise caution in relying on per-capita income as an indicator of market potential in an emerging or developing economy. There are four reasons for this caution.

First, managers must adjust the numbers for the existence of an *informal economy*—economic transactions that are not officially recorded and therefore left out of government calculations of a nation's GDP. Yet, in developing economies, the informal economy is often as large as the formal economy. These countries typically lack sophisticated taxation systems for detecting and reporting commercial transactions. Individuals and businesses often underreport income to minimize tax obligations. In addition, barter exchanges do not involve monetary transactions and, therefore, are not captured by national estimates of GDP either. Second, the great majority of the population is on the low end of the income scale in emerging markets (and developing economies). As you would remember from your statistics training, 'mean' or 'average' does not accurately represent a non-normal distribution; often, the median or the modal income would reveal a better understanding. Third, household income is several times larger than per-capita income because of multiple wage earners in these countries. Multiple-income households naturally have much greater spending power than individuals. This fact is overlooked by statistics that emphasize per-capita GDP. Fourth, governments in these countries may underreport national income so they can qualify for low-interest loans and grants from international aid agencies and development banks.

In addition to per-capita GDP, managers should examine other market potential indicators including GDP growth rate, income distribution, commercial infrastructure, the rate of urbanization, consumer expenditures for discretionary items, and unemployment rate. Managers will also find the size and growth rate of the middle class to be revealing. Let's explore this next.

Middle Class as an Indicator of Market Potential

In every country, the middle class represents the proportion of people in between the wealthy and the poor. The middle class has economic independence and includes people who work in businesses, education, government, and hourly jobs. They consume many discretionary items, including electronics, furniture, automobiles, recreation, and education. Middle-class households make up the largest proportion of households in advanced economies. In emerging markets, the size and growth rate of the middle class serve as signals of a dynamic market economy.

Exhibit 9.8 provides data for a sample of emerging markets with relatively sizeable middle-class populations.[12] For marketers of products and services, these countries are prime prospects. India and Indonesia rank at the very top, given their large populations. Note, however, the trade-off between various indicators. While India and Indonesia feature large middle-class populations in absolute terms, per-capita GDP in these countries is rather modest, especially when compared to South Korea, China, Russia, and Mexico. Note, however, that the percentage of income held by their middle classes is relatively high at 49 and 48 percent,

Country	Middle-class population (millions)	Percent of income held by middle class	Per-capita GDP, (PPP, U.S.$)
China	587	45	$8,486
India	534	49	4,031
Indonesia	105	48	4,616
Russia	67	47	13,210
Brazil	65	35	9,531
Mexico	42	41	11,761
Turkey	32	45	9,629
Thailand	28	45	9,638
South Korea	26	55	25,403

Exhibit 9.8

Magnitude of Middle-Class Population for a Sample of Emerging Markets, 2007

SOURCES: International Monetary Fund at www.imf.org, World Bank at www.worldbank.org, and globalEDGE™ at globaledge.msu.edu

respectively. Contrast this to Brazil where the middle class citizens control only about 35 percent of national income. Demographic trends indicate that, in the coming two decades, the proportion of middle-class households in emerging markets will become much bigger, acquiring enormous spending power. As incomes increase, spending patterns will evolve, fueling growth across various product and service categories.

Use of a Comprehensive Index to Measure Market Potential

While a large and growing middle class points to a promising emerging market, with growing opportunities for internationalizing firms, managers should consider other indicators as well. Exhibit 9.9 presents one such comprehensive approach, the *Emerging Market Potential Index* (EMPI). The EMPI compares emerging market countries using factors that, together, provide managers of western firms with a realistic measure of export market potential.

What makes a good market? For emerging markets, the following dimensions serve as comprehensive indicators of market potential (For a detailed discussion of the EMPI methodology, see Cavusgil, 1997):[13]

- *Market Size:* the country's population, especially those living in urban areas.
- *Market Growth Rate:* the country's real GDP growth rate.
- *Market Intensity:* private consumption and gross national income per capita represent discretionary expenditures of citizens.
- *Market Consumption Capacity:* the percentage share of income held by the country's middle class.
- *Commercial Infrastructure:* characteristics such as number of mobile phone subscribers, density of telephone lines, number of PCs, density of paved roads, and population per retail outlet.
- *Economic Freedom:* the degree to which government intervenes in business activities.[14]
- *Market Receptivity:* the particular emerging market's inclination to trade with the exporter's country as estimated by the volume of imports.
- *Country Risk:* the degree of political risk.

Countries	Market size		Market growth rate		Market intensity		Market consumption capacity		Commercial infrastructure		Economic freedom		Market receptivity		Country risk		Overall index	
	Rank	Index	Rank	Index	Rank	Index	Rank	Index	Rank	Index	Rank	Index	Rank	Index	Rank	Index	Rank	Index
China	1	100	1	100	25	23	12	59	16	45	27	1	22	3	13	49	1	100
Hong Kong	24	1	20	23	1	100	13	54	2	97	6	79	2	75	2	90	2	96
Singapore	27	1	18	27	9	59	11	62	6	83	10	71	1	100	1	100	3	93
Taiwan	12	5	6	57	11	57	–	–	1	100	8	76	5	23	3	87	4	79
Israel	25	1	12	45	2	79	4	82	3	94	3	86	4	26	5	63	5	78
S. Korea	7	12	16	30	5	63	2	99	5	90	7	78	10	13	4	65	6	75
Czech Rep.	23	2	9	48	13	55	3	97	4	91	2	93	9	15	6	63	7	73
Hungary	26	1	24	14	3	76	1	100	7	78	4	83	8	16	8	62	8	64
India	2	44	3	63	22	37	7	77	25	17	17	44	27	1	16	39	9	55
Poland	14	5	27	1	10	58	6	80	8	71	5	82	14	7	9	58	10	46
Turkey	9	8	7	55	12	57	10	67	12	51	16	45	18	5	20	27	11	37

Exhibit 9.9 Emerging Market Potential Index, 2007

Note: Data for top 11 emerging markets are provided. For the full table, visit http://globaledge.msu.edu/resourceDesk/mpi.asp

SOURCE: globalEDGE™ at globaledge.msu.edu

Managers can use the EMPI in several ways. First, they can use the rankings as an objective basis for prioritizing emerging markets in the course of planning international expansion. For example, using the data of Exhibit 9.9, a manager would conclude that China, Hong Kong, and Singapore represent highly attractive export markets. China has steadily risen in the Index in recent years, as well as the central European economies of the Czech Republic, Hungary, and Poland.

Second, online EMPI rankings are interactive, so users can rank markets on the basis on any of the eight dimensions making up the overall Index (see the EMPI at globalEDGE™, globaledge.msu.edu). Third, managers can modify the assigned weights to fit the unique characteristics of their own industry. For example, in evaluating market size, food industry firms may attach more weight to market size, while firms in the telecommunications equipment industry may attach more weight to infrastructure and country risk. Fourth, managers may add additional indicators that are not currently included in the EMPI as a way of refining the tool for greater precision, or they may add additional countries beyond the emerging markets already represented in the Index.

Risks and Challenges of Doing Business in Emerging Markets

Emerging markets exhibit certain risks that affect their viability for international business. Let's review the most common, and most detrimental, of these risks.

Political Instability

The absence of reliable or consistent governance from recognized government authorities adds to business costs, increases risks, and reduces managers' ability to forecast business conditions. Political instability is associated with corruption and weak legal frameworks that discourage inward investment and the development of a reliable business environment. In Russia, for example, evolving political conditions threaten the business activities of foreign firms. Bureaucratic practices favor well-connected, home-grown firms. Western oil companies have been denied access to Russia's energy resources. In the 2006 *Ease of Doing Business* rankings of the World Bank, Russia ranked 163rd in dealing with licenses; 159th in getting credit; and 143rd in international trade procedures (www.doingbusiness.org). These conditions have harmed foreign investor confidence.[15]

Weak Intellectual Property Protection

Even if they exist, laws that safeguard intellectual property rights may not be enforced, or the judicial process may be painfully slow. In Argentina, for example, enforcement of copyrights on recorded music, videos, books, and computer software is inconsistent. Authorities attempt to stop shipments of pirated merchandise, but have inadequate resources and slow court procedures that hamper enforcement. Laws against Internet piracy are weak and ineffective.[16] Counterfeiting—unauthorized copying and production of a product—is common in China, Indonesia, and Russia, especially with software, DVDs, and CDs. In India, weak patent laws discourage investment by foreign firms.

Bureaucracy, Red Tape, and Lack of Transparency

Burdensome administrative rules, as well as excessive requirements for licenses, approvals, and paperwork, all substantially delay business activities. As an example, one of the biggest insurance firms, American International Group (AIG), formed a joint venture with the giant Indian conglomerate Tata, to enter India's underserved $8 billion insurance market. Even with a strong local partner, it still took six years before the Indian government granted AIG permission to sell property and life insurance to Indians. For another example, the South Korean government enacted import barriers to protect the LG Group and other Korean firms from foreign competitors. Also, the Indonesian government granted an agricultural monopoly to its home-grown PT Bogasari, allowing it to become one of the world's biggest producers of instant noodles.

Excessive bureaucracy is usually associated with lack of transparency, suggesting that legal and political systems may not be open and accountable to the public. Bribery, kickbacks, and extortion, especially in the public sector, cause difficulty for managers. Where anti-corruption laws are weak, managers may be tempted to offer bribes to ensure the success of business deals. In *Transparency International's* ranking of the most corrupt countries, emerging markets such as Argentina, Indonesia, and Venezuela are among the countries that experience substantial corruption.[17]

Partner Availability and Qualifications

Foreign firms need to seek alliances with local companies in countries characterized by inadequate legal and political frameworks. Through local partners, foreign firms can access local market knowledge, establish supplier and distributor networks, and develop key government contacts. Qualified partners that can provide these advantages are not readily available in emerging markets. Especially smaller emerging market countries will have few well qualified business partners that foreign firms can retain as distributors or suppliers.

Dominance of Family Conglomerates

Family conglomerate A large, privately-owned company that is highly diversified.

Many emerging market economies are dominated by family-owned rather than publicly-owned businesses. A **family conglomerate** (FC) is a large, privately-owned company that is highly diversified. Their businesses range from manufacturing to banking to construction. FCs control the majority of economic activity and employment in emerging markets like South Korea, where they are called *chaebols*, India where they are called *business houses*, Latin America where they are called *grupos*, and Turkey where they are called *holding companies*. A typical FC may hold the largest market share in each of several industries in its home country. In South Korea, the top 30 FCs account for nearly half the assets and industry revenues in the Korean economy. Samsung, perhaps the most famous Korean FC, has annual revenues of $140 billion. In Turkey, the Koc Group accounts for about 20 percent of trading on the Istanbul Stock Exchange, and Sabanci provides over five percent of Turkey's national tax revenue. FCs enjoy various competitive advantages in their home countries, such as government protection and support, extensive networks in various industries, superior market knowledge, and access to capital. For example, Hyundai Group was an early mover in South Korea's auto industry and now holds the largest share of the country's car market. When foreign automakers tried to enter the market, they found Hyundai's advantages overwhelming.

The origin and growth of FCs are partly attributable to their special relationships with the government, which often protects FCs by providing subsidies, loans, tax incentives, and market entry barriers to competitors. In some emerging markets, the government may even launch the FC, as in the case of Siam Cement Group in Thailand. One of the largest FCs in Indonesia, the Bimantara Citra Group, got its start by selling its foreign oil allocations to the state-owned oil monopoly. The Group has long enjoyed a close relationship with the Indonesian government and secured numerous lucrative contracts. When the Hyundai Group in South Korea experienced a financial crisis, the Korean government and Hyundai's major creditors provided over $300 million in assistance, including credit extension and short-term loans.[18] FCs provide huge tax revenues and facilitate national economic development, which explains why governments are so eager to support them.

The fact that FCs dominate the commercial landscape in many emerging markets suggests they will be either formidable competitors or capable partners (possibly with much bargaining power). We return to this issue in the next section.

Strategies for Doing Business in Emerging Markets

Different market conditions abroad compel companies to devise unique approaches. For example, Toyota markets simple, low-cost car models in various low-income countries. In India, Toyota has built a large factory and aims to boost its share of the India car market to 10 percent by 2010. The "ultra-low-cost" vehicles carry a price tag of roughly $7,000.[19] Meanwhile, General Motors is building low-cost cars targeted to emerging markets such as China, India, and Russia. Renault, Volkswagen, and other big carmakers are following suit.[20] In this section, we discuss three strategies that firms employ to succeed in emerging markets.

Partnering with Family Conglomerates

As we discussed, family conglomerates are key players in their respective economies and have much capital to invest in new ventures. For example, most major FCs in Korea, as well as Koc and Sabanci in Turkey, Vitro in Mexico, and Astra in Indonesia, own their own financing operations in the form of insurance companies, banks, and securities brokers. Many FCs possess extensive distribution channels throughout their home countries. They have a deep understanding of local markets and customers.

For foreign firms that want to do business in emerging markets, FCs can make valuable venture partners.[21] By collaborating with an FC, the foreign firm can: (1) reduce the risks, time, and capital requirements of entering target markets; (2) develop helpful relationships with governments and other key, local players; (3) target market opportunities more rapidly and effectively; (4) overcome infrastructure-related hurdles; and (5) leverage FC's resources and local contacts.

There are many examples of successful FC partnering. Ford partnered with Kia to introduce the Sable line of cars in South Korea. Ford benefited from Kia's strong distribution and after-service network. Digital Equipment Corporation (DEC) designated Tatung, a Taiwanese FC, as the main distributor of its workstations and client-server products in Taiwan. DEC benefited from Tatung's local experience and distribution network. In Turkey, Sabanci entered a joint venture with Danone, the French yogurt producer and owner of the Evian brand of bottled water. Danone brought ample technical knowledge in packaging and bottling, and a reputation for healthy and environmentally friendly products, but it lacked information on the local market. As the Turkish market leader, Sabanci knows the market, retailers, and distributors. The collaboration helped make Danone the bottled water market leader in the first year.

Marketing to Governments in Emerging Markets

In emerging markets, as well as in developing economies, government agencies and state-owned enterprises are an important customer group for three reasons: First, governments buy enormous quantities of products (such as computers, furniture, office supplies, and motor vehicles) and services (such as architectural, legal, and consulting services). Second, state enterprises in areas such as railways, airlines, banking, oil, chemicals, and steel buy goods and services from foreign companies. Third, the public sector influences the procurement activities of various private or semi-private corporations. For example, in India the government is directly involved in planning housing projects. Construction firms lobby the government to gain access to promising deals to build apartments and houses for local dwellers.

Emerging market governments regularly announce **tenders**—formal offers made by a buyer to purchase certain products or services. Tender is also known as a *request for proposals* (*RFPs*). Government agencies seek bids from suppliers to procure bulk commodities, equipment, and technology or to build power plants, highways, dams, and public housing. Vendors submit bids to the government to work on these projects.

Governments in emerging markets as well as developing countries often formulate economic development plans and annual programs to build or improve national infrastructure. To

Tenders Formal offers made by a buyer to purchase certain products or services.

Emerging market governments are important potential customers for various types of products and services. Pictured here is India's parliament building in New Delhi.

find vendors, the government follows specific buying procedures that lead to large, lucrative sales to international vendors. Securing major government contracts usually requires substantial competencies and resources. Firms competing for such projects assemble a team of managers and technical experts, especially when pursuing large deals. Governments prefer dealing with vendors that offer complete sales and service packages. The most successful vendors also offer financing for major sales, in the form of low-interest loans or grants. Governments are attracted by deals that create local jobs, employ local resources, reduce import dependence, and provide other country-level advantages.

Bechtel, Siemens, General Electric, Hitachi, and other major vendors regularly participate in bidding for global tenders from emerging market governments. Some of the largest construction projects include the Panama Canal expansion and the channel tunnel between France and the United Kingdom. Another mega project, the Three Gorges Dam on the Yangtze River in China, is expected to cost about $25 billion when completed. It will be the largest hydroelectric dam in the world. Six groups of global contractors have been involved in this project, including ABB, Kvaerner, Voith, Siemens, and General Electric. The dam is expected to be fully operational in 2009, following 16 years of construction.

Skillfully Challenge Emerging Market Competitors

As the opening vignette shows, the new global challengers possess various strengths that make them formidable competitors in the global marketplace. Advantages such as low-cost labor, skilled workforce, government support, and family conglomerates are fostering the rise of firms that are capturing market share from incumbent international players. For example, the global farm equipment industry long has been dominated by venerable names such as John Deere and Komatsu. Recently, however, India's Mahindra & Mahindra has been grabbing market share with brands such as the Mahindra 5500, a powerful, high-quality tractor that sells for far less than competing models. One dealership in the state of Mississippi—a market long dominated by John Deere—sold more than 300 Mahindras in just four months.[22]

Advanced economy firms can counter in various ways. Initially, managers must conduct research to develop an understanding of the new challengers.

Workers build steel beams for a new highway in China. Large-scale infrastructure projects in emerging markets and developing economies are attractive business opportunities.

It is critical for managers to analyze the advantages of the emergent firms and how they can transform the incumbent's industry. The next step is to acquire new capabilities that improve the firm's competitive advantages. For example, many incumbents are boosting their R&D to invent new, superior products. Others are partnering with competitors in order to pool resources against emerging market rivals. Incumbent firms can also match new global challengers at their own game by leveraging low-cost labor and skilled workers in locations such as China, India, Mexico, and Eastern Europe. Many advanced economy firms partner with family conglomerates and others in emerging markets on critical value-chain activities such as R&D, manufacturing, and technical support.

Catering to Economic Development Needs of Emerging Markets and Developing Economies

In recent years, internationalizing firms have become increasingly more involved in activities that help to facilitate economic development in emerging markets and developing economies. The most important of these trends are: (1) fostering economic development with profitable modernization projects, and (2) facilitating entrepreneurship through small-scale loans. Such efforts are a form of corporate social responsibility because they help developing economies grow. In most cases they make good business sense, too.

Fostering Economic Development with Profitable Projects

International firms increasingly recognize that serving buyer needs in poor countries can be profitable. Historically, few firms targeted such countries because managers assumed there were few profitable opportunities. In reality, if firms market appropriate products and employ suitable strategies, doing business in emerging markets and developing economies can be profitable. Companies formulate innovative solutions to succeed in markets with limited spending power. For example, Unilever and P&G sell Sunsilk and Pantene shampoo in India for less than $0.02 per mini-sachet. Narayana Hrudayalaya is an Indian insurance provider that sells health insurance for less than $0.20 per person per month in India. It has signed up millions of customers. Amul, one of India's largest processed-food firms, sells a wide range of food products to millions of poor people. Such firms had to devise new business models—manufacturing, packaging, distribution, and market reach—to be profitable, but they have succeeded in profitably serving countless customers.[23]

Consider the case of Africa, where estimates indicate there are fewer telephone lines than in New York City. Between 1998 and 2004, however, the number of mobile-phone users in Africa grew to 81 million—the fastest growth worldwide. The phones were supplied by such firms as Ericsson, the Swedish telecom. Ericsson helped modernize the telecom infrastructure in rural parts of Tanzania. The firm installed phone lines and cellular systems that facilitate not only the communication needs of households and businesses, but also those of non-governmental organizations and other aid agencies.[24] The emergence of a significant cell phone market in Africa led to the development of related industries and the launch of local firms that produce accessories, such as devices for recharging cell phone batteries.

Ericsson's experience suggests that market-based solutions not only contribute to social and economic transformation, but can be profitable as well. This company has skillfully turned modernization projects into profitable operations in emerging markets. Ericsson also modernized much of Russia's antiquated phone systems; installed Hungary's digital telephone system, in partnership with local government; and was instrumental in expanding Vietnam's telecommunications network, in sales financed by the World Bank. Collaborating with government agencies and state-owned enterprises provides

Telecommunication infrastructure is improving in parts of Africa. Serving buyer needs in Africa and other developing areas can help raise local living standards. Pictured here is a Berber using a mobile phone in Morocco.

firms with competitive advantages when entering emerging markets. In India, Ericsson manufactures optical fiber cables in partnership with the Birla Group, one of India's largest family conglomerates. Ericsson entered joint ventures in Russia to navigate a tough market characterized by poor business infrastructure and significant risk.

Advanced economy firms that invest in developing economies and emerging markets support the development of infrastructure in transportation, communications, and energy systems. Firms create jobs and contribute to regional and sector development. Investment generates local tax revenues, which can be spent to improve living standards among the poor. Transferring technology and know-how promotes local innovation and enterprise. Many firms develop community-oriented social programs that foster economic and social development. For example, Novartis and Microsoft used portions of their profits to create programs in developing economies that improve living standards, reduce poverty, encourage dialog on development policy, and drive research on development concerns such as healthcare and infrastructure.

Microfinance to Facilitate Entrepreneurship

Microfinance refers to providing small-scale financial services, such as "microcredit" and "microloans," which assist entrepreneurs to start businesses in poor countries. By providing small loans, frequently less than $100, small-scale entrepreneurs accumulate sufficient capital to launch businesses that help pull them out of poverty. This concept led economics professor Muhammad Yunus to found the Grameen Bank in Bangladesh in 1974. Since then, millions of Grameen borrowers in Bangladesh have risen out of acute poverty. Aspiring entrepreneurs use the small loans to buy everything from cows that produce milk to sell in markets, to mobile phones that villagers can rent to make calls. The majority of microloan recipients are women.

Today, the World Bank estimates there are more than 7,000 microfinance institutions, serving some 16 million poor people in developing economies.[25] The Grameen Bank now has over 2,100 branches. The Bank has spun off 17 microfinance organizations in China alone. Thanks to the success of microfinance, Yunus was awarded the 2006 Nobel Peace Prize. Grameen Bank has inspired similar efforts in dozens of poor countries worldwide, often sponsored by philanthropic organizations such as the Bill and Melinda Gates Foundation and the Omidyar Network.[26] [27]

Ordinary banks do not loan money to startup entrepreneurs because such individuals lack collateral, steady employment, and a verifiable credit history. Microfinance gets around traditional practice, enabling impoverished people to develop small businesses that allow them to build wealth and exit poverty. Proponents point to how a small amount of money can have a dynamic, ripple effect on many lives in a village. They argue that microfinance might be the most effective way to tackle global poverty, bringing better lives to millions of people.

Over time, microfinance has gained credibility in the mainstream banking industry as a source of future growth. Various organizations now offer other forms of small-scale financial services, including insurance and mortgage lending in poor countries worldwide. In Mexico, Cemex's *Patrimonio Hoy* program has widened access to cement and other building materials by organizing low-income customers into groups of three families that monitor each other's progress in constructing their own homes and collectively paying off debts at regular intervals. *Patrimonio Hoy* and other Cemex programs have made home ownership a reality for tens of thousands of low-income Mexican families.[28]

Arcelik: International Aspirations of an Emerging Market Firm

Arcelik is a Turkish appliance manufacturer with 16,000 employees and sales of around $4 billion per year. The company is controlled by the Koc Group, Turkey's largest and most prestigious family conglomerate. Arcelik has over 100 home appliances in its product line. Since its founding in 1955, Arcelik has sold more than 75 million appliances, including air conditioners, dishwashers, washing machines, cooking appliances, and refrigerators. Arcelik produces more than half of Turkey's consumer durables, under brand names such as Beko, Altus, and Arcelik. As trade barriers declined in the 1980s and 1990s, several competitors from Europe entered the Turkish market, threatening Arcelik's market share. Arcelik management began to view its home market as too small and launched a plan for aggressive international expansion.

Turkey is an emerging market and has applied for membership in the European Union. Over 50 percent of Turkey's 71 million residents are under age 25. There are roughly 15 million households with an average family size of four. The younger population drives higher marriage rates, approximately 500,000 annually, which drives demand for household goods. Urbanization is increasing—people are moving to the cities to improve their living standards. Relatively low saturation levels of domestic brands promise strong annual growth in the market, significantly higher than in advanced economies. Turkey's average per-capita income is relatively low; $9,600 in 2007. Purchasing power outside urban areas like Istanbul, Ankara, Izmir, Bursa, and a handful of other cities is still very low.

The Global Household Appliance Industry

Consumers tend to view home appliances as commodities, and often value low prices over brands and features. Some home appliances, such as dishwashers and cooking equipment, carry smaller profit margins. The average life span of a major appliance is 10 to 15 years. To lower manufacturing costs, firms attempt to standardize the materials, parts, and components used to make appliances, and devise similar manufacturing processes. Manufacturing plants are becoming more automated, and the use of low-cost labor is advantageous only in the short run.

To be able to charge premium prices and increase profit margins, some appliance makers differentiate their products by incorporating innovative, value-added technology and distinctive features. However, innovation is costly. Offering appliances with the latest high-tech features requires frequent changes in production methods and regular re-training of factory workers. Passing higher prices on to customers is difficult due to substantial competition and the low spending power of buyers in emerging markets.

In the advanced economies, the household appliance industry is mature and most markets are saturated. There are many global competitors, such as BSH, Electrolux, General Electric, Haier, Merloni, National, and Whirlpool. Intense competition has triggered widespread industry consolidation. Mergers and acquisitions have created several large firms that have forced out smaller independent players. For example, where once some 400 appliance producers operated in Europe, today only five companies control over 70 percent of the market.

Although major appliance manufacturers began to globalize in the 1990's, most continued to market products specifically suited to individual markets. Because of differences in cultural, legal, technical, and economic variables, manufacturers cannot market the same products across all of Europe, North America, South America, and Asia. For example, in India, consumers prefer washing machines that offer superior cleaning power at a low price. Consumers in China and Latin America have low spending power, but still want to buy popular models with ample features. In Europe, Arcelik must contend with strict environmental rules that regulate the amount of electricity and water that washers can use. Some markets prefer front-loading models, while others emphasize top-loading models.

Increasingly, appliance firms emphasize smart business strategies. Because "hard" factors such as tooling, equipment, factory layout, materials procurement, and design do not provide a long-term competitive edge, appliance makers emphasize dynamic "soft" factors, such as innovative use of information technology, in order to achieve competitive advantages.

Market research reveals that the distribution of sales in the global household appliance industry is approximately: 34 percent for Asia/Pacific, 24 percent for Western Europe, 23 percent for North America, and 19 percent for other regions. The table on the next page indicates total sales of household appliances in millions of units. As you can see, sales prospects are especially favorable in the Asia/Pacific region, where ongoing industrialization, high population, and rising incomes promise appliance firms attractive opportunities. Latin America also offers strong growth potential due to ongoing industrialization and urbanization. Above-average gains are also expected in most of Eastern Europe and the Africa/Mideast region.

Total Sales of Household Appliances (in millions of units)

Region	1998	2003	2007
Asia / Pacific	80.1	106.4	135.1
Western Europe	64.9	69.7	73.9
North America	58.4	61.4	64.4
Eastern Europe	18.1	23.3	31.9
Latin America	18.0	21.3	25.9

Sources: *Appliance Manufacturer* and *World Market Share Reporter.*

Europe is typically segmented into Western and Eastern Europe. In Western Europe, markets are relatively saturated. Annual sales increases averaged about 3 percent, although some markets, such as Germany and the Netherlands, are very sluggish. Eastern Europe has the potential of higher market growth rates, and market demand is driven mainly by the upgrading of the installed appliance base. Sales in Eastern Europe have been brisk, increasing between 5 and 8 percent annually.

Arcelik's Aspiration: To Become a Global Player

In Europe, Whirlpool is the market leader in home laundry appliances. Electrolux is the leader in refrigerators and vacuum cleaners, and BSH is the leader in dishwashers. Outside Turkey, Arcelik's biggest markets are in Europe. Arcelik first established the *Beko* brand of appliances and TV sets in Britain in the 1990s. The firm gradually expanded into France, Germany, and Spain. In the early 2000s, Arcelik purchased well-known local European brands Blomberg (a subsidiary of Brandt) and Grundig in Germany, Elektra Bregenz and Tirolia in Austria, as well as Leisure and Flavel (appliances and TV sets) in Britain. In Romania, Arcelik acquired Arctic (washing machines, ranges, and TV sets), and immediately invested to modernize the company's operations and double its productive capacity. In 2005, the firm built a refrigerator and washing machine manufacturing plant in Russia and established sales subsidiaries in the Czech Republic, Hungary, and Italy.

Arcelik is advantaged through its knowledge of how to produce products for lower-income countries. Manufacturing plants in Turkey and Eastern Europe allow Arcelik to produce appliances less expensively than some competitors. Arcelik aims to become a leading player worldwide. One challenge is that Arcelik's brands are largely unknown outside Europe. Brand image acts as a barrier to entry and could reduce the likelihood of short-run success. Arcelik's competitors rely on both local and regional brands. Regional brands are distinguished by decades of tradition and a high degree of consumer awareness. Both local and regional brands are tailored to meet customer needs in their respective countries or regions.

To better manage sales and service, the firm established distribution centers throughout Europe, Arcelik

has an unparalleled distribution network of roughly 1,700 Arcelik dealers and Beko dealers, as well as approximately 1,700 non-exclusive agents. The network is valuable because geographic reach is critical in maintaining market leadership, and few firms can afford to build such as extensive dealership network. Arcelik also boasts a strong after-sales service network with 530 authorized service shops.

Arcelik has embraced information technology (IT) to help reduce costs and facilitate its international ambitions. Cisco aided Arcelik's e-transformation by supplying the underlying networking technology that supports the firm's key business applications. Arcelik has created a virtual networked organization online, where information and knowledge flow not only internally but also externally to business partners such as sales outlets and service centers. All of the firm's suppliers are connected over an extranet, with access to key ordering and product information. This innovative use of information technology saves the firm millions of dollars annually.

The Future

Arcelik aims to sustain continuous growth in the global marketplace and become a leading, global household appliances company. To achieve this goal, management needs to improve operational efficiency to levels that match or exceed major competitors, and increase investment in high-growth markets. Arcelik sees its best prospects in emerging, fast-growing markets in Eastern Europe, Asia, and Latin America. The firm's success will depend on lowering operating costs in manufacturing, leveraging low-cost manufacturing platforms and information technology, and producing products that appeal to foreign markets.

AACSB: Reflective Thinking, Ethical Reasoning
Case Questions

1. Arcelik has been very active in Western Europe. Do you expect Arcelik's prospects to be better in emerging market and developing economies than in advanced economies? In what ways are emerging market and developing economies attractive to Arcelik? In general terms, how can the firm reap benefits from such markets in order to maximize company performance?

2. Arcelik management is keen on entering some emerging market or developing economies. What types of risks and challenges does Arcelik likely face in doing business in emerging markets? What should management do to identify the most promising markets? How should the firm adapt its products?

3. Originating from an emerging market, Arcelik may be better poised to cater to the economic development needs of emerging market and developing economies. In what ways can Arcelik skillfully fulfill its corporate social responsibility in such countries? Suggest specific approaches that may include: developing simpler, less expensive appliances; arranging for multiple installment purchases; encouraging the development of local suppliers; and designing products that conserve water and energy. ◄

This case was prepared by Professor Zumrut Ecevit Sati of Celal Bayar University, Turkey, and Goksel Yalcinkaya of Michigan State University, under the direction of Professor S. Tamer Cavusgil.

Sources: Appliance Magazine. (2002). April, p.1; Arcelik. (2006). Corporate overview at www.Arcelik.com.tr; Freedonia Group. (2001). *World Market Share Reporter,* p. 229; Gale Group. (2003). Encyclopedia of Global Industries, 4th edition. Detroit: Gale Group; Hoover's profile of Arcelik at www.hoovers.com; Tewary, Amrit. (2004). Standard & Poor's Industry Surveys; UNCTAD. (2005). "Turkish Outward FDI." December, Geneva; Cisco Corp. (2005). "Internet Business Solutions Group," retrieved at www.cisco.com.

CHAPTER ESSENTIALS

Key Terms

advanced economies, p. 256
developing economies, p. 256
emerging markets, p. 257
family conglomerate, p. 272

global sourcing, p. 266
new global challengers, p. 262
outsourcing, p. 266
privatization, p. 261

tenders, p. 273
transition economies, p. 261

Summary

In this chapter, you learned about:

1. **The distinction between advanced economies, developing economies, and emerging markets**

   Advanced economies are post-industrial countries characterized by high per-capita income, highly competitive industries, and well-developed commercial infrastructure. They consist primarily of post-industrial societies of Western Europe, Japan, the United States, Canada, Australia, and New Zealand. The **developing economies** represent low-income countries that have not yet industrialized. Due to low buying power and limited appeal to foreign firms, their participation in international business is limited. The **emerging markets** are former developing economies well on their way to becoming advanced economies. Located mainly in Asia, Eastern Europe and Latin America, emerging markets are transforming themselves into market-driven economies by liberalizing trade and investment policies, privatizing industries, and forming economic blocs. Brazil, Russia, India, and China are examples of large emerging markets.

   Transition economies are a subset of emerging markets that have transitioned from centrally planned economies into liberalized markets. **Privatization** refers to the transfer of state-owned industries to private concerns. **New global challengers** are top firms from rapidly developing emerging markets that are fast becoming key contenders in world markets.

2. **What makes emerging markets attractive for international business**

   First, emerging markets represent promising export markets for products and services. Second, they are ideal bases for locating manufacturing activities. Low labor costs have made emerging markets major suppliers of a variety of manufactured products to the rest of the world. Finally, emerging markets are popular destinations for **global sourcing**—procurement of products and services from foreign locations. Procurement can be from either independent suppliers or company-owned subsidiaries. Sourcing from foreign suppliers has been a steadily increasing activity among firms due to the popularity of **outsourcing**—procurement of select value-adding activities, including production of intermediate goods or finished products, from independent suppliers.

3. Estimating the true potential of emerging markets

Special considerations must be taken into account to estimate the true demand in emerging markets. Managers can follow one of three approaches to more realistically assess emerging market potential. They can: rely upon per-capita income, considered the size and growth rate of the middle class, and build a more comprehensive set of indicators such as the Emerging Market Potential Index.

4. Risks and challenges of doing business in emerging markets

Emerging markets pose various risks. Political instability, inadequate legal and institutional frameworks, lack of transparency, and inadequate intellectual property protection are among the factors that add to the cost of doing business. Another complication arises from the prevalence in the emerging markets of **family conglomerates**—large, diversified, family-owned businesses. These firms dominate the respective economies and represent either formidable rivals or attractive choices for partnerships.

5. Strategies for doing business in emerging markets

Firms aspiring to do business in emerging markets need to adapt strategies and tactics to suit unique conditions. These countries are ripe for global sourcing and as export and direct investment destinations. Some firms succeed in these markets by partnering with family conglomerates. Governments are often major buyers in emerging markets. Selling to government agencies involves responding to a **tender**, a formal request for suppliers to bid on projects. Firms from advanced economies follow various approaches to skillfully challenge emerging market competitors.

6. Catering to economic development needs of emerging markets and developing economies

Leading firms display good corporate social responsibility by engaging in activities that facilitate economic development in emerging market and developing economies. Firms can serve low income countries with inexpensive, specifically-designed products and services, and community involvement. Micro-finance, emergence of financial institutions that serve emerging-market entrepreneurs with small-scale loans, has already made a big difference in terms of promoting entrepreneurial initiatives by start up companies.

Test Your Comprehension AACSB: Reflective Thinking, Ethical Reasoning

1. What are advanced economies, developing economies, and emerging markets? What are the major distinctions among these three country groups?

2. Explain the major reasons why firms would want to do business in emerging markets. What makes these markets attractive?

3. How can managers examine the true market potential of emerging markets?

4. Describe the various risks and challenges that managers encounter in emerging markets.

5. What is a family conglomerate (FC)? How are FCs different from publicly owned companies? What role do FCs play in emerging markets?

6. Describe the process for selling to foreign governments and state enterprises.

7. Doing business in emerging markets involves strategies that are often distinct from those of other international venues. What types of business approaches can firms use when doing business in emerging markets?

8. How can firms show corporate social responsibility in emerging markets and developing economies?

Apply Your Understanding AACSB: **Communication, Reflective Thinking**

1. Auto Ornaments Ltd., is a firm that makes accessories for cars, such as seat covers and window tinting. The firm has never conducted any international business. The general manager, Steve Diesel, would like to expand into foreign markets. He heard that roughly three quarters of the world's people live in developing economies and emerging markets. He figures there must be a big market in those countries for Auto Ornaments products. What should Steve know about the characteristics of developing economies and emerging markets that make them attractive targets, *and* unattractive targets, for Auto Ornaments. Make a recommendation to Steve on the advantages and disadvantages of entering these markets. Be sure to justify your answer.

2. Suppose you work at Microsoft in their Xbox video game console division. Microsoft has long targeted Xbox to the advanced economies, especially in North America and Europe. Management would like to sell more Xbox 360's to emerging markets. What are the main characteristics of emerging markets that might make them potentially good markets for Xbox? Identify the major risks and challenges that Microsoft might encounter in selling the Xbox 360 to emerging markets.

3. CBKing has been trying to export its products to various emerging markets and has enjoyed little success so far. You know a lot about emerging markets and have been anxious to share your views with CBKing's president, Mr. Roger Wilko. What strategies would you recommend Roger pursue in doing business with emerging markets? You conclude there should be some demand in the military and the government agencies. Explain how your firm should go about selling to emerging market customers.

globalEDGE Internet Exercises

AACSB: Analytical Skills, Reflective Thinking

Refer to Chapter 1, page 27, for instructions on how to access and use globalEDGE™.

1. The World Bank sponsors the *Doing Business* database (www.doingbusiness.org/), which provides measures of business regulations and their enforcement in 175 countries. Firms can use these measures to analyze specific regulations that enhance or constrain investment, productivity, and growth. Visit the site and choose two emerging markets. Then answer the following questions: (a) How well does each country rank in terms of ease of starting a business, employing workers, and trading across borders? (b) How long does it take to start a business? (c) How much time does it take to pay taxes? (d) Review other statistics and identify which country is most friendly for doing business.

2. Using globalEDGE™, find the "country commercial guide" for two emerging markets of your choice. Compare the two countries on the following dimensions: "leading sectors for exports and investment" and "marketing products and services." (a) Which of the two countries is more promising for marketing laptop computers? (b) Which of the two countries is promising for sales of portable electrical power generators? (c) Which of the two countries is promising for sales of telecommunications equipment?

3. The three groups of countries we studied in this chapter can also be contrasted in terms of degree of economic freedom. Economic freedom refers to the extent to which economic activities in a nation can take place freely and without government restrictions. The Heritage Foundation provides an *Index of Economic Freedom* (http://www.heritage.org) that considers such factors as trade policies, extent of government intervention, monetary and fiscal policies, inward foreign direct investment, property rights, and infrastructure for banking and finance. Countries are classified into various categories including 'free,' 'mostly free,' 'mostly unfree' and 'repressed.' How are emerging market and developing economies classified? What seems to be the overall relationship between market liberalization and economic development?

CKR Cavusgil Knight Riesenberger

Management Skill Builder©

Learning About and Assessing Emerging Markets

Emerging markets are rapidly industrializing and dynamic economies. When companies decide to do business in emerging markets, the first important step is to identify the most attractive countries to enter. This involves comparing almost 30 countries across various criteria.

AACSB: Reflective Thinking, Analytical Skills

Managerial Challenge

Each emerging market has its own distinctive characteristics. Managers must determine which markets to enter and learn about the characteristics of those markets. Such knowledge helps managers to avoid wasting organizational resources, and to maximize the firm's profits and competitive advantages.

Background

Emerging market countries have transformed their economies into dynamic and progressive markets. Among other things, we witness in these countries: robust private sector activity and entrepreneurship, liberalization of trade and investment, rapidly improving living standards, and a growing middle class with rising economic aspirations. Dynamic changes in these societies also make it difficult for the manager to assess their current market potential.

Managerial Skills You Will Gain

In this C/K/R Management Skill Builder©, as a prospective manager, you will:

1. Learn how to increase prospects for enhancing company performance by targeting an important group of foreign markets—emerging markets.

2. Learn about critical factors to consider when targeting emerging markets.

3. Access key information sources related to emerging markets.

4. Analyze disparate data to arrive at recommendations.

Your Task

Assume that you are a product manager of a firm that makes and markets cordless telephones. Your task is to analyze factors in leading emerging markets and choose the best one to target with exports of your product. You may also investigate information sources on the evolving status of emerging markets.

Go to the C/K/R Knowledge Portal©

www.prenhall.com/cavusgil

Proceed to the C/K/R Knowledge Portal© to obtain the expanded background information, your task and methodology, suggested resources for this exercise, and the presentation template.

The International Monetary and Financial Environment

> ## The Complex Monetary and Financial Relationship between China and the United States

China and the United States are large economies, providing nearly half the world's economic growth in recent years. The two countries represent the world's most important bilateral economic and trading relationship. Each has a distinct role: China is the world's leading product manufacturer, and the United States is one of the wealthiest consumer and industrial markets.

China owes much of its international trading success to the value of the renminbi, its national currency (also called the yuan). For years the renminbi has been cheap by world standards, making Chinese products inexpensive to foreign importers. The value of the renminbi is set at a fixed exchange rate to the U.S. dollar and other world currencies. The Chinese government intervenes regularly in currency markets to ensure that this fixed rate is maintained. The relatively low value of the renminbi has stimulated huge demand for Chinese-made products, a major cause of the United States' persistent trade deficit with China.

Large-scale exporting has led to massive capital inflows, making China the world's biggest holder of "foreign exchange reserves" (money that nations receive

from their international transactions, such as exporting). China has used much of these reserves to invest in U.S. government securities, helping to finance the United States' huge government budget deficits. In 2006, China purchased nearly half the issues of U.S. Treasury securities, totaling $87 billion and making China the world's largest investor in U.S. government debt. The United States needs Chinese capital to finance its trade and budget deficits. Simultaneously, China needs the United States to buy the exports responsible for much of China's wealth.

China's fixed exchange-rate policy is one of the hottest topics in international finance. Some economists argue that the system has been good for China, stabilizing its currency and giving foreign investors the confidence to build factories in China. But other economists have argued that China's fixed rate distorts trade and investment flows. They believe China should allow its currency to float freely in response to market forces. Partly because of pressure from the United States and other countries, China revalued the renminbi slightly in 2005 to make it more expensive relative to the dollar.

When the Chinese government increased the renminbi's value, its products became more expensive to foreigners, reducing world demand for Chinese exports.

Currency revaluations of this sort can lower a country's earnings and trigger an economic recession. Because China is highly integrated into the world economy, a Chinese recession could trigger economic problems in the United States and other countries. A slowing Chinese economy could also reduce China's appetite for U.S. imports. The effect could be substantial—China is the world's biggest consumer of pork, cotton, coal, aluminum, steel, washing machines, cell phones, and a host of other products.

China and the United States are inextricably linked in a complex relationship, critical to the economic health of both countries. How this relationship evolves over time will determine, to a great extent, the future prosperity of the world economy.

Sources: Areddy, James. (2007). "China's Rate Boost Shows Economy's Vigor," *Wall Street Journal*, March 19, p. A2; Batson, Andrew. (2007). "China Says It Won't Rattle Markets," *Wall Street Journal*, March 17–18, p. A10; *Economist*, (2004). "A Survey of the World Economy: The Dragon and the Eagle," October 2, special section; Field, Alan. (2005). "China Revalues Yuan," *Journal of Commerce*, July 21, p. 1; Morici, Peter. (2005). "Why China Should Revalue the Yuan," *Journal of Commerce*, July 4, p. 1; Norris, Floyd. (2007). "Washington Dares to Challenge the Lender It Depends Upon," *New York Times*, April 14, p. C3; *Wall Street Journal* (2005). "China's Currency Bow," July 22, p. A12.

A s the opening vignette demonstrates, international business transactions take place within the global monetary and financial systems. Understanding these systems is fundamental to company success. When people think of international trade, they invariably think of trade in products and services. However, the markets for foreign exchange and capital are much larger. Firms regularly trade the U.S. dollar, European euro, Japanese yen, and other leading currencies to meet their international business obligations. This trade requires that nations exchange currencies with each other. The exchange rate links different national currencies so that international price and cost comparisons can be made. In this chapter, we explore the monetary and financial structure that makes trade and investment possible. We explain the nature, organization, and functions of the foreign exchange market and the monetary and financial dimensions of how companies facilitate international transactions.

Currencies and Exchange Rates in International Business

Cross-border transactions occur through an exchange of currencies between buyers and sellers. A currency is a form of money and a unit of exchange. The tendency of each country to prefer to use its own unique currency complicates international business transactions. There are some 175 currencies in use around the world. When buying a product or a service from a Mexican supplier, for example, you must convert your own currency into Mexican pesos in order to pay the supplier. However, the currency regime is simplifying in some locations. Numerous countries in Europe use the euro, and a few countries, such as Panama, have adopted the U.S. dollar as their currency.

Exhibit 10.1 provides the exchange rates for the U.S. dollar and a sample of currencies on a recent day. The value of national currencies is in constant flux. The **exchange rate**—the price of one currency expressed in terms of another—varies over time. This fluctuation means you have to keep three things in mind. First is the issue of whether you and your Mexican supplier agreed on an exchange rate in advance, or if the exchange rate is to be decided on the date of the actual payment. Second, you should keep in mind whether the purchase agreement quoted the price in your currency or in the supplier's currency. Third, because several months can pass from the time you place an order to the time the order arrives, fluctua-

Exchange rate The price of one currency expressed in terms of another. It is the number of units of one currency that can be exchanged for another.

Exhibit 10.1

U.S. Dollar Exchange Rates for a
Sample of Currencies as of
October 2, 2007

SOURCE: © 2007 x-rates.com, all rights reserved.

	Currency per one U.S. dollar	U.S. dollars per unit of currency
Australian dollar	$1.130	$0.885
Brazilian real	1.822	0.549
British pound	0.490	2.042
Canadian dollar	1.000	1.000
Chinese renminbi (yuan)	7.509	0.133
Euro	0.706	1.416
Indian rupee	39.650	0.025
Japanese yen	115.830	0.009
Mexican peso	10.910	0.092
New Zealand dollar	1.314	0.761
Norwegian kroner	5.423	0.184
Singapore dollar	1.484	0.674
Saudi Arabian riyal	3.750	0.267
South African rand	6.909	0.145
Turkish lira	1.204	0.830

tions in the exchange rate during that time could cost you money or earn you money, because what you pay or receive is higher or lower than at the time of the transaction.

These and similar complications in cross-border transactions create **currency risk**, the risk that arises from changes in the price of one currency relative to another. It is one of the four types of risks encountered in international business that we illustrated in Exhibit 1.6 on page 11. If you purchase from a supplier whose currency is appreciating against yours, you face a currency risk, since you may need to hand over a larger amount of your currency to pay for your purchase. If you expect a payment from a customer whose currency is depreciating against your own, currency risk also arises, because you may receive a smaller payment amount in your currency, if the sale price was expressed in the currency of the customer. Of course, if the foreign currency fluctuates in your favor, you may gain a windfall. Nevertheless, exporters or importers are not usually in the business of making money from currency speculation; they are typically concerned about *losses* that arise from currency fluctuations.

Exporters and licensors face risk also because foreign buyers either pay in a foreign currency, or they must convert their currency into that of the vendor. Foreign direct investors face currency risk because they both receive payments and incur obligations in foreign currencies.

Currency risk Risk that arises from changes in the price of one currency relative to another.

Convertible and Nonconvertible Currencies

A *convertible currency* can be readily exchanged for other currencies. The most convertible currencies are called *hard currencies*. They are strong, stable currencies that are universally accepted, such as the U.S. dollar, Japanese yen, Canadian dollar, British pound, and the European euro. These are the currencies used most for international business transactions. Nations prefer to hold hard currencies as reserves because of their strength and stability in comparison to other currencies.

A currency is *nonconvertible* when it is used for domestic transactions and is not acceptable for international transactions. In some cases, the government may not allow it to be converted into a foreign currency. Currency convertibility is so strict in some developing economies that firms sometimes avoid using currencies altogether and receive payments in the form of products rather than cash; in other words, they engage in a form of barter. Governments impose restrictions on the convertibility of their currency in order to preserve their supply of hard currencies, such as the U.S. dollar or the euro, or to avoid the problem of *capital flight*— the possibility that residents or foreigners will sell their holdings in the nation's currency or convert it into a foreign currency. Capital flight diminishes a country's ability to service debt and pay for imports.

As an example, foreign investors sometimes drastically reduce their investments in a particular country and its currency. This occurs because people believe that their holdings are more likely to maintain their value when converted into a different currency (usually a hard currency, such as the U.S. dollar or euro) or invested elsewhere. For example, between 1979 and 1983, some $90 billion reportedly left Mexico when foreign lenders lost confidence in the Mexican economy and investors took their money out of the country. In 2007, Ecuador's president, Rafael Correa, dismissed 57 opposition members of Congress and embarked on a plan to write a new constitution and transform Ecuador's legal framework. Some Ecuadorians fear that Correa is attempting to establish a dictatorship. In 2006, Correa expropriated Occidental Petroleum, previously Ecuador's largest foreign investor. Correa's unpredictable actions have panicked foreign investors and Ecuador's wealthier citizens, who have withdrawn millions of dollars from the country's economy.[1]

Foreign Exchange Markets

A critical function of money is to facilitate payment for the products and services that the firm sells. When doing business in the home country, getting paid is straightforward—the U.S. dollar is acceptable throughout the United States, the euro is widely used in Europe, and the Japanese need only yen when buying and selling with each other. But suppose a Canadian needs to pay a Japanese, or a Japanese needs to pay an Italian, or an Italian needs to pay a Canadian. What then? The Canadian wants to be paid in Canadian dollars, the Japanese wants to be paid in yen, and the Italian wants to be paid in euros. Each of these currencies—the Canadian dollar, yen, and euro—is known as *foreign exchange*. **Foreign exchange** represents all forms of money that are traded internationally, including foreign currencies, bank deposits, checks, and electronic transfers. Foreign exchange resolves the problem of making international payments and facilitates the international investment and borrowing among firms, banks, and governments.

Currencies such as the U.S. dollar, yen, and euro are traded on the **foreign exchange market**, the global marketplace for buying and selling national currencies. The market has no fixed location. Rather, trading occurs through continuous buying and selling among banks, currency traders, governments, and other exchange agents located worldwide. International business would be impossible without foreign exchange and the foreign exchange market.

Exchange Rates Are in Constant Flux

Sometimes there are dramatic fluctuations in the exchange rate between the U.S. dollar and the euro and between numerous other currencies, as illustrated in Exhibit 10.2. In 1985, the Japanese yen was trading at 240 yen to the U.S. dollar. By 1988, the yen had fluctuated to just 125 yen to the dollar, an appreciation of almost 50 percent. Implications for international business with Japan were huge. In the span of just three years, Japanese firms witnessed a significant downturn in their exports, as Japanese products became substantially more expensive in dollar terms. Meanwhile, as the dollar buying power of the Japanese increased, U.S. firms experienced a surge in their exports to Japan.[2] Exhibit 10.2 also shows that the French franc is one of those Eurozone-country currencies that was taken out of circulation and replaced by the euro.

Foreign exchange All forms of money that are traded internationally, including foreign currencies, bank deposits, checks, and electronic transfers.

Foreign exchange market The global marketplace for buying and selling national currencies.

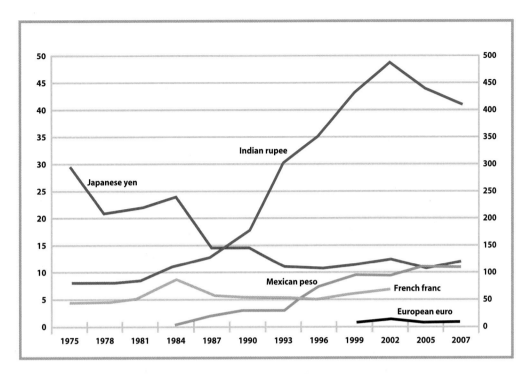

Exhibit 10.2

Selected Exchange Rates to the U.S. Dollar over Time

Notes: Right-hand scale is for Japanese yen; Left-hand scale is for all other currencies. The euro became the common currency of various countries in the European Union in 1999, replacing the French franc and other European currencies. The Mexican Peso was revalued in 1983.

SOURCE: IMF and World Bank data.

Lincoln Electric Co. in Cleveland, Ohio, has been able to export much more of its arc-welding products to Europe because of the recent weakening of the U.S. dollar relative to the euro.[3] Conversely, for U.S. consumers, the euro is relatively more expensive and may discourage them from buying European products. This has affected firms such as Volkswagen, whose U.S. sales fell off as a result of the higher cost to U.S. buyers.[4] This type of currency risk is a natural outcome of multicountry operations.

Fluctuating exchange rates affect both firms and customers. Suppose that today, the euro/dollar exchange rate is €1 = $1; that is, for a European to buy one United States dollar, she or he must pay one euro. Next, suppose that during the coming year the exchange rate goes to €1.50 = $1. Compared to before, the dollar is much more expensive to European firms and consumers—it costs 50 percent more to acquire a dollar. Let's examine the effect of this change on Europeans.[5]

Effect on European Firms:
- European firms must pay more for inputs from the United States—such as raw materials, components, and support services—that they use to produce finished products and services.
- Higher input costs reduce profitability and may necessitate firms raising prices to final customers; these higher prices lower customer demand for goods and services.
- Because the euro has become less expensive for U.S. consumers, firms can increase their exports to the United States. Firms can even raise their export prices and remain competitive in the U.S. market.
- Increased exports to the United States generate higher revenues and higher profits.

Effect on European Consumers:
- Because U.S. products and services now cost more, European consumers demand fewer of them.
- The cost of living rises for those Europeans who consume many dollar-denominated imports.
- Fewer European tourists can afford to visit the United States. Fewer European students study at U.S. universities.

Now, suppose that the euro/dollar exchange rate goes to €0.50 = $1. What are the effects on European firms and consumers? The effects are essentially the opposite of those summarized above: European firms pay less for inputs from the United States, which means the firms can drop their prices on goods and services. Because U.S. products and services now cost less, consumers demand more of them. As you can see, the effects of a fluctuating exchange rate have an affect on both sides of international transactions. Management must monitor exchange rates constantly and devise strategies to optimize firm performance in light of strong and weak currencies. We discuss these strategies in Chapter 19.

In 1999, 11 member states in the European Union switched to a single currency—the euro—eliminating the problem of exchange rate fluctuations among the participating nations (physical coins and banknotes came into circulation later, in 2002). As of January 2007, 13 member states were participating in the Eurozone. Fluctuations in exchange rates motivate countries to coordinate their monetary policies at regular meetings of the Bank for International Settlements and the G8, the group of eight major industrial countries. Governments attempt to manage exchange rates by buying and selling hard currencies and by keeping inflation in check. However, the foreign exchange market has become so huge and its movements so fluid that even major governments have difficulty controlling exchange rate movements.

 # How Exchange Rates Are Determined

In a free market, the "price" of any currency—that is, its rate of exchange—is determined by supply and demand. The levels of supply and demand for the currency, as with most commodities, will vary inversely with its price. Thus, all else being equal:

- The greater the supply of a currency, the lower its price.
- The lower the supply of a currency, the higher its price.
- The greater the demand for a currency, the higher its price.
- The lower the demand for a currency, the lower its price.

Let's assume a U.S. consumer would like to buy a German car, such as a BMW, with a nominal price of 25,000 euros. Assume further that the euro/dollar exchange rate is one euro equals $1.25. Now suppose the consumer delays six months, during which the exchange rate shifts, with the new rate becoming one euro equals $1.50. That is, due to increased demand for euros and/or decreased supply of euros, the euro has become more expensive to U.S. customers. In this case, the consumer will be less inclined to buy the BMW because, ultimately, she or he must buy expensive euros to obtain the car. By contrast, if, during the six-month period, the euro becomes cheaper to the consumer (with, say, an exchange rate of one euro equals one dollar), she or he will be more inclined to buy the BMW. As this example implies, the greater the demand for a country's products and services, the greater the demand for its currency.

Broadly speaking, there are four main factors that influence the supply and demand for a currency: economic growth, interest rates and inflation, market psychology, and government action. Let's review each of these factors next.

Economic Growth

Economic growth is the increase in value of the goods and services produced by an economy. It is usually measured as the annual increase in real GDP, in which the inflation rate is subtracted from the economic growth rate in order to obtain a more accurate measure. Economic growth results from continual economic activities, including innovation and entrepreneurship. It implies a continued increase in business activities and a corresponding increase in consumer need for money to facilitate more economic transactions. To accommodate economic growth, the central bank increases the nation's money supply. The **central bank** is the monetary authority in each country that regulates the money supply, issues currency, and manages the exchange rate of the nation's currency relative to other currencies. Economic growth is associated with an increase in the supply and demand of the nation's money supply, and by extension, the nation's currency. Thus, economic growth has a strong influence on the supply and demand for national currencies. For example, several East Asian countries have experienced rapid economic growth in recent years. This has stimulated a steadily increasing demand for the currencies of these countries by firms and individuals, both domestic and foreign.

Central bank The monetary authority in each nation that regulates the money supply and credit, issues currency, and manages the exchange rate of the nation's currency.

Interest Rates and Inflation

Inflation is an increase in the price of goods and services, so that money buys less than in preceding years. Exhibit 10.3 shows that inflation rates have reached high levels in some countries over time. Countries such as Argentina, Brazil, and Zimbabwe have had prolonged periods of *hyperinflation*—persistent annual double-digit and indeed triple-digit rates of consumer price increases. A practical effect of this hyperinflation is the need, say, for a restaurant owner to change the menu every few days in order to list the most recent prices. In a high-inflation environment, the purchasing power of the currency is constantly falling. Interest rates and inflation are closely related. In countries with high inflation, interest rates tend to be high. This occurs because investors expect to be compensated for the inflation-induced decline in the value of their money. So, if inflation is running at 10 percent, for example, banks have to pay *more* than 10 percent interest to attract customers to open savings accounts.

Fundamentally, inflation occurs when: (1) demand grows more rapidly than supply, or (2) the central bank increases the nation's money supply faster than output. When a disproportionately large amount of money is introduced into an economy, the result is too much money chasing a relatively fixed supply of goods

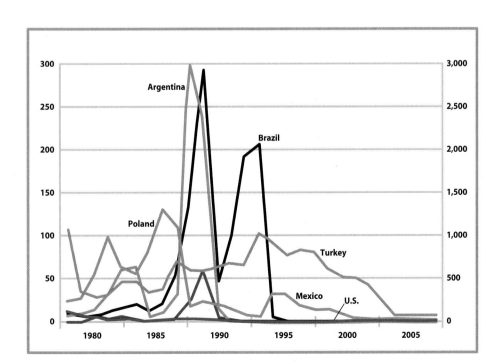

Exhibit 10.3

Inflation in Selected Countries, 1980–2005

Note: Chart shows annual percentage rate of inflation. Right-hand scale is for Argentina, Brazil, and Poland; left-hand scale is for all the other countries.

SOURCE: International Monetary Fund (www.imf.org)

In response to Argentina's financial crisis in 2001, anxious customers in Buenos Aires lined up to withdraw their money at a branch of Bank Boston. Argentina experienced massive capital flight when the government announced it would default on its international loans, which imperiled Argentine banks.

and services, which causes prices to go up. For instance, triggered by sizeable increases in the national money supply, inflation was running at over 400 percent per year in Brazil in the mid-1990s. Imagine the difficulty both buyers and sellers would have adjusting to constant decline of the currency's value, and ever-rising prices!

Inflation affects the value of the nation's currency in a major way. If inflation results from an excessive increase in the money supply, all else being equal, the price of that money (as expressed in terms of foreign currencies) will fall. In other words, an oversupply of money causes its value to fall. In this way, a rise in inflation causes the value of the national currency to fall.

The link between interest rates and inflation, and between inflation and the value of currency, implies that there is a relationship between real interest rates and the value of currency. For example, when interest rates in Japan are high, foreigners seek profits by buying Japan's interest-bearing investment opportunities, such as bonds and deposit certificates. Investment from abroad will have the effect of increasing demand for the Japanese yen.

Market Psychology

Exchange rates are often affected by *market psychology*, the unpredictable behavior of investors. Investors may engage in *herding behavior* and/or *momentum trading*. Herding refers to the tendency of investors to mimic each others' actions. It results partly because a disagreement of opinion creates anxiety and a desire to seek consensus and, thereby, follow the behavior of others. Momentum trading is a type of behavior in which investors buy stocks whose prices have been rising and sell stocks whose prices have been falling. It is usually carried out using computers that are set to do massive buying or selling when asset prices reach certain levels. Herding and momentum trading tend to occur in the wake of financial crises. A case in point is Argentina, which experienced a massive flight of capital investment when the government announced it would default on its international bank loans in 2001. Foreign investors panicked and deserted Argentina in droves.[6]

Government Action

The pricing of currencies affects company performance. When a nation's currency is expensive to foreigners, the nation's exports are likely to fall.[7] When a nation's currency is cheap to foreigners, the nation's exports increase. When the value of a nation's currency depreciates over a prolonged period, consumer and investor confidence can be undermined. A steep currency depreciation weakens the nation's ability to pay foreign lenders, possibly leading to economic and political crisis.

To minimize these effects, governments often intervene to influence the value of their own currencies. As seen in the opening vignette, the Chinese government regularly intervenes in the foreign exchange market to maintain the value of the renminbi at a desirable level. This is done to keep the renminbi undervalued, helping to ensure that Chinese exports remain strong.

An undervalued national currency can result in a **trade surplus**, which results when a nation's exports exceed its imports for a specific period of time, causing a net inflow of foreign exchange. By contrast, a **trade deficit** results when a nation's imports exceed its exports for a specific period of time, causing a net outflow of foreign exchange. The *balance of trade* is the difference between

Trade surplus The amount by which a nation's exports exceed its imports for a specific period of time.

Trade deficit The amount by which a nation's imports exceed its exports for a specific period of time.

the monetary value of a nation's exports and its imports over the course of a year. For example, if Germany exports cars to Kenya, money flows out of Kenya and into Germany, because the car importer in Kenya pays the exporter in Germany. This results in a surplus item in Germany's balance of trade and a deficit item in Kenya's balance of trade. If the total value of Kenya's imports from Germany became greater than the total value of Kenya's exports to Germany, then Kenya would have a trade deficit with Germany. Factors that can affect the level of the balance of trade include the prices of goods manufactured at home, exchange rates, trade barriers, and the method used by the government to measure the trade balance.

Many economists believe a persistent trade deficit is harmful to the national economy. When a trade deficit becomes severe or persists over a long period of time, the nation's central bank may devalue its currency. A **devaluation** is a government action to reduce the official value of its currency, relative to other currencies. It is usually accomplished by buying and selling currencies in the foreign exchange market. Devaluation aims to deter the nation's residents from importing from other countries, potentially reducing the trade deficit.[8] The *Global Trend* feature on the next page explains the large trade deficits that the U.S. economy has experienced in recent decades.

Devaluation Government action to reduce the official value of its currency, relative to other currencies.

At a broader level, governments must manage their **balance of payments**, the annual accounting of *all* economic transactions of a nation with all other nations. The balance of payments is the nation's balance sheet of trade, investment, and transfer payments with the rest of the world. It represents the difference between the *total* amount of money coming into and going out of a country. Consider the case of a Japanese MNE that builds a factory in China. In the process of investing in China to build the factory, money flows out of Japan and into China, generating a deficit item for Japan and a surplus item for China, in their respective balance of payments. The balance of payments is affected by other transactions as well, as when citizens donate money to a foreign charity, when a government provides foreign aid, or when tourists travel internationally, spending their money abroad.

Balance of payments The annual accounting of all economic transactions of a nation with all other nations.

 # Development of the Modern Exchange Rate System

Despite several decades of rising international trade, the years before World War II (1939–1945) were characterized by turmoil in the world economy. The Great Depression (1929–1939) and the war coincided with a collapse of the international trading system and of relations among nations. Following the war, some countries came together to energize international commerce and to devise a framework for stability in the international monetary and financial systems. In 1944, the governments of 44 countries negotiated and signed the Bretton Woods agreement.

The Bretton Woods accord pegged the value of the U.S. dollar to an established value of gold, at a rate of $35 per ounce. The U.S. government agreed to buy and sell unlimited amounts of gold in order to maintain this fixed rate. Each of Bretton Woods' other signatory countries agreed to establish a par value of its currency in terms of the U.S. dollar and to maintain this pegged value through central bank intervention. In this way, the Bretton Woods system kept exchange rates of major currencies fixed at a prescribed level, relative to the U.S. dollar and, therefore, to each other.

The demise of the Bretton Woods agreement began in the late 1960s when the United States government employed deficit spending to finance both the Vietnam War and expensive government programs. Rising government spending stimulated the economy and U.S. citizens began spending more on imported goods, aggravating the U.S. balance of payments. The United States acquired trade deficits with

Is the U.S. Trade Deficit Good or Bad?

The United States has posted annual trade deficits since 1971. The deficit in merchandise goods (excluding services) has grown substantially in recent years, reaching a record level of $856 billion in 2006. This represented 6.5 percent of the U.S. gross domestic product. It also meant that the country was borrowing more than $2 billion daily in order to finance its trade gap. In recent years, China has contributed to nearly a quarter of this trade deficit. But the United States also has a trade deficit with its other major trading partners, including Canada, Mexico, and the oil-producing countries in the Middle East.

Persistent trade deficits can be harmful because, like a household whose spending exceeds its income, more money flows out of a country than coming in. Trade deficits can produce higher interest rates, inflation, and general economic instability. To finance a trade deficit, the United States has to sell assets or borrow money from foreigners. For instance, the United States borrows money from China, Japan, and other governments when they invest in U.S. treasury bonds and treasury bills. A persistent deficit means the United States is accumulating a lot of foreign debt.

Each country's balance of trade is closely tied to the exchange rate of its currency. If a country has a trade surplus, there is relatively more demand for its currency and the currency can strengthen, or appreciate, over time. Conversely, if the nation has a chronic deficit position, its currency will weaken, or depreciate, over time. Big U.S. trade deficits partly explain the weakening of the U.S. dollar in foreign exchange markets.

Trade deficits are not inherently good or bad. They must be judged based on the circumstances in which they arose. For one, the deficit is not harmful if it results from imports of input goods used to manufacture higher-value finished products, many of which are exported. Second, trade deficits are generally measured in terms of *merchandise* trade. But, as the exhibit shows, the United States does have a trade *surplus* in international services, which offsets some of the merchandise trade deficit. Third, the United States attracts much inward foreign direct investment. Although inward FDI does not affect the trade deficit in the government's official accounting, it does, over time, offset a portion of the deficit.

Many factors contribute to the persistent deficit, including the tendency of many countries to use the U.S. dollar as their reserve currency, which encourages dollars to flow out of the United States. In addition, the United States is dependent on many imports, including oil, autos, and computer equipment. The trend has intensified as the United States has become a services-based economy—more than two-thirds of the U.S. GDP is now derived from the services sector—with a commensurate decrease in the size of the U.S. manufacturing sector.

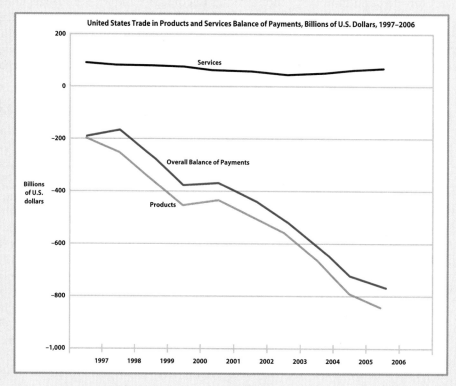

United States Trade in Products and Services Balance of Payments, Billions of U.S. Dollars, 1997–2006

Japan, Germany, and other European countries. Over time, demand for U.S. dollars so exceeded their supply that the U.S. government could no longer maintain an adequate stock of gold. This situation put pressure on governments in Europe, Japan, and the United States to revalue their currencies, a solution that none were willing to implement. As a result, President Nixon suspended the link between the U.S. dollar and gold in 1971, and withdrew the U.S. promise to exchange gold for U.S. dollars. This action essentially brought an end to the Bretton Woods system. U.S. government budget and trade deficits persist to the present day.

Bretton Woods left a legacy of principles and institutions that remain in use today. First, Bretton Woods instituted the concept of international monetary cooperation, especially among the central banks of leading nations. Second, it established the notion of fixing exchange rates within an international regime so as to minimize currency risk. Third, it created the **International Monetary Fund (IMF)** and the **World Bank**. The IMF is an international agency that attempts to stabilize currencies by monitoring the foreign exchange systems of member countries and by lending money to developing economies. The World Bank is an international agency that provides loans and technical assistance to low- and middle-income countries, with the goal of reducing poverty. Finally, Bretton Woods established the importance of currency convertibility, in which all countries adhere to a system of unfettered multilateral trade and conversion of currencies. According to this system, member countries agree to refrain from imposing restrictions on currency trading and agree not to engage in discriminatory currency arrangements. This principle is an important aspect of the trend toward global free trade that the world is experiencing today.

International Monetary Fund (IMF) An international agency that aims to stabilize currencies by monitoring the foreign exchange systems of member countries, and lending money to developing economies.

World Bank An international agency that provides loans and technical assistance to low and middle-income countries with the goal of reducing poverty.

The Exchange Rate System Today

With the collapse of Bretton Woods, almost all major currencies began to be traded freely in world markets, and their value floated according to the forces of supply and demand. The official price of gold was formally abolished and governments became free to choose the type of exchange rate system that best suited their individual needs. Fixed exchange rate systems were given equal status with floating exchange rate systems, and countries were no longer compelled to maintain specific pegged values for their currency. Instead, they were urged to pursue domestic economic policies that would support the stability of their currency relative to others. The exchange rate system today comprises two main types of foreign exchange management: the floating system and the fixed system.

The Floating Exchange Rate System. Most advanced economies use the floating exchange rate system. Under this system, governments refrain from systematic intervention and each nation's currency floats independently, according to market forces. Major world currencies—including the Canadian dollar, the British pound, the euro, the U.S. dollar, and the Japanese yen—float independently on world exchange markets. Their exchange rates are determined daily by the forces of supply and demand. The system gives governments the latitude to modify monetary policy to fit the circumstances that they face at any time. If a country is running a trade deficit, the floating rate system allows for this to be corrected more naturally than if the country uses a fixed exchange rate regime.

The Fixed Exchange Rate System. Under the fixed exchange rate system, sometimes called a *pegged* exchange rate system, the value of a currency is set relative to the value of another (or the value of a basket of currencies) at a specified rate. It is the opposite of the floating exchange rate system. As the reference value rises and falls, so does the currency pegged to it. In the past, some currencies were also fixed to some set value of gold. The fixed exchange rate system was the system used in the Bretton Woods agreement. Many developing economies and some emerging markets use this system today. For example, as noted in the opening vignette, China pegs its currency to the value of a basket of currencies. Belize pegs the value of its currency to the U.S. dollar. To maintain the peg, the governments of these countries intervene in currency markets to buy and sell dollars and other currencies, in order to maintain the exchange rate at a fixed, preset level.

A fixed regime promotes greater stability and predictability of exchange rate movements and provides greater certainty and stability within a nation's economy. The central bank must stand ready to fill any gaps between supply and demand for its currency.

Many economists believe floating exchange rates are preferable to fixed exchange rates because floating rates more naturally respond to, and represent, the supply and demand for currencies in the foreign exchange market. In some situations, however, fixed exchange rates may be preferable for their greater stability. For example, the Asian financial crisis was contained in part because of China's adherence to a fixed exchange regime. A fixed regime provided much stability to world currencies under the Bretton Woods system in the years following World War II.

At times, countries adhere to neither a purely fixed exchange rate nor a floating exchange rate system. Rather, they try to hold the value of their currency within some range against the U.S. dollar or other important reference currency, in a system often referred to as *dirty float*. That is, the value of the currency is determined by market forces, but the central bank intervenes occasionally in the foreign exchange market to maintain the value of its currency within acceptable limits relative to a major reference currency. Many Western countries resort to this type of intervention from time to time.

 ## The International Monetary and Financial Systems

We've seen how currencies facilitate international transactions and how exchange rates affect the amount of international trade. Let's now examine the two systems that determine exchange rates: the international monetary system and the global financial system.

The **international monetary system** refers to the institutional framework, rules, and procedures by which national currencies are exchanged for one another. The **global financial system** refers to the collective financial institutions that facilitate and regulate the flows of investment and capital funds worldwide. Key players in the global financial system include finance ministries, national stock exchanges, commercial banks, and central banks, as well as the Bank for International Settlements, the World Bank, and the International Monetary Fund. Thus, the global financial system incorporates the national and international banking systems, the international bond market, the collective of national stock markets, and the market of bank deposits denominated in foreign currencies.

International Monetary System

The international monetary system includes institutional arrangements that countries use to govern exchange rates. The international monetary system affects the financial activities of governments worldwide and is the basis for international financial markets. For example, if a U.S. investor wants to buy stocks on the London Stock Exchange, the exchange rate of the British pound to the U.S. dollar will affect the investor's earnings.

Of greatest importance to international business, however, is the role that the system plays in facilitating cross-border trade and investment. Firms seek to get paid for the products and services that they sell abroad. The resulting monetary flows take the form of various currencies traded between nations.

International monetary system Institutional framework, rules, and procedures by which national currencies are exchanged for one other.

Global financial system The collective of financial institutions that facilitate and regulate investment and capital flows worldwide, such as central banks, commercial banks, and national stock exchanges.

Global Financial System

The global financial system is built on the activities of firms, banks, and financial institutions, all engaged in ongoing international financial activity. The system has many linkages with national financial markets. Since the 1960s, the global financial system has grown substantially in volume and structure, becoming increasingly more efficient, competitive, and stable.

Today, the global financial system can accommodate massive cross-national flows of money and the massive foreign exchange markets that they have engendered. Initially triggered by the rapid growth in world trade and investment, the globalization of finance accelerated in the 1990s with the open-

The international monetary system provides the framework within which national currencies, including the U.S. dollar, British pound, and the euro, are exchanged for another.

ing of the former Soviet Union and China to international business. More recently, massive cross-national flows of capital—mostly in the form of pension funds, mutual funds, and life insurance investments—are driving equity markets in many countries. Firms can increasingly access a range of capital markets and financial instruments all over the world.[9]

While flows of FDI-related funds have been noteworthy since the 1960s, money flowing abroad as portfolio investments is a relatively new trend. The volume of these flows has become enormous. In 2005, for example, about 15 percent of U.S. equity funds were invested in foreign stocks.[10] Facilitation of financial flows benefits developing economies by increasing their foreign exchange reserves, reducing their cost of capital, and stimulating local development of financial markets.

The growing integration of the financial and monetary activity worldwide is due to several drivers, including:

- The evolution of monetary and financial regulations worldwide.
- The development of new technologies and payment systems and the use of the Internet in global financial activities.
- Increased global and regional interdependence of financial markets.
- The growing role of single-currency systems, such as the euro.

The globalization of financial flows has yielded many benefits. Yet by increasing the volume and speed of international capital flows, it has also led to possibilities of financial risk. Capital flows are much more volatile than FDI-type investments. It is much easier for investors to withdraw and reallocate liquid capital funds than FDI funds, which are directly tied to factories and other permanent operations that firms establish abroad.[11] Economic difficulties that one country experiences can quickly spread to other countries, like a contagion. **Contagion** refers to the tendency of a financial or monetary crisis in one country to spread rapidly to others due to the ongoing worldwide financial integration. Financial instability is worsened when governments fail to adequately regulate and monitor their banking and financial sectors.[12]

A good example of a contagion is the financial crisis in East Asia in the late 1990s, which occurred in the wake of rapid growth that the region experienced from international trade, FDI, and access to the global financial market. The crisis

Contagion The tendency of a financial or monetary crisis in one country to spread rapidly to others due to ongoing financial integration worldwide.

was caused in part by careless banking practices that resulted in vast sums being loaned out to firms and individuals who often lacked the ability to repay the loans. Foreign investors had become overly enthusiastic about the region's prospects, and poured capital into East Asia, often with little regard for high levels of risk and poor underlying fundamentals in local economies. Investors rapidly withdrew their investments once they grasped the extent of risk and instability in the region's economies and banking systems. This capital flight made an already dire economic crisis worse.[13]

Let's discuss various organizations that attempt to mitigate capital flight and manage other challenges in the global monetary and financial systems.

 Key Players in the Monetary and Financial Systems

A variety of national, international, private, and government players make up the international monetary system and the global financial system. Exhibit 10.4 highlights the major players and illustrates the relationships among them. These players operate at the levels of the firm, the nation, and the world.

The Firm

Cross-border buying and selling activities of business enterprises require them to acquire large quantities of foreign exchange. Customers make payments to firms in the course of international business transactions. The firm typically receives earnings from international operations in foreign currencies and must convert them into the currency of the home country. Firms also engage in investment, franchising, or licensing activities abroad that generate revenues that they must exchange into the home currency. For example, Jim Moran Enterprises in Florida is the largest importer of Toyota cars in the United States, and must ultimately pay for its imports in Japanese yen. Moran imports thousands of Toyotas into U.S. ports every year, and deals with the foreign exchange market to convert U.S. dollars to yen.

Some larger, more experienced MNEs with spare cash may acquire foreign currencies for speculative purposes. That is, they may hold foreign currency with a view to profiting from fluctuations in exchange rates. Other firms may acquire foreign currency in order to be able to invest in foreign stock markets and other foreign investment vehicles to obtain short-term gains.

Other private-sector players involved in the international monetary and financial system include life insurance companies, savings and loan associations, and stockbrokers that manage pensions and mutual funds. Some large MNEs have in-house finance departments that manage the foreign exchange and financial transactions of the firm. Nontraditional financial institutions like Western Union play a key role in international transfers of funds. In 2003, foreign residents in the United States used Western Union to wire billions of dollars to family members in India ($10 billion), Mexico ($9.9 billion), and Morocco ($3.3 billion). These funds were converted into local currencies.[14]

National Stock Exchanges and Bond Markets

A *stock exchange* is a facility for the trading of securities and other financial instruments. The traded securities include the shares issued by companies, trust funds, and pension funds, as well as corporate and government bonds. Stock exchanges are a major source of funds for firms to engage in international business. Information technology has revolutionized the functioning of stock markets, providing

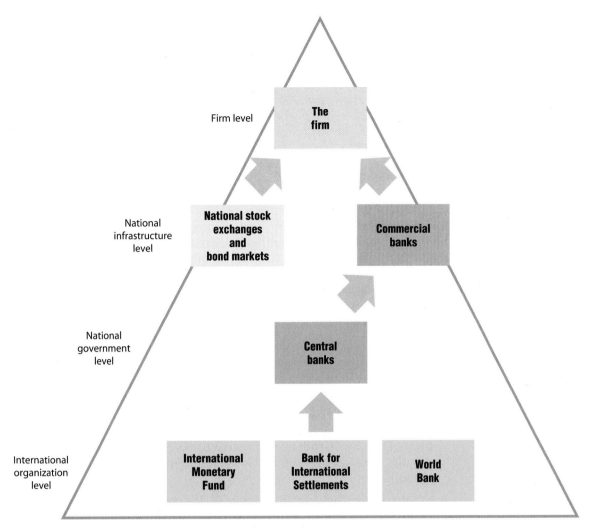

Exhibit 10.4 Key Participants and Relationships in the Global Monetary and Financial Systems

huge advances in speed and cost of transactions. Today, many exchanges are electronic networks not necessarily tied to a fixed location.

Each country sets its own rules for issuing and redeeming stock. Trade on a stock exchange is by members only. For example, the Tokyo Stock Exchange (TSE) is the home stock market to firms such as Toyota, Sony, and Canon. The TSE is the major vehicle through which some 2,000 Japanese firms raise capital to fund their business activities. Several foreign companies, such as BP and Chrysler, are also listed on the TSE. Today, MNEs often list on a number of exchanges worldwide to maximize their ability to raise capital.

The character of markets varies worldwide. For example, the majority of the shares in the Japanese market are held by corporations, while in Britain and the United States shares are held much more by individuals. Despite these differences, stock exchanges are being increasingly integrated into a global securities market.

Bonds are another type of security sold through banks and stockbrokers. They are a form of debt that corporations and governments incur by issuing interest-bearing certificates in order to raise capital. Bonds enable the issuer to finance long-term investments. For example, SK Telekom, the main wireless communications provider in South Korea, financed much of its operations by selling bonds in the global market.

Several European telecommunications providers, such as Telecom Italia, Deutsche Telecom, and France Telecom, issued international bonds to fund their activities.[15]

In many national stock and bond markets, the most important players today are the *institutional investors*—managers of pensions and mutual funds, as well as insurance companies. They have now assumed an enormous role in driving capital markets around the world. As an example, the Government Pension Investment Fund of Japan, one of the world's largest, has over $1 trillion of assets.

Commercial Banks

Banks are important players in the global financial sector. They store deposits and extend credit to households and firms. A bank raises funds by attracting deposits, borrowing money in the interbank market, or issuing financial instruments in the global money market or securities markets. Commercial banks—Bank of America, Mizuho Bank in Japan, and BBVA in Spain—are the foot soldiers of the international monetary system. They, more than any other institution, circulate money and engage in a wide range of international financial transactions. Banks are regulated by national and local governments, which have a strong interest in ensuring the solvency of their national banking system.

The many types of banks and their primary activities include:

- *Investment banks* underwrite—guarantee the sale of—stock and bond issues and advise on mergers, such as the merger of Goldman Sachs in the United States and Nomura Securities in Japan. Read this chapter's *Recent Grad in IB* feature, which highlights Chip Besse, who works in investment banking in Europe.

- *Merchant banks* provide capital to firms in the form of shares rather than loans. They are essentially investment banks especially equipped to handle international operations. The Arab-Malaysian Merchant Bank is an example.

- *Private banks* manage the assets of the very rich. Union Bank in Switzerland (UBS) and ABN AMRO Private Banking in Luxembourg are examples.

- *Offshore banks* are located in jurisdictions with low taxation and regulation, such as Switzerland or Bermuda. Banco General in Panama and Bank of Nova Scotia in the British Virgin Islands are examples.

- *Commercial banks* deal mainly with corporations or large businesses. Credit Lyonnais in France and Bank of America are examples.

In late 2006, nine foreign banks took a key step toward breaking into the Chinese retail banking industry, receiving permission to become the first international lenders to incorporate in China under World Trade Organization market-opening pledges. Here, Citibank of the United States is pictured in Shanghai.

For firms, the most important functions of banks are to lend money to finance business activity, play a key role in nations' money supplies, and exchange foreign currencies. The major world banking centers are London, New York, Tokyo, Frankfurt, and Singapore, with London having the greatest concentration of international banks in the world. Many banks are MNEs themselves, such as Citibank, Britain's HSBC, and Spain's BBVA. Smaller banks participate in international business by interacting with larger, *correspondent banks* abroad. A correspondent bank is a large bank that maintains relations with other banks around the world to facilitate international banking transactions.

Chip Besse is a natural entrepreneur. He started a waste management company while he was in college. Chip realized early that he wanted a career in finance. In his junior year, he obtained a 10-month internship with Merrill Lynch, the investment broker, where he assisted with quarterly reports on restructuring client portfolios. Chip studied on his own and became well versed in insurance sales and variable investment annuities.

In his senior year, Chip studied abroad for a semester in Valencia, Spain. The experience opened his eyes to the possibilities of an international career. A campus visit from an international bank executive motivated Chip further. He contacted the banker via e-mail and telephone for several months until, impressed by his persistence, she offered him an internship at the large international bank where she worked in London.

Chip's hard work so impressed his superiors that they let him enroll in the bank's Graduate Training Program, where he learned how to build financial models for managed buy-outs (MBOs) and leveraged buy-outs (LBOs), as well as mergers and acquisitions. Chip's work involved him in deals to buy companies, make them more profitable, and then sell them. He worked with a team that closed deals throughout Europe, the Middle East, and the United States. Chip's experience accumulated as he assisted in soliciting funds from equity investors and banks. He made numerous presentations to credit committees and transaction management teams. He researched financial data on acquisition targets in various sectors. He devised a system for monitoring budget variances on ongoing investments.

Chip's group acquired underperforming firms and restructured their strategies, with the aim of making them leading industry players. For example, Chip worked on a deal in Scandinavia to refocus a family-run firm that was losing money. Chip and his group helped negotiate a divestment of the firm, cut costs, and devised various growth strategies. Through the efforts of his team, the firm brought in proceeds from divestment of nearly $150 million and increased its profit margin from 2 to 9 percent.

In Britain, Chip worked on the LBO of a movie-theatre chain worth over $800 million. His assignments included financial modeling of the acquisition, refinancing, and optimizing the firm's capital structure. Chip negotiated with lawyers, accountants, and trade partners. In Central America, he negotiated an LBO for a solid-waste removal firm. He worked on a $30 million debt and equity fundraising deal for an Eastern European start-up, also in the waste management business, and a $600 million acquisition of a European sporting company.

After spending over a year at the bank, Chip joined his managing director and colleagues in establishing a new investment firm. In its first year, the firm acquired three companies in Europe and investigated various opportunities in North and South America, Eastern Europe, and Asia. In his spare time, Chip obtained certification in advanced financial modeling, corporate valuations, and the advanced analysis of financial statements.

Chip's majors: Bachelor's degree in Finance with a minor in Spanish

Objectives: Adventure, international perspective, career growth, self-understanding, and the opportunity to learn foreign languages

Internships during college: Merrill Lynch investment broker

Jobs held since graduating:
- A major bank in London
- A new investment firm in London

Success Factors for a Career in International Business

"I enjoy learning about new cultures and assessing investment opportunities where the common variables change drastically. My work requires an eclectic skill base. We often deal with political risk, currency risk, and cultural risk. We try to mitigate most of the risks by doing our homework, talking to local people, immersing ourselves in the culture, and being really diligent by visiting all the locations. There is no 'normal' day at the office."

Challenges

"I recommend a career in international business [even though] doing business in another country and living away from your family and friends is not easy. It takes an open mind, much hard work, and persistence."

Banking practices vary widely. In some countries, banks are owned by the state and are extensions of government. In other countries, banks face little regulation and may lack safety nets that might prevent their failure. In developing economies, private banks are usually subject to substantial government regulation.

Another distinction among national banking practices is the density of banks in individual countries. For example, Canada, Sweden, and the Netherlands each has only five banks controlling more than 80 percent of all banking assets. In Germany, Italy, and the United States, by contrast, the top five banks control less than 30 percent of all banking assets. Banks also charge different rates for their services. For a typical customer, the annual price of core banking services in Italy is over $300, and $150 in the United States. However, the annual price is about only $50 in China and the Netherlands.[16]

Central Banks

As the official national bank of each country, the central bank regulates the money supply and credit, issues currency, and manages the rate of exchange. The central bank also controls the amount of financial reserves held by private banks. It implements monetary policy by increasing or decreasing the money supply through one of the following methods: (1) buying and selling money in the banking system, (2) increasing or decreasing the interest rates on funds loaned to commercial banks, or (3) buying and selling government securities. The central bank may also function as the lender of last resort in the event of a financial crisis. Examples of central banks include the Reserve Bank of India, the Bank of England, the Banque de France, the Bank of Japan, and the Federal Reserve Bank in the United States.

Monetary intervention The buying and selling of government securities by a central bank to maintain the exchange rate of a country's currency at some acceptable level.

As an example, the Federal Reserve Bank of the United States, also known as the Fed, formulates and conducts U.S. monetary policy by influencing the money supply and credit conditions in the U.S. economy. The Fed's main goal is to keep inflation low. A central bank conducts **monetary intervention**, which involves buying and selling government securities to maintain a certain exchange rate of its currency. For example, if the Fed wants to support the value of the U.S. dollar, it might buy dollars in the foreign exchange market. The Fed supervises and regulates the nation's banking system to ensure the safety and soundness of the national financial system. The Fed also works with the International Monetary Fund, the Bank for International Settlements, the Organisation for Economic Cooperation and Development (OECD), and other international agencies to ensure sound international monetary and financial policies in global markets.

The Bank for International Settlements

The Bank for International Settlements (BIS) is an international organization established in 1930 and based in Basel, Switzerland. The mission of the BIS is to foster cooperation among central banks and other governmental agencies, with the aim of supporting stability in the global monetary and financial systems. The BIS provides banking services to central banks and assists them in devising sound monetary policy. It attempts to ensure that central banks maintain reserve assets and capital/asset ratios above prescribed international minimums. Assisting countries to maintain these minimums is important because it helps governments avoid becoming too indebted. Maintaining adequate capital is prescribed by the Basel Capital Accord, originally promulgated by the BIS.[17]

International Monetary Fund

Headquartered in Washington, D.C., the International Monetary Fund (IMF) provides the framework and determines the code of behavior for the international monetary system. The agency promotes international monetary cooperation, exchange rate stability, and orderly exchange arrangements. It also encourages countries to adopt sound economic policies. These functions are critical, because economic crises can destroy jobs, slash incomes, and cause human suffering.

Governed today by 184 countries, the IMF stands ready to provide financial assistance in the form of loans and grants to support policy programs intended to correct macroeconomic problems. For instance, during the 1997–1998 Asian financial crisis, the IMF pledged $21 billion to assist South Korea to reform its economy, restructure its financial and corporate sectors, and recover from recession.[18]

To help manage currency valuation worldwide, the IMF established a special type of international reserve known as the **Special Drawing Right (SDR)**. The SDR is a unit of account or a reserve asset, a type of currency used by central banks to supplement their existing reserves in transactions with the IMF and to manage international exchange rates. For example, a central bank might use SDRs to purchase foreign currencies to manage the value of its currency on world markets. The value of the SDR is very stable because it is based on a basket of currencies—the euro, the Japanese yen, the U.K. pound, and the U.S. dollar.

The IMF plays an important role in addressing financial and monetary crises faced by nations around the world. Typical crises fall into three major categories.

A *currency crisis* results when the value of a nation's currency depreciates sharply or when its central bank must expend substantial reserves to defend the value of its currency, thereby pushing up interest rates. Currency crises occur more commonly in smaller countries, and are sometimes the result of a sudden loss of confidence in the national economy or speculative buying and selling of the nation's currency.

A *banking crisis* results when domestic and foreign investors lose confidence in a nation's banking system, leading to widespread withdrawals of funds from banks and other financial institutions. This situation arose in the United States in the 1930s when, during the Great Depression, millions of people panicked about their savings and rushed to withdraw funds from their bank accounts. The crisis led to the failure of numerous banks. Banking crises tend to occur in developing economies with inadequate regulatory and institutional frameworks. These crises can lead to other problems, such as exchange rate fluctuations, inflation, abrupt withdrawal of FDI funds, and general economic instability.

A *foreign debt crisis* arises when a national government borrows an excessive amount of money from banks or by selling government bonds. For example, China's total foreign debt now exceeds $200 billion. However, the debt is manageable because China has a huge reserve of foreign exchange. By contrast, Argentina's foreign debt has reached roughly 150 percent of the country's GDP. In the effort to pay off the debt, financial and other resources are used that might be otherwise used for investing in more important national priorities. Governments thus draw huge sums out of the national money supply, which reduces the availability of these funds to consumers and to firms attempting to finance business activities.

The IMF assists countries to resolve crises by offering technical assistance and training. It provides assistance by setting fiscal policy, monetary and exchange rate policies, and supervising and regulating banking and financial systems. The IMF also provides loans to help distressed countries in recovery. However, the international agency is frequently criticized because its prescriptions often require national governments to undertake reforms that are painfull, at least in the short run. For example, the IMF may recommend that state economic enterprises should be downsized and workers laid off. Or, the government should give up subsidies or price supports for basic commodities. Some critics charge that the IMF harms countries by imposing too much austerity on them in

Special Drawing Right (SDR) A unit of account or a reserve asset, a type of currency used by central banks to supplement their existing reserves in transactions with the IMF.

Officials of the International Monetary Fund meet to address the needs of developing economies in international monetary affairs. The IMF promotes exchange rate stability and sound economic policies worldwide.

times of financial distress. The IMF argues that any country in an economic crisis usually must undergo substantial restructuring, such as the deregulation of national industries or privatization of state enterprises. However, it is sometimes difficult to pinpoint to what extent IMF prescriptions cause more harm than good.

World Bank

Originally known as the International Bank for Reconstruction and Development, the initial purpose of the World Bank was to provide funding for the reconstruction of Japan and Europe following World War II. Today the World Bank aims to reduce world poverty and is active in a range of development projects to bring water, electricity, and transportation infrastructure. Headquartered in Washington, D.C., the World Bank is a specialized agency of the United Nations and has more than 100 offices worldwide. It is supported by some 184 member countries that are jointly responsible for how the institution is financed and how its money is spent.

The World Bank consists of a collection of subagencies that oversee various international development activities. The International Development Association loans billions of dollars each year to the world's poorest countries. The International Finance Corporation works with the private sector to promote economic development. It invests in sustainable private enterprises in developing countries and provides equity, loans, loan guarantees, risk management products, and advisory services to needful clients. The Multilateral Investment Guarantee Agency aims to encourage FDI to developing countries by providing guarantees to foreign investors against losses caused by noncommercial risks.

The IMF and the World Bank often work together. While the IMF focuses on countries' economic performance, the World Bank emphasizes longer-term development and the reduction of poverty. While the IMF makes short-term loans to help stabilize foreign exchange, the World Bank makes long-term loans to promote economic development.

The European Union and the Euro

The European Union (EU) was established in 1993, an outgrowth of regional integration efforts in Europe since the 1950s. In the intervening years, other countries have joined, bringing the total to 27 member states in 2007. The EU's main objectives are to establish pan-European citizenship and assert Europe's economic and political role in the world. In 1989, the EU began to move toward the goal of a monetary union. The members created the European Monetary Union (EMU), which established a common currency, the euro. In 1998, the European Central Bank (ECB) was established in Germany. In 1999, the euro became the currency for large transactions of 11 EU member states, and euro banknotes and coins were issued in 2002, replacing traditional currencies such as the French franc and the German mark. As of 2007, 13 member states in the EU had adopted the euro. Illustrated in the exhibit below, these member states are: Austria, Belgium, Finland, France, Germany, Greece, Ireland, Italy, Luxembourg, Netherlands, Portugal, Slovenia, and Spain. Note that Denmark, Sweden and the United Kingdom are still not participating in the monetary union.

Sharing a single currency helps knit together the euro zone economies into a unified whole, eliminates exchange fluctuations, and simplifies trade. It is easy to compare the spectrum of prices, taxes, and required pension contributions across national borders, and thus, businesses are tempted to make new investments in countries where costs are lowest and regulation is lightest. Member governments are under continuous pressure in the EMU to cut taxes, trim red tape, and harmonize fiscal and social policies. Harmonization implies that the governments are attempting to make these policies as similar as possible, throughout all the EU member states. For example, the governments are harmonizing product standards and regulations that govern business practices. They are coordinating their economic policies and jointly devising structural reforms that apply to all the EU countries.

The Euro and Business

The introduction of the euro was a unique opportunity and a stimulus for European firms to rethink fundamentals about how they did business. Accounting transactions became cheaper and easier to carry out because there is only one currency to deal with. Firms had to undertake a range of operational preparations,

Euro Zone Member Countries

European Union member countries

Countries that use the Euro
(both as of July 2007)

particularly regarding financial and accounting operations. For example, firms had to convert all accounts to the euro.

Managers at large multinationals favor the euro because it reduces the cost of doing business in many national markets, especially by removing the effect of currency fluctuations in cross-border trade and investment. The single currency makes the job of running an MNE much easier. U.S. and Japanese companies doing business in Europe now have fewer currency exchange hassles. With the move to a single currency, there are opportunities to reduce costs that benefit firms and their customers.

Many companies found that they had to radically modify their pricing strategies. For instance, computer maker Dell considered various strategies and ultimately decided to be a leader in harmonizing prices across the EU. Use of a single currency makes prices easier to compare, which increases competition in the EU. Firms like Dell had to standardize their pricing across Europe to prevent customers from shopping the continent and making their purchases in the country with the lowest price.

Challenges for Policymakers

The ECB views the currency zone as one region, rather than as separate countries with different economic conditions. The problem is that when the countries tied themselves to the euro, their economies had not yet converged. Even today, very different economic and fiscal conditions exist among the nations that comprise the euro zone. Many countries—Belgium, France, Germany, Greece, and Italy, to name a few—have high national debts or high pension costs. For example, while the proportion of workers is declining in most countries, the number of retirees is increasing. Having fewer workers means fewer people paying taxes, which reduces options for financing national pension and retirement funds. When one country's economy is booming, with little debt and low unemployment, another country's economy may be stalled, with high unemployment. ECB governors attempt to devise monetary policy for all EU members, simultaneously, but the one-size-fits-all approach does not suit circumstances across such a wide range of national economic conditions.

Interest rates may be even more problematic. A key ECB mandate is to keep inflation at 2 percent or less. Governments seek to keep inflation low because it can discourage investment and saving, harm living standards, and complicate business planning. When the ECB cuts interest rates, banks borrow funds and more euros are released into the EU money supply. All else being equal, increasing the money supply can drive up inflation. Despite the 2-percent goal, the inflation rate varies widely across the member countries. Less-well-off countries in southern Europe, trying to catch up to wealthier countries like Germany, have inflation rates that are often above 3 percent. Inflation in other countries can be below 1 percent, prompting fears of deflation, a decline in prices. Deflation is just as harmful to an economy as inflation. Deflation can cause large drops in GDP and reduce the value of assets and income.

Another risk faced by the European Union is asymmetric shock, an economic problem that afflicts one part of the euro zone much more than any other. When such an event occurs in a currency union, the policy response is difficult, because there is little scope for independent monetary or exchange rate management. For instance, if southern Europe experiences high inflation and northern Europe experiences deflation, ECB policy that aims to fix the problem in one region is likely to make it worse in another.

ECB policy has become especially challenging with the admission into the EU of poorer eastern European countries such as Poland and the Czech Republic, whose economies are much less stable than those in western Europe. As the number of diverse EU members rises, there is an ever-greater risk of asymmetric shocks. Compared to the original EU members, living standards in the new EU countries are low. Giving up the freedom to adjust interest rates, and accepting a monetary policy that may be either too tight or too slack, could hobble their progress toward attaining higher living standards.

As the currency of continental Europe, the euro has become a symbol of Europe's values and solidarity. But Britain, fearing the threat to its national autonomy, has opted not to join the monetary union, keeping the British pound as its currency. In a poll of senior British business executives, only 35 percent thought Britain should switch to the euro as soon as possible. A British decision to join the euro zone would be seen as a powerful vote of confidence in the euro. Conversely, the decision to stay out raises questions about the EU's official view—that the single currency is both historically inevitable and unarguably beneficial for all who adopt it.

Appreciation of the Euro

If the value of the euro appreciates, it harms the foreign sales and profits of the EU's internationally active firms. A rising euro makes European products more expensive abroad, and therefore less competitive, or yields MNEs smaller earnings when they convert foreign profits into euros. The common currency was intended partly to help shield the euro bloc from currency shocks by creating a large, unified economy. Because Europe is more reliant on trade, however, the EU is still more sensitive to currency fluctuations than the United States. The ECB estimates that a one-year, 5 percent increase in the value of the euro can knock nearly 1 percent off annual GDP growth, several times the impact a similar rise in the dollar would have on the United States. The usual drawbacks of an appreciating currency, such as getting priced out of export markets, hits Europe faster and harder than it does Japan or the United States.

The euro was weak for the first several years of its existence, and the ECB fought the decline by intervening in foreign exchange markets. ECB monetary policy can do only so much for economies that remain burdened with high taxes and inflexible labor markets. For instance, in recent years, the rise of the euro against the dollar and the yen has resulted in falling international sales for European companies. A strong euro could cause problems for Europe's economy overall. It could even tip the continent into a full-blown recession—a risk that would prompt the ECB to cut interest rates. As a broad rule of thumb, a 10 percent rise in the value of the euro against the dollar causes a 3 percent fall in European corporate profits.

A moderate, controlled rise of the euro would theoretically make import prices cheaper and lower inflation, which could ease pressure on the ECB to raise interest rates. But inflation in Europe can drag down private consumption. There is one immediate advantage of a stronger euro: It helps squeeze inflation by cutting the price of imports, especially oil.

The Euro's Unifying Effect

The success of the euro as a unifying force in Europe is gradually changing the international balance of power. European governments feel more empowered to challenge U.S. policy initiatives in the wider global arena. U.S. policymakers wonder whether the euro will challenge the dollar's dominance as the world's currency of choice for international trade. In their reserves of foreign currencies, the central banks of many countries—including Canada, China, and Russia—are giving more weight to the euro. The European currency's position in global foreign currency reserves is growing, eroding the power of the dollar. Many governments are increasing their euro holdings, and Asia is now significantly less dollar-centric than in the past.

AACSB: Reflective Thinking
Case Questions

1. What types of challenges did European firms face in doing business across borders prior to adopting the euro? What types of changes did these firms make once the euro became the new currency?

2. What types of competitive advantages and disadvantages are associated with the implementation of the euro from the perspective of the firm? Was adopting the euro worth it? Why or why not?

3. Elaborate on the following statement: "Because Europe is more reliant on trade, the EU is more sensitive to currency fluctuations than the United States." Why is the EU more sensitive to currency fluctuations?

4. What is the job of a central bank, like the ECB? What is meant by the term *asymmetric shock*? Why does the ECB have to implement a one-size-fits-all monetary policy? What are the challenges and disadvantages of such a policy?

5. Why did Britain opt out of joining the euro zone? What are the potential advantages and disadvantages for Britain of being in the euro zone?

Sources: Bucci, G., and C. James. (1997). The implications of being in and out of the single European currency. *Credit Control* 18(2): 21–26; *Economist*. (2003). "Finance and Economics: Germany's Euro Test," June 14, p. 96; *Economist*. (2003). "Grappling with the Strong Euro," June 7, p. 65; Ellison, Sarah. (2002). "Revealing Price Disparities, the Euro Aids Bargain-Hunters," *Wall Street Journal*, Jan 30, p. A15; Fairlamb, D. (2003). "Super Euro: As the Currency Soars, Central Banks are Raising Their Holdings," *Business Week*, February 17, p. 54; Garnham, P. (2007). "Euro Close to Record High Against Dollar," *Financial Times*, April 26, p. 42; Marshall, M., and D. Wessel. (1997). "One Currency, One Central Bank, One Big Question" *Wall Street Journal*, May 2, p. A10; Read, T. (1997). "The Model of a Central Bank," *Euromoney*, August, pp. 55–56; Reed, S. (1997). "The Almighty Euro," *Business Week*, December 29, p.114; Sesit, M. (2002). "Euro's Launch Helps Consumers Easily Compare Cost of Goods," *Wall Street Journal*, January 18, p. C11; Walker, M., and J. Perry. (2006). "Politics & Economics: Euro Zone Economy Shows More Self-Reliance," *Wall Street Journal*, December 1, p. A6.

CHAPTER ESSENTIALS

Key Terms

balance of payments, p. 293
central bank, p. 291
contagion, p. 297
currency risk, p. 287
devaluation, p. 293
exchange rate, p. 286

foreign exchange, p. 288
foreign exchange market, p. 288
global financial system, p. 296
International Monetary Fund (IMF),
    p. 295
international monetary system, p. 296

monetary intervention, p. 302
Special Drawing Right (SDR), p. 303
trade surplus, p. 292
trade deficit, p. 292
World Bank, p. 295

Summary

In this chapter, you learned about:

1. Currencies and exchange rates in international business

Much of international trade involves exchanging currencies, such as the dollar, euro, and yen. An **exchange rate** is the price of one currency expressed in terms of another. **Currency risk** arises from the changes in the price of one currency relative to another. As exchange rates fluctuate, so do firms' international business prospects. A *convertible currency* is one that can be readily exchanged for other currencies. Some currencies are *nonconvertible* and not readily exchangeable for other currencies. **Foreign exchange** refers to all forms of money that are traded internationally, including foreign currencies, bank deposits, checks, and electronic transfers. *Capital flight* refers to the tendency of international investors to drastically reduce their investments in a currency that is losing its value. Currencies are exchanged in the **foreign exchange market**—the global marketplace for buying and selling currencies—mainly by banks and governments.

2. How exchange rates are determined

The relative values of currencies are determined by various factors. First is *economic growth*, the increase in value of the products and services produced by a country. A second factor is inflation, which is closely related to interest rates. As inflation rises, so do interest rates. This tendency is usually accompanied by a decrease in the value of the involved currency. A third determinant of exchange rates is *market psychology*, the often unpredictable behavior of investors, especially when acting en masse. Finally, governments play a major role in influencing exchange rates. **Trade deficit** refers to the amount by which a nation's imports exceed its exports for a specific period of time. **Trade surplus** is the amount by which a nation's exports exceed its imports for a specific period of time. Government action to influence exchange rates is broadly termed **monetary intervention**. When the action aims to lower the currency's value, the result is a **devaluation**—government action to reduce the official value of its currency, relative to other currencies. The **balance of payments** is the annual accounting of *all* economic transactions of a nation with all other nations.

3. Development of the modern exchange rate system

The evolution of the modern exchange rate system began with the Bretton Woods agreement in 1944, which aimed to stabilize exchange rates worldwide. But the system collapsed in 1971 as currency values were allowed to begin floating according to market forces. Currently, the value of major world currencies is based on a *floating exchange rate system*, as determined by market forces. However, some developing economies apply a *fixed exchange rate system* in which the value of the national currency is permanently pegged or set to the value of one or more other currencies.

4. The international monetary and financial systems

The **international monetary system** refers to the institutional framework, rules, and procedures by which national currencies are exchanged for each other. It includes institutional arrangements that countries put in place to govern exchange rates. The system includes the foreign exchange market as well as the central banks of each nation, national treasuries, commercial banks, and supranational agencies, such as the International Monetary Fund and World Bank. The **global financial system** is the collective of financial institutions that facilitate and regulate investment and capital flows worldwide, such as central banks, commercial banks, and national stock exchanges. It reflects the activities of companies, banks, and financial institutions, all engaged in ongoing financial activity. The system includes national and international banking systems, the international bond market, the collective of national stock markets, and the market of bank deposits denominated in foreign currencies. The global financial system now facilitates massive trading of financial assets and currencies. It also gives rise to **contagion**, the tendency of a financial or monetary crisis in one country to spread rapidly to other countries.

5. Key players in the monetary and financial systems

Key participants include firms that acquire large quantities of foreign exchange in the course of international business. These firms engage in various investment activities abroad that generate revenues and inject money into the financial system. Nations also have *national stock exchanges* and bond markets in which securities and bond trading takes place. There are various categories of banks, which perform a range of functions. Each country has a **central bank**—the monetary authority that regulates the money supply and credit, issues currency, and manages the rate of exchange. It is usually the lender of last resort, and controls the monetary policy and levels of foreign exchange within national economies. The **World Bank** is an international agency that provides loans and technical assistance to low and middle-income countries with the goal of reducing poverty. The **International Monetary Fund** (IMF) is a key international agency that aims to stabilize currencies by monitoring the foreign exchange systems of member countries and lending money to developing economies. The IMF employs **special drawing rights**, a type of international reserve, to help manage currency valuation worldwide. A *currency crisis* results when the value of the nation's currency depreciates sharply. A *banking crisis* results when investors lose confidence in a nation's banking system and massively withdraw funds. Excessive *foreign debt* can harm the stability of national financial systems.

Test Your Comprehension AACSB: Reflective Thinking

1. Distinguish the terms exchange rate and foreign exchange. What does each term mean?

2. Distinguish between convertible and nonconvertible currencies.

3. Exchange rates fluctuate constantly. What is the effect of this on companies engaged in cross-border transactions?

4. Summarize the four major factors that determine exchange rates.

5. What is the relationship between inflation, interest rates, and currency values?

6. What was the Bretton Woods agreement, and what is the legacy of Bretton Woods for international trade today?

7. Distinguish the two systems that make up the exchange rate system today.

8. What is the difference between the international monetary system and the global financial system?

9. What are the implications of contagion for the global economy today?

10. What are the key players in the international monetary and financial systems?

11. What are the aims of the World Bank and the International Monetary Fund?

Apply Your Understanding
AACSB: Reflective Thinking, Analytical Skills, Ethical Reasoning

1. Everest Company has been exporting its line of mountain-climbing equipment to distributors around the world since the late 1970s. Top markets have been France, Norway, Switzerland, India, and Japan. Everest's customers in these countries always pay in their local currency. Everest's vice president for international sales often states that the firm's biggest day-to-day challenge is dealing with foreign currencies. Why does he say this? What are the consequences of fluctuating exchange rates for Everest's sales revenue and other performance indicators?

2. Every nation has a government that implements monetary and fiscal policies. Monetary policy primarily involves management of the nation's money supply to achieve specific goals—such as constraining inflation and achieving full employment. How does a nation carry out monetary policy? What are the policy instruments that central bankers employ to alter the money supply? Central bankers go to much effort to devise sound monetary policies. Why do they do this? Why is it important to have sound monetary policies? What is the role of monetary policy in facilitating international trade?

3. The balance of trade is the nation's balance sheet of trade with the rest of the world. It represents the difference between the monetary value of a nation's exports and its imports. Some experts believe that a large trade deficit is harmful or may be a sign of economic problems. Do you agree? The United States has run a large trade deficit for many years. What are the long-term consequences of this trend for the United States?

globalEDGE Internet Exercises

(http://globalEDGE.msu.edu)

AACSB: Communication, Reflective Thinking

Refer to Chapter 1, page 27, for instructions on how to access and use globalEDGE.™

1. There are numerous foreign exchange calculators on the Internet, such as www.x-rates.com. You can find them via globalEDGE ™ or by entering the keywords "exchange rate" into a Google search. Visit one of these calculators and compare the exchange rates of various currencies, including the dollar, euro, yen, and renminbi. What is the rate for these currencies today? What was the euro–dollar exchange rate one year ago? What factors might have caused the fluctuation in this rate during the year? Does this Web site provide a way to trade foreign currencies? What is the amount of commission or other fees charged?

2. Assume that you are a manager at a firm interested in entering Russia. As part of your initial analysis, top management would like to know about the level of currency and financial risks associated with the Russian market. Using globalEDGE™ resources, write a short report on the current status of these risks, as well as the state of the Russian financial system and historical exchange rate stability. Based on your findings, what would your recommendation be?

3. The International Monetary Fund (IMF) lists its purposes as follows: (1) to promote international monetary cooperation via consultation and collaboration on international monetary problems; (2) to facilitate the expansion and balanced growth of international trade; and (3) to promote exchange stability, to maintain orderly exchange arrangements among members, and to avoid competitive exchange depreciation. Visit the IMF Web site (www.imf.org) and list several examples of how the IMF undertakes and accomplishes these goals. What kinds of specific actions has the IMF taken over the past year in order to address economic or financial crises of various nations?

CKR Cavusgil Knight Riesenberger

Management Skill Builder©

Identifying the Best Location for a Bank Branch Abroad

Banks are a leading participant in the global economy. They provide capital, foreign exchange, and money for national economies. Banks are reaching out to extend their operations to new markets around the world. Branch banking is a relatively inexpensive way to enter foreign markets, and the rise of international branch banking is part of the globalization of finance. Branch banking involves the bank in opening branches in the countries where the bank seeks to do business.

AACSB: Reflective Thinking, Analytical Skills

Managerial Challenge

The problem of choosing the best markets for locating bank branches abroad is complex. What makes a good location? What types of indicators should be considered? In advance of locating bank branches abroad, management should try to ascertain the most appropriate location to maximize bank performance. The successful international manager investigates the best locations in advance. Given the number of potential locations and the variables to consider, decisions about the best foreign locations can be challenging.

Background

Banks' international lending and borrowing activities have led to increased cross-border capital flows. Banks have developed new types of financial instruments and investment vehicles that increasing numbers of firms and depositors worldwide find attractive. Larger banks often establish foreign branches, providing essentially the same financial services as local banks abroad. The international business environment entails various risks, and when banks set up branches abroad, they seek to maximize conditions for success and to minimize risk.

Managerial Skills You Will Gain

In this C/K/R Management Skill Builder©, as a prospective manager, you will:

1. Learn how to research key monetary and financial statistics on international markets.

2. Develop skills to identify factors to consider when locating bank branches abroad.

3. Learn how these factors relate to maximizing banks' performance and competitive advantages abroad.

Your Task

Assume you are a manager at Citibank, Barclays, or some other large bank. Management wants to set up additional bank branches abroad. Your task is to identify the most appropriate foreign location for setting up a bank branch. Based on your analysis, you should make a recommendation on which countries are most promising.

Go to the C/K/R Knowledge Portal©
www.prenhall.com/cavusgil

Proceed to the C/K/R Knowledge Portal© to obtain the expanded background information, your task and methodology, suggested resources for this exercise, and the presentation template.

Global Strategy and Organization

Learning Objectives

In this chapter, you will learn about:

1. The role of strategy in international business

2. The integration-responsiveness framework

3. Distinct strategies emerging from the integration-responsiveness framework

4. Organizational structure

5. Alternative organizational arrangements for international operations

6. Building the global firm

7. Putting organizational change in motion

> IKEA's Global Strategy

Furniture retailer IKEA is a Swedish company that has transformed itself into a global organization over the past three decades. Ingvar Kamprad founded the firm in Sweden in 1943 when he was 17 years old. IKEA originally sold pens, picture frames, jewelry, and nylon stockings—any product that Kamprad could sell at a low price. In 1950, IKEA began selling furniture and housewares. In the 1970s, the company began expanding into Europe and North America. IKEA's philosophy is to offer quality, well-designed furnishings at low prices. The company designs "knock-down" furniture that the customer purchases and then assembles at home. Designs implement functional, utilitarian, and space-saving features, with a distinctive Scandinavian style.

IKEA Group sales for the fiscal year 2006 totaled 17.3 billion euros, making IKEA the largest furniture retailer in the world. Its stores, usually located in major cities, are mammoth, warehouse-style outlets, with each stocking approximately 9,500 items, including everything for the home—from sofas to plants to kitchen utensils.

IKEA is now owned by a Dutch-registered foundation controlled by the Kamprad family. Its corporate offices are in the Netherlands, Sweden, and Belgium.

Product development, purchasing, and warehousing are concentrated in Sweden. Headquarters designs and develops IKEA's global product line and branding, often in close collaboration with external suppliers. Approximately 30 percent of the merchandise is made in Asia, and two-thirds in Europe. A few items are sourced in North America to address the specific needs of that market, but 90 percent of IKEA's product line is identical worldwide. Managers at IKEA stores feed market research back to headquarters in Sweden on sales and customer preferences.

IKEA targets people all over the world, with a focus on families with limited income and limited living space. This global segment is characterized by liberal-minded, well-educated, white-collar people—including college students—who care little about status and view foreign products positively. Targeting a global customer segment allows IKEA to offer standardized products at uniform prices, a strategy that minimizes the costs of international operations. IKEA seeks scale economies by consolidating worldwide design, purchasing, and manufacturing. It distinguishes itself from conventional furniture makers that serve fragmented markets. Its designers work closely with contract suppliers around the world to ensure savings, high volume, and high standards.

Each IKEA store follows a centrally developed communications strategy. The catalogue is the most important marketing tool. In 2006, 175 million copies were printed in 27 languages, representing the largest circulation of a free publication in the world. The catalogue, also available online (www.ikea.com), is prepared in Sweden to assure conformity to the IKEA look. The catalogue conforms to IKEA's cosmopolitan style. Each product has a unique, proper name. For sofas, IKEA uses Scandinavian rivers or cities (Henriksberg, Falkenberg), women's names for fabric (Linne, Mimmi, Adel), and men's names for wall units (Billy, Niklas, Ivar).

IKEA's employees ("co-workers") across the globe are widely acknowledged as the basis for the firm's success. Corporate culture is informal. There are few titles, no executive parking spaces, and no corporate dining room. Managers fly economy class and stay in inexpensive hotels. Regional organizations are minimized so that stores maintain direct contact with IKEA in Sweden. This speeds decision making and ensures that the IKEA culture is easily globalized. Management in each store is required to speak either English or Swedish, to ensure efficient communications with headquarters.

IKEA organizes an "antibureaucratic week" each year in which managers wear sales clerks' uniforms and do everything from operating cash registers to driving forklifts. By using this system, managers stay in touch with all of IKEA's operations and remain close to suppliers, customers, and salespeople. The firm's culture emphasizes consensus-based decision making and problem solving, and managers readily share their knowledge and skills with co-workers. IKEA's distinct culture helps employees and suppliers feel they are an important part of a global organization. This culture has a strong global appeal, supporting IKEA's continued growth.

How does a company like IKEA manage its operations across 35 countries, 240 stores, more than 100,000 employees, 20 franchises, and 2,000 suppliers? Part of the complexity comes from having to adapt to local regulations on labor laws, store operations, unique supplier relationships, and shopping preferences. Among other challenges, IKEA must figure out how to:

1. Ensure valuable customer feedback (for example, design preferences) from individual markets reach decision makers at headquarters

2. Reward employees and motivate suppliers with expectations that vary from country to country

3. Achieve the real benefits of international operations—efficiency on a global scale and learning—while remaining responsive to local needs

4. Keep designs standardized across markets, yet be able to respond to local preferences and trends

5. Delegate adequate autonomy to local store managers while retaining central control

Sources: Coppola, V. (2002). "Furniture as Fashion Wins Ikea." *Adweek*, Feb. 25, pp. 12–13; Duff, M. (2003). "IKEA Eyes Aggressive Growth," *DSN Retailing Today* Jan. 27, p. 23; www.businessweek.com, "Online Extra: IKEA's Design for Growth," June 6, 2005; www.businessweek.com, "IKEA: How the Swedish Retailer became a Global Cult Brand," November 14, 2005; IKEA corporate web site at www.IKEA-group.IKEA.com; IKEA company profile at Hoovers, at *www.hoovers.com*

Globalization has increased the speed, frequency, and magnitude by which firms from diverse industries can access international markets for customers. Managers are evolving their internationalization strategies to transform their organizations into globally competitive enterprises. As the IKEA vignette shows, managers are striving to coordinate sourcing, manufacturing, marketing, and other value-adding activities on a worldwide basis. They seek to eliminate redundancy and adopt organization-wide standards and common processes. Some managers, like those at IKEA, try to nurture products that may gain the approval of a global clientele and become global brands. Nevertheless, organizing the firm on a global scale is very challenging. It requires strategic positioning, organizational capabilities, alignment of value-adding activities on a worldwide basis, a high degree of coordination and integration, attention to the needs of individual markets, and implementation of common processes.

In this chapter, we discuss the role of strategy and alternative structural arrangements in building a globally integrated enterprise. In the next chapter, we follow up with a discussion of how managers can go about identifying global market opportunities.

The Role of Strategy in International Business

Strategy is a plan of action that channels an organization's resources so that it can effectively differentiate itself from competitors and accomplish unique and viable goals. Managers develop strategies based on their examination of the organization's strengths and weaknesses relative to its competition and the opportunities it faces. Managers decide which customers to target, what product lines to offer, and with which firms to compete.

Strategy in the international context is a plan for the organization to position itself positively from its competitors and configure its value-adding activities on a global scale. It guides the firm toward chosen customers, markets, products, and services in the global marketplace, not necessarily in a particular international market.[1] As a minimum, strategy in the international context should help managers to formulate a strong international vision, allocate scarce resources on a worldwide basis, participate in major markets, implement global partnerships, engage in competitive moves in response to global rivals, and configure value-adding activities on a global scale.[2]

What is the role of strategy in creating competitive advantage in international business? It has been argued that an effective international strategy begins with developing a standardized product that can be produced and sold the same way in multiple countries.[3] Kenichi Ohmae[4] argues that delivering value to customers worldwide is the overriding goal, while other observers stress achieving strategic flexibility.[5] The idea of exploiting scale economies by building global volume and deriving synergies across the firm's different activities is also relevant.[6] Managers should also build a strong worldwide distribution system and use profits from successful products and markets to subsidize the development of other products and markets.[7]

The most widely accepted prescription for building sustainable, competitive advantage in international business is that of Bartlett and Ghoshal.[8] They argue that managers should look to "develop, *at one and the same time,* global scale efficiency, multinational flexibility, and the ability to develop innovations and leverage knowledge on a worldwide basis."[9] They propose that the firm that aspires to become a globally competitive enterprise must seek simultaneously these three strategic objectives—efficiency, flexibility, and learning. Let's review each objective.

Efficiency *The firm must build efficient international supply chains.* Efficiency refers to lowering the cost of the firm's operations and activities on a global scale. Multinational enterprises with multiple value chains around the world must pay special attention to how they organize their R&D, manufacturing, sourcing product, marketing, and customer service activities. For example, automotive companies such as Toyota strive to achieve scale economies by concentrating manufacturing and sourcing activities in a limited number of locations around the world.

Flexibility *The firm must develop worldwide flexibility to manage diverse country-specific risks and opportunities.* The diversity and volatility of the international environment is a special challenge for managers. Therefore, the firm's ability to tap

Strategy A plan of action that channels an organization's resources so that it can effectively differentiate itself from competitors and accomplish unique and viable goals.

Strategy in the international context A plan for the organization to position itself positively from its competitors and configure its value-adding activities on a global scale.

local resources and exploit local opportunities is critical. For example, managers may opt for contractual relationships with independent suppliers and distributors in one country while engaging in direct investment in another. Or, the firm may adapt its marketing and human resource management practices to suit its unique country conditions (we discuss marketing and human resource management issues in chapters 17 and 18). Changing environmental circumstances, such as exchange rate fluctuations, may prompt managers to switch to local sourcing or to adjust prices.

Learning *The firm must create the ability to learn from international exposure and exploit learning on a worldwide basis.* The diversity of the global environment presents the internationalizing firm with unique learning opportunities. Even though the firm goes abroad to exploit its unique advantages, such as technology, brand name, or management capabilities, managers can add to the stock of capabilities by internalizing new knowledge gained from international exposure. Thus, the organization can acquire new technical and managerial know-how, new product ideas, improved R&D capabilities, partnering skills, and survival capabilities in unfamiliar environments. The firm's partners or subsidiaries can capture and disseminate this learning throughout their corporate network. For example, it was Procter & Gamble's research center in Brussels that developed a special capability in water-softening technology, primarily because European water contains more minerals than water in the United States. Similarly, the company learned to formulate a different kind of detergent in Japan, where customers wash their clothes in colder water than in the United States or Europe.

In the final analysis, international business success is largely determined by the degree to which the firm achieves its goals of efficiency, flexibility, and learning. But it is often difficult to excel in all three areas simultaneously. Rather, one firm may excel at efficiency while another may excel at flexibility, and a third at learning. In the 1980s, for example, many Japanese MNEs achieved international success by developing highly efficient and centralized manufacturing systems. In Europe, numerous MNEs have succeeded by being locally responsive while sometimes failing to achieve substantial economic efficiency or technological leadership. Many MNEs based in the United States have struggled to adapt their activities to the cultural and political diversity of national environments, and instead have proven to be more skillful at achieving efficiency via scale economies.

Strategy in Multidomestic and Global Industries

Companies in the food and beverage, consumer products, and clothing and fashion industries may often resort to a country-by-country approach to marketing to specific needs and tastes, laws, and regulations. Industries in which competition takes place on a country-by-country basis are known as **multidomestic industries**. In such industries, each country tends to have a unique set of competitors.

By contrast, industries such as aerospace, automobiles, telecommunications, metals, computers, chemicals, and industrial equipment are examples of **global industries**, in which competition is on a regional or worldwide scale. Formulating and implementing strategy is more critical for global industries than multidomestic industries. Most global industries are characterized by the existence of a handful of major players that compete head-on in multiple markets. For example, Kodak must contend with the same rivals—Japan's Fuji and the European multinational, Agfa-Gevaert—wherever it does business around the world. Similarly, American Standard and Toto dominate the worldwide bathroom fixtures market. In the earthmoving equipment industry, Caterpillar and Komatsu compete head-on in all major world markets.

Multidomestic industry An industry in which competition takes place on a country-by-country basis.

Global industry An industry in which competition is on a regional or worldwide scale.

The Integration-Responsiveness Framework

Since efficiency and learning objectives are often related, they are frequently combined into a single dimension, called global integration. **Global integration** refers to the coordination of the firm's value-chain activities across countries to achieve worldwide efficiency, synergy, and cross-fertilization in order to take maximum advantage of similarities between countries. The flexibility objective is also called local responsiveness. **Local responsiveness** refers to meeting the specific needs of buyers in individual countries.

The discussion about the pressures on the firm to achieve the dual objectives of global integration and local responsiveness has become known as the *integration-responsiveness (IR) framework*.[10] The IR framework, shown in Exhibit 11.1, was developed to help managers better understand the trade-offs between global integration and local responsiveness.

In companies that are locally responsive, managers adjust the firm's practices to suit distinctive conditions in each market. They adapt to customer needs, the competitive environment, and the local distribution structure. Thus, Wal-Mart store managers in Mexico adjust store hours, employee training, compensation, the merchandise mix, and promotional tools to suit conditions in Mexico. Firms in multidomestic industries such as food, retailing, and book publishing tend to be locally responsive because language and cultural differences strongly influence buyer behavior in these industries

In contrast, global integration seeks economic efficiency on a worldwide scale, promoting learning and cross-fertilization within the global network and reducing redundancy. Headquarters personnel justify global integration by citing converging demand patterns, spread of global brands, diffusion of uniform technology, availability of panregional media, and the need to monitor competitors on a global basis. Thus, designing numerous variations of the same basic product for individual markets will only add to overall costs and should be avoided. Firms in global industries such as aircraft manufacturing, credit cards, and pharmaceuticals are more likely to emphasize global integration.

Global integration
Coordination of the firm's value-chain activities across countries to achieve worldwide efficiency, synergy, and cross-fertilization in order to take maximum advantage of similarities between countries.

Local responsiveness
Meeting the specific needs of buyers in individual countries.

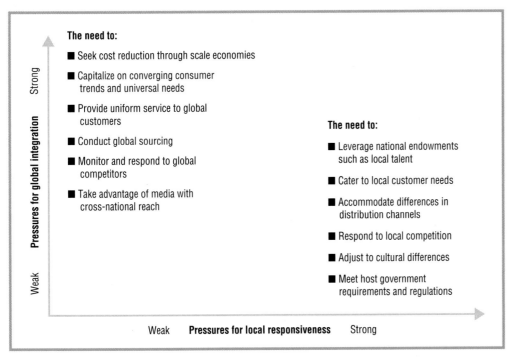

The need to:

■ Seek cost reduction through scale economies

■ Capitalize on converging consumer trends and universal needs

■ Provide uniform service to global customers

■ Conduct global sourcing

■ Monitor and respond to global competitors

■ Take advantage of media with cross-national reach

The need to:

■ Leverage national endowments such as local talent

■ Cater to local customer needs

■ Accommodate differences in distribution channels

■ Respond to local competition

■ Adjust to cultural differences

■ Meet host government requirements and regulations

Pressures for global integration (Weak / Strong)

Weak   **Pressures for local responsiveness**   Strong

Exhibit 11.1

Integration-Responsiveness Framework: Competing Pressures on the Internationalizing Firm

Pressures for Local Responsiveness

There are various factors that compel the firm to become locally responsive in the countries where it conducts business.[11] These factors are:

- *Unique natural endowments available to the firm.* Each country has national endowments that the foreign firm should access.

- *Diversity of local customer needs.* Businesses, such as clothing and food, require significant adaptation to local customer needs.

- *Differences in distribution channels.* These vary considerably from market to market and may increase the need for local responsiveness. For example, small retailers in Japan understand local customs and needs, so locally responsive MNEs use them to distribute products in that country.

- *Local competition.* When competing against numerous local rivals, centrally controlled MNEs will have difficulty gaining market share with global products that are not adapted to local needs.

- *Cultural differences.* Cultural characteristics influence consumer buying decisions. The influence of cultural differences may vary considerably, depending on the type of product. For those products where cultural differences are important, such as clothing and furniture, local managers require considerable freedom from headquarters to adapt their product and marketing practices.

- *Host government requirements and regulations.* When governments impose trade barriers or complex business regulations, they can halt or reverse the competitive threat of foreign firms. The MNE may establish a local subsidiary with substantial decision-making authority to minimize the effects of protectionism.

Pressures for Global Integration

Another set of factors compels the firm to coordinate its activities across countries in an attempt to build efficient operations.[12] These are:

- *Economies of scale.* Concentrating manufacturing in a few select locations where the firm can profit from economies of mass production motivates global integration. Also, the smaller the number of manufacturing and R&D locations, the easier it is for the firm to control quality and cost.

- *Capitalize on converging consumer trends and universal needs.* Standardization is appropriate for products with widespread acceptance and whose features, quality, and cost are similar worldwide. Examples include computer chips and electronic components. Companies such as Nike, Dell, ING, and Coca-Cola offer products that appeal to consumers everywhere.

- *Uniform service to global customers.* Services are easiest to standardize when firms can centralize their creation and delivery. Multinational enterprises with operations in numerous countries particularly value service inputs that are consistent worldwide.

- *Global sourcing of raw materials, components, energy, and labor.* Firms face an ongoing pressure to procure high-quality input goods in a cost-efficient manner. Sourcing of inputs from large-scale, centralized suppliers provides benefits from economies of scale and more consistent performance outcomes. Sourcing from a few well-integrated suppliers is more efficient than sourcing from numerous loosely connected distributors.

- *Global competitors.* Competitors that operate in multiple markets threaten firms with purely domestic operations. Global coordination is necessary to monitor and respond to competitive threats in foreign and domestic markets.

- *Availability of media that reaches consumers in multiple markets.* The availability of cost-effective communications and promotion makes it possible for firms to cater to global market segments that cross different countries. For example, firms now take advantage of the Internet and cross-national television to simultaneously advertise their offerings in numerous countries.

Distinct Strategies Emerging from the Integration-Responsiveness Framework

The integration-responsiveness framework presents four distinct strategies for internationalizing firms. Exhibit 11.2 illustrates these strategies. Internationalizing firms pursue one or a combination of four major types of strategies. In general, multidomestic industries favor home replication and multidomestic strategies, while global industries favor global and transnational strategies.

With a **home replication strategy** (sometimes called *export strategy* or *international strategy*), the firm views international business as separate from, and secondary to, its domestic business. Early in its internationalization process, such a firm may view international business as an opportunity to generate incremental sales for domestic product lines. Typically, products are designed with domestic customers in mind, and international business is sought as a way of extending the product life cycle and replicating its home-market success. The firm expects little knowledge flows from foreign operations.[13]

A second approach is **multidomestic strategy** (sometimes called *multilocal strategy*), whereby an internationalizing firm delegates considerable autonomy to each country manager, allowing him or her to operate independently and pursue local responsiveness. With this strategy, managers recognize and emphasize differences between national markets. As a result, the internationalizing firm allows

Home replication strategy An approach in which the firm views international business as separate from and secondary to its domestic business.

Multidomestic strategy An approach to firm internationalization where headquarters delegates considerable autonomy to each country manager, allowing him or her to operate independently and pursue local responsiveness.

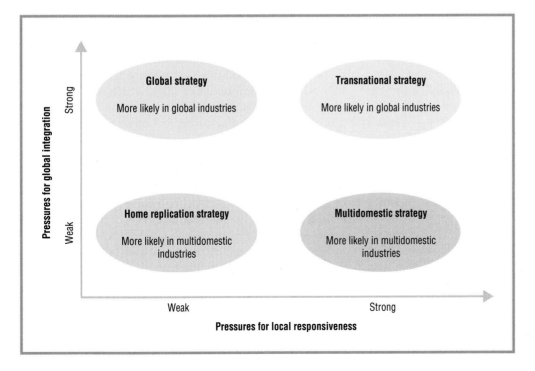

Exhibit 11.2

Four Distinct Strategies Emerging from the Integration-Responsiveness Framework

subsidiaries to vary product and management practices by country. Country managers tend to be highly independent entrepreneurs, often nationals of the host country.[14] They function independently and have little incentive to share knowledge and experience with managers in other countries. Products and services are carefully adapted to suit the unique needs of each country.

Firms that pursue a multidomestic strategy relinquish considerable autonomy to foreign subsidiaries and exercise little central control. The multidomestic approach has several advantages. If the foreign subsidiary includes a factory, locally produced goods and products can be better adapted to local markets. The approach places minimal pressure on headquarters staff because management of country operations is delegated to individual managers in each country. Firms with limited internationalization experience often find multidomestic strategy an easy option, as they can delegate many tasks to their country managers (or foreign distributors, franchisees, or licensees, where they are used).

Nevertheless, multidomestic strategy has some disadvantages. The firm's foreign subsidiary managers tend to develop strategic vision, culture, and processes that differ substantially from those of headquarters. They have little incentive to share knowledge and experience with managers in the firm's other country markets, which leads to duplication of activities and reduced economies of scale. Limited information sharing also reduces the possibility of developing a knowledge-based competitive advantage.[15] Competition may escalate between the subsidiaries for the firm's resources because subsidiary managers do not share a common corporate vision. While a multidomestic strategy results in firms having a highly responsive presence in different national markets, it leads to inefficient manufacturing, redundant operations, a proliferation of products designed to meet local needs, and generally higher cost of international operations than other strategies.[16]

These disadvantages may eventually lead management to abandon multidomestic strategy in favor of a third approach—**global strategy**. With this strategy, headquarters seeks substantial control over its country operations in an effort to minimize redundancy and achieve maximum efficiency, learning, and integration worldwide. In the extreme case, global strategy asks why not make "the same thing, the same way, everywhere?"[17] In this way, global strategy emphasizes greater central coordination and control than multidomestic strategy, with various product or business managers having worldwide responsibility. Activities such as R&D and manufacturing are centralized at headquarters, and management tends to view the world as one large marketplace.

Global strategy offers many advantages: It provides management with a greater capability to respond to worldwide opportunities, increases opportunities for cross-national learning and cross-fertilization of the firm's knowledge base among all the subsidiaries, and creates economies of scale, which results in lower operational costs. Global strategy can also improve the quality of products and processes—primarily by simplifying manufacturing and other processes. High-quality products promote global brand recognition and give rise to consumer preference and efficient international marketing programs.

The ability of firms to pursue global strategy has been facilitated by many factors, including the converging needs and tastes of consumers around the world, the growing acceptance of global brands, the increasing diffusion of uniform technology (especially in industrial markets), the integrating effects of the Internet and e-commerce, the integration of markets through economic blocs and financial globalization, and the spread of international collaborative ventures.

As in other approaches, global strategy has its limitations. It is challenging for management to closely coordinate the activities of a large number of widely dispersed international operations. The firm must maintain an ongoing communication between headquarters and its subsidiaries, as well as between the subsidiaries. When carried to an extreme, global strategy results in a loss of responsiveness and flexibility in local markets. Local managers who are stripped

Global strategy An approach where headquarters seeks substantial control over its country operations in an effort to minimize redundancy and achieve maximum efficiency, learning, and integration worldwide.

of autonomy over their country operations may become demoralized and lose their entrepreneurial spirit.

A final alternative is **transnational strategy**, a coordinated approach to internationalization in which the firm strives to be more responsive to local needs while retaining sufficient central control of operations to ensure efficiency and learning. Transnational strategy combines the major advantages of multidomestic and global strategies while minimizing their disadvantages.[18] Transnational strategy implies a flexible approach: *standardize where feasible; adapt where appropriate.* In practice, managers implement transnational strategy by:

- Exploiting scale economies by sourcing from a reduced set of global suppliers and concentrating the production of offerings in relatively few locations where competitive advantage can be maximized
- Organizing production, marketing, and other value-chain activities on a global scale
- Optimizing local responsiveness and flexibility
- Facilitating global learning and knowledge transfer
- Coordinating *competitive moves*— that is, how the firm deals with its competitors, on a global, integrated basis[19]

Transnational strategy requires planning, resource allocation, and uniform policies on a global basis. Firms standardize products as much as possible while adapting them as needed to ensure ample sales in individual markets. For example, in IKEA's case, some 90 percent of its product line is identical across more than two dozen countries. IKEA's overall marketing plan is centrally developed at company headquarters in Europe in response to convergence of product expectations. Nevertheless, the plan is implemented with local adjustments. The firm also modifies some of its furniture offerings to suit tastes in individual countries. IKEA decentralizes some of its decision making, such as the language to use in advertising, to local stores.

The British bank Standard Chartered, Procter & Gamble (P&G), Dow Chemical, and software maker Oracle are all striving for a transnational strategy. Dow Chemical created global business divisions to take charge of investment and market development. But Dow also relies on local managers to deal with regulatory issues, which can be complex in emerging markets. Procter & Gamble cut the country manager's role and handed all strategic questions about brands back to headquarters. Procter & Gamble's new model differentiates between high- and low-income countries. In high-income countries, major decisions are made at headquarters. In low-income countries, some decision making is delegated to the regional level. Local managers in these countries require more autonomy to deal effectively with difficult local issues such as sourcing and marketing.

Given the difficulty of maintaining a delicate balance between central control and local responsiveness, most firms find it difficult to implement transnational strategy. In the long run, almost all firms find that they need to include some elements of localized decision making as well, because each country has its idiosyncratic characteristics. For instance, few people in Japan want to buy a computer that has an English-language keyboard. Thus, while Dell can apply a mostly global strategy to Japan, it must incorporate some multidomestic elements as well. Even Coca-Cola,

Transnational strategy A coordinated approach to internationalization in which the firm strives to be more responsive to local needs while retaining sufficient central control of operations to ensure efficiency and learning.

This IKEA Home Furnishings store opened in Shanghai, China in April, 2003. Consistent with a global strategy, IKEA standardizes its products as much as possible.

often touted as a global brand, varies its ingredients slightly in different markets. While consumers in the United States prefer a sweeter Coca-Cola, the Chinese want less sugar.[20]

Having discussed distinct strategies that firms pursue in international expansion, let's now explore the related topic—organizational structure alternatives. While a strategy is the blueprint for action, a firm needs a structure with people, resources, and processes to implement the blueprint.

Organizational Structure

Organizational structure
Reporting relationships inside the firm that specify the linkages between people, functions, and processes.

Organizational structure refers to the reporting relationships inside the firm—"the boxes and lines"—that specify the linkages between people, functions, and processes that allow the firm to carry out its international operations. In the larger, more experienced MNE, these linkages are extensive and include the firm's subsidiaries and affiliates. A fundamental issue in organizational design is how much decision-making responsibility the firm should retain at headquarters and how much it should delegate to foreign subsidiaries and affiliates. This is the choice between *centralization* and *decentralization*. Let's examine this fundamental choice in more detail.

Centralized or Decentralized Structure?

A centralized approach means that headquarters retains considerable authority and control. A decentralized approach means that the MNE delegates substantial autonomy and decision-making authority to the country subsidiaries. There is no clear-cut best approach.

Exhibit 11.3 identifies the typical contributions of headquarters and subsidiaries. Generally, the larger the financial outlay or the riskier the anticipated result, the more involved headquarters will be in decision making. For example, decisions on developing new products or entering new markets tend to be centralized to headquarters. Decisions involving strategies for two or more countries are best left to headquarters managers who have a more regional or global perspective.[21] Decisions to source products from one country for export to another, or decisions on intracorporate transfer pricing are likely to be centralized. Decisions on global products that are marketed in several countries with common trademarks and brand names are usually the responsibility of headquarters. Conversely, decisions on local products that are sold only in single-

A subsidiary is the primary contributor to these activities:	Headquarters is the primary contributor to these activities:	Shared responsibility of subsidiary and headquarters:
• Sales • Marketing • Local market research • Human resource management • Compliance with local laws and regulations	• Capital planning • Transfer pricing • Global profitability	**With the subsidiary's lead:** • Geographic strategy • Local product and service development • Technical support and customer service • Local procurement **With the headquarters' lead:** • Broad corporate strategy • Global product development • Basic research and development • Global product sourcing • Development of global managers

Exhibit 11.3 Subsidiary and Headquarters Contributions

country markets should be the joint responsibility of corporate and respective country managers, with the latter taking the leadership role.

The choice between headquarters and subsidiary involvement in decision making is also a function of the nature of the product, the nature of competitors' operations, and the size and strategic importance of foreign operations. In the long run, no firm can centralize *all* its operations. Retaining some local autonomy is desirable. Companies need to effectively balance the benefits of centralization and local autonomy. The challenge is for companies to achieve these goals simultaneously.[22] The old phrase, "think globally, act locally," is an oversimplification of the true complexities of today's global competition; *"think globally and locally, act appropriately"* better describes the reality of today's marketplace.[23]

A worker inspects the first production of bottled Coca-Cola beverages during the opening of the new Coca-Cola plant in central Bacolod City, Philippines. While the headquarters organization of Coca-Cola will provide global brand support and broad marketing guidance to its bottlers in individual countries, the local bottler organization will assume responsibility for such activities as local sales promotion, labeling to meet local government requirements, retail support, and local customer research.

Planning, shared by managers at headquarters and subsidiaries, is vital to the design of effective strategies that take full advantage of existing worldwide operations. Highly centralized, top-down decision making ignores subsidiary managers' intimate knowledge of host countries. Conversely, highly decentralized, bottom-up decision making by autonomous subsidiary managers ignores the functional knowledge that managers at headquarters possess and fails to integrate strategies across countries and regions. Shared decision making necessitates negotiations between headquarters and subsidiary managers, with give-and-take on both sides. In the final analysis, however, all decisions are subject to headquarters approval. Senior corporate managers should employ various strategies to encourage positive, open-minded, collaborative relationships with country managers. These strategies include:

- Encouraging local managers to identify with broad, corporate objectives and make their best efforts
- Visiting subsidiaries to instill corporate values and priorities
- Rotating employees within the corporate network to develop multiple perspectives
- Encouraging country managers to interact and share experiences with each other through regional meetings
- Providing/establishing financial incentives and penalties to promote compliance with headquarters' goals

Alternative Organizational Arrangements for International Operations

There are four typical organizational structures for the internationalizing firm: export department/international division, decentralized structure, centralized structure, and global matrix structure. A long-established body of literature suggests that "structure follows strategy."[24] The organizational design a firm chooses for international operations is largely the result of how important managers consider international business and whether they prefer centralized or decentralized decision making. The firm's experience in international business also affects its organizational design. Organizational designs tend to follow an evolutionary pattern: As the firm's international involvement increases, it adopts increasingly more complex organizational designs. Let's explore the four types of organizational structures in detail.[25]

Export Department or International Division

For manufacturing firms, exporting is usually the first foreign market entry strategy. At first, it rarely involves much of a structured organizational response. As export sales reach a substantial proportion of the firm's total sales, however, senior managers will usually establish a separate **export department** whose manager may report to senior management or to the head of domestic sales and marketing. Exhibit 11.4 illustrates the export department structure.

The export department is the simplest form of organizational structure for controlling international operations. As the company develops extensive export operations, or as it initiates more sophisticated foreign market entry strategies, such as FDI, management will typically create an **international division structure**, a separate division within the firm dedicated to managing its international operations. Exhibit 11.5 illustrates this organizational structure. Typically, a vice president of international operations is appointed, who reports directly to the corporate CEO. The decision to create a separate international unit is usually accompanied by a significant shift in resource allocation and an increased focus on the international marketplace.[26] Managers in this division typically oversee the development and maintenance of relationships with foreign suppliers and distributors. The division typically undertakes more advanced internationalization options, such as licensing and small-scale foreign investment.

The international division structure offers several advantages. It centralizes management and coordination of international operations. It is staffed with international experts who focus on developing new business opportunities abroad and offering assistance and training for foreign operations. When a firm develops the division, it signals that management is committed to international operations. Nevertheless, the international division structure has several disadvantages. For one, a domestic versus international power struggle often occurs—for example, over the control of financial and human resources. There is likely to be little sharing of knowledge between the foreign units or between the foreign units and headquarters. R&D and future-oriented planning activities tend to remain domestically focused. Products continue to be developed for the domestic marketplace, with international needs considered only after domestic needs have been addressed. Because of these problems, many firms eventually evolve out of the international division structure.[27]

Firms at more advanced stages of internationalization tend to set up more complex organizational designs. The major rationale for firms to select a more complex structure is to reap economies of scale through high-volume production and economies of scope—that is, more efficient use of marketing and other strategic resources over a wider range of products and markets. There is greater emphasis on innovative potential through learning effects, pooling of resources, and

Export department A unit within the firm charged with managing the firm's export operations.

International division structure An organizational design in which all international activities are centralized within one division in the firm, separate from domestic units.

Exhibit 11.4

The Export Department Structure

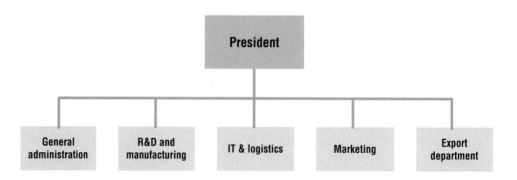

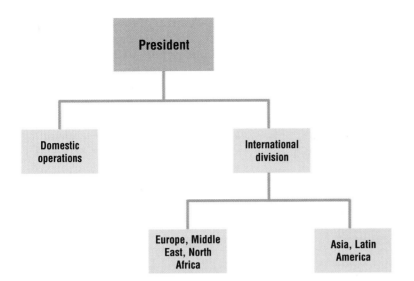

Exhibit 11.5

The International Division Structure

know-how. The integrated chain of command in this structure allows management to make rapid, cohesive decisions regarding global operations.[28]

The more complex organizational designs emphasize a decentralized structure, typically organized around geographic areas; or a centralized structure, typically organized around product or functional lines. We describe these structures next.

Decentralized Structure (Geographic Area Division)

Geographic area division is an organizational design in which control and decision making are decentralized to the level of individual geographic regions, whose managers are responsible for operations within their region. Exhibit 11.6 illustrates this type of organizational design. Firms that market relatively uniform goods across entire regions with little adaptation requirements tend to organize their international operations geographically. The structure is decentralized because management of international operations is largely delegated to the regional headquarters responsible for each geographic area. Nestlé uses such a structure. It has organized its international divisions into a South America division, North America division, Europe division, Asia division, and so forth. The firm treats all geographic locations, including the domestic market, as equals. All areas work in unison toward a common global strategic vision. Assets, including capital, are distributed with the intent of optimal return on corporate goals—not area goals. Geographic area divisions usually manufacture and market locally appropriate goods within their own areas. Firms that use the geographic area approach are often in mature industries with narrow product lines, such as the pharmaceutical, food, automotive, cosmetics, and beverage industries.

Geographic area division An organizational design in which control and decision making are decentralized to the level of individual geographic regions, whose managers are responsible for operations within their region.

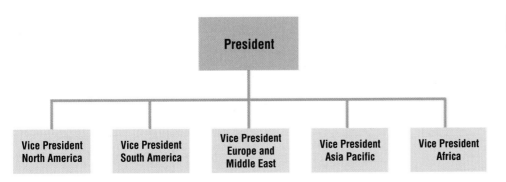

Exhibit 11.6

The Geographic Area Structure.

Nestlé chocolate bars on sale in Beijing. Nestlé uses a geographic area division structure for organizing its international operations.

Product division An arrangement in which decision making and management of the firm's international operations is organized by major product line.

Functional division An arrangement in which decision making and management of the firm's international operations are organized by functional activity (such as production and marketing).

Advantages of the geographic area structure include the ability to strike a balance between global integration while achieving local adaptation on a regional basis. The area division leadership has authority to modify products and strategy. Improved communications and coordination are possible between subsidiaries within each region, but communication and coordination with *other* area divisions and corporate headquarters may be de-emphasized. The area focus may distract the regional management team from addressing *global* issues such as product development and product management.[29]

Centralized Structure (Product or Functional Division)

A **product division** is an arrangement in which decision making and management of the firm's international operations is organized by major product line. Management creates a structure based on major categories of products within the firm's range of offerings. Each product division has responsibility for producing and marketing a specific group of products, worldwide. For instance, Motorola organizes its international operations within each of its product categories, including cell phones, consumer electronics, and satellites. Exhibit 11.7 illustrates such an organization. Each of the international product divisions operates as a stand-alone profit center with substantial autonomy. Their primary goal is to achieve a high degree of worldwide coordination within each product category. Increased coordination encourages greater economies of scale and an improved flow of product knowledge and technology across borders.

The advantage of the product division structure is that all support functions, such as R&D, marketing, and manufacturing, are focused on the product. At the same time, products are easier to tailor for individual markets to meet specific buyer needs. Nevertheless, the product division structure also causes duplication of corporate support functions for each product division and a tendency for managers to focus their efforts on subsidiaries with the greatest potential for quick returns.[30] In addition, suppliers and customers may be confused if several divisions call on them.

A variation of the centralized structure is the functional division. A **functional division** is an arrangement in which decision making and management of the firm's international operations are organized by functional activity (such as production and marketing). For example, oil and mining firms, which have value-adding processes of exploration, drilling, transportation, and storing, tend to use this type of structure. Exhibit 11.8 illustrates such an arrangement. Cruise ship lines may engage in both shipbuilding and passenger cruise marketing—two very distinctive functions that require separate departments for international production and international marketing. Thus, it makes sense to delineate separate divisions for the performance of production and marketing functions worldwide. The advantages of the

Exhibit 11.7

The Global Product Structure

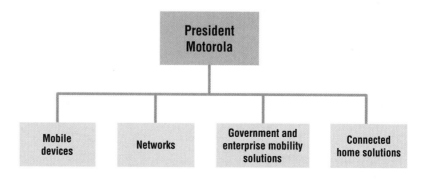

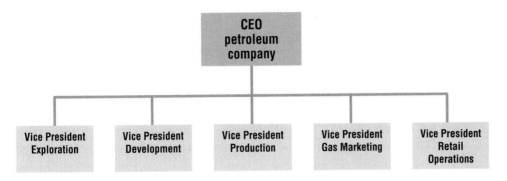

Exhibit 11.8

The Global Functional Structure

functional division are a small central staff, which provides strong central control and coordination, and a united, focused global strategy with a high degree of functional expertise. However, the functional approach may falter in coordinating manufacturing, marketing, and other functions in diverse geographic locations because the central staff lacks expertise in these areas. In addition, when the firm deals with numerous product lines, coordination can become unwieldy.[31]

Global Matrix Structure

The organizational designs described so far worked well in the 1970s and 1980s. As worldwide business moved into the early 1990s, however, a number of economic conditions began to shift. Many countries experienced increasing trade deficits and rising interest rates on foreign debt. Local governments responded by increasing restrictions on foreign companies, requiring them to invest locally, meet local content needs, and transfer technology. In some markets, local customers showed a renewed preference for local brands. Corporations began to realize that these economic forces increasingly required them to address global and local needs *simultaneously*. This realization led managers to create the global matrix structure.

A **global matrix structure** is an arrangement that blends the geographic area, product, and functional structures in an attempt to leverage the benefits of a purely global strategy and maximize global organizational learning while remaining responsive to local needs. It is an attempt to capture the benefits of the geographic area, product, and functional organization structures simultaneously while minimizing their shortcomings.

Among the four strategy alternatives we discussed so far, the global matrix structure is most closely associated with the transnational strategy. The area structure facilitates local responsiveness but can inhibit worldwide economies of scale and the sharing of knowledge and core competences among the geographic areas. The product structure overcomes these shortcomings but is weak in local responsiveness. By using the global matrix structure approach, responsibility for operating decisions about a given product is shared by the product division and the particular geographic areas of the firm. To implement the matrix approach, the firm develops a dual reporting system in which, for example, an employee in a foreign subsidiary may report on an equal basis to two managers: the local subsidiary general manager and a corporate product division manager.

In the global matrix structure, organizational capabilities and best practices are shared with all country units. This approach requires managers to think and operate along two of the following three major dimensions: geography, product, and function (cross-functional). The firm must simultaneously possess the ability to: (1) develop worldwide coordination and control, (2) respond to local needs, and (3) maximize interorganizational learning and knowledge sharing.[32]

The global matrix structure recognizes the importance of flexible and responsive country-level operations and shows firms how to link those operations to retain competitive effectiveness and economic efficiency. Managers working in this structure must make shared decisions that affect the entire organization. For most firms, the

Global matrix structure An arrangement that blends the geographic area, product, and functional structures in an attempt to leverage the benefits of a purely global strategy and maximize global organizational learning while remaining responsive to local needs.

Firms such as Unilever, which owns numerous global brands such as Lipton tea, Hellman's spreads, Slimfast, and Dove products, need to balance forces of global integration with local adaptation. Local adaptation is necessary for such marketing issues as retail distribution strategy, labeling requirements, and consumer incentives.

matrix approach represents relatively new thinking in the management of the modern MNE. How successfully firms are able to implement and maintain this approach for long-term global success remains to be seen.

Unilever—the European company with over $50 billion sales in food, beverage, cleaning, and personal care products—is an example of a firm that has benefited from a matrix organization. Originally a merger between British and Dutch firms, in recent years Unilever headquarters has moved toward coordination while retaining local responsiveness. The firm had long pursued a multidomestic approach, but this became unwieldy over time. For example, in the late 1990s, Unilever was buying more than 30 different types of vanilla for its ice cream in Europe, while its Rexona deodorant had 30 different packages and 48 distinctive formulations. Advertising and branding efforts were handled locally and often amateurishly. The firm struggled to develop global products that could compete with rivals such as Procter & Gamble and L'Oreal. These competitors, with more centralized operations, were responding faster to changing consumer tastes. They were better at coordinating their international units and had captured efficiencies by striking supplier contracts for many countries simultaneously. At the same time, giant retailers such as Wal-Mart were pressuring Unilever to cut its prices. Unilever's total sales were in line with P&G, but the firm had over 230,000 employees, twice as many as P&G. The decentralized structure of Unilever's international organization had produced needless duplication and countless obstacles to applying a more efficient global approach.

To address its problems, Unilever put in place a massive reorganization plan designed to centralize authority and reduce the power of local country bosses. To implement a global culture and organization, the firm divested hundreds of businesses, cut 55,000 jobs, closed 145 factories, and discontinued 1,200 brands. Today, Unilever has about 400 brands. The firm develops new products using global teams that emphasize the commonalities among major-country markets. Local managers are not allowed to tinker with packaging, formulation, or advertising of global brands, such as Dove soap. Unilever is well on the road to implementing a more balanced matrix approach to its international operations.[33]

As with the other organizational structures, the matrix approach has its disadvantages. For example, the chain of command from superiors to subordinates can become muddled. It is difficult for employees to receive directions from two different managers who are located thousands of miles apart and have different cultural backgrounds and business experiences. When conflict arises between two managers, senior management must offer a resolution. The matrix structure can, therefore, give rise to conflict, waste management's time, and compromise organizational effectiveness. The heightened pace of environmental change, increased complexity and demands, and the need for cultural adaptability have been overwhelming for many firms that have attempted the matrix structure.[34] For this reason, many companies that have experimented with the matrix structure have eventually returned to simpler organizational arrangements.

 Building the Global Firm

Exhibit 11.9 illustrates the requisite dimensions of a truly global firm. As highlighted earlier, management must start with an appropriate strategy and organizational structure. While critical, these dimensions by themselves are insufficient. In addition to strategy and organizational structure, management must cultivate three additional areas: visionary leadership, organizational culture, and organizational processes. We discuss these three attributes of truly global firms next.[35]

Visionary Leadership

Visionary leadership is defined as senior human capital in an organization that provides the strategic guidance necessary to manage efficiency, flexibility, and learning in an internationalizing firm.[36] Leadership is more complex in global firms than in domestic firms because valuable organizational assets—such as productive capabilities, brands, and human resources—all cross national borders. In firms with various complex international operations, visionary leadership is critical for success.

Take the example of Peter Brabeck, CEO of Nestlé. Brabeck is a keen pilot, mountain climber, and Harley-Davidson fan with a reputation for straight talking. From Nestlé's headquarters in Switzerland, he is leading Nestlé into the growing nutrition market by developing healthier, value-added products and services. Brabeck perceived a worldwide market for food products that meet consumers' growing interest in health and nutrition. To address this growing market, Nestlé recently purchased Jenny Craig, the U.S. weight management and food-products company. In Germany, Nestlé launched a nutritional institute to advise consumers on dietary issues, dispensing nutritional advice to more than 300,000 customers per month. In France, Brabeck created a nutritional home-care service, providing for patients with special dietary needs. These initiatives position Nestlé in a growing global market and generate global brand loyalty for the firm's line of healthy food products.[37]

At least four traits exemplify visionary leaders:

Global mindset and cosmopolitan values. Initially, visionary leadership requires management to acquire a **global mindset**—openness to, and awareness of, diversity across cultures. The degree of management's global outlook is critical to ultimate success.[38] Dogmatic managers—who tend to be close-minded, lack vision, and have difficulty adapting to other cultures—are likely to fail. By contrast, managers who are open minded, committed to internationalization, and adopt to other cultures are likely to succeed. Such a posture is particularly important among smaller internationalizing firms that lack substantial tangible resources.[39]

Visionary leadership Senior human capital in an organization that provides the strategic guidance necessary to manage efficiency, flexibility, and learning in an internationalizing firm.

Global mindset Openness to, and awareness of, diversity across cultures.

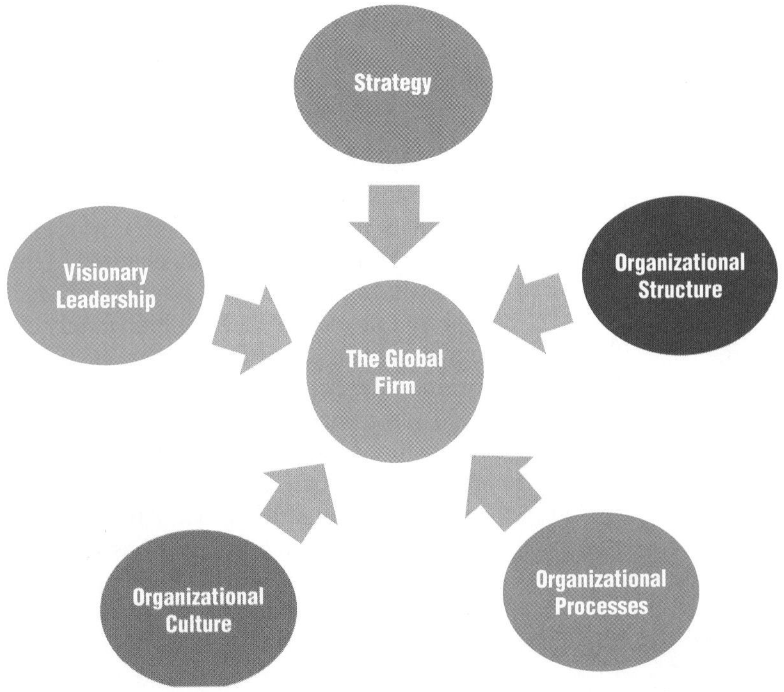

Exhibit 11.9

Dimensions of Truly Global Companies

Willingness to commit resources. Commitment drives visionary leaders to develop needed financial, human, and other resources to achieve their firms' international goals. The complexities of foreign markets imply that international ventures take more time than domestic ones to become profitable. Such conditions require high levels of managerial commitment and the unrelenting belief that the firm will eventually succeed. In the absence of such commitment, lower-level managers cannot respond adequately to foreign markets and perform the tasks necessary to ensure success. Highly committed firms engage in systematic international market expansion, allocate necessary resources, and empower structures and processes that ensure ultimate success.

Global strategic vision. Visionary leaders are effective in articulating a *global strategic vision*—what the firm wants to be in the future and how it will get there. As they develop their strategic vision, senior managers focus on the ideal picture of what the company should become. This ideal picture is the central rallying point for all plans, employees, and employee actions. This is akin to the concept of *strategic intent*, defined as an ambitious and compelling dream that energizes and provides emotional and intellectual energy.[40]

As an example of a firm with strategic vision, consider Synclayer, a Japanese SME whose senior managers have envisioned a large and growing market for new products for the elderly. By 2015, one in four Japanese—about 30 million people—will be over 65. The company has ambitions to take worldwide leadership in developing products for senior citizens. Synclayer has developed an IT-based system that allows older people still living at home to take basic medical measurements, such as blood pressure and temperature, and send them to a local health database. The medical service can then act if the measurements suggest a health problem. The firm's vision is to develop the products in Japan and then launch them into foreign markets with sizeable elderly populations.[41]

Willingness to invest in human assets. Visionary leaders must nurture the most critical asset of any organization—human capital. At the center of any globalization effort are a handful of managers who understand the world and are prepared to manage the complexity, uncertainty, and learning that the firm faces in the global marketplace. Leadership involves the ongoing effort to develop human capital that is capable of creating the organizational culture, strategy, structure, and processes of a global firm. In global firms, senior leaders adopt such human resource practices as the use of foreign nationals, promoting multicountry careers, and cross-cultural and language training to develop global supermanagers.[42]

Ratan N. Tata, the chairman of the Tata Group who transformed this Indian conglomerate into a transnational organization, and Carlos Ghosn, the CEO of Nissan and Renault, featured in this chapter's Closing Case, both exemplify visionary leadership. Tata oversees a $22 billion family conglomerate whose companies market a range of products from automobiles to watches. Since 2000, his group has made numerous international acquisitions (from Tetley Tea to the London-based steel firm Corus), reflecting a change in strategic vision from local to global. Another example is Toyota CEO Fujio Cho, who has led his firm to record sales in the intensely competitive global automobile industry. In a recent year, profits rose nearly 150 percent. His leadership style emphasizes innovation, product quality, continuous improvement, and an ability to spot future-ori-

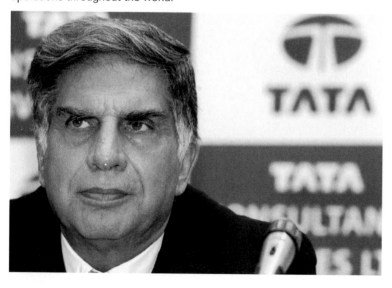

Ratan Tata is chairman of India's Tata group. Tata transformed the giant Indian conglomerate into a transnational organization, with operations throughout the world.

ented opportunities, including the Prius hybrid and the youth-oriented Scion brands of Toyota cars.[43]

Organizational Culture

Organizational culture refers to the pattern of shared values, norms of behavior, systems, policies, and procedures that employees learn and adopt. Employees acquire them as the correct way to perceive, think, feel, and behave in relation to new problems and opportunities that confront the firm.[44] Organizational culture is the "personality" of the firm. Employees demonstrate organizational culture by using the firm's common language and accepting rules and norms, such as the pace and amount of work expected and the degree of cooperation between management and employees.

As seen in the case of IKEA, in the opening vignette, organizational culture usually derives from the influence of founders and visionary leaders or some unique history of the firm. The role of the founder's values and beliefs is particularly important. Visionary leaders can transform organizational culture, as Lou Gerstner and Jack Welch radically altered the fortunes of IBM and General Electric (GE), respectively—large bureaucratic organizations that had failed to adapt to changing environments.

At the Japanese electronics giant Canon, CEO Fujio Mitarai has developed an organizational culture that emphasizes science and technology. The focus extends from product development to the way goods are made on the factory floor. Recent innovations have slashed production time and costs. Canon invests billions in R&D and is the world's second largest recipient of new U.S. patents. This orientation has allowed Canon to become a world leader in digital cameras, copiers, printers, and flat-screen TVs.[45] Similarly, focus on product quality is a pillar of Toyota's organizational culture. For instance, the gap between the hood and the grille on its Lexus luxury car is not allowed to be more than an eyelash. Toyota workers in Canada receive continuous quality-oriented training in Lexus manufacturing processes, and if no one responds to computer-detected manufacturing flaws within 15 minutes, upper management is automatically notified. Toyota performs a *triple-check* on quality at every stage of Lexus production.[46]

Today, management at firms like Canon and Toyota seek to build a *global* organizational culture—an organizational environment that plays a key role in the development and execution of corporate global strategy. Companies that proactively build a global organizational culture:[47]

- Value and promote a global perspective in all major initiatives
- Value global competence and cross-cultural skills among their employees
- Adopt a single corporate language for business communication
- Promote interdependency between headquarters and subsidiaries
- Subscribe to globally accepted ethical standards

Firms aspiring to become truly global seek to maintain strong ethical standards in all the markets where they are represented. Ultimately, senior leadership of any company must be held accountable for cultivating an organizational culture that welcomes social responsibility and is deliberate about fulfilling its role. We define **corporate social responsibility** as operating a business in a manner that meets or exceeds the ethical, legal, commercial, and public expectations of stakeholders (customers, shareholders, employees, and communities). The *Global Trend* feature elaborates on the role of corporate social responsibility in the multinational firm.

Firms combine visionary leadership with organizational culture to create processes that define how the firm will carry out day-to-day activities in order to achieve company goals. Let's examine these organizational processes next.

Organizational culture The pattern of shared values, norms of behavior, systems, policies, and procedures that employees learn and adopt.

Corporate social responsibility Operating a business in a manner that meets or exceeds the ethical, legal, commercial, and public expectations of stakeholders (customers, shareholders, employees, and communities).

Global Corporate Social Responsibility Rises to the Top of the MNE Agenda

As companies internationalize, they increasingly confront the question of how to be good global citizens. Global corporate social responsibility (CSR) affects the quality of life of customers, suppliers, workers, and other stakeholders with which the firm interacts. CSR addresses issues such as workers' rights, workers' pay sufficient to ensure a reasonable living standard, company activities that disrupt traditional communities and lifestyles, and environmental damage caused by corporate activities. A study by McKinsey & Co. found that executives worldwide overwhelmingly embrace the idea that firms have societal and environmental obligations in addition to ensuring corporate profitability.

As an example, IKEA (featured in the opening vignette) has been deliberate about promoting social and environmental responsibility. The firm employs its own specially trained auditors and environmental coordinators. IKEA products must be manufactured under acceptable working conditions by suppliers who take responsibility for the environment. IKEA and its suppliers work closely with UNICEF, Save the Children, and the WWF to prevent child labor and to support responsible forestry. All work is in conjunction with the UN Convention on the Rights of the Child (1989). All suppliers must meet the standards of the Forest Stewardship Council (FSC). In addition to these activities, the IKEA Foundation supports various charitable causes through generous contributions.

Governments and stakeholders have expectations of how multinational firms should fulfill their global CSR social contract. These expectations include contributing to a region's employment opportunities, protecting workers and communities from physical harm, providing good working conditions, avoiding discriminatory hiring practices and workplaces, maintaining transparency and avoiding corruption, reducing poverty and injustice, and improving access to quality health care and education.

Minding social and environmental accountability is increasingly part of how international business gets done. Managers must incorporate CSR into its various activities abroad. Nevertheless, the task is complex, because when companies step onto the global stage, they encounter a wide variety of stakeholders, whose expectations often appear contradictory and overwhelming. In addition, social and environmental problems commonly encountered abroad may appear baffling to management at headquarters, who have little direct international experience. It is often country managers, rather than those at headquarters, who are at the forefront of deciding what issues to address and how to address them.

How do MNEs address global CSR? The Center for Corporate Citizenship at Boston College interviewed managers worldwide and found that they are becoming more sophisticated about identifying, balancing, and prioritizing social and environmental issues. In a world ever sensitive to social and environmental issues, managers increasingly undertake the following types of activities:

- Develop closer relations with foreign stakeholders to better understand their needs and jointly work toward solutions

- Build internal and external capabilities to enhance the firm's contribution to the local community and the global environment

- Ensure that diverse voices are heard by creating organizational structures that employ managers and workers from around the world

- Develop global CSR standards and objectives that are communicated and implemented across the firm, worldwide

- Train managers in global CSR principles and integrate these into managerial responsibilities

Global CSR has firmly inserted itself into the day-to-day agenda of the executive suite, as growing MNE activities increasingly pose environmental concerns and bring firms into daily contact with a range of international activities—such as R&D, manufacturing, sales, and marketing—that can pose a variety of ethical dilemmas. The McKinsey study found that business executives should balance their obligation to shareholders with explicit contributions "to the broader public good." Eighty percent of the executives agreed that generating high returns for investors should be accompanied by a focus on providing good jobs, supporting social causes in local communities, and going beyond legal requirements to minimize pollution and other negative effects of business.

Sources: Center for Corporate Citizenship. (2005). *Going Global: Managers' Experiences Working with Worldwide Stakeholders.* Research report. Boston: Boston College; McKinsey & Co. (2006). *The McKinsey Global Survey of Business Executives: Business and Society.* Accessed January 2006 at www.mckinseyquarterly.com

Organizational Processes

Organizational processes refer to managerial routines, behaviors, and mechanisms that allow the firm to function as intended. In an international firm, typical processes include mechanisms for collecting strategic market information, assessing and rewarding employees, and budgeting for international operations.

General Electric and Toyota have gained substantial competitive advantage by emphasizing and refining the countless processes that comprise their value chains. For example, GE digitizes all key documents and uses intranets and the Internet to automate many activities and reduce operating costs. Many processes cross functional areas within the firm. For example, the new product development process involves input from R&D, engineering, marketing, finance, and operations. In global firms, processes also cut across national borders, which increase both the urgency and complexity of devising well-functioning processes.

Common Organizational Processes Designed to Achieve Coordination

Contemporary firms develop and implement common processes. Managers attempt to achieve global coordination and integration not just by subscribing to a particular organizational design, such as the global matrix structure, but by also implementing a variety of common processes or *globalizing mechanisms*. These common processes provide substantial interconnectedness within the MNE network and allow for meaningful cross-fertilization and knowledge. Together, they constitute important and powerful vehicles in the creation of truly global firms. These common processes include *global teams, global information systems,* and *global talent pools.*

Global teams Increasingly, global teams are charged with problem-solving and best-practice development within the company.[48] A **global team** is "an internationally distributed group of people . . . with a specific mandate to make or implement decisions that are international in scope."[49] Team members are drawn from geographically diverse units of the MNE and may interact entirely via corporate intranets and video conferencing, without meeting in person. A global team brings together employees with the experience, knowledge, and skills to resolve common challenges. It is assigned fairly complex tasks, represents a diverse composition of professional and national backgrounds, and has members that are distributed around the world. Often, global teams are charged with specific agendas and a finite time period to complete their deliberations and make recommendations.

The nature of global teams varies. *Strategic global teams* identify or implement initiatives that enhance the positioning of the firm in its global industry. *Operational global teams* focus on the efficient and effective running of the business across the whole network.[50] An example of a strategic global team is the Global Strategy Board at General Motors (GM). It includes GM executives who are leaders in processes such as labor relations, design-engineering, manufacturing, marketing, quality, human resource management, and purchasing. The team is charged with overseeing the development of common global processes, spreading best practices throughout GM's worldwide operations, and avoiding "reinventing the wheel" in individual regions.

The most successful teams are flexible, responsive, and innovative. To develop global strategies, it is important that the team involve culturally diverse managers whose business activities span the globe. Culturally diverse teams have three valuable roles:

1. Create a global view inside the firm while remaining in touch with local realities.
2. Generate creative ideas and make fully informed decisions about the firm's global operations.
3. Ensure team decisions are implemented throughout the firm's global operations.

Organizational processes
Managerial routines, behaviors, and mechanisms that allow the firm to function as intended.

Global team An internationally distributed group of people with a specific mandate to make or implement decisions that are international in scope.

Global information systems   The desire to create a globally coordinated company is motivated by the need for world-scale efficiency and minimal redundancy. In the past, geographic distance and cross-cultural differences served as impediments to achieving an interconnected, global company. The advent of the Internet and modern information technologies now provide the means for virtual interconnectedness within the global company network. Global IT infrastructure, together with tools such as intranets and electronic data interchange, make it feasible for distant parts of the global network to share and learn from each other.

The development of Chevrolet Equinox by General Motors illustrates the effective use of modern IT and communication technologies. When GM decided in 2001 to develop a sports utility vehicle to compete with Toyota's RAV4 and Honda's CR-V, it tapped its capabilities all over the globe. The V6 engine was built in China, with cooperation from engineers in Canada, China, Japan, and the United States. From a global collaboration room in Toronto, engineers teleconferenced almost daily with counterparts from Shanghai, Tokyo, and Warren, Ohio. They exchanged virtual-reality renderings of the vehicle and collaborated on the styling of exteriors and design of components. The SUV was built in Ontario, Canada, at a factory that GM shares with its Japanese partner, Suzuki.

Global talent pools   Developing managers and other members of the organization to think and behave globally is necessary for ultimate global success. International firms employ a combination of home-country personnel, host-country personnel, and expatriates. An **expatriate** is an employee who is assigned to work and reside in a foreign country for an extended period, usually a year or longer. For example, a U.S. firm might employ a German or U.S. manager in its subsidiary in France. In this example, both the German and American managers are expatriates. Sophisticated MNEs develop a pool of highly developed talent, regardless of nationality, to manage evolving international operations. The MNEs develop a database of skilled individuals within the firm and make it available on the corporate intranet. As an example, Citibank managers can search on the company intranet for the right recruit—with desirable qualifications—regardless of where that individual is located in the company's global network. In this way, Citibank identifies and uses the best talent worldwide for the task at hand.

Global firms invest in their employees to build needed capabilities, not just in technical or business terms, but in terms of language and cultural capabilities and types of international experience. The development of a *global talent pool* requires the creation of an environment that fosters and promotes cooperation across borders, the free exchange of information, and the development of creative managers capable of functioning effectively anywhere in the world.

Expatriate An employee who is assigned to work and reside in a foreign country for an extended period, usually a year or longer.

 Putting Organizational Change in Motion

This chapter has highlighted strategies, structures, and processes that help build truly global firms. Reorganizing the firm on a global scale is not a simple task nor can it be accomplished quickly. Take the case of Procter & Gamble's "Organization 2005" program, launched in 1998.[51] The plan called for an aggressive redesign of P&G's organizational structure, work processes, culture, and pay structures worldwide. Procter & Gamble's management sought to create a global organization that could simultaneously serve specific national needs. The firm moved from four business units based on geographical regions to seven based on global product lines, thereby changing their organizational structure significantly. It established Market Development Organizations in eight world regions to tailor its global marketing to local markets. Business processes such as human resource management, order management, and accounting were to be consolidated from separate geographic regions to one corporate organization that would serve P&G operations worldwide.

However, "Organization 2005" floundered in various ways. Efforts to make P&G a more nimble MNE did not go well in the firm's conservative corporate culture. Management laid off thousands of workers and abruptly transferred about 2,000 people to Geneva and about 200 to Singapore. These changes created resentment among key personnel. A reorganization of reporting structures created confusion. Some food and beverage managers at the U.S. headquarters had to report to the president of the Venezuela subsidiary. Managers in the U.S. household cleaning division reported to Brussels. Global marketing programs failed from insufficient research. In Germany, the name of P&G's dishwashing liquid suddenly changed from Fairy to Dawn, the U.S. brand. But since Dawn was unknown in Germany, sales plummeted. In short, while seemingly a promising plan, "Organization 2005" was based on inadequate research and poor implementation. Headquarters alienated managers and sowed anxiety and confusion among customers and employees alike.

As this example illustrates, firms must approach the development of global strategy with great care. For many firms, a truly global organization remains an ideal yet to be achieved. To ensure international business success, the firm should: (1) formulate a global strategy; (2) develop an appropriate organizational structure; (3) provide visionary leadership; (4) cultivate an organizational culture worldwide and (5) refine and implement organizational processes.

Internationalizing a company will not fully succeed unless all five of these organizational dimensions complement each other to support the desired outcomes. Success in international markets is not based on a single prescription or formula but a multidimensional and coherent set of actions. These include: participating in all major markets in the world, standardizing product and marketing programs wherever feasible, taking integrated, competitive moves across the country markets, concentrating value-adding activities at strategic locations across the world, and coordinating the value-chain activities to exploit the synergies of multinational operations. Superior global performance will result if all the dimensions of a global strategy are aligned with external industry globalization forces and internal organizational resources.[52]

In this chapter, we have described the essential dimensions of internationally effective firms. In all of its complexity, there are seemingly countless variables to consider when designing for international success. How should senior leaders proceed? Where does one start? With processes? Structure? Organizational culture? Hasty and highly ambitious efforts to transform an organization may fail. It is best for senior management to focus on only one or two dimensions at a time, tackling the most easily changed dimensions of the organization first in order to prepare the way for the more difficult changes.

Finally, transforming an organization into a truly global company can take years and involve many obstacles and uncertainty. Senior management needs to instill a sense of urgency to drive the organization toward the desired changes. Equally important is buy-in from employees for implementation—securing wholehearted participation of key individuals and groups toward common organizational goals. One CEO of a very large company, who was asked to resign by his board of directors after a bungled corporate turnaround, put it this way: ". . . we did not fail because we did not have a clever strategy. We did not fail because we did not have shrewd managers or talented engineers and scientists. We failed because I simply could not rally the troops."

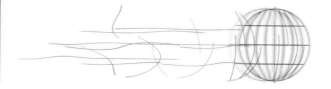

CLOSING CASE

Carlos Ghosn and Renault-Nissan: Leading for Global Success

Nissan Motor Co., based in Tokyo, is Japan's number two automobile manufacturer. The company's 2006 sales were over 10 billion Japanese yen, with an operating profit margin of 7.4 percent. In 2007, Nissan launched 11 all-new products globally. A few years ago, Nissan was on the verge of bankruptcy. The French automaker Renault stepped in, took a 44 percent stake, and installed Carlos Ghosn as Nissan's CEO. In a dramatic turnaround, Ghosn (hard *G*, rhymes with "stone") returned Nissan to profitability and became a celebrity in Japan. Born in Brazil, raised in Lebanon, and educated in France, Ghosn is a charismatic leader who speaks four languages. He is smooth in public, works constantly, and is committed to organizational goals. He is featured in Japanese comic books, mobbed for autographs during factory tours, and adored throughout Japan for saving a car company once given up for dead.

Under Ghosn's watchful eye, Nissan evolved from a troubled carmaker to a corporate success story in just a few years. He closed inefficient factories, reduced Nissan's workforce, curbed purchasing costs, shared operations with Renault, and introduced new products. Ultimately, Nissan became one of the world's most profitable automotive companies. How did Nissan do it?

Nissan's Organizational Culture

Ghosn defied Japan's often bureaucratic and clubby business culture, for example, by reducing Nissan's steel suppliers from five to three. The CEO of NKK Steel protested that "Toyota would never act in such a way." One of Ghosn's biggest tests was overcoming the denial inside Nissan about the firm's perilous condition. In Japan, large companies are viewed as too big to fail. If the *keiretsu*'s banks don't rush to the rescue, then the government will. Ghosn cut through such antiquated thinking to save Nissan.

Corporate Japan often moves slowly and reactively. Ghosn introduced a proactive style, with fast decision making. Senior management at Nissan is now proactive, operating with a sense of urgency even when the firm is not in crisis. The culture is about anticipating problems, putting them on the table, and eliminating them before they happen. Ghosn is always in a rush, relying on decisiveness and delegation—but yielding to consensus when it is passionate. In the style of a true globalist, Ghosn notes that "It's irrelevant where you are headquartered . . . the keys are where the jobs are located and where the profits go." To reinforce his global aspirations, Ghosn has made English, not Japanese, the official language of Nissan. Managers who learn English advance faster than those who speak only Japanese.

This move puts Nissan on a clear footing to change its organizational culture and become a global firm.

Ghosn's Leadership Style

Ghosn dislikes long meetings. Instead of spending a lot of time analyzing and discussing, he prefers action. At Nissan, he pushed top staff to meet tough sales targets and promised publicly that the entire management team would resign if it didn't meet the targets. He inspires the workforce by communicating with them on the factory floor. Even the most mundane events were handled like big media shows. One Nissan earnings news conference opened with loud music and dazzling video shots of zooming cars.

Renault-Nissan

On the heels of his success, Ghosn took over as CEO of Renault in 2005. He now runs *both* companies, commuting between Paris and Tokyo in his Gulfstream jet. The unusual arrangement underscores the demand for proven leaders in the global auto industry, which has suffered from oversupply and intense competition. In a typical month, he could spend the first week in Paris, focusing solely on Renault, and the third week in Japan, focusing on Nissan. He personally oversees Nissan's North America business, where 60 percent of Nissan profits are earned. He carries two agendas: one for Nissan and one for Renault.

Innovation Is Key

Renault-Nissan's long-term strategy is to continually invest substantially in R&D for breakthrough technologies and innovative products. In the 2000s, top management increased R&D by 50 percent, reinvesting 5 percent of net sales in new technologies. At its new Mississippi plant in the United States, Nissan launched five models in less than 8 months. It rolled out a small car (the "Versa"), a re-engineered Altima midsize sedan, a heavily redesigned Nissan Quest minivan, and a redesigned Infiniti G35. Nissan established a design subsidiary in Shanghai, China, to produce cars that fit that country's growing market. The firm has developed hybrid vehicles to address a growing consumer demand triggered by high gasoline prices.

Global Production

Renault-Nissan has production plants in Britain, France, and the United States, to be close to key foreign markets. It also manufactures in China, Taiwan, and the Philippines, to profit from low-cost, high-quality labor. Nissan uses modular architecture. The Maxima and Altima, built in

336

Nissan's U.S. plant in Tennessee, as well as the new Quest, Titan pickup, and Armada sport-utility vehicle are put together with single modules from parts suppliers. The finished modules are then bolted into a car or truck body rolling down the assembly line. All together, buying modules built by supplier partners save up to 30 percent of the total cost of that section of the car.

Nissan consolidated its U.S. manufacturing operations, moving thousands of jobs from southern California to Tennessee. The move centralized manufacturing and made it easier for senior management to keep tabs on U.S. operations. The Tennessee plant has been the most productive factory in North America for years, producing a car in less than 16 labor hours, several hours fewer than rival carmakers.

Additional Global Strategy Elements

Senior management set up a company in Amsterdam—Renault-Nissan BV—which offers a neutral forum where both firms can map out a common strategy for product engineering, model development, and computer systems and leverage their combined size to squeeze suppliers for lower costs. Renault-Nissan's board of directors consists of four members from each organization.

Nissan is globalizing its engineering, production, and purchasing operations. It built a $45 million engineering center near Tokyo to consolidate its global production-engineering activities. Also, Ghosn is taking the Infiniti luxury brand global. Nissan makes Infiniti dealerships conform to an interior design that gives them a uniform look and global image.

The integration of Nissan with Renault went smoothly. Renault has been building its Clio compact and Scenic minivan at Nissan plants in Mexico, while Nissan makes its Frontier pickup at a Renault factory in Brazil. The ultimate goal is to reduce the number of platforms (chassis) that the group uses to a minimum. This is important because every shared platform provides $500 million in annual savings for each carmaker. Renault also shares eight engine designs with Nissan. They share engineering and parts purchases. Roughly three-quarters of the parts used by the two automakers are jointly sourced. These moves allow both firms to slash the expense and time of introducing new models, consistently driving down purchasing costs and increasing global profits, and they shave months off development time of new vehicles. One result of shared platforms is the world's most global car, called the Nissan Versa in the United States, the Renault Clio in Europe, the Nissan Tiida in Asia, and the Renault Logan in the Middle East. In total, Nissan offers seven different vehicles based on the underpinnings that go into the Versa, creating scale economies that cut costs and improve profits.

But avoiding redundancy is not the only way for Nissan to be global. It is also critical to have a presence in the most important markets. While the United States is a relatively expensive place to make cars, it is also the world's biggest market. Thus, Toyota, Honda, BMW, Mercedes, Nissan, and Hyundai all produce there, even expanding U.S. production in recent years. Nissan now exports its U.S.-made Quest minivans to China, considered to be the next big market. It exports other U.S.-made models—the Altima sedan and Infiniti QX56 SUV—to the Middle East and Latin America.

The Future of Automobile Industry Growth—Emerging Markets

In the coming decade, hundreds of millions of Indians, Chinese, Russians, Brazilians and others will join the ranks of the middle class and will have automobiles high on their list of wanted items. Estimates indicate that the market for automobiles priced under $10,000 will grow from 12 million to 18 million cars by 2012. India's car market is forecast to double to 3.3 million cars by 2014, and China's demand will grow 140 percent, to 16.5 million cars in the same period.

The One-Lakh Car

India's Tata Motors is planning to launch a new automobile in 2008 that is targeted at a retail price of one-lakh (about U.S. $25,000). The key is the low wages of engineers in India and the firm's ability to squeeze manufacturing costs to their lowest levels. Tata's prototype has four doors, achieves a top speed of 80 mph, and has a 33-horsepower engine. Renault-Nissan CEO Ghosn announced that it plans to create its own $2,500 vehicle to compete with the new Tata Motors model.

The Logan is key to Ghosn's success in emerging markets. The Logan, built in Romania, was first launched in 2004 for about $7,500. In 2006, Renault-Nissan sold 247,000 Logans, and it is forecasting sales in excess of 1 million Logans worldwide by 2010. Many of these sales will be in China and India. The company plans to build a low-cost pickup truck based on the Logan for sale in Southeast Asia, South Africa, and the Middle East. Renault-Nissan originally planned to sell the Logan only in emerging markets, but the Logan became available for sale in Western Europe in 2005. Demand has been exceedingly strong because of the high quality and low price.

Renault-Nissan in Emerging Markets

At Renault, Ghosn is charging ahead with an ambitious restructuring plan. He is expanding Renault's potential beyond Europe, especially into Eastern Europe, India, Iran, Russia, and South Korea. He aims to increase international sales of Renault to nearly half the firm's total production. Part of the rationale for the expansion is to reduce production in France, which has become costly, in part due to strong union demands. Renault also acquired full control of Samsung Motors, making South Korea an important base for both Renault and Nissan.

Renault is a market leader in Europe, Japan, China, and in the United States. Renault-Nissan is on the verge of capturing the number three spot globally, behind Toyota and General Motors.

AACSB: Reflective Thinking
Case Questions

1. In what ways is Carlos Ghosn a visionary leader? What traits does he possess that are typical of a visionary leader?

2. What is the nature of Nissan's international strategy? Is the firm following a primarily global strategy or a multidomestic strategy? What advantages does Nissan derive from the particular strategy that it pursues? In what ways does Nissan demonstrate efficiency, flexibility, and learning?

3. Describe Nissan's organizational culture. What are the characteristics of Nissan's culture? In what ways has Carlos Ghosn contributed to Nissan's culture? Elaborate.

4. Global firms pursue a relatively centralized approach to international operations. What are the characteristics of the trend toward global integration of company operations? How does Nissan demonstrate these characteristics?

5. Examine Nissan in terms of the Integration-Responsiveness Framework. What are the pressures that Nissan faces for local responsiveness? What are the pressures that Nissan faces for global integration? What advantages do each of local responsiveness and global integration bring to Nissan?

Sources: Bremner, B., G. Edmondson, and C. Dawson. (2004). "Nissan's Boss," *Business Week,* Oct 4, pp. 50–55; Flint, J. (2003). "Too Much Globalism," *Forbes,* Feb 17, p. 96; Ghson, C., and P. Ries. (2005). *Shift: Inside Nissan's Historic Revival,* New York: Currency/Doubleday; Guthrie, A. (2005). "For Nissan, Success in Mexico Rides on Tsuru's Enduring Appeal," *Wall Street Journal,* Dec 21, p. 1; Hoovers' information web site at www.hoovers.com; Muller, J. (2006). "The Impatient Mr. Ghosn," *Forbes,* May 22, pp. 104–107; Shirouzu, N. (2006). "Ghosn's Goal for Renault: Go Global," *Wall Street Journal,* June 21, p. B3; Shirouzu, N., and N. Boudette. (2006). "What Alliance with Mr. Ghosn Could Bring GM," *Wall Street Journal,* July 7, p. B1; Welch, D. (2003). "How Nissan Laps Detroit," *Business Week,* Dec 22, p. 58; Wrighton, J. and J. Sapsford (2005), "Split Shift: For Nissan's Rescuer, Ghosn, New Road Rules Await at Renault," *Wall Street Journal,* April 26, p. A.1; www.businessweek.com. "Putting Ford In The Rearview Mirror," February 12, 2007; www.businessweek.com. "The Race To Build Really Cheap Cars," April 23, 2007; www.nissan-global.com.

CHAPTER ESSENTIALS

Key Terms

corporate social responsibility,   p. 331
expatriate,   p. 334
export department,   p. 324
functional division   p. 326
geographic area division,   p. 325
global integration,   p. 317
global mindset,   p. 329
global industry   p. 316
global matrix structure,   p. 327

global strategy,   p. 320
global team,   p. 333
home replication strategy,   p. 319
international division structure,
    p. 324
local responsiveness,   p. 317
multidomestic industry,   p. 316
multidomestic strategy,   p. 319
organizational culture,   p. 331

organizational processes,   p. 333
organizational structure,   p. 322
product division,   p. 326
strategy,   p. 315
strategy in the international context,
    p. 315
transnational strategy,   p. 321
visionary leadership,   p. 329

Summary

In this chapter, you learned about:

1. The role of strategy in international business

Strategy is a plan of action that channels an organization's resources so that it can effectively differentiate itself from competitors and accomplish unique and viable goals. **Strategy in the international context** is a plan for the organization to position itself positively from its competitors and configure its value-adding activities on a global scale.

2. The integration-responsiveness framework

The integration-responsiveness (IR) framework reduces the managerial imperatives to two key needs: the need for global integration of value-chain activities and the need for local responsiveness. **Local responsiveness** refers to meeting the specific needs of buyers in individual host countries. **Global integration** refers to the coordination of the firm's value-chain activities across countries to achieve worldwide efficiency, synergy, and cross-fertilization in order to take maximum advantage of similarities across countries. The key challenge is in deciding how locally responsive the firm should be in comparison to how far it should go in integrating its worldwide business.

3. Distinct strategies emerging from the integration-responsiveness framework

The IR framework presents four alternative strategies. Using **home replication strategy,** the firm views international business as separate from, and secondary to, its domestic business. Products are designed with domestic consumers in mind, and the firm is essentially a domestic company with some foreign activities. **Multidomestic strategy** is a more committed approach, emphasizing entry via FDI, but in which managers recognize and emphasize differences among national markets. Managers treat individual markets on a stand-alone basis, with little cross-national integration of company efforts. **Global strategy** aims to integrate the firm's major objectives, policies, and action sequences into a cohesive whole, targeted primarily to the global marketplace. Top management performs sourcing, resource allocation, market participation, and competitive moves on a global scale. Using **transnational strategy**, the firm strives to be more responsive to local needs while simultaneously retaining maximum global efficiency and emphasizing global learning and knowledge transfer. The strategy involves combining the major beneficial attributes of both multidomestic and global strategies while minimizing their disadvantages.

4. Organizational structure

Organizational structure refers to the reporting relationships in the organization between people, functions, and processes that allow the firm to carry out its international operations. Organizational structure determines where key decisions are made, the relationship between headquarters and subsidiaries, the nature of international staffing, and the degree of *centralization* and *decentralization* of decision making and value-chain activities in the firm's worldwide operations. In achieving a fine balance between the two choices, managers should recognize the unique contributions made by both headquarters and subsidiaries. The best role for corporate managers is to provide broad leadership, experience, and serve as a source of encouragement. In turn, subsidiary managers are best at dealing with customers, handling employee issues, and initiating action in the field. In this way, an ideal partnership develops and evolves.

5. Alternative organizational arrangements for international operations

There are various organizational designs for global operations. The **export department** is the simplest, in which a unit within the firm manages all export operations. Slightly more advanced is the **international division structure,** in which all international activities are centralized within one division separate from other domestic units. The decentralized structure emphasizes the **geographic area division**, in which control and decision making are decentralized to the level of individual geographic regions. The centralized structure involves either product or functional divisions. Using the **product division,** decision making and management of the firm's international operations are organized by major product line. Using the **functional division,** decision making is organized by functional activity, such as production and marketing. The **global matrix structure** blends the geographic area, product, and functional structures in an attempt to leverage the benefits of a purely global strategy and maximize global organizational learning while remaining responsive to local needs.

6. Building the global firm

Managers who exhibit **visionary leadership** possess a **global mindset**, cosmopolitan values, and a globally strategic vision. They engage in strategic thinking, committing resources and human assets to realizing a global approach to business. **Organizational culture** is the pattern of shared values, norms, systems, policies, and procedures that employees learn and adopt. Advanced international firms value global competence and cross-cultural skills, adopt a single corporate language, and promote interdependency among headquarters and the firm's subsidiaries. They subscribe to globally accepted ethical standards and responsible citizenship. **Organizational processes** refer to managerial routines, behaviors, and mechanisms that allow the firm to function as intended. International organizational processes include **global teams**, global talent pools, and global information systems.

7. Putting organizational change in motion

As a minimum, managers should formulate a global strategy, develop a suitable organizational structure, provide visionary leadership, cultivate an organizational culture worldwide, and refine and implement organizational processes. Highly ambitious efforts to rapidly transform an organization may falter. Instead, focusing on one or two dimensions at a time is prudent. It is best to tackle the most easily changed dimensions of the organization first, in order to prepare the way for the more difficult changes. Senior management needs to instill a sense of urgency to drive the organization forward.

Test Your Comprehension AACSB: Reflective Thinking

1. What are the primary strategic objectives in international business?

2. Describe the integration-responsiveness framework. What are the pressures for local responsiveness? What are the pressures for global integration?

3. What is the difference between global strategy and multidomestic strategy? Visit the web site of Dell Computer (www.dell.com). Does Dell generally apply a global strategy or a multidomestic strategy? How can you tell?

4. Define transnational strategy. Give examples of firms that apply a transnational strategy.

5. What is the difference between a centralized and a decentralized organizational structure? Why do firms often prefer to have a centralized structure?

6. What are different organizational arrangements for global operations? Which arrangement is most associated with global strategy?

7. Define visionary leadership. What are the traits of a manager who has visionary leadership?

8. Define organizational culture. What kind of organizational culture is needed to become a global firm?

9. Define organizational processes. Give and elaborate on several examples of organizational processes. What organizational processes are most salient to achieving a global approach to international business?

Apply Your Understanding AACSB: Communication, Reflective Thinking

1. Visit online sites for Toyota (www.toyota.com) and Procter & Gamble (www.pg.com). From what you can gather, how do these two firms organize their international activities? Do they seem to be applying multi-domestic strategy or global strategy in sourcing, manufacturing, product development, and marketing activities? Would you expect a firm to change its approach to internationalization over time?

2. AlumCo is a large producer of aluminum products. AlumCo now handles international operations through its export department. But top management believes this arrangement is no longer suited to the firm's growing international activities and wants to adopt a more sophisticated approach. What alternative organizational structures (international division, geographic area structure, etc.) should the firm consider? Make a recommendation to top management as to the most appropriate international structure that AlumCo should employ. For reference, check out the website of Alcan, the well-known Canadian aluminum firm, at www.alcan.com.

3. Firms with a global organizational culture have several common characteristics. They seek a global identity, value a global perspective in all undertakings, adopt a common language, promote interdependency between headquarters and subsidiaries, value input from foreign units, and subscribe to globally accepted ethical standards. Recall the opening vignette in this chapter on IKEA, the giant furniture retailer. Based on your reading, outline the various ways that IKEA exhibits these characteristics.

4. Multinational firms that apply a coordinated global strategy see the world as one large production and marketing platform and develop standardized products that are then marketed worldwide using a uniform marketing approach. In reality, however, most firms do not apply a purely global strategy. At the same time, a strictly multidomestic approach is inefficient. While a few large countries (e.g., China, Japan, and the United States) might warrant individual treatment, many firms strike a compromise by dividing the world into regions. Usually these firms apply a geographic area strategy for their international operations. What is the rationale for using a regional approach when thinking about, and devising strategy for, international business?

AACSB: Reflective Thinking, Analytical Skills, Use of Information Technology

Refer to Chapter 1, page 27, for instructions on how to access and use globalEDGE™.

1. Multinational firms play a key role in globalization. Various news organizations prepare classifications and rankings of MNEs (e.g., *Business Week, Forbes, Fortune, Financial Times*). Find two such rankings and identify the criteria used to rank the top global firms. What countries are home to the great majority of MNEs on these lists? For each list, how "global" are the top three firms? That is, in what countries do they operate? Conduct a search for 'rankings.'

2. You work for an MNE that makes and markets cellular telephones. Senior managers want to begin selling the phones in Latin America. To pursue a transnational strategy, management wants to minimize adaptation of the phones. They have asked you for a briefing. Focusing on three Latin American countries, prepare a report that identifies the *common* features of Latin American markets that management should consider when developing the cell phones that the firm will sell there. For example, what language should be used in the cell phones? What pricing should management use? You may wish to consult the country commercial guides, Country Insights, and market research reports available through globalEDGE™. In addition, the Area Studies (http://www.psr.keele.ac.uk/area.htm), and the U.S. Department of Commerce

(http://www.export.gov) portals are useful resources.

3. Global strategy is characterized by various elements. First, at its most basic level, managers who use global strategy seek to *centralize* the firm's value-chain activities around the world. Centralization helps the firm achieve economies of scale, thereby cutting the costs of operations. Second, the firm attempts to *standardize* its marketing activities by offering relatively standardized (that is, largely unadapted) products and services worldwide. Standardization is possible because world markets are being homogenized by advances in communication and transportation technologies. Customers worldwide increasingly exhibit similar preferences and demand for the same products. Finally, firms that pursue global strategy locate manufacturing and marketing subsidiaries at numerous locations around the world in order to leverage the comparative advantages of specific countries and operate on a truly global basis. globalEDGE™ is home to a large collection of articles that describe the global strategy approaches of numerous firms. Conduct a search at globalEDGE™ by entering the keyword *global strategy* to find articles on this topic. Find and describe examples of companies that apply global strategy. Based on your reading of these articles, and on the previous summary of global strategy elements, describe specific ways in which the example firms that you found employ global strategy in practice.

Management Skill Builder©

The Critical Role of Negotiations in International Business

Negotiations are a cooperative process in which two parties commit to reach an agreement via communication and interaction. Negotiations are critical in international business. In any negotiation, cultural differences between the negotiators will play a significant role in how the participants think and act. It is critical to understand the negotiating culture, customs, and other characteristics of the other party before negotiations commence. In numerous cultures, for example, it is essential to get acquainted with each other and to establish a "comfort level" before initiating the negotiation process.

AACSB: Communication, Multicultural and Diversity, Analytical Skills

Managerial Challenge

Miscommunication is a key cause of failure in the negotiation process. Miscommunication arises from various sources, but perhaps the most important is a failure to understand the mindsets and motives of the negotiating parties. A critical managerial challenge is to develop an understanding of negotiators from a variety of national and cultural backgrounds. In order to succeed, a negotiator must conduct substantial advance research.

Background

Negotiations are an essential component of all international business transactions, whether they are the sale of a product or service to a buyer, the formation of a joint venture, the acquisition of a firm, or the licensing of a technology. Communication is the lifeblood of negotiations. The potential for cross-cultural misunderstandings is ever present. Differing circumstances dictate different approaches to negotiations. Goals of the parties may differ; they may even be diametrically opposed. The parties employ a number of techniques, such as persuasion, coercion, and even manipulation. Developing skills in international negotiations can determine the success of a wide range of collaborations, contractual relations, and everyday encounters in international business.

Managerial Skills You Will Gain

In this C/K/R Management Skill Builder©, as a prospective manager, you will:

1. Learn how to increase company performance by acquiring knowledge of negotiation skills.

2. Learn to recognize important cultural dimensions, negotiating styles, and other factors in international negotiations.

3. Acquire research skills to access the information needed to prepare for and to optimize international negotiations.

Your Task

Assume you are the team leader at an international firm that will engage in negotiations with businesspeople from Mexico and Saudi Arabia. To ensure success, you are to perform advance research on the cultural characteristics of the people with whom you will be negotiating.

Go to the C/K/R Knowledge Portal©

www.prenhall.com/cavusgil

Proceed to the C/K/R Knowledge Portal© to obtain the expanded background information, your task and methodology, suggested resources for this exercise, and the presentation template.

Global Market Opportunity Assessment

Learning Objectives

In this chapter, you will learn about:

1. An overview of global market opportunity assessment

2. Analysis of organizational readiness to internationalize

3. Assessment of the suitability of products and services for foreign markets

4. Screening countries to identify target markets

5. Assessment of industry market potential

6. Selection of foreign business partners

7. Estimating of company sales potential

> Estimating Market Demand in Emerging Markets and Developing Countries

Estimating the demand for products or services in emerging markets and developing economies is a challenging task for managers. These countries have unique commercial environments and may lack reliable data, market research firms, and trained interviewers. Consumers may consider research activities an invasion of privacy, and some survey respondents may try to please researchers by telling them what they want to hear, rather than providing fully honest and accurate information.

Just three emerging markets—China, India, and Brazil—have a combined GDP of more than $15 trillion, significantly more than the United States. Africa is among the biggest worldwide markets for mobile phone sales, growing to over 100 million users in just a few years. While most Africans can't afford a cell phone, the trend illustrates an often-overlooked point: developing economies are huge markets for products and services. For instance, Unilever and Procter & Gamble are among the companies that market shampoo and other necessities in India. Narayana Hrudayalaya is an Indian firm that sells health insurance to countless customers for pennies per month.

Estimating market demand in such countries requires managers to be flexible and creative. Let's consider the case of two firms trying to estimate the demand for wallpaper and adhesive bandages (band-aids) in Morocco.

In Morocco, the wealthier people live in villas or condominiums, which are potential target markets for sales of wallpaper. Import statistics are often not very helpful, because the government usually records wallpaper imports by weight and value. Companies sell wallpaper by the roll, and different qualities and designs will have different weights. Such information is of little use in estimating the number of modern households that will buy wallpaper.

One wallpaper company used three approaches to estimate demand for wallpaper. First, managers used a recent study that reported the number of water heaters purchased in Morocco. Managers assumed that if households purchased this important, "modern" convenience, they also would likely want to purchase wallpaper. Second, managers accessed government statistics that disclosed the level of domestic wallpaper sales, discretionary income by type of household, and home construction data. Third, managers surveyed the lifestyle of a sample of local consumers. Their findings revealed that Moroccans usually shop for wallpaper as a complementary decoration to fitted carpets. Among married couples, it is generally the wife who decides the style and decoration of the home. Customers tend to be well-to-do; they include professionals, merchants, and high-ranking administrators. Each of these approaches provided this wallpaper company with separate estimates of its market size for wallpaper. The company then triangulated a single estimate. Specifically, the company was interested in the degree to which the three separate estimates converged. Researchers blended their own judgment into these findings in order to ultimately arrive at a reasonably reliable estimate of demand for wallpaper.

In the case of adhesive bandages, available data revealed that 70 percent of demand for pharmaceutical items—including adhesive bandages—was met by wholesalers concentrated in Casablanca, Morocco's capital city. The country imported all its adhesive bandages. Demand was quickly growing, due to rapid population growth, free hospitalization and medication for the needy, and reimbursement programs for medical and drug expenses. Although the government published import statistics, the information was confusing, because data on band-aid imports was mixed together with data on other types of adhesives. Moreover, the band-aid data was superficial and incomplete. Finally, widespread smuggling and gray-marketing of adhesive bandages through unofficial distribution channels complicated estimates of demand.

In an effort to gather more information, researchers interviewed band-aid sales personnel from firms such as Johnson & Johnson and Curad. Their findings revealed that consumers tend to be price sensitive when buying band-aids, and that they rely on doctors and pharmacists to recommend well-known brands. Researchers eventually arrived at a reasonable estimate of band-aid sales by assimilating data from various sources. They visited numerous retail stores to ask about sales, prevailing retail prices, competitive brands, and consumer attitudes toward prices and brands. Researchers also tallied statistics from the United Nations Development Program and other aid agencies that donate medical supplies to developing countries.

As you can see, estimating demand in foreign markets is challenging, but managers can overcome the challenges through creative use of market research. ◄

Sources: Amine, Lyn and S. Tamer Cavusgil. (1986). "Demand Estimation in a Developing Country Environment: Difficulties, Techniques, and Examples," *Journal of the Market Research Society* 28 (1): 43–65; Cavusgil, S. Tamer, P. Ghauri, and M. Agarwal. (2002). *Doing Business in Emerging Markets: Entry and Negotiation Strategies.* Thousand Oaks, CA: Sage; Prahalad, C. K. (2005). "Aid Is Not the Answer," *The Wall Street Journal* Aug 31, p. A8; Wilkes, V. (2005). "Marketing and Market Development: Dealing with a Global Issue: Contributing to Poverty Alleviation," *Corporate Governance* 5 (3): 61–69; U.S. Commercial Service and the U.S. Department of State. (2005). *Country Commercial Guide Morocco Fiscal Year 2005,* retrieved at www.buyusainfo.net.

 ## An Overview of Global Market Opportunity Assessment

The choices managers make determine the future of the firm. Making good choices depends on objective evidence and hard data about which products and services to offer, and where to offer them. The more managers know about an opportunity, the better equipped they will be to exploit it. This is particularly true in international business, which usually entails greater uncertainty and unknowns than domestic business.[1]

Central to a firm's research is identifying and defining the best business opportunities in the global marketplace to pursue. **Global market opportunity** refers to a favorable combination of circumstances, locations, or timing that offers prospects for exporting, investing, sourcing, or partnering in foreign markets. In various foreign locations, the firm may perceive opportunities to: sell its products and services; establish factories or other production facilities to produce its offerings more competently or more cost-effectively; procure raw materials, components, or services of lower cost or superior quality; or enter into collaborative arrangements with foreign partners. Global market opportunities can enhance company performance, often far beyond what the firm can normally achieve in its home market.

Global market opportunity
Favorable combination of circumstances, locations, or timing that offers prospects for exporting, investing, sourcing, or partnering in foreign markets.

In this chapter, we discuss six key tasks that the manager should perform to define and pursue global market opportunities. Exhibit 12.1 illustrates the objectives and outcomes typically associated with each task. Such a formal process is especially appropriate in pursuing a marketing or collaborative venture opportunity. As the exhibit shows, the six key tasks are:

1. Analyze organizational readiness to internationalize.

2. Assess the suitability of the firm's products and services for foreign markets.

3. Screen countries to identify attractive target markets.

4. Assess the industry market potential, or the market demand, for the product(s) or service(s) in selected target markets.

5. Select qualified business partners, such as distributors or suppliers.

6. Estimate company sales potential for each target market.

In carrying out this systematic process, the manager will need to employ objective *selection criteria* by which to make choices, as listed in the final column of Exhibit 12.1. Let's examine each task in detail.

Task One: Analyze Organizational Readiness to Internationalize

Before undertaking a substantial investment in international business, whether it is launching a product abroad or sourcing from a foreign supplier, the firm should conduct a formal assessment of its readiness to internationalize. A thorough evaluation of organizational capabilities is useful, both for firms *new* to international business and for those with considerable experience. Such a self-audit is similar to a SWOT analysis (that is, an evaluation of the firm's Strengths, Weaknesses, Opportunities, and Threats). Here, managers peer into their own organization to determine the degree to which it has the motivation, resources, and skills necessary to successfully engage in international business.

Concurrently, management also examines conditions in the *external* business environment by conducting formal research on the opportunities and threats that face the firm in the markets where it seeks to do business. Here, managers research the specific needs and preferences of buyers, as well as the nature of competing products, and the risks involved in entering foreign markets.

Management's goal in analyzing organizational readiness to internationalize is to figure out what resources the firm has and the extent to which they are sufficient for successful international operations. In this way, managers assess the firm's *readiness* to venture abroad. During this process, management considers the firm's degree of international experience, the goals and objectives that management envisions for internationalization, the quantity and quality of skills, capabilities, and resources available for internationalization, and the extent of actual and potential support provided by the firm's network of relationships. If it is discovered that the firm lacks one or more key resources, management must commit necessary personnel and time *before* allowing the contemplated venture to go forward.

As an example, consider *Home Instead, Inc.,* a small U.S. firm that provides services for the elderly who choose to live independently at home but require companionship, assistance with meal preparation, and help with shopping and housekeeping. Following an assessment of its readiness to internationalize, management perceived substantial international opportunities—particularly in Japan—but also recognized deficiencies in certain key capabilities. So, the company hired Ms. Yoshino Nakajima, who is fluent in Japanese and an expert on the Japanese market, to be vice president for international development. Ms. Nakajima

Task	Objective	Outcomes	Selection criteria
1. Analyze organizational readiness to internationalize	To provide an objective assessment of the company's preparedness to engage in international business activity.	A list of firm strengths and weaknesses, in the context of international business, and recommendations for resolving deficiencies that hinder achieving company goals.	Evaluate factors needed for international business success: • Relevant financial and tangible resources • Relevant skills and competencies • Senior management commitment and motivation
2. Assess the suitability of the firm's products and services for foreign markets	To conduct a systematic assessment of the suitability of the firm's products and services for international customers. To evaluate the degree of fit between the product or service and customer needs.	• Determination of factors that may hinder product or service market potential in each target market. • Identification of needs for the adaptations that may be required for initial and ongoing market entry.	Assess the firm's products and services with regard to: • Foreign customer characteristics and requirements • Government-mandated regulations • Expectations of channel intermediaries • Characteristics of competitors' offerings
3. Screen countries to identify target markets	To reduce the number of countries that warrant in-depth investigation as potential target markets to a manageable few.	Identification of five to six high-potential country markets that are most promising for the firm.	Assess candidate countries that the firm may enter with regard to: • Market size and growth rate • Market intensity (that is, buying power of the residents in terms of income level) • Consumption capacity (that is, size and growth rate of the country's middle class) • Country's receptivity to imports • Infrastructure appropriate for doing business • Degree of economic freedom • Political risk

Exhibit 12.1 Key Tasks in Global Market Opportunity Assessment

Task	Objective	Outcomes	Selection criteria
4. Assess industry market potential	To estimate the most likely share of industry sales within each target country. To investigate and evaluate any potential barriers to market entry.	• 3 to 5-year forecasts of industry sales for each target market • Delineation of market entry barriers in industry	Assess industry market potential in the target country by considering: • Market size, growth rate, and trends in the industry • The degree of competitive intensity • Tariff and nontariff trade barriers • Standards and regulations • Availability and sophistication of local distribution • Unique customer requirements and preferences • Industry-specific market potential indicators
5. Select qualified business partners	To decide on the type of foreign business partner, clarify ideal partner qualifications and plan entry strategy.	• Determination of value adding activities required of foreign business partners • List of attributes desired of foreign business partners • Determination of value-adding activities required of foreign business partners	Assess and select intermediaries and facilitators based on: • Manufacturing and marketing expertise in the industry • Commitment to the international venture • Access to distribution channels in the market • Financial strength • Quality of staff • Technical expertise • Infrastructure and facilities appropriate for the market
6. Estimate company sales potential	To estimate the most likely share of industry sales the company can achieve, over a period of time, for each target market.	• 3 to 5-year forecast of company sales in each target market • Understanding of factors that will influence company sales potential	Estimate the potential to sell the firm's product or service, with regard to: • Capabilities of partners • Access to distribution • Competitive intensity • Pricing and financing • Market penetration timetable of the firm • Risk tolerance of senior managers

launched the franchise in Japan, where it captured substantial market share. Next, management tapped into the global network of 1,700 trade specialists of the U.S. Commercial Service, a government agency that provided the firm with leads and contacts in countries it had identified as the best target markets. Now *Home Instead* has numerous franchises in Australia, Canada, Ireland, and Portugal. Its international operations are thriving.[2]

A formal analysis of organizational readiness to internationalize requires managers to address the following questions:

- *What does the firm hope to gain from international business?* Various objectives and goals are possible, including increasing sales or profits, following key customers who locate abroad, challenging competitors in their home markets, or pursuing a global strategy of establishing production and marketing operations at various locations worldwide.

- *Is international business expansion consistent with other firm goals, now or in the future?* The firm should manage internationalization in the context of its mission and business plan. Over time, firms have various opportunities. Managers should evaluate one venture against others that might be undertaken in the domestic market to ensure that internationalization is the best use of firm resources.

- *What demands will internationalization place on firm resources, such as management, personnel, and finance, as well as production and marketing capacity? How will the firm meet such demands?* Management must confirm that the firm has enough production and marketing capacity to serve foreign markets. Nothing is more frustrating to the management team and the international channel than not being able to fill orders due to insufficient capacity. For instance, when Cirrus Logic, Inc., a manufacturer of audio microchips, wanted to expand its ability to market chips to international customers like Bose, LG Electronics, and Sony, it had to increase its manufacturing capacity first.[3]

- *What is the basis of the firm's competitive advantage?* Here, managers evaluate the reasons for the firm's current success. Firms derive competitive advantage from doing things better than competitors. It might be based on strong R&D capabilities, sourcing of superior input goods, cost-effective or innovative manufacturing capacity, skillful marketing, or a highly effective distribution channel. It is important to understand what advantages the firm has, so that managers can apply these advantages effectively in foreign markets.

Managers can use diagnostic tools to facilitate a self-audit of the firm's readiness to internationalize. One of the best-known tools is *CORE (COmpany Readiness to Export)*, developed by Professor Tamer Cavusgil in the early 1980s (see www.globalEDGE.msu.edu). *CORE* has been adopted and used widely by individual enterprises, consultants, and the U.S. Department of Commerce. Since *CORE* has benefited from extensive research on the factors that contribute to successful exporting, it also serves as an ideal tutorial for self-learning and training.

CORE asks managers questions about their organizational resources, skills, and motivation to arrive at an objective assessment of the firm's readiness to successfully engage in exporting. It also generates assessments on both organizational readiness and product readiness. This self-assessment tool helps managers recognize the useful assets they have and the additional resources they need to make internationalization succeed. The assessment emphasizes exporting, since it is the typical entry mode for most newly internationalizing firms.

Assessing organizational readiness to internationalize is an ongoing process. Managers need to continuously verify the firm's ability to modify its products and processes to suit conditions in local markets. For example, Levi

Strauss is the world's largest manufacturer of trousers, notably denim jeans, which are sold worldwide. Countries differ in their tastes and fashions, which creates the need for firms to adapt products and services. Levi has had to assess its ability to undertake marketing adaptations in various markets. For example, in Islamic countries, women are discouraged from wearing tight-fitting attire, so Levi made a line of loose-fitting jeans. When Levi first entered Japan, local preferences and the smaller physique of many Japanese meant that the firm had to make its famous blue jeans tighter and smaller.

In addition to considering local customs, preferences, and physical makeup, Levi also adapts to local regulations. Levi often re-shot TV commercials in countries such as Australia and Brazil because local regulations insist on domestically produced commercials. Differences in climate also necessitate changes; for instance, in hot climates, customers prefer thinner denim in brighter colors, and shorts. Management has had to regularly assess the firm's capacity to accommodate the adaptations required for numerous individual markets.[4]

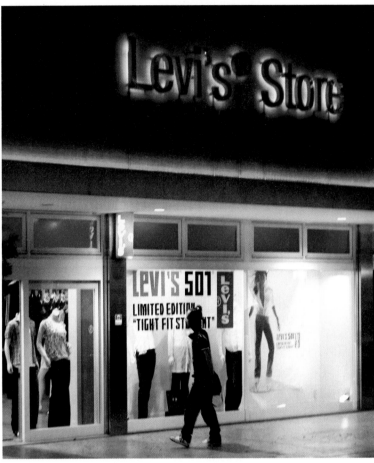

Levi makes tight-fit jeans to accommodate the Japanese physique and loose-fitting jeans to accommodate tastes in Islamic countries.

Task Two: Assess the Suitability of the Firm's Products and Services for Foreign Markets

Once management has confirmed the firm's readiness to internationalize, it next ascertains the degree to which its products and services are suitable for foreign markets. Most companies produce a portfolio of offerings, some or all of which may hold the potential for generating international sales.

Factors Contributing to Product Suitability for International Markets

There are various ways to gauge the viability of offerings in foreign markets. The products or services with the best international prospects tend to have the following four characteristics:

1. *Sell well in the domestic market.* Those products and services that are received well at home are likely to succeed abroad, especially where similar needs and conditions exist. The manager should examine why the product or service is received well at home and then identify foreign markets with similar demand requirements.

2. *Cater to universal needs.* For example, buyers all over the world demand personal-care products, medical devices, and banking services. International sales may be promising if the product or service is relatively unique or has important features that are hard to duplicate by foreign firms.

3. *Address a need not well served in particular foreign markets.* Potential may exist in developing countries or elsewhere, where the product or service does not currently exist, or where demand is just beginning to emerge.

4. *Address a new or emerging need abroad.* For some products and services, demand might suddenly emerge following a disaster or other largescale or emergent trend. For example, a major earthquake in Turkey can create an urgent need for portable housing. Rising AIDS cases in South Africa can create a need for pharmaceuticals and medical supplies. Growing affluence in various emerging markets can create a growing demand for restaurants and hospitality services. Managers need to monitor such trends, so they can be prepared to enter the right market at the right time.

Key Issues for Managers to Resolve in Determining Product Potential

Here are some of the key questions managers should answer to determine the international market potential of a particular product or service:

- Who initiates purchasing? For example, homemakers are usually the chief decision-makers for household products. Professional buyers make purchases on behalf of firms.

- Who uses the product or service? For instance, children consume various products, but their parents may be the actual buyers. Employees consume various products, but their company makes the purchases.

- Why do people buy the product or service? That is, what specific needs does the product or service fulfill? These needs vary around the world. For example, Honda sells gasoline-powered generators that consumers in advanced economies use for recreational purposes; consumers in developing economies may buy these for basic household heating and lighting.

- Where do consumers purchase the product or service? Once the researcher understands where the offering is typically purchased, it is useful to visit potential buyers to find out the extent of their potential interest. These store audits also provide useful information on whether the product or service must be adapted to specific market needs, as well as how to price, promote, and distribute it.

- What economic, cultural, geographic, and other factors in the target market can limit sales? Countries vary substantially in terms of buyer-income levels, preferences, climate, and other factors that can inhibit or facilitate purchasing behavior. Managers should investigate such factors and adapt their offers accordingly.

One of the simplest ways to find out if a product or service holds promise for generating international sales is to ask potential intermediaries in the target market about the potential of a product in their markets. A manager can also review importer or distributor lists, available from government sources, trade associations, or directories online or in libraries.

Data on the extent to which the target country has imported a product over time is also very useful for understanding current and future potential demand. Data may be available from various sources, such as http://export.gov, http://www.stat-usa.gov, or globalEDGE™. The level of exports should be investigated as well, because some countries, such as Singapore or Hong Kong, are used mainly as a transit point for international products and, therefore, may not actually be major users.

Another useful method for determining a product's marketability is to attend an industry trade fair in the target market or region and interview prospective customers or distributors. Since trade fairs often cover entire regions, such as Asia or Europe, this approach is efficient and cost effective for simultaneously learning about the market potential of several countries.

For successful international ventures, most firms focus on offering products and services that fit its resources and competitive advantages and can be produced from existing production facilities with minimal adaptation. The managers target those markets that are most likely to accept their offering and which have high profit and long-term potential growth.

 ## Task Three: Screen Countries to Identify Target Markets

Screening for the best country to target is a fundamental decision in international business, whether the firm is engaged in importing, investing, or exporting. Firms that seek to source from foreign suppliers need to identify countries where capable suppliers are located. Once a firm chooses a particular country, it needs to ensure that conditions for importing from that country are favorable. For firms looking to make a direct investment in foreign markets, it is best to focus on countries that promise long-term growth and substantial returns, while posing relatively low political risk. Finally, exporting firms should target countries with low tariff barriers, steady demand, and qualified intermediaries.

Exporters typically use trade statistics that reveal exports or imports by country and product and allow the researcher to compare the size of the market among candidate countries. Statistics on how much of the product is already being exported to the target market help gauge the market's viability for accepting sales of the offering. By examining statistics over a period of years, a manager can determine which markets are growing and which are shrinking. The exporter can purchase research reports from professional market research consultants that provide descriptions, assessments, and key statistics on particular markets. For instance, the U.S. Department of Commerce conducts and publishes numerous market surveys, such as *The Water Supply and Wastewater Treatment Market in China, Automotive Parts and Equipment Industry Guide in Europe,* and the *Country Commercial Guide for Brazil.*

The choice of country markets is particularly important in the early stages of internationalization. Failure to choose the right markets will not only result in a financial loss, but the firm will incur opportunity costs as well. That is, by choosing the wrong markets, the firm ties up resources that it might have more profitably employed somewhere else. When entry is planned through *foreign direct investment (FDI),* choosing the right market is especially critical, because FDI is very costly. As you learned in Chapter 1, FDI is an internationalization strategy in which the firm establishes a physical presence abroad through acquisition of productive assets such as capital, technology, labor, land, plant, and equipment. With FDI entry, the cost of abandoning the market and terminating relationships can easily exceed millions of dollars.

Some firms target psychically similar countries—that is, countries similar to the home country in terms of language, culture, and other factors. These countries fit management's comfort zone. For instance, Australian firms often choose New Zealand, the United Kingdom, or the United States as their first target markets abroad. Many choose the United Kingdom rather than France or Italy as their first European target. The choice is logical, because English is spoken in New Zealand, the United Kingdom, and the United States, and these cultures bear similarities to that of Australia. As their managerial experience, knowledge, and confidence increase, these firms expand into more complex and culturally distant markets, such as China or Japan.

In the contemporary era, however, firms have become more venturesome as well as more knowledgeable regarding foreign-market entry. As a result, many target non-traditional, higher-risk countries. The born-global companies exemplify this trend. Ongoing globalization tends to mitigate the foreignness of markets and—thanks to advances in communication and transportation technologies—have reduced the cost and risk of reaching out to culturally distant countries, including emerging markets.

As firms become more knowledgeable about foreign markets, they are venturing into countries with different languages and cultures. U.S.-based Motorola sells mobile phones in Vietnam. The United States imports agricultural and other products from Vietnam.

When screening countries, it is best for managers to target markets that are growing rapidly or in which the offered product or service is relatively new to the market. Markets in which there are numerous competitors or in which the product is already widely used are unattractive, because existing rivals may strongly resist the entry of newcomers.

The nature of information necessary for country screening varies by product type or industry. For example, in marketing consumer electronics, the researcher would emphasize countries with large populations of people with adequate discretionary income and ample energy production and consumption. For farming equipment, the researcher would consider countries with substantial agricultural land and farmers who enjoy relatively high incomes. For health care insurance, the researcher targets countries that have numerous hospitals and doctors.

In the process of screening for attractive country markets, managers need to monitor a range of economic, political, and cultural factors. These factors affect the international business environment in major ways, and point to various opportunities and threats that firms analyze and evaluate. Read the *Global Trend* feature to learn about a number of current trends that affect the global market environment.

Targeting Regions or Gateway Countries

Often, the firm may target a region or a group of countries rather than individual countries. Compared to targeting one country at a time, targeting a group of countries is more cost effective, particularly when the markets have similar demand conditions, business regulations, and culture. A good example is the European Union, which comprises some 27 countries that are relatively similar in terms of income level, regulations, and infrastructure. When entering Europe, firms often devise a pan-European strategy that considers many member countries of the European Union, rather than planning separate efforts in individual countries.

In other cases, the firm may target so-called *gateway countries,* or *regional hubs,* which serve as entry points to nearby or affiliated markets. For example, Singapore has traditionally served as the gateway to southeast Asian countries, Hong Kong is an important gateway to China, Turkey is a good platform for entering the central Asian republics, and Finland provides business-friendly access to the former Soviet Union. Firms base their operations in a gateway country so they can serve the larger adjacent region.

Screening Methodology for Potential Country Markets

With almost 200 countries around the world, it is neither cost effective nor practical to target all of them. Thus, management must choose markets that offer the best prospects. There are two basic methods for accomplishing this: gradual elimination and indexing and ranking.

Global Macro Trends That Affect International Business

Managers must regularly assess the long-term trends in its product markets, as well as shifting aspects of technology and globalization. Firms succeed when they ride these currents—those that swim against them usually struggle. For instance, in sectors such as banking, telecommunications, and technology, almost two-thirds of recent organic growth in western firms (that is, growth from increasing sales) has resulted from being in the right markets and regions. By identifying and analyzing key trends, it is possible to forecast long-term directional changes that affect the firm's future fortunes.

What current trends are international managers tracking that will make the future world very different from the world of today? A recent study by McKinsey, a consulting firm, identified the following macroeconomic trends as transforming the global economy.

Centers of economic activity that will undergo a major shift, not just globally, but also regionally. The locations of global economic activities are shifting due to economic liberalization, technological advances, capital market developments, and demographic shifts. Today, Asia (excluding Japan) accounts for 13 percent of world GDP, while western Europe accounts for more than 30 percent. By 2025, these proportions may reverse, as most global economic activity shifts toward Asia. Some industries and functions in Asia—manufacturing and IT services, for example—will be the major beneficiaries. Elsewhere, emerging markets are becoming centers of activity as well.

Need to increase organizational productivity. Populations are aging across the developed countries, meaning there are fewer young people to work and pay taxes. This demographic shift requires higher levels of efficiency and creativity from both the public and private sectors. Governments must perform their services less expensively and with greater efficiency. They will gradually apply private-sector approaches in the provision of social services. Otherwise, there is a risk that aging populations will reduce the overall level of global wealth. The shift is creating opportunities for firms in certain product and service sectors, such as finance and health care.

More consumers, especially in the developing economies. Almost a billion new consumers will enter the global marketplace through 2015, as economic growth in emerging markets pushes them beyond the threshold level of $5,000 in annual household income, a point when people begin to spend on discretionary goods. In the period up to 2015, consumers' spending power in emerging economies will increase to more than $9 trillion, near the current spending power of western Europe. Consumers everywhere will increasingly leverage information and communications technologies to access the same products and brands. These shifts require firms to devise new products and marketing strategies. For example, firms are increasingly employing the Internet to reach new markets and deepen relations with existing customers.

The shifting talent battlefield. The shift to knowledge-intensive industries highlights a growing scarcity of knowledge workers. Increasing integration of global labor markets (e.g., China, India, and Eastern Europe) is opening vast new talent sources. Emerging markets now have tens of millions of university-educated young professionals, more than double the number in advanced economies. To take advantage of this trend, firms increasingly leverage information and communication technologies to employ well-educated individuals located in the emerging markets and elsewhere.

Growing demand for natural resource. As economic growth accelerates, especially in emerging markets, use of natural resources will grow at unprecedented rates. Demand for oil is likely to grow by 50 percent through the year 2025. This shift portends new opportunities for firms in the global energy sector. In China, demand for copper, steel, and aluminum has tripled in recent years, suggesting new opportunities for mining companies. Meanwhile, water shortages are increasingly common in much of the world. Climate change and the gradual decay of the ozone level require attention. Addressing these challenges is costly, and will likely slow growth. Innovation in technology, regulation, and the use of resources is central to creating a world that can both drive robust economic growth and sustain environmental demands.

Widespread access to information. Knowledge is increasingly available to people worldwide. For instance, the presence of search engines such as Google makes seemingly limitless information instantly available. Knowledge production itself is growing. For example, worldwide patent applications have been rising annually at 20 percent. Companies are applying new models of knowledge production, access, distribution, and ownership.

Managers need to understand the implications of these macroeconomic trends, along with customer needs and competitive developments. In such an evolving environment, the role of market research and competitive intelligence is growing. Managers who account for these trends in their strategy development will be best placed to succeed in the global marketplace. Thinking about these trends will be time well spent for any future manager.

Sources: Davis, I., and E. Stephenson. (2006). "Ten Trends to Watch in 2006," *The McKinsey Quarterly*, retrieved January, 2006 at www.mckinsey.com; Porter, Eduardo. (2003). "Buying Power of Hispanics Is Set to Soar," *Wall Street Journal*, April 18, p. B1.

Gradual Elimination The firm that applies *gradual elimination* starts with a large number of prospective target countries and then gradually narrows its choices by examining increasingly specific information. As indicated in Exhibit 12.1 on pages 348–349, the firm aims to reduce to a manageable few the number of countries that warrant in-depth investigation as potential target markets. The objective is to identify five or six high-potential country markets that are most promising for the firm. Research can be expensive. To save time and money, it is essential to eliminate unattractive markets as quickly as possible. At the same time, it is wise to be open-minded and consider all reasonable markets. For example, targeting developing economies with a product that is not yet widely consumed may be more profitable than targeting saturated and more competitive markets in Europe, Japan, and North America.

In the early stages, market research proceeds in a stepwise manner, in which the researcher follows a funnel approach of obtaining general information first, then specific information next. The researcher initially obtains information on macro-level market-potential indicators, such as population- or income-related measures, to identify a short list of countries (perhaps five or six) that represent the most attractive markets. Such broad screening data are readily available from sources such as globalEDGE ™.

Once managers identify the most promising markets, they employ more specific and precise indicators to narrow the choices. For example, a manager may use current import statistics of the particular product to determine the potential desirability of a target market. This information is readily available, because most countries record the flow of imported and exported products to levy import duties and to determine the value of their own exports. Most countries also make these statistics available to international organizations, such as the United Nations (see www.comtrade.un.org/db/) and the Organi-

Country	Market Size		Market Growth Rate		Market Intensity		Market Consumption Capacity		
	Rank	Index	Rank	Index	Rank	Index	Rank	Index	
China	1	100	1	100	25	23	12	59	
Hong Kong	24	1	20	23	1	100	13	54	
Singapore	27	1	18	27	9	59	11	62	
Taiwan	12	5	6	57	11	57	—	—	
Israel	25	1	12	45	2	79	4	82	
South Korea	7	12	16	30	5	63	2	99	
Czech Rep.	23	2	9	48	13	55	3	97	
Hungary	26	1	24	14	3	76	1	100	
India	2	44	3	63	22	37	7	77	
Poland	14	5	27	1	10	58	6	80	

Exhibit 12.2 Application of Indexing and Ranking Methodology: Emerging Market Potential Indicators, 2007

Note: Only top 10 countries are provided here; consult www.globaledge.msu.edu for the complete list.

Source: globalEDGE™ (www.globaledge.msu.edu/ibrd/marketpot.asp).

zation for Economic Cooperation and Development (OECD; www.oecd.org). By analyzing research data and gradually narrowing the choices, the researcher identifies the one or two most promising markets for further exploration.

Indexing and Ranking The second primary method for choosing the most promising foreign markets is *indexing* and *ranking,* in which the researcher assigns scores to countries for their overall market attractiveness. For each country, the researcher first identifies a comprehensive set of market-potential indicators and then uses one or more of these indicators to represent a variable. Weights are assigned to each variable to establish its relative importance: the more important a variable, the greater its weight. The researcher uses the resulting weighted scores to rank the countries.

This indexing and ranking method is illustrated by the *Emerging Market Potential (EMP) Indicators* methodology, developed by the senior author of this book, Tamer Cavusgil,[5] and featured at globalEDGE™.[6] Exhibit 12.2 presents the resulting index. It ranks the emerging markets—some of the world's most-promising developing countries. The Exhibit highlights a collection of variables that are useful for describing the attractiveness of countries as potential target markets. Exhibit 12.3 defines the variables and relative weights used in the Exhibit.

Among the variables in Exhibit 12.3, *market size* and *market growth rate* are especially important for measuring market potential.[7] They address the question "Is the market big enough and does it have a future?" If a country's population is large and its per–capita income is substantial, it is probably a good prospect for international sales. By itself, however, a sizable market is insufficient. The market should also be growing at a stable or substantial rate, particularly in terms of population or income. Countries with robust income growth are desirable targets. For each country, a researcher examines population,

Commercial Infrastructure		Economic Freedom		Market Receptivity		Country Risk		Overall Index	
Rank	Index	Rank	Index	Rank	Index	Rank	Index	Rank	Index
16	45	27	1	22	3	13	49	1	100
2	97	6	79	2	75	2	90	2	96
6	83	10	71	1	100	1	100	3	93
1	100	8	76	5	23	3	87	4	79
3	94	3	86	4	26	5	63	5	78
5	90	7	78	10	13	4	65	6	75
4	91	2	93	9	15	6	63	7	73
7	78	4	83	8	16	8	62	8	64
25	17	17	44	27	1	16	39	9	55
8	71	5	82	14	7	9	58	10	46

Variable	Definition	Weight (out of 100)	Example Measurement Indicators
Market size	Proportion of the country's population concentrated in urban areas	20	• Urban population
Market growth rate	Pace of industrialization and economic development	12	• Annual growth rate of commercial energy use • Real GDP growth rate
Market intensity	Buying power of the country's residents	14	• Per-capita gross national income, based on purchasing power parity • Private consumption as a percentage of GDP
Market consumption capacity	Size and growth rate of the country's middle class	10	• Percentage share of middle-class income and consumption
Commercial infrastructure	Ease of access to marketing, distribution, and communication channels	14	• Telephone mainlines (per 100 habitants) • Cellular mobile subscribers per 100 inhabitants • Paved road density • Internet hosts per million people • Population per retail outlet • Television sets per capita
Economic freedom	Degree to which the country has liberalized its economy	10	• Trade and tax policies • Monetary and banking policies • Government consumption of economic output • Capital flows and foreign investment • Property rights • Extent of black market activity
Market receptivity to imports	Extent to which the country is open to imports	12	• Per-capita imports • Trade as percentage of GDP
Country risk	Level of political risk	8	• Country risk rating
Total		100	

Exhibit 12.3 Variables Used for Country Screening in the Emerging Market Potential (EMP) Indicators Index

national income, and growth statistics for the previous 3 to 5 years. A key question is whether or not market growth has been consistent year to year. In addition to large, fast-growing markets, a researcher should identify some smaller but fast-emerging markets that may provide ground-floor opportunities. There are likely to be fewer competitors in new markets than in established ones. Countries in which the product is not currently available or in which competitors have only recently entered may also be promising targets.

As we discussed in Chapter 9 on emerging markets, the *size* and *growth rate* of the middle class are critical indicators of promising targets.

The *middle class* is measured by the share of national income available to middle-income households. These middle-class consumer households are the best prospect for a typical marketer because the wealthier class in most emerging markets is relatively small and the poorest segment has little spending capacity. The relative size of the middle class, and the pace with which it is growing, also indicate how national income is distributed in that country. If income is not equally distributed, the size of the middle class will be limited and the market will not be very attractive.

While the middle class is an important indicator for estimating the size of foreign markets, as also elaborated in Chapter 9, per capita income measure may underestimate the true potential of emerging markets due to such factors as the existence of a large, informal economy.

In Exhibit 12.2, an analysis of the rankings for each of the dimensions reveals some interesting patterns. For example, China ranks first in market size, but twenty-fifth in market intensity and last in economic freedom. It also ranks low in infrastructure. As this observation reveals, there are always trade-offs in targeting country markets. No single country is attractive on all dimensions. Along with more-desirable features, the researcher must also contend with less-desirable features. For example, both Singapore and Hong Kong are favorable targets in terms of economic freedom, but they are city-states with small populations.

The top four countries in the index in Exhibit 12.2 are all in East Asia. In recent years, East Asian economies have made tremendous strides in market liberalization, industrialization, and modernization. South Korea is a champion of economic growth, with annual per-capita GDP growth of almost 6 percent. The level of per capita GDP in the past 40 years has advanced tenfold. South Korean firms have become world leaders in many industries, such as shipbuilding, mobile communications, and flat-screen televisions. The country is the world's test market for state-of-the-art wireless and Internet services and applications. South Korean firms use pioneering technologies that are years ahead of their competitors and are poised to overtake other countries in mobile technology, broadband, and other leading communications technologies. Asia's rapid economic development is a primary factor in the current phase of globalization.[8]

Country rankings of the type indicated in Exhibit 12.2 are not static. Rankings change over time as shifts occur in each country because of macroeconomic events or country-specific developments. For example, while India ranks relatively high, it may dramatically fall if a new political regime reverses market liberalization. The recent accession of Hungary and Poland into the European Union should improve the economic prospects of these countries. The introduction of modern banking systems and legal infrastructure should increase Russia's attractiveness as an export market. Chile has achieved substantial progress in economic reforms and higher living standards. However, economic stagnation has led to a drop in Argentina's market attractiveness.

A final point relates to the rather generic and broad nature of the variables suggested by ranking indicators. They are only a general guide for identifying promising country markets. The ranking and indexing methodology is intended for use in the early stages of qualifying and ranking countries. Much more detailed analysis is needed once a firm identifies a handful of target markets. The researcher will eventually need to supplement the indicators for specific industries. Indicators to emphasize when researching soft drink markets, for example, vary substantially from those used for researching medical equipment. For medical equipment, the researcher will probably gather additional data on health care expenditures, number of physicians per capita, and number of hospital beds per-capita. Firms in the financial services sector will require specific data on commercial risk. In addition, depending on the industry, researchers may apply different *weights* to each market-potential indicator. For example, population size is relatively less important for a firm that markets yachts than for one that sells footwear. Each firm must assign appropriate weights to each indicator, depending on its specific circumstances.

Screening Countries for Direct Investment and Global Sourcing

The discussion so far has taken the perspective of a firm seeking the best country markets for exporting. However, firms internationalize through other entry modes as well—such as FDI—to set up production and assembly facilities abroad, and to source goods from foreign suppliers. While the goal of delineating a handful of prospective countries remains the same in these entry modes, the researcher may employ a different set of criteria for country screening. Let's discuss how the desirable country attributes differ for FDI and global sourcing.

Country Screening for Foreign Direct Investment FDI amounts to investing in physical assets, such as a factory, marketing subsidiary, or regional headquarters, in a foreign country. Such investments are usually undertaken for the long term. Accordingly, the types of variables to consider differ from those appropriate for export entry. For example, the availability in the target market of skilled labor and managerial talent are relatively more important to consider for FDI entry than exporting. Researchers identifying the best locations for FDI entry would normally consider the following variables:

- Long-term prospects for growth
- Cost of doing business: potential attractiveness of the country based on the cost and availability of commercial infrastructure, tax rates and wages, access to high-level skills and capital markets
- Country risk: regulatory, financial, political, and cultural barriers, and the legal environment for intellectual property protection
- Competitive environment: intensity of competition from local and foreign firms
- Government incentives: availability of tax holidays, subsidized training, grants, or low-interest loans

As in the case of screening countries for export opportunities, there are several sources of publicly accessible studies for screening countries for FDI. A useful resource is provided by the United Nations Conference on Trade and Development (UNCTAD). UNCTAD's *FDI Indices* methodology benchmarks both FDI performance and potential, ranking countries by how well they perform as recipients or originators of FDI (www.unctad.org). Another resource is provided by the consulting firm, A. T. Kearney, which prepares an annual *Foreign Direct Investment Confidence Index*, (www.atkearney.com). The index tracks how political, economic, and regulatory changes affect the FDI intentions and preferences of the world's top 1,000 firms. By surveying executives at these firms, the index captures the most important variables to consider from the 65 countries that receive more than 90 percent of global FDI investments.

Exhibit 12.4 displays the results of the A. T. Kearney Index. The index reveals that advanced economies in western Europe, as well as Australia, Japan, and the United States, possess high investor confidence. In other words, firms prefer these locations for making FDI-based investments. These locations are popular due to their relative size and business-friendly infrastructure. The advanced economies engage in substantial cross-investments in each other's markets. For example,

Europe and the United States are each others' most important partners for FDI. Their transatlantic economy represents over $2.5 trillion in total foreign affiliate sales, and it mutually supports nearly a quarter of the world's entire foreign affiliate workforce employed by MNEs abroad.

Note that of the top ten destinations in the A. T. Kearney Index, six are emerging markets: China, India, Poland, Russia, Brazil, and Hong Kong. Investors prefer China because of its huge size, fast-growing consumer market, and position as an excellent site for low-cost manufacturing. China also enjoys superior access to export markets, favorable government incentives, low-cost structure, and a stable macroeconomic climate. However, executives see India as the world's leader for business process and outsourcing IT services. India has a highly educated workforce, strong managerial talent, established rule of law, and transparent transactions and rules.

Country Screening for Global Sourcing Global sourcing and offshoring refer to the procurement of finished products, intermediate goods, and services from suppliers located abroad. Sourcing is critically important to all types of firms. As with FDI decisions, the types of screening variables managers consider in sourcing are often distinct from those they consider for exporting. When seeking foreign sources of supply, managers will examine such factors as cost and quality of inputs, stability of exchange rates, reliability of suppliers, and the presence of a work force with superior technical skills.

A. T. Kearney also prepares an annual *Offshore Location Attractiveness Index* (www.atkearney.com). This index assists managers to understand and compare the factors that make countries attractive as potential locations for offshoring of service activities such as IT, business processes, and call centers. A. T. Kearney evaluates countries across 39 criteria, categorized into three dimensions:

- *Financial structure* takes into account compensation costs (for example, average wages), infrastructure costs (for electricity and telecom systems), and tax and regulatory costs (such as tax burden, corruption, and fluctuating exchange rates).

- *People skills and availability* accounts for a supplier's experience and skills, labor-force availability, education and linguistic proficiency, and employee-attrition rates.

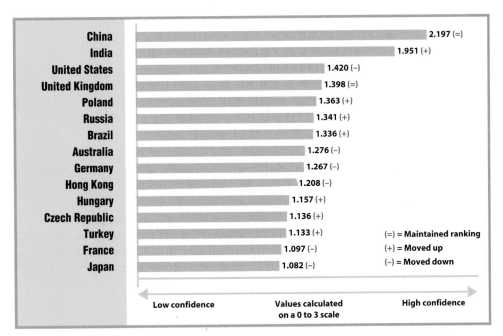

Exhibit 12.4

A. T. Kearney Foreign Direct Investment Confidence Index

SOURCE: Copyright © A.T. Kearney, 2005. All rights reserved. Reprinted with permission.

China   2.197 (=)
India   1.951 (+)
United States 1.420 (−)
United Kingdom 1.398 (=)
Poland   1.363 (+)
Russia   1.341 (+)
Brazil   1.336 (+)
Australia   1.276 (−)
Germany   1.267 (−)
Hong Kong   1.208 (−)
Hungary   1.157 (+)
Czech Republic 1.136 (+)
Turkey   1.133 (+)
France   1.097 (−)
Japan   1.082 (−)

(=) = Maintained ranking
(+) = Moved up
(−) = Moved down

Low confidence   Values calculated on a 0 to 3 scale   High confidence

- *Business environment* assesses economic and political aspects of the country, commercial infrastructure, cultural adaptability, and security of intellectual property.

Exhibit 12.5 presents the *Offshore Location Attractiveness Index.* Note that 9 of the top 10 countries in the index are emerging markets, such as India, China, and Brazil. Although important, the cost of labor is only one of several factors in the decision to source inputs from abroad. Managers also cite productivity level, technical skills, and customer service skills as important factors. The index credits India and China (and to a lesser extent Russia and the Philippines) for educational achievement. Among developed economies, the index credits New Zealand, Canada, and Ireland with other strengths, such as highly developed infrastructure, English fluency, low country risk, and high degree of global integration.

 Task Four: Assess Industry Market Potential

The methods for screening countries discussed so far are most useful for gaining comparative insights into individual markets and for reducing the complexity of choosing appropriate foreign locations. Once the number of potential countries has been reduced to a manageable number—say five or six—the next step is to conduct in-depth analysis of each of these country markets. Rather than examining broad, macro-level indicators, as done in earlier stages, the researcher narrows

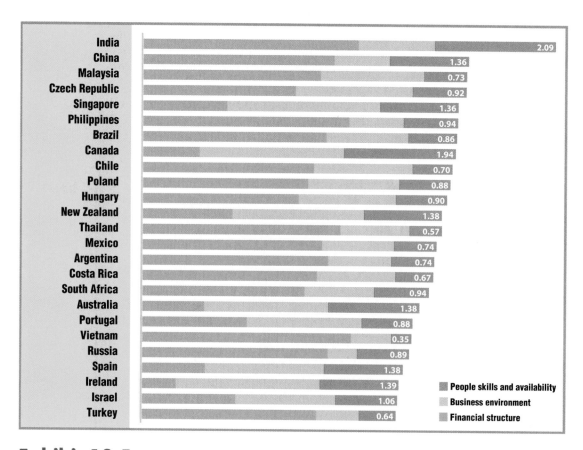

	Index value
India	2.09
China	1.36
Malaysia	0.73
Czech Republic	0.92
Singapore	1.36
Philippines	0.94
Brazil	0.86
Canada	1.94
Chile	0.70
Poland	0.88
Hungary	0.90
New Zealand	1.38
Thailand	0.57
Mexico	0.74
Argentina	0.74
Costa Rica	0.67
South Africa	0.94
Australia	1.38
Portugal	0.88
Vietnam	0.35
Russia	0.89
Spain	1.38
Ireland	1.39
Israel	1.06
Turkey	0.64

People skills and availability
Business environment
Financial structure

Exhibit 12.5 A. T. Kearney's Offshore Location Attractiveness Index

SOURCE: Copyright © A.T. Kearney, 2006. All rights reserved. Reprinted with permission.

the focus to examine *industry-level* market potential indicators, because market potential is industry specific.

In task four, the researcher estimates the current and future levels of sales expected for the particular industry as a whole. This is termed **industry market potential**—an estimate of the likely sales that can be expected for all firms in the particular industry for a specified period of time. In other words, it is an aggregate of the sales that may be realized by all companies in the industry. Industry market potential is different from *company sales potential*, which refers to the share of industry sales the focal firm itself can expect to achieve during a given year. Most firms forecast sales at least three years into the future, of both industry market potential and company sales potential.

Estimating industry market potential enables the manager to refine the analysis and identify the most attractive countries for the firm's product or service. By examining country-level characteristics more closely at this stage, the manager is able to decide which countries to retain for subsequent analysis of company sales potential. In addition to gaining industry-specific insights into the select markets, managers will be able to formulate an understanding of the degree to which the firm needs to adapt its product and marketing approaches.

To develop an estimate of industry market potential, managers need data and insights on the following variables:

- Market size, growth rate, and trends in the specific industry
- Tariff and nontariff trade barriers to enter the market
- Standards and regulations that affect the industry
- Availability and sophistication of local distribution
- Unique customer requirements and preferences
- Industry-specific market potential indicators

In addition to generic determinants of demand, each industry sector—from fire alarms to zippers—has its own *industry-specific potential indicators* or *distinctive drivers of demand.* Marketers of cameras, for instance, examine climate-related factors such as the average number of sunny days in a typical year, given that most pictures are taken outdoors. In marketing laboratory equipment, the researcher might examine data on the number of hospitals, clinics, hospital beds, and doctors, as well as the level of governmental expenditures on health care. A manufacturer of electric generators might examine the rate of industrialization and dependence on hydroelectricity. A marketer of cooling equipment and industrial filters will consider the number of institutional buyers, such as restaurants and hotels. These are all industry-specific market potential indicators.

Managers also evaluate factors that affect the marketing and use of the product, such as consumer characteristics, culture, distribution channels, and business practices. Intellectual property rights and enforcement vary around the world. Managers should therefore evaluate regulations, trademarks, and product liability, and formulate strategies for protecting the firm's critical assets. The researcher should also ascertain the existence and nature of subsidy and incentive programs, from home and foreign governments, that the firm can access to obtain capital and to reduce the cost of foreign market entry.

A key question is whether industry market growth has been consistent from year to year. In addition to large, fast-growing markets, the researcher should identify some smaller but fast-emerging markets that may provide ground-floor opportunities. There are fewer competitors in markets that are opening for the first time. For example, most of the 60,000 pubs in the United Kingdom have recently come under the ownership of big chains, which are injecting substantial capital and trying to attract new clientele by serving food, a shift that will greatly

Industry market potential
An estimate of the likely sales that can be expected for all firms in the particular industry for a specified period of time.

More British pubs are serving food, creating a new market potential for firms in the food catering industry.

increase opportunities for firms in the restaurant food industry. The market research firm Mintel International estimated that food sales to British pubs will increase several billion dollars through the late 2000s. This represents a big change in British pub culture and a large new market for firms in the food industry.[9]

Growth rates tend to be substantially higher in new industries or those undergoing rapid innovation. For each country, the researcher should bear in mind that the product is likely to be in a different phase of its product life cycle. Countries in which the product is not currently available or in which competitors have only recently introduced the product may be especially promising targets.

Practical Methods for Managers to Assess Industry Market Potential

Managers can use a variety of practical methods to estimate industry market potential:

- *Simple trend analysis.* This method quantifies the total likely amount of industry market potential by examining aggregate production for the industry as a whole, adding imports from abroad and deducting exports. This gives a rough estimate of the size of the current industry sales in the country.

- *Monitoring key industry-specific indicators.* The manager examines unique industry drivers of market demand by collecting data from a variety of sources. For example, Caterpillar, a manufacturer of earthmoving equipment, examines the volume of announced construction projects, number of issued building permits, growth rate of households, infrastructure development, and other pertinent leading indicators as a way of anticipating countrywide sales of its construction equipment.[10]

- *Monitoring key competitors.* To gain insights into the potential of a particular country, the manager investigates the degree of major competitor activity in the countries of interest. For example, if Caterpillar is considering Chile as a potential market, he or she investigates the current involvement in Chile of its number one competitor, the Japanese firm Komatsu. Caterpillar gathers competitive intelligence to anticipate Komatsu's likely future moves.

- *Following key customers around the world.* Using this approach, the firm follows its major accounts as they enter new markets. Automotive suppliers can anticipate where their services will be needed next by monitoring the international expansion of their customers, such as Honda or Mercedes Benz. Similarly, Caterpillar follows current customers in the construction industry (such as Bechtel) as these customers bid for contracts or establish operations in specific foreign markets.

- *Tapping into supplier networks.* Many suppliers serve multiple clients and can be a major source of information about competitors. Firms can gain valuable leads from current suppliers by inquiring with them about competitor activities.

- *Attending international trade fairs.* Industry trade fairs and exhibitions are excellent venues for managers to obtain a wide range of information on potential foreign markets. By attending a trade fair in the target country, a manager can learn a great deal about market characteristics that can help to estimate industry sales potential. Trade fairs are also helpful for identifying potential distributors and other business partners.

Data Sources for Estimating Industry Market Potential

For each target country, the manager seeks data that directly or indirectly report levels of industry sales and production, as well as the intensity of exports and imports in the product category of interest. A particularly useful information source is the National Trade Data Base (NTDB), available from the U.S. Department of Commerce's STAT-USA[11] and www.export.gov databases. Specific reports available from the NTDB include the following:

- *Best Market Reports* identify the top ten country markets for specific industry sectors.
- *Country Commercial Guides* analyze countries' economic and commercial environments.
- *Industry Sector Analysis Reports* analyze market potential for sectors such as telecommunications.
- *International Market Insight Reports* cover country and product-specific topics, providing various ideas for approaching markets of interest.

In developing market estimates of any kind, managers must be creative and must consult any resource that may shed light on the task at hand. Data and resources are rarely complete and precise in international market research. Consider the example of Teltone Inc. The firm wished to enter Mexico with its inexpensive brand of cellular telephones and needed to estimate industry-wide demand. It consulted numerous sources, including reports by the International Telecommunications Union (in Geneva, Switzerland), the *National Trade Data Bank,* and several United Nations publications. Managers researched the size of the Mexican upper class and its average income, the nature of support infrastructure for cellular systems in Mexico, and the nature and number of retail stores that could handle cell phones. Teltone managers also came across some statistics from the National Telecommunications Trade Association on the number of competitors already active in Mexico and their approximate sales volumes. From these sources, the company was able to arrive at a rough estimate of market size for telephones and prevailing prices in Mexico.

The *Recent Grad in IB* feature on the next page profiles Javier Estrada, who found exciting opportunities in his young career in international market research.

 ## Task Five: Select Foreign Business Partners

As we discussed in Chapter 3, business partners are critical to the success of the focal firm in international business. These partners include distribution-channel intermediaries, facilitators, suppliers, and collaborative venture partners, such as joint venture partners, licensees, and franchisees. Once a target market has been selected, the focal firm needs to decide on the type of partners it needs for its foreign-market venture. It also needs to identify suitable partner candidates, negotiate the terms of its relationship with chosen partners, and support as well as monitor the conduct of chosen partners. The firm's success depends on its ability to perform these tasks well.

There are many examples of partnering in international business. Exporters tend to collaborate with foreign-market intermediaries such as distributors and agents. Firms that choose to sell their intellectual property, such as know-how, trademarks, and copyrights, tend to work through foreign licensees. These

Javier Estrada graduated from a state university several years ago with a bachelor's degree in business. Upon graduation, Javier went to work for the United Nations World Food Programme (WFP) in Guatemala and Honduras. Fluent in Spanish, Javier was the youngest U.N. officer in Latin America. He was given the task of monitoring the functioning and execution of all WFP projects. The experience taught Javier about international management and logistics in the high-pressure environment of the various disasters the United Nations faced in Central America.

Ever adventurous, Javier next moved to the Dominican Republic, where, at the age of 24, he took a position as director of research in the local office of Bates Advertising, a global ad agency that handled accounts such as Wendy's, Purina, and Bell South. In this position, Javier investigated the local target market—how the market responded to key brands, the level of market share, and the most effective way of reaching target markets with advertising and other marketing communications tools. According to Javier, "the real challenge in international advertising is not in the large, established brands, but in the small, poorly positioned one."

A typical day for Javier included meetings with colleagues to discuss the progress of market research projects and assessing the next steps on behalf of his clients. Javier implemented consumer surveys to find out what specific benefits Latin American consumers were seeking. He used the information from this research to craft advertising campaigns ideally tailored to customer needs and attitudes. In creating surveys, Javier researched various secondary data sources on the Internet and in Bates' private library. He visited

Santa Domingo to get a more authentic feel for the market and to meet with local experts. He also used a comprehensive report prepared by the United States Department of Commerce International Trade Administration (ITA) on the target market.

Javier developed Spanish-language questionnaires to gain an even deeper understanding of the market. Javier sent out questionnaires to a random sample of typical consumers throughout the Dominican Republic. He then analyzed the completed questionnaires and presented the results to his superiors. Findings from these studies helped Javier prepare reports with recommendations on the most appropriate advertising strategies for the Dominican Republic.

Success Factors

"My parents felt strongly that our lives should be influenced not only by the quality of our education, but also by our travels. . . . In school we were far from the wealthiest kids, but we were definitely among the most traveled." Javier was lucky enough to live in several countries during his teens and twenties. He comments: "You really get to know yourself when you are completely alone in a whole new culture, and reestablishing a network of friends and work contacts." International experience contributed to Javier's independent spirit and his ability to function successfully anywhere in the world.

In his market research position, Javier enjoyed going to other countries and meeting different people.

"My job provided the chance to help companies develop marketing programs that were really appropriate for their customers. If you really understand your customer, you have tremendous responsibility to use the information

Javier's major: Business

Objectives: Integrating business skills with social planning in a public agency and pursuing a career in politics

Jobs held since graduating:

- United Nations World Food Programme in Guatemala and Honduras
- Director of Research, Bates Advertising, Dominican Republic
- Director of a major charity in Mexico

wisely and honestly. . . . Of course, I wouldn't have received the job if I hadn't worked hard in school. Good management training provided me with the skills to perform effectively. Sensitivity is important, since you need to be able to communicate with people who are culturally different from you. You need a strong empathy for your customers, and you need to try to identify exactly which research questions they are trying to address. . . ."

What's Ahead?

Javier has ever-higher goals for his career. He has been long concerned about poverty issues in Latin America, and his experiences with the United Nations had a profound effect on him. Javier pursued a master's degree in social policy and planning from the London School of Economics. Having worked in both business and development, Javier found his passion in integrating his business skills with social planning at the governmental level. Recently, Javier headed a major charity organization in Mexico. Eventually he wants to pursue a political career. He says, "I need to dream big."

licensing partners are independent businesses that apply intellectual property to produce products in their own country. In the case of internationalization through **franchising**, the foreign partner is a franchisee—an independent business abroad that acquires rights and skills from the focal firm to conduct operations in its own market (such as in the fast-food or car-rental industries). Alternatively, the focal firm may internationalize by initiating an **international collaborative venture**, which entails business initiatives undertaken jointly with other local or international partners. These collaborations may be project-based or may involve equity investments. Other types of international business partnerships include global sourcing, contract manufacturing, and supplier partnerships. We describe these partnerships in greater detail in Chapters 13 through 16.

Criteria for Selecting a Partner

Perhaps the most important decision for the focal firm is to identify the ideal qualifications of potential foreign partners. In general, the firm should seek a good fit in terms of both strategy (common goals and objectives) and resources (complementary core competencies and value-chain activities). It is helpful to anticipate the potential degree of synergy with the prospective partner for the intermediate-term, say 3 to 6 years into the future. Managers must be assured of a harmonious partnership in a dynamic environment.

Brunswick Corporation, a leading manufacturer of bowling equipment, considers the following criteria when screening for potential foreign distributors:

- Financially sound and resourceful, so that they can invest in the venture and ensure their future growth
- Competent and professional management, with qualified technical and sales staff
- Willing and able to invest in the focal firm's business and grow the business
- Possessing a good knowledge of the industry, and has access to distribution channels and end-users
- Known in the marketplace and well-connected with local government (as political clout is helpful especially in emerging markets)
- Committed and loyal in the long run

Firms also seek partners with complementary expertise. For example, while the focal firm may bring engineering and manufacturing expertise to the partnership, the local distributor may bring knowledge of local customers and distribution channels.

These and similarly desirable characteristics are not always available in prospective partners. If a company enters a foreign market late, then it may have to pick the second best or an even less-qualified partner. This implies that the firm should be ready and able to strengthen the partner's capabilities by transferring appropriate managerial and technical know-how over time.

Searching for Prospective Partners

The process of screening and evaluating business partners can be overwhelming. It is an ongoing task for most internationally-active firms. To identify prospective partners and gather background information, managers

Licensing Arrangement where the owner of intellectual property grants a firm the right to use that property for a specified period of time in exchange for royalties or other compensation.

Franchising Arrangement whereby the focal firm allows another the right to use an entire business system in exchange for fees, royalties, or other forms of compensation.

International collaborative venture Cross-border business alliance where partnering firms pool their resources and share costs and risks to undertake a new business initiative. Also referred to as an international partnership or an international strategic alliance.

Firms seeking a foreign business partner look for a variety of qualifications, including common goals and objectives and competent management.

consult various sources as well as conduct field research. Commercial banks, consulting firms, trade journals, and industry magazines, as well as country and regional business directories, such as *Kompass* (Europe) and *Dun and Bradstreet* are very helpful in developing a list of partner candidates. Many national governments offer inexpensive services that assist firms in finding partners in specific foreign markets. The knowledge portal globalEDGE™ (www.globalEDGE.msu.edu) provides additional resources, including several diagnostic tools, to help managers make systematic choices about alternative partner candidates.

Field research through onsite visits and gathering research from independent sources and trade fairs are crucial in the early stages of assessing a partner. Companies also find it useful to ask prospective partners to prepare a formal business plan before entering into an agreement. The quality and sophistication of such a plan provides insights into the capabilities of the prospective partner and serves as a test of the partner's commitment.

 Task Six: Estimate Company Sales Potential

Once managers have singled out several promising country markets, verified industry market potential, and assessed the availability of qualified business partners, the next step is to estimate company sales potential in each country. **Company sales potential** is an estimate of the share of annual industry sales that the firm expects to generate in a particular target market. Estimating company sales potential is often much more challenging than earlier tasks. It requires the researcher to obtain highly refined information from the market. The researcher needs to make certain fundamental assumptions about the market and project the firm's revenues and expenses for 3 to 5 years into the future. The estimates are never precise and require quite a bit of judgmental analysis.

Company sales potential An estimate of the share of annual industry sales that the firm expects to generate in a particular target market.

Determinants of Company Sales Potential

In arriving at an estimate of company sales potential in the foreign market, managers will collect and review various research findings and assess the following:

- *Partner capabilities.* The competencies and resources of foreign partners, including channel intermediaries and facilitators, tend to determine how quickly the firm can enter and generate sales in the target market.

- *Access to distribution channels.* The ability to establish and make best use of channel intermediaries and distribution infrastructure in the target market determines how much sales the firm can achieve.

- *Intensity of the competitive environment.* Local or third-country competitors are likely to intensify their own marketing efforts when confronted by new entrants. Their actions are often unpredictable and not easily observed.

- *Pricing and financing of sales.* The degree to which pricing and financing are attractive to both customers and channel members is critical to initial entry and to ultimate success.

- *Human and financial resources.* The quality and quantity of the firm's resources are a major factor in determining the proficiency and speed with which success can be achieved in the market.

- *Market penetration timetable.* A key decision is whether managers opt for gradual or rapid market entry. Gradual entry gives the firm time to develop and leverage appropriate resources and strategies, but may cede some advantages to competitors in getting established in the market.

Rapid entry may allow the firm to surpass competitors and obtain first-mover advantages, but it can tax the firm's resources and capabilities.

- *Risk tolerance of senior managers.* Results are a function of the level of resources that top management is willing to commit, which in turn depend on the extent of management's tolerance for risk in the market.
- *Special links, contacts, and capabilities of the firm.* The extent of the focal firm's network in the market—its existing relationships with customers, channel members, and suppliers—can have a strong effect on venture success.
- *Reputation.* The firm can succeed faster in the market if target customers are already familiar with its brand name and reputation.

Such a comprehensive assessment should lead to general estimates of potential sales, which managers can compare to actual sales results of incumbent firms in the market, when such data are available.

Thus, the process of estimating company sales is more like starting from multiple angles, then converging on an ultimate estimate that relies heavily on judgment. Exhibit 12.6 provides one framework managers may use to estimate company sales. Managers would combine information about customers, intermediaries, and competition, and see if such an analysis points to a reasonable estimate. Often, managers prepare multiple estimates based on best case, worst case, and most-likely case scenarios. Note also that arriving at such estimates will require assumptions from the manager as to the degree of firm effort, price aggressiveness, possible competitive reactions, degree of intermediary effort, and so on. Finally, note that sales prospects for a company hinges on factors both controllable by management (e.g., prices charged to intermediaries and customers), as well as uncontrollable factors (e.g., intensity of competition). Ultimately, the process of arriving at a sales estimate is more of an art than a science.

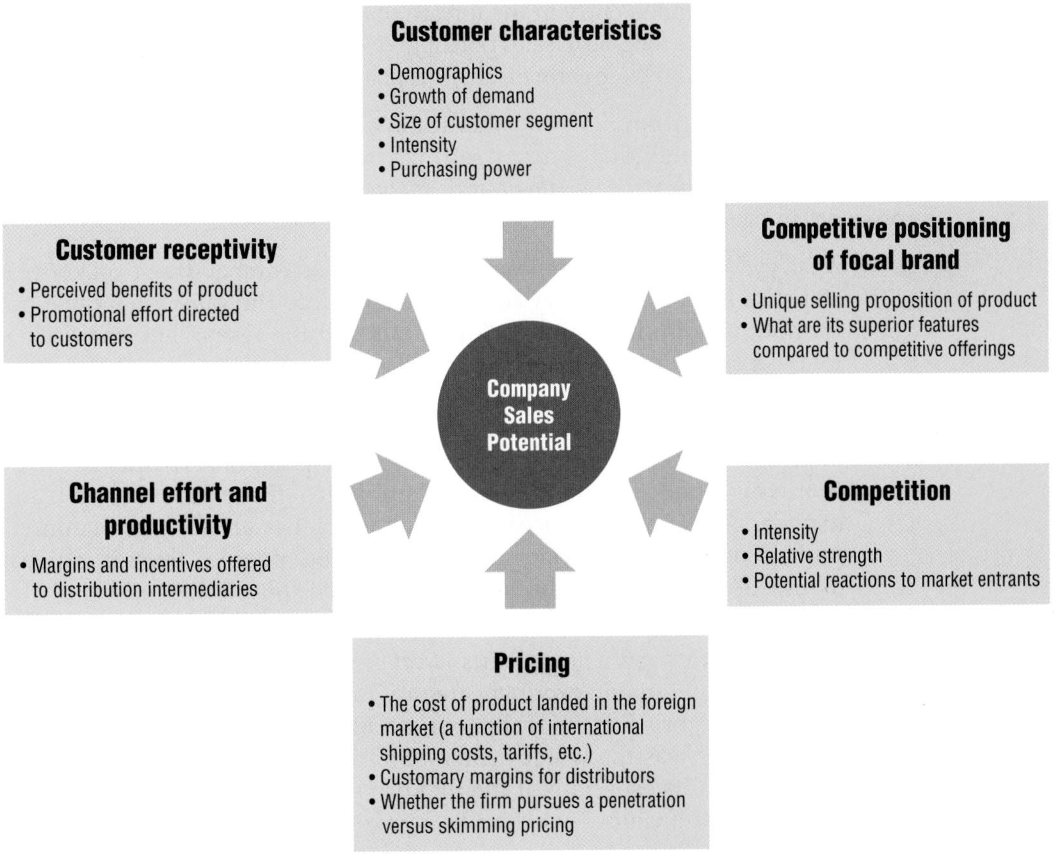

Exhibit 12.6

A Framework for Estimating Company Sales Potential in the Foreign Market

Customer characteristics
- Demographics
- Growth of demand
- Size of customer segment
- Intensity
- Purchasing power

Customer receptivity
- Perceived benefits of product
- Promotional effort directed to customers

Channel effort and productivity
- Margins and incentives offered to distribution intermediaries

Company Sales Potential

Competitive positioning of focal brand
- Unique selling proposition of product
- What are its superior features compared to competitive offerings

Competition
- Intensity
- Relative strength
- Potential reactions to market entrants

Pricing
- The cost of product landed in the foreign market (a function of international shipping costs, tariffs, etc.)
- Customary margins for distributors
- Whether the firm pursues a penetration versus skimming pricing

Practical Approaches to Estimating Company Sales Potential

It is critical for managers to begin with the factors suggested in Exhibit 12.6. In addition, experienced managers find the following activities to be especially helpful in estimating company sales potential in a foreign market:

- *Survey of end-users and intermediaries.* The firm can survey a sample of customers and distributors to determine the level of potential sales.

- *Trade audits.* Managers may visit retail outlets and question channel members to assess relative price levels of competitors' offerings and perceptions of competitor strength. In this approach, managers estimate market potential through the eyes of the trade (intermediaries) responsible for handling the product in the market. The trade audit can also indicate opportunities for new modes of distribution, identify types of alternative outlets, and provide insights into company standing relative to competitors.

- *Competitor assessment.* The firm may benchmark itself against principal competitor(s) in the market and estimate the level of sales it can potentially attract away from them. What rival firms will have to be outperformed? If key competitors in a given market are large, powerful firms, competing head-on could prove costly and lead to failure. Keep in mind, however, that even in those countries dominated by large firms, research may reveal market segments that are underserved or ignored altogether. Such market niches may be attractive, particularly for smaller firms with modest sales goals.

- *Obtaining estimates from local partners.* Collaborators such as distributors, franchisees, or licensees already experienced in the market are often best positioned to develop estimates of market share and sales potential.

- *Limited marketing efforts to test the waters.* Some companies may choose to engage in a limited entry in the foreign market—a sort of test market—as a way of gauging long-term sales potential or gaining a better understanding of the market. From these early results, it is possible to forecast longer-term sales.

In addition to these approaches, other techniques are also useful in the developing-country and emerging-market settings, where information sources are especially limited. These are *analogy* and *proxy indicators.* We illustrated these approaches in the opening vignette.

- *Analogy.* When using the *analogy* method, the researcher draws on known statistics from one country to gain insights into the same phenomenon for another, similar country. For instance, if the researcher knows the total consumption of citrus drinks in India, then—assuming that citrus-drink consumption patterns do not vary much in neighboring Pakistan—a rough estimate of Pakistan's consumption can be made, making an adjustment, of course, for the difference in population. Another illustration would be for the marketer of antibiotics. If the firm knows from experience that X number of bottles of antibiotics are sold in a country with Y number of physicians per thousand people, then it can be assumed that the same ratio (of bottles per 1,000 physicians) will apply in a similar country.

- *Proxy indicators.* By using *proxy indicators,* the researcher uses information known about one product category to infer potential about another product category. For the wallpaper marketer in the opening vignette, a useful proxy was the water heaters. This simple approach may lead to practical results especially if the two products exhibit a complementary demand relationship. For example, a proxy indicator of demand for professional hand tools in a country may be the level of construction activity in the country. Surrogate indicators of potential for a particular piece of surgical equipment in a market may include the total number of surgeries performed.

 # In Conclusion

The decision to internationalize is never easy. Some firms are attracted to foreign markets by the promise of revenues and profits; others are drawn by the prospect to increase production efficiency; still others internationalize due to competitive pressures or to keep pace with rivals. Whatever the rationale, when companies fail in their international business ventures, it is often because they neglect to conduct a systematic and comprehensive assessment of global market opportunity.

Although we present the six tasks for global market opportunity assessment in a sequential manner, firms do not necessarily pursue them in succession. Indeed, firms often pursue two or more of the tasks simultaneously. In addition, the process is highly dynamic. Market conditions change, partner performance may fluctuate, and competitive intensity will increase. These dynamic events require managers to constantly evaluate their decisions and commitments. Management must be open to making course changes as circumstances dictate.

Of the six key tasks, some of the choices that managers will make are interrelated. For example, the choice of a business partner is very much a function of the country. The type of distributor to use is likely to vary from market to market, be it the Netherlands or Nigeria. The degree of political risk firms can expect in the latter case implies a need for a politically well-connected business partner. Similarly, in a nontraditional market such as Vietnam, the firm may opt for a partner who can serve both as a distributor and cultural adviser.

The local business partner is crucial to the success of the cross-border venture. Seasoned executives contend that even the most attractive country cannot compensate for a poor partner. While the quantity and quality of market information about individual countries have increased substantially, most managers tend to struggle in their ability to identify qualified and interested business partners. This is especially true in emerging markets that may lack an abundance of competent and professional intermediaries, suppliers, joint venture partners, or facilitators. The most qualified partners are likely to be already subscribed and representing other foreign firms. This necessitates the recruitment of second- or even third-best candidates, and then committing adequate resources to upgrade their technical and managerial skills.

CLOSING CASE

Advanced Biomedical Devices: Assessing Readiness to Export

Advanced Biomedical Devices, Inc. (ABD), is headquartered in Maryland, and plans to initiate exporting activities. The company just completed the process of assessing its readiness to export, using CORE (COmpany Readiness to Export). ABD was founded by Dr. Richard Bentley, a well-known British surgeon who developed a medical device that helps the wound-healing process. Dr. Bentley was so committed to the ground-breaking technology that he left his surgery practice and founded ABD in the United States. ABD's product line includes several innovative devices called Speedheal, named because of their ability to accelerate the healing rate of wounds following surgery. Speedheal also reduces post-surgery pain because it keeps the wound area from swelling. Speedheal oxygenates the wound area by pulsing electrons through the bandage covering the wound. The devices are very small and portable. Various versions exist for different types of surgeries: hand surgery, face lifts, abdominal procedures, and so on.

Dr. Bentley launched ABD with a skillful management team. The team includes managers who have worked extensively in the European market and have traveled and worked periodically in the Pacific Rim and Latin America. In addition, ABD's manufacturing director is from Germany, and another manager had lived in France and Malaysia for several years.

Substantial demand for Speedheal helped to rapidly increase sales, approaching 20 percent annual growth in some years. Over time, employment at ABD grew to 85 people and sales expanded, primarily through medical product distributors, to hospitals and clinics throughout the United States. The firm's success had stimulated the entry of competitors offering similar products, but rivals never achieved the degree of miniaturization in ABD's products. Miniaturization remains one of Speedheal's competitive advantages. ABD management's projections for future growth remain promising.

Dreams of International Expansion

Top management turned its thoughts to internationalization and generating sales outside of the United States. ABD had received unsolicited orders from abroad and had learned a great deal about handling international transactions, including foreign exchange, letters of credit, and logistics. While ABD's plan to internationalize was in its early stages, management intended to expand beyond occasional export sales. The long-term motivation was to target key world markets.

One expected benefit of internationalization was the opportunity for ABD to learn from global competitors and markets. Many trends that start in foreign markets eventually reach the United States, and often the best way to track them is to do business internationally. Management also believed it could reduce ABD's overall risks by selling to a variety of foreign markets. Finally, management believed that by internationalizing, competitors with similar products could be preempted in specific foreign markets.

International Strategic Intent

Dr. Bentley and his management team formulated some questions about ABD's internationalization decision. They knew that the answers to these questions would represent the company's first real strategic direction for going international, ABD's strategic intent. Management wanted to develop a comprehensive strategic plan that would lay the foundation for international success. Following a series of meetings, the team reached consensus on the following key elements of ABD's initial strategic direction:

- Top management will strongly commit to internationalization, and ABD will pursue foreign markets aggressively. The firm will hire a vice president for international operations within the coming year.

- ABD will invest up to 20 percent of the firm's earnings in export opportunities.

- ABD will begin building distributor relationships in a number of countries.

- ABD will establish a marketing subsidiary in at least one foreign location within three to five years, and hire sales personnel who select and manage the distributors in their market area.

- Management will take steps to ensure that all international ventures reach profitability within two years of their launch.

- Management will develop international marketing plans for each target market, each with its own budget.

- Plans call for international sales to reach 35 percent of total sales within four years.

- ABD will establish an annual budget of $220,000 to finance international activities for each of the first three years. Of that, about $60,000 will be devoted to market research to determine the best target markets and to understand competitors.

Product Readiness for Export

Following approval of the strategic intent, Dr. Bentley and his management team addressed questions about the challenges of internationalization. The first question dealt with training sales representatives in foreign markets to sell medical devices to hospitals and clinics, the primary end-markets for ABD products. Sales reps require training because they deal with doctors, nurses, and other professionals who are deeply involved in decision making about purchases of hospital supplies. Because training costs can be high in foreign markets, Dr. Bentley wanted to ensure ABD was prepared to make this investment as part of succeeding abroad.

Dr. Bentley also raised the issue of after-sales service. Because ABD's products were seldom defective, the solution for a defective product was to replace it rather than trying to make a repair. U.S. customers counted on a ready backup stock in the event of product defects. ABD planned to employ the same solution for its foreign operations, and management assumed there would be no need for a separate staff to deal with after-sales service. Because Speedheal devices are small and lightweight but valuable, per-unit transportation costs are very low. In fact, in urgent situations abroad, ABD often solved customer service complaints by shipping a replacement device by air.

Eventually, the management team came to realize that pricing for foreign markets was complex and would require substantial market research. While pricing in the United States was well understood, management realized there was much it did not know about foreign pricing. Dr. Bentley and several managers had attended trade fairs in Europe and had concluded that ABD's prices were not too expensive, particularly since no other firms offered similar wound-healing products. In fact, ABD had filled unsolicited orders from the European Union and found that customers never challenged its pricing. Nevertheless, management decided that some research was needed to refine their pricing approach.

Next, the team discussed foreign inventory management. Because the devices are cheap to transport by air freight, distributors can replenish inventories quickly and economically. This was a significant benefit to distributors, on the one hand, because they would not have to maintain much inventory to support sales. On the other hand, Speedheal devices are sensitive to changes in temperature and humidity, and function best when warehoused in climate-controlled facilities. Such warehousing is increasingly common, so ABD should have no problem locating the right warehousing in Europe and elsewhere.

ABD's management realized that the firm's flexible packaging put them in a good position to enter foreign markets, and they were prepared to modify the product in various ways that might be required for foreign markets.

Management instinctively understood the importance of designing products that meet worldwide standards and regulations. The team knew, for example, that products targeted to Europe would have to meet two standards: the CE mark, a mandatory safety mark required of toys, machinery, and low-voltage equipment; and ISO standards, aimed at making the development, manufacturing, and supply of products and services efficient, safe, and clean.

Knowledge, Skills, and Resources

In a subsequent meeting, the ABD team considered less-tangible aspects of the firm's readiness to internationalize. Management knew that critical self-assessment was vital to the long-term success of the firm. They gradually realized that internationalization would incur numerous additional costs. For example, they needed additional working capital for foreign warehousing, longer shipping times, and maintaining larger inventories abroad. While letters of credit would be used when first opening new markets, management would opt for open-account payment systems (payable in 30 or 60 days, depending on the market).

Dr. Bentley also considered the appropriate growth rate for the firm. Management knew of companies that began exporting but were interrupted when foreign demand grew too quickly, or when an imbalance developed between domestic and international sales. In some cases, a company's business could increase rapidly, demanding the firm to supply a volume of product that greatly exceeded production capacity. In other cases, the company's domestic sales dropped sharply, requiring management to divert all efforts to rescuing domestic operations, thus disrupting the export program.

Management had much to learn about the costs ABD would incur in getting into specific foreign markets. There would be costs for legal help, freight forwarding, international transportation, and customs duties. There would also be costs for bank charges, rental costs for establishing foreign offices, and expenses for getting approvals for certain regulatory issues. ABD's management was not completely clear on the amount of these costs, but they were willing to learn.

Competitive intelligence was another concern. In fact, another incentive for internationalization was to learn more about global competitors. While some of the major medical device manufacturers were marketing in the United States, others were based strictly abroad. ABD would have to research and understand the strategies and marketing practices of the important competitors. Dr. Bentley recognized the importance of getting patent coverage on his inventions around the world, and of protecting the intellectual property rights of his firm. He plans to retain legal counsel, at home and abroad, to ensure ABD's critical assets are protected from patent infringements. ABD plans to hire lawyers to develop suitable distribution and agent agreements, sales agreements, licensing, and to deal with local employment laws.

ABD's management believed the firm's initial foreign markets would be Australia, Canada, Western Europe, and Japan, because they have the largest proportion of affluent consumers with the ability to pay for sophisticated medical care. Therefore, ABD had gathered information about the markets and competition in those countries, but recognized that it needed to do much more.

Managerial Capabilities for Long-Term Internationalization

One concern was whether management would be able to cope with deepening internationalization. In the end, the ABD team recognized that, at minimum, they were right to take painstaking efforts to determine the firm's readiness to export. Extensive meetings and preliminary research provided the basis for developing initial strategies and action programs, as well as the basis for identifying improvements to make the company stronger in the coming months and years.

This case was written by Myron M. Miller, Michigan State University (retired), in association with Professor S. Tamer Cavusgil.

AACSB: Reflective Thinking, Analytical Skills
Case Questions

1. Do you believe that ABD's products are in a state of readiness to begin exporting to Europe? Why or why not? Are the products ready for exporting to emerging markets (e.g., China, Russia, Mexico) that may have little experience with the high-tech solutions afforded by Speedheal products? What factors suggest that Speedheal products might enjoy substantial demand in all types of foreign markets?

2. Does management at ABD possess the appropriate knowledge, skills, and capabilities for internationalization? Why or why not? What steps should management take to better prepare the firm, managers, and employees to internationalize?

3. Refer to Exhibit 12.1, "Key Tasks in Global Market Opportunity Assessment" on page 348. Evaluate if ABD accomplished each task well or poorly. Did ABD achieve each of the objectives set out for the tasks?

4. If you were a member of ABD's management team, what countries would you recommend that ABD target first? As a manager, you would need to justify your recommendation. Carry out an investigation by examining characteristics of specific countries to arrive at your recommendation. ◄

CHAPTER ESSENTIALS

Key Terms

company sales potential, p. 368
franchising, p. 367
global market opportunity, p. 346

industry market potential, p. 363
international collaborative venture,
  p. 367

licensing, p. 367

Summary

In this chapter, you learned about:

1. An overview of global market opportunity assessment

Global market opportunity assessment refers to a favorable combination of circumstances, locations, or timing that offer prospects for exporting, investing, sourcing, or partnering in foreign markets. The firm may perceive opportunities to sell, establish factories, obtain inputs of lower cost or superior quality, or enter collaborative arrangements with foreign partners that support the focal firm's goals. Global market opportunities help the firm improve its performance, often far beyond what it can achieve in the home market. Managers continuously seek the most relevant data and knowledge to make the most of international opportunities. This chapter discusses six key tasks that managers perform in defining and pursuing global market opportunities. See Exhibit 12.1 for a summary of these tasks.

2. Analysis of organizational readiness to internationalize

As the first task, management assesses the firm's readiness to internationalize. Similar to a SWOT analysis (that is, an evaluation of the firm's Strengths, Weaknesses, Opportunities, and Threats), management assesses the firm's strengths and weaknesses regarding its ability to do international business. Managers assess the *external* business environment by conducting formal research on the opportunities and threats that face the firm. The objective of assessing readiness to internationalize is to figure out what resources the firm has and the extent to which they are appropriate for successful international operations. The firm must develop resources that it lacks. Diagnostic tools, such as *CORE* (**CO***mpany* **R***eadiness to* **E***xport*), facilitate a self-audit of the firm's readiness to internationalize.

3. Assessment of the suitability of products and services for foreign markets

Products and services that are good candidates for marketing successfully abroad are those that sell well in the domestic market, cater to universal needs, address a need not well served in the target market, or address a new or emergent need abroad. Management should ask specific questions to determine the product's or service's international market potential. For example, who initiates purchasing in the market? Who uses the offering? Why do people buy it? Where is the product or service purchased? What economic, cultural, geographic, and other factors can limit sales?

4. Screening countries to identify target markets

Whether the firm is engaged in importing (sourcing from abroad), investing, or exporting, the choice of country is critical, particularly in the early stages of internationalization. Failure to choose the right markets is costly not only for its own sake, but also because of opportunity costs. The best markets are those that are large and fast-growing. The nature of information necessary for country screening varies by product type and industry. There are two basic methods for screening country markets: gradual elimination and ranking and indexing.

5. Assessment of industry market potential

Once a firm reduces the number of potential country targets to a manageable number—say five or six—the next step is to conduct in-depth analyses of each of these country markets. The researcher examines industry-level market potential indicators. **Industry market potential** refers to an estimate of the likely sales that can be expected for all firms in the particular industry for a specific period of time. An estimate of industry market potential enables the manager to hone in on a few most promising countries. In addition to generic determinants of demand, each industry sector has its own *industry-specific potential indicators*. Among the methods for assessing industry market potential are simple trend analysis, monitoring key industry-specific indicators, monitoring key competitors, following key customers around the world, tapping into supplier networks, and attending international trade fairs.

6. **Selection of foreign business partners**

   International business partners include distribution channel intermediaries, facilitators, suppliers, and collaborative venture partners such as joint venture partners, licensees, and franchisees. Management in the focal firm must decide the types of partners it needs, identify suitable partner candidates, negotiate the terms of relationships with chosen partners, and support as well as monitor the conduct of chosen partners.

7. **Estimation of company sales potential**

   Company sales potential refers to the share of annual industry sales that the firm can realistically achieve. It is the best estimate of how much the firm believes it can sell in the target market over a given time period. Estimating company sales potential requires the researcher to obtain highly refined information from the market. Among the most influential determinants of company sales potential are: partner capabilities, access to distribution channels in the target market, intensity of the competitive environment, pricing and financing of sales, quality of human and financial resources, the timetable for market entry, risk tolerance of senior managers, the firm's contacts and capabilities, and being well-known in the market.

Test Your Comprehension AACSB: **Reflective Thinking**

1. What is a global market opportunity? What opportunities do firms seek abroad?

2. Identify and explain the six major tasks that managers undertake in global market opportunity assessment.

3. Identify the major issues that managers consider when they perform a formal analysis of organizational readiness to internationalize.

4. What are the typical characteristics of products or services that have the best prospects for selling in foreign markets?

5. Summarize the screening methodology for potential country markets.

6. What are the typical variables used in indexing and ranking method?

7. What types of variables should the researcher consider when screening for export markets, foreign direct investment, and global sourcing?

8. What is involved in assessing industry market potential?

9. What are the major issues to consider when selecting foreign business partners?

10. How can firms go about estimating company sales potential?

Apply Your Understanding AACSB: **Communication, Reflective Thinking**

1. Target is a large retailer with about 1,500 stores in the United States, but very few in other countries. Target has a reputation for merchandising thousands of chic yet inexpensive products for the home, including apparel, furniture, electronics, sporting goods, and toys. Management is looking to open stores in major European cities, but due to limited floor space, it is unable to offer all its usual products. Target hires you as a consultant to decide which products from the firm's U.S. product line to offer in Europe. In other words, your task is to identify Target products suitable for global business. Although a challenging task, you know of various criteria that Target can apply to identify the most appropriate products. Write a brief report in which you describe these criteria and offer some examples to back up your ideas. Be sure to justify your answer using the advice and other information included in this chapter.

2. Cuesta Corporation, an SME manufacturer of various types of scented hand and body soaps, hires Victoria Ridge to locate foreign markets. She seeks your help in deciding how to proceed. You have decided to lend Victoria a hand, before she washes out of the soap business. You advise Victoria that markets for scented soap are fairly saturated within advanced

economies. However, you are aware of numerous *emerging markets* that the industry has overlooked. Using your knowledge of Exhibit 12.2, "Emerging Market Potential Indicators," on pages 356–357 develop a list of the top five emerging markets that Victoria should target. These are the emerging markets that, based on your research, offer the greatest prospects for generating sales. Be sure to justify your choice of countries, based on indicators from this chapter such as market size, market growth rate, market intensity, and market consumption capacity.

3. Upon graduation, a company that makes and sells accessories for luxury automobiles hires you. The company hopes to expand into foreign markets. Your boss comes into your office and hands you a list of countries that he believes hold the greatest potential for international sales. You peruse the list and notice that your boss has based his analysis on per capita income levels of the target countries, reasoning that consumers with the highest incomes are most likely to own luxury cars. Nevertheless, his analysis is based on traditional per capita income, without regard to purchasing power parity. In addition, you feel that some other key indicators of demand are neglected. Mustering your courage, you decide to propose an improved methodology for picking countries. What should be the principal features of this methodology?

AACSB: Reflective Thinking, Use of Information Technology

Refer to Chapter 1, page 27, for instructions on how to access and use globalEDGE™.

1. China is an attractive market partly because of its large size and growing affluence. Before they begin exporting to China, most firms conduct market research to acquire a fuller understanding of the country's market situation. Two useful sites for conducting research are the China Business Information Center (CBIC; www.export.gov/china) and UK Trade and Investment (www.uktradeinvest.gov.uk). At the CBIC, for example, firms can find out if they are "China Ready." They can access trade leads and read current news about doing business in China. Suppose you get a job with a firm that markets various products, including: (a) breakfast cereal, (b) popular music on CDs, and (c) laptop computers, and wants to begin exporting to China. For each of these three product categories, using the Web sites given above and globalEDGE™, prepare a wish list of the information that the firm should gather prior to making a decision to export to China.

2. Wal-Mart is now the largest retailer in the United States, Canada, and Mexico. However, Wal-Mart still gets only about a quarter of its sales from outside the United States. Coles Myer is the largest retailer in Australia, and gets very little of its sales from outside Australia (its main foreign market is nearby New Zealand). Assess the international retailing sector using online resources, such as globalEDGE™ and A. T. Kearney (www.atkearney.com). Based on your research: (a) What factors should these top retailers consider in choosing countries for internationalizing their operations? (b) What are the best target markets for these companies to expand to? (c) What types of questions should management at each firm ask in assessing their readiness to internationalize?

3. The U.S. Census Bureau tracks foreign trade statistics. Visit the site at www.census.gov and find the most recent versions of the report "Profile of U.S. Exporting Companies" by entering this title in the search engine. Peruse the report and address the following questions: (a) What types of companies export from the United States? That is, what is the breakdown by company type of U.S. exporters? For example, are the exporters mainly large or small firms? Do they operate mainly in the manufacturing, agricultural, or services sectors? (b) What is the role of small and medium-sized exporters in U.S. trade? What percent of U.S. exporters are these types of firms, and what proportion of total exports do they account for? (c) What countries are the three favorite targets of U.S. exporters? According to the report, what factors make these countries the top markets for U.S. firms?

CKR Cavusgil Knight Riesenberger

Management Skill Builder©

Global Market Opportunity Assessment for Cancer Insurance

Cancer is a leading cause of premature death. Major types of cancer include skin, lung, stomach, breast, and prostate cancer. It is a life-threatening disease that is often difficult and expensive to treat, with medical bills running into the hundreds of thousands of dollars. In many countries, people buy health insurance to pay the costs of medical care. Health insurance companies such as AFLAC and American International Group (AIG) specialize in supplemental policies to cover specialized cancer care.

AACSB: Reflective Thinking, Analytical Skills

Managerial Challenge

Given limited resources, managers must identify the most appropriate countries to target with their products and services. Because decisions about which markets to enter can be very challenging, managers conduct research on the available choices. Initially, managers systematically narrow the number of potential target countries using *Global Market Opportunity Assessment*. In this exercise, your challenge is to assess markets for supplemental cancer insurance in various countries.

Background

Companies and governments often provide citizens with basic medical insurance. However, these policies may not fully cover the high cost of life-threatening ailments such as cancer. Moreover, most people lack comprehensive health insurance against cancer. Thus, people often purchase supplemental health insurance. A sizeable market for comprehensive cancer insurance exists around the world. There are numerous health insurance companies that offer cancer insurance. When seeking to sell insurance abroad, these firms need to find out what countries offer the best sales prospects. Because the choice of potential markets can be overwhelming, managers use Global Market Opportunity Assessment (GMOA).

Managerial Skills You Will Gain

In this C/K/R Management Skill Builder©, as a prospective manager, you will:

1. Learn the factors to consider when screening countries for foreign market entry.

2. Understand how these factors relate to maximizing the firm's competitive advantages.

3. Screen foreign markets to identify the most appropriate markets to target with the firm's products and services.

Your Task

In this exercise, your task is to conduct a *Global Market Opportunity Assessment* to identify the most promising country to target for sales of supplemental cancer insurance. You will examine variables that can help you estimate the size of relevant industry sales within each of four possible target countries. Your assessment of each target country will be based on industry-specific indicators of demand for cancer insurance.

Go to the C/K/R Knowledge Portal©

www.prenhall.com/cavusgil

Proceed to the C/K/R Knowledge Portal© to obtain the expanded background information, your task and methodology, suggested resources for this exercise, and the presentation template.

Exporting and Countertrade

> Exporter's Dogged Pursuit of International Customers

Is your pet having a bad hair day? Or is your horse's mane looking dull? Sharon Doherty, president of Vellus Products, Inc., can help. Vellus is a small company in the United States that makes pet grooming products such as customized shampoos, conditioners, brushing sprays, and detanglers. According to Doherty, shampoos for people don't work well on pets because animals' skin is more sensitive than humans and is easily irritated.

Vellus' first export sale was to a Taiwanese importer who purchased $25,000 worth of products to sell at Taiwan dog shows. The word was out. "I started receiving calls from people around the world who heard of our products and asked how they could get in touch with me to buy them," Doherty recalls. "But I needed a way to do market research and learn more about ways of doing business in these countries." Vellus had to adapt some of its marketing for foreign markets to meet local conditions.

Vellus has become quite familiar with the cultural aspects of pet care. In England, dog exhibitors prefer less poofed-out topknots than those in show dogs in the United States, where owners prefer more exotic topknots. In England, dog exhibitors prefer Shih-Tzus with a big head, long back, and who are somewhat lower to the ground,

while U.S. exhibitors prefer Shih-Tzus with more leg and a shorter back. These preferences determine the types of shampoos and brushes that each country needs.

Exporting benefits firms such as Vellus by increasing sales and profits and diversifying their customer base. As an entry strategy, exporting is low cost, low risk, and uncomplicated. These are big advantages for smaller firms like Vellus that typically lack substantial financial and human resources. Exporting also helps stabilize fluctuations in sales volume. For instance, because dog shows take place abroad during different parts of the year, exporting helps stabilize Vellus' sales levels.

Firms like Vellus take advantage of support provided by intermediaries located abroad. Doherty often gives advice and guidance to her foreign-based distributors, sharing her knowledge and understanding of importing along with marketing in the dog show network. She says this advice is much appreciated and goes a long way to building long-term relationships. Doherty also makes sure to do her homework on potential distributors. "Gather as much information as you can. Don't make any assumptions—the wrong choice can cost your business valuable time and money."

Exporters like Vellus locate foreign distributors using various methods. One approach is to attend a trade fair in the target country. In Vellus' case, management discovered potential distributors by attending foreign dog shows. Other companies consult country and regional business directories, foreign yellow pages, industry trade associations, and government sources.

Vellus received guidance from government agencies that support small-firm exporting. "They provided me with lots of help and an abundance of excellent information," Doherty said. Having done her homework, it's no wonder Vellus Products continues to flourish. The firm has a wide range of clients, from the rich and famous to distributors, breeders, and individual pet owners around the world. The president of the United Arab Emirates is a regular

customer; his stables buy Vellus products for his horses twice a year.

To date, Vellus has sold its products in 28 countries, including Australia, Canada, China, England, Finland, New Zealand, Norway, Singapore, South Africa, and Sweden. Roughly half the firm's revenues come from exports. All told, more than 300 breeds of pampered pooches are strutting their stuff with the help of Vellus Products. Management has registered the firm's trademark in 15 countries, and looks to expand export sales.

Sources: Judy, Jo Ann. (1998). "Worldwise Women," *Small Business News*, July 01, p. 21; Pavilkey, Susan. (2001). "Pet Product Maker Gives International Clients Royal Treatment," *Business First*, Jan 19, p. A20; U.S. Department of Commerce, at *www.export.gov/comm_svc/press_room/news/articles*

An Overview of Foreign Market Entry Strategies

As we begin Part Four of this book, let's review foreign market entry strategies that companies use to expand abroad. Recall Chapter 3, where we discussed the following three categories of internationalization strategies for the focal firm:

Global sourcing The strategy of buying products and services from foreign sources; also referred to as importing, global procurement, or global purchasing.

Exporting The strategy of producing products or services in one country (often the producer's home country), and selling and distributing them to customers located in other countries.

Countertrade An international business transaction where all or partial payments are made in kind rather than cash.

1. International transactions that involve the exchange of products are *home-based* international trade activities, such as *global sourcing, exporting,* and *countertrade.* **Global sourcing** (also known as importing, global procurement, or global purchasing) refers to the strategy of buying products and services from foreign sources. While sourcing or importing represents an inbound flow, exporting represents *outbound* international business. Thus, **exporting** refers to the strategy of producing products or services in one country (often the producer's home country), and selling and distributing them to customers located in other countries. In both global sourcing and exporting, the firm manages its international operations largely from the home country. We discuss global sourcing in greater detail in Chapter 16. **Countertrade** refers to an international business transaction where all or partial payments are made in kind rather than cash. That is, instead of receiving money as payment for exported products, the firm receives other products or commodities.

2. Contractual relationships are most commonly referred to as *licensing* and *franchising.* By using licensing and franchising, the firm allows a foreign partner to use its intellectual property in return for royalties or other compensation. Firms such as McDonalds, Dunkin' Donuts, and Century 21 Real Estate use franchising to serve customers abroad. We discuss contractual strategies for foreign market entry in Chapter 15.

3. Equity or ownership-based international business activities typically involve *foreign direct investment (FDI)* and equity-based *collaborative ventures.* In contrast to home-based international operations, the firm establishes a presence in the foreign market by investing capital and securing ownership of a factory, subsidiary, or other facility there. Collaborative ventures include joint ventures in which the firm makes similar equity investments abroad, but in partnership with another company. We discuss FDI and collaborative ventures in Chapter 14.

Each foreign market entry strategy has its advantages and disadvantages, and each places specific demands on the firm's managerial and financial resources.

Broadly, exporting, licensing, and franchising require a relatively low level of managerial commitment and dedicated resources. By contrast, FDI and equity-based collaborative ventures necessitate a high level of commitment and resources.

Managers typically consider the following six variables when selecting an entry strategy:

1. The *goals* and *objectives* of the firm, such as desired profitability, market share, or competitive positioning.

2. The particular financial, organizational, and technological *resources* and *capabilities* available to the firm.

3. *Unique conditions in the target country,* such as legal, cultural, and economic circumstances, as well as the nature of business infrastructure, such as distribution and transportation systems.

4. *Risks* inherent in each proposed foreign venture in relation to the firm's goals and objectives in pursuing internationalization.

5. The nature and extent of *competition* from existing rivals and from firms that may enter the market later.

6. The *characteristics of the product or service* to be offered to customers in the market.

The specific characteristics of the product or service, such as its composition, fragility, perishability, and the ratio of its value to its weight, can strongly influence the type of internationalization strategy that management chooses for expanding abroad. For example, products with a low value/weight ratio (such as tires, cement, and beverages) are expensive to ship long distances, suggesting that the firm should internationalize through a strategy other than exporting. Similarly, fragile or perishable goods (such as glass and fresh fruit) are expensive or impractical to ship long distances because they typically require special handling or refrigeration. Complex products (such as medical scanning equipment and computers) require substantial technical support and after-sales service, which might necessitate a substantial presence in the foreign market.

 # The Internationalization of the Firm

In this chapter, we explore home-based international trade activities: exporting, importing, and countertrade. Exporting is the typical foreign market entry strategy for most firms, and thus it deserves greater attention. Before discussing exporting in detail, let's consider the nature and characteristics of firm internationalization.

Diverse Motives for Pursuing Internationalization

When selecting an entry mode, managers must identify the firm's underlying motivation for venturing abroad. Companies internationalize for a variety of reasons.[1] Some motivations are *reactive* and others *proactive*. For example, following major customers abroad is a reactive move. When large automakers such as Ford or Toyota expand abroad, their suppliers are compelled to follow them to foreign markets. Automotive suppliers, such as Robert Bosch, Denso, Lear, TRW, and Valeo quickly set up their own international operations. By contrast, seeking high-growth markets abroad or preempting a competitor in its home market are proactive moves. Companies such as Vellus, discussed in the opening vignette, are pulled into international markets because of the unique appeal of their products. Multinational enterprises (MNEs), such as Hewlett-Packard, Kodak, Nestlé, AIG, and Union Bank of Switzerland may venture abroad to

SMEs such as Vellus Products, Inc., maker of pet-grooming products, internationalize quickly because of their unique product appeal. Here, a Great Dane is showcased at Crufts in Birmingham, England, the world's largest dog show.

enhance various competitive advantages, learn from foreign rivals, or pick up ideas about new products.

For companies that launch exporting, licensing, or franchising ventures, internationalization motives tend to be relatively straightforward. In most cases, management seeks to maximize returns from investments that the firm has made in products, services, and know-how by seeking a broader customer base located abroad. When companies such as Boston Scientific (medical instruments), Subway, and Starbucks internationalize, they are essentially exploiting their competitive assets in a broader geographic space. In contrast, FDI and collaborative ventures usually involve more complex motivations. They pose greater risks for managers and require careful consideration of the likely costs and benefits of internationalization. For example, the Swedish appliance maker Electrolux recently built assembly operations in such diverse markets as Hungary, Mexico, Poland, Russia, and Thailand. Home appliances represent a complex global industry in which profit margins are tight and competition is intense. By undertaking product development, manufacturing, supply-chain coordination, and workforce management in relatively risky markets, Electrolux has taken on formidable challenges.[2]

Characteristics of Firm Internationalization

What are typical patterns and characteristics associated with the process of international expansion?[3] Five conclusions can be reached.

1. *Push and pull factors serve as initial triggers.* Typically a combination of triggers, internal to the firm and in its external environment, is responsible for initial international expansion. *Push factors* include unfavorable trends in the domestic market that compel firms to explore opportunities beyond national borders. Examples include declining demand, falling profit margins, growing competition at home, and reliance on products that have reached a mature phase in their life cycle. *Pull factors* are favorable conditions in foreign markets that make international expansion attractive. Examples include situations in which management desires faster growth and higher profit margins, or the will to enter markets that have fewer competitors, foreign government incentives, or opportunities to learn from competitors. Often, both push and pull factors combine to motivate the firm to internationalize.

2. *Initial involvement may be accidental.* For many firms, initial international expansion is unplanned. Many companies internationalize "by accident" or because of fortuitous events. For example, DLP, Inc., a manufacturer of medical devices for open-heart surgery, made its first major sale to foreign customers that the firm's managers met at a trade fair. Without necessarily meaning to, the firm got started in international business right from its founding. Vellus Products, the firm discussed in the opening vignette, started exporting because a foreign distributor decided to showcase the firm's products at a dog show in Taiwan. Such reactive or unplanned internationalization has been typical of many firms prior to the 1980s. Today, because of growing pressures from international competitors and the increasing ease with which internationalization can be achieved, firms tend to be more deliberate in their international ventures.

3. *Balancing risk and return.* Managers weigh the potential profits, revenues, and achievement of strategic goals of internationalization against the initial investment that must be made in terms of money, time, and other company resources. The greater the anticipated returns, the more likely it is that management will pursue an international project and commit resources necessary to ensure its success. Because of increased costs and greater complexity, international ventures often take longer to become profitable than domestic ventures. Risk-taking preferences of managers determine what initial investments the firm will make and its tolerance for delayed returns. Risk-averse managers tend to prefer more conservative international projects that involve relatively safe markets and entry strategies. These managers tend to target foreign markets that are culturally close; that is, they have a similar culture and language to the home country. For example, a risk-averse U.S. company would favor Canada over China. A risk-averse Australian company would prefer Britain over Nigeria.

4. *An ongoing learning experience.* Internationalization is a gradual process that can stretch over many years and involve entry into numerous national settings. There are ample opportunities for managers to learn and adapt how they do business. If profits are attractive, management will commit increasing resources to international expansion and will seek additional foreign opportunities that, in turn, result in more learning opportunities. Eventually, internationalization develops a momentum of its own, as direct experience in each new market reinforces learning and positive results pave the way for greater international expansion.[4] Active involvement in international business provides the firm with many new ideas and valuable lessons that it can apply to the home market and to other foreign markets. For example, in the process of developing fuel-efficient automobiles for the United States, General Motors (GM) turned to its European operations, where it had been marketing smaller cars for some time. GM leveraged ideas that it had acquired in Europe to develop fuel-saving cars for the U.S. market.

5. *Firms may evolve through stages of internationalization.* Historically, most firms have opted for a gradual, incremental approach to international expansion. Even today most firms internationalize in stages, employing relatively simple and low-risk internationalization strategies early on and progressing to more complex strategies as the firm gains experience and knowledge. Exhibit 13.1 illustrates the typical firm's internationalization stages and the justifications for each stage. In the *domestic market focus* stage, management focuses on only the home market. In the *experimental stage,* management tends to target low-risk, culturally close markets, using relatively simple entry strategies such as exporting or licensing. As management gains experience and competence, it enters the *active involvement* and *committed involvement* stages. Managers begin to target increasingly complex markets, using more challenging entry strategies such as FDI and collaborative ventures.

While firms generally follow the pattern described in Exhibit 13.1 when expanding abroad, today born global firms internationalize much faster than companies did in the past. Born globals reach a stage of active involvement in international business within the first few years of their founding.

Exporting as a Foreign Market Entry Strategy

Because it entails limited risk, expense, and knowledge of foreign markets and transactions, most firms prefer exporting as their primary foreign market entry strategy. Typically, the focal firm retains its manufacturing activities in its home market but conducts marketing, distribution, and customer service activities in the export market. The focal firm can conduct the latter activities itself, or contract with an independent distributor or agent to have them performed.

Stages of internationalization	Critical management activity or orientation	How the firm behaves
Domestic market focus	Focus on home market	Firm operates only in its home market due to limited resources or lack of motivation
Preinternationalization stage	Research and evaluate the feasibility of undertaking international business activity	*Typical triggers from outside the firm:* • The firm receives unsolicited orders from customers located abroad. • Change agents (such as foreign distributors) contact the firm, seeking to represent it in their countries. *Typical triggers from inside the firm:* • Managers seek to increase the firm's performance or improve its competitive advantages. • Managers are proactive about international expansion.
Experimental involvement	Initiate limited international business activity, typically through exporting	• Managers consider foreign market opportunities attractive.
Active involvement	Explore international expansion, including entry strategies other than exporting	• Managers have accumulated experience that reinforces expectations about the benefits of international business. • Managers are willing to commit additional resources for international expansion. • Managers dedicate firm resources appropriate for expanding into new foreign markets.
Committed involvement	Allocate resources based on international opportunities	• The firm performs well in various international ventures. • The firm overcomes barriers to doing international business.

Exhibit 13.1 Typical Stages in Firm Internationalization

SOURCE: Adapted from S. Tamer Cavusgil (1980) "On the Internationalization Process of Firms," *European Research* 8 (6): 273–81.

Exporting is the entry strategy responsible for the massive inflows and outflows that constitute global trade. Exporting typically generates substantial foreign-exchange earnings for nations. Japan has benefited from massive inflows of export earnings for years. China has become the leading exporter in various sectors, providing enormous revenues to the Chinese economy. Smaller economies such as Belgium and Finland also add much to their foreign-exchange reserves from exporting, and use them to pay for their sizeable imports of foreign goods.

When government agencies cite statistics on trade deficits, trade surpluses, and the volume of merchandise trade for individual countries, these data generally refer to firms' collective exporting and importing activities. For example, the United States is the primary export market for Canadian goods, and accounts for some three-quarters of Canadian exports each year. The two-way trade between Canada and the United States represents the largest bilateral trade relationship in the world.

China recently surpassed Europe, Japan, and the United States to become the world's top exporter of information technology (IT) products. The speed of China's ascent has been startling. In 1996, China's exports of computers, mobile phones, and other IT goods amounted to only $36 billion. By 2006, the figure exceeded $300 billion. In the intervening years, almost all major Western IT firms had located much of their production in China, primarily because of its low-cost manufacturing and capable factory workers. China's success has occurred particularly at the expense of the United States, from which direct IT exports have declined substantially in recent years.[5]

Exporting is a foreign entry strategy of manufacturers such as Boeing.

Exporting: A Popular Entry Strategy

Firms venturing abroad for the first time usually use exporting as their entry strategy. Exporting is also the entry strategy most favored by small and medium-sized enterprises (SMEs), such as Vellus Products. Beyond initial entry, however, all types of firms, large and small, use exporting regardless of their stage of internationalization. For example, some of the largest exporters in the United States include big aircraft manufacturers such as Boeing and Lockheed. Big trading companies that deal in commodities, such as Cargill and Marubeni, are also large-scale exporters. Large manufacturing firms—those with more than 500 employees—typically account for the largest overall value of exports. Such firms account for about three-quarters of the total value of exports from the United States. However, the vast majority of exporting firms—more than 90 percent in most countries—are SMEs with fewer than 500 employees.

As an entry strategy, exporting is very flexible. Compared to more complex strategies such as foreign direct investment (FDI), the exporter can both enter and withdraw from markets fairly easily, with minimal risk and expense. Exporting may be employed repeatedly during the firm's internationalization process, generally at the early stages and again from production facilities that the firm eventually establishes at various foreign locations, destined for markets in other countries. Very experienced international firms usually export in combination with other strategies, such as joint ventures and foreign direct investment. For example, Toyota has used FDI to build factories in key locations in Asia, Europe, and North America. Toyota uses these production bases to export cars to neighboring countries and regions.

Exhibit 13.2 shows the degree to which various manufacturing industries, and firms within those industries, are dependent on international sales. The analysis is limited to large, publicly traded manufacturing companies in the United States. The data represent international sales from both the headquarter's country and the firm's foreign subsidiaries. The Exhibit suggests that firms in industries such as computers, chemicals, and medical equipment are more dependent on international sales than firms in industries such as electrical equipment, publishing, and autos. What are the common features of the most geographically diversified industries? Many are high value-added, high-technology industries subject to globalization. We also find, in general, the greater the tendency of

Industry	Average international sales in the industry (as percentage of total sales)	Example of a leading firm in the industry	Example firm's international sales (as percentage of total sales)
Computers & other electronic products	60%	Fairchild Semiconductor International Inc.	85%
Chemicals	44	OM Group Inc.	80
Medical instruments & equipment	42	Bio-Rad Laboratories Inc.	66
Motor vehicle parts	42	Autoliv Inc.	71
Communications equipment	40	Agere Systems Inc.	80
Pharmaceuticals	37	Schering-Plough Corp.	57
Aerospace & defense	36	Sequa Corp.	50
Food	32	Chiquita Brands International Inc.	73
Plastics	32	Tupperware Corp.	73
Apparel	31	Nike Inc.	56
Beverages	30	Coca-Cola Co.	73
Electrical equipment & appliances	28	Exide Technologies	59
Publishing & printing (including software)	27	Oracle Corp.	52
Motor vehicles	26	Paccar Inc.	55

Exhibit 13.2 International Sales Intensity of Various United States-Based Industries

SOURCE: Industry Week, www.industryweek.com/ReadArticle.aspx?Article ID=1480&Section ID=41.

the industry or the firm to retain manufacturing at home, the greater the dependence on international sales. For example, aircraft manufacturers tend to concentrate their manufacturing in Europe and the United States, yet market their products all over the world.

Service Industry Exports

In most advanced economies, services are the largest component of economic activity. Firms in virtually all services-producing industries market their offerings in foreign countries. These include industries such as travel, transportation, architecture, construction, engineering, education, banking, finance, insurance, entertainment, information, and professional business services. For example, Hollywood film studios earn billions by exporting their movies and videos. Construction firms send their employees abroad to work on major construction projects. Service professionals, such as accountants, engineers, and business consultants often provide their services via the Internet, by telephone and mail, and by visiting customers directly in their home countries. The U.S. firm PMI Mortgage Insurance Co. recently began exporting mortgage insurance packages to various foreign markets. Insurance packages can be created in a central location, such as London, and then exported via mail and the Internet to customers located in other countries. The firm enjoys considerable success in Asia and various European countries.[6]

However, services are distinct from products in certain key ways. Many *pure* services cannot be exported because they cannot be transported. For example, you cannot box up a haircut and ship it overseas. Most retailing firms, such as Carrefour and Marks & Spencer, offer their services by establishing retail stores in their target markets—that is, they internationalize via FDI because retailing requires direct contact with customers. In other cases, many services firms can export *some* of what they produce but rely on other entry strategies to provide *other* offerings abroad. For example, some aspects of professional services cannot be exported and require the firm to establish a physical presence in target markets. While Ernst & Young can export *some* accounting services by sending its employees abroad, in other cases it will establish a physical presence abroad by setting up an office. Ernst & Young then hires *local* personnel to perform local accounting services.

Overall, most services are *delivered* to foreign customers either through local representatives or agents, or marketed in conjunction with other entry strategies such as FDI, franchising, or licensing. The Internet provides the means to export some types of services, ranging from airline tickets to architectural services. The Internet is helping to make the service sector one of the fastest growing areas of exports in international business.[7]

Services can promote and maintain product exports. Many merchandise exports would not take place if they were not supported by service activities. For example, few people would want to buy a car if there were no repair services available to maintain it. Accordingly, firms that export cars must also provide a means for the vehicles to be repaired in the recipient countries. They establish customer service facilities in target markets through FDI, or they contract with local shops to provide such services.

Advantages of Exporting

Serving foreign customers through exporting has been a popular internationalization strategy throughout history because it offers firms a way to accomplish the following:

- Increase overall sales volume, improve market share, and generate profit margins that are often more favorable than in the domestic market.
- Increase economies of scale and therefore reduce per-unit cost of manufacturing.
- Diversify customer base, reducing dependence on home markets.
- Stabilize fluctuations in sales associated with economic cycles or seasonality of demand. For example, a firm can offset declining demand at home due to an economic recession by refocusing efforts toward those countries that are experiencing more robust economic growth.
- Minimize risk and maximize flexibility, compared to other entry strategies. If circumstances necessitate, the firm can quickly withdraw from an export market.
- Lower cost of foreign market entry since the firm does not have to invest in the target market or maintain a physical presence there. Thus, the firm can use exporting to test new markets before committing greater resources through foreign direct investment.
- Leverage the capabilities and skills of foreign distributors and other business partners located abroad.

The low-cost, low-risk nature of exporting, combined with the ability to leverage foreign partners, makes exporting especially suitable for SMEs. For example, small California wineries have begun to export their popular products around the world. Wine exports have reached nearly 20 percent of total output for these modest enterprises. One successful approach has been cobranding, in which California wines are bundled in packages of similar products, such as cheese and snacks, that are then sold to customers abroad. The total value of U.S. wine exports hovers near $1 billion per year and has been growing rapidly. But California wineries are being challenged in their home market by the exporting activities of cost-effective wine producers from countries like Australia, Chile, and South Africa.[8] The *Global Trend* feature describes how SMEs are increasingly active in exporting.

Disadvantages of Exporting

As an entry strategy, exporting also has some drawbacks. First, because exporting does not require the firm to have a physical presence in the foreign market (in con-

> GLOBAL TREND

The Emergence of SME Exporters

The role of small and medium-sized enterprises (SMEs) in exporting is growing. In the United States, SMEs have less than 500 employees, although the definition differs in Europe and elsewhere, where firms may have as few as 100 employees to qualify as SMEs. SMEs account for a great proportion of all U.S. exporters. From 1992 to 2004, they represented nearly 100 percent of the growth in the U.S. exporter population, swelling from about 108,000 firms in 1992 to over 225,000 firms by 2004. SMEs were responsible for nearly a third of merchandise exports from the United States in 2006. Most were wholesalers, distributors, and other nonmanufacturing firms.

In recent years, the national governments of Australia, Britain, Canada, China, New Zealand, and the United States have undertaken aggressive campaigns to help more SMEs become exporters. Governments sponsor trade fairs and trade missions that connect SMEs with distributors and other facilitators in promising foreign markets. The

World Bank assists SME exporters from emerging markets by increasing access to capital and developing their international business skills. While most SMEs export to advanced economies, an increasing number of these firms target emerging markets. These firms do not necessarily require large export markets since they tend to cater to smaller market niches.

For example, Pharmed Group, based in Florida, is a full-line distributor of medical, surgical, and pharmaceutical supplies. Looking to further expand its export sales, the firm signed a deal with Drogao, a major drug store chain in Brazil. Export sales have contributed significantly to Pharmed's growth. Another SME, Optical Xport, exports optical lenses and frames to customers in West and Central Africa from its low-cost manufacturing base in Senegal. These efforts increase the flow of medical supplies and eyeglasses to the poor in Latin America and Africa.

SME exporters have certain advantages that differentiate them from larger and more experienced firms:

- *Flexibility*—the ability to rapidly adapt to foreign market opportunities.
- *Quick response*—faster decision making and implementation of new operating methods.
- *Customization*—the ability to customize products to foreign buyers, with greater ease and smaller production runs.
- *Risk-taking*—SME managers often have an entrepreneurial spirit, high-growth aspirations, and a strong determination to succeed.

SMEs bring these advantages to bear in markets worldwide. SMEs benefit numerous emerging markets, which typically lack access to a wide range of products and services.

Sources: Dahl, Darren. (2005). "Instantly International," *Inc.*, 27(6): 44; U.S. Department of Commerce at www.export.gov/comm_svc/press_room/news/articles; Neupert, Kent, C. Christopher Baughn, and T. Dao. (2006). "SME Exporting Challenges in Transitional and Developed Economies," *Journal of Small Business and Enterprise Development* 13(4): 535–44; Prahalad, C. K. (2004). "Why Selling to the Poor Makes for Good Business," *Fortune*, Nov. 15, pp. 70-71; U.S. Department of Commerce. (2004). *Exporter Database*, Washington, DC: U.S. Department of Commerce; World Bank. (2005). *2004 Annual Review: Small Business Activities.* Washington, DC: World Bank Group.

trast to FDI), management has fewer opportunities to learn about customers, competitors, and other unique aspects of the market. A lack of direct contact with foreign customers means that the exporter may fail to perceive opportunities and threats, or may not acquire the knowledge that it needs to succeed in the market in the long term.

Second, exporting usually requires the firm to acquire new capabilities and dedicate organizational resources to properly conduct export transactions. Firms that are serious about exporting must hire personnel with competency in international transactions and foreign languages. Exporting requires management to expend the time and effort to learn about freight forwarders, documentation, foreign currencies, and new financing methods. The acquisition of such capabilities puts a strain on firm resources.

Third, compared to other entry strategies, exporting is much more sensitive to tariff and other trade barriers, as well as fluctuations in exchange rates. For example, the U.S. dollar gained 12 percent against the euro and 15 percent against the yen in 2005. This led to slower growth of U.S. exports, harming those firms that rely heavily on exporting for generating international sales. Exporters run the risk of being priced out of foreign markets if shifting exchange rates make the exported product too costly to foreign buyers.

A Systematic Approach to Exporting

The more experienced managers use a systematic approach to improve the firm's prospects for successful exporting by assessing potential markets, organizing the firm to undertake exporting, acquiring appropriate skills and competencies, and implementing export operations. Exhibit 13.3 highlights the steps involved in this process. Let's examine each of these steps in detail.

Step One: Assess Global Market Opportunity As a first step, management assesses the various global market opportunities available to the firm. It analyzes the readiness of the firm and its products to carry out exporting. In this process, managers might employ a diagnostic tool such as *CORE (COmpany Readiness to Export,* available online at globalEDGE™). Management screens for the most attractive export markets, identifies qualified distributors and other foreign business partners, and estimates industry market potential and company sales potential. It is often useful for managers to visit the most promising countries to develop a deeper understanding of customer requirements, competitive environment, capabilities of intermediaries, and government regulations. Participating in foreign trade shows and trade missions is a practical means for identifying market potential and foreign intermediaries. We explained the global market opportunity assessment (GMOA) process in detail in Chapter 12.

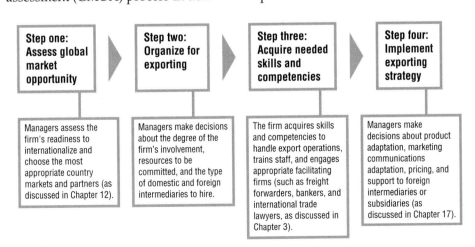

Exhibit 13.3

A Systematic Approach to Exporting

SOURCE: Adapted from S. Tamer Cavusgil and Shaoming Zou, "Marketing Strategy-Performance Relationship: An Investigation of the Empirical Link in Export Market Ventures," *Journal of Marketing 58* (January 1994): 1–21.

Step Two: Organize for Exporting Next, managers address the following questions: What types of managerial, financial, and productive resources should the firm commit to exporting? What sort of a timetable should the firm follow for achieving export goals and objectives? To what degree should the firm rely on domestic and foreign intermediaries to implement exporting?

Exhibit 13.4 illustrates alternative organizational arrangements in exporting. **Indirect exporting** is accomplished by contracting with intermediaries located in the firm's home market. Smaller exporters, or those new to international business, typically hire an export management company (EMC) or a trading company based in the exporter's home country. These channel intermediaries assume responsibility for finding foreign buyers, shipping products, and getting paid. The principal advantage of indirect exporting for most firms is that it provides a way to penetrate foreign markets without the complexities and risks of more direct exporting. The novice international firm can start exporting with no incremental investment in fixed capital, low startup costs, and few risks, but with prospects for incremental sales.

By contrast, **direct exporting** is typically achieved by contracting with intermediaries located in the *foreign* market. The local intermediaries serve as an extension of the exporter, negotiating on behalf of the exporter and assuming such responsibilities as local supply-chain management, pricing, and customer service. Compared to indirect exporting, the main advantage of direct exporting is that it gives the exporter greater control over the export process and potential for higher profits, as well as allowing a closer relationship with foreign buyers and the marketplace. However, compared to indirect exporting, the exporter must dedicate more time, personnel, and corporate resources in developing and managing export operations.

Indirect exporting Exporting that is accomplished by contracting with intermediaries located in the firm's home market.

Direct exporting Exporting that is accomplished by contracting with intermediaries located in the foreign market.

Exhibit 13.4

Alternative Organizational Arrangements for Exporting

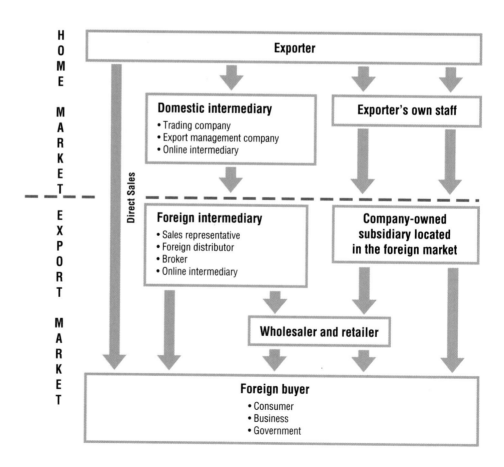

Direct and indirect exporting are not mutually exclusive, and many firms use both approaches for different foreign markets. Key considerations for deciding whether to use indirect or direct exporting are: (1) the level of resources—mainly time, capital, and managerial expertise—that management is willing to commit to international expansion and individual markets; (2) the strategic importance of the foreign market; (3) the nature of the firm's products, including the need for after-sales support; and (4) the availability of capable foreign intermediaries in the target market.

Another exporting arrangement is for the firm to set up a sales office or a **company-owned subsidiary** that handles marketing, physical distribution, promotion, and customer service activities in the foreign market. In this arrangement, the firm undertakes major tasks directly in the foreign market, such as participating in trade fairs, conducting market research, searching for distributors, and finding and serving customers. Management may decide to pursue this route if the foreign market seems likely to generate a high volume of sales or has substantial strategic importance. Management may also elect to set up regional or national distribution centers and warehouses. At the extreme, the firm may establish a full-function marketing subsidiary, staffed with a local sales force. For instance, exports of Australia-based Webspy Company's internet software now make up 80 percent of the firm's annual revenue. Initially the firm exported exclusively through independent foreign distributors. But eventually Webspy established sales subsidiaries in London and Seattle to service its two most important regional markets, Europe and North America (www.austrade.gov.au).

Company-owned subsidiary
A representative office of the exporter that handles marketing, physical distribution, promotion, and customer service activities in the foreign market.

Step Three: Acquire Needed Skills and Competencies

Export transactions are varied and often complex, requiring specialized skills and competencies. The firm may wish to launch new or adapted products abroad, target countries with varying marketing infrastructure, finance customer purchases, or contract with helpful facilitators at home and abroad. Accordingly, managers need to gain new, internationally oriented capabilities in areas such as product development, distribution, logistics, finance, contract law, and currency management. Managers may need to acquire foreign language skills and the ability to interact with customers from diverse cultures. Fortunately, numerous facilitators, such as those described in Chapter 3, are available to assist firms that lack specific skills and competencies.

Step Four: Implement Exporting Strategy

In the final stage, management formulates elements of the firm's export strategy. *Product adaptation* involves modifying a product to make it fit the needs and tastes of the buyers in the target market. For example, when Microsoft markets computer software in Germany, it must ensure the software is written in German. Even Vellus, the firm discussed in the opening vignette, must vary the dog-grooming products that it sells abroad because U.S. exhibitors prefer dogs with poofed-out topknots while British exhibitors prefer less hair. The dog brushes and shampoos that Vellus sells in the United States may not sell in Britain. In export markets with many competitors, the exporter needs to adapt its products in order to gain competitive advantage.

Marketing communications adaptation refers to modifying advertising, selling style, public relations, and promotional activities to suit individual markets. Marketing communications activities are adapted depending on the nature of the target market, the nature of the product, the firm's position in the market relative to competitors, and management's specific goals and objectives. *Price competitiveness* refers to efforts to keep foreign pricing in line with that of competitors. In markets with many competitors, the exporter may need to charge competitive prices. However, SMEs often lack the resources to compete head-to-head on pricing with larger rivals. Such firms compete not by charging low prices, but by emphasizing the nonprice benefits of their products, such as quality, reliability, and brand leadership. *Distribution strategy* often hinges on developing strong and mutually beneficial relations with foreign intermediaries.[9] Companies provide ongoing support to distributors and subsidiaries in the form of sales force training, technical assistance, marketing know-how, promotional support, and pricing incentives. In markets with numerous competitors, the exporter may need to boost the capabilities of its distributors. If the product is technologically complex, the exporter may need to increase support to intermediaries to ensure they understand how to market and service the product.

Importing

Importing Buying of products and services from foreign sources and bringing them into the home market. Also referred to as global sourcing, global procurement, or global purchasing.

The counterpart of exporting is **importing**, in which the firm chooses to buy products and services from foreign sources and bring them into the home market. Firms that import, whether they are manufacturers, wholesalers, or retailers are called importers. Importing is also referred to as *global sourcing, global procurement,* or *global purchasing.* The sourcing may be from independent suppliers abroad or from company-owned subsidiaries or affiliates.

Many manufacturers and retailers are also major importers. Manufacturing companies tend to import raw materials and parts to go into assembly. Retailers secure a substantial portion of their merchandise from foreign suppliers. For example, in the United States, retailers such as Wal-Mart, Home Depot, and Target are among the largest importers. By itself, Wal-Mart accounts for about 10 percent of U.S. imports from China, amounting to about $20 billion per year. Other large importers include chemical companies (e.g., LG), electronics firms (e.g., Phillips), and food wholesalers (e.g. Chiquita Brands International).

The fundamentals discussed in this chapter regarding exporting, payments, and financing also apply to importing. Both importing and exporting—sometimes referred to collectively as *international trade*—require the firm to follow various complex procedures, often related to clearing products through domestic ports of entry. Successful exporting and importing necessitate careful management of the focal firm's global supply chain, that is, the firm's integrated network of sourcing, production, and distribution activities, organized on a world scale. As with exporting, most importers delegate much of the mechanics of importing to *facilitators,* the specialist firms such as freight forwarders and customs house brokers that we discussed in Chapter 3. Today, many manufacturers source input goods and services from foreign suppliers worldwide. We therefore devote a separate chapter, Chapter 16, to global sourcing.

Managing Export-Import Transactions

Skillful exporters develop the ability to conceive and carry out aggressive foreign market entry and meet the demands of day-to-day export operations. In the early phase of exporting, management establishes an export group or department represented by only an export manager and a few assistants. The export department is typically subordinate to the domestic sales department and depends on other units inside the firm to fulfill customer orders, receive payments, and organize logistics. Novice international firms prefer this minimalist approach because it requires only a limited commitment of corporate resources, a key consideration when management is unsure or hesitant about getting started in international business. Assuming the firm's early export efforts are successful, management is likely to increase its commitment to internationalization by developing a specialized export staff. In large, experienced exporters, management typically creates a separate export department, which can become fairly autonomous.

When comparing domestic and international business transactions, key differences arise in the areas of documentation and shipping.

Documentation

Documentation refers to the official forms and other paperwork that are required in export transactions for shipping and customs procedures. Initially, the exporter usually issues a *quotation* or *pro forma invoice* upon request by potential customers. This can be structured as a standard form, which informs the potential buyer about the price and description of the exporter's product or service. The *commercial invoice* is the actual demand for payment issued by the exporter when a sale is concluded. It includes a description of the goods, the exporter's address, delivery address, and payment terms. The exporter may also include a *packing list,* particularly for shipments that involve numerous goods, which indicates the exact contents of the shipment.

Documentation Official forms and other paperwork required in export transactions for shipping and customs procedures.

Firms typically distribute exported goods by ocean transport, although some firms use air transport. The *bill of lading* is the basic contract between exporter and shipper. It authorizes a shipping company to transport the goods to the buyer's destination. It also serves as the importer's receipt and proof of title for purchase of the goods. The shipper's *export declaration* (sometimes called "ex-dec") lists the contact information of the exporter and the buyer (or importer), as well as a full description, declared value, and destination of the products being shipped. National customs services and other port authorities use the export declaration to ascertain the content of shipments, to control exports, and to compile statistics of which goods are entering and leaving the country. The *certificate of origin* is the "birth certificate" of the goods being shipped and indicates the country where the product originates. Exporters usually purchase an *insurance certificate* to protect the exported goods against damage, loss, pilferage (theft), and, in some cases, delay.

Documentation must be completed in a precise manner. The types of documents required vary depending on regulations of both the home and destination countries. The exporter typically entrusts the preparation of documents to an international freight forwarder. As introduced in Chapter 3, freight forwarders are among the key facilitators in international business, functioning like travel agents for cargo. In addition to documentation, the typical freight forwarder is a specialist in international shipping methods and the international trade regulations of the home and target countries. The freight forwarder assists exporters with tactical and procedural aspects of exporting such as logistics, packing, and labeling. At the foreign port, the freight forwarder arranges to have exported products cleared through customs and shipped on to the buyer. After shipment, the freight forwarder routes documentation to the seller, the buyer, or to another facilitator, such as a bank.

Another important document is the *license,* a type of permission to export. National governments sometimes require exporters to obtain a license for reasons of national security, foreign policy, or because the exported product is in short supply. For example, governments usually don't allow firms to export nuclear materials or harmful biological agents that can be used to create weapons. In addition, some governments impose sanctions on trade with certain countries as part of their foreign policy. Lastly, governments may forbid the export of certain types of essential goods, such as petroleum products, if they are in short supply in the home country.

Export transactions frequently involve shipping products through seaports, such as this one in California.

Incoterms Universally accepted terms of sale that specify how the buyer and the seller share the cost of freight and insurance in an international transaction, and at which point the buyer takes title to the goods.

Shipping and Incoterms

International shipping exposes the exporter's goods to adverse conditions and handling by various facilitators. The firm must comply with the laws and procedures specific to each market. Logistics personnel must make sure the product is packed carefully, so that it arrives in good condition at the distant target market. The shipment must be labeled correctly to ensure it is handled properly en route and arrives at the right place on time. The exporter must complete and send with the shipment the appropriate documentation that complies with regulations of the home and foreign governments.

Most export transactions involve products being shipped from the exporter's factory to a nearby seaport or airport. From there, the shipment is transported by ship or airplane to a foreign port, where it is transferred to land-based transportation and conveyed to the customer's final destination. Alternatively, in the case of shipments to neighboring countries, the exported product may be transported entirely via land-based means, such as rail or truck, to the customer's destination. Throughout the delivery process, the exporter incurs various transportation costs. In addition, the exported product is usually insured against damage or loss during transit.

In the past, disputes sometimes arose over who should pay the cost of freight and insurance in international transactions: the seller (that is, the exporter) or the foreign buyer. To eliminate such disputes, a system of universal, standard terms of sale and delivery, known as **Incoterms** (short for "International Commerce Terms") have been developed by the International Chamber of Commerce (http://www.iccwbo.org). Commonly used in international sales contracts, Incoterms specify how the buyer and the seller share the cost of freight and insurance, and at which point the buyer takes title to the goods. Exhibit 13.5 illustrates the implications of the three most commonly used Incoterms.

Methods of Payment in Exporting and Importing

Receiving payment for products sold is more complicated in international business than in domestic business. Foreign currencies may be unstable, and/or governments may be reluctant to allow funds to leave the country. In the event of disputes over payment, local laws and enforcement mechanisms may favor local citizens over foreign firms. Some customers in developing countries lack payment mechanisms such as credit cards and checking accounts. In short, getting paid in international business entails risks and potentially complex payment methods.

In countries with advanced economies, firms often extend credit to buyers with the assurance they will be paid. It is typical for exporters to allow customers in such markets several months to make payments or to structure payment on *open account*. If payment is not forthcoming, a legal system is usually in place to compel creditors to meet their obligations. By contrast, in many emerging markets and developing countries, exporters extend credit cautiously. They evaluate new customers carefully and may decline a customer's request for credit if the risk is too great.

Fortunately, there are several conventional methods for getting paid in international business. Listed roughly in order of most secure to least secure from the exporter's standpoint, these methods are: *cash in advance, letter of credit, open account, consignment,* and *countertrade.* While the last method, countertrade, can

Incoterms	Definition	Key points	Arrangement of shipping
EXW Ex works (named place)	Delivery takes place at the seller's premises or another named place (i.e., works, factory, or warehouse). Shipment is not cleared for export and not loaded on any collecting vehicle.	EXW represents minimum obligation for the seller; the buyer bears all costs and risks involved in claiming the goods from the seller's premises.	Buyer arranges shipping.
FOB Free on board (named port of shipment)	Delivery takes place when the goods pass the ship's rail at the named port of shipment.	The buyer bears all the costs and risks of loss or damage upon delivery. The seller clears the goods for export. This term is used only for sea and inland waterway transport.	Buyer arranges shipping.
CIF Cost, insurance and freight (named port of destination)	Delivery takes place when the goods pass the ship's rail in the port of shipment.	The seller must pay for insurance and freight necessary to bring the goods to the named port of destination. At that point, the risk of loss or damage to the goods is transferred from the seller to the buyer. The seller clears the goods for export.	Seller arranges shipping and insurance.

Exhibit 13.5 Incoterms: Examples of How Transport Obligations, Costs, and Risks are Shared between the Buyer and the Seller

SOURCE: International Chamber of Commerce, http://www.iccwbo.org

serve as a method of payment in international business transactions, it is also a distinct form of foreign market entry that deserves extensive treatment. Therefore, we discuss it separately in this chapter. We explain each of the other four payment methods next.

Cash in Advance

When the exporter receives cash in advance, payment is collected before the goods are shipped to the customer. The main advantage is that the exporter need not worry about collection problems and can access the funds almost immediately upon concluding the sale. Many exporters accept credit cards as payment, especially for low-value sales. From the buyer's standpoint, however, cash in advance is risky and may cause cash flow problems. The buyer may hesitate to pay cash in advance for fear the exporter will not follow through with shipment, particularly if the buyer does not know the exporter well. For these reasons, cash in advance is unpopular with foreign buyers and tends to discourage sales. Exporters who insist on cash in advance tend to lose out to competitors who offer more flexible payment terms.

Letter of Credit

Letter of credit Contract between the banks of a buyer and a seller that ensures payment from the buyer to the seller upon receiving an export shipment.

A documentary letter of credit, or simply a *letter of credit,* resolves some of the problems associated with cash in advance. Because a letter of credit protects the interests of both the seller and the buyer simultaneously, it has become the most popular method for getting paid in export transactions. Essentially, a **letter of credit** is a contract between the banks of the buyer and seller that ensures payment from the buyer to the seller upon receiving an export shipment. It amounts to a substitution of each bank's name and credit for the name and credit of the buyer and seller. The system works because virtually all banks have established relationships with correspondent banks around the world.

A letter of credit may be either *irrevocable* or *revocable.* Once established, an irrevocable letter of credit cannot be canceled without agreement of both buyer and seller. The selling firm will be paid as long as it fulfills its part of the agreement. As a bonus, the letter of credit immediately establishes trust between buyer and seller. Among the countless firms that use letters of credit is Pinewood Healthcare, a manufacturer of generic pharmaceuticals. Exports account for 70 percent of Pinewood's sales. When Pinewood first started exporting to Africa, the firm sometimes experienced difficulties in getting paid. The situation improved greatly when it began contracting sales via letter of credit.[10]

The letter of credit also specifies the documents the exporter is required to present, such as a bill of lading, commercial invoice, and a certificate of insurance. Before making a payment, the buyer's bank verifies that all documents meet the requirements the buyer and seller agreed to in the letter of credit. If not, the discrepancy must be resolved before the bank makes the payment.

Exhibit 13.6 presents the typical cycle of an international sale through a letter of credit.

1. An "Exporter" signs a contract for the sale of products to a foreign buyer, the "Importer."

2. The Importer requests its bank (the "Importer's Bank") to open a letter of credit in favor of the Exporter, the beneficiary of the credit.

3. The Importer's Bank notifies the "Exporter's Bank" that a letter of credit has been issued.

Exhibit 13.6

Letter of Credit Cycle

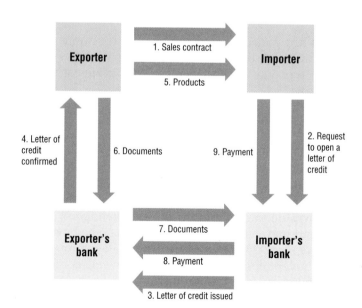

4. The Exporter's Bank confirms the validity of the letter of credit.

5. The Exporter prepares and ships the products to the Importer as specified in the letter of credit.

6. The Exporter presents the shipment documents to its bank, the Exporter's Bank, which examines them to ensure they fully comply with the terms of the letter of credit. The documents typically include an invoice, bill of lading, and insurance certificate, as specified in the letter of credit.

7. The Exporter's Bank sends the documents to the Importer's Bank, which similarly examines them to ensure they comply fully with the letter of credit.

8. Upon confirmation that everything is in order, the Importer's Bank makes full payment for the goods to the Exporter, via the Exporter's Bank.

9. The Importer makes full payment to its bank within the time period granted to it, which, in many countries, can extend to several months.

A related payment method is the *draft*. Similar to a check, the draft is a financial instrument that instructs a bank to pay a specific amount of a specific currency to the bearer on demand or at a future date. For both letters of credit and drafts, the buyer must make payment upon presentation of documents that convey title to the purchased goods, and confirm that specific steps have been taken to prepare the goods and their shipment to the buyer. Letters of credit and drafts can be paid immediately or at a later date. Drafts that are paid upon presentation are called *sight drafts*. Drafts that are to be paid at a later date, often after the buyer receives the goods, are called *time drafts* or *date drafts*. In addition, the exporter can sell any drafts and letters of credit in its possession via discounting and forfeiting to financial institutions that specialize in such instruments. Exporters do this in order to avoid having to wait weeks or months to be paid for their exports.

Open Account

When the exporter uses an *open account,* the buyer pays the exporter at some future time following receipt of the goods, in much the same way that a retail customer pays a department store on account for products he or she has purchased. Because of the risk involved, exporters use this approach only with customers of long standing or with excellent credit or a subsidiary owned by the exporter. With an open account, the exporter simply bills the customer, who is expected to pay under agreed terms at some future time. Many large MNEs make purchases only on open account. However, the lack of documents and banking channels that the exporter would normally use if selling via letters of credit can make it difficult to have claims enforced legally. The exporter might also have to pursue collection abroad (that is, undertake a legal procedure to collect its debt), which can be difficult and costly.

Consignment Sales

Under a *consignment sale,* the exporter ships products to a foreign intermediary who then sells them on behalf of the exporter. The exporter retains title to the goods until they are sold, at which point the intermediary or foreign customer owes payment to the exporter. The disadvantage of this approach is that the exporter maintains very little control over the products. The exporter may not receive payment for some time after delivery, or not at all. Thus, exporters that conduct consignment sales often carry risk insurance. Consignment sales work best when the exporter has an established relationship with a trustworthy distributor.

Cost and Sources of Export-Import Financing

The ability to finance a sale is often a factor that differentiates successful exporters from other firms. If a competitor offers better terms for a similar product, the exporter may lose sales. The ability to offer attractive payment terms is often necessary to generate sales. Four key factors determine the cost of financing for export sales.

First is the *creditworthiness of the exporter.* Firms with little collateral, minimal international experience, or those that receive large export orders that exceed their manufacturing capacity may encounter much difficulty in obtaining financing from banks and other lenders at reasonable interest rates, or may not receive financing at all. Second, *creditworthiness of the importer* is a determining factor. An export sales transaction often hinges on the ability of the buyer to obtain sufficient funds to purchase the goods. Some buyers, particularly those from developing economies or countries with currency controls, may be unable to secure financing through letters of credit.

Third is the *riskiness of the sale.* International sales are usually more risky than domestic ones. Banks are reluctant to loan funds for risky sales. Even when funds are provided, financing institutions tend to expect a higher return on loans for risky projects. Riskiness is a function of the value and marketability of the good being sold, the extent of uncertainty surrounding the sale, the degree of political and economic stability in the buyer's country, and the likelihood that the loan will be repaid.

Finally, the *timing of the sale* influences the cost of financing. In international trade, the exporter usually wants to be paid as soon as possible, while the buyer prefers to delay payment, especially until it has received or resold the goods. In some industries, the length of time to complete a sale may be considerable. A common challenge arises when the firm receives an unusually large order from a foreign buyer. In this case, the exporter needs to draw on substantial working capital to initiate and conclude production of the order. This is particularly burdensome for resource-constrained SMEs. In addition, payment periods in international sales are often long, frequently extending over several months.

These four factors strongly influence the availability and cost of funds. Ultimately, the cost of financing affects the pricing and profitability of a sale as well as the payment terms the exporter can offer the buyer. Fortunately, there are various sources for financing international sales, which we discuss next.

Commercial Banks

The same commercial banks used to finance domestic activities can often finance export sales. A logical first step for the exporter that needs financing is to approach the local commercial bank with which it already does business. Alternatively, the exporter may approach a commercial bank with an international department. Such banks are familiar with exporting and may also provide international banking services such as letters of credit. Another option is to have the bank make a loan directly to the foreign buyer to finance the sale. Such loans are available for well-established foreign buyers in stable markets.

Factoring, Forfaiting, and Confirming

Factoring is the discounting of a foreign account receivable by transferring title of the sold item and its account receivable to a *factoring house* (an organization that specializes in purchasing accounts receivable) for cash at a discount from the face value. *Forfaiting* is the selling, at a discount, of long-term accounts receivable of the seller or promissory notes of the foreign buyer. There are numerous *forfaiting houses,* companies that specialize in this practice. *Confirming* is a financial service in which an independent company confirms an export order in the seller's country and makes payment for the goods in the currency of that country. For the exporter, confirming means that the entire export transaction from plant to end user can be fully coordinated and paid for over time. Although used by many exporting firms, these financing options are less widely available than commercial bank financing.

Distribution Channel Intermediaries

In addition to acting as export representatives, some intermediaries may finance export sales. For example, many trading companies and export management companies provide short-term financing or may simply purchase products for export directly from the manufacturer, thus eliminating any risks associated with the export transaction as well as the need for financing.

Buyers and Suppliers

Foreign buyers of expensive products often make down payments that reduce the need for financing from other sources. In addition, buyers may make incremental payments as production of the goods or project is completed. Some industries use letters of credit that allow for progress payments upon inspection by the buyer's agent or receipt of a statement by the exporter that a certain percentage of the product has been completed. In addition, vendors from whom the exporter buys input goods or supplies may be willing to offer more favorable payment terms to the exporter if they are confident they will receive payment.

Intracorporate Financing

Large multinational enterprises with foreign subsidiaries have many more options for financing exports. For instance, the MNE may allow its subsidiary to retain a higher-than-usual level of its own profits, in order to finance export sales. The parent firm may provide loans, equity investments, and trade credit (such as extensions on accounts payable) as funding for the international selling activities of its subsidiaries. The parent can also guarantee loans obtained from foreign banks by its subsidiaries. Finally, large MNEs can often access equity financing by selling corporate bonds or shares in stock markets.

Government Assistance Programs

Most government agencies offer programs to assist exporters with their financing needs. These programs sometimes require that the exported goods contain substantial local content. Some programs provide loans or grants to the exporter, while others offer guarantee programs that require the participation of a bank or other approved lender. Commercial banks use government guarantee and insurance programs to reduce the risk associated with loans to exporters. Under such arrangements, the government pledges to repay a loan made by a commercial bank in the event the importer is unable to repay.

In the United States, the *Export-Import Bank* (Ex-Im Bank) is a government agency that has numerous programs to assist exporters. The bank issues credit insurance that protects firms against default on exports sold under short-term credit. Financing is available for exports, imports, and international investments. In addition, there are agencies that serve the needs of small exporters. For instance, the *U.S. Small Business Administration* helps firms that otherwise might be unable to obtain trade financing. Canada's Export Credits Insurance Corporation, India's Export Credit & Guarantee Corporation, Ltd., and Argentina's Compania Argentina de Seguros de Credito, perform services comparable to those of the Ex-Im Bank.

Multilateral Development Banks (MDBs)

Multilateral Development Banks (MDBs) International financial institutions owned by multiple governments within world regions or other groups.

Multilateral Development Banks (MDBs) are international financial institutions owned by multiple governments within world regions or other groups. Their individual and collective objective is to promote economic and social progress in their member countries—many of which are developing countries. MDBs include the African Development Bank, the Asian Development Bank, the European Bank for Reconstruction and Development, the Inter-American Development Bank, and the World Bank Group. These institutions fulfill their missions by providing loans, technical cooperation, grants, capital investment, and other types of assistance to governments and agencies in the member countries.

Identifying and Working with Foreign Intermediaries

As the opening vignette emphasizes, success in exporting usually depends on establishing strong relationships with distributors, sales representatives, and other intermediaries in foreign markets. Trade fairs are a good way to meet potential intermediaries, become familiar with key players in the industry, and pick the brains of old hands—that is, other exporters experienced in the foreign market. In addition, firms may obtain recommendations on appropriate intermediaries from freight forwarders and trade consultants. In other cases, when attempting to find suitable foreign intermediaries, exporters may consult the following sources:

- Country and regional business directories, such as *Kompass* (Europe), *Bottin International* (worldwide), *Nordisk Handelskelander* (Scandinavia), and the *Japanese Trade Directory*. Other directories include: Dun and Bradstreet, Reuben H. Donnelly, Kelly's Directory, and Johnson Publishing, as well as foreign *Yellow Pages* (often available online).

- Trade associations that support specific industries, such as the National Furniture Manufacturers Association or the National Association of Automotive Parts Manufacturers.

- Government departments, ministries, and agencies charged with assisting economic and trade development, such as Austrade in Australia, Export Development Canada, and the International Trade Administration of the U.S. Department of Commerce.

- Commercial attachés in embassies and consulates abroad.

- Branch offices of certain foreign government agencies located in the exporter's country, such as JETRO, the Japan External Trade Organization.

Often, the best method for managers to identify and qualify intermediaries is to visit the target market. On-site visits afford managers direct exposure to the market and opportunities to meet prospective intermediaries. Managers can also inspect the facilities as well as gauge the capabilities, technical personnel, and sales capabilities of prospective intermediaries. Once the choices have been narrowed to one or two intermediary candidates, experienced exporters often request a prospective intermediary to prepare a business plan for the proposed venture. The quality and sophistication of the resulting plan provides a basis for judging the true capabilities of the prospective partner.

Working with Foreign Intermediaries

In Chapter 3, we discussed the nature and role of various intermediaries in international business. In exporting, the most typical intermediary is the foreign-based independent distributor. The exporter relies on the distributor for much of the marketing, physical distribution, and customer service activities in the export market. The exporter's success greatly depends on the capabilities that the distributor brings to the venture. Therefore, effective managers go to great lengths to build *relational assets*—that is, high-quality, enduring business and social relationships with key intermediaries and facilitators abroad that provide competitive advantages. For instance, Sharon Doherty (in the opening vignette) succeeded in exporting by developing close relationships with qualified foreign distributors. While competitors can usually replicate the exporter's other competitive attributes, such as product features or marketing skills, strong ties with competent foreign intermediaries are built over time, and provide the exporter with an enduring competitive advantage.

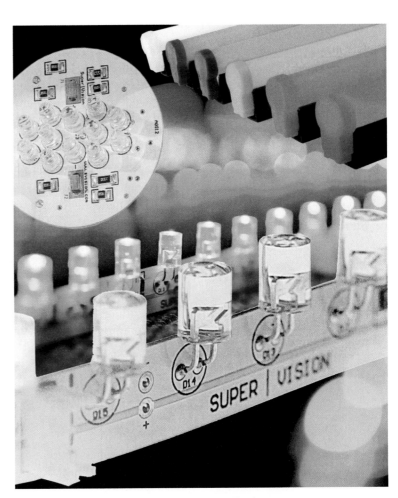

Developing relational assets with intermediaries is accomplished in various ways. The exporter can cultivate mutually beneficial, bonding relations; display genuine response to the intermediary's needs; and build solidarity with the partner, by demonstrating solid commitment, remaining reliable, and building trust.[11] As an example, Super Vision International Inc. is a manufacturer of fiber-optic lighting. When exporting to a particular country, Super Vision initially develops a close working relationship with the country's top importer, which then becomes Super Vision's conduit to smaller companies in the country. The recipe seems successful: Super Vision now receives two-thirds of its revenues from abroad, much of it from developing countries.[12]

Working closely with foreign intermediaries has helped fiber-optic lighting manufacturer Super Vision International Inc. earn significant revenue from abroad.

To create a positive working relationship, the exporter should be sensitive to the intermediary's objectives and aspirations. This requires developing a good understanding of the intermediary's needs and working in earnest to address those needs. In general, foreign intermediaries expect exporters to provide the following:

- Good, reliable products, and those for which there is a ready market
- Products that provide significant profits
- Opportunities to handle other product lines
- Support for marketing communications, such as advertising and promotions, and product warranties
- A payment method that does not unduly burden the intermediary
- Training for intermediary personnel and the opportunity to visit the exporter's facilities (at the exporter's expense), to gain first-hand knowledge of the exporter's operations
- Help establishing after-sales service facilities, including training of local technical representatives and allowances for the cost of replacing defective parts, as well as a ready supply of spare parts, to maintain or repair the products.

Meeting these expectations goes a long way in creating mutually beneficial, long-term relationships.

In turn, the exporter has expectations that its intermediaries should ideally meet. Since relationships with foreign intermediaries are so critical to the exporter's

Intermediary dimension	Evaluation criteria
Strengths	• Ability to finance initial sales and subsequent growth in the market • Ability to provide financing to customers • Quality of management team • Reputation among current and past customers • Connections with influential people or government agencies in the market
Product factors	• Familiarity with the exporter's product • Quality and sophistication of all product lines handled by the intermediary • Ability to ensure security for patents and other intellectual property rights • Willingness to drop competing product lines
Marketing skills	• Experience with target customers • Extent of geographic coverage provided in the target market • Quality and quantity of sales force • Ability to formulate and implement marketing plans
Commitment	• Percent of intermediary's business accounted by a single supplier • Willingness to maintain inventory sufficient to fully serve the market • Commitment to achieving minimum sales targets

Exhibit 13.7 Criteria for Evaluating Export Intermediaries

SOURCE: From S. Tamer Cavusgil, Poh-Lin Yeoh, and Michel Mitri (1995), "Selecting Foreign Distributors: An Expert Systems Approach," *Industrial Marketing Management*, 24 (4) pp. 298–304. Copyright © 1995, with permission from Elsevier.

success, experienced exporters implement a careful screening and selection process when first appointing distributors. Exhibit 13.7 summarizes the selection criteria that experienced exporters use to qualify prospective intermediaries.

When Intermediary Relations Go Bad

Despite good intentions, disputes can arise between the exporter and its intermediaries. Disputes may involve such issues as:

- Compensation arrangements (for example, the intermediary may wish to be compensated even if it were not directly responsible for generating a particular sales order in its territory)
- Pricing practices of the exporter's products
- Advertising and promotion practices, and the extent of advertising support expected from the manufacturer
- After-sales servicing for customers
- Policies on the return of products to the exporter
- Maintaining an adequate level of inventories
- Incentives for promoting new products
- Adapting the product for local customers

In anticipation of such disagreements, many exporters establish a contract-based, legal relationship with the partner. These exporters require the intermediary to sign a contract that binds the intermediary to achieve certain performance objectives and handle the product in a specified manner. Some firms require candidate intermediaries to undergo a courtship or probationary period during which they evaluate the intermediary's performance. At the end of the trial period, if the intermediary's performance is suboptimal or if disputes appear likely to emerge, the exporter may terminate the relationship or require the intermediary to enter a strict contractual relationship.

If the exporter decides to enter into a formal relationship with the intermediary, it must negotiate a contractual agreement that clarifies the tasks and responsibilities of both parties, specifies the duration of the relationship and the terms for its renewal, defines the intermediary's sales territory, and explains the resolution process for potential disputes. The agreement also describes the grounds and terms for terminating the intermediary. For instance, exporters typically terminate their intermediaries if the latter fall short of performance requirements, such as annual sales targets specified by the exporter. The intermediary, for its part, may ask for compensation in the form of indemnities in the event of termination.

Exporters must negotiate intermediary contracts with great care. The exporter needs to ascertain the legal requirements for termination in advance, and include contractual provisions that specify the intermediary's rights for compensation. In many countries, commercial regulations favor local intermediaries and may require the exporter to indemnify the distributor—that is, compensate the intermediary even if it can provide just cause for termination. In some countries, legal contracts may prove insufficient to protect the exporter's interests. For example, China and Russia lack strong legal institutional frameworks, which can make contracts hard to enforce.

Just as in the firm's domestic operations, exporters occasionally encounter problems with buyers or intermediaries who default on payment. As a rule, problems with bad debt are easier to *avoid* than to correct after they occur. Before entering an agreement, the exporter should perform a credit and other background check on potential intermediaries and large-scale buyers. In terms of payment mechanisms, cash in advance or a letter of credit is usually best. In addition to ensuring payment, the letter of credit encourages a high degree of trust between buyer and seller. The exporter can also buy insurance from insurance companies specialized in international transactions to cover commercial credit risks.

In all events, eventually some buyers default on payment. When this happens, the exporter's simplest and least costly recourse is to negotiate with the offending party. With patience, understanding, and flexibility, conflicts can often be resolved to the satisfaction of both sides. Although compromise may be required on certain points—perhaps even on the price of the committed goods—the exporter can save a valuable customer or intermediary, and profit in the long run. But if negotiations fail and the cost of termination is substantial, the exporter may need to seek assistance from its bank, legal counsel, and other qualified experts. At the extreme, the exporter may be forced to pursue litigation, arbitration, or other legal means for enforcing payment on a sale.

 # Countertrade

While countertrade can serve as a method of payment in international trade, it is also a distinct form of foreign market entry. Countertrade activities are especially prevalent in dealing with developing-country governments. Goods and services are traded for other goods and services when conventional means of payment are difficult, costly, or nonexistent. Thus, barter is a form of countertrade. Countertrade refers to an international business transaction where all or partial payments are made in kind rather than cash. The focal firm is engaged simultaneously in exporting and importing.

Consider the example of Caterpillar, which exported earth-moving equipment to Venezuela. In exchange, the Venezuelan government gave Caterpillar 350,000 tons of iron ore. Middle Eastern countries occasionally pay for imported goods with crude oil, as when Saudi Arabia purchased jets from Boeing. Also called *two-way* or *reciprocal* trade, countertrade operates on the principle of "I'll buy your products if you'll buy mine."

Exhibit 13.8 illustrates the multiple transactions involved in countertrade deals. Typically, the focal firm is a Western company, say General Electric, which

Exhibit 13.8

A Countertrade Transaction Where Products Are Received from the Customer as Partial or Full Payment

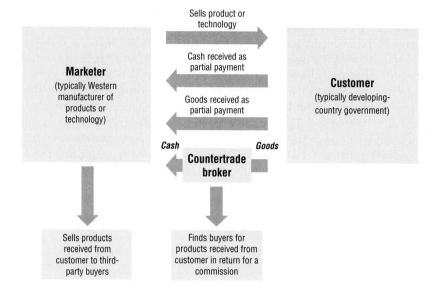

wishes to sell its products or technology (for example, jet engines) to a developing-country government. In a particular instance, the customer, the Indonesian government, was experiencing an acute shortage of convertible currencies (for example, the U.S. dollar, the euro, the yen) and was unable to pay General Electric in cash. The Indonesian government then asked General Electric to accept some local products as partial payment or in full. Typically the products developing countries offer are commodities (for example, agricultural grains, minerals, or manufactured products that may have limited international sales potential). General Electric may then agree to take these products and sell them in international markets in order to get paid. Alternatively, General Electric may ask a countertrade broker to sell these developing-country goods on its behalf, in return for a commission. In another countertrade deal, Philip Morris exported cigarettes to Russia for which it received industrial chemicals as payment. It shipped these chemicals to China and received glassware in exchange that it then sold for cash in North America. In addition to a buyer and a seller, a countertrade broker may also be involved. Multiple transactions also may take years to complete. As you can see, countertrade transactions tend to be much more complicated than conventional cash-for-goods trade.

Here are some other examples of countertrade transactions:

- Caterpillar received caskets from Columbian customers and wine from Algerian customers in return for selling them earthmoving equipment.
- Goodyear traded tires for minerals, textiles, and agricultural products.
- Coca-Cola sourced tomato paste from Turkey, oranges from Egypt, and beer from Poland in order to contribute to national exports in the countries it conducts business.
- Control Data Corporation accepted Christmas cards from the Russians in a countertrade deal.
- Pepsi-Cola acquired the rights to distribute Hungarian motion pictures in the West in a countertrade transaction.

The Magnitude and Drivers of Countertrade

Many MNEs have been pursuing nontraditional trade deals since the 1960s, not only in developing countries that lack hard currencies, but also in industrialized nations. While the exact extent of countertrade is unknown, some observers estimate that it accounts for as much as one-third of all world trade. Countertrade deals are also more prevalent in large-scale government procurement projects. For example, countertrade has been mandatory for all Australian federal government foreign purchases of more than 2.5 million Australian dollars. In South Korea, countertrade is mandated for government telecommunications and defense procurement exceeding $1 million. In Asia, Indonesia led the way early by requiring countertrade for large-scale public sector purchases. Eastern European nations and Russia have practiced barter and countertrade transactions for quite some time.

Countertrade occurs in response to two primary factors. First is the chronic shortage of hard currency in developing economies. Second is the lack of marketing expertise, adequate quality standards, and knowledge of western markets by developing-economy enterprises. Countertrade enables these enterprises to access markets that might otherwise be inaccessible, and at the same time generate hard currency.

Types of Countertrade

There are four main types of countertrade: barter, compensation deals, counterpurchase, and buy-back agreements. First, **barter**—the oldest form of trade—refers to the direct exchange of goods without any money. Though less common today, barter is still exercised (even in domestic trade) in straightforward, one-shot deals. Compared to the other forms of countertrade, barter involves a single contract (rather than two or more contracts typical of other forms), has a short time span (other countertrade deals may stretch over several years), and is less complicated (other forms generally require managerial commitment and resources are required in countertrade).

Second, **compensation deals** involve payment both in goods and cash. For example, a company may sell its equipment to the government of Brazil and receive half the payment in hard currency and the other half in merchandise.

Third, also known as a back-to-back transaction or offset agreements, **counterpurchase** involves two distinct contracts. In the first contract, the seller agrees to sell its product at a set price and receives cash payment from the buyer. However, this first deal is contingent on a second contract wherein the seller also agrees to purchase goods from the buyer for the total monetary amount or a set percentage of same. If the exchange is not of equal value, partial payment may be made in cash. Alternatively, the buyer may require that a certain proportion of the seller's goods be produced and assembled in the buyer's country. Counterpurchase is common in the defense industry, where the governments that purchase military hardware may require the defense contractor to purchase some local products or contribute to local employment.

Finally, in a product **buy-back agreement**, the seller agrees to supply technology or equipment to construct a facility and receives payment in the form of goods produced by the facility. For example, the seller might design and construct a factory in the buyer's country to manufacture tractors. The seller is compensated by receiving finished tractors from the factory it built, which it then sells in world markets. In essence, the original transaction involves goods and services that produce other goods and services, which are then received in payment. Product buy-back agreements may require several years to complete and therefore entail substantial risk.

Risks of Countertrade

There are four problems firms can encounter in reciprocal trade.

First, the goods that the customer offers may be inferior in quality, with limited potential to sell them in international markets.

Second, it is often very difficult to put a market value on goods the customer offers, because these goods are typically commodities or low-quality manufactured products. In addition, the buyer may not always have the opportunity to inspect the goods or have time to conduct a market analysis.

Barter A type of countertrade that involves the direct exchange of goods without any money.

Compensation deals A type of countertrade that involves payment both in goods and cash.

Counterpurchase A type of countertrade that involves two distinct contracts. In the first contract, the seller agrees to sell its product at a set price and receives cash payment from the buyer. This first deal is contingent on a second contract wherein the seller also agrees to purchase goods from the buyer for the total monetary amount or a set percentage of same.

Buy-back agreement A type of countertrade that involves the seller agreeing to supply technology or equipment to construct a facility and receives payment in the form of goods produced by the facility.

Third, countertrade deals are inefficient because both parties pad their prices. The seller may experience considerable difficulty in re-selling the commodities that it receives as payment. In a typical scenario, General Electric (GE) will place the products it receives as payment in countertrade (e.g., nails, furniture, tomato paste) with a broker who then sells them in world markets for a commission. Consequently, General Electric will build in the cost of disposing of the goods into the price that it quotes to the buyer. The buyer, in turn, anticipating GE's price padding, will pass the extra cost onto its customers. Thus, the resulting transaction between GE and the buyer is inefficient.

Fourth, reciprocal trade amounts to highly complex, cumbersome, and time-consuming transactions. As a result, the proportion of countertrade deals that firms are able to bring to fruition is often quite low. Fifth, rules imposed by governments can make countertrade highly bureaucratic. The rules essentially become cumbersome and often frustrating for the exporting firm.

Why Countertrade?

Although most firms are reluctant to engage in reciprocal trade, there are five circumstances when they would consider it. First, when the alternative is no trade at all, as in the case of mandated countertrade, firms will have to consider countertrade. Second, countertrade may help firms get a foothold in new markets and help them cultivate new customer relationships. For example, in the mining industry, certain types of minerals are available only in developing countries. Mining rights in these areas may be available only to firms willing to countertrade. Third, many companies use countertrade creatively to develop new sources of supply. Reciprocal trade is made more attractive if the company can secure products it would use in its own operations. The firm may develop new suppliers in the process.

Fourth, firms have used countertrade as a way of repatriating profits frozen in a foreign subsidiary operation's blocked accounts. Otherwise unable to repatriate its earnings, the firm will scout the local market for products it can successfully export to world markets. General Motors' former Motors Trading subsidiary was created to generate trade credits—that is, sell its vehicles in a market in return for contributing to exports of merchandise originating from that country.

Fifth, given their risky and cumbersome nature, firms may succeed in developing managers who are comfortable with a trading mentality. Multinational enterprises such as GM, GE, Siemens, Toshiba, and Caterpillar have set up separate divisions to foster global managers with a trading mentality, thereby becoming entrepreneurial, innovative, politically connected, and highly knowledgeable about a range of commodities and tradable goods. These firms recognize the value of such attributes for pursuing international deals and attempt to foster them by involving their global managers in countertrade. The skills that managers acquire contribute to international performance, not only in countertrade deals, but in various other cross-border transactions as well.

Barrett Farm Foods: A Small Firm's International Launch

Philip Austin, general manager of Barrett Farm Foods, was thrilled after returning from the food industry trade fair in Cologne, Germany—the largest food and beverage fair in the world. Barrett Farm Foods, based in Melbourne, Victoria, is Australia's sixth largest food company. It distributes both bulk agricultural commodities and processed food products. Among others, it sells macadamia nuts, cereal bars, garlic, ginger, dried fruits, and honey throughout Australia. Barrett has had a healthy rate of growth over the past decade, and its sales reached US$215 million last year. While Barrett is well known in the domestic market, its international experience has been limited to responding to occasional, unsolicited orders from foreign customers. In completing these export orders, Barrett has relied on intermediaries in Australia that provided assistance to international logistics and payments. Yet Austin is enthusiastic about substantially expanding the export business over the next few years.

Recognizing an Opportunity

What prompted Mr. Austin to attend the Cologne fair was a recent report from Austrade, the Australian government's trade promotion agency, which highlighted the tremendous potential of Australian exports of foodstuffs. For example, According to Austrade, Australian food exports exceeded AU$25 billion last year. Austrade believes that highly processed foodstuffs are the coming trend and wants to boost their exports.

But this raises a dilemma: much of current exports are primarily raw foods, not *processed* foods. If just 10 percent of processed food value-adding were done in Australia, the country's balance of trade would improve. For example, instead of exporting raw grains to Europe, Austrade wants Australian producers to process the grains into bread and other bakery products, thereby creating jobs for Australians. Austrade believes that meat, cereal, sugar, dairy commodities, and marine products have the most potential for food processing.

Meeting with Potential Export Customers at the Cologne Fair

At the Cologne fair, Barrett's nut- and honey-based cereal bars and butter-like spread were a hit. Luigi Cairati, a senior executive with the Italian supermarket chain Standa, was keen on doing business with Barrett. He pointed out that, over the past decade, there has been an explosion of interest among European supermarkets and food stores for exotic foods and vegetables, with each group competing to display produce from around the world. Standa was seeking new products from other countries, partly to meet off-season demand for fruit and vegetables. Gabrielle Donce, purchasing manager for French food group Fauchon, also confirmed her interest in showcasing exotic and high-quality food in Fauchon stores. She added that Europeans view Australia as a country that is exotic, pollution-free, and a producer of quality products. In addition, the market for canned fruit is opening up as the fruit crop from trees in Europe declines over time.

Mr. Austin also met Peter Telford, an agent from the United Kingdom who showed interest in representing Barrett Farm Foods in Europe. Mr. Telford talked about his knowledge of the market, extensive contacts, and prior business experience. He also noted that other Australian firms, such as Goodman Fielder Wattie, Burns Philip, Adelaide Steamship, Elders-IXL, SPC, and Southern Farmers, are already doing business in the region. He pointed to several success stories, including Sydney-based pastry manufacturer, C & M Antoniou, which has now established a small plant in Britain as a way of avoiding the considerable wall of agricultural duties surrounding the EU market. The company is now supplying several of Britain's major supermarket chains, including Marks & Spencer, Tesco, and Sainsbury's. Another Australian group, Buderim Ginger, has recently expanded its operations from Britain into continental Europe by opening an office in Germany.

Creating a Task Force

After the fair, Mr. Austin created a three-person task force among his senior managers and charged them with implementing an export drive. He felt that an export volume of US$30 million for the first year was reasonable. For products to be exported to Europe, Barrett would have to examine its current product offerings. It would appoint an agent, such as Peter Telford, to facilitate sales to European customers. The people Philip Austin met at the Cologne fair were potential customers to contact for immediate sales. The company could also forward some product and company literature to European importers, identify and appoint one or more distributors in Europe that have access to large-scale buyers such as supermarkets, and revamp its web site to attract export business.

While Barrett's senior managers shared Mr. Austin's enthusiasm about expanding to European markets, they did not share his optimism. Barrett had little internal expertise to deal with the complexities of international shipping, export documentation, and receiving payments from export customers. In addition, they knew that export transactions take a long time to complete, and the firm would have to arrange for financing of export sales. Most importantly, senior managers felt that they would have to invest in creating a small export team and quickly acquire or train employees who are proficient in export transactions.

Food is a complex business, in part because it is perishable, often requiring special equipment for distribution. In addition, Europe has many differences in national tastes, regulations, and market structures. Food products are especially susceptible to local preferences. For example, Vegemite—a dark brown, salty breakfast spread made from yeast—that is a favorite of the Australians, has little acceptance outside of Australia. Having no name recognition in the European Union, Barrett may also have to resort to store branding, which will generate lower profit margins.

Barrett will have to rely on competent foreign intermediaries with access to key supermarket chains to distribute its products. Is Peter Telford the right choice? What kind of commission will be necessary to compensate these intermediaries? With many larger, more experienced competitors in the European Union, Barrett must keep its pricing competitive, although the complexity of pricing can overwhelm inexperienced managers. Barrett's senior managers also realize that prices have a clear effect on sales and profits. The launch of Europe's common currency, the euro, simplified pricing strategy,

but numerous challenges remain. Prices are affected by transportation costs, buyer demand, exchange rates, tariffs, competitors' pricing, regulatory compliance, and the costs of marketing and physical distribution.

AACSB: **Reflective Thinking, Analytical Skills**

Case Questions

1. Do you see any problems with Mr. Austin's plan for European expansion? Do you support his entrepreneurial approach to exporting? What should be the features of a more systematic approach to exporting?

2. Why did Barrett choose exporting as its entry strategy for Europe, as opposed to foreign direct investment or licensing? What advantages does exporting provide to Barrett? What are the potential drawbacks of exporting for Barrett?

3. What challenges can Barrett expect in its export drive? What types of new capabilities does the firm need to acquire to manage its export transactions?

4. How should Barrett choose between direct and indirect exporting? What are the ideal characteristics of European intermediaries for Barrett? If it chooses to minimize its risks, which of the three most commonly used Incoterms would Barrett favor? Where can Barrett turn for financing its export sales?

CHAPTER ESSENTIALS

Key Terms

barter, p. 407
buy-back agreement, p. 407
company-owned subsidiary, p. 393
compensation deals, p. 407
counterpurchase, p. 407
countertrade, p. 382

direct exporting, p. 392
documentation, p. 395
exporting, p. 382
global sourcing, p. 382
importing, p. 394
incoterms, p. 396

indirect exporting, p. 392
letter of credit, p. 398
Multilateral Development Bank
(MDBs), p. 402

Summary

In this chapter, you learned about:

1. An overview of foreign market entry strategies

Market entry strategies consist of *exporting, sourcing,* and *foreign direct investment,* as well as *licensing, franchising,* and *non-equity alliances.* Each strategy has advantages and disadvantages and places its own demands on corporate resources. To select a market entry strategy, managers must consider the firm's resources and capabilities, conditions in the target country, risks inherent in each venture, competition from existing and potential rivals, and the characteristics of the product or service to be offered in the market. **Importing** refers to the strategy of buying products and services from sources located abroad for use at home. It is also referred to as **global sourcing**, global purchasing, or global procurement.

2. The internationalization of the firm

Firms internationalize due to *push factors* and *pull factors.* Initial internationalization may be accidental. Management must balance risk against return. Each international venture provides learning experiences that encourage further internationalization. Firms generally pass through stages of internationalization, going from relatively simple and low-risk entry strategies to more complex strategies.

3. Exporting as a foreign market entry strategy

Exporting amounts to producing at home and then shipping products abroad, to be sold and delivered to foreign customers via intermediaries. It is the strategy favored by most firms when they first internationalize. Exporting is also a relatively flexible entry strategy, allowing the firm to readily withdraw in case of substantial problems in the target market. A systematic approach to exporting requires managers to perform a global market opportunity assessment, make organizational arrangements for exporting, acquire needed skills and competencies, as well as

design and implement the export strategy. Among the organizational arrangements for exporting are **indirect exporting**, **direct exporting**, and establishing a **company-owned subsidiary**.

4. Managing export-import transactions

Management must become familiar with customs clearance, international goods transportation, and **documentation**, the required forms and other paperwork used to conclude international sales. The exporter typically entrusts preparation of documents to a freight forwarder. In addition, national governments sometimes require exporters to obtain a license, a type of permission to export. **Incoterms** are universally accepted terms of sale that effectively specify what is and what is not included in the price of a product sold internationally, particularly with regard to the cost of transporting and insuring the good. Among the most commonly used Incoterms are EXW, FOB, and CIF.

5. Methods of payment in exporting and importing

Exporting also requires knowledge of payment methods, such as cash in advance, **letter of credit**, open account, consignment sales, and countertrade. For most firms, letter of credit is best because it establishes immediate trust and protects both the buyer and seller.

6. Cost and sources of export-import financing

Intense competition in export markets mandates that exporters offer attractive payment terms to their customers. Sources of finance for export transactions include commercial banks, *factoring, forfaiting,* and *confirming,* distribution channel intermediaries, intercompany financing, government assistance programs, and **multilateral development banks.**

7. Identifying and working with foreign intermediaries

Managers can identify intermediaries, such as sales representatives and distributors, from a variety of public and private information sources. Qualified and committed foreign distributors are valuable *relational assets*. It is best to develop long-term relations with these business partners, who perform a variety of functions abroad on behalf of the exporter. Key to good relations include cultivating mutually beneficial bonds, genuinely responding to distributor needs, and encouraging loyalty. Success factors in exporting include being strongly committed to the export venture, doing market research, emphasizing strong products, developing an international business plan for each export venture, and adapting to foreign cultures.

8. Countertrade

Countertrade refers to an international business transaction where all or partial payments are made in kind rather than cash. Countertrade involves getting paid in goods or services, instead of currency. Also called two-way or reciprocal trade, countertrade operates on the principle of "I'll buy your products if you'll buy mine." There are four types of countertrade. **Barter** involves the direct exchange of goods without any money. **Compensation deals** involve payment both in goods and cash. **Counterpurchase** involves two distinct contracts. In the first contract, the seller agrees to sell its product at a set price and receives cash payment from the buyer. This first deal is contingent on a second contract wherein the seller also agrees to purchase goods from the buyer for the total monetary amount or a set percentage of same. **Buy-back agreements** involve the seller agreeing to supply technology or equipment to construct a facility and receives payment in the form of goods produced by the facility.

Test Your Comprehension AACSB: Reflective Thinking

1. What are the major foreign market entry strategies? What are the essential characteristics of each?

2. Describe the typical internationalization process that a firm may use in expanding abroad.

3. What is exporting? What are the major advantages and disadvantages of exporting?

4. Describe the organizing framework for exporting. What steps should the firm go through to ensure exporting success?

5. What are the major tasks involved in the management of export transactions?

6. Explain the primary payment methods that exporters typically use. What is the most reliable payment method, and how do exporters carry it out?

7. What are Incoterms, and why do firms follow them?

8. How would you go about identifying suitable foreign intermediaries?

9. What steps should the exporter take to ensure success in working with intermediaries?

10. Explain the nature, role, and risks involved in countertrade.

Apply Your Understanding AACSB: **Communication, Reflective Thinking**

1. Although most companies expand abroad gradually, some smaller firms internationalize at or near the firm's founding. The so-called born global firms represent a revolution in international business. Their emergence suggests that companies can participate actively in foreign markets from an early stage. Suppose you are an international business consultant and you have been contacted by management at a young firm that manufactures office furniture. The firm needs to generate more sales and wants to expand abroad. Given that internationalization is risky, particularly for smaller firms, what advice would you give them? In particular, what systematic approach to exporting and managing export-import transactions would you recommend?

2. Moose & Walrus is a manufacturer of a popular line of clothing for young people. Moose & Walrus is firmly established in its home market, which is relatively saturated and has little prospects for future sales growth. Moose & Walrus has decided to export its clothing line to Japan and various European countries. Because of the firm's strong manufacturing base in its home country, management has decided to internationalize through exporting, and has hired you to help with this effort. Prepare a briefing for senior managers and describe the advantages and disadvantages of exporting. In addition, recommend and describe payment methods.

3. Antenna Communications Technologies, Inc. (ACT) is a small satellite technology communications firm. Its product is a multibeam antenna that allows customers in the broadcast industry to receive signals from up to 35 satellites simultaneously. The firm has very limited experience in international business. ACT recently hired you as its export manager and, based on some extensive research, you have determined that substantial export markets exist for the product in Africa, China, Russia, and Saudi Arabia. You have followed most of the steps in the organizing framework for exporting and have decided that direct exporting is the most appropriate entry strategy for ACT. Your next task is to find distributors in the target markets. How would you go about this task? What resources should you access to find distributors in these markets? Once established, what is the best way to maintain solid relations with foreign distributors? Finally, what payment method should ACT use for most of its prospective markets?

AACSB: Communication, Reflective Thinking

Refer to Chapter 1, page 27, for instructions on how to access and use globalEDGE™.

1. You work for a firm that manufactures children's toys. Your firm has little international experience and wishes to get started in exporting. Your boss understands the importance of using strong distributors abroad, but knows little about how to find them. Having studied international business in college, you know that many national governments offer programs that help new exporters find appropriate intermediaries in foreign countries. Examples of such programs include trade missions, trade shows, distributor search services, and matchmaker programs (in which the exporter is matched with foreign intermediaries). In the United States, for example, the International Trade Administration (ITA) provides various services for helping exporters find foreign distributors. Visit the web site of the ITA (www.ita.doc.gov), or the main trade support agency of your country (via globalEDGE™), and see what programs are available. Then prepare a memo to your boss in which you describe specific programs that you believe would help your firm get started in exporting.

2. Suppose you work for a major trading company involved in the exporting of timber in the lumber industry in Canada; of petroleum in the oil industry in Britain; and of processed food products in the agricultural industry in the United States. To enhance your career prospects, you want to become better informed about the export of these goods from their respective countries. Visit globalEDGE™ and research current international news about the above industries in the countries indicated. Based on your findings, prepare a brief report on the current status of each of the industries in their countries in the context of your firm's exporting efforts.

3. Suppose that your employer wants to export its products and get paid through letter of credit (LC). Suppose further that no one at the firm knows much about LCs. You have volunteered to become the company's LC expert. One way to accomplish this is to visit globalEDGE™ and do a search on the keywords "letter of credit." Another approach is to visit the web sites of major banks to learn about procedures and instructions for getting paid via LC. Exemplar banks include CIBC (www.cibc.com), the National Australia Bank www.national.com.au), and Wachovia (www.wachovia.com). As a preliminary step, visit the web sites of each of these banks and see what you can learn about LCs. For each bank, what are the requirements for getting an LC? What services does the bank offer in regard to LCs? Can you get training in LCs from these banks?

CKR Cavusgil Knight Riesenberger
Management Skill Builder©

Identifying An Attractive Export Market

Exporters seek the best foreign markets for their products and services. Managers conduct market research to determine the viability of potential export markets. They examine such factors as market size, growth rate, economic status, competition, and the degree of political stability. Without this market research, firms can fail in their export ventures.

AACSB: Reflective Thinking, Use of Information Technology

Managerial Challenge

The task of choosing the best export markets is complex. What makes an ideal market? What market potential indicators should managers consider? The managerial challenge is to choose the best export markets by following a systematic process of international market research.

Background

Exporting is the most widely used entry mode. This is especially true for firms that are new to international business and for firms with substantial production facilities at home. Research is particularly important to small and medium-sized enterprises, which usually lack the resources to sustain significant losses from failed exporting efforts.

Managerial Skills You Will Gain

In this C/K/R Management Skill Builder©, as a prospective manager, you will:

1. Learn the important indicators used to assess the viability of potential export markets

2. Access information needed to develop international business plans

3. Research country-level barriers that firms face in exporting

Your Task

Assume that you work for a firm that makes and markets portable DVD players. Management has decided to begin exporting the players abroad. Your task is to conduct market research aimed at formulating a ranking of the most viable countries that your firm should target with exports of portable DVD players. As part of the exercise, you will visit several online portals and gather relevant data.

Go to the C/K/R Knowledge Portal©

www.prenhall.com/cavusgil

Proceed to the C/K/R Knowledge Portal© to obtain the expanded background information, your task and methodology, suggested resources for this exercise, and the presentation template to use.

Foreign Direct Investment and Collaborative Ventures

> ## Deutsche Post's Global Buying Spree

As cross-border trade increases, so does the demand for supply chain, logistics, and express delivery services from firms that move raw materials, parts, finished goods, packages, and documents around the world. Specialized logistics facilitators organize, coordinate, and control supply chains using technological advancements and a physical presence that spans the world. Couriers such as UPS, FedEx, and DHL have global networks of offices and warehouses, trucks and aircraft, and extensive information tracking systems to serve firms' global delivery and logistics needs.

Deutsche Post AG, previously the German state-owned postal service, was privatized in 2000. Since then, the firm has been spending billions to acquire firms worldwide, becoming the world's leading express and logistics provider. The express division combines airplanes and trucks to transport mail and parcel shipments. The logistics division manages the international transportation needs of numerous firms. Deutsche Post generates roughly half its sales in Europe, one-third in North America, and the rest from the Asia/Pacific region.

Deutsche Post's main strength is its size. With 500,000 employees and annual revenues exceeding $70 billion in 2007, Deutsche Post owns 420 aircraft, 72,000

vehicles, and 640 branch logistics offices in 200 countries. The firm established offices either through foreign direct investment (FDI) or by forming collaborative ventures with partner firms in foreign markets. Firms use FDI to establish a physical presence abroad by building or acquiring a production or assembly facility, sales office, or other type of local facility. The parent firm in this relationship may own 100 percent of the foreign operation or it may exercise only partial ownership, in collaboration with a foreign partner. The latter arrangement is known as a *joint venture,* when two or more firms create a jointly owned enterprise.

Like many other firms in recent years, Deutsche Post has used foreign acquisitions to expand internationally. For instance, in 1999 Deutsche Post acquired Danzas, the Swiss ocean and air freight firm. In 2002, it paid $2.7 billion to acquire the U.S. firm DHL. The next year Deutsche Post (through DHL) spent $1 billion for the ground delivery network of U.S.-based Airborne. The 2005 acquisition of 81 percent of the Indian express company Blue Dart strengthened Deutsche Post's ability to service customers in Asia. The 2005 acquisition of Britain's Exel, with its 110,000 employees in 130 countries, increased Deutsche Post's control of express delivery and logistics operations across Europe and the United States. DHL became

Deutsche Post's main arm for global express delivery, offering express services, international air and ocean freight, contract logistics, and value-added services, with such customers as Standard Chartered Bank, PepsiCo, BMW, and Sun Microsystems.

In addition to acquisitions, Deutsche Post entered various collaborative ventures. The firm formed an alliance with Amazon.com to handle Amazon's huge delivery needs for its export customers. DHL entered a 50/50 joint venture with Sinotrans to serve the huge Chinese market. In Japan, Deutsche Post formed a joint venture with Yamato, Japan's biggest private postal company.

Deutsche Post faced formidable challenges in absorbing acquisitions and producing strong financial returns. In the United States, it struggled to build a reliable transportation network. Late deliveries sparked customer defections and forced Deutsche Post to offer price discounts. The huge cost of absorbing DHL and Airborne reduced management's ability to make needed improvements to operations and service standards.

As a former German state enterprise, much of Deutsche Post's early success stemmed from subsidies and other support from the German government. Competitors in the United States, such as FedEx and UPS, as well as labor unions and national security bodies, argued that Deutsche Post should not be allowed to acquire major transportation infrastructure in the United States. Despite substantial legal wrangling, regulators ruled in favor of DHL and Deutsche Post. Today, Deutsche Post is a world leader in global air freight, ocean freight, and contract logistics.

Sources: Bream, Rebecca. (2004). "Deutsche Post Buys UK Mail Group," *Financial Times*, Jan. 28, p. 35; Deutsche Post corporate web site at *www.deutschepost.de*; *Direct Marketing*. (2001). "Amazon Expands Alliance with Deutsche Post Global Mail," Nov., p. 7; EIU ViewsWire. (2003). "Netherlands Industry: Deutsche Post Buys Dutch Express Provider, Feb. 20; Esterl, Mike. (2006). "Deutsche Post Struggles to Deliver in the U.S.," *Wall Street Journal*, April 12, p. C.5; Hahn, A. (2003). "Deutsche Post Unique Route: Will the Germans' Plan to Buy Part of Airborne Pave the Way for Foreign Ownership?" *The Investment Dealers' Digest*, March 31, p. 1; Hoffman, William. (2006). "Post-Merger Indigestion," *Traffic World*, March 27, p. 1; *Precision Marketing*. (2006). "Deutsche Post and Yamato in Joint Offering," May 12, p. 9; Ward, Andrew. (2006). "DHL Agrees to Buy 49% Stake in Polar Air," *Financial Times*, Oct. 17, p. 28.

An Organizing Framework for Foreign Market Entry Strategies

Foreign direct investment (FDI) An internationalization strategy in which the firm establishes a physical presence abroad through acquisition of productive assets such as capital, technology, labor, land, plant, and equipment.

International collaborative venture Cross-border business alliance in which partnering firms pool their resources and share costs and risks of the venture; also called an "international partnership" or "international strategic alliance."

The cross-border spread of capital and ownership is one of the most remarkable facets of globalization. Consider a recent example. Throughout 2005, several companies were in a bidding race to acquire Maytag Corp., based in Newton, Iowa, one of the leaders in the worldwide home appliance industry. Chief among the bidders was Haier Group, China's largest appliance maker. Haier Group bid over $1 billion with the hope of establishing a greater presence in the United States, the largest appliance market in the world. The bidding war finally culminated in early 2006 with Whirlpool, another U.S. appliance maker, emerging as the winning bidder in a deal worth about $2.6 billion. While the Chinese firm failed in this particular attempt to complete a cross-border acquisition, this example illustrates the important phenomenon of foreign direct investment and international collaborative ventures. **Foreign direct investment (FDI)** is an internationalization strategy in which the firm establishes a physical presence abroad through ownership of productive assets such as capital, technology, labor, land, plant, and equipment. An **international collaborative venture** refers to a cross-border business alliance in which partnering firms pool their resources and share costs and risks of the new venture. It is a form of FDI in which the focal firm partners with one or more other companies to establish a physical presence abroad.

Another recent example is from the beer industry. South African Breweries (SAB) established a major presence in the United States beer market through its 2002 purchase of Miller Brewing, changing its name to SABMiller plc. In 2005, the firm acquired 97 percent of Bavaria S.A., the second largest brewer in South America. In 2006, SABMiller acquired Foster's India for $120 million, gaining control of nearly 50 percent of the Indian beer market. Meanwhile, in China, the firm entered a joint venture with CR Snow Breweries, helping to make SABMiller the largest brewer in China. A **joint venture** is a form of collaboration between two or more firms to create a jointly owned enterprise. A partner in a joint venture may enjoy minority, equal, or majority ownership. Through numerous FDI and collaborative ventures in the 2000s, SABMiller has become the world's third-largest brewer, with operations in more than 60 countries.[1] Both FDI and international collaborative venture are examples of fundamental ways in which focal firms implement international expansion.

Joint venture A form of collaboration between two or more firms to create a jointly owned enterprise.

Trends in Foreign Direct Investment and Collaborative Ventures

Foreign direct investment is the most advanced and complex foreign market entry strategy, and involves establishing manufacturing plants, marketing subsidiaries, or other facilities abroad. For the firm, FDI requires substantial resource commitment, local presence and operations in target countries, and global scale efficiency. It also entails greater risk as compared to other entry modes.

In 2005, there were 141 cross-border acquisitions at valued more than $1 billion. The top three recipient countries were the United Kingdom, the United States, and Germany. Here are some examples of recent cross-border investments:

- Vodafone, a British firm, acquired the Czech telecom Oskar Mobil.
- eBay, a U.S. firm, acquired Luxembourg's Skype Technologies, a prepackaged software company.
- Japan Tobacco Inc. acquired the British cigarette maker Gallaher Group PLC for almost $15 billion.
- Dubai International Capital Group acquired the British theme park operator Tussauds Group for $1.5 billion.
- Sing Tel, a Singapore firm, acquired 49 cross-border firms worth over $36 billion over eight years, including Cable and Wireless Optus Ltd. of Australia.

These and numerous other examples illustrate several trends in the contemporary global economy. First, companies from both advanced economies and emerging markets are active in FDI. Second, destination or recipient countries for such investments include both advanced economies and emerging markets. Third, companies employ multiple strategies to enter foreign markets as investors, including acquisitions and collaborative ventures. Fourth, companies from all types of industries, including services, are active in FDI and collaborative ventures. For example, major retailers began expanding abroad in the 1970s. Leading examples include Wal-Mart (U.S.), Carrefour (France), Royal Ahold (Netherlands), Metro AG (Germany), and Tesco (UK). Finally, direct investment by foreign companies occasionally raises patriotic sentiments among citizens. For example, the possibility of a Haier takeover of Maytag Corp. in 2005 stirred anti-Chinese sentiment in the United States over East Asian companies gobbling up U.S. businesses. That same year, a bid by Chinese oil company CNOOC Ltd. to buy California-based Unocal Corp. for $18.5 billion raised concerns over national security. When the public objected to the possibility of a Chinese state enterprise gaining control in a critical sector such as energy, the U.S. Congress banned the deal.

Low, Moderate, and High-Control Foreign Market Entry Strategies

We have already noted that one of the key decisions that management makes in international business is the choice of foreign market entry strategy and the particular institutional arrangement it employs to access the foreign market. When undertaking foreign market entry, the focal firm must consider several factors, including:

- The degree of control it wants to maintain over the decisions, operations, and strategic assets involved in the venture
- The degree of risk it is willing to tolerate and the time frame within which it expects returns
- The organizational and financial resources (for example, capital, managers, technology) it will commit to the venture
- The availability and capabilities of partners in the market
- The value-adding activities it is willing to perform itself in the market, and what activities it will leave to partners
- The long-term strategic importance of the market

While all these factors are relevant, perhaps none is more critical than the first one—the degree of control the focal firm wants to maintain over the venture. *Control* refers to the ability to influence the decisions, operations, and strategic resources with respect to the foreign venture. Without control, the focal firm "will find it more difficult to coordinate actions, carry out strategies . . . and resolve the disputes that invariably arise when two parties . . . pursue their own interests."[2]

In Exhibit 3.5 (Chapter 3, page 70), we classified entry strategies into three categories, based on the nature of international transaction: (1) the trade of products, (2) contractual exchange of services or intangibles, and (3) equity ownership in foreign-based enterprises. Exhibit 14.1 illustrates another useful way to organize foreign market entry strategies based on the degree of control each strategy affords the focal firm over foreign operations.

On the continuum of control in Exhibit 14.1, the arm's-length buyer-seller relationships of exporting represent little or no control at one extreme, while FDI, through a wholly owned subsidiary, represents maximum control at the other extreme. Thus, foreign market entry strategies can be considered in three categories, based on the degree of control available to the focal firm:

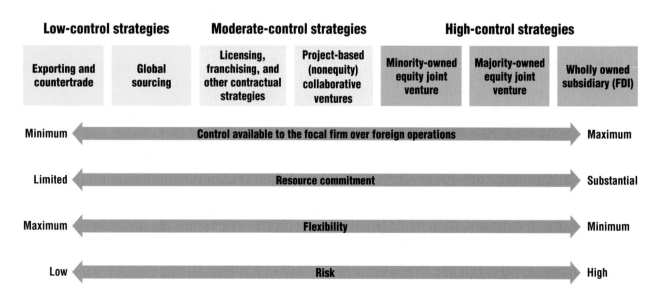

Exhibit 14.1 A Classification of Foreign Market Entry Strategies Based on Degree of Control Afforded to the Focal Firm

- *Low-control strategies* are exporting, countertrade (already discussed in Chapter 13), and global sourcing (to be discussed in Chapter 16). They provide the least control over foreign operations, since the focal firm delegates considerable responsibility to foreign partners (distributors or suppliers).

- *Moderate-control strategies* are contractual relationships such as licensing and franchising (Chapter 15) and project-based collaborative ventures (discussed in this chapter).

- *High-control strategies* are equity joint ventures and FDI (discussed in this chapter). The focal firm attains maximum control by establishing a physical presence in the foreign market.

The particular arrangement of entry strategies in Exhibit 14.1 also highlights trade-offs, other than control, that the focal firm makes when entering foreign markets. First, high-control strategies require substantial *resource commitments* by the focal firm. Second, because the firm becomes anchored or physically tied to the foreign market for the long term, it has less *flexibility* to reconfigure its operations there as conditions in the country evolve over time. Third, longer-term involvement in the market also implies considerable *risk* due to uncertainty in the political and customer environments. Especially amplified are political risk, cultural risk, and currency risk, which we discussed earlier.

Motives for Foreign Direct Investment (FDI) and Collaborative Ventures

Companies pursue FDI and international collaborative ventures for complex and overlapping reasons. The ultimate goal is to enhance firm competitiveness in the global marketplace. It is useful to classify specific motives into three categories: market-seeking motives, resource or asset-seeking motives, and efficiency-seeking motives.[3] Exhibit 14.2 illustrates these motives. They apply equally to FDI and collaborative ventures. In any one venture, several motives may apply simultaneously, with one more dominant than others. Let's examine them in greater detail.

Market-Seeking Motives

Managers may seek new market opportunities either as a result of unfavorable developments in their home market (they are pushed into international markets) or attractive opportunities abroad (they are pulled into international markets). There are three primary market-seeking motivations:

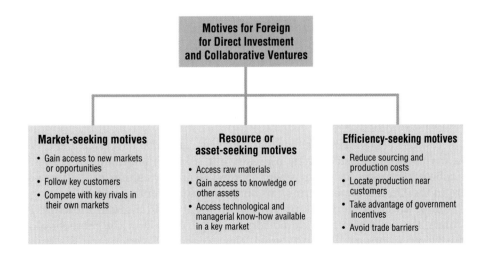

Exhibit 14.2

Firm Motives for Foreign Direct Investment and Collaborative Ventures

A Toyota Prius hybrid car on display at the Auto Mobil International trade fair in Leipzig, Germany. Toyota has demonstrated its social responsibility by investing in fuel-efficient and clean car technologies at its factories around the world.

1. *Gain access to new markets or opportunities.* The existence of a substantial market motivates many firms to produce offerings at or near customer locations. Local production improves customer service and reduces cost of transporting goods to buyer locations. Boeing, Coca-Cola, IBM, and Toyota all generate more sales abroad than they do in their home markets. The giant chip-maker Intel expects big sales from China, where incomes are rising and less than 10 percent of Chinese homes own a computer.[4]

2. *Follow key customers.* Firms often follow their key customers abroad to preempt other vendors from servicing them. One example is Tradegar Industries, which supplies the plastic that its customer Procter & Gamble uses to manufacture disposable diapers. When P&G built a plant in China, Tradegar management made the decision to establish production there as well.

3. *Compete with key rivals in their own markets.* Some MNEs may choose to confront current or potential competitors directly, in the competitors' home market. The strategic purpose is to weaken the competitor by forcing it to expend resources to defend its market. For example, in the earth-moving equipment industry, Caterpillar entered a joint venture with Mitsubishi to put pressure on the market share and profitability of Komatsu, their common rival. Expending substantial resources to defend its home market hampered Komatsu's ability to expand its activities abroad.[5]

Resource or Asset-Seeking Motives

Firms wish to acquire production factors that may be more abundant or less costly in a foreign market or seek complementary resources and capabilities of partner companies. Specifically, FDI or collaborative ventures may be motivated by the firm's desire to attain the following objectives:

1. *Access raw materials* needed in extractive and agricultural industries. For example, firms in the mining, oil, and crop-growing industries have little choice but to go where the raw materials are located. In the wine industry, companies establish wineries in areas suited for growing grapes.

2. *Gain access to knowledge or other assets.*[6] In such areas as R&D, manufacturing, and marketing, the focal firm can benefit from the partner's know-how. For instance, when Whirlpool entered Europe, it partnered with Philips to benefit from the latter firm's well-known brand name and distribution network. In another example, General Motors and Toyota first joined forces to create New United Motor Manufacturing Inc., or NUMMI, in Fremont, California. As a result, General Motors learned about Toyota's production techniques in the manufacture of high-quality vehicles. In turn, Toyota received technology and design expertise that allowed it to develop vehicles better suited to U.S. consumers.

3. *Access technological and managerial know-how available in a key market.*[7] The firm may benefit by establishing a presence in a key industrial cluster, such as the robotics industry in Japan, chemicals in Germany, fashion in Italy, or software in the United States. Firms can obtain many advantages from locating at the hub of knowledge development and innovation in a given industry. For instance, the countries considered ideal today for R&D in the biotechnology industry are Denmark, Finland, Israel, New Zealand, Sweden, and the United

States because they all have abundant pools of biotech knowledge workers.[8] In addition, many firms enter a collaborative venture abroad as a prelude to wholly owned FDI. Collaboration with a local partner reduces the risks of entry while allowing the entrant to gain local expertise prior to launching operations of its own in the market.

Efficiency-Seeking Motives

In pursuing international expansion, firms also seek to enhance the efficiency of their value-adding activities. The objective is to create economies of scale as well as economies of scope; that is, to achieve a more efficient use of corporate assets by employing them across a larger number of products and markets. For example, a firm can concentrate manufacturing in a few locations around the world as a way of optimizing production operations.[9] Or, the firm can disseminate best practice in, say, new product development, or procurement of a global network of subsidiaries. Global brands can pay better dividends for product innovation. Efficiency-seeking motives include:

1. *Reduce sourcing and production costs* by accessing inexpensive labor and other cheap inputs to the production process.[10] This motive accounts for the massive development of factories and service-producing facilities in China, Mexico, Eastern Europe, and India.

2. *Locate production near customers.* In industries that require firms to be especially sensitive to customer needs, or in which tastes change rapidly, managers often locate factories or assembly operations near important customers. For instance, in the fashion industry, Spain's Zara and Sweden's H&M locate much of their garment production in key markets such as Europe. Production is more expensive, but the clothing gets into shops faster and more closely represents the latest fashion trends.[11]

3. *Take advantage of government incentives.*[12] In addition to restricting imports, governments may offer subsidies and tax concessions to foreign firms to encourage them to invest locally. Governments encourage inward FDI because it provides local jobs and capital, increases tax revenue, and transfers skills and technologies.

4. *Avoid trade barriers.* Firms may engage in FDI to avoid tariffs and other trade barriers, as these usually apply only to exporting. By establishing a physical presence within an economic bloc, such as the EU, a foreign firm obtains the same advantages as local firms. Partnering with a local firm helps to overcome regulations or trade barriers, or to satisfy local content rules. The desire to avoid trade barriers helps explain why numerous Japanese automakers set up factories in the United States in the 1980s. However, the motive is less important today than in the past because trade barriers have declined substantially in many countries.

 Foreign Direct Investment

Foreign direct investment is a high-control strategy for entering foreign markets. The firm invests equity or capital in foreign countries for the purpose of building or acquiring manufacturing plants, subsidiaries, sales offices, or other needed facilities. Ownership abroad in brick-and-mortar facilities enables the firm to maintain a physical presence and secure direct access to customers and partners. In this sense, FDI is an equity or ownership form of foreign market entry. Local presence is especially critical when significant value-chain activities must be performed in the market. Foreign direct investment is the entry strategy most associated with the MNE. Large firms such as Sony, Nestlé, Nokia, Motorola, and Toyota have extensive FDI-based operations around the world. While certain types of foreign investment are common to both manufacturing firms and services providers, manufacturers tend to establish production facilities abroad, while service firms usually establish agency relationships and retail facilities.

Samsung, the South Korean electronics giant, first entered the United States via FDI in 1984. Over time, the firm used FDI to establish low-cost factories in Mexico, Southeast Asia, and Eastern Europe. In the 1990s, Samsung acquired capabilities via acquisition for developing and producing semiconductors. The firm used FDI to establish 10 R&D centers—in Britain, China, India, Israel, Japan, Russia, and the United States—that drive the development of leading technologies in digital media and appliances, telecommunications, and semiconductors. Most of Samsung's sales are from international operations—from Asia (42 percent), Europe (24 percent), and the United States (15 percent)—which are facilitated via the firm's roughly 38 foreign sales affiliates. Samsung also has 26 manufacturing sites and three logistics centers located abroad, all established via FDI.[13]

International portfolio investment Passive ownership of foreign securities such as stocks and bonds for the purpose of generating financial returns.

Foreign direct investment should not be confused with international or foreign portfolio investment. **International portfolio investment** refers to passive ownership of foreign securities such as stocks and bonds for the purpose of generating financial returns. It is a form of international investment, but it is not direct investment, which seeks control of a business abroad and represents a long-term commitment. The United Nations uses the benchmark of at least 10 percent ownership in the enterprise to differentiate FDI from portfolio investment. However, this percentage may be misleading because control is not usually achieved unless the investor owns more than 50 percent of a foreign venture.

Key Features of FDI

Foreign direct investment is characterized by six key features. First, FDI represents *greater resource commitment*. As the ultimate internationalization strategy, it is far more taxing on the firm's resources and capabilities than any other entry strategy.

Second, FDI implies *local presence and operations*. By using the FDI strategy, management chooses to have local presence and establish direct contact with customers, intermediaries, facilitators, and the government sector. Some firms concentrate their operations in one or a handful of locations; other firms disperse their FDI among numerous countries.

Third, FDI allows the firm to achieve *global scale efficiency*, which helps enhance the performance of the firm. Managers choose each location on the basis of comparative advantages. That is, the firm seeks to perform R&D activities in the most knowledge-intensive countries in its industry, source from suppliers that provide the best intermediate and finished goods, build production facilities at locations that provide the best ratio of productivity to labor costs, and establish marketing subsidiaries to sell its goods or services in those countries that offer the greatest sales potential.

Fourth, compared to other entry strategies, FDI entails *substantial risk and uncertainty* because establishing a permanent, fixed presence in a foreign country makes the firm vulnerable to specific circumstances in that country. Substantial local investment in plant, equipment, and human resources exposes the direct investor to political risk and intervention by local government on pricing, wages, and hiring practices. It also reduces the firm's flexibility by tying up equity capital in the foreign market. Direct investors often must contend with inflation and other local economic conditions. For example, Procter & Gamble (P&G) does a thriving business through its local subsidiary, selling consumer products in Turkey. However, Turkey has had a history of high inflation, sometimes approaching 100 percent per year. P&G has had to devise a variety of strategies to minimize its exposure to inflation's adverse effects, including ongoing wage negotiations with the local workforce, increasing prices in line with local conditions, and repatriating profits quickly.

Fifth, direct investors must *deal more intensively* with the particular social and cultural variables present in the host market. Multinational enterprises with high-profile, conspicuous operations are especially vulnerable to close public scrutiny of their actions. In order to minimize potential problems, MNEs often prefer to invest in countries that are culturally and linguistically similar to the home country. When setting up shop in Europe, for example, U.S. firms may favor Belgium or the Netherlands because English is widely spoken in these countries.[14]

Sixth, related to the last point, multinational firms increasingly strive to behave in *socially responsible* ways in host countries. Many are sensitizing their employees to be ethical abroad, investing in local communities and seeking to establish global standards of fair treatment for workers. For example, Unilever, the giant Dutch-British producer of consumer products, operates a free community laundry in a Sao Paulo slum, provides financing to assist tomato growers to convert to environmentally friendly irrigation, and recycles 17 million pounds of waste annually at a toothpaste factory. In Bangladesh, where there are just 20 doctors for every 10,000 people, Unilever funds a hospital that offers free medical care to the needy. In Ghana, the company teaches palm oil producers to reuse plant waste while providing drinkable water to deprived communities. In India, Unilever provides small loans to help women in remote villages start small-scale enterprises. In all the countries where it operates, Unilever discloses how much carbon dioxide and hazardous waste it produces.[15]

Unilever is not alone in being socially responsible in its host countries. Many other MNEs are responding to such global agendas as sustainability—meeting humanity's needs without harming future generations. For example, automakers such as Toyota, Renault, and Volkswagen are investing in fuel-efficient and clean technologies. Nokia is a leader in phasing out toxic materials. Dell was among the first to accept old PC hardware from consumers and recycle it for free. GlaxoSmithKline and Merck offer AIDS drugs at cost. Suncor Energy assists Native Americans to deal with social and ecological issues in Canada's far north.

The six features of foreign direct investment we have reviewed create formidable challenges for the firm. Even a large, well-established company like Disney experienced several failures in its foreign investing. As *Fortune* magazine noted, "The company's record in operating theme parks overseas is spottier than 101 Dalmatians".[16] When Disney established Tokyo Disneyland, its management incorrectly assumed that the Disneyland experience could not be successfully transferred to Japan. Instead of investing, Disney opted to license rights in Japan for nominal profits. But then Tokyo Disneyland proved to be a huge success. Not wanting to repeat the same mistake, management opted to retain an FDI stake in its next theme park—Disneyland Paris. But it proved to be a financial sinkhole. Having learned from these experiences, the latest theme park, Hong Kong Disneyland, is expected to be a success. However, partly due to making concessions to the Chinese government, Disney owns just 43 percent of the venture. And management is worried about intellectual property violations in China, which are likely to reduce profits from licensing Disney movies, animated characters, and other valuable properties.[17]

Who Is Active in Direct Investment?

Direct investment is the typical foreign market entry strategy for large MNEs—firms with extensive experience in international business. Exhibit 14.3 provides a sample of leading MNEs engaged in FDI,

This woman talking on her cell phone is near a Vodafone outlet in Bahrain. Vodafone is one of the most international firms due to its very extensive FDI activities.

Rank	Company	Home country	Industry	Assets (U.S.$ billions) Foreign	Assets (U.S.$ billions) Total	Sales (U.S.$ billions) Foreign	Sales (U.S.$ billions) Total	Number of subsidiaries and affiliates Foreign	Number of subsidiaries and affiliates Total
1	General Electric	United States	Electrical & electronic equipment	449	751	57	153	787	1,157
2	Vodafone	United Kingdom	Telecommun-ications	248	259	53	62	70	198
3	Ford Motor	United States	Motor vehicles	180	305	71	172	130	216
4	General Motors	United States	Motor vehicles	174	480	59	194	166	290
5	British Petroleum	United Kingdom	Petroleum	155	193	232	285	445	611
6	Exxon Mobil	United States	Petroleum	135	196	203	291	237	314
7	Royal Dutch Shell	United Kingdom and Netherlands	Petroleum	130	193	170	265	328	814
8	Toyota Motor	Japan	Motor vehicles	123	234	103	171	129	341
9	Total	France	Petroleum	99	115	123	152	410	576
10	France Telecom	France	Telecommun-ications	86	131	24	59	162	227

Exhibit 14.3 World's Most International Non-Financial MNEs, Ranked by Foreign Assets

SOURCE: UNCTAD (2006), World Investment Report 2006, New York: United Nations. The United Nations is the original author of the material. Used with permission.

arranged by the value of their foreign assets. The Exhibit shows the MNEs with the greatest amount of such foreign assets as subsidiaries and affiliates, world-wide. For example, U.K.-based Vodafone is a mobile phone supplier with numerous sales offices in most major cities around the world.

Service Multinationals

Firms must offer services, such as lodging, construction, and personal care, when and where they are consumed. This requires firms to establish either a permanent presence through FDI (for example, as in retailing), or a temporary relocation of the service company personnel (for example, as in the construction industry).[18] For instance, management consulting is a service that is usually embodied in experts who interact directly with clients to dispense advice. Thus, firms such as McKinsey and Cap Gemini generally establish offices in foreign markets. Many support services, such as advertising, insurance, accounting, the law, and overnight package delivery are also best provided at the customer's location. Overall, FDI is vital for internationalizing services.[19]

The nature of the service may necessitate establishing a physical presence in the foreign market when the offering is relatively complex, requires extensive adaptation or substantial service, or is tied to some geographic location. For exam-ple, Intrawest, Inc., is a developer that is building several ski resorts in China, which is seen as the next big market for downhill skiing. The firm, therefore, has offices in China. Likewise, banks have branches around the world because bank-

Company	Home country	Number of subsidiaries and affiliates		Number of host countries
		Total	Foreign	
GE Capital Services	United States	1,425	1,085	55
Citigroup	United States	612	347	70
UBS	Switzerland	426	363	43
Allianz Group	Germany	778	569	47
BNP Paribas	France	622	403	53
Gruppo Assicurazioni Generali	Italy	368	323	39
Zurich Financial Services	Switzerland	358	345	34
Unicredito	Italy	1,044	998	31
HSBC Bank	United Kingdom	1,076	658	47
Société Générale	France	430	253	48

Exhibit 14.4

Large International Financial MNEs, Based on Breadth of International Operations

SOURCE: UNCTAD (2006), World Investment Report 2006, New York: United Nations. The United Nations is the original author of the material. Used with permission.

ing services must be available to clients wherever they do business. Exhibit 14.4 presents a sample of the world's most international financial institutions and illustrates the breadth of their international operations. As an example, Citigroup has representative offices in 70 countries.

Leading Destinations for FDI

Advanced economies such as Australia, Belgium, Britain, Canada, Germany, Japan, Netherlands, and the United States have long been popular destinations for FDI because of their strong GDP per capita, GDP growth rate, density of knowledge workers, and superior business infrastructure, such as telephone systems and energy sources.[20] In recent years, however, emerging markets and developing economies have been gaining appeal as FDI destinations. According to A.T. Kearney's FDI Confidence Index, the top destinations for foreign investment today are China and India (www.atkearney.com).

China is popular because of its size, rapid growth rate, and low labor cost. The country is an important platform where MNEs manufacture products for export to key markets in Asia and elsewhere. India is popular because of its highly educated workforce and managerial talent. Compared to China, India is also seen as having fewer cultural barriers and as being more transparent and respectful of the rule of law.[21] China and India are also attractive for strategic reasons—locations that hold immense long-term potential as target markets and new sources of competitive advantages.

Factors to Consider in Selecting FDI Locations

Exhibit 14.5 lists the criteria that firms use to evaluate countries as potential targets for FDI projects. Suppose that Taiwan-based Acer wants to build a new computer factory abroad. Managers at Acer would research the best country in which to build the factory, based on the factors indicated in the exhibit. Acer managers would research various country candidates in terms of country and regional factors,

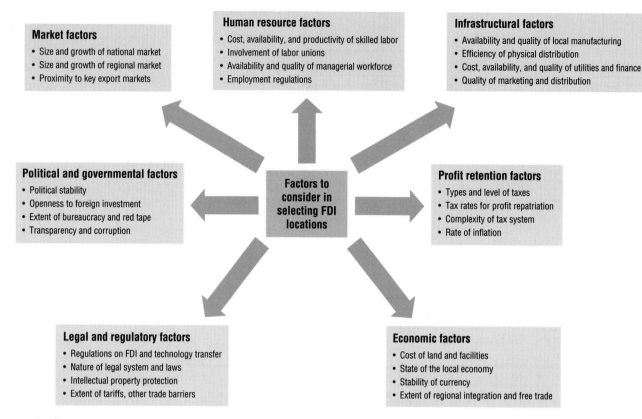

Exhibit 14.5 Factors to Consider in Selecting Foreign Direct Investment Locations

SOURCE: Reprinted by permission of John Wiley & Sons, Inc. from Entry Strategies for International Markets by Franklin R. Root. Copyright © 1994 by John Wiley & Sons, Inc.

infrastructural factors, political factors, profit retention factors, and human resource factors in order to find the best location for building the factory.

Consider the attractiveness of Eastern European nations as FDI destinations. Several of the selection criteria noted in Exhibit 14.5 have attracted foreign firms to these countries. In Slovakia, Peugeot Citroën built a factory in the tiny town of Trnava, which employs up to 3,500 people and churns out up to 300,000 compact cars a year. Low wages and superior worker quality are of importance to foreign carmakers such as Toyota, Suzuki, and Hyundai, which have rushed to build factories or acquire local auto plants in Slovakia, Poland, Hungary, and Romania. In the Czech Republic, Chinese electronics manufacturer Sichuan Changhong is building a $30 million factory that will produce up to one million flat-screen televisions per year. Such firms are gradually drawing their suppliers into the region, where they are establishing their own local production facilities. Engineers in Slovakia earn half of what Western engineers make, and assembly line workers one-third to one-fifth. East European governments offer incentives, from financing to a low flat-and-simple tax on employee wages and corporate profits, as in Slovakia, where all taxes are a simple 19 percent. By comparison, personal income tax rates vary between 15 and 42 percent in Germany. By manufacturing in the Czech Republic, Sichuan Changhong avoids the substantial tariffs that the European Union imposes on imports from China. Eastern Europe is physically and psychically close to the huge EU market (several Eastern European countries are EU members) and has emerged as a viable market for sale of various products. Meanwhile, production of automobiles and other products in Britain, France, and other Western European countries is falling due to higher manufacturing costs, taxes, and strict labor rules.[22] As you can see, usually a combination of criteria is responsible for direct investment location decisions.

Types of Foreign Direct Investment

Foreign direct investment activities can be classified by the form of FDI (greenfield versus mergers and acquisitions), nature of ownership (wholly owned versus joint venture), and level of integration (horizontal versus vertical).

Greenfield Investment versus Mergers and Acquisitions

Greenfield investment occurs when a firm invests to build a new manufacturing, marketing, or administrative facility, as opposed to acquiring existing facilities. As the name *greenfield* implies, the investing firm typically buys an empty plot of land and builds a production plant, marketing subsidiary, or other facility there for its own use. This is exactly what Ford did, for example, when it established its large factory outside Valencia, Spain.

The direct investor also has the option of merging with or acquiring an existing company in the foreign market. An **acquisition** refers to a direct investment or purchase of an existing company or facility. For example, when Home Depot entered Mexico, it acquired the stores and assets of an existing retailer of building products, Home Mart.[23] The Chinese personal computer manufacturer Lenovo internationalized rapidly via an ambitious acquisition strategy. In 2004, Lenovo acquired IBM's PC business, which accounted for about two-thirds of its revenue in 2005. The deal provided Lenovo with valuable strategic assets, such as brands and distribution networks. The acquisition helped Lenovo rapidly extend its market reach and become a global player.[24]

A **merger** is a special type of acquisition in which two firms join to form a new, larger firm. Mergers are more common between companies of similar size because they are capable of integrating their operations on a relatively equal basis. A recent example was the merger between Lucent Technologies in the United States and Alcatel in France. Their merger resulted in the creation of the world's largest company in the global telecommunications equipment business (Alcatel-Lucent). Like joint ventures, mergers can generate many positive outcomes, including interpartner learning and resource sharing, increased economies of scale, reduced costs by eliminating duplicative activities, a broader range of products and services for sale, and greater market power. Cross-border mergers confront many challenges due to national differences in culture, competition policy, corporate values, and operating methods. Success requires substantial advance research, planning, and commitment.

In some industries, intense competition and overcapacity create pressures to restructure and consolidate industries through mergers and acquisitions. The rationale behind consolidation is to eliminate redundancy and create more efficient, larger-scale operations. The *Global Trend* feature on page 430 describes the ongoing consolidation of the global automobile industry.

Multinational enterprises may favor acquisition over greenfield FDI because, by acquiring an existing company, the MNE will gain access to the acquired firm's experienced staff and obtain ownership of existing assets such as plant, equipment, and human resources, as well as access to existing suppliers and customers. In addition, acquisition provides an immediate stream of revenue and accelerates the MNE's return on investment, as compared to greenfield FDI. By contrast, host-country governments usually prefer that MNEs undertake greenfield FDI because, compared to acquisition, it creates new jobs and production capacity, facilitates technology and know-how transfer to locals, and improves linkages to the global marketplace. Many governments offer incentives to encourage greenfield investments, which may be sufficient to offset the advantages normally provided by acquisition-based entry.

Greenfield investment Direct investment to build a new manufacturing, marketing, or administrative facility, as opposed to acquiring existing facilities.

Acquisition Direct investment to purchase an existing company or facility.

Merger A special type of acquisition in which two firms join to form a new, larger firm.

The Nature of Ownership in FDI

Equity participation
Acquisition of partial ownership in an existing firm.

Wholly owned direct investment A foreign direct investment in which the investor fully owns the foreign assets.

Equity joint venture A type of partnership in which a separate firm is created through the investment or pooling of assets by two or more parent firms that gain joint ownership of the new legal entity.

Foreign direct investors also can choose the degree of control they wish to retain in the new venture. This is accomplished through full or partial ownership. Ownership suggests full or partial control over the affairs of the business—for example, decisions about new products, expansion, and profit distribution. Firms can choose between a wholly owned venture or a joint venture to secure control. The choice determines the extent of the firm's financial commitment to the foreign venture. If the focal firm is pursuing partial ownership in an existing firm, this is referred to as **equity participation**.

Wholly owned direct investment is foreign direct investment in which the investor fully owns the foreign assets. In other words, it assumes 100 percent ownership of the business and secures complete managerial control over its operations. For example, many foreign automotive firms have set up fully owned manufacturing plants in the United States in order to serve this large market from within. Exhibit 14.6 illustrates the location of Toyota's United States plants and the year of establishment. In contrast to wholly owned direct investment, an **equity joint venture** is a type of partnership in which a separate

> GLOBAL TREND

Consolidation in Global Industries

One aspect of globalization and foreign investment is the consolidation of global industries through mergers and acquisitions. Consolidation most often occurs when global overcapacity results in a glut of inventory, in which supply greatly exceeds consumer demand. When this occurs, intense competition necessitates the widespread merging of suppliers, which reduces the number of firms in an industry. Consolidation is a modern feature of several global industries, including pharmaceuticals, personal computers, telecommunications, and beer brewing.

Perhaps the leading example of consolidation is the global auto industry. During the past century, the 270 original automakers worldwide merged into seven big firms and three smaller ones. Six of these—General Motors, Toyota, Ford, Renault/Nissan, Volkswagen, and DaimlerChrysler—accounted for some 70 percent of global sales. The most recent consolidation deals all involved European firms: BMW acquired Rover, Renault

merged with Nissan, and Daimler-Benz bought Chrysler (which it subsequently sold in 2007).

Despite recent consolidations, productive capacity in the world auto industry still exceeds global demand by several million vehicles per year. Overcapacity in North America, Europe, and Japan continues to sap profitability. New automakers in China and India will account for most added production in the future. Some experts predict that more cars will be made in the period from 2005 through 2025 than in the prior 105-year history of the industry. The resultant competition will be very intense for Western carmakers, leading to more consolidation. Declining financial performance at Fiat, GM, and Ford (which owns Mazda and Volvo) means that these firms will need to offshore more of their value chains to cost-effective locations such as China, Eastern Europe, and Mexico.

Nations have historically supported the auto industry because of its remarkable ability to generate

good-paying jobs, spin-off industries, and tax revenues. Governments regularly intervene to subsidize players, even as global competitive pressures hasten their demise. For example, Japan rescued the troubled Mitsubishi Motors, which employs over 40,000 people. The bailout illustrates why the overpopulated car industry has trouble consolidating and reducing capacity. Carmakers are seen as national champions. Letting them fail is undesirable because so many jobs are at stake. Meanwhile, a few makers—Toyota, BMW, Renault-Nissan, and Honda—are proving very profitable. They are the leading exemplars of the importance of skillful company management in a complex global industry that faces numerous challenges.

Sources: *Economist.* (2004). "A Survey of the Car Industry: The New European Order," September 4, survey section; *Economist.* (2005). "The Global Car Industry: Extinction of the Predator," September 10, pp. 63–65; Sapsford, Jathon, and Norihiko Shirouzu. (2005). "Mitsubishi Group to Give Car Maker $3 Billion Bailout," *Wall Street Journal,* January 20, pp. A1 and A6.

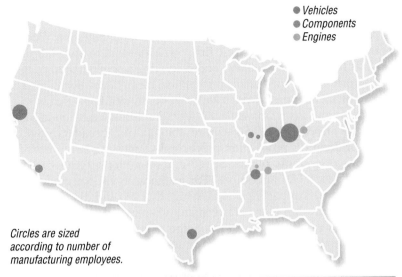

- Vehicles
- Components
- Engines

Circles are sized according to number of manufacturing employees.

Exhibit 14.6

Toyota's Direct Investments in United States Manufacturing Plants

SOURCE: Alex Taylor III (2007), "America's Best Car Company," *Fortune*, March 19, 99. 98-101. Copyright © 2007 Time Inc. All rights reserved.

Vehicle plants currently operating	Start of production	Models produced	Manufacturing employees
1. Georgetown, Kentucky	1988	Avalon, Camry, Solara, engines	6,904
2. Fremont, California	1986*	Corolla, Tacoma, Pontiac Vibe	5,173
3. Princeton, Indiana	1999	Sequoia, Sienna, Tundra	4,645
4. San Antonio, Texas	2006	Tundra	1,955
5. Long Beach, California	1972	Hino trucks, catalytic converters, parts	686
6. Blue Springs, Mississippi	2010**	Highlander	2,000

*Joint venture between General Motors and Toyota **Projected

firm is created through the investment or pooling of assets by two or more parent firms that gain joint ownership of the new legal entity.[25] A partner in a joint venture may hold majority, equal (50–50), or minority ownership. Ownership generally implies control; however, how the governing board is composed and how voting rights are distributed between the partners more accurately represents the relative power of the partners.

Many firms find the joint venture an attractive option because of the sheer complexity of foreign markets. Collaborative ventures can benefit small and medium-sized enterprises by providing them with infusion of capital. For example, Shanghai-based Tri Star International acquired a majority stake in Illinois-based Adams Pressed Metals, a manufacturer of parts for tractors and other earth-moving equipment. The cash infusion saved 40 jobs at Adams and gave Tri Star access to the U.S. market and marketing know-how.[26]

In some cases, a joint venture with a local partner may be the only entry strategy available to the focal firm. This arises when the government of a target country seeks to protect important local industries by prohibiting foreign firms from gaining 100 percent ownership in local enterprises. However, governments have relaxed such regulations over time, and they are now usually receptive to any form of FDI.

Vertical versus Horizontal FDI

Vertical integration An arrangement whereby the firm owns, or seeks to own, multiple stages of a value chain for producing, selling, and delivering a product or service.

A third classification of FDI is vertical versus horizontal integration. **Vertical integration** is an arrangement whereby the firm owns, or seeks to own, *multiple* stages of a value chain for producing, selling, and delivering a product or service. Vertical FDI takes two forms. In *forward vertical integration*, the firm develops the capacity to sell its outputs by investing in *downstream* value-chain facilities—that is, marketing and selling operations. Forward vertical integration is less common than *backward vertical integration*, in which the firm acquires the capacity abroad to provide inputs for its foreign or domestic production processes by investing in *upstream* facilities, typically factories, assembly plants, or refining operations. Firms can own both backward and forward FDI operations. For instance, in various countries Honda owns both suppliers of car parts *and* dealerships that sell and distribute cars.

Horizontal integration An arrangement whereby the firm owns, or seeks to own, the activities involved in a single stage of its value chain.

Horizontal integration is an arrangement whereby the firm owns, or seeks to own, the activities involved in a *single* stage of its value chain. For instance, Microsoft's primary business is developing computer software. In addition to producing operating systems, word processing, and spreadsheet software, it has also developed subsidiaries abroad that make other types of software. For example, Microsoft acquired a Montreal-based firm that produces the software used to create movie animations. As this example suggests, firms invest abroad in their own industry to expand their capacity and activities. A firm may acquire another firm engaged in an identical value-chain activity to achieve economies of scale, expand its product line, increase its profitability, or, in some cases, eliminate a competitor.

 # International Collaborative Ventures

A collaborative venture is essentially a partnership between two or more firms, and includes equity joint ventures as well as, project-based nonequity ventures.[27] International collaborative ventures are sometimes referred to as *international partnerships* and *international strategic alliances*.[28] A joint venture is essentially a special type of collaboration involving equity investment by the parent firms.

Collaboration helps firms overcome the often substantial risk and high costs of international business. It makes possible the achievement of projects that exceed the capabilities of the individual firm. Groups of firms sometimes form partnerships to accomplish large-scale goals such as develop new technologies, or complete major projects such as power plants. By collaborating, the focal firm can draw on a range of complementary technologies, accessible only from other firms, to innovate and develop new products. The advantages of collaboration help explain why the volume of such partnerships has grown substantially in the last few decades.[29]

While collaboration can take place at similar or different levels of the value chain, it is typically focused on R&D, manufacturing, or marketing. International collaborative ventures have been on the rise to realize joint R&D in knowledge-intensive, high-technology sectors such as robotics, semiconductors, aircraft manufacturing, medical instruments, and pharmaceuticals.

There are two basic types of collaborative ventures: equity joint ventures and project-based, nonequity ventures. Equity joint ventures are traditional types of collaboration that have been around for a long time. In recent decades, however, there has been a proliferation of the newer, project-based collaborations.

Equity Joint Ventures

Joint ventures are normally formed when no one party possesses all of the assets needed to exploit an available opportunity. In a typical international deal, the foreign partner contributes capital, technology, management expertise, training, or some type of product. The local partner contributes the use of its factory or other facilities, knowledge of the local language and culture, market navigation know-how, useful connections to the host country government, or lower-cost production factors such as labor or raw materials. Western firms often seek joint ventures to gain access to markets in Asia. The partnership allows the foreign firm to access key market knowledge, gain immediate access to a distribution system and customers, and attain greater control over local operations.

As an example, Procter & Gamble (P&G) is in a joint venture with Dolce & Gabbana, an Italian fashion house. Under the deal, P&G produces perfumes, while the Italian firm markets them in Europe, leveraging the strength of its strong local brand name.[30] Samsung, the Korean electronics firm, began internationalizing in the 1970s through joint ventures with foreign-technology suppliers such as NEC, Sanyo, and Corning Glass Works. The partnerships allowed Samsung to acquire product designs and marketing outlets and gave management increasing confidence in foreign operations. As its capabilities grew, Samsung ventured into international production. Samsung's earliest foreign manufacturing effort was via a joint venture in Portugal, launched in 1982.[31]

Project-Based, Nonequity Ventures

Increasingly common in cross-border business, the **project-based, nonequity venture** is a collaboration in which the partners create a project with a relatively narrow scope and a well-defined timetable, without creating a new legal entity. Combining personnel, resources, and capabilities, the partners collaborate until the venture bears fruit, or until they no longer consider it valuable to collaborate. Typically, partners collaborate on joint development of new technologies, products, or share other expertise with each other. Such cooperation may help them catch up with rivals in technology development. For instance, Sony developed the microprocessor used in Playstation 3 in partnership with IBM and Toshiba. The venture led to the creation of the Cell chip, which is 10 times faster than Intel's most powerful Pentium chip and which permits more graphics-intensive gaming.[32]

Project-based, nonequity ventures are especially common in technology-intensive industries. One example is IBM and NTT, who formed a strategic partnership for a limited period. Under the arrangement, IBM provided outsourcing services to NTT, Japan's dominant telecommunications carrier and, in turn, NTT provided outsourcing services and contacts for computer services sales to customers in Japan.[33] In another example, Germany's Siemens teamed with Motorola to develop the next generation of 300-mm 12-inch wafers, an important innovation in the global semiconductor industry. Semiconductors are integrated circuits used in the manufacture of computers and consumer electronics. While Motorola provided its expertise in advanced logic products and leading-edge manufacturing, Siemens contributed its superior knowledge of random access memory.

Differences between Equity versus Project-Based, Nonequity Ventures

Project-based collaborations differ from the traditional equity joint ventures in four important ways. First, no new legal entity is created. Partners carry on their activity within the guidelines of a contract. Second, parent companies do not necessarily seek ownership of an ongoing enterprise. Instead, these companies simply contribute their knowledge, expertise, personnel, and monetary resources in order to derive knowledge or access-related benefits. Third, collaboration tends to have a well-defined timetable and an end date, and partners go their separate

Project-based, nonequity venture A collaboration in which the partners create a project with a relatively narrow scope and a well-defined timetable, without creating a new legal entity.

	Advantages	*Disadvantages*
Equity joint ventures	• Afford greater control over future directions • Facilitate transfer of knowledge between the partners • Common goals drive the joint venture	• Complex management structure • Coordination between the partners may be a concern • Difficult to terminate • Greater exposure to political risk
Project-based, nonequity ventures	• Easy to set up • Simple management structure; can be adjusted easily • Takes advantage of partners' respective strengths • Can respond quickly to changing technology and market conditions • Easy to terminate	• Knowledge transfer may be less straightforward between the partners • No equity commitment; thus, puts greater emphasis on trust, good communications, and developing relationships • Conflicts may be harder to resolve • Division of costs and benefits may strain relationship

Exhibit 14.7 Advantages and Disadvantages of International Collaborative Ventures

ways once the objectives have been accomplished or the partners find no reason for continuation. Fourth, the nature of collaboration is narrower in scope, typically revolving around projects, new products, marketing, distribution, sourcing, or manufacturing.

Exhibit 14.7 highlights advantages and disadvantages associated with the two types of international collaborative ventures.

Consortium

Consortium A project-based, nonequity venture with multiple partners fulfilling a large-scale project.

A **consortium** is a project-based, usually nonequity venture with multiple partners fulfilling a large-scale project. It is typically formed with a contract, which delineates the rights and obligations of each member. Work is allocated to the members on the same basis as profits. Thus, each partner in a three-partner consortium, in which each performs one third of the work, would earn one third of the resulting profits. Consortia are popular for innovation in industries such as commercial aircraft, computers, pharmaceuticals, and telecommunications, where the costs of developing and marketing a new product often reach hundreds of millions of dollars and require sweeping expertise. For example, Boeing, Fuji, Kawasaki, and Mitsubishi joined forces to design and manufacture major components of the Boeing 767 aircraft.

Often, several firms come together to pool their resources to bid on a major project, such as to build a power plant or a high-tech manufacturing facility. Each firm brings a unique specialty to the project and, on its own, would be unable to win the project bid. No formal legal entity is created, as each firm retains its individual identity. In this way, if one party withdraws, the consortium can continue with the remaining participants. One example of a consortium is iNavSat, formed among several European firms to develop and manage Europe's global satellite navigation system (www.inavsat.com).

Cross-Licensing Agreements

Cross-licensing agreement A type of project-based, nonequity venture where partners agree to access licensed technology developed by the other, on preferential terms.

A **cross-licensing agreement** is a type of a project-based, nonequity venture where partners agree to access licensed technology developed by the other, on preferential terms. The agreement assumes each partner has or expects to have something to license. In a similar way, two firms might enter a *cross-distribution agreement*, in which each partner has the right to distribute products or services produced by the other, on preferential terms. For example, the Star Alliance is an agreement between several airlines—including Air Canada, United Airlines, Lufthansa, Scandinavian Airlines System, Air New Zealand, and Thai Airways—to market each others' airline flights and other services (www.staralliance.com).

 # Managing Collaborative Ventures

Collaborative ventures pose specific types of managerial challenges. Under FDI and exporting, the focal firm emphasizes competing skillfully against rival companies. By contrast, with collaborative ventures, the focal firm must cooperate with one or more other firms that, in different circumstances or other countries, may actually be the firm's competitors.[34] This requires managers to gain partnering skills and to be proactive about searching and consummating partnerships with other firms around the world.[35] Let's review the key tasks of the manager in successfully collaborating with foreign partners.

Understand Potential Risks in Collaboration

Collaboration implies that two or more firms have made a decision that partnering is preferred to going it alone. While partnering is often an option, managers must weigh the potential risks against the potential benefits. The following questions are relevant in this analysis:

- As a firm, are we likely to grow very dependent on our partner?
- By partnering, will we stifle growth and innovation in our own organization?
- Will we share our competencies excessively, to the point where corporate interests are threatened? How can we safeguard our core competencies?
- Will we be exposed to significant commercial, political, cultural, or currency risks?
- Will we close certain growth opportunities by participating in this venture?
- Will managing the venture place an excessive burden on corporate resources, such as managerial, financial, or technological resources?

Management in the focal firm must ensure that it is not exposing itself to excessive risk. The potential partner may be a current or potential competitor, is likely to have its own agenda, and will likely gain important competitive advantages from the relationship.[36] Management must protect its hard-won capabilities and other organizational assets. If not, its bargaining power vis-à-vis the partner and its ability to compete in other spheres will be reduced. Harmony is not necessarily the most important goal. Some degree of conflict and tension between the partners may be preferable to surrendering core skills. The firm does not want to become too dependent on its partner. For instance, Intel has been careful not to share too much of its proprietary technology with its partners in China. The firm has avoided building a chip factory in China because Intel's microprocessor devices are at the heart of the firm's intellectual property. In a country known for weak protection of intellectual property rights, management is concerned about the theft of not only its chip designs but also the design and methods of its manufacturing processes.[37]

Pursue a Systematic Process for Partnering

The initial decision in internationalization is the choice of the most appropriate target market. The chosen market determines the characteristics needed in a business partner. If the firm is planning to enter an emerging market, for example, it may want a partner with political clout or "connections." Thus, it is prudent for managers to view country targeting and partner selection as interdependent choices.

Exhibit 14.8 outlines the process for identifying and working with a suitable business partner.[38] The Exhibit reveals that managers need to draw on their cross-cultural competence, legal expertise, and financial planning skills in this process.

Initially, management evaluates whether a collaborative or a wholly owned venture is most appropriate in the particular case. When managers first contemplate internationalization via FDI, they usually think in terms of a wholly owned operation. Many firms are used to retaining control and sole access to profits that comes with 100 percent ownership. The nature of the industry or product offering may also make partnering a less desirable strategy. Nevertheless, management should always consider collaboration as an option. For example, in the global Internet service-provider industry, China is an increasingly popular venue. Both Microsoft and Google entered the huge market via joint ventures with local partners. But eBay! and Yahoo entered China primarily via wholly owned FDI. Each firm chose the entry strategy most appropriate for its particular situation.[39]

Broadly, the firm enters a collaborative venture when it ascertains that a necessary link in its value chain is somehow weak or missing. If this is the case, the

Step and Key Challenge

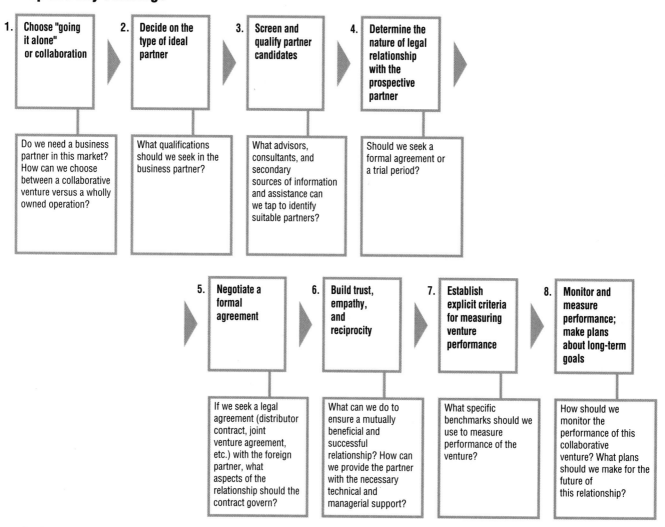

Exhibit 14.8 A Systematic Process to International Business Partnering

firm chooses a partner that can replace the function of the deficient link. In this way, the firm can meet its growth and other strategic objectives faster or more effectively. Management must evaluate the cost and benefits of full ownership versus collaboration in the context of its own industry and international markets.

Ensure Success with Collaborative Ventures

About half of all collaborative ventures fail within their first five years of operation because of unresolved disagreements, confusion about venture goals, and other problems. International ventures are particularly challenging because, in addition to involving complex business issues, managers face the additional burden of dealing across culture and language, as well as differences in political, legal, and economic systems. Collaborative ventures in developing economies are particularly complex and generally have an even higher failure rate than those in advanced economies.[40] Companies as diverse as Avis, General Mills, TRW, GM-Daewoo, and Saab-Fairchild have all experienced failed ventures.

In China in 2007, French food giant Danone's joint venture with a local Chinese partner turned sour after the Chinese firm set up a mirror business in which it sold, on the side, the same products that the joint venture was marketing. Meanwhile, the Chinese partner asserted that terms of the JV agreement were unfair and accused Danone of trying to gain control of its other businesses. Danone formed the partnership in 1996 at a time when the Chinese government often imposed such ventures on foreign firms. The incident has threatened Danone's reputation and main toehold in the huge Chinese market. [41]

Success Factors in Collaborative Ventures

Experience with collaborative ventures suggests several guidelines that managers should follow for enhancing success. Let's consider these guidelines next.

Be cognizant of cultural differences. International collaborations require the parties to learn and appreciate both partners' corporate and national cultures. Cultural incompatibility can cause anger, frustration, and inefficient relations. The partners may never arrive at a common set of values and organizational routines. The undertaking is especially complex when the parties are from very distinct cultures—say, Norway and Nigeria. Establishing cultural compatibility is a must.

Pursue common values and culture. Partners should be willing to mold a common set of values and culture. Problems arise when partners have differing goals for the venture, or goals change over time. When this occurs, managers find themselves operating at cross-purposes against the goals of the other partner. For example, Japanese firms tend to value market share over profitability, while U.S. firms value profitability over market share. Because different strategies are required to maximize each of these performance goals, a joint venture between Japanese and U.S. firms may run aground. To overcome challenges, partners need to regularly interact and communicate at three levels of the organization: senior management, operational management, and the workforce.

Give due attention to planning and management of the venture. Poor planning and subsequent organizational conflicts can hamper venture success. Firms should agree on questions of management, decision making, and control. Without this agreement, each partner may want to control the venture's operations, causing a strain on the managerial, financial, and technological resources of the partners. In some cases, equal governance and a sense of shared enterprise are best because they help partners view themselves as equals and reach consensus. In other cases, having a dominant partner in the relationship helps ensure success. When one of the partners is clearly the driver or the leader in the relationship, there is less likelihood of a stalemate and prolonged decision making due to extensive negotiations between the partners.

Safeguard core competencies. Collaboration takes place between firms that are current or potential competitors. Accordingly, the partners must walk the fine line between cooperation and competition. For example, for several years, Volkswagen and General Motors succeeded in China by partnering with the Chinese firm, Shanghai Automotive Industry Corporation (SAIC). The Western firms transferred much technology and know-how to the Chinese partner. Having learned much from VW and GM, SAIC is now poised to become a major player in the global automobile industry and a competitor to its original partners.[42]

Adjust to shifting environmental circumstances. When environmental conditions change, the rationale for a collaborative venture may weaken or disappear. Unexpected developments can unfavorably affect the venture. For example, an industry or economic downturn may shift priorities in one or both firms. Cost overruns can make the venture untenable. New government policies or regulations can increase costs or eliminate anticipated benefits. Managers should maintain flexibility to adjust to changing conditions.

The Experience of Retailers in Foreign Markets

Retailers represent a special case of international service firms that internationalize substantially through FDI and collaborative ventures. Retailing takes various forms and includes department stores (e.g., Marks & Spencer, Bay, Macy's), specialty retailers (Body Shop, Gap, Disney Store), supermarkets (Sainsbury, Safeway, Sparr), convenience stores (Circle K, 7-Eleven, Tom Thumb), discount stores (Zellers, Tati, Target), and big-box stores (Home Depot, IKEA, Toys "Я" Us). Wal-Mart now has roughly 100 stores and 50,000 employees in China. It sources almost all its merchandise locally, providing jobs for thousands more Chinese.[43]

The major drivers of retailer internationalization have been saturation of home country markets, deregulation of international investment, and opportunities to benefit from lower costs abroad. For example, Home Depot expanded abroad because the home improvement market in Canada and the United States is increasingly saturated.[44] Most emerging markets exhibit pent-up demand, fast economic growth, a growing middle class, and increasingly sophisticated consumers. In densely populated developing countries, consumers are flocking to discount retailers that sell a wide selection of merchandise at low prices.

Retailers usually choose between FDI and franchising as a foreign market entry strategy. The larger, more experienced firms, such as Carrefour, Royal Ahold, IKEA, and Wal-Mart tend to internationalize via FDI; that is, they tend to own their stores. Smaller and less experienced international firms such as Borders bookstores tend to rely on networks of independent franchisees. In franchising, the retailer adopts a business system from, and pays an ongoing fee to, a franchise operator. Still other firms may employ a dual strategy; using FDI in some markets and franchising in others. Franchising provides a fast way to internationalize. But relative to FDI, it affords the firm less control over its foreign operations, which can be risky in countries with unstable political or economic situations, or with weak intellectual property laws. Consequently, firms such as Starbucks, Carrefour, IKEA, Royal Ahold, and Wal-Mart usually internationalize through company-owned stores.

A Home Depot store in Mexico. As the home improvement markets in Canada and the United States have become saturated, the retailing giant has leveraged FDI to expand to other countries.

Foreign direct investment allows these firms to maintain direct control over their foreign operations and proprietary assets.

Many retailers have floundered in foreign markets. For example, when the French department store Galleries Lafayette opened a store in New York City, it could not compete with the city's numerous posh competitors. In its home market in Britain, Marks & Spencer succeeds with store layouts in which food and clothing offerings are blended in relatively small stores, a formula that translated poorly in Canada and the United States. IKEA experienced problems in Japan, where consumers value high-quality furnishings, not the low-cost products that IKEA offers.

Wal-Mart is the world's largest retailer but suffered dismal results in Germany because it could not compete with local competitors, and eventually exited the market. In Mexico, Wal-Mart constructed massive U.S.-style parking lots for its new super centers. But most Mexicans don't have cars, and city bus stops were beyond the huge lots, so shoppers could not haul their goods home. In Brazil, most families do their big shopping once a month, on payday. Wal-Mart built aisles too narrow and crowded to accommodate the rush. It stocked shelves with unneeded leaf blowers in urban Sao Paulo. In Argentina, Wal-Mart's red-white-and-blue banners, reminiscent of the U.S. flag, offended local tastes. Sam's Club, Wal-Mart's food discounting operation, flopped in Latin America partly because its huge multipack items were too big for local shoppers with low incomes and small apartments.[45]

Challenges of International Retailing

As these examples reveal, foreign markets pose big challenges to retailers. Retailing depends for much of its success on the store environment and the shopping experience. It is strongly affected by factors in each national environment. Four barriers stand in the way of successfully transplanting home market success to international markets.

First, *cultural and language barriers* are a special obstacle for international retailers. Compared to most businesses, retailers are particularly close to customers. They must respond to local market requirements, for example, by customizing the product and service portfolio, adapting store hours, modifying store size and layout, and meeting labor union demands.

Second, consumers tend to develop strong *loyalty to indigenous retailers*. As Galleries Lafayette in New York and Wal-Mart in Germany discovered, the foreign firm competes against local competitors that usually enjoy great loyalty from local consumers.

Third, managers must address *legal and regulatory barriers*. Some countries have idiosyncratic laws that affect retailing. For example, Germany limits store opening hours, and retailers must close on Sundays. Japan's Large-Scale Store Law meant that foreign warehouse and discount retailers needed permission from existing small retailers before setting up shop. The law, although relaxed in recent years, presented a major obstacle to the Japan entry of stores like Toys "Я" Us.

Fourth, when entering a new market, retailers must *develop local sources of supply*. They must find sources for thousands of products that local suppliers may be unwilling or unable to supply. For example, when Toys "Я" Us entered Japan, local toy manufacturers were reluctant to work with the U.S. firm. Some retailers end up importing many of their offerings, which requires establishing complex and costly international supply chains.

International Retailing Success Factors

The most successful retailers pursue a systematic approach to international expansion. First, *advanced research and planning* is essential. A thorough understanding of the target market, combined with a sophisticated business plan, allows the firm to anticipate potential problems and prepare for success. In the run-up to launching stores in China, management at the giant French retailer

Carrefour spent 12 years building up its business in Taiwan, where it developed a deep understanding of Chinese culture. It also learned how to forge alliances with local governments. These preparations helped Carrefour become China's biggest foreign retailer, rapidly developing a network of hypermarkets in 25 cities.[46]

Second, international retailers need to *establish efficient logistics and purchasing networks* in each market where they operate. Scale economies in procurement are especially critical. Retailers need to organize sourcing and logistical operations to ensure that adequate inventory is always maintained, while minimizing the cost of operations.

Third, international retailers should assume an *entrepreneurial, creative approach to foreign markets.* Virgin Megastore is a good example. Starting from one location in London in 1975, founder Richard Branson expanded Virgin to numerous markets throughout Europe, North America, and Asia. Its stores were big, well lit, and music albums were arranged in a logical order. Consequently, sales turnover was much faster than that of smaller music retailers.

Fourth, retailers must be willing to *adjust their business model to suit local conditions.* For example, Home Depot offers merchandise in Mexico that suits the small budgets of do-it-yourself builders. It has introduced payment plans for customers and promotes the do-it-yourself mindset in a country where most cannot afford to hire professional builders.[47] The major dimensions along which retailers differentiate themselves abroad include selection, price, marketing, store design, and the ways in which goods are displayed. But retailers must proceed cautiously; in the process of adapting to local conditions, the unique features that first made the firm a success can be diluted or destroyed. Management must make such adjustments with great care.

IKEA, the world's largest furniture retailer, has experienced great international success, launching over 200 furniture megastores in dozens of countries. Part of IKEA's success derives from strong leadership and skillful management of human resources. Management balances global integration of operations with responsiveness to local tastes. In each store, IKEA offers as many standardized products as possible while maintaining sufficient flexibility to accommodate specific local conditions. This is achieved in part by testing the waters and learning in smaller markets before entering big markets. For instance, IKEA perfected its retailing model in German-speaking Switzerland before entering Germany.

Interestingly, while individual retail firms have had great difficulty in transferring their home market success to foreign markets, retailing formats tend to be much easier to internationalize than retail brands. Retail formats or categories such as supermarkets, convenience stores, discount stores, catalogue-based sellers, online retailers, and outlet malls have all spread to other countries with relative ease. As an example, U.S.-style shopping malls have now spread all over the world. In Spain, for example, the number of shopping malls doubled between 1995 and 2005, with an average of 30 to 50 new malls opening every year. The country's largest is Madrid Xanadu, an 85-acre complex with an indoor ski slope, a go-cart track and 100 stores. But activists oppose the mall phenomenon in Spain, in part because intense competition has forced the closure of many Spanish mom-and-pop stores, and permanently changed the nature of Spanish retailing.[48]

 # Foreign Direct Investment, Collaborative Ventures, and Ethical Behavior

Corporate social responsibility (CSR)

Operating a business in a manner that meets or exceeds the ethical, legal, commercial, and public expectations of stakeholders (customers, shareholders, employees, and communities).

Corporate social responsibility (CSR) refers to operating a business in a manner that meets or exceeds the ethical, legal, commercial, and public expectations of stakeholders (customers, shareholders, employees, and communities). It represents a set of core values that includes avoiding human rights abuses, upholding the right to join or form labor unions, elimination of compulsory and child labor, avoiding workplace discrimination, protecting the natural environment, and guarding against corruption, including extortion and bribery. [49] Exhibit 14.9 illustrates the diversity of CSR initiatives that firms worldwide undertake.

Failure to adopt CSR behaviors can have adverse, even catastrophic, consequences. For example, efforts by the China National Petroleum Company (CNPC) to raise money on the New York Stock Exchange in 2000 were partly affected by the firm's activities in Sudan, which human rights groups had criticized. In part due to negative publicity regarding CNPC's Sudan operations, the firm raised a smaller sum than it expected.

Yet, socially responsible decisions can be costly. For example, a firm that installs antipollution equipment or improves worker conditions abroad will likely incur additional costs. It is generally easier for shareholders to measure financial returns on their investment than to assess the benefits provided by socially responsible behavior. The criticism of a firm whose costs escalate because of CSR projects often seems louder than the praise it receives from proactive ethical behavior. In countries such as the United States, firms' financial performance is evaluated on a quarterly basis, which increases the challenges of implementing CSR projects that may take years to produce positive results.

Weighing the costs and benefits of CSR, particularly in complex international environments, is a problem that bedevils managers. Some managers believe that it is sufficient to simply follow the laws and regulations in place in each country.

Company	Industry	Sample accomplishments
ABN AMRO (Netherlands)	Financial services	Finances various socially responsible projects, including biomass fuels and micro enterprises. Involved in carbon-emissions trading.
Dell (United States)	Computers	Accepts old computers from customers for recycling, free of charge.
GlaxoSmithKline (Britain)	Pharmaceuticals	Devotes substantial R&D to poor-country ailments, such as malaria and tuberculosis. Was first to offer AIDS medications at cost.
Marks & Spencer (Britain)	Retailing	Sources locally in order to cut fuel use and transportation costs. Provides good wages and benefits to retain staff.
Nokia (Finland)	Telecommunications	Makes telephones for low-income consumers. Has been a leader in environmental practices, such as phasing out toxic materials.
Norsk Hydro (Norway)	Oil and gas	Cut greenhouse gas emissions by 32 percent. Consistently measures the social and environmental impact of its projects.
Philips Electronics (Netherlands)	Consumer electronics	Top innovator of energy-saving appliances and lighting products, as well as medical devices for developing economies.
Scottish & Southern (Scotland)	Utilities	Proactively discloses the environmental risk, including air pollution and climate change, posed by its services.
Toyota (Japan)	Automobiles	The world leader in developing efficient gas-electric vehicles, such as the top-selling Prius.

Exhibit 14.9 Corporate Social Responsibility: A Sampling of MNE Accomplishments

SOURCE: Engardio, Pete. (2007). "Beyond the Green Corporation," *Business Week*, January 29, pp. 50–64.

However, many countries are characterized by weak legal and regulatory systems, and widespread corruption. *Relativism* refers to the belief that ethical truths are relative to the groups that hold them. Relativism is akin to the advice: "When in Rome, do as the Romans do." According to this view, a Japanese multinational that believes bribery is wrong might pay bribes in countries where the practice is customary and culturally acceptable. It is natural for the firm to follow the values and behaviors that prevail in the countries where it does business. *Normativism* is a belief in universal behavioral standards that firms and individuals should uphold. According to this view, the Japanese multinational that believes bribery is wrong will enforce this standard everywhere in the world. The United Nations and other CSR proponents increasingly encourage companies to follow a normative approach in their international dealings. [50]

Most firms apply a combination of relativism and normativism abroad. That is—rightly or wrongly—most firms strike a balance between corporate values developed in the home country and local standards. However, in a global business environment, such an approach puts the firm at risk of violating norms that are increasingly universal. In countries with questionable ethical standards, it is usually best to maintain environmental, workplace, and anticorruption standards that are *superior* to what is required by local laws and values. This strategy helps garner goodwill in the local market and averts potentially damaging negative publicity in the firm's other markets. Senior managers must develop a cogent and practicable code of ethics that serves as a moral compass for the firm's operations around the world. Like a mission statement, the code should be designed to guide employee behavior in all situations, so that the firm avoids behaviors that compromise corporate ethical standards wherever it does business.

One firm that attempts to implement its corporate citizenship principles universally is Petrobras, the Brazilian oil company. Its operations span 21 countries, many of which have unstable political or social environments. In Brazil, Petrobras has developed extensive CSR-oriented programs related to poverty reduction, youth education, child labor and abuse, and fundamental rights for people with physical and mental impairments. In Africa and elsewhere, Petrobras has developed CSR initiatives in areas such as reconstruction projects for schools, day-care centers, hospitals, and in rural communities. In Colombia, the firm developed a program to train community health agents. In Nigeria, Petrobras cooperates with a local nongovernmental organization to provide HIV/AIDS prevention education in secondary schools.[51]

In Britain, the supermarket chain Tesco (with 380,000 employees) uses wind-powered energy systems to provide electricity for some of its stores. In 2006, the company vowed to cut the energy use in its British buildings in half by 2008. In much of its supply chain, instead of noisy gas-powered tractor-trailer trucks, the firm uses bio-diesel trucks and state-of-the-art trains that are quieter and prevent thousands of tons of carbon dioxide emissions from polluting the atmosphere. Tesco attempts to measure the "carbon costs" of each item that it sells, in order to devise less-polluting approaches to serving customer needs. Customers are rewarded for bringing their own reusable shopping bags to stores, instead of using disposable plastic bags. The firm determines senior management bonuses partly based on meeting energy- and waste-reduction targets. In 2007, Tesco announced plans to install a massive solar-panel roof on its planned new distribution center in California. [52]

AUTOLATINA: A Failed International Partnership

Autolatina, a joint venture between Ford and Volkswagen (VW), was created in 1987 in Brazil with several goals in mind:

- Serve the highly protected car markets of Brazil and Argentina from within.
- Establish an unbeatable presence in Latin America.
- Share the risk of operating in a volatile market.
- Offer a wide range of car models to Latin American customers.

Soon after founding the venture, Autolatina's market share reached 60 percent in the Brazilian market and 30 percent in Argentina.

Germany's Volkswagen was originally founded with the goal of offering popular cars that anyone could afford. The company achieved this goal with the Beetle, which at one time was the world's best-selling car. Early on, the Beetle became a mascot of Brazil's economic miracle, accounting for nearly half of Brazilian car sales. Volkswagen launched the Gol in 1980. It was assembled at *Volkswagen do Brazil*, which employed more than 45,000 people, becoming the largest industrial corporation in Latin America. Eventually, the Gol surpassed the Beetle as Brazil's best-selling car.

Ford was the first car company to assemble in Brazil. Early on, Ford resisted government demands to establish complete automotive operations, including assembly and full manufacturing in Brazil. Ford's resistance worked to VW's advantage—the German firm eventually prevailed and became number one in Brazil.

Meanwhile, Brazil's own car industry, coddled by years of high tariffs and other protectionism, was moving quickly to modernize. For decades, the country banned imported cars or did not allow expensive and foreign parts to be fitted to locally made cars. In the 1970s, the auto industry was a symbol of the "Brazilian miracle." A ban on imports meant that Brazil's underdeveloped industry faced little foreign competition. Local manufacturers became complacent and failed to keep up with the latest car styles and technological innovations. At around the same time, Ford management was renewing its interest in Brazil and aimed to reestablish its former dominance there.

Autolatina: A Perfect Marriage

The partners' objective in the Ford-VW joint venture was to combine operations in order to overcome obstacles in the Brazilian market. By 1989, Ford and Volkswagen had a total of 15 vehicle, engine, and parts plants in Brazil and Argentina, employing 75,000 people. Their combined annual production capacity was 900,000 cars and trucks, distributed through 1,500 dealerships. Their automotive and credit operations achieved total sales of US$4 billion.

In a market protected from foreign imports, Autolatina became a big success. It offered inexpensive models, including the Escort XR3, Sierra, VW's Gol, Beetle, and midsized Ford Falcons. The partners organized plant operations by size of vehicles: VW focused on building small cars, while Ford supplied the larger Escort and a line of pickup trucks. The two partners also produced shared products. For instance, Volkswagen made the Ford Versailles (derived from the VW Santana), and Ford produced the VW Logus (derived from the Ford Escort). The firms unified their marketing and sales staffs and hired specialists and consultants to accommodate the two different company cultures.

Production of Autolatina cars grew rapidly over time. It seemed that both companies had succeeded in identifying the key factors contributing to Autolatina's success: inexpensive, noncompeting models, a growing market, and sharing manufacturing and profits. Autolatina enabled Ford and VW to serve an important region from within while reducing the partners' operational costs.

Developments: New Competition and the Emergence of MERCOSUR

Eventually, however, conditions shifted in Brazil, and Autolatina was caught unprepared by renewed economic growth. In addition to the popular car policy, Brazil reduced tariffs on car imports. Over the course of five years, import tariffs fell from 85 percent to as low as 20 percent.

In 1991, MERCOSUR (Mercado Comun del Sur, the region's free trade agreement) went into effect. Originally an agreement between Argentina, Brazil, Paraguay, and Uruguay, MERCOSUR was extended in 1996 to include Chile and, in 1997, Bolivia. With 150 million of MERCOSUR's 200 million inhabitants, Brazil was ready to become the region's carmaking center. The formation of MERCOSUR coincided with a rise in domestic demand, industrial modernization, and the internationalization of numerous firms from the region. Local companies such as Autolatina began to target the greatly enlarged market.

At the same time, MERCOSUR opened new opportunities for foreign multinationals. Numerous carmakers entered Brazil and Argentina, including Fiat, GM, Honda, Mercedes Benz, Renault, and Toyota. They used FDI to launch local production of various popular car models. Gradually Brazil became the world's tenth largest producer of motor vehicles.

443

Meanwhile, the products of Autolatina, built for a protected market, fell out of step with the rapidly evolving marketplace. Brazilian consumers began to show a preference for lower-cost small cars, and price competition intensified from the abundance of competing small cars. Both GM and Fiat launched popular cars (Corsa and Uno, respectively) for less than $7,000. The Closing Case table presents the variety of offerings by four leading firms. Although Autolatina had succeeded in reviving the VW Beetle, customers deserted the Beetle for lower-priced competing brands. With increased competition, customer's choices expanded beyond low cost, increasing the pressure on manufacturers to improve quality and offerings.

Company	Market Segment	Products
Volkswagen[1]	Small	Beetle, Gol
	Mid-sized	Logus, Pointer, Voyage
	Large	Santana
Ford	Mid-sized	Escort, Verona
	Large	Versailles
General	Small	Corsa
Motors	Mid-sized	Kadett, Monza, Vectra
	Large	Omega
Fiat	Small	Uno
	Large	Tempra

[1] Volkswagen stopped production of the Beetle in 1996 in Brazil. The new Beetle (sold in Europe and the United States) is not manufactured in Brazil.

Conflicts between the Partners

In addition to dynamic changes in the market, conflicts arose in the strategies of Ford and VW. Ford dealers in Brazil had been begging for smaller cars, better suited to Latin American consumers. But Ford avoided the erosion of Autolatina's profits by competing with VW's Gol (from which it was receiving half the profits). Volkswagen management, on the other hand, avoided sharing its subcompact designs with Ford. Mutual willingness to share technological knowledge and other key competencies declined over time.

Differences in the organizational cultures of the two partners also contributed to deteriorating relations. The German and the U.S. organizations had different history and origins, as well as differing management styles.

Within the boundaries of Autolatina, VW and Ford were reasonably well integrated operationally, even exchanging model fabrication. But outside the relationship, suppliers continued to serve the two companies independently, as well as the dealerships. Autolatina was not fully integrated with suppliers or dealers, leading to inefficiencies in the supply chain. Although consolidation reduces cost of administration and value-chain activities, the two firms failed to consolidate their supply bases and dealerships.

VW and Ford continued to compete with each other in the worldwide market, which hindered the sharing of technical knowledge and potential gains from joint R&D. Outside of the Autolatina collaboration, the partners even competed against each other by launching new cars in the same category.

The End of Autolatina

In 1995, Ford and VW dissolved their alliance. The parting was so amicable that the employees were allowed to choose the company they wanted to continue to work for.

Because the sale of subcompact vehicles, known as *popular cars* in Latin America, took off rapidly, Volkswagen's smaller cars benefited from the demise of the joint venture. Volkswagen held a third of the regional market. The firm invested $ 2.5 billion to expand capacity by one third (up to 2,500 vehicles a day), and launched a new truck plant and a line of new engines.

By contrast, Ford continued to specialize in midsized cars and was unable to respond to the regional demand for small cars. Eventually Ford's image in Brazil was hurt. It acquired a reputation for producing cars that few wanted to buy. Ford began a $1.1 billion investment on its own to build Fiestas in Brazil and Escorts in Argentina. But by then, VW, Fiat, and GM had attained big market shares in Brazil. Ford's market share fell to just 11 percent. More recently, Ford now builds the Fiesta, Focus, and a few other small cars in Brazil and Argentina. Each plant exports in large volumes to neighboring countries. Ford is undertaking new investments in Brazil, mainly to develop new products for the local market.

AACSB: Reflective Thinking

Case Questions

1. What were Ford's motives and objectives for entering its collaborative venture with Volkswagen? Evaluate the extent to which Ford accomplished these objectives.

2. What type of collaborative venture did Ford enter with Volkswagen? What were the advantages and disadvantages of this venture from Ford's perspective?

3. What strengths did Ford and VW bring to the Autolatina venture? Did these firms have any weaknesses? Elaborate.

4. Did Ford commit any blunders in its Latin American operations? Specify.

5. What can other managers learn from Ford's experience regarding international collaborative ventures? What should Ford do now?

This case was prepared by Alexandre M. Rodrigues and Elvin Zung under the direction of Professor S. Tamer Cavusgil.

Sources: Berry, B. (1987). "Volkswagen Steps up Imports from Latin America," *Iron Age*, pp. 49–51; Blumenstein, Rebecca. (1997). "Head of Ford Unit In Brazil Expects A Narrower Loss," *Wall Street Journal*, May 14, p. B8; Bradsher, K. (1997). "Messy Latin Divorce Splits Ford and VW," *International Herald Tribune*, May 18, p. 8; Cavusgil, S. T. (1998). "International Partnering: A Systematic Framework for Collaborating with Foreign Business Partners," *Journal of International Marketing* 6(1): 91–108; Corcoran, E. (1987). "Special Report—The global automobile: Cooperating to Compete," *IEEE Spectrum*, 24(10): 53–56; *Economist*. (1993). "The Bugs from Brazil", Aug 21, p. 54; *Economist*. (1994). "Brazil's Car Industry: Party Time," Sept. 17, p. 76; Guiles, Melinda G., and Roger Cohen.

(1986). "Ford, Volkswagen Plan Joint Venture To Oversee Units in Argentina, Brazil." *Wall Street Journal*, Nov. 25, p. 1; *FinancialWire*. (2007). "Ford To Invest $2.2 Billion in Brazil Through 2011," Jan. 5, p. 1; Kamm, Thomas. (1993). "Beetles Could Give Power to the People of Brazil Once Again—President Wants Autolatina To Revive the VW Bug, But Price Won't Be Retro." *Wall Street Journal*, Feb. 1, p. A1; Kamm, Thomas. (1994). "Pedal to the Metal: Brazil Swiftly Becomes Major Auto Producer As Trade Policy Shifts," *Wall Street Journal*, Apr. 20, p. A1; Katz, I., G. Smith, and A. Mandel-Campbell. "Brazil's Neighbors Are Very Nervous," *Business Week*, Nov. 17, p. 64; Kotabe, M. "MERCOSUR and Beyond." Austin: Center for International Business Education and Research, University of Texas at Austin; Moffett, M. (1996). "Bruised in Brazil: Ford Slips as Market Blooms," *Wall Street Journal*, Dec. 13, p. A10; Shapiro, H. (1991). "Determinants of Firm Entry into the Brazilian Automobile Manufacturing Industry, 1956–1968." *Business History Review* 65:876–948.

CHAPTER ESSENTIALS

Key Terms

acquisition, p. 429

consortium, p. 434

corporate social responsibility (CSR), p. 440

cross-licensing agreement, p. 434

equity joint venture, p. 430

equity participation, p. 430

foreign direct investment (FDI), p. 418

greenfield investment, p. 429

horizontal integration, p. 432

international collaborative venture, p. 418

international portfolio investment, p. 424

joint venture, p. 419

merger, p. 429

project-based, nonequity venture, p. 433

vertical integration, p. 432

wholly owned direct investment, p. 430

Summary

In this chapter, you learned about:

1. An organizing framework for foreign market entry strategies

The strategies for foreign market entry can be classified in terms of the amount of control they afford the firm in its foreign markets. Control refers to the ability to influence the decisions, operations, and strategic resources of foreign ventures. *Low-control strategies* are exporting, countertrade, and global sourcing. *High control-strategies* include joint ventures and foreign direct investment (FDI). A **joint venture** is a form of collaboration between two or more firms that leads to minority, equal, or majority ownership. **Foreign direct investment** is an internationalization strategy in which the firm establishes a physical presence abroad through ownership of productive assets such as capital, technology, labor, land, plant, and equipment. Greater control results by having a direct presence in the foreign market. *Moderate-control strategies* involve contractual relationships such as licensing and franchising. High-control strategies require sub-

stantial *resource commitments* and entail less *flexibility* in the market. Long-term involvement in the market exposes the firm to *risk*.

2. Motives for foreign direct investment (FDI) and collaborative ventures

Firms employ FDI for various reasons, including *market-seeking motives*, to enter new markets and gain new customers, *resource/asset-seeking motives*, to acquire production factors that may be cheaper or more abundant in foreign markets, and *efficiency-seeking motives*, to enhance the efficiency of the firm's value-adding activities. These motives often occur in combination. Motivations for **international collaborative ventures** include the ability to gain access to new markets, opportunities, or knowledge; to undertake international activities too costly or risky for one firm alone; to reduce costs; to meet government requirements; and to prevent or reduce competition.

3. Foreign direct investment

Foreign direct investment is the most advanced and complex entry strategy, and involves establishing manufacturing plants, marketing subsidiaries, or other facilities abroad. For the firm, FDI requires substantial resource commitment, local presence and operations in target countries, and global scale efficiency. It also entails greater risk, as compared to other entry modes. Foreign direct investment is most commonly used by MNEs—large firms with extensive international experience. Services are intangible and typically cannot be exported. Services usually are location-bound and require firms to establish a foreign presence, generally via FDI. **International portfolio investment** is passive ownership of foreign securities such as stocks and bonds.

4. Types of foreign direct investment

Foreign direct investment can be **wholly owned direct investment**, in which the firm owns 100 percent of foreign operations, or an **equity joint venture** with one or more partners. Firms may engage in **greenfield investment** by building a facility from scratch, or by acquiring an existing facility from another firm through **acquisition**. With **vertical integration**, the firm seeks to own multiple stages of its value chain. With **horizontal integration**, the firm seeks to own activities involved in a single stage of its value chain. A **merger** is a special type of acquisition in which two companies join together to form a new, larger firm.

5. International collaborative ventures

Joint ventures (JVs) are normally formed when no one party possesses all the assets needed to exploit an opportunity. Joint ventures are an example of ownership-based collaborations. The **project-based, nonequity venture** emphasizes a contractual relationship between the partners and is formed to pursue certain goals or meet an important business need while the partners remain independent. A **consortium** is a project-based, nonequity venture in which a group of firms undertake a large-scale activity that is beyond the capabilities of the individual members.

6. Managing collaborative ventures

Collaboration requires management to clearly define its goals and strategies. It requires much research and analysis up front, as well as strong negotiation skills. Decisions are made regarding allocation of responsibilities in management, production, finance, and marketing, as well as how to handle day-to-day operations and plans for the future. At least half of all collaborative ventures fail because of cultural differences, weak underlying venture rationale, differing partner objectives, poor planning, lack of control, asymmetric partner contributions, shifting environmental conditions, or the risk of creating a competitor. Firms should choose their partners carefully and follow a systematic process for managing ventures.

7. The experience of retailers in foreign markets

International retailing has greatly expanded in recent years. Because retailing involves intensive customer interaction, it is particularly susceptible to culture, income levels, and other conditions abroad. Success depends on adapting to local conditions while maintaining the retailer's unique features and value proposition. International retailers face various challenges, including cultural and language barriers, strong loyalty to local retailers, legal and regulatory barriers, and the necessity to develop local supply sources. Retailer success also depends on advanced research and planning, establishing efficient logistics and purchasing networks, using an entrepreneurial, creative approach to foreign markets, and adjusting the business model to suit local needs.

8. Foreign direct investment, collaborative ventures, and ethical behavior

Corporate social responsibility (CSR) refers to operating a business in a manner that meets or exceeds the ethical, legal, commercial, and public expectations of stakeholders (customers, shareholders, employees, and communities).

Test Your Comprehension AACSB: Reflective Thinking, Analytical Skills

1. What are the various types of foreign direct investment? Distinguish between acquisition and greenfield.

2. What are the major motivations for undertaking FDI?

3. Delineate the types of firms involved in FDI. Are there any types of companies that can internationalize *only* via FDI? Elaborate.

4. What are the different types of collaborative ventures? What type of venture should a firm choose for entering a culturally distant market like Malaysia? For developing the next generation of products in its industry? For undertaking a short-term project, such as building infrastructure (e.g., highway, dam, airport terminal) abroad?

5. What are the major motives for undertaking FDI for a small firm whose sales are dwindling in its home market? For a firm that wants to enter a country with high trade barriers? For a firm with high manufacturing costs in its home market? For a hotel chain? For a large, diversified firm that wants to enter various markets worldwide for a variety of reasons?

6. What factors should management consider when deciding where in the world to establish a production or assembly facility? A marketing subsidiary? A regional headquarters?

7. Governments frequently provide incentives to encourage foreign firms to invest within their national borders. Why would a government encourage inward FDI?

8. What steps should the firm take to ensure the success of its international collaborative ventures?

9. Explain what steps a firm should take to successfully launch a collaborative venture with a foreign partner.

10. What are the risks of international retailing? What can a retailer—such as a department store or a restaurant—do to maximize its chances of succeeding in foreign markets?

Apply Your Understanding AACSB: Communication, Reflective Thinking

1. Suppose you get a job at MobileTV, a small manufacturer of TV sets installed in cars and boats. Business has been dwindling recently and management is worried. Part of the problem is the growing volume of cheap imports from emerging markets. Because MobileTV does all its manufacturing in Britain and Canada, it lacks cost advantages and so its prices are relatively high. You decide to study the problem. You believe MobileTV should move much of its manufacturing to Mexico. But top management knows almost nothing about FDI. Prepare a report to management detailing the advantages of establishing a production base in Mexico. Why should the firm be interested in foreign manufacturing? Finally, make a recommendation as to which type of FDI MobileTV should use in Mexico.

2. Collaborative ventures are a major trend in international business. Complexity in foreign markets has led many firms to search for more flexibility in foreign market entry. Suppose you work for the Aoki Corporation, a producer of processed foods. Your boss, Hiroshi Aoki, has heard there is a big market for processed foods in continental Europe but does not know how to enter or do business there. You recommend entering Europe through a joint venture with a local European firm. Prepare a memo to Mr. Aoki explaining the objectives and risks of internationalizing via collaborative ventures. Explain why a collaborative venture might be a better entry strategy than wholly owned FDI. Keep in mind that processed food is a culturally sensitive product that entails various complexities in marketing and distribution. What type of European partner do you believe Aoki should seek?

3. While taking an introductory class in international business, you get a part-time job at Javaheads, a start-up chain of coffee shops. Business is booming and the far-sighted owner of Javaheads, Mr. Ralph Caffeen, wants to open some shops in the Caribbean, where he likes to vacation. You recently learned that replicating retail success at home in foreign markets is difficult, and many retailers have failed in international expansion. As an assertive business student, you decide to share your knowledge of international retailing with Ralph. What are the risks in international retailing? What recommendations can you offer to Ralph in order to improve Javaheads' chances for international success?

globalEDGE Internet Exercises

AACSB: Communication, Reflective Thinking, Use of Information Technology

Refer to Chapter 1, page 27, for instructions on how to access and use globalEDGE™.

1. Your future employer would like to establish a factory in Latin America to make and sell products in the region. It has narrowed the pool of candidate countries to Argentina, Brazil, and Chile. Your task is to write a report that compares the FDI environments of these countries. One approach is to obtain the *Country Fact Sheet* for each nation from UNCTAD (www.unctad.org), the United Nations Conference on Trade and Development, an agency that gathers FDI data. You can access this data either through globalEDGE™ or the UNCTAD site. By examining the fact sheets, answer each of the following questions individually for Argentina, Brazil, and Chile:

   a. Who are the major trading partners of each country in the region? (This indicates the size and stability of existing trading relationships with key partners.)
   b. Which are the leading firms now doing FDI in each country? (This can identify key competitors.)
   c. What is each country's rating on the FDI Performance Index? (This rating indicates the performance that typical firms have experienced when investing in each country.)
   d. What is the level of merger and acquisition activity in each country? (This shows the maturity of each country for acquisition-based FDI.)

2. Suppose your firm aims to identify prospective countries for direct investment. Your boss has requested a report on the attractiveness of alternative locations based on their potential FDI return. A colleague mentions a tool called the "FDI Confidence Index." Consult this resource and write a report in which you identify the top FDI destinations, as well as the criteria used to construct the index. The Confidence Index is published by the consulting firm A.T. Kearney, based on an annual survey of CEOs at the world's top MNEs. Access the index by entering "FDI Confidence Index" at globalEDGE™ or directly at www.atkearney.com. Download the PDF file to do your research.

3. Assume you own a company that manufactures medical products in the biotechnology industry. You want to establish a foreign plant to manufacture your products and are seeking countries with a high concentration of knowledge workers. Therefore, you decide to collect information regarding the "knowledge economy" abroad. The *World Bank Development Gateway* (www.developmentgateway.org) highlights the state of knowledge in various countries. Visit the site and prepare a report on the knowledge economy in Singapore, South Korea, and Spain. You will be able to find numerous articles and retrieve information regarding these countries.

Selecting a Site for a Manufacturing Plant

Manufacturing is an important stage in many firms' value chains. It involves a range of activities, including development of product and process technologies, managing inflows of input materials, organizing inbound and outbound logistics, maintaining quality and reliability standards of manufactured outputs, and actual manufacturing operations. Firms use foreign locations to manufacture the products that they sell around the world. For firms that manufacture abroad, the most important first step is finding the right location to build the manufacturing plant.

AACSB: Reflective Thinking, Analytical Skills

Managerial Challenge

Decisions regarding where to locate factories are complex. For large production projects, numerous decisionmakers at MNEs perform complex analyses to find the best manufacturing location abroad. Building or acquiring a foreign factory involves FDI, usually the most expensive foreign entry strategy. Given limited resources, managers set up factories in locations that maximize the firm's competitive advantage. The best approach to selecting a location is to narrow the possible countries to one ideal location, using a systematic research process.

Background

In searching for ideal foreign manufacturing sites, managers account for numerous factors, including those related to each country's economy, political system, level of government intervention, legal protection, quality and cost of labor, presence of labor unions, and level of infrastructure.

Managerial Skills You Will Gain

In this C/K/R Management Skill Builder©, as a prospective manager, you will:

1. Learn the factors to consider when evaluating countries for locating a foreign manufacturing plant.

2. Understand how these factors relate to maximizing the firm's competitive advantage.

3. Analyze business conditions in Eastern Europe.

4. Select the location for a foreign manufacturing plant.

Your Task

Assume you work for a company that makes bathroom fixtures (e.g., sinks, bathtubs, shower systems), such as American Standard or Toto. Your firm wants to enter the huge European market with these products. With over 450 million relatively affluent consumers in a concentrated area, the European Union is highly attractive. To better serve this region, foreign companies build manufacturing plants in Europe via direct investment. But, production costs are high in Western Europe. A recent trend has been to establish factories in Eastern Europe because of the lower-cost, high-quality labor there. Your task is to identify the most suitable Eastern European country to establish a manufacturing plant.

Go to the C/K/R Knowledge Portal©

www.prenhall.com/cavusgil

Proceed to the C/K/R Knowledge Portal© to obtain the expanded background information, your task and methodology, suggested resources for this exercise, and the presentation template.

Licensing, Franchising, and Other Contractual Strategies

> Harry Potter: The Magic of Licensing

One of the hottest properties in merchandise licensing is Harry Potter, valued at over $1 billion. Not bad for a bespectacled 11-year-old boy. Potter has come a long way since he first appeared in the 1997 children's book by J. K. Rowling. Potter evolved from an unhappy orphan to a confident trainee wizard. The stories appeal to both children and adults. Kids love Potter because he is a fantastic combination of cool kid and good kid. Adults like the classical theme of good versus evil. Licensing deals have benefited immensely from the Warner Bros. production and release of major Harry Potter movies.

Warner Bros. purchased exclusive licensing rights for Harry Potter. Warner allows firms all over the world to use Potter images on their manufactured products—such as game software, children's furniture, and clothing—in exchange for a royalty. The royalty is a flat percentage of the sale generated by the licensed product that the manufacturer pays to the licensor. The ability to associate Potter with manufactured products greatly increases the sale of licensed products, allowing them to command high prices. Such deals have made Rowling one of the wealthiest women in England.

Warner licenses Harry Potter to a number of firms. Some firms produce *artefacts*—products seen in the films that do not have Potter's name on them. For example, Califor-

nia's Jelly Belly Candy Company creates Potter's favorite candy, Bertie Bott's Every Flavour Beans, in flavors such as earwax, sardine, and vomit. LEGO is making construction kits that allow kids to build their own Hogwarts castle, and Mattel is making Harry Potter toys.

Electronic Arts, the largest independent software game producer, paid Warner for a license to develop and market video games. The license covers games played on the Internet, video game consoles such as Sony's PlayStation 2, and cellular telephones. Fans can play a virtual version of Quidditch, which is a bit like aerial polo but with contestants flying on broomsticks. Mattel, Electronic Arts, and other licensees pay a royalty to Warner for the right to use the Potter image to sell their merchandise.

Goodwin Weavers, a home furnishings company, also has a Harry Potter license. The company produces Potter tapestry throws, wall hangings, decorative pillows, "pillow buddies," and fleece. P. J. Kids made a line of Potter loft beds that sold extremely well, despite a nearly $2,000 price tag. Such products command high prices through the magic of licensing a very popular brand.

The licensing process is self-generating—each Harry Potter book sets the stage for a film, which boosts book sales, which promotes sales of Potter-licensed products.

Globally, the first four Potter books sold over 200 million copies in 55 languages. The first two Potter movies grossed over $1.8 billion at the box office. Meanwhile, Rowling and Warner have exercised restraint. They don't want to license Potter to just anyone. Experts estimate that the hot property could have generated 200 to 300 product licenses in the United States alone. Warner wants to make sure that overexposure doesn't kill the golden goose.

One of the risks that licensors such as Warner face is intellectual property violations. These occur when a firm or individual uses the licensed item to generate profits without permission of the property's owner. For instance, over 80 percent of recorded music and business software in China is counterfeit. Pirated DVD versions of Potter movies are sold on the streets of Chinese cities for as little as one dollar, often before the film's official premiere in China. Unauthorized translations of one of the Potter books have been posted on the Internet. Such postings affect future sales because people may not bother to buy the book if an online version is available. Chinese bookstores recently released a boxed set of Harry Potter novels, but even before release, kiosks around China were selling unauthorized versions of the books. To combat counterfeiting, the official Chinese publisher printed the Potter books on special light green paper and advised the local media—newspapers, magazines, television—how to recognize the real version. Licensees hope that Harry Potter will generate the same magic in China that he has in the rest of the world. ◀

Sources: Derrick, Stuart. (2005). "Brands Cash In on Literary Scene," *Promotions & Incentives*, July/August, pp. 13–14; *DSN Retailing Today*. (2000). "Harry Potter: Is Warner Bros. Brewing Licensing Magic," August 21, pp. A8; *Economist.com / Global Agenda*. (2003). "Harry Potter and the Publishing Goldmine," June 23, p. 1; Forney, Matt. (2000). "Harry Potter, Meet 'Ha-li Bo-te'—Children's Books Hit China, But Price and Piracy Could Put Crimp in Sales," *Wall Street Journal*, Sept 21, p. B1; Jardine, Alexandra. (2001). "Marketing Magic," *Marketing*, November 15, p. 20; O'Mara, Sheila. (2002). "Harry—Licensing's Golden Child," *Home Textiles Today*, January/February, p. 10; *Wall Street Journal*. (2000). "Electronic Arts Gets Rights to Develop Harry Potter Games," August 11, p. A4

The Nature of Contractual Entry Strategies in International Business

Contractual entry strategies in international business Cross-border exchanges where the relationship between the focal firm and its foreign partner is governed by an explicit contract.

Intellectual property Ideas or works created by firms or individuals such as patents, trademarks, and copyrights.

Licensing Arrangement in which the owner of intellectual property grants another firm the right to use that property for a specified period of time in exchange for royalties or other compensation.

Franchising Arrangement in which the firm allows another the right to use an entire business system in exchange for fees, royalties, or other forms of compensation.

In this chapter, we address various types of cross-border contractual relationships, including licensing and franchising. **Contractual entry strategies in international business** refer to cross-border exchanges where the relationship between the focal firm and its foreign partner is governed by an explicit contract. **Intellectual property** refers to ideas or works created by firms or individuals, such as patents, trademarks, and copyrights. It incorporates such knowledge-based assets of the firm or individuals as industrial designs, trade secrets, inventions, works of art, literature, and other "creations of the mind."[1]

Two common types of contractual entry strategies are *licensing* and *franchising*. **Licensing** is an arrangement in which the owner of intellectual property grants another firm the right to use that property for a specified period of time in exchange for royalties or other compensation. **Franchising** is an arrangement in which the firm allows another the right to use an entire business system in exchange for fees, royalties, or other forms of compensation.

Contractual relationships are fairly prevalent in international business. Manufacturers as well as service firms routinely transfer their knowledge assets to foreign partners. For example, pharmaceutical manufacturers engage in cross-licensing practices where they exchange scientific knowledge about producing specific products, as well as the rights to distribute these products in certain geographic regions. Professional service firms such as those in architecture, engineering, advertising, and consulting extend their international reach through contracts with foreign partners. Similarly, service firms in retailing, fast food, car rentals, television programming, and animation rely on licensing and franchising agreements. As an example, 7-Eleven runs the world's largest chain of convenience stores, with about 26,000 stores in 18 countries. While the parent firm in Japan owns most of the stores, several thousand in Canada, Mexico, and the United States are operated through franchising arrangements.

Unique Aspects of Contractual Relationships

Cross-border contractual relationships share six common characteristics. They are:

- *Governed by a contract that provides the focal firm a moderate level of control over the foreign partner.* A formal agreement specifies the rights and obligations for both partners. Control refers to the ability of the focal firm to influence the decisions, operations, and strategic resources of a foreign venture and ensure that foreign partners undertake assigned activities and procedures. The focal firm also maintains ownership and jurisdiction over its intellectual property. However, as Exhibit 14.1 on page 420 relies on shows, contractual agreements do not afford the same level of control as foreign direct investment, since the focal firm relies on independent businesses abroad.

- *Typically involve exchange of intangibles (intellectual property) and services.* Examples of intangibles that firms exchange include technical assistance and know-how. (See Exhibit 3.5 on page 70 for a complete list). Along with intangibles, however, firms may also exchange products or equipment to support the foreign partner.

- *Can be pursued independently or in conjunction with other foreign market entry strategies.* Firms can engage in contractual agreements as an alternative way of responding to international opportunities. In other cases, contractual relationships may accompany and support FDI and exporting.[2] Their use is context specific; that is, a focal firm may pursue a contractual relationship with certain customers, countries, or products, but not others.

- *Provide for a dynamic, flexible choice.* Over time the focal firm may switch to another way of servicing foreign markets. For example, franchisors such as McDonald's or Coca-Cola often find it desirable to acquire some of their franchisees and bottlers. In doing so, they would be switching from a contractual to an ownership-based entry strategy.

- *Often reduce local perceptions of the focal firm as a foreign enterprise.* Since the focal firm partners with a local firm, it may attract less of the criticism often directed at foreign MNEs.

- *Generate a predictable level of earnings from foreign operations.* In comparison to FDI, contractual relationships imply reduced volatility and risk.[3]

Types of Intellectual Property

A *patent* provides an inventor with the right to prevent others from using, selling, or importing an invention for a fixed period—typically, up to 20 years.[4] It is granted to any firm or individual that invents or discovers any new and useful process, device, manufactured product, or any new and useful improvement on these. A *trademark* is a distinctive design, symbol, logo, word, or series of words placed on a product label. It identifies a product or service as coming from a common source and having a certain level of quality. Well-known trademarks include British Petroleum's "BP" acronym, McDonald's golden arches, and Nike's swoosh symbol. A *copyright* protects original works of authorship, giving the creator the exclusive right to reproduce the work, display and perform it publicly, and to authorize others to perform these activities. Copyrights cover works from music, art, literature, films, and computer software.

An *industrial design* refers to the appearance or features of a product. The design is intended to improve the aesthetics and usability of a product in order to increase its production efficiency, performance, or marketability. The thin Apple iPod with the company logo is a well-known industrial design. A *trade secret* is confidential know-how or information that has commercial value.[5] Trade secrets include information such as production methods, business plans, and customer lists. For example, the formula to produce Coca-Cola is a trade secret. A *collective mark* is a logo belonging to an association or group whose members retain the right to use the mark identifying the origin of a product or service. Typically, the members use the marks to identify themselves and their products with a level of quality or accuracy, geographical origin, or other characteristics established by the organization. For example, DIN is the collective mark for the German Institute for Standardization, typically found on home appliances in Europe.

Intellectual property rights (IPRs) refer to the legal claim through which the proprietary assets of firms and individuals are protected from unauthorized use by other parties. The availability and enforcement of these rights varies from country to country. The fundamental rationale for IPRs is to provide inventors with a monopoly advantage for a specified period of time, so that they can exploit their inventions and create commercial advantage. Such legal rights enable inventors not only to recoup investment costs, but also to acquire power and dominance in markets by granting a period of years in which the inventor need not face direct competition from competitors producing the same product. Without legal protection and the assurance of commercial rewards, most firms and individuals would have little incentive to invent.

> **Intellectual property rights (IPRs)** The legal claim through which the proprietary assets of firms and individuals are protected from unauthorized use by other parties.

 Licensing

A licensing agreement specifies the nature of the relationship between the licensor (owner of intellectual property) and the licensee (the user). High-technology firms routinely license their patents and know-how to foreign companies. For example, Intel has licensed the right to a new process for manufacturing computer chips to a chip manufacturer in Germany. As revealed in the opening vignette, Warner licenses images from the Harry Potter books and movies to companies worldwide. Disney licenses the right to use its cartoon characters in the production of shirts and hats to clothing manufacturers in Hong Kong. Disney also licenses its trademark names and logos to manufacturers of apparel, toys, and watches for sale worldwide. Licensing allows Disney to create synergies with foreign partners who adapt materials, colors, and other design elements to suit local tastes. Licensing allows the licensee to produce and market a product similar to the one the licensor may already produce in its home country. By gaining an association with a famous name like Disney, the licensee can generate substantial sales.

Exhibit 15.1 illustrates the nature of the licensing agreement between the licensor and the licensee.[6] Upon signing a licensing contract, the licensee pays the licensor a fixed amount up front *and* an ongoing **royalty** of typically 2 to 5 percent on gross sales generated from using the licensed asset. The fixed amount covers the licensor's initial costs of transferring the licensed asset to the licensee, including consultation, training in how to deploy the asset, engineering, or adaptation. However, certain types of licensable assets, such as copyrights and trademarks, have much lower transfer costs.

> **Royalty** A fee paid periodically to compensate a licensor for the temporary use of its intellectual property; often based on a percentage on gross sales generated from using the licensed asset.

The licensing contract typically runs from 5 to 7 years and is renewable at the option of the parties. While the licensor usually must provide technical information and assistance to the licensee, once the relationship is established and the licensee fully understands its role, the licensor has little or no additional role. The licensor typically plays an advisory role, but has no direct involvement in the mar-

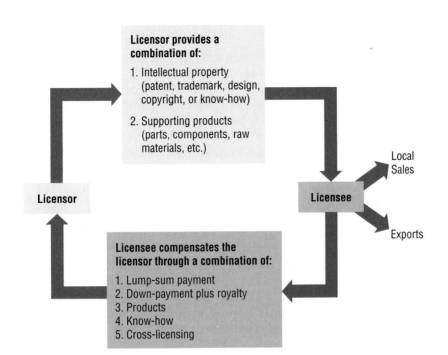

Exhibit 15.1

Licensing as a Foreign Market
Entry Strategy

SOURCE: Adapted from Welch and Welch (1996)
and personal correspondence with Lawrence Welch.

ket and provides no ongoing managerial guidance. Most firms enter into *exclusive agreements*, implying that the licensee is *not* permitted to share the licensed asset with any other company within a prescribed territory. In addition to operating in its domestic market, the licensee may also be permitted to export to third countries.

If the licensor is an MNE, it may enter a licensing arrangement with its own wholly or partly-owned foreign affiliate. In this case, licensing is an efficient way to compensate the foreign affiliate and transfer intellectual property to it within a formal legal framework. Typically, the firm uses this form of licensing when the foreign affiliate is a separate legal entity, a common scenario in many countries. Multinational firms often use licensing as an innovative way to compensate or transfer intellectual property to their foreign subsidiaries or affiliates. Some firms view licensing as a supplementary strategy to other entry strategies, such as exporting or FDI.

In the fashion industry, firms with strong brands such as Bill Blass, Hugo Boss, and Pierre Cardin generate substantial profits from licensing deals for jeans, fragrances, and watches. Saks Inc., the first foreign luxury department store in China, entered the country by licensing its Saks Fifth Avenue name for a flagship department store in Shanghai. Saks generates revenue from the licensing agreement and controls which merchandise is sold there, but has no other involvement. Licensing brings greater awareness of Saks Fifth Avenue to Asia without requiring Saks itself to operate the store, thereby reducing its risk.[7]

The national origin of popular brands might surprise you. In the food industry, Peter Paul Mounds and Almond Joy are owned by the British food firm Cadbury Schweppes and produced in the United States through a licensing agreement with Hershey Foods. Planters, Sunkist, and Budweiser brands are owned by U.S. companies and sold in Britain, Japan, and Singapore through licensing agreements with local companies. Coca-Cola has a licensing agreement to distribute Evian bottled water in the United States on behalf of the brand's owner, French company Danone. Indeed, a review of annual reports from 120 of the largest multinational food companies revealed that at least half are involved in some form of international product licensing.[8]

There are two major types of licensing agreements: (1) trademark and copyright licensing, and (2) know-how licensing. Let's review each in detail.

Disney licenses its trademark characters to apparel and consumer products manufacturers worldwide, generating substantial licensing revenue. These girls in Tokyo, Japan are dressed like Disney princess characters Cinderella and Snow White and Minnie Mouse.

Trademark and Copyright Licensing

Trademark licensing involves a firm granting another firm permission to use its proprietary names, characters, or logos for a specified period of time in exchange for a royalty. Trademarks appear on such merchandise as clothing, games, food, beverages, gifts, novelties, toys, and home furnishings. Organizations and individuals with name brand appeal benefit from trademark licensing, such as Coca Cola, Harley-Davidson, Laura Ashley, Disney, Michael Jordan, and even your favorite university! Playboy Enterprises successfully licensed its logo and other marketing assets to clothing manufacturers in other countries. As revealed in the opening vignette, a famous trademark like Harry Potter generates millions of dollars to the owner, with little effort. U.S. companies derive trademark-licensing revenues well in excess of $100 billion annually.

In the United States and a number of other countries, firms acquire rights to trademarks through first use and continuous usage. In other countries, however, rights to trademarks are acquired through registration with government authorities, and many countries require local use of the registered mark to maintain the registration. When a firm registers its trademark, it formally notifies government authorities that it owns the trademark and is entitled to intellectual property protection. The convention of gaining ownership to a trademark simply through registration has caused concerns for many firms. For example, when it wanted to enter South Africa in 1993, McDonald's was frustrated to learn that a local businessperson had already applied to register the McDonald's trademark for his own use and to have the company's rights to the trademark withdrawn.[9] When McDonald's protested in court to establish its ownership, the South African Supreme Court actually ruled in favor of the local entrepreneur.

Winnie the Pooh is one of trademark licensing's biggest success stories. Developed as a children's literary character in 1926, Pooh evolved into a multi-billion dollar licensing property. Acquired by Disney in 1961, Pooh is the second-highest earning fictional character of all time, behind only Mickey Mouse. The Pooh image is licensed to many manufacturers for inclusion on a range of products, from baby merchandise to textiles to gardening products. There are roughly 1,000 Pooh licensees in Europe alone.[10]

In many countries, a *copyright* gives the owner the exclusive right to reproduce the work, prepare derivative works, distribute copies, or perform or display the work publicly. Original works include art, music, and literature, as well as computer software. The term of protection varies by country, but the creator's life plus 50 years is typical. However, because many countries offer little or no copyright protection, it is wise to investigate local copyright laws before publishing a work abroad.[11]

Know-how agreement
Contract in which the focal firm provides technological or management knowledge about how to design, manufacture, or deliver a product or a service.

Know-How Licensing

Gaining access to technology is an important rationale for licensing. A **know-how agreement** is a contract in which the focal firm provides technological or management knowledge about how to design, manufacture, or deliver a product or a service. The licensor makes its patents, trade secrets, or other know-how available to a licensee in exchange for a royalty. The royalty may be a lump sum, a *running royalty* based on the volume of products produced from the know-how, or a combination of both.

In some industries, such as pharmaceuticals, chemicals, and semiconductors, technology is acquired in reciprocal licensing arrangements between firms from the same or similar industries. This is known as *cross-licensing.* In industries where the rate of technological advances is rapid and where innovations often build on each other, technology licensing from competitors provides key advantages. It reduces the cost of innovation by avoiding duplication of research, while reducing the risk of excluding any one firm from access to new developments.

For example, AT&T once held most of the key patents in the semiconductor industry. As more firms entered the industry and the pace of R & D quickened, AT&T was at risk of being surpassed by competitors. In Europe, Japan, and the United States, thousands of semiconductor patents were eventually awarded. In such a complex network of patents, it would have been nearly impossible for any one firm to operate in the industry without licenses from competitors. Thus, AT&T, Intel, Siemens, and numerous other competitors began licensing their patents to each other. The collective licensing activities of these firms greatly accelerated innovation in semiconductors.

A similar observation can be made of the pharmaceutical industry. Because the R & D to develop a new drug can reach hundreds of millions of dollars, and new drugs require time-consuming government approval processes, pharmaceutical firms want to launch their discoveries as quickly as possible. To reduce cost and increase the speed of new drug development, pharmaceutical firms license inventions to each other.[12] In other industries, firms may license technology and knowhow from competitors to compensate for insufficient knowledge, fill gaps in their product line-ups, or enter new businesses. It is often more efficient to acquire technology from other firms through licensing than to invest potentially huge sums in R & D. Typically, there is an understanding that the firm that acquires technology in this way will, in turn, license some of its own technology to others.

Who Are the Top Licensing Firms?

Exhibit 15.2 lists the world's top licensing firms by annual revenues. All but one (Sanrio) are based in the United States. Among them, the greatest amount of licensing occurs in the apparel, games, and toy industries. Licensing sales have benefited immensely from the emergence of large-scale retailers, such as Wal-Mart and Carrefour, and Internet-based selling.

 **Advantages and Disadvantages of Licensing**

Exhibit 15.3 summarizes the advantages and disadvantages of licensing from the perspective of the licensor. Let's highlight some of the key points.

Advantages of Licensing

As an entry strategy, licensing requires neither substantial capital investment nor involvement of the licensor in the foreign market. Licensing allows the firm to gain market presence without FDI. For this reason, it is a preferred strategy of small and medium-sized enterprises (SMEs), which may lack the resources to internationalize through more costly entry strategies. Licensing also allows the firm to exploit the fruits of research and development that it has already conducted. Once the licensing relationship is established, the licensor needs to invest little additional effort while it receives a stream of royalty income. Thus, unlike

Rank	Firm Name	Annual Licensing Revenues (U.S.$ billions)	Typical Deals
1	Disney Consumer Products	$21.0	Toy and apparel licensing for Disney movies such as *The Little Mermaid* and *The Lion King*, and characters such as Winnie the Pooh and Mickey Mouse
2	Warner Bros. Consumer Products	6.0	Toy and apparel licensing from movies such as *Superman Returns*, *Scooby-Doo*, and *Harry Potter*
3	Nickelodeon & Viacom Consumer Products	5.2	Toy and apparel licensing for TV programs such as *SpongeBob SquarePants*; video game licensing from *The Godfather* movie
4	Marvel Entertainment	5.0	Toy, game, and apparel licensing for *Ghost Rider*, *Fantastic Four*, *Captain America*, and *X-Men*
5	Major League Baseball	4.7	Baseball-related video games, apparel, toys
6	Sanrio (Japan)	4.2	Toys and apparel tied to the *Hello Kitty* character
7	The Cherokee Group	4.1	Apparel and shoes tied to Cherokee and Sideout brands
8	National Football League	3.5	American football-related apparel and equipment
9	General Motors	3.0	Toys and apparel based on popular car models
10	Lucasfilm Ltd.	3.0	Toys, games, and apparel based on the *Star Wars* and *Indiana Jones* movies

Exhibit 15.2

Leading Licensors Ranked by Licensing Revenues

SOURCE: Wilensky, Dawn, (2006). "101 Leading Licensors," License, April, pp.22–37, accessed at www.licensemag.com

other foreign entry strategies, the licensor bears no cost of establishing a physical presence in the market or maintaining inventory there. Meanwhile, the licensee benefits by gaining access to a key technology at a much lower cost than if it had developed the technology on its own.[13]

Licensing makes entry possible in countries that restrict foreign ownership in specific industries, such as defense and energy, that may be considered critical for national security. Licensing enables firms to enter smaller markets or those that are difficult to enter because of trade barriers, such as tariffs and bureaucratic requirements. For example, drug manufacturer Roche entered a licensing agreement with Chugai Pharmaceuticals in Japan in order to expand its presence in the Japanese patented medication market. Success in Japan requires substantial market know-how and a deep knowledge of the local drug approval process. The relationship accelerated Roche's penetration of the huge Japanese market.[14]

Licensing can also be used as a low-cost strategy to test the viability of foreign markets. By establishing a relationship with a local licensee, the foreign firm can learn about the target market and devise the best future strategy for establishing a more substantive presence there. A firm may use licensing as a strategy to pre-

Advantages	Disadvantages
• Does not require capital investment or presence of the licensor in the foreign market	• Revenues are usually more modest than with other entry strategies
• Ability to generate royalty income from existing intellectual property	• Difficult to maintain control over how the licensed asset is used
• Appropriate for entering markets that pose substantial country risk	• Risk of losing control of important intellectual property, or dissipating it to competitors
• Useful when trade barriers reduce the viability of exporting or when governments restrict ownership of local operations by foreign firms	• The licensee may infringe the licensor's intellectual property and become a competitor
• Useful for testing a foreign market prior to entry via FDI	• Does not guarantee a basis for future expansion in the market
• Useful as a strategy to preemptively enter a market before rivals	• Not ideal for products, services, or knowledge that are highly complex
	• Dispute resolution is complex and may not produce satisfactory results

Exhibit 15.3

Advantages and Disadvantages of Licensing to the Licensor

empt the entry of competitors in a target market. That is, by establishing a licensing presence in a market, the firm develops its brand name and familiarity there, hindering competitors who enter the market later.

Disadvantages of Licensing

Because royalties are based on the licensee's sales volume, the licensor depends on the licensee's sales and marketing prowess for its profits. A poor partner may be unable to generate substantial sales. As a moderate-control entry strategy, the licensor is limited in its ability to control the manner in which its asset is used. If the licensee uses the asset carelessly, such as by producing a substandard product, the licensor's reputation can be harmed. For this reason, experienced firms usually require foreign licensees to meet minimum quality standards. For example, U.S.-based Anheiser-Busch Brewing Company markets Budweiser beer in Japan through a licensing arrangement with Kirin, a strong local brewer. One of the most reputable brewers in Japan, Kirin produces Bud and other beers according to Anheiser-Busch's strict standards.

If the licensee is very successful, the licensor may wish it had entered the market through a more lucrative entry strategy. This was the case that Disney faced when it developed Disneyland Tokyo through a licensing arrangement with a Japanese partner. When the theme park proved much more successful than originally thought, Disney management wished it had developed Disneyland Tokyo itself. In Mexico, Televisa experienced the same problem. The largest producer of Spanish-language TV programming, Televisa opted for a licensing arrangement with California-based Univision to enter the U.S. market, where over 35 million people speak Spanish as their primary language. For its part, the Mexican company receives only 9 percent of Univision's advertising revenue. Licensing profits tend to be substantially lower than those possible from exporting or FDI entry. Moreover, licensing does not guarantee a basis for future expansion. The licensor's options for internationalizing by other means are usually restricted in the licensing agreement.

Can you tell the difference between these two dolls? Licensors run the risk of creating competitors, as Mattel discovered when it granted a license to a Brazilian firm to market Barbie doll. The latter firm went on to create a competitor to Barbie, the Susi doll (on the left).

A focal firm should ensure that its valued intellectual assets do not fall into the hands of individuals or companies that are likely to become competitors. Licensing is more viable in industries in which technological changes are frequent and affect many products. Rapid technological change means that the licensed technology becomes obsolete before the licensing contract expires. Otherwise, in cases where loss of the licensor's technical knowledge or other know-how to a potential competitor is the major concern, it is often best for a firm to avoid licensing as an entry strategy.

Because licensing requires sharing intellectual property with other firms, the risk of creating the future competitor is substantial.[15] The rival may go on to exploit the licensor's intellectual property for entering third countries or creating products that differ somewhat from those prescribed in the licensing contract. Licensees can leverage the licensed know-how to become strong competitors and, eventually, industry leaders. This scenario has played out in the auto, computer chip, and consumer electronics industries in Asia as Western firms have transferred process technologies to firms in China, Japan, and South Korea.

For instance, Japan's Sony originally licensed the technology associated with the transistor from inventor Bell Laboratories in the United States. Bell had advised Sony to use the transistors to make hearing aids. But instead, Sony used the technology to create small, battery-powered transistor radios. Based on this advantage, Sony and other Japanese companies soon became the global leaders in transistor radios. Bell squandered a huge opportunity. Sony subsequently became the first Japanese company listed on the New York Stock Exchange and one of the world's biggest consumer electronics firms.[16]

In another example, the U.S. toymaker Mattel licensed rights to distribute the Barbie doll to the Brazilian toymaker Estrela. Once the agreement expired, Estrela developed its own Barbie look-alike doll—"Susi"—which eclipsed Brazilian sales of Barbie dolls. Estrela then launched the Susi doll in Argentina, Chile, Paraguay, and Uruguay to great success. In Japan, Mattel entered a licensing agreement with local toymaker Takara, which adapted the doll to suit the tastes of Japanese girls. When the agreement expired, Takara continued to sell the doll under a different name, "Jenny," becoming a competitor to Mattel in the world's second biggest toy market.[17]

 Franchising

Franchising is an advanced form of licensing in which the focal firm (the *franchisor*) allows an entrepreneur (the *franchisee*) the right to use an entire business system in exchange for compensation. As with licensing, an explicit contract defines the terms of the relationship. McDonald's, Subway, Hertz, and FedEx are well-established international franchisors. Others that use franchising to expand abroad include Benetton, Body Shop, Yves Rocher, and Marks & Spencer. As these examples suggest, franchising is very common in international retailing. Nevertheless, some retailers, such as IKEA and Starbucks, have a strong preference for expanding abroad through company-owned outlets. In such a case, these companies are opting for greater control over foreign operations forgoing the possibility of more rapid expansion abroad.

Although there are various types of franchising, the most typical arrangement is *business format franchising* (sometimes called *system franchising*).[18] Exhibit 15.4 shows the nature of the franchising agreement. In this arrangement, the franchisor transfers to the franchisee a total business method, including production and marketing methods, sales systems, procedures, and management know-how, as well as the use of its name and usage rights for products, patents, and trademarks.[19] The franchisor also provides the franchisee with training, ongoing support, incentive programs, and the right to participate in cooperative marketing programs. In return, the franchisee pays some type of compensation to the franchisor, usually a royalty representing a percentage of the franchisee's revenues. The franchisee may be required to purchase certain equipment and supplies from the franchisor to ensure standardized products and consistent quality. For instance, Burger King and Subway require franchisees to buy food preparation equipment from specified suppliers. Some franchisors, such as McDonald's, also lease property (especially land) to franchisees.

While licensing relationships are often short-lived, the parties to franchising normally establish an ongoing relationship that may last many years. Accordingly, compared to licensing, franchising is usually a much more stable, long-term entry strategy. In addition, franchisors often combine franchising with other entry strategies. For instance, about 70 percent of the more than 2,000 Body Shop stores worldwide are operated by franchisees, while the rest are owned by Body Shop headquarters. Large retailers such as IKEA and Carrefour often employ both franchising and FDI when expanding abroad.

Franchising is more comprehensive than licensing because the franchisor prescribes virtually all of the business activities of the franchisee. The franchisor tightly controls the business system to ensure consistent standards. International franchisors employ globally recognized trademarks and attempt

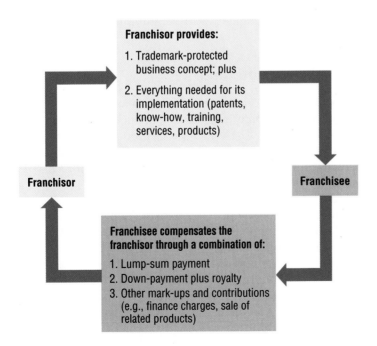

Franchisor provides:

1. Trademark-protected business concept; plus

2. Everything needed for its implementation (patents, know-how, training, services, products)

Franchisor   **Franchisee**

Franchisee compensates the franchisor through a combination of:

1. Lump-sum payment
2. Down-payment plus royalty
3. Other mark-ups and contributions (e.g., finance charges, sale of related products)

Exhibit 15.4

Franchising as a Foreign Market Entry Strategy

SOURCE: Adapted from Welch (1992) and personal correspondence with Lawrence Welch.

to guarantee the customer a uniform and consistent retail experience and product quality. Completely standardized business activities, however, are difficult to replicate across diverse markets. Differences in areas such as key ingredients, worker qualifications, and physical space may necessitate changes to the franchise formula. For example, space restrictions in Japan forced KFC to reconfigure its cooking equipment from a wide horizontal design, common in the United States, to a narrower, more vertical design that saves space. In addition, Japanese KFCs tend to be multistoried restaurants, in order to save on the high cost of land. The challenge is to strike the right balance, adapting the format to respond to local markets without affecting the overall image and service of the franchise.[20]

McDonald's is perhaps the leading example of business format franchising. Its worldwide franchisee network is remarkably successful. The opening of the first Russian McDonald's outlet in Moscow in January 1990 had political implications as well, coming soon after the collapse of the communist regime in the former Soviet Union. The store seated 700 inside, had 27 cash registers, and was enormously popular. About 80 percent of McDonald's 30,000-plus restaurants worldwide are owned and run by franchisees. These restaurants serve over 50 million customers daily and employ 1.5 million people.

Master franchise

Arrangement in which an independent company is licensed to establish, develop, and manage the entire franchising network in its market and has the right to subfranchise to other franchisees, thus assuming the role of local franchisor.

Some focal firms may choose to work with a single, coordinating franchisee in a particular country or region. In this **master franchise** arrangement, an independent company is licensed to establish, develop, and manage the entire franchising network in its market. The master franchisee has the right to subfranchise to other independent businesses and thus assume the role of the local franchisor. McDonald's is organized this way in Japan. From the focal firm's perspective, the arrangement is the least capital- and time-intensive. However, the trade-off is that, by delegating the responsibilities of identifying and working with its franchisees directly, the focal firm gives up considerable control over its foreign market operations.

Franchisees prefer the arrangement because it provides an exclusive, large, predefined territory (often an entire country) and substantial economies of scale from operating numerous sales outlets simultaneously. It gains access to a proven retailing and marketing concept, and partnership with a corporate headquarters and master franchisees in other territories, which typically provide support, know-how, and the latest innovations in the field. Master franchising accounts for as much as 80 percent of international franchising deals. Sbarro, Inc., the Italian pizza chain, operates via master franchises in Belgium, Britain, Canada, Guatemala, Kuwait, and the Philippines.[21]

Who Are the Top Franchisors?

Franchising is a global phenomenon and accounts for a large proportion of international trade in services. Many product and service categories lend themselves to international franchising. These include fast food outlets, health and fitness, professional business services, and home improvement products and services and various types of retailers.[22] (See Exhibit 3.6 on page 72 for a list of the world's top franchisors).

The United States is home to the largest number of franchisors and dominates international franchising. U.S. franchisors and their franchisees account for roughly $1 trillion in annual U.S. retail sales—an astonishing 40 percent of total U.S. retail sales. Approximately 1 in every 12 retail establishments in the United States is a franchised business.[23] Other countries are also active in franchising. For instance, annual franchised sales of fast foods in England are said to account for 30 percent of all foods eaten outside the home. The internationalization of franchising systems is a major trend that became popular beginning in the 1970s.

Information and communications technologies have accelerated the pace of international franchising. The ability to exchange information instantaneously through the Internet enhances the franchisor's ability to control international operations. Some franchisees use electronic point-of-sale equipment that links their sales and inventory data to the franchisor's central warehouse and distribution network. Information technology also allows the franchisor to serve customers or franchisees with central accounting and other business process functions.

Advantages and Disadvantages of Franchising

The relationship between the franchisor and franchisee is characterized by complementary functions. While franchisors provide vital assets, franchisees perform functions in foreign markets, such as marketing and distribution, which the franchisor usually cannot perform. The franchisor possesses economies of scale, a wealth of intellectual property, and know-how about its own industry, while the franchisee has entrepreneurial drive and substantial knowledge about the local market and how to run a business there. Franchising combines centralized control over foreign operations and a standardized business approach with the skills of local entrepreneurs who have enough flexibility to deal with local market conditions. In other words, franchising provides an effective blending of skill centralization and operational decentralization.

When economic and cultural conditions in the target market vary greatly from those of the franchisor's home market, the franchisor relies much more on the franchisee's expertise in the market. A large pool of well-chosen franchisees can greatly enhance the speed and quality of the franchisor's performance abroad.[24] For example, KFC internationalized quickly and performed well worldwide by developing franchisees in 90 countries.

The Franchisor Perspective

Exhibit 15.5 highlights the advantages and disadvantages of franchising to the franchisor. Firms prefer franchising when they lack the capital or international experience to get established abroad through FDI, or when offering the product abroad through independent distributors or traditional licensing is ineffective as

Advantages	Disadvantages
• Entry into numerous foreign markets can be accomplished quickly and cost effectively	• Maintaining control over franchisee may be difficult
• No need to invest substantial capital	• Conflicts with franchisee are likely, including legal disputes
• Established brand name encourages early and ongoing sales potential abroad	• Preserving franchisor's image in the foreign market may be challenging
• The firm can leverage franchisees' knowledge to efficiently navigate and develop local markets	• Requires monitoring and evaluating performance of franchisees, and providing ongoing assistance
	• Franchisees may take advantage of acquired knowledge and become competitors in the future

Exhibit 15.5

Advantages and Disadvantages of Franchising to the Franchisor

an internationalization strategy. Foreign markets often provide greater profitability than the home market. For example, the Beijing KFC store has generated more sales than any other KFC outlet worldwide due, in part, to the novelty of the offering, absence of direct competition, and huge pedestrian traffic. Governments in host countries often encourage franchising by foreigner entrants because most of the profits and investment remain in the local economy.

For the franchisor, franchising is a low-risk, low-cost entry strategy. It offers the ability to develop new and distant international markets relatively quickly and on a larger scale than possible for most nonfranchise firms. The franchisor can generate additional profit with only small, incremental investments in capital, personnel, production, and distribution.

However, the major disadvantages to the franchisor include the need to maintain control over potentially thousands of outlets worldwide. When dealing in numerous, complex international markets, the risk of creating competitors is substantial. The franchisor must disclose business secrets and detailed knowledge. When the franchising agreement is terminated, some franchisees leverage their newly acquired knowledge to remain in business, often by slightly altering the franchisor's brand name or trademark. There is also the risk that existing franchisees will jeopardize the franchisor's image by not upholding its standards. For instance, Dunkin' Donuts experienced problems in Russia when it discovered that some franchisees were selling vodka along with donuts.

A major challenge for franchisors is to become familiar with foreign laws and regulations. As an example, the European Union has strict laws that favor the franchisee, which sometimes hamper the franchisor's ability to maintain control over franchisee operations. Laws and foreign exchange circumstances affect the payment of royalties.

Franchising emphasizes standardized products and marketing. But this does not imply 100 percent uniformity. Local franchisees exercise some latitude in tailoring offerings to local needs and tastes. For example, McDonald's offers a McPork sandwich in Spain, a spicy chicken burger in China, teriyaki burgers in Japan, and wine in France. In its Beijing outlets, KFC offers shredded carrots, fungus, and bamboo shoots instead of the coleslaw that it sells in Western countries. Also in China, Starbucks offers a Green Tea Cream Frappuccino, TCBY sells sesame-flavored frozen yogurt, and Mrs. Fields markets mango muffins.[25]

The Franchisee Perspective

Exhibit 15.6 highlights the advantages and disadvantages of franchising to the franchisee. From the perspective of the franchisee, franchising is especially beneficial to the SME. Most small firms lack substantial resources or strong managerial skills. The big advantage of franchising to the franchisee is the ability to launch a business using a tested business model. In essence, franchising amounts to cloning best practices. It greatly increases the small firm's chances for success by duplicating a tried-and-true business format.[26]

 Other Contractual Entry Strategies

In addition to licensing and franchising, there are several other types of contractual agreements in international business. These international agreements involve major construction projects, manufacturing products under contract, providing management and marketing services, or leasing major assets. We devote Chapter 16 to global sourcing, a specific form of international con-

Advantages	Disadvantages
• Gain a well-known, recognizable brand name	• Initial investment or royalty payments may be substantial
• Acquire training and know-how; receive ongoing support from the franchisor	• Franchisee are required to purchase supplies, equipment, and products from the franchisor only
• Operate an independent business	• The franchisor holds much power, including superior bargaining power
• Increase likelihood of business success	• Franchisor's outlets may proliferate in the region, creating competition for the franchisee
• Become part of an established international network	• Franchisor may impose inappropriate technical or managerial systems on the franchisee

Exhibit 15.6

Advantages and Disadvantages of Franchising to the Franchisee

tracting. Here, we discuss the following contracting strategies: turnkey contracting, build-operate-transfer arrangements, management contracts, and leasing.

Turnkey Contracting

Turnkey contracting refers to an arrangement where the focal firm or a consortium of firms plans, finances, organizes, manages, and implements all phases of a project abroad and then hands it over to a foreign customer after training local personnel. Contractors are typically firms in construction, engineering, design, and architectural services. In a typical turnkey project, a major facility (such as a nuclear power plant or a subway system) is built, put into operation, and then handed over to the project sponsor, often a national government. The arrangement involves construction, installation, and training, and may include follow-up contractual services, such as testing and operational support.

Among the most popular turnkey projects are extensions and upgrades to metro systems, such as bridges, roadways, and railways. Turnkey projects are also used to construct airports, harbors, refineries, and hospitals. One of the world's largest publicly funded turnkey projects is in Delhi, India. The estimated $2.3 billion project was commissioned by Delhi Metro Rail Ltd. to build roads and tunnels that run through the city's central business district. The turnkey consortium includes local firms and Skanska AB, one of the world's largest construction firms, based in Sweden.[27]

In recent years, firms in the construction, engineering, architecture, and design industries have become major players in global contract services. These firms include Hochtief AG of Germany and Skanska AB of Sweden. (See Exhibit 3.7 on page 74 for a list of leading firms). They have undertaken some of the world's most important construction projects, such as the Three Gorges Dam in China and the Chunnel linking England to France. California-based Bechtel participated in projects such as the renovation of London's 140-year-old subway, the cleanup of the Chernobyl nuclear plant in Russia, and construction of nuclear power plants in South Korea.[28] In Hong Kong, a consortium of firms, including the French giant Bouygues, signed a $550 million contract to build the main highway running from Hong Kong into mainland China.[29] Bovis Lend Lease of the United Kingdom was responsible for building the Petronas Towers in Kuala Lumpur, Malaysia.

Turnkey contracting
Arrangement where the focal firm or a consortium of firms plans, finances, organizes, manages, and implements all phases of a project abroad and then hands it over to a foreign customer after training local personnel.

Build-Operate-Transfer Arrangements (BOT)

Build-operate-transfer (BOT)
Arrangement in which the firm or a consortium of firms contracts to build a major facility abroad, operate it for a specified period, and then hand it over to the project sponsor, typically the host-country government or public utility.

Under a **build-operate-transfer (BOT)** arrangement, a firm contracts to build a major facility abroad, such as a dam or water treatment plant, operates the facility for a specified period, and then transfers its ownership to the project sponsor, typically the host-country government or public utility. This is a variation of turnkey contracting. Instead of turning the completed facility over to the project sponsor, in a BOT deal, the builder operates it for a number of years, sometimes a decade, before transferring ownership to the sponsor.

In a typical deal, a consortium of private multinational financiers, contractors, and advisors joins together to finance, design, construct, and operate the facility. During the time that the consortium operates the facility, it can charge user fees, tolls, and rentals to recover its investment and generate profits. Alternatively, the host-country government may pay the BOT partner for services provided by the facility, such as water from a treatment plant, at a price calculated over the life of the contract, to cover its construction and operating costs and provide a reasonable return.

Governments often grant BOT concessions to get needed infrastructure built cost-effectively. Typical projects include sewage treatment plants, highways, airports, bridges, tunnels, mass transit systems, and telecommunications networks. In Vietnam, for example, rapid growth in industry and tourism has greatly increased demand for electric power. The Vietnamese government commissioned the construction of the 720 megawatt Phu My 3 Power Plant, the country's first privately owned major energy facility. It was built as a BOT project by Siemens Power Generation (Germany) and is owned by a consortium that includes BP (Britain) and Kyushu Electric Power (Japan).[30]

Management Contracts

Management contract
Arrangement in which a contractor supplies managerial know-how to operate a hotel, resort, hospital, airport, or other facility in exchange for compensation.

Under a **management contract**, a contractor supplies managerial know-how to operate a hotel, resort, hospital, airport, or other facility in exchange for compensation. In contrast to licensing or franchising, management contracts involve specialized know-how as well as actual operation of a facility. The contractor provides its unique expertise in running a facility without actually owning it.

In a management contract, the client organization receives assistance in managing local operations while the management company generates revenues without having to make a capital outlay. For instance, much of Disney's income from its theme parks in France and Japan comes from providing management services for the parks, which are largely owned by other interests. In another example, BAA Limited manages the retailing and catering operations of various airports in Europe and the United States. As an entry strategy, the use of management contracts traces back to the 1950s. Both the Marriott and Four Seasons corporations run numerous luxury hotels around the world through management contracts, without owning the hotels that they manage.

Management contracts can help foreign governments with infrastructure projects when the country lacks local people with the skills to run the projects. Occasionally the offering of a management contract is the critical element in winning a bid for other types of entry strategies, such as BOT deals and turnkey operations. A key disadvantage of management contracts is that they involve training foreign firms that may become future competitors.[31]

Leasing

International leasing is another contractual strategy, in which a focal firm (the lessor) rents out machinery or equipment to corporate or government clients abroad (lessees), often for several years at a time. International leasing plays an important role in developing economies that may lack the financial resources to purchase needed equipment. The lessor retains ownership of the property throughout the lease period and receives regular lease payments from the lessee. From the perspective of the lessee, leasing helps reduce the costs of using needed machinery and equipment. A major advantage for the lessor is the ability to gain quick access to target markets, while putting assets to use earning profits. Leasing may be more profitable for the lessor in international business than in domestic markets because of tax regulations.[32]

For example, Amsterdam-based ING Lease International Equipment Management owns and leases Boeing commercial aircraft to clients such as Brazil's Varig airlines. Dubai-based Oasis Leasing leases aircraft to Air New Zealand, Airtours, Gulf Air, Go, Virgin Express, and Macedonian Airlines. One of the leading leasing firms is ORIX. Based in Japan, ORIX leases everything from computers and measuring equipment to aircraft and ships. The firm operates over 1,300 offices worldwide and generated sales of nearly $7 billion in 2006.

One industry sector active in international leasing is composed of firms manufacturing capital goods such as elevators and escalators. Read the *Recent Grad in IB* feature on page 468 feature to learn about an international business career working for a capital goods company. The feature also illustrates that you can acquire valuable experience in international business by working for a foreign-owned company in your native country.

Leasing has become an important, contract-based internationalization strategy. ING Lease International Equipment Management of the Netherlands leases Boeing aircraft to Brazil's Varig airlines, such as this jet landing in Rio de Janeiro.

The Special Case of Internationalization by Professional Service Firms

Professional services include accounting, advertising, market research, consulting, engineering, legal counsel, and IT services. Firms in these industries have rapidly internationalized their activities over the past three decades. They use both direct investment (company-owned foreign branches) as well as independent contractors to gain a foothold in the foreign market. Some professional service firms internationalize by simply following their key clients abroad. The Internet has greatly aided the international spread of some business process services such as software engineering. As a result, their value-adding is increasingly centralized in cost-effective locations such as India and Eastern Europe.

Professional service firms encounter three unique challenges when going international. First, professional qualifications that allow firms to practice law, dentistry, medicine, or accounting in the home country are rarely recognized by other countries. For example, if you are certified as a Certified Public Accountant in the United States and would like to practice accounting in Argentina, you must earn local certification in that country. Second, professionals who work abroad for long periods generally must obtain employment visas in the countries where they are employed. Third, professional services often require intensive interaction with the local public, which necessitates language and cultural skills.[33]

What market entry strategies do professional service firms employ when going international? Typically, a mix of direct investment and contractual strategies are used concurrently. As we noted earlier, explicit contracts can coexist with other entry modes. For example, an advertising agency such as Publicis Groupe, based in France, will maintain a network of company-owned branches around the world while simultaneously entering into contractual relationships with independent

Jennifer Knippen's interest in international business was confirmed when she participated in a study abroad program in Valencia, Spain as an undergraduate. She returned from Spain with a renewed focus for an international career. She graduated with dual degrees in economics and international business, and immediately headed back to Spain for five months of intensive language training in Spanish. While in Spain, she traveled through various regions to broaden her education.

When Jennifer returned home, she attended a career fair, which led to a sales engineer position with the United States subsidiary of KONE, Inc., a leading manufacturer of elevators and escalators based in Finland. Her experience at KONE was incredibly challenging and uplifting. Jennifer had to learn a technical product in the demanding construction industry.

Her job description as sales engineer encompassed various tasks. She consulted architects in the design stages of a project—cost analysis, equipment specifications, building integration, and code compliance. She then generated a proposal to the general contractor working on the project. If her proposal was accepted, she would then manage the project through completion (usually more than a year). Jennifer managed multiple projects at a time while still meeting annual and quarterly sales budgets.

Managers at KONE praised Jennifer's strong presentations and relationship-building skills. She began working on high-rise projects with some of the top architectural and construction firms. Through pre-selling, with KONE's global support and resources, Jennifer stimulated substantial demand. Eventually she was awarded "Best in Class" for the highest-volume sales in her region.

Jennifer experienced the benefits and challenges that come with working for a local subsidiary of an international parent company. KONE has been extremely successful in Europe and other parts of the world and has applied a similar approach in the United States. One of the challenges that Jennifer faced was strict U.S. building code regulations. She also had to monitor fluctuations in the euro–dollar exchange rate, as this greatly affects the sales price of imported equipment.

Jennifer's majors: Economics and international business
Jobs held since graduating:
Sales Engineer, KONE, Inc.

What's Ahead?

The elevator business has its ups and downs, and eventually Jennifer decided to return to school to pursue an International MBA. She thought that the experience she had gained, coupled with an advanced degree in international management, would position her well for an exciting international career. Jennifer is excited about what lies ahead.

Success Factors for a Career in International Business

Foreign travel and a study abroad program in college inspired Jennifer to pursue an international career. Learning Spanish enhanced her credentials to secure an international business job. Jennifer set career goals and worked hard to achieve them.

local firms. Focal firms in professional services are likely to serve their major markets with direct investment; that is, they will opt for company-owned representative offices in these markets. In numerous small markets, however, they will enter into contractual relationships with independent partner firms in the same line of business. These independent contractors are sometimes known as *agents, affiliates,* or *representatives.* For example, PriceWaterhouseCooper, a leading international accounting firm, can contract with indigenous accounting firms in smaller markets where it chooses not to have its own offices. Those focal firms with limited international experience are also more likely to rely upon foreign partners.

Read the *Global Trend* feature to learn how a management consulting firm internationalizes.

 ## Management of Licensing and Franchising

Licensing and franchising are complex undertakings and they require skillful research, planning, and execution. The focal firm must conduct advance research on the host country's laws on intellectual property rights, repatriation of royalties, and contracting with local partners. Key challenges of the focal firm include: establishing whose national law takes precedence for interpreting and enforcing the contract, deciding whether to grant an exclusive or nonexclusive arrangement, and determining the geographic scope of territory to be granted to the foreign partner.

> GLOBAL TREND

Internationalization of Management Consulting Firms

The internationalization of U.S. management consulting firms began in the 1950s during the economic growth period following World War II. These firms were often attracted abroad by their clients. For example, IBM World Trade hired McKinsey to undertake a major reorganization study, and McKinsey launched its first international office in London in 1959. Expanding into South America and continental Europe in the 1960s, McKinsey established offices in the Netherlands, Germany, Italy, France, and Switzerland, as well as Canada and Australia. In smaller markets, the firm entered into contractual relationships with local consulting firms. Management consulting firms from the United States played a major role in the development of local management thinking and business approaches in foreign markets. For example, Unilever, an Anglo-Dutch consumer products company and one of Europe's largest firms, hired McKinsey to review its corporate structure. McKinsey recommended Unilver change from geographic divisions to product divisions.[34]

McKinsey was not the only consulting firm to internationalize. Arthur D. Little opened its first European office in Zürich in 1957. Booz Allen Hamilton broadened its reach to Europe, the Philippines, and elsewhere during the 1960s and 1970s. The Boston Consulting Group (BCG)—which developed the *growth share matrix* to assist its clients categorize their products into stars, cash cows, question marks, and dogs—had also internationalized relatively early, opening its first international office in Tokyo. Bain & Co. began its operations in London and Tokyo.

Management consulting firms faced various challenges in international expansion. Because management consulting is a knowledge-intensive business and the critical resource—experienced consultants—is scarce, opening multiple offices around the world proved difficult. In addition to opening new offices abroad, these firms pursued two other internationalization strategies. First, some consulting firms acquired local consulting firms as a means of quickly getting established in the target market. A. T. Kearney first entered Britain by acquiring a local consulting firm,

Norcross and Partners. Second, some consulting firms chose to contract with local consultancies, commissioning projects for them to fulfill. This approach—developing a contractual relationship with indigenous consulting firms—proved to be a practical strategy to serve smaller markets that did not warrant a company-owned office. Through such a contractual relationship, foreign firms transferred their standard operating procedures and best practices to local partners to ensure high-quality project fulfillment.

Today, management consulting firms are spread around the world through an international network of company-owned offices, affiliates, and contractual partners. For instance, McKinsey has more than 80 offices in 44 countries. It provides a full range of consulting services to corporations, government agencies, and foundations, including leadership training, operations analysis, and strategic planning.

SOURCES: Hoovers corporate profile of McKinsey at http://www.hoovers.com, Jones, Geoffrey and Alexis Lefort (2006), "McKinsey and the Globalization of Consultancy," Case Study 9-806-035, Boston: Harvard Business School Press; McKinsey corporate website at www.mckinsey.com

With contractual entry strategies, success also requires patience and the ability to remain in the market despite setbacks. As an example, Pizza Hut's initial entry in China failed. One early partner was the Chinese government, which lacked entrepreneurial drive and business expertise. Low-quality food and poor service initially undermined Pizza Hut's image in China. To address the problem, Pizza Hut repurchased all the licenses it had granted to local franchisees. It then revised its entry strategy by developing corporate-owned restaurants until the franchising market matured. This approach is also useful when the franchisor is not well known in the market. In this case, the franchisor invests time and money to develop its reputation and brand name before contracting with local franchisees.

Careful Selection of Qualified Partners

As with other entry strategies, the most critical success factor in contracting is often finding the right partner abroad. The focal firm should carefully identify, screen, and train potential contractors who are unlikely to become competitors in the future.

Selecting a strong partner is especially important in international franchising because it speeds up market entry and helps minimize start-up costs. The most qualified franchisees tend to have entrepreneurial drive, access to capital and prime real estate, a successful business track record, good relationships with local and national government agencies, strong links to other firms (including facilitators), a pool of motivated employees, and a willingness to accept oversight and to follow company procedures. In emerging markets, a knowledgeable, locally connected partner can help sort through various operational problems. In China and Russia, partnering with a state-owned enterprise may be necessary to gain access to key resources and navigate complex legal and political environments.

Choosing the right partner for master franchisees is critical. Master franchising contracts are of long duration (usually 10 to 20 years), resulting in ongoing problems if the master franchisor performs poorly. To ensure success, franchisors often partner with established firms abroad. For example, in Japan, KFC's franchise partner is Mitsubishi and Burger King's partner is Japan Tobacco.

For franchisors, developing capable partners in local supply chains is also a prerequisite. Franchisees need a reliable supply chain in order to obtain input products and supplies. In developing economies and emerging markets, host-country suppliers may be inadequate for providing a sufficient quantity or quality of input goods. In Turkey, Little Caesars pizza franchisees found it difficult to locate dairy companies that could produce the cheese varieties required for pizza. In other countries, KFC developed its own supply-chain network, ensuring dependable delivery of chicken and other critical inputs. In Russia and Thailand, McDonald's had to develop its own supply lines for potatoes in order to ensure the quality of its french fries. When McDonald's first entered India, management faced resistance from the government. Eventually government authorities came to understand that McDonald's would work with Indian farmers to improve the country's agricultural practices and production. Relations improved as the government recognized that McDonald's was committed to being a good corporate citizen.

Managerial Guidelines for Protecting Intellectual Property

As we noted earlier in the chapter, working with independent partners through contractual arrangements provides the focal firm with only moderate control over foreign partners. Therefore, safeguarding intellectual property and foreign operations becomes a challenge. Laws that govern contractual relations are not always clear, conflicts arise due to cultural and language differences, and contract enforcement abroad is often costly or unattainable. Thus, in addition to devising a detailed contract, the focal firm should emphasize developing a close, trusting relationship with foreign partners. Management in the focal firm can enhance the relationship by providing the foreign partner with superior resources and strong support. A satisfied partner is more likely to comply with contractual provisions and produce successful outcomes.

Infringement of intellectual property is the unauthorized use, publication, or reproduction of products and services that are protected by a patent, copyright, trademark, or other intellectual property right. Such a violation amounts to *piracy*. Infringement of intellectual assets often results in the production and distribution of *counterfeit*, or fake, products or services that imitate the original produced by the asset's owner. See Exhibit 6.10 on page 185 for a listing of losses from piracy in selected countries. For example, annual piracy losses are $177 million in Brazil in records and music, and $1,433 million in Russia in business software in a recent year.

> **Infringement of intellectual property** Unauthorized use, publication, or reproduction of products or services that are protected by a patent, copyright, trademark, or other intellectual property right.

The total value of counterfeit and pirated goods crossing borders and traded online worldwide is approximately $600 billion annually, a figure equivalent to about five percent of the United States GDP.[35] Counterfeiters create knockoffs of products that include clothing, fashion accessories, watches, medicines, and appliances. Some counterfeiters use a product name that differs only slightly from a well-known brand, but is close enough that buyers associate it with the genuine product. They alter the name or design of a product just enough so that prosecution is hampered. While firms such as Rolex and Tommy Hilfiger are well-known victims, counterfeiting is common in such industrial products as medical devices and car parts (e.g., brake pads, fan belts, and batteries). In China, counterfeiters have even produced entire fake motor vehicles.[36]

Cisco Systems sued its Chinese joint venture partner, Huawei Technologies Co., for pirating its networking software and infringing several patents. The lawsuit also cited Huawei, the largest telecommunications equipment manufacturer in China, for illegally using technical documentation that Cisco copyrighted in its own product manuals.[37] In China, fake versions of computer software are widely available for only a few dollars, while the cost of legitimate products can exceed a typical worker's monthly salary. Although Microsoft's Windows and Office products dominate the software market, the firm never gets paid when its software is copied and distributed by unauthorized parties. In Russia, up to 90 percent of computer software may be pirated. As a result, Microsoft has decided to focus on corporate customers only. The firm battles piracy even among the employees in its Russian subsidiary.[38]

The Internet has added a new dimension to international counterfeiting. In Russia, web sites sell popular music downloads for as little as 5 cents each, or less than one dollar for an entire CD. The illegal sites use low prices to attract music fans worldwide. The sites are easily accessed by shoppers in countries where they are outlawed under IPR laws.[39]

Counterfeiting and piracy are particularly troublesome in emerging markets and developing economies where intellectual property right laws are weak or poorly enforced. When piracy occurs, the firm's competitive advantage and brand equity are eroded.[40] Small and medium-sized enterprises are particularly vulnerable as they typically lack the resources to litigate intellectual property rights violators.

In advanced economies, intellectual property is usually protected within established legal systems and methods of recourse. A firm can initiate legal action against someone who infringes its intellectual assets and will usually achieve a satisfactory remedy. In recent years, advanced economies have taken the lead in signing treaties that support the international protection of IPRs. Key international treaties include The Paris Convention for the Protection of Industrial Property, The Berne Convention for the Protection of Literary and Artistic Works, and The Rome Convention for the Protection of Performers and Broadcasting Organizations. The World Intellectual Property Organization (WIPO; www.wipo.int)—an agency of the United Nations—administers these multilateral agreements.

Recently, the World Trade Organization (WTO) created the Agreement on Trade Related Aspects of Intellectual Property Rights (TRIPS), a comprehensive international treaty that lays out remedies, dispute-resolution procedures, and enforcements to protect intellectual property. The WTO is pressuring member countries to comply with the accord, and can discipline violators through the dispute settlement mechanism. At the same time, TRIPS provides exceptions that benefit developing economies, such as the ability to access needed patent medication for ailments such as AIDS, which is widespread in Africa.

Firms that are working in countries that are not signatories to WIPO, TRIPS, or other treaties still face challenges. Rights granted by a patent, trademark registration, or copyright apply only in the country where they are obtained; they confer no protection abroad. Moreover, on top of rewarding and promoting innovation, foreign governments often have additional priorities, such as gaining access to new technologies. In each country, intellectual property protection varies as a function of local laws, administrative practices, and treaty obligations. IPR enforcement depends on the attitudes of local officials, substantive requirements of the law, and court procedures. As a result, former licensees and franchisees can launch illicit businesses using proprietary knowledge that they are no longer entitled to.

A focal firm should have a proactive and comprehensive set of strategies to reduce the likelihood of IPR violations and help avoid their adverse effects, especially in countries with weak property rights. Exhibit 15.7 illustrates such a set of strategies:[41]

- Understand local intellectual property laws and enforcement procedures, especially when exposed assets are very valuable. For each target country, determine how easily licensed assets can be replicated. Avoid countries with weak intellectual property laws.
- Register patents, trademarks, trade secrets, and copyrights with the government in each country where the firm does, or intends to do, business. Also register in countries known to be sources of counterfeit products.
- Ensure that licensing and franchising agreements provide for oversight to ensure intellectual property is used as intended.
- Include a provision in licensing contracts that requires the licensee to share any improvements or technological developments on the licensed asset with the licensor. In this way, the licensee never acquires any advantages that allow it to surpass the licensor.[42]
- Pursue criminal prosecution or litigation against those who infringe on protected assets, such as logos and proprietary processes. For example, Mead Data Central, Inc., owner of the Lexis-Nexis brand of computerized legal research services, sued Toyota when the Japanese firm began selling its new luxury automobiles under the name "Lexus." The suit failed, but shows how Mead is resolute in protecting its assets.[43]

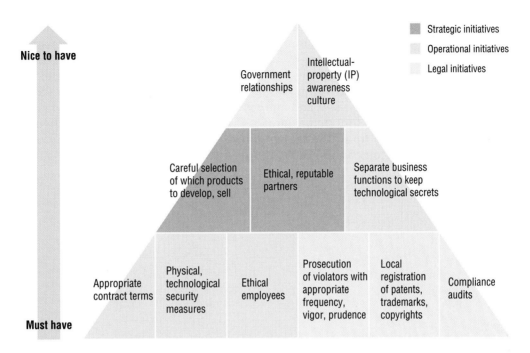

Exhibit 15.7 The Pyramid of Intellectual Property Protection

SOURCE: Meagan Dietz, Sarena Shao-Tin Lin, and Lei Yang. (2005). "Protecting Intellectual Property in China," *The McKinsey Quarterly*, number 3.

- Monitor franchisee, distribution, and marketing channels for any asset infringements. Monitor the activities of local business partners for potential leaks of vital information and assets.[44]

- Include in franchise contracts a requirement that the franchisee, suppliers, and distributors report infringements of products or processes, if discovered.

- Guard trade secrets closely. Use password-based security systems, surveillance, and firewalls to limit access to intellectual property. Intel and Microsoft release only limited information about key technologies to partner firms, especially in locations such as China, where intellectual property violations are rife.

- Train employees to use registered assets correctly and to preserve desired protection levels. In emerging markets, some firms emphasize hiring managers with international work and educational experience, as this tends to foster a healthy respect for intellectual property.

- Include noncompete clauses in employee contracts for all positions to prevent employees from serving competitors for up to three years after leaving the firm.[45]

- Use contemporary technology to minimize counterfeiting. For example, many firms include biotech tags, electronic signatures, or holograms with their products, to differentiate them from fakes.

- Continuously update technologies and products. The firm that regularly renews its technology can stay ahead of counterfeiters by offering products that counterfeiters cannot imitate fast enough. Differentiate products by emphasizing a strong brand name. When available, customers usually prefer established brands that feature the latest technology.

In the long run, the best way to cope with the consequences of infringement is to sustain competitiveness through innovation and constant technological advances. Then, even when licensing violations occur the firm is protected, as the stolen intellectual property rapidly becomes obsolete. Firms also lobby national governments and international organizations for stronger intellectual property laws and more vigilant enforcement, with limited success. Ultimately, when contractual strategies prove undesirable or ineffective, focal firms may step up to the higher-control entry strategy of acquiring ownership, which accompanies FDI.

Subway and the Challenges of Franchising in China

Subway, the fast-food marketer of submarine sandwiches and salads, has roughly 28,300 shops in 86 countries and generates over $10 billion in annual revenues. The franchising chain opened its first international restaurant in Bahrain in 1984. Since then, Subway has expanded worldwide, and generates about one fifth of its annual revenues abroad. The firm expects foreign markets to contribute to much of its future growth.

In China, Subway is the third-largest U.S. fast food chain, after McDonald's and KFC. Fish and tuna salad sandwiches are the top sellers. Despite China's huge potential, however, by 2005 Subway had opened only 19 stores there. The franchise had its share of initial setbacks. Subway's master franchisor in Beijing, Jim Bryant, lost money to a scheming partner and had to teach the franchising concept to a country that had never heard of it. Until recently, there was no word in Chinese for "franchise."

According to his agreement with Subway's corporate office, Bryant is authorized to recruit local entrepreneurs, train them to become franchisees, and act as a liaison between them and Subway headquarters. For this work, he receives half of their $10,000 initial fee and one third of their 8 percent royalty fees. This kind of arrangement made a billionaire out of McDonald's master franchisor in Japan. Nevertheless, multinational franchisors face significant challenges, particularly in dealing with China's ambiguous legal environment, finding appropriate partners, and identifying the most suitable marketing, financing, and logistics strategies. Famous brands like A&W, Dunkin' Donuts, and Rainforest Cafe all stumbled in their initial forays into China.

Cultural problems are an ongoing challenge. After Bryant opened his first Subway shop, customers stood outside and watched for a few days. When they finally tried to buy a sandwich, they were so confused that Bryant had to print signs explaining how to order. They didn't believe the tuna salad was made from fish because they could not see the head or tail. They did not like the idea of touching their food, so they would gradually peel off the paper wrapping and eat the sandwich like a banana. To make matters worse, few customers liked sandwiches.

But Subway—or Sai Bei Wei (Mandarin for "tastes better than others")—is forging ahead. Bryant managed to recruit a few highly committed franchisees that he monitors closely to maintain quality. One franchisee lost about $6,000 in her first 8 months but is now profitable and recently bought a second outlet. In addition to the stores in Beijing, numerous more are under construction.

Why China for Franchising?

On the surface, franchising in China is very attractive because of its huge market, long-term growth potential, and the dramatic rise in disposable income among its rapidly expanding urban population. The market for fast food is estimated at $15 billion per year. China's urban population, the target market for casual dining, has expanded at a 5 percent compound annual growth rate over the past several years, a trend expected to continue. Increasingly hectic lifestyles also have led to an increase in meals the Chinese eat outside the home. Furthermore, surveys reveal that Chinese consumers are interested in sampling non-Chinese foods.

Market researchers have identified several major benefits to franchising in China:

- *A win-win proposition.* Restaurants were one of the first industries the government opened to private ownership in the early 1980s. Franchising in China combines the Western know-how of franchisors with the local market knowledge of franchisees. Many Chinese have strong entrepreneurial instincts and are eager to launch their own businesses.

- *Minimal entry costs.* Because much of the cost of launching a restaurant is borne by local entrepreneurs, franchising minimizes the costs to franchisors of entering the market.

- *Rapid expansion.* By leveraging the resources of numerous local entrepreneurs, the franchisor can get set up quickly. Franchising is superior to other entry strategies for rapidly establishing many outlets throughout any new market.

- *Brand consistency.* Because franchisors are required to strictly adhere to company operating procedures and policies, brand consistency is easier to maintain.

- *Circumvention of legal constraints.* Franchising allows the focal firm to avoid trade barriers associated with exporting and FDI, common barriers in China.

Challenges of Franchising in China

China's market also poses many challenges for franchisors:

- *Knowledge Gap.* Despite the likely pool of potential franchisees, realistically, few Chinese have significant knowledge about how to start and operate a business. There is still much confusion about franchising among lawmakers, entrepreneurs, and consumers. Focal firms must educate government officials, potential franchisees, and creditors on the basics of franchising, a process that consumes energy, time, and money.

- *Ambiguous Legal Environment.* Franchisors need to closely examine China's legal system regarding contracts and intellectual property rights. The Chinese government introduced regulations permitting franchising in 1997. The legal system is evolving and is full of loopholes and ambiguities. Some critical elements are not covered. The situation has led to diverse interpretations of the legality of franchising in China. Franchisors must be vigilant about protecting trademarks. A local imitator can quickly dilute or damage a trademark a focal firm has built up through much expense and effort. Branding is important to franchising success, but consumers become confused if several similar brands are present. For instance, Starbucks fought a Shanghai coffee shop, which had copied its logo and name. The fast-food hamburger chain "Merry Holiday" uses a yellow color scheme and emphasizes the letter "M" in its signage, similar to McDonald's. There have been reports about fake Burger King restaurants operating in China. Large franchisors such as KFC and Pizza Hut are struggling to root out counterfeiters.

- *Escalating Start-Up Costs.* Ordinarily, entry through franchising is cost-effective. However, various challenges, combined with linguistic and cultural barriers, can increase the up-front investment and resource demands of new entrants in China and delay profitability. Given the shortage of restaurant equipment in China, the franchisor may have to invest in store equipment and lease it to the franchisee, at least until the franchisee can afford to buy it. Franchisors must be patient. For instance, McDonald's has been in China since the early 1990s and has devoted substantial resources to building its brand. But few firms have the resources of McDonald's.

Perhaps the biggest challenge of launching franchises in China is finding the right partners. It is paradoxical that entrepreneurs with the capital to start a restaurant often lack the business experience or entrepreneurial drive, while entrepreneurs with sufficient drive and expertise often lack the start-up capital. Subway's franchise fee of $10,000 is equivalent to more than two year's salary of the average Chinese. China lacks an adequate system of banks and other capital sources for small business. Entrepreneurs often borrow funds from family members and friends to launch business ventures. Fortunately, Chinese banks are increasingly open to franchising. For example, the Bank of China established a comprehensive credit line of $12 million for Kodak franchisees.

Availability and financing of suitable real estate are major considerations as well, particularly for initial show-case stores where location is critical. According to real estate laws enacted in 1990, local and foreign investors are allowed to develop, use, and administer real estate. But in many cases, the Chinese government owns real estate that is not available for individuals to purchase. Private property laws are underdeveloped and franchisees occasionally risk eviction. Fortunately, a growing number of malls and shopping centers are good locations for franchised restaurants.

The Chinese authorities maintain restrictions on the repatriation of profits to the home country. Strict rules discourage repatriation of the initial investment, making this capital rather illiquid. To avoid this problem, firms make initial capital investments in stages to minimize the risk of not being able to withdraw overinvested funds. Fortunately, China is gradually relaxing its restrictions on repatriated profits. To alleviate the burden of these restrictions, franchisors have been reinvesting their profits back into China to continue to fund the growth of their operations. Reinvesting profits also provides a natural hedge against exchange rate fluctuations.

Learning from the Success of Others

Experience has shown that new entrants to China often benefit from establishing a presence in Hong Kong and then moving inland toward the southern provinces. Before it was absorbed by mainland China, Hong Kong was one of the world's leading capitalist economies. It is an excellent probusiness location to gain experience for doing business in China. In other cases, franchisors have launched stores in smaller Chinese cities, gaining experience there before expanding into more costly competitive urban environments such as Beijing and Shanghai.

Adapting offerings to local tastes appears to be a prerequisite. Suppliers and business infrastructure in the country are often lacking. Franchisors spend much money to develop supplier and distribution networks. They may also need to build logistical infrastructure to move inputs from suppliers to individual stores. McDonald's has replicated its supply chain, bringing its key suppliers, such as potato supplier Simplot, to China. There is no one best approach in China. For instance, TGI Friday's imports roughly three-quarters of its food supplies, which helps maintain quality. But heavy importing is expensive and exposes profitability to exchange rate fluctuations.

AACSB: **Reflective Thinking, Multicultural and Diversity**

Case Questions

1. Subway brings to China various intellectual property in the form of trademarks, patents, and an

entire business system. What are the specific threats to Subway's intellectual property in China? What can Subway do to protect its intellectual property in China?

2. What do you think about Subway's method and level of compensating its master franchisee and regular franchisees in China? Is the method satisfactory? Is there room for improvement?

3. What are the advantages and disadvantages of franchising in China from Jim Bryant's perspective? What can Bryant do to overcome the disadvan-

tages? From Subway's perspective, is franchising the best entry strategy for China?

4. Subway faces various cultural challenges in China. What are these challenges and what can Subway and its master franchisee do to overcome them?◄

Source: Adler, Carlye. (2005). "How China Eats a Sandwich," *Fortune*, March 21, pp. F210[B]–[D]; Alon, Ilan. (2001). "Interview: International Franchising in China with Kodak," *Thunderbird International Business Review*, 43(6), pp. 737–46; Bugg, James. (1994). "China: Franchising's New Frontier," *Franchising World*, 26(6) pp. 8–10; Burke, Bob, and Carol Wingard. (1997), "The Big Chill." *China Business Review*, 24(4), pp. 12–18; Clifford, Mark. (1998). "Companies: And They're Off," *Far Eastern Economic Review*, 156(48), pp. 76–79; Dayal-Gulati, A., and Angela Lee. (2004). *Kellogg on China: Strategies for Success.* Evanston, IL: Northwestern University Press; Subway corporate Web site at www.subway.com.

CHAPTER ESSENTIALS

Key Terms

build-operate-transfer (BOT), p. 466
contractual entry strategies in
   international business, p. 452
franchising, p. 452
infringement of intellectual
   property, p. 471

intellectual property, p. 452
intellectual property
   rights (IPRs), p. 454
know-how agreement, p. 456
licensing, p. 452
management contract, p. 466

master franchise, p. 462
royalty, p. 454
turnkey contracting, p. 465

Summary

In this chapter, you learned about:

1. The nature of contractual entry strategies in international business

Contractual entry strategies in international business refer to granting permission to use intellectual property to a foreign partner in exchange for a continuous stream of payments. **Intellectual property rights** refer to the legal claim through which the proprietary assets of firms and individuals are protected from unauthorized use by other parties. Firms run the risk of disclosing their intellectual property to outside parties. **Licensing** is an arrangement in which the owner of intellectual property grants a firm the right to use that property for a specified period of time in exchange for royalties or other compensation. **Franchising** is an arrangement in which the firm allows another the right to use an entire business system in exchange for fees, royalties, or other forms of compensation. A **royalty** is a fee paid to the licensor at regular intervals to compensate for the temporary use of intellectual property. Under a

know-how agreement, the focal firm provides technological or managerial knowledge about how to design, manufacture, or deliver a product or service.

2. Licensing

The agreement between the licensor and the licensee is for a specific time period, in a specific country or region. The licensor may enter an *exclusive agreement* with the licensee to minimize competition with other licensees in the same territory. Once the relationship is established and the licensee fully understands its role, the licensor has little additional input. Licensing is widely used in the fashion and toy industries.

3. Advantages and disadvantages of licensing

The main advantage of licensing to the licensor is that it does not require substantial capital investment or physical presence in the foreign market. Licensing allows the firm to gain market presence without making an equity investment. The licensor can avoid political risk, government regulations, and other risks associated with *FDI*. Licensing enables firms to enter markets that have high trade barriers or to test market viability. But licensing generates lower profits and limits the firm's ability to control its intellectual property. There is a risk that the licensee will become a competitor once the licensing agreement expires.

4. Franchising

Franchisors employ widely identifiable trademarks and attempt to guarantee the customer a consistent retail experience and product quality. A **master franchise** is an arrangement whereby a franchisee obtains the rights to, and is responsible for, developing franchised outlets to serve a country or a region. Franchising is common in international retailing, but is difficult to replicate across diverse markets.

5. Advantages and disadvantages of franchising

Franchising allows franchisees to gain access to well-known, well-established brand names and business systems, allowing them to launch successful businesses with minimal risk. The franchisor can rapidly internationalize by leveraging the drive and knowledge of local franchisees. But as with licensing, franchisors risk dissipating their intellectual property to unauthorized parties.

6. Other contractual entry strategies

Under **build–operate–transfer (BOT)** arrangements, the firm contracts to build a major facility, such as a power plant, which it operates for a period of years and then transfers to the host-country government or other public entity. **Turnkey contracting** involves one or several firms planning, financing, organizing, and managing all phases of a project which, once completed, they then hand over to a host-country customer. **Management contracts** occur when a company contracts with another to supply management know-how in the operation of a factory or service facility, such as a hotel. With *leasing*, the firm rents machinery or equipment, usually for a long period, to clients located abroad.

7. Management of licensing and franchising

Infringement of intellectual property rights takes place through counterfeiting and piracy, which cost companies billions of dollars per year. Managers must proactively safeguard their proprietary assets by registering patents, trademarks, and other assets in each country and minimize operating in major counterfeiting countries and countries with weak intellectual property laws. Firms must also train employees and licensees in the proper legal use of intellectual property and vigilantly track down and prosecute intellectual property violators. Licensors and franchisors should carefully investigate individuals or firms seeking a contractual relationship. The best franchisee candidates are trustworthy and willing to follow company procedures. They also have a successful business record and vigorous entrepreneurial spirit.

Test Your Comprehension AACSB: Reflective Thinking

1. Distinguish between the major types of intellectual property: trademarks, copyrights, patents, industrial designs, and trade secrets.

2. What are the major characteristics of licensing? What are the major characteristics of franchising?

3. What are the advantages and disadvantages of licensing?

4. What are the advantages and disadvantages of franchising from the perspective of franchisors and franchisees?

5. What industry sectors are more likely to rely on franchising to tap foreign markets?

6. Define and distinguish the following contractual entry strategies: build-operate-transfer, turnkey projects, management contracts, and leasing.

7. What are best practices in managing international contractual relationships?

8. Suppose you work for a firm that holds valuable intellectual property and is contemplating various international business projects. What strategies would you recommend to management for protecting the firm's intellectual property?

Apply Your Understanding AACSB: Communication, Reflective Thinking

1. The licensing of intellectual property is now a global business. As revealed in the opening vignette, Warner Bros. is doing a thriving business by licensing images of Harry Potter characters on its manufactured products, such as software, games, and clothing. However, safeguarding intellectual property is a big challenge in many countries. Illicit operators worldwide produce their own books, shirts, games, and other products that feature the Potter images—without entering a licensing agreement with Warner. What steps can Warner take to address this problem? That is, what types of strategies can Warner use to protect Harry Potter from intellectual property infringement around the world?

2. In addition to licensing and franchising, there are various other contractual entry strategies. Suppose upon graduation you get a job with Hitachi America, Ltd. (www.hitachi.us)—the U.S. subsidiary of the giant Japanese firm. Hitachi is involved in various contractual entry strategies in its international operations. These include build-operate-transfer and turnkey projects in the infrastructure development sector, management contracts to run nuclear power plants, and leasing of heavy earthmoving equipment to foreign governments. Suppose that Hitachi America wants to extend its reach into Latin America. Prepare a report for your senior managers in which you explain the various ways for Hitachi to implement these entry strategies.

3. Suppose you own a "flying doctor" business in Australia in which you employ physicians to travel by air to ranches and rural communities in Australia's Outback to care for the sick and wounded. Your business has thrived and you've been able to add numerous employees. You've decided that, given your success, you can extend your service to rural areas in the Asia-Pacific region beyond Australia. There are numerous nations in Southeast Asia and the South Pacific characterized by populations concentrated in remote areas, many of which are underserved by medical care. There are various ways to internationalize professional services, including *licensing, franchising*, and FDI. For the professional services sector, differentiate between these three entry strategies: (a) what are the advantages and disadvantages of each? (b) What are the main differences between franchising and FDI?

AACSB: Reflective Thinking

Refer to Chapter 1, page 27, for instructions on how to access and use globalEDGE™.

1. You have just started working in the office of the International Intellectual Property Alliance (IIPA; www.iipa.com). You learn that worldwide piracy of products is rampant. Your boss assigns you the task of drafting a brief policy memo in which you address the following questions:

   • What is the worldwide scope of piracy? What industries are most affected by piracy, and what is the financial loss from piracy in each of these industries?
   • What are the top five countries that are the greatest sources of piracy?
   • What strategies do you recommend for combating piracy?

   In addition to globalEDGE™ and the IIPA portal, other useful sites for this exercise are the Office of the United States Trade Representative (www.ustr.gov), United Nations (www.un.org), and the Business Software Alliance (www.bsa.org).

2. Suppose you are an international entrepreneur and want to open your own franchise somewhere in Europe. You decide to conduct research to identify the most appropriate franchise and to learn how to become a franchisee. Entrepreneur.com publishes an annual list of the top 200 franchisors seeking international franchisees. Visit www.entrepreneur.com for the list or search for "franchising" at globalEDGE™. Choose the franchise that interests you most (for example, Subway, ServiceMaster, Century 21), and visit its corporate Web site. Based on information from the Web site, as well as globalEDGE™ and Hoovers.com, address the following questions:

   • How many franchised operations does this firm have outside its home country?
   • What are the major countries in which the firm has franchises? Are there any patterns in terms of the countries where this firm is established?
   • According to the application information provided at the corporate site, what qualifications is the firm seeking in new franchisees?
   • What types of training and support does the firm provide for its franchisees?

3. The International Licensing Industry Merchandisers' Association (LIMA; www.licensing.org) is an organization with offices worldwide. It fosters the growth and expansion of licensing by helping members network, educating members about licensing, and establishing standards of ethical and professional conduct in intellectual property licensing. Suppose you work for a small animation company that has developed several popular cartoon characters that have licensing potential, in the same way that Disney licenses its cartoon characters. Management would like to learn more about becoming a licensor of its cartoon characters. To begin licensing the characters to interested garment makers, school supply manufacturers, and similar firms, visit the LIMA Web site and write a memo that addresses the following:

   • Who are the major members of LIMA?
   • What are the major trade shows that your firm can attend to exhibit its licensable products and learn more about licensing?
   • What types of seminars and training are available to learn more about becoming a licensor?
   • Based on the information provided at the site, what can you learn about anticounterfeiting activities and challenges in licensing?

CKR Cavusgil Knight Riesenberger

Management Skill Builder©

Choosing the Best Entry Strategy

As firms pursue internationalization, managers must select the most suitable entry strategy from among exporting, FDI, licensing, franchising, and the other strategies described in this and previous chapters. Managers should carefully consider all the costs and benefits—especially the possible expenses and revenues—involved with each potential entry strategy. The ultimate objective of internationalization is usually to maximize profits and market share. Failure to choose the best entry strategy can lead to suboptimal performance.

AACSB: Reflective Thinking, Analytical Skills

Managerial Challenge

This C/K/R Management Skill Builder© examines the case of Gliders, a firm that makes tennis shoes with an embedded wheel that allows the wearer to skate. Gliders is facing growing competition from low-cost producers in countries such as China. In order to confront this threat and increase sales, Gliders management wants to begin selling the tennis shoes abroad and has targeted Germany as its initial market. Because Gliders is a small firm with limited human and financial resources, management must choose the best strategy to enter Germany in order to maximize company performance.

Background

Gliders's target market is primarily children. Kids love to wear Gliders to dance, play street hockey, and just glide around town. Preteens love them as alternative transportation. The firm has an established brand name and is constantly retooling and churning out upgraded wheel varieties, fashions, and comfort features. It also offers various accessories, such as helmets and kneepads, that feature the Gliders logo. The firm owns other intellectual property, such as designs, trademarks, and patents. Branding is extremely important, and management wants to maintain the shoes' image as quality and cool.

Managerial Skills You Will Gain

In this C/K/R Management Skill Builder©, as a prospective manager, you will:

1. Understand the various types of foreign market entry strategies, including the costs and benefits associated with each.

2. Learn how to improve a company's prospects for increasing sales and profits in foreign markets.

3. Appreciate an important component of international business planning and strategy.

Your Task

Assume you are a recently hired, first-line manager at Gliders. Top management wants to begin selling Gliders in Germany and has given you the task of conducting an analysis to determine the most appropriate entry strategy, choosing among exporting, licensing, FDI, and joint venture.

Go to the C/K/R Knowledge Portal©

www.prenhall.com/cavusgil
Proceed to the C/K/R Knowledge Portal© to obtain the expanded background information, your task and methodology, suggested resources for this exercise, and the presentation template.

chapter

16

Global Sourcing

Learning Objectives

In this chapter, you will learn about:

1. Trends toward outsourcing, global sourcing, and offshoring
2. Evolution of global sourcing
3. Benefits and challenges of global sourcing for the firm
4. Implementing global sourcing through supply-chain management
5. Risks in global sourcing
6. Strategies for minimizing risk in global sourcing
7. Implications of global sourcing for public policy and corporate citizenship

> Global Sourcing of Pharmaceutical Drug Trials

Nearly 40 percent of clinical trials for new drugs in the pharmaceutical industry are now conducted in emerging markets such as China and Russia. It is estimated that by 2010, some two million people in India will take part in clinical trials. Where drug testing was once conducted mostly in developed economies, pharmaceutical firms such as Pfizer increasingly prefer emerging markets because they offer clear advantages: (1) lower costs for recruitment of physicians and patients, (2) large potential patient populations, (3) diversity of patient populations and medical conditions, and (4) less likelihood of patients taking other medicines that could interact with the drug under study.

It costs an average of $900 million to develop and bring a new drug to market in the United States. More than half the cost relates to confirming drug safety and effectiveness in trial phases on humans, as required by the U. S. Food and Drug Administration (FDA) and similar agencies worldwide. Recruiting patients accounts for 40 percent of the trial budget. Testing in emerging markets greatly reduces recruitment costs. According to GlaxoSmithKline, a drug trial costs about $30,000 on a per-patient basis in the United States and about $3,000 in Romania.

Firms typically outsource the trials to contract research organizations, which in turn hire physicians in local communities and hospitals to find patients. For example, subcontractors tested Merck's Vioxx and Zocor drugs and many of Pfizer's billion-dollar drugs in Russia and other developing countries before gaining approval in the United States. Almost every major Western pharmaceutical firm is conducting clinical trials in hospitals across Russia. In a poor country with a dysfunctional medical system, patients often consider the trials a way to access medical treatment. Russia's centralized hospital system recruits patients for trials quickly, which shaves millions of dollars and several months off the drug development process.

Nevertheless, offshoring of clinical trials raises questions about ethics and oversight of this critical stage in the development of new medications. While the vast majority of trials in emerging markets have been conducted without problems, some breakdowns in ethical and scientific processes have occurred. For example, Pfizer was sued for testing a meningitis drug on Nigerian children without their parents' consent, resulting in five deaths. Some trials endangered patients or were conducted without proper ethical review. Better oversight of this critical stage in the development of new medications is warranted, but conducting drug trials properly can be challenging. Emerging markets may lack the resources the FDA normally requires. One official asks "How do you meet procedures required by the FDA in settings where electricity is going off two hours a day?"

In one case, the Nigerian trial for an antiretroviral drug was shut down amid concerns that researchers did not store the drugs or handle the scientific data properly. Where physicians in Russia normally earn $200 per month, a trial investigator there can make 10 times that amount by recruiting patients into trials. This financial incentive raises potential conflicts for doctors, some of whom may bribe patients to ensure their participation in trials.

In emerging markets, some drug trials do not receive adequate attention from ethics review committees. One study found that a quarter of all trials in developing economies did not receive any local official review. Still, the U.S. approval process places a great burden on local review. The FDA is required to inspect a certain proportion of trial sites. Nevertheless, in a recent year, despite more than 500 drug trials in Russia alone at some 3,000 sites, the FDA inspected only about 100 sites worldwide. Of the international sites inspected, the FDA criticized more than 30 percent for failure to follow protocol, and cited nearly 10 percent for failure to report adverse patient reactions to trial drugs.

While the FDA is working closely with local governments with hopes that world ethical standards will catch up with its regulations, pharmaceutical firms are increasing their outsourcing of drug trials abroad. Trials will continue to shift to emerging markets in search of more patients with faster recruitment at lower cost.

Sources: Bloch, M., A. Dhankhar, and S. Narayanan. (2006). "Pharma Leaps Offshore," *McKinsey Quarterly*, July, p. 12; Engardio, Pete. (2006). "The Future of Outsourcing: How It's Transforming Whole Industries and Changing the Way We Work," *Business Week*, January 30, p. 58; *Economist Intelligence Unit*. (2007). "U.K. Regulations: Tougher on Drugs," April 11. Retrieved from www.viewswire.com; A. T. Kearney. (2007). *Country Attractiveness Index for Clinical Trials*, A. T. Kearney Company. Retrieved from www.atkearney.com; Lustgarten, Abrahm. (2005). "Drug Testing Goes Offshore," *Fortune*, August 8, pp. 66–71; PhRMA. (2007, March). *Pharmaceutical Industry Profile 2007*. March.

 # Trends Toward Outsourcing, Global Sourcing, and Offshoring

As noted in the opening vignette, companies in the pharmaceutical industry cut product development costs and hasten speed to market by sourcing drug-testing processes from emerging markets. Focal firms shop around the world for inputs or finished products to meet efficiency and strategic objectives and remain competitive.

The search for the best sources of products and services is an ongoing task for managers. In some cases, firms have moved entire value-chain activities such as manufacturing to foreign locations. Nike Inc., along with competitors Reebok and Adidas in the athletic shoe industry, contracts out nearly all of its athletic shoe production to foreign suppliers. These firms are best described as brand owners and marketers today, not as manufacturers. Similarly, Apple Inc. sources some 70 percent of its production abroad while focusing its internal resources on improving its operating system and other software platforms. This approach allows Apple to optimally utilize its limited capital resources and focus on its core competences. Dell Inc. is another firm that relies extensively on a global manufacturing network, composed largely of independent suppliers. See Exhibit 16.1 to learn how Dell assembles components from suppliers in numerous locations for its Dell Inspiron notebook computer.[1]

Global sourcing is the procurement of products or services from independent suppliers or company-owned subsidiaries located abroad for consumption in the home country or a third country. Also called *global procurement* or *global purchasing*, global sourcing amounts to *importing*—an inbound flow of goods and services. It is an entry strategy that involves a contractual relationship between the buyer (the

Global sourcing The procurement of products or services from independent suppliers or company-owned subsidiaries located abroad for consumption in the home country or a third country.

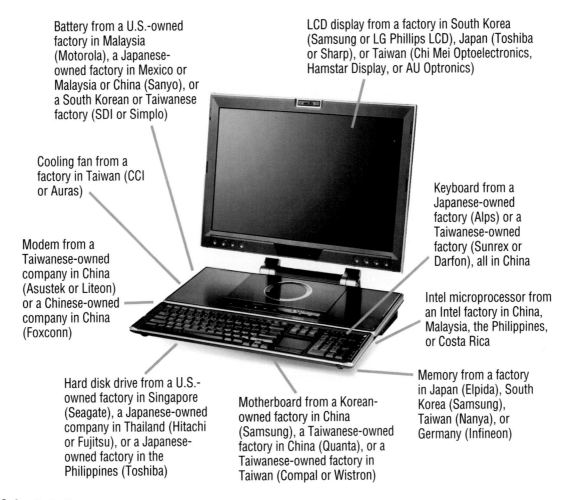

Battery from a U.S.-owned factory in Malaysia (Motorola), a Japanese-owned factory in Mexico or Malaysia or China (Sanyo), or a South Korean or Taiwanese factory (SDI or Simplo)

LCD display from a factory in South Korea (Samsung or LG Phillips LCD), Japan (Toshiba or Sharp), or Taiwan (Chi Mei Optoelectronics, Hamstar Display, or AU Optronics)

Cooling fan from a factory in Taiwan (CCI or Auras)

Keyboard from a Japanese-owned factory (Alps) or a Taiwanese-owned factory (Sunrex or Darfon), all in China

Modem from a Taiwanese-owned company in China (Asustek or Liteon) or a Chinese-owned company in China (Foxconn)

Intel microprocessor from an Intel factory in China, Malaysia, the Philippines, or Costa Rica

Hard disk drive from a U.S.-owned factory in Singapore (Seagate), a Japanese-owned company in Thailand (Hitachi or Fujitsu), or a Japanese-owned factory in the Philippines (Toshiba)

Motherboard from a Korean-owned factory in China (Samsung), a Taiwanese-owned factory in China (Quanta), or a Taiwanese-owned factory in Taiwan (Compal or Wistron)

Memory from a factory in Japan (Elpida), South Korea (Samsung), Taiwan (Nanya), or Germany (Infineon)

Exhibit 16.1 Sourcing for the Dell Inspiron Notebook Computer

SOURCE: Adapted from Friedman, Thomas. (2005). *The World is Flat*, New York: Farrar, Straus, & Giroux

focal firm) and a foreign source of supply. Global sourcing involves subcontracting the performance of specific manufacturing or services tasks to the firm's own subsidiaries or independent suppliers. As illustrated in Exhibit 14.1 on page 420, global sourcing is a low-control strategy in which the focal firm sources from independent suppliers through contractual agreements, as opposed to buying from company-owned subsidiaries.

Although global sourcing has been an established international business activity since the 1980s, it has gained new momentum in the current phase of globalization. Four key drivers are especially responsible for the growth of global sourcing in recent years:

- Technological advances, including instant Internet connectivity and broadband availability
- Declining communication and transportation costs
- Widespread access to vast information, including growing connectivity between suppliers and the customers that they serve
- Entrepreneurship and rapid economic transformation in emerging markets

While firms had their early experience with the sourcing of merchandise goods, in recent years they have increasingly subcontracted the performance of business processes and other services to subsidiaries and independent suppliers located worldwide.[2] For example, contractors such as Softtek in Mexico help U.S. banks to develop customized software, manage their IT systems, and perform support and maintenance for commercial finance operations. Softtek has 3,500 employees, mostly engineers, and outsourcing facilities in Brazil, Colombia, Peru, and Venezuela. Argentina, which boasts one of the best-educated workforces in Latin America, is aggressively promoting software development centers. The low salaries of software engineers (typically less than $12,000 a year) has persuaded such companies as Walt Disney, Peugeot, and Repsol to have web site design and software development performed in Argentina.

In undertaking global sourcing, managers face two key decisions: (1) which value-chain activities should be outsourced; and (2) where in the world these activities should be performed. Let's consider these two managerial choices.

Decision 1: Outsource or Not?

Managers must decide between *internalization* and *externalization*—whether each value-adding activity should be conducted in house or by an external, independent supplier. In business, this is traditionally known as the *make or buy* decision: "Should we make a product or perform a particular value-chain activity ourselves, or should we source it from an outside contractor?" Firms usually internalize those value-chain activities that they consider part of their *core competence*, or which involve the use of proprietary knowledge and trade secrets that they want to control. For example, Canon uses its core competencies in precision mechanics, fine optics, and microelectronics to produce some of the world's best cameras, printers, and copiers. Canon usually internalizes value-chain activities such as R&D because they yield improvements in these competencies. By contrast, firms will usually source from *external* suppliers those products or services that are peripheral to the firm's main offerings, have a lower cost, or when the supplier specializes in providing the specific offerings. By contrast, firms will usually source from *external* suppliers when the sourced products or services are peripheral to the firm's main offerings, can be obtained at lower cost, or can be provided by suppliers specialized in providing the specific offerings.

By contrast, firms will usually source from external suppliers, products, or services that: are peripheral to the firm's main offerings; can be obtained at lower cost; or can be provided by suppliers specialized in providing the specific offerings. More formally, **outsourcing** refers to the procurement of selected value-adding activities, including production of intermediate goods or finished products, from external independent suppliers. Firms outsource because they generally are not superior at performing *all* primary and support activities. Most value-adding activities—from manufacturing to marketing to after-sales service—are candidates for outsourcing.

Historically, outsourcing involved the acquisition of raw materials, parts, and components from independent suppliers. More recently, outsourcing has extended to include the procurement of services as well.[3] The typical firm will outsource services such as accounting, payroll, and some human resource functions, as well as travel services, IT services, customer service, and technical support. This type of outsourcing is known as **business process outsourcing (BPO)**.[4] Firms contract with third-party service providers to perform specific business tasks, usually as a means of reducing the cost of performing tasks that are not part of the firm's core competencies or critical to maintaining the firm's competitive position in the marketplace. BPO can be divided into two categories: *back-office activities*, which includes internal, upstream business functions such as payroll and billing, and *front-office activities*, which includes downstream, customer-related services such as marketing or technical support.

Today in Europe, North America, Japan, and other advanced economies, few firms produce an entire product. Most firms contract out their peripheral activities to outside suppliers.

Outsourcing The procurement of selected value-adding activities, including production of intermediate goods or finished products, from independent suppliers.

Business process outsourcing (BPO) The outsourcing of business functions to independent suppliers, such as accounting, payroll, human resource functions, IT services, customer service, and technical support.

Decision 2: Where in the World Should Value-Adding Activities Be Located?

For each value-adding activity, managers have the choice of either keeping the activity at home or locating it in a foreign country. **Configuration of value-adding activity** refers to the pattern or geographic arrangement of locations where the firm carries out value-chain activities.[5] For instance, to run its global network of package shipping, DHL established offices in countries and cities worldwide. It also set up high-tech tracking centers in Arizona, Malaysia, and the Czech Republic. This configuration allows DHL staffers to track the locations of shipments worldwide, 24 hours a day. DHL management chose these specific locations for shipment tracking because, in a world of 24 time zones, they are each about 8 hours distant from each other.

Instead of concentrating value-adding activities in their home country, many firms configure these activities across the world to save money, reduce delivery time, access factors of production, and extract maximal advantages relative to competitors. This helps explain the migration of manufacturing industries from Europe, Japan, and the United States to emerging markets in Asia, Latin America, and Eastern Europe. Depending on the firm and the industry, management may decide to concentrate certain value-adding activities in just one or a handful of locations, while dispersing others to numerous countries.

For example, the German automaker Bayerische Motoren Werke AG (BMW) employs 70,000 factory personnel at 23 sites in 13 countries to manufacture sedans, coupes, and convertibles. Workers at the Munich plant build the BMW 3 Series and supply engines and key body components to other BMW factories abroad. In the United States, BMW has a plant in South Carolina that makes over 500 vehicles daily for the world market. In northeast China, BMW makes cars in a joint venture with Brilliance China Automotive Holdings Ltd. In India, BMW has a manufacturing presence to serve the needs of the rapidly growing South Asia market. However, BMW's profits have suffered in recent years due to higher cost of raw materials such as plastics and steel. Management must configure BMW's sourcing at the best locations worldwide in order to: minimize costs (for example, by producing in China), access skilled personnel (by producing in Germany), remain close to key markets (by producing in China, India, and the United States), and succeed in the intensely competitive global car industry.

Global Sourcing from Subsidiaries versus Independent Suppliers

The two strategic choices we just discussed lead us to the framework in Exhibit 16.2. The focal firm can source from independent suppliers, from company-owned subsidiaries and affiliates, or from both. In the Exhibit, Cells C and D represent the global sourcing scenarios. While global sourcing implies procurement from foreign locations, in some cases the focal firm may source from its own wholly owned subsidiary or an affiliate jointly owned with another firm (Cell C). This is known as **captive sourcing**, which refers to sourcing from the firm's own production facilities located abroad. In this scenario, production is carried out at a foreign facility that the focal firm owns through direct investment. For example, Genpact (formerly Gecis Global) was a captive sourcing unit of General Electric (GE). With annual revenues of about $500 million and more than 19,000 employees worldwide, Genpact is one of the largest providers of business-process outsourcing services. GE sold Genpact in 2005, and the supplier became an independent firm. While maintaining its work for GE, Genpact is now free to seek other customers worldwide.[6]

Configuration of value-adding activity The pattern or geographic arrangement of locations where the firm carries out value-chain activities.

Captive sourcing Sourcing from the firm's own production facilities located abroad.

Exhibit 16.2

The Nature of Outsourcing and Global Sourcing

	Value-adding activity is internalized	Value-adding activity is externalized (outsourced)
Value-adding activity kept in home country	*A* Keep production in-house, in home country	*B* Outsource production to third party provider at home
Value-adding activity conducted abroad (global sourcing)	*C* Delegate production to foreign subsidiary or affiliate (captive sourcing)	*D* Outsource production to a third-party provider abroad (contract manufacturing or global sourcing from independent suppliers)

Alternatively, the focal firm can procure intermediate goods or finished products from independent suppliers (Cell D), an increasingly likely scenario. The firm externalizes its production to foreign partners to harness their capabilities. Global sourcing requires the firm to identify qualified suppliers, develop necessary organizational and technological capabilities to relocate specific tasks, and coordinate a geographically dispersed network of activities.

Contract Manufacturing: Global Sourcing from Independent Suppliers

Contract manufacturing An arrangement in which the focal firm contracts with an independent supplier to manufacture products according to well-defined specifications.

The typical relationship between the focal firm and its foreign supplier (Cell D in Exhibit 16.2) may take the form of **contract manufacturing**, an arrangement in which the focal firm contracts with an independent supplier to manufacture products according to well-defined specifications. Often, an explicit contract spells out the terms of the relationship. The supplier is responsible for production and adheres to the focal firm's specifications. Once the products are manufactured, the supplier turns them over to the focal firm, which then markets, sells, and distributes them. In essence, the focal firm "rents" the manufacturing capacity of the foreign contractor.

In a typical scenario, the focal firm approaches several suppliers with product designs or specifications and asks for quotations on the cost to produce the merchandise, accounting for cost of labor, processes, tooling, and materials. Once the bidding process is complete, the focal firm contracts with the most qualified manufacturer. Contract manufacturing is especially common in the apparel, shoe, furniture, aerospace, defense, computer, semiconductor, energy, medical, pharmaceutical, personal care, and automotive industries.

Patheon is one of the world's leading contract manufacturers in the pharmaceutical industry. The company provides drug development and manufacturing services to pharmaceutical and biotechnology firms worldwide. Patheon operates 11 production facilities in North America and Europe, producing over-the-counter drugs and several of the world's top-selling prescription drugs on contract for most of the world's 20 largest pharmaceutical firms. Patheon generates about half its sales in North America and the other half in Europe.[7] Benetton employs contract manufacturers to produce clothing, and IKEA uses contract manufacturers to produce furniture. Contract manufacturing also allows firms to enter target countries quickly, especially when the market is too small to justify significant local investment.

You have probably never heard of Taiwan's Hon Hai Precision Industry Co., a leading contract manufacturer in the global electronics industry. Hon Hai works under contract for well-known companies, churning out iPods and iPhones for Apple, PlayStations for Sony, printers and PCs for Hewlett-Packard, and thousands of other products. In 2007, Hon Hai's sales surpassed $40 billion. The firm employs some 360,000 people in scores of contract factories worldwide, from Malaysia to Mexico.[8]

One advantage of contract manufacturing is that the focal firm—for example, Apple, Hewlett-Packard, or Sony—can concentrate on product design and marketing while transferring manufacturing responsibility to an independent contractor. The contract manufacturer is likely to be located in a low-wage country and have strengths in terms of scale economies, manufacturing prowess, and specific knowledge about the engineering and development processes of products that it handles for its clients.[9] A major drawback of contract manufacturing is that the focal firm has limited control over the supplier. Lack of direct ownership implies limited influence over the manufacturing processes of the supplier, potential vulnerability to the supplier's acting in bad faith, and limited ability to safeguard intellectual assets.

Offshoring

Offshoring is a natural extension of global sourcing. **Offshoring** refers to the relocation of a business process or entire manufacturing facility to a foreign country. Large multinational companies are particularly active in shifting production facilities or business processes to foreign countries to enhance their competitive advantage. Offshoring is especially common in the service sector, including banking, software code writing, legal services, and customer-service activities. For example, large legal hubs have emerged in India that provide services such as drafting contracts and patent applications, conducting research and negotiations, as well as performing paralegal work on behalf of Western clients. With lawyers in North America and Europe costing $300 an hour or more, Indian firms can cut legal bills by 75 percent.[10]

Firms generally offshore certain tasks or subactivities of business functions. In each of the business functions—human resources, accounting, finance, marketing, and customer service—certain tasks are routine and discrete. These functions are candidates for offshoring, as long as their performance by independent suppliers does not threaten or diminish the focal firm's core competencies or strategic assets. Examples of successful offshoring to foreign providers include billing and credit card processing in finance, creating customer databases and recording sales transactions in marketing, and payroll maintenance and benefits administration in human resources.

India receives the bulk of advanced economies' relocated business services. This sector in India has grown by as much as 50 percent per year during the 2000s. The country's emergence as a major offshoring destination results from its huge pool of qualified labor who work for wages as little as 25 percent of comparable workers in the West, combined with the worldwide economic downturn of the early 2000s, which triggered multinational firms to seek ways to shave costs.[11] But India is not the only destination of substantial outsourcing work. Firms in Eastern Europe perform support activities for architectural and engineering firms from Western Europe and the United States. Accountants in the Philippines perform support work for major accounting firms. Accenture has back-office operations and call centers in Costa Rica. Many IT support services for customers in Germany are actually based in the Czech Republic

Offshoring The relocation of a business process or entire manufacturing facility to a foreign country.

Workers at a call center in Bangalore support international customers. India has received the bulk of outsourced business process services in recent years.

and Romania. Boeing, Motorola, and Nortel do much of their R&D in Russia. South Africa is the base for technical and user-support services for English, French, and German-speaking customers throughout Europe.[12]

Limits to Global Sourcing

Not all business activities or processes lend themselves to offshoring. Jobs most conducive to being offshored tend to be in industries with the following characteristics:

- Large-scale manufacturing industries whose primary competitive advantage is efficiency and low cost
- Industries such as automobiles that have uniform customer needs and highly standardized processes in production and other value-chain activities
- Service industries that are highly labor intensive, such as call centers and legal transcription
- Information-based industries whose functions and activities can be easily transmitted via the Internet, such as accounting, billing, and payroll
- Industries such as software preparation, whose outputs are easy to codify and transmit over the Internet or by telephone, such as routine technical support and customer service activities.

In contrast, many jobs in the services sector cannot be separated from their place of consumption. This limits the types of service jobs that firms can move abroad. Personal contact is vital at the downstream end of virtually all value chains. Other services are consumed locally. For example, people normally do not travel abroad to see a doctor, dentist, lawyer, or accountant.[13] Consequently, many service jobs will never be offshored. For example, through 2005, only about 3 percent of jobs in the United States that require substantial customer interaction (for example, those in the retailing sector) have been transferred to low-wage economies. By 2008, less than 15 percent of all service jobs have moved from advanced economies to emerging markets.[14]

In addition, many companies, such as Harley-Davidson in the United States, have their own reasons to keep production at home. A great proportion of the value added by Harley-Davidson is local. Harley-Davidson both assembles its motorcycles and procures key components such as the engine, transmission, gas tank, brake system, and the headlight assembly in the United States.[15] Harley's customers view the product as an American icon and tend to not tolerate production abroad. Another factor is labor union contracts, which limit management's ability to transfer core production abroad without union consent.

Strategic Implications of Outsourcing and Global Sourcing

Exhibit 16.3 explains the strategic implications of the two choices firms face: whether to perform specific value-adding activities themselves or to outsource them, *and* whether to concentrate each activity in the home country or disperse it abroad. The Exhibit portrays a typical value chain, ranging from R&D and design, to customer service. The first row indicates the degree to which management considers each value-adding activity a strategic asset to the firm. The second row indicates whether the activity tends to be internalized inside the focal firm or outsourced to a foreign supplier. The third row indicates where management typically locates an activity.

These decisions depend largely on the strategic importance of the particular activity to the firm. For example, companies typically consider R&D and design activities central to their competitive advantage. As a result, they are more likely to internalize these functions and less likely to outsource. In con-

	R&D Design	Component Manufacturing	Manufacturing or Assembly	Marketing and Branding	Sales, Distribution and Logistics	Customer Service
Importance of this activity to the firm as a strategic asset	Very important	Low importance	Low to medium importance	Very important	Medium importance	Medium importance
Likelihood of internalizing rather than outsourcing this activity	High	Low	Low to Medium	High	Low to Medium	Low to Medium
Geographic configuration: Overall tendency to locate activity at home or abroad	Usually concentrated at home	Usually dispersed across various markets	Usually concentrated in a few markets	Branding concentrated at home; Marketing concentrated or dispersed to individual markets	Dispersed to individual markets	Dispersed to individual markets, except call centers, which are often concentrated

Exhibit 16.3 Typical Choices of Outsourcing and Geographic Dispersion of Value-Chain Activities among Firms

trast, manufacturing, logistics, and customer service activities tend to be more readily outsourced and geographically dispersed. The decision will also be a function of the firm's experience with international business and availability of qualified suppliers.

 Evolution of Global Sourcing

Global sourcing by the private sector now accounts for more than half of all imports by major countries.[16] Global sourcing has changed the way companies do business in all kinds of industries. For example, Steinway procures parts and components from a dozen foreign countries to produce its grand pianos. Similarly, retailers do extensive global sourcing: Most of the products sold by Best Buy, Target, Wal-Mart, and Carrefour are sourced from suppliers in emerging markets. These retailers benefit by importing good-quality consumer products at low prices.

Phases in the Evolution: From Global Sourcing of Inputs to Offshoring Value-Adding Activities

The first major wave of global sourcing emphasized the *manufacturing* of input *products* and began in the 1960s with the shift of European and United States manufacturing to low-cost countries as geographically diverse as Mexico and Spain. Early observers pointed to the emergence of the *modular* corporation and the *virtual* corporation in the context of global sourcing.[17] Eventually, managers began to realize that tasks within most functions and value-chain activities are subject to externalization if such a move serves to facilitate efficiency, productivity, quality, and higher revenues.

The next wave of global sourcing began in the 1990s with offshoring, in which firms began to outsource specific value-adding activities in the services sector to locations such as India and Eastern Europe. In addition to IT services (software, applications, and technical support) and customer-support activities (technical support, call centers), many other service sectors became part of the offshoring trend. For example, in the health care sector, procedures such as CT scans and radiology evaluation are conducted in offshore locations. Consumers also are engaged in so-called *medical tourism*, in which they travel to countries such as India and Thailand for such medical procedures as bypass surgery or appendix removal.

Today, business-process outsourcing in product development, human resources, and finance/accounting services has become very common.[18] For example, Microsoft has invested billions in India to add to its existing R&D and technical-support operations there. Both Intel and Cisco Systems have invested billions to develop R&D operations in India as well. JP Morgan, a large investment bank, has several thousand employees in India who have evolved from performing simple back-office tasks, such as data entry to settling structured-finance and derivative deals—highly sophisticated banking transactions. India has reached a more mature stage in its development than other emerging countries. It first served as a center for software application development and maintenance. Subsequently, Indian firms and local captive operations of numerous MNEs began offering low-cost back-office services. Most recently, India has developed a strong industrial base of its own in IT and other high value-added business processes. Wipro, Infosys, and Tata Consultancy are among the most prominent players in global sourcing in the business services, software development, and call center industries. Note India's prominence in this activity is in addition to that of the United States. While many of the firms are headquartered in the United States, much of their work is actually performed in India or other emerging markets.

Magnitude of Global Sourcing

The magnitude of global sourcing is considerable. In 2005, India alone booked $22 billion worth of business in answering customer phone calls, managing far-flung computer networks, processing invoices, and writing custom software for MNEs from all over the world.[19] Global sourcing has created more than 1.3 million jobs during the past decade for India. Meanwhile, between 2000 and 2004, the United States outsourced some 100,000 service jobs each year.[20] In 2006, information-technology and business-process outsourcing exceeded $150 billion worldwide.

Diversity of Countries That Initiate and Receive Outsourced Work

Clearly, China and India are major players in global sourcing. The *Global Trend* feature highlights the ongoing rivalry between these two countries as they compete to be the world's leading destinations for global sourcing. Nevertheless, as noted in the opening vignette, numerous other countries are active players as well. In terms of buyer countries, global sourcing is practiced by firms all around the world. U.S. firms have led the trend with nearly two-thirds of total offshore service projects. In 2003, firms in the United States offshored $87 billion of business services. In the same year, companies in other nations offshored to the United States $134 billion of business services. This insourcing supported a variety of relatively high-skilled U.S. jobs in engineering, management consulting, banking, and legal services.

China: Rivaling India in the Global Sourcing Game

For services, India is perhaps the world's leading offshoring destination. India is a popular destination for software development and back-office services, such as telephone call centers and financial accounting activities. India is one of the world's leading centers in the IT industry, thanks in part to the emergence of indigenous MNEs such as Infosys and Wipro. Infosys rivals Microsoft as one of the top software development firms worldwide.

Compared to India, however, China's history as a supplier to the world is longer. China is the center of manufacturing for countless Western firms. For example, the U.S. firm Keurig manufactures single-serving coffee machines. After Keurig management found that its coffee-makers were overpriced at $250 each because of high manufacturing costs, the firm outsourced manufacturing to a partner in China. The move allowed Keurig to begin offering new models for as little as $99. As a result, Keurig has greatly increased its sales.

China aims to surpass India in services outsourcing, and the Chinese government is making huge investments to upgrade worker training and the quality of its universities. China has three major advantages. First, the country is home to a large amount of skilled, low-cost labor. It produces 350,000 graduate engineers every year, almost four times that of the United States. Second, China has a huge domestic market with rapid and sustainable economic growth. Third, the attitude of the Chinese government, long an obstacle to foreign firms, is increasingly probusiness. The government has been developing a range of policies that favor foreign firms that manufacture in China.

Nevertheless, China still has numerous pitfalls. The country is weak in intellectual property protection, has a language and culture that foreign firms find challenging, and lacks quality infrastructure. Dealing with the Chinese government is complicated because of substantial bureaucracy and infighting among its various agencies. The resulting chaos hampers the ability of Chinese entrepreneurs to launch and manage companies.

By contrast, India has better intellectual property protection, a workforce with English language skills, and infrastructure that, although poor by advanced-economy standards, is often superior to that of China. India is likely to remain the global-sourcing leader in the services sector for some time to come.

Sources: *Economist.* (2005b). "The Myth of China Inc.," September 3, pp. 53–54; Farrell, Diana, Noshir Kaka, and Saacha Sturze. (2005). "Ensuring India's Offshoring Future," *The McKinsey Quarterly*, Special Edition: Fulfilling India's Promise; Hagel, John. (2004). Offshoring Goes on the Offensive: Cost Cutting is Only the First Benefit, *The McKinsey Quarterly*, no. 2, online journal; *Inc. Magazine.* (2006). "Singling Out a New Market," January, p. 46; Overby, Stephanie. (2005). "It's Cheaper in China," *CIO Magazine*, September 15. Retrieved from www.cio.com/archive/091505/nypro.html, December 10, 2005.

In Europe, forty percent of large firms report that they have outsourced services to other countries. The biggest European outsourcing deal of 2005—a $7 billion, 10-year contract to manage 150,000 computers and networking software for the British military—was awarded to a consortium led by EDS, a Texas-based company.[21] In Japan's IT industry, 23 percent of firms have outsourced services abroad.

Exhibit 16.4 identifies key players in global sourcing by four geographic regions. For example, Cairo-based Xceed Contact Center handles calls in Arabic and European languages for Microsoft, General Motors, Oracle, and Carrefour. Russia is aiming at high-end programming jobs. With its strong engineering culture, Russia has an abundant pool of underemployed talent available at wages about one-fifth those of the United States.

Singapore and Dubai have declared that their safety and advanced legal systems give them an edge in handling high-security and business-continuity services. The Philippines draws on longstanding cultural ties and solid English skills to attract call-center work. Central and South American countries use their Spanish skills to seek call-center contracts for the Hispanic market in the United States.[22]

	Central and Eastern Europe	*China and South Asia*	*Latin America and the Caribbean*	*Middle East and Africa*
Top-Ranked Countries	Czech Republic, Bulgaria, Slovakia, Poland, Hungary	India, China, Malaysia, Philippines, Singapore, Thailand	Chile, Brazil, Mexico, Costa Rica, Argentina	Egypt, Jordan, United Arab Emirates, Ghana, Tunisia, Dubai
Up-and-Comers	Romania, Russia, Ukraine, Belarus	Indonesia, Vietnam, Sri Lanka	Jamaica, Panama, Nicaragua, Colombia	South Africa, Israel, Turkey, Morocco
Emerging Local Providers	Luxoft (Russia), EPAM Systems (Belarus), Softline (Ukraine), DataArt (Russia)	NCS (Singapore), Bluem, Neusoft Group, BroadenGate Systems (China)	Softtek (Mexico), Neoris (Mexico), Politec (Brazil), DBAccess (Venezuela)	Xceed (Egypt), Ness Technologies (Israel), Jeraisy Group (Saudi Arabia)

Exhibit 16.4

Key Players in Global Sourcing by Region

SOURCE: Engardio, Pete. (2006). "The Future of Outsourcing: How It's Transforming Whole Industries and Changing the Way We Work," *Business Week*, January 30, p. 58.

In addition to low labor costs, other attractions of offshoring include the ability to increase productivity, improve service, and access superior technical skills. Recently, Vietnam has attracted considerable offshored business. With Europe as its largest export market, outscored production in Vietnam doubled in the early 2000s because it offers modern but low-cost operations, skilled but less expensive labor, and access to local sources unencumbered by trade restrictions.

A.T. Kearney's Global Services Location Index (www.atkearney.com) is topped by emerging markets only, including: India, China, Malaysia, Thailand, Brazil, Indonesia, Chile, and the Philippines. The United States is the only advanced economy ranked in the top 21 destinations. To help firms identify countries for outsourcing value-chain activities, the index emphasizes various criteria: the country's financial structure (compensation costs, infrastructure costs, tax and regulatory costs), the availability and skills of people (cumulative business-process experience and skills, labor force availability, education and language, and worker attrition rates), and the nature of the business environment (the country's political and economic environment, physical infrastructure, cultural adaptability, and security of intellectual property).

 ## Benefits and Challenges of Global Sourcing for the Firm

As with other international entry strategies, global sourcing offers both benefits and challenges for the firm. Exhibit 16.5 provides an overview of these benefits and challenges.

In terms of challenges, firms should pay special attention to the seven concerns mentioned in Exhibit 16.5. Many of these challenges arise if the focal firm is sourcing from independent suppliers abroad. The low-control nature of global sourcing implies that the issues of identifying, screening, negotiating, and monitoring partner activities become highly critical to the success of the firm. We elaborated on these issues earlier in the book, in Chapters 13 through 15. An additional challenge is the vulnerability to adverse currency fluctuations. Potential cost savings from global sourcing can be offset by a weakening home currency. In this scenario, foreign-sourced products cost more to import. For example, if China allowed its currency to appreciate, then its exports are

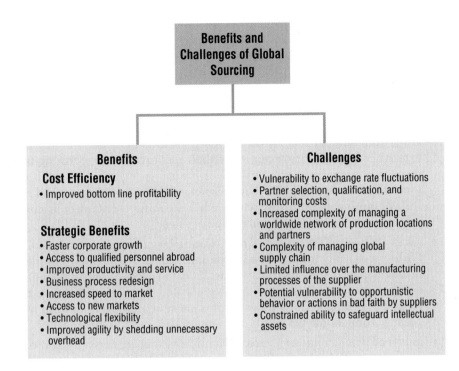

Exhibit 16.5

Benefits and Challenges of Global Sourcing

likely to slow down, as it will be relatively more expensive for customers to continue to source from China.

In terms of benefits of global sourcing to the focal firm, there are two primary reasons to pursue global sourcing: cost efficiency and the achievement of strategic goals. Let's consider these in turn.

Cost Efficiency

Cost efficiency is the traditional rationale for sourcing abroad. The firm takes advantage of "labor arbitrage"—the large wage gap between advanced economies and emerging markets. One study found that firms expect to save an average of more than 40 percent off baseline costs as a result of offshoring.[23] These savings tend to occur particularly in R&D, product design activities, and back-office operations such as accounting and data processing. For example, a programmer in the United States with an IT-related college degree and five years of JAVA programming experience can expect to earn over $60,000 a year, plus benefits. In Bangalore, the salary is likely to be around $6,000 including benefits. A Ph.D. statistician in India earns up to $40,000 annually, compared with $200,000 in the United States. Most of the work that such Indian information workers perform can be transmitted instantly over the Internet. This wage discrepancy explains why firms like IBM, HP, Accenture, Dell, HSBC, Citicorp, and JP Morgan have been growing their India operations by 30 to 50 percent a year during the 2000s.[24]

Achievement of Strategic Goals

In addition to helping save the firm money, global sourcing can also help it achieve longer-term goals. This strategic view of global sourcing—called *transformational outsourcing*—suggests that a firm can achieve gains in efficiency, productivity, quality, and revenues much more effectively by leveraging offshore talent.[25] Global sourcing can provide the means to speed up innovation, fund development projects that are otherwise unaffordable, or turn around failing businesses. Firms leverage global sourcing to free expensive analysts, engineers, and sales personnel from routine tasks so they can spend more time innovating and working with customers.[26] Global sourcing can be a catalyst to overhaul outdated office operations and prepare for new competitive battles.

Often, both types of rationale—cost efficiency and achieving strategic goals—are present and are not mutually exclusive in a particular global sourcing activity. Whatever the primary motivation, the firm engaged in global sourcing can expect a variety of specific benefits, including:

- *Faster corporate growth.* By outsourcing various peripheral activities to external suppliers, firms can focus their resources on performing more profitable activities such as R&D or building relationships with customers. For example, global sourcing enables companies to expand their staff of engineers and researchers while keeping constant their cost of product development as a percentage of sales.[27]

- *Access to qualified personnel abroad.* Countries such as China, India, the Philippines, and Ireland offer abundant pools of educated engineers, managers, and other specialists. The ability to access a larger pool of talented individuals, wherever they are located, helps firms achieve their goals. For example, Disney has much of its animation work done in Japan because some of the world's best animators are located there.

- *Improved productivity and service.* Manufacturing productivity and other value-chain activities can be improved by global sourcing to suppliers that specialize in these activities. For example, Penske Truck Leasing improved its efficiency and customer service by outsourcing dozens of business processes to Mexico and India. Global sourcing enables firms to provide 24/7 coverage of customer service, especially for customers who need around-the-clock support.

- *Business process redesign.* By reconfiguring their value-chain systems or reengineering their business processes, companies can improve their production efficiency and resources utilization. Multinational firms see offshoring as a catalyst for a broader plan to overhaul outdated company operations.[28]

- *Increased speed to market.* By shifting software development and editorial work to India and the Philippines, the U.S.-Dutch publisher Walters Kluwer was able to produce a greater variety of books and journals and publish them faster. As the opening vignette describes, big pharmaceutical firms get new medications to market faster by global sourcing of clinical drug trials.

- *Access to new markets.* Firms can tap emerging markets and technologies in other countries, which not only helps them better understand foreign customers, but also facilitates their marketing activities there. Firms can also use global sourcing to service countries that may be otherwise closed due to protectionism. For example, by moving much of its R&D operations to Russia, the telecommunications firm Nortel gained an important foothold in a market that desperately needs telephone switching equipment and other communications infrastructure.

- *Technological flexibility.* By switching suppliers at a time when new, less expensive technology becomes available, firms are no longer as tied to specific technologies as they would be if they produced the technology themselves. Sourcing provides greater organizational flexibility and faster responsiveness to evolving consumer needs.

- *Improved agility by shedding unnecessary overhead.* Unburdened by a large bureaucracy and administrative overhead, companies can be more responsive to opportunities and adapt more easily to environmental changes, such as new competitors.

Combined, these benefits give firms the ability to continuously renew their strategic postures. For example, Genpact, Accenture, and IBM Services are outsourcing specialists that dispatch teams to meticulously dissect the workflow of other firms' human resources, finance, or IT departments. This helps the specialists build new IT platforms, redesign all processes, and administer programs, acting as a virtual subsidiary to their client firms. The contractor then disperses work among global networks of staff from Asia to Eastern Europe and elsewhere.[29]

Industries that particularly benefit from global sourcing include those in labor-intensive sectors such as garments, shoes, and furniture, those that use relatively standardized processes and technologies such as automotive parts and machine tools, and those that make and sell established products with a predictable pattern of sales, such as components for consumer electronics. For example, diamond processing is a labor-intensive industry that uses standardized processes that result in diamond rings and equipment used for fine cutting. The diamond cutting industry has been concentrated in Antwerp, Belgium, for the past five centuries. Recently, however, diamond cutting is being outsourced to firms in India that perform the work more cost-effectively and provide other advantages. China is also emerging as an important participant in diamond cutting.

Implementing Global Sourcing through Supply-Chain Management

A major reason why sourcing products from distant markets has become a major business phenomenon today is the efficiency with which goods can be physically moved from one part of the globe to another. This efficiency is due to the sophisticated processes and strategies involved in moving products from one point—such as from manufacturer to intermediaries—to another point—such as intermediaries to customers.

Global supply chain refers to the firm's integrated network of sourcing, production, and distribution, organized on a worldwide scale and located in countries where competitive advantage can be maximized. Global supply-chain management involves both upstream (supplier) and downstream (customer) flows.

Note that the concepts of the supply chain and the value chain are related but distinct. Recall that the value chain is the collection of activities intended to design, produce, market, deliver, and support a product or service. The supply chain is the collection of logistics specialists and activities that provides inputs to manufacturers or retailers. Skillful supply-chain management serves to optimize value-chain activities. Sourcing from numerous suppliers scattered around the world would be neither economical nor feasible without an efficient supply-chain system. Even as a casual observer, one has to be impressed when seeing the vast collection of products in a supermarket or department store that originated from dozens of different countries. The speed with which these products are delivered to end users is equally impressive.

Consider a striking example of how global supply-chain management is making global sourcing feasible and, at the same time, contributing to firm competitiveness. The roll-out of the first Boeing 787 Dreamliner jet in Everett, Washington, in July, 2007, marked a new beginning for this aircraft maker. Several features of the new aircraft are unique. It is a fuel-saving, medium-sized passenger jet that uses carbon composite for the fuselage (instead of aluminum). It is lightweight and has spacious interiors and higher cabin pressure than other models—for a more comfortable journey. However, the most remarkable aspect of the Boeing 787 Dreamliner jet is the extent of outsourcing. Boeing itself is responsible for only about 10 percent of the value added of this new aircraft—the tail fin and final assembly. Some 40 suppliers worldwide contribute the

Global supply chain The firm's integrated network of sourcing, production, and distribution, organized on a worldwide scale and located in countries where competitive advantage can be maximized.

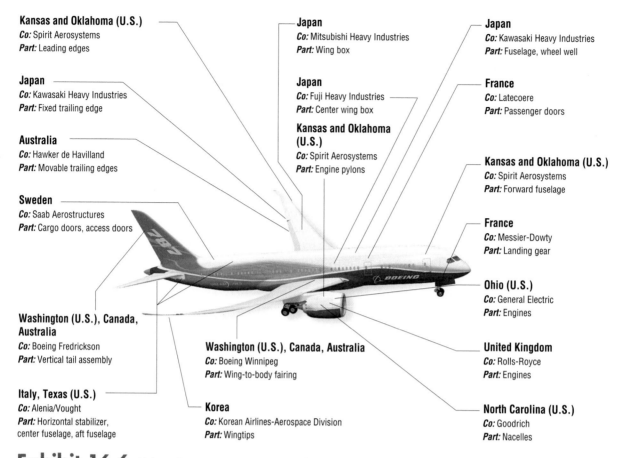

Kansas and Oklahoma (U.S.)
Co: Spirit Aerosystems
Part: Leading edges

Japan
Co: Kawasaki Heavy Industries
Part: Fixed trailing edge

Australia
Co: Hawker de Havilland
Part: Movable trailing edges

Sweden
Co: Saab Aerostructures
Part: Cargo doors, access doors

Washington (U.S.), Canada, Australia
Co: Boeing Fredrickson
Part: Vertical tail assembly

Italy, Texas (U.S.)
Co: Alenia/Vought
Part: Horizontal stabilizer, center fuselage, aft fuselage

Japan
Co: Mitsubishi Heavy Industries
Part: Wing box

Japan
Co: Fuji Heavy Industries
Part: Center wing box

Kansas and Oklahoma (U.S.)
Co: Spirit Aerosystems
Part: Engine pylons

Washington (U.S.), Canada, Australia
Co: Boeing Winnipeg
Part: Wing-to-body fairing

Korea
Co: Korean Airlines-Aerospace Division
Part: Wingtips

Japan
Co: Kawasaki Heavy Industries
Part: Fuselage, wheel well

France
Co: Latecoere
Part: Passenger doors

Kansas and Oklahoma (U.S.)
Co: Spirit Aerosystems
Part: Forward fuselage

France
Co: Messier-Dowty
Part: Landing gear

Ohio (U.S.)
Co: General Electric
Part: Engines

United Kingdom
Co: Rolls-Royce
Part: Engines

North Carolina (U.S.)
Co: Goodrich
Part: Nacelles

Exhibit 16.6 Where Boeing Company Sources the Components for its New 787 Aircraft

SOURCE: Tatge, Mark (2006), "Global Gamble," Forbes, (April 17), pp. 78–80.

remaining 90 percent of the value. For example, the wings are built in Japan, the carbon composite fuselage is made in Italy, and the landing gear is manufactured in France. As illustrated in Exhibit 16.6, components for the new 787 originate from distant parts of the world. The global dispersion of manufacturing responsibility allows Boeing to transform itself into a systems integrator and focus on its core capabilities—design, marketing, and branding. Boeing also reduces the chance of a bottleneck at one plant holding up production of the aircraft. It is no longer at the mercy of the weakest link in the chain, which was often one of Boeing's own plants.[30]

Networks of supply-chain hubs and providers of global delivery service are an integral part of global supply chains. Many focal firms delegate supply-chain activities to such independent logistics service providers as DHL, FedEx, TNT, and UPS. Consulting firms that manage the logistics of other firms are called *third party logistics providers (3PLs)*. Using a 3PL is often the best solution for international logistics, especially for firms that produce at low volumes or lack the resources and the expertise to create their own logistics network.

A good example of how global supply-chain management has evolved can be taken from the ongoing European Union integration. The removal of border controls allowed supply-chain managers to redraw the maps of their sourcing and distribution activities throughout Europe. Warehousing and distribution centers were consolidated and centralized. Intel reduced shipping costs by at least 7 percent by consolidating its worldwide freight expenditures into four transportation firms. As a result, from its 14 manufacturing sites around the world, Intel improved on-time delivery and customer-service performance substantially.[31]

A global supply-chain network consolidates a firm's sourcing, manufacturing, and distribution in a few strategic locations worldwide so the firm can *concentrate* these activities in countries where it can maximize its competitive advantages. Exhibit 16.7 illustrates the stages, functions, and activities in the supply chain. It reveals how suppliers interact with the focal firm and how these, in turn, interact with distributors and retailers. Each stage in the global supply chain encompasses functions and activities that involve the focal firm in sourcing and distribution. When the focal firm deals with multiple products and demanding customers spread around the world, managing supply chains becomes more complex.

Costs associated with physically delivering a product to an export market may account for as much as 40 percent of the total cost. Skillful supply-chain management reduces this cost while increasing customer satisfaction. Experienced firms make optimal use of information and communications technology (ICT), which streamlines supply chains, reducing costs and increasing distribution efficiency. For example, managers use *Electronic Data Interchange (EDI)*, which passes orders directly from customers to suppliers automatically through a sophisticated ICT platform. The UK-based supermarket chain Tesco greatly reduced inventory costs by using an EDI system to link point-of-sale data to logistics managers. Technology allows Tesco to track product purchases down to the minute. Many canned foods that used to sit in Tesco's warehouses for days or weeks are now received directly from suppliers.[32]

Supply-chain applications software enhances information sharing and improves efficiency by helping the manufacturer and focal firm track international shipments and clear customs. Many firms digitize key documents such as customs declarations and invoices, which improves speed and reduces order processing costs and shipping procedures. Spain-based retailer Zara is a good example of firms that use EDI technology to optimize supply-chain management, inventory management, and responsiveness to consumer demands. The firm uses

	Suppliers	Focal Firm	Intermediaries and/or Retailers
Stage in supply chain	Sourcing, from home country and abroad	Inbound materials; outbound goods and services	Distribution to domestic customers or foreign customers (exports)
Major functions	Provide raw materials, parts, components, supplies, as well as business processes and other services to focal firms	Manufacture or assemble components or finished products, or produce services	Distribute and sell products and services
Typical activities	Maintain inventory, process orders, transport goods, deliver services	Manage inventory, process orders, manufacture or assemble products, produce and deliver services, distribute products to customers, retailers, or intermediaries	Manage inventory, place or process orders, produce services, manage physical distribution, provide after-sales service

Exhibit 16.7

Stages, Functions, and Activities in the Global Supply Chain

wireless personal digital assistants (PDAs) and instantaneous communications with its stores to carry out ongoing market research. These technologies have allowed Zara to become a leader in rapid-response retailing. Like Zara's, the best global supply chains consist of reliable, capable partners all connected through automated, real-time communications. In an efficient global supply chain, the focal firm and its supply-chain partners continuously communicate and share information in order to meet the demands of the marketplace.

Logistics and Transportation

Logistics involves physically moving goods through the supply chain. It incorporates information, transportation, inventory, warehousing, materials handling, and similar activities associated with the delivery of raw materials, parts, components, and finished products. Managers seek to reduce moving and storage costs by using just-in-time inventory systems. Internationally, logistics are complex due to greater geographic distance, multiple legal and political environments, and the often inadequate and costly nature of distribution infrastructure in individual countries. The more diverse the firm's global supply chain, the greater the cost of logistics.

Competent logistics management is critical. For example, the California ports of Los Angeles and Long Beach handle over 40 percent of imports into the United States. Although the two California ports process over 24,000 containers per day, infrastructure deficiencies and increasing demand combine to result in long delays, which translate into longer transit times and higher costs for U.S. importers. Because of delays, Toys "Я" Us had to build 10 extra days into its supply chain, and MGA Entertainment lost $40 million in revenues when it could not deliver its bestselling Bratz dolls on time to retailers.[33] As a result of poor supply-chain planning, Microsoft's Xbox 360 games console sold out soon after launch. Their scarcity led to high prices in unofficial channels. On eBay, Xbox consoles sold for as much as $1,000, compared with the official price of about $400.[34]

Transportation Modes

International logistics typically involves multiple *transportation modes*. Land transportation is conducted via highways and railroads. Ocean transportation is handled through large container ships. Air transportation involves commercial or cargo aircraft. Ocean and air transport are common in international business because of long shipping distances. Ships are the most common transportation mode, even among countries connected by land bridges. Sea transport was revolutionized by the development of 20- and 40-foot shipping containers, the big boxes that sit atop ocean-going vessels. Sea transportation is very cost effective because one ship can carry thousands of these containers at a time.

The transportation modes involve several trade-offs. There are three considerations in choosing a particular mode: *transit time* is the amount of time it takes for the goods to be delivered, *predictability* is the reliability of anticipated transit time versus actual transit time, and the *cost* of transportation. For example, ocean transport is far slower, but also far cheaper, than air transport. Air transport is fast and extremely predictable, but costly. Given its high cost, air transport is the preferred transportation mode in three common situations: to transport perishable products, such as food and flowers, to transport goods with a high value-to-weight ratio, such as jewelry and laptop computers, and to make emergency shipments, such as when a foreign customer urgently needs a missing part.

The use of air freight has increased dramatically since the 1970s, as the cost of air transport has declined. Air freight accounts for only about one percent of the total volume but more than a third of the total value of international shipments.

Land transport is usually more expensive than ocean transport but cheaper than air freight. Ocean shipping from, for example, China to the United States, or from East Asia to Europe, takes two to four weeks, including customs clearance. While timeconsuming, the cost of ocean freight is quite low, often accounting for less than one percent of a product's final price.

Risks in Global Sourcing

Global sourcing is carried out by small and large firms alike. In many firms, initial involvement in international business takes the form of global sourcing (which, for such firms, can be viewed as *inward internationalization*). Based on the experience gained through global sourcing, a firm may then progress to exporting, direct investment, or collaborative ventures (*outward internationalization*). Global sourcing often leads to increased company awareness of international opportunities. In this way, global sourcing expands managers' horizons by showing the way to expand sales and other activities.

However, as with other business activities, global sourcing also involves unexpected complications. In fact, studies reveal that as many as half of all outsourcing arrangements are terminated earlier than planned. Specifically, global sourcing involves seven major risks.[35]

1. *Less-than-expected cost savings.* International transactions are often more complex and costly than expected. Conflicts and misunderstandings arise because of differences in the national and organizational cultures between the focal firm and foreign supplier. Such factors give rise to cost savings that are less than what management had originally anticipated.

2. *Environmental factors.* Numerous environmental challenges confront focal firms, including exchange rate fluctuations, labor strikes, adverse macroeconomic events, high tariffs and other trade barriers, as well as high energy and transportation costs. Firms sometimes find that the cost to set up a foreign outsourcing facility is far greater than planned, due to the need to upgrade poor infrastructure or because the facility must be located in a large city to attract sufficient skilled labor. As noted in the opening vignette, for example, inadequate energy systems and other infrastructure problems in Africa compromised the testing of new medications developed by big pharmaceutical firms.

3. *Weak legal environment.* Many of the popular locations for global sourcing (for example, China, India, and Russia) have weak laws and enforcement regarding intellectual property, which can lead to the erosion of key strategic assets. Many countries are characterized by inadequate legal systems, red tape, convoluted tax systems, and complex business regulations that complicate local operations.

4. *Risk of creating competitors.* As the focal firm shares its intellectual property and business-process knowledge with foreign suppliers, it also runs the risk of creating future rivals. For example, Schwinn, long the leader in the global bicycle industry, created competitors by transferring much of its production and core expertise to foreign suppliers. The suppliers acquired sufficient knowledge, became lower-cost competitors, and eventually forced Schwinn into bankruptcy (from which it eventually recovered).

Firms that undertake global sourcing may encounter problematic environmental factors, such as poor infrastructure in transportation systems, as suggested by this street scene in India.

5. *Inadequate or low-skilled workers.* Some foreign suppliers may be staffed by employees who lack appropriate knowledge about the tasks with which they are charged. Other suppliers suffer rapid turnover of skilled employees, who find jobs with more desirable firms. For instance, typical Indian operations in business processing lose 20 percent or more of their workers each year and good managers are often in short supply. Customer complaints about the quality of service led Dell to move its corporate call center from India back to the United States in 2003.

6. *Over-reliance on suppliers.* Unreliable suppliers may put earlier work aside when they gain a more important client. Suppliers occasionally encounter financial difficulties or are acquired by other firms with different priorities and procedures. When such events occur, management at the focal firm may find itself scrambling to find alternative suppliers. Overreliance can shift control of key activities too much in favor of the supplier. As more and more tasks are performed by the supplier, the focal firm may lose control of important value-chain tasks. Focal firm management should strive to maintain an appropriate balance of power between itself and foreign suppliers.

7. *Erosion of morale and commitment among home-country employees.* Global sourcing can create a situation in which employees are caught in the middle between their employer and their employer's clients. At the extreme, workers find themselves in a psychological limbo, unclear about who their employer really is. When outsourcing causes retained and outsourced staff to work side by side, tensions and uncertainty may arise, evolving into a sort of "us-versus-them" syndrome and diminished employee commitment and enthusiasm.

One firm that experienced problems in its early phases of global sourcing is the London-based bank HSBC. Starting with one software-development center in Pune, a satellite city of Bombay, the bank established development centers in China and Brazil. When departments with tech needs at HSBC headquarters would order large jobs from India, the outsourcing staff in Pune would comply but occasionally realize they had bitten off more than they could chew. While the center had technical skills, it lacked specific knowledge in the banking industry. For instance, HSBC asked the Pune staff to build an insurance product but soon discovered the staff was unfamiliar with the insurance industry. HSBC management solved the problems by requiring bank experts from London to sit alongside the technical experts in Pune during project development.

Strategies for Minimizing Risk in Global Sourcing

The experience of firms with global sourcing so far reveals six managerial guidelines for strategic global sourcing.

1. *Go offshore for the right reasons.* The best rationale is strategic. The vast majority of companies cite cost-cutting as the main reason for global sourcing. After the first year, however, most firms encounter diminishing returns in the amount of money saved. Cost-cutting is often a distraction from more beneficial, long-term goals such as enhancing the quality of offerings, improving overall productivity, and freeing up knowledge workers and other core resources that can be redeployed to improve long-term performance. To maximize returns, management should engage in substantive planning that examines tasks and subactivities in each of the firm's value chains. The analysis should aim to outsource those tasks in which the firm is relatively weak, that offer relatively little value to the bottom line, or that can be performed more effectively by others, yet are not critical to the firm's core competencies.

2. *Get employees on board.* Global sourcing tends to invite opposition from employees and other organizational stakeholders. Disaffected middle managers can undermine projects and other goals that offshoring seeks to achieve. Poorly planned sourcing projects can create unnecessary tension and harm employee morale. Thus, management should seek to gain employee support for outsourcing projects. The decision to outsource should be based on reaching a consensus of middle managers and employees throughout the firm. Management should be diligent about developing alternatives for redeploying laid-off workers, and involve employees in selecting foreign partners. Where labor unions are involved, management should seek their counsel and incorporate their views. For example, when management at Dutch bank ABN Amro decided to offshore numerous accounting and finance functions, it took great pains to prepare the firm's large base of employees in advance. The bank set up a full-time communications department to explain the move to middle managers and staff. Senior executives held town hall meetings with employees and involved unions in managing the shift.[36]

3. *Choose carefully between a captive operation and contracting with outside suppliers.* Managers should be vigilant about striking the right balance between the organizational activities that it retains inside the firm and those that are sourced from outside suppliers. An increasing number of firms are establishing their own sourcing operations abroad. By owning the offshored facility, management maintains complete control of outsourced activities and retains control of key technologies and processes. For example, when Boeing wanted to outsource key value-chain tasks, management established a company-owned center in Moscow where it employs 1,100 skilled but relatively low-cost aerospace engineers. The Russian team is working on a range of projects, including the design of titanium parts for the new Boeing 787 Dreamliner jet.[37]

4. *Emphasize effective communications with suppliers.* A common reason for global sourcing failure is that both buyers and suppliers tend not to spend enough time up front to get to know each other well. They rush into a deal before clarifying partner expectations, which can give rise to misunderstandings and inferior results. Partners need to maintain active communication and oversight. For instance, because production quality in an emerging market may vary over time, managers at the focal firm may need to closely monitor manufacturing processes. When partners do not share necessary information with each other, vagueness and ambiguity emerge, followed by misunderstanding and frustration in outsourcing projects.[38] Poor cultural fit is also a potential problem. Guided by different business philosophies and practices, partners tend to approach the same issue differently. Effective communication is necessary to minimize misunderstandings that can diminish relationships between buyers and suppliers.

5. *Invest in supplier development and collaboration.* When a business function is delegated to a supplier, the parties need to exchange information, transfer knowledge, troubleshoot, coordinate, and monitor. Over the long haul, various benefits emerge when the focal firm adjusts its processes and product requirements to match the capabilities of foreign suppliers. Management should collaborate closely with suppliers in codevelopment and codesign activities. Close supplier cooperation also enables the focal firm to tap into a stream of ideas for new products, processes, technologies, and improvements. Efforts to build strong relationships help create a moral contract between the focal firm and the supplier, which is often more effective than a formal legal contract.

6. *Safeguard interests.* The focal firm should take specific actions to safeguard its interests in the supplier relationship. First, it can encourage the supplier to refrain from engaging in potentially destructive acts that jeopardize the firm's reputation. Second, it can escalate commitments by making partner-specific investments (such as sharing knowledge with the supplier) on an *incremental* basis, allowing for ongoing review, learning, and adjustment. Third, it can share costs and revenues by building a stake for the supplier so that, in case of failure to conform to expectations, the supplier also suffers costs or foregoes revenues. Fourth, it can maintain flexibility in selecting partners by keeping options open to find alternative partners in case a particular supplier does not work out. Finally, the focal firm can hold the partner at bay by withholding access to intellectual property and key assets in order to safeguard the firm's interests for the long term. If conflicts with the supplier become an ongoing problem, unresolved by negotiations, one option for the firm is to acquire full or partial ownership of the supplier.

Implications of Global Sourcing for Public Policy and Corporate Citizenship

Global sourcing is controversial. The business community sees global sourcing as a way of maintaining or increasing business competitiveness. Others view it negatively, focusing on the loss of jobs. After IBM workers in Europe went on strike against offshoring, shareholders at IBM's annual meeting argued for an anti-offshoring resolution. If the resolution had passed, it would have limited IBM's options to manage the firm, threatening company performance.

The general public is equally likely to be critical of offshoring. When the state of Indiana awarded a $15 million IT services contract to a supplier that planned to use technicians from India to do some of the work, the Indiana Senate intervened and cancelled the deal. Indiana is one of many public sector players that are contracting out services to foreign vendors in order to save tax dollars. The state recently leased the management of the Indiana Toll Road to an Australian-Spanish partnership for 75 years for $3.8 billion.

Global sourcing has sparked protests in many countries. Here, a union member protests IBM's policies of job outsourcing.

Concerns about outsourcing and offshoring are not new. In the 1970s and 1980s, when manufacturing jobs were outsourced, labor unions protested about "runaway corporations." Fortunately, bleak forecasts of job losses proved wrong as a result of economic expansion and job growth in the 1990s. In the United States, the proportion of jobs outsourced abroad each year is still less than 0.1 percent of total U.S. employment.

Potential Harm to Economies from Global Sourcing

Concerns about the consequences of global sourcing deserve serious attention. Critics of global sourcing point to three major problems. Global sourcing can result in (1) job losses in the home country, (2) reduced national competitiveness, and (3) declining standards of living. Regarding the last two concerns, critics worry that, as more tasks are performed at lower cost with comparable quality in other countries, high-wage countries will eventually lose their national competitiveness. Critics fear that long-held knowledge and skills will eventually drain away to other countries, and the lower wages paid abroad to perform jobs that were previously done in high-wage countries will eventually pull down wages in the latter countries, leading to lower living standards.

The biggest worry is job losses. For example, the number of U.S. jobs in the legal industry outsourced to foreign contractors now exceeds 25,000 jobs per year.[39] Some estimate that more than 400,000 jobs in the IT industry that were previously performed in the United States have moved offshore.[40] One study predicts that by the year 2017, 3.3 million U.S. service jobs—with a value of $136 billion—will be sent abroad.[41] Critics say all of this amounts to exporting jobs.

Moreover, job losses result when companies increase their sourcing of input and finished goods from abroad. For instance, Wal-Mart sources as much as 70 percent of its merchandise from China. This has led public officials and concerned citizens to form a protest group called Walmartwatch.com. The group claims that millions of U.S. jobs have been lost due to Wal-Mart's sourcing from foreign instead of U.S. suppliers.[42] In addition to the advanced economies, however, job losses are occurring in developing economies as well. For instance, El Salvador, Honduras, Indonesia, Morocco, and Turkey are restructuring as jobs in the textile industry are gradually transferred to China, India, and Pakistan, where multinational clothiers can operate more efficiently.[43]

Consider the potentially devastating effect of wholesale job losses on a small community. Recently, Electrolux, one of the world's largest household-appliance manufacturers, closed its factory in Michigan and moved production to Mexico. The company had been producing refrigerators in Greenville, Michigan, for nearly 40 years, providing 2,700 jobs. From the company's viewpoint, closing the plant made economic sense. Once the world's largest refrigerator factory, it had developed weak financial performance and costly labor. By establishing a *maquiladora* plant in Juarez, Mexico, Electrolux sought to profit from low wages and take advantage of the El Paso Foreign Trade Zone just across the border in Texas. Management believed it was acting in the firm's best interest and strengthening its global competitiveness.

From the local community's standpoint, however, the decision was devastating. How could so many jobs be replaced in such a small community? What would happen to the town's social and economic landscape? Assistance from labor unions and the State of Michigan were to no avail. Concessions in terms of lower wages by the labor union, and over $100 million from Michigan to Electrolux in tax breaks and grants were insufficient for Electrolux to change its mind. It did not help that Electrolux is a foreign-owned company headquartered in Sweden. Residents perceived the company had little loyalty to their community. In 2007, the Greenville plant was demolished. The town hopes to redevelop the site for mixed usage, as riverfront condominiums, commercial space, and parkland. Most former workers found other jobs in the service sector, although typically for less pay.[44]

Also recall the Boeing 787 Dreamliner aircraft. In the process of transforming itself from a manufacturer into a systems integrator, the company shed about 38,000 jobs in the United States. It was also criticized for transferring technology to foreign partners.

From these examples, it is easy to see the clash of interests between MNEs and local communities. Proponents of global sourcing argue that workers who lose their jobs due to offshoring can find new work. But this may be overly optimistic. It takes considerable time for laid-off workers to find new jobs. According to one estimate, as much as one-third of U.S. workers who have been laid off cannot find suitable employment within a year.[45] Older workers are particularly vulnerable. Compared to younger workers, they find it more difficult to learn the skills needed for new positions. The rate of redeployment is likely to be even lower in Europe, where unemployment rates are already high, and in Japan, where employment practices are less flexible. In Germany, the percentage of

Workers at a Nike factory in Vietnam, where Nike is the largest private employer. Following charges that its foreign contract factories were run like "sweatshops," Nike took steps to improve working conditions.

workers who are not reemployed within a year of losing their jobs is as high as 60 percent. Under such circumstances, global sourcing may increase the overall unemployment rate, reduce overall income level, and harm the national economy. Even workers who do find new jobs may be unable to achieve wages and work levels that equal those of their former positions.

Ethical and Social Implications of Global Sourcing

The prevalence of global sourcing has also raised public debate about the role of MNEs in protecting the environment, promoting human rights, and improving labor practices and working conditions. In other words, the bar for global corporate citizenship has been raised. Consider, for example, the case of foreign suppliers that operate *sweatshops*—factories in which people may work long hours for very low wages, often in harsh conditions.[46] Sweatshops may employ child labor, a practice that has been outlawed in much of the world. Those who defend moving production to low-wage facilities abroad point to a lower standard of living as an explanation for the low wages, and argue that their operations benefit the community by providing needed jobs. They point out that the choice for local workers is often between low-paying work or no work at all. Others argue that the alternatives available to such workers are even less desirable, such as poverty, prostitution, and social problems.

Opponents of sweatshops argue that corporations that sell their products in wealthy countries have a responsibility to pay their workers according to basic Western standards, especially when their products command high prices in advanced-economy markets. Another argument is that the foreign companies that establish factories destroy the preexisting agricultural market that may have provided a better life for laborers. In response to public pressure, some companies have reduced or ended their use of such cheap labor. For example, apparel makers Gap, Nike, and New Balance are notable for changing their policies after intense pressure from campus anti-sweatshop groups.

Potential Benefits to National Economy

Those in favor of global sourcing call attention to the benefits that it provides to the national economy. Proponents advance four key arguments. First, by reconfiguring value chains to the most cost-efficient locations, companies reduce their production costs and enhance their performance in an increasingly competitive global marketplace. For example, Roamware Inc., a U.S. firm that sells computer systems to cell phone providers, saved thousands of dollars on a project to create an electronic database by hiring Pangea3, an Indian firm, to do the job instead of relying on a nearby supplier.[47] As individual firms enhance their competitiveness, the national economy should strengthen as well.

Second, cost reductions and enhanced competitiveness allow firms to reduce the prices that they charge their customers. This benefits not only buyers but also the firms themselves, which become more price-competitive and enjoy greater market demand, which in turn stimulates job creation, offsetting much of the employment lost to outsourcing.

Third, by leveraging a flexible labor market and strong economic growth, countries that outsource may be able to shift their labor force to higher-value activities. This transformation has the effect of boosting the nation's productivity and industrial efficiency. By concentrating resources in higher-value activities, firms create better jobs. Large software firms Microsoft and Oracle have simultaneously increased both outsourcing and their domestic payrolls for higher-value jobs.[48]

Finally, declining wages may be offset by lower prices secured for outsourced products or services. Hence global sourcing tends to indirectly increase consumers' purchasing power and lift their living standards.[49] For instance, Wal-Mart has been roundly criticized for sourcing most of its merchandise from China. But the practice allows Wal-Mart to resell the goods at low prices, which translates into higher living standards for Wal-Mart customers.

Public Policy toward Global Sourcing

The consequences of global sourcing for the national economy and workers are not yet fully known. A recent comprehensive study, carried out for the United States, argues that the official statistics understate the impact of offshoring on the national economy.[50] Digging deeper into the statistics, the study finds that import growth, adjusted for inflation, is faster than the official numbers show. The author concluded that more of the gain in living standards in recent years has come from cheap imports, less from an increase in domestic productivity. This suggests that real GDP (gross domestic product) may be overstated. In contrast, the benefits that U.S. consumers gain from trade are actually understated. An implication is that the United States' living standards depend in part on the ability of foreign factories to boost output and cut costs.

In short, the findings suggest that U.S. consumers may enjoy an even better deal from imports than previously thought. From a public-policy standpoint, it is simply impractical for a nation to prohibit global sourcing. A more enlightened approach is to mitigate the harm that global sourcing can cause.[51] Offshoring amounts to a process of *creative destruction*, a concept first proposed by Austrian economist Joseph Schumpeter.[52] According to this view, over time, firms' innovative activities tend to make mature products obsolete. For example, the introduction of personal computers essentially wiped out the typewriter industry, the DVD player eliminated the VCR industry, and so on. Similarly, just as offshoring results in job loss and adverse effects for particular groups and economic sectors, it also creates new advantages and opportunities for firms and consumers alike. New industries created through the process of creative destruction will create new jobs and innovations.

If the loss of certain jobs is inevitable as a result of offshoring, public-policy makers are better off guiding employment toward higher value-added jobs by stimulating innovation, for example. Admittedly, this implies greater government intervention and is likely to produce positive outcomes only in the long run. The public sector can reduce the unfavorable consequences of global sourcing. One of the best ways would be to keep the cost of doing business relatively low. Governments can use economic and fiscal policies to encourage the development of new technologies by helping entrepreneurs reap the financial benefits of their work and keeping the cost of capital needed to finance R&D relatively low. Another useful policy is to ensure that the nation has a strong educational system, including technical schools and well-funded universities that supply engineers, scientists, and knowledge workers. A strong educational system helps to ensure that firms can draw from a high-quality pool of qualified labor. As firms restructure through global sourcing efforts, increased worker flexibility ensures that many who lose jobs can be redeployed in other positions.

CLOSING CASE

Good Hopes for Global Outsourcing

Good Hope Hospitals of California, Inc. ("Good Hope") is a chain of nine hospitals in or near Los Angeles, San Diego, and San Francisco. Founded in 1976, Good Hope is run on a for-profit basis and management continuously strives for efficient operations. Andy Delgado is Good Hope's Vice President for Finance and Accounting, and Joy Simmons is the senior manager in Information Technology. The two executives needed to make significant cuts in operational costs in their respective areas. Extremely reluctant to lay off workers, they mutually agreed on a plan to outsource some work now done by contractors in California to suppliers located abroad.

Delgado and Simmons believed that some of Good Hope's ongoing business processes could be outsourced, including data processing for accounts receivable and accounts payable, certain customer service applications, transcription of medical records, and some data processing. Both managers had heard about the benefits of global sourcing but neither knew how to proceed. So, they began to research their options.

The Downside of Global Sourcing

In the course of their research, Delgado and Simmons also learned that services are frequently more challenging to outsource than manufacturing. This is partly because it is usually more difficult to judge the quality of services than that of manufactured products. Firms that use global sourcing sign legal contracts with suppliers binding themselves to deliver promised levels of service. In reality, there is much variation in the quality of services delivered. To achieve satisfactory outcomes, the contracting firm should emphasize developing trust and understanding with the supplier, especially critical in cross-cultural settings. Delgado and Simmons wondered about the enforceability of legal agreements in different country settings.

Another potential concern was the quality of workers. Some foreign suppliers cannot hire a sufficient number of skilled managers to oversee the work performed by their staffs. Workers must be trained, supervised, and properly motivated. Could Good Hope provide such support and technical assistance?

Delgado and Simmons also read troubling stories about firms whose offshore operations proved to be more costly than originally planned. They read about firms that lost customers and jeopardized their reputations because of poor customer service received from abroad. Delgado and Simmons also worried about breach of confidentiality—to what extent could they rely on foreign organizations to keep patient data confidential? The various risks implied that Good Hope would need to interact closely and frequently with the external supplier, which would add substantial costs in terms of negotiating, transacting, and monitoring, as well as international travel. Delgado and Simmons realized they would need to approach global sourcing very carefully.

Offshoring Destinations

Delgado and Simmons next focused their research on identifying the most promising foreign locations for offshoring. Their investigation revealed that India was the most popular choice for many types of services. The country's outsourcing sector had been growing at 25 to 50 percent per year. India's labor costs are 25 to 40 percent of those in the United States and English is widely spoken. The team learned that reputable firms such as IBM, Dell, and Citicorp had offshored numerous service operations to India.

Their investigation revealed that China was also a potential destination. The country has millions of suitable workers and soon is expected to rival India as a provider of services such as insurance underwriting and back-office operations. Outsourcing costs are currently lower in China than in India. However, a concern is China's reputation for excessive regulation and bureaucracy. Delgado and Simmons wondered if they could develop sufficient trust and understanding with partners in an unfamiliar and distant culture with language differences.

Eastern Europe also emerged as a promising location. The region is culturally similar to the United States, and wages in much of the region are on par with those in India. For example, while Indian accountants earn roughly $10 an hour, wages are substantially lower in Bulgaria and Romania. The Czech Republic is a popular location and is the site of business-process centers for firms such as DHL, Siemens, and Lufthansa. One expert claimed the quality of work in the Czech Republic sometimes surpasses the best available in India. Even Infosys, the giant Indian IT firm, has major support operations in the Czech Republic. But Eastern European countries sometimes have a shortage of qualified labor, particularly among middle managers. As the region's economies develop, social and health insurance costs are also increasing. Taxes can be high and bureaucratic governments hinder efficient business operations. Corruption is a problem in some countries.

Delgado and Simmons also considered sites in Latin America such as Chile, Mexico, and Costa Rica. Latin America offered various attractions. In addition to being cost effective, it is much closer to the United States and generally in the same time zone. Outsourcing customer service to Latin America also makes sense to Californians, many of whom speak Spanish as their first language. But Latin America's outsourcing infrastructure is still young, and Delgado and Simmons worried about whether they could find an appropriate supplier. Numerous other outsourcing locations were possible around the world. For Delgado and Simmons, the number of options was bewildering. Somehow they had to reach a decision.

Help from an Outsourcing Broker

The executives sought the assistance of an outsourcing broker, a consultant with expertise in finding subcontractors and services suppliers abroad. Brokers are especially useful for firms new to outsourcing or those that lack the resources to find foreign suppliers on their own. Eventually the broker found a supplier in India that appeared well suited to meet Good Hope's needs. For example, for transcribing doctor's notes and other medical documents, Simmons learned that Good Hope would pay 12 cents per word, 5 cents less than charged by the firm's current supplier in California. Simmons determined that Good Hope would save about $640,000 a year on medical transcriptions alone. When the accounting and customer service work were added to the mix, the executives discovered that Good Hope would save roughly $1.4 million annually. Delgado was elated: "How else could we shave so much from our expenses with so little effort? And best of all, we don't have to lay off any of our own workers."

The Supplier Firm

To meet all their outsourcing needs, Delgado and Simmons settled on a firm in Bangalore, India, known as BangSource. According to the outsourcing broker, BangSource had a good reputation and was already handling accounting, data processing, transcription, and customer service operations for several large U.S. hospitals. BangSource expects to pick up many new accounts in Australia, Canada, and Europe. BangSource is located in one of the fastest-growing areas of Bangalore and buses in workers from all around the region. The outsourcing broker confided that although BangSource's employee turnover rate was 25 percent, this was consistent with the rate at other outsourcing firms.

The consultant put Good Hope in touch with Mr. Singh, a manager at BangSource and recent graduate of one of India's numerous MBA programs. Mr. Singh explained that BangSource had been in business for about 4 years and had quickly achieved considerable expertise in various business processes. BangSource had recently begun to hire computer engineers and marketing personnel, as the firm was planning to increase its outsourcing capabilities to include software development and telemarketing.

The Situation One Year Later

In the year following the signing of a contract with Bang-Source, Good Hope encountered various problems. The cost of BangSource's services proved to be significantly higher than what Mr. Singh had originally forecast. Processing of accounting and other data was more complex than anticipated, so costs had escalated. Also, BangSource proved less efficient in addressing Good Hope's customer service queries, and required more telephone time and phone calls to address customer needs. Although the Indian customer service workers generally spoke perfect English, some had hard-to-understand accents and a few of Good Hope's customers had complained. Various misunderstandings arose between BangSource and Good Hope as management at the respective firms attempted to refine activity processing. The problem was exacerbated by recent fluctuations in the rupee-dollar exchange rate, which sometimes inflated the cost of BangSource's services even further.

In addition, while BangSource's business had increased substantially in the previous year, provision of electrical power by the local energy utility had not kept pace, and BangSource occasionally experienced power outages and downtime of computer systems. Growing demand for workers in the Bangalore area delayed hiring efforts, and BangSource was sometimes late in performing promised services due to a shortage of skilled workers. BangSource also faced problems hiring enough qualified managers, which further impaired the quality of its accounting and call-center services.

Delgado and Simmons were disappointed and unsure whether Good Hope was better off today than a year earlier. Top management was pressing the team to solve the problems. As the pair prepared to fly to India to meet with BangSource management, they knew that outsourcing could succeed but they had to figure out how to overcome the various challenges.

AACSB: Reflective Thinking, Ethical Reasoning

Case Questions

1. What motives and specific strategic goals can Good Hope achieve by outsourcing to India? Identify strategic goals that Good Hope could potentially achieve in the future.

2. What are the specific risks that Good Hope faced and potentially faces in outsourcing the activities to India?

3. What specific guidelines should management at Good Hope have taken into account as it ventured into global sourcing? What should Good Hope do now to resolve the problems it faces in outsourcing to BangSource?

4. Suppose that thousands of additional firms in California decided to outsource their back-office activities (such as accounting, finance, and data analysis) to India. What would be the implications of such a trend to California's workers and economy? What steps could California take to reduce the potential harm to its citizens of widespread global sourcing?

Sources: Dahl, Darren. (2005). "Outsourcing the Outsourcing," *Inc. Magazine*, December, pp. 55–56; *Economist*. (2004). "A World of Work: A Survey of Outsourcing," November 13, special section; *Economist*. (2005). "The Rise of Nearshoring," December 3, pp. 65–67; *Economist*. (2005). "India: The Next Wave," December 17, pp. 57–58; Engardio, Pete. (2006). "The Future of Outsourcing: How It's Transforming Whole Industries and Changing the Way We Work," *Business Week*, January 30, p. 58; Ewing, Jack, and Gail Edmondson. (2005). "The Rise of Central Europe," *Business Week*, December 12, pp. 50–56; Human Resources Outsourcing Association Europe. (2007). "Outsourcing's Future Holds Major Surprises for Global Providers," April 13, at www.hroaeurope.com.

Key Terms

business process outsourcing (BPO), p. 486

captive sourcing, p. 487

configuration of value-adding activity, p. 487

contract manufacturing, p. 488

global sourcing, p. 484

global supply chain p. 497

offshoring, p. 489

outsourcing, p. 486

Summary

In this chapter, you learned about:

1. Trends toward outsourcing, global sourcing, and offshoring

Global sourcing refers to the procurement of products or services from suppliers or company-owned subsidiaries located abroad for consumption in the home country or a third country. **Outsourcing** is the procurement of selected value-adding activities, including production of intermediate goods or finished products, from external independent suppliers. **Business process outsourcing** refers to the outsourcing of business functions such as finance, accounting, and human resources. Procurement can be from either independent suppliers or via company-owned subsidiaries or affiliates. **Offshoring** refers to the relocation of a business process or entire manufacturing facility to a foreign country. Managers make two strategic decisions regarding value-adding activities: whether to *make or buy* inputs and where to locate value-adding activity—that is, the geographic **configuration of value-adding activity**. **Contract manufacturing** is an arrangement in which the focal firm contracts with an independent supplier to have the supplier manufacture products according to well-defined specifications.

2. Evolution of global sourcing

Today much of the growth in global sourcing is in the services sector, in areas such as IT, customer support, and professional services. India has received the bulk of outsourced business services, while China is favored for manufacturing. But other countries, mostly emerging markets, are viable outsourcing destinations as well. Hundreds of billions of dollars of business services are outsourced to foreign suppliers annually. The potential for global sourcing remains huge. Certain conditions make countries popular recipients of outsourced activity, including workers' mastery of English, a skilled labor force, low labor costs, and strong intellectual-property protections.

3. Benefits and challenges of global sourcing for the firm

Global sourcing aims to reduce the cost of doing business or to achieve other strategic goals. For some entrepreneurs, global outsourcing has provided the means to turn around failing businesses, speed up the pace of innovation, or fund development projects that are otherwise unaffordable. Other benefits of global sourcing include faster corporate growth, the ability to access qualified personnel, improved productivity and service, redesigned business processes, faster foreign market entry, access to new markets, and technological flexibility. Global sourcing also allows firms to focus on their core activities and continuously renew their strategic assets.

4. Implementing global sourcing through supply-chain management

The efficiency with which goods can be physically moved from one part of the globe to another makes global sourcing feasible. **Global supply chain** refers to the firm's integrated network of sourcing, production, and distribution, organized on a world scale, and located in countries where competitive advantage can be maximized.

5. Risks in global sourcing

Global sourcing involves business risks, including failure to realize anticipated cost savings, environmental uncertainty, the creation of competitors, engaging suppliers with insufficient training, overreliance on suppliers, and eroding the morale of existing employees. Firms should approach global sourcing very carefully, with meticulous planning.

6. Strategies for minimizing risk in global sourcing

Firms should develop a strategic perspective in making global sourcing decisions. Although cost cutting is usually the first rationale, global sourcing is also a means to create customer value and improve the firm's competitive advantages. It is a tool to enhance the quality of offerings, improve productivity, and free up resources that can be redeployed to improve long-term performance. To make global sourcing succeed, management should gain employee cooperation, emphasize strong supplier relations, safeguard its interests in the supplier relationship, and choose the right foreign suppliers.

7. **Implications of global sourcing for public policy and corporate citizenship**

   Global sourcing is a means to sustain or enhance firm competitiveness, but can also contribute to job losses and declining living standards. Some firms outsource to suppliers that employ sweatshop labor. But attempts to prohibit global sourcing are impractical. Governments should enact policies in the home country that encourage job retention and growth by reducing the cost of doing business and by encouraging entrepreneurship and technological development. Public policy should aim to develop a strong educational system and upgrade the modern skills of the population.

Test Your Comprehension AACSB: Reflective Thinking, Ethical Reasoning

1. What are the differences between outsourcing, global sourcing, and offshoring?

2. What is business process outsourcing? What are its implications for company strategy and performance?

3. What are the two strategic decisions that managers face regarding the firm's international value chain, and what are their implications for company performance?

4. Identify the various benefits that companies receive from global sourcing. Why do firms outsource to foreign suppliers?

5. What two countries are the most important global sourcing destinations today? What are the basic differences between these two countries, and what activities are typically outsourced to each?

6. What are the characteristics that make countries attractive as global sourcing destinations?

7. In what service industries are jobs commonly outsourced to foreign suppliers?

8. What are the risks that firms face in global sourcing?

9. What steps can managers take to minimize the risks of global sourcing?

10. What are the major guidelines for strategic global sourcing? What actions can management take to make global sourcing succeed?

11. What are the advantages and disadvantages of global sourcing to the nation? What public policy initiatives are likely to reduce the disadvantages of global sourcing?

Apply Your Understanding AACSB: Reflective Thinking, Ethical Reasoning

1. Revisit the opening vignette at the beginning of this chapter. Assume you have started a new job as a junior manager at a pharmaceutical firm. Management is considering outsourcing some of the firm's value chain to suppliers located abroad. Which activities is the firm most likely to outsource? Identify the benefits that your firm can obtain and the specific strategic goals that it could potentially achieve by undertaking global sourcing.

2. Suppose your new job is at Intel, the world's largest semiconductor company and the inventor of the microprocessors found in many personal computers. Intel combines advanced chip design capability with a leading-edge manufacturing capability. The firm is well known for advanced R&D and innovative products. Intel has much of its manufacturing done in China, to take advantage of low-cost labor and an educated workforce capable of producing Intel's knowledge-intensive products. Intel has been stepping up its R&D activity in China and collaborates with Chinese firms in new-technology development. Identify the risks that Intel faces in its operations in China. What strategies and proactive measures can Intel management take to safeguard its interests? What long-term strategic goals does Intel achieve by offshoring from China?

3. Global sourcing helps firms increase their business competitiveness. But it also contributes to job losses in the home country. Some firms outsource to suppliers that employ sweatshop labor. Attempts to prohibit global sourcing are impractical, so governments take other steps to reduce its limitations. What policies should a government adopt to minimize the harm of global sourcing? What can governments in advanced-economy countries do to minimize job loss or encourage job retention and growth? What can such governments do to reduce the problems associated with sweatshops?

globalEDGE Internet Exercises
(http://globalEDGE.msu.edu)

AACSB: Reflective Thinking, Ethical Reasoning, Use of Information Technology, Analytical Skills

Refer to Chapter 1, page 27, for instructions on how to access and use globalEDGE™.

1. You work for a software company that aims to outsource some of its software development to a foreign supplier. At present, you are considering three countries: Hungary, Mexico, and Russia. You need to learn more about the capabilities of these countries as sites for the outsourcing of software development and production. One approach is to visit the research section of the World Bank (www.worldbank.org). At the World Bank Web site, go to Topics, then on Information & Communication Technologies (ICT), then on Tables. For each of the three countries, find and examine variables that indicate the quality of the local software and IT environment. Based on your findings, which country appears strongest for meeting the needs of your firm?

2. International labor standards are complex and closely related to global sourcing. In particular, the use of sweatshops has attracted much attention. A sweatshop is a factory characterized by very low wages, long hours, and poor working conditions. Some sweatshops employ children in unsafe conditions. Various prolabor groups advocate for minimum labor standards in foreign fac-

tories. Suppose your future employer wants to outsource a portion of its production to certain developing countries, but is concerned about the possibility of employing sweatshop labor. Visit the Web sites of groups that encourage minimum standards in labor conditions (for example, www.sweatshopwatch.org, www.aworldconnected.org, www.corpwatch.org, or enter the keywords "labor conditions" at globalEDGE™) and prepare a memo to your employer that discusses the major concerns of those who advocate minimum labor standards.

3. Your firm just decided to outsource to India such back-office operations as accounting and basic finance functions. Unclear on how to proceed, management has asked you to find candidate suppliers in India. As a first step, you decide to check the online Yellow Pages (such as yahoo.com or superpage.com) and search for appropriate Indian firms. Find three firms in India that specialize in business-process outsourcing and examine their Web sites. Describe and compare the business-process services that each firm provides. What selection criteria should you use? Which firm seems most qualified and reputable for providing outsourcing of business-process services?

CKR Cavusgil Knight Riesenberger
Management Skill Builder©

A Smarter Approach to Global Sourcing

Firms now increasingly outsource many of their service activities in much the same way as manufacturing firms outsource parts and components production. While the main motive for global sourcing is to reduce costs, other motives include the ability to achieve strategic goals and concentrate on the firm's core competencies, allowing management to redirect resources to the most profitable uses.

AACSB: Reflective Thinking

Managerial Challenge

Undertaking global sourcing is risky and potentially expensive. Choosing the wrong sourcing partner can lead to unexpected costs and complications. Management at the focal firm must deal with foreign legal systems, tax laws, and bureaucratic regulations. In some countries corruption is commonplace, and the firm may struggle to protect its core technologies and know-how.

Background

The top global sourcing locations include major cities in India, China, the Philippines, and Eastern Europe. But these locations increasingly suffer from shortcomings, particularly shortages of qualified workers, which are pushing up wages. High demand is straining local infrastructure and has led to severe traffic congestion, frequent power outages, and communications blackouts. Other locations—such as Turkey, Thailand, South Africa, Brazil, Mexico, Botswana, and Indonesia—are increasingly attractive outsourcing destinations. Many companies are now seeking new foreign locations to outsource their value-chain activities.

Managerial Skills You Will Gain

In this C/K/R Management Skill Builder©, as a prospective manager, you will:

1. Learn the factors to consider when evaluating countries as potential locations for global sourcing.

2. Understand how these factors relate to maximizing corporate competitive advantages.

3. Use the methodology of screening countries for sourcing potential.

4. Build research skills for planning company operations.

Your Task

Assume that you work for a large investment brokerage firm, such as Merrill Lynch, AIG, Goldman Sachs, or UBS Financial Services. Your firm performs various business process activities (such as accounting, financial analysis, account reconciliation, data entry) that result in substantial ongoing expenses. To reduce costs, management has decided to outsource some of these activities to a foreign business-process subcontractor. Management sought the advice of a global sourcing consultant, who advised that two countries—Russia and Mexico—are particularly good locations for meeting the firm's needs. Your task is to complete the final stages of the analysis by researching Russia and Mexico and recommending which country better meets the brokerage's sourcing needs.

Go to the C/K/R Knowledge Portal©

www.prenhall.com/cavusgil
Proceed to the C/K/R Knowledge Portal© to obtain the expanded background information, your task and methodology, suggested resources for this exercise, and the presentation template.

chapter

17

Marketing in the Global Firm

> Zara's Unique Model for International Marketing Success

The Spanish multinational Inditex has transformed itself into Europe's leading apparel retailer. Inditex's flagship store is Zara, the fashion chain that specializes in up-to-date clothing at affordable prices. Headquartered in northern Spain, Zara generated about $5 billion in sales in 2006 across its stores in some 60 countries. In Asia, Zara has some 40 stores from Bangkok to Tokyo, and opened its first shop in Shanghai in 2006. In the United States, the firm plans to double its store count to more than 50 by 2009.

Zara is a leader in rapid-response retailing. In-house teams produce fresh designs twice a week. While competitors typically have up to an 11–month lead time to move a garment from design to manufacturing, total turn-around time at Zara is just 2 weeks. None of its styles last in stores more than a month. Zara is fast and flexible in meeting market needs by integrating design, production, distribution, and sales within its own stores. Zara created about 20,000 different items in 2006, roughly triple what Gap produced. Because textiles are a labor-intensive business, most retailers source from low-cost shops in Asia. Zara, on the other hand, produces its most fashionable items—50 percent of all its merchandise—at a dozen company-

owned factories in Spain. Clothes with longer shelf life are outsourced to low-cost suppliers in Turkey and Asia.

Zara's supply chain is lightning fast. Once clothing is produced, it is shipped to stores in 24 to 36 hours. Using the latest information technology, garments are continuously scanned as they pass through the distribution channel. Distributors immediately know what is needed for restocking. Predetermined fabrics await design instructions, and suppliers provide other needed materials, such as thread, zippers, and buttons just-in-time. Rapid-response retailing means fashions go straight from the factory to stores. Nevertheless, the Spain-based production and distribution model has its limitations. Rapid-response retailing becomes harder to manage the farther away from Spain the firm's outlets are located.

Stores are both uncluttered and colorful, creating a high-end luxury shopping environment. Management emphasizes product innovation and value pricing. Adapted to individual markets, prices are higher in high-income countries and more competitive in low-income or low-demand countries. Much of the firm's promotional activities depend on creating buzz, generating word-of-mouth, and setting up stores in prominent locations. Zara's flashy outlets are on some of the world's priciest streets: Fifth Avenue in New York, Ginza in Tokyo, Via Condotti in Rome, and the Champs-Elysees in Paris.

Zara's positioning differentiates the firm from key competitors based on pricing (low to moderate) and fashion (slightly formal, chic). For instance, the United States-based chain Gap and Italy's Benetton are positioned as moderately high-priced but not particularly fashion-forward. Sweden's H&M offers merchandise that is casual and targeted to younger people. A key competitive advantage of Zara is that it stays at the very leading edge of fashion.

The retailer follows a unique approach to eliciting consumer feedback. Management reacts quickly to daily sales figures. Using wireless organizers, managers and salespeople in Zara's stores advise headquarters daily about constantly changing consumer tastes. Stores employ retail specialists with a strong sense of fashion who advise on which items move fastest. Fast-moving items are replicated quickly, in a myriad of colors or styles, and slow-moving

items are removed. Zara's researchers also visit college campuses, clubs, and other hotspots. Magazines like Vogue as well as fashion shows provide additional inspiration.

In a fickle industry, often characterized by sluggish growth, Zara has been growing fairly rapidly. The firm is expanding in Asia and North America and penetrating deeper into Europe. Managers intend to apply the same strategies that have proven successful thus far.

Sources: *Business Week*, (2007). "Retailers Need to Boost Product Turnover," January 16. Retrieved from www.businessweek.com; *Business Week*, (2006). "Fashion Conquistador,'" September 4. Retrieved from www.businessweek.com; *Business Week*, (2006). "Zara: Taking the Lead in Fast-Fashion," April 4. Retrieved from www.businessweek.com; Echikson, William. (2000). "The Mark of Zara," *Business Week*, May 29, pp. 98–100; *Economist*, (2005). "The Future of Fast Fashion," June 18, p. 63; Fraiman, Nelson, and Medini Singh. (2002). *Zara*. Case study. New York: Columbia Business School, Columbia University; Heller, Richard. (2001). "Galician Beauty," *Forbes*, May 28, p. 98; Hoovers.com entry on Zara International, Inc.; Inditex press kit, June 2007. www.inditex.com; Inditex Press Release "Business Week Ranks Inditex as the Seventh Best Performing European Company," May 14, 2007; Maitland, Alison. (2005). "Make Sure You Have Your Christmas Stock In," *Financial Times*, December 19, p. 11.

 # Global Marketing Strategy

Marketing brings the customer focus to the firm's cross-border business. Marketing in the internationalizing firm is concerned with identifying, measuring, and pursuing market opportunities abroad. Exhibit 17.1 provides a framework for these activities and previews the topics of this chapter. The outer layer represents the cultural, social, political, legal, and regulatory environment of foreign markets. These environmental conditions constrain the firm's ability to price, promote, and distribute a product. For example, the firm will need to review prices frequently in high-inflation countries, adapt the positioning of the product to suit customer expectations, and ensure products comply with mandated government standards.

Working with the diversity of individual country markets, managers then will need to formulate a global marketing strategy. The middle layer in Exhibit 17.1 represents the **global marketing strategy**—a plan of action that guides the firm in: (1) how to position itself and its offerings in foreign markets and which customer segments to target, and (2) the degree to which its marketing program elements should be standardized and adapted.[1]

Before we turn to the second aspect of global marketing strategy (standardization/adaptation), let's discuss the first function: targeting customer segments and positioning.

Targeting Customer Segments and Positioning

Market segmentation refers to the process of dividing the firm's total customer base into homogeneous clusters in a way that allows management to formulate unique marketing strategies for each group. Within each market segment, customers exhibit similar characteristics regarding income level, lifestyle, demographic pro-

Global marketing strategy A plan of action that guides the firm in how to position itself and its offerings in foreign markets, which customer segments to target, and the degree to which its marketing program elements should be standardized and adapted.

Exhibit 17.1

Organizing Framework for
Marketing in the International Firm

The Environment of International Business
Diverse Cultural, Political, Legal, Monetary, and Financial
Environment of the Firm

Global Marketing Strategy
Targeting Customer Segments and Positioning

**International Marketing Program
Standardization and Adaptation**

Global Branding and Product Development	International Pricing
International Distribution	International Marketing Communications

file, or desired product benefits. As an example, Caterpillar targets its earthmoving equipment by applying distinct marketing approaches to several major market segments, such as construction firms, farmers, and the military. For each of these customer segments, Caterpillar devises a distinct marketing program, for example, creating value-priced tractors for farmers, moderately priced earthmoving equipment for construction firms, and high-priced, heavy-duty trucks and other vehicles for the military.

In international business, firms frequently form market segments by grouping countries together based on macrolevel variables, such as level of economic development or cultural dimensions. For example, many MNEs group the Latin American countries together based on a common language (Spanish or Portuguese), or the European countries together based on similar economic conditions. The approach has proven most effective for product categories in which governments play a key regulatory role (such as telecommunications, medical products, and processed foods) or where national characteristics prevail in determining product acceptance and usage.[2]

Today, firms increasingly target *global* customer or market segments. A **global market segment** represents a group of customers that share common characteristics across many national markets. Firms target these buyers with relatively uniform marketing programs. For example, MTV and Levi Strauss both target a largely homogenous youth market that exists around most of the world. In fact, consumer product

Global market segment A group of customers that share common characteristics across many national markets.

MTV has a global market segment of young adults who enjoy music. Here, members of the Mexican band, Mana, hold their MTV Legend Award at the MTV Video Music Awards Latin America 2006 in Mexico City.

companies are targeting the youth market across advanced and emerging economies. This segment generally follows global media, is quick to embrace new fashions and trends, and has significant disposable income. Another global market segment is jet-setting business executives. They have much disposable affluence and are eager consumers of premium products that represent luxury and sophisticated style.

The firm's objective in pursuing global market segments is to create a unique positioning of its offerings in the minds of target customers. *Positioning* is an aspect of marketing strategy in which the firm develops both the product and its marketing to evoke a distinct impression in the customer's mind, emphasizing differences from competitive offerings. For example, in the international construction industry, Bechtel positions itself as providing sophisticated technical solutions for major infrastructure projects worldwide. In the theme park business, Disney positions itself as standing for family values and "good, clean fun" to attract families to its theme parks around the world.[3]

Positioning may also involve the images of specific product *attributes* held by consumers. For example, Diet Coke elicits an image of someone who needs to lose or maintain weight compared to regular Coca-Cola. When Coca-Cola first entered Japan, research revealed that Japanese women do not like products labeled as "diet," nor is the population considered overweight. Thus, management altered the product's positioning in Japan by changing the name of Diet Coke to Coke Light.

Internationalizing firms aim for a *global positioning strategy*, that is, one in which the offering is positioned *similarly* in the minds of buyers worldwide. Starbucks, Volvo, and Sony are good examples of companies that successfully use this approach. Consumers around the world view these strong brands in the same way. Global positioning strategy is beneficial because it reduces international marketing costs by minimizing the extent to which management must adapt elements of the marketing program for individual markets.[4]

 ## Standardization and Adaptation of the International Marketing Program

In addition to guiding the process of targeting and positioning, global marketing strategy also articulates the degree to which the firm's marketing program should vary across foreign markets. In the innermost layer in Exhibit 17.1, we identify the key elements of the marketing program (sometimes referred to as the *marketing mix*) that are subjected to the standardization/adaptation decision, given the international context. These elements are: global branding and product development, international pricing, international marketing communications, and international distribution. Domestic marketing strategy is concerned with the marketing program elements in a single country. In the international context, marketing strategy takes on additional complexity because of local competitors, as well as cross-national differences in culture, language, living standards, economic conditions, regulations, and quality of business infrastructure. In addition, the firm needs to keep abreast of *global* competitors and optimize its value-chain activities across its various markets. Accordingly, the firm's key challenge is how to resolve the trade-offs between standardizing the firm's marketing program elements *and* adapting them for individual international markets. Since the firm is typically involved in more than a single foreign market, management also must grapple with how best to coordinate marketing activities across national markets.

Adaptation refers to the firm efforts to modify one or more elements of its international marketing program to accommodate specific customer requirements in a particular market. In contrast, **standardization** refers to the firm efforts to make its marketing program elements uniform, with a view to targeting entire regions, or even the global marketplace, with a similar product or service.

Achieving a balance between adaptation and standardization is part of a broader corporate strategy that has the firm debating its position between *global integration* and *local responsiveness*. As we discussed in Chapter 11, global integration seeks worldwide efficiency, synergy, and cross-fertilization in the firm's value-chain activities, while local responsiveness objectives seek to meet the specific needs of buyers in individual countries. How the firm resolves the balance between global integration and local responsiveness affects how it makes standardization and adaptation decisions in its marketing program elements.

Exhibit 17.2 highlights the trade-offs between standardization and adaptation in international marketing. Let's now examine the arguments for, and advantages of, each strategy.

Adaptation Firm efforts to modify one or more elements of its international marketing program to accommodate specific customer requirements in a particular market.

Standardization Firm efforts to make its marketing program elements uniform, with a view to targeting entire regions, or even the global marketplace, with a similar product or service.

Standardization

Representing a tendency toward global integration, standardization is more likely to be pursued in global industries such as aircraft manufacturing, pharmaceuticals, and credit cards. Boeing, Pfizer, and MasterCard are examples of firms that use standardized marketing strategy with great success. Their offerings are largely uniform across many markets worldwide. A standardized marketing approach is most appropriate when:

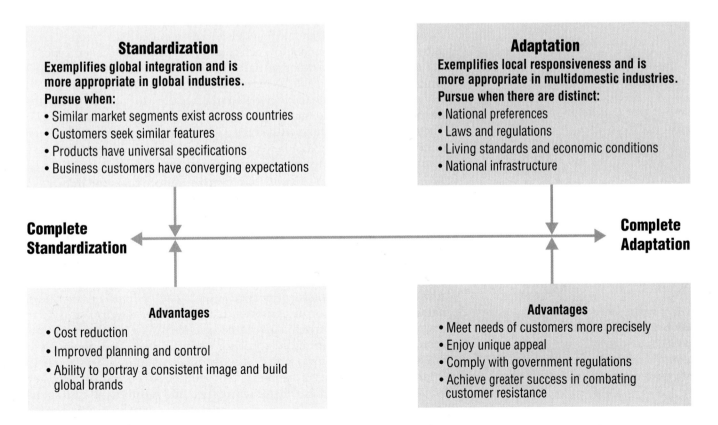

Exhibit 17.2 Tradeoffs between Adaptation and Standardization of International Marketing Program

Popular consumer electronics such as Apple's iPod can gain a worldwide following and require little adaptation from country to country.

- Similar market segments exist across countries.
- Customers seek similar features in the product or service.
- Products have universal specifications.
- Business customers have converging expectations such as quality and performance.

The viability of standardization varies across industries and product categories. For example, commodities, industrial equipment, and high-technology products lend themselves to a high degree of standardization. Popular consumer electronics (e.g., Sony's PlayStation, Apple's iPod, and Canon digital cameras) and several well-known fashion accessories (e.g., Rolex watches and Louis Vuitton handbags) are largely standardized around the world. Automotive parts, building materials, dinnerware, and basic food ingredients are other examples of products that require little or no adaptation.

When managers build on commonalities in customer preferences and attempt to standardize their international marketing program, they can expect at least three types of favorable outcomes.

- *Cost Reduction.* Standardization reduces costs by enabling economies of scale in design, sourcing, manufacturing and marketing. Offering a similar marketing program to the global marketplace or across entire regions is more efficient than having to adapt products for each of numerous individual markets. For example, the appliance manufacturer Electrolux once made hundreds of refrigerator models to accommodate the diverse tastes and regulatory requirements of each country in Europe. However, as product standards and tastes gradually harmonized across the European Union, Electrolux was able to reduce the number of its refrigerators to a few dozen models. The move allowed management to consolidate manufacturing facilities and streamline its marketing activities across the EU. The resulting consolidation saved Electrolux millions of euros. With fewer offerings, the company can better concentrate on incorporating advanced features and superior technology into its products.

- *Improved Planning and Control.* Standardization provides for improved planning and control of value-adding activities. In the case of Electrolux, for example, fewer offerings mean that management can simplify quality control and reduce the number of parts that it stocks for repairing defective products. Marketing activities are also simplified. Instead of designing a unique marketing campaign for each country in Europe, the firm is able to standardize its campaigns.

- *Ability to Portray a Consistent Image and Build Global Brands.* A *brand* is a name, sign, symbol, or design intended to identify the firm's product and differentiate it from those of competitors. A **global brand** is a brand whose positioning, advertising strategy, look, and personality are standardized worldwide. Standardization allows the firm to establish and project a globally recognized corporate or product brand that helps increase customer interest and reduces the confusion that arises from the proliferation of numerous adapted products and marketing programs.[5] Marketing is more effective and efficient because the firm can serve larger global market segments that transcend multiple countries.

Global brand A brand whose positioning, advertising strategy, look, and personality are standardized worldwide.

As an example, Gillette, the U.S. shaving products company recently acquired by Procter & Gamble, sells the same products using uniform marketing in all the countries where it does business, often engaging in a simultaneous global launch. The firm has successfully launched its line of shavers (such as Trak II, Sensor, and Fusion) across multiple countries. Results have been impressive. While achieving 70 percent market share in the world shaver market, Gillette's global approach allows management to minimize the cost of marketing and distribution.[6]

Adaptation

While standardizing where they can, firms will also engage in adaptation. Adaptation of an international marketing program exemplifies local responsiveness. It is a strategy used in *multidomestic industries*, which tailor their offerings to suit individual markets. Examples include publishing and software industries, where books, magazines, and software must be translated into the language of the target country. Adaptation may be as simple as translating labels and instructions into a foreign language, or as complex as completely modifying a product to fit the needs of unique market conditions. Local adaptation can provide the marketer with important advantages. Let's explore the major reasons why firms may adapt marketing program elements.

Differences in National Preferences. Adaptation makes the offering more acceptable to customers in individual markets. Differences in consumer behavior around the world are a major driver of local adaptation. For example, when targeting China, the dairy producer New Zealand Milk adds ginger and papaya flavoring to its milk products to suit the tastes of local customers. The Netherlands' Foremost Friesland Co. sells green tea-flavored fresh milk in Thailand. Japan's Meiji Co. is selling a pandan-flavored milk in Singapore.[7] When *The Simpsons* cartoon series was broadcast in Saudi Arabia, it was substantially adapted for language and local Islamic sensibilities. The show was renamed *Al Shamshoon*, Homer Simpson's name was changed to "Omar," and Bart Simpson became "Badr." The program aims to win coveted young viewers, who constitute a large proportion of the population in the Arab world. In addition to translating the show into Arabic, producers had to deal with the way the Simpson daughter and mother dress. Producers removed references to practices forbidden by the Qur'an or considered potentially offensive, such as consuming pork and beer. Producers changed Homer Simpson's Duff beer to soda, hot dogs to Egyptian beef sausages, and donuts to the popular Arab cookies called *kahk*. Moe's Bar was completely written out of the show. As one Arab viewer told ABC News "It's different. . . . we are a totally different culture, so you can't be talking about the same subject and in the same way."[8]

McDonald's has been able to standardize its hamburgers across most world markets, but not all. Because some people do not eat beef—for example, Hindus in India—the company substitutes lamb in its burgers in some markets, while adding to its menu additional items such as Kofte burgers (hamburger with special spices) in Turkey. In Japan, McDonald's offers shrimp burgers, as well as miso soup and rice. McDonald's outlets in Norway serve "McLaks"—a grilled salmon sandwich with dill sauce. In Berlin, consumers can savor a beer with their double cheeseburgers and fries. In some Arab countries, the "McArabia"—a flatbread, spicy chicken filet—has been a success.[9]

Differences in Laws and Regulations. The promotion of certain products is restricted in some countries. For example, laws in Europe, including Germany, Norway, and Switzerland, restrict advertising directed at children. Packaged foods in Europe are often labeled in several different languages, including English, French, German, and Spanish. In Quebec, Canada's French-speaking province, local law requires product packaging to be in both English and French. The use of some sales promotion activities—for example, coupons and sales contests—is restricted or just not customary in some markets.

Differences in Living Standards and Economic Conditions. Because income levels vary substantially around the world, firms typically adjust both the pricing and the complexity of their product offerings for individual markets. For example, Microsoft has had to lower the price of its software for some markets (e.g., Thailand, Malaysia, and Indonesia) in order to bring it in line with local purchasing power.[10] Dell sells simplified versions of its computers in developing economies to accommodate lower local spending power. Inflation and economic recessions also influence pricing policy. A recession signals a drop in consumer confidence, and the firm may need to reduce prices in order to generate sales. High inflation can rapidly erode profits, even as prices rise. Exchange rate fluctuations also necessitate adjustments. When the importing country currency is weak, the buying power of its consumers is reduced. But when the importing country currency is strong, buyers can afford to pay higher prices for imported products.

Differences in National Infrastructure. The quality of transportation networks, marketing institutions, and overall business infrastructure particularly influences the alternatives and quality of marketing communications and distribution systems that firms employ abroad. Infrastructure is especially poor in the rural parts of developing economies, which necessitates innovative approaches for getting products to customers. For example, the density of roads and rail networks in western China is underdeveloped. Firms use small trucks to reach retailers in outlying communities. Deficiencies in media require substantial adaptations to promotional activities. In rural Vietnam, most consumers cannot access television, magazines, or the Internet. Radio, billboards, and brochures are favored for targeting low-income buyers.

What can managers expect when they accommodate these differences by customizing international marketing program elements? Primary advantages of adapting an international marketing program to the individual market include the following:

- Meeting needs of customers more precisely
- Creating unique appeal for the product
- Complying with such government regulations as health and technical standards
- Achieving greater success in combating customer resistance

In addition, adaptation provides managers with an opportunity to explore alternative ways of marketing the product or service. Such knowledge of market reactions to customized offerings can guide the firm in its R & D efforts, often leading to superior products for sale abroad and at home. In fact, products developed or modified for foreign markets sometimes prove so successful that they are launched as new products in the firm's home market. For example, Toyota originally designed the Lexus for the U.S. market. After perfecting the luxury car during 15 years in the United States, the firm launched Lexus in Japan in 2005.[11]

Standardization and Adaptation: A Balancing Act

A managerial decision about the degree of standardization and adaptation is not an either/or decision, but, rather, a balancing act. There are good arguments and outcomes in favor of both standardization and adaptation; it is up to the manager to sort out the trade-offs in light of the unique circumstances of the international business environment and the firm's chosen strategy.

Perhaps the most important distinction between standardization and adaptation is that standardization helps the firm reduce its costs, while adaptation helps the firm more precisely cater to local needs and requirements, thereby increasing its revenues. While there are many reasons for firms to engage in adaptation of their international marketing program, adaptation is costly. Adaptation may require substantial redesign of products, modifications to manufacturing operations, lower pricing, and overhauled distribution and communications strategies. The costs add up when these changes simultaneously multiply in numerous national markets. Therefore, whenever possible, managers usually err on the side of standardization because it is easier and less costly than adaptation. Others adapt marketing program elements *only when necessary,* to respond to local customer preferences and mandated regulations. For instance, the Anglo-Dutch MNE Unilever streamlined the number of its brands from over 1,600 to about 400 and focused attention on a dozen or so global brands. However, the firm had to retain many local adaptations to suit individual markets. In nutrition-conscious countries, Unilever is adapting its food products by lowering the levels of sugar, salt, trans-fats, and saturated fats.

Often managers will engage in standardization and adaptation simultaneously, at varying degrees. They will make adjustments to some elements of the marketing program while keeping others intact. For example, IKEA will maintain product design uniformity across markets while making modifications to, say, the size of beds or drawers it sells in individual countries. Similarly, it will emphasize its catalog as the principal promotional tool but supplement it with TV advertising in a mass-media oriented market such as the United States.

It is also rarely feasible or practical to follow a "one offering-one world" strategy across *all* dimensions of the marketing program. For example, automotive companies tried for years to market a "world car" that meets customer preferences everywhere as well as complying with various government-imposed safety specifications. Ambitious experiments such as the Ford Mondeo failed to meet the approval of customers and regulatory bodies around the world. Flexibility and adaptability in design became necessary due to climate and geography (for example, engine specifications), government regulations (emissions standards), customer preferences (e.g., cupholders), and gas prices.

As a compromise, some firms will pursue standardization as part of a *regional* strategy, where international marketing program elements are formulated to exploit commonalities across a geographic region instead of across the world. For example, General Motors markets distinctive car models for China (e.g., Buick), Europe (Opel, Vauxhall), and North America (Cadillac, Saturn). Convergence of regional preferences, regional economic integration, harmonization of product standards, and growth of regional media and distribution channels all make regional marketing more feasible than pursuing global marketing approaches.[12]

Global Branding and Product Development

Global marketing strategy poses unique challenges and opportunities for managers, particularly in the marketing program elements of global branding and global product development. Let's review these specific topics.

Global Branding

A key outcome of global positioning strategy is the development of a global brand. Well-known global brands include Hollywood movies (for example, Star Wars), pop stars (Shakira), sports figures (David Beckham), personal care products (Gillette Sensor), toys (Barbie), credit cards (Visa), food (Cadbury), beverages (Heineken), furniture (IKEA), and consumer electronics (iPod).[13] Consumers prefer globally branded products because branding provides a sense of trust and confidence in the purchase decision.[14] A strong global brand enhances the efficiency and effectiveness of marketing programs, stimulates brand loyalty, facilitates the ability to charge premium prices, increases the firm's

Well-known celebrities such as Shakira are considered global brands because they command worldwide appeal and premium value.

Exhibit 17.3

Top Global Brands, by Region, 2007

SOURCE: *Business Week* (www.businessweek.com/brand) and *Interbrand* (www.interbrand.com)

Company	Brand Value U.S.$ billions	Country of Origin	Main Product or Service
Asian Brands			
Toyota	24.8	Japan	Cars
Honda	15.8	Japan	Cars
Samsung	15.0	South Korea	Consumer electronics
Sony	10.7	Japan	Consumer electronics
Canon	9.0	Japan	Copiers, cameras
European Brands			
Nokia	26.5	Finland	Cell phones
Mercedes-Benz	20.0	Germany	Cars
BMW	17.1	Germany	Cars
Louis Vuitton	16.1	France	Fashion accessories
Nescafé	12.2	Switzerland	Coffee
U.S. Brands			
Coca-Cola	67.5	United States	Soft drinks
Microsoft	59.9	United States	Software
IBM	53.4	United States	IT services and consulting
GE	47.0	United States	Appliances, jet engines
Intel	35.6	United States	Computer chips

leverage with intermediaries and retailers, and generally enhances the firm's competitive advantage in global markets.[15] The firm can reduce its marketing and advertising costs by concentrating on a single global brand instead of a number of national brands.

The strength of a global brand is best measured by its brand equity—the market value of a brand. Exhibit 17.3 provides brand equity figures for selected global brands, as calculated by Interbrand (www.interbrand.com), a European-based company. *Business Week* devotes a special issue each year to Interbrand's list of the top 100 global brands (www.businessweek.com/brand). To qualify for Interbrand's list, a brand must first generate worldwide sales exceeding $1 billion, at least a third of which should come from outside the home market. Then, Interbrand estimates the projected brand earnings and deducts a charge for the cost of owning the tangible assets from these earnings. Finally, Interbrand calculates the net present value of future brand earnings, ending with an estimate of brand value.

You may wish to look up the entire list of 100 global brands on the *Business Week* portal. What makes these brands so successful in capturing such a worldwide following? Here are the underlying features that make these brands special:

- Some are highly visible, conspicuous consumer products, such as consumer electronics and jeans.
- Some serve as status symbols worldwide, such as cars and jewelry.
- Many have widespread appeal because of innovative features that seem to fit everyone's lifestyle, such as mobile phones, credit cards. and cosmetics.
- Some are identified with the country of origin and command a certain degree of country appeal, such as Levi's (American style) and IKEA furniture (Scandinavian style).

Still, in other cases, global brands are reaping the benefits of first-mover advantages in offering new and novel products or services. For example, in 1971 the first

Starbucks opened in Seattle, Washington, and offered freshly-brewed coffee in a comfortable setting that encouraged people to sit and relax. Nokia, originally founded as a Finnish wood-processing plant in 1865, reengineered itself in the 1990s to become one of the world's leading telephone exchange and mobile phone companies. It has distanced itself from competitors by investing in new technologies and design. Samsung Electronics, part of a larger South Korean conglomerate, also propelled itself into consumer electronics with unique design and leading-edge technology. Interestingly, Sony—a long-time leader in consumer electronics—turned to Samsung in 2004 to help it gain a foothold in the flat-panel TV market.

Developing and maintaining a global brand name is the best way for firms to build global recognition and maximize the effectiveness of their international marketing program. For example, the Eveready Battery Co. consolidated its various national brand names—such as Ucar, Wonder, and Mazda—into one global brand name, Energizer. The move greatly increased the efficiency of Eveready's marketing efforts around the world. While most managers conceive brands for a national market and then internationalize them, the preferred approach is to build a global brand from the beginning. Several firms have succeeded in this approach, including Japan's Sony Corporation. "Sony" was derived from the Latin for "sound." Another Japanese firm, Datsun, switched to Nissan worldwide to create a unified global brand.[16]

Global branding also helps the MNE compete more effectively with local brands, which are often quite popular because they appeal to buyers' sense of local tradition, pride, and preference. For example, market leaders Coca-Cola and Pepsi face many local brands around the world. In Europe, popular local brands include Virgin Cola (Britain), Afri-Cola (Germany), Kofola (Czech Republic), and Cuba Cola (Sweden). Cola Turka was developed to help retain soft drink profits in its native Turkey and challenged the dominance of Coca-Cola and PepsiCo. In Peru, Inca Kola was long a successful local brand that established itself as "Peru's Drink." But Inca Kola's experience revealed how local brands can be vulnerable to the market power of strong global brands. In 1999, Coca-Cola purchased 50 percent of the Inca Kola Corporation. Inca Cola and Coke each have about 30 percent of the Peruvian market, giving Coke an edge since it owns half of the former local brand.

Global Product Development

In developing products with multicountry potential, managers emphasize the commonalities across countries rather than the differences between them.[17] A basic product will incorporate only core features into which the firm can inexpensively implement variations for individual markets. For example, while the basic computers that Dell sells worldwide are essentially identical, the letters on its keyboards and the languages used in its software are unique to countries or major regions. Everything else in the computers is largely identical. Firms design many products using *modular architecture,* a collection of *standardized* components and subsystems that can be rapidly assembled in various configurations to suit the needs of individual markets. Honda and Toyota design models like the Accord and Corolla, respectively, around a standardized platform to which modular components, parts, and features are added to suit specific needs and tastes.

General Motors has been relying on its *Global Product Development Council* in Detroit to improve efficiency. Concerned about duplication of effort across its divisions, GM top management took authority away from regional engineering operations and charged the council with overseeing $7 billion annual spending on new model development. The council promotes company-wide use of GM's best car platforms, wherever they are developed, worldwide. For example, it adapted the Holden Monaro from its Australian subsidiary for North American use as the GTO rather than creating a totally new model. As a result, development cost was a modest $50 million instead of the $500 million it would typically cost to create a new model.

A *global team* is a group within a firm that develops common solutions and global products. As we discussed in Chapter 11, global teams are assigned to formulate best practices that a firm would implement in all of its worldwide units. Global teams assemble employees with specialized knowledge and expertise from various geographically diverse units of the MNE, who collaborate in a project to develop workable solutions to common problems.

The *Global Trend* feature highlights the increasing use of global teams in the development of global products and designs. You may wish to do a quick on-line search for creative product designs that benefited from global teams. For example, the iRobot Roomba Discovery Floorvac, designed by iRobot Corporation, performs domestic chores by navigating its way through rooms without falling down stairs. The iXi Bike was designed in Britain, France, and the United States for France's iXi Bicycle Company. The bike fits easily into the trunk of a small car. Lenovo Smartphone ET960 was designed by a team from East Asia. The lightweight telephone is an MP3 and media player, a game console, and can receive television transmissions. PerfectDraft was developed for Belgium's Inbev Company.

A special feature of global development is the opportunity for a firm to engage in global product launch—simultaneous roll-out of a new product across multiple markets. Simultaneous launch of products that cater to a global clientele has also become increasingly common because it provides scale economies in R&D, product development, production, and marketing. IT products (for example, Apple computers), software (Microsoft), pharmaceuticals (Viagra), movies (*The Matrix*), and many consumer products (Gillette's razor series) are often introduced simultaneously across several countries or geographic regions.

 International Pricing

Pricing is complex and generally subjective in domestic business. It is even more difficult in international business, with multiple currencies, trade barriers, additional cost considerations, and typically longer distribution channels. Managers readily acknowledge the critical role of prices in international markets' success.[18] After all, prices do have a measurable effect on sales and directly affect profitability. Prices often invite competitive reaction, which can drive down a price. Conversely, prices can escalate to unreasonable levels because of tariffs, taxes, and higher markups by foreign intermediaries. Price variations among different markets can lead to **gray market activity**—legal importation of genuine products into a country by intermediaries other than authorized distributors (also known as parallel imports). We discuss gray markets later in this chapter.

Pricing interacts with and affects all other marketing program elements. Prices influence customers' perception of value, determine the level of motivation to expect from foreign intermediaries, have an impact on promotional spending and strategy, and compensate for weaknesses in other elements of the marketing mix. Let's explore the unique aspects of international pricing.

Factors Affecting International Pricing

Factors that influence pricing for international customers fall into four categories. First is the *nature of the product or industry*. A specialized product, or one with a technological edge, gives a company greater price flexibility. When the firm holds a relative monopoly in a given product (such as Microsoft's operating system software), it can generally charge premium prices.

The second factor is the *location of the production facility*. Locating manufacturing in countries with low-cost labor enables a firm to charge cheaper prices. Locating factories in or near major markets cuts transportation costs and may eliminate problems created by foreign exchange fluctuations. During the 1980s, for example,

Gray market activity Legal importation of genuine products into a country by intermediaries other than authorized distributors (also known as parallel imports).

Designing Global Products with Global Teams

Until the 1990s, product development and design was a sequential process, usually based in a single country. Marketers and engineers agreed on a set of technical specifications and they developed a product and sent it to the factory for manufacturing. However, development in a single national environment meant that the product required much adaptation for selling abroad. Today, many more firms develop global products that are intended for world markets from the outset. Product designers work in virtual global teams, held together by information and communications technologies. Firms usually draw global team members from various functional areas in subsidiaries around the globe. The firm identifies members based on their comparative advantages rather than on their physical location.

Consider how Verifone develops its latest telecommunications products at its development centers in France, India, Singapore, Taiwan, and the United States. Management emphasizes a strong global culture of interpersonal communications and information sharing among the centers and team members. The firm uses international rotational assignments, ongoing training, videoconferencing, and crossnational social events to facilitate cross-fertilization of knowledge. As another example, the Boeing 777 was developed by design teams composed of experts from Europe, Japan, and the United States. The company separated the jet design plans into tail, fuselage, wings, and other modular sections. A global team developed and designed each section. Boeing management prefers the team approach because it leverages comparative advantages provided by designers and engineers in specific countries as well as the core competencies of the best subcontractors and experienced personnel, wherever they are located worldwide.

While the global team approach requires careful cross-national coordination, it results in offerings that are both cost effective and suitable for major markets worldwide. Design and development occur simultaneously, and many companies co-opt suppliers and customers. Such teams allow firms to optimize their global resources, run their design and development operations on a 24–hour clock, and launch new products in record time.

Modern communications technology enables global teams. Groupware and Web-enabled design and product development applications allow multinational teams to seamlessly manage product development and design. Teams use computer-aided design (CAD)—which facilitates three-dimensional design on compatible computer systems—to integrate contributions from their counterparts from around the world. Sophisticated software allows the team to pilot various product configurations at virtually no cost. Rapid prototyping means that a firm can test new designs on global customers and modify them based on market research.

How do companies organize the global design process? Best-in-class firms manage the global team effort centrally, typically from company headquarters. Success depends on obtaining and sharing the latest data on customer needs and circumstances and continuously measuring product development performance internally and with partners. International market research is critical. To continuously learn what customers are thinking, many firms use online communities and *blogs* (*weblogs*), a user-generated portal where entries are made and displayed in journal style. Blogs combine text, images, Internet links, and the ability for members to leave interactive comments.

Sources: Aberdeen Group. (2005). *The Global Product Design Benchmark Report: Managing Complexity as Product Design Goes Global,* December, Boston: Aberdeen Group; *BusinessWeek Online.* (2006). "Special Report: Innovation," April 24. Retrieved from www.businessweek.com; *Business Week,* (2005). "The Best Product Designs of 2005," July 4. Retrieved from www.businessweek.com; Galbraith, Jay. (2000). *Designing the Global Corporation.* San Francisco: Jossey-Bass; Keller, Robert. (2001). "Cross-Functional Project Groups in Research and New Product Development," *Academy of Management Journal,* 44(3), pp. 547–555; Murray, Janet, and Mike C. H. Chao. (2005). "A Cross-Team Framework of International Knowledge Acquisition on New Product Development Capabilities and New Product Market Performance," *Journal of International Marketing,* 13(3), pp. 54–73.

Toyota and Honda built car factories in the United States, their most important foreign market. But Mazda retained much of its manufacturing in Japan, exporting its cars to the United States. As the Japanese yen appreciated against the dollar, Mazda had to raise its prices, which hurt its U.S. sales.

The third factor that influences international pricing is the *type of distribution system.* Exporting firms rely on independent distributors based abroad, who occasionally modify export pricing to suit their own goals. Some distributors mark up prices substantially—up to 200 percent in some countries—which may harm the manufacturer's image and pricing strategy in the market. By contrast, when the firm internationalizes via FDI by establishing company-owned marketing subsidiaries abroad, management can maintain control over pricing strategy. Firms that make direct sales to end users also control their pricing and can make rapid adjustments to suit evolving market conditions.

The fourth factor is *foreign market considerations.* Such foreign market factors as climate and other natural conditions may require the firm to spend money to modify a product or its distribution. Food items shipped to hot climates require refrigeration, which drives up costs. In countries with many rural residents, or those with a poor distribution infrastructure, delivering products to widely dispersed customers necessitates higher pricing because of higher shipping costs. Foreign government intervention is also a critical factor. Governments impose tariffs that lead to higher prices. Many governments also impose limits on prices. For example, Canada imposes price limits on prescription drugs, which reduces the firm's pricing flexibility. Health rules, safety standards, and other regulations increase the cost of doing business locally, which necessitates higher prices.

Exhibit 17.4 provides a comprehensive list of the factors, both internal and external to the firm, that influence how firms set international prices. Ini-

Exhibit 17.4

Internal and External Factors That Affect International Pricing

---

Internal to the Firm

- Management's profit and market share expectations
- Cost of manufacturing, marketing, and other value-chain activities
- The degree of control management desires over price setting in foreign markets

External Factors

- Customer expectations, purchasing power, and sensitivity to price increases
- Nature of competitors' offerings, prices, and strategy
- International customer costs:
  - Product/package modification; labeling and marking requirements
  - Documentation (certificate of origin, invoices, banking fees)
  - Financing costs
  - Packing and container charges
  - Shipping (inspection, warehousing, freight forwarder's fee)
  - Insurance
- Landed cost
  - Tariffs (customs duty, import tax, customs clearance fee)
  - Warehousing charges at the port of import; local transportation
- Importer's cost
  - Value-added tax and other applicable taxes paid by the importer
  - Local intermediary (distributor, wholesaler, retailer) margins
  - Cost of financing inventory
- Anticipated fluctuations in currency exchange rates

tially, management must account for its own objectives. Most firms seek to maximize profits abroad. However, many companies focus on market share, often charging low prices in order to gain the largest number of customers. Earlier in this chapter we discussed other factors, such as control issues and the cost of production and marketing. Many countries in Europe and elsewhere charge value-added taxes (VATs) on imported products. Unlike a sales tax, which is calculated off of the retail sales price, the VAT is determined as a percentage of the gross margin—the difference between the sales price and the cost to the seller of the item sold. In the EU, for example, VAT rates range between 15 and 25 percent.

A Framework for Setting International Prices

Managers examine the suitability of prices at several levels in the international distribution channel—importers, wholesalers, retailers, and end users—and then set prices accordingly. Exhibit 17.5 presents a systematic approach for managers to use to set international prices at various levels.[19]

Let's illustrate the international pricing framework with an example. Suppose that a leading musical instrument manufacturer, Melody Corporation, wants to begin exporting electric guitars to Japan and needs to set prices. Initially, Melody will export its "John Mayer" line of guitars, which normally retail at around $2,000 in the United States. Initial research reveals that added costs of shipping, transportation insurance, and a 5 percent Japanese tariff will add a total of $300 to the price of each guitar, bringing the total landed price to $2,300. Melody has identified an importer in Japan, Aoki Music Wholesalers, which wants to add a 10 percent profit margin to the cost of each imported guitar. Thus, the total price once a

---

Step 1. Estimate the "landed" price of the product in the foreign market by totaling all costs associated with shipping the product to the customer's location.

Step 2. Estimate the price the importer or distributor will charge when it adds its profit margin.

Step 3. Estimate the target price range for end users. Determine:
- Floor price (lowest acceptable price to the firm, based on cost considerations)
- Ceiling price (highest possible price, based on customer purchasing power price sensitivity and competitive considerations)

Step 4. Assess the company sales potential at the price the firm is most likely to charge (between the floor price and ceiling price).

Step 5. Select a suitable pricing strategy based on corporate goals and preferences from:
- Rigid cost-plus pricing
- Flexible cost-plus pricing
- Incremental pricing

Step 6. Check consistency with current prices across product lines, key customers, and foreign markets (in order to deter potential gray market activity).

Step 7. Implement pricing strategy and tactics, and set intermediary and end-user prices. Then, continuously monitor market performance and make pricing adjustments as necessary to accommodate evolving market conditions.

Exhibit 17.5

Key Steps in International Price Setting

guitar leaves Aoki's Japan warehouse is $2,530, which is also the lowest acceptable price to Melody (the floor price), since management doesn't want Japanese earnings to dip below those in the United States.

Next, market research on per capita (per person) income levels and competitor prices reveals that Japanese musicians are willing to pay prices about 20 percent above typical U.S. prices for high-quality instruments. Given this information, Melody management believes that Japan can sustain a ceiling price for the Mayer guitar of 10 percent above the floor price—that is, $2,783. Next, management commissions a report from a Japanese market research firm that estimates Melody's sales potential at the floor price and at the ceiling price. Managers eventually decide on a suggested price of $2,560, representing a desire to get established quickly in the Japanese market. This price is also consistent with other factors in the target market, such as Japanese purchasing power, market growth, Japan's large musician population, competitors' prices, and Japanese attitudes on the relationship of price to product quality. Management also feels the price is reasonable given the Melody's pricing in other markets, such as Hawaii and Australia. Accordingly, the firm implements the price level for end users and the corresponding price for its importer, Aoki. Melody begins shipping guitars to Japan and monitors the marketplace, paying close attention to actual demand and the need to make any pricing adjustments in coming months.

Let's review the three pricing strategies in Step 5 of Exhibit 17.5. *Rigid cost-plus pricing* refers to setting a fixed price for all export markets. It is an approach favored by less experienced exporters. In most cases, management simply adds a flat percentage to the domestic price to compensate for the added costs of doing business abroad. The export customer's final price includes a mark-up to cover transporting and marketing the product, as well as profit margins for both intermediaries and the manufacturer. This method often fails to account for local market conditions, such as buyer demand, income level, and competition.

In *flexible cost-plus pricing,* management includes any added costs of doing business abroad in its final price. At the same time, management adjusts prices as needed to accommodate local market and competitive conditions, such as customer purchasing power, demand, competitor prices, and other external variables, as identified in Exhibit 17.4. This approach is more sophisticated than rigid cost-plus pricing because it accounts for specific circumstances in the target market. In the opening vignette, Zara uses this approach, adapting prices to suit conditions in each of the countries where it does business.

In highly competitive markets, the firm may set prices to cover only its variable costs, not its fixed costs. This is known as *incremental pricing.* Here, management assumes that fixed costs are already paid from sales of the product in the firm's home country or other markets. The approach enables the firm to offer very competitive prices, but must be pursued carefully because it may result in suboptimal profits.

When carried to an extreme, incremental pricing may invite competitors to accuse a firm of dumping. As discussed in Chapter 7, *dumping* is the practice of charging a lower price for exported products, sometimes below manufacturing cost—potentially driving local suppliers out of business. The seller may compensate for the low price by charging higher prices in other markets. Many national governments regard dumping as a form of unfair competition and, consequently, may impose antidumping duties or initiate legal action with the World Trade Organization.

Managing International Price Escalation

International price escalation The problem of end-user prices reaching exorbitant levels in the export market caused by multilayered distribution channels, intermediary margins, tariffs, and other international customer costs.

International price escalation refers to the problem of end-user prices reaching exorbitant levels in the export market caused by multilayered distribution channels, intermediary margins, tariffs, and other international customer costs (identified in Exhibit 17.4). International price escalation may mean that the retail price in the export market may be two or three times the domestic price, creating a competitive disadvantage for the exporter. Managers can use five key strategies to combat export price escalation abroad.[20]

First, the exporter can attempt to *shorten the distribution channel.* The exporter can set up a more direct route to reach the final customer by bypassing some intermediaries in the channel. With a shorter channel, there are fewer intermediaries to compensate, which reduces the product's final price. Second, the *product can be redesigned* to remove costly features. For example, Whirlpool developed a no-frills, simplified washing machine that it can produce inexpensively and which it sells for a lower price in developing economies. Third, the firm can *ship its products unassembled,* as parts and components, qualifying for lower import tariffs. The firm will then perform final assembly in the foreign market, often by low-cost labor. Some firms have their product assembled in Foreign Trade Zones, where import costs are lower and government incentives may be available.[21] Fourth, some firms explore whether the product can be *re-classified using a different tariff classification* to qualify for lower tariffs. Suppose that Motorola faces a high tariff when exporting "telecommunications equipment" to Bolivia. By having the product reclassified as "computer equipment," Motorola might be able to export the product under a lower tariff. The practice is possible because imported products often fit more than one product category for determining tariffs. Finally, the firm may decide to *move production or sourcing to another country* to take advantage of lower production costs or favorable currency rates.

Managing Pricing under Varying Currency Conditions

The strength of the home-country currency vis-à-vis its trading partners affects the firm's pricing abroad. For example, when the U.S. dollar is strong, it costs Europeans more to purchase U.S. products. Conversely, when the U.S. dollar is weak, it costs Europeans relatively less to purchase U.S. products. In export markets, a strong domestic currency can deter competitiveness, while a weakening domestic currency makes the firm's pricing more competitive. Examine Exhibit 17.6 for strategies firms can use to react to either weakening or appreciating domestic currencies.[22]

Transfer Pricing

Also known as intracorporate pricing, **transfer pricing** refers to the practice of pricing intermediate or finished products exchanged among the subsidiaries and affiliates of the same corporate family located in different countries.[23] For example, when Ford's factory in South Africa sells parts and components to the Ford manufacturing plant in Spain, it charges a transfer price for this intracorporate transaction. These prices, for products transferred within the Ford corporate family, generally differ from the market prices that Ford charges its external customers.

MNEs like Ford attempt to manage internal prices primarily for two reasons. First, companies use transfer pricing to repatriate—that is, to bring back to the home country the profits from countries that restrict MNEs from taking their earnings out of the country. Occasionally, a foreign government may block the transfer of funds out of the country, often due to a shortage of its own currency. When this happens, the MNE might opt to charge high prices to its foreign affiliate as an alternative means of transferring money out of the affiliate's country. In this way, the affiliate transfers substantial funds to the parent, by paying high prices for goods imported from the parent. The strategy works because controls imposed on money transferred in this way are not normally as strict as controls imposed on straight repatriation of profits. Second, transfer pricing can serve as a vehicle for MNEs to shift profits out of a high corporate income-tax country into a low corporate

Transfer pricing The practice of pricing intermediate or finished products exchanged among the subsidiaries and affiliates of the same corporate family located in different countries.

Exhibit 17.6

Strategies for Dealing with Varying Currency Conditions

When the exporter gains a price advantage because its home-country currency is WEAKENING relative to the customer's currency, then it should:	When the exporter suffers from a price disadvantage because its home-country currency is APPRECIATING relative to the customer's currency, then it should:
Stress the benefits of the firm's low prices to foreign customers.	Accentuate competitive strengths in nonprice elements of its marketing program, such as product quality, delivery, and after-sales service.
Maintain normal price levels, expand the product line, or add more costly features.	Consider lowering prices by improving productivity, reducing production costs, or redesigning the product to eliminate costly features.
Exploit greater export opportunities in markets where this favorable exchange rate exists.	Concentrate exporting to those countries whose currencies have not weakened in relation to the exporter.
Speed repatriation of foreign-earned income and collections.	Maintain foreign-earned income in the customer's currency and delay collection of foreign accounts receivable (if there is an expectation that the customer's currency will regain strength over a reasonable time period).
Minimize expenditures in the customer's currency (for example, for advertising and local transportation).	Maximize expenditures in the customer's currency.

income-tax one and thereby increase company-wide profitability. When this occurs, the MNE may opt to maximize the expenses (and therefore minimize the profits) of the foreign-country affiliate by charging high prices for goods sold to the affiliate. MNEs typically centralize transfer pricing under the direction of the chief financial officer at corporate headquarters.

Consider Exhibit 17.7 for a simple illustration of transfer pricing. A subsidiary may buy or sell a finished or intermediate product from another affiliate at below cost, at cost, or above cost. Suppose that the MNE treats Subsidiary A as a favored unit. That is, Subsidiary A is allowed to *source at or below cost* and *sell at a relatively high price* when transacting with other subsidiaries. When consistently applied over a period of time, Subsidiary A will produce relatively more favorable financial results, at the expense of Subsidiaries B, C, and D. Why would the MNE headquarters allow this? In this scenario, the favored Subsidiary A is likely to be in a country that has:

- Lower corporate income-tax rates
- High tariffs for the product in question
- Favorable accounting rules for calculating corporate income
- Political stability
- Little or no restrictions on profit repatriation
- Strategic importance to the MNE

While the subsidiary's financial performance has been boosted in an artificial way, the earnings of the MNE as a whole are optimized. Nevertheless, this benefit

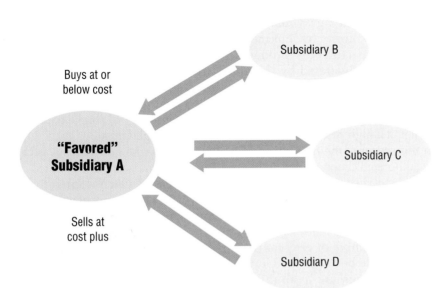

often comes at a cost. First, there is the complication of internal control measures. Manipulating transfer prices makes it very difficult to determine the true profit contribution of a subsidiary. Second, morale problems typically surface at a subsidiary whose profit performance has been made to look worse than it really is. Third, some subsidiary managers may react negatively to price manipulation. Fourth, there is the concern about local accounting regulations. Subsidiaries, as local businesses, must abide by the rules. Legal problems will arise if the subsidiary follows accounting standards that are not approved by the host government. Indeed, many governments closely scrutinize transfer pricing practices of multinational companies to ensure that foreign companies pay their fair share of taxes by reporting accurate earnings.

Gray Market Activity (Parallel Imports)

What do companies such as Caterpillar, Duracell, Gucci, Mercedes-Benz, and Sony have in common? They are MNEs with established brand names that have been the target of gray market activity. Exhibit 17.8 illustrates the nature of flows

Exhibit 17.8 Illustration of Gray Market Activity

and relationships in a gray market activity—the legal importation of genuine products into a country by intermediaries other than authorized distributors.[24] Consider a manufacturer that produces in the source country and exports its products to another, illustrated by the green arrow between countries A and B in Exhibit 17.8. If the going price of the product happens to be sufficiently lower in Country B, then gray market brokers can exploit arbitrage opportunities—buy the product at a low price in Country B, import it into the original source country, and then sell it at a high price there, illustrated by the orange arrow.

In this scenario, the first transaction, illustrated by the green arrow, is carried out by authorized channel intermediaries. The second transaction, illustrated by the red arrow, is carried out by unauthorized intermediaries. Often referred to as *gray marketers,* the unauthorized intermediaries are typically independent entrepreneurs. Because their transactions parallel those of authorized distributors, gray market activity is also called *parallel importation.*

A recent example of gray marketing activity can be drawn from the pharmaceutical trade between the United States and Canada where, in the latter, prescription drugs are available at a lower cost. Some consumers in the United States purchase their prescription drugs from online pharmacies in Canada, at a considerable saving. The gray market opportunity arises because the Canadian provinces negotiate with pharmaceutical companies in establishing a wholesale price—often lower than the prevailing price in the United States. Though the U.S. Federal Drug Administration discourages importation of drugs from other countries since their authenticity or efficacy cannot be verified, consumers continue to fill their prescriptions through Internet pharmacies in Canada. Gray market activity is especially common among premium brands of automobiles, cameras, watches, computers, perfumes, and even construction equipment. It also occurs in international buying and selling of commodities, such as light bulbs and car parts.

You can see that the root cause of gray market activity is a sufficiently large difference in price of the same product between two countries. Such a price difference may be due to either: (1) the manufacturer's inability to coordinate prices across its markets, or (2) a conscious effort on the part of the firm to charge higher prices in some countries when competitive conditions permit. Exchange rate fluctuations may also exacerbate gray market activity by widening the price gap between products priced in two different currencies.

Manufacturers of branded products have good reason to be concerned. Substantial gray market activity complicates at least three aspects of their business. First, there is the risk of a tarnished brand image when customers realize that the product is available at a lower price through alternative channels—particularly less-prestigious outlets. Second, manufacturer-distributor relations can be strained because parallel imports result in lost sales to authorized distributors. Third, gray market activity can disrupt regional sales forecasting, pricing strategies, merchandising plans, and other marketing efforts.

In the United States, the legality of parallel imports had not been initially clarified (hence the term *gray* markets) until the U.S. Supreme Court ruled in 1988 that trademark owners cannot prevent parallel importation. By ruling in favor of the gray market brokers, the Supreme Court acted to serve the best interests of the consumer, who has access to *genuine* (not counterfeit) products at substantially lower prices. Since lobbying by the COPIAT (The Coalition to Preserve the Integrity of American Trademarks) has not produced adequate legislation to stop gray market imports, companies are now compelled to develop their own solutions to combat such activity.

Companies can pursue at least four strategies to cope with gray market imports.[25] First, they can counter through aggressive *price-cutting* in countries and regions targeted by gray market brokers. Second, they can interfere with the flow of products into markets where gray market brokers procure the product. For example, the U.S. firm Pfizer could substantially reduce the shipment of its cholesterol drug Lipitor to Canada to levels that would be just sufficient for local use by Canadian patients. Third, companies can publicize the limitations of gray market channels. Trademark owners such as pharmaceutical companies could flood the media with messages that tactfully build doubt about gray market products. Consumers who fill their prescriptions via online Canadian pharmacies have been warned that the products they receive through these channels may be counterfeits. Indeed, this is a legitimate concern, since counterfeit drugs do make their way into pharmacies in Canada and the United States.[26] Finally, firms can design products with exclusive features that strongly appeal to customers. Adding safety, luxury, or functional features that are unique to each market reduces the likelihood that products will be channeled elsewhere.

 # International Marketing Communications

Companies use *marketing communications* (also known as *promotion*) to provide information to and communicate with existing and potential customers, with the ultimate aim of stimulating demand. International marketing communications emphasize advertising and promotional activities. The nature of these activities can vary substantially around the world. Let's examine them in more detail.

International Advertising

Firms conduct advertising via *media*, which includes direct mail, radio, television, cinema, billboards, transit, print media, and the Internet. *Transit* refers to ads placed in buses, trains, and subways, and is particularly useful in large cities. *Print media* refer to newspapers, magazines, and trade journals. We can assess media availability by examining the amount of advertising spending by region. In 2006, advertising expenditures on major media (newspapers, magazines, television, radio, cinema, billboards, and Internet) amounted to approximately U.S. $100 billion in each of Western Europe and Asia-Pacific. In the United States, advertising expenditures totaled almost U.S. $200 billion.

The availability and quality of media closely determine the feasibility and nature of marketing communications. Exhibit 17.9 provides statistics on media

	Literacy Rate (percentage of population)	Percentage of Households with Television	Radio Stations per one Million People	Newspapers per one Million People
Argentina	97	97	6.5	2.7
Australia	99	96	30.0	2.4
China	91	91	0.5	0.7
India	60	37	0.2	4.8
Japan	99	99	9.2	0.9
Mexico	92	92	13.0	2.9
Netherlands	99	99	15.2	2.1
Nigeria	68	26	0.9	0.2
South Africa	86	54	13.7	0.4
United States	99	99	46.7	5.0

Note: Data are for the most recent year available.

Exhibit 17.9

Media Characteristics in Selected Countries

SOURCES: CIA World Factbook at www.cia.gov; World Bank at www.worldbank.org

Many firms use a standardized approach to international advertising. Benetton's standardized 'United Colors of Benetton' ad has enjoyed much success worldwide.

for various countries. The literacy rate indicates the number of people who can read—a critical ability for understanding most ads. Other data reveal the diversity of communication media in selected countries. Media are widely available in advanced economies. In developing economies, however, TV, radio, the Internet, and newspapers may be limited. The firm must use creative approaches to advertise in countries with low literacy rates and limited media infrastructure. Certain media selections make sense for some countries but not for others. For example, Mexico and Peru emphasize television advertising, Kuwait and Norway concentrate on print media, and Bolivia uses a lot of outdoor advertising on billboards and buildings.

At the firm level, international advertising expenditures vary depending on the size and extent of the firm's foreign operations. For instance, smaller firms often lack the resources to advertise on TV or develop a foreign sales force. Differences in culture, laws, and media availability mean that it is seldom possible to duplicate in foreign markets the type and mix of advertising used in the home market. For example, the Italian government limits television advertising on state channels to 12 percent of airtime per hour and 4 percent per week. Mexico and Peru require that firms produce commercials for the local audience in their respective countries and use local actors.

Advertising conveys a message encoded in language, symbols, colors, and other attributes, each of which may have distinctive meanings. Buyer receptiveness differs as a function of culture and language. Culture determines buyer attitudes toward the role and function of advertising, humor content, the depiction of characters (such as the role of men and women), and decency standards. In China, Nike Inc. ran an ad produced for the U.S. audience in which NBA basketball star LeBron James battles—and defeats—a computer-generated Chinese Kung Fu master. Chinese consumers were offended and China's national government banned the ad.[27]

Many MNEs succeed in applying a relatively standardized approach to international advertising. Benetton, the Italian clothing manufacturer, has run essentially the same and highly successful, "United Colors of Benetton" ad campaign, which features interracial harmony, in markets worldwide. Levi Strauss' advertising approach is similar around the world, stressing the all-American image of its jeans. One TV ad in Indonesia showed teenagers cruising around a small U.S. town in 1960s convertibles. In Japan, Levi's frequently used James Dean, the 1950s U.S. film star, as the centerpiece of its advertising. The dialogue in Levi's ads is often in English, worldwide.[28] The most effective ad campaigns are based on a full understanding of the target audience's buying motivations, values, behavior, purchasing power, and demographic characteristics.

Most MNEs employ advertising agencies to create promotional content and select media for foreign markets. The choice is usually between a home-country-based agency with international expertise, a local agency based in the target market, and a *global ad agency* that also has offices in the target market. Exhibit 17.10 identifies the leading global advertising agencies. Such agencies maintain networks of affiliates and local offices around the world. Consequently, they can create advertising that is both global and sensitive to local conditions while offering a range of additional services such as market research, publicity, and package design.

Rank	Agency	Headquarters	Parent Company
1	McCann Erickson Worldwide	U.S.	Interpublic Group, U.S.
2	Ogilvy & Mather	U.S.	WPP Group, U.K.
3	Grey Worldwide	U.S.	WPP Group, U.K.
4	Euro RSCG Worldwide	U.S.	Havas, France
5	Saatchi & Saatchi	U.S.	Publicis Groupe, France
6	BBDO Worldwide	U.S.	Omnicom Group, U.S.
7	Publicis	France	Publicis Groupe, France
8	JWT	U.S.	WPP Group, U.K.
9	Y&R Advertising	U.S.	WPP Group, U.K.
10	Lowe Worldwide	U.K.	Interpublic Group, U.S.

Exhibit 17.10 The Largest Global Ad Agencies, 2005

SOURCE: Adapted from Endicott, R. Craig. (2005). "Ad Age Global Marketing Report 2005," *Advertising Age*, Nov. 14.

International Promotional Activities

Promotional activities are short-term marketing activities intended to stimulate an initial purchase of the product, immediate purchase, or increased purchases, as well as to improve intermediary effectiveness and cooperation. They include tools such as coupons, point-of-purchase displays, demonstrations, samples, contests, gifts, and Internet interfacing. Some promotional activities (for example, couponing) are illegal or restricted abroad. For instance, Greece, Portugal, and Spain permit virtually every type of promotion, but Germany, Norway, and Switzerland forbid or restrict some. Other promotional activities, such as giveaways, may be considered unethical. Depending on the country, some consumers may be turned off by particular activities. In much of the world, promotional activities are relatively uncommon and may be misunderstood. For example, receiving a free gift is difficult to interpret in some societies. Promotional activities usually require a high level of intermediary or retailer sophistication in order to succeed.

Global Account Management

With more transparent markets, global customers demand uniform and consistent prices, quality, and customer service. **Global account management (GAM)** refers to servicing a key global customer in a consistent and standardized manner, regardless of where in the world it operates. For example, Wal-Mart is a key global account for Procter & Gamble as it purchases a substantial amount of products from P&G. Wal-Mart expects consistent service, including uniform prices for the same product from P&G regardless of where in the world they are delivered. Key accounts such as Migros, Zellers, and Wal-Mart typically purchase from a collection of preferred suppliers who meet their specifications. Suppliers target these key customers by shifting resources from national, regional, and function-based operations to GAM, whose programs feature dedicated cross-functional teams, specialized coordination activities for specific accounts, and formalized structures and processes. Private IT-based portals facilitate the implementation of such systems. Each global customer is assigned a global account manager, or team, who provides the customer with coordinated marketing support and service across various countries.[29]

Global account management (GAM) Servicing a key global customer in a consistent and standardized manner, regardless of where in the world it operates.

International Distribution

Distribution refers to the processes of getting the product or service from its place of origin to the customer. Distribution is the most inflexible of the marketing program elements—once a firm establishes a distribution channel, it may be difficult to change it. As we discussed in chapters 3 and 13, the most common approaches to international distribution include engaging independent intermediaries (for exporting firms), or establishing marketing and sales subsidiaries directly in target markets (an FDI-based approach).

For exporters, intermediaries typically include foreign distributors, agents, trading companies, and export management companies. Many exporters prefer a full stocking distributor because it possesses product knowledge, expert personnel, physical facilities (such as warehousing), and financial resources. When the firm enters a market with direct investment, it will establish a subsidiary. This implies investing directly in the market to lease, acquire, or set up a sales office, production facilities, warehouse, or an entire distribution channel. Entering a new market as a foreign direct investor provides various advantages. First, it helps ensure control over marketing and distribution activities in the target market. Second, it facilitates monitoring the performance of employees and other actors in the local market. Third, it allows the firm to get close to the market, which is especially helpful when the market is complex or rapidly changing.

Some firms bypass traditional distribution systems altogether by using *direct marketing*—selling directly to end users. To supplement direct marketing efforts, many firms use the Internet to provide detailed product information and the means for foreigners to buy offerings. Some firms, such as Amazon.com, are entirely Internet-based, with no retail stores. Others, such as Carrefour, Coles, and Tesco, combine direct marketing with traditional retailing.

The international distribution channel differs for the exporter and the foreign subsidiary. The exporter ships goods to its intermediary, who moves the product through customs and the foreign distribution channel to retail outlets or end users. By contrast, the foreign subsidiary may function as its own distributor, working directly with customers and retailers to move offerings through the channel into the local marketplace. *Channel length* refers to the number of distributors or other intermediaries that it takes to get the product from the manufacturer to the market. The longer the channel, the more intermediaries the firm must compensate, and the costlier the channel. For example, Japan is characterized by long distribution channels involving numerous intermediaries. High channel costs contribute to international price escalation, creating a competitive disadvantage for the firm.

 # Ethical Dimensions of International Marketing

Because of market globalization, firms' marketing activities strongly influence the buying decisions of consumers worldwide. MNEs now recognize that their customers and other stakeholders expect them to act in a socially responsible manner and display corporate citizenship in their international operations. Many MNEs are proactively developing policies aimed at meeting higher expectations of the public. An important dimension of corporate citizenship is the way firms develop and align their products and services to create greater value for society. In marketing, ensuring that suppliers earn a sustainable income, providing needed products to poor consumers, and disposing of used products responsibly are examples of issues that are high on the corporate social responsibility (CSR) agenda.

For example, in its 7,400 outlets throughout Europe, McDonald's in 2007 began selling coffee sourced only from growers certified by the Rainforest Alliance. The nonprofit organization aims to ensure a sustainable income to the world's poorest coffee growers, mostly in Africa.[30] In a similar move, Nestlé in 2005 joined the Fair Trade movement and began offering a brand of coffee that is sourced from farmers who receive a guaranteed price above world market levels.

Meanwhile, some firms are developing products to serve the needs of the world's poor, such as a bicycle rigged to carry heavy loads, and simple pumps for irrigating crops during the dry season. Such products help people who cannot afford labor-saving and technological products ordinarily targeted to customers in advanced economies. For example, Quanta Computers Inc. makes a laptop computer that is inexpensive enough—around U.S. $100—to help ensure that children in poor countries have access to the information technologies that drive the world economy. The computer is aimed at the nearly 2 billion children in developing economies who receive little or no education.[31]

Motorola has developed various initiatives to promote greater access to mobile communications in developing economies where fixed-line telecommunications are often inadequate or nonexistent, and hinder productivity and economic development. Telephone service is a critical vehicle that promotes increased entrepreneurship and improved GDP. Many countries leapfrogged into fixed-line infrastructure and developed mobile phone networks to support national telecommunication needs. Between 2006 and 2010, it is estimated that the number of mobile customers in developing economies will double, surpassing two billion users. To support this growth, Motorola delivered more than 16 million low-cost (under $30) mobile phones to more than 50 developing countries. In 2006, the firm helped develop a mobile phone-based system for disease management in Africa, where field health workers file patient reports and check drug supplies by mobile phone. Cellular connectivity helps professionals in poor areas deal more effectively with disease outbreaks, medicine shortages, and health maintenance.[32]

A critical environmental issue in marketing is the proper disposal of used products. In the United States, for example, consumers own more than three billion electronic products, ranging from cellular telephones to computers and television sets. Rapid technological changes mean that the life expectancy of these goods is growing shorter. They are usually discarded not because they are broken, but because better versions become available. Products that could be recycled instead end up in landfills, harming the natural environment. In Europe, national governments have passed legislation to deal with the problem. The Waste Electrical and Electronic Equipment (WEEE) directive of the European Union makes companies responsible for collecting and recycling unwanted electronic goods. Similar legislation has been passed in some U.S. states. European law also restricts the types of materials (e.g., harmful substances such as lead and mercury) that can be used to manufacture electronic products. Meanwhile, Cisco and other firms have created incentive programs that encourage consumers to return their old equipment, often for credit toward the purchase of new products. Cisco's program is designed as a financial incentive to prevent old equipment from piling up in landfills.[33]

MTV India: Balancing Global and Local Marketing

MTV Networks (www.mtv.com), a division of Viacom, has a big audience among young people in Asia, Australia, Canada, Europe, and Latin America. In total, MTV is broadcast in more than 170 countries in 32 languages. Only 20 percent of all MTV viewers live in the United States, the company's home market. There are 136 distinct MTV channels and 230 Web sites, and they are more widely viewed than any other global network, including CNN. Originally created as a basic cable channel dedicated to music, MTV now encompasses an array of media services and even licensed consumer products.

MTV first went international in 1987 when it launched MTV Europe. With the U.S. market near saturation, management decided to target the huge and growing youth market abroad. Indeed, about one in four people around the world is between 15 and 34 years old. Despite being a global media giant, MTV maintains its international strategy of "Think globally and locally, act appropriately." Management requires that about 70 percent of its programming be developed or adapted for each of the youth segments that it targets abroad. But while most MTV channels have flourished, especially in Brazil and the United Kingdom, others have struggled to find a niche, especially in Asia, and more specifically, in India.

With 470 million people between the ages of 10 and 34, India seems like a huge potential market. India's middle class is rapidly expanding, and the number of households with TV sets has skyrocketed in recent years to 100 million, half of which receive cable. Economic liberalization has made it easier for foreign businesses to enter India. Nevertheless, the Indian market poses various challenges. There are roughly 100 distinctive cable channels vying for advertising dollars. Competition for cable subscribers is intense, and profit margins are often razor thin. There is also corruption and theft, including cable cutting, piracy, and theft of subscriber fees. Indian families typically watch TV as an entire household, which makes it difficult for advertisers to isolate target audiences.

MTV first entered India through a low-risk licensing agreement with Hong Kong's Star TV. Initially MTV was responsible only for programming, while Star TV focused on negotiating deals with local cable companies and advertisers. Because individual markets remained small and undeveloped, MTV management developed a regional marketing strategy by delivering a pan-Asian music channel.

Later, Star TV was sold to the News Corporation, the media giant owned by Rupert Murdoch. News Corporation had its own music channel, known simply as [V], so Star TV ended its partnership with MTV and even hired key staffers away from MTV to develop a new music channel specifically for India. As MTV continued to follow a regional marketing approach, targeting all of Asia and employing English-speaking hosts, management at [V] pursued a different approach. It decided to adapt its music channel to accommodate the preferences of customers in individual Asian markets. This approach paid off, as [V] managed to capture much of MTV's market share. Over time, as [V] flourished, MTV struggled to gain share using its more standardized programming.

MTV also committed some blunders that hurt its prospects in Asia. MTV's Indian staff initially insisted that widely popular Bollywood music (Bollywood is the Indian equivalent of the Hollywood movie industry) wasn't "cool" enough for the teen market. However, the Indian audience disagreed, and MTV's ratings suffered. Gradually, several other music channels emerged, hosted in a variety of local dialects in the population.

Finally, in the late-1990s MTV management opted for a more localized approach and began adapting its programming. It launched MTV India, based in Mumbai, and broadcast across Bangladesh, Nepal, Pakistan, Sri Lanka, and the Middle East as well. MTV India utilized new technologies, such as digital compression, to achieve its goals of increased local programming. When MTV began including more Bollywood music in its programming, ratings soared by 700 percent. Hosts began to speak a mix of both English and Hindi, dubbed "Hinglish." MTV also targeted Indian youth with cricket matches and fashion shows. As the sophistication of its strategy improved, MTV grabbed more market share and eventually surpassed its main rival, [V]. On a worldwide basis, however, MTV's Indian profitability was still low compared to the firm's other international subsidiaries, mainly due to poor advertising revenue.

MTV needed to be creative to become profitable. Initially, it established relationships with advertisers. Instead of merely selling time slots to advertisers, MTV developed programming that incorporates a particular product or brand. For example, the firm worked with Honda to develop "Roadies," a series that documents the experiences of seven young people traveling across India on Honda motorbikes. MTV also created the "World's Longest Dance Party," sponsored by Axe deodorant, and a fashion awards show, sponsored by Lycra.

Ultimately, MTV management discovered that it could not simply export U.S. programming to India. Shows that were extremely popular in the United States, such as "The Osbournes," floundered in India. MTV catered increasingly to the Indian audience, developing costly programming tailored to specific cultural traits and other characteristics.

Localization of TV programming seems to have worked well for MTV. Nevertheless, MTV managers are concerned that the firm may not be reaping the benefits of a global marketing strategy. Programming is broadcast worldwide, but many channels are highly localized, reducing potential gains from economies of scale. Thus, the latest strategic initiative is to develop uniform programming that sells in multiple countries. Therefore, MTV has greatly increased funding of international programming and has developed a jointly based team out of London and New York to develop ideas.

In addition, suspecting that it is missing out on opportunities to cater to the youth market with alternative products and services such as video games, MTV also wishes to explore the feasibility of becoming a one-stop shop for companies hoping to reach global youth markets. For instance, in an advertising relationship with Motorola, MTV aired commercials in Europe, Latin America, and Asia. To supplement revenues, MTV is also considering launching a line of consumer products—fragrances, CDs, and clothing—designed for the youth market.

MTV continues to seek international growth from emerging markets such as China and Mexico, where strong per capita income gains are expected. Management believes that international operations are capable of earning 40 percent of total revenue in the near term. Yet, the goal of sustaining a profitable organization by striking an ideal balance between local adaptation and global standardization has been very elusive.

AACSB: **Reflective Thinking**

Case Questions

1. What strategies and tactics in marketing program elements are most important in MTV's international operations?

2. What is MTV's main international market segment? What are the characteristics of this segment? How did management position MTV for this segment in India?

3. Describe the evolution of MTV's international marketing strategy in India. What approach did it apply in the early years compared to the later years? Has MTV been able to articulate a clear global marketing strategy in India? What other opportunities can it pursue with the youth market in addition to broadcasting music?

4. Is it feasible for MTV to reach an ideal balance between standardization of programming and local adaptation? If so, how? Thinking in terms of the marketing program elements and marketing strategy, what can management do now to make MTV succeed around the world?

This case was written by Kelly Nealis under the supervision of Dr. Gary Knight. Sources: Capell, Kerry. (2002). "MTV's World," *Business Week*, February 18, pp. 81–86; *Economist.com*, (1998). "Star Woes," April 9. Retrieved from www.economist.com/displaystory.cfm?story_id=159806; Goldsmith, Charles. (2003). "MTV Seeks Global Appeal," *Wall Street Journal*, July 21, p. B1; Gunther, Marc. (2004). "MTV's Passage to India," *Fortune*, August 9, pp.117–121; "MTV: Music Television." Retrieved from www.viacom.com; "MTV Launches Innovative Web Site in India." Retrieved from www.viacom.com; "MTV Announces International Expansion Plans for Europe, Asia, and Latin America." Retrieved from www.viacom.com; (2007). "MTV Networks India." Retrieved from www.mtvindia.com; (2007). "MTV Property Counts." Retrieved from www.viacom.com.

CHAPTER ESSENTIALS

Key Terms

adaptation, p. 519

global account management (GAM), p. 537

global brand, p. 520

global market segment, p. 517

global marketing strategy, p. 516

gray market activity, p. 526

international price escalation, p. 530

standardization, p. 519

transfer pricing, p. 531

Summary

In this chapter, you learned about:

1. Global marketing strategy

Developing a marketing strategy requires managers to assess the unique foreign market environment and then make choices about market segments, targeting, and positioning. A **global marketing strategy** is a plan of action that guides the firm in: how to position itself and its offerings in foreign markets, which customer segments to pursue, and the degree to which its marketing program elements should be standardized and adapted.

2. Standardization and adaptation of the international marketing program

How the firm balances **adaptation** and **standardization** determines the extent to which the firm must modify a product and its marketing to suit foreign markets. When possible, firms prefer to standardize their products to achieve scale economies and minimize complexity. A **global market segment** is a group of customers that share common characteristics across many national markets. *Positioning* strategy involves using marketing to create a particular image of a product or service, especially relative to competitor offerings, among the firm's customers worldwide.

3. Global branding and product development

A **global brand** is perceived similarly in all the firm's markets and increases marketing strategy effectiveness, allowing the firm to charge higher prices and deal more effectively with channel members and competitors. In developing products with multicountry potential, managers emphasize the commonalities across countries rather than the differences. The development of global products facilitates economies of scale in R&D, production, and marketing. Innovation and design in international product development are increasingly performed by *global teams*—an internationally distributed group of people with a specific mandate to make or implement decisions that are international in scope.

4. International pricing

International prices are determined by factors both internal and external to the firm, which often cause prices to inflate abroad. A special challenge for exporters in pricing is **international price escalation**—the problem of end-user prices reaching exorbitant levels in the export market, caused by multilayered distribution channels, intermediary margins, tariffs, and other international customer costs. **Transfer pricing** is the practice of pricing intermediate or finished products exchanged among the subsidiaries and affiliates of the same corporate family located in different countries. **Gray market activity**, also known as parallel imports, refers to legal importation of genuine products into a country by intermediaries other than authorized distributors.

5. International marketing communications

International marketing communications involves the management of advertising and promotional activities across national borders. Managers are often compelled to adapt their international communications due to unique legal, cultural, and socioeconomic factors in foreign markets. Firms must also accommodate literacy levels, language, and available media. In working with key business customers, firms may follow **global account management (GAM)** practices—the servicing of a key global customer in a consistent and standardized manner, regardless of where in the world they operate.

6. International distribution

Firms usually engage foreign intermediaries or foreign-based subsidiaries to reach customers in international markets. When designing the international channel, management must account for various factors, including the nature of the product and the market. Some firms bypass traditional distribution systems altogether by using *direct marketing*. *Channel length* refers to the number of distributors or other intermediaries that it takes to get the product from the manufacturer to the market. The longer the channel, the more intermediaries must be compensated, and the costlier the distribution function.

7. Ethical dimensions of international marketing

Firms increasingly recognize that their international marketing activities are closely scrutinized by the public. In response, firms put in place corporate social responsibility programs such as ensuring that suppliers earn a sustainable income, providing needed products to poor consumers, and disposing of used products responsibly. Firms are becoming more proactive in corporate citizenship, but much more remains to be accomplished.

Test Your Comprehension AACSB: Reflective Thinking, Ethical Reasoning

1. Describe the marketing program elements and how each influences sales and performance in international business.

2. Audrey Corp. has historically adapted its offerings for all its foreign markets, leading to a proliferation of product variations. Explain why Audrey Corp. might want to consider global marketing strategy. What are the benefits of global marketing strategy?

3. Distinguish between adaptation and standardization in international marketing.

4. Consider Toshiba's laptop computer division. In terms of the marketing program elements, what attributes of laptop computers does the firm need to adapt and which attributes can it standardize for international markets?

5. What is the role of market segmentation and positioning in international marketing? What is a global market segment?

6. William Corporation is a manufacturer of high-quality men and women's fashions. What steps should you take to transform William into a well-recognized global brand?

7. What are the most important factors to consider when formulating international pricing strategies? What steps would you follow in arriving at international prices?

8. Export customers of a consumer products firm tend to be highly sensitive to price. However, the firm is experiencing substantial price escalation in these markets. What factors may be causing this situation? What can management do to reduce the detrimental impact of international price escalation?

9. What are the most important factors to consider when designing strategy for international marketing communications?

10. Describe the role of distribution and logistics in international business.

11. Summarize the key ethical issues that characterize international marketing.

Apply Your Understanding AACSB: Reflective Thinking, Analytical Skills

1. One manifestation of global marketing strategy is the increased tendency of MNEs to launch new products simultaneously around the world. For example, many movies—such as *The Matrix* and *Harry Potter*—are introduced at the same time in markets worldwide, using essentially the same marketing program. Visit the Web sites of the *Matrix* and the *Harry Potter* movies. What global market segments do these movies appear to target? Describe the specific aspects of global marketing strategy that you can detect in the international marketing of these films.

2. Products must be adapted to accommodate national differences arising from customer preferences and each market's economic conditions, climate, culture, and language. Think about the following products: packaged flour, swimsuits, textbooks, and automobiles. For each of these products, describe how a firm would need to adapt different marketing program elements to suit conditions in China, Germany, and Saudi Arabia. Keep in mind that China is an emerging market with low per capita income, Saudi Arabia is an emerging market with a conservative culture rooted in Islam, and Germany is an advanced and liberal economy. In developing your answer for each product, think especially about the nature of the product, its pricing and distribution, and how a firm would promote it in the market.

3. Office Depot, the supplier of office equipment and supplies, has stores in countries throughout Asia, Europe, and Latin America. Suppose the firm has decided to launch its own line of notebook computers and wants to know how to price them in various markets. What would be the most important factors Office Depot should consider when setting prices in foreign markets? Suggest a step-by-step approach to international pricing.

globalEDGE Internet Exercises

AACSB: Reflective Thinking

Refer to Chapter 1, page 27, for instructions on how to access and use globalEDGE™.

1. Global branding is key to international marketing success. Every year *Business Week* and *Interbrand* publish a ranking of the top 100 global brands. The ranking can be accessed by searching the term "global brand" at globalEDGE™, or by entering "global brands scorecard" in a Google search. For this exercise, locate and retrieve the most current ranking and answer the following questions:

   a. What do you consider are the strengths and weaknesses of the methodology *Interbrand* uses to estimate brand equity?

   b. What patterns do you detect in terms of the countries and industries most represented in the top 100 list?

   c. *Business Week* publishes an article in conjunction with the ranking. According to *Business Week,* what managerial guidelines are helpful in order for a company to develop a strong global brand?

2. Procter and Gamble (P&G) and Unilever are the two leading firms in the consumer products industry for products such as soap, shampoo, and laundry detergent. P&G (www.pg.com) is based in the United States and Unilever (www.unilever.com) is based in Europe. What are the major regional markets of each firm? What products does each firm offer through a global marketing strategy? Structure your answer in terms of the elements of the marketing program. That is, what global strategy approaches does each firm apply for the product, its pricing, promotion, and distribution?

3. A *third-party logistics provider* (3PL) provides outsourced or "third party" logistics services to companies for part or all of their distribution activities. Examples include C.H. Robinson Worldwide, Maersk Logistics, and FedEx. Your firm needs to find a 3PL to handle its distribution efforts abroad. Your task is to locate two 3PLs online and address the following questions:

   a. What logistical services does each firm provide?

   b. What types of customers does each 3PL serve?

   c. Where are their headquarters and branch offices located?

   d. Based on the information provided, which of the two 3PLs would you most likely choose? Why?

CKR Cavusgil Knight Riesenberger
Management Skill Builder©

Developing a Distribution Channel in Japan

A critical step in developing international marketing operations is the creation of the foreign distribution channel. The distribution channel provides the means to convey products (and many services) from their point of production to a convenient location where they can be purchased by customers. In the absence of a well-conceived distribution channel, efforts in formulating the other marketing program elements—product, pricing, and communications—may prove fruitless.

AACSB: Reflective Thinking, Multicultural and Diversity

Managerial Challenge

The firm should establish a reliable distribution channel in the foreign market from the very beginning. Channels are often costly to set up, and once established, may be difficult to change. Because buyers may view the distributor as the originator of the product or service, the firm must use a systematic approach to choose the right distributor. In this C/K/R Management Skill Builder©, your challenge is to investigate the nature of distribution channels in Japan for a firm that manufactures medical equipment.

Background

The market in Japan for medical equipment and supplies is very promising. Japan's medical device market is the second largest in the world and is one of the few product markets that have achieved steady growth despite the sluggish performance of the Japanese economy in recent years. The value of the market exceeds $10 billion annually, and imported products are popular. Foreign firms see bright sales prospects in such product categories as pacemakers, artificial implants, and catheters, as well as software and other products used in medical information and communications systems.

Managerial Skills You Will Gain

In this C/K/R Management Skill Builder©, as a prospective manager, you will:

1. Design a channel in a promising foreign market to increase firm performance.
2. Learn the factors to consider when making international channel arrangements.
3. Research alternative channels to reach end users.
4. Explore the types of country-level barriers that firms encounter in setting up distribution channels within foreign markets.

Your Task

Investigate establishing a distribution channel in Japan for a firm in your home country that makes medical equipment.

Go to the C/K/R Knowledge Portal©

www.prenhall.com/cavusgil

Proceed to the C/K/R Knowledge Portal© to obtain the expanded background information, your task and methodology, suggested resources for this exercise, and the presentation template.

545

Human Resource Management in the Global Firm

> ## International Human Resource Management at Johnson & Johnson

Johnson & Johnson (J&J) is a manufacturer of pharmaceutical and consumer health care products, with well-known brands such as Band-Aid, Tylenol, Neutrogena, Listerine, Sudafed, and Rolaids. In 2006, worldwide sales topped $53 billion, about half of which came from North America, one quarter from Europe, 14 percent from Asia-Pacific and Africa, and the rest from Latin America and other regions. J&J's decentralized workforce includes more than 116,000 employees in over 250 business units worldwide.

J&J pays special attention to the care and management of human resources. The firm's Credo, an internal document that has been around for over six decades, articulates a commitment to company employees. A section of the Credo reads:

We are responsible to our employees worldwide. Everyone must be considered as an individual. We must respect their dignity and recognize their merit. They must have a sense of security in their jobs. Compensation must be fair and adequate, and working conditions clean, orderly and safe. We must be mindful of our employees' family responsibilities. Employees must feel free to make suggestions and complaints. There must be equal opportunity for employment, development and advancement. We must provide competent, ethical management.

Riddhi Parikh, Assistant Manager for Human Resources at J&J in India, relies on the Credo whenever employee action is needed. She can authorize employee travel, expenses, and many benefits without permission from her manager. Riddhi can focus on what she would like as an employee—to be free, to be able to learn and advance in the company and to have the power to make decisions. Thanks to J&J's high regard for human resources, the average tenure of employees at the Indian subsidiary is 15 years. More broadly, J&J managers worldwide are empowered to make important decisions within their scope of operations.

Johnson & Johnson claims to hire "the best and the brightest" people to fill its leadership pipeline. All J&J leaders are responsible for developing managers for global operations. As part of his performance evaluation, J&J's chairman is measured on his ability to develop managers. The J&J executive committee spends 20 percent of its time figuring out ways to find and nurture talent. In Canada, J&J's Leadership Development Program drives company culture and superior business performance. As part of the development process, employees often need to learn new skills in order to move across functional boundaries and take up new international assignments.

In salary packages, firms link merit increases and discretionary bonuses to the new skills managers acquire. J&J uses a "total rewards" compensation approach, in which management considers all the rewards available in the workplace, including opportunities for learning and development. J&J uses a sophisticated personnel evaluation system that can account for a variety of elements that employees might value within their compensation packages, across the firm's operations worldwide.

The firm also takes pride in providing opportunities for employees to acquire new skills. For example, most units can send employees to the J&J Law School Online, an Internet-based program. J&J's two-year Finance Leadership Development Program rotates trainees through a combination of classroom and structured on-the-job training that exposes them to various parts of the business.

As part of the hiring process, J&J also emphasizes diversity. Management compensa-tion is linked to efforts to hire minorities, women, and people from varied cultural backgrounds. In a diverse global marketplace, the effort is a crucial step toward expanding the firm's markets. J&J's vice president for human resources is a woman, Kaye Foster-Cheek, a native of Barbados. J&J is driving the Women's Leadership Initiative in its international units, even in emerging markets such as India.

Sources: Byron, Ellen. (2001). "E-Business: The Web @ Work / Johnson & Johnson," *Wall Street Journal*, Nov. 19, p. B4; Cameron, Carolynn. (2007). "Johnson & Johnson Canada's Design, Development and Business Impact of a Local Leadership Development Program," *Organization Development Journal*, 25(2), pp. 65–70; Johnson & Johnson company profile. Retrieved from Hoovers.com; Heffes, Ellen. (2005). "J&J: 'Quality of People Is Key to Growth'," *Financial Executive*, July/August, pp. 19–20; Keenan, William. (1993). "Measuring Skills That Improve Performance," *Sales and Marketing Management*, December, pp. 29–30; Lath, Shivani. (2006). "Johnson & Johnson: Living By Its Credo," *Business Today*, November 5, p. 126; Marquez, Jessica. (2006). "Business First," *Workforce Management*, October 23, 2006, pp. 1–6; Maxey, Daisy. (2007). "CEO Compensation Survey," *Wall Street Journal*, April 9, p. R.4; Rumpel, Steven, and John Medcof. (2006). "Total Rewards: Good Fit For Tech Workers," *Research Technology Management*, September/October, pp. 27–36.

The Strategic Role of Human Resources in International Business

How sustainable is firm competitiveness without the employees and their knowledge and experience? Imagine especially the knowledge-intensive sectors such as management consulting, banking, advertising, engineering, and architecture. Without the creative people, designers, problem solvers, and other knowledge workers, firms such as McKinsey, Saatchi & Saatchi, Pixar, Gucci, Herman Miller, Nokia, and many others would hardly survive. Today, firms often refer to employees as "human talent," "human capital," or "intangible assets," suggesting that they represent an investment rather than a cost.

Managers at Johnson & Johnson appear to recognize that the employees and the knowledge they possess may be their most strategic asset. Recruiting, managing, and retaining human resources at a firm with global operations are especially challenging. Take the global organization of Siemens, the German MNE. In 2005, Siemens had 460,800 employees in some 190 countries. It employed 290,500 throughout Europe, 100,600 in North and South America, 58,000 in the Asia-Pacific region, and 11,900 in Africa, the Middle East, and Russia. Like Siemens, firms such as Volkswagen, Hutchison Whampoa, Nestlé, IBM, Anglo American, Unilever, Wal-Mart, Deutsche Post, McDonald's, Matsushita, and Mittal Steel have more than 150,000 employees working outside of their home country. Management grapples with a wide range of challenges in hiring and managing workers within the distinctive cultural and legal frameworks that govern employee practices around the world. **International human resource management (IHRM)** can be defined as the planning, selection, training, employment, and evaluation of employees for international operations.[1] International human resource managers serve in an advisory or support role to line managers by hiring, training, and evaluating employees, and by providing IHRM guidelines.

International human resource management (IHRM) The planning, selection, training, employment, and evaluation of employees for international operations.

When Toshiba develops a laptop computer that is lighter, more powerful, and less expensive than competing models, other companies can usually reverse engineer and develop their own version of the computer. However, how the firm recruits, trains, and places skilled personnel in its worldwide value chains sets it apart from the competition. The combined knowledge, skills, and experiences of employees are distinctive and provide myriad advantages to the firm's operations worldwide.

Three Employee Categories

International human resource managers work at three different levels in a firm that has multicountry operations:

1. **Host-country nationals (HCNs).** These employees are citizens of the country where the subsidiary or affiliate is located. Typically, HCNs make up the largest proportion of the employees that the firm hires abroad. The firm's labor force in manufacturing, assembly, basic service activities, clerical work, and other non-managerial functions largely consists of HCNs.

2. **Parent-country nationals (PCNs).** Also known as *home-country nationals,* PCNs are citizens of the country where the MNE is headquartered.

3. **Third-country nationals (TCNs).** These are employees who are citizens of countries other than the home or host country. Most TCNs work in management and are hired because they possess special knowledge or skills.[2]

To give an example, a Canadian MNE may employ Italian citizens in its subsidiary in Italy (HCNs), may send Canadian citizens to work in Asia-Pacific on assignment (PCNs), or send Swiss employees on assignment to its subsidiary in Turkey (TCNs). Thus, in addition to where the individual is employed, the nationality of the employee is important, especially with respect to compensation policies.

You can see that in a global organization, it is very common for employees to move across national boundaries to take up responsibilities that others cannot fulfill. These employees on international assignments are traditionally called *expatriates.* An **expatriate** is an employee who is assigned to work and reside in a foreign country for an extended period, usually a year or longer. Note that any one of the three categories of employees can be considered an expatriate, depending on the location of the assignment. For example, an HCN who is transferred into parent country operations also resides outside of his or her home country.[3] While expatriates comprise only a small percentage of the workforce in most MNEs, they perform critical functions abroad, such as managing a subsidiary.

For IHRM managers, the ultimate challenge is to ensure that the right person is in the right position at the right location with the right pay scale. Today, human resources are highly mobile. For example, the information technology, financial services, and telecom sectors in the southern part of India are currently experiencing a shortage of mid- and senior level managerial talent. As a result, managers from distant places such as Eastern Europe are being posted to India to take advantage of compensation packages that have become highly competitive by advanced-economy standards. Heads of national subsidiaries are now commanding salaries up to $400,000.[4]

Host-country national (HCN) An employee who is a citizen of the country where the MNE subsidiary or affiliate is located.

Parent-country national (PCN) An employee who is a citizen of the country where the MNE is headquartered.

Third-country national (TCN) An employee who is a citizen of a country other than the home or host country.

Expatriate An employee who is assigned to work and reside in a foreign country for an extended period, usually a year or longer.

Differences between Domestic and International HRM

Compared to human resource management in the domestic context, IHRM is more complex. Exhibit 18.1 illustrates six factors that increase the complexity of human resource management in the international context.[5] Let's discuss each in turn.

Exhibit 18.1

Factors Contributing to the Complexity of Human Resource Management in the International Context

1. *New HR responsibilities.* Several activities that are not necessarily encountered in the domestic market include: international taxation, international relocation and orientation, administrative services for expatriates, host government relations, and language translation services. An Australian national posted to Brazil as an expatriate is often subject to taxation by both governments, and may incur double taxation. Therefore, the issue of tax equalization—ensuring that there is no tax disincentive associated with any particular international assignment—is one of the complicating aspects of IHRM.

2. *The need for a broader, international perspective in compensation policy.* Recall that, at any one time, the human resources manager provides guidance in such issues as compensation policy for a mix of PCNs, HCNs, and TCNs, who are nationals of numerous countries. Establishing a fair and comparable compensation scale, regardless of nationality, is one of the challenges in a large MNE.

3. *Greater involvement in the employees' personal lives.* The HR professionals in the firm are concerned about the welfare of the expatriates and their families for such matters as housing arrangements, health care, schooling of children, safety, and security, as well as proper compensation in view of the higher cost of living in some locations around the world.

4. *Managing the mix of expatriates versus locals.* Organizations must be staffed in each national location with personnel from the home country, the host country, or third countries. The mix of staff depends upon several factors, including the international experience of the firm, cost of living in the foreign location, and availability of qualified local staff.

5. *Greater risk exposure.* When employee productivity falls below acceptable levels or an expatriate returns prematurely from an international assignment, the consequences are even more pronounced in international business. Exposure to political risk and terrorism is also a major concern for HR professionals and may require an increased compensation package and security arrangements for the employee and her or his family.

6. *External influences of the government and national culture.* External to the firm is the broader context of the host country environment. Especially notable is the influence of the government and national culture.

Let's explore this last factor in greater detail. First, excessive regulations or bureaucratic hurdles that host governments may impose are often a concern for the firm. Personnel must be evaluated and compensated in ways that are consistent with local standards and customs. The degree to which labor is unionized and the nature of labor-management relations in the host country also have implications for human resource management. For example, in many European countries, labor unions are actively involved in the management of the firm. In France, Germany, and Spain, employees may work no more than a set number of hours per week (sometimes as few as 35).

Similarly, as we discussed in Chapter 5, national culture has a profound impact on the effectiveness of employees and firms. Human resource managers have the responsibility to prepare employees and their families to live and work effectively in a new cultural environment. Employees need to be trained in ways that account for local standards, cultural norms, and language differences. Firms also increasingly emphasize the importance of workforce diversity and the need to develop employees with global mindsets.[6] Prohibitions against gender discrimination in Australia, Europe, and North America conflict with practices in some countries, where women are underrepresented in the workplace.

For all these reasons, managers at firms with extensive international operations pay attention to planning, selecting, training, employing, and evaluating international human resources. Adjustments will be made to human resource policies as local conditions dictate. For example, in an emerging market such as Vietnam, benefits will need to include allowances for housing, education, and other facilities that are not readily available there. Subsidiary managers will need to become familiar with local customs and establish codes of conduct with respect to such issues as gift giving, rewards, and providing meals to employees during the workday. At the same time, the firm will attempt to organize IHRM on a global scale so the organization applies integrated, uniform IHRM policies.

Key Tasks in International Human Resource Management

Exhibit 18.2 outlines six key tasks of international human resource managers. First is international staffing policy—activities directed at recruiting, selecting, and placement of employees. Second is preparation and training of personnel. Third is international performance appraisal, providing feedback necessary for employees' professional development. Fourth is compensation of personnel, including formulation of benefits packages that may vary greatly from country to country. Fifth is international labor relations, involving interaction with labor unions and collective bargaining. Sixth is achieving diversity in the international workforce.

The remainder of this chapter is devoted to IHRM tasks identified in Exhibit 18.2.

 International Staffing Policy

One of the critical tasks the firm performs is determining the ideal mix of employees in the firm's international subsidiaries and affiliates.[7] The optimal mix varies by location, industry, stage in the value chain, and availability of qualified personnel. In addition, local laws prescribe the proportion of employees the firm can employ from nonlocal sources.

Exhibit 18.3 illustrates the various criteria and rationale for hiring each type of employee.[8] In general, firms post PCNs abroad to take advantage of their specialized knowledge, especially in upstream value-chain operations, and/or when management wants to maintain substantial control over foreign operations. The subsidiary is more likely to comply with MNE objectives and policies when PCNs are at the helm. PCNs can also assist in developing local managers. By contrast, firms prefer HCNs when the host-country environment is complex and their specialized knowledge or local connections are required in the local marketplace. Firms tend to employ HCNs to perform downstream value-chain activities such as marketing and sales that require extensive local knowledge.[9] One advantage with HCNs is that the cost of compensating them is usually much lower than

Exhibit 18.2

Key Tasks and Challenges of International Human Resource Management

Task	Strategic Goals	Illustrative Challenges
International staffing policy	• Choose between home-country nationals, host-country nationals, and third-country nationals • Develop global managers • Recruit and select expatriates	• Avoid country bias, nepotism, and other local practices • Cultivate global mindsets
Preparation and training of employees	• Increase effectiveness of international employees, leading to increased company performance • Train employees with an emphasis on area studies, practical information, and cross-cultural awareness	• Minimize culture shock and the occurrence of early departure by expatriates
International performance appraisal	• Assess, over time, how effectively managers and other employees perform their jobs abroad	• Establish uniform, organizationwide performance benchmarks while remaining sensitive to customary local practices; for example, instituting explicit and nonambiguous performance metrics
Compensation of employees	• Develop guidelines and administer compensation e.g., base salary, benefits, allowances, and incentives	• Avoid double taxation of employees
International labor relations	• Manage and interact with labor unions, collective bargaining, handling strikes and other labor disputes, wage rates, and possible workforce reduction	• Reduce absenteeism, workplace injuries due to negligence, and the occurrence of labor strikes
Diversity in the international workforce	• Recruit talent from diverse backgrounds to bring experience and knowledge to firm problems and opportunities	• Achieve gender diversity

Staff with *Parent Country* Nationals (PCNs) When. . .	Staff with *Host-Country* Nationals (HCNs) When. . .	Staff with *Third-Country* Nationals (TCNs) When. . .
Headquarters wants to maintain strong control over its foreign operations.	The country is distant in terms of culture or language (such as Japan), or when local operations emphasize downstream value-chain activities such as marketing and sales, as HCNs usually understand the local business environment best.	Top management wants to create a *global* culture among the firm's operations worldwide.
Headquarters wants to maintain control over valuable intellectual property that is easily dissipated when accessible by HCNs or TCNs.	Local connections and relations are critical to operational success (such as relations with the government in Russia).	Top management seeks unique perspectives for managing host-country operations.
Knowledge sharing is desirable among headquarters and the subsidiaries, particularly for developing local managers or the host-country organization.	The local government requires the MNE to employ a minimum proportion of local personnel, or tough immigration requirements prevent the long-term employment of expatriates.	Headquarters wants to transfer knowledge and technology from third countries to host-country operations.
Foreign operations emphasize R&D and manufacturing, because PCNs are usually more knowledgeable about such upstream value-chain activities.	Cost is an important consideration; Salaries of PCNs, especially those with families, can be up to four times those of HCNs.	The firm cannot afford to pay the expensive compensation typical of PCNs.

Exhibit 18.3

Criteria for Selecting Employees for Foreign Operations

PCNs or TCNs. On the other hand, firms prefer TCNs when top management wants to transfer knowledge or corporate culture from third countries to host-country operations. Worldwide staffing with TCNs helps firms develop an integrated global enterprise, while excessive use of HCNs may lead to a collection of autonomous subsidiaries—a federation of national units.

Searching for Talent

Hiring and placing people in appropriate positions is a critical IHRM task. *Recruitment* involves searching for and locating potential job candidates to fill the firm's needs. *Selection* involves gathering information to evaluate and decide who should be employed in particular jobs. Successful MNEs are led by managers with substantial international and functional experience.

A western family and a young Muslim woman feed pigeons in front of an Istanbul mosque. Successful expatriates have family members who cope well in new environments.

One of the most challenging IHRM tasks is finding and developing exceptional leaders and other human resource talent. Managers must identify potential candidates and groom them to become corporate leaders, train personnel to meet the firm's evolving business needs, and generally ensure that the talent supply keeps pace with the growth of the firm. Hiring and developing the best talent is critical to long-term, superior performance, but many firms fail to invest adequately in developing employees.

Some senior executives believe that there is currently a shortage of talent willing and qualified to work outside of their home countries. They contend that there simply are not enough good employees to go around. For example, Schlumberger Ltd., a Texas oil company with operations worldwide, cannot find enough engineers. Schlumberger is one of the rare firms that has turned its human resources department into a strategic asset in order to find and develop talent around the world. Among other initiatives, Schlumberger has assigned high-level executives as "ambassadors" to 44 important engineering schools, such as Kazakhstan's Kazakh National Technical University, Beijing University, Massachusetts Institute of Technology, and Universidad Nacional Autonoma de Mexico. Dell, IBM, Nokia, and Unilever are also among the firms that are proactive in finding and developing international talent.

Developing talent is a multistep process, so human resource managers, in collaboration with executive management, need to:

1. Analyze the firm's growth strategies and the mission-critical roles needed to achieve those strategies.

2. Define the requirements for each role in terms of desired skills, behaviors, and experiences.

3. Examine the firm's current supply of talent and create a plan to acquire needed talent.

4. Develop talent internally and acquire existing or potential talent from outside the firm.

5. Assess current and potential talent according to each individual's performance over time, willingness to learn, learning skills, and commitment to career advancement.[10]

What about the employees sent abroad by firms for international assignments? Not all personnel are suited for expatriate positions. Some employees prefer to remain at home and avoid international positions. Others are sent abroad only to discover they are not cut out for international work. Thus, the firm must choose carefully. Employees who are adept at working effectively in foreign environments tend to have the following characteristics:[11]

- *Technical competence.* In distant locations, managers should have sufficient managerial and technical capabilities to fulfill the firm's goals and objectives.

- *Self-reliance.* Having an entrepreneurial orientation, a proactive mindset, and a strong sense of innovativeness is important because expatriate managers often must function with considerable independence abroad, with limited support from headquarters.

- *Adaptability.* The manager should possess an ability to adjust well to foreign cultures. The most important traits are cultural empathy, flexibility, diplomacy, and a positive attitude for overcoming stressful foreign situations.

- *Interpersonal skills.* The best candidates get along well with others. Building and maintaining relationships is key, particularly for managers who interact with numerous colleagues, employees, local partners, and government officials.[12]

- *Leadership ability.* The most successful managers view change positively and manage threats and opportunities that confront the firm. They collaborate with employees to implement strategies and facilitate successful change.

- *Physical and emotional health.* Living abroad can be stressful. Most expatriates experience culture shock and other traumas, and medical care is often lacking. Thus, excellent physical and mental health are critical.

- *Spouse and/or dependents prepared for living abroad.* The candidate should have suitable family attributes—the ability of the spouse and other family members to cope with new environments. In the opening vignette, Johnson & Johnson HR managers put much emphasis on family well-being in international assignments.

How can you build an international career? As young adults, future global managers typically learn one or more foreign languages and acquire a facility for international travel by visiting or living abroad. They develop an optimistic, open-minded outlook about the world and an interest in international issues. Many seek study and internship opportunities abroad. As they develop professionally within their firms, they seek out international work assignments to enhance their knowledge of international business.[13]

Expatriate Failure and Culture Shock

What happens when things go awry for the employee while on an international assignment? **Expatriate failure** is the premature return of an employee from an international assignment. It occurs when the employee is unable to perform well or to meet company expectations while on a foreign assignment. Expatriate failure is costly because it results in lost productivity and failure to achieve company goals, as well as expenditures associated with relocating the employee abroad, such as training and international travel. Failure can also affect expatriates themselves, leading to diminished careers or problems in their family lives.

A leading cause of expatriate failure is **culture shock**—the confusion and anxiety, often akin to mental depression, that can result from living in a foreign culture for an extended period.[14] Culture shock may affect the expatriate or family members. An expatriate's stress is due to his or her inability to interpret the large number of new cues in the foreign environment. The expatriate or family members generally overcome culture shock, usually within a few months, but some give up and return home early. Inadequate language or cross-cultural skills tend to exacerbate expatriate failure. The employee may prove unable to function in unfamiliar surroundings or to communicate well with locals.[15] Whatever the cause, as many as a third of foreign assignments end prematurely due to expatriate failure. The rate is particularly high among employees assigned to countries with culture and language very different from those at home.

Employees deal with culture shock in various ways, including regular exercise, relaxation techniques, or keeping a detailed journal of their experiences. Culture shock and expatriate failure can also be reduced through advance preparation, training, and by developing a deep interest in the new surroundings.

Expatriate failure The premature return of an employee from an international assignment.

Culture shock The confusion and anxiety, often akin to mental depression, that can result from living in a foreign culture for an extended period.

Preparation and Training of Personnel

What can firms do to help employees better understand, adapt, and perform well in foreign environments?[16] Proper preparation and training are crucial. Training is the process of modifying employee attitudes and knowledge in ways that increase the likelihood of attaining organizational goals. Exhibit 18.4 highlights key features of preparation and training programs for international personnel.

Firms should provide training for all employees posted outside their home countries. Training is also a factor for the nonmanagerial workforce abroad, such as engineers, hourly workers, or those who perform business process services. HR managers must assess the training needs of host-country workers and devise training programs that ensure they can do their jobs, whether in manufacturing, marketing, sales, after-sales services, or business processes such as accounting and records management.

For employees on international assignment, training tends to have three components: (1) **area studies**—factual knowledge of the historical, political, and economic environment of the host country, (2) **practical information**—knowledge and skills necessary to function effectively in a country, including housing, health care, education, and daily living, and (3) **cross-cultural awareness**—the ability to interact effectively and appropriately with people from different language and cultural backgrounds.[17]

Training methods vary. In order of increasing rigor, they include: videos, lectures, assigned readings, case studies, books, Web-based instruction, critical incident analyses, simulations, role-playing, language training, field experience, and long-term immersion. Role-playing and simulations involve the employee acting out typical encounters with foreigners. As you'll recall from Chapter 5, critical incident analysis involves examining an episode between an employee and a foreign counterpart in which tension has arisen due to a cross-cultural misunderstanding. With field experience, the manager visits the host country for usually one or two weeks. Long-term immersion places the employee in the country for several months or more, often for language and cultural training. In deciding which training methods to use, the firm must strike a balance between the rigor of training versus the degree of interaction required abroad and the cultural distance between the employee's native and new culture.[18]

Area studies Factual knowledge of the historical, political, and economic environment of the host country.

Practical information Knowledge and skills necessary to function effectively in a country, including housing, health care, education, and daily living.

Cross-cultural awareness Ability to interact effectively and appropriately with people from different language and cultural backgrounds.

Goal	Desirable Employee Qualities	Training emphasizes	Training methods
Increase manager's effectiveness abroad; Increase company performance	Technical competence, self-reliance, adaptability, interpersonal skills, leadership ability, physical and emotional health, spouse and dependents prepared for living abroad	• *Area studies*–host-country historical, political, economic, and cultural dimensions • *Practical information*–skills necessary to work effectively in host country • *Cultural awareness*–cross-cultural communication; negotiation techniques; reduction of ethnocentric orientation and self-reference criterion; language skills	Videos, lectures, assigned readings, case studies, critical incident analysis, simulations and role-playing, language training, field experience, long-term immersion

Exhibit 18.4 Key Features of Preparation and Training for International Personnel

Preparing Employees for Repatriation

Repatriation is the return of the expatriate to his or her home country following completion of a lengthy foreign assignment. Like expatriation, repatriation requires advance preparation. Unless managed well, the expatriate is likely to encounter problems upon returning home. Some returning employees find their international experience is not valued, and they may be placed in lesser or ill-suited positions relative to what they held abroad. Some expatriates report financial difficulties upon returning, such as inflated housing prices or cuts in pay. Many experience "reverse culture shock," readjustment to home-country culture. For the employee and family members who have spent several years abroad, psychological readjustment to life in the home country can be stressful. Interestingly, as many as one quarter of expatriates may leave their firm within one year of returning home.[19] Others refuse to undertake subsequent international assignments.

Training methods for these IBM employees cover issues of people management, HR policies and programs, and leadership development issues.

Human resource managers can provide counseling on the types of problems that employees face upon returning home. While the expatriate is abroad, the firm can monitor the employee's compensation and career path. After returning home, the firm can provide bridge loans and other interim financial assistance, as well as counseling, to address both career and psychological needs. The firm needs to ensure that the expatriate has a job in place that is equal to, or better than, the one held before going abroad. It is likely that, while abroad, the employee has accumulated considerable knowledge and contacts that the firm can leverage.[20]

Repatriation The return of the expatriate to his or her home country following the completion of a lengthy foreign assignment.

Cultivating Global Mindsets

Ethnocentric views are common in some MNEs, where headquarters staff often believe their ways of doing business are superior and can be readily transferred to other countries.[21] The more progressive MNEs today subscribe to a *geocentric orientation*, staffing headquarters and subsidiaries with the most competent personnel, regardless of national origin. As we discussed in Chapter 5, a geocentric orientation is synonymous with a global mindset, where the employee is able to understand a business or market or country boundaries. A *global mindset* is characterized by an openness to, and articulation of, multiple cultural and strategic realities on both global and local levels.[22] Employees come from diverse international backgrounds, bringing a holistic perspective to decision making on the firm's operations worldwide. Senior managers are expected to be committed to hiring, developing, nurturing, and recognizing employees who possess a global mindset and offer global leadership potential.

Cross-cultural awareness training can go a long way in increasing intercultural sensitivity and effectiveness. Individuals need to be well versed in how best to supervise and communicate with local employees, to negotiate with customers and suppliers, and to generally adapt to the local culture. Training should aim to help the employee avoid the self-reference criterion—the tendency to view other cultures through the lens of one's own culture.

Employees also benefit from training in the host-country language. Learning the local language allows the employee to interact more effectively with local colleagues and workers, communicate with suppliers and customers, monitor competitors, recruit local talent, and improve relations with host-country officials and organizations. Language ability also increases the employee's insights and enjoyment of the local culture.[23]

A firm can deliberately seek to enhance the cultural intelligence of its employees. **Cultural intelligence** refers to the capability of an employee to function effectively in

Cultural intelligence The capability of an employee to function effectively in situations characterized by cultural diversity.

situations characterized by cultural diversity.[24] It incorporates four dimensions: (1) *strategy* refers to how an employee makes sense of cross-cultural experiences through his or her judgments; (2) *knowledge* is the employee's understanding of cultural dimensions such as values, social norms, religious beliefs, and language; (3) *motivation* emphasizes the employee's interest in interacting with people from different cultures, as well as a sense of confidence in functioning effectively in culturally diverse settings; (4) *behavioral flexibility* refers to an employee's capability to adopt verbal and nonverbal behaviors that are appropriate in different cultures.[25]

Charting Global Careers for Employees

Successful firms give high-potential employees adequate opportunity to gain experience not just in their home country but at headquarters and in other countries as well. This approach broadens the pool of global talent for managerial positions and visibly shows top management's commitment to global strategy. For example, at Unilever, employees cannot advance very far in the firm without substantial international experience. The Anglo-Dutch firm has numerous programs to develop international leadership skills. Managers are rotated through various jobs and locations around the world, especially early in their careers. Unilever maintains a **global talent pool**—a searchable database of employees, profiling their international skill sets and potential for supporting the firm's global aspirations. HR managers search the database for the right recruit, with ideal qualifications, regardless of where in its global network the individual is located. In this way, the best talent is identified and tapped for each task, from anywhere in the world.[26]

The career path of the global manager provides for recurring local and international assignments. Firms such as Nestlé, ABB, and Citibank develop a pool of talented employees, regardless of nationality, with deep knowledge of the firm's worldwide operations.

Employees with a global mindset strive to understand organizational and group dynamics in order to create consensus among divergent members.[27] They lead and participate effectively in global teams. As we discussed in Chapter 11, a **global team** is an internationally distributed group of people with a specific mandate to make or implement decisions that are international in scope. Members of a global team will require training in order to work well with others. Firms employ innovative approaches so that the team members work cohesively. For example, one team with members from the United States and Latin America had to negotiate with a supplier from Japan. In meetings, the Japanese would often discuss matters among themselves, speaking in Japanese. The members from the United States and Latin America decided to respond by having discussions of their own in Spanish, with even those who didn't speak Spanish pretending to do so. Using this approach, the Japanese got the message that their exclusionary caucuses were annoying.[28]

International Performance Appraisal

Performance appraisal is a formal process of assessing how effectively employees perform their jobs. Appraisals help a manager identify problem areas where an employee needs to improve and where additional training is warranted. It is an ongoing process that determines the employee's compensation and firm's performance.

Firms may give PCNs, HCNs, and TCNs a variety of organizational goals that vary from unit to unit. For example, a new foreign subsidiary might be charged with establishing relations with key customers and rapidly increasing sales. A manufacturing plant might be tasked with ensuring high productivity

Global talent pool A searchable database of employees, profiling their international skill sets and potential for supporting the firm's global aspirations.

Global team An internationally distributed group of people with a specific mandate to make or implement decisions that are international in scope.

Performance appraisal The formal process of assessing how effectively employees perform their jobs.

or maintaining quality output. Occasionally a subsidiary performs poorly, and the local manager's goal is simply to resolve local problems and get the unit back on track.

In the course of appraising performance, managers compare expected outcomes with actual performance. MNEs typically devise diagnostic procedures to assess the performance of individual employees, ascertain if any problems are attributable to inadequate skill levels, provide additional training and resources as needed, and terminate employees who consistently fail to achieve prescribed goals.

The following factors make performance evaluations more complex in the international context:[29]

- The problem of *noncomparable outcomes* arises because of differences in economic, political, legal, and cultural variables. For example, one does not punish a Mexican subsidiary manager because worker productivity is half that of the average in home-country operations. Firms need to take into account worker conditions and other factors in Mexico that result in lower productivity levels.[30] Differing accounting rules may result in financial results that appear more favorable than results evaluated according to stricter accounting rules that the firm uses at home.

- *Incomplete information* results because headquarters is separated from foreign units by both time and distance. Performance evaluation may become clouded because headquarters' superiors usually cannot directly observe employees working in the host country. To address this problem, subsidiary managers may be assessed by two evaluators—one from headquarters and one based abroad. The firm may send managers to visit subsidiaries directly to meet staff and observe local conditions firsthand. Firms often create an intranet, which provides a degree of interconnectedness among the firm's employees scattered around the world. Such a resource can serve as a growing clearinghouse of knowledge, experiences, and best practices within the firm.

- Performance outcomes may be affected by the *maturity* of foreign operations. Relatively new subsidiaries usually do not achieve the same level of results as older subsidiaries staffed with experienced personnel. New international operations usually require more time to achieve results than the norm in the home market.

Management needs to consider these factors when appraising the performance of foreign subsidiaries, affiliates, and personnel.[31] In the absence of such awareness, the headquarters staff may arrive at inaccurate or biased assessments.

Compensation of Personnel

Compensation packages vary across nations because of differences in legally mandated benefits, tax laws, cost of living, local tradition, and culture. Employees posted at foreign sites expect to be compensated at a level that allows them to maintain their usual standard of living, which can add substantially to the cost. Exhibit 18.5 presents the cost of living in selected cities. You can see that major business capitals around the world are especially costly, including Tokyo, Paris, London, Seoul, and Hong Kong.

When developing compensation packages for employees working internationally, there are generally four elements for managers to consider: base remuneration or wages, benefits, allowances, and incentives. The *base remuneration* is based on

Exhibit 18.5

Cost of Living in Selected Cities, 2006 (New York = 100)

SOURCE: Adapted from *Economist* (2006), "The Cost of Living," July 20, p. 76.

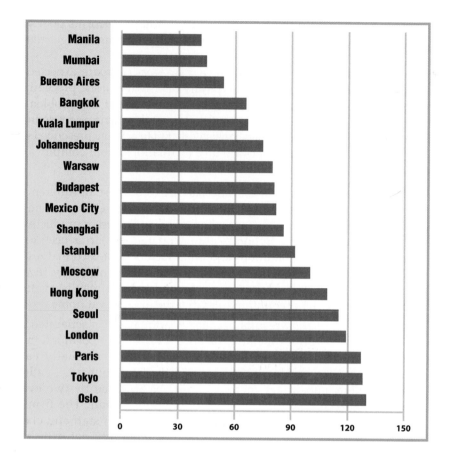

the salary or wages that the employee typically receives in his or her home country. Thus, a local factory worker in Poland would receive wages equivalent to what average factory workers receive in the particular industry in Poland. A Dutch manager working in the United States would receive a base salary comparable to that paid to managers at the same level in the Netherlands. Expatriate salaries are usually paid in the home currency, the local currency, or some combination of both.

Benefits include health care plans, life insurance, unemployment insurance, and a certain number of paid vacation days. Benefits vary greatly from country to country to the extent that they may make up a substantial proportion of the total compensation package—typically, a third of total compensation. Local regulations and industry practice tend to determine the nature of benefits. Benefits may also vary in terms of whether they are tax deductible. Expatriates receive the benefits normally accorded to home-country employees.

Allowance is an additional payment that allows the expatriate to maintain a standard of living similar to home. The allowance is usually used to pay for housing, and sometimes food and clothing. Additional support may be provided to cover expenses such as relocation and children's education, as well as business-related entertainment and travel. Housing can be very costly in major commercial centers around the world. For example, the cost of a Western-style four-bedroom apartment in Tokyo may exceed $5,000 per month. International relocation is also potentially costly, particularly if the employee insists on shipping major furniture, clothing, and other personal items abroad. Firms also provide hardship allowances to compensate employees who work in countries with civil strife or other conflicts or developing countries that lack essential housing, education, and other facilities and services.[32]

Given the potential hardships of working abroad, many MNEs also provide *incentives* to expatriate employees. The incentive is like a bonus intended to motivate the employee to undertake extraordinary efforts to accomplish company goals abroad, particularly in new foreign markets. The incentive is typically a one-time, lump-sum payment.[33]

In expatriate compensation, tax equalization is a special consideration. Expatriates may face two tax bills for the same pay, one from the host country and one from the home country. Most parent-country governments have devised regulations that allow the expatriate to minimize double taxation. Often, the expatriate may need to pay income tax in only one country. In cases where additional taxes are incurred by the employee, the employer will usually reimburse the employee for this extra tax burden.

International Labor Relations

Labor relations is the process through which management and workers identify and determine the job relationships that will be in effect at the workplace. *Labor unions* (also called trade unions) provide a means for **collective bargaining**—collective negotiations between management and hourly labor and technical staff regarding wages and working conditions. When the firm and labor union negotiate a relationship, they formalize it with a contract. Most countries maintain minimum labor standards under local law. Labor regulations vary substantially, with minimum regulations in Africa and the Indian subcontinent to highly detailed labor regulations and laws embedded in countries such as Germany and Sweden.

Union membership varies widely by country. Exhibit 18.6 illustrates the percentage of workers in each country that have formal union memberships. Note the

Collective bargaining
Collective negotiations between management and hourly labor and technical staff regarding wages and working conditions.

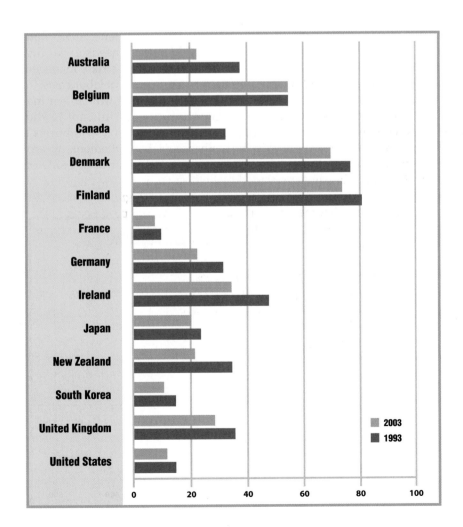

Exhibit 18.6

Percentage of Workers Who Belong to Labor Unions, 1993 and 2003

SOURCE: Adapted from Blanchflower. David, (2007), "International Patterns of Union Membership," *British Journal of Industrial Relations*, 45(1), pp. 1–28.

gradual decline, in recent years, of union membership in many advanced economies. Union membership has fallen to less than 15 percent of workers in France, South Korea, and the United States. The figure is less than 25 percent for Australia, Germany, Japan, and New Zealand. However, union membership is relatively high in Belgium, Denmark and Finland, where more than 50 percent of the workforce are unionized. In most of these countries, the majority of union members are government workers.[34]

In Central and Eastern Europe, the dissolution of the Soviet Union meant the end of mandatory union membership.[35] In many countries, younger workers are less interested in joining unions and labor laws have become less union-friendly than in the past.[36] The trend toward outsourcing of manufacturing and business processes to foreign suppliers also contributes to declining membership in trade unions. For example, Germany, a nation with a strong tradition of unionized labor, has seen a net outflow of FDI in recent years as German firms have established manufacturing in Eastern Europe and Southeast Asia.

When management and labor fail to reach agreement, the union may declare a *strike*—an organized, collective refusal to work, in order to pressure management to grant union demands. Exhibit 18.7 shows the average annual number of days not worked per 1,000 employees due to strikes and other labor disputes for various countries. Worldwide, the incidence of strikes has declined over the last decade, but strikes remain a powerful weapon for persuading management to agree to union demands. For example, French workers at Perrier, the premium bottled water producer, recently called a strike to protect wages and jobs. The left-leaning CGT (Confédération Générale du Travail) labor union represents 93 percent of Perrier's 1,650 workers, who earn an average annual salary of US$32,000, considered reasonable in southern France. Owned by Nestlé since 1992, management argued that it earns very little profit on the brand and needs to cut costs in order to improve corporate performance. In response to the strike, management threatened to move Perrier production to Eastern Europe to cut labor costs.[37]

If a strike persists for more than a few days, a *mediator* or an *arbitrator* may be called in to negotiate between labor and management in an attempt to end the strike. A mediator is an expert in labor-management relations who brings both sides together and helps them reach a mutually acceptable settlement. An arbitrator is an expert third party who delivers a judgment in favor of one side or the other, by assessing arguments presented by both sides.

Exhibit 18.7

Average Annual Days Not Worked Due to Labor Disputes (per 1,000 employees, 1996–2005)

SOURCE: Adapted from Hale, D., (2007), "International Comparisons of Labour Disputes in 2005," *Economic & Labour Market Review*, 1(4): pp. 23–31 and International Labour Organization at www.ilo.org.

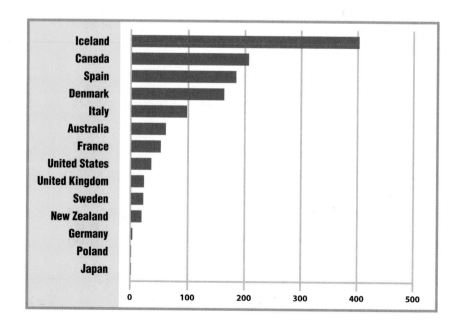

Distinctive Features of Labor around the World

Each world region has a distinctive approach to labor that is influenced by history, tradition, and other local factors. In the United States, unionization is concentrated in such industries as automobiles and steel, and is strong among public sector employees such as police and teachers. Union membership in the United States peaked in the 1950s; however, the unionized labor force in automobiles, steel, and other traditional industries has fallen dramatically in recent years. Globalization, capital mobility, and mass immigration from Mexico have substantially affected the power of organized labor, leading to continued workforce restructuring. Nevertheless, U.S. labor unions remain an important political force. In the United States, most employers accepted the 8–hour workday by 1912 and the 40–hour work week by 1950. Discrimination based on age or race has been illegal since the 1960s. Labor union activity centers on collective bargaining over wages, benefits, and workplace conditions, and on representing their members if management attempts to violate contract provisions.[38]

China's experience with collective bargaining is very recent. Given the close ties between labor and government, Western managers usually deal with the Chinese government extensively, at the national and local levels, when managing labor relations. Wal-Mart had to officially recognize unions in China—something it does not normally do. Meanwhile, China has a developing independent labor movement. In Guangzhou, 300 workers sent a letter to their factory manager demanding wage increases from less than $60 per month to the legal minimum of $69. In a recent year, Chinese workers staged some 57,000 strikes and protests to demand better wages and working conditions. The Chinese government is pushing for better conditions for China's 169 million factory workers, but progress is slow.[39] Labor activism and the number of labor disputes channeled through formal dispute resolution processes have grown significantly in recent years. The national government has undertaken several initiatives to better protect workers' rights, including new legislation and a campaign by the All-China Federation of Trade Unions aimed at unionizing workers in foreign enterprises.[40]

In Europe, labor unions have a long history. In addition to factory workers, unions often represent white-collar workers such as physicians, engineers, and teachers. Unions often hold much political power and may be allied with a particular political party—usually the Labor Party. A unique feature of the European labor union scene, especially evident in Germany and the Scandinavian countries, is the participation of labor unions in decision making about wage rates, bonuses, profit sharing, holiday leaves, dismissals, and plant expansions and closings. In 2006, the European Union passed new legislation that requires even small enterprises to inform and consult employees about a range of business, employment, and work organization issues. The legislation aimed to increase worker participation in the management of firms.[41] For example, in Sweden, labor plays a significant role in shop-floor decisions and participates in issues such as product quality standards and how to organize the factory for greater efficiency and safety. In Sweden and Germany, labor participation may be mandated, and workers often sit on corporate boards, a practice known as **codetermination**.[42] By contrast, in South Korea, the United Kingdom, and the United States, labor unions and management often hold adversarial roles.

Codetermination An industrial relations practice where labor representatives sit on the corporate board and participate in company decision making.

The Cost and Quality of Labor

Worker wages vary greatly worldwide. Advanced economies tend to pay relatively high wages, typically in the range of US$15 to $30 per hour. Wages are particularly high in Northern Europe. In developing economies, by contrast, wages

Exhibit 18.8

Cost of Labor, 2005: State-Mandated Minimum Wage Plus Social-Security Contributions as a Percentage of the Labor Cost of the Average Worker

SOURCE: Adapted from *Economist* (2005), "Cost of Labor," April 2, p. 92.

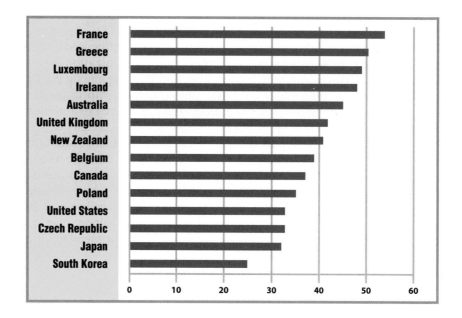

often amount to only a few dollars per day. To provide a sense of the cost of labor around the world, Exhibit 18.8 displays the state-mandated minimum wage plus social security contributions as a percentage of the labor cost of the average worker, for various countries. Note that wages constitute a relatively high proportion of labor cost in France. France's statutory minimum wage and its mandatory social security contributions amount to 54 percent of the average labor cost. In Japan, by contrast, the minimum wage plus statutory social security contributions reach only 32 percent of the cost of the average worker.

Keep in mind that the cost of labor is not the sole consideration for a firm. The quality and productivity of labor are equally important considerations. Quality and trainability of labor are highly variable around the world. Educational and training systems differ and may inhibit the availability of qualified personnel. Well-educated and skilled labor pools are scarce in some countries. Many workers require training and adaptation to the firm's culture in order to meet management's requirements. Training is a critical factor, particularly for companies that outsource business processes to emerging markets. The cost of training is likely to offset some of the cost savings that outsourcing aims to produce.

Firms must consider wages in the context of worker productivity. Low-cost labor provides little value if its productivity is commensurately low. Productivity is the value of the output produced by a unit of labor (often measured as output per hour). The more productive a worker is, the more his or her output at a given wage rate. For example, an autoworker in Canada might produce 50 radiators per day, while a worker in Mexico might produce only 30 radiators per day. Firms often outsource or offshore work abroad only to discover that the local level of productivity is less than expected. For example, all else being equal, a worker in Romania who is paid half the wage of a comparable worker in Germany provides no additional value if the Romanian worker is only half as productive as the German worker. Accordingly, when outsourcing work to foreign vendors, managers must take care to ensure that worker productivity in the host country meets acceptable levels.

Workforce Reduction

When firms experience downturns or rising input costs, they may have to resort to workforce reduction. Laying off workers (or making them "redundant," as it is referred to in the United Kingdom) is difficult in much of the world due to local norms, regulations, or strong labor unions. For example, in Japan, local custom obligates firms to avoid lay-offs or find positions for dismissed workers in supplier organizations. Most European countries have regulations that restrict management's ability to lay off workers.

Managers need to gain a full understanding of local labor laws and regulations regarding worker dismissal. In the United States, the ability to declare Chapter 11 bankruptcy enables firms to shed labor in the process of reorganization. For example, this legislation enabled auto parts manufacturer Delphi Corporation to gain concessions from the United Auto Workers union on wages, benefits, and plant closings in 2007. Delphi was able to reduce hourly wages from about $27 per hour to a $14–$18.50 range.

The firm should avoid hiring large numbers of employees until managers understand the type of workforce it needs. For some needs, part-time employees and contract workers may be a better alternative. Many countries require "just cause" to terminate an employee. If just cause cannot be demonstrated, the courts may require the employer to pay termination indemnities, a sum of money upon termination that can be substantial. In most cases, just cause is satisfied if the employee becomes permanently disabled, is terminated within a probationary period (usually between 1 and 6 months), or is guilty of incompetence, theft, or disclosure of confidential information. In most countries, the employee is almost always considered the weaker party; thus, ambiguous cases are usually settled in favor of the employee.[43]

Trends in International Labor

Several trends are affecting the international workforce. Among these is the increasing mobility of labor across national borders. Factors that are driving this trend include the growing interconnectedness of national economies, rapid expansion of multinational firms, the rise of international collaborative ventures as an internationalization strategy, and greater emphasis on global teams to accomplish organizational tasks.

Many countries are coping with an influx of immigrants, both legal and illegal, who compete with established workers by providing low-cost labor. Some nations, particularly those with labor shortages or rapidly growing economies, encourage immigration in order to access an adequate pool of workers. For example, Canada encourages immigration to bolster its pool of skilled labor. In Europe, the inflow of immigrant workers has expanded rapidly due to expansion of the European Union. For example, several million Polish workers sought employment in the United Kingdom since Poland became a member of the European Union. Persian Gulf countries have long retained large labor pools from abroad. By contrast, Japan has been reluctant to encourage worker immigration, a policy that, combined with a low birthrate, will produce labor shortages in the near future.

Formation of global alliances by national labor unions is another recent trend. To help counter weakening union power, labor organizations have lobbied supranational organizations, such as the International Labour Office (a United Nations agency) to require MNEs to comply with labor standards and practices worldwide. Some national labor unions are joining forces with unions in other countries, forming global labor/trade unions in order to equalize compensation and working conditions for workers in different geographical areas.[44] Subsidiaries of European firms in the United States have signed union-organizing agreements that compel their U.S. units to comply with European labor standards.[45] A few unions have succeeded in creating global agreements that affect all the subsidiaries of numerous MNEs. Union Network International (UNI), formed in 2000, represents 900 unions with 15 million members around the world. Firms that have signed global agreements with the UNI include Carrefour (France), Hennes & Mauritz (Sweden; owner of H&M retail stores), Metro AG (Germany), and Telefonica (Spain).

Firm Strategy in International Labor Relations

Today, complex cross-border linkages are creating sensitive interactions among differing national labor systems. Wage levels or labor unrest in one country affect the firm's activities in other countries. For example, a strike in Canada may force General Motors to shut down an engine plant in the United States for lack of parts from its Canadian subsidiary. Maintaining cohesive labor relations is critical because unions influence the cost of labor, productivity, worker morale, and firm performance.

Because national differences produce markedly different labor relations across countries, MNEs usually delegate the management of labor relations to their foreign subsidiaries. However, this can be a mistake because of the potential *global* impact of labor relations in any one country. Labor agreements made by foreign subsidiaries can affect the MNE's international plans or create precedents for negotiations in other countries. Assigning responsibility for international human resources policy to a senior executive at headquarters can help ensure consistent, systematic human resource policies.

Headquarters needs to manage the firm's labor pool worldwide. Initially, management should establish an information system that provides continuous data on labor developments. The best approach is to use the company intranet and to centralize data from subsidiaries worldwide. This information system can help managers anticipate employee concerns and devise solutions to potential threats in cross-national labor relations. A company intranet can also serve as an effective vehicle for communicating with employees worldwide and regularly informing them of the firm's mission and objectives as well as ongoing challenges and future threats. It is often easier to negotiate with labor unions when they understand the threats and challenges confronting the firm.

Another major task for IHRM is to ensure that the firm is fulfilling its corporate social responsibility in each of the countries it conducts business. The *Global Trend* feature details how one firm, Nike, is rising to this challenge.

 ## Diversity in the International Workforce

The more progressive firms in cross-border business include employees from diverse backgrounds who bring a wealth of experience and knowledge to addressing the firm's problems and opportunities. For example, Johnson & Johnson links managers' compensation to efforts to hire minorities, women, and people from varied cultural backgrounds. J&J sponsors the Women's Leadership Initiative in its various international units. Diverse groups are active in the international workforce and are accepted around the world. Nevertheless, cultural diversity increases the complexity of interaction. Language and communication styles differ from country to country, as can traditional views of hierarchy and decision-making processes. The potential for misunderstanding, bungled efforts, and ill will is substantial.

Women in International Business

In most advanced economies, men and women tend to have equal opportunity in the workplace, and working women have become the norm. In general, however, all societies impose roles on men and women. In some countries, women are

Global Corporate Citizenship in International Human Resource Management

Heightened interest in the impact of business activity on society is compelling firms to become better corporate citizens abroad. Corporate social responsibility (CSR) implies that the firm should be responsive to all its stakeholders and operate in socially acceptable ways. While managers strive to enhance firm competitiveness, they have a responsibility to serve society and to be mindful of personnel at all levels of the firm, including non-nationals. Corporate actions affect employees, regardless of whether they work directly or indirectly for the firm. Firms must behave responsibly when hiring, contracting with, and managing personnel.

Apparel and footwear has long been a low-tech industry, employing low-cost labor in emerging markets and developing economies. Firms such as Nike, Reebok, and Adidas are primarily designers, marketers, and distributors of athletic footwear, apparel, and accessories, outsourcing nearly all production to independent contractors located around the world. In the case of Nike, production is carried out by numerous suppliers that employ some 800,000 workers. Most suppliers are located in Argentina, China, India, Indonesia, Malaysia, Mexico, Portugal, South Korea, Sri Lanka, Taiwan, Thailand, Turkey, and Vietnam. Approximately 80 percent of these contract workers are women between the ages of 18 to 24. They tend to be poorly educated and desperate for jobs, leaving them vulnerable to violation of basic rights. Many supplier organizations do not yet have adequate human resource policies, leading to potential exploitation of labor.

Nike long had been accused of caring little for the welfare of its contract workers abroad. For example, in the early 1990s, workers in some Nike factories in Asia were paid wages that were insufficient to sustain even basic nutritional needs. Many supplier facilities were operated like sweatshops, where workers labored for long hours in difficult conditions. Nike executives deflected the accusations by arguing that the factories were not owned or operated by Nike and therefore Nike was not responsible for conditions in them or for worker wages.

By the early 1990s, Nike was producing hundreds of millions of shoes per year. As its global sourcing came under greater scrutiny, NGOs—non-governmental organizations, groups that undertake charitable activities—and labor advocates claimed that the workshops were rife with worker exploitation, poor working conditions, and various human rights violations. Negative publicity became a major public relations problem and made Nike a major target for the antiglobalization and antisweatshop movements.

To better understand conditions in its contract factories, Nike began performing systematic assessments in its operations abroad. In the mid-2000s, Nike improved working conditions in supplier organizations. Initially, to increase transparency, Nike disclosed the location of its more than 700 contract factories around the world. It announced CSR goals for the period through 2011 that aim to integrate corporate responsibility into the firm's business strategies and long-term growth. Management set benchmarks to improve labor conditions and eliminate excessive worker overtime. Auditing tools were developed that measure compliance with new labor standards. The firm approved plans to invest in worker development and to ensure its standards are clearly understood and followed.

The firm also has developed an approval process to ensure compliance with acceptable working conditions and to select or reject suppliers based on compliance with environmental, health, and safety assessments that require factories to meet minimum standards. Once Nike signs a contract with a factory to manufacture its products, it monitors the factory to ensure it maintains Nike standards. In 2006, Nike approved 81 new contract factories, mostly in Asia. As part of the assessment process, the firm also examines country-level factors such as quality of infrastructure, human rights, adherence to the rule of law, and economic and political conditions. Nike has sought the assistance of outside auditors in this process.

Nike management wants to ensure that workers are treated as craftspeople, not commodities. In traditional manufacturing, Nike trained workers on one task that represented one step in the process. Under the new model, Nike is retraining workers to produce in teams. Workers will be cross-trained in different skill sets and empowered to manage the production process, immediately addressing quality problems and other issues. The firm has begun training foreign suppliers in these techniques. In the process, it hopes to increase wages and improve working conditions. Nike's goals include making sure that workers at every stage of the supply chain are rewarded with locally relevant and fair wages. The firm is also introducing collective bargaining training in all contract factories. Minimum wages are to be determined through negotiations between workers and management.

Despite all these efforts, a recent Nike survey in 2006 indicated that substantial improvements were still needed in its contract factories regarding wages, benefits, and communication between local management and workers. Audits revealed that treatment of workers was at times abusive, mandated benefits were not provided, and management training was insufficient. In factories in countries such as China, Thailand, and Indonesia, local managers were not complying with Nike's improving standards. Factory management sometimes denied access to Nike's compliance inspectors and local factories often provided false information regarding working conditions. Some employees were working more than 70 hours per week or more than 2 weeks at a time without a break. Some suppliers were employing child labor and workers under the minimum legal age. In some cases, the auditors found evidence of physical abuse.

Sources: Birchall, Jonathan. (2007). "Nike to Resume Football Production in Pakistan," Financial Times, May 26–27, p. 5; Locke, Richard. (2007). The Promise and Perils of Globalization: The Case of Nike. Cambridge: Massachusetts Institute of Technology; Nike, Inc. (2007). "Nike CSR." Press release. Retrieved June 8, 2007, from www.nike.com; Nike, Inc. (2007). Workers in Contract Factories. Company report. Retrieved from www.nike.com; Skapinker, Michael. (2005). "Nike Ushers in a New Age of Corporate Responsibility," Financial Times, April 20, p. 11; Wall Street Journal, (2007). "Nike Cites Efforts to Promote Labor, Environmental Issues," June 1, p. B3

restricted to a limited set of work roles, and may have fewer legal rights than men. Economically, they are often dependent on men. Women are expected to fill prescribed traditional roles and may be excluded from commercial activities.

For example, in Latin America, a woman's marital status may be considered in the hiring process. A firm may consider a young married woman with no children a risky investment because of the perception she may soon leave the job to start a family. In Asia and the Middle East, female managers are often mistaken as the wife or secretary of a male manager. Women may have fewer opportunities to work outside the home and advance their own economic interests.

Female managers in international business are still much more the exception than the norm.[46] Consider, for example, the proportion of women working in top management positions. Exhibit 18.9 provides comparative statistics on the proportion of women in senior management. The data are based on an annual survey of 7,200 privately held medium-sized firms headquartered in 32 mostly advanced economies, representing 81 percent of total world GDP.[47] Note the unique position of the Philippines, where representation by women in senior management is highest. Interestingly, the Philippines is characterized as a country where women's rights have never been a big issue, religious practices do not clash with the right of a woman to work outside the home, and females have refined their entrepreneurial and leadership skills over many decades.

Nevertheless, the Exhibit suggests that women, as a percentage of senior management positions, still occupy a low representation in most countries. Even in the advanced economies, women are not usually afforded the same opportunities as their male colleagues for education and training. Although evidence suggests that just as many women seek international positions as men, relatively few women are asked to fill expatriate positions.[48]

There are several reasons for the relatively low representation of women in international managerial positions. First, senior managers may assume that women do not make suitable leaders abroad or that foreign men do not like reporting to female managers. Firms are reluctant to send women to locations where the demarcation between male and female roles is sharper. Even obtaining a work visa may prove problematic in such countries as Saudi Arabia. In most countries, male managers drink together, go to sports events, or enjoy the night life. Many women feel uncomfortable in all-male settings.[49]

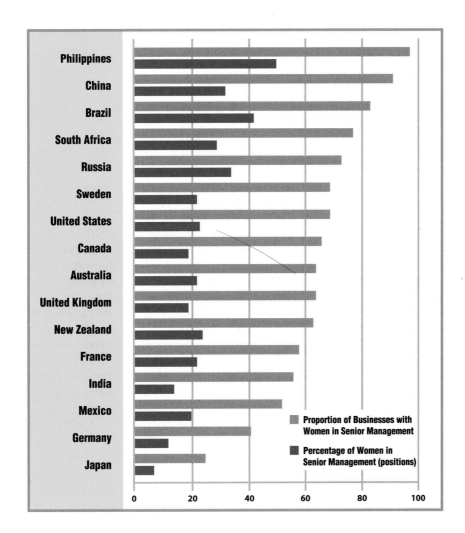

Exhibit 18.9

Comparative Statistics on Representation of Women in Senior Management

SOURCE: Adapted from Grant Thornton International Business Report, 2007, at www.grantthorntonibos.com.

In addition, some female managers prefer to remain in their home countries, to fulfill family obligations or avoid disrupting their partner's career. Disruption of children's education and caring for aging parents may be important considerations. Flexible and part-time work policies are crucial to women's progress up the corporate ladder, but few companies provide such opportunities. Finally, because women currently occupy relatively few top management positions (in Europe, women occupy only 15 percent of senior executive posts), there are fewer women with sufficient experience to be sent abroad for important jobs.[50]

More recently, we have seen several positive trends. Many more women are obtaining university degrees in business. Women account for about one-third of students in European MBA programs, and some 50 percent of recruits joining European firms are female graduates.[51] In the United States, 140 women enroll in higher education each year for every 100 men; in Sweden, the number is as high as 150.[52] Also, businesswomen increasingly form their own networks. In the United Kingdom, for example, a group of women established *Women Directors on Boards*, which aims to improve prospects for women to reach top management jobs. *The Alliance of Business Women International* is a U.S. organization that encourages and supports businesswomen involved in international business (www.abwi.org).

A recent survey by Mercer Human Resource Consulting found that companies in Asia-Pacific had 16 times more females on foreign assignments in 2006 than in 2001. Companies in North America had nearly four times as many, while those in Europe had about twice as many. About half the surveyed firms believe the number of female expatriates will continue rising in the future. At the same time,

15 percent of companies said they would not send women to hardship locations such as the Middle East. The survey involved more than 100 multinational companies with nearly 17,000 male and female expatriates.[53]

Success Strategies for Women Managers in International Business

In many countries, being a female expatriate can be an advantage. Experienced international women executives have learned and regularly take advantage of this fact. They develop and leverage their strengths as women and as managers. Women stand out more, and competent women earn much respect. In the long run, managerial competence wins out over prejudice.

Many women have found ways of overcoming senior management bias against sending females abroad. It is easier to get foreign assignments if you speak a foreign language or have other international skills. Gaining substantial experience as a domestic manager or in short international assignments can greatly improve prospects for working abroad. Garnering strong support from senior management increases credibility. Once abroad, most women report that the first reaction of surprise is often replaced by professionalism and respect. Some of the female graduates highlighted in the *Recent Grads in IB* feature in this book fit this trend.

Firms can take steps to ensure women achieve greater equality in international business. They can fill leadership roles in foreign assignments with qualified women. They can adopt guidelines where a minimum percentage of senior executive posts and selection committees are made up of women employees. They can set targets for the number of women on the executive board. A larger number of female executives are now serving as mentors and role models for aspiring women. Progressive firms appear to understand the need to forge a new paradigm of diversity and internationally successful female managers. Organizations like Accenture, Ernst & Young, and Vinson & Elkins all sponsor programs that assist women to advance in the workplace.

Sony's Evolving Human Resource Challenges

Sony employs 168,000 people worldwide, making and marketing the PlayStation home video game systems, televisions, digital and video cameras, laptop computers, personal music players, and semiconductors. The firm has several entertainment divisions, including Epic, Sony Pictures Entertainment, Sony Pictures Home Entertainment, and Sony Pictures Television. This MNE generates about 30 percent of its sales from its home-country, Japan, and roughly 23 percent from each of Europe, North America, and other regions.

Sony underwent a major management shake-up in 2005, hiring Sir Howard Stringer as chairman and CEO, the first non-Japanese to head the firm. Stringer instituted a reorganization plan to close 11 factories, cut more than 10,000 jobs, and shift component manufacturing to low-cost locations such as China. In 2006, Sony announced it would cease making Walkmans in Japan and move its production to lower-cost Malaysia and China. At the same time, the firm is building a leading-edge plant in Japan to develop and manufacture knowledge-intensive products such as semiconductors. The superior training and discipline of Japanese labor means Sony can justify the higher cost of manufacturing in Japan. In addition to Japan, Malaysia, and China, Sony's other main manufacturing plants are in Britain, Mexico, Spain, and the United States.

The national environments where Sony operates differ sharply in terms of culture, legal systems, economic conditions, technology levels, and infrastructure. In 1999 in Tijuana, Mexico, for example, a Sony executive barely escaped with his life following a carjacking. An executive at another Japanese firm in Mexico was killed during a bungled carjacking. Fortunately such incidents are rare, but expatriates must prepare for all kinds of risks.

In China, many Sony expatriates live and work in Wuxi, an industrial cluster south of Shanghai, where the firm has four subsidiaries and an R&D center. In Dalian, China, Sony has a center to develop application software. The firm was initially attracted to China because of its low-cost labor, but today it also benefits from the superior skills of the local workforce, particularly for high-technology projects. For instance, Dalian has some 26,000 experienced software engineers, and its 22 universities and technical institutes churn out thousands more software engineering grads per year.

The high concentration of foreign firms in China (such as Dell, Hitachi, Matsushita, IBM, NEC, and Hewlett-Packard) has created much competition for local talent because many firms face a shortage of new hires.

Human Resource Philosophy

Sony aims to be progressive in international human resource management. When recruiting new employees, the firm looks for candidates who have an entrepreneurial spirit, think creatively, and have strong communications skills. The firm's pursuit of diverse talent is exemplified by the firm's former chairman, Norio Ohga, who was also an opera singer, a licensed jet pilot, and an orchestral conductor. Ohga's education in music and the arts, alongside science and engineering, enabled him to advise Masaru Ibuka and Akio Morita, Sony's cofounders, on the technical advances necessary to develop the company's first tape recorders and other audio devices that resulted in some of the firm's most successful products. In all areas, Sony encourages employees to structure their roles to make best use of their individual strengths.

In Sony's foreign subsidiaries, human resource managers spend quality time with employees, linking the firm's objectives and strategies to the employee capabilities that are needed to achieve important tasks. Senior managers identify the jobs that are key to realizing the firm's objectives and analyze whether they have the best people in the most strategically important jobs and what talent they need to hire.

For example, in 2003, Sony Europe needed to restructure and reinvent itself in a difficult market due to increasing competition from South Korea and China. Human resource managers focused on identifying and leveraging the key strengths of managers and other employees as a means to enhance corporate performance. The firm introduced mentoring projects that encouraged employees to focus on what they do best and maximize their contribution to increasing firm performance.

Training and Talent Development

Sony offers management trainee programs for its most promising recruits. Trainees are counseled to do what they are passionate about and find ways to use their talents to advance the firm. Promising candidates complete formal courses, such as Sony's 2-year, eight-module program that covers all aspects of firm operations and its business practices. As the candidate progresses, the training is increasingly tailored to individual demands and career aspirations. The firm established a mentoring and coaching network across all its talent pools. Incumbent executives coach their potential successors who, in turn, act as mentors to younger upper-management candidates. Much of the training is done online. For example, for technical personnel, Sony uses an online system, TrainNet, that streamlines the development of personnel worldwide.

Sony implemented an extensive talent pipeline running vertically through the organization, developing and supporting high-potential personnel from entry level all the way to incumbent executives at senior levels of the firm. Management has a system of exhaustive interviews and assessments for identifying potential talent within the firm's own ranks. Executive fast-track candidates must be fluent in English and two other languages, have significant international experience, and possess the drive and ambition to take on international leadership roles.

Senior managers are required to continuously scan the employee pool to identify and groom potential talent. The resultant coaching system has effectively created an internal market for talent, removing the talent management function from the human resource department and establishing it as an effective tool through which the business improves. Ensuring an organization's leadership requires a strategic long-term view. Some of the talent entering Sony this year will be leading the company in 15 years. Senior managers ensure that they know employee strengths and are placed where they can be best utilized. Sony also emphasizes skillful management of its nonmanagerial workforce.

The Manufacturing Workforce

In 2001, the Japanese yen's appreciation against the dollar and the euro, combined with the costly development and launch of PlayStation2, led to a persistent decline in profitability. In response, Sony management decided to downsize design and production operations. In all, worldwide restructuring reduced the number of Sony factories from 70 to 54.

In 2003, Sony closed an audio-equipment plant in Indonesia, laying off some 1,000 workers. Industry insiders say Sony's decision was spurred by local labor unrest. The workers virtually halted manufacturing for more than 2 months while protesting a production change that required some of them to work while standing. They took to the streets with placards comparing Sony with the Japanese army that occupied Indonesia during World War II.

In the majority of cases, however, Sony management has tried to avoid laying off workers. In Britain, two Sony factories that once employed 4,000 workers making cathode ray tubes (CRTs) gradually lost their competitiveness following introduction of the flat screen TV. Sony took pains to reduce the workforce with care, working with unions to create enhanced packages and find new job opportunities in the region. Over time, management restructured the plants to produce high-definition broadcast cameras. Sony built strong customer relationships, developed new talent, created a new corporate culture, and aligned employees to the new strategy. The plants reinvented themselves by emphasizing best-in-class efforts to achieve preferred supplier status. The workforce had become much more entrepreneurial, and

one of the plants became Sony's only recognized digital center of excellence outside Japan.

Sony outsources much work to independent companies, and employs temporary workers to assist with production when product demand is high. For example, orders for PlayStation game consoles peak during Christmas. The use of temporary workers helps meet peak demand needs, keeps wage and benefit costs low, and avoids complex workforce reductions. Older employees and others often prefer seasonal work because it leaves them free during other parts of the year. For instance, at one of its U.S. plants, Sony hires 500 full-time temporary workers from August to January. Workers are offered a fair wage, health-care benefits, paid vacation, and the company's 401(k) retirement plan. In the off-season, workers have the option to extend health-care benefits. Most of the workers return year after year and provide a strong pool from which to recruit full-time staff. Temporary workers are often students seeking internships.

Corporate Social Responsibility

Sony pursues an "integrity approach" to foreign manufacturing operations and attempts to maintain workplace standards that exceed local requirements. As the firm expands internationally, management knows that actions today may be crucial for entry to new markets tomorrow. Exploiting low workplace standards in one country can ruin a reputation and jeopardize entry to new markets. For example, Sony learned a lesson from its experiences in Mexico, where human rights groups accused it of violating workers' rights to organize and associate freely.

Managers appear to have learned that simply doing what is required by the standards of the host country can result in inconsistencies in firm operations. The result may be fragmentation and difficulty in establishing effective quality control. The firm has taken steps to standardize workplace norms so that management can benchmark internal performance, transfer expertise between countries, and provide coherent management to worldwide operations. It is attempting to establish a universal standard of employment, offering superior working conditions and locally relevant wages and benefits at all locations. Managers want to ensure that wages in foreign factories provide a livable, fair standard of living to workers.

AACSB: **Reflective Thinking, Ethical Reasoning, Multicultural and Diversity**

Case Questions

1. Japanese MNEs usually follow an *ethnocentric* orientation in international staffing, in which managers from headquarters hold key subsidiary positions. Sony is shifting away from this model. What approach should Sony follow for staffing its subsidiaries? When

recruiting expatriates for foreign operations, what characteristics should Sony emphasize in order to ensure it has managers who are most adept at working abroad? What steps should the firm take to ensure its expatriate candidates are adequately prepared for long-term international assignments?

2. Sony faces challenges in finding suitable talent for its operations in China and Europe. What steps should Sony take to ensure it has an adequate pool of international managers and other talent for worldwide operations? What should Sony do to promote global mindsets?

3. What is your view of Sony's training efforts? What steps could Sony take to improve its training in light of its multicountry operations?

4. Sony has experienced labor relations problems in Indonesia and elsewhere. What strategies should management follow to improve labor relations? What can top management do to reduce the number and severity of labor difficulties that Sony might face in the future?

5. What is your view of Sony's efforts at corporate social responsibility (CSR) in international operations? What steps can Sony take to improve CSR in organizing and managing its operations around the world, particularly in developing countries and emerging markets?

Sources: Balfour, Frederik, and Hiroko Tashiro. (2005). "Golf, Sushi-and Cheap Engineers," *Business Week*, March 28, p. 54; Bream, Rebecca, and Alexandra, Harney. (2000). "Sony Plans to Streamline Its Operations," *Financial Times*, July 27, p. 32; Dhume, Sadanand. (2002). "Sony Signs Off," *Far Eastern Economic Review*, December 12, p. 19; Donkin, Richard. (2002). "Changing Lifestyles for True Fulfilment," *Financial Times*, October 10, p. 12; EIU ViewsWire. (2005). *China Finance: Japanese and South Korean Investment Migrates South*, February 11, London: Economist Intelligence Unit; Harney, Alexandra. (2000). "Japanese Fall Foul of Rise in Mexico Costs," *Financial Times*, December 21, p. 12; Hoover's profile of Sony at Hoovers.com; Kent, Simon. (2005). "Pooling Its Resources," *Personnel Today*, September, pp. 23-24; Maher, Kris. (2005). "Seasonal Hiring Expands," *Wall Street Journal*, June 20, p. A2; *Personnel Today*, (2005). "How to Keep Them Keen," June 28, p. 19; Pinkerfield, Hayley. (2007). "The Survivors," *Human Resources*, January, pp. 29-30; Rosenzweig, Philip. (1998). "How Should Multinationals Set Global Workplace Standards?" *Financial Times*, March 27, p. 11; Stewart, Graeme, and Jon French. (2005). "Creating a Corporate Shield," *Business Mexico*, October, pp. 18-25; Turner, David. (2005). "Personality, Not University, Key to Job Hunting in Japan," *Financial Times*, September 22, p. 7; *Wall Street Journal*, (1994), "Labor Department to Study Complaint Against Sony," October 20, p. B2; White, Roy. (2006). "Building on Employee Strengths at Sony Europe," *Strategic HR Review*, July/August, pp. 28-31.

CHAPTER ESSENTIALS

Key Terms

area studies, p. 556
codetermination, p. 563
collective bargaining, p. 561
cross-cultural awareness, p. 556
cultural intelligence, p. 557
culture shock, p. 555
expatriate, p. 549
expatriate failure, p. 555
global talent pool, p. 558
global team, p. 558
host-country national (HCN), p. 549
international human resource management (IHRM), p. 548
parent-country national (PCN), p. 549
performance appraisal, p. 558
practical information, p. 556
repatriation, p. 557
third-country national (TCN), p. 549

Summary

In this chapter, you learned about:

1. **The strategic role of human resources in international business**

International human resource management **(IHRM)** is the selection, training, employment, and motivation of personnel for international operations. IHRM is more complex than its domestic counterpart. The firm must develop procedures, policies, and processes appropriate for each country where it does business. A **host-country national (HCN)** is an employee who is a citizen of the country where the MNE subsidiary or affiliate is located. A **parent-country national (PCN)** is an employee

who is a citizen of the country where the MNE is headquartered. A **third-country national (TCN)** is an employee who is a citizen of a country other than the home or host country. An **expatriate** is an employee who is assigned to work and reside in a foreign country for an extended period, usually a year or longer.

There are six key tasks in IHRM: staffing, training and developing employees, performance appraisal, compensation or remuneration of employees including formulation of benefit packages that vary greatly from country to country, management of labor unions and collective bargaining processes, and achieving diversity in the workplace.

2. International staffing policy

IHRM managers determine the ideal mix of employees to work in the firm's subsidiaries and affiliates abroad. Managers best suited for working abroad typically have technical competence, self-reliance, adaptability, interpersonal skills, leadership ability, physical and emotional health, and, if present, a family prepared for living abroad. **Expatriate failure** is the unplanned early return home of an employee or the failure of an expatriate to function effectively abroad. It is not unusual for expatriates to experience culture shock.

3. Preparation and training of personnel

Proper training and orientation of managers improves firm performance. Training for foreign assignments includes **area studies, practical information,** and **cross-cultural awareness.** Training includes methods such as videos, lectures, readings, simulations, and field experience. Acquiring language skills provides managers with numerous advantages. **Repatriation** is the return of the expatriate to the home country and requires advance preparation. Training is also important for the nonmanagerial workforce abroad.

4. International performance appraisal

International performance appraisals involve providing feedback on how well employees are doing their jobs, identifying problems and areas where more training is needed, and providing a basis to reward superior performance. Firms must develop systems for measuring the performance of foreign units. Various factors in the foreign environment can impede effective performance appraisal.

5. Compensation of personnel

Compensation packages vary internationally because of differences in legally mandated benefits, tax laws, cost of living, local tradition, and culture. Expatriates expect to be compensated at a level that allows them to maintain their usual standard of living, which can be very costly in some locations. Typical expatriate compensation includes four components: base salary, benefits, allowances, and incentives. Tax equalization must be considered because expatriates may face two tax bills for the same pay, from the host and home countries.

6. International labor relations

MNEs employ many nonmanagerial employees abroad, often represented by *labor unions,* to work in factories and perform other tasks. Management must ensure effective labor relations and take care when reducing the workforce. Along with the cost of labor, the quality and productivity of the workforce are important considerations. **Codetermination,** the participation of workers on boards of directors, is common in some countries. Labor unions are sometimes at odds with the realities of global competition and the influx of immigrants in many countries. Leading MNEs establish an information system on labor developments, communicate with all employees, and formulate a standard policy on employment and working conditions worldwide.

7. Diversity in the international workforce

Progressive MNEs include personnel from diverse backgrounds, nationalities, and gender who bring a wealth of experience and knowledge to addressing the firm's problems and opportunities. Employee cultural diversity increases the complexity of interaction. Success comes from understanding and accepting differences, and then using them to enhance planning, strategy, and the firm's operations. In most countries, women are restricted to less responsible work roles. Female managers in international business are still somewhat rare. Firms can take several steps to ensure women achieve more equality in international business.

Test Your Comprehension AACSB: **Reflective Thinking, Ethical Reasoning**

1. What is international human resource management (IHRM)? Why is it important to internationalizing firms? What is the role of IHRM in company strategy?

2. Under what circumstances would an MNE staff itself with each of parent-country nationals, host-country nationals, and third-country nationals?

3. What steps can senior managers take to develop global managers?

4. What are the characteristics of managers adept at working abroad?

5. In what ways might an employee experience expatriate failure?

6. What are the major components of training for foreign assignments?

7. What approaches can human resource managers follow to prepare expatriates for returning home?

8. What factors should human resource managers consider when appraising the performance of an employee working abroad?

9. Suppose you are working abroad as an expatriate for an MNE. What are typical components you would expect to have in your compensation package?

10. What are some key trends affecting international labor?

11. What measures can firms take to enhance the prospects of placing women in international business jobs?

Apply Your Understanding
AACSB: **Communication, Reflective Thinking, Ethical Reasoning**

1. Nissan Motor Co. is Japan's second-largest automotive company, with annual sales of around US$100 billion. The firm makes Maxima and Sentra cars, Altima and Infiniti upscale sedans, Frontier pickups, and the Xterra and Pathfinder SUVs. A few years ago, Nissan was on the verge of bankruptcy. Then Carlos Ghosn was installed as the firm's CEO. He closed inefficient factories, curbed purchasing costs, and introduced new products. Suppose Nissan asked you to advise them on IHRM issues. What specific human resource strategies would you recommend to Nissan top management to further enhance the firm's performance? In particular, how would you advise top management on international staffing policy, developing global managers, preparation and training of employees, and company strategy for international labor?

2. Global Wannabe (GW), a manufacturer of musical instruments, is very eager to internationalize. While it conducts almost no international business now, the board of directors believes that in the coming four years, GW should generate at least a third of its sales from abroad by establishing foreign marketing subsidiaries and by setting up production bases in low-cost countries to reduce manufacturing costs. GW's president, Larry Gerber, has placed you on the task force charged with recruiting managers who can run GW's operations abroad. What guidelines would you offer to GW for recruiting and selecting expatriates, avoiding the problem of expatriate failure, and evaluating the performance of employees posted abroad?

3. You are looking forward to a job interview next week with Mercer, one of the larger employment consulting firms. Mercer is interested in hiring you to work in the area of international labor relations. If you get the job, you will be advising multinational firms on how to manage international labor relations, the distinctive features of labor around the world, and strategies for working with labor unions abroad. In preparing for this interview, you decide to prepare a set of systematic notes that capture the key points. Based on your research, what principles should guide firms' labor relations abroad?

globalEDGE Internet Exercises

AACSB: Communication, Reflective Thinking, Use of Information Technology

Refer to Chapter 1, page 27, for instructions on how to access and use globalEDGE™.

1. The cost of living and other lifestyle factors vary considerably around the world. It is critical to develop an appropriate compensation package for managers working abroad. The U.S. Department of State provides information that firms can use to calculate compensation around the world. Prepare a report on the factors relevant to developing a compensation package for expatriates working in Prague and Tokyo, including "Living Costs Abroad," by accessing the State Department via globalEDGE™ keywords "Travel/Living Abroad") or directly at aoprals.state.gov/.

2. Stryker Corp., a manufacturer of medical devices based in the United States, wishes to establish an assembly facility in France, Germany, or the Netherlands, so that it can better serve its European customers. You have the task of choosing the most appropriate country from the three choices by researching the following statistics: the cost of labor ("manufacturing hourly compensation index") and level of productivity ("manufacturing output per hour"). Essentially, management wants to pick the country that has the best overall profile of low labor cost and high productivity. An excel-

lent source for this data is the United States Department of Labor, Bureau of Labor Statistics (www.bls.gov). After conducting your research and analysis, prepare a recommendation as to which country—France, Germany, or the Netherlands—would be the best choice to locate the factory. (Note: Normally, such decisions are much more complex than implied in this exercise; but such a preliminary analysis could serve as a starting point for decision making.)

3. Executive Planet™ is just one of numerous portals that provide information for traveling managers and expatriates on how to live and do business in various countries. Suppose that you work for Virgin, the British airline, and you have been assigned to work in Virgin's office in an emerging market (choose an emerging market such as Argentina, India, Russia, Mexico, South Africa, or Turkey). You need to learn how to be effective in your dealings with customers and colleagues in the chosen country. Select three topics (such as making appointments, business dress guidelines, or gift giving) and prepare an executive summary on how to behave regarding the topics that you have selected for your chosen country. You can find "Executive Planet™" online via globalEDGE™ or by visiting the site directly www.executiveplanet.com.

CKR Cavusgil Knight Riesenberger

Management Skill Builder©

Evaluating International Locations for Quality of Life

Multinational firms establish regional headquarters and various subsidiaries abroad to manage company operations. Consequently, MNEs often require employees to live and work abroad for extended periods. MNEs must employ a systematic approach for relocating expatriates abroad. When identifying locations for transferring managers abroad, there are numerous factors to consider.

AACSB: Reflective Thinking

Managerial Challenge

Employees are sometimes reluctant to relocate abroad unless the quality of life is adequate. An employee may leave the company if assigned to an undesirable location. Before moving employees to a country or world region, the firm should research and consider various factors that will ensure transferred employees assimilate into the local culture. Success is determined by whether a transferee remains in the new position. An employee who returns home early or quits the firm is an expensive failure in human resource terms. The managerial challenge is to identify the most appropriate foreign locations in terms of variables such as quality of life, climate, and cost of living.

Background

National economies are more and more interconnected and the number of expatriates is on the rise. Expatriates expect to maintain a standard of living abroad similar to the one that they enjoy at home. When identifying locations for transferring managers abroad, there are numerous variables to consider. With the enlargement of the European Union, Europe has become one of the world's most attractive markets. Eastern Europe now enjoys numerous advantages, including low-wage, high-quality workers. Many firms are anxious to relocate their employees to the European continent. However, management should make such moves carefully. A failed expatriate relocation is potentially disastrous for the employee and very costly for the firm. A number

of measurable features, such as commuting times, tax rates, and housing cost can affect the ease with which an expatriate moves to a foreign city and the ease of settling into life there.

Managerial Skills You Will Gain

In this C/K/R Management Skill Builder©, as a prospective manager, you will:

1. Learn the important indicators used to assess the quality of life in various international locations.
2. Understand the types of information needed about living conditions abroad.
3. Understand factors that firms consider when relocating managers abroad for establishing a regional headquarters or subsidiary.

Your Task

Assume that you work for an MNE that is relocating some of its management staff to Europe. Your task is to conduct market research aimed at identifying the most attractive European cities, based on quality of life and other factors.

Go to the C/K/R Knowledge Portal©

www.prenhall.com/cavusgil

Proceed to the C/K/R Knowledge Portal© to obtain the expanded background information, your task and methodology, suggested resources for this exercise, and the presentation template to use.

Financial Management and Accounting in the Global Firm*

> ## How a Small Firm Rides Foreign-Exchange Waves

Markel Corporation is a Pennsylvania-based SME that makes Teflon-like tubing and insulated lead wire for the automotive industry. The family-owned firm began exporting in the mid-1980s to Germany, Spain, and Japan, and generates 40 percent of its roughly $30 million annual sales from abroad.

Markel faces daily challenges dealing with fluctuating international currencies. Every morning, CEO Kim Reynolds scans the financial news to stay abreast of how exchange rates are affecting his profits. It is a routine born of experience. In the early 2000s, an appreciating dollar made Markel's products more expensive to European and Japanese customers, which cut deeply into Markel's bottom line and forced Mr. Reynolds and other executives to take pay cuts. But the currency game works both ways. By the mid-2000s, the euro had strengthened, increasing the buying power of European customers and boosting Markel's sales revenues.

When the euro was first introduced, its value relative to the U.S. dollar sank like a rock, bottoming out at nearly $0.82 cents in the fall of 2000. That meant that each euro Markel received in sales was worth far less in U.S. dollars than the company expected. In 2001 and 2002 combined, Markel suffered more than $625,000 in currency losses, and the company posted overall losses in each year. The crisis forced management to

rethink its strategies and become more efficient. For example, Markel paid $250,000 to buy a new extruder that generates 25 percent more footage of wire per work shift. Managers cut waste material by 6 percent in the production of high-temperature oxygen-sensor wires. In these and other ways, Markel rode out the bad times as best as it could.

To small companies like Markel, swings in the $3 trillion-a-day world currency market can make or break the firm. The problem arises because Markel quotes its prices in the customer's currency. Local-currency pricing has helped Markel capture 70 percent of the world market for high-performance, Teflon-coated cable-control tubes and wires. For international sales, Markel uses a three-part strategy:

- Quote prices in the customer's currency, which translates to more consistent prices for the customer and helps Markel gain market share
- Purchase forward contracts to stabilize future dollar-denominated revenues
- Emphasize efficient company operations to make it through the times when exchange rates move in the wrong direction and hurt sales

*The authors gratefully acknowledge the valuable contributions of Professor Hakan Saraoglu, Bryant University, in the preparation of this chapter. Thanks are also due to Professors Raj Aggarwal of the University of Akron, Kirt Butler of Michigan State University, Chuck Kwok of the University of South Carolina, and Betty Yobaccio of Bryant University for reviewing earlier drafts.

A *forward contract* is an agreement to buy or sell currency at an agreed-upon exchange rate for delivery at a specific future date. Firms such as Markel buy forwards from banks in order to hedge exchange-rate exposure. The goal of *hedging* is to balance purchases and sales of foreign currencies to minimize exposure to future currency risk. Suppose that Markel sells merchandise to its Spanish importer for €50,000, payable in 90 days. Because there is a delay in getting paid, Markel is exposed to currency risk: If the euro depreciates during the 90-day period, Markel will receive fewer dollars. To counteract this risk, Markel enters a forward agreement to sell €50,000, 90 days in the future, at an exchange rate agreed upon today, ensuring that it receives a known dollar amount.

When Markel's chief financial officer thinks the dollar is on its way up, he hedges his expected euro revenue stream with a forward contract. But his estimate isn't always correct. For instance, suppose Markel buys a €50,000 contract at $1.05 per euro, or $52,500. Next, suppose that when the contract is exercised at the end of the 90-day period, the euro is actually trading at $1.08. Had Markel estimated correctly, it could have made an extra $1,500. Like most international firms, Markel is not in the business of trying to make money on foreign exchange trading. Management just wants to minimize its international currency risks. ◄

Source: Phillips, Michael M. (2003). "How a Small Firm Rides Foreign-Exchange Waves," *Wall Street Journal*, February 7, accessed July 7, 2006 at http://online.wsj.com/article/0,SB104458055572499453,00.html

International *financial management* refers to the acquisition and use of funds for cross-border trade, investment, and other commercial activities. Financial management is a major business function that is more complex for firms engaged in international business. The firm must learn to carry out transactions in a multitude of foreign currencies and operate in diverse environments characterized by restrictions on capital flows, country risk, and varying accounting and tax systems.

Imagine the relatively new challenges for the contemporary firm: increasing globalization, the integration of financial markets, the rise of global e-commerce, and expanding opportunities to profit from financial activities. The firm's ability to minimize risk and seize opportunities depends on its financial management skills. Financial managers access funds from a variety of sources—foreign bond markets, local stock exchanges, foreign banks, venture capital firms, and intracorporate financing—based on wherever in the world capital is cheapest.

Firms engaged in international business need capital to fund such activities as R&D, manufacturing, and marketing, pay for products and services sourced from abroad, and set up and run foreign operations and subsidiaries. Access to funding is critical for smaller firms that receive large product orders from abroad and must finance the production of goods as they wait for payment from foreign customers. These funds often come from investors. Investors acquire stakes in foreign firms by buying corporate bonds from banks and other intermediaries, investing in foreign stock markets, or investing directly in promising international firms. International financial activity also takes the form of speculation in foreign currency and stock markets and buying and selling of foreign exchange contracts.

 ## Primary Tasks in International Financial Management

Consider the managers at a multinational company such as Motorola, which has facilities in nearly 50 countries and raises funds in financial markets worldwide. The firm's managers must therefore be familiar with the laws and regulations that govern the financial exchanges worldwide. The financial dimensions of Motorola's activities are managed globally, through a network of subsidiaries and strategic business units. The units are a complex web of financial coordination and control processes supplemented by investment analysis, capital structure optimization, risk reduction, and the mobilization of global financial resources.

The international financial manager is involved in the acquisition and allocation of financial resources for the firm's current and future activities and projects, with the primary objective of maximizing the firm's value. These managers need to be competent in carrying out six major financial management tasks critical to firms engaged in international business. Exhibit 19.1 highlights these tasks:

1. *Decide on the capital structure*—determine the ideal long-term mix of debt versus equity financing for the firm's international operations.

2. *Raise funds for the firm*—acquire equity, debt, or intracorporate financing for funding value-adding activities and investment projects.

3. *Working capital and cash flow management*—manage funds passing in and out of the firm's value-adding activities.

4. *Capital budgeting*—assess the financial attractiveness of major investment projects (e.g., foreign market expansion and entry).

5. *Currency risk management*—manage the multiple-currency transactions of the firm and the exposure to risk created by exchange rate fluctuations.

6. *Manage the diversity of international accounting and tax practices*—learn to operate in a global environment with diverse accounting practices and international tax regimes.

You should note that, the greater the scale of international operations for the firm, the greater is the relevance of these international financial management tasks. In other words, an MNE with a large number of subsidiaries and affiliates around the world will need to dedicate considerably more attention to efficient handling of cross-border acquisition and use of funds than a smaller exporter. Yet, it is precisely this scale of global operations that gives the firm the strategic flexibility that we discussed in Chapter 11. Geographic diversification gives the firm the opportunity to tap capital at a lower cost, minimize overall tax obligations, achieve efficient scale of financial operations, and gain greater bargaining power with lenders.

The six international financial management tasks also serve as the basis for organizing the content of this Chapter. Let's delve more deeply into each task.

Exhibit 19.1

International Financial Management Tasks

Equity financing The issuance of shares of stock to raise capital from investors and the use of retained earnings.

Debt financing The borrowing of money from banks or other financial intermediaries, or selling corporate bonds to individuals or institutions to raise capital.

 Task One: Decide on the Capital Structure

A *capital structure* is the mix of long-term *equity financing* and *debt financing* firms use to support their international activities. The capital structure affects the profitability and stability of the firm and its international operations. The firm obtains **equity financing** by selling shares of stock to investors or by retaining earnings, which is profit reinvested in the firm rather than paid to investors. Shares of stock provide an investor with an ownership interest—that is, equity—in the firm. In new companies, founders often provide equity financing through personal savings. **Debt financing** comes from either of two sources: loans from banks and other financial intermediaries or money raised from the sale of corporate bonds to individuals or institutions.

Debt service payments—the periodic principal and interest payments to pay off a loan—are a fixed cost. Using debt financing can add value to the firm because some governments allow firms to deduct interest payments from their taxes. To maintain a good credit rating and minimize the possibility of going bankrupt, most MNEs keep the debt proportion of their capital structure below a maximum threshold that they can service even when facing adverse conditions. Too much debt can force companies into financial distress, possibly bankruptcy. This was exemplified by the Asian financial crisis of 1997. Inadequate equity markets in Indonesia, Malaysia, and Thailand forced firms in those countries to rely excessively on debt to finance business growth. Worse, banks in the region borrowed U.S. dollars from Western banks and then loaned the money as local currencies in their home markets. When the value of the Asian currencies fell against the U.S. dollar, thousands of banks and other firms in the region could not service their debt obligations and went bankrupt.[1]

In the United Kingdom and the United States, one study found that firms' average debt ratio—debt divided by total assets—is about 0.55.[2] In other words, the capital structure is composed of roughly equal amounts of debt and equity financing. How much debt a firm should hold partly depends on the nature of its industry and target markets. For instance, a company with relatively stable sales (e.g., an insurance company) that sells mainly to affluent foreign markets can sustain a higher debt ratio in its capital structure than a consumer goods firm that sells to a range of mostly poor countries with highly cyclical sales.

Not all countries view substantial debt as risky. For example, the average debt ratio is 0.62 in Germany, 0.76 in Italy, and occasionally even higher in Japan and some developing countries.[3] This view arises for a couple of reasons. First, the country may lack a well-developed stock market or other systems for obtaining capital from equity sources. Hence, firms may have little choice but to borrow money from banks. Second, a nation's firms may have much closer relationships with banks. In Japan, large MNEs are often part of a conglomerate or a holding company that also includes a bank. For instance, Japan's Sony Corporation has its own bank, Sony Bank.

Global money market The collective financial markets where firms and governments raise short-term financing.

Global capital market The collective financial markets where firms and governments raise intermediate-term and long-term financing.

 Task Two: Raise Funds for the Firm

There are various ways for firms to raise funds to finance company operations. Lufthansa Airlines recently raised several hundred million euros by issuing stock shares to acquire A380 airplanes, the new double-decker aircraft from Airbus. Grupo Mexico, a giant producer of copper and silver, issued millions of peso-denominated shares to honor debts and other commitments incurred by its foreign subsidiaries. Stanley Works, the U.S. toolmaker, funds part of its Japanese operations by selling shares on the Tokyo Stock Exchange.

Firms can obtain financing in the **global money market**, which are the collective financial markets where firms and governments raise short-term financing, and the **global capital market**, which are the collective financial markets where firms and governments raise intermediate- and long-term financing. Since funding for most projects comes from instruments whose maturity period is over one year, we refer to all such funding as *capital.* We focus on the global capital market because it is the meeting point of those who want to invest money and those who want to raise funds.

The key advantage of participating in the global capital market is the ability to access funds from a larger pool of sources at a competitive cost. The great advantage for international investors is the ability to access a much wider range of investment opportunities than is available in the domestic capital market. This can result in higher prices for securities in international markets, and hence lower capital costs for MNEs with access to international capital markets. In one study, top managers at MNEs in France suggested that access to capital is one of the main criteria they consider when deciding where to expand internationally.[4]

Financial Centers

The global capital market is concentrated in major *financial centers:* New York, London, and Tokyo. Major secondary centers include Frankfurt, Hong Kong, Paris, San Francisco, Singapore, Sydney, and Zurich. At these locations, firms can access the major suppliers of capital—banks, stock exchanges, and venture capitalists. Exhibit 19.2 lists the share of major financial markets held by Europe, the United States, and the rest of the world. For example, Europe is home to the

Exhibit 19.2

Share of Financial Markets in Major World Regions

SOURCE: From *Financial Times,* October 12, 2005. Data from International Financial Services.

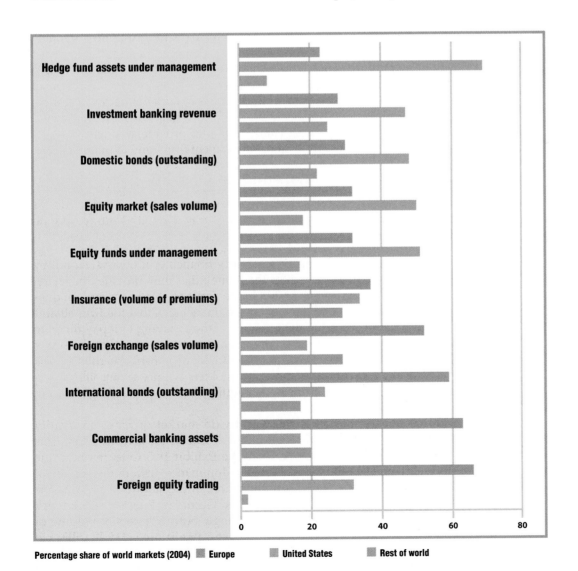

Percentage share of world markets (2004) ▪ Europe ▪ United States ▪ Rest of world

largest volume of outstanding international bonds (59 percent of the world total), the United States is home to the largest volume of investment banking revenue (47 percent), and countries outside Europe and the United States have sizeable markets in insurance and foreign exchange (29 percent for both). Europe's global share of financial markets has been rising in recent years, although the United States remains dominant in many markets.

The global capital market is huge and growing rapidly. In 2006:

- International issues of equity in world securities markets amounted to about $380 billion, up from $83 billion in 1996 and just $14 billion in 1986.
- The stock of cross-national bank loans and deposits was $18,916 billion, up from $7,205 billion 10 years earlier.
- There were some $17,574 billion in outstanding international bonds and notes, up from $3,081 billion in 1996.[5]

What are the causes of the rapid rise in the global capital markets? There are at least four reasons. First, the deregulation of financial markets by national governments has led to easier movement of capital across national borders. Second, innovation in information and communication technologies has accelerated the ease and pace of global financial transactions. Third, the globalization of business activity compels firms to seek new and more cost-effective ways to finance global operations and to be innovative in financial management activities. Fourth is the widespread *securitization* of financial instruments. Securitization is the process of converting an illiquid financial instrument, such as a bank loan, into a tradable security, such as stocks.

The global capital market provides three key advantages for the firm. First, compared to being restricted to financial markets in their home countries, the global market provides a broader base from which the firm can draw its financing needs. Second, the greater breadth of financing sources means that firms can often access funding at substantially reduced cost. Third, the market provides a variety of investment opportunities for MNEs, professional investment firms, and individuals.

Sources of Funds for International Operations

Let's now consider, in greater detail, the three primary sources of funds for international operations: equity financing, debt financing, and intracorporate financing.

Equity Financing When the firm uses equity financing, it obtains capital by selling shares of stock. In exchange for the money that they provide, the shareholders obtain a percentage of ownership in the firm and, often, a stream of dividend payments. The main advantage of equity financing is that the firm obtains needed capital without incurring debt; that is, without having to repay funds to the providers at any particular time. The main disadvantage is that the firm's ownership is diluted whenever new equity is sold. Management also runs the risk of losing control in the event one or more shareholders acquire a controlling interest in the firm. Internationally, firms obtain equity financing by selling shares in the global equity market.

Global equity market The worldwide market of funds for equity financing—the stock exchanges throughout the world where investors and firms meet to buy and sell shares of stock.

The **global equity market** is the worldwide market of funds for equity financing—the stock exchanges throughout the world where investors and firms meet to buy and sell shares of stock. Examine Exhibit 19.3 to learn about the largest stock exchanges in the world. Note the dominance, in both the volume of shares traded as well as the market capitalization, of the stock exchanges in the United States, the United Kingdom, Japan, and Germany. The New York Stock Exchange (NYSE) is clearly the largest exchange, both in terms of volume of shares traded ($21.79 trillion in 2006) and market capitalization ($15.42 trillion in 2006). Among the roughly 3,600 firms listed, about 450 are foreign-owned firms from Europe, Canada, Asia, and Latin America. Apart from accessing new

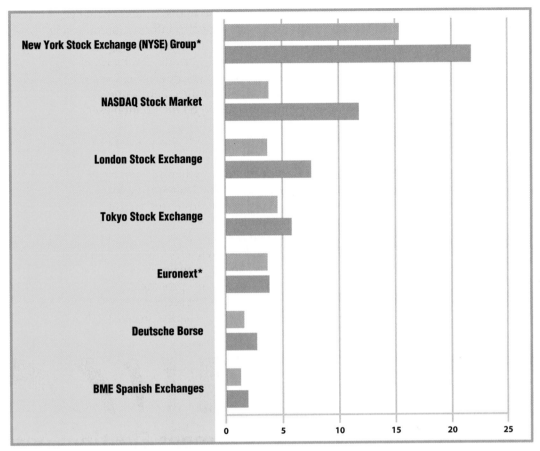

New York Stock Exchange (NYSE) Group*

NASDAQ Stock Market

London Stock Exchange

Tokyo Stock Exchange

Euronext*

Deutsche Borse

BME Spanish Exchanges

0   5   10   15   20   25

■ Domestic Equity Market Capitalization (trillions of U.S. dollars)
■ Total Value of Share Trading (trillions of U.S. dollars)

*Note: NYSE and Euronext completed a merger in April 2007 to form the NYSE Euronext.

Exhibit 19.3 Largest Stock Exchanges in the World by Value of Shares Traded, 2006

SOURCE: From *The Economist* (2006), "Battle of the Bourses," May 27, 2006. Copyright © 2006 The Economist. Used with permission.

investors, firms that cross-list their shares in other exchanges may actually derive higher valuations than those that don't. One study found that firms that cross-listed their shares enjoyed a valuation premium of about 14 percent; for those non-US firms that have listed on a major exchange such as the NYSE, the premium is about 31 percent.[6]

As an investor, you are by no means limited to buying equity in firms listed in the stock exchanges of your home country. In fact, an important trend today is that of investors who buy stocks on foreign exchanges. The trend has greatly accelerated in recent years due to the large-scale activities of institutional investors.[7] Pension funds—funds that manage the investments of employee savings for retirement—represent the largest portion of this trend. The size of these funds has reached remarkable proportions in the advanced economies. For example, in 2005, the cumulative value of pension funds exceeded the respective GDPs in the Netherlands (125 percent) and Switzerland (117 percent). They amounted to more than 60 percent of the GDPs of the United States, United Kingdom, and Finland.[8] When combined with invested life insurance assets, the global pension assets exceed $10 trillion.[9] The origin of much of these investments is foreign. In 2000, for instance, foreign investment amounted to about 40 percent of the pension sectors in Belgium and France and 60 percent in the Netherlands.[10] At one point, CALPERS, the pension fund of the state of California, accounted for 5 percent of the French stock exchange.[11]

The marriage of technology and trading has allowed stock exchanges to grow rapidly. The Internet has vastly improved access to information on foreign markets and trading on international exchanges. Investing in foreign markets makes sense for two main reasons: diversification and opportunity. By investing internationally, investors can minimize losses during slumps in the local economy and take advantage of foreign investment opportunities. For example, Britons invest in the several hundred foreign companies listed on the London exchange, including Canon, Fujitsu, and South African Breweries.[12]

Growing mergers and collaborations between exchanges in European countries facilitate international trading. The 2006 merger of the NYSE and the Euronext exchange—a Paris-based pan-European stock exchange with subsidiaries in Belgium, France, the Netherlands, Portugal, and the United Kingdom—contributed to increased transatlantic trading.[13] Many recent advances are due to the Internet, which facilitates online trading. In contrast to the past, when traders depended on expensive stock brokers, almost anyone can now trade on world stock markets at very low cost. Even a small market like the Cayman Islands Stock Exchange offers full online investing opportunities. Typical of the new breed of small technology-driven virtual exchanges, the Cayman's exchange provides a listing facility for Caribbean offshore mutual funds and specialist debt securities. Read the *Global Trend* feature to learn about the development of stock exchanges in emerging markets.

>GLOBAL TREND

Emerging Markets as International Investment Destinations

Many investors view stocks in emerging markets as a good bet because of the formation in these countries of numerous, fast-growing firms, and their competitive advantages of low-cost labor and superior products. While some of the emerging markets still have political regimes that do not consistently follow the rule of law and shareholder rights, their economies often are geared for global growth.

Nevertheless, emerging market stocks are not without considerable risk. Investors were badly burned by a series of crises and poor returns in the 1990s. In 1994, the "tequila crisis" in Mexico hurt investors when the Mexican government devalued its currency.

The tequila crisis was followed by the Asian financial crisis in 1997, when countries such as Thailand and Malaysia saw their currencies severely devalued as banks in the region could not service their debt obligations. The interconnected nature

of financial markets worldwide, made possible by modern information and communications technologies, also meant that the Asian financial crisis produced global shockwaves and prompted a sell-off in world stock markets.[14]

As recently as 1998, the Russian government devalued its currency and defaulted on its debt. Equity markets in Argentina and Turkey also have experienced considerable volatility. Share-price indices on the Shanghai and Shenzhen exchanges have been extremely volatile, and the Chinese government has yet to develop a sound regulatory system and institutions for securities trading.

As opportunities arise in emerging markets to invest in stock markets and undertake FDI, firms and governments in these countries increasingly understand that the cost of capital goes hand in hand with good governance and respect for shareholder rights. Companies that abuse shareholders by not providing

periodic earnings reports find it hard to raise money from the public.

In order to accommodate the growing demand to invest in emerging markets, local stock exchanges are becoming increasingly sophisticated. Stock exchanges in Brazil, China, and South Korea each have several hundred corporate listings, worth hundreds of billions of dollars. In smaller countries, the stock exchange may be a one-room operation with a blackboard and a telephone. Thus, nations such as Bhutan, Oman, and Kazakhstan have established primitive exchanges in the hope of becoming the next Chile or Singapore.

Sources: Burgess, Kate. (2002). "The Wheel Is Spinning, Once Again: Don't Be Seduced by Siren Calls to Invest in Emerging Markets," *Financial Times,* March 30, p. 01; *Economist.* (2005). "China's Stockmarket: A Marginalized Market," February 26, pp. 71–72; *Forbes.* (2006). "Global Markets," March 27, p. 150; Gunn, Eileen. (1997). "Emerging Markets," *Fortune,* August 18, pp. 23–24.

Debt Financing

In debt financing, a firm borrows money from a creditor in exchange for repayment of principal and an agreed-upon interest amount in the future. The primary advantage of debt financing over equity financing is that the firm does not sacrifice any ownership interests to obtain needed capital. As noted earlier, debt financing is obtained from two sources: loans and the sale of bonds.

International Loans. The firm may borrow money from banks in its home market or in foreign markets. It may borrow funds denominated in the home currency or in foreign currencies. However, borrowing internationally is complicated by cross-national differences in banking regulations, inadequate banking infrastructure, shortage of loanable funds, macroeconomic difficulties, and fluctuating currency values.[15] Banks are often reluctant to extend credit to small and medium-sized enterprises (SMEs), so these firms may turn to government agencies such as the Export Import (Ex-IM) Bank, a federal agency in the United States for direct loans, working capital loans, and loan guarantees. Similarly, governments in the developing world often provide loans to promote inward foreign direct investment (FDI) projects such as the construction of dams, power plants, and airports. Finally, many subsidiaries of large MNEs obtain loans from their parent firm or a sister subsidiary.

The Eurocurrency Market. Another key source of loanable funds is money deposited in banks outside its country of origin. Although its role has declined somewhat in favor of the euro, the U.S. dollar accounts for the largest proportion of these funds.[16] **Eurodollars** are U.S. dollars held in banks outside the United States, including foreign branches of U.S. banks. Thus, a U.S. dollar-denominated bank deposit in Barclays Bank in London or Citibank in Tokyo is a Eurodollar deposit. More broadly, any currency deposited in a bank outside its country of origin is called a **Eurocurrency**. Eurodollars account for roughly two-thirds of all Eurocurrencies. Interestingly, more than two-thirds of U.S. banknotes are often held outside the United States as a reserve currency. The firms Matsushita and Hitachi borrowed Eurodollars in Japan to finance much of their worldwide operations. Other Eurocurrencies include euros, yen, and British pounds, as long as they are banked outside their home country.

The Eurocurrency market is attractive to firms because these funds are not subject to the same government regulations as in their home-country banking systems. For instance, U.S. dollars on deposit in French banks and euros on deposit in U.S. banks are not subject to the same reserve requirements of their home countries. Compared to local currencies, banks offer higher interest rates on Eurocurrency deposits and charge lower interest rates for Eurocurrency loans. These differences contributed to the emergence of a huge Eurocurrency market.

Eurodollars are deposited in banks such as Barclays Plc., Britain's third-largest bank. Eurocurrencies, funds banked outside their country of origin, are a key source of loanable funds for international business.

Eurodollars U.S. dollars held in banks outside the United States, including foreign branches of U.S. banks.

Eurocurrency Any currency deposited in a bank outside its country of origin.

Bond A debt instrument that enables the issuer (borrower) to raise capital by promising to repay the principal along with interest on a specified date (maturity).

Global bond market The international marketplace in which bonds are bought and sold, primarily through banks and stockbrokers.

Foreign bond A bond sold outside the issuer's country and denominated in the currency of the country in which it is issued.

Eurobond A bond sold outside the issuer's home country but denominated in its own currency.

Intracorporate financing Funds provided from sources inside the firm (both the headquarters and subsidiaries) such as equity, loans, and trade credits.

Bonds. A major source of debt financing is bonds. A **bond** is a debt instrument that enables the issuer (borrower) to raise capital by promising to repay the principal along with interest on a specified date (maturity). Along with firms, governments, states, and other institutions also sell bonds. Investors purchase bonds and redeem them at face value in the future. The **global bond market** is the international marketplace in which bonds are bought and sold, primarily through banks and brokers.

Foreign bonds are sold outside the bond issuer's country and denominated in the currency of the country in which they are issued. For example, when Mexican cement giant Cemex sells dollar-denominated bonds in the United States, it is issuing foreign bonds. **Eurobonds** are sold outside the bond issuer's home country but denominated in its own currency. For example, when Toyota sells yen-denominated bonds in the United States, it is issuing Eurobonds. The telecommunications giant AT&T has issued hundreds of millions of dollars in Eurobonds to support its international operations. Pharmaceutical firms Eli Lilly and Merck have funded much of their multinational operations from Eurobonds. Eurobonds are typically issued in denominations of $5,000 or $10,000, pay interest annually, and are sold in major financial centers, especially London.

Intracorporate Financing

Funding for international operations can also be obtained from within the firm's network of subsidiaries and affiliates. Where some units at times are cash rich, others are cash poor and need capital. Consequently, members of the MNE family—both headquarters and subsidiaries—can provide financing to one another. **Intracorporate financing** refers to funds provided from sources inside the firm in the form of equity, loans, and trade credits. Trade credit arises when a supplier of goods and services grants the customer the option to pay at a later date.

There are several advantages associated with the practice of MNEs loaning funds to their foreign subsidiaries. First, because interest payments are often tax deductible, the borrowing subsidiary's income tax burden is reduced. Second, an intracorporate loan has little effect on the parent's balance sheet when financial results are consolidated into the parent's financial statements, because the funds are simply transferred from one area of the firm to another. Third, a loan within the MNE may save transaction costs (fees charged by banks to exchange foreign currencies and transfer funds between locations) of borrowing funds from banks. Finally, a loan avoids the ownership-diluting effects of equity financing.

As an example, IBM's global financing division invests in international financing assets and obtains and manages international debt, all aimed at supporting IBM's global operations. The division provides loan financing to internal users for terms generally between two and five years. It provides inventory and accounts receivable financing to IBM's dealers and subsidiaries in various countries.[17]

 ## Task Three: Working Capital and Cash Flow Management

Recall that *working capital* refers to the current assets of a company. *Net working capital* is the difference between current assets and current liabilities. As part of working capital management, firms manage all current accounts, such as cash, accounts receivable, inventory, and accounts payable. An important component of working capital management in the MNE is cash flow management, which ensures that cash is available where and when it is needed. Cash flow needs arise from everyday business activities, such as paying for labor and materials or resources, servicing interest payments on debt, paying taxes, or paying dividends to shareholders. Cash is generated from various sources, including the sale of goods and services, and often needs to be transferred from one part of the MNE to another. International finance managers devise various strategies for transferring funds within the firm's worldwide operations in order to optimize global operations.

The number of sources of intracorporate transfers is a function of the number of subsidiaries, alliances, and business relationships worldwide. For firms with extensive international operations, the network of potential intracorporate fund transfers is both vast and complex. For example, the 2002 bankruptcy of the energy giant Enron resulted, in part, from the enormous amount of debt that management had hidden in the firm's various subsidiaries worldwide. Remarkably, roughly a third of world trade results from the collective trading activities represented within the MNE network, composed of the headquarters and its subsidiaries. In other words, a considerable proportion of world trade is the result of intracorporate transfers.

Methods for Transferring Funds within the MNE

For MNEs with extensive international operations, like Siemens, Johnson & Johnson, and Kyocera Corporation, intracorporate fund transfers are very important. Financial managers must be aware of the different methods of transferring funds within the MNE so that they can move funds most efficiently, minimizing transaction costs and tax liabilities while maximizing the returns that can be earned with those funds.

MNEs employ a variety of systems for cross-national funds movement. This is illustrated in Exhibit 19.4, which depicts a typical firm with subsidiaries in Mexico and Taiwan. Within its network, this firm can transfer funds through trade credit, dividend remittances, royalty payments, fronting loans, transfer pricing, and multilateral netting. Here is how each works:

- Through *trade credit*, a subsidiary can defer payment for goods and services received from the parent company. Credit terms tend to be longer in foreign markets, compared to the United States. Where the 30-day credit is the norm in the United States, 90-day credit is more typical in Europe, with even longer terms elsewhere.

- *Dividend remittances* are a common method for transferring funds from foreign subsidiaries to the parent, but vary for each subsidiary depending on factors such as tax levels and currency risks. For instance, some host governments levy high taxes on dividend payments, which discourages

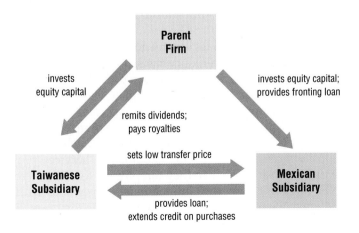

Exhibit 19.4

Typical Methods for Transferring Funds Within the MNE

MNEs from using this approach. Governments can also limit how much MNEs can remit.

- *Royalty payments* are remuneration paid to the owners of intellectual property, as we saw in Chapter 15. Assuming the subsidiary has licensed technology, trademarks, or other assets from the parent or other subsidiaries, royalties can be an efficient way to transfer funds. Also, because they may be viewed as an expense, royalties are tax deductible in many countries. A parent MNE can collect royalties from its own subsidiaries as a way of generating funds.

Fronting loan A loan between the parent and its subsidiary, channeled through a large bank or other financial intermediary.

- A **fronting loan** is a loan between the parent and its subsidiary, channeled through a large bank or other financial intermediary. Using this approach, the parent deposits a large sum in a foreign bank, which then transfers the funds to the subsidiary in the form of a loan. Fronting allows the parent to circumvent restrictions that foreign governments impose on direct intracorporate loans. For one, if the loan is made through a bank in a **tax haven**—a country hospitable to business and inward investment because of its low corporate income taxes—the parent can minimize taxes that might otherwise be due if the loan were made directly. In addition, while some countries restrict the amount of funds that can be transferred abroad within the MNE in order to preserve foreign exchange, such restrictions usually do not apply to the repayment of bank loans.

Tax haven A country hospitable to business and inward investment because of its low corporate income taxes.

- *Transfer pricing* (also known as *intracorporate pricing*) refers to prices that subsidiaries and affiliates charge one another as they transfer goods and services within the same MNE. As you will recall from Chapter 17, firms can use transfer pricing to shift profits out of high-tax countries into low-tax countries, minimize foreign exchange risks, for example, by moving funds out of countries where a currency devaluation is forecast, and optimize the management of internal cash flows.[18] Keep in mind the drawbacks of transfer pricing, however, as we discussed in Chapter 17.[19]

Multilateral netting, another method of funds transfer within the MNE, requires a more detailed discussion, which we provide next.

Multilateral Netting

In the past, cash usually was held in each foreign subsidiary that was responsible for funding its own short-term needs. However, MNE managers increasingly understand the value of concentrating the firm's financial operations at some central location, known as a *centralized depository*. Using a method known as *pooling*, MNEs bring together surplus funds into either regional or global depositories. They then direct these funds to needful subsidiaries or invest the funds to generate income.

A centralized depository provides several advantages. First, by pooling funds in a central location, managers can reduce the size of highly liquid accounts and use the funds in longer-term investments that can provide higher returns. Second, interest rates on large deposits are normally higher than rates for small investments. Third, if the depository is based in a financial center (for example, London, New York, Sydney, or Toronto), then management can more easily access a variety of financial instruments for short-term investments that pay higher rates of return. Finally, the depository centralizes expertise and financial services, providing more benefits to the firm's subsidiaries than they can provide for themselves.

Large MNEs carry out numerous international transactions within their network of subsidiaries. Each transaction generates transaction costs. For example, suppose a firm's Japanese subsidiary owes the Spanish subsidiary $8 million and, simultaneously, the Spanish subsidiary owes the Japanese subsidiary $5 million. The firm could handle these outstanding balances in separate transactions, by having the Japanese subsidiary pay $8 million to the Spanish subsidiary, and the Spanish subsidiary pay $5 million to the Japanese subsidiary. A more intelligent solution, however, would be to reduce transaction costs by having the Japanese subsidiary make a net payment of $3 million to the Spanish subsidiary. In this way, the remaining debt is canceled by transferring an amount that is considerably less than either of the two original amounts, with a commensurate reduction in transactions costs such as fees and delays in funds transfers.

Accordingly, **multilateral netting** refers to the strategic reduction of cash transfers within the MNE family through the elimination of offsetting cash flows. It involves three or more subsidiaries that hold accounts payable or accounts receivable with one other subsidiary. MNEs with numerous subsidiaries usually establish a netting center that headquarters supervises. For example, Philips, a leading Dutch consumer electronics firm, has operating units in some 60 countries. Philips has a netting center to which subsidiaries regularly report all intracorporate balances on the same date. The center subsequently advises each subsidiary of the amounts to pay and receive from other subsidiaries on a specified date. Philips avoids considerable transaction costs because of multilateral netting.

Multilateral netting Strategic reduction of cash transfers within the MNE family through the elimination of offsetting cash flows.

Task Four: Capital Budgeting

The major decisions in international business include which foreign markets to enter and what to accomplish in each market. Firms must decide whether to invest in ventures as diverse as launching a major exporting effort, acquiring a distribution center, building a new factory, or refurbishing industrial equipment. Since firms have limited resources, they cannot afford to invest in every project that comes their way. The purpose of *capital budgeting* is to help managers decide which international expansion projects are economically desirable.

The ultimate decision to accept or reject an investment project depends on the project's initial investment requirement, its cost of capital, and the amount of incremental cash flow or other advantages that the proposed project is expected to provide. Internationally, such decisions are complex, because managers must consider many variables, each of which can strongly affect the potential profitability of a venture. For example, when doing the capital budgeting for locating foreign restaurants in the fast food industry, managers consider such variables as the cost of alternative locations and the level of local competition, as well as the effect on projected revenue of the distance to highways, availability of public transportation, and the amount of traffic at each location.[20]

Net Present Value Analysis of Capital Investment Projects

Managers typically employ net present value (NPV) analysis to evaluate international capital investment projects. NPV is the difference between the present value of a project's incremental cash flows and its initial investment requirement.[21]

Four special considerations complicate international capital budgeting for financial managers

This McDonald's franchise is in Wuhan, China. MNEs such as McDonald's conduct capital budgeting to determine which foreign locations are economically desirable. Managers account for various cost and revenue factors, including land prices, personnel development, marketing costs, and the amount of traffic at each location.

of an MNE. First, project cash flows are in a currency other than the reporting currency of the parent firm. Second, tax rules in the locality of the project and in the parent's country may be significantly different. Third, there may be limitations to the transfer of funds from the foreign project to the parent company. Finally, the project may be exposed to country or political risks above and beyond its regular business risk (which may include high inflation or adverse shifts in exchange rates).

To address these complexities, managers rely on one of two different approaches. One approach in the NPV analysis of a multinational project is to estimate the incremental after-tax operating cash flows in the local currency of the subsidiary and *then* discount them at the project's cost of capital, which is the required rate of return from the project, appropriate for its risk characteristics. If the NPV is positive, then the project is expected to earn its required return in the subsidiary's country and add value to the subsidiary. This approach is called the *project's perspective* in capital budgeting, and managers can use it as a first screen for evaluating the acceptability of an international capital investment project.[22]

Another approach, called the *parent's perspective* in capital budgeting, involves estimating the future cash flows from the project that will eventually be repatriated to the parent company. Using this approach requires managers to convert the expected cash flow values to the *functional currency* of the parent—that is, the currency of the primary economic environment in which it operates. Thus, for U.S.-based firms the functional currency is the U.S. dollar; for Japan-based firms the functional currency is the yen. This conversion involves forecasting *spot exchange rates*, or forward rates, and calculating their present value using a discount rate in line with the required return on projects of similar risk. Managers can then compute the NPV in the parent's functional currency by subtracting the initial investment cash flow from the present value of the project cash flows. For a project to be eventually acceptable, it must add value to the parent company, and therefore should have a positive NPV from the parent's perspective. NPV analysis is widely used in evaluating international capital investment projects.

Estimating project cash flows is complex and requires forecasting a range of variables that contribute to anticipated revenues and costs, often several years into the future. For most firms, the largest component of revenue will be from sales. Initial and ongoing costs typically include R&D, development of essential project resources, personnel, factor inputs, and marketing.

 Task Five: Currency Risk Management

Recall Markel, the firm featured in the opening vignette. Shifting currency values are among the greatest day-to-day challenges facing firms like Markel. Therefore, a major task facing firms is managing currency risk—the risk of adverse unexpected fluctuations in exchange rates. Exporters and licensors face currency risk because foreign buyers typically pay in their own currency. Foreign direct investors face currency risk because they receive both payments and incur obligations in foreign currencies. Managers of foreign investment portfolios face currency risk as well; for example, a Japanese stock might gain 15 percent in value, but if the yen falls by 15 percent, the stock gain is eliminated. Moreover, currency crises usually affect other local asset prices as well, including debt, equipment, and real estate markets. Even smaller Mexican companies were affected by the collapse of the Mexican peso in the mid-1990s. Firms in Indonesia, Malaysia, and Thailand were hurt by the collapse of local currencies in the Asian financial crisis.[23]

Changes in the value of a currency result from a significant increase or decline in demand for the currency relative to its supply, or a significant increase or decline in supply of the currency relative to its demand. Declining demand causes the value of the currency, and hence its purchasing power, to fall on world markets. When demand for the currency falls, its value depreciates.

Firms face exposure to currency risk when their cash flows and the value of their assets and liabilities change as a result of unexpected changes in foreign exchange rates. If the firm could quote its prices and get paid in its home-country currency, then from its perspective, currency risk would be eliminated. However, the risk would still exist for foreign customers. To accommodate foreign buyers, many firms like Markel quote their prices in the currency of the buyer. To cope with the resulting exposure to currency risk and potential losses, these firms then monitor and attempt to forecast the movement of exchange rates. In other words, in an international transaction, either the buyer or the seller incurs a currency risk.

Three Types of Currency Exposure

Currency fluctuations result in three types of exposure for the firm: transaction exposure, translation exposure, and economic exposure.[24] **Transaction exposure** refers to currency risk that firms face when outstanding accounts receivable or payable are denominated in foreign currencies. Suppose that Gateway imports three million Taiwan dollars' worth of computer keyboards and pays in the foreign currency. At the time of the initial purchase, suppose that the exchange rate was US$1 = T$30, but that Gateway pays on credit terms of 3 months after the purchase. If during the 3-month period the exchange rate shifts to US$1 = T$27, Gateway will have to pay an extra US$11,111 as a result of the rate change ([3,000,000/27] –[3,000,000/30]). From Gateway's standpoint, the Taiwan dollar has become more expensive. Such gains or losses are real: they affect the firm's value directly by affecting its cash flows.

Translation exposure is the currency risk that results when an MNE translates financial statements denominated in a foreign currency into the functional currency of the parent firm, as part of consolidating international financial results. It results from exchange rate fluctuations that negatively affect the financial results of a firm with extensive international operations.

MNEs with multicountry operations consolidate financial results in order to generate organization-wide reports. **Consolidation** is the process of combining and integrating the financial results of foreign subsidiaries into the financial records of the parent firm. Accounting practices also require the firm to report consolidated financial results in the functional currency.

Translation exposure occurs because, as exchange rates fluctuate, so do the functional-currency values of exposed assets, liabilities, expenses, and revenues. Translating quarterly or annual foreign financial statements into the parent's functional currency results in gains or losses on the date when foreign financial statements are consolidated into those of the parent. For example, when translated into the dollar, the quarterly net income of the Japanese subsidiary of a U.S. MNE may be affected negatively if the Japanese yen depreciates against the dollar during the quarter. It should be noted that in the case of translations, the gains or losses are "paper" or "virtual"; translation exposure does not affect cash flows directly. In contrast, in the case of transactions, the gains and losses are real.

Economic exposure (also known as *operating exposure*) is the currency risk that results from exchange rate fluctuations affecting the pricing of products, the cost of inputs, and the value of foreign investments. Economic exposure is the risk that exchange rate fluctuations will distort or diminish long-term financial results. When a firm prices its products, exchange rate fluctuations help or hurt sales by making those products relatively more or less expensive from the standpoint of foreign buyers. For example, if the yen appreciates against the euro, then a European firm can expect to sell more goods in Japan because the Japanese have

Transaction exposure The currency risk that firms face when outstanding accounts receivable or payable are denominated in foreign currencies.

Translation exposure The currency risk that results when a firm translates financial statements denominated in a foreign currency into the functional currency of the parent firm, as part of consolidating international financial results.

Consolidation The process of combining and integrating the financial results of foreign subsidiaries into the financial statements of the parent firm.

Economic exposure The currency risk that results from exchange rate fluctuations affecting the pricing of products, the cost of inputs, and the value of foreign investments.

stronger buying power when purchasing euros. But if the yen weakens against the euro, then the European firm's sales will likely drop in Japan unless management lowers its Japanese prices by an amount equivalent to the fall in the yen. Similarly, when sourcing inputs, the firm may be harmed by currency shifts that raise the price of those inputs. The value of foreign investments can also fall, in home currency terms, with exchange rate changes.

Economic exposure is distinct from transaction exposure. Transaction exposure involves the effect of exchange rate fluctuations on ongoing contractual transactions.[25] Economic exposure involves the effect of exchange rate fluctuations on long-term profitability resulting from changes in revenues and expenses. These effects appear in the firm's financial statements. For instance, the weakening of the U.S. dollar relative to the euro in the early 2000s gradually reduced the value of U.S. investments in Europe, increased the cost of Euro-denominated input goods, but improved the prospects for U.S. firms to sell their dollar-denominated products in the EU.

The three types of currency exposure we discussed can also produce positive results when the relevant exchange rate fluctuates in the direction favorable to the firm. However, as a manager, you are more concerned with fluctuations that produce undesirable outcomes. The existence of such problems explains why most member countries in the European Union use a single currency, the euro. With a single medium of exchange, currency risk is eliminated. For international firms operating outside the euro zone, however, currency risk is still a significant problem.

Foreign Exchange Trading

Centuries ago, people used only a few precious metals, such as gold and silver, as a medium of exchange as well as reserve currencies. In 2006, two Swedish farmers digging holes on a farm in Gotland—an island off the Swedish coast—discovered a pile of 10th-century silver coins, weighing about seven pounds. The silver coins were minted in Baghdad, Iraq—about 2,100 miles from Sweden—and apparently served as a source of currency for Vikings.[26] Today, a relatively limited number of currencies still facilitate cross-border trade and investment. Some two-thirds of foreign reserves are in U.S. dollars, 25 percent in euros, 7 percent in yen and British pounds, and only 2 percent in the world's remaining 150 national currencies.

What is different today is the sheer volume of currencies that are exchanged as well as the speed with which these transactions can be consummated. As of 2007, some $3 trillion worth of currency is traded every day.[27] To put things in perspective, this figure is 10 times the value of daily stock and bond turnover, and a hundred times the value of daily goods and services trade. A third of all currency trading, about $1 trillion per day, takes place in London.

Also impressive is the computerized nature of foreign exchange trade. Consider the UBS, one of the world's largest investment banks, based in Switzerland, that offers a range of currency-related products. The bank's clients transact nearly all their spot, forward, and currency-swap trades online using UBS's leading-edge computer platforms in dozens of countries. Technology allows customers in remote areas to enjoy the currency trading services that until recently were accessible only in large cities via big banks.[28] Citibank leverages its comprehensive customer portal—CitiFX Interactive—to provide clients a wide range of services, including library research, currency trading, and ana-

About $3 trillion worth of currency is traded every day. Computer technology has spurred the speed of trades. In 2005, Indian finance Minister P. Chidambaram (right) launched the issue of on-line payment of Central Excise and Service Tax through the Internet portals of various banks during a conference with Cherian Varghese, Chairman and Managing Director of the Union Bank of India (left).

lytical tools. Online bill payment is increasingly important to executives and others who frequently travel abroad.[29]

Large banks are the primary dealers in the currency markets, and they quote the prices at which they will buy or sell currencies. For example, if an importer wishes to buy $100,000 of euros to finance a purchase from Austria, the currency exchange will typically be handled through the importer's bank. Large banks such as Citibank maintain reserves of major currencies and work with foreign correspondent banks to facilitate currency buying and selling. Currency transactions between banks occur in the *interbank market*.

Currency also can be bought and sold through brokers that specialize in matching up buyers and sellers. Currency traders are especially active in major financial centers such as London, New York, Frankfurt, and Tokyo. Trading is also increasingly conducted through online brokers and dealers at sites such as www.openforex.com and Everbank (www.everbank.com).

The foreign exchange market uses a specialized terminology to describe the functions that currency dealers perform. The **spot rate** is the exchange rate applicable to the trading of foreign currencies in which the current rate of exchange is used and delivery is considered "immediate." It is the exchange rate obtainable for immediate receipt of a currency. The spot rate applies to transactions between banks for delivery within 2 business days, or immediate delivery for over-the-counter transactions involving nonbank customers—for example, when you buy currencies at airport kiosks.

The **forward rate** refers to the exchange rate applicable to the collection or delivery of foreign currencies at some future date. It is the exchange rate quoted for future delivery of a currency. The forward rate is a contractual rate between the currency dealer and the dealer's client. Dealers in the forward exchange market deal in promises to receive or deliver foreign exchange at a specified time in the future, but at a rate determined at the time of the transaction. The primary function of the forward market is to provide protection against currency risk.

Dealers quote currency exchange rates in two ways. The **direct quote** is the number of units of the domestic currency needed to acquire one unit of the foreign currency, also known as the *normal* or *American quote*. For example, on September 21, 2007, it cost $1.41 to acquire one euro. The **indirect quote** is the number of units of the foreign currency obtained for one unit of the domestic currency (also known as the *reciprocal* or *European/Continental terms*). For example, 'for 1 dollar, I can receive 0.71 euros.[30]

You may have observed at airports, for example, that when foreign-exchange dealers quote prices, they always quote a *bid* (buy) rate and an *offer* (sell) rate at which they will buy or sell any particular currency. The difference between the bid and offer rates—*the spread*—is the margin on which the dealer earns a profit.

Types of Currency Traders

There are three main types of currency traders: hedgers, speculators, and arbitragers. **Hedgers** seek to minimize the risk of exchange rate fluctuations, often by buying forwards or similar financial instruments. Hedgers typically include MNEs and other firms whose main business is international trade or investment. They are not necessarily interested in profiting from currency.

Speculators refer to currency traders who seek profits by investing in currencies with the expectation that they will rise in value in the future. Speculators seek to make a profit from currency trading by predicting future shifts in a currency's value. For example, they may buy a currency today whose value they expect to rise at some future time. A speculator might purchase a certificate of deposit denominated in Mexican pesos or a money market account tied to the Chinese

Spot rate The exchange rate applicable to the trading of foreign currencies in which the current rate of exchange is used and delivery is considered immediate.

Forward rate The exchange rate applicable to the collection or delivery of a foreign currency at some future date.

Direct quote The number of units of the domestic currency needed to acquire one unit of the foreign currency (also known as the normal or American quote).

Indirect quote The number of units of the foreign currency obtained for one unit of the domestic currency (also known as the reciprocal or European/Continental terms).

Hedgers Currency traders who seek to minimize the risk of exchange rate fluctuations, often by buying forwards or similar financial instruments.

Speculators Currency traders who seek profits by investing in currencies with the expectation that they will rise in value in the future.

外国為替

🇺🇸 ドル　　　112. 15-20　円
🇪🇺 ユーロ　　138. 59-72　円
🇬🇧 ポンド　　206　　　　円
🇨🇭 スイスフラン　8　　　　円
🇦🇺 豪ドル　　　84　　　　円
🇨🇦 カナダドル　84

Major foreign currency rates are displayed in a trading room in Tokyo. Successful cross-national operations require skillful currency management.

yuan, believing that the value of these currencies will rise in the future. The speculator can also bet on the downside of a currency; this would be considered short selling. Speculators attempt to profit from forecast changes in prices through time, and take risks in the process because the future spot prices are unknown.

Arbitragers are currency traders who buy and sell the same currency in two or more foreign-exchange markets to take advantage of differences in the currency's exchange rate. They trade in foreign-exchange markets to generate profits. But unlike the speculator who bets on the future price of a currency, the arbitrager attempts to profit from a current disequilibrium in currency markets based on known prices. For example, if the euro-dollar exchange rate quoted in New York on Monday morning is €1 = $1.25, but the quoted exchange-rate in London at that moment is €1 = $1.30, a trader could make a profit by buying €1 million for $1.25 million in New York, and then simultaneously selling those euros in London for $1.3 million, yielding a riskless profit of $50,000 on the sale, before commission and expenses. Don't get too excited, however! When such arbitrage opportunities exist, they quickly disappear as the very actions of the arbitragers force the exchange rates to adjust to the equilibrium level. Arbitrage opportunities in today's markets typically involve exotic positions in illiquid contracts, such as credit derivatives in emerging markets, and are seldom true arbitrage because they involve some risk. Such risky positions are sometimes called risk arbitrage.

Exchange Rate Forecasting

A loss incurred due to fluctuating exchange rates is a common international business occurrence. In the 1980s, for example, the Japanese automotive company Subaru manufactured nearly all of its vehicles in Japan, despite the fact that three-quarters of its sales were in the United States. Subsequently, between 1985 and 1987, the Japanese yen appreciated almost 50 percent against the dollar. This caused the dollar price of Subaru cars to rise substantially, and Subaru's U.S. sales fell off.[31] Hence, an important objective of managers is to protect against currency risk. The first step managers take is to forecast movements in exchange rates.

Initially, the financial manager needs to be aware of the trends in factors that influence currency fluctuations. He or she also needs to monitor currency trading daily, paying particular attention to the potential for herding behavior and momentum trading. Herding is the tendency of investors to mimic each others' actions. Momentum trading is accomplished via computers that are programmed to conduct massive buying or selling when prices reach certain levels. For example, the massive sell-off of the Mexican peso in 1995 was anticipated by forecasters in 1994, following indications that the Mexican government could no longer support the currency's artificially high value. In most countries, exchange rates respond immediately to economic information, such as the election of a new government, labor disputes, and major supply shocks (for example, as when oil-exporting countries suddenly announce a drop in supply). Accurate forecasting also requires managers to assess the likely actions of foreign-exchange traders.

Arbitragers Currency traders who buy and sell the same currency in two or more foreign-exchange markets to take advantage of differences in the currency's exchange rate.

Firms with extensive international operations develop sophisticated in-house capabilities to forecast exchange rates. These operations combine in-house forecasting with reports provided by major banks and professional forecasters. For example, Citibank provides services to help customers with forecasting and the development of risk-minimization strategies. Banks and firms rely on *technical analysis* to analyze recent movements in exchange rates and *fundamental analysis* to analyze evolving macroeconomic data.

SMEs usually lack the resources to do substantial in-house forecasting. They rely on forecasts provided by banks and from business news sources. For example, each weekly issue of the *Economist* features a table that describes recent historical trends of major exchange rates. Other information sources are available online: the Bank for International Settlements (www.bis.org), the World Bank (www.worldbank.org), and the European Central Bank (www.ecb.int).

Management of Exposure to Currency Risk through Hedging

Suppose you decided to buy a Toyota at a local car dealership. The dealer insists that you pay in Japanese yen. You would hesitate to buy the car, partly because of the need to acquire yen, and partly because alternative dealers let you pay in your own currency. All around the world, customers prefer to deal in their own currency. If firms insist on quoting prices and getting paid in their own currency, then the burden is placed on foreign buyers to monitor and manage foreign exchange. As revealed in the opening vignette case of Markel, to remain competitive, even small exporters must learn to operate in foreign currencies. In so doing, however, they must also learn how to minimize their exposure to currency risk.

The most common method for managing exposure is *hedging,* which refers to efforts to compensate for a possible loss from a bet or investment by making offsetting bets or investments. In international business, **hedging** refers to using financial instruments and other measures to reduce or eliminate exposure to currency risk. Hedging allows the firm to limit potential losses by locking in guaranteed foreign exchange positions. If the hedge is perfect, the firm is protected against the risk of adverse changes in the price of a currency. Banks offer various financial instruments, such as forward contracts, options, and swap agreements to facilitate hedging.

Hedging Using financial instruments and other measures to reduce or eliminate exposure to currency risk.

Hedging entails various costs, such as bank fees and interest payments on the amounts borrowed to carry the hedging transactions. The firm must balance these costs against the expected benefits. In addition, the firm can use active or passive hedging strategies. In *passive hedging,* each exposure is hedged as it occurs and the hedge stays in place until maturity. In *active hedging,* total exposure is reviewed frequently and the firm only hedges a subset of its total exposures, usually those that pose the greatest potential harm. Hedges may be withdrawn before they reach maturity. Some active hedgers seek to profit from hedging, even to the point of maintaining active in-house trading desks. Most firms, however, are conservative in their approach. They simply try to cover all exposures—or their most important ones—and the hedges stay in place until maturity. They do not try to generate profits from speculation.

Hedging Instruments Once managers have assessed the level of currency exposure and determined which exposure is critical, they can hedge against potential exchange rate changes. Using various financial instruments, the firm attempts to establish a balanced position in which exposed assets equal exposed liabilities. The four most common hedging instruments are described next.

Forward Contracts. A **forward contract** is a financial instrument to buy or sell a currency at an agreed-upon exchange rate at the initiation of the contract for future delivery and settlement. In the forward market, trades are made for future delivery at an agreed-upon date and an agreed-upon price on the day of the hedging

Forward contract A financial instrument to buy or sell a currency at an agreed-upon exchange rate at the initiation of the contract for future delivery and settlement.

transaction. Until the delivery date, no money changes hands. Banks quote forward prices in the same way as spot prices—with bid and ask prices at which they will buy or sell currencies. The bank's bid-ask spread is a cost for its customers.

Forward contracts are especially appropriate for hedging transaction exposure. For example, suppose that Dow Chemical sells merchandise to a German importer for €100,000, payable in 90 days. Because of the time interval involved in getting paid, Dow has a transaction exposure to currency risk. That is, if the euro depreciates during the 90-day period, Dow will receive fewer dollars. To hedge against this risk, Dow enters into a forward contract with a bank to sell €100,000, 90 days from now, at an exchange rate agreed upon today, ensuring that it receives a known dollar amount in the future. There will be a gain or loss resulting from a forward contract, but it is known up front when the contract is signed.

Futures Contracts. Similar to a forward contract, a **futures contract** represents an agreement to buy or sell a currency in exchange for another at a prespecified price and on a prespecified date. One difference between a forward contract and a futures contract is that the latter is standardized to enable trading in organized exchanges, such as the Chicago Mercantile Exchange (CME). While the terms of forward contracts are negotiated between a bank and its customer, futures contracts come in standardized maturity periods and contract sizes. For example, a CME British pound futures contract has a contract size of £62,500 and matures in the months that are in the March quarterly cycle (March, June, September, and December). Futures contracts are especially useful for hedging transaction exposure.

Currency Options. A **currency option** differs from forwards and futures in that it gives the purchaser the right, but not the obligation, to buy a certain amount of foreign currency at a set exchange rate within a specified amount of time. The seller of the option must sell the currency at the buyer's discretion, at the price originally set. Currency options typically are traded on organized exchanges, such as the Philadelphia Stock Exchange (PHLX). As such, they are available only for the major currencies.

There are two types of options. A *call option* is the right, but not the obligation, to buy a currency at a specified price within a specific period (called an American option) or at a specific date (called a European option).[32] A *put option* is the right to sell the currency at a specified price. Each option is for a specific amount of currency. For example, on a recent date, Australian dollar option contracts were offered with a contract size of 50,000 Australian dollars each on the PHLX. Options are useful as an insurance policy or disaster hedge against adverse currency movements.

Currency Swaps. A **currency swap** involves the exchange of one currency for another currency according to a specified schedule. The two parties agree to exchange a given amount of one currency for another and, after a specified period of time, to give back the original swapped amounts. Thus, a swap is a simultaneous spot and forward transaction. When the agreement is activated, the parties exchange principals at the current spot rate. Usually each party must pay interest on the principal as well. For instance, if Party A loaned dollars and borrowed euros, Party A pays interest in euros and receives interest in dollars. At a future date, the original principal amounts are returned to the original holders. Consider the following example. An agreement by an MNE to pay 4 percent compounded annually on a euro principal of €1,000,000 and receive 5 percent compounded annually on a U.S. dollar principal of $1,300,000 every year for 2 years constitutes a currency swap. As a result of this agreement, the MNE will receive €1,000,000 and pay $1,300,000 today. It will then pay €40,000 annual interest and receive $65,000 annual interest for 2 years. At the end of the second year, the MNE will receive $1,300,000 and pay €1,000,000.

Futures contract An agreement to buy or sell a currency in exchange for another at a prespecified price and on a prespecified date.

Currency option A contract that gives the purchaser the right, but not the obligation, to buy a certain amount of foreign currency at a set exchange rate within a specified amount of time.

Currency swap An agreement to exchange one currency for another, according to a specified schedule.

Best Practice in Minimizing Currency Exposure

Managing currency risk across many countries is challenging because management must keep abreast of the firm's evolving exposures, as well as shifting laws, regulations, and market conditions. Managers need to pursue a systematic approach in order to minimize currency risk.

Exhibit 19.5 presents guidelines managers can use to minimize currency risk. The last recommendation, one of maintaining strategic flexibility in manufacturing and sourcing, is an ultimate solution. To the extent that the firm operates in a portfolio of markets, each with varying degrees of currency, economic, and political stability, it can then attempt to optimize its operations. For example, in terms of optimizing its sourcing activities, Compaq Computer has secondary suppliers for all its critical input components in multiple countries. When the need arises, management can quickly shift production from one country to another. Similarly, Dell outsources inputs from various countries and can emphasize certain suppliers over others, depending on the favorability of exchange rates and other factors.

Task Six: Manage the Diversity of International Accounting and Tax Practices

In international business, firms have to record the transactions and list the assets and liabilities related to each operation. Developing accounting systems to identify, measure, and communicate this financial information is

Exhibit 19.5

Managerial Guidelines for Minimizing Currency Risk

1. **Seek expert advice.** Initially, management should get expert help from banks and consultants to establish programs and strategies that minimize risk.
2. **Centralize currency management within the MNE.** While some currency management activities may be delegated to local managers, company headquarters should set basic guidelines for the subsidiaries to follow.
3. **Decide on the level of risk the firm can tolerate.** The level varies depending on the nature of the project, amount of capital at risk, and management's risk tolerance.
4. **Devise a system to measure exchange rate movements and currency risk.** The system should provide ongoing feedback to facilitate the timely development of appropriate risk-minimizing strategies.
5. **Monitor changes in key currencies.** Exchange rates fluctuate constantly. Continuous monitoring of currency rates can avert potentially costly mistakes.
6. **Be wary of unstable currencies or those subject to exchange controls.** The manager should deal in stable, readily convertible currencies. Be wary of government restrictions that affect the ability to exchange currencies that, in turn, affect the value of assets, liabilities, income, and expenses.
7. **Monitor long-term economic and regulatory trends.** Exchange rate shifts usually follow evolving trends such as rising interest rates, inflation, labor unrest, and the coming to power of new governments.
8. **Distinguish economic exposure from transaction and translation exposures.** Managers often focus on reducing transaction and translation exposures. However, the long-run effects of economic exposure on company performance can be more detrimental.
9. **Emphasize flexibility in international operations.** A flexible production and outsourcing strategy means the firm can shift production and outsourcing to various nations. For example, in the long run, management might shift production to countries with currencies that are weak compared to the home-country currency.

especially challenging in multicountry operations where substantial variations in accounting systems exist. As an example, there are dozens of approaches for determining the cost of goods sold, return on assets, R&D expenditures, net profits, and other outcomes in different countries.[33] Balance sheets and income statements vary internationally, primarily with regard to language, currency, format, and the underlying accounting principles that are applied or emphasized. Financial statements prepared according to the rules of one country may be difficult to compare with those prepared in another country.

Transparency in Financial Reporting

Transparency The degree to which companies regularly reveal substantial information about their financial condition and accounting practices.

Local accounting practices determine the degree of transparency in the reporting of financial information. **Transparency** is the degree to which companies regularly reveal substantial information about their financial condition and accounting practices. The more transparent a nation's accounting systems, the more regularly and comprehensively the nation's public firms report their financial results to creditors, stockholders, and the government in a reliable manner. Transparency is important because it improves the ability of investors to accurately evaluate company performance, thereby improving managerial decision making. Chile, Costa Rica, Hungary, and the Czech Republic are examples of the numerous countries that have attracted greater FDI by enhancing their regulatory environments, resulting in reduced uncertainty. In many developing and emerging market economies, the accounting systems have low transparency, financial statements may not become available until many months after the relevant accounting period, and published information may be incomplete or unreliable.

In the United States, The Sarbanes-Oxley Act of 2002 was enacted to rein in accounting and managerial abuses among corporations and investors. The Act emerged in the wake of accounting fraud scandals at large corporations such as Enron, Worldcom, and Tyco. Sarbanes-Oxley makes corporate CEOs and CFOs personally responsible for the accuracy of annual reports and other financial data. Foreign affiliates of U.S. firms and foreign firms with significant U.S. operations are also required to comply with the Sarbanes-Oxley provisions. In addition, government agencies are strengthening their supervision of banks and other financial intermediaries in the wake of the Asian financial crisis, Citibank's problems in Japan, and similar experiences. Banks worldwide are taking steps to increase the stability and transparency of their financial systems. Read the *Recent Grad in IB* feature for Maria Keeley's thoughts on the Sarbanes-Oxley Act.

Accounting reforms in the United States are being extended into Europe and other regions. A major challenge, however, is the cost of compliance to firms, estimated at tens of billions of dollars and millions of work hours to change or install systems for internal accounting controls in large, publicly traded firms. In an effort to avoid rigid financial requirements, some European firms are reducing their business in the United States, and several have de-registered from U.S. stock markets. European legislators, however, are moving to increase the transparency and strictness of their own accounting standards.[34]

Trends toward Harmonization

The growth of international trade and investment has pressured multinational firms and international organizations such as the International Accounting Standards Board (IASB), the United

The Sarbanes-Oxley Act of 2002 has increased CEO and CFO responsibility to ensure the accuracy of their annual reports. Pictured here is the stock exchange in Santiago, Chile, one of several countries that have strengthened their accounting regulations.

In college, Maria Keeley spent a year in Spain and served as the president of her university's international business club. She majored in Finance, International Business, and Spanish. Following graduation, she took a job as a credit analyst with Motorola (www.motorola.com), a leading manufacturer of cell phones and other wireless handsets. In her first job, Maria used analytical, problem solving, and communication skills that she developed in college to serve Motorola clients and subsidiaries in Central and South America and Mexico.

At Motorola, Maria carried out analyses to assess risk levels of various customers and countries. She performed account maintenance and managed accounts receivables for the Latin America personal communications division. She conducted audits of Motorola subsidiaries for compliance with established controls and procedures. These duties required Maria to travel frequently to Latin America. Within her first year on the job, her responsibilities expanded and she became the primary contact for financial analysis support to northern Latin America, the Caribbean, and Central America. Her new tasks included the analysis, tracking, and reconciliation of Motorola's funds for regional marketing activities.

Eager to gain experience in Europe, Maria volunteered to transfer to Motorola's London operations. In London, she served as a finance manager in the firm's $160 million mobile phone business for the Middle East, North Africa, and Turkey. She also sought her CIMA Certification—the British equivalent of a certified public accountant. After two years in London, Maria

was transferred to Dubai, the United Arab Emirates, as Financial Controller for Motorola's Middle East, North Africa, and Turkey region. In her new role, Maria coordinated the management of Motorola's financial activities in the Islamic world.

Lessons Learned so Far

Here are some of Maria's comments on her experience so far in the world of international financial management.

"One of the biggest challenges that I face is increased regulations—in particular, the Sarbanes-Oxley legislation, which requires stricter auditing of financial records in the wake of accounting scandals. It's critical to ensure that all of Motorola's legal entities are compliant worldwide. There are also local regulations that must be assimilated and integrated. As a result, the focus and time that I must allocate to compliance activities has greatly increased. Simultaneously, competition in the mobile devices industry is growing exponentially, and the level of support that I must provide to our sales and marketing operations needs to be enhanced as well.

"I am currently based in England. However, I support a big region with multiple time zones and work schedules. The work week in the Middle East varies from Saturday to Thursday, or from Sunday to Friday. Due to time differences, the region starts the day at least 3 hours before the United Kingdom. In order to ensure that business decisions are not held up, I respond to requests quickly and make myself accessible. This means I am often on the phone

Maria's majors: Finance, International Business, and Spanish

Objectives: Obtain a law degree and move into the executive suite at Motorola or other multinational firm

Jobs held since graduating college:

- Credit Analyst, Motorola, U.S.
- Finance Manager, Motorola, U.K.
- Financial Controller, Motorola, United Arab Emirates

with colleagues in the Middle East at 6 A.M. London time.

"In the region that I supervise, the spoken languages are French (North Africa), Arabic (Middle East), and Turkish (Turkey). Although I'm currently studying Arabic, I still am unable to carry a business conversation in Arabic, and only manage to use my Spanish while visiting a particular distributor in Morocco that is partially owned by Telefonica (www.telefonica.com), Spain's telecom provider. Luckily, most of our business partners speak English.

"There is definitely a disadvantage to not speaking the local language. In Turkey, for instance, some of our business partners do not speak English and, as a result, I rely on the sales team to translate conversations. There is definitely a drawback to receiving important information secondhand. Even when colleagues speak fluent English, particularly in North Africa, there is a tendency to revert to their most comfortable language, in this case French. When I go to lunch with

601

business associates in Morocco or Algeria, for instance, the parties will revert to their most comfortable language and it is almost never English.

"Much of the Islamic world has specific norms for women, who usually do not participate in professional business activities. To my surprise, I am pleased that people generally treat me with respect. Only occasionally, usually during the first encounter, will a business partner entirely disregard me in a business meeting. I have found that, if I establish myself as a knowledgeable professional, people in the Middle East generally treat me as well as they do their male colleagues.

"There is one last cultural difference that puts me at a disadvantage: being a non-smoker in countries where people still smoke a lot. Most of the debriefing after a challenging meeting or conference call happens during cigarette breaks. Given the relaxed atmosphere, the parties are more likely to discuss issues in a candid manner. It is not culturally acceptable for a nonsmoker to join, because the purported reason for the break is to smoke, and if you don't smoke it would appear that you were just wasting time from work. Nevertheless, I'm not willing to take up smoking just to be more effective in my job. It is a cultural difference that I accept."

Maria's Advice for an International Business Career

When asked what qualities have contributed most to her success, she replies "hard work, having a deliberate career strategy, and cultivating relationships with helpful people both when I was in college and in the professional world. One thing I would say to college students today is that you really have to plan. Set goals for yourself and then work hard to meet them."

What's Ahead?

As for the future, Maria hopes to obtain a law degree and then gradually move into the executive suite at Motorola or some other multinational firm. But having a career, especially an international one, is still challenging these days for women who also want to start a family. Maria Keeley is up to the task and looks forward to fulfilling both her career and personal goals.

Nations, the European Union, and the Asociación Interamericana de Contabilidad to harmonize world accounting systems, particularly regarding measurement, disclosure, and auditing standards. For example, the IASB has been working to develop a single set of high-quality, understandable, and enforceable global accounting standards that emphasize transparent and comparable information.

The IASB favors harmonization for a number of reasons. First, it increases the comparability and transparency of accounting practices, which enhances reliability of foreign financial statements. Second, it helps reduce the cost of preparing financial statements. Third, it increases the efficiency of consolidating financial information from various countries. Fourth, it facilitates investment analysis for both investors and managers, which reduces risk for investors and helps managers make better decisions.

Harmonization is particularly important to MNEs that seek to attract potential foreign investors by listing on foreign stock exchanges. Imagine that you are managing a European firm that wishes to list on the NYSE. While the idea makes sense, the process of producing and reporting your financial statement according to the U.S. Generally Accepted Accounting Practices (GAAP), as required by the U.S. Securities and Exchange Commission (SEC), is a costly and time-consuming bureaucratic ordeal. In Europe, you have been using the International Financial Reporting Standards (IFRS), which now have been adopted by more than 100 countries. A remarkable milestone was reached early in 2007 when the SEC announced that it will no longer require foreign firms to reconcile their accounts to the U.S. system, beginning with the 2009 fiscal year.[35] Indeed, the two organizations on both sides of the Atlantic, Europe's IASB and the U.S. Financial Accounting Standards Board, had been working closely over the previous six years for the convergence of the two systems. The next ambitious goal is to permit U.S. companies that operate globally to file only under the IFRS.

Consolidating the Financial Statements of Subsidiaries

A special challenge in international accounting is *foreign currency translation*—translating data denominated in foreign currencies into the firm's functional currency. It is a critical task, because the financial records of subsidiaries are normally maintained in the currencies of the countries where the subsidiaries are located. When the results of the subsidiaries are consolidated into headquarters' financial statements, they must be expressed in the parent's functional currency. Top management also undertakes translation to plan, evaluate, integrate, and control overseas activities.

When headquarters consolidates foreign financial records, it uses one of two methods to translate foreign currencies into the parent's functional currency: the current rate method and the temporal method. By using the **current rate method**, all foreign currency balance sheet and income statement items are translated at the current exchange rate—the spot exchange rate in effect on the day (in the case of balance sheets), or for the period (in the case of income statements), the statements are prepared. This method is typically used when translating records of foreign subsidiaries that are considered separate entities, rather than part of the parent firm's operations. Consider the case of Computershare Limited, an Australian firm that markets financial software through its worldwide network of subsidiaries. The company translates the financial statements of its subsidiaries using the current rate method, because these subsidiaries are considered stand-alone legal entities. Amounts payable and receivable in foreign currencies are converted to Australian dollars at the exchange rate in effect on the day of consolidation.[36]

One feature of the current rate method is that it results in gains and losses, depending on the exchange rates in effect during the translation period. For instance, the value of income received in a foreign currency six months earlier may differ substantially from its value on the day it is translated. For firms with extensive international operations, the accounting translation method can strongly influence company performance. As mentioned earlier, in the case of translations, the gains or losses are "paper," or "virtual," while in the case of transactions, they are real. Nevertheless, paper gains or losses affect the valuation of a firm.

With the **temporal method**, the choice of exchange rate depends on the underlying method of valuation. If assets and liabilities are normally valued at historical cost, then they are translated at the historical rates—that is, the rates in effect when the assets were acquired. If assets and liabilities are normally valued at market cost, then they are translated at the current rate of exchange. Thus, monetary items such as cash, receivables, and payables are translated at the current exchange rate. Nonmonetary items such as inventory and property, plant, and equipment are translated at historical rates.

According to U.S. accounting standards, if the functional currency of the subsidiary is that of the local operating environment (for example, if the yen is the main currency used by the Japanese subsidiary of a U.S. multinational firm), the company must use the current rate method. If the functional currency is the parent's currency, the MNE must use the temporal method. The choice of method can give rise to very different profitability and other performance outcomes, and firms must adhere to accepted accounting practices and laws.

Current rate method Translation of foreign currency balance sheet and income statements at the current exchange rate—the spot exchange rate in effect on the day, or for the period when the statements are prepared.

Temporal method Translation of foreign currency balance sheet and income statements at an exchange rate that varies with the underlying method of valuation.

International Taxation

In cross-border business, taxes include direct taxes, indirect taxes, sales taxes, and value-added taxes. A *direct tax* is imposed on income derived from business profits, intracorporate transactions, capital gains, and sometimes royalties, interest, and dividends. The tax may also be imposed on the acquisition or sale of real estate and other assets. An *indirect tax* applies to firms that license or franchise products and services or who charge interest. In effect, the local government withholds some percentage of royalty payments or interest charges as tax. A *sales tax* is a flat percentage tax on the value of goods or services sold, paid by the ultimate user. A *value-added tax* (VAT) is payable at each stage of processing in the value chain of a product or service. VAT is calculated as a percentage of the difference between the sale and purchase price of a good. This tax is common in Canada, Europe, and Latin America. Each business in the value chain involved in the production of a good is required to bill the VAT to its customers and pay the tax on its purchases, crediting the amounts it paid against the amounts due on its own activities. The net result is a tax on the added value of the produced good.

The most common form of direct tax is the *corporate income tax*. Exhibit 19.6 provides corporate income tax rates for a sample of countries. Called "corporation tax" in some localities, corporate income tax is a major factor in international planning because it encourages managers to organize business operations in ways that minimize this tax. Firms can usually reduce the amount of tax by deducting business expenses from the revenues that they earn. Thus, income tax influences the timing, magnitude, and composition of company investment in plant and equipment, R&D, inventories, and other business assets. As you can gather from the Exhibit, the recent trend in many countries has been toward falling tax rates, because governments recognize that high taxes can discourage investment.[37] For example, the corporate income tax rate in Russia has decreased from 43 percent to 24 percent. In Canada, the rate has decreased from 42 percent to 36 percent. Ireland has the lowest income tax rate, 13 percent—one of the pillars of its economic revitalization policy in the 1980s and 1990s.

Historically, companies that earned income in more than one country would have been required to pay direct taxes in each country on the same earnings. Because multiple taxation reduces company earnings, and may even eliminate profitability, most countries have signed tax treaties with their trading partners that help ensure firms pay the appropriate taxes. A typical tax treaty between country A and country B states that, if the firm pays income tax in A, it need not pay the tax in B, if they are similar in amount. If it pays income tax in B, it need not pay the tax in A. This is often accomplished with a system of foreign tax credits—a type of automatic reduction in tax liability that the firm receives when it can prove that it has already paid income tax abroad. Alternatively, the firm may be liable to pay tax in each country, but the amount is prorated so that the total tax paid is no more than the maximum tax in either of the two countries. Tax treaties also usually obligate nations to assist each other in tax enforcement; that is, assuring that international firms pay taxes in one country or the other. In this way, tax treaties help prevent tax evasion.

Tax Havens As discussed earlier, tax havens are countries that are hospitable to business and inward investment because of their low corporate income taxes. Among the many tax havens worldwide are the Bahamas, Luxembourg, Monaco, Singapore, and Switzerland. Tax havens exist in part because tax systems vary greatly around the world. MNEs have an incentive to structure their global activities in ways that minimize taxes. MNEs take advantage of tax havens either by establishing operations in them or by funneling business transactions through them. For example, Accenture, a management consultancy operating in dozens of countries, moved its headquarters to Bermuda to minimize its U.S. tax obliga-

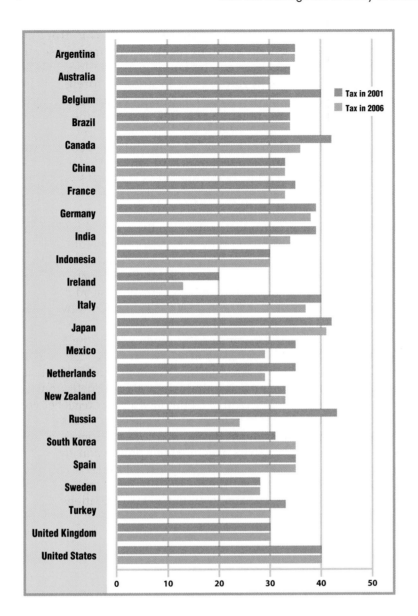

Exhibit 19.6

Corporate Income Tax Rates Around the World (as a percent of corporate income, rounded to the nearest whole percent)

SOURCE: Table reprinted from *KPMG's Corporate Tax Rate Survey: An International Analysis of Corporate Tax Rates from 1993 to 2006.*
Copyright © 2006 KPMG International. KPMG International is a Swiss cooperative of which all KPMG firms are members. KPMG International provides no services to clients. Each member firm is a separate and independent legal entity and each describes itself as such. All rights reserved. Printed in U.S.A. Reprinted with permission of KPMG International.

tions. Similarly, the U.S. oil firm Halliburton announced in 2007 that it would move its corporate headquarters to Dubai, one of the United Arab Emirates known for its business friendly environment and tax incentives. While the use of tax havens is generally legal, governments often pass laws that restrict their use. For instance, the U.S. government imposed restrictions on the ability of firms to move major operations to tax havens. [38] When employed appropriately, tax havens are a legal means for reducing income taxes. Their use will likely continue as long as substantial differences in tax rates persist among nations. Corporations sometimes use tax havens to "park" revenues until needed somewhere else for trade or investment purposes.

The Organization for Economic Cooperation and Development (OECD), World Bank, and other international organizations discourage the wrongful use of tax havens by lobbying countries to develop transparent tax systems. The EU and OECD also pressure countries to reduce harmful tax competition. In Europe, for example, foreign investors tend to establish operations in countries with low taxes, and avoid countries with high taxes. Because this tendency can harm greater European unity and economic development, the EU wants to minimize tax differences and increase transparency.

Managing International Finance to Minimize Tax Burden While domestic tax systems are usually complex, dealing with taxes in several countries simultaneously is much more challenging. In the long run, taxation affects managerial decisions regarding the location of foreign investments, type of entry modes used, the legal form of foreign operations, approaches to transfer pricing, methods for obtaining capital, and even the choice of target markets.

Financial managers seek to minimize international taxes. For example, in the beer industry in Japan, the government imposes high taxes on malt, a key brewing ingredient. The malt tax is one of the highest in the world, roughly 20 times greater than in Europe. Accordingly, foreign firms that brew beer in Japan have begun to employ a new distillation technology for making beer that eliminates the need for malt. The end product tastes like beer, but is actually a type of liquor. Occasionally, governments may create tax breaks on income earned abroad. For example, in the United States, the American Jobs Creation Act of 2005 provided a one-time opportunity for U.S. MNEs to repatriate foreign subsidiary earnings at the maximum rate of 5.25 percent, instead of the typical 35 percent. It was estimated that as much as $300–$350 billion were repatriated in 2005–2006.

Many of the techniques for transferring funds within the MNE and company management of currency exposure described in this chapter are useful for minimizing the firm's tax burdens as well. For example, minimizing taxes is typically the main goal of transfer pricing strategies. MNEs benefit from a strategy that takes advantage of differences in taxation rates and systems between countries. MNEs establish holding companies or finance corporations in particular countries or operate in government designated low-tax zones (Foreign Trade Zones) within countries. The MNEs structure their production and selling activities in ways that minimize their tax obligations. As long as taxes reduce company profitability, and as long as substantial tax differences exist among nations, firms will develop strategies that aim to minimize tax obligations.

International Financial Operations at Tektronix

An oscilloscope is a measuring device with a display screen that checks the condition of electronic equipment. In 1946, the founders of United States-based Tektronix, Inc. built their first oscilloscope out of electronic parts purchased from government surplus sales. TEK, as Tektronix is known to employees and customers, went public in 1963. The firm is now the world's largest maker of oscilloscopes and the second largest maker of test and measurement equipment. TEK's oscilloscopes and other measuring devices have contributed immensely to the development of computers and communications equipment.

TEK employs several thousand employees in about 30 countries worldwide. The firm receives roughly half its sales from North America, 25 percent from Europe, 15 percent from Japan, and the rest from other countries. Total annual sales now exceed $1 billion per year. TEK owes part of its original success to venture capital funding. However, the great majority of its capital comes from equity financing, with additional capital from debt sources. The firm's stock is listed on the New York Stock Exchange under the symbol TEK.

International Operations

TEK launched its first foreign distributor in Sweden in 1948. In later years, the firm set up many sales subsidiaries abroad. It developed joint ventures in Japan (with Sony, called "Sony-Tek") and in China to distribute TEK products in those countries. It also established manufacturing plants in Germany, Italy, and Malaysia. However, TEK still manufactures some three-quarters of its products in the United States. By contrast, TEK competitor Hewlett Packard has manufacturing plants in some 20 countries. Other major TEK competitors—Xerox, Kodak, and Compaq—similarly have multiple manufacturing plants around the world. TEK management prefers to centralize manufacturing, as this optimizes quality control and provides economies of scale and the opportunity to synchronize production with R&D.

Because TEK does most of its manufacturing in the United States and gets more than half its sales from abroad, the firm has substantial foreign exchange exposure. For instance, the yen-dollar exchange rate has experienced big swings after multigovernment intervention in the mid-1980s succeeded in strengthening the Japanese currency. Most of TEK's foreign sales are invoiced in local currencies. So when the U.S. dollar strengthens against other currencies, TEK's profits take a hit when revenues are converted into dollars. When sales are denominated in dollars, prices can become prohibitively expensive for foreign customers. TEK also sources many inputs from abroad, which creates currency risks in its accounts payable.

In addition, for financial accounting, almost all of TEK's non-U.S. subsidiaries use their local currencies as the functional currency. Thus, assets and liabilities are translated into U.S. dollars at end-of-period exchange rates. Income and expense items are translated at the average rate during the accounting period. To minimize currency risk, management has to deal proactively with transaction, translation, and economic exposures.

Tax-Related Decisions

One goal of every MNE is to minimize domestic and foreign taxes while avoiding too much government scrutiny. In recent years, however, foreign tax authorities have been aggressively monitoring the intracompany pricing policies of multinationals doing business in their respective jurisdictions to ensure that relevant tax revenues stay on their home turf. Countries such as Australia, France, Canada, Germany, Japan, Mexico, and the United Kingdom have increased their tax audits of foreign firms.

To help address these and other tax challenges, TEK devised a long-term tax strategy. For its European operations, all treasury functions, including cash management, inventory, and receivables are centralized to TEK's subsidiary in England. The approach creates efficiencies in TEK's financial activities and simplifies tax preparation. In addition, worldwide pricing for TEK's thousands of products and components are set by the parent company in the United States. The goal is to lower TEK's global tax rate, which had been running at 32 percent in the past. The new structure also enhances TEK's ability to use foreign tax credits.

Currency Risk Management

TEK uses currency hedging on a selective basis rather than a 100 percent hedging approach. Financial managers hedge specific currency exposures to minimize the effect of harmful exchange rate fluctuations. But not all risks can be hedged, because of the cost of banking fees and interest charges. As a result, TEK has experienced big foreign exchange losses in the past. To help minimize these losses, management has established a unit at headquarters responsible for assessing and managing currency risk. TEK managers obtain intelligence from online sources and the forecasting departments of large banks. They monitor changes in key currencies on a regular basis. Among the approaches that TEK has used to minimize risk are multilateral netting, offsetting cash flows, a centralized depository, forward contracts, and currency options.

Multilateral Netting

TEK has many ongoing transactions with and among its various subsidiaries. The firm's financial managers can strategically reduce the number of cash transfers between these entities by eliminating offsetting cash flows between headquarters and the subsidiaries. This approach helps reduce transaction costs, such as bank charges. TEK performs a monthly multilateral netting process to minimize exposures. Specifically, all subsidiaries report to headquarters what is owed in foreign currencies to other subsidiaries, customers, suppliers, and to headquarters itself. Financial managers then advise each subsidiary how much to pay other subsidiaries in a way that minimizes the overall number and amount of intersubsidiary cash transfers. Management also matches hedging instruments with the firm's most pressing currency exposures. The netting process helps reduce the cost and hassle of dealing with many small internal transfers of cash. Fortunately, the 2002 launch of the euro greatly simplified international transactions and reduced the need for some netting operations.

Offsetting Cash Flows

Whenever possible, management consolidates accounts receivable and accounts payable, matching them against one another. For example, if TEK owes a French supplier 800,000 euros, it can grant a trade credit in the amount of 800,000 euros to a German customer, making the receivable and payable both offset each other in the same currency. TEK also has some flexibility to change the invoicing currency of its subsidiaries and affiliates—for example, by having some invoices from its Japan subsidiary denominated in yen instead of dollars. Offsetting cash flows is also accomplished with counterbalanced investments in Asia and Europe, as well as skillful transfer pricing and other types of intracorporate financing activities. For instance, if headquarters wants to spend $1 million to establish a new subsidiary in Europe, it will request existing European subsidiaries to retain a similar amount of their earnings in euros. Then, instead of converting the foreign earnings into U.S. dollars, TEK uses the retained euro earnings to build the new subsidiary.

Centralized Depository

TEK centralizes management of currency risk at company headquarters. While some currency management is delegated to local managers, headquarters in the United States is in charge and sets basic guidelines for the subsidiaries to follow. Management pools funds into centralized depositories and directs these funds where needed to subsidiaries or invests them to generate income. Management also pools accounts receivable for some European subsidiaries into a regional depository.

The practice makes the receipt and dispersal of cash more manageable, allows the firm to benefit from economies of scale in the investment and other uses of excess cash, and helps reduce the amount of local borrowing that European subsidiaries would normally undertake. The centralized approach also concentrates managerial expertise and financial services at a central location, which provides more benefits to the subsidiaries. Finally, TEK employs a reinvoicing center that invoices foreign subsidiaries in the local currency but receives invoices in U.S. dollars.

Forward Contracts and Currency Options

TEK hedges against currency risk by selectively taking positions in forward contracts. These instruments allow financial managers to buy or sell currency at a specific future date at an agreed-upon exchange rate; they are especially useful for hedging transaction exposure that involves large foreign amounts. In this way, whenever management is concerned about the value of a receivable in the future, it can guarantee a fixed exchange rate and minimize the possibility of currency risk. The firm also employs currency options, a contract that grants the holder the right to buy or sell currency at a specified exchange rate during a specified period of time. In addition, TEK uses currency futures contracts with maturities of 1 to 3 months to mitigate currency risk. At any given time, TEK's currency contracts can exceed $100 million. The downside is that TEK must pay substantial trading fees and other costs for its currency hedging activities.

Other Financial Developments

A few years ago, TEK undertook a major restructuring of company operations. The sale of a major division generated proceeds of more than $900 million. Management had to decide whether to return these funds to shareholders or pay down the firm's corporate debt. TEK's equity financing is far greater than its debt. In comparison to its equity holdings, TEK's debt is modest and quite manageable, based on expected cash flows. Management has long favored a low debt-to-equity ratio.

TEK earnings suffered in the late 1990's due to the Asian financial crisis and the associated downturn in Asian markets. Like all international firms, TEK's sales are subject to ups and downs in the economies of its major markets abroad, as well as fluctuations in the various currencies in which the firm does business. Still, TEK management has shown itself capable of weathering even the most difficult of challenges. Careful planning and implementation of financial operations will help the firm to continue to reign as the leader in oscilloscopes and other measuring equipment.

AACSB: Reflective Thinking, Analytical Skills

Case Questions

1. What are the implications for currency risk of TEK focusing its manufacturing in the United States but generating most of its sales abroad? Are competitors, such as HP, Xerox, and Eastman Kodak geographically more diversified in their sourcing activities? If so, what advantages does this create for them?

2. The case lists various approaches that TEK follows to minimize its exposure to currency risk. If you were hired by TEK, what other strategies and tactics would you recommend top management use to reduce the firm's exposure even further? Justify your answer.

3. Visit TEK's Web site at www.tektronix.com and review the summary of the company's financial data. Based on this information, does TEK's debt-to-equity ratio appear to be excessive? Do you

think TEK can sustain a higher level of debt? Why or why not? What other approaches could TEK use to generate financing for its international operations?

4. The case describes approaches that TEK follows to minimize its international tax liability. Based on your reading of the chapter, how would you advise TEK management to further reduce its taxes around the world?

Sources: Epstein, Joseph. (1996). "Did Rip Van Winkle Really Lift Its Head?" Financial World, April 8, pp. 42–45; Hoyem, George, and Bart Schachter. (2004). "Forget India, Outsource to Oregon!" Venture Capital Journal, December 1, p. 1; Ioannou, Lori. (1995). "Taxing Issues," International Business, March, pp. 42–45; Lee, Marshall. (1986). Winning with People: The First 40 Years of Tektronix. Beaverton, OR: Tektronix, Inc.; Maturi, Richard J. (1990). "Take the Sting Out of the Swings," Industry Week, September 3, p. 96; McElligott, Tim. (2001). "This Way Out: Rick Wills, Tektronix," Telephony, June 4, pp. 190–191; Stonehill, Arthur, Jerry Davies, Randahl Finnessy, and Michael Moffett. (2004). "Tektronix (C)," Thunderbird International Business Review, July/August, 46(4), pp. 465–469; Sony Corp. History of Sony, retrieved from www.sony.net/Fun/SH/1-32/h1.html; Tektronix corporate profile, retrieved from www.hoovers.com; Tektronix corporate Web site, at www.TEK.com; Tektronix, Inc. (2000), Annual Report, Beaverton, OR; Tektronix, Inc. (2005). Form 10-K to U.S. Securities and Exchange Commission. Beaverton, OR: Tektronix, Inc.

CHAPTER ESSENTIALS

Key Terms

Summary

In this chapter, you learned about:

1. Primary tasks in international financial management

International financial management involves the acquisition and use of funds for cross-border trade and investment activities. Participants include firms, banks, and brokerage houses. Managers such as Chief Financial Officers (CFOs) organize financial activities inside the

focal firm. CFOs decide on the firm's capital structure, raise capital, manage working capital and cash flows, do capital budgeting, manage currency risk, and deal with diverse accounting and tax practices.

2. How firms set up their international capital structure from equity and debt

The *capital structure* is the mix of long-term financing—**equity financing** and **debt financing**—that the firm uses to support its international activities. Equity financing is obtained by selling shares in stock markets and by retaining earnings. Debt financing is obtained by borrowing money from banks and other financial institutions or by selling **bonds**.

3. How financial managers raise capital to fund international value-adding activities and investment projects

Companies can raise money in the **global capital market**. Equity financing can be obtained in the **global equity market**—the stock exchanges throughout the world where investors and firms meet to buy and sell shares of stock. In terms of debt financing, firms may borrow in the **Eurocurrency** market, which uses currency banked outside its country of origin. Firms also sell bonds—often **foreign bonds** or **Eurobonds**— in the **global bond market**. MNEs can also support the operations of their subsidiaries through **intracorporate financing**.

4. The management of working capital and cash flow for international operations

Net working capital is the difference between current assets and current liabilities. Firms often manage intracorporate funds by developing a *centralized depository,* into which funds are pooled from the firm's network of subsidiaries and affiliates to distribute to units that need funds. There are various methods for transferring funds within the MNE, including *dividend remittances, royalty payments, transfer pricing,* and *fronting loans*. A **fronting loan** is a loan from a parent firm to its subsidiary, channeled through a bank or other financial intermediary. **Multilateral netting** is the process of strategically reducing the number of cash transfers between the parent and subsidiaries by eliminating the offsetting cash flows between these entities.

5. Capital budgeting: decision-making on international capital expenditures

Capital budgeting rests on analyses that management undertakes to evaluate the viability of proposed international projects. Management calculates the *net present value* of a proposed project to decide whether it should be implemented.

6. Currency risk: exposure, forecasting, and management

There are three main types of currency exposure: transaction exposure, economic exposure, and translation exposure. A firm faces **transaction exposure** when outstanding accounts receivable or payable are denominated in foreign currencies. **Economic exposure** results from exchange rate fluctuations affecting the pricing of products, the cost of inputs, and the value of foreign investments. **Translation exposure** arises as the firm combines the financial statements of foreign subsidiaries into the parent's financial statements, a process called **consolidation**. Currency trading takes place between banks and currency brokers, often on behalf of multinational firms. Currency traders include **hedgers, speculators,** and **arbitragers**. Managers attempt to forecast exchange rates to minimize their firm's exposure to currency risk. They rely on various analyses and information technology to predict the future value of currencies. There are various approaches for minimizing exposure to currency risk, including centralizing currency management, measuring currency risk, monitoring long-term trends, and emphasizing flexibility in international operations. A key tool for minimizing exposure to currency risk is **hedging**, which is the use of specialized financial instruments to balance positions in foreign currencies. Key hedging tools include **forward contracts, futures contracts, currency options,** and **currency swaps**.

7. Managing international accounting practices and taxation issues

Financial statements prepared in one country may be difficult to compare with those prepared in another country. Accounting practices are based on one of several models. Through **transparency**, firms regularly and comprehensively reveal reliable information about their financial condition and accounting practices. Various factors account for differences in national accounting systems. Several international organizations are seeking to harmonize cross-national accounting practices. Managers use the **current rate method** and the **temporal method** for currency translation. Internationally, firms seek to minimize taxes, which consist of direct taxes, indirect taxes, sales taxes, and value-added taxes. Governments use two major methods for eliminating multiple taxation: the foreign tax credit and tax treaties. **Tax havens** are countries with low taxes that are friendly to business and inward investment.

Test Your Comprehension AACSB: **Reflective Thinking**

1. What international financial management tasks should managers handle on a long-term basis?

2. What are the components of the capital structure in the typical MNE? What about MNEs in Japan? What about a typical firm in your country?

3. From a managerial perspective, what are the advantages and disadvantages of financing obtained from each of the following: equity, debt, and intra-corporate sources?

4. Suppose you had to raise capital to fund international value-adding activities and investment projects. From what types of sources (e.g., stock markets) would you most likely obtain each type of financing? What are financial centers and where are they located?

5. What are the major tasks involved in managing working capital and cash flow for international operations?

6. What are the major steps involved in capital budgeting? For what types of ventures do international managers typically need to engage in capital budgeting?

7. What are the types of currency exposure? Why is currency exposure potentially harmful to the firm's international operations? How can managers go about forecasting currency exposure? What steps could you take to minimize currency exposure?

8. Who are the major players involved in foreign-exchange trading?

9. What are the major methods for translating foreign-currency denominated financial statements into the financial statements of the parent firm?

10. As an international tax consultant to an MNE, what steps would you take to minimize tax obligations around the world?

Apply Your Understanding AACSB: **Reflective Thinking, Analytical Skills**

1. Marite Perez is CEO of Havana, Inc., a large manufacturer of high-tech medical equipment, based in North Miami Beach, Florida. The firm makes vital signs monitors, MRIs, X-ray machines, and other equipment for exploratory medical diagnostics. Marite wants to rapidly expand the firm into foreign markets. To accomplish this, she plans to invest a lot of money in developing new products and establishing production and marketing subsidiaries abroad. To whom can Marite possibly turn in order to raise capital for these projects? What is the relevance of various methods of raising capital (e.g., equity financing, debt financing, and intracorporate financing) for her firm? What are the advantages and disadvantages associated with each?

2. Michael Norton is the president of Liberty Enterprises, a large MNE based in Singapore that makes computers and related peripherals. The firm has many subsidiaries around the world. Demand for Liberty's products has been growing in Asia and Europe, especially in Indonesia, Japan, France, and Spain. Michael has always used external sources to finance the firm's working capital needs. Currently, with rapidly expanding business, he needs to access more working capital. What is the feasibility of raising funds through intracorporate sources? What should Michael know about the process of multilateral netting?

3. Emi Aoki, the treasurer at a major Canadian MNE, considers dealing with foreign currencies as one of the biggest challenges of her job. She uses a lead or lag strategy to minimize transaction and translation currency risks. If the particular foreign currency is expected to weaken, Emi's firm tries to collect foreign-currency receivables before they are due (a lead strategy), and pay foreign-currency payables late (a lag strategy). If the foreign currency is expected to strengthen, she attempts to delay receiving receivables and speed up payables. If Emi's firm is operating in a high-inflation country, then she tries to collect receivables early. How sound is this strategy? To what extent is the strategy feasible?

4. You have just returned from a seminar on doing business in developing countries. Many of these countries are suffering from weak currencies. One of the suggestions you heard is to keep cash and receivables to a minimum when currency depreciation is expected. In a weak-currency situation, you are advised to remit cash from subsidiaries to the parent as rapidly as possible or invest it locally in assets that can appreciate in value, such as real estate. Similarly, your local subsidiary in such a country should confine its dealings to the local currency as much as possible, minimizing the need to translate it into other currencies. To the extent that the cost of local debt is not excessive, the subsidiary may obtain needed capital from local sources. Evaluate these two guidelines for minimizing currency exposure.

globalEDGE Internet Exercises
(http://globalEDGE.msu.edu)

AACSB: Reflective Thinking, Analytical Skills

Refer to Chapter 1, page 27, for instructions on how to access and use globalEDGE™.

1. The *World Federation of Exchanges* is the organization that represents major stock exchanges around the world. Visit the online portal at: www.world-exchanges.org and use the annual report of the Federation as well as detailed statistics available on individual exchanges to answer the following questions:

   a. What percentage of the world market capitalization is represented by the top 10 exchanges?

   b. For the most recent year, what exchanges accounted for the largest increases in market capitalization?

   c. Which exchanges have seen the greatest increase over the recent past in the number of firms that are listed?

   d. Worldwide consolidation trends have also affected the stock exchanges. A good example is the merger of Paris-based Euronext with the NYSE. What are the underlying causes of these cross-border mergers?

2. Suppose your job is to ensure that your firm has enough foreign exchange on hand to pay outstanding accounts payable. Assume your firm owes 1,000,000 yen to a Japanese supplier, which is due exactly 60 days from now. Your task is to exchange dollars for the right amount of yens. To do this, you can enter a contract with a bank today to buy 1,000,000 yen 60 days forward, or wait 60 days and buy 1,000,000 yen at the then-prevailing spot exchange rate. Which alternative do you prefer, and why? If you expect that the spot rate 60 days from now will be the same as the spot rate today, what is the expected dollar cost of buying 1,000,000 yen in the spot market 60 days from now? How many dollars will it cost you to obtain 1,000,000 yen if you entered the forward contract? You can use the following online sites to obtain the spot exchange rates: go to www.ft.com and click on "market data, currencies," or go to globalEDGE™ and enter "exchange rates" in the search engine.

3. Many corporate Web sites provide financial information (including financial statements), as well as other information about companies' status and progress. As an institutional investor, you are thinking of investing in one of the following firms: Diageo (www.diageo.com), the premium drinks firm; Vivendi (www.vivendi.com), a French telecom; Grupo Carso (www.gcarso.com.mx), a major Mexican retailing conglomerate and SK Telecom (www.sktelecom.com), the largest wireless communication services provider in South Korea. Look up each firm's corporate Web site. Based on the information provided, answer the following questions:

   a. How would you rate the transparency of each firm?

   b. How inclined are you to invest in each firm, based on the information provided? Justify your answer.

   c. In terms of transparency and investor-oriented information, which site is best?

   d. Based on the best site, what recommendations would you make to the firm that owns the weakest site to improve its transparency and attract investors?

Understanding Currencies: Big Macs and Dell Computers

There are more than a hundred currencies in use worldwide, most of which fluctuate daily due to a wide range of macroeconomic and political conditions. In today's integrated global economy, dealing with foreign currencies requires managers to forecast currency values and proactively manage currency risk. Currency risk dramatically affects the revenues and expenses of firms. The problem is especially acute for accounts payable, accounts receivable, and other assets and obligations that endure for more than a few weeks.

AACSB: Reflective Thinking, Use of Information Technology

Managerial Challenge

Properly forecasting currency values and managing currency risk are essential activities for the international firm. The management challenge is to assess the relative cost of identical Dell computer models across a number of countries using the *Economist*'s "Big Mac" Index of currency values.

Background

Currency values fluctuate in response to many interacting factors. In this C/K/R Management Skill Builder©, you will work with the *Economist's* Big Mac Index of currency values. The index tracks the prices of McDonald's Big Mac hamburgers, produced in 120 countries. It is a useful gauge of international pricing because Big Macs are one of the relatively few goods that are available almost everywhere. Another widely available product is Dell computers. In this exercise, you will assess the relative cost of identical Dell computer models across a number of countries using the Big Mac Index.

Managerial Skills You Will Gain

In this C/K/R Management Skill Builder©, as a prospective manager, you will:

1. Learn about the "real" value of international currencies.

2. Understand the difference between foreign prices interpreted via exchange rates and interpreted via purchasing power parity.

3. Learn about translating and dealing with foreign currencies.

4. Interpret prices expressed in Purchasing Power Parity terms.

5. Examine factors in addition to simple market forces that influence currency values.

6. Explore different currencies around the world.

Your Task

Your task is to recreate the Big Mac Index, using the price of a single model of Dell computers. You will pick several countries and replicate the table found on the C/K/R Knowledge Portal© by accessing an exchange rate table and Web sites for Dell computers worldwide. At each Dell Web site the local price is given for various computer models. Generally, Dell sells the same computer models worldwide.

Go to the C/K/R Knowledge Portal©

www.prenhall.com/cavusgil

Proceed to the C/K/R Knowledge Portal© to obtain the expanded background information, your task and methodology, suggested resources for this exercise, and the presentation template.

> Appendix

The Math of Currency Trading

News outlets such as the *Financial Times* and the *Wall Street Journal*, as well as online sources, publish bilateral exchange rate tables that list currency values in terms of other currencies. These tables report bid-ask midpoints and so do not represent prices that can actually be traded in the market. Here is an example.

	£	€	¥	$
U.K. pound (£)	1	0.7333	0.004954	0.5735
Euro (€)	1.3637	1	0.006755	0.7820
Japanese yen (¥)	201.875	148.032	1	115.768
U.S. dollar ($)	1.7438	1.2787	0.008638	1

The cells above the diagonal contain the number of units of the currency in the left-hand column that equal one of the currencies along the top row of the table (e.g., £0.7333/€). Conversely, the cells below the diagonal contain the number of units of the currency in a particular column of the table that equals the value of one unit of currency from that row (e.g., €1.3637/£).

Rather than trying to remember this convention, it is usually easier to infer the convention used in these tables from the values of your domestic currency. In the example above, Japanese and U.S. residents are likely to know that the dollar/yen price of 115.768 reflects a yen-per-dollar exchange rate of ¥115.768/$, rather than a dollar-per-yen price. This is a direct price for a U.S. resident and an indirect price for a Japanese resident. The yen-per-dollar price is then simply the reciprocal of the dollar-per-yen price:

$$1/(¥115.768/\$) = \$0.008638/¥.$$

Note that the values in this table are internally consistent. Thus, the yen-per-pound exchange rate must equal the yen-per-dollar rate times the dollar-per-pound rate:

$$¥201.875/£ = (¥115.768/\$) (\$1.7438/£).$$

Alternatively, the yen-per-pound rate can be calculated by dividing the yen-per-dollar rate by the pound-per-dollar rate:

$$¥201.875/£ = (¥115.768/\$) / (£0.5735/\$).$$

Keeping track of the currency units ensures that the answer has the correct units.

Exchange rates that do not involve the domestic currency are called **cross rates**. Cross rates for infrequently traded currencies can be calculated by comparing them against an actively traded currency such as the dollar. For example, the cross rate between the Chilean peso (CLP) and Japanese yen can be calculated by combining the CLP-per-dollar rate with the yen-per-dollar rate. If one U.S. dollar is worth 559.51 Chilean pesos, then the CLP-per-yen rate must be

$$(CLP\ 559.51/\$) / (¥115.768/\$) = CLP\ 4.8330/¥.$$

Again, it is important to keep track of the currency units to ensure the desired result.

> Glossary

Absolute advantage principle A country benefits by producing only those products in which it has absolute advantage, or can produce using fewer resources than another country.

Acculturation The process of adjusting and adapting to a culture other than one's own.

Acquisition Direct investment to purchase an existing company or facility.

Adaptation Firm efforts to modify one or more elements of its international marketing program to accommodate specific customer requirements in a particular market.

Advanced economies Post-industrial countries characterized by high per-capita income, highly competitive industries, and well-developed commercial infrastructure.

Agent An intermediary (often an individual or a small firm) that handles orders to buy and sell commodities, products, and services in international business transactions for a commission.

Antidumping duty A tax imposed on products deemed to be dumped and causing injury to producers of competing products in the importing country.

Arbitragers Currency traders who buy and sell the same currency in two or more foreign-exchange markets to take advantage of differences in the currency's exchange rate.

Area studies Factual knowledge of the historical, political, and economic environment of the host country.

Balance of payments The annual accounting of all economic transactions of a nation with all other nations.

Barter A type of countertrade that involves the direct exchange of goods without any money.

Bond A debt instrument that enables the issuer (borrower) to raise capital by promising to repay the principal along with the interest on a specified date (maturity).

Born global firm A young entrepreneurial company that initiates international business activity very early in its evolution, moving rapidly into foreign markets.

Build-operate-transfer (BOT) Arrangement in which the firm or a consortium of firms contracts to build a major facility abroad, operate it for a specified period, and then hand it over to the project sponsor, typically the host-country government or public utility.

Business process outsourcing (BPO) The outsourcing of business functions to independent suppliers, such as accounting, payroll, human resource functions, IT services, customer service, and technical support.

Buy-back agreements A type of countertrade that involves the seller agreeing to supply technology or equipment to construct a facility and receives payment in the form of goods produced by the facility.

Captive sourcing Sourcing from the firm's own production facilities located abroad.

Central bank The monetary authority in each nation that regulates the money supply and credit, issues currency, and manages the exchange rate of the nation's currency.

Codetermination An industrial relations practice where labor representatives sit on the corporate board and participate in company decision making.

Collective bargaining Collective negotiations between management and hourly labor and technical staff regarding wages and working conditions.

Commercial risk Firm's potential loss or failure from poorly developed or executed business strategies, tactics, or procedures.

Common market A stage of regional integration in which trade barriers are reduced or removed, common external barriers are established, and products, services, and factors of production are allowed to move freely among the member countries.

Company-owned subsidiary A representative office of the exporter that handles marketing, physical distribution, promotion, and customer service activities in the local market.

Company sales potential An estimate of the share of annual industry sales that the firm expects to generate in a particular target market.

Comparative advantage Superior features of a country that provide it with unique benefits in global competition typically derived from either natural endowments or deliberate national policies.

Comparative advantage principle It can be beneficial for two countries to trade without barriers as long as one is more efficient at producing goods or services needed by the other. What matters is not the absolute cost of production, but rather the relative efficiency with which a country can produce the product.

Compensation deals A type of countertrade that involves payment both in goods and cash.

Competitive advantage Distinctive assets or competencies of a firm—typically derived from cost, size, or innovation strengths—that are difficult for competitors to replicate or imitate.

Configuration of value-adding activity The pattern or geographic arrangement of locations where the firm carries out value-chain activities.

Consolidation The process of combining and integrating the financial results of foreign subsidiaries into the financial statements of the parent firm.

Consortium A project-based, nonequity venture with multiple partners fulfilling a large-scale project.

Contagion The tendency of a financial or monetary crisis in one country to spread rapidly to others due to ongoing financial integration worldwide.

Contract manufacturing An arrangement in which the focal firm contracts with an independent supplier to manufacture products according to well-defined specifications.

Contractual entry strategies in international business Cross-border exchanges where the relationship between the focal firm and its foreign partner is governed by an explicit contract.

Corporate social responsibility (CSR) Operating a business in a manner that meets or exceeds the ethical, legal, commercial, and public expectations of stakeholders (customers, shareholders, employees, and communities).

Counterpurchase A type of countertrade that involves two distinct contracts. In the first contract, the seller agrees to sell its product at a set price and receives cash payment from the buyer. This first deal is contingent on a second contract wherein the seller also agrees to purchase goods from the buyer for the total monetary amount or a set percentage of same.

Countertrade An international business transaction where all or partial payments are made in kind rather than cash.

Countervailing duty A duty imposed on products imported into a country to offset subsidies given to producers or exporters in the exporting country.

Country risk Potentially adverse effects on company operations and profitability caused by developments in the political, legal, and economic environment in a foreign country.

Critical incident analysis (CIA) An analytical method for analyzing awkward situations in cross-cultural interactions by developing empathy for other points of view.

Cross-border contractual relationships Cross-border exchanges where the relationship between the focal firm and its foreign partner is governed by an explicit contract.

Cross-cultural awareness Ability to interact effectively and appropriately with people from different language and cultural backgrounds.

Cross-cultural risk A situation or event where a cultural miscommunication puts some human value at stake.

Cross-licensing agreement A type of project-based, usually nonequity venture where partners agree to access licensed technology developed by the other, on preferential terms.

Cultural intelligence The capability of an employee to function effectively in situations characterized by cultural diversity.

Cultural metaphor A distinctive tradition or institution strongly associated with a particular society.

Culture The learned, shared, and enduring orientation patterns in a society. People demonstrate their culture through values, ideas, attitudes, behaviors, and symbols.

Culture shock The confusion and anxiety, often akin to mental depression, that can result from living in a foreign culture for an extended period.

Currency control Restrictions on the outflow of hard currency from a country, or the inflow of foreign currencies.

Currency option A contract that gives the purchaser the right, but not the obligation, to buy a certain amount of foreign currency at a set exchange rate within a specified amount of time.

Currency risk Risk that arises from changes in the price of one currency relative to another.

Currency swap An agreement to exchange one currency for another, according to a specified schedule.

Current rate method Translation of foreign currency balance sheet and income statements at the current exchange rate—the spot exchange rate in effect on the day, or for the period when the statements are prepared.

Customs Checkpoints at the ports of entry in each country where government officials inspect imported products and levy tariffs.

Customs brokers Specialist enterprises that arrange clearance of products through customs on behalf of importing firms.

Customs union A stage of regional integration in which the member countries agree to adopt common tariff and nontariff barriers on imports from nonmember countries.

Debt financing The borrowing of money from banks or other financial intermediaries, or selling of corporate bonds to individuals or institutions to raise capital.

Devaluation Government action to reduce the official value of its currency, relative to other currencies.

Developing economies Low-income countries characterized by limited industrialization and stagnant economies.

Direct Exporting Exporting that is accomplished by contracting with intermediaries located in the foreign market.

Direct quote The number of units of the domestic currency needed to acquire one unit of the foreign currency (also known as the *normal* or *American quote*).

Distribution channel intermediary A specialist firm that provides a variety of logistics and marketing services for focal firms as part of the international supply chain, both in the home country and abroad.

Documentation Official forms and other paperwork required for export sales to transport goods and clear customs.

Dumping Pricing exported products at less than their normal value, generally for less than their price in the domestic or third-country markets, or at less than production cost.

Economic exposure The currency risk that results from exchange rate fluctuations affecting the pricing of products, the cost of inputs, and the value of foreign investments.

Economic union A stage of regional integration in which member countries enjoy all the advantages of early stages, but also strive to have common fiscal and monetary policies.

Emerging markets Subset of former developing economies that have achieved substantial industrialization, modernization, and rapid economic growth since the 1980s.

Equity financing The issuance of shares of stock to raise capital from investors and the use of retained earnings.

Equity joint venture A type of partnership in which a separate firm is created through the investment or pooling of assets by two or more parent firms that gain joint ownership of the new legal entity.

Equity participation Acquisition of partial ownership in an existing firm.

Ethnocentric orientation Using our own culture as the standard for judging other cultures.

Eurobond A bond sold outside the issuer's home country and denominated in its own currency.

Eurocurrency Any currency deposited in a bank outside its country of origin.

Eurodollars U.S. dollars held in banks outside the United States, including foreign branches of U.S. banks.

Exchange rate The price of one currency expressed in terms of another. It is the number of units of one currency that can be exchanged for another.

Expatriate An employee who is assigned to work and reside in a foreign country for an extended period, usually a year or longer.

Expatriate failure The premature return of an employee from an international assignment.

Export control A government measure intended to manage or prevent the export of certain products or trade with certain countries.

Export department A unit within the firm charged with managing the firm's export operations.

Exporting The strategy of producing products or services in one country (often the producer's home country), and selling and distributing them to customers located in other countries.

Export management company (EMC) An intermediary that acts as an export agent on behalf of a (usually inexperienced) client company.

Extraterritoriality Application of home-country laws to persons or conduct outside of national borders.

Facilitator A firm or an individual with special expertise in legal advice, banking, customs clearance, or related support services, that assists focal firms in the performance of international business transactions.

Family conglomerate A large, privately-owned company that is highly diversified.

Focal firm The initiator of an international business transaction, including MNEs and SMEs, that conceives, designs, and produces the offerings intended for consumption by customers worldwide.

Foreign bond A bond sold outside the issuer's country and denominated in the currency of the country in which it is issued.

Foreign direct investment (FDI) An internationalization strategy in which the firm establishes a physical presence abroad through acquisition of productive assets such as capital, technology, labor, land, plant, and equipment.

Foreign distributor A foreign market-based intermediary that works under contract for an exporter, takes title to, and distributes the exporter's products in a national market or territory, often performing marketing functions such as sales, promotion, and after-sales service.

Foreign exchange All forms of money that are traded internationally, including foreign currencies, bank deposits, checks, and electronic transfers.

Foreign exchange market The global marketplace for buying and selling national currencies.

Foreign trade zone (FTZ) An area within a country that receives imported goods for assembly or other processing, and re-export. For customs purposes, the FTZ is treated as if it is outside the country's borders.

Forward contract A financial instrument to buy or sell a currency at an agreed-upon exchange rate at the initiation of the contract for future delivery and settlement.

Forward rate The exchange rate applicable to the collection or delivery of a foreign currency at some future date but at a rate specified at the time of the initial transaction.

Franchising Arrangement whereby the focal firm allows another the right to use an entire business system in exchange for fees, royalties, or other forms of compensation.

Franchisor A firm that grants another the right to use an entire business system in exchange for fees, royalties, or other forms of compensation.

Freight forwarder A specialized logistics service provider that arranges international shipping on behalf of exporting firms, much like a travel agent for cargo.

Free trade Relative absence of restrictions to the flow of goods and services between nations.

Free trade agreement A formal arrangement between two or more countries to reduce or eliminate tariffs, quotas, and barriers to trade in products and services.

Free trade area A stage of regional integration in which member countries agree to eliminate tariffs and other barriers to trade in products and services within the bloc.

Fronting loan A loan between the parent and its subsidiary, channeled through a large bank or other financial intermediary.

Functional division An arrangement in which decision making and management of the firm's international operations are organized by functional activity (such as production and marketing).

Futures contract An agreement to buy or sell a currency in exchange for another at a prespecified price and on a prespecified date.

Geocentric orientation A global mindset where the manager is able to understand a business or market without regard to country boundaries.

Geographic area division An organizational design in which control and decision making is decentralized to the level of individual geographic regions, whose managers are responsible for operations within their region.

Global account management (GAM) Servicing a key global customer in a consistent and standardized manner, regardless of where in the world it operates.

Global bond market The international marketplace in which bonds are bought and sold, primarily through banks and stockbrokers.

Global brand A brand whose positioning, advertising strategy, look, and personality are standardized worldwide.

Global capital market The collective financial markets where firms and governments raise intermediate-term and long-term financing.

Global equity market The worldwide market of funds for equity financing—the stock exchanges throughout the world where investors and firms meet to buy and sell shares of stock.

Global financial system The collective of financial institutions that facilitate and regulate investment and capital flows worldwide, such as central banks, commercial banks, and national stock exchanges.

Global industry An industry where competition is on a regional or worldwide scale.

Global integration Coordination of the firm's value-chain activities across countries to achieve worldwide efficiency, synergy, and cross-fertilization in order to take maximum advantage of similarities between countries.

Globalization of markets Ongoing economic integration and growing interdependency of countries worldwide.

Global marketing strategy A plan of action that guides the firm in how to position itself and its offerings in foreign markets, which customer segments to pursue, and the degree to which its marketing program elements should be standardized and adapted.

Global market opportunity Favorable combination of circumstances, locations, or timing that offers prospects for exporting, investing, sourcing, or partnering in foreign markets.

Global market segment A group of customers that share common characteristics across many national markets.

Global matrix structure An arrangement that blends the geographic area, product, and functional structures in an attempt to leverage the benefits of a purely global strategy and maximize global organizational learning while remaining responsive to local needs.

Global mindset Openness to, and awareness of, diversity across cultures.

Global money market The collective financial markets where firms and governments raise short-term financing.

Global sourcing The strategy of buying products and services from sources located abroad for use at home. Also referred to as importing, global procurement, or global purchasing.

Global strategy An approach where headquarters seeks substantial control over its country operations in an effort to minimize redundancy and achieve maximum efficiency, learning, and integration worldwide.

Global supply chain The firm's integrated network of sourcing, production, and distribution, organized on a world scale and located in countries where competitive advantage can be maximized.

Global talent pool A searchable database of employees, profiling their international skill sets and potential for supporting the firm's global aspirations.

Global team An internationally distributed group of people with a specific mandate to make or implement decisions that are international in scope.

Gray market activity Legal importation of genuine products into a country by intermediaries other than authorized distributors (also known as parallel imports).

Greenfield investment Direct investment to build a new manufacturing, marketing, or administrative facility, as opposed to acquiring existing facilities.

Hedgers Currency traders who seek to minimize the risk of exchange rate fluctuations, often by buying forwards or similar financial instruments.

Hedging Using financial instruments and other measures to reduce or eliminate exposure to currency risk.

High-context culture A culture that emphasizes nonverbal messages and views communication as a means to promote smooth, harmonious relationships.

Home replication strategy An approach in which the firm views international business as separate from and secondary to its domestic business.

Horizontal integration An arrangement whereby the firm owns, or seeks to own, the activities involved in a single stage of its value chain.

Host-country national (HCN) An employee who is a citizen of the country where the MNE subsidiary or affiliate is located.

Idiom An expression whose symbolic meaning is different from its literal meaning.

Import license Government authorization granted to a firm for importation of a product.

Importing or Global sourcing Buying of products and services from foreign sources and bringing them into the home market. Also referred to as global sourcing, global procurement, or global purchasing.

Incoterms Universally accepted terms of sale that specify how the buyer and the seller share the cost of freight and insurance in an international transaction, and at which point the buyer takes title to the goods.

Indirect exporting Exporting that is accomplished by contracting with intermediaries located in the firm's home market.

Indirect quote The number of units of the foreign currency obtained for one unit of the domestic currency (also known as the *reciprocal* or *European/Continental terms*).

Individualism versus collectivism Describes whether a person functions primarily as an individual or within a group.

Industrial cluster A concentration of businesses, suppliers, and supporting firms in the same industry at a particular location, characterized by a critical mass of human talent, capital, or other factor endowments.

Industry-market potential An estimate of the likely sales that can be expected for all firms in the particular industry for a specified period of time.

Infringement of intellectual property Unauthorized use, publication, or reproduction of products or services that are supported by a patent, copyright, trademark, or other intellectual property rights.

Intellectual property Ideas or works created by people or firms, such as patents, trademarks, and copyrights.

Intellectual property rights The legal claim through which the proprietary assets of firms and individuals are protected from unauthorized use by other parties.

International business Performance of trade and investment activities by firms across national borders.

International collaborative venture Cross-border business alliance where partnering firms pool their resources and share costs and risks of the new venture. Also referred to as an international partnership or international strategic alliance.

International division structure An organizational design in which all international activities are centralized within one division in the firm, separate from domestic units.

International human resource management (IHRM) The planning, selection, training, employment, and evaluation of employees for international operations.

International investment The transfer of assets to another country or the acquisition of assets in that country.

International Monetary Fund (IMF) An international agency that aims to stabilize currencies by monitoring the foreign exchange systems of member countries, and lending money to developing economies.

International monetary system Institutional framework, rules, and procedures by which national currencies are exchanged for each other.

International portfolio investment Passive ownership of foreign securities such as stocks and bonds for the purpose of generating financial returns.

International price escalation The problem of end-user prices reaching exorbitant levels in the export market caused by multilayered distribution channels, intermediary margins, tariffs, and other international customer costs.

Internalization theory An explanation of the process by which firms acquire and retain one or more value-chain activities "inside" the firm, minimizing the disadvantages of dealing with external partners and allowing for greater control over foreign operations.

International trade Exchange of products and services across national borders, typically through exporting and importing.

Intracorporate financing Funds provided from sources inside the firm (both the headquarters and subsidiaries) such as equity, loans, and trade credits.

Investment incentive Transfer payment or tax concession made directly to foreign firms to entice them to invest in the country.

Joint venture A form of collaboration between two or more firms to create a jointly owned enterprise.

Joint venture partner A focal firm that creates and jointly owns a new legal entity through equity investment or pooling of assets.

Know-how agreement Contract in which the focal firm provides technological or management knowledge about how to design, manufacture, or deliver a product or a service.

Legal system A system for interpreting and enforcing laws.

Letter of credit Contract between the banks of a buyer and a seller that ensures payment from the buyer to the seller upon receiving an export shipment.

Licensing Arrangement where the owner of intellectual property grants a firm the right to use that property for a specified period of time in exchange for royalties or other compensation.

Licensor A firm that enters a contractual agreement with a foreign partner that allows the latter the right to use certain intellectual property for a specified period of time in exchange for royalties or other compensation.

Local responsiveness Meeting the specific needs of buyers in individual countries.

Logistics service provider A transportation specialist that arranges for physical distribution and storage of products on behalf of focal firms, also controlling information between the point of origin and the point of consumption.

Long-term versus short-term orientation Denotes the degree to which people and organizations defer gratification to achieve long-term success.

Low-context culture A culture that relies on elaborate verbal explanations, putting much emphasis on spoken words.

Management contract Arrangement in which a contractor supplies managerial know-how to operate a hotel, airport, or other facility in exchange for compensation.

Manufacturer's representative An intermediary contracted by the exporter to represent and sell its merchandise or services in a designated country or territory.

Maquiladoras Export-assembly plants in northern Mexico along the U.S. border that produce components and typically finished products destined for the United States.

Masculinity versus femininity Refers to a society's orientation, based on traditional male and female values. Masculine cultures tend to value competitiveness, assertiveness, ambition, and the accumulation of wealth. Feminine cultures emphasize nurturing roles, interdependence among people, and taking care of less fortunate people.

Master franchise Arrangement in which an independent company is licensed to establish, develop, and manage the entire franchising network in its market and has the right to subfranchise to other franchisees, thus assuming the role of local franchisor.

Mercantilism The belief that national prosperity is the result of a positive balance of trade, achieved by maximizing exports and minimizing imports.

Merger A special type of acquisition in which two firms join to form a new, larger firm.

Monetary intervention The buying and selling of government securities by a central bank to maintain the exchange rate of a country's currency at some acceptable level.

Monochronic A rigid orientation to time, in which the individual is focused on schedules, punctuality, and time as a resource.

Multidomestic industry An industry where competition takes place on a country-by-country basis.

Multidomestic strategy An approach to firm internationalization where headquarters delegates considerable autonomy to each country manager, allowing him or her to operate independently and pursue local responsiveness.

Multilateral Development Banks (MDBs): International financial institutions owned by multiple governments within world regions or other groups.

Multilateral netting Strategic reduction of cash transfers within the MNE family through the elimination of offsetting cash flows.

Multinational enterprise (MNE) A large company with substantial resources that performs various business activities through a network of subsidiaries and affiliates located in multiple countries.

National industrial policy A proactive economic development plan initiated by the public sector, often in collaboration with the private sector, that aims to develop or support particular industries within the nation.

New global challengers Top firms from rapidly developing emerging markets that are fast becoming key contenders in world markets.

Nontariff trade barrier A government policy, regulation, or procedure that impedes trade through means other than explicit tariffs.

Offshoring The relocation of a business process or entire manufacturing facility to a foreign country.

Organizational culture The pattern of shared values, norms of behavior, systems, policies, and procedures that employees learn and adopt.

Organizational processes Managerial routines, behaviors, and mechanisms that allow the firm to function as intended.

Organizational structure Reporting relationships inside the firm that specify the linkages between people, functions, and processes.

Outsourcing The procurement of selected value-adding activities, including production of intermediate goods or finished products, from independent suppliers.

Parent-country national (PCN) An employee who is a citizen of the country where the MNE is headquartered.

Performance appraisal The formal process of assessing how effectively employees perform their jobs.

Political system A set of formal institutions that constitute a government.

Polycentric orientation A host-country mindset where the manager develops a greater affinity with the country in which she or he conducts business.

Polychronic A flexible, nonlinear orientation to time, in which the individual takes a long-term perspective and is capable of attending to multiple tasks simultaneously.

Power distance Describes how a society deals with the inequalities in power that exist among people.

Practical information Knowledge and skills necessary to function effectively in a country, including housing, health care, education, and daily living.

Privatization Transfer of state-owned industries to private concerns.

Product division An arrangement in which decision making and management of the firm's international operations is organized by major product line.

Project-based, nonequity venture A collaboration in which the partners create a project with a relatively narrow scope and a well-defined timetable, without creating a new legal entity.

Project-based, nonequity venture partners Focal firms that collaborate through a project, with a relatively narrow scope and a well-defined timetable, without creating a new legal entity.

Protectionism National economic policies designed to restrict free trade and protect domestic industries from foreign competition.

Quota A quantitative restriction placed on imports of a specific product over a specified period of time.

Regional economic integration The growing economic interdependence that results when two or more countries within a geographic region form an alliance aimed at reducing barriers to trade and investment.

Regional economic integration bloc A geographic area consisting of two or more countries that have agreed to pursue economic integration by reducing barriers to the cross-border flow of products, services, capital, and, in more advanced states, labor.

Repatriation The return of the expatriate to his or her home country following the completion of a lengthy foreign assignment.

Royalty A fee paid periodically to compensate a licensor for the temporary use of its intellectual property; often based on a percentage of gross sales generated from using the licensed asset.

Rule of law The existence of a legal system where rules are clear, publicly disclosed, fairly enforced, and widely respected by individuals, organizations, and the government.

Self-reference criterion The tendency to view other cultures through the lens of one's own culture.

Small and Medium-sized Enterprise (SME) A company with 500 or fewer employees in the United States, although this number may need to be adjusted downward for other countries.

Socialization The process of learning the rules and behavioral patterns appropriate to one's given society.

Special Drawing Right (SDR) A unit of account or a reserve asset, a type of "currency" used by central banks to supplement their existing reserves in transactions with the IMF.

Speculators Currency traders who seek profits by investing in currencies with the expectation that they will rise in value in the future.

Spot rate The exchange rate applicable to the trading of foreign currencies in which the current rate of exchange is used and delivery is considered immediate.

Standardization Firm efforts to make its marketing program elements uniform, with a view to targeting entire regions of countries, or even the global marketplace, with a similar product or service.

Stereotype Generalization about a group of people that may or may not be factual, often overlooking real, deeper differences.

Strategy A plan of action that channels an organization's resources so that it can effectively differentiate itself from competitors and accomplish unique and viable goals.

Strategy in the international context A plan for the organization to position itself positively from its competitors and configure its value-adding activities on a global scale.

Subsidy Monetary or other resources a government grants to a firm or group of firms, usually intended to ensure their survival by facilitating the production and marketing of products at reduced prices or to encourage exports.

Tariff A tax imposed on imported products, effectively increasing the cost of acquisition for the customer.

Tax haven A country hospitable to business and inward investment because of its low corporate income taxes.

Temporal method Translation of foreign currency balance sheet and income statements at an exchange rate that varies with the underlying method of valuation.

Tenders Formal offers made by a buyer to purchase certain products or services.

Third-country national (TCN) An employee who is a citizen of a country other than the home or host country.

Trade deficit The amount by which a nation's imports exceed its exports for a specific period of time.

Trade surplus The amount by which a nation's exports exceed its imports for a specific period of time.

Trading company An intermediary that engages in import and export of a variety of commodities, products, and services.

Transaction exposure The currency risk that firms face when outstanding accounts receivable or payable are denominated in foreign currencies.

Translation exposure The currency risk that results when an MNE translates financial statements denominated in a foreign currency into the functional currency of the parent firm, as part of consolidating international financial results.

Transfer pricing The practice of pricing intermediate or finished products exchanged among the subsidiaries and affiliates of the same corporate family located in different countries.

Transition economies Subset of emerging markets that have transformed from centrally planned economies into liberalized markets.

Transnational strategy A coordinated approach to internationalization in which the firm strives to be more responsive to local needs while retaining sufficient central control of operations to ensure efficiency and learning.

Transparency The degree to which companies regularly reveal substantial information about their financial condition and accounting practices.

Turnkey contracting Arrangement in which the focal firm or a consortium of firms plan, finance, organize, manage, and implement all phases of a project abroad and then hand it over to a foreign customer after training local personnel.

Turnkey contractors Focal firms or a consortium of firms that plans, finances, organizes, manages, and implements all phases of a project and then hands it over to a foreign customer after training local personnel.

Uncertainty avoidance The extent to which people can tolerate risk and uncertainty in their lives.

Value chain The sequence of value-adding activities performed by the firm in the process of developing, producing, marketing, and servicing a product.

Vertical integration An arrangement whereby the firm owns, or seeks to own, "multiple" stages of a value chain for producing, selling, and delivering a product or service.

Visionary leadership Senior human capital in an organization that provides the strategic guidance necessary to manage efficiency, flexibility, and learning in an internationalizing firm.

Wholly-owned direct investment A foreign direct investment in which the investor fully owns the foreign assets.

World Bank An international agency that provides loans and technical assistance to low and middle-income countries with the goal of reducing poverty.

World Trade Organization (WTO) A multilateral governing body empowered to regulate international trade and investment.

> Notes

Chapter 1

1. We use the term *international business* to refer to the cross-border business activities of individual firms, while economists use *international trade* to refer to aggregate cross-border flows of products and services between nations. While international business describes an enterprise-level phenomenon, international trade describes the macrophenomenon of aggregate flows between nations.

2. Nick Wingfield, "eBay Sets Sights on Indian Market with Acquisition," *Wall Street Journal*, June 23, 2004.

3. "Desert Song,"*Economist*, October 7, 2004.

4. Marc A. Miles et al., *2005 Index of Economic Freedom* (Washington, DC: The Heritage Foundation).

5. OECD, *Globalization and Small and Medium Enterprises (SMEs)*, (Paris: Organisation for Economic Co-operation and Development, 1997).

6. Gary Knight and S. Tamer Cavusgil, "Innovation, Organizational Capabilities, and the Born-Global Firm," *Journal of International Business Studies* 35, no. 2 (2004): 124–41; Patricia McDougall, Scott Shane, and Benjamin Oviatt, "Explaining the Formation of International New Ventures: The Limits of Theories from International Business Research," *Journal of Business Venturing* 9, no. 6 (1994): 469–87; OECD (1997).

7. U.S. Department of Commerce (2004), at http://www.commerce.gov.

8. World Bank, *World Development Indicators* (Washington, DC: The World Bank, 2004).

9. Sidney Weintraub, *NAFTA at Three: A Progress Report* (Washington, DC: Center for Strategic and International Studies, 1997).

10. Christopher Bartlett and Sumantra Ghoshal, *Transnational Management: Text, Cases, and Readings in Cross-Border Management* (Homewood, IL: Irwin, 1992).

11. Kerry Capell, "McDonald's Offers Ethics with Those Fries," *Business Week*, January 9, 2007.

Chapter 2

1. Thomas L. Friedman, "It's a Flat World, After All," *New York Times Magazine*, April 3, 1990, 33–37.

2. Ibid.

3. Ibid.

4. Thomas L. Friedman, *The Lexis and the Olive Tree* (New York: Anchor Books, 2000).

5. This discussion is based on Lawrence Beer, *Tracing the Roots of Globalization, It's Not A New Event,* unpublished manuscript, W. P. Carey School of Business, Arizona State University, 2006. An abbreviated version of the paper is available at the C/K/R Knowledge Portal©.

6. The word *trade* comes from the Anglo-Saxon term *trada,* which means to walk in the footsteps of others. Ancient trade routes were the foundation for a high level of cross-cultural exchange of ideas that led to the development of religion, science, economic activity, and government. The phrase "all roads lead to Rome" is not so much a metaphorical reference to Rome's dominance of the world 2,000 years ago, but to the fact that Rome's territorial colonies were constructed as commercial resource centers to serve the needs of the Roman Empire and increase its wealth. In an empire that stretched from England to Israel and from Germany to Africa, the Romans created more than 300,000 kilometers of roads. Roman roads were the lifeblood of the state that allowed trade to flourish. The Roman Empire was so concerned with the interruption of its shipping lanes for imported goods that it dispatched army legions to protect those lanes.

In the middle ages, the Knights Templar acted as guardians for pilgrims making the hazardous journey to pay homage to the birthplace of the Christian religion. In addition to protecting tourists, this warrior order created the first international banking system with the use of rudimentary traveler's checks, eliminating the need for travelers to carry valuables on their person.

In 1100, Genghis Khan not only united the Mongols but created an empire beyond the Chinese border that included Korea and Japan in the East, Mesopotamia (modern day Iraq and Syria), Russia, Poland, and Hungary. He instituted common laws and regulations over his domain, most notably the preservation of private property, to enhance and protect international trade.

Arab merchants traded in spices along land routes reaching from northern Arabia across modern day Turkey, through Asia Minor, and finally reaching China. By concealing the origins of cinnamon, pepper, cloves, and nutmeg, traders gained a monopoly and controlled prices. Europeans came to believe that the spices came from Africa, when in fact they had merely changed hands in the region. Under the traditional trading system, spices, linen, silk, diamonds, pearls, and opium-based medicines reached Europe via indirect routes over land and sea. Representing one of the earliest systems of international distribution, the products passed through many hands on their long voyage. At every juncture, prices increased several fold. (This discussion is based on Lawrence Beer, Arizona State University.)

7. C. Chase-Dunn, Yukio Kawano, and Benjamin D. Brewer, "World Globalization Since 1795: Waves of Integration in the World-System," *American Sociological Review* 65, no. 1 (2000): 77–95.

8. Lawrence Franko, *The European Multinationals* (Stamford, CN: Greylock Publishers, 1976).

9. Louis Emmerij, "Globalization, Regionalization, and World Trade," *Columbia Journal of World Business* 27, no. 2 (1992): 6–13.

10. "The Death of Distance: A Survey of Telecommunications," *The Economist*, September 30, 1995; Company profile of Vodafone, 2007, at http://www.hoovers.com/.

11. "The Phenomenal Growth of Vodafone: Rapid Rise through an Aggressive Leadership Style," *Strategic Direction* 19, no. 7 (2003): 25–26.

12. Marcos Aguiar et al., *The New Global Challengers: How Top 100 Rapidly Developing Economies Are Changing the World*, Boston Consulting Group, May 25, 2006.

13. GNI refers to the total value of goods and services produced within a country after taking into account payments made to, and income received from, other countries.

14. Jeremy Siegel, *The Future for Investors* (New York: Crown Business, 2005).

15. Richard Nelson and Sidney Winter, *An Evolutionary Theory of Economic Change* (Cambridge, MA: Belknap Press, 1982).

16. Michael E. Porter and Victor E. Millar, "How Information Gives You Competitive Advantage," *Harvard Business Review* 63 (July–August 1985): 149–60; S. Tamer Cavusgil, "Extending the Reach of E-Business," *Marketing Management* 11, no. 2 (2002): 24–29; Janice Burn and Karen Loch, The Societal Impact of the World Wide Web—Key Challenges for the 21st Century," *Information Resources Management Journal* 14, no. 4 (2001): 4–12.

17. Cliff Wymbs, "How E-Commerce Is Transforming and Internationalizing Service Industries," *Journal of Services Marketing* 14, no. 6 (2000): 463—71.

18. Friedman (2005).

19. Ibid.

20. Martin Wolf, *Why Globalization Works* (New Haven, CN: Yale University Press, 2004).

21. "The Day the Factories Stopped," *The Economist*, October 23, 2004.

22. Pete Engardio et al., "The New Global Job Shift," *Business Week*, February 3, 2003, 50.

23. Tara Radin and Martin Calkins, "The Struggle Against Sweatshops: Moving Toward Responsible Global Business," *Journal of Business Ethics* 66, no. 2–3 (2006): 261—69.

24. S. L. Bachman, "The Political Economy of Child Labor and Its Impacts on International Business," *Business Economics* July 2000, 30–41.

25. Wolf (2004).

26. Michael Smith, "Trade and the Environment," *International Business* 5, no. 8 (1992): 74.

27. "Rise of the Sushi King," *Business 2.0* December 1, 2004, 80.

Chapter 3

1. Carol Matlack, "Europe: Go East, Young Man," *Business Week*, October 30, 2006.

2. Alison Coleman, "How to Be an Expert at Export," *Financial Times*, October 26, 2005.

3. Farok Contractor, Chin-Chun Hsu, and Sumit Kundu, "Explaining Export Performance: A Comparative Study of International New Ventures in Indian and Taiwanese Software Industry," *Management International Review* 45, Special Issue no. 3 (2005): 83–110; G. Knight & S. T. Cavusgil, "The Born Global Firm: A Challenge to Traditional Internationalization Theory," in *Advances in International Marketing* vol. 8, ed. Tage Koed Madsen (Greenwich, CN: JAI Press, 1996): 11–26; A. Rebecca Reuber and Eileen Fischer, "The Influence of the Management Team's International Experience on the Internationalization Behaviors of SMEs," *Journal of International Business Studies* 28, no. 4 (1997): 807–19.

4. Y. Ono, "Beer Venture of Anheuser, Kirin Goes Down Drain on Tepid Sales," *Wall Street Journal*, November 3, 1999.

5. C. Macdonald, "Toy Story," *Canadian Plastics* 61, no. 2 (2003): 17–18.

6. Carlye Adler, "How China Eats a Sandwich," *Fortune Small Business*, March 2005.

7. Peter M. Reina, "Public Funds and Turnkey Contracts Fuel Growing Global Subway Work," *ENR*, October 25, 2004: 32.

8. "BOT Group Awards Major Hong Kong Road Contract," *ENR*, July 3, 1995: 30.

9. "Hitachi Ltd.: Joint Venture to Promote Smart-Card Operating System," *Wall Street Journal*, November 26, 2005.

10. "BP Sets India Venture, Explores China Tie-Ups," *Wall Street Journal*, October 14, 2005.

11. Charles Waltner, "Cisco Forms Strategic Alliance with Fujitsu," December 5, 2004, http://www.newsroom.cisco.com/dlls/2004/prod_120604c.html; Cisco, "China's ZTE Forms Strategic Alliance With Cisco Systems," http://www.newsroom.cisco.com/dlls/2004/prod_120604c.html; Italtel, "Italtel and Cisco Systems Alliance Mission," http://www.italtel.com/ShowContent?item=1028.

12. U.S. Department of Commerce, *A Basic Guide to Exporting* (Washington, DC: U.S. Government Printing Office, 1992).

13. S. Tamer Cavusgil, Lyn S. Amine, and Robert Weinstein, "Japanese Sogo Shosha in the U.S. Export Trading Companies," *Journal of the Academy of Marketing Science* 14, no. 3 (1986): 21–32.

14. D. Willmott, "Disintermediation: The Buzzword from Hell," *PC Magazine*, September 10, 1997.

15. A. Chircu and R. Kauffman, "Strategies for Internet Middlemen in the Intermediation/Disintermediation/Reintermediation Cycle," *Electronic Markets* 9, no. 2 (1998): 109–17.

16. Brian Grow et al., "Bitter Pills," *Business Week*, December 18, 2006.

Chapter 4

[1] David Ricardo, *Principles of Political Economy and Taxation* (London: Everyman Edition, 1911; first published in 1817).

[2] John Romalis, "Factor Proportions and the Structure of Commodity Trade," *The American Economic Review* 94, no.1 (2004): 6–97.

[3] Raymond Vernon, "International Investment and International Trade in the Product Cycle," *Quarterly Journal of Economics* 80 (May 1966): 19–207.

[4] Michael Porter, *The Competitive Advantage of Nations* (New York: Free Press, 1990).

[5] Mourad Dakhli and Dirk De Clercq, (2004), "Human Capital, Social Capital, and Innovation: A Multi-Country Study," *Entrepreneurship and Regional Development* 16, no. 2 (2004), 10–115.

[6] Clyde Prestowitz, *Trading Places* (New York: Basic Books, 1989); Lester Thurow, *Head to Head: The Coming Economic Battle Among Japan, Europe, and America* (New York: William Morrow, 1992).

[7] "The Luck of the Irish: A Survey of Ireland," *The Economist,* special section, (October 16, 2004).

[8] Warren J. Bilkey, "An Attempted Integration of the Literature on the Export Behavior of Firms," *Journal of International Business Studies* 9 (Summer, 1978): 3–46; S. Tamer Cavusgil, "On the Internationalization Process of Firms," *European Research* 8, no. 6 (1980): 27–81; Jan Johanson and Jan-Erik Vahlne, "The Internationalization Process of the Firm—A Model of Knowledge Development and Increasing Foreign Commitments," *Journal of International Business Studies* 8 (Spring/Summer, 1977): 2–32; Cavusgil, 1980.

[9] G. Knight and S. T. Cavusgil, "The Born Global Firm: A Challenge to Traditional Internationalization Theory," in *Advances in International Marketing* vol. 8, ed. S. Cavusgil and T. Madsen (Greenwich, CT: JAI Press, 1996).

[10] Ibid.

[11] Gary A. Knight and S. Tamer Cavusgil, (2004). "Innovation, Organizational Capabilities, and the Born-Global Firm." *Journal of International Business Studies* 35, no. 2 (2004):12–41; Benjamin Oviatt and Patricia McDougall, "Toward a Theory of International New Ventures," *Journal of International Business Studies* 25, no. 1 (1994):4–64; Michael Rennie, "Born Global," *McKinsey Quarterly* no. 4 (1993): 4–52.

[12] UNCTAD, *World Investment Report 2005* (New York: United Nations, 2005).

[13] "The Beer Wars Come to a Head: Can SABMiller Stay Ahead of Busch as the Global Market Merges?" *Business Week,* May 24, 2004: 68.

[14] Stephen Hymer, *The International Operations of National Firms* (Cambridge, MA: MIT Press, 1976).

[15] Peter Buckley and Mark Casson, *The Future of the Multinational Enterprise* (London: MacMillan, 1976).

[16] Dunning, John (1988), "The Eclectic Paradigm of International Production: A Restatement and Some Possible Extensions," *Journal of International Business Studies,* 19: 1-31; Rugman, Alan (1980), "A New Theory of the Multinational Enterprise: Internationalization Versus Internalization," *Columbia Journal of World Business,* 15 (1): 23–24.

[17] Dunning, (1988).

[18] Ibid.

[19] Bruce Kogut, "Joint Ventures: Theoretical and Empirical Perspectives," *Strategic Management Journal* 9 (1988): 31–332. P. Rajan Varadarajan and Margaret H. Cunningham, "Strategic Alliances: A Synthesis of Conceptual Foundations," *Journal of the Academy of Marketing Science* 23 (1995): 28–296.

[20] "For Starbucks, There's No Place Like Home," *Business Week,* June 9 (2003) :48.

[21] James Lincoln, Christina Ahmadjian, and Eliot Mason, "Organizational Learning and Purchase-Supply Relations in Japan," *California Management Review* 40 no. 3 (1998) :24–264.

[22] Hakan Hakansson, *International Marketing and Purchasing of Industrial Goods: An Interaction Approach* (New York: Wiley, 1982).

Chapter 5

[1] R. Rosmarin, "Mountain View Masala," *Business 2.0* (March 2005): 54–56.

[2] Howard Perlmutter, "The Tortuous Evolution of the Multinational Corporation," *Columbia Journal of World Business* 4, no.1 (1969): 9–18.

[3] V. Govindarajan and A. Gupta, *The Quest for Global Dominance* (San Francisco: Jossey-Bass/Wiley, 2001).

[4] Robert Boyd and Peter Richerson, *Culture and Evolutionary Process* (Chicago: University of Chicago Press, 1985).

[5] Harry C. Triandis, *Culture and Social Behavior* (New York: McGraw-Hill, 1994).

[6] M. J. Herskovits, *Cultural Anthropology* (New York: Knopf, 1955).

[7] Geert Hofstede, *Culture's Consequences* (Beverly Hills, CA: Sage, 1980).

[8] Harry C. Triandis, *Culture and Social Behavior* (New York: McGraw-Hill, 1994).

[9] Sengun Yeniyurt and Janell Townsend, "Does Culture Explain Acceptance of New Products in a Country? An Empirical Investigation," *International Marketing Review* 20, no. 4 (2003): 377–96; Yong Zhang and James Neelankavil, "The Influence of Culture on Advertising Effectiveness in China and the USA: A Cross-Cultural Study," *European Journal of Marketing* 31, no. 2 (1997): 134–42.

[10] David A. Griffith, Michael Y. Hu, and John K. Ryans, Jr., "Process Standardization across Intra- and Inter-cultural Relationships," *Journal of International Business Studies* 31, no. 2 (2000): 303–24; Thomas Head, Clara Gong, Chunhui Ma et al., "Chinese Executives' Assessment of Organization Development Interventions," *Organization Development Journal* 24, no. 1 (2006): 28–40; Joel D. Nicholson and Yim-Yu Wong, "Culturally Based Differences in Work Beliefs," *Management Research News* 24, no. 5 (2001): 1–10.

[11] David Aviel, "American Managers and Their Asian Counterparts," *Industrial Management* 38, no. 2 (1996): 1–2; Richard Linowes, Yoshi Tsurumi, and Toro Nakamura, "The Japanese Manager's Traumatic Entry into the United

States: Understanding the American Japanese Cultural Divide; Executive Commentary," *Academy of Management Executive* 7, no. 4 (1993): 21–40.

12. Vern Terpstra and Kenneth David, *The Cultural Environment of International Business* 3rd ed. (Cincinnati, OH: Southwestern, 1991).

13. M. J. Gannon and Associates, *Understanding Global Cultures: Metaphorical Journeys through 17 Countries* (Thousand Oaks, CA: Sage, 1994).

14. Nancy Adler, *International Dimensions of Organizational Behavior* (Cincinnati, OH: South-Western, 2002).

15. Edward T. Hall, *Beyond Culture* (New York: Anchor, 1976).

16. Richard Priem, Leonard Love, and Margaret Shaffer, "Industrialization and Values Evolution: The Case of Hong Kong and Guangzhou, China," *Asia Pacific Journal of Management* 17, no. 3 (2000): 473–82.

17. F. Kluckhohn and F. Strodbeck, *Variations in Value Orientations* (Evanston, IL: Row Peterson, 1961).

18. Alice Eagly and Shelly Chaiken, *The Psychology of Attitudes* (New York: Harcourt Brace Jovanovich, 1993).

19. Joyce Osland, Silvio De Franco, and Asbjorn Osland, "Organizational Implications of Latin American Culture: Lessons for the Expatriate Manager," *Journal of Management Inquiry* 8, no. 2 (1999): 219–38.

20. Roger Axtell, *The DO's and TABOO's of International Trade* (New York: Wiley, 1994).

21. Meg Carter, "Muslims Offer a New Mecca for Marketers," *Financial Times,* August 11, 2005.

22. *Economist,* "Babel Runs Backwards," January 1, 2005.

23. Edward T. Hall, *The Silent Language* (Garden City, NY: Anchor, 1981).

24. P. Dicken, *Global Shift: Transforming The World Economy* (New York: Guilford, 1998).

25. T. Clark and D. Rajaratnam, "International Services: Perspectives at Century's End," *Journal of Services Marketing* 13, nos. 4/5 (1999): 298–302.

26. B. Kogut, "Country Capabilities and the Permeability of Borders," *Strategic Management Journal* 12 (Summer, 1991): 33–47.

27. T. Clark, D. Rajaratnam, and T. Smith, "Toward a Theory of International Services: Marketing Intangibles in a World of Nations," *Journal of International Marketing* 4, no. 2 (1996): 9–28.

28. S. Lorge, "Federal Express," *Sales and Marketing Management* 149, no. 11 (1997): 63.

29. J. M. Greig, "The End of Geography?: Globalization, Communications, and Culture in the International System," *The Journal of Conflict Resolution* 46, no. 2 (2002): 225–44.

30. R. Rosmarin, "Text Messaging Gets a Translator," *Business 2.0* (March, 2005): 32; Nitish Singh, Vikas Kumar, and Daniel Baack, "Adaptation of Cultural Content: Evidence from B2C E-Commerce Firms," *European Journal of Marketing* 39, nos. 1/2 (2005): 71–86.

31. Russell Belk, "Hyperreality and Globalization: Culture in the Age of Ronald McDonald," *Journal of International Consumer Marketing* 8, nos. 3/4 (1996): 23–37.

32. Tyler Cowen, *Creative Destruction: How Globalization Is Changing the World's Cultures* (Princeton, NJ: Princeton University Press, 2002).

33. Laszlo Tihanyi, David A. Griffith, and Craig J. Russell, "The Effect of Cultural Distance on Entry Mode Choice, International Diversification, and MNE Performance: A Meta-Analysis," *Journal of International Business Studies* 36, no. 3 (2005): 270–83.

34. Tomasz Lenartowicz and James P. Johnson, "A Cross-National Assessment of the Values of Latin America Managers: Contrasting Hues or Shades of Gray?" *Journal of International Business Studies* 34, no. 3 (2003): 266–81.

35. James Johnson, Tomasz Lenartowicz, and Salvador Apud, "Cross-Cultural Competence in International Business: Toward a Definition and a Model," *Journal of International Business Studies* 37, no. 4 (2006): 525–35; Soon Ang, Linn Van Dyne, and Christine Koh, "Personality Correlates of the Four-Factor Model of Cultural Intelligence," *Group & Organization Management* 31, no. 1 (2006): 100–123.

Chapter 6

1. Jack Ewing, "Germany: A Cold Shoulder for Coca-Cola," *Business Week,* May 2, 2005, 52.

2. S. Tamer Cavusgil, Pervez Ghauri, and Milind Agarwal, *Doing Business in Emerging Markets* (Thousand Oaks, CA: Sage, 2002). Further citations to this work are given in the text.

3. *Economist,* "Country Risk," February 26, 2005, 102.

4. *Business Week,* "Getting Past Yukos," Sept. 13, 2004, 52.

5. Cavusgil, Ghauri, Agarwal 2002.

6. Steven Soper, *Totalitarianism: A Conceptual Approach* (Lanham, MD: University Press of America, 1985); Carl J. Friedrich and Zbigniew Brzezinski, *Totalitarian Dictatorship and Autocracy,* 2d ed. (Cambridge, MA: Harvard University Press, 1965).

7. Milton Friedman and Rose Friedman, *Free to Choose* (New York: Harcourt Brace Jovanovich, 1980); Martin Schnitzer and James Nordyke, *Comparative Economic Systems* (Cincinnati, OH: Southwestern, 1983).

8. Milton Friedman, "The Battle's Half Won," *Wall Street Journal,* December 9, 2004: A16; *Statistical Abstract of the United States,* Economics and Statistics Administration, (Washington, DC: U.S. Census Bureau, 2004).

9. Christopher Swan, "$400 Billion Industry: Japan's First Islamic Bond," (*Bloomberg,* April, 2007).

10. Phyllis Berman, "The Three Marketeers," *Forbes,* July 25, 2005, 78.

11. Raman Kumar, William Lamb, and Richard Wokutch, "The End of the South African Sanctions, Institutional Ownership, and the Stock Price Performance of Boycotted Firms," *Business and Society* 41, no. 2 (2002): 133–65.

12. Seth Lubove, "Gas Attack," *Forbes,* May 23, 2005, 54–56.

13. Javier Blas and Carola Hoyos, "Oil Wrestling," *Financial Times,* May 5, 2006, 15.

14. Yonah Alexander, David Valton, and Paul Wilkinson, *Terrorism: Theory and Practice* (Boulder, CO: Westview, 1979).

15. Jonathan Laing, "Aftershock," *Barron's,* September 9, 2002, 23.

16. International Chamber of Commerce, "Policy Statement: Extraterritoriality and Business," Paris: ICC, July 13, 2006.

17. Kurt Stanberry, Barbara C. George, and Maria Ross, "Securities Fraud in the International Arena," *Business and Society* 30, no. 1 (1991): 27–36.

18. Randall Hess and Edgar Kossack, "Bribery as an Organizational Response to Conflicting Environmental Expectations," *Academy of Marketing Science* 9, no. 3 (1981): 206–226; Judith Scott, Debora Gilliard, and Richard Scott, "Eliminating Bribery as a Transnational Marketing Strategy," *International Journal of Commerce & Management* 12, no. 1 (2002): 1–17.

19. Anindya Bhattacharya, "Multiculturalism and the Accounting Profession: Enhancing Employee Productivity and Client Satisfaction," *The National Public Accountant* 46, no. 3 (2001): 13–14, 21.

20. Hank Boerner, "Europe Faces Eagle Eye of U.S. Financial Regulation," *European Business Forum* 21 (2005): 46–49.

21. Transparency International, (2005), at www.transparency.org.

22. David Zussman, "Fighting Corruption Is a Global Concern," *Ottawa Citizen,* October 11, 2005, A15.

23. John Hongxin Zhao, Seung Kim, and Jianjun Du, "The Impact of Corruption and Transparency on Foreign Direct Investment: An Empirical Analysis," *Management International Review* 43, no. 1 (2003): 41–62.

24. Transparency International, (2005), at www.transparency.org.

25. Marco Celentani, Juan-Jose Ganuza, and Jose-Luis Peydros, "Combating Corruption in International Business Transactions," *Economica* 71, no. 283 (2004): 417–49.

26. *Economist,* "The Good Company: A Survey of Corporate Social Responsibility," January 22, 2005, special section; Kathleen Rehbein, Sandra Waddock, and Samuel Graves, "Understanding Shareholder Activism: Which Corporations Are Targeted?" *Business and Society* 43, no. 3 (2004): 239–67.

27. Lawrence Koslow and Robert Scarlett, *Global Business* (Houston, TX: Cashman Dudley, 1999).

28. Michael Schuman and Jeffrey Ressner, "Disney's Great Leap Into China," *Time,* July 18, 2005: 52–54.

29. Vara Vauhini, "Russian Web Sites Offer Cheap Songs, But Piracy is Issue," *Wall Street Journal,* Jan 26, 2005: D10.

Chapter 7

1. Jeffrey D. Sachs and Andrew Warner, "Economic Reform and the Process of Global Integration," *Brookings Papers on Economic Activity,* Issue no. 1: Washington, DC: Brookings Institute (1995); Heritage Foundation. Accessed at the Heritage Foundation Web site at www.heritage.org/research/features/index/

2. David Dollar and Aart Kraay, "Trade, Growth, and Poverty," Policy Research Working Paper no. WPS 2615, June, 2001. Washington DC: World Bank, Development Research Group; United Nations, *World Economic and Social Survey,* accessed 2005 at www.un.org.

3. *Financial Times,* "Bush Move Marks U.S. Trade Policy Turning Point," March 6 (2002): 6.

4. Jim Carlton, "U.S. Nears Mexican Cement Pact," *Wall Street Journal.* August 29, 2005, A7.

5. Stefanie Lenway, Kathleen Rehbein, and Laura Starks, "The Impact of Protectionism on Firm Wealth: The Experience of the Steel Industry," *Southern Economic Journal* 56, no. 4 (1990): 1079–93.

6. G. Chazan and G. White, "Kremlin Weighs on Growth," *Wall Street Journal,* October 17, 2005, A16.

7. Robert Reich, *The Work of Nations: Preparing Ourselves for 21st Century Capitalism* (New York: Knopf, 1991); Lester Thurow, *Head to Head: The Coming Economic Battle Among Japan, Europe, and America* (New York: William Morrow, 1992).

8. United Nations, accessed 2007 at the United Nations Web site on financial statistics at www.un.org/reports/financing/profile.htm.

9. Dustin Smith, "The Truth About Industrial Country Tariffs," *Finance and Development* 39, no. 3 (2002), Washington DC, International Monetary Fund, accessed at http://www.imf.org

10. *Economist,* "Textiles: Knickers in a Twist," August 27, 2005, 50.

11. United States Trade Representative, "National Trade Estimate Report." Accessed 2004 at www.ustr.gov.

12. Frederik Balfour, "The State's Long Apron Strings." *Business Week,* August 22, 2005, 74.

13. World Trade Organization (WTO), Glossary. Geneva, Switzerland. Accessed 2007 at www.wto.org.

14. Ibid.

15. William Beach and Marc Miles, "Explaining the Factors of the Index of Economic Freedom," *2005 Index of Economic Freedom* (Washington, DC: Heritage Foundation). Accessed 2006 at www.heritage.org.

16. Heritage Foundation. *2007 Index of Economic Freedom* (Washington, DC: Heritage Foundation). Accessed 2007 at www.heritage.org.

17. Smith 2002.

18. *Economist,* "In the Shadow of Prosperity." January 20, 2007, 32–34.

19. Chacholidades, Militiades (1990), *International Economics,* New York: McGraw Hill.

20. James Ingram, *International Economics* (New York: Wiley, 1983).

21. Thurow 1992.

22. Eugene Salorio, Jean Boddewyn, and Nicolas Dahan, "Integrating Business Political Behavior with Economic and Organizational Strategies." *International Studies of Management & Organization* 35, no. 2 (2005): 28–35.

23. N. King, "Tale of the Tuna: Grocery Rivalry Fuels Tariff Spat," *Wall Street Journal*, April 20, 2002, B1.

24. William McDaniel and Edgar Kossack, "The Financial Benefits to Users of Foreign-Trade Zones." *Columbia Journal of World Business* 18, no. 3 (1983): 33–41.

25. Scott Kennedy, "The Barbarians Learn How to Lobby at the Gates of Industry." *Financial Times*, September 28, 2005, 5.

Chapter 8

1. Balassa, Bela, *The Theory of Economic Integration* (Homewood, IL: Irwin, 1961); Jacob Viner, *The Customs Union Issue* (New York: Carnegie Endowment for International Peace, 1950).

2. J. Crawford and R. Fiorentino, *The Changing Landscape of Regional Trade Agreements*, Discussion Paper no. 8 (Geneva, Switzerland: World Trade Organization, 2005)

3. European Union (2005), Web site of the European Union at http://europa.eu.int.

4. *Economist*, "Transformed: EU Membership has Worked Magic in Central Europe," June 25, 2005, 6–8.

5. *Economist*, "European Carmakers: Driving Out of the East," March 5, 2005, 60.

6. R. Smyser, "The Core of the Global Economy," *The World & I* April, 2001, 26–31.

7. World Trade Organization (2006), statistics from the WTO Web site at www.wto.org.

8. *Business Week*, "Happy Birthday, NAFTA," December 22, 2003, 112.

9. Alan Rugman, *The End of Globalization: Why Global Strategy is a Myth and How to Profit from the Realities of Regional Markets* (New York: American Management Association, 2001).

10. Central Intelligence Agency, (2007), CIA World Factbook, at odci.gov/cia/publications/factbook.

11. George Garman and Debora Gilliard (1998), "Economic Integration in the Americas: 1975–1992," *The Journal of Applied Business Research* 14(3): 1–12.

12. Jacob Viner, (1950), *The Customs Union Issue* New York: Carnegie Endowment for International Peace; Franklin Root, (1984), *International Trade and Investment*, 5th ed. Cincinnati, OH: South-Western Publishing Co.

13. Ibid.

14. Emile Dreuil, James Anderson, Walter Block, and Michael Saliba, (2003), "The Trade Gap: The Fallacy of Anti World-Trade Sentiment," *Journal of Business Ethics* 45 (3): 269–78.

15. *Economist*, "A Divided Union," September 23, 2004, 64.

16. Subhash Jain, and John K. Ryans, "A Normative Framework for Assessing Marketing Strategy Implications of Europe 1992," in *Euromarketing*, E. Kaynak and P. Ghauri, eds. (New York: International Business Press, 1994).

17. *Economist*, "Transformed: EU Membership has Worked Magic in Central Europe," June 25, 2005, 6–8.

18. European Union (2005), Web site of the European Union at http://europa.eu.int.

Chapter 9

1. Boston Consulting Group. (2006) The New Global Challengers. Boston: The Boston Consulting Group, Inc.; Engardio, Pete. (2006). "Emerging Giants." *Business Week*, July 31, pp. 40–42.

2. Ted London and Stuart Hart (2004), "Reinventing Strategies for Emerging Markets: Beyond the Transnational Model," *Journal of International Business Studies* 35 (2004): 350–63.

3. *Economist*, "The Luck of the Irish: A Survey of Ireland," October 16, 2004.

4. World Bank, *World Bank Development Indicators* (Washington DC: World Bank, 2007).

5. Ibid.

6. World Bank, (2007), *Doing Business: Benchmarking Business Regulations*, at www.doingbusiness.org.

7. Jack Behrman and Dennis Rondinelli, "The Transition to Market-Oriented Economies in Central and Eastern Europe," *European Business Journal* 12 (2000): 87–99.

8. Stanley Reed, "This Mobile Upstart Really Gets Around," *Business Week*, July 31, 2006, 49.

9. Alex Wang, "The Downside of Growth: Law, Policy and China's Environmental Crisis," *Perspectives* 2 (2000), Rockville, MD: Overseas Young Chinese Forum, available at www.oycf.org.

10. Michael Deneen, and Andrew Gross, "The Global Market for Power Tools," *Business Economics* July, 2006, 66–73.

11. S. Tamer Cavusgil and Lyn S. Amine (1986), "Demand Estimation in a Developing Country Environment: Difficulties, Techniques, and Examples," *Journal of the Market Research Society* 28 (1986): 43–65.

12. The "percent of income held by middle class" refers to percentile distribution of income in a nation. In particular, it represents the proportion of national income earned by the middle 60 percentile of the population when the top 20 percentile (the wealthiest) and the bottom 20 percentile (the poorest) are excluded. For example, the middle class— 60 percent of the population sandwiched between the wealthiest and the poorest—in Brazil accounted for only 35 percent of national income, suggesting a relatively unequal distribution of national income.

13. S. Tamer Cavusgil, "Measuring the Potential of Emerging Markets: An Indexing Approach," *Business Horizons* 40 (1997): 87–91.

14. The Index of Economic Freedom, prepared by The Heritage Foundation (http://www.heritage.org/research/features/index/) measures and ranks over 150 countries across 10 specific freedoms such as tax rates and property rights.

15. Ariel Cohen, "Putin's Crisis: Dealing with Russia's Political Upheaval," WebMemo #671, February 20, 2005, at www.heritage.org.

16. United States Trade Representative (2006), *National Trade Estimate Report on Foreign Trade Barriers*, at www.ustr.gov.

17. Transparency International (2005), at www.transparency.org.

18. Daekwan Kim, Destan Kandemir, and S. Tamer Cavusgil, "The Role of Family Conglomerates in Emerging

Markets: What Western Companies Should Know," *Thunderbird International Business Review* 46 (2004): 13–20.

19. Peter Marsh, "Toyota Gears Up for Production Drive in India," *Financial Times* March 5, 2007, 21.

20. John Reed, "GM Plans to Build Low-Priced Small Vehicle, *Financial Times* March 5, 2007, 21.

21. Jeffrey Garten, *The Big Ten: The Big Emerging Markets and How They Will Change Our Lives* (New York: Basic Books, 1997). G. Kolodko, ed., *Emerging Market Economics: Globalization and Development* Aldershot, Hants, England: Ashgate, 2003); Daekwan Kim, Destan Kandemir, and S. Tamer Cavusgil, "The Role of Family Conglomerates in Emerging Markets: What Western Companies Should Know," *Thunderbird International Business Review* 46 (2004): 13–20.

22. Pete Engardio, "Emerging Giants," *Business Week,* July 31, 2006, 40–49.

23. C. K. Prahalad, "Aid is Not the Answer," *Wall Street Journal,* August 31, 2005, A8; C. K. Prahalad, *The Fortune at the Bottom of the Pyramid: Eradicating Poverty Through Profits* (Philadelphia: Wharton School Books, 2005).

24. Simon Elegant, "Comeback Kid," *Far Eastern Economic Review,* September 3, 1998, 10–14; Azziz Panni, "Sweden's Mobile Leader," *International Management* 49 (1994): 24–29.

25. Brigit Helms, *Access For All: Building Inclusive Financial Systems* (Washington, DC: The World Bank, 2006).

26, 27. Jay Greene, "Taking Tiny Loans to the Next Level," *Business Week* November 27, 2006, 76–82.

28. Christopher Beshouri, (2006), "A Grassroots Approach to Emerging-Market Consumers," *The McKinsey Quarterly* no. 4, at www.mckinseyquarterly.com.

Chapter 10

1. *Economist,* "The Americas: Tightening His Grip; Ecuador's Rafael Correa," April 21, 2007, 60.

2. *Federal Reserve Bulletin,* various years, at www.federalreserve.gov.

3. Timothy Aeppel, "Weak Dollar, Strong Sales," *Wall Street Journal,* January 20, 2005, p. B1.

4. *Economist,* "Volkswagen: Higher Wages or More Job Security," September 18, 2004, 66–67.

5. Richard A. Ajayi, and Mbodja Mougoue, "On the Dynamic Relation Between Stock Prices and Exchange Rates," *The Journal of Financial Research* 19 (1996): 193–207.

6. *Business Mexico,* "Fractured Argentina," 13 (2003): 54.

7. Abdul-Hamid Sukar and Seid Hassan, "US Exports and Time-Varying Volatility of Real Exchange Rate," *Global Finance Journal* 12 (2001): 109–14.

8. Josef Brada, Ali Kutan, and Su Zhou, "The Exchange Rate and the Balance of Trade: The Turkish Experience," *The Journal of Development Studies* 33 (1997): 675–84.

9. International Monetary Fund (2004), *Global Financial Stability Report,* at www.imf.org.

10. *Financial Planning,* "Foreign Intrigue: Planners Need a Passport to Follow the Money that's Flooding into Overseas Mutual Funds, but the Wave may be about to Break," 1 (May, 2005): 1.

11. Alan Greenspan, (1997), "The Globalization of Finance," *The Cato Journal* 17 (1997) at www.cato.org.

12. International Monetary Fund (2003), "Effects of Financial Globalization on Developing Countries: Some Empirical Evidence" International Monetary Fund, at www.imf.org.

13. C. Bulent Aybar and Claudia Milman, "Globalization, emerging market economies and currency crisis in Asia," *Multinational Business Review* 7 (1999): 37–44.

14. G. Zachary, "Give Me Your Tired, Your Hungry, our Cash. . . ," *Business 2.0* October, 2004, 66–69.

15. *Corporate Finance,* "Telcos Offer Incentives to Lure Bond Investors," July 2000, 4.

16. *Economist,* "Open Wider: A Survey of International Banking," May 21, 2005, special section.

17. Bank for International Settlements (2001), *Consultative Document: The New Basel Capital Accord,* at www.bis.org.

18. *Economist,* "America's Current Account Deficit: The O'Neill Doctrine," April 27, 2002, 12.

Chapter 11

1. G. T. Hult, S. Deligonul, and S. Tamer Cavusgil, "The Hexagon of Market-Based Globalization: An Empirical Approach Towards Delineating The Extent of Globalization In Companies," in *New Perspectives in International Business Thought,* A. Lewin, ed., (London: Palgrave, 2006); George Yip, *Total Global Strategy II,* (Upper Saddle River, NJ: Prentice Hall, 2003).

2. S. Tamer Cavusgil, Sengun Yeniyurt, and Janell Townsend, "The Framework of a Global Company: A Conceptualization and Preliminary Validation," *Industrial Marketing Management* 33 (2004): 711–16; George Yip, (2003), *Total Global Strategy II,* (Upper Saddle River, NJ: Prentice Hall, 2003).

3. Theodore Levitt, "The Globalization of Markets," *Harvard Business Review* 61 (May–June, 1983): 92–102.

4. Kenichi Ohmae, "Planning for a Global Harvest," *Harvard Business Review* 67 (1989): 136–45.

5. Bruce Kogut, "Designing Global Strategies: Profiting from Operational Flexibility," *Strategic Management Journal* 27 (1985): 27–38.

6. T. Hout, Michael Porter, Michael, and E. Rudden, "How Global Companies Win Out," *Harvard Business Review* 60 (September–October, 1982): 98–105.

7. Gary Hamel and C. K. Prahalad, "Do You Really Have a Global Strategy?" *Harvard Business Review* 63 (1985): 139–49.

8. Christopher A. Bartlett and Sumantra Ghoshal, *Managing Across Borders: The Transnational Solution* (Boston, MA: Harvard Business School Press, 1989).

9. Christopher A. Bartlett and Sumantra Ghoshal, *Transnational Management: Text, Cases, and Readings in Cross-Border Management,* 3rd ed. (Boston, MA: Irwin/McGraw-Hill, 2000).

10. Christopher Bartlett, and Sumantra Ghoshal, *Managing Across Borders: The Transnational Solution* (Boston, MA: Harvard Business School Press, 1989); Timothy M. Devinney, David F. Midgley, and Sunil Venaik, "The Optimal Performance and the Global Firm: Formalizing and Extending the Integration-Responsiveness Framework," *Organization*

Science 11 (2000): 674–95; Yves L. Doz, Christopher Bartlett, and C. K. Prahalad, "Global Competitive Pressures and Host Country Demands: Managing Tensions in MNCs," *California Management Review* 23 (1981): 63–74; Yadong Luo, "Determinants of Local Responsiveness: Perspectives from Foreign Subsidiaries in an Emerging Market," *Journal of Management* 26 (2001): 451–77; C. K. Prahalad, *The Strategic Process in a Multinational Corporation,* Unpublished doctoral diss. (Graduate School of Business Administration, Harvard University Cambridge, MA, 1975).

11. Christopher Bartlett and Sumantra Ghoshal, *Managing Across Borders: The Transnational Solution* (Boston, MA: Harvard Business School Press, 1989); Robert T. Moran, and John R. Riesenberger, *The Global Challenge* (London: McGraw-Hill, 1994).

12. Bartlett and Ghoshal 1989; Moran and Riesenberger 1994.

13. Christopher A. Bartlett and Sumantra Ghoshal, *Transnational Management: Text, Cases, and Readings in Cross-Border Management,* 3rd ed. (Boston, MA: Irwin/McGraw-Hill, 2000).

14. Ibid.

15. Robert T. Moran and John R. Riesenberger, *The Global Challenge* (London: McGraw-Hill, 1994).

16. Christopher A. Bartlett and Sumantra Ghoshal, *Transnational Management: Text, Cases, and Readings in Cross-Border Management,* 3rd ed. (Boston, MA: Irwin/McGraw-Hill, 2000).

17. Theodore Levitt, "The Globalization of Markets," *Harvard Business Review* 61 (May-June, 1983): 92–102.

18. Christopher A. Bartlett and Sumantra Ghoshal. *Transnational Management: Text, Cases, and Readings in Cross-Border Management,* 3rd ed. (Boston, MA: Irwin/McGraw-Hill, 2000).

19. Shaoming Zou and S. Tamer Cavusgil, "The GMS: A Broad Conceptualization of Global Marketing Strategy and Its Effect on Firm Performance," *Journal of Marketing* 58 (January, 2002): 1–21; George Yip, *Total Global Strategy II* (Upper Saddle River, NJ: Prentice Hall, 2003).

20. Robert T. Moran and John R. Riesenberger *The Global Challenge* (London: McGraw-Hill, 1994).

21. Pankaj Ghemawat, (2005), "Regional Strategies for Global Leadership," *Harvard Business Review* 83, (December, 2005): 98–106.

22. Robert T. Moran and John R. Riesenberger, *The Global Challenge* (London: McGraw-Hill, 1994); Franklin Root, *Entry Strategies for International Markets* (San Francisco: Jossey-Bass, 1998).

23. Moran and Riesenberger (1994).

24. Alfred D. Chandler, *Strategy and Structure* (Cambridge, MA: MIT Press, 1962).

25. Bartlett and Ghoshal (1992).

26. Ibid.

27. Ibid.

28. Ibid.

29. Ibid.

30. Ibid.

31. Ibid.

32. Christopher A. Bartlett and Sumantra Ghoshal, *Managing Across Borders: The Transnational Solution* (Boston, MA: Harvard Business School Press, 1989); Robert T. Moran and John

R. Riesenberger, *The Global Challenge* (London: McGraw-Hill, 1994); G. T. Hult, S. Deligonul, and S. Tamer Cavusgil, "The Hexagon of Market-Based Globalization: An Empirical Approach Towards Delineating The Extent of Globalization In Companies," in *New Perspectives in International Business Thought,* A. Lewin, ed. (London: Palgrave, 2006).

33. Deborah Ball, "Despite Revamp, Unwieldy Unilever Falls behind Rivals," *Wall Street Journal,* January 3, 2005, A1, A5.

34. Robert T. Moran and John R. Riesenberger, *The Global Challenge* (London: McGraw-Hill, 1994).

35. S. Tamer Cavusgil, Sengun Yeniyurt, and Janell Townsend, "The Framework of a Global Company: A Conceptualization and Preliminary Validation," *Industrial Marketing Management* 33 (2004): 711–16; G. T. Hult, S. Deligonul, and S. Tamer Cavusgil, "The Hexagon of Market-Based Globalization: An Empirical Approach Towards Delineating The Extent of Globalization In Companies," in *New Perspectives in International Business Thought,* A. Lewin, ed. (London: Palgrave, 2006); George Yip, *Total Global Strategy II* (Upper Saddle River, NJ: Prentice Hall, 2003).

36. G. T. Hult, S. Deligonul, and S. Tamer Cavusgil, "The Hexagon of Market-Based Globalization: An Empirical Approach Towards Delineating The Extent of Globalization In Companies," in *New Perspectives in International Business Thought,* A. Lewin, ed. (London: Palgrave, 2006); Ben L. Kedia and Akuro Mukherji, "Global Managers: Developing a Mindset for Global Competitiveness," *Journal of World Business* 34 (1999): 230–51.

37. Haig Simonian, "Climber Scales the Health Peak," *Financial Times,* August 21, 2006, 8.

38. Stephen Rhinesmith, *A Manager's Guide to Globalization* (Homewood, IL: Business One Irwin, 1998).

39. Gary A. Knight and S. Tamer Cavusgil, "Innovation, Organizational Capabilities, and the Born-Global Firm," *Journal of International Business Studies* 35(2004): 124–41; Jeffrey Covin and Dennis Slevin, "Strategic Management of Small Firms in Hostile and Benign Environments," *Strategic Management Journal* 10 (January, 1989): 75–87; G. T. Lumpkin and Gregory Dess, "Clarifying the Entrepreneurial Orientation Construct and Linking it to Performance," *Academy of Management Review* 21(1996): 135–72.

40. Gary Hamel and C. K. Prahalad, "Strategic Intent," *Harvard Business Review* (May–June, 1989): 63–76.

41. *Economist,* "The Grey Market: Hey, Big Spender," December 3, 2005, 59–60.

42. S. Tamer Cavusgil, Sengun Yeniyurt, and Janell Townsend, "The Framework of a Global Company: A Conceptualization and Preliminary Validation," *Industrial Marketing Management* 33 (2004): 711–16.

43. *Business 2.0,* "What You Can Learn from Toyota," (January/February, 2005): 67–72.

44. Joel D. Nicholson and Yim-Yu Wong "Culturally Based Differences in Work Beliefs," *Management Research News* 24, no. 5 (2001): 1–10; Edgar H. Schein, *Organizational Culture and Leadership* 2nd ed. (San Francisco: Jossey-Bass, 1997).

45. Clay Chandler, "Canon's Big Gun," *Fortune,* February 6, 2006, 92–98.

46. *Business 2.0,* "What You Can Learn from Toyota," January-February, 2005, 67–72.

47. S. Tamer Cavusgil, Sengun Yeniyurt, and Janell Townsend, "The Framework of a Global Company: A Conceptualization and Preliminary Validation," *Industrial Marketing Management* 33 (2004): 711–16; Stephen Rhinesmith, *A Manager's Guide to Globalization* (Homewood, IL: Business One Irwin, 1998); George S. Yip, Johny K. Johansson, and J. Roos, "Effects of Nationality on Global Strategy," *Management International Review* 37 (1997): 365–385.

48. Björn Ambos and Bodo Schlegelmilch, "In Search of Global Advantage," *European Business Forum* 21 (Spring, 2005): 23–24; Chen, Stephen, Ronald Geluykens, and Chong Ju Choi (2006), "The Importance of Language in Global Teams," *Management International Review,* 46(6), pp. 679–696. Jay R. Galbraith, *Designing the Global Corporation* (San Francisco: Jossey-Bass, 2000); Robert T. Keller, "Cross-Functional Project Groups in Research and New Product Development: Diversity, Communications, Job Stress, and Outcomes," *Academy of Management Journal* 44 (2001): 547–55; Mary Maloney and Mary Zellmer-Bruhn, "Building Bridges, Windows and Cultures," *Management International Review* 46 (2006): 697–720.

49. Martha L. Maznevski and Nicholas A. Athanassiou, "Guest Editors' Introduction to the Focused Issue: A New Direction for Global Teams Research," *Management International Review* 46 (2006): 631–46.

50. Terence Brake, *Managing Globally* (New York: Dorling Kindersley, 2002).

51. CNN Money, "P&G CEO Quits Amid Woes," June 8, 2000; Galuszka, Peter "Is P&G's Makeover Only Skin-Deep?" *Business Week,* November 15, pg. 52; Procter & Gamble, "Organization 2005 Drive for Accelerated Growth Enters Next Phase," press release, June 9, 1999, at www.pg.com, on page 63.

52. Linda Shi, Shaoming Zou, J. Chris White, Regina McNally, and S. Tamer Cavusgil, "Executive Insights: Global Account Management Capability," *Journal of International Marketing* 13 (2005): 93–113.

Chapter 12

1. Jeen-Su Lim, Thomas Sharkey, and Ken Kim, "Competitive Environmental Scanning and Export Involvement: An Initial Inquiry," *International Marketing Review* 13 (1996): 65–80.

2. F. Cunningham, "Commerce Department Helps Franchisors Go Global," *Franchising World,* December, 2005, 63–67.

3. S. Silverman, "Chipping Away," *International Business,* March, 1995, 54–57.

4. D. Vrontis and P. Vronti, "Levis Strauss: An International Marketing Investigation," *Journal of Fashion Marketing and Management* 8 (2004): 389–98.

5. S. Tamer Cavusgil, "Measuring the Potential of Emerging Markets: An Indexing Approach," *Business Horizons* 40 (January–February, 1997): 87–91.

6. globalEDGE [2005], "Market potential indicators for emerging markets," available at ciber.bus.msu.edu/publicat/mktptind.htm.

7. Sundar Bharadwaj, Terry Clark, and Songpol Kulviwat, "Marketing, Market Growth, and Endogenous Growth Theory: An Inquiry into the Causes of Market Growth," *Journal of the Academy of Marketing Science* 33 (2005): 347–59.

8. Moon Ihlwan and Amey Stone, "Special Report: Emerging Tech Markets: South Korea: Tech's Test Market," *Business Week,* March 4, 2003.

9. *Business Week,* "Britain: Beyond Beer and Peanuts," September 19, 2005, 110.

10. S. Tamer Cavusgil, "Guidelines for Export Market Research," *Business Horizons* 28 (November–December, 1985): 27–33.

11. U.S. Department of Commerce, *A Basic Guide to Exporting* (Washington, DC: U.S. Government Printing Office, 1992).

Chapter 13

1. Tao Gao, "The Contingency Framework of Foreign Entry Mode Decisions: Locating and Reinforcing the Weakest Link," *Multinational Business Review* 12 (2004): 37–68.

2. McKinsey Quarterly, "Escaping the Middle Market Trap: An Interview with the CEO of Electrolux," 4 (2006): 73–79.

3. S. Tamer Cavusgil, "On the Internationalization Process of Firms," *European Research* 8 (1980): 273–81.

4. Jan Johanson and J.-E. Vahlne, "The Internationalization Process of the Firm—A Model of Knowledge Development and Increasing Foreign Commitments," *Journal of International Business Studies* 8 (Spring–Summer, 1977): 23–32; Robert Salomon and J. Myles Shaver, "Learning by Exporting: New Insights from Examining Firm Innovation," *Journal of Economics & Management Strategy* 14 (2005): 431–42.

5. *Economist,* "Digital Dragon," December 17, 2005, 58.

6. David Liu, "Exporting Mortgage Insurance Beyond the United States," *Housing Finance International* 14 (2000): 32–41.

7. Rajshekhar, Javalgi, Charles Martin, and Patricia Todd, (2004), "The Export of E-Services in the Age of Technology Transformation: Challenges and Implications for International Service Providers," *The Journal of Services Marketing* 18 (2004): 560–73.

8. Institute for International Business, "The Global vs. Domestic Wine Industry," *Global Executive Forum* (Spring–Summer, 2005): 12.

9. S. Tamer Cavusgil and Shaoming Zou, "Marketing Strategy-Performance Relationship: An Investigation of the Empirical Link in Export Market Ventures," *Journal of Marketing* 58 (January, 1994): 1–21.

10. M. O'Flanagan, "Case Study: Exporting Gives Businesses a Healthy Outlook," *Sunday Business Post,* April 6, 2003.

11. Chun Zhang, S. Tamer Cavusgil, and Anthony Roath, "Manufacturer Governance of Foreign Distributor Relationships: Do Relational Norms Enhance Competitiveness in the Export Market?" *Journal of International Business Studies* 34 (2003): 550–63.

12. *Business Week,* "So You Think the World Is Your Oyster," June 9, 1997, 4.

Chapter 14

1. Bhavna, "The Beer Market in India," *Just—Drinks,* March, 2007, 65–87; Hoovers.com company profile of SAB-Miller at www.hoovers.com.

2. Erin Anderson and Hubert Gatignon, "Modes of Foreign Entry: A Transaction Cost Analysis and Propositions," *Journal of International Business Studies* 17 (Fall, 1986): 1–26: William H. Davidson, *Global Strategic Management* (New York: Wiley, 1982).

3. John Dunning, *International Production and the Multinational Enterprise* (London, Allen and Unwin, 1981).

4. Fred Vogelstein, "How Intel Got Inside," *Fortune,* October 4, 2004, 127–36.

5. Farok Contractor and Peter Lorange, eds. *Cooperative Strategies in International Markets* (Lexington, MA, Lexington Books, 1988); Gary Hamel, Yves Doz, and C. K. Prahalad, "Collaborate with Your Competitors—and Win," *Harvard Business Review* 67 (January–February, 1989): 133–39; Katherine Harrigan, "Strategic Alliances: Their New Role in Global Competition." *Columbia Journal of World Business* 22 (Summer, 1987): 67–69; Vern Terpstra and Bernard Simonin, "Strategic Alliances in the Triad," *Journal of International Marketing* 1 (1993): 4–25.

6. Lilach Nachum and Srilata Zaheer, "The Persistence of Distance? The Impact of Technology on MNE Motivations for Foreign Investment," *Strategic Management Journal,* 26 (2005): 747–67.

7. Wilbur Chung, and Juan Alcacer, "Knowledge Seeking and Location Choice of Foreign Direct Investment in the United States," *Management Science* 48 (2002): 1534–42.

8. Anders Lotsson, "Tomorrow: A Sneak Preview," *Business 2.0* (August, 2005): 77–84.

9. Lilach Nachum and Cliff Wymbs, "Product Differentiation, External Economies and MNE Location Choices: M&As in Global Cities," *Journal of International Business Studies* 36 (2005): 415–23.

10. Lilach Nachum and Srilata Zaheer, "The Persistence of Distance? The Impact of Technology on MNE Motivations for Foreign Investment," *Strategic Management Journal* 26 (2005): 747–67.

11. *Economist,* "Retailing: Storm Clouds Over the Mall," October 8, 2005, 71–72.

12. Barbara Katz and Joel Owen, "Should Governments Compete for Foreign Direct Investment?" *Journal of Economic Behavior & Organization* 59 (2006): 230–38.

13. UNCTAD, *World Investment Report 2006* (New York: United Nations Conference on Trade and Development, 2006).

14. Thomas C. Head and P. Sorensen, "Attracting Foreign Direct Investment: The Potential Role of National Culture," *The Journal of American Academy of Business* 6 (205): 305–309.

15. *Business Week,* "Beyond the Green Corporation," January 29, 2007, 50–64.

16. Clay Chandler, "Mickey Mao," *Fortune,* April 18, 2005, 170–78.

17. Ibid.

18. M. K. Erramilli and C. P. Rao, "Service Firms' International Entry-Mode Choice: A Modified Transaction-Cost Analysis Approach," *Journal of Marketing* 57 (July, 1993): 19–38; J. Li and S. Guisinger, "The Globalization of Service Multinationals in the 'Triad' Regions: Japan, Western Europe, and North America," *Journal of International Business Studies* 23 (1992): 675–96; United Nations, *The Transnationalization of Service Industries* (New York: Transnational Corporations and Management Division, Department of Economic and Social Development, 1993).

19. Rajshekhar Javalgi, David A Griffith, and D Steven White, "An Empirical Examination of Factors Influencing the Internationalization of Service Firms," *Journal of Services Marketing* 17 (2003): 185–201.

20. UNCTAD, (2006).

21. A.T. Kearney, Inc., *FDI Confidence Index* (Alexandria, VA: Global Business Policy Council, 2004).

22. John Tagliabue, "Would Stalin Drive a Peugeot?," *New York Times,* November 25, 2006, B1, B9; David Rocks, "Made in China—Er, Veliko Turnovo," *Business Week,* January 8, 2007, 43.

23. Andrew Ward, "Home Depot in Mexico," *Financial Times,* April 6, 2006, 8.

24. UNCTAD, (2006)

25. In this book, we adopt the customary definition of joint venture where it is assumed to carry equity interest by the parent firms that founded it. That is, a joint venture is always an equity venture. Nevertheless, in the popular literature the term "equity venture" is incorrectly used to refer to all types of collaborative ventures, including project-based collaborations. Therefore, we will use the term "equity joint venture" rather than simply "joint venture' in order to avoid miscommunication.

26. Paul Kaihla, "Why China Wants to Scoop Up Your Company," *Business 2.0,* June, 2005, 29–30.

27. Farok Contractor and Peter Lorange, *Cooperative Strategies and Alliances,* (Oxford: Elsevier Science, 2002).

28. Janell Townsend, "Understanding Alliances: A Review of International Aspects in Strategic Marketing," *Marketing Intelligence & Planning* 21 (2003): 143–58.

29. Donald Fites, "Make Your Dealers Your Partners," *Harvard Business Review* 74 (1996): 84–91; Masaaki Kotabe, Hildy Teegen, Preet Aulakh, Maria Cecilia Coutinho de Arruda, Roberto Santillan-Salgado, and Walter Greene, "Strategic Alliances in Emerging Latin American: A View

from Brazilian, Chilean, and Mexican Companies," *Journal of World Business* 35 (2000): 114–32.

30. *Wall Street Journal*, "Procter & Gamble Co.: Company to Produce Perfumes For Dolce & Gabbana of Italy," December 15, 2005, C11.

31. UNCTAD, (2006)

32. Daniel Lyons, "Holy Chip!" *Forbes*, January 30, 2006, 76–82.

33. Robert A. Guth, "IBM Announces Deal With Japan's NTT," *Wall Street Journal*, November 1, 2000, A.23.

34. Farok Contractor and Peter Lorange, *Cooperative Strategies and Alliances* (Oxford: Elsevier Science, 2002); Gary Hamel, (1991), "Competition for Competence and Inter-Partner Learning Within International Strategic Alliances," *Strategic Management Journal* Special Issue: Global Strategy, 12 (Summer, 1991): 83–103; Gary Hamel, Yves Doz, and C. K. Prahalad, "Collaborate with Your Competitors—and Win," *Harvard Business Review* 67 (January–February, 1989): 133–39.

35. S. Tamer Cavusgil, "International Partnering: A Systematic Framework for Collaborating with Foreign Business Partners," *Journal of International Marketing* 6 (1998): 91–107; Destan Kandemir, Attila Yaprak, and S. Tamer Cavusgil, "Alliance Orientation: Conceptualization, Measurement and Impact on Market Performance," *Journal of the Academy of Marketing Science* 34 (2006): 324–40.

36. Bruce Heimana and Jack Nickerson, "Empirical Evidence Regarding the Tension Between Knowledge Sharing and Knowledge Expropriation in Collaborations," *Managerial and Decision Economics* 25 (2004): 401–20.

37. Fred Vogelstein, "How Intel Got Inside," *Fortune*, October 4, 2004, 127–36.

38. S. Tamer Cavusgil, "International Partnering: A Systematic Framework for Collaborating with Foreign Business Partners," *Journal of International Marketing* 6 (1998): 91–107.

39. *Business Week*, "China: The Great Internet Race," June 13, 2005, 54–55.

40. Sing Keow Hoon-Halbauer, "Managing Relationships within Sino-Foreign Joint Ventures," *Journal of World Business* 34 (1999): 334–70.

41. James Areddy, "Danone's China Deal Turns Sour," *Wall Street Journal*, April 12, 2007, A10.

42. Alex Taylor, "Shanghai Auto Wants to be the World's Next Great Car Company," *Fortune*, October 4, 2004, 103–10.

43. Dorinda Elliott and Bill Powell, "Wal-Mart Nation," *Time*, June 27, 2005, 37–39.

44. Andrew Ward, "Home Depot in Mexico," *Financial Times*, April 6, 2006, 8.

45. Adrienne Sanders, "Yankee Imperialist," *Forbes*, December 13, 1999, 56.

46. Clay Chandler, "The Great Wal-Mart of China," *Fortune*, July 25, 2005, 104–16.

47. Andrew Ward, "Home Depot in Mexico," *Financial Times*, April 6, 2006, 8.

48. Dale Fuchs, "Spaniards Making the Shift to the Mall," *New York Times*, December 31, 2005, accessed 2/2/06 at www.nytimes.com.

49. UNCTAD, (2006)

50. Ibid.

51. Ibid.

52. Ibid.; Jonathon Birchall, "Sun Rises Over Wal-Mart's Power Policy," *Financial Times*, January 22, 2007, 8.

Chapter 15

1. International Center for Trade and Sustainable Development (ICTSD) (2003), *Property Rights: Implications for Development Policy, Policy Discussion Paper*, ICTSD and UNCTAD (2003), Intellectual Property Rights & Sustainable Development Series.

2. Farok J. Contractor, (1999), "Strategic Perspectives for International Licensing Managers: The Complementary Roles of Licensing, Investment and Trade in Global Operations," Working Paper no. 99.002 (Rutgers University, 1999).

3. Ibid.

4. International Center for Trade and Sustainable Development, (2003).

5. Kay Millonzi and William Passannante, "Beware of the Pirates: How to Protect Intellectual Property, *Risk Management*, 43(1996): 39–42.

6. D. E. Welch and L. S. Welch, "In the Internationalization Process and Networks: A Strategic Management Perspective," *Journal of International Marketing* 4 (1996): 11–28.

7. Vanessa O'Connell and Mei Fong, "Saks to Follow Luxury Brands Into China," *Wall Street Journal*, April 18, 2006, B1.

8. Dennis Henderson, Ian Sheldon, and Kathleen Thomas, "International Licensing of Foods and Beverages Makes Markets Truly Global," *FoodReview* (September, 1994): 7–12.

9. *Economist*, "Management Brief: Johannesburgers and Fries," 27 September, 1997, 113–14.

10. U.S. Department of Commerce, *A Basic Guide to Exporting* (Washington D.C.: U.S. Government Printing Office, 1992).

11. Graham Pomphrey, "Pooh at 80," *License Europe!*, April 1, 2006, accessed at www.licensemag.com/licensemag.

12. Piero Telesio, *Technology Licensing and Multinational Enterprises* (New York: Praeger, 1979).

13. Ibid.

14. *Chemical Market Reporter*, "Roche Gains a Stronghold in Elusive Japanese Market," December 17, 2001, 2.

15. Telesio (1979).

16. Akio Morita, Edwin Reingold, and Mitsuko Shimomura, *Made in Japan: Akio Morita and Sony* (New York: EP Dutton, 1986).

17. Jan Golab, "King Barbie: How I Gussied Up America's Favorite Toy and Turned My Struggling Company into a Megatoyopoly," *Los Angeles Magazine*, August 1, 1994, 66; Mattel, Inc. annual reports (various years).

18. F. Burton and A. Cross, "International Franchising: Market versus Hierarchy," in *Internationalisation Strategies*, G. Chryssochoidis, C. Millar, and J. Clegg, eds., 135–52 (New York: St. Martin's Press, 2001).

19. L. S. Welch, "Internationalization by Australian Franchisors," *Asia Pacific Journal of Management* 7 (1990): 101–21.

20. K. Fladmoe-Lindquist, "International Franchising," in *Globalization of Services*, Y. Aharoni and L. Nachum, eds., 197–216 (London: Routledge, 2000).

21. Ibid.; C. Steinberg, "A Guide to Franchise Strategies," *World Trade* 7 (1994): 66–70.

22. John Stanworth and Brian Smith, *The Barclays Guide to Franchising for the Small Business* (Oxford, UK: Basil Blackwell, 1991).

23. David Kaufmann, "The Big Bang: How Franchising Became an Economic Powerhouse the World Over—Franchise 500®," *Entrepreneur,* January, 2004.

24. Barry Quinn and Anne Marie Doherty, (2000), "Power and Control in International Retail Franchising," *International Marketing Review* 17 (2000):354–63.

25. Carlyle Adler, "How China Eats a Sandwich,"*Fortune,* March 21, 2005, F210.

26. Stanworth (1991).

27. *ENR*, "Public Funds and Turnkey Contracts Fuel Growing Global Subway Work," October 25, 2004, 32.

28. *Euromoney*, "Full Steam Ahead with Nuclear Power," December, 1980, 36.

29. *ENR*, "BOT Group Awards Major Hong Kong Road Contract," July 3, 1995, 30.

30. Robert Peltier, "Phu My 3 Power Plant, Ho Chi Minh City, Vietnam," *Power*, August, 2004, 42.

31. Farok Contractor and Sumit Kundu, "Modal Choice in a World of Alliances: Analyzing Organizational Forms in the International Hotel Sector," *Journal of International Business Studies* 29 (1998): 325–56; V. Panvisavas and J. S. Taylor, (2006) "The Use of Management Contracts by International Hotel Firms in Thailand," *International Journal of Contemporary Hospitality Management* 18 (2006): 231–40.

32. David A. Ricks and Saeed Samiee-Esfahani, (1974), "Leasing: It May be Right Abroad Even When It is Not at Home," *Journal of International Business Studies* 5(1974): 87–90.

33. Lloyd Downey, "Marketing Services: How TPOs Can Help," *International Trade Forum* 4 (2005): 7–8.

34. Geoffrey Jones and Alexis Lefort, "McKinsey and the Globalization of Consultancy," Harvard Business School case study 9–806–035 (Cambridge, MA: Harvard Business School, 2006).

35. International Chamber of Commerce, "OECD Study a Vital Step to Understanding the Global Scope of Counterfeiting," (Paris: International Chamber of Commerce, accessed at www.iccwbo.org, 2007).

36. Murray Hiebert, "Chinese Counterfeiters Turn Out Fake Car Parts," *Wall Street Journal*, March 3, 2004, A14 Joon Muller, "Stolen Cars," *Forbes*, February 16, 2004, 58.

37. Hamblen, Matthew, "Cisco, Huawei Look to Settle Software-Copying Lawsuit," *Computer World,* Oct. 6, 2003, p. 19.

38. B. Cassell, "Microsoft Battles Piracy in Developing Markets," *Wall Street Journal,* December 23, 2004, B4.

39. Vauhini (2005), 59; Jack Goldsmith and Tim Wu, *Who Controls the Internet: Illusions of a Borderless World* (Oxford University Press, 2006).

40. Xiaobai Shen, "Developing Country Perspectives on Software," *International Journal of IT Standards & Standardization Research*, 3 (2005): 21–43.

41. Meagan Dietz, Sarena Shao-Tin Lin, and Lei Yang, "Protecting Intellectual Property in China," *The McKinsey Quarterly* 3 (2005): 6–10.

42. Dayal-Gulati, A. and Angela Lee (2004), *Kellogg on China: Strategies for Success*, Evanston, IL: Northwestern University Press.

43. Millonzi and Passannante (1996).

44. Dietz, Shao-Tin Lin, and Yang (2005).

45. Ibid.

Chapter 16

1. Thomas Friedman, *The World Is Flat* (New York: Farrar, Straus, & Giroux, 2005)

2. Geri Smith, "Can Latin America Challenge India?," *Business Week*, January 30, 2006, 'Online Extra,' retrieved at www.businessweek.com.

3. Masaaki Kotabe, Janet Murray, and Rajshekhar Javalgi, "Global Sourcing of Services and Market Performance: An Empirical Investigation," *Journal of International Marketing,* 6 (1998): 10–31; Masaaki Kotabe and Janet Murray, "Outsourcing Service Activities," *Marketing Management* 10 (2001): 40–46.

4. *Economist*, "Outsourcing: Time to Bring it Back Home?" March 5, 2005, 63.

5. Michael E. Porter, *Competition in Global Industries* (Boston: Harvard Business School Press, 1986).

6. Andrew Baxter, "GE Unit Plugs into the Outside World," *Financial Times*, September 28, 2005, 8.

7. Shareowner, "Patheon Inc.: Contract Drug Manufacturing and Development," November–December, 2003, 36.

8. Bruce Einhorn, "A Juggernaut In Electronics," *Business Week,* June 18, 2007, 46.

9. Benito Arrunada, and Xose H. Vazquez, "When Your Contract Manufacturer Becomes Your Competitor, *Harvard Business Review* (September, 2006): 135–45.

10. *Economist*, "India: The Next Wave," December 17, 2005, 57–58.

11. Institute for International Business, "Globalization of Work: Outsourcing and Offshoring," *Global Executive Forum*, Spring–Summer, 2005, 6–7.

12. *Business Week*, "Is Your Job Next?" February 3, 2003, accessed on January 14, 2006, at www.businessweek.com.

13. Murray Weidenbaum, "Outsourcing: Pros and Cons," *Executive Speeches* 19 (2004): 31–35.

14. Peter Marsh, "Foreign Threat to Service Jobs 'Overblown'," *Financial Times,* June 16, 2005.

15. *New York Times* "If You Can Make It Here. . . How Some Companies Manage to Keep Building Things in America," September 4, 2005, section 3, 1.

16. United Nations, 2005, p. 10.

17. *Fortune,* "The Modular Corporation," February 8, 1993, 106.

18. Duke University CIBER/Archstone Consulting, *Second Biannual Offshore Survey Results,* 2005.

19. *Business Week,* 2006, on p. 29.

20. Abdul Rasheed and K. Matthew Gilley, "Outsourcing: National- and Firm-Level Implications," *Thunderbird International Business Review* 47 (2005): 513–28.

21. *Economist,* "Outsourcing: Time to Bring it Back Home?" March 5, 2005, 63.

22. *Business Week,* 2006, p. 30.

23. Duke University CIBER/Archstone Consulting, *Second Biannual Offshore Survey Results,* 2005.

24. Institute for International Business, "Globalization of Work: Outsourcing and Offshoring," *Global Executive Forum* (Spring-Summer, 2005): 6–7.

25. *Business Week,* 2006, p. 21.

26. Pete Engardio, "The Future of Outsourcing," *Business Week,* January 30, 2006, 50–64.

27. Duke University CIBER/Archstone Consulting, *Second Biannual Offshore Survey Results,* 2005.

28. *Business Week,* 2006, p. 22.

29. Pete Engardio, "The Future of Outsourcing," *Business Week,* January 30, 2006, 50–64.

30. Doug Cameron, "Boeing: Manufacturing Enters a New Era," *Financial Times,* June 18, 2007, 6; John Gapper, "A Cleverer Way to Build a Boeing," *Financial Times,* July 8, 2007.

31. George Yip, *Total Global Strategy II* (Upper Saddle River, NJ: Prentice Hall, 2003).

32. James Womack and Daniel Jones, *Lean Solutions* (New York: Free Press, 2005).

33. Barney Gimbel, "Yule Log Jam," *Fortune,* December 13, 2004, 164–70.

34. Alison Maitland, "Make Sure You Have Your Christmas Stock In," *Financial Times,* December 19, 2005, 11.

35. Masaaki Kotabe Janet Murray, "Global Sourcing Strategy and Sustainable Competitive Advantage," *Industrial Marketing Management* 33 (2004): 7–14.

36. Manjeet Kripalani, "Five Offshore Practices that Pay Off," *Business Week,* January 30, 2006, 60–61.

37. *Business Week,* 2006, p. 40.

38. David Craig and Paul Willmott, "Outsourcing Grows Up," *The Mckinsey Quarterly,* (February, 2005), Web exclusive.

39. Eric Bellman and Nathan Koppel, "More U.S. Legal Work Moves to India's Low-Cost Lawyers," *Wall Street Journal,* September 28, 2005, B1.

40. Murray Weidenbaum, (2004), "Outsourcing: Pros and Cons," *Executive Speeches,* 19 (2004): 31–35.

41. J. McCarthy, "3.3 Million U.S. Service Jobs to Go Offshore," *Forrester Research, Inc.,* 2002. Retrieved December 4, 2005, from www.forrester.com.

42. *USA Today,* "To Start Up Here, Companies Hire Over There," February 11, 2005, 1B-2B.

43. *Economist,* "The Looming Revolution," November 13, 2004, 75–77.

44. Ryan Jeltema, "Electrolux Plant Walls Come Tumbling Down," *The Daily News,* June 7, 2007.

45. L. D. Tyson, "Offshoring: The Pros and Cons for Europe," *Business Week,* December 6, 2004, 32.

46. Tara Radin and Martin Calkins, "The Struggle Against Sweatshops: Moving Toward Responsible Global Business," *Journal of Business Ethics* 66 (2006): 261–68.

47. Eric Bellman and Nathan Koppel, "More U.S. Legal Work Moves to India's Low-Cost Lawyers," *Wall Street Journal,* September 28, 2005, B1.

48. Murray Weidenbaum, "Outsourcing: Pros and Cons," *Executive Speeches* 19 (2004): 31–35.

49. Paul Krugman, (1994), "Does Third World Growth Hurt First World Prosperity?" *Harvard Business Review* 72 (1994): 113–21.

50. Michael Mandel, "The Real Cost of Offshoring," *Business Week,* June 18, 2007.

51. L. D. Tyson, (2004), "Offshoring: The Pros and Cons for Europe," *Business Week,* December 6, 2004, 32.

52. Schumpeter, Joseph A. (1942) *Capitalism, Socialism, and Democracy,* New York, Harper & Brothers Publishers.

Chapter 17

1. Shaoming Zou and S. Tamer Cavusgil, "The GMS: A Broad Conceptualization of Global Marketing Strategy and Its Effect on Firm Performance," *Journal of Marketing* 66 (2002): 40–56.

2. H. Gatignon, J. Eliashberg, and T. Robertson, "Modeling Multinational Diffusion Patterns: An Efficient Methodology," *Marketing Science* 8 (1989): 231–43.

3. G. Fowler and M. Marr, "Disney's China Play," *Wall Street Journal,* June 16, 2005, B1, B7.

4. George Yip, *Total Global Strategy II* (Upper Saddle River, NJ: Prentice Hall, 2003).

5. Roger Calantone, S. Tamer Cavusgil, Jeffrey Schmidt, and Geon-Cheol Shin, (2004), "Internationalization and the Dynamics of Product Adaptation—An Empirical Investigation," *Journal of Product Innovation Management* 21 (2004): 185–98.

6. George Yip, *Total Global Strategy II* (Upper Saddle River, NJ: Prentice Hall, 2003).

7. Cris Prystay, "Milk Industry's Pitch in Asia: Try the Ginger or Rose Flavor," *Wall Street Journal,* August 9, 2005, B1.

8. J. Tapper and A. Miller, (2005), "'The Simpsons' Exported to Middle East," Oct. 18, *ABC News,* accessed at abcnews.go.com/wnt.

9. Brian Bremner, "McDonald's Is Loving It in Asia," *BusinessWeek.com,* January 24, 2007.

10. *Wall Street Journal,* "Microsoft To Offer Budget Windows Program In Asia," August 11, 2004, B2.

11. Ian Rowley, "Will Japan Fall in Love with Lexus?" *Business Week,* July 11, 2005, 49.

12. George Yip, *Total Global Strategy II* (Upper Saddle River, NJ: Prentice Hall, 2003).

13. Douglas B. Holt, John A. Quelch, and Earl Taylor, "How Global Brands Compete," *Harvard Business Review* (September, 2004): 68–75.

14. Rajshekhar Javalgi, Virginie Pioche Khare, Andrew Gross, and Robert Scherer, (2005), "An Application of the Consumer Ethnocentrism Model to French Consumers," *International Business Review* 14 (2005): 325–44.

15. David A. Aaker, *Managing Brand Equity* (New York: The Free Press, 1991); James Gregory and Jack Wiechmann, *Branding Across Borders* (Chicago: McGraw-Hill, 2002).

16. George Yip, *Total Global Strategy II* (Upper Saddle River, NJ: Prentice Hall, 2003).

17. Ibid.

18. Matthew B. Myers, "Implications of Pricing Strategy-Venture Strategy Congruence: An Application Using Optimal Models in an International Context," *Journal of Business Research* 57 (2004): 591–690.

19. S. Tamer Cavusgil, "Pricing for Global Markets," *Columbia Journal of World Business* (Winter, 1996): 66–78.

20. S. Tamer Cavusgil, "Unraveling the Mystique of Export Pricing," *Business Horizons* 31 (1988): 54–63.

21. William McDaniel and Edgar Kossack, "The Financial Benefits to Users of Foreign-Trade Zones," *Columbia Journal of World Business* 18 (1983): 33–41.

22. S. Tamer Cavusgil, "Unraveling the Mystique of Export Pricing," *Business Horizons* 31 (1988): 54–63.

23. Thomas Pugel and Judith Ugelow, "Transfer prices and Profit Maximization in Multinational Enterprise Operations," *Journal of International Business Studies* 13 (Spring–Summer, 1982): 115–19.

24. S. Tamer Cavusgil and Ed Sikora, "How Multinationals Can Counter Gray Market Imports," *Columbia Journal of World Business* 23 (1988): 75–86. Also see: Reza Ahmadi and B. Rachel Yang, "Parallel Imports: Challenges from Unauthorized Distribution Channels," *Marketing Science* 19 (Summer, 2000): 281; Matthew B. Myers, "Incidents of Gray Market Activity Among U.S. Exporters: Occurrences, Characteristics, and Consequences, *Journal of International Business Studies* 30 (1999): 105–26.

25. S. Tamer Cavusgil and Ed Sikora, "How Multinationals Can Counter Gray Market Imports," *Columbia Journal of World Business* 23 (1988): 75–86.

26. Chris Hansen, "Inside the World of Counterfeit Drugs," June 9, 2006, *MSNBC Interactive* article, accessed at www.msnbc.msn.com.

27. F. Balfour and D. Kiley, "Ad Agencies Unchained," *Business Week,* April 25, 2005, 50–51.

28. George Yip, *Total Global Strategy II* (Upper Saddle River, NJ: Prentice Hall, 2003).

29. Linda Shi, Shaoming Zou, J. Chris White, Regina McNally, and S. Tamer Cavusgil, "Executive Insights: Global Account Management Capability," *Journal of International Marketing* 13 (2005): 93–113; Sengun Yeniyurt, S. Tamer Cavusgil, and Tomas Hult, "A Global Market Advantage Framework: The Role of Global Market Knowledge Competencies," *International Business Review* 14 (2005): 1–19.

30. Kerry Capell, "McDonald's Offers Ethics with Those Fries," *Business Week,* January 9, 2007, accessed at online edition at www.businessweek.com.

31. Cynthia Wagner, "Designing for the 'Other 90 Percent," *The Futurist,* May–June, 2007, 34–35.

32. Center for Corporate Citizenship, "In Good Company: Motorola," Boston, MA: Boston College, Carroll School of Management, 2007, accessed at http://www.bcccc.net.

33. Sarah Murray, "Manufacturers Take on Greater Responsibility," *Financial Times,* April 18, 2007, 3.

Chapter 18

1. Dowling, Peter, Festing, Marion and Allen Engle (2008), *International HRM: Managing People in a Multinational Context, 5th Ed,* London: Thomson Learning.

2. Ibid

3. Ibid

4. Johnson, Jo (2007), "More Westerners Take Top Posts in India as Locals' Pay Demand Soars," *Financial Times,* May 30, p. 1

5. Dowling, Festing and Engle.

6. Levy, Orly, Schon Beechler, Sully Taylor, and Nakiye Boyacigiller (2007) "What we talk about when we talk about 'Global Mindset;' Managerial Cognition in Multinational Corporations,", *Journal of International Business Studies,* volume 38, number 2, 231– 258.

7. Neelankavil, James, Anil Mathur, and Yong Zhang (2000), "Determinants of Managerial Performance: A Cross-Cultural Comparison of the Perceptions of Middle-Level Managers in Four Countries," *Journal of International Business Studies,* 31(1), pp. 121–41

8. Dowling, Festing, and Engle (2007); Harzing, Anne-Wil (2001), "Of Bears, Bumble-Bees, and Spiders: The Role of Expatriates in Controlling Foreign Subsidiaries," *Journal of World Business,* 36(4), pp.366–79

9. Harzing, Anne-Wil (2001), "Who's in Charge? An Empirical Study of Executive Staffing Practices in Foreign Subsidiaries," *Human Resource Management,* 40(2), pp. 139–45

10. Byrnes, Nanette (2005), "Star Search," *Business Week,* Oct 10, pg. 68; Pollitt, David (2006), "Unilever "Raises The Bar" In Terms of Leadership Performance," *Human Resource Management International Digest,* 14(5), pp. 23–25; Philip Harris, Robert Moran, and Sarah Moran, *Managing Cultural Differences, 6th ed.* (Burlington, MA: Elsevier Buttermann-Heinemann, 2007)

11. Dowling, Festing, and Engle (2007)

12. Harris, Moran, and Moran (2007)

13. Kedia, Ben L. and Akuro Mukherji (1999), "Global Managers: Developing a Mindset for Global Competitiveness," *Journal of World Business,* 34 (3): 230–251

14. Dowling, Festing, and Engle (2007)

15. Harzing, Anne-Wil and Claus Christensen (2004) "THINK PIECE: Expatriate Failure: Time to Abandon the Concept?" *Career Development International*, 9(6/7), pp. 616–20

16. Mendenhall, M., E. Dunbar, and G. Oddou (1987), "Expatriate Selection, Training and Career Pathing: A Review and Critique," *Human Resources Management*, 26, pp. 331–45

17. Harris, Moran, and Moran (2007)

18. Tung, Rosalie (1987), "Expatriate Assignments: Enhancing Success and Minimizing Failure," *Academy of Management Executive*, 1, pp. 117–26

19. Black, J., H. Gregersen, and M. Mendenhall (1992), "Toward a Theoretical Framework of Repatriation Adjustment," *Journal of International Business Studies*, 23, pp. 737–60

20. Harris, Moran, and Moran (2007)

21. Moran, Robert T. and John R. Riesenberger (1994), *The Global Challenge*, London: McGraw-Hill

22. Levy, Orly, Schon Beechler, Sully Taylor, and Nakiye Boyacigiller (2007) "What we talk about when we talk about 'Global Mindset;' Managerial Cognition in Multinational Corporations,", *Journal of International Business Studies*, volume 38, number 2, 231– 258.

23. Rhinesmith, Stephen (1998), *A Manager's Guide to Globalization*, Homewood, IL: Business One Irwin

24. Ang, S., Van Dyne, L., and Koh, C.K.S. (2006), "Personality correlates of the four factor model of cultural intelligence," *Group and Organization Management*, 31, 100–123.

25. Ibid

26. Yip, George (2003), *Total Global Strategy II*, Upper Saddle River, NJ: Prentice Hall

27. Brett, Jeanne, Kristin Beyfar, and Mary Kern (2006), "Managing Multicultural Teams," *Harvard Business Review*, 84(11), pp. 84–92

28. Holland, Kelley (2007), "How Diversity Makes a Team Click," *New York Times*, April 22, p. 16

29. Dowling, Peter, Denice Welch, and Randall Schuler (1999), *International Human Resource Management*, 3rd. ed., Cincinnati: South-Western.

30. Ibid

31. Ibid

32. Hodgetts, Richard and Fred Luthans (2003), *International Management: Culture, Strategy, and Behavior, 5th ed.*, Boston: McGraw-Hill Irwin

33. Ibid

34. Blanchflower, David (2007), "International Patterns of Union Membership," *British Journal of Industrial Relations*, 45(1), pp. 1–28

35. Economist (2006), "Europe: There's Life in the Old Dinosaurs Yet," February 18, pg. 41 Waddington, Jeremy (2005), "Trade Unions and the Defence of the European Social Model," *Industrial Relations Journal*, pg. 518–24

36. Blanchflower, David (2007), "International Patterns of Union Membership," *British Journal of Industrial Relations*, 45(1), pp. 1–28; Meardi, Guglielmo (2006), "Multinationals' Heaven? Uncovering and Understanding Worker Responses to Multinational Companies in Post-Communist Central Europe," *International Journal of Human Resource Management*, 17(8), pp. 1366–1378

37. Tomlinson, Richard (2004), "Troubled Waters at Perrier," *Fortune*, Nov. 29, pp. 173–76

38. Dubofsky, M and F.R. Dulles (2004), *Labor in America: A History, 7th ed*, Wheeling, IL: Harlan Davidson

39. Roberts, Dexter (2005), "Waking Up to Their Rights," *Business Week*, August 22/29, pp. 123–128

40. Wu, Victorien (2006), "Labor Relations in Focus," *The China Business Review*, 33(6), pp. 40–44

41. "'Breaking the ICE': Workplace Democracy in a Modernized Social Europe," Hardy, Stephen and Nick Adnett (2006), *The International Journal of Human Resource Management* 17(6), pp. 1021–31

42. Alesina, Alberto and Francesco Giavazzi (2006), *The Future of Europe: Reform or Decline*, Boston: MIT Press

43. Koslow, Lawrence and Robert Scarlett (1999), *Global Business*, Houston, TX: Cashman Dudley

44. Mako C., P. Csizmadi, and M. Illessy (2006), "Labour Relations in Comparative Perspective," *Journal for East European Management Studies*, 11(3), pp. 267–87

45. Marquez, Jessica (2006), "Unions' Global End Run," *Workforce Management*, January 30, pp. 1–4

46. Dowling, Welch, and Schuler (1999); *Economist* (2005), "The Conundrum of the Glass Ceiling," July 23, pp. 63–65; Price Waterhouse (1997) *International Assignments: European Policy and Prejudice 1997/1998*, Europe

47. Grant Thornton (2007) *Grant Thornton International Business Report 2007*, accessed at www.grantthorntonibos.com

48. Adler, Nancy (2002), *International Dimensions of Organizational Behavior, 4th ed.*, Cincinnati, OH: South-Western; Harris, Moran, and Moran (2007)

49. Moran, Robert T., Phillip R. Harris, and Sarah V. Moran (2007), *Managing Cultural Differences, Global Leadership Strategies for the 21st Century, 7th ed.*, Oxford, UK: Elsevier.

50. Gratton, Lynda (2007), "Steps that Can Help Women Make it to the Top," *Financial Times*, May 23, p. 13

51. Ibid.; *Economist* (2005), "The Conundrum of the Glass Ceiling," July 23, pp. 63–65

52. *Economist* (2006), "Women and the World Economy: A Guide to Womenomics," April 12, p. 80

53. Mercer Human Resource Consulting (2006), "More Females Sent on International Assignment than ever Before, Survey Finds," October 12, accessed at www.mercerhr.com

Chapter 19

1. Henry Sender, "Financial Musical Chairs," *Far Economic Review* (July, 1999): 30–36.

2. W. Sekely and J. Collins, (1988), "Cultural Influences in International Capital Structure," *Journal of International Business Studies* (Spring, 1988): 87–100.

3. Ibid.

4. Ernst and Young, "Globalisation Act II: Team Europe Defends Its Goals," results of 2006 survey on the attractiveness of Europe (Paris: Ernst & Young, 2006).

5. Bank for International Settlements, Statistics division, accessed at www.bis.org.

6. Andrew Karolyi, Craig Doidge, and René Stulz, "Foreign Firms Cross-Listed in the United States Valued Higher : Study Shows Average Premium of 13.9 Percent," *The Exchange* 12 (2005).

7. K. Lewis, "Trying to Explain Home Bias in Equities and Consumption," *Journal of Economic Literature* 37 (1999): 571–608.

8. OECD, *Institutional Investors: Statistical Yearbook, Organization for Economic Cooperation and Development* (Paris: OECD, 2001).

9. Ibid.

10. Ibid.

11. Daniel Yergin and Joseph Stanislaw, *The Commanding Heights: The Battle for the World Economy* (New York: Touchstone, 2002).

12. Alicia Wyllie, (2002), "Have Portfolio Will Travel," *The Sunday Times*, January 20, 2002, 1.

13. *Economist*, "Battle of the Bourses," May 27, 2006, 83–85.

14. Bank of England, "E-Commerce and the Foreign Exchange Market—Have the Promises Been Met?" *Bank of England, Quarterly Bulletin, London* 44 (2004): 97–101; Alan Greenspan, "The Globalization of Finance," *The Cato Journal* 17 (1997) at www.cato.org.

15. Robert Cottrell, "Thinking Big: A Survey of International Banking," *Economist*, May 20, 2006, survey section.

16. Michael Sesit and Craig Karmin, "How One Word Haunts the Dollar," *Wall Street Journal*, 2005 March 17, C16.

17. IBM, Inc., *2003 Annual Report*, 2004, accessed at www.ibm.com.

18. Here is an example of how transfer pricing works. Consider an MNE with a subsidiary in three countries. Suppose that subsidiary A operates in country A with high corporate income taxes, and subsidiary B operates in country B, a tax haven. One way to minimize taxes is for subsidiary A to sell merchandise to subsidiary B for a low transfer price. Subsidiary B then resells the merchandise to subsidiary C in the third country at a high transfer price. This results in lower overall taxes for subsidiary A because of its low profits, for subsidiary B because of country B's low tax rates, and for subsidiary C because the high cost of its purchase reduces its profits.

19. While this approach to transferring funds within the MNE is quite common, transfer pricing has some drawbacks. First, while transfer pricing between members of the corporate family is legal when carried out within reasonable limits, governments strongly disapprove of the practice of avoiding tax obligations. Thus, many governments impose policies that restrict transfer pricing. Coca-Cola's Japan subsidiary was fined 15 billion yen ($145 million) for making royalty payments from trademarks and products to its U.S. parent that Japan's National Tax Administration judged as too high. Second, transfer pricing can distort the financial results of foreign subsidiaries. For instance, a subsidiary that is required to charge low prices for its exports may experience unusually low profitability, which harms its performance and can demoralize local staff. Third, some MNEs use artificial transfer prices to hide the poor results of a badly performing subsidiary, or achieve other goals aimed at concealing the true performance of the firm.

20. Timor Mehpare and Seyhan Sipahi, "Fast-Food Restaurant Site Selection Factor Evaluation by the Analytic Hierarchy Process," *The Business Review* 4 (2005): 161–67.

21. Here is an illustration of net present value analysis. A U.S.-based MNE is considering an expansion project through its subsidiary in Mexico. The project requires an initial investment of 220 million Mexican pesos (MXP) and has an economic life of 5 years. The project is expected to generate annual after-tax cash flows of MXP120 million, MXP125 million, MXP150 million, MXP155 million, and MXP200 million, which will be remitted to the parent company during the next 5 years. The current spot exchange rate is MXP11/$ and the spot rates are expected to be MXP11.10/$, MXP11.25/$, MXP11.50/$, MXP11.55/$, and MXP11.75/$ for the next 5 years. Assuming that the appropriate discount rate for this project is 10 percent, what is the NPV of the project from the parent company's perspective? Should the MNC accept this project based on its NPV? Let's analyze.

The U.S. cash flows of the project can be calculated as follows:

	0	1	2	3	4	5
Mexican peso cash flows	MXP 220 million	MXP 120 million	MXP 125 million	MXP 150 million	MXP 155 million	MXP 200 million
Prevailing spot exchange rate	MXP 11/$	MXP 11.10/$	MXP 11.25/$	MXP 11.50/$	MXP 11.55/$	MXP 11.75/$
U.S. dollar cash flows	$20,000,000	$10,810,811	$11,111,111	$13,043,478	$13,419,913	$17,021,277

The NPV of the project can be calculated as follows:

$$NPV = -\$20,000,000 + \$10,810,811/(1+0.10)^1 + \$11,111,111/(1+0.10)^2 + \$13,043,478/(1+0.10)^3 + \$13,419,913/(1+0.10)^4 + \$17,021,277/(1+0.10)^5$$

$$NPV = \$28,545,359$$

The MNC can accept the project because it has a positive NPV.

22. The discount rate used in the NPV analysis of international projects may be higher due to a premium for additional risks involved in doing business internationally. Management may insist on a higher level of required return in the net present value calculation because higher country/political and currency risks indicate a higher probability of venture failure. A firm might apply a 7 percent discount rate to potential investments in Germany and Japan because those countries enjoy political and economic stability. But the same firm might use a 14 percent discount rate for similar potential investments in Pakistan and Russia because those countries experience political

and economic turmoil. The higher the discount rate, the higher the projected net cash flows must be for the investment to have a positive net present value contribution. Occasionally, the discount rate for international projects can be lower than for domestic ones. Risk arises from various sources and management must systematically assess the range of potentially influential factors.

23. Peter Drucker, *Management Challenges for the 21st Century* (New York: Harper Collins, 1999).

24. Robert Aliber, *Exchange Risk and International Finance* (New York: Wiley, 1979).

25. Donald R. Lessard, "Finance and Global Competition," *Midland Corporate Finance Journal* (Fall, 1987).

26. *Trade Fact of the Week,* "Currency Trading Totals $3 Trillion a Day," March 14, 2007.

27. Ibid.

28. Gordon Platt, "World's Best Foreign Exchange Banks 2005," *Global Finance* 19 (2005): 24–33.

29. Adam Rombel, "The World's Best Internet Banks," *Global Finance* 16 (2002): 37–38.

30. See Appendix for Chapter.

31. Richard Rescigno, "At the Crossroads: Subaru Strives to Get Back Into Gear," *Barron's,* March 28, 1988, 15–19.

32. Here is a simple example of an option transaction from a familiar context. Say you are in the market to buy a house. You find one that you like but you are not sure if you want to buy it. At this stage, you opt to put a deposit down to have the seller keep his for-sale house for you for two weeks. Later, if you buy the house, the deposit counts toward the purchase price. If you do not buy the house, you lose your deposit. You had the option to buy the house at an agreed-upon price but not the obligation to do so.

33. W. Wallace and J. Walsh, "Apples to Apples: Profits Abroad," *Financial Executive* (May–June, 1995): 28–31.

34. Hank Boerner, "Europe Faces Eagle Eye of US Financial Regulation," *European Business Forum* 21 (2005): 46–49.

35. Robert Bruce, "Giant Step Is Taken Towards a Single Global Standard," *Financial Times*, May 3, 2007.

36. Computershare, *2003 Annual Report,* accessed at www.computershare.com, (2003).

37. Alan J. Auerbach and Martin Feldstein, *Handbook of Public Economics,* 3rd ed. (Amsterdam: North-Holland, 2001).

38. Brody Mullins, "Accenture Lobbyists Near Big Win On Securing Tax-Haven Status," *Wall Street Journal,* July 14, 2005, A2.

> Photo Credits

Cover

Imagebroker/Alamy

Chapter 1

page 2: Rita Ariyoshi/PacificStock.com; page 16: Digital Archive Japan/Alamy.com; **page 18:** Kevin Foy/Alamy.com; **page 19:** © Jack Hollingsworth/CORBIS All Rights Reserved; **page 21:** Fredrik Renander/Alamy.com; **page 22:** Ashley Lumb;

Chapter 2

page 28: © Steve Raymer/CORBIS All Rights Reserved; **page 36**: © Daniel Karmann/CORBIS All Rights Reserved; **page 44**: Jeff Greenberg/PhotoEdit Inc.; **page 46**: Fabrice Bettex/Alamy.com; **page 51**: Frederic J. Brown/Agence France Presse/Getty Images.

Chapter 3

page 60: Mike Caldwell/Getty Images Inc.-Stone Allstock; **page 69**: ERG Group; **page 73**: Guang Niu/Corbis/Reuters America LLC; **page 76**: David Pearson/Alamy.com; **page 82**: Cynthia Asoka; **page 83**: G P Bowater/Alamy.com.

Chapter 4

page 92: G P Bowater/Mira.com; **page 97**: The Granger Collection, New York; **page 101**: AP Wide World Photos; **page 105**: © Steve Raymer/CORBIS All Rights Reserved; **page 106**: G P Bowater/Mira.com; **page 115**: G P Bowater/Alamy.com.

Chapter 5

page 124: AP Wide World Photos; **page 127**: Alamy.com; **page 128**: Maurice Dancer; **page 133**: Zhibo Yu; **page 140**: ERIKO SUGITA/Corbis/Reuters America LLC; **page 148**: Getty Images-Photodisc.

Chapter 6

page 158: Demetrio Carrasco © Dorling Kindersley; **page 166**: Jeff Greenberg/The Image Works; **page 171**: Hasan Sarbakhshian/AP Wide World Photos; **page 174**: Philippe Bataille/AP Wide World Photos; **page 176**: Fujifotos/The Image Works.

Chapter 7

page 192: G P Bowater/Creative Eye/MIRA.com; **page 198**: Ric Francis/AP Wide World Photos; **page 204**: Andrew Winning/Corbis/Reuters America LLC; **page 206**: Jim Young/Corbis/Reuters America LLC; **page 210**: Jorgen Schytte/Peter Arnold, Inc.

Chapter 8

page 222: © Guido Cozzi/CORBIS All Rights Reserved; **page 239**: © Krista Kennell/ZUMA/ CORBIS All Rights Reserved; **page 240**: © Adrian Sifon/Reuters/CORBIS All Rights Reserved; **page 241**: © Rolf Haid/dpa/CORBIS All Rights Reserved;

Chapter 9

page 254: Dennis Cox /AGE Fotostock America, Inc.; **page 266**: Rainer Unkel/Alamy.com; **page 273**: ANCIENT ART & ARCHITECTURE/DanitaDelimont.com; **page 274**: © Michael Reynolds/CORBIS All Rights Reserved; **page 275**: Charles O. Cecil/Alamy.com.

Chapter 10

Page 284: Hartmut Schwarzbach /argus/Peter Arnold, Inc.; **page 292**: Enrique Marcarian/Corbis/Reuters America LLC; **page 297**: ZAP ART/Getty Images, Inc.–Taxi; **page 300**: Eugene Hoshiko/AP Wide World Photos; **page 301**: Chip Besse; **page 303**: Hyungwon Kang/Corbis/Reuters America LLC.

Chapter 11

page 312: ©Hans-Jürgen Burkard/Bilderberg; **page 321**: © Paul Souders/CORBIS All Rights Reserved; **page 323**: ROMEO GACAD /Agence France Presse/ Getty Images; **page 326**: Greg Baker/AP Wide World Photos; **page 328**: Missing**page 330**: Punit Paranjpe/Corbis/Reuters America LLC;

Chapter 12

page 344: Dannielle Hayes/Omni-Photo Communications, Inc.; **page 351**: Jason McDonald; **page 354**: DB/PB/Reuters Limited; **page 364**: © Steve Raymer/CORBIS All Rights Reserved; **page 366**: Javier Estrada; **page 367**: Bob Daemmrich/PhotoEdit Inc.;

Chapter 13

page 380: Bill Bachman/Alamy.com; **page 384**: Richard Olsenius/National Geographic Image Collection; **page 387**: © Louie Psihoyos/CORBIS All Rights Reserved; **page 396**: © Macduff Everton/CORBIS All Rights Reserved; **page 403**: Nexxus Lighting, Inc.;

Chapter 14

page 416: Alamy.com; **page 422**: Eckehard Schulz/AP Wide World Photos; **page 425**: © Hamad I. Mohammed/ Reuters/CORBIS All Rights Reserved; **page 438**: Home Depot Inc.;

Chapter 15

page 450: AP Wide World Photos; **page 456**: © YOSHIKAZU TSUNO/AFP/Getty Images; **page 460**: © 2007 Hans Georg; **page 467**: Sergio Moraes/Reuters Limited.; **page 468**: Jennifer Knippen;

Chapter 16

page 482: DPI PHOTO/Philip Teuscher; **page 489**: CRASTO/Reuters/Corbis/Bettmann; **page 501**: Mira/ Alamy.com; **page 504**: Stew Milne/AP Wide World Photos; **page 506**: AP Wide World Photos.

Chapter 17

page 514: Peter Wilson © Dorling Kindersley; **page 518**: Henry Romero/Corbis/Reuters America LLC; **page 520**: © Glow Images/Alamy; **page 523**: David Young-Wolff/PhotoEdit Inc.; **page 536**: Courtesy of United Colors of Benetton;

Chapter 18

page 546: Bob Daemmrich/The Image Works; **page 554**: © Owen Franken/CORBIS All Rights Reserved; **page 557**: © Najlah Feanny/CORBIS All Rights Reserved;

Chapter 19

Page 578: Katsumi Kasahara/AP Wide World Photos; **page 587**: © Andy Rain/CORBIS All Rights Reserved; **page 591**: Tina Manley/Alamy.com; **page 596** © Yuriko Nakao/CORBIS All Rights Reserved; **page 594**: Manish Swarup/AP Wide World Photos; **page 600**: Atlantide S.D.F./AGE Fotostock America, Inc.; **page 601**: Maria Keely.

Author Index

This index includes names of authors cited.

For names of companies, *see* the Companies Index. For terms and topics, see the Subject Index.

Page references with "e" refer to exhibits, page references with "f" refer to footnotes, and page references with "n" refer to notes cited by number.

> Company Index

> Subject Index

This index includes terms and topics. For names of companies, *see* the Companies Index. For authors cited, see the Authors Index. Page numbers with "e" refer to exhibits.

A

Absolute advantage principle, theory of international trade, 97–98, 100, 615
Accounting and reporting laws, as country risk, 179
Accounting, international, management of:
about, 599–606
financial statements of subsidiaries, 603
international taxation, 604–606 (*See also* Taxation)
as task in financial management, 581
transparency in financial reporting, 600
trends toward harmonization, 600, 602, 603
Accounting practices and standards, 179
Accounting reforms, 600
Acculturation, 130, 615
Acquired advantages, 99, 109
Acquisition, as type of foreign direct investment, 429, 615. *See also* Mergers and acquisitions (M&A)
Active hedging, 597
Active involvement stage, of internationalization process model, 110, 385, 386e
Adaptability, in cross-cultural success, 149
Adaptation, in international marketing program, 519, 521–522, 522–523, 615
Adhesive bandages, market demand for, 346
Administrative procedures, 199e, 203–204, 271
Ad valorem tariffs, 200
Advanced economies. *See also* Developed economies
about, 256, 257
compared to emerging and developing economies, 256–257, 260e, 261e, 262e
defined, 256, 615
payment methods and credit from exporters, 396
world map of, 258e, 259e
Advertising, 145, 535–536
Affiliates, 13, 468
Africa:
developing economies, and poverty, 257, 260
economic development with cell phone market, 275
global sourcing countries and firms, 494e
regional economic integration blocs, 239
African Development Bank, 402
African Union for Regional Cooperation, 239
Agencies for international trade, 206
Agents. *See also* Manufacturer's representative
defined, 75, 615
as distribution channel intermediaries, 75–76
professional service firms as, 468
Aggregate activities, 36

Aging populations, macroeconomic trends for, 355
Agreement on Subsidies and Countervailing Measures (ASCM), 215–216
Agreement on Trade in Large Civil Aircraft, 215
Agreement on Trade-Related Aspects of Intellectual Property Rights (TRIPS), 187, 472
Agricultural commodities, 77
Agricultural industries, resource-seeking motives and, 422
Agricultural subsidies, 205, 206, 233–234
Agricultural trade barriers, 211, 242
AIDS, 53, 187, 257
Air freight/transport, 500–501
Airline industry, 435, 467. *See also* Boeing in Companies index
Airbus *versus* Boeing, 215–216
supply-chain management in Boeing, 497–498
Alabama, U.S., sock manufacturing in, 246
Algeria, as Maghreb Union member, 238
All-China Federation of Trade Unions, 563
Alliance of Business Women International (U.S.), 569
Allowance, in compensation of personnel, 560
Amae, Japanese indulgent dependence, 132
Ambiguity attitudes, as cross-cultural difference, 131, 149
American Jobs Creation Act (2005), 606
American option, 598
American quote, 595
Analogy method, estimating company sales potential with, 370–371
Andean Pact, 237
Antiboycott regulations, as country risk, 179
Antidumping duty, as government intervention, 200e, 206, 615
APEC (Asia Pacific Economic Cooperation), 36, 212, 237
Apocalypse Now movie, 151
Apparel industry, 246–248
Appliance industry, 277–279, 384, 505
Arab League, 239
Arab Maghreb Union, 238–239
Arab merchants, ancient, 623
Arbitrage opportunities, 596
Arbitragers, 596, 615
Arbitration, 184
Arbitrator, in labor strikes, 562
Area studies, 556, 615
Argentina:
capital flight from, 292
Compania Argentina de Seguros de Credito, 401
corruption in, 180, 271
hyperinflation in, 291
intellectual property rights in, 271
as MERSOSUR member, 236
risk as investment destination, 586
software development center, 486
Artefacts, 450
ASEAN (Association of Southeast Asian Nations), 172, 237

Asian countries, as high-context cultures, 136–137
Asian Development Bank, 402
Asian financial crisis of 1990s:
earnings reduced at Tektronix, 608
effect of global integration, 36
effect of international financial systems on, 296, 297–298
equity and bond markets, and debt ratios, 582, 586
IMF and South Korea, 302
risk in internationalization, 13
Asia Pacific Economic Cooperation (APEC), 36, 212, 237
Asociación Interamericana de Contabilidad, 602
Asoka, Cynthia, 82
Asset-based services, 146
Asset-seeking motives, 421e, 422–423
Association of Southeast Asian Nations (ASEAN), 172, 237
Asymmetric shock, 306
A. T. Kearney Foreign Direct Investment Confidence Index, 360–361, 361e
A. T. Kearney Offshore Location Attractiveness Index, 361, 362e
Attitudes, in culture, 139
Australia:
as advanced economy, 256
as APEC member, 237
Austrade, 402, 409
as CER member, 238
countertrade, mandatory, 407
Austria, as European Union member, 233e
Automatic teller machines (ATMs), internationalization of, 16
Automobile industry:
adaptation of marketing program, 523
Autolatina partnership in Brazil, 443–444
competing firms' role in host country, 173
consolidation of firms, 430
foreign exchange management by parts supplier, 578–580
government intervention in, 196
Hyundai's struggle for success, 117–119
management of government intervention, 214
visionary leadership at Renault-Nissan, 336–338

B

Back-office activities, 486
Back-to-back transaction, as countertrade, 407
Backward vertical integration, 432
Bahamas, as tax haven, 604
Bahrain, as GCC member, 238
Balance of payments, 293, 615
Balance of trade, 292–293
Bangalore, India:
high country risk for KFC in, 163
industrial cluster of knowledge-intensive firms, 105
national comparative advantage of, 109
as new Silicon Valley, 28–30